Consumer Behavior
Building Marketing Strategy

FOURTEENTH EDITION

David L. Mothersbaugh
University of Alabama

Del I. Hawkins
University of Oregon

Susan Bardi Kleiser
Texas Christian University

Contributing Authors

Linda L. Mothersbaugh
Integrated Solutions, LLC

Carolyn (Casey) Findley Watson
Indiana University Southeast

CONSUMER BEHAVIOR: BUILDING MARKETING STRATEGY

Published by McGraw-Hill Education, 2 Penn Plaza, New York, NY 10121. Copyright ©2020 by McGraw-Hill Education. All rights reserved. Printed in the United States of America. No part of this publication may be reproduced or distributed in any form or by any means, or stored in a database or retrieval system, without the prior written consent of McGraw-Hill Education, including, but not limited to, in any network or other electronic storage or transmission, or broadcast for distance learning.

Some ancillaries, including electronic and print components, may not be available to customers outside the United States.

This book is printed on acid-free paper.

1 2 3 4 5 6 7 8 9 LWI 24 23 22 21 20 19

ISBN 978-1-260-56648-2
MHID 1-260-56648-X

Cover Image: ©*alice-photo/shutterstock*

mheducation.com/highered

Preface

Marketing attempts to influence the way consumers behave. These attempts have implications for the organizations making them, the consumers they are trying to influence, and the society in which these attempts occur. We are all consumers, and we are all members of society, so consumer behavior, and attempts to influence it, is critical to all of us. This text is designed to provide an understanding of consumer behavior. This understanding can make us better consumers, better marketers, and better citizens.

MARKETING CAREERS AND CONSUMER BEHAVIOR

A primary purpose of this text is to provide the student with a usable, managerial understanding of consumer behavior. Most students in consumer behavior courses aspire to careers in marketing management, sales, or advertising. They hope to acquire knowledge and skills that will be useful to them in these careers. Unfortunately, some may be seeking the type of knowledge gained in introductory accounting classes; that is, a set of relatively invariant rules that can be applied across a variety of situations to achieve a fixed solution that is known to be correct. For these students, the uncertainty and lack of closure involved in dealing with living, breathing, changing, stubborn consumers can be very frustrating. However, if they can accept dealing with endless uncertainty, utilizing an understanding of consumer behavior in developing marketing strategy will become tremendously exciting.

It is our view that the utilization of knowledge of consumer behavior in the development of marketing strategy is an art. This is not to suggest that scientific principles and procedures are not applicable; rather, it means that the successful application of these principles to particular situations requires human judgment that we are not able to reduce to a fixed set of rules.

Let us consider the analogy with art in some detail. Suppose you want to become an expert artist. You would study known principles of the visual effects of blending various colors, of perspective, and so forth. Then you would practice applying these principles until you developed the ability to produce acceptable

paintings. If you had certain natural talents, the right teacher, and the right topic, you might even produce a masterpiece. The same approach should be taken by one wishing to become a marketing manager, a salesperson, or an advertising director. The various factors or principles that influence consumer behavior should be thoroughly studied. Then, one should practice applying these principles until acceptable marketing strategies result. However, while knowledge and practice can in general produce acceptable strategies, great marketing strategies, like masterpieces, require special talents, effort, timing, and some degree of luck (what if Mona Lisa had not wanted her portrait painted?).

The art analogy is useful for another reason. All of us, professors and students alike, tend to ask, "How can I use the concept of, say, social class to develop a successful marketing strategy?" This makes as much sense as an artist asking, "How can I use blue to create a great picture?" Obviously, blue alone will seldom be sufficient for a great work of art. Instead, to be successful, the artist must understand when and how to use blue in conjunction with other elements in the picture. Likewise, the marketing manager must understand when and how to use a knowledge of social class in conjunction with a knowledge of other factors in designing a successful marketing strategy.

This book is based on the belief that knowledge of the factors that influence consumer behavior can, with practice, be used to develop sound marketing strategy. With this in mind, we have attempted to do three things. First, we present a reasonably comprehensive description of the various behavioral concepts and theories that have been found useful for understanding consumer behavior. This is generally done at the beginning of each chapter or at the beginning of major subsections in each chapter. We believe that a person must have a thorough understanding of a concept in order to successfully apply that concept across different situations.

Second, we present examples of how these concepts have been utilized in the development of marketing strategy. We have tried to make clear that these examples are not "how you use this concept." Rather, they are presented as "how one organization facing a particular marketing situation used this concept."

Third, at the end of each chapter and each major section, we present a number of questions, activities, or cases that require the student to apply the concepts.

CONSUMING AND CONSUMER BEHAVIOR

The authors of this book are consumers, as is everyone reading this text. Most of us spend more time buying and consuming than we do working or sleeping. We consume products such as cars and fuel, services such as haircuts and home repairs, and entertainment such as television and concerts. Given the time and energy we devote to consuming, we should strive to be good at it. A knowledge of consumer behavior can be used to enhance our ability to consume wisely.

Marketers spend billions of dollars attempting to influence what, when, and how we consume. Marketers not only spend billions attempting to influence our behavior but also spend hundreds of millions of dollars studying our behavior. With a knowledge of consumer behavior and an understanding of how marketers use this knowledge, we can study marketers. A television commercial can be an annoying interruption of a favorite program. However, it also can be a fascinating opportunity to speculate on the commercial's objective, its target audience, and the underlying behavior assumptions. Indeed, given the ubiquitous nature of commercials, an understanding of how they are attempting to influence us or others is essential to understand our environment.

Throughout the text, we present examples that illustrate the objectives of specific marketing activities. By studying these examples and the principles on which they are based, one can develop the ability to discern the underlying logic of the marketing activities encountered daily.

SOCIAL RESPONSIBILITY AND CONSUMER BEHAVIOR

What are the costs and benefits of regulating the marketing of food to children? How much more needs to be done to protect the online privacy of children? Of adults? What are the appropriate type and size of warning label for cigarettes that should be mandated by the federal government? These issues are currently being debated by industry leaders and consumer advocacy groups. As educated citizens, we have a responsibility to take part in these sorts of debates and work toward positive solutions. However, developing sound positions on these issues requires an understanding of such factors as information processing as it relates to advertising—an important part of our understanding of consumer behavior.

The debates described above are just a few of the many that require an understanding of consumer behavior. We present a number of these topics throughout the text. The objective is to develop the ability to apply consumer behavior knowledge to social and regulatory issues as well as to business and personal issues.

AREAS OF ONGOING CHANGE AND FOCUS

Marketing and consumer behavior, like the rest of the world, are changing at a rapid pace. Both the way consumers behave and the practices of studying that behavior continue to evolve. In order to keep up with this dynamic environment, the fourteenth edition includes a number of important features.

Internet, Mobile, and Social Media

The Internet, mobile marketing, and social media are dramatically changing how and where consumers shop and buy. This edition integrates the latest research, practices, and examples concerning technology throughout the text and the cases.

Global Marketing

Previous editions have included a wealth of global material, and this edition is no exception. Multiple global examples can be found woven into the text across the chapters. In addition, Chapter 2 and several of the cases are devoted to global issues.

Ethnic Subcultures

This edition continues our emphasis on the exciting issues surrounding marketing to ethnic subcultures. Ethnic diversity is increasing, and we draw in the latest research and emerging trends to shed light on this important topic.

Strategic Application

This edition continues our emphasis on the application of consumer behavior concepts and theory to exciting marketing problems and important emerging trends. We do this through our heavy emphasis on segmentation schemes, as well as opening examples, featured consumer insights, and cases. This edition contains many segmentation schemes that provide insights into the development of marketing strategy. The opening examples, in-text examples, and consumer insights provide additional strategic insight by showing how specific companies utilize various consumer behavior concepts in developing effective marketing strategies. Finally, cases provide an opportunity to apply consumer behavior concepts to real-world problems.

UNIQUE FEATURES AND NEW TO THIS EDITION

Integrated Coverage of Ethical/Social Issues

Marketers face numerous ethical issues as they apply their understanding of consumer behavior in the marketplace. We describe and discuss many of these issues. These discussions are highlighted in the text via an "ethics" icon in the margin. In addition, Chapter 20 is devoted to social and regulation issues relating to marketing practice. Several of the cases also are focused on ethical or regulatory issues, including all of the cases following Part Six.

Consumer Insights

These boxed discussions provide an in-depth look at a particularly interesting consumer study or marketing practice. Each has several questions within it that are designed to encourage critical thinking by the students. Many of the consumer insights are new to the fourteenth edition.

New to This Edition

As with our prior editions, we strive to keep pace with the changing environment surrounding consumer behavior by updating each chapter with the latest research, as well as current and relevant examples from industry. Fresh, new ads, photos, and screenshots have been added throughout the text relating to the discussion of various consumer behavior concepts. We detail below the specific revisions made throughout the fourteenth edition.

CHAPTER 1

- New Consumer Insight on market segmentation based on product-related needs

CHAPTER 2

- New Consumer Insight on Coca-Cola's glocalization strategy (adapting locally, marketing globally)
- Updated tables related to global demographics

CHAPTER 3

- New Chapter Opener on the reversal of gender roles
- Updated tables on gender-based activities, including social media usage

CHAPTER 4

- New Chapter Opener on changing U.S. living situations, with the rise of multigenerational households
- New Consumer Insight on the segmentation of the Generation Y market, using demographic identifiers
- New term (multigenerational household), new section on generations (Generation Alpha) added to the chapter
- Updated tables throughout, especially those referencing the Simmons National Consumer Survey

CHAPTER 5

- New Consumer Insight on ethnic subcultures
- Updated figures and tables, including those referencing the Simmons National Consumer Survey

CHAPTER 6

- New Consumer Insight on American family structures

CHAPTER 7

- New Chapter Opener on brand communities with lululemon
- New Consumer Insight related to the impact on a brand of consumer-generated content posted online about that brand
- Updated Consumer Insight related to online marketing, buzz, and WOM that deals with "astroturfing"
- New term added (brand ambassador)

PART II CASES (new or updated)

- IKEA Uses Market Research to Adapt for Global Markets
- How Social Media Nearly Brought Down United Airlines
- *Grace and Frankie:* The Invisibility of Baby Boomer Women

CHAPTER 8

- New Chapter Opener on brands' use of product placement in video games, movies, video streaming services, and music videos to reach consumers
- Updated Consumer Insight on the effectiveness of advertising in the DVR and "cord-cutting" era
- Updated tables, especially those referencing the Simmons National Consumer Survey

CHAPTER 9

- New Consumer Insight on a brand's repositioning to attract a new consumer segment

CHAPTER 10

- New Chapter Opener on brand personalities, based on Gap Inc.'s brands

CHAPTER 11

- New Chapter Opener on changing consumer attitudes, using avocados as the example

CHAPTER 12

- New Chapter Opener on lifestyles, as related to Cooking Enthusiasts
- Updated figures and tables related to lifestyle segments, such as VALS and Global Mosaic

PART III CASES (new or updated)

- Repositioning McDonald's
- Let's Move! Campaign Celebrities Endorsing Soda?!
- Meal Kits Are Shifting How Consumers Shop for Food
- The Tale of Two Emotional Ads
- The World Shares a Coke

CHAPTER 13

- New Chapter Opener on rituals

CHAPTER 14

- Updates throughout for accuracy and currency

CHAPTER 15

- Updated Consumer Insight on the personalization of the online search experience
- New table on segments of smartphone consumers

CHAPTER 16

- Updated Consumer Insight on context effects

CHAPTER 17

- Major restructuring of "The Evolving Retail Scene" section of the chapter, including learning objective 2, emphasizing omni-channel shopping and mobile retailing
- New Consumer Insight on mobile retailing
- New terms added (showrooming, webrooming)
- New tables on online buying behavior, including smartphone shopping and shopping app downloads
- Updated table on shopping orientations

CHAPTER 18

- Updates throughout for accuracy and currency

PART IV CASES (new or updated)

- Nissan Goes after the Dog Lover Niche
- WAWA Dominates with Its Mobile App

CHAPTER 19

- New Chapter Opener on the role of technology in business relationship marketing
- New Consumer Insight on organizational culture

PART V CASES (new or updated)

- Cuties: How Commodity Fruits Became a Branded Sensation
- Farmers' Brand Loyalty for Heavy Farm Equipment Machinery

CHAPTER 20

- Updates on government regulations and online marketing to children, including social media marketing

PART VI CASES (new or updated)

- Is Crude Puppet Movie Hitting a Dead End on *Sesame Street?*
- COPPA Evolves, but Technology Industries Evolve Faster

END OF CHAPTER ACTIVITIES

Review Questions

The review questions at the end of each chapter allow students or the instructor to test the acquisition of the facts contained in the chapter. The questions require memorization, which we believe is an important, though insufficient, part of learning.

Discussion Questions

These questions can be used to help develop or test the students' understanding of the material in the chapter. Answering these questions requires the student to utilize the material in the chapter to reach a recommendation or solution. However, they can generally be answered without external activities such as customer interviews; therefore, they can be assigned as in-class assignments.

Application Activities

The final learning aid at the end of each chapter is a set of application exercises. These require the students to utilize the material in the chapter in conjunction with external activities such as visiting stores to observe point-of-purchase displays, interviewing customers or managers, or evaluating ads. They range in complexity from short evening assignments to term projects.

ADDITIONAL LEARNING MATERIALS

Three useful sets of learning material are presented outside the chapter format—cases, an overview of consumer research methods, and a format for a consumer behavior audit.

Cases

There are cases at the end of each major section of the text except the first. Many of the cases are new to the fourteenth edition. Many of the cases can be read in class and used to generate discussion of a particular topic. Students like this approach, and many instructors find it a useful way to motivate class discussion.

Other cases are more complex and data intense. They require several hours of effort to analyze. Still others can serve as the basis for a term project. We have used several cases in this manner with success (the assignment is to develop a marketing plan clearly identifying the consumer behavior constructs that underlie the plan).

Each case can be approached from a variety of angles. A number of discussion questions are provided with each case. However, many other questions can be used. In fact, while the cases are placed at the end of the major sections, most lend themselves to discussion at other points in the text as well.

Consumer Research Methods Overview

Appendix A provides a brief overview of the more commonly used research methods in consumer behavior. While not a substitute for a course or text in marketing research, it is a useful review for students who have completed a research course. It can also serve to provide students who have not had such a course with relevant terminology and a very basic understanding of the process and major techniques involved in consumer research.

Consumer Behavior Audit

Appendix B provides a format for doing a consumer behavior audit for a proposed marketing strategy. This audit is basically a list of key consumer behavior questions that should be answered for every proposed marketing strategy. Many students have found it particularly useful if a term project relating consumer behavior to a firm's actual or proposed strategy is required.

AACSB TAGGING   𝕀𝕀𝕀 AACSB INTERNATIONAL

McGraw-Hill Education is a proud corporate member of AACSB International. Understanding the importance and value of AACSB accreditation, *Consumer Behavior: Building Marketing Strategy* recognizes the curricula guidelines detailed in the AACSB standards for business accreditation by connecting selected questions in the text and the test bank to the six general knowledge and skill guidelines in the AACSB standards. The statements contained in *Consumer Behavior: Building Marketing Strategy* are provided only as a guide for the users of this textbook. The AACSB leaves content coverage and assessment within the purview of individual schools, the mission of the school, and the faculty. While the *Consumer Behavior: Building Marketing Strategy* teaching package makes no claim of any specific AACSB qualification or evaluation, we have labeled selected questions according to the six general knowledge and skills areas.

You're in the driver's seat.

Want to build your own course? No problem. Prefer to use our turnkey, prebuilt course? Easy. Want to make changes throughout the semester? Sure. And you'll save time with Connect's auto-grading too.

65%
Less Time Grading

Laptop: McGraw-Hill Education

They'll thank you for it.

Adaptive study resources like SmartBook® 2.0 help your students be better prepared in less time. You can transform your class time from dull definitions to dynamic debates. Find out more about the powerful personalized learning experience available in SmartBook 2.0 at **www.mheducation.com/highered/connect/ smartbook**

Make it simple, make it affordable.

Connect makes it easy with seamless integration using any of the major Learning Management Systems— Blackboard®, Canvas, and D2L, among others—to let you organize your course in one convenient location. Give your students access to digital materials at a discount with our inclusive access program. Ask your McGraw-Hill representative for more information.

Padlock: Jobalou/Getty Images

Solutions for your challenges.

A product isn't a solution. Real solutions are affordable, reliable, and come with training and ongoing support when you need it and how you want it. Our Customer Experience Group can also help you troubleshoot tech problems— although Connect's 99% uptime means you might not need to call them. See for yourself at **status. mheducation.com**

Checkmark: Jobalou/Getty Images

FOR STUDENTS

Effective, efficient studying.

Connect helps you be more productive with your study time and get better grades using tools like SmartBook 2.0, which highlights key concepts and creates a personalized study plan. Connect sets you up for success, so you walk into class with confidence and walk out with better grades.

Study anytime, anywhere.

Download the free ReadAnywhere app and access your online eBook or SmartBook 2.0 assignments when it's convenient, even if you're offline. And since the app automatically syncs with your eBook and SmartBook 2.0 assignments in Connect, all of your work is available every time you open it. Find out more at **www.mheducation.com/readanywhere**

> *"I really liked this app—it made it easy to study when you don't have your text-book in front of you."*
>
> - Jordan Cunningham, Eastern Washington University

No surprises.

The Connect Calendar and Reports tools keep you on track with the work you need to get done and your assignment scores. Life gets busy; Connect tools help you keep learning through it all.

Calendar: owattaphotos/Getty Images

Learning for everyone.

McGraw-Hill works directly with Accessibility Services Departments and faculty to meet the learning needs of all students. Please contact your Accessibility Services office and ask them to email accessibility@mheducation.com, or visit **www.mheducation.com/about/accessibility** for more information.

Top: Jenner Images/Getty Images, Left: Hero Images/Getty Images, Right: Hero Images/Getty Images

Acknowledgments

We enjoy studying, teaching, consulting, and writing about consumer behavior. Most of the faculty we know feel the same. As with every edition of this book, our goal for the fourteenth edition has been to make a book that students enjoy reading and that excites them about a fascinating topic.

Numerous individuals and organizations helped us in the task of writing this edition. We are grateful for their assistance. At the risk of not thanking all who deserve credit, we would like to thank Dr. Sijun Wang at Loyola Marymount University, Dr. Junwu Dong at Guangdong University, Patricia Breman at Strategic Business Insights, Dr. Nancy Sirianni at The University of Alabama, and Dr. Edward Bardi, Professor Emeritus at The University of Toledo. Thanks also to Maggie Kleiser at The University of Oklahoma for her research assistance.

We would also like to thank the many members of the McGraw-Hill Higher Education team, including Editorial Coordinator Christian Lyon, Freelance Developer Gabriela Velasco, Product Development Manager Kelly Delso, Executive Portfolio Manager Meredith Fossel, Content Project Manager Vicki Krug, Assessment Content Project Manager Katie Reuter, Content Licensing Specialist Carrie Burger, and Executive Marketing Manager Nicole Young.

Finally, to our families and colleagues at Alabama, Oregon, and TCU—Thanks for your ongoing support, encouragement, patience, and friendship.

David L. Mothersbaugh
Del I. Hawkins
Susan Bardi Kleiser

Brief Contents

Part One
Introduction 2

CHAPTER ONE
Consumer Behavior and Marketing Strategy 4

Part Two
External Influences 34

CHAPTER TWO
Cross-Cultural Variations in Consumer Behavior 36

CHAPTER THREE
The Changing American Society: Values 78

CHAPTER FOUR
The Changing American Society: Demographics and Social Stratification 110

CHAPTER FIVE
The Changing American Society: Subcultures 150

CHAPTER SIX
The American Society: Families and Households 186

CHAPTER SEVEN
Group Influences on Consumer Behavior 218

● Part Two Cases
   Cases 2–1 through 2–8 259

Part Three
Internal Influences 278

CHAPTER EIGHT
Perception 280

CHAPTER NINE
Learning, Memory, and Product Positioning 322

CHAPTER TEN
Motivation, Personality, and Emotion 364

CHAPTER ELEVEN
Attitudes and Influencing Attitudes 396

CHAPTER TWELVE
Self-Concept and Lifestyle 432

● Part Three Cases
   Cases 3–1 through 3–9 458

Part Four
Consumer Decision Process 484

CHAPTER THIRTEEN
Situational Influences 486

CHAPTER FOURTEEN
Consumer Decision Process and Problem Recognition 512

CHAPTER FIFTEEN
Information Search 534

CHAPTER SIXTEEN
Alternative Evaluation and Selection 566

CHAPTER SEVENTEEN
Outlet Selection and Purchase 596

CHAPTER EIGHTEEN
Postpurchase Processes, Customer Satisfaction, and Customer Commitment 640

● Part Four Cases
   Cases 4–1 through 4–8 674

Part Five
Organizations as Consumers   690

CHAPTER NINETEEN

Organizational Buyer Behavior   692

● Part Five Cases
  Cases 5–1 and 5–2   722

Part Six
Consumer Behavior and Marketing
Regulation   728

CHAPTER TWENTY

Marketing Regulation and Consumer
Behavior   730

● Part Six Cases
  Cases 6–1 and 6–2   757

Appendix A Consumer Research Methods   761
Appendix B Consumer Behavior Audit   772

Indexes   778

Contents

Part One
Introduction   2

CHAPTER ONE
Consumer Behavior and Marketing
Strategy   4

Applications of Consumer Behavior   8
  Marketing Strategy   8
  Regulatory Policy   8
  Social Marketing   8
  Informed Individuals   9
Marketing Strategy and Consumer
Behavior   9
Market Analysis Components   11
  The Consumers   12
  The Company   12
  The Competitors   12
  The Conditions   13
Market Segmentation   13
  Product-Related Need Sets   14
  Customers with Similar Need Sets   15
  Description of Each Group   16
  Attractive Segment(s) to Serve   16
Marketing Strategy   17
  The Product   17
  Communications   18
  Price   19
  Distribution   20
  Service   20
Consumer Decisions   20
Outcomes   21
  Firm Outcomes   21
  Individual Outcomes   22
  Society Outcomes   23
The Nature of Consumer Behavior   24
  External Influences (Part II)   24
  Internal Influences (Part III)   25
  Self-Concept and Lifestyle   26
  Consumer Decision Process (Part IV)   27
  *Organizations (Part V) and Regulation
    (Part VI)   27*

The Meaning of Consumption   27
Summary   29

Part Two
External Influences   34

CHAPTER TWO
Cross-Cultural Variations in Consumer
Behavior   36

The Concept of Culture   40
Variations in Cultural Values   43
  Other-Oriented Values   44
  Environment-Oriented Values   49
  Self-Oriented Values   51
Cultural Variations in Nonverbal
Communications   53
  Time   54
  Space   56
  Symbols   56
  Relationships   57
  Agreements   58
  Things   59
  Etiquette   59
  *Conclusions on Nonverbal
    Communications   60*
Global Cultures   60
  A Global Youth Culture?   61
Global Demographics   62
Cross-Cultural Marketing Strategy   64
  Considerations in Approaching a Foreign Market   65
Summary   69

CHAPTER THREE
The Changing American Society:
Values   78

Changes in American Cultural Values   80
  Self-Oriented Values   80
  Environment-Oriented Values   84
  Other-Oriented Values   88

Marketing Strategy and Values   90
  Green Marketing   90
  Cause-Related Marketing   91
  Marketing to Gay and Lesbian Consumers   93
  Gender-Based Marketing   96
Summary   103

CHAPTER FOUR
The Changing American Society:
Demographics and Social Stratification   110

Demographics   112
  Population Size and Distribution   112
  Occupation   114
  Education   114
  Income   116
  Age   117
Understanding American Generations   119
  Pre-Depression Generation   120
  Depression Generation   120
  Baby Boom Generation   122
  Generation X   123
  Generation Y   125
  Generation Z   128
  Generation Alpha   130
Social Stratification   130
Social Structure in the United States   131
  Upper Americans   131
  Middle Americans   134
  Lower Americans   137
The Measurement of Social Class   138
Social Stratification and Marketing Strategy   139
Summary   142

CHAPTER FIVE
The Changing American Society:
Subcultures   150

The Nature of Subcultures   152
Ethnic Subcultures   154
African Americans   155
  Consumer Segments and Characteristics   156
  Media Usage   156
  Marketing to African Americans   158
Hispanics   160
  Acculturation, Language, and Generational Influences   161
  Marketing to Hispanics   164

Asian Americans   166
  Consumer Segments and Characteristics   168
  Marketing to Asian Americans   169
Native Americans   170
Asian Indian Americans   172
Arab Americans   172
Religious Subcultures   173
  Christian Subcultures   174
  Non-Christian Subcultures   176
Regional Subcultures   177
Summary   179

CHAPTER SIX
The American Society: Families
and Households   186

The Nature and Influence of American Households   188
  The Influence of Households   188
  Types of Households   189
The Household Life Cycle   192
Marketing Strategy Based on the Household
Life Cycle   200
Family Decision Making   202
  The Nature of Family Purchase Roles   202
  Determinants of Family Purchase Roles   204
  Conflict Resolution   205
Marketing Strategy and Family Decision Making   206
Consumer Socialization   207
  The Ability of Children to Learn   207
  The Content of Consumer Socialization   208
  The Process of Consumer Socialization   208
  The Supermarket as a Classroom   210
Marketing to Children   210
Summary   211

CHAPTER SEVEN
Group Influences on Consumer
Behavior   218

Types of Groups   220
  Consumption Subcultures   221
  Brand Communities   224
  Online Communities and Social Networks   226
Reference Group Influences on the Consumption
Process   228
  The Nature of Reference Group Influence   228
  Degree of Reference Group Influence   229

Marketing Strategies Based on Reference Group
Influences   231
   Personal Sales Strategies   231
   Advertising Strategies   232
Communications within Groups and Opinion
Leadership   233
   Situations in Which WOM and Opinion
      Leadership Occur   237
   Characteristics of Opinion Leaders   238
   Marketing Strategy, WOM, and Opinion Leadership   239
Diffusion of Innovations   242
   Categories of Innovations   243
   Diffusion Process   246
   Marketing Strategies and the Diffusion Process   249
Summary   251

Part Two Cases
2–1 IKEA Uses Market Research to Adapt for Global
     Markets   259
2–2 CVS Caremark Discontinues the Sale of
     Tobacco Products   261
2–3 Beats by Dre's Rise to the Top   263
2–4 How Social Media Nearly Brought Down
     United Airlines   265
2–5 *Grace and Frankie:* The Invisibility of Baby
     Boomer Women   268
2–6 American Beagle Outfitters: April Fool's Joke
     Turned Reality   270
2–7 Tide Goes after Green with New Pods   272
2–8 Hispanic Marketing in Online and Mobile
     Formats   274

Part Three
Internal Influences   278

CHAPTER EIGHT
Perception   280

The Nature of Perception   282
Exposure   282
   Selective Exposure   284
   Voluntary Exposure   287
Attention   287
   Stimulus Factors   288
   Individual Factors   294
   Situational Factors   295
   Nonfocused Attention   295

Interpretation   297
   Individual Characteristics   298
   Situational Characteristics   301
   Stimulus Characteristics   301
   Consumer Inferences   304
Perception and Marketing Strategy   306
   Retail Strategy   306
   Brand Name and Logo Development   307
   Media Strategy   308
   Advertisements   310
   Package Design and Labeling   310
Summary   311

CHAPTER NINE
Learning, Memory, and Product
Positioning   322

Nature of Learning and Memory   324
Memory's Role in Learning   325
   Short-Term Memory   325
   Long-Term Memory   327
Learning under High and Low Involvement   330
   Conditioning   330
   Cognitive Learning   335
   Learning to Generalize and Differentiate   336
   Summary of Learning Theories   337
Learning, Memory, and Retrieval   337
   Strength of Learning   339
   Memory Interference   345
   Response Environment   346
Brand Image and Product Positioning   347
   Brand Image   347
   Product Positioning   348
   Product Repositioning   350
Brand Equity and Brand Leverage   351
Summary   355

CHAPTER TEN
Motivation, Personality, and Emotion   364

The Nature of Motivation   366
   Maslow's Hierarchy of Needs   366
   McGuire's Psychological Motives   367
Motivation Theory and Marketing Strategy   372
   Discovering Purchase Motives   373
   Marketing Strategies Based on Multiple
      Motives   374

Motivation and Consumer Involvement   375

Marketing Strategies Based on Motivation Conflict   375

Marketing Strategies Based on Regulatory Focus   376

Personality   377

Multitrait Approach   378

Single-Trait Approach   379

The Use of Personality in Marketing Practice   380

Communicating Brand Personality   381

Emotion   382

Types of Emotions   383

Emotions and Marketing Strategy   384

Emotion Arousal as a Product and Retail Benefit   384

Emotion Reduction as a Product and Retail Benefit   385

Consumer Coping in Product and Service Encounters   385

Emotion in Advertising   386

Summary   388

CHAPTER ELEVEN

Attitudes and Influencing Attitudes   396

Attitude Components   398

Cognitive Component   398

Affective Component   401

Behavioral Component   402

Component Consistency   403

Attitude Change Strategies   405

Change the Cognitive Component   405

Change the Affective Component   406

Change the Behavioral Component   408

Individual and Situational Characteristics That Influence Attitude Change   409

Cue Relevance and Competitive Situation   409

Consumer Resistance to Persuasion   410

Communication Characteristics That Influence Attitude Formation and Change   411

Source Characteristics   411

Appeal Characteristics   415

Message Structure Characteristics   420

Market Segmentation and Product Development Strategies Based on Attitudes   421

Market Segmentation   421

Product Development   421

Summary   423

CHAPTER TWELVE

Self-Concept and Lifestyle   432

Self-Concept   434

Interdependent/Independent Self-Concepts   434

Possessions and the Extended Self   435

Measuring Self-Concept   437

Using Self-Concept to Position Products   438

Marketing Ethics and the Self-Concept   439

The Nature of Lifestyle   441

Measurement of Lifestyle   442

General versus Specific Lifestyle Schemes   443

The VALS™ System   445

The VALS™ Segments   447

Geo-Lifestyle Analysis (Claritas PRIZM®)   448

Claritas PRISM Premier: Social and Lifestage Groups   448

Sample PRIZM Segments   449

An Application of PRIZM   450

International Lifestyles   450

Summary   452

Part Three Cases

3–1 Patagonia's Eco-Fashion Push   458

3–2 Repositioning McDonald's   461

3–3 *Let's Move!* Campaign Celebrities Endorsing Soda?!   462

3–4 Attention, Millennials! Automobile Manufacturers Adapt for You   466

3–5 Meal Kits Are Shifting How Consumers Shop for Food   469

3–6 Hello Kitty Mania   473

3–7 Xerox's Ongoing Battle to Reposition   476

3–8 The Tale of Two Emotional Ads   479

3–9 The World Shares a Coke   481

Part Four

Consumer Decision Process   484

CHAPTER THIRTEEN

Situational Influences   486

The Nature of Situational Influence   488

The Communications Situation   488

The Purchase Situation   489

The Usage Situation   490

The Disposition Situation   490

Situational Characteristics and Consumption Behavior   491
    Physical Surroundings   491
    Social Surroundings   496
    Temporal Perspectives   498
    Task Definition   498
    Antecedent States   499
Ritual Situations   501
Situational Influences and Marketing Strategy   502
Summary   505

CHAPTER FOURTEEN
Consumer Decision Process and Problem Recognition   512

Types of Consumer Decisions   514
    Nominal Decision Making   516
    Limited Decision Making   516
    Extended Decision Making   517
The Process of Problem Recognition   517
    The Nature of Problem Recognition   518
    Types of Consumer Problems   520
Uncontrollable Determinants of Problem Recognition   521
Marketing Strategy and Problem Recognition   522
    Discovering Consumer Problems   523
    Responding to Consumer Problems   525
    Helping Consumers Recognize Problems   526
    Suppressing Problem Recognition   529
Summary   530

CHAPTER FIFTEEN
Information Search   534

The Nature of Information Search   536
Types of Information Sought   536
    Evaluative Criteria   537
    Appropriate Alternatives   537
    Alternative Characteristics   540
Sources of Information   540
    Internet Search   541
    Mobile Search   548
    Marketing Strategy and Mobile Search   549
Amount of External Information Search   550
Costs versus Benefits of External Search   552
    Market Characteristics   552
    Product Characteristics   553
    Consumer Characteristics   553
    Situation Characteristics   554

Marketing Strategies Based on Information Search Patterns   555
    Maintenance Strategy   555
    Disrupt Strategy   555
    Capture Strategy   556
    Intercept Strategy   557
    Preference Strategy   557
    Acceptance Strategy   558
Summary   559

CHAPTER SIXTEEN
Alternative Evaluation and Selection   566

Consumer Choice and Types of Choice Process   568
    Types of Consumer Choice Processes   569
Evaluative Criteria   572
    Nature of Evaluative Criteria   573
    Measurement of Evaluative Criteria   575
Individual Judgment and Evaluative Criteria   577
    Accuracy of Individual Judgments   577
    Use of Surrogate Indicators   578
    The Relative Importance and Influence of Evaluative Criteria   579
    Evaluative Criteria, Individual Judgments, and Marketing Strategy   579
Decision Rules for Attribute-Based Choices   580
    Conjunctive Decision Rule   581
    Disjunctive Decision Rule   582
    Elimination-by-Aspects Decision Rule   583
    Lexicographic Decision Rule   584
    Compensatory Decision Rule   585
    Summary of Decision Rules   587
Summary   590

CHAPTER SEVENTEEN
Outlet Selection and Purchase   596

The Evolving Retail Scene   599
    Online Retailing   600
    Mobile Retailing   602
    Store-Based Retailing   603
    Omni-Channel Retailing for the Omni-Channel Shopper   606
Attributes Affecting Retail Outlet Selection   611
    Outlet Image   611
    Retailer Brands   613
    Retail Advertising   614
    Outlet Location and Size   616

Consumer Characteristics and Outlet Choice   617

   Perceived Risk   617

   Shopping Orientation   619

In-Store and Online Influences on Brand Choices   620

   The Nature of Unplanned Purchases   620

   Point-of-Purchase Materials   622

   Price Reductions and Promotional Deals   623

   Outlet Atmosphere   624

   Stockouts   626

   Website Functioning and Requirements   627

   Mobile and Mobile Apps   627

   Sales Personnel   628

Purchase   629

Summary   629

CHAPTER EIGHTEEN

Postpurchase Processes, Customer Satisfaction, and Customer Commitment   640

Postpurchase Dissonance   642

Product Use and Nonuse   644

   Product Use   644

   Product Nonuse   645

Disposition   647

   Product Disposition and Marketing Strategy   648

Purchase Evaluation and Customer Satisfaction   650

   The Evaluation Process   650

Dissatisfaction Responses   653

   Marketing Strategy and Dissatisfied Consumers   654

Customer Satisfaction, Repeat Purchases, and Customer Commitment   657

   Repeat Purchasers, Committed Customers, and Profits   659

   Repeat Purchasers, Committed Customers, and Marketing Strategy   662

Summary   665

Part Four Cases

4–1 Scent Marketing Reaches Consumers' Emotions   674

4–2 Amazon Prime Air Prepares for Takeoff   676

4–3 Nissan Goes after the Dog Lover Niche   678

4–4 WAWA Dominates with Its Mobile App   680

4–5 Macy's Embraces Beacon Technology   681

4–6 Tesla's Novel and Environmental Approach Drives Amazing Brand Loyalty   683

4–7 Gilt Groupe's Innovative Approach to Loyalty Programs   685

4–8 Albertsons Ditches Self-Checkout in Favor of Human Contact   687

Part Five
Organizations as Consumers   690

CHAPTER NINETEEN
Organizational Buyer Behavior   692

Organizational Purchase Process   694

   Decision-Making Unit   694

   Purchase Situation   696

   Steps in the Organizational Decision Process   698

   The Role of the Internet and Mobile in the Organizational Decision Process   703

Organizational Culture   704

External Factors Influencing Organizational Culture   705

   Firmographics   705

   Culture/Government   708

   Reference Groups   708

Internal Factors Influencing Organizational Culture   709

   Organizational Values   709

   Perception   711

   Learning   713

   Motives and Emotions   713

Organizational Buyer Segments and Marketing Strategy   714

Summary   717

Part Five Cases

5–1 Cuties: How Commodity Fruits Became a Branded Sensation   722

5–2 Farmers' Brand Loyalty for Heavy Farm Equipment Machinery   724

Part Six
Consumer Behavior and Marketing Regulation   728

CHAPTER TWENTY
Marketing Regulation and Consumer Behavior   730

Regulation and Marketing to Children   732

   Concerns about the Ability of Children to Comprehend Commercial Messages   733

   Concerns about the Effects of the Content of Commercial Messages on Children   735

Controversial Marketing Activities Aimed at Children   737

Children's Online Privacy Issues   739

Regulation and Marketing to Adults   741

Consumer Privacy   741

Marketing Communications   742

Product Issues   749

Pricing Issues   750

Summary   751

Part Six Cases

6–1 Is Crude Puppet Movie Hitting a Dead End on *Sesame Street?*   757

6–2 COPPA Evolves, but Technology Industries Evolve Faster   759

Appendix A Consumer Research Methods   761

Appendix B Consumer Behavior Audit   772

Indexes   778

Introduction

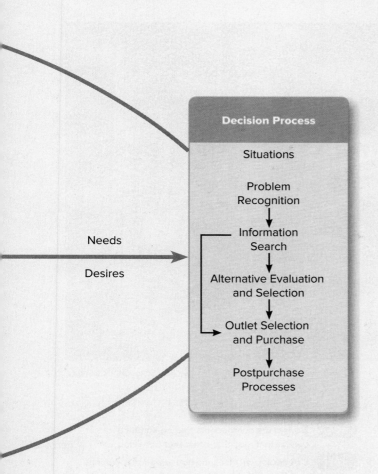

Decision Process

Situations

Problem
Recognition

↓

Information
Search

↓

Alternative Evaluation
and Selection

↓

Outlet Selection
and Purchase

↓

Postpurchase
Processes

Needs

Desires

What is consumer behavior? Why should we study it? Do marketing managers, regulators, and consumer advocates actually use knowledge about consumer behavior to develop strategies and policy? How? Will a sound knowledge of consumer behavior help you in your career? Will it enable you to be a better citizen? How does consumer behavior impact the quality of all of our lives and of the environment? How can we organize our knowledge of consumer behavior to understand and use it more effectively?

Chapter 1 addresses these and a number of other interesting questions, describes the importance and usefulness of the material to be covered in this text, and provides an overview of the text. Chapter 1 also explains the logic of the model of consumer behavior shown here, which is presented again in Figure 1–3 and discussed toward the end of the chapter.

chapter

1

Consumer Behavior and Marketing Strategy

Source: Starbucks Corporation

LEARNING OBJECTIVES

LO1 Define consumer behavior.

LO2 Summarize the applications of consumer behavior.

LO3 Explain how consumer behavior can be used to develop marketing strategy.

LO4 Explain the components that constitute a conceptual model of consumer behavior.

LO5 Discuss issues involving consumption meanings and firm attempts to influence them.

Marketers face exciting and daunting challenges as the forces that drive and shape consumer behavior rapidly evolve. Here are just a few examples.

Evolution of Marketing and Customer Experience—Marketers offer different ways for consumers to get their cup of coffee. Consumers can buy coffee beans and make a cup of coffee. They can buy K-Cup® pods and brew a single cup of coffee. They can opt to go to a coffee shop and buy a cup of coffee. Or they can go to Starbucks and buy a cup of coffee. Which option do you think is more expensive? Likely you would say that the first option is the least expensive and the final option the most expensive—and generally you would be correct! But why is that so? The answer lies in the layers of value that marketers can add to "commodity-like" products. These layers include services and experiences that consumers have indicated are of value to them. Thus, as products move from being a commodity to a good to a service to an experience, consumers are likely to pay more. The success of Starbucks attests to consumer willingness to pay more for a cup of coffee from Starbucks that layers the core product with service and experience. And Starbucks is going further. For example, it recently opened a store in New Orleans that is one of its portfolios of "local relevancy" stores. These *hyper local* stores are designed to provide intense experiential aspects that reflect the historical and cultural ambience of the store's locale.[1] This Starbucks in New Orleans pictured at the beginning of this chapter is a great example of this hyper local approach.

Marketing 2 Consumers versus Marketing 4 Consumers—Marketing has evolved not only in its offerings, but also in its relationship to consumers. A power shift away from marketers to consumers has changed the landscape. Succinctly stated, Marketing 2 Consumers has shifted to Marketing 4 Consumers. Marketing 2 Consumers used mass marketing, a scattered approach to reach as many consumers as possible including unavoidably wasting resources on consumers who have no interest in the product offering. Marketing 2 Consumers saturated consumers with advertisements, repeatedly and frequently, in an effort to gain consumer attention. In contrast, Marketing 4 Consumers uses a more targeted approach in an effort more likely to reach only the consumers who want the marketer's offering. Marketing 4 Consumers recognizes that consumers have the power to choose whether or not they will allow marketers' permission (say with a click on the Internet) to start a dialogue. Product creation is no longer exclusively in the hands of marketers. Consumers can initiate and participate in product innovation by pitching an idea and/or funding a pitch (e.g., Kickstarter, Etsy). Consumers can verify marketers' promises of competitive prices for all nature of things from air fare (e.g., Kayak) to products (e.g., NexTag). And consumers do not have to take marketers at their word because they easily can access customer reviews (e.g., Amazon.com).[2]

Social Media—The power shift from marketers to consumers has been further amplified by the rise of social media—Facebook, Pinterest, Snapchat, Twitter—which place user-generated, consumer-to-consumer(s) communication outside of the direct control and influence of marketers. A humorous example is the more than 8,000 Tweets (on Twitter) reporting the abnormally long receipts CVS gives its customers. Tweets show photos of consumers holding up CVS receipts that stretch above their heads and wrap around their waists. The motivation behind these long receipts is big data. CVS collects data on each customer purchase via the customer's CVS card. When customers check out, the cash register prints out on each consumer's receipt custom coupons mined from the history of previous purchases. CVS was both fortunate and savvy. They noticed the trend (social media allows for this to be done quickly and efficiently), noted

the negativity (consumers' perception of waste and lack of environmental concern), and are reacting (moving more of their coupons and rewards direct to consumer cards). Such "real-time" trend tracking was simply not possible in most cases prior to social and digital media.

This shift in power from Marketing 2 Consumers to Marketing 4 Consumers and the rise of social media have made it all the more crucial for marketers to understand consumer behavior. Marketers' use of crowdsourcing to give voice to their consumers' needs and wants exemplifies marketers' understanding of the need to place consumers at the center of marketing. Examples of online crowdsourcing include Amazon Studios' Amazon Preview, Lay's "Do Us A Flavor," and Lego's LEGO Ideas. These examples show how valuable it can be when marketers talk "with" their customers rather than simply talk "to" them.[3]

LO1

The field of **consumer behavior** is *the study of individuals, groups, or organizations and the processes they use to select, secure, use, and dispose of products, services, experiences, or ideas to satisfy needs and the impacts that these processes have on the consumer and society.* This view of consumer behavior is broader than the traditional one, which focused more narrowly on the buyer and the immediate antecedents and consequences of the purchasing process. Our broader view will lead us to examine more indirect influences on consumption decisions as well as far-reaching consequences that involve more than just the purchaser and the seller.

The opening examples above summarize some attempts to apply an understanding of consumer behavior in a rapidly evolving environment that includes changes in technology and how consumers interact and communicate with firms. Throughout this text, we will explore the factors and trends shaping consumer behavior and the ways marketers and regulators can use this information. Four key aspects regarding consumer behavior are highlighted in this text.

- *Consumer behavior is a complex, multidimensional process.* Consumer decisions often involve numerous steps and are influenced by a host of factors including demographics, lifestyle, and cultural values. Consumer decisions are further complicated when the needs and wants of multiple individuals or groups are considered, as when families must make decisions about where to eat for dinner or where to go on vacation.
- *Successful marketing decisions by firms, nonprofit organizations, and regulatory agencies require an understanding of the processes underlying consumer behavior.* This relates to

Source: Air France

Source: Flexjet

understanding theories about when and why consumers act in certain ways. Whether they realize it or not, organizations are making decisions every day based on explicit or implicit assumptions about what processes drive consumer behavior. Examine the Air France and Flexjet ads in Illustration 1-1. *What assumptions about consumer behavior underlie each ad? Which approach is best? Why?*

- *Successful marketing decisions require organizations to collect information about the specific consumers involved in the marketing decision at hand.* Consumer decisions are heavily influenced by situation and product category. Thus, consumer research is necessary to understand how specific consumers will behave in a specific situation for a given product category. Appendix A examines various consumer research approaches.

- *Marketing practices designed to influence consumer behavior involve ethical issues that affect the firm, the individual, and society.* The issues are not always obvious and many times involve trade-offs at different levels. The fast-food industry is currently dealing with such issues. While their products are highly desirable to many consumers in terms of taste and affordability, they also tend to be high in calories, fat, and sodium. These health-related issues have grabbed the attention of government and consumer groups.

Sufficient knowledge of consumer behavior exists to provide usable guidelines. However, applying these guidelines effectively requires monitoring the environment for changes and factoring those changes into marketing decisions. It also requires practice. We provide a variety of such opportunities in the form of (a) questions and exercises at the end of each chapter, (b) short cases at the end of each main part of the text, and (c) a consumer behavior audit for developing marketing strategy (Appendix B) at the end of the text.

APPLICATIONS OF CONSUMER BEHAVIOR

Marketing Strategy

LO2

Marketing decisions based on explicit consumer behavior theory, assumptions, and research are more likely to be successful than those based on hunches or intuition, and thus create a competitive advantage. An accurate understanding of consumer behavior can greatly reduce the odds of failures such as:

> S.C. Johnson pulled the plug on its Ziploc TableTops, a line of semi-disposable plates. TableTops was one of the company's most expensive launches with $65 million spent on marketing. A number of factors appear to have contributed to the failure including relatively high prices (which made consumers less likely to throw them away) and the fact that the products really weren't all that disposable. As one retailer explained, "There are no repeat purchases. The things last forever."[4]

Thus, a primary goal of this book is to help you obtain a usable managerial understanding of consumer behavior to help you become a more effective marketing manager. Before we take a look at marketing strategy and consumer behavior, let's examine regulatory policy, social marketing, and the importance of being an informed individual.

Regulatory Policy

Various regulatory bodies exist to develop, interpret, and/or implement policies designed to protect and aid consumers. For example, the Food and Drug Administration (FDA) administers the Nutrition Labeling and Education Act (NLEA). Among other things, NLEA requires that packaged foods prominently display nutrition information in the form of the Nutrition Facts panel.

Has NLEA succeeded? One study suggests that it depends. For example, the Nutrition Facts panel is of most benefit to highly motivated consumers who are low in nutritional knowledge. Demonstrating such benefits is important in light of the estimated $2 billion in compliance costs. However, such cost–benefit comparisons are complicated because placing a dollar value on individual and societal benefits is often difficult.[5]

Clearly, effective regulation of many marketing practices requires an extensive knowledge of consumer behavior. We will discuss this issue throughout the text and provide a detailed treatment in Chapter 20.

Social Marketing

Social marketing is *the application of marketing strategies and tactics to alter or create behaviors that have a positive effect on the targeted individuals or society as a whole.*[6] Social marketing has been used in attempts to reduce smoking, to increase the percentage of children receiving their vaccinations in a timely manner, to encourage environmentally sound behaviors such as recycling, to reduce behaviors potentially leading to AIDS, to enhance support of charities, to reduce drug use, and to support many other important causes.

Just as for commercial marketing strategy, successful social marketing strategy requires a sound understanding of consumer behavior. For example, Amazon's "I Love Reading" Kindle campaign (see Illustration 1–2) uses an emotional-based appeal. In Chapter 11, we will analyze the conditions under which such campaigns are likely to succeed.

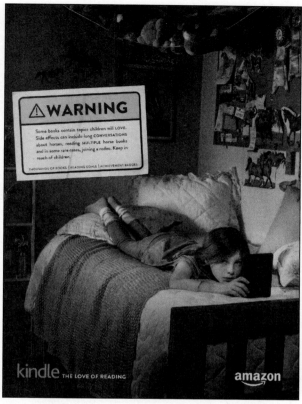

Source: Amazon

Informed Individuals

Most economically developed societies are legitimately referred to as consumption societies. Most individuals in these societies spend more time engaged in consumption than in any other activity, including work or sleep (both of which also involve consumption). In addition, marketers spend billions to influence consumer decisions. These attempts occur in ads, in websites, on packages, as product features, in sales pitches, and in store environments. They also occur in the content of many TV shows, in the brands that are used in movies, and in the materials presented to children in schools.

It is important that consumers accurately understand the strategies and tactics being used so they can be more effective consumers. It is equally important that, as citizens, we understand the consumer behavior basis of these strategies so we can set appropriate limits when required. That is, an understanding of consumer behavior can establish a foundation for reasoned business ethics.

MARKETING STRATEGY AND CONSUMER BEHAVIOR

The applications of consumer behavior involve the development, regulation, and effects of marketing strategy. We now examine marketing strategy in more depth.

Marketing strategy, as described in Figure 1–1, is conceptually very simple. It begins with an analysis of the market the organization is considering. On the basis of the consumer analysis undertaken in this step, the organization identifies groups of individuals, households,

LO3

FIGURE   1-1   Marketing Strategy and Consumer Behavior

or firms with similar needs. These market segments are described in terms of demographics, media preferences, geographic location, and so forth. Management then selects one or more of these segments as target markets on the basis of the firm's capabilities relative to those of its competition (given current and forecasted economic and technological conditions).

Next, marketing strategy is formulated. To survive in a competitive environment, an organization must provide its target customers more value than is provided to them by its competitors. **Customer value** is *the difference between all the benefits derived from a total product and all the costs of acquiring those benefits.* It is critical that a firm consider value *from the customer's perspective.* Ziploc's TableTops failed because consumers felt the benefit of being semi-disposable did not outweigh the cost of the product itself or the guilt they felt about eventually throwing it away. Thus, marketing strategy seeks to provide the customer with more value than the competition while still producing a profit for the firm.

Marketing strategy is formulated in terms of the marketing mix; that is, it involves determining the product features, price, communications, distribution, and services that will provide customers with superior value. This entire set of characteristics is often referred

©ChameleonsEye/Shutterstock

to as the **total product.** The total product is presented to the target market, which is consistently engaged in processing information and making decisions designed to maintain or enhance its lifestyle (individuals and households) or performance (businesses and other organizations).

Look at Illustration 1–3. What is the total product? Clearly, it is much more than food and beverages. It also involves an experience. Increasingly, marketers sell experiences as much as or more than actual products and services. An "experience" occurs when a company intentionally creates a memorable event for customers. While products and services are to a large extent external to the customer, an experience is largely internal to each customer. The experience exists in the mind of an individual who has been engaged on an emotional, physical, intellectual, or even spiritual level.

Outcomes based on the execution of a marketing strategy occur for the firm, the individual, and society. Firms expect to establish an image or position in the marketplace among target customers, generate sales, and ultimately create satisfied customers who are the key to long-term profits. For the individual, the process results in some level of need satisfaction, financial expenditure, attitude creation or change, and/or behavioral changes. Note that some of these behaviors may involve injurious consumption. For society, the cumulative effect of the marketing process affects economic growth, pollution, and social welfare, the latter of which creates many ethical implications.

We detail each phase of Figure 1–1 next.

MARKET ANALYSIS COMPONENTS

Market analysis requires a thorough understanding of the consumption process of potential customers; the organization's own capabilities; the capabilities of current and future competitors; and the economic, physical, and technological environment in which these elements will interact.

The Consumers

It is not possible to anticipate and react to customers' needs and desires without a complete understanding of consumer behavior. Discovering customers' needs is a complex process, but it often can be accomplished by marketing research. For example, Target wanted to tap into the $210 billion college market. In particular, Target was looking at the furnishings and accessories market and was interested in the specific needs and motivations of students making the transition from home to college dorm life. Jump Associates conducted the research for Target and took a unique approach:

> [Jump Associates] sponsored a series of "game nights" at high school grads' homes, inviting incoming college freshmen as well as students with a year of dorm living under their belts. To get teens talking about dorm life, Jump devised a board game that involved issues associated with going to college. The game naturally led to informal conversations—and questions—about college life. Jump researchers were on the sidelines to observe, while a video camera recorded the proceedings.

On the basis of this research (which is a variation of focus groups—see Appendix A), Target successfully launched the Todd Oldham Dorm Room line, which included such products as Kitchen in a Box and Bath in a Box—all-in-one assortments of the types of products needed by college freshmen.[7] Target continues to appeal to the college market with logo merchandise and other dorm products.

Knowing the consumer requires understanding the behavioral principles that guide consumption behaviors. These principles are covered in depth in the remainder of this text.

The Company

A firm must fully understand its own ability to meet customer needs. This involves evaluating all aspects of the firm, including its financial condition, general managerial skills, production capabilities, research and development capabilities, technological sophistication, reputation, and marketing skills. Marketing skills would include new-product development capabilities, channel strength, advertising abilities, service capabilities, marketing research abilities, market and consumer knowledge, and so forth.

Failure to fully understand strengths and weaknesses can cause serious problems. IBM's first attempt to enter the home computer market, with the PC Jr., was a failure in part for that reason. Although IBM had an excellent reputation with large business customers and a very strong direct sales force for serving them, these strengths were not relevant to the household consumer market. Its move into high-end business consulting, through IBM Services, has been a major success and, interestingly, moves IBM back to a focus on its earlier core strengths.

The Competitors

It is not possible to consistently do a better job than the competition of meeting customer needs without a thorough understanding of the competition's capabilities and strategies. This understanding requires the same level of knowledge of a firm's key competitors that is required of one's own firm. In addition, for any significant marketing action, the following questions must be answered:

1. If we are successful, which firms will be hurt (lose sales or sales opportunities)?
2. Of those firms that are injured, which have the capability (financial resources, marketing strengths) to respond?
3. How are they likely to respond (reduce prices, increase advertising, introduce a new product)?
4. Is our strategy (planned action) robust enough to withstand the likely actions of our competitors, or do we need additional contingency plans?

The Conditions

The state of the economy, the physical environment, government regulations, and technological developments affect consumer needs and expectations as well as company and competitor capabilities. The deterioration of the physical environment has produced not only consumer demand for environmentally sound products but also government regulations affecting product design and manufacturing.

International agreements such as NAFTA (North American Free Trade Agreement) have greatly reduced international trade barriers and raised the level of both competition and consumer expectations for many products. And technology is changing the way people live, work, deal with disease, and so on. Corporate websites, social media such as Twitter and Facebook, and mobile apps are just some of the ways technology is changing the way consumers communicate and access media.

Clearly, a firm cannot develop a sound marketing strategy without anticipating the conditions under which that strategy will be implemented.

MARKET SEGMENTATION

Perhaps the most important marketing decision a firm makes is the selection of one or more market segments on which to focus. A **market segment** is *a portion of a larger market whose needs differ somewhat from the larger market.* Because a market segment has unique needs, a firm that develops a total product focused solely on the needs of that segment will be able to meet the segment's desires better than a firm whose product or service attempts to meet the needs of multiple segments.

To be viable, a segment must be large enough to be served profitably. However, it should be noted that technology advances such as flexible manufacturing and customized media are allowing for mass customization such that firms can target smaller segments and even individuals profitably. *Behavioral targeting,* in which consumers' online activity is tracked and specific banner ads are delivered based on that activity, is another example of how technology is making individualized communication increasingly cost-effective.

Market segmentation involves four steps:

1. Identifying product-related need sets.
2. Grouping customers with similar need sets.
3. Describing each group.
4. Selecting an attractive segment(s) to serve.

Source: FCA US LLC

Source: Honda Motor Co., Ltd.

Both the Ram and
Honda ads are for
the same basic prod-
uct. Yet, as these ads
show, the products
are designed to
meet different sets of
needs beyond their
basic function.

Product-Related Need Sets

Organizations approach market segmentation with a set of current and potential capabilities. These capabilities may be a reputation, an existing product, a technology, or some other skill set. The first task of the firm is to identify need sets that the organization is capable, or could become capable, of meeting. The term **need set** is used to reflect the fact that most products in developed economies satisfy more than one need. Thus, a watch can meet more needs than just telling time. Some customers purchase watches to meet status needs, while others purchase them to meet style needs, and so on. Illustration 1-4 shows two truck ads—one for Ram, the other for Honda. Even though these ads are for the same general product, *what needs are these different ads appealing to?*

Identifying the various need sets that the firm's current or potential product might satisfy typically involves consumer research, particularly focus groups and depth interviews, as well as logic and intuition. These need sets often are associated with other variables such as age, stage in the household life cycle, gender, social class, ethnic group, or lifestyle, and many firms start the segmentation process focusing first on one or more of the groups defined by one of these variables. Thus, a firm might start by identifying various ethnic groups and then attempt to discover similarities and differences in consumption-related needs across these groups. While better-defined segments will generally be discovered by focusing first on needs and then on consumer characteristics associated with those needs, both approaches are used in practice and both provide a useful basis for segmentation.

Need sets exist for products and services and can include needs related to various shopping venues. Consumer Insight 1-1 examines the need sets of holiday shoppers.

Need Sets of Holiday Shoppers

What kind of holiday shopper are you? Do you value finding cheap deals? Is convenience important to you? Not all holiday shoppers are equal in terms of what they value. A recent study by Cardlytics, a marketing technology and analytics company, analyzed year-over-year holiday spending from 2015 and 2016 to better understand holiday shoppers. Based on this research, Cardlytics created a typology of four different segments of holiday shoppers based on their needs and purchase behaviors.[8]

As you can see, each of these segments of shoppers has a different need set that is reflected in their shopping behavior as far as timing and retail outlet selection. According to Dani Cushion, Chief Marketing Officer at Cardlytics:

> While a lot of marketers have put all of their eggs in the Black Friday basket, the spend has really flattened out. . . . There are four distinct holiday shopper timing segments, running three weeks each. Each segment contributes to the overall holiday spend.

Marketers should take care to tailor marketing strategies in different ways to target each of these segments.

Critical Thinking Questions

1. Think about yourself and a couple of people you know. Can you match yourselves with one of the four types of holiday shoppers described here? Please discuss.

2. This typology relates specifically to shoppers in the holiday season? How do you think the need sets and purchase behaviors compare/differ for those shopping in general?

3. What advice would you give marketers when they are attempting to target each of these four segments?

Segment	Percent of Holiday Spending (2016)	Needs	Timing of Purchases	Retail Outlet Preferences
Steady Shoppers	46%	Variety and options	Shop throughout holiday season	Online and in-store, from many retailers
Last-Minute Shoppers	28%	Convenience and time savings	Wait to shop until just before the holiday	Online
Black Friday Shoppers	16%	Deals and bargains	Make most purchases on Black Friday	Online and in-store
Early Bird Shoppers	10%	Efficiency and stress reduction	Finish shopping well in advance of holiday	A select few stores

Customers with Similar Need Sets

The next step is to group consumers with similar need sets. For example, the need for moderately priced, fun, sporty automobiles appears to exist in many young single individuals, young couples with no children, and middle-aged couples whose children have left home. These consumers can be grouped into one segment as far as product features and perhaps even product image are concerned despite sharply different demographics. Consumer Insight 1–1 provides an additional example of "clustering" or grouping consumers with similar need sets. For example, those who are early shoppers are all similar in that their need set includes efficiency and stress reduction while holiday shopping.

This step generally involves consumer research, including focus group interviews, surveys, and product concept tests (see Appendix A). It could also involve an analysis of current consumption patterns.

Description of Each Group

Once consumers with similar need sets are identified, they should be described in terms of their demographics, lifestyles, and media usage. Designing an effective marketing program requires having a complete understanding of the potential customers. It is only with such a complete understanding that we can be sure we have correctly identified the need set. In addition, we cannot communicate effectively with our customers if we do not understand the context in which our product is purchased and consumed, how it is thought about by our customers, and the language they use to describe it. Thus, while many young single individuals, young couples with no children, and middle-aged couples whose children have left home may want the same features in an automobile, the media required to reach each group and the appropriate language and themes to use with each group would likely differ.

Attractive Segment(s) to Serve

Once we are sure we have a thorough understanding of each segment, we must select our **target market**—*the segment(s) of the larger market on which we will focus our marketing effort.* This decision is based on our ability to provide the selected segment(s) with superior customer value at a profit. Thus, the size and growth of the segment, the intensity of the current and anticipated competition, the cost of providing the superior value, and so forth are important considerations. Table 1–1 provides a simple worksheet for use in evaluating and comparing the attractiveness of various market segments.

TABLE 1-1   Market Segment Attractiveness Worksheet

Criterion	Score
Segment size	_____
Segment growth rate	_____
Competitor strength	_____
Customer satisfaction with existing products	_____
Fit with company image	_____
Fit with company objectives	_____
Fit with company resources	_____
Distribution available	_____
Investment required	_____
Stability/predictability	_____
Cost to serve	_____
Sustainable advantage available	_____
Communications channels available	_____
Risk	_____
Segment profitability	_____
Other (_____)	_____

*Score on a 1–10 scale, with 10 being most favorable.

As Table 1–1 indicates, segments that are sizable and growing are likely to appear attractive. However, profitability cannot be ignored. After all, a large unprofitable segment is still unprofitable. Finding profitable segments means identifying a maximal fit between customer needs and the firm's offerings. This means that some customers and segments will be unprofitable to serve and may need to be "fired." While firing customers may be difficult, it can lead to greater profits, as Australia-based ING Direct has found. ING Direct is a bare-bones bank. It has limited offerings (no checking) and does most of its transactions online. ING Direct wants "low-maintenance" customers who are attracted by its higher interest rates. As their CEO notes:

> The difference between ING Direct and the rest of the financial industry is like the difference between take-out food and a sit-down restaurant. The business isn't based on relationships; it's based on a commodity product that's high-volume and low-margin. We need to keep expenses down, which doesn't work when customers want a lot of empathetic contact.[9]

ING Direct keeps costs lower and profits higher by identifying high-cost customers and (nicely) letting them go by suggesting they might be better served by a "high-touch" community bank. *Can you think of any potential risks of "firing" customers?*

It is important to remember that each market segment requires its own marketing strategy. Each element of the marketing mix should be examined to determine if changes are required from one segment to another. Sometimes each segment will require a completely different marketing mix, including the product. At other times, only the advertising message or retail outlets may need to differ.

MARKETING STRATEGY

It is not possible to select target markets without simultaneously formulating a general marketing strategy for each segment. A decisive criterion in selecting target markets is the ability to provide superior value to those market segments. Because customer value is delivered by the marketing strategy, the firm must develop its general marketing strategy as it evaluates potential target markets.

Marketing strategy is basically the answer to the question, *How will we provide superior customer value to our target market?*

The answer to this question requires the formulation of a consistent marketing mix. The **marketing mix** is *the product, price, communications, distribution, and services provided to the target market.* It is the combination of these elements that meets customer needs and provides customer value. For example, in the chapter opener, we see that Starbucks creates value through a combination of products, service, and a superior experience.

The Product

A **product** is *anything a consumer acquires or might acquire to meet a perceived need.* Consumers are generally buying need satisfaction, not physical product attributes.[10] As the former head of Revlon said, "in the factory we make cosmetics, in the store we sell hope." Thus, consumers don't purchase quarter-inch drill bits but the ability to create quarter-inch holes. FedEx lost much of its overnight letter delivery business not to UPS or Airborne but to fax machines and the Internet because these technologies could meet the same consumer needs faster, cheaper, or more conveniently.

We use the term *product* to refer to physical products and primary or core services. Thus, an automobile is a product, as is a transmission overhaul or a ride in a taxi. Packaged goods alone (food, beverages, pet products, household products) account for over 30,000 new product introductions each year.[11] Obviously, many of these will not succeed. To be successful, a product must meet the needs of the target market better than the competition's product does.

Product-related decisions also include issues of packaging, branding, and logos, which have functional and symbolic dimensions. When Starbucks changed its logo by eliminating the words "Starbucks Coffee" and the circle around their emblematic "Siren," there was some consumer backlash on social media against this new logo. *Do you think Starbucks' new logo is effective? What factors underlie your judgment?*

Communications

Marketing communications include *advertising, the sales force, public relations, packaging, and any other signal that the firm provides about itself and its products.* An effective communications strategy requires answers to the following questions:

1. *With whom, exactly, do we want to communicate?* While most messages are aimed at the target-market members, others are focused on channel members, or those who influence the target-market members. For example, pediatric nurses often are asked for advice concerning diapers and other nonmedical infant care items. A firm marketing such items would be wise to communicate directly with the nurses.

    Often it is necessary to determine who within the target market should receive the marketing message. For a children's breakfast cereal, should the communications be aimed at the children or the parents, or both? The answer depends on the target market and varies by country.

2. *What effect do we want our communications to have on the target audience?* Often a manager will state that the purpose of advertising and other marketing communications is to increase sales. While this may be the ultimate objective, the behavioral objective for most marketing communications is often much more immediate. That is, it may seek to have the audience learn something about the product, seek more information about the product, like the product, recommend the product to others, feel good about having bought the product, or a host of other communications effects.

3. *What message will achieve the desired effect on our audience?* What words, pictures, and symbols should we use to capture attention and produce the desired effect? Marketing messages can range from purely factual statements to pure symbolism. The best approach depends on the situation at hand. Developing an effective message requires a thorough understanding of the meanings the target audience attaches to words and symbols, as well as knowledge of the perception process. Consider the Weber ad in Illustration 1–5. Some female consumers may not relate to the approach of this ad. However, it communicates clearly to its intended male market.

4. *What means and media should we use to reach the target audience?* Should we use personal sales to provide information? Can we rely on the package to provide needed information? Should we advertise in mass media, use direct mail, or rely on consumers to find us on the Internet? If we advertise in mass media, which media (television, radio, magazines, newspapers, Internet) and which specific vehicles (television programs, specific magazines, websites, banner ads, and so forth) should we use? Is it necessary or desirable to adjust the language used? With respect to the media and language issues, MasterCard's approach is instructive. They indicate that

    > Hispanics are the largest and fastest growing ethnic group in the U.S. . . . As we continue to bring value to Hispanic consumers, it is important for MasterCard to be speaking their language in the channels that are relevant to them.[12]

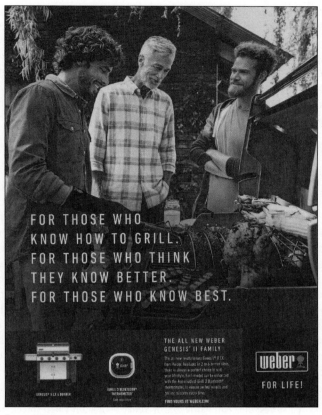

Source: Weber

FOR THOSE WHO KNOW HOW TO GRILL.
FOR THOSE WHO THINK THEY KNOW BETTER.
FOR THOSE WHO KNOW BEST.

THE ALL NEW WEBER GENESIS' II FAMILY

weber
FOR LIFE!

5. *When should we communicate with the target audience?* Should we concentrate our communications near the time that purchases tend to be made or evenly throughout the week, month, or year? Do consumers seek information shortly before purchasing our product? If so, where? Answering these questions requires knowledge of the decision process used by the target market for this product.

Price

Price is *the amount of money one must pay to obtain the right to use the product.* One can buy ownership of a product or, for many products, limited usage rights (i.e., one can rent or lease the product, as with a car). Economists often assume that lower prices for the same product will result in more sales than higher prices. However, price sometimes serves as a signal of quality. A product priced "too low" might be perceived as having low quality. Owning expensive items also provides information about the owner. If nothing else, it indicates that the owner can afford the expensive item. This is a desirable feature to some consumers. Starbucks charges relatively high prices for its coffee. Yet it understands that the Starbucks brand allows consumers to "trade up" to a desired image and lifestyle without breaking the bank. Therefore, setting a price requires a thorough understanding of the symbolic role that price plays for the product and target market in question.

It is important to note that the price of a product is not the same as the cost of the product to the customer. **Consumer cost** is *everything the consumer must surrender in order to* *receive the benefits of owning/using the product.* As described earlier, the cost of owning/using an automobile includes insurance, gasoline, maintenance, finance charges, license fees, parking fees, time and discomfort while shopping for the car, and perhaps even discomfort about increasing pollution, in addition to the purchase price. One of the ways firms seek to provide customer value is to reduce the nonprice costs of owning or operating a product. If successful, the total cost to the customer decreases while the revenue to the marketer stays the same or even increases.

Distribution

Distribution, *having the product available where target customers can buy it,* is essential to success. Only in rare cases will customers go to much trouble to secure a particular brand. Obviously, good channel decisions require a sound knowledge of where target customers shop for the product in question. Today's distribution decisions also require an understanding of cross-channel options. Savvy retailers are figuring out ways to let each distribution channel (e.g., online versus offline) do what it does best. For example, retailers often are challenged to balance appropriate types and levels of in-store inventory with interactive kiosks. Obviously, retailers who adopt this approach have to choose an appropriate merchandising strategy where fast-moving, high-profit, seasonal items are in-store to attract customers while other merchandise is available online.[13] Finally, retailer characteristics need to be understood and delivered upon. Disney is in the process of renovating its stores to be more interactive, and this has driven increased store visits and sales. The remodel seems to focus on entertainment that is especially appropriate in light of its brand and customer. Specifically,

> In the newly designed stores, kids can battle Darth Vader on a giant video screen, or interact with other characters from the Disney, Pixar, "Star Wars" and Marvel franchises. . . . The same screen will show live feeds of parades at Disney theme parks.[14]

Service

Earlier, we defined *product* to include primary or core services such as haircuts, car repairs, and medical treatments. Here, **service** refers to *auxiliary or peripheral activities that are performed to enhance the primary product or primary service.* Thus, we would consider car repair to be a product (primary service), while free pickup and delivery of the car would be an auxiliary service. Although many texts do not treat service as a separate component of the marketing mix, we do because of the critical role it plays in determining market share and relative price in competitive markets. A firm that does not explicitly manage its auxiliary services is at a competitive disadvantage.

Auxiliary services cost money to provide. Therefore, it is essential that the firm furnish only those services that provide value to the target customers. Providing services that customers do not value can result in high costs and high prices without a corresponding increase in customer value.

CONSUMER DECISIONS

As Figure 1–1 illustrated, the consumer decision process intervenes between the marketing strategy (as implemented in the marketing mix) and the outcomes. That is, the outcomes of the firm's marketing strategy are determined by its interaction with the consumer decision process. The firm can succeed only if consumers see a need that its product can solve, become aware of the product and its capabilities, decide that it is the best available solution, proceed to buy it, and become satisfied with the results of the purchase. A significant part of this text is devoted to the understanding of the consumer decision process.

OUTCOMES

Firm Outcomes

Product Position   The most basic outcome of a firm's marketing strategy is its **product position**—*an image of the product or brand in the consumer's mind relative to competing products and brands.* This image consists of a set of beliefs, pictorial representations, and feelings about the product or brand. It does not require purchase or use for it to develop. It is determined by communications about the brand from the firm and other sources, as well as by direct experience with it. Most marketing firms specify the product position they want their brands to have and measure these positions on an ongoing basis. This is because a brand whose position matches the desired position of a target market is likely to be purchased when a need for that product arises.

The Lunchables ad in Illustration 1–6 is positioning the brand as a fun brand. This image and personality are facilitated and enhanced by the color and imagery used.

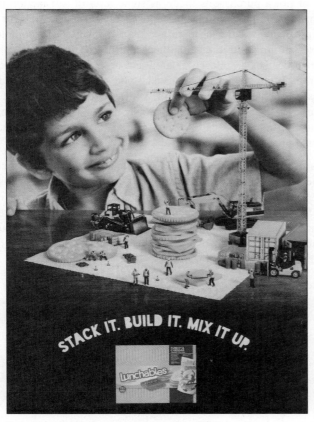

Source: Kraft Foods, H.J. Heinz Company Brands LLC

ILLUSTRATION 1-6

This Lunchables ad positions the brand as fun.

Sales and Profits   Sales and profits are critical outcomes, as they are necessary for the firm to continue in business. Therefore, virtually all firms evaluate the success of their marketing programs in terms of sales revenues and profits. As we have seen, sales and profits are likely to occur only if the initial consumer analysis was correct and if the marketing mix matches the consumer decision process.

Customer Satisfaction   Marketers have discovered that it is generally more profitable to maintain existing customers than to replace them with new customers. Retaining current customers requires that they be satisfied with their purchase and use of the product. Thus, **customer satisfaction** is a major concern of marketers.

As Figure 1–2 indicates, convincing consumers that your brand offers superior value is necessary in order to make the initial sale. Obviously, one must have a thorough understanding of the potential consumers' needs and of their information acquisition processes to succeed at this task. However, *creating satisfied customers,* and thus future sales, requires that customers continue to believe that your brand meets their needs and offers superior value *after they have used it.* You must deliver as much or more value than your customers initially expected, and it must be enough to satisfy their needs. Doing so requires an even greater understanding of consumer behavior.

Individual Outcomes

Need Satisfaction   The most obvious outcome of the consumption process for an individual, whether or not a purchase is made, is some level of satisfaction of the need that initiated the consumption process. This can range from no satisfaction (or even a negative level if a purchase increases the need rather than reduces it) to complete satisfaction. Two key processes are involved: the actual need fulfillment and the perceived need fulfillment. These two processes are closely related and are often identical. However, at times they differ. For example, people might take food supplements because they believe the supplements are enhancing their health, while in reality they could have no direct health effects or even negative effects. One objective of government regulation, and a frequent goal of consumer groups, is to ensure that consumers can adequately judge the extent to which products are meeting their needs.

 Injurious Consumption   Although we tend to focus on the benefits of consumption, we must remain aware that consumer behavior has a dark side. **Injurious consumption** occurs *when individuals or groups make consumption decisions that have negative consequences for their long-run well-being.* Examples can include (a) overspending due to aggressive marketing efforts and cheap credit; (b) consuming products that are not healthy including fast foods, cigarettes, alcohol, and so on; and (c) engaging in activities such as gambling that can have devastating financial consequences for some.

FIGURE   1-2   Creating Satisfied Customers

One product that caught the attention of the FDA was caffeinated alcohol beverages. They tend to be large in volume and also contain high levels of alcohol and caffeine. It is estimated that one can of these new caffeinated alcohol beverages has the same impact on people as drinking five to six beers. These beverages also increase the chances that people engage in dangerous behaviors such as driving under the influence, in part because the caffeine causes them to misgauge how intoxicated they are.[15]

Although these are issues we should be concerned with, and we will address them throughout this text, we also should note that alcohol consumption seems to have arisen simultaneously with civilization, and evidence of gambling is nearly as old. Consumers smoked and chewed tobacco long before mass media or advertising as we know it existed, and illegal drug consumption continues to grow worldwide despite the absence of large-scale marketing, or at least advertising. Thus, though marketing activities based on knowledge of consumer behavior undoubtedly exacerbate some forms of injurious consumption, they are not the sole cause, and, as we will see shortly, such activities may be part of the cure.

Society Outcomes

Economic Outcomes   The cumulative impact of consumers' purchase decisions, including the decision to forgo consumption, is a major determinant of the state of a given country's economy. Consumers' decisions on whether to buy or to save affect economic growth, the availability and cost of capital, employment levels, and so forth. The types of products and brands purchased influence the balance of payments, industry growth rates, and wage levels. Decisions made in one society—particularly large, wealthy societies such as those of the United States, Western Europe, and Japan—have a major impact on the economic health of many other countries.

Physical Environment Outcomes   Consumers make decisions that have a major impact on the physical environments of both their own and other societies. The cumulative effect of U.S. consumers' decisions to rely on relatively large private cars rather than mass transit results in significant air pollution in American cities as well as the consumption of nonrenewable resources from other countries. The decisions of people in most developed and in many developing economies to consume meat as a primary source of protein result in the clearing of rain forests for grazing land; the pollution of many watersheds due to large-scale feedlots; and an inefficient use of grain, water, and energy to produce protein. It also appears to produce health problems for many consumers. Similar effects are being seen as ethanol (made from corn, sugar cane, or rice) becomes a more popular alternative to oil as a source of fuel for automobiles. The high cost of fuel, along with the diversion of grain from food to fuel, is driving up food costs and threatens to increase poverty levels around the world.[16] Such outcomes attract substantial negative publicity. However, these resources are being used because of consumer demand, and consumer demand consists of the decisions you and I and our families and our friends make!

As we will see in Chapter 3, many consumers now recognize the indirect effects of consumption on the environment and are altering their behavior to minimize environmental harm.

Social Welfare   Consumer decisions affect the general social welfare of a society. Decisions concerning how much to spend for private goods (personal purchases) rather than public goods (support for public education, parks, health care, and the like) are generally made indirectly by consumers' elected representatives. These decisions have a major impact on the overall quality of life in a society.

Injurious consumption, as described above, affects society as well as the individuals involved. The social costs of smoking-induced illnesses, alcoholism, and drug abuse are staggering. To the extent that marketing activities increase or decrease injurious consumption, they have a major impact on the social welfare of a society. Consider the following:

> According to the U.S. Public Health Service, of the 10 leading causes of death in the United States, at least 7 could be reduced substantially if people at risk would change just 5 behaviors: compliance (e.g., use of antihypertensive medication), diet, smoking, lack of exercise, and alcohol and drug abuse. Each of these behaviors is inextricably linked with marketing efforts and the reactions of consumers to marketing campaigns. The link between consumer choices and social problems is clear.[17]

However, the same authors conclude: "Although these problems appear daunting, they are all problems that are solvable through altruistic [social] marketing." Thus, marketing and consumer behavior can both aggravate and reduce serious social problems.

THE NATURE OF CONSUMER BEHAVIOR

LO4

Figure 1–3 shows the model that we use to capture the general structure and process of consumer behavior and to organize this text. It is a **conceptual model.** It does not contain sufficient detail to predict particular behaviors; however, it does reflect our beliefs about the general nature of consumer behavior. Individuals develop self-concepts (their view of themselves) and subsequent lifestyles (how they live) based on a variety of internal (mainly psychological and physical) and external (mainly sociological and demographic) influences. These self-concepts and lifestyles produce needs and desires, many of which require consumption decisions to satisfy. As individuals encounter relevant situations, the consumer decision process is activated. This process and the experiences and acquisitions it produces in turn influence the consumers' self-concept and lifestyle by affecting their internal and external characteristics.

Of course, life is rarely so structured as Figure 1–3 and our discussion of it so far may seem to suggest. Consumer behavior is hardly ever so simple, structured, conscious, mechanical, or linear. A quick analysis of your own behavior and that of your friends will reveal that, on the contrary, consumer behavior is frequently complex, disorganized, nonconscious, organic, and circular. Remember—Figure 1–3 is only a model, a starting point for our analysis. It is meant to aid you in thinking about consumer behavior. As you look at the model and read the following chapters based on this model, continually relate the descriptions in the text to the rich world of consumer behavior that is all around you.

The factors shown in Figure 1–3 are given detailed treatment in the subsequent chapters of this book. Here we provide a brief overview so that you can initially see how they work and fit together. Our discussion here and in the following chapters moves through the model from left to right.

External Influences (Part II)

Dividing the factors that influence consumers into categories is somewhat arbitrary. For example, we treat learning as an internal influence despite the fact that much human learning involves interaction with, or imitation of, other individuals. Thus, learning also could be considered a group process. In Figure 1–3, the two-directional arrow connecting internal and external influences indicates that each set interacts with the other.

We organize our discussion of external influences from large-scale macrogroups to smaller, more microgroup influences. *Culture* is perhaps the most pervasive influence on consumer behavior. We begin our consideration of culture in Chapter 2 by examining

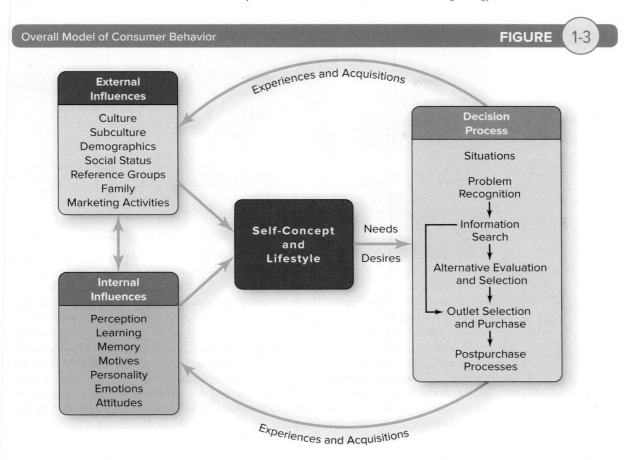

FIGURE 1-3

Overall Model of Consumer Behavior

differences in consumption patterns across cultures. In Chapters 3 through 7, we focus on American culture in detail. In Chapter 3, we examine cultural values. As we will see, while Americans share many values and consumption behaviors, there are also rich diversity and ongoing change in this society that create both marketing opportunities and unique social energy. The Tommy Hilfiger ad in Illustration 1-7 shows how marketers are embracing this diversity in their advertisements.

Chapter 4 continues our examination of American society by analyzing its demographics (the number, education, age, income, occupation, and location of individuals in a society) and social stratification. Chapter 5 considers ethnic, religious, and regional subcultures. Chapter 6 analyzes families, households, and household decision making. Finally, in Chapter 7, we look at the processes by which groups influence consumer behavior and group communication, including the role of groups in the acceptance of new products and technologies. Taken together, Chapters 2 through 7 provide a means of comparing and contrasting the various external factors that influence consumer behavior in America—and around the world. Cross-cultural variations are highlighted when possible throughout the text.

Internal Influences (Part III)

Internal influences begin with perception, the process by which individuals receive and assign meaning to stimuli (Chapter 8). This is followed by learning—changes in the content or structure of long-term memory (Chapter 9). Chapter 10 covers three closely related

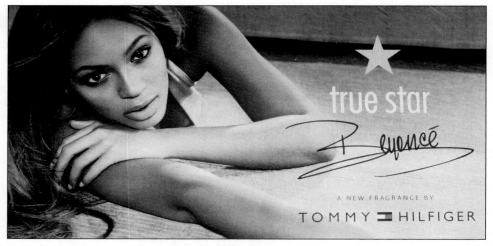

Source: Tommy Hilfiger

topics: motivation—the reason for a behavior; personality—an individual's characteristic response tendencies across similar situations; and emotion—strong, relatively uncontrolled feelings that affect our behavior. We conclude our coverage of internal influences by examining attitudes in Chapter 11. An attitude is an enduring organization of motivational, emotional, perceptual, and cognitive processes with respect to some aspect of our environment. In essence, an attitude is the way a person thinks, feels, and acts toward some aspect of his or her environment, such as a retail store, television program, or product. As such, our attitudes are heavily influenced by the external and internal factors that we will have discussed in the preceding chapters.

Self-Concept and Lifestyle

Chapter 12 concludes Part III with a detailed discussion of the key concepts of self-concept and lifestyle around which our model revolves. As a result of the interaction of the internal and external variables described earlier, individuals develop a self-concept that is reflected in a lifestyle. **Self-concept** is *the totality of an individual's thoughts and feelings about him- or herself.* **Lifestyle** is, quite simply, *how one lives,* including the products one buys, how one uses them, what one thinks about them, and how one feels about them. Lifestyle is the manifestation of the individual's self-concept, the total image the person has of him- or herself as a result of the culture he or she lives in and the individual situations and experiences that comprise his or her daily existence. It is the sum of the person's past decisions and future plans.

Both individuals and families exhibit distinct lifestyles. We often hear of "career-oriented individuals," "outdoor families," or "devoted parents." One's lifestyle is determined by both conscious and unconscious decisions. Often we make choices with full awareness of their impact on our lifestyle, but generally we are unaware of the extent to which our decisions are influenced by our current or desired lifestyle. Our model shows that consumers' self-concepts and lifestyles produce needs and desires that interact with the situations in which consumers find themselves to trigger the consumer decision process.

We do not mean to imply that consumers think in terms of lifestyle. None of us consciously think, "I'll have an Evian bottled water in order to enhance my lifestyle." Rather, we make decisions consistent with our lifestyles without deliberately considering lifestyle. Most consumer decisions involve very little effort or thought on the part of the consumer. They are what we call *low-involvement decisions.* Feelings and emotions are as important in many consumer decisions as logical analysis or physical product attributes. Nonetheless, most consumer purchases involve at least a modest amount of decision making, and most are influenced by the purchaser's current and desired lifestyle.

Consumer Decision Process (Part IV)

Consumer decisions result from perceived problems ("I'm thirsty") and opportunities ("That looks like it would be fun to try"). We will use the term *problem* to refer both to problems and to opportunities. Consumer problems arise in specific situations and the nature of the situation influences the resulting consumer behavior. Therefore, we provide a detailed discussion of situational influences on the consumer decision process in Chapter 13.

As Figure 1–3 indicates, a consumer's needs/desires may trigger one or more levels of the consumer decision process. It is important to note that for most purchases, consumers devote very little effort to this process, and emotions and feelings often have as much or more influence on the outcome as do facts and product features. Despite the limited effort that consumers often devote to the decision process, the results have important effects on the individual consumer, the firm, and the larger society. Therefore, we provide detailed coverage of each stage of the process: problem recognition (Chapter 14); information search (Chapter 15); alternative evaluation and selection (Chapter 16); outlet selection and purchase (Chapter 17); and use, disposition, and purchase evaluation (Chapter 18). The increasing role of technology, particularly the Internet, in consumer decision making is highlighted throughout these chapters.

Organizations (Part V) and Regulation (Part VI)

Organizations or businesses also can be consumers as when Mercedes-Benz purchases dashboard subcomponents from a supplier. This type of marketing often is termed business-to-business (B2B) marketing to differentiate it from business-to-consumer (B2C) marketing that is the focus of much of this text. The special nature of organizations and how they behave warrant special attention. In Chapter 19, we show how our model of individual and household consumer behavior can be modified to help understand the consumer behavior of organizations.

Regulation is an aspect of consumer behavior that permeates marketer actions relating to all parts of our model and it warrants special attention as well. Chapter 20 focuses our attention on the regulation of marketing activities, especially those targeting children. We pay particular attention to the role that knowledge of consumer behavior plays or could play in regulation.

THE MEANING OF CONSUMPTION

LO5

As we proceed through this text, we will describe the results of studies of consumer behavior, discuss theories about consumer behavior, and present examples of marketing programs designed to influence consumer behavior. While reading this material, however, do not lose sight of the fact that consumer behavior is not just a topic of study or a basis for developing marketing or regulatory strategy. Consumption frequently has deep meaning for the consumer.[18]

Consumption Meaning and Motivation

Consumer behavior is the study of why consumers buy. Understanding consumer behavior is at the heart of marketing strategy and a major focus of this text. Government agencies must "sell" ideas and services (e.g., The Affordable Care Act, tax increases) to citizens. Nonprofits must convince consumers to contribute to their organizations (e.g., Salvation Army). Companies must persuade consumers to buy their products and services. Some products and services are essential. However, much of consumption is not need-based, at least in a functional sense. Many companies spend considerable money and effort convincing consumers to buy products, services, or brands they don't really need. And consumers often want products and services they cannot afford, which, if acted on, can lead to negative financial consequences such as crushing credit card debt. In this insight we explore some of the factors driving consumer purchases that drive at the deeper meaning of consumption beyond mere function and necessity.

Meaning in the mundane—Sometimes consumers know what they want—from simple and relatively inexpensive everyday things like milk, bread, and socks, which require little decision effort, to more expensive items such as cars, TVs, and homes, which require considerable decision effort. Even in these situations where products meet basic needs, there can be far more meaning in the objects purchased than might meet the eye. Cars and homes can take on important meanings over time when they are associated with major events such as a first date, a child's first step, and so on. Even truly mundane products can attain heightened meaning if associated with important events or people in one's life. Chapter 12 deals with this idea of products becoming a part of the extended self and as a consequence taking on much deeper meanings than might initially seem possible.

Meaning in avoidance—Consumers often know what they don't want—at least at the broadest level—and make consumption choices accordingly. Consumers don't want fear of physical harm in their lives—so they buy cars with safety enhancements and products such as smoke alarms and carbon monoxide detectors to reduce physical risk. Consumers don't want financial risk in their lives—so they buy insurance and extended warranties, and hire financial planners. Risk and risk avoidance are an important part of consumer behavior and decision making, as discussed in Chapter 3 and Chapter 16.

Meaning in innovative brands—The iPhone is unquestionably a marketing success. It has helped to make Apple one of the most profitable companies in the world.[19]

Consider the example of a man named Andre Hank. Andre, just escaping homelessness, proudly states that he was able to save for and buy a pair of Nikes. He could undoubtedly have purchased a different brand that would have met his physical needs just as well as the Nikes for much less money. Although Andre does not state why he bought the more expensive Nikes, a reasonable interpretation is that they serve as a visible symbol that Andre is back as a successful member of society. In fact, Nike is sometimes criticized for creating, through its marketing activities, symbols of success or status that are unduly expensive. *Consider this issue as you read about the various meanings and motives underlying Consumer Insight 1-2.*[20]

As you read the chapters that follow, keep in mind that the decisions consumers make are the result of a complex set of forces, often reflecting meaning and motivations that are powerful, nuanced, and beyond mere function.

Consumers willingly wait in long lines for hours to have the chance to buy a new version of the iPhone. And yet, consumers didn't know they wanted that product until it already existed. The iPhone is clearly more than just a phone. It has many meanings to consumers—including innovative, cutting-edge, sophisticated, intellectual—that consumers buy as much as or more than the phone. In fact, a brand's personality can be as much a driver of purchase as how well it meets functional requirements, as discussed in Chapter 10.

The more radical the innovation, the more marketers must be able to see the match between customer core needs and the possibilities created by emerging technology. Below are a few quotes about the challenges of *innovating ahead of the customer*.

> You can't just ask customers what they want and then try to give that to them. By the time you get it built, they'll want something new.[21]
>
> —Steve Jobs

> It's really hard to design products by focus groups. A lot of times, people don't know what they want until you show it to them.[22]
>
> —Steve Jobs

The iPhone is a marketer's dream. However, most new products do not succeed. Why this is so and how marketers can adapt their strategies is a key aspect of Chapter 7.

Meaning beyond function—Women's hair removal is highly popular in the United States and has led to a thriving industry including razors, chemical depilatories, and electrolysis. However, women in other parts of the world—France, Italy, China—do not shave.[23] Crest's introduction of "Whitestrips" in 2001 created a new over-the-counter product to whiten teeth that has since grown to a multimillion-dollar market.[24] Such examples highlight the fact that "needs" come in various forms. While being hair-free under one's arms or having whiter teeth may not improve one's physical well-being, in many countries and cultures, such attributes are related to the need to belong or to be respected, as discussed in Chapter 10. Some consumer groups argue that marketers create unnecessary needs on the part of the consumer and worry about their consequences for both the individual and society, as discussed in Chapter 20.

Critical Thinking Questions

1. How and why do you think products acquire meaning to consumers?
2. Can you see any potential negative consequences to marketing attempts to encourage purchases of products consumers don't need?
3. Do marketers create needs?

SUMMARY

LO1: Define consumer behavior.

The field of *consumer behavior* is the study of individuals, groups, or organizations and the processes they use to select, secure, use, and dispose of products, services, experiences, or ideas to satisfy needs and the impacts that these processes have on the consumer and society.

LO2: Summarize the applications of consumer behavior.

Consumer behavior can be applied in four areas: (a) marketing strategy, (b) regulatory policy, (c) social marketing, and (d) creation of informed individuals. Developing marketing strategy involves setting levels of the marketing mix based on an understanding of the market and segments involved to create desirable outcomes. Developing regulatory guidelines involves developing policies, guidelines, and laws to protect and aid consumers. *Social marketing* is the application of marketing strategies and tactics to alter or create behaviors that have a positive effect on the targeted individuals or society as a whole. Creating more informed individuals involves educating consumers about their own consumption behaviors as well as marketers' efforts to influence them in such a way as to create a more sound citizenship, effective purchasing behavior, and reasoned business ethics.

LO3: Explain how consumer behavior can be used to develop marketing strategy.

The interplay between consumer behavior and marketing strategy involves five stages. First is market analysis, which involves gathering data and tracking trends related to the company, competitors, conditions, and consumers. Second is market segmentation. A *market segment* is a portion of a larger market whose needs differ somewhat from the larger market. Firms segment their markets and choose a segment or segments that best fit their capabilities and market conditions. Third is marketing strategy, which involves setting appropriate levels for the marketing mix as a function of the segments being targeted and the market conditions that exist. Fourth is the consumer decision process, which is a series of steps starting with problem recognition and moving through information search, alternative evaluation, purchase, use, and postpurchase evaluation. Marketing efforts can be targeted to these different stages. Fifth is outcomes at the individual, firm, and societal levels. And while profit maximization is often a goal at the firm level, possible adverse effects at the individual and societal level are of importance to firms, government organizations, and regulators. An understanding of consumer behavior theory and concepts is critical at each stage as marketers gather information, develop marketing strategies to influence consumer decisions, and evaluate the effects of their marketing efforts.

LO4: Explain the components that constitute a conceptual model of consumer behavior.

The conceptual model of consumer behavior developed here can be broken into four interrelated parts. External and internal influences affect the consumer's self-concept and lifestyle, which, in turn, affects the decision process. External influences (Part II of the text) include culture, reference groups, demographics, and marketing activities. Internal influences (Part III) include perception, emotions, attitudes, and personality. *Self-concept* is the totality of an individual's thoughts and feelings about him- or herself. *Lifestyle* is, quite simply, how one lives, including the products one buys, how one uses them, what one thinks about them, and how one feels about them. External and internal factors operate to influence self-concept and lifestyle, which, in turn, influences the decision process (Part IV). Overlaying these basic components is organizations (Part V) and regulation (Part VI). Organizations or businesses also can be consumers, as when Mercedes-Benz purchases dashboard subcomponents from a supplier. This type of marketing often is termed business-to-business (B2B) marketing to differentiate it from business-to-consumer (B2C) marketing, which is the focus of much of this text. The special nature of organizations and how they behave warrant special attention. Regulation is an aspect of consumer behavior that permeates marketer actions relating to all parts of our model and it warrants special attention as well.

LO5: Discuss issues involving consumption meanings and firm attempts to influence them.

Consumption has meaning beyond the satisfaction of minimum or basic consumer needs. Thus, consumers might purchase Nike sneakers not only to satisfy the functional needs associated with safety and support, but also for symbolic needs associated with status, identity, and group acceptance. Some criticize marketers for their attempts to instill in, or amplify, consumer desires for products beyond minimum functional aspects. And while this criticism may hold true, it also seems likely that such desires and symbolic meanings are naturally assigned to objects even in the relative absence of marketing. Nonetheless, the ethical implications of marketers' actions in this regard are important to consider.

KEY TERMS

Conceptual model 24
Consumer behavior 6
Consumer cost 19
Customer satisfaction 22
Customer value 10
Distribution 20
Injurious consumption 22

Lifestyle 26
Marketing communications 18
Marketing mix 17
Marketing strategy 17
Market segment 13
Need set 14
Price 19

Product 17
Product position 21
Self-concept 26
Service 20
Social marketing 8
Target market 16
Total product 11

REVIEW QUESTIONS

1. How is the field of consumer behavior defined?
2. What conclusions can be drawn from the examples at the beginning of this chapter?
3. What are the four major uses or applications of an understanding of consumer behavior?
4. What is *social marketing?*
5. What is *customer value,* and why is it important to marketers?
6. What is required to provide superior customer value?
7. What is a *total product?*
8. What is involved in the *consumer* analysis phase of market analysis in Figure 1–1?
9. What is involved in the *company* analysis phase of market analysis in Figure 1–1?
10. What is involved in the *competitor* analysis phase of market analysis in Figure 1–1?
11. What is involved in the *conditions* analysis phase of market analysis in Figure 1–1?
12. Describe the process of *market segmentation.*
13. What is *marketing strategy?*
14. What is a *marketing mix?*
15. What is a *product?*
16. What does an effective communications strategy require?
17. What is a *price?* How does the price of a product differ from the *cost of the product to the consumer?*
18. How is *service* defined in the text?
19. What is involved in creating satisfied customers?
20. What are the major outcomes for the firm of the marketing process and consumers' responses to it?
21. What are the major outcomes for the individual of the marketing process and consumers' responses to it?
22. What are the major outcomes for society of the marketing process and consumers' responses to it?
23. What is *product position?*
24. What is meant by *injurious consumption?*
25. What is meant by *consumer lifestyle?*
26. Describe the consumer decision process.

DISCUSSION QUESTIONS

27. Why would someone shop on the Internet? Buy an iPad? Eat at Chili's frequently?
    a. Why would someone else not make those purchases?
    b. How would you choose one outlet, brand, or model over the others? Would others make the same choice in the same way?
28. Respond to the questions in Consumer Insight 1–1.
29. Of what use, if any, are models such as the one in Figure 1–3 to managers?
30. What changes would you suggest in the model in Figure 1–3? Why?
31. Describe your lifestyle. How does it differ from your parents' lifestyle?
32. Do you anticipate any changes in your lifestyle in the next five years? What will cause these changes? What new products or brands will you consume because of these changes?
33. Describe a recent purchase you made. To what extent did you follow the consumer
decision-making process described in this chapter? How would you explain any differences?
34. Describe several *total products* that are more than their direct physical features.
35. Describe the needs that the following items might satisfy and the total cost to the consumer of obtaining the benefits of the total product.
    a. Digital video recorder (e.g., TiVo)
    b. Lasik eye surgery
    c. Motorcycle
    d. SUV
36. How would you define the product that the Hard Rock Cafe provides? What needs does it meet?
37. To what extent, if any, are marketers responsible for injurious consumption involving their products?
38. How could social marketing help alleviate some of society's problems?
39. Respond to the questions in Consumer Insight 1–2.

40. Is the criticism of Nike for creating a shoe that is symbolic of success to some groups valid? Why or why not?

41. Robert's American gourmet snack foods produced herbal-based snacks such as Spirulina Spirals and St. John's Wort Tortilla Chips, and now makes Pirate's Booty baked snacks. According to the company president, "We're selling like crazy. We don't do research. We react as sort of a karma thing."[25] How would you explain the firm's success? What are the advantages and risks of this approach?

APPLICATION ACTIVITIES

42. Interview the manager or marketing manager of a retail firm. Determine how this individual develops the marketing strategy. Compare this person's process with the approach described in the text.

43. Interview the managers of a local charity. Determine what their assumptions about the consumer behavior of their supporters are. To what extent do they use marketing strategy to increase support for the organization or compliance with its objectives?

44. Interview five students. Have them describe the last three restaurant meals they consumed and the situations in which they were consumed. What can you conclude about the impact of the situation on consumer behavior? What can you conclude about the impact of the individual on consumer behavior?

45. Visit one or more stores that sell the following items. Report on the sales techniques used (point-of-purchase displays, store design, salesperson comments, and so forth). What beliefs concerning consumer behavior appear to underlie these techniques? It is often worthwhile for a male and a female student to visit the same store and talk to the same salesperson at different times. The variation in salesperson behavior is sometimes quite revealing.
    a. Books and magazines
    b. Cellular phones
    c. Pet supplies
    d. Expensive art
    e. Expensive jewelry
    f. Personal computers

46. Interview individuals who sell the items listed below. Try to discover their personal models of consumer behavior for their products.
    a. Expensive jewelry
    b. Pets
    c. Golfing equipment
    d. Plants and garden supplies
    e. Flowers
    f. Car insurance

47. Interview three individuals who recently made a major purchase and three others who made a minor purchase. In what ways were their decision processes similar? How were they different?

REFERENCES

1. Sources for "Evolution of Marketing" section: J. B. Pine and J. H. Gilmore, *The Experience Economy* (Boston, MA: Harvard Business Press, 1999); M. Rhodes, "Starbucks Channels Old-World Mysticism in New Big Easy Store," *FastCompany.com,* December 13, 2013, www.fastcodesign.com, accessed July 13, 2014.

2. Sources for "Marketing 2 Consumers" section: S. Godin, *Permission Marketing* (New York: Simon & Schuster, 1999); P. Fuller and K. Hein, "A Two-Way Conversation," *Brandweek,* February 24, 2002, pp. 20–28.

3. Sources for the "Social Media" section: J. Howe, "The Rise of Crowdsourcing," *Wired Magazine,* June 2006, http://archive.wired.com/wired/archive/14.06/crowds.html, accessed July 13, 2014; J. Howe, *Crowdsourcing* (New York: Three Rivers Press, 2008); T. Smith, "The Social Media Revolution," *International Journal of Market Research* 51, no. 4 (2009), pp. 559–61;

H. Simula, A. Tollinen, and H. Karjaluoto, "Crowdsourcing in the Social Media Era," *Journal of Marketing Development and Competitiveness,* May 2013, pp. 122–37; T. Luna, "Long CVS Receipts Spark Social Media Sensation," *Boston Globe,* August 31, 2013, www.bostonglobe.com, accessed July 13, 2014; G. Buchanan, "5 Examples of Companies Innovating with Crowdsourcing," blog.innocentive.com, January 11, 2018, accessed May 15, 2018.

4. J. Neff, "S.C. Johnson Likely to Bag Ziploc TableTops," *Advertising Age,* November 25, 2002, p. 3; J. Neff, "S.C. Johnson Faces a Clean-up Job," *Advertising Age,* November 29, 2004, p. 8.

5. See W. I. Ghani and N. M. Childs, "Wealth Effects of the Passage of the Nutrition Labeling and Education Act of 1990 for Large U.S. Multinational Food Corporations," *Journal of Public Policy and Marketing,* Fall 1999, pp. 147–58; S. K. Balasubramanian and

C. Cole, "Consumers' Search and Use of Nutrition Information," *Journal of Marketing,* July 2002, pp. 112–27.

6. See A. R. Andreasen, "Social Marketing," *Journal of Public Policy & Marketing,* Spring 1994, pp. 108–14; P. Kotler, N. Roberto, and N. Lee, *Social Marketing* (Thousand Oaks, CA: Sage, 2002).

7. A. S. Wellner, "The New Science of Focus Groups," *American Demographics,* March 2003, pp. 29–33.

8. This insight based on: B. Bartlett, "Here Are the 4 Types of Shoppers You'll See This Holiday Season," www.adweek.com/sponsored/here-are-4-types-shoppers-you-ll-see-holiday-season-174610/, accessed May 1, 2018; D. Cushion, "The Four Distinct Holiday Shopper Segments—And How to Reach Them," www.huffingtonpost.com/entry/the-four-distinct-holiday-shopper-segments-and-how_us_59c05474e4b0f96732cbc895, September 18, 2017, accessed May 1, 2018; D. Cushion, "The Four Distinct Holiday Shopper Segments—And How to Reach Them," www.cardlytics.com/blog/four-distinct-holiday-shopper-segments-reach/, September 26, 2017, accessed May 1, 2018; A. Gesenhues, "2017 Holiday Shopping Trends: How Consumers Plan to Research & Purchase Gifts This Season," https://marketingland.com/2017-holiday-shopping-trends-consumers-plan-research-purchase-gifts-season-228212, November 10, 2017, accessed May 1, 2018; C. Salpini, "4 Types of Holiday Shoppers Marketers Need to Reach," www.retaildive.com/news/4-types-of-holiday-shoppers-marketers-need-to-reach/507068/, October 13, 2017, accessed May 1, 2018.

9. E. Esfahani, "How to . . . Get Tough with Bad Customers," *Business 2.0,* October 2004, p. 52.

10. T. F. McMahon, "What Buyers Buy and Sellers Sell," *Journal of Professional Services Marketing* 2 (1996), pp. 3–16.

11. Productscan Online, "'Build a Better Mousetrap': 2004 New Product Innovations of the Year," press release, December 27, 2004; C. Mims, "Why There Are More Consumer Goods Than Ever," *Wall Street Journal,* April 25, 2016.

12. "MasterCard Launches Marketing, Education Campaign for Hispanics," *Payment News,* May 18, 2009.

13. See, e.g., J. Weber and A. T. Palmer, "How the Net Is Remaking the Mall," *BusinessWeek Online,* May 9, 2005.

14. "Disney Hits New Markets with Retail Makeover," *Reuters,* January 11, 2011; L. Richwine, "Disney Tests New Store Design as Shoppers Go Online," www.reuters.com, September 26, 2017, accessed May 15, 2018.

15. P. Wingert, "Why It's So Risky," *Newsweek,* November 22, 2010, p. 14.

16. "Price Rises Threaten Progress on Poverty," *Financial Times,* April 10, 2008, p. 8.

17. R. E. Petty and J. T. Cacioppo, "Addressing Disturbing and Disturbed Consumer Behavior," *Journal of Marketing Research,* February 1996, pp. 1–8.

18. See M. L. Richins, "Special Possessions and the Expression of Material Values," *Journal of Consumer Research,* December 1994, pp. 522–33.

19. "Apple Becomes Most Valuable Company Ever," *CBS News (online),* August 20, 2012, www.cbsnews.com/news/apple-becomes-most-valuable-company-ever/, accessed July 21, 2014.

20. C. Miller, "The Have-Nots," *Marketing News,* August 1, 1994, pp. 1–2; P. Mergenhagen, "What Can Minimum Wage Buy?," *American Demographics,* January 1996, pp. 32–36; and A. Hank, "Hank Finds Two Families," *StreetWise,* May 16–31, 1996, p. 7. See also R. P. Hill, "Disadvantaged Consumers," *Journal of Business Ethics* 80 (2008), pp. 77–83.

21. B. Burlingham and G. Gendron, "The Entrepreneur of the Decade," *Inc. Magazine,* April 1, 1989, www.inc.com/magazine/19890401/5602.html, accessed July 21, 2014.

22. A. Reinhardt, "Steve Jobs on Apple's Resurgence," *BusinessWeek,* May 25, 1998, www.businessweek.com/bwdaily/dnflash/may1998/nf80512d.htm, accessed July 21, 2014.

23. C. Hope, "Caucasian Female Body Hair and American Culture," *Journal of American Culture,* Spring 1982, pp. 93–99; Y. Ren, "Why Chinese Women Like Me Aren't Ashamed of Our Body Hair," www.telegraph.co.uk, June 24, 2015, accessed May 15, 2018.

24. K. Higgins, "P&G Reinvents Itself," *Marketing Management,* November/December 2002, pp. 12–15; A. Dutra, J. Frary, and R. Wise, "Higher-Order Needs Drive New Growth in Mature Consumer Markets," *Journal of Business Strategy* 25, no. 5 (2004), pp. 26–34.

25. M. W. Fellman, "New Age Dawns for Product Niche," *Marketing News,* April 27, 1998, p.1; www.piratesbooty.com, accessed May 15, 2018.

External Influences

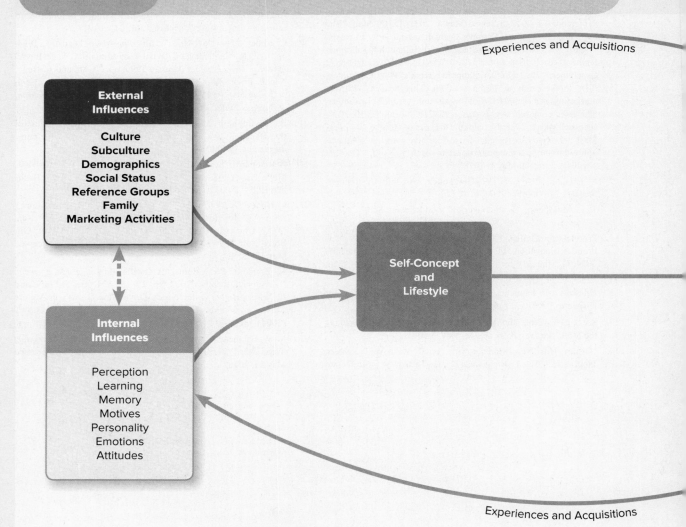

External Influences

Culture
Subculture
Demographics
Social Status
Reference Groups
Family
Marketing Activities

Internal Influences

Perception
Learning
Memory
Motives
Personality
Emotions
Attitudes

Self-Concept and Lifestyle

Experiences and Acquisitions

Experiences and Acquisitions

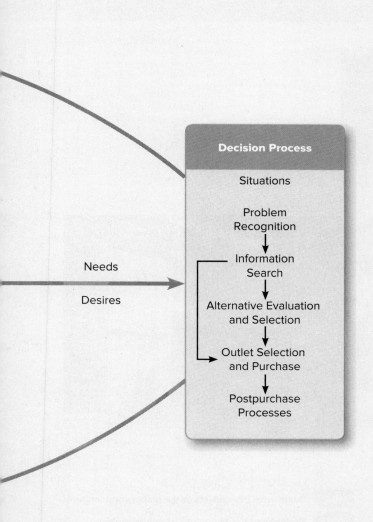

Decision Process

Situations

Problem
Recognition

↓

Information
Search

↓

Alternative Evaluation
and Selection

↓

Outlet Selection
and Purchase

↓

Postpurchase
Processes

Needs

Desires

The external influence area of our model shown at the left is the focal point of this part of the text. Any division of the factors that influence consumer behavior into separate and distinct categories is somewhat arbitrary. For example, we will consider learning in Part III of the text, which focuses on internal influences. However, a substantial amount of learning involves interaction with, or imitation of, other individuals. Thus, learning clearly involves external influences such as family and peers. Our focus in this part is on the functioning of the various external groups, not the processes by which individuals react to these groups.

In this part, we begin with large-scale, macrogroup influences and move to smaller, more microgroup influences. As we progress, the nature of the influence exerted changes from general guidelines to explicit expectations for specific behaviors. In Chapter 2, we examine how cultures cause differing behaviors across countries and other cultural units. Chapters 3 through 6 focus primarily on the American society, examining its values, demographics, social stratification, subcultures, and family structure. Chapter 7 examines the mechanisms by which groups influence consumer behaviors. In combination, these chapters allow for a comparison and contrast of how external influences operate in America and around the world.

Cross-Cultural Variations in Consumer Behavior

©TK Kurikawa/Shutterstock

©unitysphere/123RF

LEARNING OBJECTIVES

LO1 Define the concept of culture.

LO2 Describe core values that vary across culture and influence behaviors.

LO3 Understand cross-cultural variations in nonverbal communications.

LO4 Summarize key aspects of the global youth culture.

LO5 Understand the role of global demographics.

LO6 List the key dimensions in deciding to enter a foreign market.

Firms often aspire to be global. The benefits can be significant, but the challenges are staggering. The adaptations, adjustments, and considerations necessary when doing business across country and cultural borders are numerous. The following examples (Target, Bunnies, and Apple) illustrate the branding and logo issues created by global trademark law.

Target: United States versus Australia— Target, the 1,800-store Minneapolis-based retailer, recently established its first non-U.S. stores in Canada.[1] Although this is Target's first venture beyond its American borders, since 1968 there have been Target department stores in Australia. Target Australia (300 stores, $3.8B annual revenue) bears an uncanny resemblance to the U.S. Target, with the same (a) "Target" name in the same font; (b) red and white bull's-eye logo on its storefront, website, and ads; (c) tagline "Expect more, Pay less"; as well as a mix of products that consumers likely would find indistinguishable from those offered in Target U.S.

The explanation for this seemingly odd occurrence can be found in trademark law and the historical development of regional and local brands at a time when globalization was less prevalent. Trademarks for the most part can be established only in one country at a time. A company doing business in multiple countries must obtain trademarks for its name separately for each country (Target U.S. did so in 1966–67; Target Australia did so in 1968). Why Target U.S. would have allowed this is speculative, but one expert suggests:

> . . . the two Targets [likely] had some sort of informal, handshake agreement. Fifty years ago,

retail was primarily a local business and there were very few, if any, truly global brands. The idea that Target U.S. and Target Australia would somehow cross paths seemed remote at best.

Currently, Target U.S. and Target Australia are not directly competing. But the globalized nature of consumer buying, the permeability of country boundaries provided by Internet access, and Target U.S.'s desire to grow beyond its borders paints a scenario that could create challenges and conflict moving forward.

Pink Bunnies: Energizer versus Duracell— The localized nature of trademark laws also explains the existence of two battery bunnies, the Energizer Bunny in the United States and Canada and the Duracell Bunnies in Europe and Australia. In 1973, Duracell created the Duracell Bunny to personify the long life of its batteries. In a worldwide advertisement campaign from 1973 to 1980, the drum-beating bunny powered by Duracell batteries outlasted all the drum-beating bunnies powered by rival batteries. However, in 1987 when Duracell failed to renew its trademark Duracell Bunny in the United States, Energizer seized the lapse to trademark its Energizer Bunny, sporting sunglasses and wearing flip-flop sandals with a noticeably brighter shade of pink fur, beating on a noticeably larger drum. Today, consumers in the United States and Canada are familiar with the fuzzy, pink-furred, sunglass-wearing, drum-beating Energizer Bunny that "keeps on going and going" while an equally iconic fuzzy, pink-furred "coppertop" Duracell Bunny exists only in Europe and Australia.[2]

Apple: Computers and Music—Apple Computer, now known as Apple, Inc., is at the apex of the technology world as well as an iconic global brand. Apple Corporation is the holding company for the Beatles. Both Apple Computer and Apple Corporation have an apple as their logo, and as long as the two companies excelled in their own separate realms (computers versus music), the two companies were able to work out their trademark differences. However, things became murky when Apple Computer entered the realm of music via iTunes. In 2006, the courts ruled in favor of Apple Computer and the two companies reached a licensing agreement in 2007.[3]

As we will see throughout this chapter and the remainder of the text, names, signs, and symbols generate imagery, beliefs, and attitudes about brands that are important drivers of consumer behavior. The local and global laws governing how brand names and logos operate across country borders is critical in light of how important the embodied meaning of such names and symbols is to the consumers who buy those brands.

As the opening vignette suggests, marketing across country and cultural boundaries is difficult and challenging. As Figure 2–1 indicates, cultures (and countries) may differ in demographics, language, nonverbal communications, and values. The success of global marketers depends on how well they understand and adapt to these differences.

In this chapter, we focus on cultural variations in *values* and *nonverbal communications*. In addition, we briefly describe how *demographic variations* across countries and cultures influence consumption patterns.

Before dealing with specifics, we must consider the broader issues of cross-cultural marketing, including globalization, attitudes toward multinational brands, and ethical considerations. Globalization means more than product exports and imports. Globalization can involve

FIGURE 2-1   Cultural Factors Affect Consumer Behavior and Market Strategy

exporting and importing values, lifestyles, and attitudes. Historically, such influence has been thought of as primarily going one way—that is, large American and other Western multinational companies and brands influencing the values and lifestyles of the countries they enter. And, no doubt, such effects occur. For example, television advertising in countries such as China and India is extensive and reflects many Western values, such as individualism and an emphasis on youth. Over time, such advertising would be expected to influence not only how some Chinese and Indians choose to live (lifestyle), but also what they value and how they think and feel.[4]

Increasingly, however, globalization means mutual influence as products, brands, cultures, and values move back and forth across the world. So, while Western brands such as Mercedes still have cachet as luxury symbols in Eastern countries such as Japan, Eastern brands such as Japan's Lexus now have developed similar luxury status in Western countries such as the United States. Additional examples include the following:[5]

- Soccer is being imported into the United States, particularly as symbolized by U.K. star David Beckham, while American-style football (termed *olive ball*) is being exported to China. Olive ball is gaining acceptance, as evidenced by the creation of The Amercan Football League of China and a football clinic for Chinese youth coached by Peyton Manning, a retired National Football League quarterback.
- Harajuku, a broad term for the "street" fashion developed by style-conscious Japanese youth, which often incorporates elements of Western style but in unique and creative ways, has become popular around the world, as shown in Illustration 2–1.
- Brazilian products and fashion became all the rage in London as "Brazilian chic" was marketed through department stores, cultural events, and positive media coverage. Similar trends are occurring worldwide not only in the United States but also in Portuguese-speaking Angola.

Although globalization can influence cultural values, it would be a mistake to think that all cultures are becoming homogenized; while younger generations of consumers appear

©Sean Pavone/123RF

to be more similar, modern, and, in some cases, Western, older consumers in those same markets cling to traditional values that must be respected. For example, China appeared to eagerly (and profitably) copy TV contest shows like *American Idol* (*Supergirl* is a Chinese version). However, lawmakers there have clamped down with regulations to make the contestants act more conservatively and to keep the judges from embarrassing the contestants. According to one expert:

> The authorities are reacting against the sensationalistic, slightly rebellious nature of the contest programs, which promote individualism and personal achievement. The winners become idols with extreme influence on Chinese citizens. "Supergirl" also introduced Chinese to the concept of voting.[6]

Beyond elders and authorities attempting to maintain traditional cultural values, consumers across the globe often hold strong pride in their local heritage and sometimes mistrust or resent international brands, seeing them as irresponsible and hurtful to local culture and business. Indeed, a recent study indicates that regardless of country, there are four basic types of world citizens:[7]

- Global citizens (55 percent)—Positive toward international brands and view them as a signal of higher quality; most concerned about corporate responsibility to the local country. Prominent in Brazil, China, and Indonesia. Rare in the United States and the United Kingdom.
- Global dreamers (23 percent)—Positive toward international brands and buy into their positive symbolic aspects; less concerned about corporate responsibility to the local country. Equally distributed across countries.
- Antiglobals (13 percent)—Negative toward international brands; don't like brands that preach American values; don't trust multinationals. Higher in the United Kingdom and China. Lower in Egypt and South Africa.
- Global agnostics (9 percent)—Don't base decisions on global brand name; evaluate as they would local brands; don't see global brands as special. Higher in the United States and South Africa. Lower in Japan, Indonesia, China, and Turkey.

 Corporate responsibility and ethical issues can span from labor policies to influences on consumption of products linked to negative consequences. One example is American tobacco companies, which are aggressively marketing their products in the developing countries of Asia, Latin America, Africa, and Eastern Europe. Smoking-related deaths are now a leading killer in Asia, where increases in female smoking are a major concern.[8] As one World Health Organization (WHO) official notes:

> Here in Japan we see Western cigarette brands marketed as a kind of liberation tool. We see cigarette companies calling on young Japanese women to assert themselves, shed their inhibitions and smoke.[9]

Clearly, there are both subtle and direct ethical issues involved in international marketing.

THE CONCEPT OF CULTURE

LO1

Culture is *the complex whole that includes knowledge, belief, art, law, morals, customs, and any other capabilities and habits acquired by humans as members of society.*

Several aspects of culture require elaboration. First, culture is a comprehensive concept. It includes almost everything that influences an individual's thought processes and behaviors. Although culture does not determine the nature or frequency of biological drives such as hunger or sex, it does influence if, when, and how these drives will be gratified. It influences not only our preferences but how we make decisions[10] and even how we perceive the world around us. Second, culture is acquired. It does not include inherited responses and predispositions. However, because much of human behavior is learned rather than innate, culture does affect a wide array of behaviors.

Third, the complexity of modern societies is such that culture seldom provides detailed prescriptions for appropriate behavior. Instead, in most industrial societies, culture supplies boundaries within which most individuals think and act. Finally, the nature of cultural influences is such that we are seldom aware of them. One behaves, thinks, and feels in a manner consistent with that of other members of the same culture because it seems "natural" or "right" to do so.

Imagine sweet corn. Most Americans think of it as a hot side dish. However, uses vary by country. Consider the following:

> Instead of being eaten as a hot side dish, the French add it to salad and eat it cold. In Britain, corn is used as a sandwich and pizza topping. In Japan, school children gobble down canned corn as an after-school treat. And in Korea, the sweet corn is sprinkled over ice cream.[11]

Some of these uses probably seem strange or disgusting to you but are perfectly natural to members of other cultures. This is the nature of culture. We don't think about the fact that many of our preferences are strongly influenced by our culture.

Culture operates primarily by setting rather loose boundaries for individual behavior and by influencing the functioning of such institutions as the family and mass media. Thus, culture provides the framework within which individual and household lifestyles evolve.

The boundaries that culture sets on behavior are called **norms**, which are simply *rules that specify or prohibit certain behaviors in specific situations.* Norms are derived from **cultural values,** or *widely held beliefs that affirm what is desirable.* Violation of cultural norms results in **sanctions,** or *penalties ranging from mild social disapproval to banishment from the group.* Thus, as Figure 2-2 indicates, cultural values give rise to norms and associated sanctions, which in turn influence consumption patterns.

The preceding discussion may leave the impression that people are aware of cultural values and norms and that violating any given norm carries a precise and known sanction. This is seldom the case. We tend to "obey" cultural norms without thinking because to do otherwise would seem unnatural. For example, we are seldom aware of how close we stand to other individuals while conducting business. Yet this distance is well defined and adhered to, even though it varies from culture to culture.

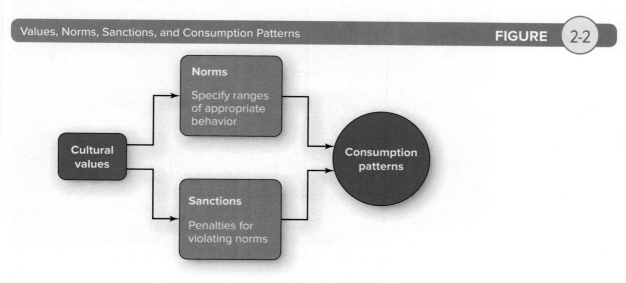

FIGURE **2-2**

Values, Norms, Sanctions, and Consumption Patterns

Norms

Specify ranges of appropriate behavior

Cultural values

Consumption patterns

Sanctions

Penalties for violating norms

Cultures are not static. They typically evolve and change slowly over time. Marketing managers must understand both the existing cultural values and the emerging cultural values of the societies they serve. A failure to understand cultural differences can produce negative consequences, such as the following:

- Mattel closed its "House of Barbie"—the company's first flagship store—in Shanghai just two years after its opening. The six-story store, which showcased a fashion runway, spa, café, and the world's largest collection of Barbie dolls and products including a Chinese Barbie named "Ling," did not impress Chinese consumers. Some analysts found Barbie to be "too sexy" for the Chinese market, with one analyst going so far as to say that the local consumers prefer "Hello Kitty cute to Barbie sexy."[12]

- In one of its London supermarkets, Tesco promoted "Smokey Bacon Flavour" Pringles in connection with the celebration of Ramadan. This holy month of fasting is practiced by Muslims, who also do not consume pork-based products. Although these Pringles do not actually contain pork, the store quickly issued an apology for the mistake and moved the Pringles to another part of the store.[13]

- Lipton created a line of instant meals named *Side Dishes*. The meals sold well in the United States but not in Latin America, a large market that Lipton had hoped would fuel growth for the line. Latin American housewives, with more traditional views of their family role, felt that "instant" meals implied they were lazy or poor caretakers for their families.[14]

Starbucks' CEO offers this cautionary note for American businesses going global: "The biggest lesson is not to assume that the market or the consumers are just like Americans, even if they speak English or otherwise behave as if they were."[15] However, with appropriate strategies and an eye toward the needs and wants of local consumers, sophisticated retailers and manufacturers can and do succeed throughout the world, as shown in Illustration 2-2.

ILLUSTRATION 2-2

Many companies offer a mix of standard and customized products in their locations around the world.

©StreetVJ/Shutterstock

VARIATIONS IN CULTURAL VALUES

Cultural values are widely held beliefs that affirm what is desirable. These values affect behavior through norms, which specify an acceptable range of responses to specific situations. A useful approach to understanding cultural variations in behavior is to understand the values embraced by different cultures.

LO2

Numerous values vary across cultures and affect consumption. We will present a classification scheme consisting of three broad forms of cultural values: *other-oriented, environment-oriented,* and *self-oriented.* The cultural values that have the most impact on consumer behavior can be classified in one of these three general categories.

Other-oriented values reflect a society's view of the appropriate relationships *between individuals and groups* within that society. These relationships have a major influence on marketing practice. For example, if the society values collective activity, consumers will look toward others for guidance in purchase decisions and will not respond favorably to promotional appeals to "be an individual."

Environment-oriented values prescribe a society's relationship *to its economic and technical as well as its physical environment.* As a manager, you would develop a very different marketing program for a society that stressed a problem-solving, risk-taking, performance-oriented approach to its environment than you would for a fatalistic, security- and status-oriented society.

Self-oriented values reflect the objectives and approaches to life *that the individual members of society find desirable.* Again, these values have strong implications for marketing management. For instance, the acceptance and use of credit is very much determined by a society's position on the value of postponed versus immediate gratification.

Table 2–1 provides a list of 18 values that are important in most cultures. Most of the values are shown as dichotomies (e.g., materialistic versus nonmaterialistic). However, this

Cultural Values of Relevance to Consumer Behavior	TABLE 2-1

Other-Oriented Values

- *Individual/Collective.* Are individual activity and initiative valued more highly than collective activity and conformity?
- *Youth/Age.* Is family life organized to meet the needs of the children or the adults? Are younger or older people viewed as leaders and role models?
- *Extended/Limited family.* To what extent does one have a lifelong obligation to numerous family members?
- *Masculine/Feminine.* To what extent does social power automatically go to males?
- *Competitive/Cooperative.* Does one obtain success by excelling over others or by cooperating with them?
- *Diversity/Uniformity.* Does the culture embrace variation in religious belief, ethnic background, political views, and other important behaviors and attitudes?

Environment-Oriented Values

- *Cleanliness.* To what extent is cleanliness pursued beyond the minimum needed for health?
- *Performance/Status.* Is the culture's reward system based on performance or on inherited factors such as family or class?
- *Tradition/Change.* Are existing patterns of behavior considered to be inherently superior to new patterns of behavior?
- *Risk taking/Security.* Are those who risk their established positions to overcome obstacles or achieve high goals admired more than those who do not?
- *Problem solving/Fatalistic.* Are people encouraged to overcome all problems, or do they take a "what will be, will be" attitude?
- *Nature.* Is nature regarded as something to be admired or overcome?

Self-Oriented Values

- *Active/Passive.* Is a physically active approach to life valued more highly than a less active orientation?
- *Sensual gratification/Abstinence.* To what extent is it acceptable to enjoy sensual pleasures such as food, drink, and sex?
- *Material/Nonmaterial.* How much importance is attached to the acquisition of material wealth?
- *Hard work/Leisure.* Is a person who works harder than economically necessary admired more than one who does not?
- *Postponed gratification/Immediate gratification.* Are people encouraged to "save for a rainy day" or to "live for today"?
- *Religious/Secular.* To what extent are behaviors and attitudes based on the rules specified by a religious doctrine?

is not meant to represent an either/or situation but a continuum. For example, two societies each can value tradition, but one may value it more than the other. For several of the values, a natural dichotomy does not seem to exist. For a society to place a low value on cleanliness does not imply that it places a high value on dirtiness. These 18 values are described in the following paragraphs.

Other-Oriented Values

Individual/Collective   Does the culture emphasize and reward individual initiative, or are cooperation with and conformity to a group more highly valued? Are individual differences appreciated or condemned? Are rewards and status given to individuals or to groups? Answers to these questions reveal the individual or collective orientation of a culture. Individualism is a defining characteristic of American culture. Australia, the United Kingdom, Canada, New Zealand, and Sweden are also relatively individualistic. Taiwan, Korea, Hong Kong, Mexico, Japan, India, and Russia are more collective in their orientation.[16]

This value is a key factor differentiating cultures, and it heavily influences the self-concept of individuals. Not surprisingly, consumers from cultures that differ on this value differ in their reactions to foreign products,[17] advertising,[18] and the Internet.[19] Examples include

- Consumers in more collectivist countries care more about how they are treated in terms of respect and concern after a service failure than do consumers in more individualistic countries.[20]
- Consumers from more collectivist countries tend to be more imitative and less innovative in their purchases than those from individualistic cultures.[21] Thus, ad themes such as "be yourself" and "stand out" are often effective in the United States but generally not in Japan, Korea, or China.
- Advertising in collectivist countries such as Korea contains more celebrity appeals than does advertising in individualistic countries such as the United States.[22]

Interestingly, you might expect luxury items to be less important in collectivist cultures. However, they are quite important, but for different reasons. In individualistic cultures, luxury items are purchased as a means of self-expression or to stand out.[23] This is often not the case in more collectivist Asian societies, such as China, where the majority of young consumers are willing to pay a premium for luxury goods.[24] As one expert describes:

> Brands take on roles as symbols that extend well beyond the intrinsic features of the category. One is not buying a watch, or even a status brand, one is buying club membership, or an "I am just like you" (symbol).[25]

Similarly, the notion of conspicuous consumption is often associated with individualistic societies. However, a recent study finds that brand reputation influences decisions more for conspicuously consumed products in collectivist countries.[26] Another study finds that concern for appearance is 40 percent higher for those in collectivist countries. One explanation is that a given behavior is used for different reasons in different cultures. As one expert notes:

> Dressing well . . . might convey a sense of individuality in individualist cultures. However, it might be interpreted by collectivist-culture consumers as a way to demonstrate their in-group identity, show their concerns with in-group norms, follow in-group trends and avoid loss of face in front of in-group members.[27]

As useful as such generalizations are, it is important to realize that cultural values can and do evolve. This is particularly true among young, urban consumers in the developed and developing countries of Asia, where individualism is on the rise.[28] For example, 26 percent of Chinese teens consider individuality an important trait, more than double the rate of older Chinese.[29] Although this number is substantially lower than that of Western cultures, it represents an important shift. Consider the following description of the new young single woman in Japan:

> [T]he young single woman in Japan is now on an odyssey. The stereotyped office lady of the 80s was a junior office clerk. Today, though, Japanese women are climbing higher up the corporate career ladder, which is in turn bringing out a more independent streak. Women now are going out and finding their own path in life . . . and more are saying, "I don't want to follow the trend all the time, I can find my own way."[30]

In the face of such changes, traditional appeals may not work as they once did. For example, in the late 1980s, Shiseido Co. launched its very successful Perky Jean makeup line with the theme, "Everyone is buying it." "That would never work now," says a company executive.

The different values held by younger and older Asian consumers illustrate that few cultures are completely homogeneous. Marketers must be aware of differences both *between* cultures and *within* cultures.[31]

Youth/Age   To what extent do the primary family activities focus on the needs of the children instead of those of the adults? What role, if any, do children play in family decisions? What role do they play in decisions that primarily affect the child? Are prestige, rank, and important social roles assigned to younger or older members of society? Are the behavior, dress, and mannerisms of the younger or older members of a society imitated by the rest of the society?

While American society is clearly youth oriented, many Asian cultures have traditionally valued the wisdom that comes with age. Thus, mature spokespersons would tend to be more successful in these cultures than would younger ones. However, some Asian cultures are becoming increasingly youth oriented with increases in youth-oriented ads designed to target them.[32] Consider the following description of Taiwan:

> Taiwan is very, very youth-oriented, and it is a very hip culture. . . . You have a consumer-based economy that is quite potent, and pitching to the youth is a good way of ensuring that your products are going to be bought.[33]

Illustration 2–3 demonstrates 7-Up's use of a youth theme in China. These unique outdoor "light pole" signs are common in China's major cities.

This youth trend also can be seen in Arab countries. One study of Arab consumers from Saudi Arabia, Bahrain, Kuwait, and the United Arab Emirates shows the rapid emergence of several youth segments. The largest (35 percent) consists of younger, more liberal, individualistic married couples living in nuclear (versus communal) families in which women are more likely to work outside the home and thus demand a greater voice in family decisions.[34] This youth trend may explain why recent research finds numerous similarities in values such as independence and respect for the elderly reflected in Arab and American television ads.[35]

Children's influence on purchases and the tactics they use vary according to the youth-versus-age value, and this has implications for marketers.[36] For example, one study compared the tactics used by children in the Fiji Islands with those used in the United States. The Fiji Islands (and other Pacific Island nations) can be characterized as less individualistic and higher in respect for authority and seniority. As a consequence, Fiji children were more likely to "request" than "demand," and Fiji parents responded more favorably

©Marie Hornbein

(i.e., bought the item) to "requests." In contrast, American children were more likely to demand than to request, and American parents responded more positively to demands.[37]

China's policy of limiting families to one child has produced a strong focus on the child, a shift toward youth, and increasing Westernization of children's commercials. In fact, many Chinese children receive so much attention that they are known in Asia as "little emperors."[38] Consider the following description of the Zhou family and their 10-year-old daughter Bella, who live in Shanghai:

> Under traditional Confucian teachings, respecting and obeying one's elders were paramount. In today's urban China, it is increasingly children who guide their parents through a fast-changing world. When the Zhous bought a new television set last year, Bella chose the brand. When they go out to eat, Bella insists on Pizza Hut.[39]

Obviously, while changes to traditional cultures such as those in Asia and the Gulf are occurring, it is important to remember that traditional segments and values still remain and that marketers must adapt not only across but within cultures.

Extended/Limited Family The family unit is the basis for virtually all societies. Nonetheless, the definition of the family and the rights and obligations of family members vary widely across cultures. As we will see in Chapter 6, our families have a lifelong impact on us, both genetically and through our early socialization, no matter what culture we come from. However, cultures differ widely in the obligations one owes to other family members at various stages of life as well as who is considered to be a member of the family.

In the United States, the family is defined fairly narrowly and is less important than in many other cultures. In general, strong obligations are felt only to immediate family members, and these diminish as family members establish new families. In many other countries and regions, including South America, Fiji, Israel, and Asia, the role of the family is much stronger. Families, and obligations, often extend to cousins, nieces, nephews, and beyond. The following description indicates the complexity and extent of the extended Chinese family:

> The family is critically important in all aspects of Chinese life and there is a distrust of nonfamily members. In response to this, the Chinese have developed family-like links to a greater extent than almost any other culture. It stretches to the furthest horizons, from close family, to slightly distant, to more distant, embracing people who are not really family but are connected to someone in one's family and to all their families. As such, the family is really a system of contacts, rather than purely an emotional unit as in the west.[40]

Clearly, marketers need to understand the role of families in the cultures they serve and adapt accordingly. For example:

- Adolescents and young adults in Mexico and Thailand (compared to the United States) are more influenced by parents and family in terms of consumption values and purchases.[41]
- Because Indian consumers tend to shop in groups and with their families, Biyani (a large discounter similar to Walmart) has U- and C-shaped aisles to provide private corners where families can discuss their purchase decisions.[42]

Masculine/Feminine   Are rank, prestige, and important social roles assigned primarily to men? Can a female's life pattern be predicted at birth with a high degree of accuracy? Does the husband, wife, or both make important family decisions? Basically, we live in a masculine-oriented world, yet the degree of masculine orientation varies widely, even across the relatively homogeneous countries of Western Europe.

This value dimension influences both obvious and subtle aspects of marketing. For example, the roles and manner in which one would portray women in ads in Muslim countries would differ from those in the United States.[43] Indeed, when the U.S. military worked with an Afghan agency to create ads featuring pictures of babies that were designed to promote Afghan pride and discourage suicide bombings, they found that ". . . the babies all had to be boys, and the ad copy focused on males."[44]

However, roles of women are changing and expanding throughout much of the world.[45] This is creating new opportunities as well as challenges for marketers.[46] For example, the increasing percentage of Japanese women who continue to work after marriage has led to increased demand for time-saving products as well as other products targeted at the working woman. And during a recent U.K. election cycle, the major parties heavily targeted educated women through Mumsnet, the largest online parenting site in the United Kingdom, with 1.2 million users who are predominantly higher-income, college-educated women.[47]

Participation in sports and exercise is another aspect strongly influenced by the masculinity dimension. There tends to be a wide disparity between men and women participation rates (men higher) in countries and cultures high in masculine orientation such as South Korea, Mexico, Brazil, and France. However, as always, modern trends must be considered. In Brazil, for example, women's soccer has been embraced by the country's many soccer fanatics, both men and women, young and old. Marta, the soccer superstar known only by one name like soccer great Pelé, has inspired a movement towards gender equality in her nation, as shown in memes with taglines like "fight like a woman."[48] And women from South Korea and China are now a dominant force in women's professional golf, winning six of the LPGA's last 12 major titles. Illustration 2–4 shows the changing role of women as represented by their ever-increasing participation in professional sports.

ILLUSTRATION 2-4

The changing role of women around the world creates new marketing opportunities. The popularity and participation of women in sports is increasing in many cultures.

©Erik Isakson/Blend Images/Getty Images

Again, it is important to remember that traditional segments and values certainly do still remain and that marketers must adapt not only across but within cultures. For example, a recent study of women in mainland China found both traditionalist and modern segments.[49] In Hong Kong, however, the traditional values are not necessarily giving way when economic and social independence are gained. Instead, the conflict is internalized, as indicated by the following quote:

> Women in Hong Kong, who are faced with both traditional Chinese culture and Western culture, are at a crossroads of modernism and traditionalism. On one hand, they are having increasing amount of financial and decision power within the family and in the society. On the other hand, they are still under the pressure of traditional expectations on females as being a good wife and mother.[50]

For marketers, this conflict creates challenges in some cases to segment consumers into modern and traditional markets. In other cases the challenge is to help consumers (through products, positioning, advertising, and so on) deal with tensions between traditional and modern values.

Competitive/Cooperative   Is the path to success found by outdoing other individuals or groups, or is success achieved by forming alliances with other individuals or groups? Does everyone admire a winner? Cultures with more masculine and individualistic orientations, such as the United Kingdom, the United States, and Australia, tend to value competitiveness and demonstrate it openly. Collectivist cultures, even if high in masculinity (e.g., Japan), tend to find *openly* competitive gestures offensive as they cause others to "lose face."[51]

Variations on this value can be seen in the ways different cultures react to comparative advertisements. For example, the United States encourages them, while their use in other cultures can lead to consumer (and even legal) backlash. As one would expect, the more collectivist Japanese have historically found comparative ads to be distasteful, as do the Chinese, although Pepsi found Japanese youth somewhat more receptive if comparisons are done in a frank and funny way.[52] As a rule, comparative ads should be used with care and only after considerable testing.

Diversity/Uniformity   Do members of the culture embrace variety in terms of religions, ethnic backgrounds, political beliefs, and other important behaviors and attitudes? A culture that values diversity not only will accept a wide array of personal behaviors and attitudes but also is likely to welcome variety in terms of food, dress, and other products and services. In contrast, a society valuing uniformity is unlikely to accept a wide array of tastes and product preferences, though such a society may be subject to fads, fashions, and other changes over time.

Collectivist cultures tend to place a strong value on uniformity and conformity,[53] whereas more individualistic cultures tend to value diversity. For example, "in-group" influence (e.g., wanting to see the same movies as everyone else) tends to be higher in China and Japan than in the United Kingdom and the United States.[54] Obviously, however, economic and social changes associated with the youth movement in many collectivist societies mean relatively more acceptance of diversity than has been traditionally found, even if absolute levels trend lower than in their individualistic counterparts.

Environment-Oriented Values

Cleanliness   Is cleanliness next to godliness, or is it a rather minor matter? Are homes, offices, and public spaces expected to be clean beyond reasonable health requirements? In the United States, a high value is placed on cleanliness, where germ-fighting liquid soaps alone are a multi-billion-dollar market.[55] In fact, people from many other cultures consider Americans to be paranoid on the subject of personal hygiene.

Although there are differences in the value placed on cleanliness among the economically developed cultures, the largest differences are between these cultures and those of many of the underdeveloped nations. In many poorer countries, cleanliness is not valued at a level sufficient to produce a healthy environment. This is true even in large parts of rapidly developing countries such as China and India, where a lack of basic hygiene still causes significant health problems.[56] While often criticized for having a negative impact on local cultures, McDonald's has been credited with introducing more hygienic food preparation and toilets in several East Asian markets, including China.[57]

Performance/Status   Are opportunities, rewards, and prestige based on an individual's performance or on the status associated with the person's family, position, or class? Do all people have an equal opportunity economically, socially, and politically at the start of life, or are certain groups given special privileges? Are products and brands valued for their ability to accomplish a task or for the reputation or status of the brand?

A status-oriented society is more likely to prefer "quality" or established and prestigious brand names and high-priced items to functionally equivalent items with unknown brand names or lower prices (e.g., private label or store brands).[58] As a result, compared with that in the United States, advertising in Japan, China, and India tends to involve more appeals to status or wealth.[59] According to a Levi's executive in charge of their new global dENiZEN™ brand targeting emerging markets:

> We've realized a new consumer has emerged, status-seekers in rapidly emerging middle classes. This is primarily a developing-market phenomenon—they exist outside the U.S. in markets like China, India, Indonesia, Mexico, and Brazil.[60]

Performance/status is closely related to the concept of **power distance,** which refers to *the degree to which people accept inequality in power, authority, status, and wealth as* *natural or inherent in society.*[61] India, China, Brazil, Mexico, France, Hong Kong, and Japan are relatively high in their acceptance of power. Austria, Denmark, New Zealand, Sweden, and the United States are relatively low. Expert sources in ads have a greater impact in a high-power-distance country than in a low one.[62] In addition, consumers in high-power-distance countries are more likely to seek the opinions of others in making decisions.[63]

How power is used may depend on other cultural factors, however. In the United States, power is seen in terms of coercion and in Japan as relational. As a consequence, in negotiations where the buyer has more power, buyers are more likely to use that power to extract higher prices and profits in the United States, whereas that is not true in Japan. Marketers need to understand such nuances when negotiating with partners in other countries.[64]

Tradition/Change   Is tradition valued simply for the sake of tradition? Is change or "progress" an acceptable reason for altering established patterns? Compared with Americans, Korean and Chinese consumers have traditionally been much less comfortable dealing with new situations or ways of thinking.[65] Britain, too, has a culture laden with tradition. This value is reflected in their advertising, where, compared to ads in America, those in Britain and China are more likely to emphasize tradition and history.[66]

It is important to note once again that change can and does live alongside traditional values. For example, both the Korean and Chinese cultures are now enthusiastically embracing change. In China, "modernness" (often symbolized by a Western name) is an important product attribute, particularly among younger, urban Chinese. A recent study found that advertisers in China segment their advertising depending on audience. For the mainstream audiences targeted by television, traditional appeals are used more often. In magazines targeted at younger Chinese (e.g., *Elle, Cosmopolitan,* and *Ray Li*), modern appeals focusing on technology, fashion, and leisure are used more often.[67] Younger urban Korean, Japanese, and more recently Chinese consumers often lead the way in technology adoption and usage and are highly demanding.[68] Vodafone found out just how much after their market share in Japan plummeted when they failed to innovate and stay on the cutting edge.[69]

Risk Taking/Security   Do the "heroes" of the culture meet and overcome obstacles? Is the person who risks established position or wealth on a new venture admired or considered foolhardy? This value relates to tolerance for ambiguity and uncertainty avoidance. It has a strong influence on entrepreneurship and economic development as well as new-product acceptance. A society that does not admire risk taking is unlikely to develop enough entrepreneurs to achieve economic change and growth. New-product introductions, new channels of distribution, advertising themes, and reliance on brand name are affected by this value.[70]

Problem Solving/Fatalistic   Do people react to obstacles and disasters as challenges to be overcome, or do they take a "what will be, will be" attitude? Is there an optimistic, "we can do it" orientation? Fatalists tend to feel they don't have control over the outcome of events. This has been shown to reduce consumer expectations of quality and decrease the likelihood that consumers make formal complaints when faced with an unsatisfactory purchase.[71]

Western Europe and the United States tend to fall toward the problem-solving end of the continuum, whereas Mexico and most Middle Eastern countries fall toward the fatalistic end. As with many of the values we have discussed, traditional and modern approaches can live alongside each other. Consider the following examples:[72]

Traditional: In the Asia-Pacific region, supernatural beliefs traditionally are believed to have a strong influence on product sales performance. In particular, name giving . . . has a strong perceived connection to fate. In more than 50 percent of the [brand names] we studied, the creation . . . was based, in part, on a "lucky" number of total strokes drawn in the creation of the characters that spelled out the brand name. [And lucky names] were more common in high-uncertain than low-uncertain market environments.

Modern: Tiger leadership is a current leadership style prowling around Southeast Asia which combines the brashness of a Western entrepreneurial style with a tireless Asian work ethic.

Nature   Is nature assigned a positive value, or is it viewed as something to be overcome, conquered, or tamed? Americans historically considered nature as something to be overcome or improved. Most northern European countries place a high value on the environment. Packaging and other environmental regulations are stronger in these countries than in America. In fact, a British company recently developed a zero-emissions motorcycle that runs on hydrogen. They worry, however, because it also makes no sound! *Would you want a motorcycle that didn't growl when you revved it up?*[73]

In turn, Americans and Canadians appear to place a higher value on the environment than the southern European countries and most developing countries, though this may reflect variations in the knowledge or financial ability to act on this value rather than the value itself.[74] These differences in attitudes are reflected in consumers' purchase decisions, consumption practices, and recycling efforts.[75]

As with all the values we are discussing, there are wide ranges within as well as between countries, which create market opportunities. For example, overall, China does not have a strong environmental orientation. However, there are segments of the country that do have such an orientation and the means to buy products and services that reflect this focus.[76]

Self-Oriented Values

Active/Passive   Are people expected to take a physically active approach to work and play? Are physical skills and feats valued more highly than nonphysical performances? Is emphasis placed on doing? Americans are much more prone to engage in physical activities and to take an action-oriented approach to problems. "Don't just stand there; do something" is a common response to problems in America. Participation in active exercise varies widely across countries, especially for women, as discussed earlier. While this obviously limits the market for exercise equipment in certain countries, it also affects advertising themes and formats. For example, an exercise or sports theme for bottled water would not be appropriate in a country such as Japan, where 60 percent of the population does not engage in physical activity.[77]

Sensual Gratification/Abstinence   Is it acceptable to pamper oneself, to satisfy one's desires for food, drink, or sex beyond the minimum requirement? Is one who forgoes such gratification considered virtuous or strange? Muslim cultures are extremely conservative on this value, as are many Asian cultures, including Hong Kong and India. A full 37 percent of Saudis indicated modesty is important, compared with 9 percent in the United States.[78] Perhaps not surprisingly, compared with U.S. and Australian ads, ads in Hong Kong and India contain fewer sex appeals.[79] And China has put legal restrictions on the use of sex appeals in ads.[80]

In Arab countries, advertisements, packaging, and products must carefully conform to Muslim standards. Polaroid's instant cameras gained rapid acceptance because they allowed Arab men to photograph their wives and daughters without fear that a stranger in a film laboratory would see the women unveiled.

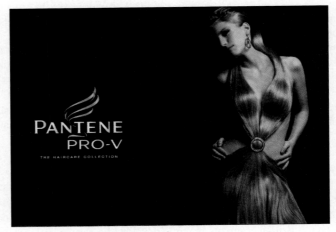

Source: The Procter & Gamble Company

In contrast, Brazilian and European advertisements contain nudity and blatant (by U.S. standards) appeals to sensual gratification. The Pantene ad shown in Illustration 2–5 provides a great example of how marketers make use of sensuality. While quite appropriate for some cultures, it would not be successful in a culture that did not accept sensual gratification.

Material/Nonmaterial   Is the accumulation of material wealth a positive good in its own right? Does material wealth bring more status than family ties, knowledge, or other activities?

There are two types of materialism. **Instrumental materialism** is *the acquisition of things to enable one to do something.* Skis can be acquired to allow one to ski. **Terminal materialism** is *the acquisition of items for the sake of owning the item itself.* Art is generally acquired for the pleasure of owning it rather than as a means to another goal. Cultures differ markedly in their relative emphasis on these two types of materialism.[81]

Increased wealth, exposure to international media and brands, and modernization appear to be increasing materialism in places generally thought to be less materialistic. For example, in more collectivist China, where family and relationships might be thought to trump possessions, Chinese youth now demonstrate greater materialism than their U.S. counterparts.[82] Beyond the youth trend, there are also subtle differences in the types of materialism across cultures. For example, while U.S. consumers place a higher value on the importance of obtaining possessions (called the centrality dimension of materialism), Korean consumers place a higher value on possessions as a means for demonstrating success (the success dimension) because it is seen as uplifting the family unit.[83]

Hard Work/Leisure   Is work valued for itself, independent of external rewards, or is work merely a means to an end? Will individuals continue to work hard even when their minimum economic needs are satisfied, or will they opt for more leisure time? For example, in parts of Latin America, work traditionally has been viewed as a necessary evil. However, generational gaps exist. For example, in Mexico, 100 percent of the older generation agreed with the statement "Today's emphasis on work is a bad thing," compared with only 28 percent of the younger generation. The trend was just the opposite in the United Kingdom, Netherlands, France, Canada, and Australia, where agreement by the older generation was around 55 percent, while agreement by the younger generation was around 80 percent. In the United States and Hong Kong, younger and older generations were roughly the same (about 50 percent agreeing) on this value.[84]

These attitudes do not necessarily reflect *actual* work patterns. For example, hours actually worked per week are highest in Mexico (43.4 hours) and lowest in Germany (26.2) and Denmark (27.1).[85] Nonetheless, this value has important consequences for lifestyle and demand for leisure activities.

Postponed Gratification/Immediate Gratification   Is one encouraged to "save for a rainy day," or should one "live for today"? Is it better to secure immediate benefits and pleasures, or is it better to suffer in the short run for benefits in the future, or in the hereafter, or for future generations? The United States, the United Kingdom, and Australia tend to have short-term orientations, while India, Hungary, Brazil, Hong Kong, and China have long-term orientations. This value has implications for business strategies, efforts to encourage savings, and the use of credit. For example, valued business goals in short-term cultures tend to include "this year's profits," while those in long-term cultures included "profits 10 years from now."[86] In addition, use of credit is lower in long-term-oriented cultures, where cash and debit card usage are more common.[87]

Religious/Secular   To what extent are daily activities determined by religious doctrine? The United States is relatively secular. Many Islamic cultures as well as some Catholic cultures are much more religiously oriented.[88] In contrast, religion plays a very small role in Chinese culture. However, even in a country such as China, where few are actively involved with a formal religion, many of the culture's values were formed in part by historical religious influences. The same is true for the secular nations of the West. Understanding the extent and type of religious influences operating in a culture is essential for effectively designing all elements of the marketing mix.[89]

Clearly, the preceding discussion has not covered all the values operating in the various cultures. However, it should suffice to provide a feel for the importance of cultural values and how cultures differ along value dimensions.

CULTURAL VARIATIONS IN NONVERBAL COMMUNICATIONS

LO3

Differences in **verbal communication systems** (languages) are immediately obvious to anyone entering a foreign culture. An American traveling in Britain or Australia will be able to communicate, but differences in pronunciation, timing, and meaning still will occur. For example, Dogpile, a U.S.-based metasearch engine (www.dogpile.com), changed its name in Europe to WebFetch after realizing that in the United Kingdom "pile" refers to hemorrhoids or the result of a dog relieving itself![90]

Attempts to translate marketing communications from one language to another can result in ineffective communications, as shown in Table 2–2.

The problems of literal translations and slang expressions are compounded by symbolic meanings associated with words, the absence of some words from various languages, and the difficulty of pronouncing certain words:[91]

* In Japan, a global soft-drink company wanted to introduce a product with the attribute "creaminess." However, research showed that there was no corresponding word in Japan for this attribute, so the company had to find something comparable, which turned out to be "milk feel."[92]
* Mars addressed the problem of making the M&M's name pronounceable in France, where neither ampersands nor the apostrophe "s" plural form exists, by advertising extensively that M&M's should be pronounced "aimainaimze."
* To market its Ziploc food storage bags in Brazil, Dow Chemical had to use extensive advertising to actually create the word *zipar,* meaning "to zip," because there was no such term in Portuguese.
* Literal translation was not the problem facing Gerber when introducing its baby food, with the cute baby picture on the label, to the African market. Products sold in countries like Ethiopia show pictures on the label of what is inside because many consumers are unable to read.[93] Gerber soon fixed the packaging.

TABLE 2-2   Translation Problems in International Marketing

- Colgate's Cue toothpaste had problems in France, as *cue* is a crude term for "butt" in French.
- Parker Pen mistook *embarazar* (to impregnate) to mean to embarrass and ran an ad in Mexico stating, "it won't leak in your pocket and make you pregnant."
- Pet milk encountered difficulties in French-speaking countries where *pet* means, among other things, "to break wind."
- Kellogg's Bran Buds translates to "burned farmer" in Swedish.
- United Airlines' in-flight magazine cover for its Pacific Rim routes showed Australian actor Paul Hogan in the outback. The caption stated, "Paul Hogan Camps It Up." "Camps it up" is Australian slang for "flaunts his homosexuality."
- China attempted to export Pansy brand men's underwear to America.
- Braniff Airlines introduced its new leather first-class seats in Mexico with the theme "Fly in Leather" which, when translated literally, read "Fly Naked."

Additional communication factors that can cause problems include humor, style, and pace, for which preferences vary across cultures, even those speaking the same basic language.[94] Nonetheless, verbal language translations generally do not present major problems as long as we are careful. What many of us fail to recognize, however, is that each culture also has nonverbal communication systems or languages that, like verbal languages, are specific to each culture. **Nonverbal communication systems** are *the arbitrary meanings a culture assigns actions, events, and things other than words.*

The following discussion examines the seven variables shown in Figure 2–3, all of which influence nonverbal communications: time, space, symbols, relationships, agreements, things, and etiquette.

Time

The meaning of time varies between cultures in two major ways. First is what we call time perspective, that is, a culture's overall orientation toward time.[95] The second is the interpretations assigned to specific uses of time.

Time Perspective   Most Americans, Canadians, Western Europeans, and Australians tend to view time as inescapable, linear, and fixed in nature. It is a road reaching into the

FIGURE 2-3   Factors Influencing Nonverbal Communications

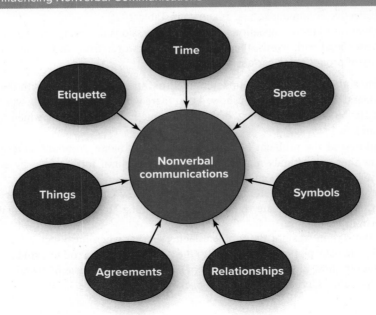

future with distinct, separate sections (hours, days, weeks, and so on). Time is seen almost as a physical object; we can schedule it, waste it, lose it, and so forth. Believing that a person does one thing at a time, we have a strong orientation toward the present and the short-term future. This is known as a **monochronic time perspective.**

Most Latin Americans, Asians, and Indians tend to view time as being less discrete and less subject to scheduling. They view simultaneous involvement in many activities as natural. People and relationships take priority over schedules, and activities occur at their own pace rather than according to a predetermined timetable. Such cultures have an orientation toward the present and the past. This is known as a **polychronic time perspective.**

Some important differences between individuals with a monochronic perspective and those with a polychronic perspective are listed below.[96]

Individuals in a Monochronic Culture	Individuals in a Polychronic Culture
Do one thing at a time	Do many things at once
Concentrate on the job	Are highly distractible and subject to interruptions
Take deadlines and schedules seriously	Consider deadlines and schedules secondary
Are committed to the job or task	Are committed to people and relationships
Emphasize promptness	Base promptness on the relationship
Are accustomed to short-term relationships	Prefer long-term relationships

How would marketing activities vary between monochronic and polychronic cultures? Personal selling and negotiation styles and strategies would need to differ, as would many advertising themes. Contests and sales with deadlines would generally be more effective in monochronic than in polychronic cultures. Convenience foods frequently fail when positioned in terms of time saving and convenience in polychronic cultures, where "saving time" is not part of the cultural thought processes. For example, in countries like Argentina with more polychronic views, fast-food restaurants often are seen as more expensive and modern and as representing modern and liberated value systems. The time-saving aspect is not as prominent there as it is in countries like the United States that are more monochronic.[97]

Interestingly, even within a culture, time perspectives can vary by age and by situation. For example, in Japan, work is approached in terms of monochronic time, whereas leisure is approached, as their culture might suggest, in terms of polychronic time.[98] Also, while Americans have tended to be monochronic, younger consumers appear to demonstrate elements of polychronic time. This so-called generation of "digital natives" seems to have no attention span—around 8 seconds—and may simultaneously be found working on the computer, watching TV, and surfing the net on their smartphones![99] Not surprisingly, U.S. advertisers find it hard to capture and hold the attention of this audience.

Meanings in the Use of Time   Specific uses of time have varying meanings in different cultures. In much of the world, the time required for a decision is proportional to the importance of the decision. Americans, by being well prepared with ready answers, may adversely downplay the importance of the business being discussed. Likewise, both Japanese and Middle Eastern executives are put off by Americans' insistence on coming to the point directly and quickly in business transactions.

Promptness is considered very important in America and Japan. Furthermore, promptness is defined as being on time for appointments, whether you are the person making the call or the person receiving the caller. According to one expert:

Time is money and a symbol of status and responsibility. To be kept waiting is offensive in monochronic cultures, it is perceived as a message. It is not in polychronic cultures.[100]

What is meant by "being kept waiting" also varies substantially by culture. Thirty minutes might seem like an eternity in the United States, but it may seem like very little time in other countries, such as those in the Middle East. As you can see, understanding such differences *prior* to doing business in a given country is critical.

Space

The use people make of space and the meanings they assign to their use of space constitute a second form of nonverbal communication.[101] In America, "bigger is better." Thus, office space in corporations generally is allocated according to rank or prestige rather than need. The president will have the largest office, followed by the executive vice president, and so on.

A second major use of space is **personal space.** It is the nearest that others can come to you in various situations without your feeling uncomfortable. In the United States, normal business conversations occur at distances of 3 to 5 feet and highly personal business from 18 inches to 3 feet. In parts of northern Europe, the distances are slightly longer; in most of Latin America, they are substantially shorter.

An American businessperson in Latin America will tend to back away from a Latin American counterpart in order to maintain his or her preferred personal distance. In turn, the host will tend to advance toward the American in order to maintain his or her personal space. The resulting "chase" would be comical if it were not for the results. Both parties generally are unaware of their actions or the reasons for them. Furthermore, each assigns a meaning to the other's actions according to what the action means in his or her own culture. Thus, the North American considers the Latin American to be pushy and aggressive. The Latin American, in turn, considers the North American to be cold, aloof, and snobbish.

Symbols

An American seeing a baby wearing a pink outfit would most likely assume the child to be female. If the outfit were blue, the assumed gender would be male. These assumptions would be accurate most of the time in the United States but not in many other parts of the world, such as Holland. Colors, animals, shapes, numbers, and music have varying meanings across cultures. Failure to recognize the meaning assigned to a symbol can cause serious problems:

- AT&T had to change its "thumbs-up" ads in Russia and Poland, where showing the palm of the hand in this manner has an offensive meaning. The change was simple. The thumbs-up sign was given showing the back of the hand.
- Mont Blanc has a white marking on the end of its pens, meant to represent the snow-capped Alpine mountain peaks. However, Arab consumers reacted negatively because it looked like the "Star of David," which is Israel's national symbol. Mont Blanc worked to clear up the misunderstanding.[102]
- In the United States, blond hair color in women is often perceived as a symbol of beauty. In a study of seven European cities, the hair color most symbolic of beauty varied from dark brown (Madrid, Paris, and London), to black (Milan), to blond (Hamburg).[103]

Table 2-3 presents additional illustrations of varying meanings assigned to symbols across cultures.[104] Despite frequent cultural differences in symbols, many symbols work well across a wide range of cultures. Kellogg's Tony the Tiger works in the United States, China (see Illustration 2-6), and many other cultures.

The Meaning of Numbers, Colors, and Other Symbols	TABLE 2-3

• White	Symbol for mourning or death in the Far East; purity in the United States
• Purple	Associated with death in many Latin American countries
• Blue	Connotation of femininity in Holland; masculinity in Sweden, United States
• Red	Unlucky or negative in Chad, Nigeria, Germany; positive in Denmark, Romania, Argentina
• Yellow flowers	Sign of death in Mexico; infidelity in France
• White lilies	Suggestion of death in England
• 7	Unlucky number in Ghana, Kenya, Singapore; lucky in Morocco, India, Czechoslovakia, Nicaragua, United States
• Triangle	Negative in Hong Kong, Korea, Taiwan; positive in Colombia
• Owl	Wisdom in United States; bad luck in India
• Deer	Speed, grace in United States; homosexuality in Brazil

Relationships

The rights and obligations imposed by relationships and friendship are another nonverbal cultural variable. Americans, more so than those in most other cultures, form relationships and make friends quickly and easily and drop them easily also. In large part, this may be because America has always had a great deal of both social and geographic mobility. People who move every few years must be able to form friendships in a short time period and depart from them with a minimum of pain. In many other parts of the world, relationships and friendships are formed slowly and carefully because they imply deep and lasting

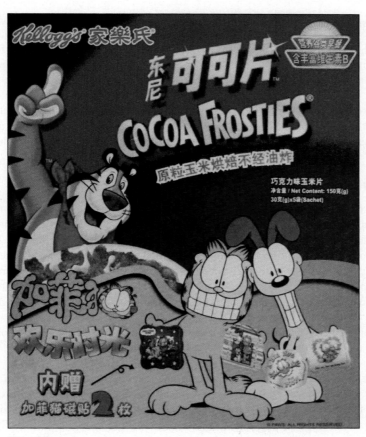

©Sijun Wang

obligations. As the following quote indicates, friendship and business are deeply intertwined in many cultures around the globe, including Latin America and Asia.

> In many cultures, the written word is used simply to satisfy legalities. In their eyes, emotion and personal relations are more important than cold facts.[105]

In addition, long-run success in many cultures involves more than just "getting to know" someone in the Western sense of the expression. For example, Chinese relationships are complex and described under the concept of **guanxi:**

> *Guanxi* is literally translated as personal connections/relationships on which an individual can draw to secure resources or advantages when doing business as well as in the course of social life. Its main characteristics are (1) the notion of a continuing reciprocal relationship over an indefinite period of time, (2) favors are banked, (3) it extends beyond the relationship between two parties to include other parties within the social network (it can be transferred), (4) the relationship network is built among individuals not organizations, (5) status matters—relationships with a senior will extend to his subordinates but not vice versa, and (6) the social relationship is prior to and a prerequisite to the business relationship.[106]

It should be noted quickly, however, that in an increasingly intertwined, modern, and global setting, even traditional notions like *guanxi* are being challenged. The following excerpt suggests the tensions felt by modern professionals in China:

> It is a bit strange but even as we almost act the part of the dynamic, modern, assertive business person, we still—underneath—still look for something deeper—far deeper—a more traditional and emotionally driven sense of trust, respect and guanxi—but we realize that in today's fast paced living (environment), it is often not possible to achieve this deeper level of relationship formation in a business climate—but to us, underneath it all, this is still the ultimate.[107]

Internet-based companies offer these professionals opportunities to interact and grow globally without relying on these deep personal connections.[108] Thus, different approaches therefore may be necessary depending on the depth and length of relationship desired.

Agreements

Americans rely on an extensive and, generally, highly efficient legal system for ensuring that business obligations are honored and for resolving disagreements. Many other cultures have not developed such a system and rely instead on relationships, friendship, and kinship; local moral principles; or informal customs to guide business conduct. For example, the Chinese "tend to pay more attention to relationships than contracts."[109] Under the American system, we would examine a proposed contract closely. Under the Chinese system, we would examine the character of a potential trading partner closely. In the words of an American CEO based in China:

> Relationships are everything in China, more so than in the United States, which is more focused on business. The Chinese want to know and understand you before they buy from you.[110]

Americans generally assume that, in almost all instances, prices are uniform for all buyers, related to the service rendered, and reasonably close to the going rate. We order many products such as taxi rides without inquiring in advance about the cost. In many Latin American, Asian, and Middle East countries, the procedure is different. Virtually all prices are negotiated prior to the sale, including those for industrial products.[111]

Things

The cultural meaning of things leads to purchase patterns that one would not otherwise predict. One observer noted a strong demand for expensive, status brands whose absolute cost was not too high among those Russians beginning to gain economically under capitalism. He concluded:

> They may stick to their locally produced toothpaste, but they want the Levi's, the Mont Blanc pens, the Moët & Chandon champagne to establish their self-esteem and their class position.[112]

The differing meanings that cultures attach to things, including products, make gift giving a particularly difficult task.[113] For example, giving a Chinese business customer or distributor a nice desk clock—a common gift in many countries—would be inappropriate. Why? In China, the word for *clock* is similar to the word for *funeral,* making clocks inappropriate gifts. When does receipt of a gift "require" a gift in return? In China, this depends on the closeness of the relationship between the parties—the closer the relationship, the less a return gift is required.[114]

The business and social situations that call for a gift, and the items that are appropriate gifts, vary widely. For example, a gift of cutlery is generally inappropriate in Russia, Japan, Taiwan, and Germany. In Japan, small gifts are required in many business situations, yet in China, they are less appropriate. In China, gifts should be presented privately, but in Arab countries, they should be given in front of others.

Etiquette

Etiquette represents generally accepted ways of behaving in social situations. Assume that an American is preparing a commercial that shows people eating an evening meal, with one person about to take a bite of food from a fork. The person will have the fork in the right hand, and the left hand will be out of sight under the table. To an American audience this will seem natural. However, in many European cultures, a well-mannered individual would have the fork in the left hand and the right hand on the table.

Behaviors considered rude or obnoxious in one culture may be quite acceptable in another. The common and acceptable American habit, for males, of crossing one's legs while sitting, such that the sole of a shoe shows, is extremely insulting in many Eastern cultures. In these cultures, the sole of the foot or shoe should never be exposed to view. While most Americans are not hesitant to voice dissatisfaction with a service encounter, many Asians are. This also appears to be true of the British, who have traditionally been characterized by their reserved nature. Such factors can lead U.S. managers to misjudge customer response to their services abroad.[115]

Normal voice tone, pitch, and speed of speech differ among cultures and languages, as does the use of gestures. Westerners often mistake the seemingly loud, volatile speech of some Asian cultures as signifying anger or emotional distress (which it would if it were being used by a Westerner) when it is normal speech for the occasion.

As American trade with Japan increases, we continue to learn more of the subtle aspects of Japanese business etiquette. For example, a Japanese executive will seldom say "no" directly during negotiations; doing so would be considered impolite. Instead, he might say, "That will be very difficult," which would mean "no." A Japanese responding "yes" to a request often means, "Yes, I understand the request," not "Yes, I agree to the request." Many Japanese find the American tendency to look straight into another's eyes when talking to be aggressive and rude.

Another aspect of Japanese business etiquette is *meishi,* epitomized by "A man without a *meishi* has no identity in Japan." The exchange of *meishi* is the most basic of social rituals in a nation where social ritual matters very much. The act of exchanging *meishi* is weighted with meaning. Once the social minuet is completed, the two know where they stand in relation to each other and their respective statures within the hierarchy of corporate or government bureaucracy. What is *meishi?* It is the exchange of business cards when two people meet! A fairly common, simple activity in America, it is an essential, complex social exchange in Japan.

Other cultures also find it necessary to learn about the subtleties of doing business with Westerners. Business leaders in China are developing training programs to help sensitize Chinese businesspeople to other cultures. According to Jack Ma, who runs one such program:

> Chinese businessmen are shrewd, but they need to learn to be more polished. At a World Economic Forum held in Bejing, Mr. Ma was depressed at how many conducted themselves, noting—Many smoked constantly and held loud cellphone conversations, even during meetings.[116]

The importance of proper, culture-specific etiquette is obvious. Although people recognize that etiquette varies from culture to culture, there is still a strong emotional feeling that "our way is natural and right."

Conclusions on Nonverbal Communications

Can you imagine yourself becoming upset or surprised because people in a different culture spoke to you in their native language, say Spanish or German, instead of English? Of course not. We all recognize that verbal languages vary around the world. Yet we generally feel that our nonverbal languages are natural or innate. Therefore, we misinterpret what is being "said" to us because we think we are hearing English when in reality it is Japanese, Italian, or Russian. It is this error that marketers can and must avoid.

GLOBAL CULTURES

An important issue facing marketers is the extent to which one or more global consumer cultures or segments are emerging. Evidence suggests that there is indeed movement in this direction.[117] Such a culture would have a shared set of consumption-related symbols with common meaning and desirability among members. One such proposed global culture is that portion of local cultures thats view itself as cosmopolitan, knowledgeable, and modern. Such individuals share many values and consumption-related behaviors with similar individuals across a range of national cultures.

Such cultures are being created by the globalization of mass media, work, education, and travel. Some product categories (cell phones, Internet) and brands (Sony, Nike) have become symbolically related to this culture. This does not imply that these brands use the same advertising globally but rather that the underlying theme and symbolism may be the same. Thus, a combined shampoo and conditioner could be positioned as a time-saver for the time-pressured modern career woman. The advertisement might portray the shampoo being used in the context of a gym in the United States or Germany, where many females exercise, but in a home context in Japan, where few women visit gyms. Philips Electronic is one firm that has developed a global positioning strategy based on such a global culture.[118]

Perhaps the closest thing to a global culture today is urban youth, which we examine next.

A Global Youth Culture?

Consider _____, a 19-year-old hip-hop music producer scouting for a new pair of Air Force 1 sneakers at the Nike shop. . . . _____, who prefers to be addressed by his street name, "Jerzy King"—moved to _____ three years ago. . . . A music school dropout who has never set foot outside of _____, he totes a mini-disc player loaded with Eminem, Puff Daddy, and Fabolous. On this particular day he's looking phat in a blue-and-white fleece jacket bearing the logo of the Toronto Maple Leafs.[119]

Can you fill in the blanks with any degree of confidence? The young man is Wang Qi and he lives in Beijing. However, many of his behaviors and possessions echo those of millions of other teenagers in Europe, North and South America, and Asia. And as we discussed earlier, it is incorrect to think of the youth influence as a one-way street from America to the rest of the world with entities like Levi's, Coke, and Taylor Swift leading the way:

Now it's a two-way street. Americans are learning Bollywood dance steps at their local health clubs. M.I.A., an up-and-coming pop singer who has Sri Lankan roots and was brought up in London, intermingles hip-hop, reggae, and South Asian influences. And Japanese *anime* has swept the globe.[120]

Similarities and convergence of lifestyles, values, and purchases make this global youth market compelling for companies, particularly given its large size. For example, a survey of global youth (age 14–29) across six countries found that 86 percent believe that products help to define and communicate their personality. It also found compelling similarities in the top three spending categories, as follows:[121]

	First Category	Second Category	Third Category
Amsterdam	Going out	Clothing	Food
Hong Kong	Clothing	Food	Transportation
Malaysia	Transportation	Food	Going out
Singapore	Food	Clothing	Entertainment
South Korea	Food	Clothing	Entertainment
United Kingdom	Going out	Clothing	Phone
United States	Clothing	Food	Music

What is causing this convergence? The largest single influence is worldwide mass media, including the Internet, and, more recently, mobile devices. Music, sports, and fashion appear to be major points of convergence, although the convergence often goes far beyond this to underlying values such as independence and risk taking. Marketers are using the similarities among youth across cultures to launch global brands or to reposition current brands to appeal to this large market. Levi's, reacting to the growing online trend among global teens, launched an online campaign in Asia targeted at "young, tech-savvy trendsetters." The website played heavily on Western music and style to promote its Levi's re-cut 501 Re-Born jeans. The theme emphasized that the jeans have been re-cut for today, with one page showing a teen being "reborn" or transformed by the new Levi's jeans.[122] Illustration 2–7 provides another example of an ad using a global youth appeal.

Several recent trends in the global youth market are critical for global marketers to understand. These include the following:[123]

- *Technology is mainstream.* Wired teens are a global phenomenon not restricted to developed countries. Sixty-six percent of teens globally are "superconnectors," meaning they use two or more electronic devices (e.g., cell phone and the Internet) daily.

This ad campaign uses a global youth appeal to target style leaders around the world.

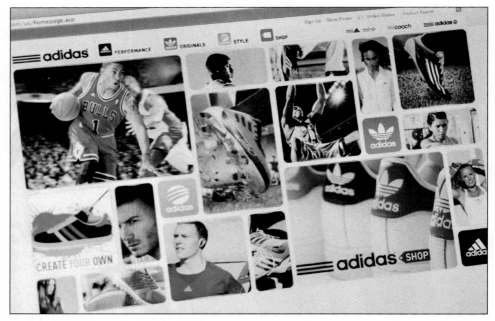

©NetPhotos/Alamy

- *U.S. teens no longer lead the way.* Now it's more about mind-set and the "creatives" are leading the way. Creatives are most prevalent in Europe (not the United States), are open to new ideas, and like expressing themselves in various ways, including personal web pages and art.
- *U.S. brands are not currently the leaders.* U.S. brands used to be the leaders among global teens. Now leading brands are Sony (Japan), H&M (Sweden), and Adidas (Germany).

As the global youth culture moves increasingly away from U.S. influence and brands, marketers in the United States must find ways to understand and connect with the trends and trendsetters across the globe. In addition, it is critical to understand that global youth also have a great many culturally unique behaviors, attitudes, and values. As one expert states, "European teens resent being thought of as Americans with an accent."[124] Global teens have gone so far as to say that their favorite brand "is me" and expect brands to enhance their individuality.[125]

Although this group has grown up with technology at their fingertips, these teenagers worldwide prefer to buy products in stores, as opposed to online. Whether living in a economically growing or mature market, the reason appears to be the same. In-store purchases are more common because this consumer group does not have access to credit cards. Where do they get their money? These creative and entrepreneurially spirited teens receive allowances, make money online, or work for themselves.[126]

The economic status of countries is discussed further in the global demographics section.

GLOBAL DEMOGRAPHICS

Economies such as India and China have seen rapid growth, which has led to increased personal disposable income and strong and growing middle classes that are the envy of marketers worldwide.[127] Concerns about the extent to which economic growth in these and other countries will continue at current rates are beginning to appear due to rising fuel and food costs.[128] To the extent that growth continues at a relatively rapid pace, such expansion not only creates opportunities, but also can present challenges.

Examine Illustration 2-8. The rapid increase in ownership of automobiles as replacements for bicycles in China has provided many with the freedom to travel greater distances. However, elevated emissions and traffic congestion have also become areas of concern.[129]

©McGraw-Hill Education/Barry Barker

ILLUSTRATION 2-8

The rapid growth in personal income in China has led to an explosion in car ownership. This has resulted in increased personal freedom but also concerns about congestion and emissions.

Disposable income is one aspect of demographics. **Demographics** *describe a population in terms of its size, structure, and distribution. Size refers to the number of individuals in the society. Structure describes the society in terms of age, income, education, and occupation. Distribution refers to the physical location of individuals in terms of geographic region and rural, suburban, and urban location.*

Demographics are both a result and a cause of cultural values. Densely populated societies are likely to have more of a collective orientation than an individualistic one because a collective orientation helps such societies function smoothly. Cultures that value hard work and the acquisition of material wealth are likely to advance economically, which alters their demographics both directly (income) and indirectly (families in economically advanced countries tend to be smaller).

A critical aspect of demographics for marketers is income, particularly the distribution of income. One country with a relatively low average income can have a sizable middle-income segment, while another country with the same average income may have most of the wealth in the hands of a few individuals. As shown below, Brazil's average per capita income is slightly lower than Romania's.[130] However, the distribution of that income differs sharply. Forty-two percent of the income generated in Brazil goes to just 10 percent of the population. In contrast, the top 10 percent of households in Romania command only 22 percent of that country's income. *How will these and the other differences shown below affect consumption?*

	Per Capita Income	Percent of Total Income to Top 10 Percent of Population	Per Capita PPP
Brazil	$ 8,840	42	$14,810
Canada	46,660	25	43,320
Chile	13,530	38	23,270
China	8,260	31	15,500
Egypt	3,460	26	11,110
France	38,520	26	42,380
India	1,680	30	6,490
Japan	36,190	25	42,870
Kenya	1,380	39	3,310
Mexico	9,040	39	17,740
Romania	9,470	22	22,950
United Kingdom	42,390	25	42,100
United States	56,180	30	58,030

Note: Per Capita Income is reported in US$; Per Capita Purchasing Power Parity (PPP) in International $.

Source: The World Bank, World Development Indicators Database: Gross National Income Per Capita 2016, Atlas Method and PPP (April 17, 2017); The World Bank, World Development Indicators Database: Income Share Held by Highest 10% (November 11, 2017).

Marketers increasingly use **purchasing power parity (PPP)** rather than average or median income to evaluate markets. PPP is based on the cost of a standard market basket of products bought in each country. An average household in one country may have a lower income in U.S. dollars. However, that household may be able to buy *more* than a household in other countries with higher income in U.S. dollars because of a lower local cost structure, government-provided health care, and so forth. The World Bank annually describes all countries in terms of PPP.[131] Notice how Chile's purchasing power is substantially higher than its per capita income would suggest. *How might an understanding of PPP change marketer decisions about such things as market potential and entry?*

The estimated age distributions of the United States, the Philippines, Japan, and Canada are shown below.[132] Note that over 35 percent of the populations of the Philippines and of India are under 20, compared with no more than one-fourth for the United States and Canada, and less than 20 percent for Japan. In the Middle East, a massive baby boom is underway, with two-thirds of the population under 25, fueling the youth movement in this region, which we discussed earlier.[133] *What product opportunities do this and the other age differences among these countries suggest?*

Age	United States (%)	Philippines (%)	Japan (%)	Canada (%)	India (%)
Under 10	12.5	22.6	8.5	10.2	18.4
10–19	12.9	20.9	9.3	10.8	18.4
20–29	14.0	17.4	9.9	13.2	17.0
30–39	13.1	14.3	12.1	13.2	15.1
40–49	12.6	10.3	14.4	12.9	12.6
50–59	13.6	7.3	12.0	14.9	9.1
60 and over	21.3	6.9	33.8	24.7	9.2

CROSS-CULTURAL MARKETING STRATEGY

As we have seen throughout the chapter, cross-cultural variations in such factors as values and demographics may make it necessary to adapt products and services to local considerations. One term for this adaptation is **glocalization,** which is generally taken to mean *global localization.*[134] There is continuing controversy over the *degree* to which cross-cultural marketing strategies should be standardized versus customized.[135] Standardized strategies can result in substantial cost savings. Maybelline's Manhattan line of cosmetics designed for the Asian market used one ad campaign in China, Taiwan, Hong Kong, Thailand, and Singapore. The ads featured an attractive Asian model in a low-cut, short dress against the Manhattan skyline at night. This combination of appeals to youth, beauty, and sophistication could be used in many other countries, though this ad would be inappropriate, and probably banned, in most Islamic countries.

Uniformity is sometimes possible, but companies often must adapt to cultural differences. Consider McDonald's:

> McDonald's used to strive for uniformity around the Globe. Now it adapts its products as appropriate— adding fried eggs to burgers in Japan and offering Samurai Pork Burgers with a sweet barbecue sauce in Thailand. However, its most dramatic changes were made when it entered India for the first time. So, instead of the all-beef Big Macs, the menu featured the mutton [lamb] Maharaja Mac.[136]

McDonald's also adapts its store layout. As shown in Illustration 2–9, separate sections for families and singles are provided in Muslim countries.

In addition to values and demographics, attitudes toward international brands can influence the need to customize offerings. For example, higher levels of patriotism and ethnocentrism appear to drive more negative views of international brands and may require more extreme forms of local customization.[137] Miller beer uses such customization to develop

©Hasan Jamali/AP Photo

ILLUSTRATION 2-9

McDonald's offers both family and singles sections in Muslim countries to accommodate the cultural norms governing interactions between men and women. The singles section is for single men only.

what it calls "local intimacy" by creating specific local brands of beer for very specific markets. For example, in Peru:

> . . . bottles of its Cusquena brand feature replica stones of an Incan wall that pay tribute to the elite standard of Inca craftsmanship that continues to this day in every bottle.[138]

Alternatively, higher levels of internationalism and cosmopolitanism appear to drive more positive views of international brands and thus allow for more standardization. In general, most companies will blend standardization and customization and a critical success factor in achieving the right balance.

Considerations in Approaching a Foreign Market

There are seven key considerations for each geographic market that a firm is contemplating. An analysis of these seven variables provides the background necessary for deciding whether or not to enter the market and to what extent, if any, an individualized marketing strategy is required. A small sample of experts, preferably native to the market under consideration, often will be able to furnish sufficient information on each variable.

Is the Geographic Area Homogeneous or Heterogeneous with Respect to Culture?   Marketing efforts are generally directed at defined geographic areas, primarily political and economic entities. Legal requirements and existing distribution channels often encourage this approach. However, it also is supported by the implicit assumption that geographical or political boundaries coincide with cultural boundaries. As we have seen, country boundaries represent general tendencies, but differences *within* a given country are also critical to consider. For example, research suggests that strategies in Latin America need to consider not only cross-country (e.g., Brazil vs. Chile) but also within-country (e.g., regional; urban vs. rural) differences.[139]

LO6

Likewise, China has strong regional cultures, urban and rural cultures, as well as sharp differences associated with income, age, and education.[140] Thus, marketing campaigns must be developed for cultural and demographic groups, not just countries.

What Needs Can This Product or a Version of It Fill in This Culture?   Most firms examine a new market with an existing product or product technology in mind. The question they must answer is what needs their existing or modified product can fill in the culture involved. For example, bicycles and motorcycles serve primarily recreational needs in the United States, but they provide basic transportation in many other countries.

Can Enough of the People Needing the Product Afford the Product?   An initial demographic analysis is required to determine the number of individuals or households that might need the product and who can actually afford it. For example, although China has over 1.4 billion consumers, the effective market for most Western goods is estimated to be considerably smaller than this total.[141] Future economic expansion in countries like China and India is expected to enhance their market potential in coming years. In addition, the possibilities of establishing credit, obtaining a government subsidy, or making a less expensive version should be considered. This latter approach is being used by P&G in China, where a tiered pricing system was designed to help reach consumers with relatively low incomes.[142] Indeed, many marketers are seeing growth in lower-middle-class markets. For example, Brazil's "Class C" customer, who earns $600 to $2,600 per month, is now its largest segment, and car sales to this group has pushed Brazil to one of the top five global markets in car ownership.[143]

What Values or Patterns of Values Are Relevant to the Purchase and Use of This Product?   The first section of this chapter focused on values and their role in consumer behavior. The value system should be investigated for influences on purchasing the product, owning the product, using the product, and disposing of the product. Much of the marketing strategy will be based on this analysis.

What Are the Distribution, Political, and Legal Structures for the Product?   The legal structure of a country can have an impact on each aspect of a firm's marketing mix. China has banned sex appeals during family view time and is tightening regulations on the opening of new Internet cafés. The United Kingdom has banned junk-food ads targeted at kids under the age of 16 and has tightened regulations on paid tweets. And Brazil has put laws in place that limit the amount of alcohol advertising.[144] Such legal restrictions limit the ability of companies to use standardized approaches to their marketing efforts. *What effect would China's ban on sex appeals have on Maybelline's advertising in Asia for its Manhattan line?*

Distribution challenges also exist. Companies like GM, Nike, and Procter & Gamble are finding this out as they move into so-called second-tier cities in China such as Chanchun. Here, distribution practices are different and require adaptation compared to first-tier cities like Bejing.[145]

In What Ways Can We Communicate about the Product?   This question requires an investigation into (1) available media and who attends to each type, (2) the needs the product fills, (3) values associated with the product and its use, and (4) the verbal and nonverbal communications systems in the culture(s). All aspects of the firm's promotional mix—including packaging, nonfunctional product design features, personal selling techniques, and advertising—should be based on these four factors.

The Internet seems like a natural medium through which to communicate to consumers. However, Internet access varies widely across countries, as does the percentage of consumers who will actually buy online. Moreover, tailoring websites to specific countries and content to specific online platforms is critical to online marketing success because of cultural variations in website dimensions driving purchase and loyalty.[146]

What Are the Ethical Implications of Marketing This Product in This Country?   All marketing programs should be evaluated on ethical as well as financial dimensions. As discussed at the beginning of the chapter, international marketing activities raise many ethical issues. The ethical dimension is particularly important and complex in marketing to third-world and developing countries. Consider Kellogg's attempt to introduce cold cereal as a breakfast food in a developing country. An ethical analysis would consider various factors, including the following:

If we succeed, will the average nutrition level be increased or decreased?

If we succeed, will the funds spent on cereal be diverted from other uses with more beneficial long-term impacts for the individuals or society?

If we succeed, what impact will this have on the local producers of currently consumed breakfast products?

Such an ethical analysis not only is the right thing to do but also may head off conflicts with local governments or economic interests. Understanding and acting on ethical considerations in international marketing is a difficult task. However, it is also a necessary one.

Consumer Insight 2–1 provides an illustration of how Coca-Cola has dealt with a number of these cross-cultural considerations in marketing its products globally.

CONSUMER INSIGHT **2-1**

Glocalization at Coca-Cola: Adapting Locally While Marketing Globally

BRIEF HISTORY

Coca-Cola is a brand that is extremely well-known the world over to the point that it may even be one of the more ubiquitous brands in existence. Coca-Cola began building its global network in the 1920s and has grown its reach to over 200 countries with nearly 450 brands. The brand has a rich history of global emotional advertising strategies while maintaining a degree of differentiation and specialization at a local level.[147]

GLOBAL STRATEGY

The company's global advertising strategy notably took off in 1971 with the "I'd Like to Buy the World a Coke" campaign, which featured young people of many nationalities gathering on a hilltop drinking Coke and singing together. Throughout the following decades, Coca-Cola continued advertising campaigns with emotional roots that had global appeal, such as "Have a Coke and a Smile," "Can't Beat the Feeling," "Can't Beat the Real Thing," "Always Coca-Cola," and "The Coke Side of Life."

In 2016, Coca-Cola took its global marketing to a new height by unifying all four of its trademarked brands (Coke Zero, Diet Coke, Coke Life, and Coca-Cola) under one message, strategy, and budget with the "Taste the Feeling" campaign. An international network of four advertising agencies produced a series of advertisements that would be shown all over the world. According to Chief Marketing Officer Marcos de Quinto, the goal was to "reinforce that Coca-Cola is for everybody." Furthermore, Rodolfo Echeverria, VP of global creative, connections, and digital at The Coca-Cola Company, reiterated:

The universal moments and storytelling depicted in the campaign were created to resonate with our consumers globally. The same images and TV creative in Japan will also be seen in Italy, in Mexico and around the world.

LOCALIZATION STRATEGY

At the same time, a large part of Coca-Cola's success in such a broad variety of international markets has been its historical multilocal approach. While there has been universal branding to some degree, the organizational structure is geographic and is divided into the various operating groups: North America, Latin America, Europe, Eurasia and Africa, and Pacific. Coca-Cola allows for differences in packaging, distribution, and media as they best fit with the needs, tastes, and cultural preferences of each geographic area. This approach is emphasized by late CEO Roberto Goizueta's "Think global, Act local" strategy and has allowed Coca-Cola to remain locally relevant. Ahmet C. Bozer, president of the Coca-Cola Company's Eurasia and Africa Group, stated, "We may be giving the same happiness message, the same brand architecture may be communicated, but it has to be done differently in each country."

- **Localized messages:** Often, advertising and promotional messages are customized to local geographic markets through use of models that mirror the local ethnicities and cultural preferences. For example, during the FIFA World Cup, Coca-Cola maintained a consistent brand message and image, but the web page for each country was locally customized with the use of local celebrities and culture. In addition, during the Arab Spring of 2011, Egypt was wrought with turmoil. Market research showed that, particularly among young consumers, people wanted to create a bright future despite the current political and social uncertainties. Coca-Cola put together a marketing communication that showed Egyptian people in Tahir Square in Cairo throwing ropes over dark clouds and pulling them to open up the clouds and reveal the sun. This particular advertisement, based in local consumer insights paired with the global strategy, was particularly effective.
- **Customized Products:** Coca-Cola does not just customize marketing communications to local markets. Across the globe, a wide variety of differences in tastes and preferences exist and Coca-Cola adapts the product offerings in local markets to meet them as well. Some flagship brands are present in each

market, such as Coca-Cola Classic and Sprite. Even still, there are differences from region to region. Coca-Cola utilizes local bottling and distribution operations, which may use slightly different methods and inputs such as sweeteners. Some countries use cane sugar, and some use high-fructose corn syrup. There are also differences in the amount of sugar between regions. One study showed that Sprite in Thailand has 47 g of sugar per 330 ml, while in Poland and Austria it has 19 g. The local bottlers sometimes innovate new products as well. For example, in India, Coca-Cola already produced Maaza Juice. The local team came up with the idea to produce Maaza Milk Shakes because dairy is a very popular drink category in India. The mango-flavored dairy milk shakes were wildly successful. Marketing communications and product innovations that are popular in one local market are often spread to similar local markets with like cultural tastes and preferences. For example, a Ramadan campaign to celebrate the Muslim holy month in Turkey was replicated in various other Muslim countries. And Minute Maid's Pulpy, China's innovation of an orange juice with lots of pulp, was successful in other countries with shared tastes.

As you can see, Coca-Cola's widespread success across the globe in so many countries and cultures is strongly rooted in both global strategy and local strategies. In other words, Coca-Cola is a prime example of glocalization at its finest!

Critical Thinking Questions:

1. Which of the core values discussed in the chapter might Coca-Cola encounter when entering various new markets?
2. Think about the seven global considerations when entering a foreign market that are discussed in the chapter and evaluate Coca-Cola on each of them (cultural homogeniety, needs, affordability, relevant values, infrastructure, communication, and ethical implications).
3. Do you have any experience with finding different sorts of beverages in different countries or even regions of the same country? If so, please share.

SUMMARY

SMARTBOOK

LO1: Define the concept of culture.

Culture is defined as the complex whole that includes knowledge, beliefs, art, law, morals, customs, and any other capabilities acquired by humans as members of society. It includes almost everything that influences an individual's thought processes and behaviors. Culture operates primarily by setting boundaries for individual behavior and by influencing the functioning of such institutions as the family and mass media. The boundaries, or *norms*, are derived from *cultural values*. Values are widely held beliefs that affirm what is desirable.

LO2: Describe core values that vary across culture and influence behaviors.

Cultural values are classified into three categories: other, environment, and self. *Other-oriented values* reflect a society's view of the appropriate relationships between individuals and groups within that society. Relevant values of this nature include *individual/collective, youth/age, extended/limited family, masculine/feminine, competitive/cooperative,* and *diversity/uniformity. Environment-oriented values* prescribe a society's relationships with its economic, technical, and physical environments. Examples of environment values are *cleanliness, performance/ status, tradition/change, risk taking/security, problem solving/fatalistic,* and *nature. Self-oriented values* reflect the objectives and approaches to life that individual members of society find desirable. These include *active/passive, sensual gratification/abstinence, material/nonmaterial, hard work/leisure, postponed gratification/immediate gratification,* and *religious/ secular.*

LO3: Understand cross-cultural variations in nonverbal communications.

Nonverbal communication systems are the arbitrary meanings a culture assigns actions, events, and things other than words. Major examples of nonverbal communication variables that affect marketers are *time, space, symbols, relationships, agreements, things,* and *etiquette.*

LO4: Summarize key aspects of the global youth culture.

There is evidence that urban youth around the world share at least some aspects of a common culture. This culture is driven by worldwide mass media and common music and sports stars. Emerging aspects include the importance of technology and the fact that U.S. teens and brands are no longer leading the way.

LO5: Understand the role of global demographics.

Demographics describe a population in terms of its size, structure, and distribution. Demographics differ widely across cultures and influence cultural values (and are influenced by them) as well as consumption patterns.

LO6: List the key dimensions in deciding to enter a foreign market.

Seven questions are relevant for developing a cross-cultural marketing strategy: (1) Is the geographic area homogeneous or heterogeneous with respect to culture? (2) What needs can this product fill in this culture? (3) Can enough of the people needing the product afford the product? (4) What values or patterns of values are relevant to the purchase and use of this product? (5) What are the distribution, political, and legal structures for the product? (6) In what ways can we communicate about the product? (7) What are the ethical implications of marketing this product in this country?

KEY TERMS

Cultural values 41
Culture 40
Demographics 63
Environment-oriented values 43
Glocalization 64
Guanxi 58
Instrumental materialism 52

Monochronic time perspective 55
Nonverbal communication
  systems 54
Norms 41
Other-oriented values 43
Personal space 56
Polychronic time perspective 55

Power distance 49
Purchasing power parity (PPP) 64
Sanctions 41
Self-oriented values 43
Terminal materialism 52
Verbal communication systems 53

REVIEW QUESTIONS

1. What are some of the ethical issues involved in cross-cultural marketing?
2. What is meant by the term *culture?*
3. What does the statement "Culture sets boundaries on behaviors" mean?
4. What is a *norm?* From what are norms derived?
5. What is a *cultural value?*
6. What is a *sanction?*
7. Cultural values can be classified as affecting one of three types of relationships—other, environment, or self. Describe each of these, and differentiate each one from the others.
8. How does the first of the following paired orientations differ from the second?
   a. Individual/Collective
   b. Performance/Status
   c. Tradition/Change
   d. Limited/Extended family
   e. Active/Passive
   f. Material/Nonmaterial
   g. Hard work/Leisure
   h. Risk taking/Security
   i. Masculine/Feminine
   j. Competitive/Cooperative
   k. Youth/Age
   l. Problem solving/Fatalistic
   m. Diversity/Uniformity
   n. Postponed gratification/Immediate gratification
   o. Sensual gratification/Abstinence
   p. Religious/Secular
9. What is meant by *nonverbal communications?* Why is this a difficult area to adjust to?
10. What is meant by each of the following as a form of nonverbal communication?
    a. Time
    b. Space
    c. Symbols
    d. Relationships
    e. Agreements
    f. Things
    g. Etiquette
11. What is *guanxi?*
12. What is the difference between *instrumental* and *terminal* materialism?
13. What are the differences between a *monochronic* time perspective and a *polychronic* time perspective?
14. What forces seem to be creating a global youth culture?
15. What are *demographics?* Why are they important to international marketers?
16. What is *purchasing power parity?*
17. What is *glocalization?* What factors affect the need to adapt to local considerations?
18. What are the seven key considerations in deciding whether or not to enter a given international market?

DISCUSSION QUESTIONS

19. Why should we study foreign cultures if we do not plan to engage in international or export marketing?
20. Is a country's culture more likely to be reflected in its art museums or its television commercials? Why?
21. Are the cultures of the world becoming more similar or more distinct?
22. Why do values differ across cultures?
23. The text lists 18 cultural values (in three categories) of relevance to marketing practice. Describe and place into one of the three categories two additional cultural values that have some relevance to marketing practice.
24. Select two cultural values from each of the three categories. Describe the boundaries (norms) relevant to that value in your society and the sanctions for violating those norms.
25. What are the most relevant cultural values affecting the consumption of each of the following? Describe how and why these values are particularly important.
    a. Internet
    b. Video games/consoles
    c. Milk
    d. Fast food
    e. Luxury cars
    f. Cell phones
26. What variations between the United States and other societies, *other than cultural variations,* may affect the relative level of usage of the following?
    a. Internet
    b. Video games/consoles
    c. Milk

   d. Fast food
   e. Luxury cars
   f. Cell phones

27. Why is materialism higher in Korea than in the United States, where given its collectivist culture one might expect materialism to be lower?

28. What values underlie the differences between Fiji Island and U.S. children in terms of the strategies they use to influence their parents' decisions? What marketing implications emerge?

29. What are the marketing implications of the differences in the *masculine/feminine orientation* across countries?

30. Respond to the questions in Consumer Insight 2–1.

31. Why do nonverbal communication systems vary across cultures?

32. Which, if any, nonverbal communication factors might be relevant in the marketing of the following?
   a. Watches
   b. Jewelry
   c. Facial tissue
   d. Laundry detergent
   e. Lip balm
   f. Women's clothing

33. What are the implications of *guanxi* for a Western firm entering the Chinese market?

34. To what extent do you think youth are truly becoming a single, global culture?

35. Will today's youth still be a "global culture" when they are 40? Why or why not?

36. How do demographics affect a culture's values? How do a culture's values affect its demographics?

37. What causes the differences between purchasing power parity and income, as shown in the text?

38. The text provides a seven-step procedure for analyzing a foreign market. Using this procedure, analyze your country as a market for
   a. Laptop computers from Japan.
   b. Automobiles from Korea.
   c. Sunglasses from Italy.
   d. Wine from Chile.

39. What are the major ethical issues in introducing prepared foods such as fast foods to developing countries?

40. Should U.S. tobacco firms be allowed to market cigarettes in developing countries? Why or why not?

41. How can developing countries keep their cultures from being overly Westernized or Americanized?

APPLICATION ACTIVITIES

42. Interview two students from two different cultures. Determine the extent to which the following are used in those cultures and the variations in the values of those cultures that relate to the use of these products:
   a. Gift cards
   b. Energy drinks (like Red Bull)
   c. Fast-food restaurants
   d. Exercise equipment
   e. Music
   f. Internet

43. Interview two students from two different cultures. Report any differences in nonverbal communications they are aware of between their culture and your culture.

44. Interview two students from two different cultures. Report their perceptions of the major differences in cultural values between their culture and your culture.

45. Interview a student from India. Report on the advice that the student would give an American firm marketing consumer products in India.

46. Interview two students from Southeast Asia regarding their perceptions of materialism and conspicuous consumption. Report on how their responses reinforce or conflict with the traditional value systems found in their countries.

47. Imagine you are a consultant working with your state's or province's tourism agency. You have been asked to advise the agency on the best promotional themes to use to attract foreign tourists. What would you recommend if Germany and Australia were the two target markets?

48. Analyze a foreign culture of your choice, and recommend a marketing program for a brand of one of the following made in your country:
   a. Automobile
   b. Beer
   c. MP3 player
   d. Discount retailer
   e. Movies
   f. Cosmetics

REFERENCES

1. T. Lee, "Target Has a Twin in Australia, but They're Not Related," *Star Tribune,* August 24, 2013, www.startribune.com/business/220867991.html, accessed August 24, 2014; as well as company websites at (Target U.S.) www.target.com/ and (Target Australia) www.target.com.au/#!.

2. K. Kovalchik, "Easter with . . . the Duracell Bunny?," Mentalfloss.com, http://mentalfloss.com/article/24372/easter-duracell-bunny, accessed August 24, 2014; "Duracell Bunny vs. Energizer Bunny," blog post on September 30, 2013, at www.budgetbatteries.co.uk/blog/?p523, accessed August 24, 2014.

3. I. Paul, "The Beatles and iTunes: A Complicated History," *PC World,* September 9, 2009; S. Tibken, "Apple Now Officially Owns Beatles' Apple Corps Logo," *CNET News,* October 25, 2012, http://news.cnet.com/8301-13579_3-57540017-37/apple-now-officially-owns-beatles-apple-corps-logo/, accessed August 24, 2014; S. Crawford, "Why Weren't The Beatles on iTunes?," *HowStuffWorks,* http://electronics.howstuffworks.com/beatles-itunes2.htm, accessed August 24, 2014.

4. See, e.g., M. Fielding, "Special Delivery," *Marketing News,* February 1, 2007, pp. 13–14; T. Sangkhawasi and L. M. Johri, "Impact of Status Brand Strategy on Materialism in Thailand," *Journal of Consumer Marketing* 24, no. 5 (2007), pp. 275–82.

5. Examples from G. Burton, "Brazilian Lessons on Coolness and Imagination," *Brazzil,* April 2005, accessed April 27, 2008; N. Madden, "How the NFL Intends to Push 'Olive Ball' in China," *Advertising Age,* October 2, 2006, p. 45; I. Rowley, "Lexus," *BusinessWeek,* March 31, 2008, p. 72; P. Cloud, "Tokyo Style–Harajuku Streets," *McClatchy-Tribune Business News,* February 1, 2010; J. Kaiman, "American Football Is Gaining Traction in China," *Los Angeles Times,* October 4, 2016; L. Tran, "Why Brazilian Fashion Is All the Rage across the Atlantic in Angola," *Conversation,* August 6, 2017.

6. N. Madden, "China Cracks Down on TV Talent Competitions," *Advertising Age,* April 3, 2006, p. 14.

7. D. Holt, J. A. Quelch, and E. L. Taylor, "How Global Brands Compete," *Harvard Business Review,* September 2004, pp. 1–8.

8. See S. Mulley, "Young Women's Smoking Crisis Declared in Asia," *Medical Post,* January 11, 2000, p. 68; J. Mackay and M. Eriksen, *The Tobacco Atlas* (Brighton, U.K.: World Health Organization, 2002), pp. 31, 89; M. E. Goldberg and H. Baumgartner, "Cross-Country Attraction as a Motivation for Product Consumption," *Journal of Business Research* 55 (2002), pp. 901–906; http://tobaccoatlas.org/consumption.html, accessed January 29, 2011.

9. Mulley, "Young Women's Smoking Crisis Declared in Asia."

10. See, e.g., J. L. Aaker and J. Sengupta, "Additivity versus Attenuation," *Journal of Consumer Psychology* 2 (2000), pp. 67–82; D. A. Briley, M. W. Morris, and I. Simonson, "Reasons as Carriers of Culture," *Journal of Consumer Research,* September 2000, pp. 157–77.

11. T. Parker-Pope, "Custom-Made," *Wall Street Journal,* September 26, 1996, p. R22; see also M. Fielding, "Walk the Line," *Marketing News,* September 1, 2006, pp. 8–10.

12. A. Groth, "Best Buy's Overseas Strategy Is Failing in Europe and China," *Business Insider,* November 4, 2011; H. Wang, "Why Barbie Stumbled in China and How She Could Re-invent Herself," *Forbes,* October 24, 2012; W. Bryan, "Shanghai Barbie Palace Closes Doors as Mattel Changes Tack in China," *NPR News,* March 8, 2011, www.npr.org, March 8, 2011, accessed November 27, 2017.

13. S. Cockroft, "Tesco Underfire after Selling Smokey Bacon Flavour Pringles as Part of a Special Ramadan Promotion," *Daily Mail,* June 24, 2015; M. Fromowitz, "Hall of Shame: More Multicultural Brand Blunders," *Campaign Live,* February 10, 2017, www.campaignlive.com, accessed December 4, 2017.

14. For this and other global missteps, see M. D. White, *A Short Course in International Marketing Blunders* (Petaluma: World Trade Press, 2002).

15. "It's a Grande-Latte World," *Wall Street Journal,* December 15, 2003, p. B1.

16. G. Hofstede, *Culture's Consequences,* 2nd ed. (Thousand Oaks, CA: Sage, 2001).

17. Z. Gurhan-Canli and D. Maheswaran, "Cultural Variations in Country of Origin Effects," *Journal of Marketing Research,* August 2000, pp. 309–17.

18. C. Pornpitakpan and J. N. P. Francis, "The Effect of Cultural Differences, Source Expertise, and Argument Strength on Persuasion," *Journal of International Consumer Marketing* 1 (2001), pp. 77–101.

19. H. Ko, M. S. Roberts, and C. Cho, "Cross-Cultural Differences in Motivations and Perceived Interactivity," *Journal of Current Issues and Research in Advertising,* Fall 2006, pp. 93–104.

20. K. Schoefer, "Cultural Moderation in the Formation of Recovery Satisfaction Judgments," *Journal of Service Research* 13, no. 1 (2010), pp. 52–64.

21. J. E. M. Steenkamp, F. Ter Hofstede, and M. Wedel, "A Cross-National Investigation into the Individual and National Cultural Antecedents of Consumer Innovativeness," *Journal of Marketing,* April 1999, pp. 55–69; I. S. Yaveroglu and N. Donthu, "Cultural Differences on the Diffusion of New Products," *Journal of International Consumer Marketing* 14, no. 4 (2002), pp. 49–63.

22. S. M. Choi, W. Lee, and H. Kim, "Lessons from the Rich and Famous," *Journal of Advertising,* Summer 2005, pp. 85–98.

23. N. Y. Wong and A. C. Ahuvia, "Personal Taste and Family Face," *Psychology & Marketing,* August 1998, pp. 423–41.

24. K. Chan and X. Wang, "Exploring the Antecedents and Consequences of Ming Pái Kóng (Brand-Name Fanaticism) among China's Generation Y," *Journal of Global Marketing* 8, no. 2 (2015), pp. 67–82.

25. C. Robinson, "Asian Culture," *Journal of the Market Research Society,* January 1996, pp. 55–62.

26. T. Erdem, J. Swait, and A. Valenzuala, "Brands as Signals," *Journal of Marketing,* January 2006, pp. 34–49.

27. T. Sun, M. Horn, and D. Merritt, "Values and Lifestyles of Individualists and Collectivists," *Journal of Consumer Marketing* 21, no. 5 (2004), pp. 318–31.

28. See, e.g., J. Zhang and S. Shavitt, "Cultural Values in Advertisements to the Chinese X-Generation," *Journal of Advertising* 32, no. 1 (2003), pp. 23–33.

29. "Global Teen Culture," *Brand Strategy,* January 2003, pp. 37–38.

30. J. Bowman, "Asian Women Put on a New Face," *Media,* April 17, 2008, p. 22.

31. See, e.g., K. C. C. Yang, "The Effects of Allocentrism and Idiocentrism on Consumers' Product Attribute Evaluation," *Journal of International Consumer Marketing* 16, no. 4 (2004), pp. 63-84.

32. B. Barak et al., "Perceptions of Age-Identity," *Psychology & Marketing,* October 2001, pp. 1003-29; C. A. Lin, "Cultural Values Reflected in Chinese and American Television Advertising," *Journal of Advertising,* Winter 2001, pp. 83-94; D. H. Z. Khairullah and Z. Y. Khairullah, "Dominant Cultural Values," *Journal of Global Marketing* 16, no. 1/2 (2002), pp. 47-70.

33. P. L. Andruss, "Groups Make Fruits Apple of Taiwan's Eye," *Marketing News,* December 4, 2000, p. 5.

34. H. Fattah, "The New Arab Consumer," *American Demographics,* September 2002, p. 58.

35. M. Kalliny and L. Gentry, "Cultural Values Reflected in Arab and American Television Advertising," *Journal of Current Issues and Research in Advertising,* Spring 2007, pp. 15-32.

36. A. Shoham and V. Dalakas, "Family Consumer Decision Making in Israel," *Journal of Consumer Marketing* 20, no. 3 (2003), pp. 238-51; M. Laroche et al., "How Culture Matters in Children's Purchase Influence," *Journal of the Academy of Marketing Science* 35 (2007), pp. 113-26.

37. J. S. Wimalasiri, "A Comparison of Children's Purchase Influence and Parental Response in Fiji and the United States," *Journal of International Consumer Marketing* 4 (2000), pp. 55-73. See also J. S. Wimalasiri, "A Cross-National Study on Children's Purchasing Behavior and Parental Response," *Journal of Consumer Marketing* 21, no. 4 (2004), pp. 274-84.

38. M. F. Ji and J. U. McNeal, "How Chinese Children's Commercials Differ from Those of the United States," *Journal of Advertising,* Fall 2001, pp. 79-92; K. Chan and J. U. McNeal, "Parent-Child Communications About Consumption and Advertising in China," *Journal of Consumer Marketing* 20, no. 4 (2003), pp. 317-34; "Little Emperors," *Fortune,* October 4, 2004, pp. 138-50.

39. L. Chang, "The New Stresses of Chinese Society Shape a Girl's Life," *Wall Street Journal,* December 4, 2003, pp. A1, A13.

40. P. Kotler, S. W. Ang, and C. T. Tan, *Marketing Management: An Asian Perspective* (Singapore: Prentice Hall Pergamon, 1996), p. 524. But see M. Liu, "China's Empty Nest," *Newsweek,* March 10, 2008, p. 41, for evidence of how this is changing among younger generations of Chinese.

41. M. Viswanathan, T. L. Childers, and E. S. Moore, "The Measurement of Intergenerational Communication and Influence on Consumption," *Journal of the Academy of Marketing Science,* Summer 2000, pp. 406-24.

42. M. Kripalani, "Here Come the Wal-Mart Wannabes," *BusinessWeek,* April 4, 2005, p. 56.

43. See F. S. Al-Olayan and K. Karande, "A Content Analysis of Magazine Advertisements from the United States and the Arab World," *Journal of Advertising,* Fall 2000, pp. 69-82.

44. L. Wentz, "U.S. Military Goes Native in Afghanistan Ad Push," *Advertising Age,* April 12, 2010, pp. 1, 20.

45. S. M. Sidin et al., "The Effects of Sex Role Orientation on Family Purchase Decision Making in Malaysia," *Journal of Consumer Marketing* 21, no. 6 (2004), pp. 381-90; "Rate of Chinese Businesswomen Higher Than World Average," *China Daily,* March 20, 2005, www.chinadaily.com.

46. L. M. Milner and J. M. Collins, "Sex-Role Portrayals and the Gender of Nations," *Journal of Advertising,* Spring 2000, pp. 67-78; G. Fowler, "China Cracks Down on Commercials," *Wall Street Journal,* February 19, 2004, p. B7.

47. E. Hall, "U.K. Politicians Court Mommy Bloggers," *Advertising Age,* February 18, 2010.

48. V. Bevins, "Marta and Rafaela: Brazil's Olympic Heroes May Be a Sign of the Nation's Shifting Attitudes," *Los Angeles Times,* August 11, 2016.

49. L. Y. Sin and O. H. Yau, "Female Role Orientation and Consumption Values," *Journal of International Consumer Marketing* 13, no. 2 (2001), pp. 49-75.

50. L. Y. M. Sin and O. H. M. Yau, "Female Role Orientation of Chinese Women," *Psychology & Marketing,* December 2004, pp. 1033-58.

51. For a related discussion, see M. de Mooij, *Global Marketing and Advertising* (Thousand Oaks, CA: Sage, 1998), pp. 252-53.

52. See K. L. Miller, "You Just Can't Talk to These Kids," *BusinessWeek,* April 19, 1993, pp. 104-106; P. Sellers, "Pepsi Opens a Second Front," *Fortune,* August 8, 1994, pp. 70-76; N. Donthu, "A Cross-Country Investigation of Recall of and Attitude toward Comparative Advertising," *Journal of Advertising,* Summer 1998, pp. 111-22.

53. See M. de Mooij, *Consumer Behavior and Culture* (Thousand Oaks, CA: Sage, 2004), pp. 162-64. For a discussion of how language can influence accessibility of cultural values, see D. A. Briley, M. W. Morris, and I. Simonson, "Cultural Chameleons," *Journal of Consumer Psychology* 15, no. 4 (2005), pp. 351-62.

54. Sun, Horn, and Merritt, "Values and Lifestyles of Individualists and Collectivists."

55. L. Shannahan, "Bugging Out over Germs," *Brandweek,* November 22, 2004, p. 17.

56. See, e.g., V. Kurian, "'Hand Wash' Campaign in Kerala Raises a Stink," *Businessline,* November 6, 2002, p. 1.

57. J. L. Watson, *Golden Arches East* (Stanford, CA: Stanford University Press, 1997).

58. R. Mandhachitara, R. M. Shannon, and C. Hadjicharalambous, "Why Private Label Grocery Brands Have Not Succeeded in Asia," *Journal of Global Marketing* 20, no. 2/3 (2007), pp. 71-87.

59. Lin, "Cultural Values Reflected in Chinese and American Television Advertising"; Khairullah and Khairullah, "Dominant Cultural Values"; S. Okazaki and B. Mueller, "An Analysis of Advertising Appeals Employed in Japanese and American Print Advertising–Revisited," Working Paper, San Diego State University (San Diego, 2008); S. Biswas, M. Hussain, and K. O'Donnel, "Celebrity Endorsements in Advertisements and Consumer Perceptions," *Journal of Global Marketing* 22 (2009), pp. 121-37.

60. N. Madden, "In China, Multinationals Forgo Adaptation for New-Brand Creation," *Advertising Age,* January 17, 2011.

61. For a related dimension, see S. Shavitt et al., "The Horizontal/Vertical Distinction in Cross-Cultural Consumer Research," *Journal of Consumer Psychology* 16, no. 4 (2006), pp. 325-56.

62. Pornpitakpan and Francis, "The Effect of Cultural Differences, Source Expertise, and Argument Strength on Persuasion"; see also B. R. Barnes et al., "Investigating the Impact of International

Cosmetics Advertising in China," *International Journal of Advertising* 23 (2004), pp. 361–87.

63. C. Pornpitakpan, "Factors Associated with Opinion Seeking," *Journal of Global Marketing* 17, no. 2/3 (2004), pp. 91–113.

64. N. R. Buchan, R. T. A. Croson, and E. J. Johnson, "When Do Fair Beliefs Influence Bargaining Behavior?," *Journal of Consumer Research,* June 2004, pp. 181–90.

65. D. Kim, Y. Pan, and H. S. Park, "High- versus Low-Context Culture," *Psychology & Marketing,* September 1998, pp. 507–21.

66. Z. Caillat and B. Mueller, "The Influence of Culture on American and British Advertising," *Journal of Advertising Research,* May–June 1996, pp. 79–88; Lin, "Cultural Values Reflected in Chinese and American Television Advertising."

67. Zhang and Shavitt, "Cultural Values in Advertisements to the Chinese X-Generation."

68. C. Riegner, "Wired China," *Journal of Advertising Research,* December 2008, pp. 496–505.

69. G. Parker, "Going Global Can Hit Snags," *Wall Street Journal,* June 16, 2004, p. B1.

70. Steenkamp, Ter Hofstede, and Wedel, "A Cross-National Investigation into the Individual and National Cultural Antecedents of Consumer Innovativeness"; Pornpitakpan and Francis, "The Effect of Cultural Differences, Source Expertise, and Argument Strength on Persuasion"; J. M. Jung and J. J. Kellaris, "Cross-National Differences in Proneness to Scarcity Effects," *Psychology & Marketing,* September 2004, pp. 739–53; Erdem, Swait, and Valenzuala, "Brands as Signals."

71. See, e.g., P. Raven and D. H. B. Welsh, "An Exploratory Study of Influences on Retail Service Quality," *Journal of Services Marketing* 18, no. 3 (2004), pp. 198–214.

72. W. L. Chang and P. Lii, "Luck of the Draw," *Journal of Advertising Research,* December 2008, pp. 523–30; E. Coggins, "The New Asian Tiger Leadership Style," http://suite101.com, accessed February 5, 2011.

73. "Quiet Motorcycle Seeks Added Vroom," *CNN.com,* March 17, 2005, www.cnn.com.

74. L. Scott and D. Vigar-Ellis, "Consumer Understanding, Perceptions, and Behaviours with Regard to Environmentally Friendly Packaging in a Developing Nation," *International Journal of Consumer Studies* 38 (2014), pp. 642–49.

75. T. S. Chan, "Concerns for Environmental Issues," *Journal of International Consumer Marketing* 1 (1996), pp. 43–55.

76. R. Y. K. Chan, "Determinants of Chinese Consumers' Green Purchase Behavior," *Psychology & Marketing,* April 2001, pp. 389–413; K. Lee, "Gender Differences in Hong Kong Adolescent Consumers' Green Purchase Behavior," *Journal of Consumer Marketing* 26, no. 2 (2009), pp. 87–96.

77. P. Hallal et al., "Global Physical Activity Levels: Surveillance Progress, Pitfalls, and Prospects," *Lancet* 380 (2012), pp. 247–57.

78. "Saudis and Americans," *NOP World* (New York: United Business Media), January 6, 2003, www.nopworld.com.

79. S. L. M. So, "A Comparative Content Analysis of Women's Magazine Advertisements from Hong Kong and Australia on Advertising Expressions," *Journal of Current Issues and Research in Advertising,* Spring 2004, pp. 47–58; Khairullah and Khairullah, "Dominant Cultural Values."

80. K. Chen and L. Chang, "China Takes Aim at Racy, Violent TV Shows," *Wall Street Journal,* May 24, 2004, p. B1.

81. C. Webster and R. C. Beatty, "Nationality, Materialism, and Possession Importance," in *Advances in Consumer Research,* vol. 24, ed. M. Brucks and D. J. MacInnis (Provo, UT: Association for Consumer Research, 1997), pp. 204–10.

82. K. Chan and G. P. Prendergast, "Social Comparison, Imitation of Celebrity Models and Materialism among Chinese Youth," *International Journal of Advertising* 27, no. 5 (2008), pp. 799–826; J. S. Podoshen, L. Li, and J. Zhang, "Materialism and Conspicuous Consumption in China," *International Journal of Consumer Studies* 35 (2011), pp. 17–25.

83. J. E. Workman and S. H. Lee, "Materialism, Fashion Consumers, and Gender," *International Journal of Consumer Studies* 35 (2011), pp. 50–57.

84. P. Paul, "Global Generation Gap," *American Demographics,* March 2002, pp. 18–19.

85. Organisation for Economic and Co-Operation Development (OECD), Hours Worked Indicator (2016), www.oecd.org, accessed December 8, 2017.

86. G. Hofstede et al., "What Goals Do Business Leaders Pursue?," *Journal of International Business Studies* 33, no. 4 (2002), pp. 785–803.

87. M. de Mooij and G. Hofstede, "Convergence and Divergence in Consumer Behavior: Implications for International Retailing," *Journal of Retailing* 78 (2002), pp. 61–69; S. Strother, "The Consumer Market in New China," *Journal of Global Business Studies* 8, no. 2 (2014), pp. 9–17.

88. See S. S. Al-Makaty, "Attitudes toward Advertising in Islam," *Journal of Advertising Research,* May–June 1996, pp. 16–25; "Saudis and Americans."

89. See, e.g., D. S. Waller, K. S. Fam, and B. Z. Erdogan, "Advertising of Controversial Products," *Journal of Consumer Marketing* 22, no. 1 (2005), pp. 6–18.

90. "Dogpile," *Kwintessential,* www.kwintessential.co.uk/translation/articles/cross-cultural-issues.htm, accessed March 20, 2005.

91. See S. Zhang and B. H. Schmitt, "Creating Local Brands in Multilingual International Markets," *Journal of Marketing Research,* August 2001, pp. 313–25.

92. D. L. Vence, "Proper Message, Design in Global Markets Require Tests," *Marketing News,* September 1, 2006, pp. 18, 24.

93. G. James, "Epic Fails in Global Branding," *Inc.,* October 29, 2014, www.inc.com, accessed November 29, 2017.

94. See M. F. Toncar, "The Use of Humor in Television Advertising," *International Journal of Advertising* 20 (2001), pp. 521–39.

95. See N. Spears, X. Lin, and J. C. Mowen, "Time Orientation in the United States, China, and Mexico," *Journal of International Consumer Marketing* 1 (2001), pp. 57–75.

96. L. A. Manrai and A. K. Manrai, "Effect of Cultural-Context, Gender, and Acculturation on Perceptions of Work versus Social/Leisure Time Usage," *Journal of Business Research,* February 1995, pp. 115–28; J. D. Lindquist and C. F. Kaufman-Scarborough, "Polychronic Tendency Analysis," *Journal of Consumer Marketing* 21, no. 5 (2004), pp. 332–42; G. H. Brodowsky et al., "If Time Is Money Is It a Common Currency?," *Journal of Global Marketing* 21, no. 4 (2008), pp. 245–57.

97. M. Lee and F. M. Ulgado, "Consumer Evaluations of Fast-Food Services," *Journal of Services Marketing* 1 (1997), pp. 39–52; G. H. Brodowsky and B. B. Anderson, "A Cross-Cultural Study of Consumer Attitudes toward Time," *Journal of Global Marketing* 3 (2000), pp. 93–109.

98. de Mooij, *Global Marketing and Advertising.*

99. K. McSpadden, "You Now Have a Shorter Attention Span Than a Goldfish," *Time,* May 14, 2015; M. Prensky, "Digital Natives, Digital Immigrants," *On the Horizon* 9, no. 5 (2001), pp. 1–6; D. Schawbel, "Fighting for the Young Consumer's Attention," www.americanexpress.com, April 24, 2012, accessed December 15, 2017.

100. de Mooij, *Global Marketing and Advertising,* p. 71.

101. See M. Chapman and A. Jamal, "Acculturation," in *Advances in Consumer Research,* vol. 24, ed. Brucks and MacInnis, pp. 138–44.

102. From White, *A Short Course in International Marketing Blunders,* p. 39.

103. R. Bjerke and R. Polegato, "How Well Do Advertising Images of Health and Beauty Travel across Cultures?," *Psychology & Marketing,* October 2006, pp. 865–84.

104. See also de Mooij, *Global Marketing and Advertising;* T. J. Madden, K. Hewett, and M. S. Roth, "Managing Images in Different Cultures," *Journal of International Marketing* 8, no. 4 (2000), pp. 90–107.

105. P. A. Herbig and H. E. Kramer, "Do's and Don'ts of Cross-Cultural Negotiations," *Industrial Marketing Management* 4 (1992), p. 293; see also P. Fan and Z. Zigang, "Cross-Cultural Challenges When Doing Business in China," *Singapore Management Review* 26, no. 1 (2004), pp. 81–90.

106. M. Ewing, A. Caruana, and H. Wong, "Some Consequences of Guanxi," *Journal of International Consumer Marketing* 4 (2000), p. 77. See also F. Balfour, "You Say Guanxi, I Say Schmoozing," *BusinessWeek,* November 19, 2007, pp. 84–85.

107. M. Willis, "Tradition versus Change," *Journal of Global Marketing* 22 (2009), pp. 67–89. See also F. F. Gu, K. Hung, and D. K. Tse, "When Does Guanxi Matter?," *Journal of Marketing,* July 2008, pp. 12–28.

108. K. Hope, "Doing Business the Chinese Way," *BBC,* October 8, 2014, www.bbc.com, accessed December 15, 2017.

109. Fan and Zigang, "Cross-Cultural Challenges When Doing Business in China," p. 85; N. J. White and J. Lee, "Dispute Resolution in the Korean and U.S. Markets," *Mid-American Journal of Business* 19, no. 2 (2004), pp. 23–30.

110. G. Brewer, "An American in Shanghai," *Sales and Marketing Management,* November 1997, p. 42.

111. See H. McDonald, P. Darbyshire, and C. Jevons, "Shop Often, Buy Little," *Journal of Global Marketing* 4 (2000), pp. 53–72; A. G. Abdul-Muhmin, "The Effect of Perceived Seller Reservation Prices on Buyers' Bargaining Behavior in a Flexible-Price Market," *Journal of International Consumer Marketing* 3 (2001), pp. 29–45.

112. C. Miller, "Not Quite Global," *Marketing News,* July 3, 1995, p. 9.

113. S. Y. Park, "A Comparison of Korean and American Gift-Giving Behaviors," *Psychology & Marketing,* September 1998, pp. 577–93.

114. A. Joy, "Gift Giving in Hong Kong and the Continuum of Social Ties," *Journal of Consumer Research,* September 2001, pp. 239–54.

See also J. Wang, F. Piron, and M. V. Xuan, "Faring One Thousand Miles to Give Goose Feathers," in *Advances in Consumer Research,* vol. 28, ed. M. C. Gilly and J. Meyers-Levy (Provo, UT: Association for Consumer Research, 2001), pp. 58–63.

115. M. K. Hui and K. Au, "Justice Perceptions of Complaint Handling," *Journal of Business Research* 52 (2001), pp. 161–73; C. A. Voss et al., "A Tale of Two Countries' Conservatism, Service Quality, and Feedback on Customer Satisfaction," *Journal of Service Research,* February 2004, pp. 212–30.

116. M. Fong, "Chinese Charm School," *Wall Street Journal,* January 13, 2004, pp. B1, B6.

117. B. D. Keillor, M. D'Amico, and V. Horton, "Global Consumer Tendencies," *Psychology & Marketing,* January 2000, pp. 1–19; F. Ter Hofstede, M. Wedel, and J. E. M. Steenkamp, "Identifying Spacial Segments in International Markets," *Marketing Science,* Spring 2002, pp. 160–77.

118. C. Edy, "The Olympics of Marketing," *American Demographics,* June 1999, pp. 47–48.

119. "Little Emperors," p. 143.

120. S. Hamm, "Children of the Web," *BusinessWeek,* July 2, 2007, pp. 50–58.

121. "Global Youth Panel," *NGT,* www.nextgreatthing.com, accessed May 5, 2008.

122. N. Madden, "Levi's Enjoys 'Rebirth' on the Web in Asia," *Advertising Age,* April 19, 2004, p. N-10.

123. C. Walker, "Six Seismic Shifts in Global Teen Culture," *Chief Marketer,* www.chiefmarketer.com, accessed February 6, 2011; IBM Institute for Business Value, "Uniquely Generation Z: What Brands Should Know About Today's Youngest Consumers," January 2017.

124. L. Bertagnoli, "Continental Spendthrifts," *Marketing News,* October 22, 2001, p. 15.

125. Z. Brooke, "'My Favorite Brand Is Me': Survey Reveals Power, Preferences of Global Youths," *American Marketing Association,* March 7, 2016, www.ama.org, accessed December 15, 2017.

126. See IBM Institute for Business Value.

127. See, e.g., L. Tong, "Consumerism Sweeps the Mainland," *Marketing Management,* Winter 1998, pp. 32–35; J. Slater, "In India, a Market Unleashed," *Wall Street Journal,* March 12, 2004, p. A13; N. Madden, "China Passes Japan as Second-Largest Economy," *Advertising Age,* August 25, 2010.

128. "Picturing a World of Want," *Newsweek,* May 5, 2008, p. 7.

129. J. L. Lee, "China Senses Need for Cleaner Fuel," *Wall Street Journal,* December 11, 2003, p. A16.

130. The World Bank, World Development Indicators Database (Gross National Income per Capita 2016, Atlas Method and PPP), April 17, 2017, www.database.worldbank.org, accessed November 29, 2017; The World Bank, World Development Indicators Database (Income Share Held by Highest 10%), November 11, 2017, www.database.worldbank.org, accessed November 29, 2017.

131. The World Bank, World Development Indicators Database (Gross National Income Per Capita 2016, Atlas Method and PPP).

132. U.S. Census Bureau, International Programs, 2016, www.census.gov/population/international/data, accessed November 29, 2017.

133. H. Fattah, "The Middle East Baby Boom," *American Demographics,* September 2002, pp. 55–60; D. Blair, "Iran's Rulers Urge a Baby Boom to Double Population by 2050," *The Telegraph,* July 30, 2015.

134. A. Esser, "The Transnationalization of European Television," *Journal of European Area Studies* 10, no. 1 (2002), pp. 13–29.

135. See, e.g., de Mooij and Hofstede, "Convergence and Divergence in Consumer Behavior"; A. Kanso and R. A. Nelson, "Advertising Localization Overshadows Standardization," *Journal of Advertising Research,* January–February 2002, pp. 79–89.

136. "When in Rome . . . ," *Businessline,* April 15, 2004, p. 1.

137. I. Vida and J. Reardon, "Domestic Consumption," *Journal of Consumer Marketing* 25, no. 1 (2008), pp. 34–44; L. Dong and K. Tian, "The Use of Western Brands in Asserting Chinese National Identity," *Journal of Consumer Research,* October 2009, pp. 504–23; M. O. Lwin, A. Stanaland, and J. D. Williams, "Exporting America," *International Journal of Advertising* 29, no. 2 (2010), pp. 245–77; A. A. Maher, P. Clark, and A. Maher, "International Consumer Admiration and the Persistence of Animosity," *Journal of Consumer Marketing* 27, no. 5 (2010), pp. 415–24.

138. E. J. Schultz, "MillerCoors Thinks Globally, but Gets 'Intimate' Locally," *Advertising Age,* October 4, 2010, pp. 1, 19.

139. C. Rubel, "Survey," *Marketing News,* July 15, 1996, p. 5; D. Barros, "Create Unique Strategy for Each Brazilian Culture," *Marketing News,* September 1, 2004, pp. 17–18.

140. G. Cui, "Segmenting China's Consumer Market," *Journal of International Consumer Marketing* 1 (1999), pp. 55–76; T. Sun and G. Wu, "Consumption Patterns of Chinese Urban and Rural Consumers," *Journal of Consumer Marketing* 21, no. 4 (2004), pp. 245–53.

141. P. L. Andruss, "Slow Boat to China," *Marketing News,* September 10, 2001, p. 11.

142. N. Madden and J. Neff, "P&G Adapts Attitude toward Local Markets," *Advertising Age,* February 23, 2004, p. 28.

143. C. Penteado, "Emerging Lower Middle Class Fires Up Marketers in Brazil," *Advertising Age,* June 14, 2010, p. 12; Mintel Group Ltd., "Travel and Tourism—Brazil—August 2013—Transport," www.mintel.com, accessed December 18, 2017.

144. Examples come from Chen and Chang, "China Takes Aim at Racy, Violent TV Shows"; G. A. Fowler, "China Cracks Down on Commercials," *Wall Street Journal,* February 19, 2004, p. B7; "Molson Airs Ad under New Rules," *Advertising Age,* February 23, 2004, p. 12; "China Bans Opening New Internet Cafes," *CNN.com,* March 2006, www.cnn.com; E. Hall, "In Europe, the Clash over Junk-Food Ads Heats Up," *Advertising Age,* March 5, 2007, p. 32; and E. Hall, "U.K. to Tighten Regulations for Paid Tweets, Sponsored Posts," *Advertising Age,* January 13, 2011.

145. N. Madden, "Lower-Tier Cities Offer Most Growth," *Advertising Age,* June 23, 2010.

146. P. D. Lynch, R. J. Kent, and S. S. Srinivasan, "The Global Internet Shopper," *Journal of Advertising Research,* May/June 2001, pp. 15–23; see also Brooke, "'My Favorite Brand Is Me.'"

147. Insight sources include R. Arthur, "Fizzy Drink Sugar Levels Vary Dramatically between Countries, Says Survey," *Beverage Daily,* October 1, 2015, www.beveragedaily.com/Article/2015/10/01/Fizzy-drink-sugar-levels-vary-dramatically-between-countries-says-survey, accessed December 9, 2017; K. Ashmall, "The Importance of Localization (and How Coca-Cola Localizes Successfully)," *Global Marketing Culture,* September 28, 2014, http://globalmarketingculture.com/the-importance-of-localization/, accessed December 9, 2017; R. Baker, "Coca-Cola Makes Biggest Ever Shift to Global Marketing," *Ad News,* January 13, 2016, www.adnews.com.au/news/coca-cola-makes-biggest-ever-shift-to-global-marketing#dfzgQdlT54QAvRuU.99, accessed December 9, 2017; T. Hobbs, "Coca-Cola Takes 'One Brand' Marketing Strategy Global with 'Taste The Feeling' Campaign," *Marketing Week,* January 19, 2016, www.marketingweek.com/2016/01/19/coca-cola-takes-one-brand-marketing-strategy-global-as-it-unveils-new-tagline/, accessed December 9, 2017; H. Holstein, "How Coca-Cola Manages 90 Emerging Markets," *Strategy + Business,* November 7, 2011, www.strategy-business.com/article/00093?gko=f3ca6, accessed December 9, 2017; J. Moye, "'One Brand' Strategy, New Global Campaign Unite Coca-Cola Trademark," *Coca-Cola Journey,* January 19, 2016, www.coca-colacompany.com/stories/taste-the-feeling-launch, accessed December 9, 2017; "The Chronicle of Coca-Cola: A Global Business," *Coca-Cola Journey,* January 1, 2012, www.coca-colacompany.com/stories/the-chronicle-of-coca-cola-a-global-business, accessed December 9, 2017.

3

The Changing American Society: Values

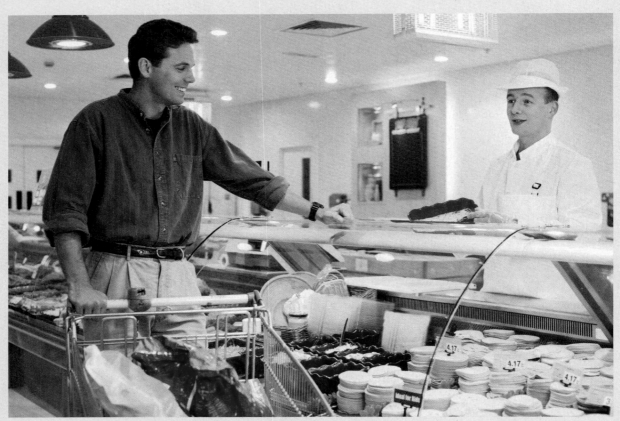

©Stockbyte/Getty Images

LEARNING OBJECTIVES

LO1 Understand core American cultural values.

LO2 Summarize changes in self-, environment-, and other-oriented values.

LO3 Discuss values as they relate to green marketing.

LO4 Discuss values as they relate to cause-related marketing.

LO5 Discuss values as they relate to marketing to gay and lesbian consumers.

LO6 Discuss values as they relate to gender-based marketing.

Gender roles continue to evolve in the United States with more women taking on traditionally male-oriented tasks and more men taking on traditionally female-oriented tasks.[1]

In recent years, there has been growth in the number of "stay-at-home dads," a role traditionally played by mothers. The Great Recession of 2007–09, which led to a greater increase in unemployment for men, propelled the trend of nonworking dads. While the number of stay-at-home dads has decreased from 2.2 million since the peak of this "Mancession," the father's household involvement has not diminished. Fathers, especially those who are Millennials, have expanded their home and childcare responsibilities, as well as decision-making power, regardless of their employment status. And marketers have taken notice.

Recent Mintel studies found that dads with multiple children are more likely to take charge of what their kids are watching on TV or how much time their children spend on the computer. And these men are more involved in what toys or games are purchased for their kids, and more likely to play video games and go to movies with their children. Dads use sports and fitness to engage with their children. Fathers are more involved with grocery shopping too, with 80 percent of Millennial fathers claiming primary or shared responsibility.

Gone are the days when "dopey dad" roamed the aisles of the supermarket, aimlessly following "mom's list." Millennial dads—dubbed supermarket natives—make their own choices.

In terms of general purchasing habits, dads prioritize value, product safety, and nutrition. Dads are thinking more about the chemicals in food and are spending time reading nutrition labels when shopping. But these priorities only go so far. These dads, nonworking especially, are not going to buy organic or locally grown products. Also, they are more impulsive at the time of purchase and are not likely to use coupons, which provides opportunities for brands to target dads through point-of-purchase marketing.

Marketers have capitalized on this emerging "involved dad" market. Using sports and fitness, brands have created programs to target dads directly. Kellogg's developed the "Share What You Love" campaign to inspire dads to share their passion for sports with their children, and Clorox promoted their "Play 2 Day" outdoor play campaign to dads. Going beyond fitness, but encouraging play, Mattel recently launched its "Dads Who Play Barbie" campaign, which highlights, among many things, Barbie's modern image as well as contemporary father–daughter interactions.

Even as stay-at-home dads begin to work outside the home, their involvement at home continues and should not be ignored. Yoplait was criticized for its recent ad "Whisper," in which it typecast mom as "the boss," even though household responsibilities and decisions, including shopping, are being shared by both parents. Brands, to be effective, cannot rely on these stereotypes anymore.

What can brands do then to appeal to these "involved dads"? As more dads shop, brands can guide fathers through their shopping experiences. At the grocery store, for example, brands can offer demonstrations to help with meal preparations. Brands should avoid using coupons as a way to attract dads, as more than a third of Millennial dads claim coupons make them look cheap. Last, appreciating the importance of a dad's time with family, brands can build loyalty by showing how the brand can help a dad cherish his family time.

Chapter 2 discussed how variations in values influence consumption patterns *across* cultures. Here, we describe how changes in values *within* culture over time influence consumption patterns, with a specific focus on the United States. The changing role of men and women in American society, highlighted in the chapter opener, reflects changes in the "masculine/feminine" value described in Chapter 2. As this example makes clear, cultural values are not constant. Rather, they evolve over time.[2] We begin by examining the evolution of American values in general. Next, we examine four marketing trends that have evolved in response to changing values: green marketing, cause-related marketing, marketing to gay and lesbian consumers, and gender-based marketing.

CHANGES IN AMERICAN CULTURAL VALUES

LO1

Observable shifts in behavior, including consumption behavior, often reflect shifts in **cultural values,** *widely held beliefs that affirm what is desirable.* Therefore, it is necessary to understand the underlying value shifts to understand current and future consumer behavior. Although we discuss American values as though every American has the same values, in fact there is substantial variance in values across individuals and groups. In addition, changes in values tend to occur slowly and unevenly across individuals and groups. While traumatic events such as the 9/11 attacks and the recent Great Recession can produce value shifts, a slow evolution is more common. Caution should be used in assuming that short-term behavioral or attitudinal changes in response to such events represent long-lasting value shifts.

Figure 3–1 presents our estimate of how American values are changing. These are the same values used to describe different cultures in Chapter 2. It must be emphasized that Figure 3–1 is based on the authors' subjective interpretation of the American society. You should feel free, indeed compelled, to challenge these judgments.

Self-Oriented Values

LO2

Traditionally, Americans have been active, materialistic, hardworking, religious people inclined toward abstinence and postponed gratification. Beginning after the end of World War II and accelerating rapidly during the 1970s and early 1980s, Americans placed increased emphasis on leisure, immediate gratification, and sensual gratification. While these changes have remained relatively intact, we discuss what role, if any, the Great Recession has had on specific values such as materialism and immediate gratification.

Religious/Secular   America is basically a secular society. A religious group does not control the educational system, government, or political process, and most people's daily behaviors are not guided by strict religious guidelines. Nonetheless, roughly 77 percent of American adults claim a religious affiliation, 36 percent claim to attend a religious service at least once a week, and 53 percent state that religion is very important in their lives.[3]

Traditional, Current, and Emerging American Values   FIGURE 3-1

Self-Oriented

Religious	T EC	Secular
Sensual gratification	E C T	Abstinence
Postponed gratification	T C E	Immediate gratification
Material	T C E	Nonmaterial
Hard work	T C E	Leisure
Active	ECT*	Passive

Environment-Oriented

Maximum cleanliness	TC E	Minimum cleanliness
Tradition	EC T	Change
Risk taking	T E C	Security
Problem solving	T CE	Fatalistic
Admire nature	E C T	Overcome nature
Performance	T E C	Status

Other-Oriented

Left	Scale	Right
Individual	T CE	Collective
Diversity	E C T	Uniformity
Limited family	TEC	Extended family
Youth	T C E	Age
Competition	T C E	Cooperation
Masculine	T C E	Feminine

*T = Traditional, E = Emerging, and C = Current.

While Americans often profess to be more religious than their behaviors would suggest, religious-based beliefs do influence decisions.[4] Many Americans for whom religion is especially important are conservative in their beliefs. They are quite active politically and as consumers. Their political activism involves attempts to regulate various marketing activities, including products (particularly "sin" products such as liquor, gambling, and pornography) and advertising.[5] Their consumption patterns include both positive consumption (purchasing religious objects and books) and negative consumption (avoiding or boycotting products and companies).

Although conservative religious groups generate substantial publicity and have considerable political power, the culture remains relatively secular. Indeed, increasing secularism is cited as one reason for the increase in interfaith marriages.[6] However, religious commitment (daily prayer, weekly attendance at services, and importance of religion) in the U.S. has not decreased over time.[7] And advertising to this group requires a nuanced approach—advertisers can't simply put a religious symbol on all products and think that it will have a positive effect. Only when there is a product-religion match (e.g., a counseling center) does the inclusion of a religious symbol such as a cross have a positive influence on purchasing. When there is a perceived lack of fit (e.g., alcohol), the inclusion of a religious symbol has a negative effect. In addition, the more religious a person is, the more pronounced these effects are.[8] We treat religion and its impact on our society in considerable depth in Chapter 5 when we discuss subcultures.

Sensual Gratification/Abstinence   Closely tied to America's traditional religious orientation was a belief in the virtue of abstinence. As American society became more secular, sensual gratification became more acceptable. This trend appears to remain strong,

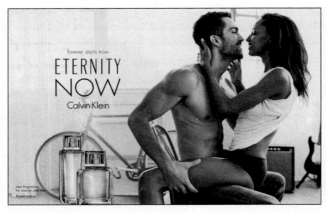

Source: Calvin Klein

even as consumer and government agencies have tried to push back and curb violence, indecency, and nudity in such venues as ads, movies, and video games.[9] For example, Axe body spray is the number one brand in its category and relies heavily on sex appeals targeting young men. And while the United States is not the highest in its use of nudity in ads, it outranked Brazil, China, South Korea, and Thailand in a recent study. However, the effectiveness of sexual appeals in ads has limits. First, the old adage "sex sells" may not hold anymore. Recent research shows that people may remember the ads with sexual appeal, but their intention to buy the brand in the ad does not change. As such, we are seeing brands like Carl's Jr. and Hardee's, who have relied on sexualized ads to sell their burgers, change their appeal to emphasize product quality—"food, not boobs."[10] Nevertheless, the ad may work depending on the viewer's gender. Men tend to react more positively than women to sex appeals involving female nudity. However, women with more liberal attitudes toward sex view sexually explicit ads just as positively as men.[11]

Other evidence of the greater value placed on sensual gratification comes from a recent study showing that one of the biggest value shifts in the United States is in the greater importance placed on fun and excitement. That is, people today, more than ever, want to lead a "pleasurable, happy life; to experience stimulation and thrills."[12] The food industry certainly relies on consumer desires for sensual gratification by selling the pleasure, happiness, and thrills that various foods can deliver. According to one Pepperidge Farm executive, their premium cookies offer a "small indulgence anytime, anywhere."[13]

Illustration 3-1 shows an ad for Calvin Klein Eternity Now that appeals to sensual gratification. How do you feel this ad would be received by men? By women?

Postponed/Immediate Gratification   In line with the value they generally place on sensual gratification, Americans seem unwilling to delay pleasures, even in the face of discomfort over spending levels and debt. For a time, there was hope that the Great Recession would usher in a new frugality among consumers and a willingness to postpone gratification by delaying or eliminating purchases. And, to some degree, it has. Americans are now saving more and paying down debt. However, recently these trends have begun to recede as once again U.S. consumers get back to "spending as usual." Consider the following quote:

> The truth is that spending may be hard to contain. Entire generations of consumers have grown up with the idea of instant gratification and the credit culture that comes with it.[14]

It is really quite difficult, therefore, to say whether U.S. consumer values relating to instant gratification have truly been affected (it does appear that they have somewhat, as represented in Figure 3–1), or whether the behavioral changes related to spending and saving had more to do with the economic constraints imposed by the recession. As a consequence, we show an emerging trend back toward instant gratification, as the "American skimper" is now shopping more freely again.[15]

Material/Nonmaterial   Americans have maintained a strong material orientation. An outcome of America's focus on materialism is a consumption-driven society. As we will see, Americans are working longer hours, in part, to afford material possessions. That is, Americans are trading time and energy for things and services such as cars and travel. Factors found to influence materialism are social media and television. As one group of researchers note:

> Television is a powerful medium . . . consumers often use information from television to construct perceptions of social reality including the prevalence of affluence. Heavier viewers tend to believe luxury products and services to be more commonplace than they actually are.[16]

As we have seen, the recent recession has curtailed spending to some degree. However, at least some of that frugality appears to have been more economically than value-related. Indeed, one expert notes that consumers are going through "frugality fatigue," which suggests that consumers are acting due to an external constraint more than an internal value change. And consider the following quote from a young woman who simply got fed up with trying to save and began spending again, which led to her eviction and caused her to have to move back in with her parents:

> After awhile, I just decided, "Screw it. I need some new clothes. I'm going to get them." My mamma's not happy, but I don't care. You stop spending and you stop living.[17]

While materialism appears to be the norm, a movement away from materialism in the United States is occurring among a select group of consumers. Role overload, burnout, and emotional exhaustion are causing some to rethink priorities and simplify their lives. Consider the following:

> I had all the stuff that was supposed to make me successful—my car and my clothes, the house in the right neighborhood and belonging to the right health club. All the external framework was excellent and inside I kind of had this pit eating away at me.[18]

Consumers' efforts to reduce their reliance on consumption and material possessions have been termed **voluntary simplicity.** Voluntary simplicity can span a continuum from minor life adjustments and reduced spending to drastic lifestyle adjustments, including downsized jobs, incomes, houses, and spending. The key is that it is a conscious and voluntary decision, not one brought on by economic necessity. Major factors in the decision to simplify appear to be reduced stress and increased life satisfaction, although other motivations, including environmentalism, can be involved. While the voluntary simplicity movement appears to represent a relatively small proportion of the U.S. population, the growth in "downshifting" certainly holds economic and marketing consequences, including the market for secondhand products and green products.[19]

Hard Work/Leisure   Americans continue their strong tradition of hard work, leading much of the industrialized world in hours worked. Average weekly hours worked is around 34 hours, longer than employees in other Group of Seven (G7) countries. Full-time workers work on average 47 hours per week, and almost 40 percent work at least 50 hours a week.[20] The percentage of women who work outside the home for wages has increased almost 45 percent since WWII, from 33 to 57 percent of all women, and 70 percent of mothers with children under the age of 18, working outside the home.[21] Americans work long hours for many reasons. One is clearly their material orientation. Americans work to have such things as a large home, two cars, and a nice vacation. Others work long hours because they lack the skills or job opportunities to provide even a moderate lifestyle without doing so. However, Americans also work long and hard because work is meaningful and valuable to them, in part because of the self-esteem and respect they gain from the work they do.[22]

Partly in response to the increase in work hours, the value placed on work relative to leisure has dropped over the past several decades. Clearly, work is still important, and higher unemployment during the recent recession has put this into even greater perspective. However, a recent study finds that for working women with children, the percentage who indicated that full-time work was ideal for them has decreased by 11 percent since 1997, while the percentage who indicated part-time work was ideal for them has increased by 12 percent.[23] And yet, over two-thirds of married women with children work outside the home for wages. Together, these statistics suggest such factors as time pressures and role conflict associated with the fact that work competes with other important aspects of one's life. This opens up opportunities for marketers who can deliver convenience. Still, we can't seem to get away from work. One study finds that between 51 and 65 percent of U.S. workers with work e-mail check it during off hours including nights, weekends, and while on vacation.[24] Thus, we have a situation in which hard work and leisure are both valued (often by the same people) and commingled in people's lives.

Active/Passive   Americans continue to value an active approach to life. Although less than half of all American adults exercise regularly, most Americans take an active approach to both leisure and problem-solving activities. Television viewing as a primary form of entertainment has dropped sharply from its peak in the mid-1980s (young men [18 to 24 years of age] seem to be moving away from TV faster than any other group).[25] Alternative activities, including surfing the net, sports, cooking, and gardening, are popular. And the amount of time children spend in scheduled activities continues to increase.[26] The following quote illustrates that Americans differ on this value, but most would agree more with the second speaker than the first.

> My idea of a vacation is a nice oceanfront resort, a beach chair, and a piña colada. Mine too. For a day or two. Then I'd go bug spit. I'd feel like I was in prison. I'd *do* something.[27]

Illustration 3–2 describes how Royal Caribbean cruises are designed for active leisure.

Environment-Oriented Values

LO2

Environment-oriented values prescribe a society's relationship with its economic, technical, and physical environments. Americans have traditionally admired cleanliness, change, performance, risk taking, problem solving, and the conquest of nature. While this cluster of values remains basically intact, there are some important shifts occurring.

Cleanliness   Americans have long valued cleanliness. This strong focus seems to be declining somewhat, particularly in terms of our homes. Likely due to increased time demands caused by work, messier homes are more acceptable.[28] However, such shifts don't

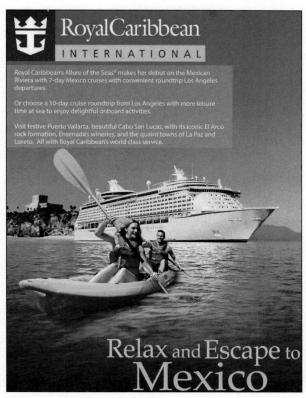

Source: Royal Caribbean International

appear to suggest major changes. The popularity of TV shows like *Hoarders* on the A&E network suggests that while Americans may accept messier homes, they are not happy about them. This obviously presents marketing opportunities.[29] For example, the development of robotic vacuum cleaners such as iRobot's Roomba taps the desire for cleanliness while offering much-needed convenience and time savings.

Personal hygiene, another aspect of cleanliness, remains very important to most Americans. One study shows that antibacterial hand sanitizers such as Purell are an important part of the arsenal of products carried around by mothers.[30] Illustration 3–3 demonstrates how Clorox emphasizes cleanliness, which is in line with the importance that Americans place on personal hygiene.

Tradition/Change   Americans always have been very receptive to change. *New* has traditionally been taken to mean *improved.* While still very appreciative of change, Americans are now less receptive to change for its own sake. New-product recalls, the expense and the failure of various government programs, and the energy required to keep pace with rapid technological changes are some of the reasons for this shift. Another reason is the aging of the American population. As we will see in the next chapter, the average age of the population is increasing, and people generally become somewhat less accepting of change as they age. Still, much of America continues to embrace change, as evidenced by a growing segment of workers that one expert calls the *creative class.* The creative class includes those who work in such professions as architecture, science, engineering, and health care as well as business and who generate new ideas and technologies for a living or engage in complex problem solving. This group now constitutes about 33 percent of the workforce, compared

ILLUSTRATION 3-3

Americans continue
to place a high value
on cleanliness,
as this Clorox ad
demonstrates.

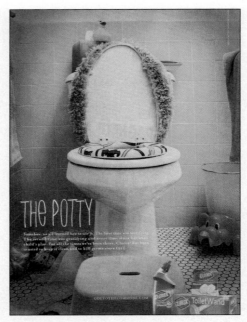

Source: The Clorox Company

with just 10 percent in 1900. Fiat, in re-launching its brand in the United States, indicated that it was targeting the creative class with a campaign heavy on digital, viral, and event-marketing approaches it felt would work best with this segment.[31]

Risk Taking/Security Americans' risk-taking orientation seems to have changed somewhat over time. There was an increased emphasis on security during the period from 1930 through the mid-1980s. This attitude was a response to the tremendous upheavals and uncertainties caused by the Depression, World War II, and the cold war. However, risk taking remains highly valued and is gaining appreciation as Americans look to entrepreneurs for economic growth and to smaller firms and self-employment to obtain desired lifestyles. Figure 3–1 indicates that there currently seems to be a greater emphasis on security, driven at least in part by the recent economic recession. However, a long-term study of the importance that Americans place on security shows that the desire for security has seen one of the largest declines over the last several decades. This suggests that the short-term focus on security may give way once again to risk taking as the economy recovers.[32]

Problem Solving/Fatalistic Americans take great pride in being problem solvers, and as we saw earlier, as a percentage of the workforce, problem solvers and creative types are on the increase. By and large, Americans believe that virtually anything can be fixed given sufficient time and effort. For example, even in the midst of the Great Recession, nearly two-thirds of Americans agreed that "[a]s Americans, we can always find ways to solve problems."[33] Marketers introduce thousands of new products each year with the theme that they will solve a problem better than existing products will. We will examine the results of this value later in this chapter in the sections on green marketing and cause marketing.

Admire/Overcome Nature Traditionally, nature was viewed as an obstacle. Americans attempted to bend nature to fit their desires without realizing the negative consequences this could have for both nature and humanity. However, this attitude has shifted dramatically over the past 30 years.

Experts have been concerned that environmentalism is dead. Some cite the fact that the percentage of Americans who call themselves environmentalists dropped from

73 to 47 percent between 1990 and 2000. Part of the decline may be real, but part of the decline may simply be in how people define *environmentalism.* For example, a recent survey conducted by Pew Research shows that 75 percent of Americans are particularly concerned with helping the environment as they go about their daily lives, but only one in five are making an effort to live in ways that help protect the environment. Nevertheless, concern for the environment remains strong for Americans:

- More than half bring their own shopping bags to the store to help the environment at least some of the time.
- Close to 60 percent purchase cleaning products to help the environment at least sometimes.
- Two-thirds of American homeowners have recycling bins at home, and 43 percent have vegetable gardens.
- Over 70 percent have at least some close friends and family who are environmentally conscious.
- Americans are bothered when others are wasteful at least some of the time: leaving on lights (76 percent), not recycling (73 percent), and driving places close enough to walk (52 percent).[34]

Table 3–1 shows eight segments, identified by IRI/TNS, based on consumer attitudes and behaviors toward the environment.[35]

Firms that convince environmentally concerned consumers that their products are environmentally sound can reap huge rewards. Such an approach has been termed **enviropreneurial marketing.** Enviropreneurial marketing is *environmentally friendly marketing practices, strategies, and tactics initiated by a firm to achieve a competitive differentiation.* Research shows that such a marketing approach can lead to increased new-product success and increased market share.[36]

We describe the marketing response to this value in the section of this chapter on green marketing.

Performance/Status   Americans are shifting back to a focus on performance rather than status. Although consumers are still willing to purchase "status" brands, these brands

Shades of Green Segmentation™ Scheme by IRI/TNS	TABLE 3-1
Eco-Centrists (16 percent): Highly committed to and concerned about environment. Beliefs reflected in their consumption behaviors across a wide range of products. Will pay more for eco-friendly products. Cynical about corporate green efforts—viewed as merely marketing tactics. High education and income; Urban South and West.	
Respectful Stewards (7 percent): Most highly concerned about environment. Beliefs reflected in their consumption behaviors. Will pay more for eco-friendly products. Not cynical about corporate green marketing efforts. Focused on community and culture. Lower education and income; Hispanic; Urban.	
Proud Traditionalists (14 percent): Environmental efforts focused on keeping home running efficiently and effectively (insulation and water-efficient products). Focused on family and hard work. Rural Midwest.	
Frugal Earth Mothers (18 percent): Environmental efforts focused on running a more efficient home to save money (buy used, wash in cold water, air-dry clothes). Focused on practicality and lowering day-to-day costs. Lower income; Rural; Female.	
Skeptical Individuals (13 percent): Believe in environmental issues like global warming and carbon emission concerns. Skeptical of corporate green efforts. Very high income and education; Urban coasts; Male.	
Eco-Chic (14 percent): Environmentally concerned, but actions don't match beliefs. More interested in appearing to be green to "ride the wave of environmental consciousness." May try eco-friendly products but tend to return to their favorite nongreen brands. Young adults.	
Green Naives (11 percent): Environmental issues have not registered with this group in terms of beliefs or actions. Sedentary; Lower income.	
Eco-Villians (7 percent): Highly dismissive of environmental concerns. Don't believe global warming exists. Highly negative of corporate green efforts—seen as marketing ploys. Middle income; Male, Smaller metro areas.	

must provide style and functionality in addition to the prestige of the name. This has led to substantial increases in sales at stores that combine price, service, and quality, such as Walmart and Target stores, and for quality retailer private-label brands such as those offered by Kroger, Target, and Walmart. In contrast, outlets with inappropriate cost structures or images, such as Kmart and Montgomery Ward, have struggled or failed.[37]

Other-Oriented Values

L02.

Other-oriented values reflect a society's view of the appropriate relationships between individuals and groups within that society. Historically, American society has been oriented toward individualism, competitiveness, masculinity, youth, limited families, and uniformity. However, several aspects of this orientation are undergoing change.

Individual/Collective   A strong emphasis on individualism is one of the defining characteristics of American society. Watch any American hit movie. The leading character will virtually always behave as an individual, often despite pressures to conform to the group. Americans believe in "doing your own thing." Even the "uniforms" that each generation of teenagers invents for itself allow ample room for individual expression. This value affects incentive systems for salespeople, advertising themes, product design, and customer complaining behavior.[38] For example, consumers higher in individualism are more likely to complain, switch, or engage in negative word-of-mouth when faced with poor service performance.[39] Individualism is also evident in the customization craze for cars, trucks, and motorcycles, a market worth over $2 billion a year. The Discovery Channel and others have tapped into this trend with shows such as *Fast 'N Loud* and *Top Gear,* which attract the highly elusive younger male audience.[40]

Diversity/Uniformity   While American culture always has valued individualism, it also has valued a degree of uniformity, particularly with respect to groups. America was founded in part by people seeking religious freedom or fleeing from various forms of persecution. The Constitution and many laws seek to protect diverse religions, political beliefs, and so forth. Nonetheless, Americans historically insisted that immigrants quickly adopt the language, dress, values, and many other aspects of the majority. Those who did not often were subject to various forms of discrimination. This was particularly true for racial and some religious minorities.

Since World War II, Americans have increasingly valued diversity. Consider the following:

Etsy, an online marketplace, recently launched a global campaign, "#DifferenceMakesUs," to promote the uniqueness of individuals. This online site has done very well lately by remaining "small and quirky." According to Etsy's CEO, "It has the feel of a farmers market instead of a supermarket."[41]

Researchers speculate that the market for diversity and individualism like Etsy is "*cultural creatives,*" the "26% of adult Americans who are concerned with self-actualization, spirituality, and self-expression and who like things that are foreign and exotic."[42] Cultural creatives, regardless of ethnicity, are more likely to cross traditional ethnic boundaries in seeking out products.

Although far from being free of racial, religious, ethnic, or class prejudice, American culture is evolving toward valuing diversity more than uniformity, as reflected in the L'Oréal ad shown in Illustration 3–4. And a recent study shows that 61 percent of Americans think that the increased racial and ethnic diversity "has been a change for the better." This percentage is higher for younger generations.[43] We examine one aspect of America's increasing acceptance of diversity—marketing to gay and lesbian consumers—later in this chapter.

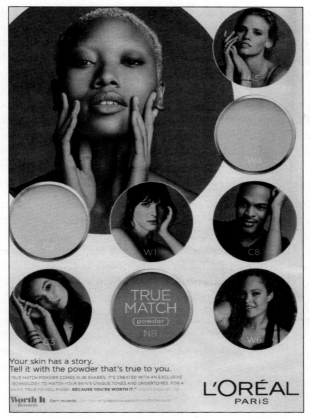

Source: The L'Oréal Group

ILLUSTRATION 3-4

Americans increasingly value diversity. As a result, a diversity approach is used in many ads, such as in this L'Oréal ad.

Limited/Extended Family America was settled by immigrants, people who left their extended families behind. As the nation grew, the western movement produced a similar phenomenon. Even today, frequent geographic moves as well as differential rates of social mobility mean that few children grow up in close interaction with aunts, uncles, cousins, nieces, or nephews.[44] It is also common for children to leave their hometowns and parents once they begin their own careers. The physical separation of traditional family members often reduces the sense of family among those members. This, in turn, reduces the impact that the family has on the individual.

This is not to say that Americans do not love their family members or that how an American is raised does not influence the person for life. Rather, it means that a 35-year-old American is unlikely to have a cousin who would feel obligated to respond positively to a loan request (this is not the case in many other cultures). Likewise, this 35-year-old would be unlikely to have one or more cousins, aunts, or nephews live with him or her for an extended time period. The role of families in the American culture is covered in depth in Chapter 6.

Youth/Age Traditionally, older people were considered wiser than young people and, therefore, were looked to as models and leaders in almost all cultures. This has never been as true in American culture, probably because transforming a wilderness into a new type of producing nation required characteristics such as physical strength, stamina, youthful vigor, and imagination. The value on youth continued as America became an industrial nation. Since World War II, it has increased to such an extent that products such as cars, clothing, cosmetics, and hairstyles seem designed for and sold only to the young. For example, youth appeals in American advertising still appear to outstrip appeals to age and tradition.[45]

But a slow reversal of this value on youth seems to be occurring. Because of their increasing numbers and disposable income, older citizens have developed political and economic clout and are beginning to use it. Cosmetics, medicines, and hair care products are being marketed specifically to older consumers, and ads for these products increasingly feature more mature celebrities, such as Jennifer Aniston, who are closer in age to the target audience. However, most of these products still have either a direct or indirect appeal of creating a younger appearance.

Age portrayal in advertising is a difficult issue. Because people often feel younger than their actual age, ads using younger models might generate a more positive reaction. In addition, for youth-oriented or conspicuously consumed products, using older models in ads may alienate younger consumers. These two factors help explain the overrepresentation of younger models in ads.[46] There is the worry, however, that at some point older consumers may feel ignored by ads that portray overly young users. Clearly, marketers have a lot to learn in this area.

Competition/Cooperation   America has long been a competitive society, and this value remains firmly entrenched. It is reflected in our social, political, and economic systems. We reward particularly successful competitors in business, entertainment, and sports with staggering levels of financial compensation. Although the focus on cooperation and team-work in schools and businesses has increased, teamwork is generally instituted so that the team or group can outperform some other team or group. It is no wonder that America was one of the first countries to allow comparative advertising.

Masculine/Feminine   American society, like most others, has reflected a masculine orientation for a long time. But as indicated by this chapter's opening vignette, this orientation is changing, as are gender roles. Although American society is becoming less masculine oriented, it still leans clearly in that direction. For example, 37 percent of parents indicate that they would prefer a boy if they could have only one child, compared with 28 percent who would opt for a girl.[47] And textbooks aimed at children still depict physical activity more often for boys (65 percent) than for girls (35 percent).[48] Still, there is a shift taking place in this value. For example, preference for male bosses continues to decline dramatically while preference for female bosses continues to increase, such that the majority have no preference of boss's gender.[49] The marketing implications resulting from evolving gender roles are discussed later in this chapter.

MARKETING STRATEGY AND VALUES

We have examined a number of marketing implications of American values and changes in these values. It is critical that all aspects of the firm's marketing mix be consistent with the value system of its target market. We now will examine marketing responses to four evolving American values: green marketing, cause-related marketing, marketing to gay and lesbian consumers, and gender-based marketing.

Green Marketing

LO3

Marketers have responded to Americans' increasing concern for the environment with an approach called **green marketing**.[50] Green marketing generally involves (1) developing products whose production, use, or disposal is less harmful to the environment than the traditional versions of the product; (2) developing products that have a positive impact on the environment; or (3) tying the purchase of a product to an environmental organization or event. For example:[51]

- Coca-Cola developed the "PlantBottle"—made from sugar cane waste products—as part of the company's "Live Positively" campaign.
- Ford's Escape and Focus car models are built out of 80 percent recycled material. And the automaker launched "The Living Roof" green initiative. This roof is a 10.4-acre

garden that helps to insulate the building and clean storm water.

- CBS created the "EcoAd" program whereby 10 percent of a company's ad buy goes to local environmental causes. Participation is signaled with a "green-leaf" eco-ad logo.

Environmental concerns don't guarantee purchase of green products. Even among those who are environmentally concerned, negative perceptions are on the rise, including beliefs that green products are too expensive, of lower quality, and not better for the environment, and that green claims can't be trusted.[52] In addition, the stereotypes associated with "green consumers" can be detrimental to the purchase of these products, as users are often seen—negatively—as "greenies" or "tree huggers." And men may be less likely to buy environmentally friendly products because of the belief that green consumers are typically more feminine.[53]

ILLUSTRATION 3-5

Environmentally friendly products such as the Audi TDI diesel also must provide consumer benefits to be successful.

Overcoming these obstacles is critical to the success of green marketing (see the Audi TDI Clean Diesel ad in Illustration 3–5). For example, Honda discontinued its Accord hybrid in 2007. Poor sales were likely due to the fact that highway mileage for the hybrid was only 1 mpg higher than the gas-only Accord, but it cost nearly $15,000 more![54]

The FTC shares consumer skepticism about green claims. Amid substantial increases in green marketing and green claims by companies, the FTC has made the first modifications in over a decade to its voluntary guidelines called the "Green Guides." The Green Guides provide guidance on acceptable and unacceptable practices relating to environmental claims. Several issues motivated the FTC to make the modifications:[55]

- First, terms such as *eco-friendly* appear to be misleading to consumers who believe that such products have "far-reaching benefits in almost all environmental areas without having any substantial drawbacks." According to the FTC, few products can live up to the perceptions that consumers have of them.
- Second is a practice termed **greenwashing** whereby a firm promotes environmental benefits that are unsubstantiated and on which they don't deliver.

Prominent among the modifications to the Green Guides are (a) a focus on qualifying claims so that it is clear in what way the product is environmentally friendly and (b) a crackdown on third-party certifications and seals. This crackdown reflects the fact that some companies have created their own seals or utilize third-party vendors that don't do anything to substantiate the claims being made (to learn more about Green Guides, visit www.ftc.gov).[56]

Cause-Related Marketing

The term *cause marketing* is sometimes used interchangeably with *social marketing*. However, the two are different. As noted in Chapter 1, social marketing is marketing done to enhance the welfare of individuals or society without direct benefit to a firm. In contrast, cause marketing, or **cause-related marketing (CRM),** is *marketing that ties a company and its*

LO4

Source: JDRF

Welcome to the Dove Self-Esteem Project

Source: Unilever

ILLUSTRATION 3-6

The One Walk ad on the left promotes a benefit to the world community without advancing the profits or image of a commercial firm. That ad is an example of social marketing. The Dove "Self-Esteem" ad on the right represents cause-related marketing. It not only benefits a cause but also enhances the image and sales of a commercial firm.

products to an issue or cause with the goal of improving sales or corporate image while providing benefits to the cause.[57] Companies associate with causes to create long-term relationships with their customers, building corporate and brand equity that eventually should lead to increased sales. A good example of CRM is Dove's "Self-Esteem Project."

Examine the two ads in Illustration 3-6. The ad on the left in Illustration 3-6 is an example of social marketing; it promotes a benefit to the world community without advancing the profits or image of a commercial firm. The ad on the right in Illustration 3-6 is an example of cause-related marketing; it attempts to benefit a cause *and* to enhance the image and sales of a commercial firm.

The foundation of CRM is marketing to consumers' values, and it can be very effective. Cause-related marketing is often effective because it is consistent with strongly held American values.[58] For example, a common theme in most CRM programs taps America's problem-solving orientation by presenting a problem, such as breast cancer, AIDS, or pollution, and an action that individuals can take to help solve the problem. Thus, consumer expectations, acceptance of CRM, and response to CRM have increased dramatically over the past decade.

Research shows that many consumers will travel out of their way to find stores and brands that support the causes they care about and also pay more for those products. In addition:

- Seventy-one percent have purchased a cause-related brand.
- Eighty-eight percent think companies should try to accomplish their business goals while simultaneously working to improve society.
- Seventy-four percent claim that a company's commitment to a social issue is important when deciding which products and services to recommend to other people.
- Eighty-six percent are likely to switch brands based on CRM when price and quality are equal.[59]

Given consumer receptivity to CRM, it is not surprising that corporate spending on it is on the rise. One area of spending, cause-related sponsorship, has grown from $120 million in 1990 to $1.5 billion, which represents the third-largest area of corporate sponsorship![60] Consumer skepticism and apathy remain a challenge. When consumers feel that the company is engaged in CRM due to positive values (they feel morally obligated), corporate trust is enhanced, which increases word-of-mouth and purchases. Alternatively, when consumers feel the company is engaged in CRM simply to enhance its own image or because stock-holders expect it, corporate trust is reduced, which decreases positive word-of-mouth and purchases.[61] CRM skepticism and apathy are demonstrated in the following descriptions and quotes of four consumer types based on their responses to CRM:[62]

Skeptic (doubts sincerity or effectiveness of CRM): "I think those are fake, most of them. Because what they give is so little it doesn't amount to anything."

Balancer (believes in CRM but generally doesn't act accordingly): "I hate to say this, but, as far as grocery stores, I go to the one that is closest to me. It makes me feel better . . . about Food Lion that they were willing to do this (participate in CRM) . . . but sometimes I don't put out that extra effort, but I guess I really should."

Attribution-oriented (concerned about motives behind CRM): "I always approach them with a skeptical eye, but I try and use good judgment and common sense based on who they are, what they're doing and try to see the end result."

Socially concerned (driven by desire to help): "I mean, as long as they're doing it, the motives can be questionable as far as I'm concerned. . . . Even if there are questionable motives, it's that much more important to support companies who do those things. Just to reinforce that good behavior."

CRM results can be improved if consumers see a "fit" between the company and the cause.[63] For example, ConAgra (a food marketing company) launched *Feeding Children Better* to combat child hunger.[64] In addition, a long-term commitment by the company to the cause can be beneficial. McDonald's Ronald McDonald House has been helping families with sick children for over 40 years. Employee involvement in the cause is also important "not just because they may contribute on their own, but because they become evangelists for the cause."[65]

A unique approach to cause-related marketing is being used with success by Toms Shoes, as discussed in Consumer Insight 3–1. *Do you think its approach overcomes some of the challenges faced by cause-related marketing?*

Marketing to Gay and Lesbian Consumers

As Americans in general are shifting to valuing diversity, they are increasingly embracing ethnic, religious, and racial diversity. Another group gaining increased public acceptance is the lesbian, gay, bisexual, transgender, and queer (LGBTQ) community (we follow business press convention and refer to LGBTQ consumers as the gay or LGBTQ market). Overall, 63 percent of Americans feel that gay and lesbian relations are morally acceptable, up from 40 percent in 2001. The strongest support comes from younger men (62 percent) and women (59 percent), supporting our earlier observation that shifts on the diversity value appear to be strongest among younger generations.[66] Interestingly, the value that Americans place on individual rights and protection appears to transcend personal opinions about lifestyle. For example, over 70 percent support hate-crime protection laws and same-sex couple rights such as hospital visitation, and 60 percent favor allowing gays and lesbians to serve openly in the military. These numbers are even stronger among younger consumers.[67] The emergence and popularity of TV shows with openly gay or lesbian characters, such as *Modern Family* and *Empire,* are additional evidence of increased public acceptance.

State and federal actions also have increased in the direction of protecting and expanding the rights of gays and lesbians on a number of fronts including open service in the

LO5

Cause Marketing "Baked into the Brand" at Toms Shoes

A Target store popped up on Times Square in New York City, one of the most expensive pieces of real estate in the country. The store interior was blanketed in a sea of pink products—pink bicycles, sweaters, flip-flops, tee shirts. Outside a coffee cart served pink donuts. All proceeds during the store's short one-month existence went to the Breast Cancer Research Foundation.[68] For every home Habitat for Humanity builds for the homeless in North America, Whirlpool donates a range and a refrigerator.[69] Hand in hand with the Red Cross, P&G Tide's "Loads of Hope" provides mobile laundromats to victims of natural disasters (e.g., New Orleans after Hurricane Katrina).[70]

These cause-marketing campaigns establish a partnership between a corporation and a nonprofit and often result in "doing well by doing good." Marketers increase their bottom line amid a halo of goodwill, while nonprofits receive needed contributions and public attention, and consumers purchase goods for themselves and thus contribute to a worthy cause. Despite the benefits of a win-win-win, critics have pointed out the downside of cause marketing. Corporations may come to lose consumer trust if consumers perceive the corporate–cause relationship as exploitation of the charity. Rather than contribute directly to nonprofits, cause marketing may be teaching consumers to contribute only when they receive something in return and at no cost to themselves. Unlike the unfettered contributions received directly from the public, the contributions charities receive in partnership with corporations may come with strings and obligations.[71]

However, the success of Toms Shoes puts a new twist on cause marketing. Toms Shoes does not partner with a nonprofit or charity. Rather, Toms Shoes is a "for profit" company with the cause "one for one" *baked into the brand.* For each pair of Toms shoes consumers buy, the company donates a pair of Toms shoes to children who need shoes but cannot afford them. In spring 2013 Toms Shoes donated 13 million pairs of shoes in 59 countries. It is now expanding its efforts to eyeglasses in 15 countries. The "baked in brand" strategy of Toms Shoes has been described as a metastory—storytelling through action. The consumer act of buying Toms shoes tells the story about the brand and the consumer. The story came first. The "for profit" status of the firm makes doing the right thing sustainable.[72]

Critical Thinking Questions

1. Should marketers, whose primary motivation is to increase the bottom line, deserve the goodwill and burnished reputation that arise through partnerships with nonprofit organizations?

2. Cause marketing teaches consumers that they can improve the world by their consumption, to contribute only when they receive something in return and at no additional cost. Do you agree with that statement?

3. Do the concerns that surround cause marketing apply to the new form of cause marketing such as Toms Shoes?

military and rights as couples, including legalizing gay marriage. In addition, nearly nine out of ten Fortune 500 companies protect workers based on sexual orientation.[73]

Before we begin, it is important to emphasize that gay consumers, like heterosexuals, vary in terms of ethnicity, geographic region, occupation, and age. These and other factors influence their behavior and, in most instances, play a much larger role in their consumption process than does their sexual orientation.

The gay market is substantial in both size and purchasing power. The size of the LGBTQ market is estimated to be about 4 percent of the adult U.S. population, or roughly 10 million people over the age of 18. Purchasing power is estimated at over $900 billion.[74]

Not surprisingly, many companies have concluded that the gay market is a highly attractive segment to pursue. Examples include[75]

- American Airlines created a page on its website specifically for LGBTQ consumers. Wyndham Hotels partnered with the airline by giving a 20 percent discount on all reservations made through the page.
- IBM has a "sales team dedicated to bringing LGBT decision-makers in contact with IBM."
- Recent LGBTQ-themed advertisements that have enjoyed success include:
  - Tiffany and Co.'s "Will You": A same-sex couple engagement ring campaign.
  - Wells-Fargo's "Learning Sign Language": Two women learning sign language to communicate with their soon-to-be-adopted child.

Any firm that desires to capture the loyalty of the gay community must have internal policies that do not discriminate against gay employees. A recent survey found that 82 percent of gay consumers are more likely to buy from companies they know are gay friendly.[76] The Human Rights Campaign Foundation (www.hrc.org) helps provide such information through its corporate equality index (CEI), which measures how equitably a company treats its LGBTQ employees, customers, and investors.

Product Issues   In many cases, the lifestyles of gay consumers do not differ sufficiently from those of other consumers to require product modifications. For example, three of the top four reasons for choosing a hotel were the same for LGBTQ customers as for heterosexuals. In order of importance, they were convenience, customer service, and recommendations from friends or family.[77] However, product modification opportunities are sometimes possible and beneficial. For example, in the realm of television, content that targets news, concerns, programs, and movies of specific interest to LGBTQ audiences is increasingly popular. The Logo network was launched in response to this growing demand. In addition, with the increased focus on same-sex marriage, companies such as Pottery Barn and Tiffany and Co. are modifying their bridal registries to be gender neutral, and websites such as Gayweddings (www.gayweddings.com) are emerging to serve this market.

Another area in which product modifications are often necessary is financial services. As the director of segment marketing for American Express explains:

> Often, gay couples are very concerned about issues like Social Security benefits and estate planning, since same-sex marriages often are not recognized under the law.[78]

Ameriprise has a LGBTQ web page devoted to this market and consistently scores 100 percent on the CEI index. As their website states:

> Ameriprise Financial was one of the first financial services firms to offer dual client analysis for domestic partners and single people in relationships. Dual client analysis allows financial advisors to help domestic partners create a shared plan for the future. Our financial advisors use a comprehensive approach to financial planning that includes tax, protection, estate, retirement and investment planning strategies.

Communication Issues   There are a large number of gay-oriented print media in the United States and Canada. Given the size and spending power of the gay market, it is not surprising that spending in gay-oriented print media has more than tripled since 1997 to its current level of over $350 million. And a large and increasing number of Fortune 500 companies now advertise in gay media.[79]

Compared with the general population, gay consumers tend to be more tech savvy and more likely to search online for information.[80] Marketers are taking this into account in developing their websites.[81] For example, iTunes offers LGBTQ podcasts, Orbitz has a gay and lesbian page on its travel site, and, as we have seen, Ameriprise has a dedicated web page for the LGBTQ community. In addition, marketers such as Virgin Mobile are using targeted banner ad campaigns to promote their products through websites that target the LGBTQ community such as OutTraveler.com and pride.com.

Because most products don't require alteration for the gay market, firms may decide to approach the market by placing one of their standard ads in gay-oriented media. Anheuser-Busch, Miller Brewing, Baileys Original Irish Cream, and American Express are among the firms that first approached this market with standard ads. However, a majority of ads (62 percent) in gay print media now are created specifically for gay consumers.[82] The ads may portray a gay couple instead of a heterosexual couple in a standard ad. Or the entire ad may contain a gay theme, such as the Tylenol ad shown in Illustration 3–7.

It has been estimated that roughly half of the gay community rarely or never read gay-oriented publications and spend considerable time using standard media.[83] As one gay man stated, "We are not only reading *Out* and *The Advocate* all the time. If you go into any gay man's apartment you're very likely to see *Vanity Fair* and *People* as well."[84] This is also true online, where eight of the ten top websites visited by gay consumers are general sites such as Yahoo!, Google, Amazon, CNN, and eBay, which are not specifically devoted to gay issues.[85]

Using ads with gay themes in standard mass media can generate concerns regarding backlash from the portion of the market that does not accept the gay community, as well as the desire to have ads that directly appeal to the largest number of viewers.[86] A recent study compared mainstream ads (heterosexual couples in the ad) with explicitly gay and lesbian ads (male or female couples) or implicit gay and lesbian ads (ads that had gay symbolic icons, such as the rainbow flag, pink triangle, and freedom rings). The study found that gays and heterosexuals equally liked the mainstream ads. In addition, although heterosexuals disliked explicit gay and lesbian ads, their attitudes were not negatively influenced by the implicit gay and lesbian ads. Finally, both explicit and implicit gay and lesbian ads were liked more than mainstream ads by those who identified themselves as gay or lesbian.[87] For marketers wanting to move into the mainstream market with appeals that are as broad as possible and still target gay consumers, this research suggests that using symbolic gay icons (which the mainstream market tends to be relatively unknowledgeable of) appears to be an effective tactic. This is important because research shows that gay consumers reward companies that advertise in gay media outlets and/or use gay themes in their advertising.

Finally, in addition to advertising in gay media, support of gay community events such as Gay Pride week is another important avenue firms use in approaching this market.

Gender-Based Marketing

LO6

As we saw in the chapter's opening vignette, gender roles in the United States are shifting. The shift is going both ways, with more women taking on traditionally male-oriented tasks and more men taking on traditionally female-oriented tasks. It's hard to imagine that just a few generations ago, the prevailing stereotype of an automobile purchase involved a male making the purchase alone. Today, women influence 80 percent of all vehicles sold, make over half of all new vehicle purchases (up from 20 percent in 1984), and purchase 40 percent of all SUVs.[88]

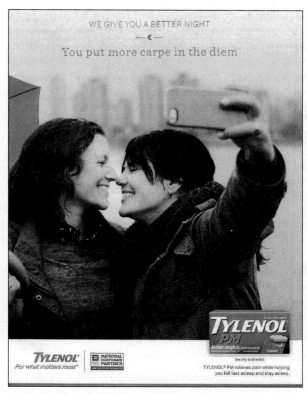

WE GIVE YOU A BETTER NIGHT

— ❦ —

You put more carpe in the diem

TYLENOL
PM
Acetaminophen
Caplets

TYLENOL®
For what matters most™

**NATIONAL
CORPORATE
PARTNER**

Use only as directed.
TYLENOL® PM relieves pain while helping
you fall fast asleep and stay asleep.

Source: Johnson & Johnson Consumer Inc

Changes in gender roles for women have been dramatic, with increased participation in the workforce, increased wealth and purchasing power, and increased participation in active lifestyles, to name just a few. Marketers of products and services ranging from automobiles, to sportswear, to financial services clearly understand the importance of women as a market segment. Consider the following examples:

- Ram trucks and Jim Beam bourbon both target women with celebrities Miranda Lambert and Mila Kunis as the brands' respective spokespeople.
- Harley Davidson has a page on its website called *Women Riders* and sponsors Garage Party events for women, who are an increasing proportion of Harley's customer base.[89]
- Nike has an entire golf and apparel line targeted to women, along with an entire section on its website featuring these products as well as the Nike Training Club app available through iTunes.

The terms *sex* and **gender** are used interchangeably to refer to *whether a person is biologically a male or a female.* **Gender identity** refers to *the traits of femininity* (expressive traits such as tenderness and compassion) *and masculinity* (instrumental traits such as aggressiveness and dominance). These traits represent the ends of a continuum, and individuals have varying levels of each trait, with biological males tending to be toward the masculine end of the continuum and biological females toward the feminine end.[90]

Gender roles are *the behaviors considered appropriate for males and females in a given society.* As the previous discussion of automobile purchasing indicates, gender roles in

America have undergone massive changes over the past 30 years. Much of this shift has been for behaviors previously considered appropriate primarily for men to be acceptable for women too. But also, as we saw in the opener, there is a shift for behaviors previously considered appropriate primarily for women to be acceptable for men too. However, marketers need to be careful when the roles are switched. For example, stay-at-home dads should not be viewed as the same as their mom counterparts. Their roles and behaviors are different. Australian researcher Jennifer Baxter commented that

"Our analysis showed that stay-at-home-dad families were not simply the reverse 'mirror' image of stay-at-home-mum families, just with the gender roles reversed."[91]

Gender roles are ascribed roles. An **ascribed role** is based on *an attribute over which the individual has little or no control.* This can be contrasted with an **achievement role,** which is based on *performance criteria over which the individual has some degree of control.* Individuals can, within limits, select their occupational role (achievement role), but they cannot generally determine their gender (ascribed role).

It can be useful to distinguish **traditional** or **modern gender orientations** on the basis of preference for one or the other of two contrasting married lifestyles:

- *Traditional.* A marriage in which the husband assumes the responsibility for providing for the family and the wife runs the house and takes care of the children.
- *Modern.* A marriage in which husband and wife share responsibilities. Both work, and they share homemaking and childcare responsibilities.

Americans have certainly moved toward a *preference* for a modern lifestyle, from only 35 percent in 1977 to 71 percent in the most recent polls.[92] In addition, only 25 percent agree that women should return to their traditional roles and 87 percent agree that fathers are just as capable as mothers of caring for their children.[93] However, while males and females both express strong preferences for the modern lifestyle as a general concept, most recognize that it comes with a cost. For example, 80 percent of mothers with children age five or under would prefer to stay home with their children if it were totally up to them,[94] and nearly half of both men and women believe that it was easier when "women stayed at home and men went to work."[95]

As the opener indicated, men's participation in household duties is on the rise. It is important to realize, however, that the focus there was on all men, whether married or single. However, for married men, while participation in household tasks has increased, the general pattern still follows more traditional gender roles. The following results from the Bureau of Labor Statistics' "American Time Use" survey show the time spent on household activities by gender.

Activity	Women (minutes/day)	Men (minutes/day)
Maintenance, repair, decoration	4	11
Lawn, garden, houseplants	7	17
Kitchen and food cleanup	13	4
Household management	13	9
Laundry	17	5
Interior cleaning	29	10
Food and drink preparation	37	17
Other household activities	15	12
Total	2 hours, 15 minutes	1 hour, 25 minutes

Source: Bureau of Labor Statistics, American Time Use Survey, 2015, accessed January 22, 2018.

Source: Ball Corporation

Source: Alikay Naturals

ILLUSTRATION 3-8

Women fulfill a multitude of roles today and have a wide range of attitudes about their roles in society. The Fuga Energy and Alikay Naturals ads take radically different approaches to the portrayal of women and women's attitudes.

These numbers highlight that women spend more than twice as much time performing more traditionally female chores (e.g., cleaning the house and preparing meals). Given that 62 percent of married women believe that "sharing household chores" is very important to a successful marriage,[96] this can lead to strong resentments, as the following quote demonstrates:

> "It's a blowout fight every month," Hope (32 and a book editor) confesses. "It's the only thing we fight about." Hope says getting Cohen (34 and a medical resident) to do his agreed-upon tasks requires constant reminders. "He'll tell me he'll wash the dishes before we go to bed, and maybe he will," she says. "But by around 9:30, with dirty dishes still in the sink, I'm broiling."[97]

With high levels of role overload and stress associated with dual-income families, many Americans are realizing that they can't have it all, and where there is a choice, some are opting for change. Sometimes the change is toward the nontraditional, as in the increasing numbers of stay-at-home dads, discussed earlier.[98] Sometimes the change is toward the traditional, as in the recent increase in stay-at-home moms.[99]

As we have seen, women have a variety of role options and a range of attitudes concerning their gender roles. The Fuga Energy and Alikay Naturals ads in Illustration 3–8 reflect two sharply contrasting views of the female role. Next, we examine some of the marketing implications of the changing roles of women in American society.

Market Segmentation   Neither the women's nor the men's market is as homogeneous as it once was. At least four significant female market segments exist:[100]

1. *Traditional housewife.* Generally married. Prefers to stay at home. Very home and family centered. Desires to please husband and children. Seeks satisfaction and meaning from household and family maintenance as well as volunteer activities. Experiences strong pressure to work outside the home and is well aware of forgone income opportunity. Feels supported by family and is generally content with role.

2. *Trapped housewife.* Generally married. Would prefer to work but stays at home because of young children, lack of outside opportunities, or family pressure. Seeks satisfaction and meaning outside the home. Does not enjoy most household chores. Has mixed feelings about current status and is concerned about lost opportunities.

3. *Trapped working woman.* Married or single. Would prefer to stay at home but works because of economic necessity or social or family pressure. Does not derive satisfaction or meaning from employment. Enjoys most household activities but is frustrated by lack of time. Feels conflict about her role, particularly if younger children are home. Resents missed opportunities for family, volunteer, and social activities. Is proud of financial contribution to family.

4. *Career working woman.* Married or single. Prefers to work. Derives satisfaction and meaning from employment rather than, or in addition to, home and family. Experiences some conflict over her role if younger children are at home but is generally content. Views home maintenance as a necessary evil. Feels pressed for time.

Although the above descriptions are oversimplified, they indicate the diverse nature of the adult female population. Notice that women may move in and out of these categories over their lifetimes. For example, an otherwise career working woman may feel more like a trapped working woman if she finds it necessary to work while her children are young. And while the career working woman category has grown significantly over the past three decades, the other segments are still sizable, unique, and important.

The male market is likewise diverse in both its attitudes and behaviors toward gender roles, work, and household chores. One classification distinguishes between modern and traditional men, whereby modern men are more focused on such factors as (a) fashion, (b) shopping, and (c) cooking.[101]

Product Strategy   Many products are losing their traditional gender typing. Guns, cars, motorcycles, computer games and equipment, golf equipment, financial services, and many other once masculine products are now designed specifically with women in mind. The expanding wealth, independence, and purchasing power of women, and the time pressure on them, make them an important target market. Consider the following:

- Women-headed households represent roughly 28 percent of all households. The Barbara K tool line (now DIYVA by Barbara K) targeted at women was launched in 2003 and has been highly successful. According to CEO Barbara Kavovit, "Women have made so many strides but can't fix things in their homes." The tools are designed to be stylish and functional, and have special features targeting women, such as cushioned handles.[102]

- Assaults against women are a major social problem. Smith & Wesson launched LadySmith, a line of guns designed specifically for women. They found that "if a woman is going to pull out a gun for personal protection, she doesn't want a cute gun." So rather than "feminize" men's guns with colored handles, Smith & Wesson targeted a key success criterion by redesigning its guns to fit women's hands.

- The high percentage of women working outside the home, particularly when coupled with children, can lead to high levels of time pressure and a resulting need for convenience products and services.[103] A wealth of such products and services have emerged to meet this need, as shown in this Barilla ad in Illustration 3–9.

As women's roles have expanded, the consumption of potentially harmful products has become socially acceptable for women. This, of course, raises the ethical issue of targeting groups that have not historically been heavy users of products such as alcohol or tobacco.

Marketing Communications A considerable amount of research suggests that males and females process and respond differently to various communications elements, including sexual appeals, music, verbal style, and so forth.[104] As just one example, females respond more favorably to a "help-others" type of appeal for a charity, whereas males respond best to a "self-help" appeal.[105] This is caused by differing worldviews that affect a range of communications responses as well as consumption behaviors.

Men and women also consume different media and use the same media differently. For example, in social media, information is a more prominent goal for men (36 percent) than women (28 percent), while finding coupons and promotions is a more prominent goal for women (47 percent) than men (33 percent).[106] As of late, though, these differences have become less pronounced. Men still prefer online discussion forums more than women do, but usage on the business networking platform LinkedIn is comparable. The usage of various platforms by those on online is provided below:

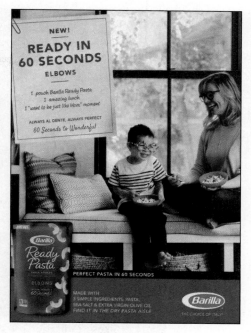

Source: Barilla G. & R. Fratelli

ILLUSTRATION 3-9

Firms such as Barilla have responded to increased time pressure with new products and positioning strategies.

Social Media Platform	Women (%)	Men (%)
Facebook	77	66
Pinterest	44	16
Instagram	31	24
LinkedIn	25	26
Twitter	21	25
Reddit, Digg or Slashdot	11	20
Tumblr	11	10

Source: M. Anderson, "Men Catch Up with Women on Overall Social Media Use," *Pew Research,* August 28, 2015, www.pewresearch.org.

Because women are quite diverse as a group, marketers also must consider such factors as ethnicity, age, life stage, and employment status differences when designing marketing communications. Ads portraying women must be careful about offending any of the various segments.[107] For example, an ad that implied that housework was unimportant or that women who work outside the home are somehow superior to those who do not could insult traditional housewives. Ads that show women primarily as decoration or as clearly inferior to males tend to produce negative responses across all female segments.[108] Despite such negative reactions, many ads still use these tactics.[109] However, some companies are hitting this issue straight on. As mentioned earlier, Dove launched its "Self-Esteem" campaign, which features realistic depictions of women, in response to idealized and unrealistic portrayals of women in advertising that have been shown to reduce self-esteem.

Finally, in terms of gender role portrayal, there are still relatively few ads showing men using products traditionally designed for women or performing tasks traditionally

ILLUSTRATION 3-10

The Centrum ad is still somewhat unusual in that it portrays a male involved in a traditional female task. Although gender roles are changing, it is much more common to portray women performing traditional male tasks than the reverse.

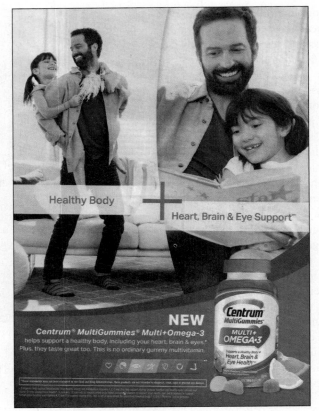

Source: Pfizer Inc.

performed by women. And according to one study, only one in four men feels that consumer product ads are designed to speak to them.[110] However, this is changing. JIF has moved away from the "Choosy mothers choose JIF," to "Choosy moms and dads choose JIF," along with positive depictions of father and child interactions in their ads. Recent Super Bowls have been home to "Dadvertising" with ads by Toyota, Nissan, and Dove for Men that portray more caring, engaged fathers.[111] The Centrum vitamins ad in Illustration 3-10 also demonstrates these changing roles. Such portrayals will likely continue to increase over time.

Retail Strategy   As we saw in the chapter opener, men and women have different purchasing habits. Differences in loyalty, brand switching, coupon usage, and shopping styles within the store all need to be accounted for by retailers as more men take on the grocery shopping task.

In addition, men and women react differently to various aspects of retail and service environments. For example, when there is a service failure, men appear to focus mostly on problem resolution, whereas women also focus on the process by which the problem is resolved. Being able to have a voice in the resolution process is much more important for women than men. Such differences need to be built into employee training programs.[112]

SMARTBOOK

LO1: Understand core American cultural values.

Cultural values are widely held beliefs that affirm what is desirable. Three categories of values that affect behaviors are those related to the self, others, and the environment. Sometimes numerous values are at work in affecting a given trend, as is the case with organic consumption, which is affected by values relating to family and nature.

LO2: Summarize changes in self-, environment-, and other-oriented values.

In terms of *self-oriented* values, we place somewhat less emphasis on hard work as an end in itself, although we continue to work some of the longest hours among industrialized nations. We are trending toward greater emphasis on sensual gratification. And, while the recent recession may have tempered spending, there appears to be a move back toward greater emphasis on immediate gratification. Finally, while religion is important, America remains a relatively secular culture.

Values that affect our relationship to our *environment* have become somewhat more performance oriented and slightly less oriented toward change. There is a strong and growing value placed on protecting the natural environment, and we increasingly value risk taking.

In terms of those values that influence an individual's relationship with *others,* Americans remain individualistic. We have substantially less of a masculine orientation now than in the past. We also place a greater value on older persons and diversity.

LO3: Discuss values as they relate to green marketing.

Americans have shifted their view from one of overcoming nature to more of admiring nature. This translates into greater concerns regarding the protection of our environment and the emergence of green marketing. *Green marketing* involves (1) developing products whose production, use, or disposition is less harmful to the environment than the traditional versions of the product; (2) developing products that have a positive impact

on the environment; or (3) tying the purchase of a product to an environmental organization or event.

LO4: Discuss values as they relate to cause-related marketing.

Americans are high on the value of problem solving. This makes us prone to want to put efforts toward causes that are important to us in an attempt to fix or improve the situation. *Cause-related marketing* is marketing that ties a company and its products to an issue or cause with the goal of improving sales and corporate image while providing benefits to the cause. Companies associate with causes to create long-term relationships with their customers, building corporate and brand equity that eventually should lead to increased sales.

LO5: Discuss values as they relate to marketing to gay and lesbian consumers.

The value placed on diversity continues to increase, including openness to alternative lifestyles and family structures including same-sex couples. The *LGBTQ* or *gay market* is estimated at roughly 10 million people over the age of 18 with purchasing power over $900 billion. Many companies view the gay market as highly attractive and have committed considerable resources to targeting this market with specific products and promotional efforts. Supportive internal policies toward gay employees as well as support for important gay causes are among the critical factors in approaching this market.

LO6: Discuss values as they relate to gender-based marketing.

The ongoing shift from a traditionally masculine view toward a balanced masculine-feminine view has resulted in changing gender roles. *Gender roles* have undergone radical changes in the past 30 years. A fundamental shift has been for the female role to become more like the traditional male role. Male roles also are evolving, with men beginning to take on what have traditionally been considered female tasks. Virtually all aspects of our society, including marketing activities, have been affected by these shifts.

KEY TERMS

Achievement role 98
Ascribed role 98
Cause-related marketing
  (CRM) 91
Cultural values 80

Enviropreneurial marketing 87
Gender 97
Gender identity 97
Gender role 97
Green marketing 90

Greenwashing 91
Modern gender orientation 98
Traditional gender orientation 98
Voluntary simplicity 83

REVIEW QUESTIONS

1. What is a *cultural value?* Do all members of a culture share cultural values?

2. Describe the current American culture in terms of each of the 18 values discussed in this chapter.

3. How is *voluntary simplicity* related to the materialism value? What are the marketing implications of voluntary simplicity? Do these implications vary by product class?

4. What is *green marketing?*

5. What values underlie green marketing?

6. How is *enviropreneurial marketing* related to new product success and market share? Link this to the value of green marketing in creating a competitive advantage.

7. Describe the basic conflict between the environmental movement and many businesses.

8. What is *cause-related marketing?* Why is it often successful?

9. What are the major decisions a firm faces with respect to the gay market?

10. What is meant by *gender?*

11. What is *gender identity?*

12. What is a *gender role?*

13. How does an *ascribed role* differ from an *achievement role?*

14. What is happening to male and female gender roles in America?

15. What are the differences between a traditional and a modern gender role orientation?

16. Describe a segmentation system for the female market based on employment status and gender role orientation.

17. What are some of the major marketing implications of the changing role of women?

DISCUSSION QUESTIONS

18. Describe additional values you feel could, or should, be added to Figure 3-1. Describe the marketing implications of each.

19. Pick the three values you feel the authors of this book were most *in*accurate about in the chapter in describing the *current* American values. Justify your answers.

20. Pick the three values you feel the authors were most *in*accurate about in describing the *emerging* American values. Justify your answers.

21. Respond to the questions in Consumer Insight 3-1.

22. Which values are most relevant to the purchase or use of the following? Are they currently favorable or unfavorable for ownership/use? Are they

shifting at all? If so, is the shift in a favorable or unfavorable direction?
   a. Dietary supplements
   b. The Salvation Army
   c. Financial investments (stocks, mutual funds, etc.)
   d. Home theater systems
   e. Tanning salon
   f. Expensive jewelry

23. Do you believe Americans' concern for the environment is a stronger value than their materialism?

24. What ethical issues do you see relating to green marketing?

25. Explain greenwashing and its possible role in the FTC's revision of the Green Guides.

26. Cause-related marketing is done to enhance a firm's sales or image. Some critics consider such marketing to be unethical. What is your position?

27. In which of the four categories of responders to cause-related marketing are you? Why?

28. Suppose AT&T showed a gay couple using its cell service plan or P&G showed a gay couple using one of its laundry products in ads on network television. Is a backlash by those who do not accept the gay community a likely response? How are such consumers likely to respond? Why?

29. Do you think housewives may be defensive or sensitive about not having employment outside of the home? If so, what implications will this have for marketing practice?

30. Develop an advertisement for the following for each of the four female market segments described in the chapter.
    a. Bicycles
    b. iPad
    c. Exercise equipment
    d. Breakfast cereal
    e. Vacation cruises
    f. Cosmetics

APPLICATION ACTIVITIES

31. Find and copy or describe an advertisement for an item that reflects Americans' position on the following values:
    a. Active/Passive
    b. Material/Nonmaterial
    c. Hard work/Leisure
    d. Postponed/Immediate gratification
    e. Sensual gratification/Abstinence
    f. Religious/Secular
    g. Cleanliness
    h. Performance/Status
    i. Tradition/Change
    j. Risk taking/Security
    k. Problem solving/Fatalistic
    l. Admire/Overcome nature
    m. Individual/Collective
    n. Limited/Extended family
    o. Diversity/Uniformity
    p. Competition/Cooperation
    q. Youth/Age
    r. Masculine/Feminine

32. Interview a person who consumes one or more organic food items. What values influence this consumption pattern?

33. Interview a salesperson who has been selling the following for at least 10 years. See if this individual has noticed a change in the purchasing roles of women over time.
    a. Electric guitars
    b. Cell phones
    c. Computers
    d. Homes
    e. Financial services

34. Interview a career-oriented working wife and a traditional housewife of a similar age. Report on differences in attitudes toward shopping, products, and so forth.

35. Form a team of five. Have each team member interview five married adult males. Based on these interviews, develop a typology that classifies them by their attitude toward and participation in household or child-rearing activities.

36. Pick two different environmental segments from Table 3–1. Find one advertisement you think is particularly appropriate or effective for each. Copy or describe each ad and justify its selection.

37. Interview a salesperson for each of the following. Ascertain the interest shown in the item by males and females. Determine if males and females are concerned with different characteristics of the item, and if they have different purchase motivations.
    a. Art
    b. Automobiles
    c. Golf clubs
    d. Personal care items
    e. Clothing
    f. Gardening tools

38. Interview 10 male and 10 female students. Ask each to describe the typical owner or

consumer of the following. If they do not specify, ask for the gender of the typical owner. Then probe to find out why they think the typical owner is of the gender they indicated. Also determine the perceived marital and occupational status of the typical owner and the reasons for these beliefs.

a. Pet snake
b. Pasta maker
c. Large life insurance policy
d. Power tools
e. Habitat for Humanity contributor
f. Personal fitness trainer

REFERENCES

1. Opener based on K. Bruno, "Millennial Dads Are Real, and So Is Their Spending Power," *Ad Age,* March 27, 2015, www.adage.com; T. Nudd, "Dads Play Barbie with Their Daughters in the Doll's Latest Charming Effort to Modernize," *AdWeek,* January 23, 2017, www.adweek.com; G. Livingston, "Growing Number of Dads Home with the Kids," *Pew Research Center,* June 5, 2014, www.pewsocialtrends.org; Mintel Group, "Millennial Dads–US–August 2017," www.mintel.com, accessed January 12, 2018; Mintel Group, "Marketing to Dads–March 2012," www.mintel.com, accessed January 12, 2018.

2. E. Gurel-Atay et al., "Changes in Social Values in the United States," *Journal of Advertising Research,* March 2010, pp. 57–67.

3. Numbers are from the 2014 Religious Landscape Study conducted by the Pew Research Center, reported at www.pewforum.org/religious-landscape-study/, accessed January 20, 2018.

4. W. H. Henley et al., "The Effects of Symbol Product Relevance and Religiosity on Consumer Perceptions of Religious Symbols in Advertising," *Journal of Current Issues and Research in Advertising,* Spring 2009, pp. 89–103.

5. Public Agenda, "New Survey Shows Religious Americans Less Likely to Support Compromise," press release, January 23, 2005, www.publicagenda.org.

6. R. Gardyn, "Breaking the Rules of Engagement," *American Demographics,* July–August 2002, p. 35.

7. See 2014 Religious Landscape Study by Pew Research Center.

8. Henley et al., "The Effects of Symbol Product Relevance and Religiosity on Consumer Perceptions of Religious Symbols in Advertising."

9. J. Flint, "Angry NFL Slams ABC's 'Desperate Housewives' Promo," *Wall Street Journal Online,* November 17, 2004, www.wsj.com.

10. J. G. Wirtz, J. V. Sparks, and T. M. Zimbres, "The Effect of Exposure to Sexual Appeals in Advertisements on Memory, Attitude, and Purchase Intention: A Meta-Analytic Review," *International Journal of Advertising* 37, no. 2 (2018), pp. 168–98; interview with J. Wirtz, www.news.illinois.edu, accessed January 20, 2018; T. L. Stanley, "Burgers, Not Boobs: Carl's Jr. Brilliantly Flips the Scripts by Tearing Down Its Own Smutty Ads," *Ad Week,* March 29, 2017, www.adweek.com.

11. L. Petrecca, "Axe Ads Turn up the Promise of Sex Appeal," *USAToday,* April 18, 2007, www.usatoday.com, accessed February 20, 2011; H.-J. Paek et al., "A Cross-Cultural and Cross-Media Comparison of Female Nudity in Advertising," *Journal of Promotion Management* 13, no. 1/2 (2007), pp. 145–67; J. Sengupta and D. W. Dahl, "Gender-Related Reactions to Gratuitous Sex Appeals in Advertising," *Journal of Consumer Psychology* 18 (2008), pp. 62–78; J. Feifer, "How Axe Built a Highly Scientific, Totally Irresistible Marketing Machine Built on Lust," *Fast Company,* August 8, 2012, www.fastcompany.com, accessed January 20, 2018.

12. Gurel-Atay et al., "Changes in Social Values in the United States."

13. S. Thompson, "Minor Indulgence Keeps Cookies from Tanking," *Advertising Age,* June 28, 2004, p. S-18.

14. S. Theil, "The Urge to Splurge Is Creeping Back," *Newsweek,* November 29, 2010, www.newsweek.com/urge-splurge-creeping-back-70101.

15. "How American Consumers Shop Now," *Consumer Reports,* September 2014, www.consumerreports.org, accessed January 20, 2018.

16. L. J. Shrum, J. E. Burroughs, and A. Rindfleisch, "Television's Cultivation of Material Values," *Journal of Consumer Research,* December 2005, pp. 473–79; S. Kamal, S. Chu, and M. Pedram, "Materialism, Attitudes, and Social Media Usage and Their Impact on Purchase Intention of Luxury Fashion Goods among American and Arab Young Generations," *Journal of Interactive Advertising* 13, no. 1 (2013), pp. 27–40.

17. Theil, "The Urge to Splurge Is Creeping Back."

18. S. Zavestoski, "The Social-Psychological Bases of Anticonsumption Attitudes," *Psychology & Marketing,* February 2002, p. 155.

19. A. Etzioni, "Voluntary Simplicity," *Journal of Economic Psychology* 19 (1998), pp. 619–43; Zavestoski, "The Social-Psychological Bases of Anticonsumption Attitudes"; M. Craig-Lees and C. Hill, "Understanding Voluntary Simplifiers," *Psychology & Marketing,* February 2002, pp. 197–210; S. McDonald et al., "Toward Sustainable Consumption," *Psychology & Marketing,* June 2006, pp. 515–34; A. Livingston, "How to Simplify Your Life with Voluntary Simplicity–Benefits and Challenges," *Money Crashers,* June 29, 2016, www.moneycrashers.com, accessed January 20, 2018.

20. L. Saad, "The '40-Hour' Workweek Is Actually Longer–by Seven Hours," Gallup, August 29, 2014, www.gallup.com; C. Isidore & T. Luhby, "Turns Out Americans Work Really Hard–But Some What to Work Harder," *CNN Money,* July 9, 2015, www.cnnmoney.com; Organisation for Economic Co-operation and Development, Hours Worked, 2016, https://data.oecd.org/emp/hours-worked.htm, accessed January 20, 2018.

21. These statistics drawn from M. DeWolf, "12 Stats About Working Women," *U.S. Department of Labor,* March 1, 2017, https://blog.dol.gov, accessed January 20, 2018.

22. A. C. Brooks, "I Love My Work," *American,* September/October 2007, accessed February 21, 2011.

23. "Fewer Mothers Prefer Full-Time Work," *PewResearchCenter Publications,* July 12, 2007.

24. "New Survey from Xobni on Email Overload Shows There Is No Such Thing as a Day Off for Americans and Brits," *PR Newswire,* September 2, 2010.

25. See P. Paul, "Targeting Boomers," *American Demographics,* March 2003, pp. 24–26; J. Consoli, "Where Have All the Young Men Gone?," *Mediaweek,* October 20, 2003, pp. 4–5.

26. M. Slatalla, "Overscheduled?," *Time,* July 24, 2000, p. 79.

27. T. Cahill, "Exotic Places Made Me Do It," *Outside,* March 2002, p. 60.

28. See J. P. Robinson and M. Milke, "Dances with Dust Bunnies," *American Demographics,* January 1997, pp. 37–40; A. Miller, "The Millennial Mind-Set," *American Demographics,* January 1999, pp. 62–63.

29. P. Tyre, "Clean Freaks," *Newsweek,* June 7, 2004, p. 42.

30. "Cash and Carry," *American Demographics,* May 2000, p. 45.

31. "Creativity at Work," *American Demographics,* December 2002–January 2003, pp. 22–23; D. Kiley, "It's Back . . . Fiat Launches 500, Slights Mass for Creative Class," *Advertising Age,* January 31, 2011, pp. 1, 8.

32. Gurel-Atay et al., "Changes in Social Values in the United States."

33. "Public Worried but Not Panicked about Economy," *PewResearchCenter Publications,* October 15, 2008.

34. R. E. Dunlap, "The State of Environmentalism in the U.S.," *Gallup,* 2007, www.gallup.com, accessed May 25, 2008; J. M. Jones, "In the U.S., 28% Report Major Changes to Live 'Green,'" *Gallup,* 2008, www.gallup.com, accessed May 25, 2008; *Public Agenda Online,* www.publicagenda.org, accessed May 25, 2008; J. Loechner, "Consumers Want Proof It's Green," *MediaPost,* April 9, 2009, www.mediapost.com, accessed February 19, 2011; C. Funk & B. Kennedy, "Everyday Environmentalism," *Pew Research Center,* October 4, 2016, www.pewinternet.org, accessed January 20, 2018.

35. TNS News Center, "TNS Global Study 'The Green Life' Reveals Spectrum of Environmental Attitudes across United States and the World," press release, April 30, 2008, www.tnsglobal.com, accessed February 20, 2011; J. Gartner, "Consumer Shades of Green Identified," *Matter Network,* June 9, 2008, http://matternetwork.com, accessed February 21, 2011; "Do 'Green' Conscious Consumers Practice What They Preach?," *BusinessWire,* September 29, 2008; "IRI/TNS Shades of Green Segmentation™," *Data Sheet,* www.infores.com, accessed February 21, 2011.

36. W. E. Baker and J. M. Sinkula, "Environmental Marketing Strategy and Firm Performance," *Journal of the Academy of Marketing Science* 33, no. 4 (2005), pp. 461–75; F. Ross, T. Martinez, and M. Molina, "How Green Should You Be?," *Journal of Advertising Research,* December 2008, pp. 547–63.

37. A. C. Cuneo, "What's in Store," *Advertising Age,* February 25, 2002, p. 1.

38. M. J. Dutta-Bergman and W. D. Wells, "The Values and Lifestyles of Idiocentrics and Allocentrics in an Individualistic Culture," *Journal of Consumer Psychology* 12, no. 3 (2002), pp. 231–42.

39. B. S. C. Liu, O. Furrer, and D. Sudharshan, "The Relationship between Culture and Behavioral Intentions toward Services," *Journal of Service Research,* November 2001, pp. 118–29.

40. J. Halliday, "Tuners Fit In with Customizer Fare," *Advertising Age,* May 31, 2004, p. S-8; R. Kissell, "Ratings; Discovery Channel Delivers Biggest May Ever," *Variety,* June 5, 2015, www.variety.com, accessed January 21, 2018.

41. K. Maney, "Mass Indvidualism Makes Life Tough for Consumer Product Giants," *Newsweek,* July 10, 2014; S. Homewood, "Etsy Celebrates Individualism in Major Global Brand Push," *AdNews,* September 2016, www.adnews.com.au, accessed January 21, 2018.

42. S. A. Grier, A. M. Brumbaugh, and C. G. Thornton, "Crossover Dreams," *Journal of Marketing,* April 2006, pp. 35–51.

43. "Millennials' Judgments about Recent Trends Not So Different," *Pew Research Center Publications,* January 7, 2010.

44. R. Suro, "Movement at Warp Speed," *American Demographics,* August 2000, pp. 61–64.

45. See, e.g., C. A. Lin, "Cultural Values Reflected in Chinese and American Television Advertising," *Journal of Advertising,* Winter 2001, pp. 83–94.

46. C. R. Wiles, J. A. Wiles, and A. Tjernlund, "The Ideology of Advertising," *Journal of Advertising Research,* May–June 1996, pp. 57–66. See also P. Simcock and L. Sudbury, "The Invisible Majority?," *International Journal of Advertising* 25, no. 1 (2006), pp. 87–106.

47. F. Newport, "Americans Continue to Express Slight Preference for Boys," *Gallup,* July 5, 2007, www.gallup.com, accessed May 26, 2008.

48. *Women's Sports and Physical Activity Facts and Statistics* (EastMeadow: Women's Sports Foundation, May 17, 2008).

49. D. W. Moore, "Americans More Accepting of Female Bosses Than Ever," *Gallup,* May 10, 2002, www.gallup.com, accessed May 26, 2008; M. Brenan, "Americans No Longer Prefer Male Boss to Female Boss," *Gallup,* November 16, 2017, www.gallup.com, accessed January 21, 2018.

50. J. Ottman, "Innovative Marketers Give New Products the Green Light," *Marketing News,* March 1998, p. 10; "Investors, Big Businesses See Green in Being Green," *CNN.com,* August 20, 2007, www.cnn.com, accessed December 1, 2008.

51. M. Gunther, "The Green Machine," *Fortune,* August 7, 2006, pp. 42–57; B. Steinberg, "Buy a Spot, Save the Planet," *Advertising Age,* January 11, 2011, pp. 1, 18; W. Parish, "Corporations That Went All Out on 'Green Marketing' Initiatives," *Marketing Dive,* February 24, 2015, www.marketingdive.com; information available through corporate websites.

52. J. Neff, "Has Green Stopped Giving?," *Advertising Age,* November 8, 2010, pp. 1, 19; J. Loechner, "Consumers Want Proof It's Green," *MediaPost,* April 9, 2009.

53. P. Antonetti and S. Maklan, "Hippies, Greenies, and Tree Huggers: How the 'Warmth' Stereotype Hinders the Adoption of Responsible Brands," *Psychology and Marketing* 33, no. 10 (October 2016), pp. 796–813; A. Brough et al., "Is Eco-Friendly Unmanly? The Green-Feminine Stereotype and Its Effect on

Sustainable Consumption," *Journal of Consumer Research* 43, no. 4 (December 2016), pp. 567–82.

54. M. Glover, "Why Honda Accord Hybrid Ran Out of Gas," *Knight Ridder Tribune Business News,* June 13, 2007, p. 1.

55. J. Neff, "FTC Goes After Broad Environmental Clams in Long-Awaited Guideline Revision," *Advertising Age,* October 6, 2010; "Green Means Go on the Enforcement Highway," *Consumer Advertising Law Blog,* www.consumeradvertisinglawblog.com, accessed February 19, 2011.

56. Federal Trade Commission, "Green Guides: Summary of Proposal," www.ftc.gov, accessed February 18, 2011; Federal Trade Commission, "FTC Issues Revised 'Green Guides,'" press release, October 1, 2012, www.ftc.gov/news-events/press-releases/2012/10/ftc-issues-revised-green-guides, accessed January 22, 2018.

57. See, e.g., P. S. Bronn and A. B. Vrioni, "Corporate Social Responsibility and Cause-Related Marketing," *International Journal of Advertising* 2 (2001), pp. 207–21.

58. M. J. Barone, A. D. Miyazaki, and K. A. Taylor, "The Influence of Cause-Related Marketing on Consumer Choice," *Journal of the Academy of Marketing Science,* Spring 2000, pp. 248–62; S. Sen and C. B. Bhattacharya, "Does Doing Good Always Lead to Doing Better?," *Journal of Marketing Research,* May 2001, pp. 225–43.

59. Cone Incorporated, "Multi-Year Study Finds 21% Increase in Americans Who Say Corporate Support for Social Issues Is Important in Building Trust," press release, December 8, 2004, www.coneinc.com; "The Do Well Do Good Public Opinion Survey on Cause-Marketing: Summary Report," www.dowelldogood.net, accessed February 24, 2011.

60. "The Growth of Cause Marketing," *Cause Marketing Forum,* www.causemarketingforum.com, accessed May 26, 2008.

61. P. A. Vlachos et al., "Corporate Social Responsibility," *Journal of the Academy of Marketing Science* 37 (2009), pp. 170–80.

62. D. J. Webb and L. A. Mohr, "A Typology of Consumer Responses to Cause-Related Marketing," *Journal of Public Policy & Marketing,* Fall 1998, pp. 226–38.

63. J. W. Pracejus and G. D. Olsen, "The Role of Brand/Cause Fit in the Effectiveness of Cause-Related Marketing Campaigns," *Journal of Business Research* 57 (2004), pp. 635–40; N. J. Rifon et al., "Congruence Effects in Sponsorship," *Journal of Advertising,* Spring 2004, pp. 29–42; X. Nan and K. Heo, "Consumer Responses to Corporate Social Responsibility (CSR) Initiatives," *Journal of Advertising,* Summer 2007, pp. 63–74.

64. Additional information about these programs can be found on each company's website. See also the Cause Marketing Forum at www.causemarketingforum.com.

65. A. Semons, "4 Keys to Creating Cause Marketing That Benefits Both Brands and Nonprofits," *Ad Week,* March 12, 2017, www.adweek.com.

66. L. Saad, "Americans' Acceptance of Gay Relations Crosses 50% Threshold," *Gallup Annual Values and Beliefs Survey,* www.gallup.com, accessed February 24, 2011; "Gay and Lesbian Rights," *Gallup Historical Trends,* May 2017, http://news.gallup.com/poll/1651/gay-lesbian-rights.aspx, accessed January 22, 2018.

67. "Gay Rights: Seven in 10 Americans Say They Would Favor Hate Crime Laws to Protect Gays and Lesbians," *Public Agenda Online,* www.publicagenda.org, accessed April 18, 2005; "Most Continue to Favor Gays Serving Openly in Military," *PewResearchCenter Publications,* November 29, 2010, www.pewresearch.org, accessed February 20, 2011.

68. C. Hays, "Stores That Pop UP and Go Away, on Purpose," *New York Times,* December 7, 2004, www.nytimes.com/2004/12/07/business/businessspecial/07HAYS.html?_r=0, accessed August 25, 2014. See also S. Hallock, "Taking Aim at Breast Cancer," *Time Magazine,* October 4, 2004, http://content.time.com/time/magazine/article/0,9171,995259,00.html#ixzz2nffbml4b, accessed August 25, 2014.

69. Habitat for Humanity, "Whirlpool Brand and Habitat for Humanity Announce House Build Locations for 2013," press release, February 27, 2013, www.habitat.org/newsroom/2013archive/02_27_2013_Whirlpool_Habitat.aspx, accessed August 25, 2014.

70. P&G, "Bringing Loads of Hope to Colorado," press release, September 20, 2013, http://news.pg.com/blog/sustainability/bringing-loads-hope-colorado, accessed August 25, 2014.

71. S. Rozensher, "The Growth of Cause Marketing: Past, Current, and Future Trends," *Journal of Business & Economics Research (online)* 11, no. 4 (2013), p. 181. For the possible downside effects, see A. Eikenberry, "The Hidden Costs of Cause Marketing," *Stanford Social Innovation Review* 7, no. 3 (2009), pp. 51–56.

72. J. Chu, "Toms Sets Out to Sell a Lifestyle, Not Just Shoes," *Fast Company,* June 17, 2013, www.fastcompany.com/3012568/blake-mycoskie-toms, accessed August 25, 2014; T. Montague, "The Rise of Storydoing," *Fast Company,* August 5, 2013, www.fastcompany.com/3015209/leadership-now/the-rise-of-storydoing-inside-the-staggering-success-of-toms-shoes, accessed August 25, 2014.

73. "The Gay and Lesbian Market in the U.S.," *Packaged Facts,* July 2010; G. Gates, "In U.S., More Adults Identifying as LGBT," *Gallup,* January 11, 2017, www.gallup.com, accessed January 22, 2018.

74. "The Gay and Lesbian Market in the U.S."; Witeck Communications, "LGBT 2015 Buying Power Study," press release, July 20, 2016, www.witeck.com, accessed January 22, 2018.

75. "The Gay and Lesbian Market in the U.S.," pp. 181–82; M. Gunther, "Wal-Mart Becomes Gay-Friendly," *CNN Money,* November 30, 2006, www.cnnmoney.com, accessed May 27, 2008; N. Madov, "See the Top 10 LGBT-Themed Ads of the Year," *Ad Age,* December 28, 2015, www.adage.com.

76. D. L. Vence, "Pride Power," *Marketing News,* September 1, 2004, pp. 1, 13.

77. "The Gay and Lesbian Market in the U.S.," *Packaged Facts,* February 2007.

78. L. Koss-Feder, "Out and About," *Marketing News,* May 25, 1998, pp. 1, 20.

79. *2009 Gay Press Report* (Mountainside, NJ: 11th Annual Report by Prime Access Inc. and Rivendell Media Company Inc., 2004), available at www.gaymarket.com/agency_reports.html. See also M. Gunther, "Courting the Gay Consumer," *CNN Money,* December 7, 2006, www.cnnmoney.com.

80. "The Gay and Lesbian Market in the U.S." (2010).

81. R. Greenspan, "Advertisers May Find Gay Dollars Online," *ClickZ,* July 30, 2003, www.clickz.com.

82. *2009 Gay Press Report.*

83. "The Gay and Lesbian Market in the U.S." (2007).

84. R. Gardyn, "A Market Kept in the Closet," *American Demographics,* November 2001, pp. 37–42; see also J. J. Burnett, "Gays," *Journal of Advertising Research,* January 2000, pp. 75–83.

85. R. Greenspan, "Gays Access News, Influenced by Ads," *ClickZ,* May 17, 2004, www.clickz.com.

86. J. L. Aaker, A. M. Brumbaugh, and S. A. Grier, "Nontarget Market and Viewer Distinctiveness," *Journal of Consumer Psychology* 3 (2000), pp. 127–40; G. Oakenfull and T. Greenlee, "The Three Rules of Crossing Over from Gay Media to Mainstream Media Advertising," *Journal of Business Research* 57 (2004), pp. 1276–85.

87. G. K. Oakenfull and T. B. Greenlee, "Queer Eye for a Gay Guy," *Psychology & Marketing,* May 2005, pp. 421–39. See also G. K. Oakenfull, M. S. McCarthy, and T. G. Greenlee, "Targeting a Minority without Alienating the Majority," *Journal of Advertising Research,* June 2008, pp. 191–98.

88. For these and other statistics, go to the *About 4-Wheel Drive/ Offroading* website at http://4wheeldrive.about.com.

89. C. Krauss, "Harley Woos Female Bikers," *New York Times,* July 25, 2007; K. Monllos, "5 Ways Historically Male Brands Are Now Reaching Out to Women," *Ad Week,* April 24, 2016, www.adweek.com.

90. E. Fischer and S. J. Arnold, "Sex, Gender Identity, Gender Role Attitudes, and Consumer Behavior," *Psychology & Marketing,* March 1994, pp. 163–82; see also K. M. Palan, C. S. Areni, and P. Kiecker, "Gender Role Incongruity and Memorable Gift Exchange Experiences," in *Advances in Consumer Research,* ed. M. Gilly and J. Meyers-Levy (Provo, UT: Association for Consumer Research, 2001), pp. 51–57.

91. Mintel Group, "Millennial Dads—US—August 2017."

92. J. S. Grigsby, "Women Change Places," *American Demographics,* November 1992, p. 48; "Gender Equality Universally Embraced, but Inequalities Acknowledged," *Pew Global Attitudes Project,* July 1, 2010, www.pewglobal.org, accessed March 1, 2011.

93. "Child Care: Most People Say Fathers Can Be Just as Caring as Mothers and That Women Should Not Return to Their Traditional Roles," *Public Agenda Online,* www.publicagenda.org, accessed April 24, 2005.

94. "Child Care: Most Women Say That Mothers Who Work Outside the Home Are under More Stress Than Mothers Who Stay Home and Most Mothers Say They Would Prefer to Stay at Home," *Public Agenda Online,* www.publicagenda.org, accessed April 24, 2005.

95. "The Reality of the Working Woman," *Ad Age Insights White Paper,* June 7, 2010, p. 6.

96. "As Marriage and Parenthood Drift Apart Public Is Concerned About Social Impact," *PewResearchCenter Publications,* July 1, 2007.

97. P. Paul, "Whose Job Is This Anyway?," *Time,* October 4, 2004, p. 83.

98. A. Taylor, "Many Fathers Begin to Stay at Home with Children," *Knight Ridder Tribune Business News,* June 20, 2004, p. 1.

99. A. Rock, "From Two Incomes to One," *Money,* January 2005, p. 34.

100. These segments are similar to the four categories popularized by Bartos. See C. M. Schaninger, M. C. Nelson, and W. D. Danko, "An Empirical Evaluation of the Bartos Model," *Journal of Advertising Research,* May 1993, pp. 49–63; R. Bartos, "Bartos Responds to 'The Bartos Model,'" *Journal of Advertising Research,* January 1994, pp. 54–56.

101. "The U.S. Men's Market," *Packaged Facts,* November 2007.

102. A. Tsao, "Retooling Home Improvement," *BusinessWeek Online,* February 15, 2005, www.businessweek.com.

103. See, e.g., M. Posig and J. Kickul, "Work-Role Expectations and Work Family Conflict," *Women in Management Review* 19, no. 7/8 (2004), pp. 373–86; J. Warner, "Mommy Madness," *Newsweek,* February 21, 2005, p. 42; "The Female Midlife Crisis," *Wall Street Journal,* April 7, 2005, p. D1.

104. See, e.g., L. D. Wolin, "Gender Issues in Advertising," *Journal of Advertising Research,* March 2003, pp. 111–29; S. Putrevu, "Communicating with the Sexes," *Journal of Advertising,* Fall 2004, pp. 51–62.

105. F. F. Brunel and M. R. Nelson, "Explaining Gender Responses to 'Help-Self' and 'Help-Others' Charity Ad Appeals," *Journal of Advertising,* Fall 2000, pp. 15–28.

106. R. H. Levey, "Survey Shows Gender Differences in Retail Social Media Use," *Chief Marketer,* January 4, 2011.

107. See R. Widgery, M. G. Angur, and R. Nataraajan, "The Impact of Employment Status on Married Women's Perceptions of Advertising Message Appeals," *Journal of Advertising Research,* January 1997, pp. 54–62; S. Feiereisen, A. J. Broderick, and S. P. Douglas, "The Effect and Moderation of Gender Identity Congruity," *Psychology and Marketing* 26, no. 9 (2009), pp. 813–43.

108. M. S. LaTour, T. L. Henthorne, and A. J. Williams, "Is Industrial Advertising Still Sexist?," *Industrial Marketing Management,* 1998, pp. 247–55; M. Y. Jones, A. J. S. Stanaland, and B. D. Gelb, "Beefcake and Cheesecake," *Journal of Advertising,* Summer 1998, pp. 33–51.

109. For a cross-cultural meta-analysis of this topic, see M. Eisend, "A Meta-Analysis of Gender Roles in Advertising," *Journal of the Academy of Marketing Science* 38 (2010), pp. 418–40.

110. J. Neff, "Time to Rethink Your Message," *Advertising Age,* January 17, 2011.

111. D. Bukszpan, "'DADvertising': How Realistic Images of Dads Took over TV Ads," *Fortune,* June 19, 2016, www.fortune.com.

112. J. R. McColl-Kennedy, C. S. Daus, and B. A. Sparks, "The Role of Gender in Reactions to Service Failure and Recovery," *Journal of Service Research,* August 2003, pp. 66–82; see also A. S. Mattila, A. A. Grandey, and G. M. Fisk, "The Interplay of Gender and Affective Tone in Service Encounter Satisfaction," *Journal of Service Research,* November 2003, pp. 136–43.

chapter

4

The Changing American Society: Demographics and Social Stratification

Homes that help your family live in harmony

Lennar's Next Gen® - The Home Within A Home® is designed to comfortably accommodate your parents, kids who've returned home, or any other dual living arrangement you may have.

Source: Lennar Corporation

Source: Lennar Corporation

LEARNING OBJECTIVES

LO1 Understand the critical role that demographics play in influencing consumer behavior.

LO2 Define the concept of generations and discuss the generations that exist in America.

LO3 Explain the concept of social stratification and the role that socioeconomic factors play.

LO4 Identify and discuss the major social classes in America.

LO5 Understand how social class is measured.

LO6 Discuss the role of social class in developing marketing strategies.

The **multigenerational household** is on the rise.[1] Pew Research, in analyzing U.S. Census Data, reported that in 2014, close to one-fifth of Americans lived in a household with either two or more adult generations, or with both grandparents and grandchildren under the same roof. The last time the United States saw this high of a percentage was in 1950, the post-WWII era. The number began to rise with the Great Recession (2007–2009) and has continued its upward trajectory, hitting a record high 60 million Americans who live in a multigenerational family structure.

Multigenerational Households over Time

Year	Percent of Population	Number of People (millions)
1950	21%	32.2
1960	15	26.8
1970	13	25.8
1980	12	27.5
1990	14	35.4
2000	15	42.4
2009	17	51.5
2014	19	60.6

Source: Pew Research Center (2016).

Why the increase in multigenerational households? The Pew data suggest that the growing ethnic diversity in the U.S. population may be a contributing factor. Asians and Hispanics, whose populations are both seeing rapid growth in the U.S., account for 28 and 25 percent, respectively, of the multigenerational households. In addition, multigenerational family structures exist because more and more adult children are living at home. As of late, young adults (ages 18–34) are found living with their parents more so than in any other type of living situation, which is a first in over 130 years! This two-generation household, parents and adult children, is the most common type of multigenerational family structure, followed closely by the three-or-more-generation (e.g., grandparents, parents, and grandchildren) household.

Companies are capitalizing on this family structure trend. Homebuilders like Lennar Homes are designing houses and communities for the multigenerational family. The builder's slogans of "The Home Within a Home" and "Two homes, one price," for its NextGen communities are attracting this growing segment of homebuyers. It is not surprising to see interested homebuyers arrive at the listing appointment with all family members present. The buying decision is being made by everyone, young and old, who will be living in the home, especially if multiple family members are contributing financially to the purchase. Homebuilders are not alone in their appeal to multigenerational households. Nintendo targets video games to grandparents, such as Wii Bowling and Brain Age, on its DS handheld and Wii Console. Also, Disney purposefully designs marketing strategies to attract and interest all generations in a family, with movies like *Toy Story* and the company's cruise line. According to one expert:

> The trend could have big implications for marketers virtually across the board from housing to autos, insurance to package goods, necessitating a rethinking of everything from product sizes to how to reach these households and what member within them to market to.

Lennar, Nintendo, and Disney are successfully engaging these households spanning multiple generations. Understanding and meeting the unique needs of these families are becoming increasingly important as this segment continues to grow.

Marketers must segment and understand their markets. Demographics are an important aspect in this process, as the opening example, on age and generations, suggests. In this chapter, we will discuss the closely related concepts of demographics and social status. As we will see, several demographic variables—income, education, and occupation—serve as dimensions of social status, and they combine with others to determine social class. We first will take a broad look at the demographics of the American society, with particular attention to age and its related concept, generations. Then we will consider social status and the role that demographics play in social status.

DEMOGRAPHICS

LO1

Demographics *describe a population in terms of its size, distribution, and structure* (see also Chapter 2). Demographics influence consumption behaviors both directly and by affecting other attributes of individuals, such as their personal values and decision styles.[2] Consider the demographics of the devoted high-end coffee shop crowd:

> Today's most devoted coffee shop patrons are 18- to 34-year-olds and those with annual incomes over $75,000. Forty-two percent of the 18- to 34-year-olds and 46 percent of those who earn more than $75,000 say that when they drink coffee away from home, they head straight for Starbucks-like shops, compared with just 32 percent of all away-from-home coffee drinkers. The younger folks are attracted to the coffee-bar atmosphere, music selections, and what tends to be a younger customer base, while the wealthy simply want the best.[3]

Not surprisingly, marketers frequently segment and describe their markets on the basis of demographics and use that information to select appropriate media and develop effective promotional themes. As the opening example suggests, demographics often are related to values, lifestyles, and media patterns in important ways.

Population Size and Distribution

The population of the United States is over 320 million and is expected to surpass 340 million by 2020. The population has grown steadily since 1960 despite birthrates that were on a strong decline through the mid-1970s and birthrates that have held relatively steady since. This steady overall growth can be attributed to longer life expectancies, the large baby boom generation moving through the child-bearing years, and significant immigration. Population growth is expected to remain relatively steady over the next several decades, but the increasing number of deaths due to the aging of the population is expected to result in reduced population growth of about 20 percent over the next five decades. That is, the overall U.S. population will continue to grow, just at a slower rate over time.[4]

Population growth has not been even throughout the United States, nor is it expected to be so in the future. For example, based on U.S. Census population estimates from 2010 to 2017, states like Texas, North Dakota, Utah, Florida, Colorado, and Nevada have enjoyed more than 10 percent growth. Growth in many of these states is being attributed to the energy sector. In contrast, states like West Virginia, Illinois, and Northeast states including Vermont and Connecticut have experienced negligible, if any, growth. These patterns are expected to continue.[5]

As we discuss in the next chapter, regions of the country serve as important subcultures whose members have unique tastes and preferences. Several examples of these differences are shown in Figure 4–1.

A Tale of Three Cities   FIGURE   4-1

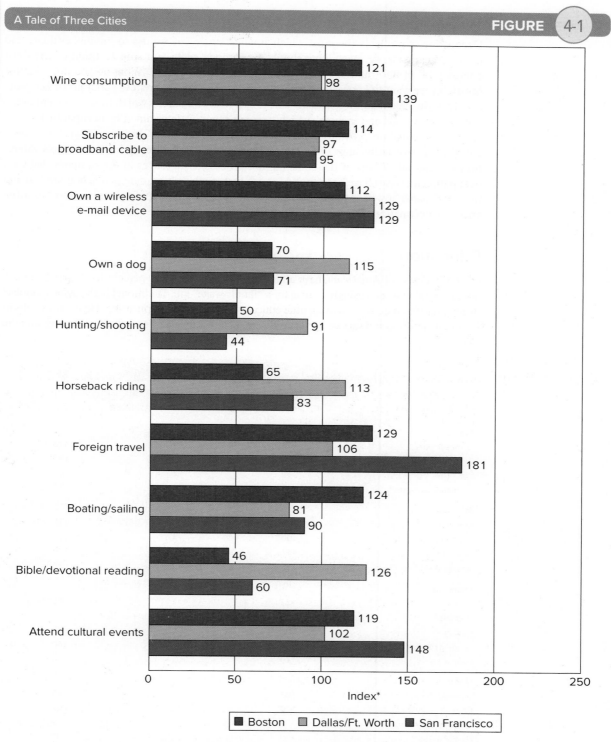

*An Index of 100 represents the average for the entire United States

Occupation

Occupation is probably the most widely applied single cue we use to initially evaluate and define individuals we meet. This should be obvious when you stop to think of the most common bit of information we seek from a new acquaintance: "What do you do?" Almost invariably we want to know someone's occupation to make inferences about his or her probable lifestyle. Occupation is strongly associated with education (which to some extent determines occupation) and income (which to some extent is determined by occupation).

One's occupation provides status and income. In addition, the type of work one does and the types of individuals one works with over time also directly influence one's values, lifestyle, and all aspects of the consumption process. Differences in consumption between occupational classes have been found for products such as beer, detergents, dog food, shampoo, and paper towels. Media preferences, hobbies, and shopping patterns also are influenced by occupational class (see Table 4–1).

Education

Over 87 percent of Americans have a high school degree, and 31 percent have completed college. Education is increasingly critical for a "family wage" job. Traditional high-paying manufacturing jobs that required relatively little education are rapidly disappearing. High-paying jobs in the manufacturing and service sectors today require technical skills, abstract reasoning, and the

TABLE 4-1   Occupational Influences on Consumption

	Wholesale and Retail Trade	Professional, Scientific, and Technical	Mining and Construction
Products			
Domestic beer	100	143	148
Cigarettes	96	69	196
Diet colas	89	117	81
Satellite radio system	103	85	115
Activities			
Sailing	108	155	125
Hunting	100	74	187
Football	111	79	138
Movies (last 6 months)	110	112	95
Shopping			
Target	123	117	85
Walmart	95	77	101
Costco	104	138	85
Academy Sports & Outdoors	84	79	160
Lowe's	79	102	144
Media			
Comedy Central	107	89	75
CNN	100	116	52
The Wall Street Journal	112	144	69
Food & Wine	120	142	99

Note: 100 = Average level of use, purchase, or consumption

Source: Simmons Research, *National Consumer Study 2018.*

ability to read and learn new skills rapidly. Individuals without these skills are generally forced into minimum-wage and often part-time jobs, which rarely will keep a family above the poverty level.[6] As the following data show, education clearly drives income in today's economy.

Because individuals tend to have spouses with similar education levels, these differences are magnified when spousal income is considered.

Income: Workers 25 and Older[7]			
Education Level	Males	Females	Males & Females
Less than high school graduate	$25,943	$16,618	$21,839
High school graduate	35,247	23,010	29,969
Some college or associate's degree	42,071	29,854	35,406
Bachelor's degree	63,113	43,047	51,676
Graduate or professional degree	86,879	58,724	70,121
Overall	**44,611**	**31,711**	**37,842**

Education influences what one can purchase by partially determining one's income and occupation. It also influences how one thinks, makes decisions, and relates to others.[8] Those with a limited education are generally at a disadvantage.

Not surprisingly, education has a strong influence on one's tastes and preferences, as shown in Table 4–2. However, education seldom provides a complete explanation for consumption patterns. For example, a lawyer earning $30,000 per year as a public defender will

Education Level Influences on Consumption				TABLE 4-2
	Graduated College	Attended College	Graduated High School	Did Not Graduate High School
Products				
Cocktails	96	108	96	81
Beer	120	88	97	75
Motorcycles	68	122	122	74
iPad (Apple)	164	99	57	29
Activities				
Waterskiing	112	87	83	130
Visiting museums	162	105	49	41
Foreign travel (last 3 years)	132	98	75	74
Registered to vote	112	87	92	64
Shopping				
Neiman Marcus	127	91	92	90
Kentucky Fried Chicken	71	108	120	109
California Pizza Chicken	166	89	54	36
Media				
Forbes	138	101	74	59
People	114	102	96	64
Nick at Nite	50	74	148	170
Fox News Channel	97	99	111	90

Note: 100 = Average level of use, purchase, or consumption

Source: Simmons Research, *National Consumer Study 2018.*

have a different lifestyle from a lawyer earning $250,000 per year in private practice, despite similar educational backgrounds.

Income

A household's income level combined with its accumulated wealth determines its purchasing power. While many purchases are made on credit, one's ability to buy on credit ultimately is determined by one's current and past income (wealth).

Most of American history has been characterized by consistently increasing real per capita income. For most middle- and lower-income Americans, this increasing trend stopped in the 1980s, and household incomes were stagnant or declining until they increased again in the mid-1990s.[9] Several notable economic expansions have taken place from the mid-1990s through 2006. The first was from 1993 through 2000 and the second from 2002 through 2006. Economic expansion results in higher incomes and spending power. A major concern, however, is the growing income divide. One study shows that during the 1993–2000 expansion, real incomes of the top 1 percent grew by 10.1 percent while the remaining 99 percent grew by only 2.4 percent. Even more striking, during the 2002–2006 expansion, the top 1 percent of incomes grew by 11 percent compared with just 0.9 percent for the remaining 99 percent. In the first three years of the current expansion (which began in mid-2009), the bottom 90 percent of earners actually lost income, while those in the top 10 percent experienced income growth.[10] Such increases in wealth concentration mean that not all Americans are benefiting equally from economic expansion in the United States.[11]

Just as Americans have not shared equally in prosperous times, neither have they shared equally in the most recent recession. For example, while the United States lost 1.2 million people previously earning over $100,000, roughly twice that (2.1 million) dropped below $35,000. And while the economy has shown positive signs, consumers are still being affected by the housing market, the high price of gas, and continued economic and global uncertainty. In response, many consumers are buying smaller cars and homes, building fewer new homes, and remodeling less.[12] Target has actually gained business in this environment by repositioning itself more toward value, in part by creating their 5% Rewards program.[13]

How long these trends hold remains to be seen. Consumers with modest incomes often want to "trade up" to luxury brands. Companies, in a strategy termed **class to mass,** have responded by expanding opportunities for less affluent consumers to afford luxury. However, today more than ever, this may require trade-offs. As one retail expert notes:

> Consumers are still willing to trade up. But if someone wants the designer jeans, they'll cut back on something else.[14]

Income *enables* purchases but *does not generally cause or explain them.* For example, a college professor or lawyer may have the same income as a truck driver or plumber. Nonetheless, it is likely that their consumption processes for a variety of products will differ. Occupation and education directly influence preferences for products, media, and activities; income provides the means to acquire them.[15] Thus, income is generally more effective as a segmentation variable when used in conjunction with other demographic variables.

How wealthy one feels may be as important as actual income for some purchases.[16] **Subjective discretionary income (SDI)** is *an estimate by the consumer of how much money he or she has available to spend on nonessentials.* Several studies show that SDI adds considerable predictive power to actual total family income (TFI) measures.[17]

Age

Proper age positioning is critical for many products. Age carries with it culturally defined behavioral and attitudinal norms.[18] It affects our self-concept and lifestyles.[19] Not surprisingly, age influences the consumption of products ranging from beer to toilet paper to vacations. Our age shapes which media we use, where we shop, how we use products, and how we think and feel about marketing activities.[20] Table 4–3 illustrates some consumption behaviors that vary with age. Numbers above (below) 100 indicate above (below) average use, purchase, or consumption in the age group. Also, Illustration 4–1 shows a Covergirl ad spotlighting a social media celebrity liked by many young adults.

The estimated age distributions (millions in each age category) of the U.S. population for 2010 and 2020 are shown in the following table.[21]

Age Category	2010	2020	Percentage Change
Under 10	42,132	45,496	+8.0%
10–19	41,103	43,392	+5.6
20–29	43,051	43,112	+0.1
30–39	40,408	44,847	+11.0
40–49	43,638	40,892	−6.3
50–59	41,680	42,578	+2.2
60–69	28,851	38,474	+33.4
Over 69	28,071	37,013	+31.9

Age Influences on Consumption   TABLE 4-3

	18–24	25–34	35–44	45–54	55–64	65+
Products						
Tequila	76	155	130	100	88	53
Scotch whisky	48	140	104	88	99	103
Botox	7	81	109	196	114	71
Blu-ray	102	142	141	119	78	32
Activities						
Skateboarding	300	170	96	60	29	22
Backpacking/Hiking	129	148	122	100	90	30
Participating in civil protest	112	104	101	91	101	94
Visiting museums	93	129	122	88	94	76
Shopping						
Belk	83	82	96	97	97	133
Victoria's Secret	167	145	121	89	66	45
Chuck E. Cheese's	101	194	155	73	62	29
The Cheesecake Factory	123	135	117	99	83	59
Media						
Reader's Digest	31	38	43	95	109	233
GQ	137	123	88	138	90	46
AARP, The Magazine	16	8	19	72	161	263
Fortune	83	58	50	132	134	130

Note: 100 = Average level of use, purchase, or consumption
Source: Simmons Research, *National Consumer Study 2018.*

Source: Coty Inc.

Even a quick look at these age distributions indicates important changes. Some of the marketing implications include

- Demand for children's products, such as toys, diapers, and clothes, will grow moderately, as the population under 10 years of age will grow 8 percent over this period.
- The teen market is growing again at a modest rate after a decade in which growth had been minimal or negative. This signals a growth in demand for fashion, music, and technology targeting the teen market.
- Given that marriage and childbirth often occur in the twenties but are increasingly delayed until the thirties, growth in the 30–39 market should provide growth in homes, childcare products and services, family cars, and insurance to offset the lack of growth in the 20–29 age group.
- Products consumed by those aged 40 to 49 will decline as this population group grows smaller. This will have significant implications for such industries as financial services, for which this is a key age group.
- The largest growth area is in the 60 and over groups, which will grow at greater than 30 percent. The 60–69 age group will be primarily one- or two-person households, with many retired or near retirement. Vacations, restaurants, second homes, and financial services aimed at this market should flourish. Growth in the 69 and over group will create many opportunities for marketers ranging from beauty aids and travel and leisure to retirement homes and health care.

Age groups, as defined by the census and as presented above, can be useful as a means of understanding and segmenting a market. For example, L'Oréal Paris launched its Age Perfect Golden Age cream, targeting older female consumers. With its tagline "Gold, Not Old!" L'Oréal Paris chose Helen Mirren as the brand's ambassador. The actress, often considered "bold, confident and sassy," fit with the brand's values, according to the company's chief marketing officer, Hugh Pile:

Brands should celebrate [older consumers] because from a strict marketing perspective they are a highly valuable audience. They are loyal, cash-rich and quite frankly there is so much to celebrate from their lives and experiences.[22]

These comments suggest an important distinction between chronological age (how old you are) and cognitive age (how old you feel). **Cognitive age** is defined as *one's perceived age, a part of one's self-concept.*[23] It is measured by asking people what age they would associate with how they look, feel, and behave. For older consumers, cognitive age is often 10 to 15 years less than chronological age. Similar results have been found for cognitive age in Japan.[24] Better health and higher education, income, and social support lead to reductions in cognitive age. And for many behaviors, cognitive age is more important than chronological age, making age perception a critical marketing consideration. Generational influences, which provide additional richness and insight beyond standard age categories, are discussed next.

UNDERSTANDING AMERICAN GENERATIONS

LO2

A **generation,** or **age cohort,** is *a group of persons who have experienced a common social, political, historical, and economic environment.* Age cohorts, because their shared histories produce unique shared values and behaviors, often function as unique market segments.[25]

Cohort analysis is the process of describing and explaining the attitudes, values, and behaviors of an age group as well as predicting its future attitudes, values, and behaviors.[26] A critical fact uncovered by cohort analysis is that each generation behaves differently from other generations as it passes through various age categories. For example, in 2011 the leading edge of the baby boom generation was eligible to retire at the traditional age of 65. Some opted for earlier retirement, some retired when eligible, and some continue to work, though eligible to retire. However, it would be a mistake to assume that retiring baby boomers will behave like the Depression generation does today. The forces that shaped the lives of these generations were different, and their behaviors will differ throughout their life cycles. As just one example, the computer and Internet skills that baby boomers have acquired will make them much heavier Internet users in their retirement years than is currently true of their parents, who in many cases were bypassed by the most recent technology revolution.

In the following sections, we will examine the seven generations that compose the primary American market.[27] The generations, along with their birth years, age range, and approximate size as of 2016, are shown in the table below and described in detail in the sections that follow.

Generation	Birth Years	Age Range	Approximate Size	Percent of Population
Pre-Depression	Prior to 1930	87+	5 M	1%
Depression	1930 to 1945	71–86	25 M	8
Baby Boom	1946 to 1964	52–70	74 M	23
Generation X	1965 to 1976	40–51	49 M	15
Generation Y	1977 to 1994	22–39	79 M	25
Generation Z	1995 to 2009	7–21	63 M	19
Generation Alpha	2010–present	6 and under	28 M	9

It is important to emphasize that generation is only one factor influencing behavior and the differences within generations are often larger than the differences across generations. In addition, generations do not have sharp boundaries. Those near the age breaks between generations often do not belong clearly to either generation.

Pre-Depression Generation

Born before 1930, this generation represents close to 5 million Americans as of 2016. High mortality accounts for the rapid reduction in the size of this group (from 12 million in 2010). These individuals grew up in traumatic times. Most were children during the Depression and entered young adulthood during World War II. They have witnessed radical social, economic, and technological change. As a group, they are conservative and concerned with financial and personal security.

As with all generations, the pre-Depression generation is composed of distinct segments, and marketing to it requires a strategy that incorporates such factors as gender, ethnicity, and social class.[28] This generation is part of the broader **mature market,** generally defined as consumers 55 years of age and over. **Gerontographics** is *one segmentation approach to the mature market that incorporates aging processes and life events related to the physical health and mental outlook of older consumers.* Four segments have been identified. *Healthy Indulgers* are physically and mentally healthy and are thus active, independent, and out to enjoy life. *Ailing Outgoers* have health problems that limit their physical abilities, but their positive outlook means they remain active within financial constraints. *Healthy Hermits* are physically healthy, but life events, often the death of a spouse, have reduced their self-concept and they have become withdrawn. *Frail Recluses* have accepted their old-age status and have adjusted their lifestyles to reflect reduced physical capabilities and social roles. *Can you see the marketing implications of these market segments for targeting the mature market?*

The pre-Depression generation faces numerous consumption-related decisions. Products related to the unique needs of this segment range from health services to single-serving sizes of prepared foods. As this generation continues to age, assisted-living services are growing rapidly. As more members of this generation experience reduced mobility, shopping will become an increasing problem. Although Internet shopping would seem a good solution, relatively few members of this generation use the Internet.

Depression Generation

Born between 1930 and 1945, this generation represents roughly 8 percent of Americans as of 2016. These people were small children during the Depression or World War II. They matured during the prosperous years of the 1950s and early 60s. They discovered both Sinatra and Presley. They "invented" rock and roll and grew up with music and television as important parts of their lives.

Most in this generation have retired or will soon do so. Many have accumulated substantial wealth in the form of home equity and savings, although the most recent economic downturn has eroded the wealth of many in terms of decreased home equity and retirement portfolio values. Those who still work often dominate the top positions in both business and government. Members of this generation are also grandparents with sufficient incomes to indulge their grandchildren, making them a major market for upscale children's furniture, toys, strollers, car seats, and clothing.

Many, particularly those in the younger part of this generation, are still in good health and are quite active. Active lifestyles translate into demand for recreational vehicles, second homes, new cars, travel services, and recreational adult education.[29] Perhaps a bit surprising to younger generations, over half of this generation are online and over half of those online have used the Internet to make travel reservations, and a full three-quarters have used the Internet to look up health information.[30] So-called active adult communities such as Sun City in Phoenix, Arizona, are a major growth arena and will continue to be so as the baby boomers enter their retirement years. These age-restricted communities offer an amazing array of activities and attract relatively wealthy households, many of whom can pay cash for their homes.[31]

Marketers targeting this segment are increasingly using themes that stress an active lifestyle and breaking with stereotypical portrayals of older consumers. A good example of this is Campbell's Healthy Request ads (as shown in Illustration 4–2). Campbell's is appealing to the "healthy indulger" segment described earlier.

Nonetheless, this generation is dealing with the physical effects of aging. In terms of clothing, comfort is important, as attested to by the success of Levi's Action Slacks and Easy Spirit shoes in targeting this segment. However, style simply cannot be overlooked as it plays an important role in maintaining a positive self-concept. Consider the thoughts of Susan, a 71-year-old who shops in department stores:

WHEN ONE HEART GOES HEART HEALTHY, TWO HEARTS CELEBRATE.

It's amazing what soup can do.

Source: The Procter & Gamble Company

ILLUSTRATION 4-2

The mature market is composed of many distinct segments. The Campbell's Healthy Request ad would appeal to the "healthy indulger" segment, which is healthy, content, and out to enjoy life.

> Lately, I have found a hard time finding the right clothes. Clothes that I used to wear, that younger people wear, don't look like they used to on me. My body is naturally changing so things don't look good. Please listen to this one. The stuff they have for people over sixty is really horrible . . . and I refuse to wear it. It's old lady looking, very old, and dated. I like stylish slacks and pretty sweaters and nice blouses.[32]

Clearly, nursing home stays and in-home care are more likely for those with serious health issues and those in the older part of this generation[33] and health care is a major concern and a major expenditure. In addition, as this group ages, declines in information processing, memory, and cognitive performance must be considered in creating communications strategies, as also seen with the pre-Depression generation.[34] The rapid, brief presentation of information that younger consumers respond to is generally not appropriate for older consumers.[35]

Asset management is important to this group, and firms such as MetLife have developed products and services to meet these needs.[36] Lawyers, accountants, and financial planners also have been attracted to the "wealth transfer" that is expected to occur as the baby boomers inherit the wealth accumulated by their parents. Numbers vary dramatically due to stock market fluctuations and rising health care costs. However, current estimates put the number between $6 and $8 trillion in the coming decades.[37]

In addition, this group of consumers is downsizing homes and possessions just like the pre-Depression generation. And increasing numbers are becoming more *tech savvy,* even to the point of using eBay to help them downsize! As one such eBay user jokes:

> The end of the bidding cycle is quite exciting, especially for older people whose lives like mine are not that exciting anymore.

SeniorNet is a nonprofit group that helps older consumers learn about computers by offering classes in nursing homes and recreation centers, and eBay has been a strong supporter of their efforts.[38]

Baby Boom Generation

Born during the dramatic increase of births between the end of World War II and 1964, this generation represents nearly 75 million Americans as of 2016. The large size of this generation makes them very important to marketers. Most of this group grew up during the prosperous 1950s and 1960s. They were heavily influenced by the Kennedy assassination, the Vietnam War, recreational drugs, the sexual revolution, the energy crisis, the rapid growth of divorce, and the cold war, as well as rock and roll and the Beatles. Although there are significant differences between the boomers born early in this generation and those born later, boomers are considered to be more self-centered, individualistic, economically optimistic, skeptical, suspicious of authority, and focused on the present than are previous generations.[39]

Baby boomers are characterized by high education levels, high incomes, and dual-career households. They also often are characterized by time poverty (particularly young boomers) as they try to manage two careers and family responsibilities. TV is still a major route through which to target this generation. However, baby boomers are more tech savvy than previous generations. More than 60 percent own a smartphone, and most use it daily.[40] Also, the Internet offers the convenience and customization that this generation demands, with roughly two-thirds of boomers using the Internet to make product purchases. Internet usage among boomers is roughly 80 percent, and their use of social networking sites is substantially higher than that of previous generations.[41]

The "empty nest" is increasingly common for this generation, a circumstance that is providing them with both increased discretionary income and time. In fact, baby boomers are 48 percent more likely than the average adult to earn $100,000 or more.[42] Their attitudes reflect their wish to remain active and vital, with money to spend. The perspectives on which brands can capitalize include boomers' desires to[43]

- Experience places such as The Great Wall before they disappear.
- Treat dogs and cats as members of the family, not just as pets.
- Be seen as fit and "not old."
- Indulge in, but not flaunt, luxury items.

As a result, sales of adventure vacations, expensive restaurant meals, second homes, recreational vehicles, maintenance-free homes, personal chefs, and personal trainers should continue to grow.[44] However, boomers also are facing the major challenge of being the caretaker of their parents. One result of this is the rapid growth of assisted-living centers as boomers often don't want their parents living with them and their parents don't want to be a burden.[45]

Retirement is no longer something in the distant future, and many already have made that step. However, surveys indicate that boomers plan to continue and expand the concept of "active retirement" begun by the Depression generation. In one study, two-thirds of 50- to 75-year-olds selected as a definition of retirement: To begin a new, active, and involved chapter in life, starting new activities and setting new goals.[46] Being a grandparent has or will become a major part of this active retirement period for many boomers. The substantial wealth and spending power of this generation make them prime targets for a whole host of categories including toys, vacations, gift cards, and school supplies.[47]

Retired or not, however, as boomers age, their physical needs are changing. Particularly among older boomers, major or chronic health problems, like incontinence, are increasingly

Source: Kimberly-Clark Corporation

ILLUSTRATION 4-3

The baby boom generation is entering its 50s and 60s. As it matures, it is creating demand for bladder-control products that do not disrupt an active lifestyle such as this Depend undergarment for women.

likely and will hamper their active lifestyles. Even for healthy boomers, however, issues of appearance are critical and demand for plastic surgery, baldness treatments, health clubs, cosmetics for both men and women, hair coloring, health foods, and related products continue to expand as this group ages. How well do you feel the baby boom generation is targeted by Depend in Illustration 4–3?

As the boomers age out of the younger demographic coveted by marketers, companies should not forget this group. In reference to brands, one boomer lamented:[48]

> They're all missing it. We're here in the millions, and we have more disposable income, time and want to spend money. Yet they don't give us the consideration that they should.

Boomers buy, while younger generations may not. And brands that strive to make a profit should not dismiss this large cohort.

Generation X

Born between 1965 and 1976, this generation represents roughly 50 million Americans as of 2016. It is a smaller generation than the generations before and after it. Generation X reached adulthood during difficult economic times. It is the first generation to be raised mainly in dual-career households, and 40 percent spent at least some time in a single-parent household before the age of 16. The divorce of their parents is often a cause of stress and other problems for the children involved. However, these changes also have caused many members of Generation X to have a very broad view of family, which may include parents, siblings, stepparents, half-siblings, close friends, live-in lovers, and others.

This is the first American generation to seriously confront the issue of reduced expectations. These reduced expectations are based on reality for many in this generation as wages and job opportunities for young workers were limited until the economic boom that started in the mid-1990s. This relative lack of opportunity was in part responsible for this generation's tendency to leave home later and also to return home to live with their parents as younger adults. Not only has the path to success been less certain for this generation, but many Generation Xers do not believe in sacrificing time, energy, and relations to the extent the boomers did for the sake of career or economic advancement.[49]

Many Generation X consumers are now parents and companies, such as Johnson's, are targeting their needs in this area.

Source: Johnson & Johnson Consumer Inc

This generation faces a world racked by regional conflicts and terrorism, an environment that continues to deteriorate, and an AIDS epidemic that threatens their lives. Members of this group tend to blame the Me Generation and the materialism associated with the baby boom generation for the difficult future they see for themselves. Given their early economic challenges, it is perhaps not surprising that this generation appears to be more entrepreneurial in its approach to jobs and less prone to devote their lives to large public corporations. For example, half of all Xers aspire to own their own business, which is 13 percent higher than the average adult.[50]

Generation X is highly educated, with more college attendance and graduates than previous generations. And Xer women are more highly educated than men, giving them increased leverage in the workforce. This is having interesting repercussions in terms of family dynamics, where increasingly Xer women are earning more than their husbands. Given the underlying masculine value predominant for much of America's history, this can be uncomfortable for some couples, although most are finding ways to navigate this change. As one analyst observes:

> At one point, the stereotype was a man might feel inferior to a woman who is at a higher point in her career than he is. I think that's dissipated a bit, where there aren't these built-in expectations of who should be above.[51]

The empowerment of Xer women extends beyond their careers. One study shows that across all generations, Xer women are the highest viewers of home improvement media and the most likely to engage in home improvement projects, including adding a room onto the house.[52]

This generation is now in its 40s, and although they tended to delay marriage and children, nearly half of Xer households are now married with children under 18.[53] This helped keep the housing market strong during the economic downturn in the early 2000s. It is also the reason that this generation increasingly feels the time crunch typical of child-rearing years. This generation is a major force in the market for cars, appliances, children's products, and travel. The Johnson's ad in Illustration 4–4 targets Xer parents.

While an important market, Generation X is not always easy to reach. It is both cynical and sophisticated about products, ads, and shopping. It is materialistic and impatient. In many aspects, its tastes are "not baby boom." Thus, it created the grunge look and snowboarding. Magazines such as *Maxim* were created for this generation, as were the X Games. It responds to irreverence in advertising but not always as well to traditional approaches. Generation Xers want products and messages designed uniquely for their tastes and lifestyles.

Xers are more diverse and open to diversity than previous generations. For example, Gen Xers are evenly spread across the different ethnic groups, with 25 percent Asian, 22 percent

Hispanic, 21 percent black, and 20 percent white.[54] Xers are also more likely to accept alternative lifestyle choices such as gay couples raising children, mothers working outside the home, living together without getting married, and people of different races getting married than are those of previous generations.[55] This generation is also more tech savvy than prior generations, with 86 percent using the Internet, and more than half engaging in online activities such as texting, video streaming, and using social media.

Examples of companies that have targeted the Generation X segment include

- Volvo redesigned its marketing mix for the S40 sedan to go after the Generation X market and some older Generation Yers. The automaker did tie-ins with Microsoft's Xbox and Virgin Group and created commercials with a hip-hop feel.[56]
- Learn & Master Guitar has a target demographic that is predominantly Generation X men who are increasingly users of Facebook. Learn & Master utilized an ad on Facebook with a visual of a 40-something male and it has done well.[57]

These ads show that successful marketers are adapting to this audience in ways that play not only to their heritage but also to their current life stage and technology use.

Generation Y

Born between 1977 and 1994, this generation represents roughly 79 million Americans as of 2016, thus surpassing the baby boom generation. This segment has grown over the past decade in part due to immigration, as evidenced by the fact that at 26 percent, the Hispanic segment of this market is larger than in any previous generation.[58] These children of the original baby boomers are sometimes referred to as the "echo boom." Overall, it is the first generation to grow up with virtually full-employment opportunities for women, dual-income households as the standard, a wide array of family types seen as normal, significant respect for ethnic and cultural diversity, computers in the home and schools, and the Internet. It also has grown up with divorce as the norm,[59] AIDS, visible homelessness (including many teenagers), drug abuse, gang violence, and economic uncertainty. The Columbine shootings, the Oklahoma City bombing, the Clinton–Lewinsky scandal, the collapse of the Soviet Union, and Kosovo were key events for this generation.[60]

Generation Y, also known as Millennials, is characterized by a strong sense of independence and autonomy. They are assertive, self-reliant, emotionally and intellectually expressive, innovative, and curious. They understand that advertisements exist to sell products and are unlikely to respond to marketing hype. They prefer ads that use humor or irony and have an element of truth about them. They like the ability to customize products to their unique needs. Recent research shows that more than half of these Millennials have no real preference between national brands and store (or private-label) brands, unlike their parents' generation who are brand loyal.[61] Factors they believe make their generation unique include (a) technology use, (b) music and pop culture, (c) tolerance, (d) intelligence, and (e) clothes. Gen Yers are diverse and embrace that diversity with the highest tolerance of any previous generation for alternative lifestyles.[62]

Younger Gen Yers are finishing college and starting careers. Older Gen Yers are starting to get married and have children, with a third falling into that category. Still, this generation has the lowest marriage rates of any prior generation as it passed through this age range, while alternative arrangements such as living together increase.[63] Younger Gen Yers have been hit harder by the most recent economic downturn, requiring some to get assistance from family or move back in with parents. This could create longer-term differences between older and younger Gen Yers because coming of age in a down economy can lead to suppressed earnings for a decade or more and also to reduced expectations.[64]

Segmenting the Generation Y Market

Generation Y, or Millennials, have a reputation for some basic traits that are commonly used to describe the generation, such as being tech-savvy, having preferences for instant gratification, relying on word-of-mouth over corporate messages, being socially and environmentally conscious, and displaying a sense of entitlement. Many companies lump American Generation Y consumers into one market segment based on these and similar descriptors, yet they continue to find difficulties in effectively marketing to them. A logical explanation is that this generation is a massive group at almost 80 million people, spanning two decades of births. There are many differences among the members that can be used to further segment these consumers into smaller, more meaningful groups that could be more effectively targeted. Boston Consulting Group and Barkley USA, an integrated marketing agency, performed a large-scale survey of 4,000 members of Generation Y and 1,000 consumers in older generations to better understand the differences. This research project resulted in six discrete segments of Generation Y members based on a variety of psychographic and key demographic attributes, which are described below:[65]

- **Hip-ennial:** The largest segment, representing 29 percent, feels that they can have a positive impact and make the world a better place. They are very informed of what is going on globally and locally through regular consumption, but not creation, of news and information on social media. The majority of this segment is underemployed females, usually students and homemakers.

- **Millennial Mom:** This is another large female-oriented segment, at 22 percent, who are confident, love to work out, travel, and pamper their children. This group skews to the older part of Generation Y and is the wealthiest of the six segments. They are very tech-savvy and active in social media, but they often feel isolated from others by their daily routines.

- **Anti-Millennial:** This segment, which accounts for 16 percent, is much more traditional and conservative than the other groups. These consumers are focused on their own business and family and do not spend extra money on green products or services. Unlike the others, they are uncomfortable with change and excitement, opting instead for the comfort of the familiar. While this group contains members of both sexes, it tends to be more female.

- **Gadget Guru:** This segment, at 13 percent, is dominated by single males. They are wired and

Despite the economic downturn, the size and market potential of Generation Y continue to attract the attention of marketers. Apparel is a major focus because young adults (younger Gen Yers) spend more on apparel than does any other age group.[66] The key is adapting to the tastes and shopping preferences of these young adults. Fast fashion and off-price retailers such as H&M and TJ Maxx appeal to the preferences of Gen Yers, who are attracted by merchandise that is affordable, yet stylish. Also, half of this group shop in brick-and-mortar stores. Nevertheless, Gen Yers practice "showrooming," whereby they go to stores to try out the product and then purchase online. We discuss showrooming in more detail in Chapter 17.

While complete statistics are not yet available, this generation is expected to be at least as highly educated as Generation X, if not more so. In addition, data for older Gen Yers show that the trend of women being more educated than men continues, reflecting ongoing changes in values and gender roles.[67]

place great importance on consuming cutting-edge technological innovations. This group is generally very confident, successful, and free spirited. They also are known for actively contributing content to social media.

- **Clean and Green Millennial:** This segment accounts for 10 percent and is male-dominated, younger, and likely to be full-time students. They are cause-driven, environmentally conscious, and health conscious and maintain generally positive outlooks. This group generates quite a bit of social media content, which often is related to supporting their philanthropic causes of choice.

- **Old-School Millennial:** This segment, which covers the remaining 10 percent, is quite different from the other five segments. They are the least likely to spend much time consuming or generating online content, instead preferring to read books and meet social contacts in person. They are also much more charitable than the other segments. This group is independent and self-directed, whereas other Gen Y members prefer mentors and managerial feedback. This group tends to be older than the other segments.

Clearly Generation Y is large and diverse, and marketers should consider the differences in these segments in designing appropriate and effective marketing strategies.

Critical Thinking Questions:

1. Market segmentation can be based on a variety of segmentation bases.
   a. After reading the descriptions of these segments of the Generation Y market, name a few of the variables that you can see the researchers used for their segmentation racial bases.
   b. What might some other useful variables have been that would have helped better describe the segments?
2. Perhaps you are a member of Generation Y. If not, you may know some others who are. Into which of the segments would you and/or other people you know be categorized? Explain why.
3. Do you feel that these segments are mutually exclusive, meaning there is no overlap and a particular person should fit only into one segment? Do you feel they are exhaustive, meaning that together they cover everyone? Explain.
4. Imagine you are a marketer of some type of consumer packaged good. Choose a product and choose one of the segments. How would you best communicate about your chosen product with your chosen segment?

Gen Y is more technologically immersed than any previous generation, with 95 percent being online, 66 percent sending IMs, and 83 percent using social network sites.[68] This group also is accustomed to media and TV programs designed for them, such as Facebook, *Girls,* and *Scandal,* and appreciate programming focused on social issues, like *Degrassi: The New Class* and *Black-ish.*[69] Ads targeting this generation must be placed in appropriate magazines and on appropriate Internet sites, television and radio programs, and video games—a strategy called "advergaming."[70] Consumer Insight 4–1 discusses some of the insights gained in segmenting the Gen Y market, along dimensions including technology.

As described in Consumer Insight 4–1, demographics (such as gender) and lifestyle are consideration factors in segmenting the Gen Y market. The portrayal of modern female gender roles and alternative lifestyles is more common and important to this group given its diversity and acceptance of that diversity. Similarly, the portrayal of multiple racial and ethnic groups in ads aimed at this generation is common and important given their multi-ethnic nature. Traditional mass-marketing approaches that were so successful with older generations often don't work well with Generation Y. Companies must continually push the creative envelope with respect to media and promotional themes to capture this audience. Tapping into consumer-generated buzz is particularly appropriate for this group given their high levels of participation in social media. As seen earlier, music and fashion are often key touch points as well. Illustration 4–5 shows how Dollar Shave Club appeals to the unique aspects of Generation Y.

Generation Z

Born between 1995 and 2009, this generation represents roughly 63 million Americans as of 2016. This generation also has been labeled the Digital Natives, Generation @, and the Net Generation due to the fact that none of the members of this cohort can recall a time before computers, the Internet, and cell phones. This generation is dealing with global unrest, economic uncertainty, terrorism, the Virginia Tech massacre, cyber-bullying, and global warming.[71] Ethnic diversity is high among this group and comparable to that of Generations X and Y. They embrace multiculturalism, having grown up with the first black president and the legalization of same-sex marriage.[72]

Most in this group are in their tweens (8 to 14) and teens. According to recent research, Generation Z values safety and privacy, yet is adaptable and tech-savvy. Having grown up in the aftermath of the September 11 attacks, Gen Zers are avoiding risky behaviors, such as underage drinking, and older members are willing to give up passion for sensibility in choosing careers. And unlike their Generation Y predecessors, Gen Zers are not compelled to share their lives publicly. As such, Snapchat is a more popular social media platform, due to its anonymity and user control, than is Facebook. This group claims to be the "first true digital natives," who are unfamiliar with a world without smartphones. They expect social progress and reject notions of a perfect, flawless world. One expert sums up Gen Zers as follows: "Alex [Dunphy from 'Modern Family'] is a true Gen Z: conscientious, hard-working, somewhat anxious and mindful of the future."[73]

Expectations placed on this generation are high and that has produced anxiety to excel at a younger and younger age. One expert indicates of this generation:

We are seeing an erosion of childhood. Kids aren't allowed to be kids for very long and they're made into little consumers at a very young age. They've grown up in a world which is focused on achievement and outcomes, and some are suffering anxiety about what they do when they finish school already.[74]

Dollar Shave Club is designed to attract Generation Y through its unique and creative marketing approach.

Source: Unilever

Personal ramifications aside, these pressures are expected to result in even higher levels of education for this group compared to previous generations and the gender divide shows no sign of weakening, although it is much too early to make firm predictions. What is known is that teens and tweens, which make up much of this generation, account for an estimated $200 billion in purchasing power.[75] Some of their purchasing power is direct and based on their own earnings, gift money, and allowances. Some of their purchasing power is indirect and based on spending by their parents on items for them. And while the economic downturn has hurt, a recent survey finds that for the teen market[76]

- While 40 percent have not been affected, the remainder have been negatively affected.
- Teens are shopping smarter (sales and comparison shopping) to weather the economic storm.
- Teens who work do so to buy clothes, save for college, and buy a car.

Beyond spending power, the teenage market is attractive to marketers because preferences and tastes formed during the teenage years can influence purchases throughout life. As the Ford Focus brand manager states, "Although very few of [teenagers] are car buyers now, it is vital to create a relationship with them so they'll think of Ford when it is time to buy a car."[77]

Honesty, humor, diversity, and information appear to be important to teens. Gen Zers care about authenticity and expect brands to be real, not fake. American Eagle's "no Photoshop" policy, of no digitally altered pictures of models, was a success and led to sales growth for the company.[78] Reaching this group using social media poses a challenge for brands, in finding the right platform to capture their attention. These teens have an attention span less than 10 seconds, use more digital platforms than older generations, and are known to switch among five screens simultaneously.[79] Illustration 4-6 shows the home page of Snapchat, a social media platform preferred by Generation Z. This platform provides users the ability to control who sees their communications.[80]

Examples of companies that are taking advantage of the tech-savvy nature of Generation Z include

- Tumblr is a micro-blogging site that allows easy access to blogging from any device, anywhere. It allows posting of photos, video, self-recording audio statements, and IMs and allows posts from Tumblr to be fed to Facebook and Twitter.[81]
- Gatorade knew the teen market was key to its current and future success. So it redesigned its marketing approach toward teens and teen athletes to include a Mobile Locker Room tour, Facebook, and Twitter.[82]

Source: Snap Inc.

ILLUSTRATION 4-6

The Snapchat social media platform appeals to the highly attractive Generation Z market.

Generation Alpha

Born starting in 2010, this generation (unofficially named Alpha by demographer Mark McCrindle) comprises 9 percent of the American population as of 2016. They are the children of Generation Y and likely to be an only child to their Millennial parents. Consequently, Alphas may expect instant gratification, much like their parents' generation does. They are tech-savvy. They are introduced to technology through smartphones or tablets at a much earlier age than were earlier generations. Consequently, Alphas are better equipped to integrate technology into their young lives. Not surprisingly, marketers are taking note of Generation Alpha's buying power. Although the oldest members of this cohort are six years old and just starting school, it is estimated that this group spends $18 billion a year on purchases for themselves and others. And over $10 billion is spent annually in the U.S. by companies advertising to children.[83]

We discuss marketing to children in more detail in Chapter 6 in our discussion of families.

SOCIAL STRATIFICATION

LO3

We are all familiar with the concept of social class, but most of us would have difficulty explaining our class system to a foreigner. The following quote illustrates the vague nature of social class:

> Like it or not, all of us are largely defined, at least in the eyes of others, according to a complex set of criteria—how much we earn, what we do for a living, who our parents are, where and how long we attended school, how we speak, what we wear, where we live, and how we react to the issues of the day. It all adds up to our socioeconomic status, our ranking in U.S. society.[84]

The words *social class* and *social standing* are used interchangeably to mean **societal rank**—*one's position relative to others on one or more dimensions valued by society.* How do we obtain a social standing? Your social standing is a result of characteristics you possess that others in society desire and hold in high esteem. Your education, occupation, ownership of property, income level, and heritage (racial or ethnic background, parents' status) influence your social standing, as shown in Figure 4–2. Social standing ranges from the lower class, those with few or none of the socioeconomic factors desired by society, to the upper class, who possess many of the socioeconomic characteristics considered by society as desirable. Individuals with different social standings tend to have different needs and consumption patterns. Thus, a **social class system** can be defined as *a hierarchical division of a society into relatively distinct and homogeneous groups with respect to attitudes, values, and lifestyles.*

FIGURE 4-2   Social Standing Is Derived and Influences Behavior

Socioeconomic factors	Social standing	Unique behaviors
Occupation	Upper class	Preferences
Education	Middle class	Purchases
Ownership	Working class	Consumption
Income	Lower class	Communication
Heritage		

"Pure" social classes do not exist in the United States or most other industrialized societies. However, it is apparent that these same societies do have hierarchical groups of individuals and that individuals in those groups do exhibit unique behavior patterns that are different from behaviors in other groups.

What exists is *not a set of social classes* but a *series of status continua.*[85] These status continua reflect various dimensions or factors that the overall society values. In an achievement-oriented society such as the United States, *achievement-related factors* constitute the primary status dimensions. Thus, education, occupation, income, and, to a lesser extent, quality of residence and place of residence are important status dimensions in the United States. Race and gender are *ascribed* dimensions of social status that are not related to achievement but still influence status in the United States. Likewise, the status of a person's parents is an ascribed status dimension that also exists in the United States. However, heritage is a more important factor in a more traditional society such as England.[86]

The various status dimensions are clearly related to each other. In a functional sense, the status of one's parents influences one's education, which in turn influences occupation that generates income, which sets limits on one's lifestyle, including one's residence. Does this mean that an individual with high status based on one dimension will have high status based on the other dimensions? This is a question of **status crystallization.** The more consistent an individual is on all status dimensions, the greater the degree of status crystallization for the individual. Status crystallization is moderate in the United States. For example, many blue-collar workers (such as plumbers and electricians) earn higher incomes than many professionals (such as public school teachers).

SOCIAL STRUCTURE IN THE UNITED STATES

LO4

The moderate level of status crystallization in the United States supports the contention that a social class system is not a perfect categorization of social position. However, this does not mean that the population cannot be subdivided into status groups whose members share similar lifestyles, at least with respect to particular product categories or activities. Furthermore, there are many people with high levels of status crystallization who exhibit many of the behaviors associated with a class system. It is useful for the marketing manager to know the characteristics of these relatively pure class types, even though the descriptions represent a simplified abstraction from reality.

A number of different sets of social classes have been proposed to describe the United States. We will use the one developed by Coleman and Rainwater.[87] In their system, shown in Table 4–4, the *upper class* (14 percent) is divided into three groups primarily by differences in occupation and social affiliations. The *middle class* (70 percent) is divided into a middle class (32 percent) of average-income white- and blue-collar workers living in better neighborhoods and a working class (38 percent) of average-income blue-collar workers who lead a "working-class lifestyle." The *lower class* (16 percent) is divided into two groups, one living just above the poverty level and the other visibly poverty-stricken.

The percentage of the American population assigned to each class in the Coleman–Rainwater system closely parallels the way Americans classify themselves.[88] The Coleman–Rainwater groups are described in more detail in the following sections.

Upper Americans

The Upper-Upper Class   Members of the upper-upper social class are aristocratic families who make up the social elite. Members with this level of social status generally are the nucleus of the best country clubs and sponsors of major charitable events. They provide

TABLE 4-4 The Coleman–Rainwater Social Class Hierarchy

Upper Americans

- Upper-Upper (0.3%). The "capital S society" world of inherited wealth, aristocratic names.
- Lower-Upper (1.2%). The newer social elite, drawn from current professional, corporate leadership.
- Upper-Middle Class (12.5%). The rest of college graduate managers and professionals; lifestyle centers on careers, private clubs, causes, and the arts.

Middle Americans

- Middle Class (32%). Average pay white-collar workers and their blue-collar friends; live on "the better side of town," try to "do the proper things."
- Working Class (38%). Average pay blue-collar workers; lead "working-class lifestyle" whatever the income, school background, and job.

Lower Americans

- Upper-Lower (9%). "A lower group of people but not the lowest"; working, not on welfare; living standard is just above poverty.
- Lower-Lower (7%). On welfare, visibly poverty-stricken, usually out of work (or have "the dirtiest jobs").

		Typical Profile		
Social Class	Percent	Income*	Education	Occupation
Upper Americans				
Upper-upper	0.3%	$1,460,000	Master's degree	Board chair
Lower-upper	1.2	1,100,000	Master's degree	Corporate president
Upper-middle	12.5	365,000	Medical degree	Physician
Middle Americans				
Middle class	32.0	68,000	College degree	High school teacher
Working class	38.0	36,500	High school	Assembly worker
Lower Americans				
Upper-lower	9.0	21,900	Some high school	Janitor
Lower-lower	7.0	12,200	Grade school	Unemployed

* Income is December 2017 inflation-adjusted dollars of original source income (December 1983) using U.S. Consumer Price Index (CPI) data.

Source: R. P. Coleman, "The Continuing Significance of Social Class in Marketing," *Journal of Consumer Research,* December 1983, p. 267.

leadership and funds for community and civic activities and often serve as trustees for hospitals, colleges, and civic organizations.

The Kennedy family is a national example of the upper-upper class. Most communities in America have one or more families with significant "old money." These individuals live in excellent homes, drive luxury automobiles, own original art, and travel extensively. They generally stay out of the public spotlight unless it is to enter politics or support a charity or community event.

The Lower-Upper Class The lower-upper class is often referred to as "new rich—the current generation's new successful elite." These families are relatively new in terms of upper-class social status and have not yet been accepted by the upper crust of the community. In some cases, their incomes are greater than those of families in the upper-upper social strata. Bill Gates, founder of Microsoft, and Ted Turner, founder of CNN, are national examples of the lower-upper class. Most communities have one or more families who have acquired great wealth during one generation, many from the high-tech and dotcom boom of the 1990s.

Many members of this group continue to live lifestyles similar to those of the upper-middle class. Other members of the lower-upper class strive to emulate the established upper-upper class. Entrepreneurs, sports stars, and entertainers who suddenly acquire substantial wealth often engage in this type of behavior. However, they are frequently unable to join the same exclusive clubs or command the social respect accorded the true "blue bloods." Many respond by aggressively engaging in **conspicuous consumption;** that is, they purchase and use automobiles, homes, yachts, clothes, and so forth primarily to demonstrate their great wealth.[89] Thus, it is not unusual to read about a star professional athlete who owns five or ten luxury cars, multiple homes, and so forth. These individuals are referred to as the **nouveaux riches.** Doing the "in thing" on a grand scale is important to this group. High-status brands and activities are actively sought out by the nouveaux riches.

Although small, these groups serve as important market segments for some products and as a symbol of "the good life" to the upper-middle class. The TAG Heuer ad in Illustration 4–7 shows a product that would appeal to the upper classes.

The Upper-Middle Class   The upper-middle class consists of families who possess neither family status derived from heritage nor unusual wealth. Occupation and education are key aspects of this social stratum, as it consists of successful professionals, independent businesspeople, and corporate managers. As shown in Table 4–4, members of this social class are typically college graduates, many with professional or graduate degrees.

Source: TAG Heuer

ILLUSTRATION 4-7

The upper classes are willing and able to pay for products and services that not only enhance the quality of their lives but are symbolic of their status, such as TAG Heuer.

This ad for Louis Vuitton would appeal to the upper-middle class. It emphasizes elegance and sophistication.

Source: LVMH

Upper-middle-class individuals tend to be confident and forward-looking. They worry about the ability of their children to have the same lifestyle they enjoy. They realize that their success depends on their careers, which in turn depend on education. As a result, having their children get a sound education from the right schools is very important to them.

This group is highly involved in the arts and charities of their local communities. They belong to private clubs where they tend to be quite active. They are a prime market for financial services that focus on retirement planning, estate planning, and college funding issues. They consume fine homes, expensive automobiles, quality furniture, good wines, and nice resorts. Illustration 4–8 contains an advertisement for Louis Vuitton that is aimed at this group.

This segment of the U.S. population is highly visible, and many Americans would like to belong to it. Because it is aspired to by many, it is an important positioning variable for some products. Figure 4–3 describes the upward-pull strategy often associated with the *class to mass* approach discussed earlier in the chapter. The Bosch ad in Illustration 4–9 is an example of the upward-pull strategy as it provides "affordable luxury."

Middle Americans

The Middle Class   The middle class is composed of white-collar workers (office workers, school teachers, lower-level managers) and high-paid blue-collar workers (plumbers, factory supervisors). Thus, the middle class represents the majority of the white-collar group and the top of the blue-collar group. The middle-class core typically has some college education though not a degree, a white-collar or a factory supervisor position, and an average income. Many members of this class feel very insecure because of downsizing, outsourcing, and fluctuations in the economy.[90]

The middle class is concerned about respectability. They care what the neighbors think. They generally live in modest suburban homes. They are deeply concerned about the quality of public schools, crime, drugs, the weakening of "traditional family values," and their

FIGURE 4-3   Upward-Pull Strategy Targeted at Middle Class

| Middle class | Aspirations
To belong to upper-middle class | Prefer
Products consumed by upper-middle class | Positioning
Upper-class symbolism for middle-class products |

Source: Robert Bosch GmbH

family's financial security. Retirement is an increasing concern as firms reduce pension plans and health care costs escalate.

Members of the middle class are likely to get involved in do-it-yourself projects. They represent the primary target market for the goods and services of home improvement centers, garden shops, automotive parts houses, as well as mouthwashes and deodorants. With limited incomes, they must balance their desire for current consumption with aspirations for future security. Illustration 4–10 shows an ad for The Home Depot that would appeal to this segment with its "More Saving. More Doing." campaign.

CLASSIC WOOD LOOK WITHOUT THE WOOD WORRY.

LET'S DO THIS.

Shown: Montagna Rustic Bay

Let's wow with a real wood look. Montagna 6"x 24" wood-look porcelain tile by Marazzi now comes in three new colors—Rustic Bay, Smoky Black, and Dapple Gray. These classic tiles are more durable than wood, so they can be used in rooms where real wood can't. The Home Depot® has everything you need for a gorgeous tile floor on a basic budget. **Let's do this.**
Visit **homedepot.com/tilescapes** for more great ideas and inspiration.

More saving. More doing.

Source: Home Depot Product Authority, LLC

The Working Class   The working class consists of skilled and semiskilled factory, service, and sales workers. Though some households in this social stratum seek advancement, members are more likely to seek security for and protection of what they already have. This segment suffered seriously during the first half of the 1990s as their average real earnings declined. Automation and the movement of manufacturing activities to developing countries also led to economic insecurity. Few of these individuals benefited from the stock market boom of the late 1990s, and many appear to have suffered the consequences of the most recent economic downturn.

Working-class families live in modest homes or apartments that are often located in marginal urban neighborhoods, decaying suburbs, or rural areas. They are greatly concerned about crime, gangs, drugs, and neighborhood deterioration. They generally cannot afford to move to a different area should their current neighborhood or school become unsafe or otherwise undesirable. With modest education and skill levels, the more marginal members of this class are in danger of falling into one of the lower classes.

Many **working-class aristocrats** dislike the upper-middle class and prefer products and stores positioned at their social-class level.[91] These individuals are proud of their ability to do "real work" and see themselves as the often-unappreciated backbone of America. They are heavy consumers of pickups and campers, hunting equipment, power boats, and beer. Miller Brewing Company gave up attempts to attract a broad audience for its Miller High Life beer. Instead, it is targeting working-class aristocrats with ads that feature bowling alleys, diners, and country music. The Home Depot's Husky Tools are clearly targeted to this segment, as shown in Illustration 4–11.

This Husky Tools product and ad would appeal to the working class, particularly the working-class aristocrats.

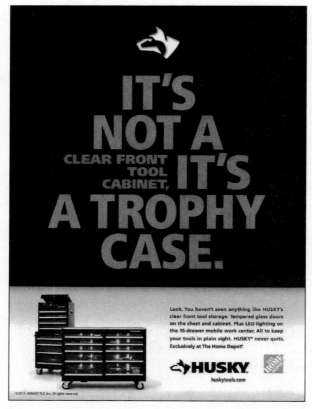

Source: Home Depot Product Authority, LLC

Lower Americans

The Upper-Lower Class   The upper-lower class consists of individuals who are poorly educated, have very low incomes, and work as unskilled laborers.[92] Most have minimum-wage jobs. The Fair Minimum Wage Act of 2007 took an important step in helping this group by moving the minimum wage to $7.25 per hour by 2009. This was a substantial improvement, but it still means that a full-time, 50-week-a-year minimum-wage job is not enough to keep a family of three above the poverty line. This is a major change from the late 1960s, when the minimum wage would support a family of three. Compounding the problem is that many of these jobs are part-time and few provide benefits such as health insurance or a retirement plan. Consider John Gibson, a 50-year-old part-time janitor in Nashville who makes somewhat more than minimum wage:

"I'd like to work more," John says. However, he is not qualified for many jobs. "I have to make sacrifices but I get by. When I get my check, the first thing I do is pay my rent." John lives alone in a small efficiency apartment. One of the things John sacrifices in order to get by is eating at fast-food restaurants. Although he likes the food and the convenience, a co-worker convinced him that it was much cheaper to prepare food at home. He minimizes his expenses on clothing by shopping at thrift stores such as the one operated by the Salvation Army.

As a part-time employee, he has no company health insurance, but he is now eligible for some coverage from the state of Tennessee. A few years before he had this coverage he was hospitalized. Afterward, his wages were garnished to cover his bills, and he was forced to rely on social service agencies. Today he spends a great deal of his spare time volunteering at these same agencies. He would enjoy golf but is seldom able to play. He has no pension plan or personal insurance and wonders what his retirement years will be like.[93]

Lack of education tends to be a defining characteristic of this group.[94] Members of the upper-lower class live in marginal housing that often is located in depressed and decayed neighborhoods. Crime, drugs, and gangs are often close at hand and represent very real threats. They are concerned about the safety of their families and their children's future. The lack of education, role models, and opportunities often produces despair that can result in harmful consumption, such as cigarettes and alcohol. It also may produce inefficient purchasing and a short-term time focus.[95]

The marketing system has not served this group effectively. They have a particularly difficult time securing financial services, and many do not have bank accounts. This means that they generally must pay a fee for cashing paychecks and other checks. However, research indicates substantial marketing opportunities in this group. They tend to be value-oriented rather than just cost-focused. They tend to be very brand loyal. Firms such as Walmart and Dollar General have done a good and profitable job serving these consumers.[96]

The Lower-Lower Class   Members of the lower-lower social stratum have very low incomes and minimal education. This segment of society often is unemployed for long periods of time and is the major recipient of government support and services provided by nonprofit organizations. Andre Hank, as described in Chapter 1, is an example of an individual who was in the upper-lower class and then wound up in the lower-lower class when he lost his job.

Marketing to the lower classes is frequently controversial. The rent-to-own business flourishes by renting durable goods, such as televisions and refrigerators, to lower-class households who frequently cannot afford to acquire them for cash and lack the credit rating to charge the purchases at regular outlets. While this service appears to meet a real need, the industry is frequently criticized for charging exorbitant interest rates on the purchases.[97]

The marketing of "sin" products to this group is even more controversial. Malt liquors and fortified wines sell heavily in lower-class neighborhoods. However, firms that actively promote such products to this market risk significant negative publicity. When R. J. Reynolds tried to market its Uptown cigarettes to lower-class urban blacks, public protests became so strong that the product was withdrawn. Although some might applaud this outcome, the unstated assumption of the protest is that these individuals lack the ability to make sound consumption decisions and thus require protections that other social classes do not require—an assumption that is certainly controversial.

Other firms are criticized for not marketing to the lower classes. Major retail chains, particularly food chains, and financial firms seldom provide services in lower-class neighborhoods. Critics argue that such businesses have a social responsibility to locate in these areas. The businesses thus criticized respond that this is a problem for all of society and the solution should not be forced on a few firms. However, a few sophisticated chain retailers such as Dollar General Corporation have begun to meet the unique needs of this segment. As one specialist in this area said:

> People with lower household incomes are still consumers. They still have to buy food. They still wear clothing. They still have to take care of their kids.[98]

The challenge for business is to develop marketing strategies that will meet the needs of these consumers efficiently and at a reasonable profit to the firm.

THE MEASUREMENT OF SOCIAL CLASS

LO5

There are two basic approaches to measuring social status: a single-item index and a multi-item index. **Single-item indexes** estimate social status on the basis of a single dimension such as education, income, or occupation. Because an individual's overall status is influenced by several dimensions, single-item indexes are generally less accurate. **Multi-item indexes** take into account numerous variables simultaneously and weight these according to a scheme that reflects societal views. We focus here on the classic multi-item approach of Hollingshead.[99]

The Hollingshead **Index of Social Position (ISP)** is a two-item index that is well developed and widely used. The item scales, weights, formulas, and social-class scores are shown in Table 4–5. Notice how, in the United States, occupation is given a higher weight than education. *Why is this?*

It is important to note that multi-item indexes were designed to measure or reflect *an individual's or family's overall social position within a community.* Because of this, it is possible for a high score on one variable to offset a low score on another. Thus, the following three individuals would all be classified as middle class on the ISP scale: (1) someone with an eighth-grade education who is a successful owner of a medium-sized firm; (2) a four-year-college graduate working as a salesperson; and (3) a graduate of a junior college working in an administrative position in the civil service. All of these individuals may well have similar standing in the community. However, it seems likely that their consumption processes for at least some products will differ, pointing out the fact that overall status may mask potentially useful associations between individual status dimensions and the consumption process for particular products.

Another important aspect of these measures is that *they were developed before the rapid expansion of the role of women.* No scale has been developed that fully accounts for the new reality of dual sources of status (both men and women) for a household.

Finally, it is important to realize that in some cases, the individual demographic variables that make up social status (multi-item indexes) may be of more relevance in answering a

| Hollingshead Index of Social Position (ISP) | TABLE 4-5 |

Occupation Scale (Weight of 7)	
Description	Score
Higher executives of large concerns, proprietors, and major professionals	1
Business managers, proprietors of medium-sized businesses, and lesser professionals	2
Administrative personnel, owners of small businesses, and minor professionals	3
Clerical and sales workers, technicians, and owners of little businesses	4
Skilled manual employees	5
Machine operators and semiskilled employees	6
Unskilled employees	7

Education Scale (Weight of 4)	
Description	Score
Professional (MA, MS, ME, MD, PhD, LLD, and the like)	1
Four-year college graduate (BA, BS, BM)	2
One to three years of college (also business schools)	3
High school graduate	4
Ten to 11 years of school (part high school)	5
Seven to nine years of school	6
Less than seven years of school	7

ISP score = (Occupation score $\times$ 7) + (Education score $\times$ 4)

Classification System	
Social Strata	Range of Scores
Upper	11–17
Upper-middle	18–31
Middle	32–47
Lower-middle	48–63
Lower	64–77

Source: Adapted from A. B. Hollingshead and F. C. Redlich, *Social Class and Mental Illness* (New York: John Wiley & Sons, 1958).

specific marketing question. For example, media habits might relate most closely to education while leisure activities might relate most closely to occupation. In these instances, marketers are better off using these direct measures of demographics than the more global measures of status. Only when an overall indication of an individual's or family's status is of particular relevance should measures such as the ISP be used. Recent research does suggest that social class is still an important determinant of various consumer behaviors in the United States.[100]

SOCIAL STRATIFICATION AND MARKETING STRATEGY

While social stratification does not explain all consumption behaviors, it is certainly relevant for some product categories. For clear evidence of this, visit a furniture store in a working-class neighborhood and then an upper-class store such as Ethan Allen. Another

LO6

example is the jeans market and, in particular, Levi Strauss. Figure 4-4 illustrates how Levi Strauss attempts to cover a large portion of the U.S. population by positioning various brands in such a way as to target different social class categories. *How effective do you feel Levi's has been in differentiating and positioning its brands for various social class segments?*

While social class is clearly useful, sometimes looking at overall social class can mask underlying mechanisms and resulting behavioral barriers. The challenge for marketers and consumer advocates is often to dig deeper for the more fundamental aspects *associated with* social class, as discussed in Consumer Insight 4-2.

FIGURE 4-4   Levi Straus Positioning to Social Class Segments

Social Class, Diet Quality, and the 99 Cent Store

Questions about the link between social class and diet quality have been examined in a number of ways, including in the medical community.[101] A recent article indicates:

> A large body of epidemiological data shows that diet quality follows a socioeconomic gradient. Whereas higher-quality diets are associated with greater affluence, energy-dense diets that are nutrient-poor are preferentially consumed by persons of lower socioeconomic status (SES) and of more limited economic means.

The article goes on to point out that it is critical to "dig deeper" into the underlying causes associated with social class. In the case of diet, these include the facts that nutritional foods often cost more and physical access to affordable nutritional foods for disadvantaged groups is often limited. The reason a search for underlying causes is so important is that it has consequences for how groups market high-quality diets to lower-SES/lower-income groups. That is, simply recommending high-cost (but nutritional) foods to low-income consumers is likely to be ineffective because the desire to consume a better diet among lower-SES/lower-income consumers would be hindered by inability to pay and limited access (no or few stores nearby that carry such foods).

The following relates the story of a lower-income consumer who was overweight. His access to lower-priced but nutritious foods through the 99 Cent Store became the answer to both of the barriers listed above, as you will see.

> Papa Joe Aviance, a Los Angeles clothing designer and musician who weighed 450 pounds, decided he had to lose weight when he saw a video of himself. "I was 450 pounds—I was two cheeseburgers away from diabetes or high cholesterol, I have been big for pretty much all my life, and I was sick of hating myself. It was now or never." Not able to afford the prices of the vegetables and fruits from high-end food stores like Trader Joe's or Whole Foods, he took up the suggestion of his friend to shop at the 99 Cent Store. His weekly $50 purchase at the 99 Cent Store, which included oatmeal, tuna fish, eggs, salad dressing, vegetables, and fruits, coupled with exercise of daily walks led to a weight loss of 250 pounds over 18 months.

The story confirms the medical article in showing that it is not social class per se that causes poor diet, but other key underlying mechanisms. Faced with inflexible food budgets, persons of lower SES find the relative high price of fruits and vegetables to be a barrier to their diet and choose the lower-priced, energy-dense foods that are high in fats and sugars. These dietary factors contribute to the observed health inequities. Individuals from lower-SES/lower-income groups have higher rates of obesity, diabetes, cardiovascular disease, and dental issues than individuals from higher-SES/higher-income groups.

The Papa Joe Aviance story highlights the key issues that (a) it is not enough to look only at social class in the abstract; (b) marketers and policymakers must look for deeper underlying factors, and address those; and (c) companies such as the 99 Cent Store can play a key role in helping lower-SES groups deal with serious health-related issues by dealing with the underlying factors rather than simply telling everyone that they should eat a healthy diet.

Awareness may be the first key. Generally speaking, Americans tend to (incorrectly) believe that wealth is distributed more equally than it is. Moreover, a general awareness of the lack of physical availability of healthy food alternatives is likely lacking as well. A broader understanding of these challenges may be necessary for there to be more companies like the 99 Cent Store that tackle the hurdles facing those on the lower social strata.

Critical Thinking Questions

1. Why is it important for marketers to focus less on social class and more on the underlying mechanisms related to social class that might affect consumers and their behaviors?

2. What challenges are faced by corporations in reducing the barriers to a healthy diet faced by those consumers of lower SES?

3. How might general misperceptions of wealth distribution help to produce well-meaning but misguided approaches to encouraging healthier diets among lower-SES consumers?

Finally, moving beyond brands per se to cities and communities can bring up social class issues. For example, many cities are trying to reverse so-called urban blight by working to attract higher-end developers and retailers to revitalize their neighborhoods. One example is Harlem, which has attracted an increasing number of upscale boutique shops, many owned by the "new black middle class," which has enhanced the appeal of Harlem. At the same time these boutiques have displaced local stores that have traditionally catered to the "long-term, lower class residents."[102] *What are the societal implications of such urban revitalization efforts?*

SUMMARY

LO1: Understand the critical role that demographics play in influencing consumer behavior.

American society is described in part by its *demographics,* which include a population's size, distribution, and structure. The structure of a population refers to its age, income, education, and occupation makeup. Demographics are not static. At present, the rate of population growth is moderate, average age is increasing, and the southern and western regions are growing. In addition to actual measures of age and income, subjective measures can provide additional understanding of consumption in the form of *cognitive age* and *subjective discretionary income.*

LO2: Define the concept of generations and discuss the generations that exist in America.

An *age cohort* or *generation* is a group of persons who have experienced a common social, political, historical, and economic environment. *Cohort analysis* is the process of describing and explaining the attitudes, values, and behaviors of an age group as well as predicting its future attitudes, values, and behaviors. There are seven major generations functioning in America today: pre-Depression, Depression, baby boom, Generation X, Generation Y, Generation Z, and Generation Alpha.

LO3: Explain the concept of social stratification and the role that socioeconomic factors play.

A *social class system* is defined as the hierarchical division of a society into relatively permanent and homogeneous groups with respect to attitudes, values, and lifestyles. A tightly defined social class system does not exist in the United States. What does seem to exist is a series of status continua that reflect various

dimensions or factors that the overall society values. Education, occupation, income, and, to a lesser extent, type of residence are important status dimensions in this country. *Status crystallization* refers to the consistency of individuals and families on all relevant status dimensions (e.g., high income and high educational level).

LO4: Identify and discuss the major social classes in America.

Although pure social classes do not exist in the United States, it is useful for marketing managers to know and understand the general characteristics of major social classes. Using Coleman and Rainwater's system, we described American society in terms of seven major categories: *upper-upper, lower-upper, upper-middle, middle, working class, upper-lower,* and *lower-lower.*

LO5: Understand how social class is measured.

There are two basic approaches to the measurement of social classes: (1) use a combination of several dimensions, a *multi-item index,* or (2) use a single dimension, a *single-item index.* Multi-item indexes are designed to measure an individual's overall rank or social position within the community.

LO6: Discuss the role of social class in developing marketing strategies.

Although social class may not play a role in all products or brands, it is obviously relevant in many situations. Brands such as Levi's appear to use social class as a segmenting tool. Targeting those in lower social classes can have ethical implications and choices regarding what products to offer, and what actions to take in this regard must be considered carefully.

SMARTBOOK

KEY TERMS

Age cohort 119
Class to mass 116
Cognitive age 119
Cohort analysis 119
Conspicuous consumption 133
Demographics 112
Generation 119

Gerontographics 120
Index of Social Position
 (ISP) 138
Mature market 120
Multigenerational household 111
Multi-item indexes 138
Nouveaux riches 133

Single-item indexes 138
Social class system 130
Societal rank 130
Status crystallization 131
Subjective discretionary income
 (SDI) 116
Working-class aristocrats 136

REVIEW QUESTIONS

1. What are demographics?
2. Why is population growth an important concept for marketers?
3. What trend(s) characterizes the occupational structure of the United States?
4. What trend(s) characterizes the level of education in the United States?
5. What trend(s) characterizes the level of income in the United States?
6. What is meant by *subjective discretionary income?* How does it affect purchases?
7. What trend(s) characterizes the age distribution of the American population?
8. What is cognitive age? How is it measured?
9. What is an age cohort? A cohort analysis?
10. Describe each of the major generations in America.
11. What is a social class system?
12. What is meant by the statement, "What exists is not a set of social classes but a series of status continua"?

13. What underlying cultural value determines most of the status dimensions in the United States?
14. What is meant by *status crystallization?* Is the degree of status crystallization relatively high or low in the United States? Explain.
15. Briefly describe the primary characteristics of each of the classes described in the text (assume a high level of status crystallization).
16. What is meant by the phrase *class to mass* and how does it relate to *upward-pull?*
17. What ethical issues arise in marketing to the lower social classes?
18. What are the two basic approaches used by marketers to measure social class?
19. What are the advantages of multi-item indexes? The disadvantages?
20. Describe the Hollingshead Index of Social Position. Why is occupation weighted more heavily? Would this weighting hold in other cultures?

DISCUSSION QUESTIONS

21. Which demographic shifts, if any, do you feel will have a noticeable impact on the market for the following in the next 10 years? Justify your answer.
    a. Upscale restaurants
    b. Botox treatments
    c. Prescription drugs
    d. Internet shopping
    e. Green products
    f. Newspapers
    g. Charitable contributions

22. Given the projected changes in America's demographics, name five products that will face increasing demand and five that will face declining demand.
23. Why do the regional differences shown in Figure 4–1 exist? What are the implications of such differences for marketers of products such as soft drinks?
24. Will the increasing median age of our population affect the general tone of our society? In what ways?

25. Respond to the questions in Consumer Insight 4–1.

26. Which demographic variable, if any, is most related to the following?
    a. Watching extreme sports on TV
    b. Scuba diving
    c. International travel
    d. In-home chef
    e. Spa treatments
    f. Going to a NASCAR event

27. Describe how each of the following firm's product managers should approach the (*i*) pre-Depression generation, (*ii*) Depression generation, (*iii*) baby boom generation, (*iv*) Generation X, (*v*) Generation Y, (*vi*) Generation Z, and (*vii*) Generation Alpha.
    a. Pepsi
    b. Panera Bread
    c. The Golf Channel
    d. dotdash.com
    e. The Humane Society
    f. iPad
    g. Facebook
    h. Crest Whitener System

28. Respond to the questions in Consumer Insight 4–2.

29. How will your lifestyle differ from your parents' when you are your parents' age?

30. How could a knowledge of social stratification be used in the development of a marketing strategy for the following?
    a. Jeans
    b. Expensive jewelry
    c. Fishing
    d. Organic milk
    e. Museum attendance
    f. Habitat for Humanity

31. Do you think the United States is becoming more or less stratified over time?

32. Do your parents have a high or low level of status crystallization? Explain.

33. Based on the Hollingshead two-item index, what social class would your father be in? Your mother? What class will you be in at their age?

34. Name two products for which each of the three following demographic variables would be most influential in determining consumption. If you could combine two of the three, which would be the second demographic you would add to each? Justify your answer.
    a. Income
    b. Education
    c. Occupation

35. Name three products for which subjective discretionary income might be a better predictor of consumption than actual income. Justify your answer.

36. How do you feel about each of the ethical issues or controversies the text describes with respect to marketing to the lower classes? What other ethical issues do you see in this area?

37. Is it ethical for marketers to use the mass media to promote products that most members of the lower classes and working class cannot afford?

38. Would your answer to Question 37 change if the products were limited to children's toys?

39. Name five products for which the upward-pull strategy shown in Figure 4–3 would be appropriate. Name five for which it would be inappropriate. Justify your answers.

40. What ethical implications arise from urban renewal efforts such as those in Harlem?

APPLICATION ACTIVITIES

41. On the basis of the demographics of devoted coffee shop patrons, select two magazines in which the industry should advertise (use Standard Rate and Data [SRDS], Mediamark, or Simmons Research Bureau data). Justify your answer.

42. Interview a salesperson at the following locations and obtain a description of the average purchaser in demographic terms. Are the demographic shifts predicted in the text going to increase or decrease the size of this average-purchaser segment?
    a. Mercedes dealership
    b. Electronics store
    c. Vacation cruise
    d. Children's apparel

e. Harley-Davidson dealership

f. Pet store

43. Using Standard Rate and Data, Mediamark, or Simmons Research Bureau studies, pick three magazines that are oriented toward the different groups listed below. Analyze the differences in the products advertised and in the types of ads.

a. Income groups

b. Age groups

c. Occupation groups

d. Education levels

44. Interview three people over 50. Measure their cognitive age and the variables that presumably influence it. Do the variables appear to "cause" cognitive age? Try to ascertain if cognitive age or their chronological age is more influential on their consumption behavior.

45. Interview two members of the following generations. Determine the extent to which they feel the text description of their generation is accurate and how they think their generation differs from the larger society. Also determine what they think about how they are portrayed in the mass media and how well they are served by business today.

a. Pre-Depression

b. Depression

c. Baby boom

d. Generation X

e. Generation Y

f. Generation Z

46. Interview a salesperson from an expensive, a moderate, and an inexpensive outlet for the following. Ascertain their perceptions of the social classes or status of their customers. Determine if their sales approach differs with differing classes.

a. Men's clothing

b. Women's clothing

c. Furniture

d. Wine

47. Examine a variety of magazines/newspapers and clip or copy an advertisement, from the magazines/newspapers or online, that positions a product as appropriate for each of the seven social classes described in the text (one ad per class). Explain how each ad appeals to that class.

48. Interview an unskilled worker, a schoolteacher, a retail clerk, and a successful businessperson all in their 30s or 40s. Measure their social status using one of the multi-item measurement devices. Evaluate their status crystallization.

49. Visit a bowling alley and a golf course parking lot. Analyze the differences in the types of cars, dress, and behaviors of those patronizing these two sports.

50. Volunteer to work two days or evenings at a homeless shelter, soup kitchen, or other program aimed at very-low-income families. Write a brief report on your experiences and reactions.

REFERENCES

1. This opener is based on B. S. Bulik, "Boom in Multigenerational Households Has Wide Implications for Ad Industry," *AdAge,* August 23, 2010, www.adage.com; B. Cohn and J. Passell, "A Record 60.6 Million Americans Live in Multigenerational Households," *Pew Research Center,* August, 16, 2016, www.pewresearch.org; S. Snelling, "Multigenerational Living Is Back and That's a Good Thing," *Forbes,* October 9, 2016, www.forbes.com; "NextGen: The Home Within a Home," *Lennar Homes,* www.lennar.com/nextgen, accessed January 28, 2018.

2. See, e.g., M. I. M. Rosa-Diaz, "Price Knowledge," *Journal of Product and Brand Management* 13, no. 6 (2004), pp. 406-28; L. Eagle, "Commercial Media Literacy," *Journal of Advertising,* Summer 2007, pp. 101-10.

3. K. Dawidowska, "Caffeine Overload," *American Demographics,* April 2002, p. 16.

4. D. Cohn and G. Livingston, "U.S. Birth Rate Decline Linked to Recession," *Pew Social & Demographic Trends,* April 6, 2010, http://pewsocialtrends.org, accessed March 10, 2011; U.S. Census figures.

5. Population Division, U.S. Census Bureau, "Annual Estimates of the Resident Population for the United States, Regions, and Puerto Rico 2010-2017," *Table 1,* December 2017.

6. "Poverty Thresholds by Size of Family Units: 1980-2008," *Income, Expenditures, Poverty, and Wealth* (Washington, DC: U.S. Census Bureau, 2011), tab. 709; U.S. Census Bureau, American Community Survey, "Educational Attainment," 2016, tab. S1501.

7. U.S. Census Bureau, American Community Survey, "Median Earnings in the Past 12 Months (In 2016 Inflation-Adjusted Dollars) by Sex by Educational Attainment for the Population 25 Years and Over," 2016, tab. B20004.

8. See, e.g., M. Mittila, H. Karjaluoto, and T. Pento, "Internet Banking Adoption among Mature Consumers," *Journal of Services Marketing* 17, no. 5 (2003), pp. 514-28; V. Mittal, W. A. Kamakura, and R. Govind, "Geographic Patterns in Customer

Service and Satisfaction," *Journal of Marketing,* July 2004, pp. 48–62.

9. S. Fulwood III, "Americans Draw Fatter Paychecks," *(Eugene, OR) Register-Guard,* September 27, 1996, p. 1; E. Kacapyr, "Are You Middle Class?," *American Demographics,* October 1996, pp. 31–35.

10. N. Irwin, "The Benefits of Economic Expansions Are Increasingly Going to the Richest Americans," *New York Times,* September 26, 2014, www.nytimes.com.

11. E. Saez, "Striking It Richer: The Evolution of Top Incomes in the United States," *Pathways Magazine* (Stanford Center for the Study of Poverty and Inequality), Winter 2008, pp. 6–7; updates and data tables available at http://elsa.berkeley.edu/~saez.

12. D. Gross, "The Latte Era Grinds Down," *Newsweek,* October 22, 2007, pp. 46–47.

13. N. Zmuda, "Why the Bad Economy Has Been Good for Target," *Advertising Age,* October 4, 2010.

14. Gross, "The Latte Era Grinds Down."

15. For an example, see F. J. Mulhern, J. D. Williams, and R. P. Leone, "Variability of Brand Price Elasticities across Retail Stores," *Journal of Retailing* 3 (1998), pp. 427–45.

16. Consumer confidence indexes also consider the subjective nature of spending and represent "leading indicators" of consumer spending. For a discussion, see M. J. Weiss, "Inside Consumer Confidence Surveys," *American Demographics,* February 2003, pp. 22–29.

17. T. C. O'Guinn and W. D. Wells, "Subjective Discretionary Income," *Marketing Research,* March 1989, pp. 32–41; see also P. L. Wachtel and S. J. Blatt, "Perceptions of Economic Needs and of Anticipated Future Income," *Journal of Economic Psychology,* September 1990, pp. 403–15; J. R. Rossiter, "'Spending Power' and the Subjective Discretionary Income (SDI) Scale," in *Advances in Consumer Research,* vol. 22, ed. F. R. Kardes and M. Sujan (Provo, UT: Association for Consumer Research, 1995), pp. 236–40.

18. P. L. Alreck, "Consumer Age Role Norms," *Psychology & Marketing,* October 2000, pp. 891–909.

19. P. Henry, "Modes of Thought That Vary Systematically with Both Social Class and Age," *Psychology & Marketing,* May 2000, pp. 421–40.

20. For example, see R. Gardyn, "Shopping Attitudes by Life Stage," *American Demographics,* November 2002, p. 33; D. M. Phillips and J. L. Stanton, "Age-Related Differences in Advertising," *Journal of Targeting, Measurement and Analysis for Marketing* 13, no. 1 (2004), pp. 7–20.

21. "Resident Population Projections by Sex and Age: 2010 to 2050," *Statistical Abstract of the United States 2008* (Washington, DC: U.S. Bureau of the Census, 2008), tab. 10.

22. M. Chahal, "Over-50s Marketing Should Stop Focusing on Age," *Marketing Week,* October 26, 2016, www.marketingweek.com; L'Oréal Paris, www.loreal-paris.com.uk, accessed February 2, 2018.

23. See K. P. Gwinner and N. Stephens, "Testing the Implied Mediational Role of Cognitive Age," *Psychology & Marketing,* October 2001, pp. 1031–48; A. Mathur and G. P. Moschis, "Antecedents of Cognitive Age," *Psychology & Marketing,* December 2005, pp. 969–94.

24. S. Van Auken, T. E. Barry, and R. P. Bagozzi, "A Cross-Country Construct Validation of Cognitive Age," *Journal of the Academy of Marketing Science,* Summer 2006, pp. 439–55.

25. See A. S. Wellner, "Generational Divide," *American Demographics,* October 2000, pp. 53–58.

26. A. Rindfleisch, "Cohort Generational Influences on Consumer Socialization," in *Advances in Consumer Research,* vol. 21, ed. C. T. Allen and D. R. John (Provo, UT: Association for Consumer Research, 1994), pp. 470–76; R. T. Rust and K. W. Y. Yeung, "Tracking the Age Wave," in *Advances in Consumer Research,* vol. 22, ed. Kardes and Sujan, pp. 680–85.

27. For a detailed treatment, see J. W. Smith and A. Clurman, *Rocking the Ages* (New York: Harper Business, 1997). See also *Generations 2010* (Washington, DC: Pew Research Center, December 2010); M. Moring, "Catching Some Z's," *Facts & Trends,* September 29, 2017, www.factsandtrends.net; C. M. Carter, "The Complete Guide to Generation Alpha, The Children of Millennials," *Forbes,* December 23, 2016; U.S. Census Bureau, "Annual Estimates of the Resident Population by Single Year of Age and Sex for the United States: April 1, 2010 to July 1, 2016," www.census.gov, accessed February 2, 2018.

28. See N. Long, "Broken Down by Age and Sex," *Journal of the Market Research Society,* April 1998, pp. 73–91; G. P. Moschis, "Life Stages of the Mature Market," *American Demographics,* September 1996, pp. 44–51.

29. P. Francese, "The Exotic Travel Boom," *American Demographics,* June 2002, pp. 48–49; *Growing Old in America* (Bethesda, MD: National Institute on Aging, 2007).

30. *Generations 2010.*

31. J. Schleimer, "Active Adults Uncovered," *Builder,* February 2001, pp. 336–40.

32. J. B. Thomas and C. Peters, "Exploring the Self-Concept, Lifestyles, and Apparel Consumption of Women over Age 65," *International Journal of Retailing & Distribution Management* 37, no. 12 (2009), pp. 1018–40.

33. M. J. Weiss, "Great Expectations," *American Demographics,* May 2003, pp. 26–35.

34. *Growing Old in America.* See also C. Yoon, C. Cole, and M. P. Lee, "Consumer Decision Making and Aging," *Journal of Consumer Psychology* 19 (2009), pp. 17–22.

35. See C. Yoon, "Age Differences in Consumers' Processing Strategies," *Journal of Consumer Research,* December 1997, pp. 329–40; S. Law, S. A. Hawkins, and F. I. M. Craik, "Repetition-Induced Belief in the Elderly," *Journal of Consumer Research,* September 1998, pp. 91–107; G. P. Moschis, "Consumer Behavior in Later Life," *Research in Consumer Behavior* 9 (2000), pp. 103–28; G. P. Moschis, "Marketing to Older Adults," *Journal of Consumer Marketing* 20, no. 6 (2003), pp. 516–25.

36. See, e.g., R. G. Javalgi, E. G. Thomas, and S. R. Rao, "Meeting the Needs of the Elderly in the Financial Services Market," *Journal of Professional Services Marketing* 2, no. 2 (2000), pp. 87–105.

37. *Inheritance and Wealth Transfer to Baby Boomers* (Westport, CT: MetLife Mature Market Institute, 2010).

38. J. Saranow, "Online Deaccessioning," *Wall Street Journal,* June 28, 2004, pp. B1–B2.

39. See, e.g., T. Reisenwitz and R. Iyer, "A Comparison of Younger and Older Baby Boomers," *Journal of Consumer Marketing* 24, no. 4 (2007), pp. 202-13.

40. J. Morrissey, "Baby Boomers to Advertisers: Don't Forget About Us," *New York Times,* October 15, 2017.

41. *Generations 2010.*

42. *U.S. Baby Boomer Attitudes and Opportunities* (Rockville, MD: Packaged Facts, June 2008).

43. S. Ward, "Small Business Ideas for the Baby Boomer Market," *Balance,* September 29, 2017, www.thebalance.com, accessed February 2, 2018.

44. J. Raymond, "The Joy of Empty Nesting," *American Demographics,* May 2000, pp. 49-54; P. Francese, "Big Spenders," *American Demographics,* September 2001, pp. 30-31; P. Francese, "The Coming Boom in Second-Home Ownership," *American Demographics,* October 2001, pp. 26-27; S. Yin, "More at Home on the Road," *American Demographics,* June 2003, pp. 26-27; S. Yin, "Full Speed Ahead," *American Demographics,* September 2003, pp. 20-21.

45. J. Raymond, "Senior Living," *American Demographics,* November 2000, pp. 58-63.

46. See R. Gardyn, "Retirement Redefined," *American Demographics,* November 2000, pp. 52-57; H. Schau, M. C. Gilly, and M. Wolfinbarger, "Consumer Identity Renaissance," *Journal of Consumer Research,* August 2009, pp. 255-76.

47. H. Tootelian and S. B. Varshney, "The Grandparent Consumer," *Journal of Consumer Marketing* 27, no. 1 (2010), pp. 57-63.

48. Morrissey, "Baby Boomers to Advertisers: Don't Forget About Us."

49. *Generational Market Research Bundle* (Rockville, MD: Packaged Facts, 2008).

50. *Study of Media and Markets* (Deerfield Beach, FL: Simmons Market Research Bureau, Fall 2005).

51. S. Chen, "Women Marrying Men with Less Education, Income," *CNN.com,* accessed May 17, 2010.

52. "Farther ALONG the X Axis," *American Demographics,* May 2004, pp. 20-24.

53. "Family Households with Own Children under 18 by Type of Family, 2000 and 2009, and by Age of Householder, 2009," *Statistical Abstract of the United States* (Washington, DC: U.S. Census Bureau, 2011), tab. 65.

54. E. Patten, "The Nation's Latino Population Is Defined by Its Youth," *Pew Hispanic,* April 20, 2016, www.pewhispanic.org, accessed February 7, 2018.

55. "Millenials," *PewResearchCenter Social and Demographic Trends,* February 24, 2010.

56. J. Halliday, "Volvo Goes after Younger Buyers," *Advertising Age,* January 19, 2004, p. 12.

57. "Facebook Targeting," *Affiliate Marketing Blog,* August 4, 2010, www.legacyaffiliateblog.com, accessed March 13, 2011.

58. *Study of Media and Markets* (Deerfield Beach, FL: Simmons Market Research Bureau, Fall 2007); Patten, "The Nation's Latino Population Is Defined by Its Youth."

59. For a discussion of the consequences of this, see A. Rindfleisch, J. E. Burroughs, and F. Denton, "Family Structure, Materialism, and Compulsive Consumption," *Journal of Consumer Research,* March 1997, pp. 312-25.

60. P. Paul, "Getting inside Gen Y," *American Demographics,* September 2001, pp. 43-49.

61. A. Pasquarelli, "Marketers' Millennial Dilemma; Bad News for All You Out There Who Spend Your Careers Building Brands," *Advertising Age,* August 21, 2017.

62. "Millenials."

63. C. Dougherty, "For Many Adults, Marriage Can Wait, Census Shows," *Wall Street Journal,* September 28, 2010.

64. R. J. Samuelson, "The Real Generation Gap," *Newsweek,* March 15, 2010; S. De Hauw and A. De Vos, "Millennials' Career Perspective and Psychological Contract Expectations," *Journal of Business and Psychology,* June 2010, pp. 293-303.

65. Insight is based on "At Last, a Millennial Segmentation," *Millennial Marketing,* www.millennialmarketing.com/2012/04/at-last-a-millennial-segmentation/, accessed January 19, 2018; C. Barton, J. Fromm, and C. Egan, "The Millennial Consumer: Debunking Stereotypes," *BCG Perspectives,* April 16, 2012, www.bcgperspectives.com/content/articles/consumer_insight_marketing_millennial_consumer/, accessed January 19, 2018; J. Fromm, "Forget What You Think You Know About Millennials," *Barkely,* April 16, 2012, www.barkleyus.com/insights/forget-what-you-think-you-know-about-millennials/, accessed January 19, 2018; D. Schawbel, "The Six Gen-Y Consumer Segments Explained," *Millennial Branding: Navigating You to Future Success,* April 25, 2012, http://millennialbranding.com/2012/gen-y-consumer-segments-explained/, accessed January 19, 2018.

66. P. Paul, "Echo Boomerang," *American Demographics,* June 2001, pp. 45-49; A. Merrick, "Gap's Greatest Generation?," *Wall Street Journal Online,* September 15, 2004, www.wsj.com.

67. Computed from U.S. Census data.

68. *Generations 2010.*

69. J. Nededog, "These Are the TV Shows Millennials Love, According to a Brand Expert," *Business Insider,* June 15, 2016, www.businessinsider.com.

70. C. La Ferle, S. M. Edwards, and W. Lee, "Teens' Use of Traditional Media and the Internet," *Journal of Advertising Research,* May 2000, pp. 55-65; H. Fattah and P. Paul, "Gaming Gets Serious," *American Demographics,* May 2002, pp. 38-43.

71. A. Walliker, "Generation Z Comes of Age," *Herald Sun,* February 25, 2008; L. Schmidt and P. Hawkins, "Children of the Tech Revolution," *Sydney (Australia) Morning Herald,* July 15, 2008; *Sparxoo 2010 Report: Generation Analysis* (Rochester, NY: Sparxoo, 2010).

72. R. Scott, "Get Ready for Generation Z," *Forbes,* November 28, 2016; "Youth Movement: Gen Z Boasts the Largest, Most Diverse Media Users Yet," *Nielsen,* July 12, 2017, www.nielsen.com, accessed February 7, 2018.

73. See R. Bernstein, "Move Over Millennials—Here Comes Gen Z," *Ad Age,* January 21, 2015, www.adage.com; A. Williams, "Move Over, Millennials, Here Comes Generation Z," *New York Times,* September 18, 2015; Scott, "Get Ready for Generation Z"; L. Kane, "Meet Generation Z, the 'Millennials on Steroids' Who Could Lead the Charge for Change in the US," *Business Insider,* December 4, 2017, www.businessinsider.com, accessed February 7, 2018.

74. Walliker, "Generation Z Comes of Age."

75. "Marketing to Tweens and Teens," product brochure, *Research and Markets,* www.researchandmarkets.com, accessed March 10, 2011.

76. "Teen Spending," money-management-works.com, accessed March 10, 2011.

77. N. Shepherdson, "New Kids on the Lot," *American Demographics,* January 2000, p. 47.

78. D. Patel, "5 Differences Between Marketing To Millennials vs. Gen Z," *Forbes,* November 27, 2017.

79. Ibid.

80. Kane, "Meet Generation Z, the 'Millennials on Steroids' Who Could Lead the Charge for Change in the US."

81. *Generations 2010; Sparxoo 2010 Report.*

82. J. Zegler, "Gatorade Repositions from Sports Drink to Sports Performance," *Brand Packaging,* September 2010.

83. C. Sterbenz, "Here's Who Comes after Generation Z—and They'll Be the Most Transformative Age Group Ever," *Business Insider,* December 5, 2015, www.businessinsider.com, accessed January 28, 2018; C. M. Carter, "The Complete Guide to Generation Alpha, the Children of Millennials," *Forbes,* December 21, 2016.

84. K. Labich, "Class in America," *Fortune,* February 7, 1994, p. 114.

85. J. E. Fisher, "Social Class and Consumer Behavior," in *Advances in Consumer Research,* vol. 14, ed. M. Wallendorf and P. Anderson (Provo, UT: Association for Consumer Research, 1987), pp. 492–96.

86. See R. P. Heath, "The New Working Class," *American Demographics,* January 1998, pp. 51–55.

87. R. Coleman, "The Continuing Significance of Social Class in Marketing," *Journal of Consumer Research,* December 1983, p. 265. For a recent discussion of social class in America, see J. Scott and D. Leonhardt, "Shadowy Lines That Still Divide," *New York Times,* May 15, 2005, www.nytimes.com, accessed May 28, 2008.

88. See Heath, "The New Working Class." See also E. Sivadas, G. Mathew, and D. J. Curry, "A Preliminary Examination of the Continuing Significance of Social Class to Marketing," *Journal of Consumer Marketing* 14, no. 6 (1997), pp. 463–79.

89. See A. M. Kerwin, "Brands Pursue Old, New Money," *Advertising Age,* June 11, 2001, p. S1.

90. See, e.g., R. J. Samuelson, "The End of Entitlement," *Newsweek,* May 26, 2008, p. 39.

91. See J. P. Dickson and D. L. MacLachlan, "Social Distance and Shopping Behavior," *Journal of the Academy of Marketing Science,* Spring 1990, pp. 153–62.

92. See also D. Watson, "In Search of the Poor," *Journal of Economic Psychology* 21 (2000), pp. 495–515.

93. P. Mergenhagen, "What Can Minimum Wage Buy?," *American Demographics,* January 1996, pp. 32–36.

94. H. Fattah, "The Rising Tide," *American Demographics,* April 2001, pp. 48–53.

95. For a theoretical examination, see P. Henry, "Hope, Hopelessness, and Coping," *Psychology & Marketing,* May 2004, pp. 375–403.

96. Fattah, "The Rising Tide."

97. R. H. Hill, D. L. Ramp, and L. Silver, "The Rent-to-Own Industry and Pricing Disclosure Tactics," *Journal of Public Policy & Marketing,* Spring 1998, pp. 1–10.

98. C. Miller, "The Have-Nots," *Marketing News,* August 1, 1994, p. 2.

99. See A. B. Hollingshead, *Elmstown's Youth* (New York: Wiley, 1949); W. L. Warner, M. Meeker, and K. Eels, *Social Class in America: A Manual of Procedure for the Measurement of Social Status* (Chicago: Science Research Associates, 1949).

100. Sivadas, Mathew, and Curry, "A Preliminary Examination of the Continuing Significance of Social Class to Marketing"; T. G. Williams, "Social Class Influences on Purchase Evaluation Criteria," *Journal of Consumer Marketing* 19, no. 3 (2002), pp. 249–76; R. M. Carey and H. R. Markus, "Understanding Consumer Psychology in Working-Class Contexts," *Journal of Consumer Psychology* 26, no. 4 (2016), pp. 568–82; S. Shavitt, D. Jiang, and H. Cho, "Stratification and Segmentation: Social Class in Consumer Behavior," *Journal of Consumer Psychology* 26, no. 4 (2016), pp. 583–93.

101. Insight sources include N. Darmon and A. Drewnowski, "Does Social Class Predict Diet Quality?," *American Journal of Clinical Nutrition* 87 (2008), pp. 1107–17; D. Ariely, "Americans Want to Live in a Much More Equal Country," *Atlantic,* August 2, 2012, www.theatlantic.com/business/archive/2012/08/americans-want-to-live-in-a-much-more-equal-country-they-just-dont-realize-it/260639/, accessed August 27, 2014; R. Dillon, "99 Cent Diet Helps Man Lose 250 Pounds with Foods from 99 Cent Store," *Examiner,* June 4, 2013, www.examiner.com/article/99-cent-diet-helps-man-lose-250-pounds-with-foods-from-99-cent-store, accessed August 27, 2014.

102. S. Zukin, "New Retail Capital and Neighborhood Change," *City & Community,* March 2009, pp. 47–64.

©Brad Barket/Getty Images for Essence

LEARNING OBJECTIVES

LO1 Understand subcultures and their influence on unique market behaviors.

LO2 Analyze the African American subculture and the unique marketing aspects it entails.

LO3 Analyze the Hispanic subculture and the unique marketing aspects it entails.

LO4 Analyze the Asian American subculture and the unique marketing aspects it entails.

LO5 Analyze the Native American, Asian Indian American, and Arab American subcultures and the unique marketing aspects they entail.

LO6 Describe the various religious subcultures and their implications for marketing.

LO7 Explain the role of geographic regions as subcultures.

American ethnic subcultures continue to lead the way today in fashion, music, and culture.[1] While we are all Americans, those from specific ethnic subcultures bring with them values, heritage, and culture that influence their choices in ways that are different from so-called mainstream America. African Americans, for example, feel a strong need to embrace their specific ethnic subculture as it relates to activities and family traditions. They also are very likely to support retailers that affirm and respect their cultural heritage by carrying ethnic items and employing people who "look like me."

Sponsorship of ethnic events offers marketers the opportunity to support and nourish the ethnic community in authentic ways. An example of one such effort is the Essence Music Festival. Originally launched in 1995 as a one-time event to celebrate the 25th anniversary of *ESSENCE,* a magazine targeted towards African American women, the event has thrived to become an annual, massive, multiday festival. Held in the New Orleans Mercedes-Benz Superdome since 1995, the Essence Music Festival is one of the biggest events of African American culture and music in the United States, drawing hundreds of thousands of people.

Although the superstar music headliners are a draw, the Essence Music Festival is more than a music fest. Themed from its inception as "the party with a purpose," the Essence Music Festival is designed to give back to the community. It may be the only musical themed event where not only musicians, but motivational speakers are featured. A lineup of empowerment seminars and panels on education, careers, beauty, and family are held at a nearby convention center. Included in the program is #YesWeCode "hackathon," which "will bring together nearly 200 of the tech industry's brightest developers, designers, and influential business professionals working alongside 50 high potential youth to solve problems with the goal of transforming their neighborhoods into thriving communities where everyone experiences success regardless of race, gender, abilities or other factors."

Sponsors include Coca-Cola, Ford, McDonald's, My Black Is Beautiful, P&G, State Farm, Walmart, Verizon, AARP, American Cancer Society, Chevron, Colgate, and We tv. According to a company spokesperson for Essence:

> The solution the festival provides is allowing our brand marketers to engage our audience with their brand in relevant ways. For them, the magazine delivers one solution and the website delivers another. The festival really rounds that out with an experiential marketing solution. Whenever we go in to speak with our clients, it's not just with a magazine solution. It's with a full 360, yearlong plan.

Some companies have stumbled in their efforts to market to, and engage, ethnic subcultures. Fully understanding an ethnic group and presenting authentic, respectful, and appropriate messages is critical to success, as demonstrated so well by Essence.

In the previous chapter, we described how changes in American demographics are creating challenges and opportunities for marketers. Another extremely important aspect of the American society is its numerous subcultures, such as the African American subculture described above. Although American society always has contained numerous subcultures, until recently, many marketers treated it as a homogeneous culture based primarily on Western European values. This view of America was never very accurate, and it is even less so today as non-European immigration, differential birthrates, and increased ethnic identification accentuate the heterogeneous nature of our society.

An array of racial, ethnic, nationality, religious, and regional groups or subcultures characterize American society today. These subcultures are growing at different rates and are themselves undergoing change. In this chapter, we describe a number of important subcultures in America. We also highlight the marketing strategy implications of a heterogeneous rather than a homogeneous society.

THE NATURE OF SUBCULTURES

LO1

A **subculture** is *a segment of a larger culture whose members share distinguishing values and patterns of behavior.* The unique values and patterns of behavior shared by subculture group members are based on the social history of the group as well as its current situation. Subculture members are also part of the larger culture in which they exist, and they generally share most behaviors and beliefs with the core culture. As Figure 5-1 indicates, the degree to which an individual behaves in a manner unique to a subculture depends on the extent to which the individual identifies with that subculture.

America has traditionally been viewed as a melting pot or a soup bowl. Immigrants from various countries came to America and quickly (at least by the second generation) surrendered their old languages, values, behaviors, and even religions. In their place, they acquired American characteristics that were largely a slight adaptation of Western European, particularly British, features. The base American culture was vast enough that new immigrants did not change the flavor of the mixture to any noticeable extent. Although this is a reasonable approximation of the experience of most Western European immigrants, it isn't very accurate for African, Hispanic, Asian, or Arab immigrants. Nor does it accurately describe the experience of Native Americans.

Today, America is perhaps better described as a salad rather than a melting pot or a soup bowl. When a small amount of a new ingredient is added to a soup, it generally loses its identity completely and blends into the overall flavor of the soup. In a salad, each ingredient retains its own unique identity while adding to the color and flavor of the overall salad.

FIGURE 5-1 Identification with a Subculture Produces Unique Market Behaviors

©Teh Eng Koon/AFP/Getty Images

However, even in the salad bowl analogy, we should add a large serving of salad dressing, which represents the core American culture and blends the diverse groups into a cohesive society.

Ethnic groups are the most commonly described subcultures, but religions and geographic regions are also the bases for strong subcultures in the United States. Generations, as described in the previous chapter, also function like subcultures. Thus, *we are all members of several subcultures.* Each subculture may influence different aspects of our lifestyle. Our attitudes toward new products or imported products may be strongly influenced by our regional subculture, our taste in music by our generation subculture, our food preferences by our ethnic subculture, and our alcohol consumption by our religious subculture. These subculture influences often result in the need for marketers to adapt one or more aspects of their marketing mix, as seen in the Coca-Cola ad in Illustration 5-1.

Identifying which subculture, if any, is an important determinant of behavior for a specific product is a key task for marketing managers. In the sections that follow, we describe the major ethnic, religious, and regional subcultures in America. While we will describe the general nature of these subcultures, it must be emphasized that *large variations exist within each subculture.* Our focus in this chapter is on America, but all countries have a variety of subcultures that marketers must consider.

ETHNIC SUBCULTURES

We define **ethnic subcultures** broadly as *those whose members' unique shared behaviors are based on a common racial, language, or national background.* In this chapter, we describe the major ethnic subcultures separately. However, there are many Americans who identify with more than one ethnic group. Romona Douglas, of white, black, and American Indian descent, described her feelings as follows:

> The assumption is that black people are a certain way, and white people are a particular way, and Asians are a certain way. Well, what about multi-racial families? I don't appreciate a McDonald's commercial with a street-wise black person. That is not me, that is not my upbringing. A lot of marketing campaigns are based on stereotypes of mono-racial communities.[2]

We describe the general characteristics of the major ethnic subcultures as a starting point, recognizing that further understanding can be gained by examining multiethnic groups as well. Figure 5–2 provides the current and projected sizes of the major ethnic groups in America.[3] As this figure makes clear, non-European ethnic groups constitute a significant and growing part of our population, from 40 percent in 2020 to 48 percent by 2040. The percentages shown in the figure understate the importance of these ethnic groups to specific geographic regions.[4] Thus, Hispanics are the largest population group in parts of Arizona, California, Florida, New Mexico, and Texas; Asian Americans are the largest group in Hawaii; and African Americans are a majority in parts of the South and urban areas such as Washington, D.C. In contrast, Northeast states such as Maine, Vermont, and New Hampshire, as well as West Virginia, are more than 90 percent white.[5]

The relatively faster growth rate of non-European groups is due to a higher birthrate among some of these groups and to greater immigration. Immigration has accounted for over a third of the U.S. population growth over the past several decades. Roughly one

---

FIGURE 5-2   Major Ethnic Subcultures in the United States: 2020–2040

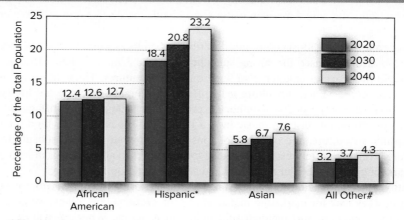

* May be of any race

\# Includes American Indian, Alaskan Native, Native Hawaiian, Pacific Islander, and two or more races

Source: U.S. Census Bureau, 2014 National Population Projections Tables: Table 11. Percent Distribution of the Projected Population by Hispanic Origin and Race for the United States: 2015 to 2060, revised May 2017, www.census.gov.

million legal immigrants enter the U.S. population each year. In 2016, the predominant sources of these immigrants were as follows:[6]

Latin America	41.6%
Asia	39.1
Europe	7.9
Africa	9.6

The influx of ethnic immigrants not only increases the size of ethnic subcultures, but also reinforces the unique behaviors and attitudes derived from the group's home culture. In the following sections, we describe the major ethnic subcultures. It is critical to remember that *all subcultures are very diverse, and general descriptions do not apply to all of the members.*

Although one's ethnic heritage is a permanent characteristic, its influence is situational. That is, the degree to which a person's consumption is influenced by his or her ethnicity depends on such factors as whom he or she is with, where he or she is, and other physical and social cues.[7] Thus, one's ethnicity might play no role in a decision to grab a quick bite for lunch during a business meeting and a large role in deciding what to prepare for a family dinner.

In addition, ethnicity is only one factor that influences an individual's behavior. As we saw in the previous chapter, demographic factors also play a role. For example, a 45-year-old black doctor earning $150,000 per year and a 45-year-old white doctor with the same income would probably have more consumption behaviors in common than they would with members of their own race who were low-income service workers. As shown below, the various ethnic groups have distinct demographic profiles.[8] Thus, one must use caution in assuming that observed consumption differences between ethnic groups are caused by their ethnicity. These differences often disappear when demographic variables such as income are held constant.

	Whites	Blacks	Hispanics	Asians
Median age (in 2015)	43	34	28	36
Median age of labor force (in 2016)	43	39	38	41
High school or more (25 or older)	92%	93%	74%	94%
Bachelor's or more (25 or older)	39%	29%	20%	61%
Families with children under 18	47%	61%	71%	51%
Growth rate (2010–2030)	16%	22%	73%	64%
Median household income	$65,041	$39,490	$47,675	$81,431

Examine Table 5-1. Which of these differences are caused mainly by ethnicity or race, and which are caused by other factors?

Astute marketers are aggressively pursuing opportunities created by increased ethnic diversity. However, successful marketing campaigns targeted at different ethnic groups must be based on a thorough understanding of the attitudes and values of each group, which are discussed next.

AFRICAN AMERICANS

African Americans, or blacks (surveys do not indicate a clear preference for either term among African Americans),[9] constitute roughly 13 percent of the American population. Concentrated in the South and the major metropolitan areas outside the South, African Americans are, on average, younger than the white population and tend to have less education and lower household income levels. However, given the diversity of this segment, opportunities exist for marketers to target diverse members of this group in terms of education and income. For example, the top 20 percentile of black households earn over $155,000 or more and the top 5 percent earn approximately $280,000.[10] In addition, African Americans

LO2

TABLE 5-1 Ethnic Subcultures and Consumption

	White	Black	Hispanic
Products			
Diet colas	111	56	72
Iced tea	95	137	103
Charcoal	87	168	125
Electric espresso/cappuccino maker	105	68	134
Activities			
Dining out (not fast food)	106	79	77
Mountain/Rock climbing	90	74	129
Soccer	88	78	210
Record/CD clubs (music)	74	210	172
Shopping			
Dollar General	101	133	91
Talbots	88	136	108
Starbucks	99	79	124
TGI Friday's	88	184	89

Note: 100 = Average level of use, purchase, or consumption.
Source: Simmons Research, *National Consumer Study 2018.*

represent $1.1 trillion in buying power, which is expected to grow by over 25 percent to $1.4 trillion in 2020, which is higher than the growth rate for whites.[11] Thus, it is not surprising that marketers are very interested in this group. For example, Coca-Cola, the leading beverage among African American consumers, recently launched a digital cooking series, "The Kitchen Table," geared toward African American mothers. Hosted by a famous chef and well-known moms, these black celebrities demonstrate how to prepare their recipes, rooted in family history, and pair them with Coke products. In addition, Apple paid $3 billion to buy Dr. Dre's Beats Electronics and Beats Music, a company known for promoting its brands with prominent black celebrities like Serena Williams. Apple made this move to reach African American consumers, specifically the more than 70 percent who own smartphones.[12]

Consumer Segments and Characteristics

It would be a mistake to treat African Americans as a single segment. A study of 3,400 African Americans between 13 and 74 years of age identified 11 distinct segments. These segments, described in Table 5-2, show the diversity of this group in terms of numerous factors including demographics, lifestyle, and technology use.[13]

Given the diversity suggested in Table 5-2, marketing strategies that target African Americans as a single market are likely to fail.

Media Usage

African Americans make greater use of mass media than do whites, have different preferences, and report more influence by mass media ads than do whites.[14] African Americans consume more information and content than does the general population across many platforms:[15]

African American Segments Identified by Yankelovich			TABLE 5-2
Segment	**Percent**	**Age**	**Additional Segment Characteristics**
New Middle Class	5	Younger (25–44)	Highest education and income (1 in 4 earns $100K or more), most suburban, high tech use (55 hours a week of Internet), positive about future, self-describe as Black, feel "Black slang" should be avoided
Broadcast Blacks	17	Middle age (2 in 3 over 44)	Female, lowest income (71 percent under $25K), urban, single parent, lowest tech (4 percent online), confident, independent, value education, self-describe as African American, feel "Black slang" should be avoided, strongly support "Buying Black"
Black Is Better	11	Middle age (35–54)	Upper-middle income; urban; trend single parent; confident and positive; self-identify as African American; strong emphasis on faith, career, and family; prefer being around people of their own ethnicity; highest spenders on clothing
Black Onliners	7	Younger (18–34)	Male; middle/upper income; brand conscious; place strongest importance on being around people of own ethnicity; most stressed about work, family, academics, and straddling Black and White worlds; heaviest users of such technology as blogs and IM
Digital Networkers	7	Younger (teens and early twenties)	School or early career phase, unmarried, male, suburban, middle/upper income, heavy tech including social networking and IM, less in touch with Black solidarity, less confident attitudes, less religious, prefer to shop online
Connected Black Teens	12	Teens living at home	Over half raised by single parent, embrace Black media, tech savvy, brand conscious and want brands popular with their culture, music focused, positive life attitude, respect elders, not as focused on only interacting with those of same ethnicity
Boomer Blacks	6	Oldest segment (average age is 52)	Upper middle class, heavily (90 percent) online, prefer Black advertising, religious, high mistrust in institutions and high awareness of prejudice, prefer being around people of their own ethnicity, strongly support "Buying Black"
Faith Fulfills	10	Trend older (35+)	Female, parents, married, highly religious, spend most time volunteering for religious and nonprofit groups, upper middle class, have positive attitude about future, don't feel they have to hide their Blackness, use Internet but not tech forward
Sick and Stressed	8	Trend older (45–65)	Male, suburban, parents, lower-middle income (40 percent earn less than $25K), less optimistic, stressed about health and finances, least likely to lead healthy lifestyle and have health insurance
Family Struggles	10	Broad age group	Mostly female, parents, lower income status (half earn under $25K), heaviest TV, are mostly online but lighter users, associate heavily with those of same ethnicity, lower use of social network sites, price but not brand conscious
Stretched Black Straddlers	7	Young (18–34)	Female; middle income; trend unmarried; exposed to the greatest racial discrimination; self-identify as Black; report acting differently when around Blacks than around other ethnicities; high stress over work, family, and money; newer to technology

Source: *Black America Today Study* (Radio One and Yankelovich, 2008).

	African Americans	**All**
Magazine readership	52%	22%
TV viewing	200 hours per month	140 hours per month
Time spent on social media	Over 6 hours per week	Over 5 hours per week

Black adults watch nearly 200 hours of TV a month, more so than any other group, and more than one-fourth consider themselves TV "addicts."[16] The type of TV programming viewed by blacks and whites has evidenced some convergence in the past several decades. However, differences in TV viewing exist that relate to shows dealing with African American themes, concerns, and issues. Consider comments from an advertiser in the automobile industry who has worked with Black Entertainment Television (BET):

> What we like about BET is that it has continued to evolve and diversify its programming. The African American market isn't really one big monolithic market, even though that's what people think. There's a lot of diversity in the market.[17]

Although African Americans have historically lagged behind the population as a whole in terms of computer ownership and Internet usage, this is no longer the case. One recent estimate is that 87 percent of African American adults are online, which is only slightly lower than the overall rate of 89 percent. Factors like education play a major role (indeed education is a much stronger determinant of Internet use than is ethnicity), with black college graduates having some of the highest Internet usage.[18] In addition, African American web users[19]

- Spend close to 56 hours a month on smartphones using apps or browsers.
- Are more likely than the general population to access the web for news and information across a number of categories, including general news, health, finances, and sports.
- Prefer a black perspective on news and information, such as Black Twitter, and are willing to pay extra for content that is relevant to them.

Because black consumers prefer relevant content, it is not surprising to see black-focused websites such as Madame Noire (www.MadameNoire.com) and The Root (www.theroot.com) attracting advertisers such as AT&T, Wells Fargo, L'Oréal, and McDonald's. BlackPlanet.com is currently the largest online community for African Americans. It features news, entertainment, and career information from a black perspective.

Finally, African Americans are more likely than whites to use their mobile devices for a variety of activities including text messaging, using social networking sites such as Twitter, interacting with brands on social media, and so on.[20] Clearly, companies such as P&G that utilize social networking approaches in their marketing efforts toward African Americans are tapping into these trends.

Marketing to African Americans

Marketing to African Americans should be based on the same principles as marketing to any other group. Adaptation to fit the requirements of the unique segments identified in Table 5–2 often may be needed, although sometimes a general market approach will be appropriate. Overall, careful use of generalizations (often seen as stereotypes) is important. Consider the following quote by Pepper Miller, president of Hunter-Miller Group, an African American consulting firm:

> Black Generation Xers spawned one of the greatest marketing and lifestyle phenomena: the Hip Hop Culture. However, not all African American Generation Xers are Hip Hoppers. Yet marketing communications targeting the African American Generation X segment continue to reflect typical and often stereotypical images of Hip Hop's rap culture.[21]

Products   African Americans have different skin tones and hair from white Americans. Cosmetics and similar products developed for white consumers are often inappropriate for black consumers. Recognition of this fact by major firms has created aggressive competition for the billions that African Americans spend each year on personal care products and services, including cosmetics, hair care, and skin care. L'Oréal created its SoftSheen–Carson Laboratories division specifically to serve women in this market. Iman's line of cosmetics, which is sold through such retailers as Walgreens, is similarly targeted to this market (www.imancosmetics.com). Illustration 5–2 shows two ads: the As I Am ad is an example of a product designed specifically for the unique needs of the African American market; the Ford ad is an example of a product designed to meet the needs of all ethnic groups but that is being promoted to African Americans.

Numerous companies have found it worthwhile to alter their products and target them specifically to African Americans. Beyond hair and skin care, examples include[22]

- Hallmark has a Mahogany line of greeting cards that feature black characters and sayings.
- Barbie offers African American dolls.
- GM has designed the Escalade and other models specifically with African Americans in mind.

Communications   A common mistake when communicating with any ethnic group is to assume that its members are the same as the larger culture except for superficial differences. Failure to recognize this often results in commercials targeted at African Americans that simply place the firm's standard ad in black media or that replace white actors with black actors, without changing the script, language, setting, or culturally relevant symbols.[23] Jaguar provides a positive example in this regard in that its direct-mail campaign to affluent African Americans (a) modified the race of the actors (black husband and wife), (b) projected positive career images (wife was a surgeon, husband was a sculptor), (c) drew on historically important cultural symbols (they lived in Harlem, historically a mecca of black culture and music), and (d) projected a positive work-related theme in its tagline: "It's not luck that got you where you are." Notice how some aspects of the campaign (black actors and Harlem) are specific to the African American community, while other aspects (professional careers and the "hard-work" theme) would be effective to the broader American consumer.

The extent to which messages targeted to African Americans need to differ from those targeting other groups varies by situation. For example, sometimes advertisers can simply change the race of the models in the ads and perhaps the consumption setting to help indicate that the product is appropriate for the needs of African Americans. This works when the product, the appeal, and the appropriate language are the same for the black target market and the other groups being targeted. The ad on the right side in Illustration 5–2 is a good example of this approach. In other cases, more specific changes need to be made to communicate how the product is designed to meet the specific needs of African Americans, as in the case of the ad on the left side in Illustration 5–2. In general, the use of black actors and spokespersons is important.[24] This is particularly the case for ethnically relevant products such as cosmetics and for those with strong ethnic identities.[25] Ads such as those in Illustration 5–2 can be run effectively in both black media and general media with a substantial black audience.

Another means of communicating with the African American and other ethnic communities is **event marketing,** which involves *creating or sponsoring an event that has a particular appeal to a market segment.* For example, church is a major force in the lives of many African Americans. To tap into black churchgoers, McDonald's sponsors the "Inspiration Celebration Gospel Tour," an annual concert series started in 2007. The national tour, which is part of the corporation's 365 Black Initiative, has raised over $500,000 since 2012 for the Ronald McDonald House Charities.[26]

ILLUSTRATION 5-2

African American consumers have both unique and shared needs relative to other ethnic groups, as shown by the As I Am and Ford ads.

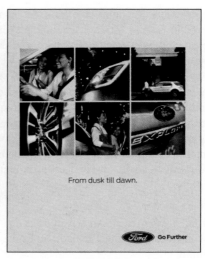

Source: Salon Commodities, Ltd.   Source: Ford Motor Company

Retailing   Retailers often adjust the merchandising mix to meet the needs of African American shoppers. For example, Albertson's, a national grocery retailer, adapts its merchandising mix in African American neighborhoods.[27] Surveys reveal that three major store-selection factors for blacks are that the store carries ethnic products (51 percent say that is important), employs people who "look like me" (40 percent), and treats customers of all races and ethnicities with respect (84 percent).[28] This focus on respect is caused by the sad fact that many black shoppers still encounter obviously disrespectful acts such as being closely watched while shopping as well as more subtle discrimination such as slower service.[29] The need for cultural sensitivity training for retail and service employees is clear.[30]

African Americans also use shopping as a form of recreation more than whites.[31] This suggests that stores with black customers should pay particular attention to providing a pleasant and fun shopping environment. Yet, online shopping is still important to black consumers. Wealthy African Americans are more likely to buy groceries and movie tickets online than are white consumers with comparable income.[32] Blacks also respond to sales differently than do whites and have differing desires with respect to credit card, cash, and check payments.[33] In addition, research suggests that African Americans are more prone to buy national brands than store brands as a way to signal status, although results in Table 5–2 show that differences in brand consciousness exist across different segments of black consumers.[34] Thus, all aspects of the shopping experience need to be carefully aligned to the needs of the target shoppers.

HISPANICS

LO3

The U.S. Census Bureau defines **Hispanic** as *a person of Cuban, Mexican, Puerto Rican, South or Central American, or other Spanish culture or origin regardless of race.* Hispanics are, on average, younger than the white non-Hispanic population and tend to have less education and lower household income levels. However, given the diversity of this segment, opportunities exist for marketers to target diverse members of this group in terms of education and income. For example, approximately 40 percent of Hispanic households earn $75,000 or more and the top 5 percent earn over $300,000.[35] In addition, Hispanics represent $1.3 trillion in buying power, more than the gross domestic product (GDP) of some countries including Australia. This buying power is expected to grow to $1.7 trillion in 2020.[36]

The Hispanic market is now the largest and fastest-growing ethnic subculture in the United States. By 2040 Hispanics are expected to represent 24 percent of the U.S. population. Marketers are definitely taking notice. Hispanics are also the youngest of the large ethnic subcultures. Like the other ethnic groups in America, Hispanics are diverse. Many marketers feel that the Hispanic subculture is not a single ethnic subculture but instead is three main and several minor nationality subcultures: Mexican Americans (63 percent), Puerto Ricans (10 percent), Cubans (4 percent), and other Latinos, mainly from Central and South America (14 percent).[37] Each group speaks a slightly different version of Spanish and has somewhat distinct values and lifestyles. Further, each group tends to live in distinct regions of the country: Mexican Americans in the Southwest and California; Puerto Ricans in New York, New Jersey, and Florida; Cubans in Florida; and other Latinos in California, New York, and Florida. Income levels also vary across the groups, with those of Cuban and Puerto Rican descent having somewhat higher incomes than those of Mexican descent.

Others argue that while one must be sensitive to nationality-based differences, the common language, the common religion (Roman Catholic for most Hispanics), and the emergence of national Spanish-language media and entertainment figures create sufficient cultural homogeneity for most products and advertising campaigns. However, at a minimum, the decision to treat Hispanics as a single ethnic subculture needs to take into consideration factors relating to acculturation, language, and generational influences, which we discuss next.

Acculturation, Language, and Generational Influences

Given that roughly 34 percent of growth in the Hispanic population is attributable to immigration, the level of acculturation plays a major role in the attitudes and behaviors of Hispanic consumers. **Acculturation** is *the degree to which an immigrant has adapted to his or her new culture.*[38] Acculturation is highly related to language use and both are strongly influenced by generational factors. A study by the Pew Hispanic Center identifies three generations of Hispanic adults:

First-generation adults (63 percent) are those born outside the United States. This generation has the lowest income and education, is most likely to identify themselves as Hispanic (including country of origin), is most likely to have Spanish as their primary language (72 percent), and is most likely to possess traditional values including a masculine view of the family decision hierarchy.

Second-generation adults (19 percent) are those born in the United States to immigrant parents. Compared to the first generation, this generation has higher income and education, is more likely to identify themselves as Americans (though 62 percent still identify as Hispanic), is equally split between being bilingual and having English as the primary language, and is somewhat less likely to ascribe to traditional values.

Third-generation (and beyond) adults (17 percent) are those born in the United States to U.S.-born parents. This group has the highest education and income, is most likely to identify as Americans (57 percent, versus 41 percent who identify themselves as Hispanic), is most likely to have English as the primary language (only 22 percent are bilingual; none are Spanish only), and is also somewhat less likely to ascribe to traditional values.[39]

As this discussion indicates, income, education, language, and identification with Hispanic culture change across generations. However, it is also important to note that most Hispanic adults identify more or less strongly with a Hispanic culture.[40] Interestingly, Hispanics are unique in this respect. As one media executive notes:

Hispanics live an ambicultural reality. Unlike other immigrant groups, Hispanics are 200%ers™— 100% American and 100% Latino—and this is more prevalent among younger demos.[41]

The Mighty, Powerful, and Influential Latina

Latinas (or Hispanic women) represent an increasingly influential segment of the Hispanic subculture. They are creating dramatic cultural shifts within the Hispanic, as well as mainstream, culture. As of 2017, the U.S. Hispanic female population was at 28 million, which is 17 percent of the total female population. This percentage should continue to rise as Hispanics are projected to account for 65 percent of the total U.S. population growth between now and 2060. Latinas are increasingly the primary breadwinners and key economic decision makers in their households.[42]

According to Stacie de Armas, Vice President of Strategic Initiatives & Consumer Engagement at Nielsen:

Latinas are coming into their own, and this new-found confidence will have an undeniable impact on our consumer-driven society. Hispanic women are increasingly the catalysts in an intercultural market-place. . . . Ambicultural Latinas move fluidly between their cultures, driving intercultural affinity by sharing her root culture with friends, family and co-workers. . . .

Furthermore, Ms. de Armas offers the following marketing implications:

Not only are they the cornerstone of the Latino family, keeping language and traditions alive, but they are also forging a wider path in the mainstream and using technology to serve as brand and culture influencers. Marketers need to know how to tap this cohort in order to stay relevant and drive consumer engagement in the future.

Here are some key points from recent research that set today's Latinas apart from other demographic groups, as well as the Latinas from the past:

- *Origins:* The population of U.S. Latinas has grown 27 percent between 2005 and 2015, of which 77 percent of that growth has come from Hispanic girls born in the U.S., not immigration. Almost half of U.S.-born Latinas are under the age of 18. In some cities, such as New York City, Latinas compose the majority of the female population.
- *Education:* Latinas are reaching greater heights of educational attainment than ever before. Nearly half of Latinas have completed at least some college education. And 74 percent of recent Latina high school graduates are currently enrolled in college versus 72 percent of non-Hispanic females.
- *Entrepreneurship:* There are approximately 1.5 million Latina majority—owned companies in the U.S., representing an 87 percent growth rate in the last five years. This is in stark contrast to the 39 percent growth rate of Hispanic male

This strong cultural identity carries over to Hispanic women, many of whom were born in the United States and thus would be classified as second- and third-generation. As discussed in Consumer Insight 5-1, Hispanic women, or Latinas, are setting cultural trends and becoming quite influential in purchase decisions.

The Hispanic culture is heavily influenced by the Roman Catholic religion. It is family oriented, with the extended family playing an important role across generations (unlike the general U.S. population in which extended family has lost its importance). It is also a masculine culture, and sports are very important to Hispanics, particularly boxing, baseball, and soccer. This masculine orientation manifests itself in many ways, including husband-dominant household decision making.[43]

As indicated in Consumer Insight 5-1, cultural changes are occurring over time, particularly among the younger members of the group. However, the Hispanic culture continues to have a fairly traditional view of the appropriate role of women. For example, the wife is expected to prepare the food for the family. As a result, food marketers such as Sara Lee and General Mills are engaging in a number of efforts to target Hispanic women. For example, General Mills' website *Que Rica Vida (What a Rich Life)* targets its various brands majority–owned companies and 27 percent growth rate of all female majority–owned companies. The volume of sales of Latina majority–owned companies also outpaced all female majority–owned companies during the last five years, at 41 percent and 19 percent respectively.

- *Marital Status:* Latinas are less likely to ever have been married than non-Hispanic whites (at 39 percent and 25 percent). The increased emphasis on education and entrepreneurship could be a driver here. However, foreign-born Latinas are twice as likely to marry as the U.S.-born Latinas. Of married Latinas, over 20 percent are married to non-Hispanic spouses, which makes them catalysts of intercultural exchange.
- *Cultural Traditions:* Latinas enjoy maintaining their cultural traditions, such as language and cuisine. Even though only 34 percent of Latinas are born outside the U.S., 74 percent (over age five) speak a language other than English in their homes. Compared to non-Hispanic white women, Latinas say they enjoy being creative in the kitchen at a higher rate (79 percent versus 70 percent).
- *Mobile Devices:* Latinas place great importance on communication and are heavy users of mobile devices. They are 15 percent more likely than non-Hispanic whites to own smartphones and smartwatches. They average 22 hours per week using their smart devices to watch videos, use apps, play games, download/purchase music, and surf the Internet.
- *Social Media:* Similarly, Latinas are more likely than non-Hispanic white women to engage on social media sites, where they spend on average five hours per day. Over 57 percent of Latinas indicate they are more likely to purchase from a brand that promotes social media content that reflects Hispanic culture, and 65 percent feel it is important for brands to generate Latina-specific content. Additionally, Latinas are more likely than non-Hispanic white women to recommend or review products and show support for brands on social media.

In conclusion, Latinas are a significant, growing, and influential segment of consumers. Marketers will do well to pay attention.

Critical Thinking Questions

1. What challenges might a marketer encounter when targeting the Latina market?

2. This insight tells us that Latinas are intercultural influencers. Think about your personal life experience and brainstorm some instances where you see this in action in areas such as products, entertainment, and celebrities.

3. Imagine you are a marketer of some type of consumer packaged good. Choose a product and choose one of the segments. How would you best communicate about your chosen product with your chosen segment?

to Hispanic women and deals with issues of food, family, and Hispanic-oriented recipes. However, because acculturation can affect gender-role views, it is critical that companies understand their target market on this dimension.[44]

Language is clearly important to the Hispanic market and often strongly intertwined with cultural identity. Less than 30 percent of Hispanics (over the age of five) speak English exclusively in the home. Thus, a large majority—close to 40 million—of Hispanics speak Spanish in the home. While more than half of those living in bilingual households feel that they speak English "very well," the presence of the Spanish language in the home cannot be ignored.[45] Perhaps even more important is that Spanish-language ads are often more effective.[46] Consider the following:

When asked about advertising effectiveness, 38% of Hispanics surveyed found English language ads less effective than Spanish ads in terms of recall and 70% less effective than Spanish ads in terms of persuasion. Many younger and acculturated Latinos mix languages in the form of "Spanglish," in which they speak English peppered with Spanish words. But, when it comes to selling, 56% of Latino adults respond best to advertising when it is presented in Spanish.[47]

Orbit advertises
its gum in both
English and Spanish.
Although Spanish-
language ads are
often more effective
when marketing to
Hispanics, this effect
may depend on
acculturation level.

Source: WM. Wrigley Jr. Company   Source: WM. Wrigley Jr. Company

Consider the two Orbit ads in Illustration 5–3. Why do you feel Orbit uses both Spanish and English language ads to target the Latino market?

Given these numbers, it should not be surprising that Univision, a Spanish-language network, is the fifth-largest network in the United States and the top three most watched networks by Hispanics are Spanish-language networks. Specifically, less than one-third of Hispanic adults prefer to watch TV in English only.[48]

Marketing to Hispanics

Hispanic consumers tend to be highly brand loyal, particularly to marketers whom they feel are working to adapt their products and services to meet their distinctive needs. Price is important, but so too is the availability of high-quality national brands. Hispanics tend to be less receptive than the general market to store brands.[49] Marketers are responding with adaptations to various aspects of their marketing mix.

Communications   As we saw earlier, Hispanics often speak Spanish and often prefer Spanish-language media. Therefore, although it is possible to reach part of this market using mass media, serious attempts to target Hispanics often will involve Spanish-language media as well. Univision, Telemundo, and UniMás are the top three Spanish-language TV networks in the United States. Spanish-language radio is widespread, with both local and network stations. And there are numerous Spanish-language magazines, including Spanish versions of such magazines as *People (People en Español), Sports Illustrated,* and *Cosmopolitan (Cosmopolitan for Latinas).* There are also many Spanish-language newspapers.

With respect to communication and media, it is important to note that a youth trend is emerging, which will likely shape the future of Hispanic media strategy. Specifically, the 14-to-24-year-old demographic (which will grow rapidly over the next decade)[50] spends more time viewing English-language TV, radio, and print media than Spanish. This group tends to be U.S.-born and more English-dominant in terms of language. In addition, the

Source: RockYou, Inc.

ILLUSTRATION 5-4

Use of the Internet by Hispanics is exploding. Sites such as www.mamáslatinas .com are being developed to appeal to the unique needs of this market.

18-to-34 demographic views Spanish- and English-language media about equally. In response, Telemundo is offering both bilingual and Spanish-language programming and is developing shows more in touch with the younger Hispanic market, such as the "Super Series" telenovelas like *El Señor de los Cielos.*

Internet use among Hispanics depends greatly on language, age, education, and nativity (where they were born)—reflective of acculturation. For English-speaking Hispanics, Internet use is at 94 percent, compared to 74 percent usage among Hispanics who primarily speak Spanish. Ninety percent of Hispanics under the age of 50 use the Internet, but as they age, usage plummets to 67 percent (aged 50 to 64) and 42 percent (those over 65). Approximately two-thirds of Hispanics with less than a high school education use the Internet, compared to 95 percent of those with some college education. For those born outside the United States and thus typically less acculturated, Internet use is at about 78 percent, higher than in past years, but not at the usage rate (91 percent) of U.S.-born Hispanics.[51]

Due to the extensive reach of the Internet, online and social network sites are clearly important to companies seeking to target Hispanics. For example, Facebook has 85 percent reach among Hispanics.[52] Online sports are available through such sites as ESPN Deportes .com, and Spanish-language versions of Yahoo! and AOL have been developed. Online Spanish-language communities such as Mamás Latinas (www.mamáslatinas.com) also are emerging. Hispanic Internet users tend to be relatively young, frequent both English- and Spanish-language sites, and, in many cases, prefer English-language media. As with traditional media providers, online Hispanic providers will be challenged to deliver content that is relevant to acculturated Hispanics, regardless of language (see Illustration 5-4).[53]

Language translation is a challenge. Examples of translation difficulties include the following:

- Tang introduced itself in its Spanish ads as *jugo de chino,* which worked well with Puerto Ricans, who knew it meant orange juice, but the phrase had no meaning to most other Hispanics.
- A Coors campaign used the word "guey," which in modern slang terms can mean the equivalent of "dude." However, the word also can be used as slang for "idiot" or "stupid." According to one expert, whether or not consumers get the humor is generational.[54]

Successful marketing to Hispanics moves beyond accurate translations into unique appeals and symbols. It requires marketers to be "in-culture," that is, to understand the value system and the overall cultural context of the various Hispanic groups. In fact, value congruence has been found to overcome persuasion shortfalls for second-language ads (e.g., English-language ads to bilingual Hispanics).[55]

- Ram Trucks worked with Colombian singer Juanes to promote the company's 1500 truck with its "*A Todo, Con Todo*" ("To Everything, With Everything") campaign. The ads, in both Spanish and English, feature Juanes and the stage crew hauling his equipment from city to city in the Ram Truck 1500.[56]
- Best Buy created a TV spot designed to bridge the gap between younger, tech-savvy Hispanic teens and their older, less-acculturated fathers who often are uncomfortable with technology but, given the patriarchal hierarchy, must "sign off" on the purchase. The slogan reads, "If you're far away, get closer with Best Buy." Best Buy says they designed the spot to get kids and their fathers talking.[57]

Products   Historically, other than specialty food products, few marketers developed unique products or services for the Hispanic market. However, given the size and growth of this market, that is changing. For example:

- Macy's launched a clothing line, "Thalia Sodi," by Mexican singer Thalía. This exclusive merchandise was targeted to Latinas and designed with these women in mind.[58]
- In Colorado, Walmart created Denver Bronco T-shirts specifically targeting Hispanic consumers. One version had the phrase "de todo corazón," meaning "with all my heart" in Spanish. Walmart's goal was to combine American sports tradition with symbols of Hispanic culture. The T-shirts became the most popular Denver Bronco's merchandise of the season.[59]
- In addition, marketers have captured the loyalty developed with their products in Central and South America by distributing them in areas of the United States with large Hispanic populations. For example, Colgate-Palmolive first began distributing its Mexican household cleaner Fabuloso in Los Angeles and Miami. Its popularity led to its current offering nationally.

Some attempts at adapting products to the Hispanic market have failed because of a failure to truly understand the needs of this market. For example, many Hispanics find the current trend in houses of having the kitchen open onto the family room to be repugnant (Hispanics tend to be uncomfortable having strangers in their kitchens) and find the homes built for Hispanic buyers to be too stereotypical.[60]

Retailing   The primary retailing responses to this market have been an increase in the number of bilingual salespeople; the use of Spanish-language signs, directions, and point-of-purchase displays; and merchandise assortments that reflect the needs of the local Hispanic community. The following provide specific examples:

- Target launched the campaign "Sin Traduccíon," which curiously translates to "Without Translation," to connect more deeply and emotionally with its Hispanic customers. With this campaign, Target aimed to highlight moments and terms that are unique to Hispanics.[61]
- Hispanic malls, such as La Gran Plaza in Fort Worth, Texas, and The Desert Sky Mall in Phoenix, are enjoying success because the environment caters to the local community and culture. These shopping centers not only include Hispanic retailers but also provide Hispanic entertainment year-round to attract families on the weekends.[62]

ASIAN AMERICANS

LO4

Asian Americans represent an important subculture. Although relatively small in size, this group will continue to grow, with increasingly rapid growth projected over the coming decades.[63] Of particular importance to marketers is that Asian Americans are the highest-educated and highest-income group, with substantial purchasing power. Asian American

Source: Singapore Press Holdings Limited

purchasing power is estimated at $825 billion and is expected to grow by 32 percent through 2020, which is higher than the growth for whites.[64] However, Asian Americans are also the most diverse group, with numerous nationalities, languages, and religions. The U.S. Census includes Asian Indians in its summary figures for this group. However, we will discuss them separately in a later section.

Asian Americans are not a single subculture. Consider the Zaoboa.sg website (www .zaoboa.com.sg) in Illustration 5-5. Ads on this site are probably quite effective with many of the Chinese members of this subculture. However, as Figure 5-3 shows, the Chinese represent only a little over a fourth of all Asian Americans, and they share neither a common language nor culture with most of the other groups.

As with Hispanics, language is a major factor. One estimate is that 80 percent of Asian Americans can be reached with "in-language" promotions. Two-thirds of Asian Americans

National Background of Asian Americans* **FIGURE** 5-3

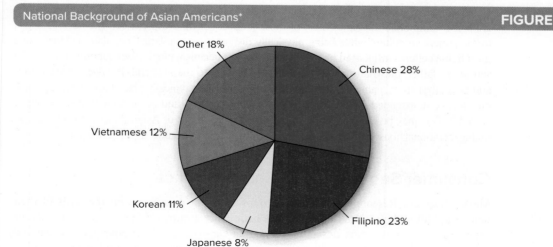

* Excludes Asian Indian Americans from count

Source: U.S. Census Bureau, "Universe: Total Asian Alone or in Any Combination Population," *2015 American Community Survey* (2016).

are immigrants, and the percentage of each nationality group that uses primarily its native language is generally high.[65] While language use and proficiency are clearly a function of acculturation and age, the following shows a wide variation in English use and proficiency across national backgrounds as well:

Country	Nativity	English Only at Home (%)	Non-English at Home, but English Spoken "Very Well" (%)	Non-English at Home, but English Spoken Less Than "Very Well" (%)
China	U.S.-born	43	47	11
	Foreign-born	10	31	59
	All	**19**	**35**	**46**
Japan	U.S.-born	84	12	4
	Foreign-born	16	33	51
	All	**56**	**20**	**23**
Korea	U.S.-born	43	48	9
	Foreign-born	16	29	54
	All	**23**	**34**	**43**
Philippines	U.S.-born	77	19	4
	Foreign-born	14	55	31
	All	**34**	**44**	**22**
Vietnam	U.S.-born	29	56	15
	Foreign-born	7	26	67
	All	**14**	**35**	**52**

Source: U.S. Census Bureau, "American FactFinder," *2011–2015 American Community Survey* (2017).

Clearly, this information suggests the need for "in-language" communications, particularly for those from national backgrounds where English proficiency is lower, or those not born in the United States. In addition to proficiency, there is research suggesting that overall, a majority of Asian Americans prefer either in-language or bilingual communication, with only 17 percent preferring English only.[66]

More than languages differ among the groups. In fact, the concept and term *Asian American* was developed and used by marketers and others who study these groups rather than the members themselves. Members of the various nationalities involved generally refer to themselves by their nationality without the term *American,* that is, Vietnamese, not Vietnamese American. An exception is Japanese Americans.[67]

While each nationality group is a distinct culture with its own language and traditions, there are some commonalities across most of these groups. All have experienced the need to adjust to the American culture while being physically distinct from the larger population. Most come from home cultures influenced by Confucianism. Confucianism emphasizes subordination of the son to the father, the younger to the elder, and the wife to the husband. It values conservatism and prescribes strict manners. Their base cultures also have typically placed a very strong value on traditional, extended families. Education, collective effort, and advancement also are highly valued.[68] This may be a contributing factor to the larger share of Asian Americans who live in multigenerational households compared to the overall U.S. population, as discussed in Chapter 4.[69]

Consumer Segments and Characteristics

Market Segment Research found three groups of Asian Americans on the basis of their demographics and attitudes that cut across nationality groups. Such commonalities can be useful starting points when designing marketing campaigns even if language and cultural symbols must be adapted. *Traditionalists* are older, are often retired, and have strong identification with their original culture; the native language tends to be the primary language;

and they are not concerned about status. *Established* are older, conservative professionals; are well educated, with strong incomes; have relatively weak identification with their native culture; have less need or desire for native-language programming; and will pay premium prices for high quality. *Living for the Moment* are younger, have moderate identification with their native culture, tend to be bilingual, and are spontaneous, materialistic, and impulsive shoppers who are concerned with status and quality.[70]

Several aspects of the Asian American population may make it easier to target. The first is geographic concentration: 45 percent of both the Asian American population and their spending power reside in the West, with over 30 percent of Asian Americans in California.[71] The second aspect is a trend toward an increase in skilled workers from Mandarin-speaking regions of mainland China. This trend appears to be causing a "gradual shift to Mandarin from Cantonese in Chinese communications."[72]

A final aspect of the Asian American community that may make it easier to target is one that is common to all subcultures, and that is the youth trend. Almost half of Asian Americans are under the age of 35, with 21 percent under 18.[73] In addition, this second generation (sometimes referred to as Generation 2.0), which was born in the United States, is, like the African American and Hispanic youth, still tied to its roots but blending languages and cultures, influencing general U.S. culture, and fueling trends in fashion and music. As in the Hispanic market, English-language media options with Asian American content targeted at this second generation are increasing. Pepsi aired ads in English on one such venue called *Stir* TV.[74] Also consider the Honda initiative:

Honda Motor Co. chose to piggyback on Boba, a beverage developed in Taiwan that is all the rage in Asian youth circles. The beverage, also known as bubble tea, consists of "pearls" of black, gummy, tapioca balls that float in the mixture of sweetened iced tea. It has quickly caught on as the soft drink of Asian youth. Honda's idea was to develop drink sleeves that surround hot beverages in the U.S. to promote its youth-oriented cars, like the Civic and Acura RSX. Ponce (manager of emerging markets) got the idea from one of her young Asian co-workers who frequents Boba stores and noticed the number of young Asians who pulled up in Hondas.[75]

Marketing to Asian Americans

As we've seen, there are several Asian American markets, based primarily on nationality and language. Each of these in turn can be further segmented on degree of acculturation,[76] social class, generation, lifestyle, and other variables. And while this creates challenges for marketers, the purchase power of this group and its various segments is increasingly attractive to marketers and causing them to address these niche markets with creative product, merchandising, and media approaches. Importantly, with their higher median income, Asian Americans are more likely to have recently purchased luxury goods than the overall population and are willing to pay more for name brands.[77]

Geographic concentration increases marketing efficiency because targeted nationalities can be reached through specialized media channels. For example, in San Francisco, station KTSF offers in-language news and entertainment programming for Chinese viewers. Many KTSF advertisers, such as McDonald's, dub their existing ads in Cantonese. Others, such as Colgate-Palmolive, run the ads they are using for the same products in Asia. Major U.S. brands such as Southwest Airlines, Ford, and AT&T sponsored KTSF's coverage of the San Francisco Lunar New Year's Parade.

Direct broadcast satellite (DBS) is also an important TV option. DBS provides a means of reaching virtually all the native-language speakers of any nationality nationwide. For example, DISH Network offers a "Chinese Package" called the "Mandarin Great Wall TV

ILLUSTRATION 5-6

The Walmart ad shown here demonstrates how marketing to Asian Americans involves more than translating ads into the appropriate languages. Acknowledgment of special celebrations and symbols are also important.

Source: Walmart Inc.

Package," with over 20 channels. DirecTV offers the gamut of language options to the Asian American audience, including offerings in Vietnamese, Cantonese, and Mandarin, which allow customers to enjoy "a world of entertainment right at home."[78]

Asian Americans are highly tech-savvy and heavy users of the Internet. Internet penetration of Asian Americans is estimated at 91 percent.[79] They are also heavy users of social media.[80] Internet-based marketing to the Asian community is growing rapidly. Firms can reach Chinese consumers in their native language on sites such as that shown in Illustration 5-5. Similar sites are gaining popularity among other Asian nationality groups, and firms such as Charles Schwab are using them as communications channels.

Marketing to the various Asian nationality groups should follow the same basic guidelines discussed earlier for Hispanics. Thus, effective communication is more than simply translating ad copy. It also requires adopting and infusing ads with cultural symbols and meanings relevant to each nationality segment. Examine the Walmart ad in Illustration 5-6. This ad is targeted toward a particular Asian nationality group. Notice the various elements that have been incorporated to focus attention on and communicate with this segment.

Other examples of successful marketing to Asian Americans include

- A Los Angeles chain selected four outlets with large numbers of Chinese and Vietnamese customers. At the time of the Moon Festival (an important holiday in many Asian cultures), the store ran ads and distributed coupons for free moon cakes and lanterns. Sales increased by 30 percent in these stores during the promotion. Likewise, Sears advertises the Moon Festival in Mandarin, Cantonese, Vietnamese, or Korean, depending on the population near each outlet. It provides nationality-relevant gifts and entertainment such as traditional dances.
- Western Union sponsors numerous Asian cultural events, such as the Asian-American Expo for the Chinese New Year in Los Angeles. A majority of Asian Americans attend cultural events relevant to their national heritage, so this is an effective strategy.[81] It also partnered with *World Journal* to publish the *Chinese Immigrant Handbook* to offer practical guidance to new immigrants. These represent grassroot, community-based efforts to target the very specific needs of various nationality groups. These efforts supplement their more traditional mass-media approaches using TV, radio, and magazines.[82]

NATIVE AMERICANS

LO5

The number of Native Americans (American Indians and Alaska Natives, in U.S. Census terms) depends on the measurement used. The Census Bureau reports three numbers for Native Americans: (1) one tribe only, (2) one tribe only or in combination with another tribe, and (3) number 2 plus in combination with any other race. The first definition produces an estimate of 4.4 million Native Americans; the total jumps to 6.6 million when the third definition is used. While many Native Americans live on or near reservations, others are dispersed throughout the country. More than 100,000 Native Americans reside in over 20 states, from Alaska to Florida.[83]

There are close to 570 Native American tribes, each with its own language and traditions. Many of the tribes have reservations and quasi-independent political status. In general, Native Americans have limited incomes,[84] but this varies widely by tribe. Native Americans are more likely to buy generic brands and check prices more frequently.[85] Nevertheless, the overall buying power of this group is estimated at $96 billion and is expected to grow by 28 percent through 2018, which is higher than the rate for whites.[86] The larger tribes by population size are as follows:[87]

Tribes	One Tribe Only	Multiracial
Navajo	310,000	369,000
Cherokee	280,000	1,108,000
Sioux	125,000	207,000
Chippewa	113,000	194,000
Mexican American Indian	104,000	181,000
Choctaw	94,000	238,000
Apache	69,000	141,000
Pueblo	57,000	72,000

In recent years, Native Americans have taken increasing pride in their heritage and are less tolerant of inaccurate stereotypes of either their history or their current status. Thus, marketers using Native American names or portrayals must ensure accurate and appropriate use. Native American cuisine is making its way into the American mainstream with efforts from Native American chefs like Freddie Bitsoie and Sean Sherman. Bitsoie, the executive chef at Mitsitam Café in the National Museum of the American Indian, stresses the importance for authenticity in Native American cooking. As such, more Native American chefs are opening their own restaurants, supporting Native American businesses for ingredients, and hiring Native American employees. Sherman, known as The Sioux Chef, focuses his cuisine on healthy, indigenous food such as maple red corn pudding. As American interest in and acceptance of diversity continue to grow, unique Native American offerings such as this will become increasingly relevant and popular.[88]

The larger tribes have their own newspapers and radio stations. In addition, there are national Native American–oriented newspapers, radio shows, and magazines.[89] Although each tribe is small relative to the total population, the geographic concentration of each tribe provides easy access for marketers. Sponsorship of tribal events and support for tribal colleges, training centers, and community centers can produce good results for firms that do so over time. For example:

- Indian Summer Inc. is an organization that holds a festival each year to "educate, preserve and promote American Indian cultures, showcase the diversity that exists within tribal cultures, provide economic opportunities to our people and strengthen communication and understanding." Harley Davidson and Pepsi are among the corporate sponsors working to support this event and build a relationship with this market.[90]
- Nike has teamed up with the Indian Health Service to set up educational programs to teach and promote health and fitness on reservations. Also, Nike's Native American Network provides support, professional development as well as health and wellness programs for the company's Native American employees.[91]

ASIAN INDIAN AMERICANS

There are approximately 3.7 million Americans of Indian heritage (from India). This segment of the population is growing rapidly as a result of immigration. Asian Indian Americans are concentrated in New York and California, with significant numbers in New Jersey, Illinois, and Texas as well. As a group, they are well educated, affluent, and fluent in English; yet most retain cultural ties to their Indian background.

Those unfamiliar with India often assume that it is a homogeneous country. However, in some ways it is more like Europe than America. It has 28 states, six union territories, 15 official languages, and dozens of other languages and dialects. Thus, while those who immigrate to America have much in common, they also have many differences based on their background in India.

Although diverse in many ways, most share a number of important cultural traits:

- They place great value on education, particularly their children's education. Children are guided to career paths in medicine, law, or engineering.[92]
- They are concerned with financial security and save at a rate much higher than the average American.
- They do not have a "throw-away" mentality. They shop for value and look for quality and durability.
- Husbands tend to have a dominant role in family decisions.

Asian Indian Americans attend to the general mass media. They also can be targeted via specialty magazines such as *Silicon India* and *Little India,* online sites such as IndiaAbroad.com, as well as cable TV, radio stations, and newspapers in regions with significant populations. For example, Western Union advertises to this segment on Eye on Asia, a cable channel focused on this group. National reach is now possible through DISH Network's South Asia Package with various channels from India. Long-term involvement in the Indian community is an effective way to gain support from this segment:

> Metropolitan Life was a major sponsor of a Navaratri, a religious festival that attracted 100,000 participants from around New York and New Jersey. As one participant said, "One of the chief executives of the company attended the festival, and the company took out a series of ads in the souvenir program. Now we feel we should reward the company for taking an interest in us."[93]

The Internet is also an effective way to market to these consumers. However, such an effort requires a sound knowledge of the community:

> It's December but Namaste.com's holiday rush has been over for two months. Christmas is not the big season for its customers. "To suggest gifting to Indians around Christmas time doesn't make sense. It's the wrong marketing message. Diwali [a festival of lights that happens in late October] is the Indian 'Christmas.'"[94]

ARAB AMERICANS

The 2010 Census identified 1.7 million self-identified Arab Americans in the United States. However, the Arab American Institute (the Census Bureau's official designee for analyzing data related to Arab Americans) has estimated the Arab American population, based on additional research, at about 3.7 million. Perhaps no group in America has a more inaccurate stereotype. For example: What is the most common religion of Arab Americans? Sixty-six percent identify themselves as Christians (up from about 50 percent in the early 1990s), and 24 percent are Muslim (down from about 50 percent in the early 1990s).

Arab Americans come from a variety of countries, including Morocco, Algeria, Egypt, Lebanon, Jordan, Saudi Arabia, and Kuwait. They share a common Arabic heritage and the Arabic language. Since World War II, many Arab immigrants have been business proprietors, landowners, or influential families fleeing political turmoil in their home countries. Many of these individuals attended Western or Westernized schools and were fluent in English before arriving.

More than 80 percent of Arab Americans are U.S. citizens, with a majority having been born in the United States. They are somewhat younger than the general population, are better educated, and have a higher-than-average income. They are also much more likely to be entrepreneurs. Big concentrations of Arab Americans can be found in California, Michigan, New York, Florida, and Texas.

Most Arab Americans are tired of negative stereotyping and misrepresentations about their culture. Even the film *Aladdin* contained insults and mistakes. Aladdin sings about the "barbaric" country from which he came. A guard threatened to cut off a young girl's hand for stealing food for a hungry child. Such an action would be contrary to Islamic law. The storefront signs in the mythical Arab land had symbols that made no sense in Arabic or any other language. The aftermath of the September 11, 2001, attacks on the World Trade Center and the Pentagon has aroused some prejudice against these citizens—as well as some enhanced knowledge of their backgrounds and beliefs.

The first rule in reaching this market is to treat its members with respect and accuracy. There are specialized newspapers, magazines, and radio and television stations focused on this market. DISH Network offers an Arabic-language package. And Walmart has begun to adjust its product selection in areas with strong Arab American populations with offerings such as falafel, olives, and Islamic greeting cards. One such area, Dearborn, Michigan, is home to many diverse Arab restaurants and markets for its community, heavily populated (over 40 percent) by Arab Americans. Attention to the unique traditions and tastes of this community can pay large dividends.[95]

RELIGIOUS SUBCULTURES

As discussed in Chapter 3, America is basically a **secular society.** That is, the educational system, government, and political process are not controlled by a religious group, and most people's daily behaviors are not guided by strict religious guidelines. Nonetheless, roughly 77 percent of American adults claim a religious affiliation, 36 percent claim to attend a religious service at least once a week, and two-thirds of religiously affiliated adults state that religion is very important in their lives.[96] Interestingly, while some are leaving religion altogether, which accounts for the ongoing decrease in those identifying with a religious affiliation over time, others are switching. A recent study indicates that 42 percent of adults have moved to another religion, with growth in unaffiliated Christian faiths and non-Christian faiths.[97]

The fact that the American culture is largely secular is not viewed as optimal by all of society. Many conservative Christians would prefer a society and legal system more in line with their faith. The intense debates over abortion, prayer in schools, the teaching of evolution versus creationism, homosexual rights, and a host of other issues are evidence of this division in American society.

Religion is important to, and directly influences the behaviors of, many Americans. This includes consuming religiously themed products[98] and avoiding the consumption of other products such as alcohol. The different religions in America prescribe differing values and behaviors. Thus, a number of **religious subcultures** exist in America.

LO6

ILLUSTRATION 5-7

The Not Of This World clothing line would appeal to the "young religious" segment identified by Yankelovich.

Source: Mardel

Christian Subcultures

Much of the American value system and the resultant political and social institutions are derived from the Christian, and largely Protestant, beliefs of the early settlers. Although American culture is basically secular, many of its traditions and values are derived from the Judeo-Christian heritage of the majority of Americans. Most of the major American holidays, including Christmas, Easter, and Thanksgiving, have a religious base. However, except for Easter, the pure religious base of these holidays is no longer the central theme that it once was.

Although the United States is predominantly Christian, the percentage of American adults claiming Christianity as their religion was 71 percent in 2014, down from 78 percent in 2007.[99] However, Yankelovich has been tracking a psychographic segment it calls the "young religious," composed of Gen X and Gen Y. Following up on the huge success of the movie *The Passion of the Christ,* clothing firms have begun marketing trendy fashions with an edge to this younger audience, including T-shirts with the slogan "Jesus Saves Bro" from brands like Not Of This World. Some retailers, like Mardel (which owns Not Of This World), have embraced this trend, while others, concerned about offending customers, have declined.[100] The Not Of This World clothing line shown in Illustration 5–7 appears to be targeting this group.

Chick-fil-A is a rarity among national fast-food chains in that they are not open on Sunday as a matter of Christian principle based on the beliefs of its founder, Truett Cathy. The following is an excerpt from the company's Vice President of Marketing regarding this decision:

> We've always had pressure from our customers, even landlords. But ultimately, we feel like it's a fundamental business issue to us . . . and we're not tempted to open on Sunday. Ironically, a lot of people respect the fact that we put something ahead of making another dollar in life. . . .[101]

Christianity takes many forms in this country, each with some unique beliefs and behaviors, as discussed next.

Roman Catholic Subculture Roughly 21 percent of American adults are Roman Catholic. The Catholic Church is highly structured and hierarchical. The pope is the central religious authority, and individual interpretation of scripture and events is minimal. A basic tenet of the Catholic Church is that a primary purpose of a marital union is procreation. Therefore, the use of birth control devices is prohibited, though many Catholics deviate from this. A result of this is a larger average family size for Catholics than for Protestants or Jews. The larger family size makes economic gains and upward social mobility more difficult. It also has a major influence on the types of products consumed by Catholics relative to many other religions.

The Catholic Church is ethnically diverse, with some 41 percent of its adult membership coming from ethnic subcultures. Recall from our earlier discussion that the predominant religion among Hispanics is Catholicism. Hispanics have fueled much of the Catholic growth since 1960. Thirty-four percent of adult Catholics are Hispanic, 3 percent are African American, and 3 percent are Asian.[102] Perhaps even more telling, almost 50 percent of Catholics under the age of 30 are Hispanic.[103] Catholics tend to be concentrated in the Northeast and in areas with large Hispanic populations. *Encuentro 2000: Many Faces in God's House* was a special event that embraced people of all ethnic and racial backgrounds for the first time at a national level. The conference included Latin music, an ethnic village, workshops reflecting the Asian experience, and speakers from various ethnic backgrounds.[104] This was just one step. The U.S. Conference of Catholic Bishops has a Hispanic Affairs section on its website devoted to issues of education and outreach to the Hispanic community, including the Encuentro, which continues today. On a more local level, the Archdiocese of Baltimore holds an annual Mass for Our Lady of Guadalupe, who was said to have appeared to an Indian peasant in 1531 near what is now Mexico City.

Like Protestants, Catholics vary in their commitment and conservatism. The more conservative members share many values and behaviors with Protestant religious conservatives. Catholics have few consumption restrictions or requirements associated with their religion. Marketers targeting this group can reach the more committed members through specialized magazines, radio programs, and community events.

Protestant Subcultures   Approximately 47 percent of American adults identify themselves as Protestant. While there are many types of Protestant faiths, with significant differences between them, most emphasize direct individual experience with God as a core tenet. In general, Protestant faiths emphasize individual responsibility and control. This focus has been credited with creating a strong work ethic, a desire for scientific knowledge, a willingness to sacrifice for the future, and relatively small families. These characteristics in turn have created upward social mobility and produced the majority of the ruling elite in America.

Protestant values and attitudes have tended to shape the core American culture. This is particularly true for white Protestants of Western European heritage—WASPs (white Anglo-Saxon Protestants). This group has historically dominated America in terms of numbers, wealth, and power, with power historically belonging to the male members of this group.

Although Protestants constitute the basic core culture of America, the diversity across and within denominations creates numerous subcultures within the larger group. Many of these religious groups have unique beliefs of direct relevance to marketers. These generally involve the consumption of products containing stimulants such as caffeine (prohibited by the Mormon Church) or alcohol (prohibited by the Southern Baptist church, among others). However, the basic distinction among Protestants, as among Catholics, is the degree of conservatism in their religious beliefs. Many Protestants are middle-of-the-road in terms of conservatism. This is consistent with America's dominant cultural values. However, a sizable and growing number are very conservative and, along with conservative Catholics, represent a significant subculture.

The Born-Again Christian Subculture   Born-again Christians have been referred to as the Christian Right, Religious Right, Conservative Christians, Evangelical Christians, and Fundamentalist Christians. **Born-again Christians** are *characterized by a strong belief in the literal truth of the Bible, a very strong commitment to their religious beliefs, having had a "born-again" experience, and encouraging others to believe in Jesus Christ.*

Born-again Christians tend to have somewhat lower education and income levels than the general population. They tend to have a more traditional gender role orientation. Born-again Christians are best known for their political stands on issues such as abortion, homosexual rights, and prayer in the schools.

Their beliefs also influence their consumption patterns. They generally oppose the use of alcohol and drugs. They do not consume movies or television programs that are overly focused on sex or other activities that they consider to be immoral. In fact, various groups of born-again Christians have organized or threatened boycotts against advertisers that sponsor shows they find inappropriate or corporations whose policies and procedures (e.g., those relating to same-sex couples) run contrary to their beliefs.

In contrast, they are very receptive to programs, books, and movies that depict traditional (i.e., Protestant) family (husband, wife, children) values. Firms with a reputation for supporting similar values are well received by this segment.

Non-Christian Subcultures

Jewish Subculture   Judaism represents 2 percent of American adults and is unique in that historically it has been an inseparable combination of ethnic and religious identity. Historically, Jews in America tended to marry other Jews, although that has changed somewhat over time.[105] In fact, a study of Match.com members found that 81 percent of Jewish single men and 72 percent of Jewish single women said they would date outside their race, ethnicity, or religion (these percentages were similar to those found for most other religions).[106] Nevertheless, Jewish dating apps such as JSwipe and JMatch appeal to younger Jews interested in dating and marrying within the Jewish faith.

Jews are heavily concentrated in the Northeast but are increasingly dispersing throughout the United States, particularly into the Sunbelt.[107] American Jews tend to have higher-than-average incomes and education levels. In most ways, Jewish consumption patterns are similar to those of other Americans with similar education and income levels.

Like other religious groups, the committed, conservative Jews represent a subculture distinct from mainstream Jews. Orthodox Jews have strict dietary rules that prohibit some foods such as pork and specify strict preparation requirements for other foods. In the U.S., national doughnut chain Krispy Kreme uses kosher ingredients and many stores have been certified kosher.[108] Orthodox Jews also strictly observe Jewish holidays, and many do not participate in even the secular aspects of the major Christian holiday Christmas. Reform Jews and Jews less committed to the strict interpretations of Judaism are less influenced by these practices.[109]

Muslim Subculture   It is important to recall from our earlier discussion that Arab Americans are often not Muslims, and by the same token Muslims in America are not necessarily Arabs. Muslims in America (representing roughly 1 percent of the American adult population) are culturally diverse, including Arab Americans, African Americans, Asian Americans, and Hispanics. This group is projected to replace Judaism as the second-largest religious group (behind Christianity) in the U.S. by 2040.[110] Like the Protestants, there are a variety of Muslim sects with varying belief patterns, though all are based on the Koran. As with Protestants, Catholics, and Jews, the most obvious division among Muslims is the degree of conservatism and the importance attached to the literal teachings of the religion.

As with the other religious groups in America, most Muslims' lives are centered on work, family, school, and the pursuit of success and happiness.

In general, Muslims tend to be conservative with respect to drug and alcohol use and sexual permissiveness. In fact, many oppose dating. They also place considerable emphasis on the family, with the eldest male as the head of the family, and on respect for elders. The more devout Muslims avoid not only pork products but also any foods that have not been prepared in accordance with the strict rules of Islam. The following quote from a devout Pakistani Muslim on why he does not eat in Western restaurants illustrates the stress this can cause:

> Well, how can I be sure that the cook who has cooked pork or bacon in a pan did not cook my vegetables in the same pan? How can I be sure that even if he used different pans he washed his hands in between cooking bacon and a vegetable? I do not think there is any way I can get a pure food out there.[111]

These beliefs conflict with the practices in the larger society and the images portrayed on television and in the movies and are also a source of conflict between older Muslims who immigrated to America and their children who were raised here.[112] Muslims in America have their own magazines, schools, social clubs, marriage services, and bookstores. There are more than 2,600 Muslim mosques and sanctuaries in America, up from 1,200 in 2000.[113] Despite the growth in this group, in general, this subculture has not attracted the attention of marketers except as it overlaps with the Arab American subculture.

Buddhist Subculture   There are nearly as many Buddhists in America as there are Muslims. They are primarily Asian American or white, although Asian Americans are more likely to be Christian (34 percent) than Buddhist (14 percent). Over 40 percent of Buddhists earn $50,000 or more, and Hawaii is home to the largest concentration of Buddhists (8 percent).[114]

There are a variety of Buddhist sects in America. All emphasize the basic idea that all beings are caught in *samsara,* a cycle of suffering and rebirth that is basically caused by desire and actions that produce unfavorable *karma.* Samsara can be escaped and a state of *nirvana* reached by following the noble *Eightfold Path.* This combines ethical and disciplinary practices, training in concentration and meditation, and the development of enlightened wisdom.

Thus far, marketers have largely ignored this market. Its small size and diverse ethnic composition make it difficult to target. However, as specialized media evolve to serve Buddhists, opportunities will exist for astute marketers.

REGIONAL SUBCULTURES

Distinct **regional subcultures** arise as a result of climatic conditions, the natural environment and resources, the characteristics of the various immigrant groups that have settled in each region, and significant social and political events. These distinct subcultures present numerous opportunities and challenges for marketers. Examples include[115]

`LO7`

- Smashburger offers customized menu items in cities to appeal to local taste. For example, the toppings on the San Diego smashburger include avocado, fresh cilantro, and sour cream, while fried pickles with ranch dressing are sold in Tulsa, Oklahoma.
- Many national magazines run regional editions. *Sports Illustrated,* for example, had four different regional covers for their recent NFL preview issue.
- Skyline Chili, a restaurant based in Cincinnati, Ohio, offers a unique chili recipe that is served alone or in combination with either pasta or a hotdog, along with toppings like grated cheddar cheese, onions, and beans, as seen in Illustration 5–8. The "3-way" (or "5-way") and "Coney" may sound a bit odd to some, but they are popular among residents of Ohio, Kentucky, and Indiana.

Skyline Chili provides menu items that appeal to customers in the Midwest region.

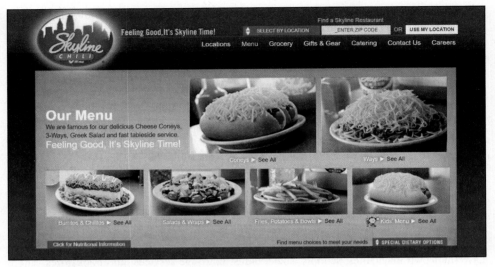

Source: Skyline Chili, Inc.

Although the most effective regional marketing strategies often are based on small geographic areas, we can observe significant consumption differences across much larger regions. Table 5–3 illustrates some of the consumption differences across the four U.S. census regions. Given such clear differences in consumption patterns, marketers realize that,

TABLE 5-3	Regional Consumption Differences			
	Northeast	**Midwest**	**South**	**West**
Products				
Imported beer	116	87	94	110
Tooth whiteners	98	94	106	97
Breakfast pastries	98	103	105	91
Bagels	128	98	87	102
Activities				
Going to concerts/music festivals	105	98	94	108
Fly fishing	91	83	98	126
Skateboarding	87	82	97	131
College football fan	74	113	113	88
Shopping				
Staples	194	43	82	109
H&M	139	64	81	133
Domino's Pizza	77	78	122	101
Chili's Grill & Bar	70	84	127	92
Media				
The New Yorker	143	97	70	120
American Rifleman	96	121	108	71
The Amazing Race (CBS)	107	97	96	105
The Simpsons (FOX)	103	108	109	75

Note: 100 = Average level of use, purchase, or consumption

Source: Simmons Research, *National Consumer Study 2018.*

for at least some product categories, the United States is no more a single market than is the European Union. Because specialized (regional) marketing programs generally cost more than standardized (national) programs, marketers must balance potential sales increases against increased costs. This decision process is exactly the same as described in the section on multinational marketing decisions in Chapter 2.

SUMMARY

LO1: Understand subcultures and their influence on unique market behaviors.

The United States is becoming increasingly diverse. Much of this diversity is fueled by immigration and an increase in ethnic pride and by identification with non-European heritages among numerous Americans. Most members of a culture share most of the core values, beliefs, and behaviors of that culture. However, most individuals also belong to several subcultures. A *subculture* is a segment of a larger culture whose members share distinguishing patterns of behavior. An array of ethnic, nationality, religious, and regional subcultures characterizes American society. The existence of these subcultures provides marketers with the opportunity to develop unique marketing programs to match the unique needs of each.

Ethnic subcultures are defined broadly as those whose members' unique shared behaviors are based on a common racial, language, or nationality background. Non-European ethnic groups constitute a significant and growing part of the U.S. population, from 40 percent in 2020 to 48 percent by 2040.

LO2: Analyze the African American subculture and the unique marketing aspects it entails.

African Americans represent a substantial non-European ethnic group at roughly 13 percent of the U.S. population. Although African Americans are younger and tend to have lower incomes than the general population, their rapidly growing education, income, purchasing power, and cultural influence continue to attract marketers to this large and diverse subculture.

LO3: Analyze the Hispanic subculture and the unique marketing aspects it entails.

Hispanics represent the largest and fastest-growing ethnic subculture in the United States. Even though Hispanics have a variety of national backgrounds (Mexico, Puerto Rico, Cuba, and so on), the Spanish language, a common religion (Roman Catholicism), and national Spanish-language media and entertainment figures have created a somewhat homogeneous Hispanic subculture.

LO4: Analyze the Asian American subculture and the unique marketing aspects it entails.

Asian Americans are the most diverse of the major ethnic subcultures. They are characterized by a variety of nationalities, languages, and religions. From a marketing perspective, it is not appropriate to consider Asian Americans as a single group. Instead, Asian Americans are best approached as a number of nationality subcultures.

LO5: Analyze the Native American, Asian Indian American, and Arab American subcultures and the unique marketing aspects they entail.

Native Americans, Asian Indian Americans, and *Arab Americans* are smaller but important subcultures. Each is diverse yet shares enough common values and behaviors to be approached as a single segment for at least some products. Geographic concentration and specialized media allow targeted marketing campaigns.

LO6: Describe the various religious subcultures and their implications for marketing.

Although the United States is a relatively secular society, roughly 77 percent of American adults claim a religious affiliation, and a majority state that religion is important in their lives. A majority of American adults identify themselves as Christian, although the percentage has declined over time. And a variety of *religious subcultures* exist both within and across the Christian faiths and the Jewish, Muslim, and Buddhist faiths. Within each faith, the largest contrast is the degree of conservatism of the members.

LO7: Explain the role of geographic regions as subcultures.

Regional subcultures arise as a result of climatic conditions, the natural environment and resources, the characteristics of the various immigrant groups that have settled in each region, and significant social and political events. Regional subcultures affect all aspects of consumption behavior, and sophisticated marketers recognize that the United States is composed of numerous regional markets.

KEY TERMS

Acculturation 161
Born-again Christians 176
Ethnic subcultures 154

Event marketing 159
Hispanic 160
Regional subcultures 177

Religious subcultures 173
Secular society 173
Subculture 152

REVIEW QUESTIONS

1. What is a *subculture?*
2. What determines the degree to which a subculture will influence an individual's behavior?
3. Is the American culture more like a soup or a salad?
4. What is an *ethnic subculture?*
5. How large are the major ethnic subcultures in America? Which are growing most rapidly?
6. What regions are the major sources of America's immigrants?
7. Are the various ethnic subcultures homogeneous or heterogeneous?
8. Describe the influence of education on the Internet use of African Americans. What are the marketing implications?
9. Describe the African American consumer groups found by the Yankelovich group.
10. What are the basic principles that should be followed in marketing to an African American market segment?

11. To what extent is the Spanish language used by American Hispanics? How do language and acculturation affect Internet use among Hispanics?
12. Can Hispanics be treated as a single market?
13. Describe the three Hispanic generational groups identified by the Pew Hispanic Center.
14. How homogeneous are Asian Americans?
15. To what extent do Asian Americans use their native language?
16. Describe three emerging aspects that may make the Asian American population somewhat easier to target.
17. Why is the United States considered to be a *secular society?*
18. Describe the *Roman Catholic subculture.*
19. Describe the *born-again Christian subculture.*
20. Describe the *Jewish subculture.*
21. Describe the *Muslim subculture.*
22. Describe the *Buddhist subculture.*
23. What is a regional subculture? Give some examples.

DISCUSSION QUESTIONS

24. Examine Table 5–1. Which of these differences are mainly caused by ethnicity or race, and which are caused by other factors?
25. Do you agree that America is becoming more like a salad than a soup in terms of the integration of ethnic groups? Is this good or bad?

26. Do you agree with the following statement regarding ethnicity made at one point in time by a Miller Brewing representative? For what types of products is this view most correct? Least correct?

    We used to have an ethnic marketing department up until several years ago. . . .

[But now we believe] the things that young Hispanic or young African American or young white people have in common are much stronger and more important than any ethnic difference.

27. Most new immigrants to America are non-European and have limited English-language skills. What opportunities does this present to marketers? Does this raise any ethical issues for marketers?

28. Does a firm's social responsibility play a role in marketing to consumers from various ethnic subcultures whose incomes fall below the poverty line? If so, what?

29. Respond to the questions in Consumer Insight 5–1.

30. Although some of the following have very limited incomes, others are quite prosperous. Does marketing to prosperous members of these groups require a marketing mix different from the one used to reach other prosperous consumers?
    a. African Americans
    b. Hispanics
    c. Asian Americans

31. Describe how each of the following firms' product managers should approach (*i*) the African American, (*ii*) the Hispanic, (*iii*) the Asian American, (*iv*) the Asian Indian American, (*v*) the Arab American, or (*vi*) the Native American markets.
    a. Pepsi
    b. Target

c. NBA
d. *Sports Illustrated* magazine
e. The United Way
f. Dell laptops
g. Google.com
h. Coach handbags

32. What, if any, unique ethical responsibilities exist when marketing to ethnic subcultures?

33. Do you agree that the United States is a secular society? Why or why not?

34. Describe how each of the following firms' product managers should approach the (*i*) Catholic, (*ii*) Protestant, (*iii*) born-again Christian, (*iv*) Jewish, (*v*) Muslim, and (*vi*) Buddhist subcultures.
    a. Red Bull
    b. Wendy's
    c. The NBA
    d. *Maxim* magazine
    e. The United Way
    f. Dell laptops
    g. Facebook
    h. Estée Lauder makeup

35. Will regional subcultures become more or less distinct over the next 20 years? Why?

36. Select one product, service, or activity from each category in Table 5–3 and explain the differences in consumption for the item across the regions shown.

APPLICATION ACTIVITIES

37. Watch two hours of prime-time major network (ABC, CBS, FOX, or NBC) television. What subculture groups are portrayed in the programs? Describe how they are portrayed. Do these portrayals match the descriptions in this text? How would you explain the differences? Repeat these tasks for the ads shown during the programs.

38. Pick a product of interest and examine the Simmons Market Research Bureau or MediaMark studies on the product in your library (these are often in the journalism library on CD-ROM). Determine the extent to which its consumption varies by ethnic group and region. Does consumption also vary by age, income, or other variables? Are the differences in ethnic and regional consumption due primarily to ethnicity

and region or to the fact that the ethnic group or region is older, richer, or otherwise different from the larger culture?

39. Examine several magazines or newspapers aimed at a non-European ethnic or nationality group. What types of products are advertised? Why?

40. Interview three members of the following subcultures and ascertain their opinions of how their ethnic or nationality group is portrayed on network television shows and in national ads.
    a. African Americans
    b. Asian Americans
    c. Hispanics
    d. Arab Americans
    e. Asian Indian Americans
    f. Native Americans

41. Interview three members of the following subcultures and ascertain the extent to which they identify with the core American culture, their ethnic subculture within America, or their nationality subculture. Also determine the extent to which they feel others of their ethnic/race group feel as they do and the reasons for any differences.
    a. African Americans
    b. Asian Americans
    c. Hispanics
    d. Arab Americans
    e. Asian Indian Americans
    f. Native Americans

42. Interview three members of the following religious subcultures and determine the extent to which

their consumption patterns are influenced by their religion.
    a. Catholics
    b. Protestants
    c. Born-again Christians
    d. Jews
    e. Muslims
    f. Buddhists

43. Interview two students from other regions of the United States and determine the behavior and attitudinal differences they have noticed between their home and your present location. Try to determine the causes of these differences.

REFERENCES

1. Chapter opener is based on L. M. Keefe, "P&G's Multicultural Marketing DNA," *Marketing News,* March 1, 2004, pp. 13–14; T. Nudd, "Nivea Apologizes for Wanting to 'Re-Civilize' Black Man," *Ad Week,* August 18, 2011, www.adweek.com/adfreak/nivea-apologizes-wanting-re-civilize-black-man-134226, accessed August 29, 2014; F. Kelley, "Essence in New Orleans," *NPR The Record,* July 9, 2012, www.npr.org/blogs/therecord/2012/07/09/156494248/essence-in-new-orleans-a-festival-that-knows-its-audience, accessed August 29, 2014; D. Ramsey, "Essence Music Festival," *Grio,* July 4, 2013, http://thegrio.com/2013/07/04/essence-music-festival-the-magic-and-the-business-behind-this-summers-hottest-ticket/2/, accessed August 29, 2014; information from Essence website at www.essence.com.

2. C. Fisher, "It's All in the Details," *American Demographics,* April 1998, p. 45.

3. The 2010 percentages are from the 2010 Census and are found at U.S. Census Bureau, "Overview of Race and Hispanic Origin: 2010," *2010 Census Briefs* (March 2011). All other data are from U.S. Census Bureau, 2008 National Population Projections Tables: Table 4. "Projections of the Population by Sex, Race, and Hispanic Origin for the United States: 2010 to 2050," August 2008.

4. W. H. Frey, "Micro Melting Pots," *American Demographics,* June 2001, pp. 20–23.

5. M. Maciag, "A State-by-State Look at Growing Minority Populations," www.governing.com, June 25, 2015, accessed February 19, 2018.

6. R. Baugh, "U.S. Lawful Permanent Residents: 2016," U.S. Department of Homeland Security, December 2017.

7. M. R. Forehand and R. Deshpande, "What We See Makes Us Who We Are," *Journal of Marketing Research,* August 2001, pp. 336–48.

8. *Statistical Abstract of the United States: 2011* (Washington, DC: U.S. Census Bureau, 2011); *2008 ASEC Supplement* (Washington, DC: U.S. Census Bureau, 2009); *Statistical Portrait of Hispanics in the United States, 2015* (Washington, DC: Pew Hispanic Center, July 2017); M. Gil and S. Rosenberg, "The Multicultural Edge: Rising Super Consumers," *Nielsen Company,* 2015; U.S. Census Bureau, "Income and Earnings Summary Measures by Selected Characteristics: 2015 and 2016," *Current Population Survey 2016,* March 2017; "Labor Force Characteristics by Race and Ethnicity, 2016," *U.S. Bureau of Labor Statistics,* October 2017.

9. E. Morris, "The Difference in Black and White," *American Demographics,* January 1993, p. 46.

10. U.S. Census Bureau, "Table H-3. Mean Household Income Received by Each Fifth and Top 5 Percent, Black Households:1967–2016," *Current Population Survey, Annual Social and Economic Supplements,* August 19, 2017.

11. J. M. Humphreys, *The Multicultural Economy 2013* (Athens, GA: Selig Center for Economic Growth, University of Georgia, 2013); J. Boschma, "Black Consumers Have 'Unprecedented Impact' in 2015," *Atlantic,* February 2, 2016.

12. Next America Staff, "5 Companies That Recognize Black Consumer Power," *Atlantic,* November 11, 2015.

13. Table 5-2 was derived from results presented in *Black America Today Study* (Radio One and Yankelovich, June 2008); information found on BlackAmericaStudy.com, accessed April 23, 2011.

14. Y. K. Kim and J. Kang, "The Effects of Ethnicity and Product on Purchase Decision Making," *Journal of Advertising Research,* March 2001, pp. 39–48.

15. J. Krogstad, "Social Media Preferences Vary by Race and Ethnicity," *Pew Research,* February 5, 2015, www.pewresearch.org, accessed February 23, 2018; "Multifaceted Connections: African-American Media Usage Outpaces across Platforms," *Nielsen,* February 3, 2015, www.nielsen.com, accessed February 23, 2018; "A New Megaphone: Social Media Gives Consumers a Chance to Be Heard on What They Watch," *Nielsen,* January 17, 2017, www.nielsen.com, accessed February 23, 2018; Mintel, "Black Consumers' Content Consumption and Sharing—US—January 2018," www.mintel.com, accessed February 23, 2018.

16. See "Multifaceted Connections: African-American Media Usage Outpaces across Platforms," *Nielsen,* February 3, 2015, www.nielsen.com; Simmons Market Research Bureau, *Summer 2017 NHCS Adult Survey,* accessed from Mintel.

17. J. Adler, "Marketers, Agencies Praise BET's Savvy," *Advertising Age,* April 11, 2005, p. B16.

18. *Demographics of Internet Users* (Washington, DC: Pew Internet & American Life Project, May 2010); "Demographics of Internet and Home Broadband Usage in the United States: Internet/Broadband Fact Sheet," *Pew Internet,* February 5, 2018, www.pewinternet.org, accessed February 23, 2018.

19. E. Burns, "African American Online Population Is Growing," *The ClickZ Network,* October 10, 2005, www.clickz.com, accessed June 7, 2008; "AOL: Some 80 Percent of African-Americans Online," *MarketingVOX,* October 17, 2005, www.marketingvox.com, accessed June 7, 2008; *Black America Today Study,* 2008; "Top U.S. Web Brands and Parent Companies for September 2009," *Nielsen Wire,* http://blog.nielsen.com/nielsenwire/online, accessed April 24, 2011. See "Multifaceted Connections: African-American Media Usage Outpaces across Platforms"; see also Mintel, "Black Consumers' Content Consumption and Sharing—US—January 2018."

20. A. Smith, *Technology Trends among People of Color* (Washington, DC: Pew Internet & American Life Project, September 17, 2010); see Boschma, "Black Consumers Have 'Unprecedented Impact' in 2015."

21. P. Miller, "African Americans Are a Heterogeneous, Not a Homogeneous, Market," *Cablevision Advertising Bureau,* 2005, www.onetvworld.org.

22. See, e.g., L. Sanders, "How to Target Blacks?," *Advertising Age,* July 3, 2006, p. 19.

23. See, e.g., B. DeBerry-Spence, "Consumer Creations of Product Meaning in the Context of African-Style Clothing," *Journal of the Academy of Marketing Science* 36 (2008), pp. 395–408.

24. E. M. Simpson et al., "Race, Homophily, and Purchase Intentions and the Black Consumer," *Psychology & Marketing,* October 2000, pp. 877–99. See also L. A. Perkins, K. M. Thomas, and G. A. Taylor, "Advertising and Recruitment," *Psychology & Marketing,* March 2000, pp. 235–55.

25. C. L. Green, "Ethnic Evaluations of Advertising," *Journal of Advertising,* Spring 1999, pp. 49–63; O. Appiah, "Ethnic Identification on Adolescents' Evaluations of Advertisements," *Journal of Advertising Research,* September 2001, pp. 7–21; T. E. Whittler and J. S. Spira, "Model's Race," *Journal of Consumer Psychology* 12, no. 4 (2002), pp. 291–301.

26. See Next America Staff, "5 Companies That Recognize Black Consumer Power"; A. Brown, "McDonald's Free Concert Series, the Inspiration Celebration Gospel Tour, Heads to 15 Cities," *Madame Noire,* April 14, 2017, www.madamenoire.com.

27. D. Howell, "Albertson's Caters to Different Ethnic Markets," *DSN Retailing Today,* October 1, 2001, p. 18.

28. Keefe, "P&G's Multicultural Marketing DNA."

29. T. L. Ainscough and C. M. Motley, "Will You Help Me Please?," *Marketing Letters,* May 2000, pp. 129–36; T. L. Baker, T. Meyer, and J. D. Johnson, "Individual Differences in Perceptions of Service Failure and Recovery," *Journal of the Academy of Marketing Science* 36 (2008), pp. 552–64.

30. See V. D. Bush et al., "Managing Culturally Diverse Buyer–Seller Relationships," *Journal of the Academy of Marketing Science,* Fall 2001, pp. 391–404.

31. See, e.g., *The African-American Market in the U.S.* (New York: Packaged Facts, 2008).

32. See Boschma, "Black Consumers Have 'Unprecedented Impact' in 2015."

33. See, e.g., ibid.

34. R. J. Wyatt, B. D. Gelb, and S. Geirger-Oneto, "How Social Insecurity and the Social Meaning of Advertising Reinforce Minority Consumers' Preference for National Brands," *Journal of Contemporary Issues and Research in Advertising* 30 (Spring 2008), pp. 61–70.

35. U.S. Census Bureau, "Table H-3."

36. Demographics, "Hispanic Influence Reaches New Heights in the U.S.," *Nielsen,* August 23, 2016, www.nielsen.com, accessed February 26, 2018.

37. *The American Community Survey* (Washington, DC: U.S. Census Bureau, 2016).

38. See *Assimilation and Language* (Washington, DC: Pew Hispanic Center, 2004); *Latino Shoppers* (Rockville, MD: Packaged Facts, 2011).

39. *Generational Differences* (Washington, DC: Pew Hispanic Center, March 2004); *Statistical Portrait of Hispanics in the United States, 2009* (Washington, DC: Pew Hispanic Center, February 2011). See also R. Villarreal and R. A. Peterson, "Hispanic Identity and Media Behavior," *Journal of Advertising Research,* June 2008, pp. 179–90.

40. G. Berman, *Portrait of the New America* (Coral Gables, FL: Market Segment Group, 2002), p. 21.

41. Demographics, "Hispanics, Transforming the Consumer Landscape," *Nielsen,* August 18, 2016, www.nielsen.com, accessed February 26, 2018.

42. Insight is based on "Hispanic Women Are Cultural Catalysts as Entrepreneurship, Education Rates Rise, According to New Nielsen Report," *Nielsen,* September 12, 2017, www.nielsen.com/us/en/press-room/2017/hispanic-women-are-cultural-catalysts-as-entrepreneurship-education-rates-rise.html, accessed February 11, 2018; A. C. Howe, "Young, Bilingual, Bicultural: Latinas Gaining Consumer Power," *NBC News,* September 12, 2017, www.nbcnews.com/news/latino/new-purchasing-power-latinas-n800366, accessed February 11, 2018; C. Lancaster, "Engaging the Evolving US Latina Consumer," *Stylus,* November 18, 2016, www.stylus.com/ccknxs, accessed February 11, 2018; "Latina Buying Power Is on the Rise," *LanguageLine Solutions,* September 27, 2017, http://blog.languageline.com/8-notable-numbers-on-the-increase-in-u.s.-latina-buying-power, accessed February 11, 2018; Nielsen Company, *Latina 2.0: Fiscally Conscious, Culturally Influential & Familia Forward* (2017), www.nielsen.com/content/dam/corporate/us/en/reports-downloads/2017-reports/Latina%202.0.pdf, accessed February 11, 2018; M. Weeks, "UGA Report: Minority Groups Driving U.S. Economy," *UGA Today,* March 2, 2017, https://news.uga.edu/Multicultural-economy-report-17/, accessed February 11, 2018.

43. C. Webster, "The Effects of Hispanic Identification on Marital Roles in the Purchase Decision Process," *Journal of Consumer Research,* September 1994, pp. 319–31.

44. See, e.g., *Gender Norms and the Role of Extended Family* (Washington, DC: Hispanic Healthy Marriage Initiative, 2006), www.acf.hhs.gov/healthymarriage/pdf/Gender_Norms.pdf, accessed May 6, 2011; *Latino Shoppers.*

45. *The American Community Survey.*

46. *The U.S. Hispanic Market* (New York: Packaged Facts, October 2003); J. Noriega and E. Blair, "Advertising to Bilinguals," *Journal of Marketing,* September 2008, pp. 69–83.

47. L. Sonderup, "Hispanic Marketing," *Advertising & Marketing Review,* April 2004, www.ad-mkt-review.com.

48. *Hispanic Fact Pack 2010* (New York: Advertising Age, 2010), p. 31; *Hispanic Fact Pack 2017* (New York: Crain Publications, August 2017), p. 18.

49. *The U.S. Hispanic Market.*

50. L. Wentz, "Rapid Change Sweeps Hispanic Advertising Industry," *Advertising Age,* May 3, 2005, www.adage.com.

51. *Demographics of Internet Users;* A. Brown, "Internet Use among Hispanics," *Pew Hispanic,* July 20, 2016, www.pewhispanic.org, accessed February 26, 2018.

52. *Hispanic Fact Pack 2017.*

53. *Hispanics Online* (New York, NY: eMarketer, May 2010).

54. For these and other examples, see "Marketing to Hispanics," *Advertising Age,* February 8, 1987, p. S23; M. Westerman, "Death of the Frito Bandito," *American Demographics,* March 1989, pp. 28–32; L. Wentz, "Debate Swirls over Slang in Coors Spot," *Advertising Age,* May 17, 2004, p. 6.

55. See D. Luna, L. A. Peracchio, and M. D. de Juan, "The Impact of Language and Congruity on Persuasion in Multicultural E-Marketing," *Journal of Consumer Psychology* 13, no. 1/2 (2003), pp. 41–50; see also R. Gardyn, "Habla English," *American Demographics,* April 2001, pp. 54–57.

56. M. Hernandez, "Big Brands Target Hispanic Consumers," *USA Today,* September 22, 2013; M. Yardley, "Juanes and Ram Truck Launch A Todo, Con Todo Ad Campaign," *The News Wheel,* March 11, 2014, www.thenewswheel.com, accessed February 26, 2018.

57. L. Wentz, "Best Buy Targets Hispanic Patriarchs," *Advertising Age,* August 2, 2004, p. 20.

58. A. Rodriguez, "Retailers Duke It Out for Hispanic Shoppers' Dollars," *Advertising Age,* April 6, 2015, p. 26.

59. J. Garcia and R. Gerdes, "To Win Latino Market, Know Pitfalls, Learn Rewards," *Marketing News,* March 1, 2004, pp. 14, 19.

60. A. S. Wellner, "Gen X Homes in," *American Demographics,* August 1999, p. 61.

61. See Rodriguez, "Retailers Duke It Out for Hispanic Shoppers' Dollars."

62. C. Cartagena, "'Hispanic Malls' Drawing Crowds by Being Culturally in Tune," *Advertising Age,* May 22, 2013, www.adage.com.

63. Demographics, "Asian-Americans Are Expanding Their Footprint in the U.S. and Making an Impact," *Nielsen,* May 19, 2016, www .nielsen.com, accessed February 28, 2018.

64. Ibid.

65. See B. Edmundson, "Asian Americans in 2001," *American Demographics,* February 1997, pp. 16–17; "90 Percent of Asian Americans Go Online," *BizReport,* May 10, 2007; *The Asian-American Market in the U.S.* (Rockville, MD: Packaged Facts, October 2008).

66. "90 Percent of Asian Americans Go Online."

67. M. C. Tharp, *Marketing and Consumer Identity in Multicultural America* (Thousand Oaks, CA: Sage, 2001), p. 259.

68. Ibid., pp. 253–57.

69. G. Lopez, N. Ruiz, and E. Patten, "Key Facts About Asian Americans, a Diverse and Growing Population," *Pew Research Center,* September 8, 2017.

70. *The 1993 Minority Market Report* (Coral Gables, FL: Market Segment Research, 1993).

71. Lopez, Ruiz, and Patten, "Key Facts About Asian Americans, a Diverse and Growing Population."

72. "Asia Rising," *American Demographics,* July–August 2002, pp. 38–43.

73. G. Gao, "Biggest Share of Whites in U.S. Are Boomers, but for Minority Groups It's Millennials or Younger," *Pew Research Center,* July 7, 2016.

74. D. L. Vence, "Growth in Asian-Am. Spending Fuels Targeted Marketing," *Marketing News,* June 1, 2004, pp. 11–13.

75. "Reaching Generation 2.0," *Advertising Age,* July–August 2002, p. 42.

76. See, e.g., Y.-K. Kim and J. Kang, "Effects of Asian-Americans' Ethnicity and Acculturation on Personal Influences," *Journal of Current Issues and Research in Advertising,* Spring 2001, pp. 43–53.

77. Demographics, "Significant, Sophisticated and Savvy: The Profile of the Asian American Shopper," *Nielsen,* December 3, 2013, www.nielsen.com; Mintel, "The Asian Premium Brand and Luxury Consumer," November 2016, www.mintel.com, accessed February 28, 2018.

78. Information accessed from corporate websites.

79. "Annual Asian American Consumer Behavior Study Reveals Key Findings in Retail, Automobile, Insurance, and Telecom Industries," *Diversity Business,* March 7, 2007, www.diversitybusiness.com, accessed June 8, 2008; Nielsen Staff, *Significant, Sophisticated and Savvy: The Asian American Consumer 2013 Report* (New York: The Nielsen Company, 2013), p. 21.

80. F. Korzenny, "Multicultural Marketing and the Reasons Why," *Journal of Advertising Research,* June 2008, pp. 173–76.

81. *New Study Reveals Lifestyle Habits and Industry Specific Consumption Behavior among Asian Americans* (Long Beach, CA: interTrend Communications, November 2005).

82. Vence, "Growth in Asian-Am. Spending Fuels Targeted Marketing."

83. U.S. Census Bureau, "American Indian and Alaska Native Heritage Month: November 2016," *Profile America Facts for Features,* November 2016.

84. "Diversity in America," *American Demographics,* November 2002, p. S17.

85. L. F. Muller, P. H. Wilson, and L. Keup, "Three Attitudinal Factors of Native American Purchase Behavior: A Study of the Plains Indian Consumer of North Dakota," in *Minority Marketing: Research Perspectives for the 1990s;* Developments in Marketing Science: Proceedings of the 1993 Academy of Marketing Science, ed. R. L. King (New York: Springer, 2015), pp. 78–80.

86. Humphreys, *The Multicultural Economy 2013.*

87. U.S. Census Bureau, "American FactFinder: American Indian and Alaska Native by Selected Tribal Groupings," *2015 American Community Survey,* tabs. B02017, B02014, accessed February 28, 2018.

88. "Native American Food Goes Haute Cuisine," *CNN.com,* September 30, 2004, www.cnn.com; E. Deruy, "Why Isn't Native American Food Hip?," *Atlantic,* June 30, 2016, www.theatlantic.com; M. Judkis, " 'This Is Not a Trend': Native American Chefs Resist the 'Columbusing' of Indigenous Foods," *Washington Post,* November 22, 2017.

89. See A. S. Wellner, "Discovering Native America," *American Demographics,* August 2001, p. 21.

90. Information from website at www.indiansummer.org/, accessed March 1, 2018.

91. A. M. Peterson, "Nike Boosts Indians' Health, Its Reputation," *Marketing News,* June 1, 2004, p. 10; Indian Health Service, "IHS/Nike Sign Agreement to Promote Healthy Lifestyles," press release, 2014, www.ihs.gov, accessed March 1, 2018; C. Luger, "Business Meets Culture at Nike's Native American Network," *Indian Country Today,* February 1, 2016.

92. A. F. Campbell, "The Overlooked Consumer Group with Billions to Spend," *The Atlantic,* August 24, 2016, www.theatlantic.com.

93. This section is based on M. Mogelonsky, "Asian Indian Americans," *American Demographics,* August 1995, pp. 32–39. See also M. M. Cardona, "Segment Marketing Grows as Tool for Financial Services Leaders," *Advertising Age,* November 20, 2000, p. S1.

94. A. S. Wellner, "Every Day's a Holiday," *American Demographics,* December 2000, p. 63.

95. "Arab Americans" section is based on S. El-Badry, "The Arab-American Market," *American Demographics,* January 1994, pp. 22–30; L. P. Morton, "Segmenting to Target Arab Americans," *Public Relations Quarterly,* Winter 2001, pp. 47–48; Arab American Institute, "Survey Reveals Arab American Experiences and Reactions Following 9/11," press release, August 19, 2002; Arab American Institute, "Arab American Demographics," www.aaiusa.org/demographics.htm, accessed May 14, 2005; K. Naughton, "Arab-America's Store," *Newsweek,* March 10, 2008, p. 42; D. Sands, "Dearborn's Arab American Markets Offer a Diverse Taste of the Middle East," *Second Wave Media,* January 19, 2017, www.secondwavemedia.com, accessed March 2, 2018; Arab American Institute website, http://aaiusa.org, accessed March 2, 2018.

96. "2014 Religious Landscape Study," *Pew Research Center,* reports released May and November 2015, accessed March 2, 2018.

97. M. Lipka, "10 Facts About Religion in America," *Pew Research,* August 27, 2015, www.pewresearch.org, accessed March 2, 2018.

98. See R. Cimino and D. Lattin, "Choosing My Religion," *American Demographics,* April 1999, pp. 60–65.

99. See Lipka, "10 Facts About Religion in America."

100. B. Ebenkamp, "The Young and Righteous," *Brandweek,* April 5, 2004, p. 18; S. Kang, "Pop Culture Gets Religion," *Wall Street Journal,* May 5, 2004, pp. B1, B2.

101. K. Wheaton, "Chick-fil-A for Sunday Lunch?," *Advertising Age,* July 12, 2010, p. 3.

102. Information on ethnic diversity from ARIS research briefs, www.gc.cuny.edu; "2014 Religious Landscape Study."

103. Information from website of The Archdiocese of Baltimore at www.archbalt.org/news, accessed May 7, 2011; update provided by B. McGill, "Catholicism in the U.S.," *Wall Street Journal,* September 18, 2015, www.wsj.com, accessed March 2, 2018.

104. Information on *Encuentro 2000* from press releases by the U.S. Conference of Catholic Bishops (Washington, DC), including "Growing Asian Impact on Church to Be Felt at *Encuentro 2000,*" May 22, 2000; "Latin Music, Movie on Cuba, Hispanic Cultural Expressions Part of *Encuento 2000* Celebration of Multiethnic Church," May 30, 2000; and "Bishops' Agenda Includes Pastoral Framework for Hispanic Ministry," October 11, 2002, www.usccb.org, website again accessed March 2, 2018.

105. B. A. Kosmin and P. Lachman, *One Nation under God* (New York: Harmony Books, 1993), p. 245.

106. "Breaking the Rules of Engagement," *American Demographics,* July–August 2002, p. 35.

107. R. Thau, "The New Jewish Exodus," *American Demographics,* June 1994, p. 11.

108. See company website at www.krispykreme.com/About/Nutritional-Info.

109. Kosmin and Lachman, *One Nation under God,* p. 12.

110. Estimates here have been hotly debated. For an excellent discussion, see "The Largest Religious Groups in the United States of America," *Adherents,* www.adherents.com. Current estimate provided by "2014 Religious Landscape Study."

111. M. Chapman and A. Jamal, "The Floodgates Open," *Enhancing Knowledge Development in Marketing* (Chicago: American Marketing Association, 1996), p. 198.

112. See S. El-Badry, "Understanding Islam in America," *American Demographics,* January 1994, p. 10.

113. Sinclair Broadcast Group, "Mosques Experiencing Growth in U.S.," *WJLA,* April 12, 2016, www.wjla.com, accessed March 2, 2018.

114. See "2014 Religious Landscape Study."

115. See company websites.

6

The American Society: Families and Households

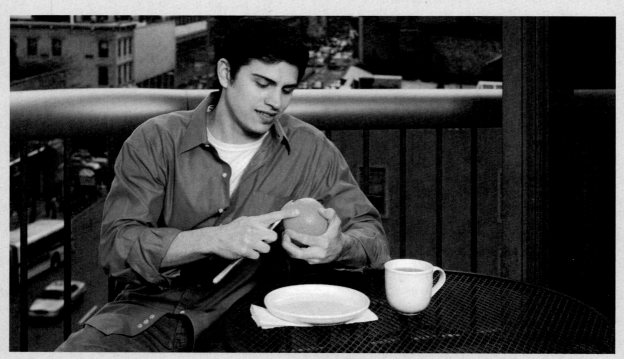

©Image Source/Alamy

LEARNING OBJECTIVES

LO1 Explain the concept of household types and their influence on consumption.

LO2 Summarize the household life cycle's various stages and marketing implications.

LO3 Understand the family decision process.

LO4 Describe the role that households play in child socialization.

LO5 Explain the sources of ethical concern associated with marketing to children.

Solo living is on the rise. According to the latest census figures, 27 percent of all households now consist of one person (a 10 percent increase from 1970). Approximately 32 million people live alone. At no other time in history have so many people opted to live alone. According to one expert, the extraordinary upsurge in solo living is the "greatest social change since the baby boom."[1]

Although delaying marriage, divorcing in greater numbers, and living longer as solitary widows or widowers are certainly part of the picture, there is an attitudinal component to it that cuts across age, social, and ethnic distinctions. Specifically, there is a growth in the number of people who *want* to live alone and can afford to do so. Single-person households are more common in metropolitan areas. Over 40 percent of households in San Francisco; Seattle; Minneapolis; Washington, D.C.; Atlanta; and Denver have one occupant. The rise of single-person households is also a global phenomenon, including countries such as France, Japan, Brazil, and China.

The market and marketing implications of single-person households is powerful. Single-person households (average annual discretionary expenditures of $34,471) have a total buying power of $1.9 trillion. They spend 49 percent more than the most affluent "families with children" households ($23,179) and 23 percent more than "married with no children" households ($28,017). From micro-apartments, to single-serving meals, to communal dining, to "solo travel packages" by cruise lines, marketers are adjusting. Indeed, real estate shortages in the metro areas where the "living single" phenomenon has taken hold are pushing the trend toward and development of small living spaces such as micro-apartments. New York City plans to build eighty 300-square-foot micro-apartments, renting at $2,000 a month. To do this, it first must change its current zoning law requiring apartments to be at least 400 square feet. Micro-apartments that are 220 square feet are already available in San Jose, California, a city in the heart of technology-heavy, hard-to-find-an-affordable-place-to-rent Silicon Valley. Nearby San Francisco will follow suit, having successfully enacted legislation to change its building code. Small-space dwellings, in turn, have sparked a need for space-saving, multipurpose furniture that retailers such as IKEA and Itsy Bitsy Ritzy Shop are filling.

The rise of single-person households is perhaps the most significant lifestyle trend in the last 50 years and will profoundly influence marketing and the design and delivery of products and service.

Single households, though important and growing, represent just one type of household. This chapter examines the nature and influence of households in American society, the household life cycle, the family decision process, consumer socialization, and marketing to children.

THE NATURE AND INFLUENCE OF AMERICAN HOUSEHOLDS

The Influence of Households

LO1

The household is the basic consumption unit for most consumer goods. Major items such as housing, automobiles, and appliances are consumed more by household units than by individuals. Furthermore, the consumption patterns of individual household members seldom are independent from those of other household members. For example, deciding to grant a child's request for a bicycle may mean spending discretionary funds that could have been used to purchase a weekend away for the parents or new clothing for a sister or brother, or otherwise used by another member of the household. Therefore, it is essential that marketers understand the household as a consumption unit, as shown in Figure 6–1.

Households are important not only for their direct role in the consumption process but also for the critical role they perform in socializing children. The family household is the

FIGURE 6-1 The Household Influences Most Consumption Decisions

Family and Nonfamily Households

TABLE 6-1

Type of Household	Number (000)	Percentage
All households	**126,224**	**100.0%**
Family households	**82,827**	**65.6**
Married couples	60,804	48.2
Children under 18 at home	*23,651*	*18.7*
No children under 18 at home	*37,153*	*29.4*
Male householder (children under 18 at home)	2,395	1.9
Female householder (children under 18 at home)	8,246	6.5
Other families	11,382	9.0
Nonfamily households	**43,396**	**34.4**
Male householder	20,539	16.3
Living alone	*15,764*	*12.5*
Female householder	22,858	18.1
Living alone	*19,488*	*15.4*

Source: *America's Families and Living Arrangements: 2017*, U.S. Census Bureau, Tables H1, F1 and AVG1.

primary mechanism whereby cultural and subcultural values and behavior patterns are passed on to the next generation. Purchasing and consumption patterns are among those attitudes and skills strongly influenced by the family household unit.

Types of Households

There are a variety of types of households. The U.S. Census Bureau defines a **household** as *all the people who occupy a housing unit* (a house, apartment, group of rooms, or single room designed to be occupied as separate living quarters). It defines a **family household** as one having *at least two members related by birth, marriage, or adoption, one of whom is the house-holder* (a householder owns or rents the residence). A **nonfamily household** is a *householder living alone or exclusively with others to whom he or she is not related.* Table 6-1 indicates the current distribution of household types in the United States.[2]

Historically, the family household—and, in particular, the traditional family household—has been an important focus for marketers. The term **traditional family** is typically used to refer to *a married opposite-sex couple and their own or adopted children living at home.* However, this type of family has clearly declined over time, particularly if one considers a traditional family to be one headed by a never-divorced couple. Today, less than 20 percent of all households are married couples with children living at home, down from 40 percent in 1970.[3] Some of this decline is due to the increase in *single-parent households.* Much of the decline is due to an increase in the number of *single-person households,* which is a function of (a) young people pushing back marriage until their late 20s (rather than getting married in their early 20s as they did in 1970) and (b) the increase in sole survivors as our population ages. Consumer Insight 6-1 discusses the changing family structure in the United States.

As discussed in Consumer Insight 6-1, step, or blended, families are also important and growing. The U.S. Census Bureau defines a **step family** as *a married-couple family household with at least one child under the age of 18 who is a stepchild (i.e., a son or daughter through marriage).* High divorce and remarriage rates mean that a substantial number of American children grow up with stepparents and stepsiblings and often have two such families,

The Evolving American Household

Decades ago, the typical American family structure was fairly straightforward. It usually consisted of a household made up of two parents in their first marriage and multiple children. This is no longer the case. American households are both shrinking and evolving. Americans are having fewer children and the conditions for having children are changing. The table below illustrates some of the shifts in family structure over time, and no household arrangement currently crosses a 50 percent threshold.[4]

Shifting American Households with Children			
	1960	1980	2014
Two parents in a first marriage	73%	64%	46%
Two parents in a remarriage	14	16	15
Cohabiting parents*	–	–	7
Single parent	9	19	26
No parent	4	4	5

*Unmarried couples living together.

The table highlights the:

- **Rise of single-parent families:** Single-parent households have significantly increased over time. The most common composition of single-parent households consists of children living with the mother.
- **Rise in cohabitation with children involved:** In recent years, cohabiting parent households have become a significant category. Sometimes the mother has never been married and enters a cohabiting relationship, while other times the mother enters a cohabiting relationship after a divorce. In any case, current estimates are that 39 percent of children by the age of 12 and 46 percent of children by the age of 16 have experience with a cohabiting mother.

These trends may be more pronounced for some ethnic groups than others, as shown in the table below. Single-parent families in black households outpace the overall American average, and the percent of cohabiting parents in Hispanic households exceeds that of the overall average. The family structure of two parents in their first marriage is still quite evident in Asian households (71 percent). As pointed out in Chapter 5, the large differences in household structure across ethnic subculture seem likely to be a function, at least in part, of the underlying differences in demographic factors such as income and education.

Ethnic Breakdown of Households with Children (in 2014)				
	Asian	White	Hispanic	Black
Two parents in a first marriage	71%	52%	43%	22%
Two parents in a remarriage	11	19	12	9
Cohabiting parents	3	6	11	7
Single parent	13	19	29	54
No parent	2	4	5	8

one formed by their mother and the other by their father. One study finds that half of all young adults have at least one step relative.[5] Creating and revising relationship identities is critical and difficult and can revolve around consumption activities. Consider the following quote about the challenges of step relationships:

> When mom and dad got divorced and mom remarried, everything changed. We, my father and I, had to find a way to create a sense of who we are without mom. We found that a passion for adventure is something we share, that mom and my sister don't, and we took up scuba diving. Although my stepdad is certainly a part of our family, my mom, sister, and I are a different "we" with many different stories to tell and a distinct history of sharing experiences.[6]

Other insights about American family structure shifts are as follows:

- **Blended families are on the rise:** Many households include children from previous relationships, or blended families. In fact, 63 percent of remarried women are in blended families with nearly half with stepchildren living in the same household. Asian children are least likely to be living in blended families (7 percent), compared with white, black, and Hispanic children (17, 15, and 15 percent, respectively).
- **Family size is shrinking:** Families also are having fewer children. In the mid-1970s, 40 percent of mothers had four or more children, compared with only 14 percent in recent times. Again, there are differences among the ethnic groups. Near the end of their child-bearing years, Hispanics (50 percent) and blacks (40 percent) are more likely to have three or more children than are whites and Asians (both 27 percent).
- **Multipartner fertility is increasing:** Of women near the end of their child-bearing years, currently 28 percent have had biological children with more than one partner, either outside or within marriages.
- **Mothers' demographics are shifting:** Since 1970, the average age of a new first-time mother has risen from 21 years old to 26 years old. This shift is largely due to a decrease in teen births

to about 7 percent from 13 percent in 1990. In addition, mothers are much better educated than in the past. Today, 67 percent of women with infants have some college, compared to 18 percent in 1960.

- **Mothers are moving into the workforce:** Increasing numbers of mothers are entering the workforce. For example, the data have been recorded only since 1975, when 47 percent of mothers with children under 18 were in the workforce, compared to 70 percent in 2014.
- **Mothers are breadwinners:** In 1960, 11 percent of families with children had a mother who was the primary income provider. By 2000, that number had risen to 34 percent and most recently has risen to 40 percent. About 37 percent of those breadwinning mothers are married and making more than their husbands, while the other 63 percent are unmarried mother households.

Critical Thinking Questions

1. What are some possible reasons for the dropping average number of children in households today?
2. Multipartner fertility is increasing. What are some reasons that you suppose could be driving this shift?
3. What new challenges might marketing managers face in targeting various types of consumer households today versus several years ago?

Recognizing the difficult dynamics of step family relationships, Café Press offers cards, T-shirts, mugs, and other products that celebrate step families. One card reads, "It's Love Not Blood That Makes a Forever Family."

In addition, while the U.S. Census Bureau defines a family in terms of marriage, birth, or adoption, many unmarried couples clearly view themselves as families. There are roughly 6.2 million *unmarried-partner* (opposite and same-sex) households in the United States. In many ways, their needs are the same as those of married couples with similar demographics. However, there are exceptions, such as finding knowledgeable assistance with legal and financial issues concerning joint home ownership, estate planning, and so forth. While same-sex couples can be targeted via specialized media (see Chapter 3), opposite-sex couples can be more difficult to reach because targeted media are lacking.

Clearly, as American households and families evolve away from the traditional family model, marketers must adapt. As discussed in Chapter 4, multigenerational families have

This Campbell's Soup ad is attempting to appeal to the needs of different family members and the different household types in which they reside.

Source: CSC Brands, L.P.

generated a need for specialized housing to accommodate this type of household. In addition, Kraft recognizes the diversity and importance of families, with ads that portray various family types in scenarios revolving around food. A recent spot features a father and his daughter enjoying a quiet conversation.

Recognizing and adapting to the differing needs of various types of families or the different needs of members within the same family can be a critical success factor. *How well does Campbell's "One Soup Fits All" campaign (see Illustration 6-1) meet the differing needs of today's diverse household?*

THE HOUSEHOLD LIFE CYCLE

The traditional view of the American household life cycle was quite simple. People married by their early 20s; they had several children;

LO2

these children grew up and started their own families; the original couple retired; and the male eventually would die, followed after a few years by the female. This was known as the *family life cycle,* and it was a useful tool for segmenting markets and developing marketing strategy. The basic assumption underlying the family-life-cycle approach is that most families pass through an orderly progression of stages, each with its own characteristics, financial situations, and purchasing patterns.

However, as described earlier, American households follow much more complex and varied cycles today. Therefore, researchers have developed several models of the **household life cycle (HLC)**.[7] All are based on the age and marital status of the adult members of the household and the presence and age of children. A useful version is shown in Figure 6–2.

The HLC assumes that households move into a variety of relatively distinct and well-defined categories over time. There are a variety of routes into most of the categories shown in Figure 6–2, and movement from one category into another frequently occurs. For example, it is common for singles to marry and then divorce within a few years without having children (moving from single to young married back to young single). Or one can become a single parent through divorce or through birth or adoption without a cohabiting partner.

Each category in the household life cycle poses a set of problems that household decision makers must solve. The solution to these problems is bound intimately to the selection and maintenance of a lifestyle and, thus, to consumption. For example, all young couples with no children face a need for relaxation or recreation. Solutions to this common problem differ, with some opting for an outdoors-oriented lifestyle and others choosing a sophisticated urban lifestyle. As these families move into another stage in the HLC, such as the "full nest I" stage, the challenges they face change. The amount of time and resources available for recreation usually diminish. New issues related to raising a child become more urgent.

Stages of Household Life Cycle   FIGURE 6-2

Stage	Marital Status		Children at Home		
	Single	Married	None	<6 years	>6 years
Younger (<35)					
Single I	×		×		
Young married		×	×		
Full nest I		×		×	
Single parent I	×			×	
Middle-aged (35–64)					
Single II	×		×		
Delayed full nest I		×		×	
Full nest II		×			×
Single parent II	×				×
Empty nest I		×	×		
Older (>64)					
Empty nest II		×	×		
Single III	×		×		

Each stage presents unique needs and wants as well as financial conditions and experiences. Thus, the HLC provides marketers with relatively homogeneous household segments that share similar needs with respect to household-related problems and purchases, as discussed in Consumer Insight 6–2.

While Figure 6–2 categorizes households into married and unmarried, it is "coupleness" rather than the legal status of the relationship that drives most of the behavior of the household. Committed couples, of the same sex or of opposite sexes, tend to exhibit most of the category-specific behaviors described below whether or not they are married.

Single I   This group consists of young (ages 18 to 34), unmarried individuals.[8] There are roughly 73 million people in this age group, with 70 percent unmarried. Of those, 74 percent of men and 66 percent of women are single. Single I is basically the unmarried members of the Generation Yers, as described in Chapter 4. The aging of the larger Generation Y cohort along with continued delay of marriage has fueled growth in this market.[9] During this time, individuals generally leave home and establish their own distinct identities. It is a time of growth and change, both exciting and positive, and frightening and painful.

This group can be subdivided into those who live with one or both parents and those who live alone or with other individuals. The roughly 53 million single individuals in this age range live as follows:

	Males (%)	Females (%)	Total (%)
Live alone	12	11	11
Live with parent(s)	45	39	42
Live with others	43	50	47

Consumer Life Cycles and Homeowner Remodeling Decisions

Consumers and households move through somewhat predictable phases.[10] As they do so, changes occur in consumption based on these shifts in household characteristics and needs and wants. Housing, of course, is needed at all the household life stages, and a relationship between the type of housing and the consumers' household life stage exists. Consumers who are single and entering the workforce are more likely to rent than own. And while home ownership is an aspiration and reality for many Americans, the challenges associated with changes in the household life cycle can generate the need to either move or remodel. Renovations are costly and can lead to unexpected and hidden costs. Two factors play into renovation decisions:

- Family (and friends) are the single most influential factors in renovation decisions.
- Household life-cycle stage changes can trigger the need for home renovations.

A recent article shows that movements across stages (e.g., from no children to children, from children to no children) can generate the need to renovate and remodel. Some of the mechanisms are as follows:

Prioritizing—Do households balance competing and, at times, conflicting commitments in how they manage and use space at home?

Embodying—Do household members have particular physical needs, either currently or in the anticipated future, that might affect how the home is arranged?

Adapting—Are households aware of a need to adapt the physical arrangement or material surroundings of their homes?

Clearly these mechanisms can be triggered by a number of factors, but household life-cycle stage and stage changes will have a major (if not *the* major) influence.

An interesting corollary effect involved in remodeling is called the Diderot effect, which, in effect, means that one change leads to a cascade of other needed or desired changes. The following quote illustrates this effect:

I think of my parents, who a year ago remodeled a powder room and redecorated the living room. That work served to highlight the age of the rest of the home, and they have since replaced the garage door and redecorated the guest room, and are now in the process of planning to remodel the kitchen and master bath, finish the basement and redecorate another bedroom. They are neither materialistic nor extravagant, but they want the house to look nice—to be updated and well maintained.

The Diderot effect is a warning to consumers of the hidden costs subsequent to the remodeling, upgrading, and replacement of goods. To the remodeler, the Diderot effect is a promise of possible repeat business from current customers who find, to their surprise, the need for additional remodeling and serves as a reminder to provide quality work.

Critical Thinking Questions

1. Why might the Diderot effect be of interest to marketers?

2. Choose two phases of the household life cycle and describe how one of the mechanisms might be involved in triggering a need for home remodeling.

3. What decision barriers must marketers overcome if consumers are aware of the Diderot effect?

Those who live with parents tend to be younger, with 59 percent being under 25. A significant number are in school or have recently graduated from high school or college and are beginning their working careers. Though people in this group have lower relative incomes, they also have few fixed expenses. They lead active, social lives. They go to bars, movies, and concerts, and purchase sports equipment, clothes, and personal care items.

Although some of those who live with others are involved with a partner, many share quarters with one or more housemates. These individuals have more fixed living expenses than do those who live with their parents, but they generally have ample disposable income as they share rent and other fixed housing costs.

These singles are a good market for the same types of products as those who live at home as well as for convenience-oriented household products. They are also a prime market for nice apartments, sports cars, clothing, travel, and similar activities. They are beginning to develop financial portfolios such as life insurance, savings, and stocks or mutual funds. The Levi's ad shown in Illustration 6–2 would appeal to both groups.

Source: Levi Strauss & Co.

ILLUSTRATION 6-2

Young singles are active and often have significant discretionary income. They are an excellent market for a wide array of recreational and leisure items. This Levi's ad would appeal to their desire for action and romance.

Singles who live alone or with others (not parents) are older, with 75 percent being over 25. In general, they have higher incomes than the others but also higher expenses because they have no one with whom to share the fixed cost of a house or apartment. They are a good market for most of the same products and services as the other singles.

Young Married: No Children   The decision to marry, or to live together, brings about a new stage in the household life cycle. Marriage is much more likely for the 25- to 34-year-olds (45 percent) than it is for the under-25 crowd (9 percent). The lifestyles of two young singles are greatly altered as they develop a shared lifestyle. Joint decisions and shared roles in household responsibilities are in many instances new experiences.[11] Savings, household furnishings, major appliances, and more comprehensive insurance coverage are among the new areas of problem recognition and decision making to which a young married couple must give serious consideration. Like the young single stage, the time spent by a young couple in this stage of the HLC has grown as couples either delay their start in having children or choose to remain childless.

Most households in this group have dual incomes and thus are relatively affluent. Compared with full nest I families, this group spends heavily on theater tickets, expensive clothes, luxury vacations, restaurant meals, and alcoholic beverages. They can afford nice cars, stylish apartments, and high-quality home appliances.

The Sandals site in Illustration 6–3 would appeal to this group as well as to some members of the single I and full nest I segments. Note that romance plays a major role in the ad. It also plays on the desire to escape worries and everyday responsibilities.

Sandals Resort is positioned as ideal for couples to escape the pressure of a hectic work schedule for relaxation and romance.

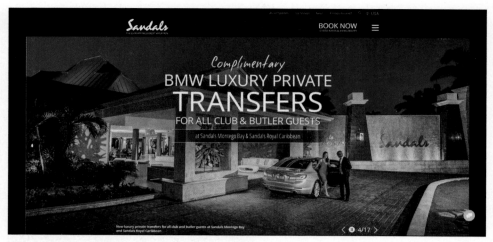

Source: Sandals Resorts

Full Nest I: Young Married with Children   Roughly 7 percent of households are young married couples with children. The addition of the first child to a family creates many changes in lifestyle and consumption. Naturally, new purchases in the areas of baby clothes, furniture, food, and health care products occur in this stage. Lifestyles are also greatly altered. The wife may withdraw fully or partly from the labor force (in roughly 60 percent of married couples with a child under three, the wife works outside the home)[12] for several months to several years, with a resulting decline in household income. The couple may have to move to another place of residence because their current apartment may not be appropriate for children. Likewise, choices of vacations, restaurants, and automobiles must be changed to accommodate young children.

Some of the changes in income and annual expenditures that occur as a household moves from childless to the young child stage in their late 20s and early 30s include the following:[13]

Expenditure	Percentage Change
Income	−9.4%
Food at home	24.3
Meals out	−9.6
Alcoholic beverages	−25.0
Adult apparel	−8.3
Children's apparel	215.7
Health care	16.1
Education	−28.8
Personal care products	−2.6

As shown above, discretionary and adult expenditures are reduced by the need to spend on child-related products such as food, health care, and children's apparel as well as to offset the decline in income. Furthermore, married couples can expect to pay almost an additional $400 a year in overall expenses per child.[14]

Obtaining competent child care becomes an issue at this stage and remains a major concern of parents at all HLC stages. Households with a stay-at-home spouse confront this issue mainly for evenings out or weekends away. Single-parent and dual-earner households generally require daily child care, which is expensive and often requires parents to make trade-offs from their ideal situation.

Moms across the HLC possess $2.4 trillion in spending power and make 85 percent of purchases in the household.[15] These women strive to find a balance between household responsibilities and enjoying time with their children, which can lead to eating meals in the car or having snacks instead of meals. Examples of companies going after moms in full nest I are given below.[16]

- Red Baron frozen pizza, in order to connect with this market, introduced a new character, the Baroness, who "embraces the messiness and chaos of motherhood."
- Dove launched its new baby line of soaps and shampoos using the campaign #RealMoms to highlight that there are "no perfect moms only real ones."

The Red Baron ad in Illustration 6–4 highlights the unique challenges facing the moms in full nest I.

Single Parent I: Young Single Parents   Birth or adoption by singles is increasingly common. Roughly 40 percent of children are born to unmarried mothers, a number that has risen by 13 percentage points since 1990. However, as many as 40 percent of these children actually may be born to cohabiting unmarried parents.[17] Divorce, while on the decline since 1980, continues to be a significant part of American society, with 44 percent of first marriages ending in divorce.[18] Most divorced individuals remarry and most women who bear children out of wedlock eventually get married. Yet, 27 percent of children under 18 live with one parent, and of those, 84 percent live with their mother.

The younger members of this group, particularly those who have never been married, tend to have a limited education and a very low income. These individuals are often members of one of the lower social classes, as described in Chapter 4. The older members of this segment and the divorced members receiving support from their ex-spouses are somewhat better off financially, but most are still under significant stress as they raise their young children without the support of a partner who is physically present.

This type of family situation creates many unique needs in the areas of child care, easy-to-prepare foods, and recreation. The need to work and raise younger children creates enormous time pressures and places tremendous demands on the energy of these parents. Most are renters and so are not a major market for home appliances and improvements. Their purchases focus on getting by, and on time- and energy-saving products and services that are not overly expensive.

Single II: Middle-Aged Single   The middle-aged single category is made up of people who have never married and those who are divorced and have no child-rearing responsibilities.

Source: Red Baron Pizza

ILLUSTRATION 6-4

Parenthood brings both great pleasures and great responsibilities. Red Baron's Baroness provides the mealtime solution to this trade-off.

These individuals are in the 35-to-64 age category, which is primarily the Generation X and baby boomers (Chapter 4), although older Generation Y consumers are moving into this category as well.

Middle-aged singles often live alone. In fact, living alone is increasingly viewed as a lifestyle choice that many are willing and able to make, given higher incomes. Middle-aged singles who live alone represented over 15 million households, which is about 44 percent of all single-person households. Middle-aged singles have higher incomes than young singles. However, all live-alone singles suffer from a lack of scale economies. That is, a couple or family needs only one dishwasher, clothes dryer, and so forth for everyone in the household, but the single-person household needs the same basic household infrastructure even though only one person uses it. Likewise, many foods and other items come in sizes inappropriate for singles, or the small sizes are disproportionately expensive. Thus, opportunities appear to exist to fill unmet needs among this important and growing market.[19]

The needs of middle-aged singles in many ways reflect those of young singles. But middle-aged singles are likely to have more money to spend on their lifestyles and are willing to indulge themselves. Thus, they may live in nice condominiums, frequent expensive restaurants, own a luxury automobile, and travel often. They are a major market for gifts, and the males buy significant amounts of jewelry as gifts.

Empty Nest I: Middle-Aged Married with No Children   Lifestyle changes in the 1980s and 1990s influenced many young couples to not have children.[20] In other cases, these households represent second marriages in which children from a first marriage are not living with the parent. This group also includes married couples whose children have left home. These three forces have produced a huge market consisting of middle-aged couples without children at home. Over 50 percent of married couples in this age group (35 to 64) don't have children under the age of 18. This segment has grown as baby boomers have moved through the latter stages of middle age and into retirement.

Both adults typically will have jobs, so they are very busy. However, the absence of responsibilities for children creates more free time than they have enjoyed since their youth.

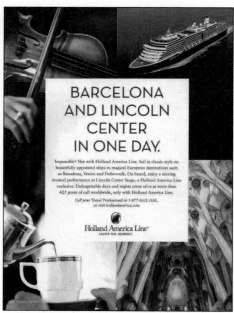

Source: Holland America Line

They also have money to spend on dining out, expensive vacations, second homes, luxury cars, and time-saving services such as housecleaning, laundry, and shopping. They are a prime market for financial services. Less obvious, they are also heavy purchasers of upscale children's products, as gifts for nieces, nephews, grandchildren, and friends' children.

The Holland America ad and product offering in Illustration 6–5 would appeal to this group.

Delayed Full Nest I: Older Married with Young Children   Many members of the baby boom generation and Generation X delayed having their first child until they were in their mid-30s. This produced the new phenomenon of a large number of middle-aged, established families entering into parenthood for the first time. Recall from Table 6–1 that married couples with children under 18 make up 18.7 percent of all households. And young married couples with children make up only 7 percent of all households. However, middle-aged (35 to 64) married couples with children (both delayed full nest I and full nest II) make up close to 15 percent of all households and represent 75 percent of all married couples with children under 18.

A major difference between delayed full nest I and younger new parents is income. Older new parents' incomes are significantly larger than those of younger new parents. They have had this income flow longer and so have acquired more capital and possessions. They spend heavily on child care, mortgage payments, home maintenance, lawn care, and household furnishings. In addition, they want only the best for their children and are willing and able to spend on them. For example, the specialty diaper and toiletries market is expected to have double-digit growth. And traditional mass marketers such as Kimberly-Clark are pushing high-end products like "pull-up" diapers with glow-in-the-dark animated characters.[21] In addition, delayed full nest I also can spend more on nonchild expenditures such as food, alcohol, and entertainment, and can make more savings and retirement contributions than can younger new parents.

Full Nest II: Middle-Aged Married with Children at Home   A major difference between this group and delayed full nest I is age of the children. The children of full nest II are generally six years and older and are becoming more independent. The presence of older children creates unique consumption needs, however. Families with children six and older are the primary consumers of lessons of all types (piano, dance, gymnastics, and so on), dental care, soft drinks, presweetened cereals, and a wide variety of snack foods.

Greater demands for space create a need for larger homes and cars. Transporting children to multiple events places time demands on the parents and increases transportation-related expenditures. These factors, coupled with heavy demand for clothing and an increased need to save for college, create a considerable financial burden on households in this stage of the HLC. This is offset somewhat by the tendency of the wife to return to work as the children enter school. This return to work usually entails greater time pressures. Meal-kit delivery programs, like Plated, have found great success tapping parents' desire to simplify mealtime with their meals delivered to the door, which have all the needed ingredients for an easy-to-prepare dinner ready to eat in the evening with minimal hassle.[22]

As we saw in Chapter 4, the teenage members (the older part of Generation Z) in these households, as well as teens in the single parent II segment, are important consumers in their own right as well as important influencers on household consumption decisions.

Single Parent II: Middle-Aged Single with Children at Home   Single individuals in the 35-to-64 age group who have children often are faced with serious financial pressures. The same demands that are placed on the middle-aged married couple with children are present in the life of a middle-aged single with children. However, the single parent often lacks some or all of the financial, emotional, and time support that the presence of a spouse generally provides. Many individuals in this position are thus inclined to use time-saving alternatives such as ready-to-eat food, and they are likely to eat at fast-food restaurants. The children of this segment are given extensive household responsibilities.

It is important to note that becoming a single parent (through adoption or conception) is increasingly viewed as a lifestyle choice for older, more financially secure women who may or may not plan to marry in the future. Single Mothers by Choice is an organization that recognizes this and offers support and assistance. According to the organization, single women by choice are well-educated, career-oriented women in their 30s and 40s. As a consequence, they often have higher income and financial security than many single parents.[23]

As consumers mature, their financial situation, free time, and physical and social needs change. This hayneedle.com ad would appeal to active members of the Empty Nest II segment.

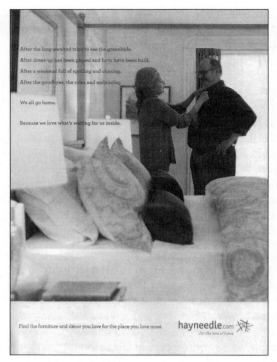

Source: Hayneedle Inc.

Empty Nest II: Older Married Couples

There are about 15 million households in this segment, and it is expected to grow rapidly over the next 10 years as baby boomers age. Many couples in the over-64 age group are either fully or partially retired. However, as we discussed in Chapter 4, improvements in health care and longevity, desire to stay active, and changes in Social Security likely will push retirement age upward over the decades to come. The younger members of this group are healthy, active, and often financially well-off. They have ample time. They are a big market for RVs, cruises, and second homes. They also spend considerable time and money on grandchildren. Increasingly, they take their grandchildren and occasionally their children on vacations. As described in Chapter 4, as they advance in age, health care and assisted living become more important. At this stage and the next, distribution of valued family assets such as family heirlooms, property, and money also becomes important.[24] Illustration 6–6 shows an ad for hayneedle.com that is designed to meet one of this segment's needs.

Single III: Older Single   There are around 20 million older singles in the United States, and this group will continue to grow as baby boomers age. Approximately 71 percent of all older singles are female, and roughly two-thirds of all older singles live alone. The conditions of being older, single, and generally retired create many unique needs for housing, socialization, travel, and recreation. Many financial firms have set up special programs to work with these individuals. They often have experienced a spouse's death and now are taking on many of the financial responsibilities once handled by the other person. A recent study labeled consumers who were single as the result of the death of a spouse as "single by circumstance" rather than single by choice. Many older singles would fall into the single by circumstance category. Results of the research suggest that older singles who are single by circumstance will be less innovative, more risk averse, more price sensitive, and more likely to engage in coping behaviors, such as spending more time watching television, than their single by choice counterparts.[25] *What are the social and ethical issues involved in marketing to older consumers who are single by circumstance?*

MARKETING STRATEGY BASED ON THE HOUSEHOLD LIFE CYCLE

The HLC is an important segmentation tool given its relation to differences in the needs, wants, constraints, and consumption patterns that are unique to each stage. However, because individuals within each stage may vary on a host of other important factors such as education or income, the HLC becomes more powerful in terms of market segmentation and strategy formulation when it is combined with these factors.

For example, think of how the need for vacations differs as one moves across the stages of the household life cycle. Young singles often desire vacations focused on activities, adventure, and the chance for romance. Young married couples without children would have similar needs but without the desire to meet potential romantic partners. Full nest I and single parent I families need vacations that allow both parents and young children to enjoy themselves. The manner in which these needs will be met will vary sharply across occupational, income, and educational categories. For example, a young professional couple may vacation in Paris or at a resort in the Caribbean. A middle-class couple may visit a domestic ski resort or visit Hawaii on a package deal. A young working-class couple may visit family or go camping.

Table 6–2 presents the **HLC/occupational category matrix.** The vertical axis is the particular stage in the HLC, which determines the problems the household will likely encounter; the horizontal axis is a set of occupational categories, which provide a range of acceptable solutions. This version has been found to be useful across a range of products in segmenting the market and developing appropriate marketing strategies for targeted segments (variables other than or in addition to occupation should be used when appropriate).

An effective use of the matrix is to isolate an activity or problem of interest to the firm, such as preparing the evening meal or providing nutritious snacks, scheduling weekend recreation, or planning a summer vacation. Research, often in the form of focus group interviews, is used to determine the following information for each relevant cell in the matrix:

1. What products or services are now being used to meet the need or perform the activity?
2. What, if any, symbolic or social meaning is associated with meeting the need or using the current products?
3. Exactly how are the current products or services being used?
4. How satisfied are the segment members with the current solutions, and what improvements are desired?

HLC/Occupational Category Matrix					TABLE 6-2
	Occupational Category				
HLC Stage	Executive/Elite Professional	Administrative/ Professional	Technical/Sales/ Clerical	Service/Trade/ Craft	Unskilled/ Manual
Single I					
Young married					
Full nest I					
Single parent I					
Single II					
Delayed full nest I					
Full nest II					
Single parent II					
Empty nest I					
Empty nest II					
Single III					

Attractive segments are those that are large enough to meet the firm's objectives and that have needs that current products are not fully satisfying. This approach has been used successfully for movies, regional bakeries, and financial services.[26] *What type of automobile would be best suited for each cell, and what type of ad should promote it?*

FAMILY DECISION MAKING

LO3

Family decision making is *the process by which decisions that directly or indirectly involve two or more family members are made.* Decision making by a group such as a family differs in many ways from decisions made by an individual. Consider the purchase of a breakfast cereal that children, and perhaps the adults, will consume. Who recognizes the need for the product? How are the type and brand selected? Does everyone consider the same attributes? A parent typically makes the actual *purchase;* does that mean that the parent also makes the *choice?* Or is the choice made by the children, the other parent, or some combination? Which parents are involved, and how does this change across products and over time? How does it differ by stage in the HLC?

Family purchases often are compared with organizational buying decisions. Although this comparison can produce useful insights, it fails to capture the essence of family decision making. Organizations have relatively objective criteria, such as profit maximization, that guide purchases. Families generally lack such explicit, overarching goals. Most industrial purchases are made by strangers or have little impact on those not involved in the purchase. Most family purchases directly affect the other members of the family.

Most important, *many family purchases are inherently emotional and affect the relationships between the family members.*[27] The decision to buy a child a requested toy or new school clothes is more than simply an acquisition. It is a symbol of love and commitment to the child. The decision to take the family to a restaurant for a meal or to purchase a new television has emotional meaning to the other family members. Disagreements about how to spend money are a major cause of marital discord. The processes families use to make purchase decisions and the outcomes of those processes have important effects on the well-being of the individual family members and the family itself. Thus, while family decision making has some things in common with organizational decision making, it is not the same.

The Nature of Family Purchase Roles

Figure 6–3 illustrates the six roles that frequently occur in family decision making, using a cereal purchase as an example.[28] It is important to note that individuals will play various roles for different decisions.

- *Initiator(s).* The family member who first recognizes a need or starts the purchase process.
- *Information gatherer(s).* The individual who has expertise and interest in a particular purchase. Different individuals may seek information at different times or on different aspects of the purchase.
- *Influencer(s).* The person who influences the alternatives evaluated, the criteria considered, and the final choice.
- *Decision maker(s).* The individual who makes the final decision. Of course, joint decisions also are likely to occur.
- *Purchaser(s).* The family member who actually purchases the product. This is typically an adult or a teenager.
- *User(s).* The user of the product. For many products there are multiple users.

The Household Decision-Making Process for Children's Products   **FIGURE** 6-3

Marketers must determine who in the family plays which role. Crayola shifted its advertising budget from children's television to women's magazines because its research revealed that mothers rather than children were more likely to recognize the problem, evaluate alternatives, and make the purchase. Kraft Lunchables, as shown in Illustration 6–7, is a product designed for use by children that is selected by both the children and the parents and purchased by the parents.

Family decision making has been categorized as *husband-dominant, wife-dominant, joint,* or *individualized.* A moment's reflection will reveal that the above four categories omit critical participants in many family decisions. Until recently, most studies have ignored the influence of children.[29] Yet children, particularly teenagers, often exert a substantial influence on family purchase decisions.[30] Thus, we need to recognize that *child-dominant* and various combinations of *husband, wife,* and *child joint decisions* are also common.

Husband-dominant decisions traditionally have occurred with the purchase of such products as automobiles, liquor, and life insurance. Wife-dominant decisions were more common in the purchase of household maintenance items, food, and kitchen appliances. Joint decisions were most likely when buying a house, living room furniture, and vacations. These patterns are much less pronounced today. As women's occupational roles have expanded, so has the range of family decisions in which they participate or dominate.[31] In fact, recent research suggests that the balance

Source: Kraft Foods, H.J. Heinz Company Brands LLC

ILLUSTRATION 6-7

Children often determine the products and brands they use. At other times, they influence these choices, but parents play the dominant role. In such cases, as with Kraft Lunchables, the marketer must meet the needs of both the child and the parents.

has tipped away from husband-dominant decisions even for traditionally male-dominated categories. Interestingly, more and more women feel that they solely make the decisions in a household, whereas men think that the decisions are shared.[32] Across a set of four categories, results are shown in the following table:[33]

	Family Weekend Activities	Large Household Purchases	Household Finances	TV Remote Control
Wife	28%	30%	38%	27%
Husband	16	19	30	26
Share	48	46	28	25

*Numbers don't add to 100 because couples could opt for "don't know" or "it depends" responses.

It is also important to recognize both direct and indirect influences. Parents might choose a Disney vacation without directly consulting their young children, but clearly would be influenced by their perceptions of the children's desires. Different family members often become involved at different stages of the decision process. For example, a child might be the primary initiator of a decision to go to McDonald's, while the parents might be more involved in the timing of that trip and most likely make the purchase itself. Finally, different family members often focus on different attributes. For example, a child may evaluate the color and style of a bicycle while one or both parents evaluate price, warranty, and safety features.

Determinants of Family Purchase Roles

How family members interact in a purchase decision is largely dependent on the *culture and subculture* in which the family exists, the *role specialization* of different family members, the degree of *involvement* each has in the product area of concern, and the *personal characteristics* of the family members.[34]

Today, America has less of a masculine orientation than many other cultures. As one would expect, wives are more involved in a wider range of decisions in the United States than they are in cultures with a more masculine focus.[35] However, subcultures and other groups in the United States vary on this value. As we saw in Chapter 5, the Hispanic subculture tends to be more of a masculine orientation than the broader culture. Research indicates that Hispanics who identify strongly with the Hispanic culture tend to make more husband-dominant decisions than do others.

Over time, each spouse develops more specialized roles as a part of the family lifestyle and family responsibilities. Whether the roles that are adopted are traditional or modern, role specialization still tends to evolve over time because it is much more efficient.

Involvement or expertise in a product area is another major factor that affects how a family purchase decision will be made. Naturally, the more involved a spouse or other family member is with a product area, the more influence this person will have. For example, when children are the primary users of a product (e.g., toys, snacks, breakfast cereal), they tend to have more influence. Teenagers who are involved with computers often strongly influence the decision for a family computer or the choice of an Internet service provider.[36]

Several personal characteristics have an effect on the influence individuals will have on purchase decisions.[37] Education and income are two such personal characteristics. The higher a wife's education and income, the more she will participate in or dominate major decisions.[38] Figure 6–4 shows that when a husband earns more than his wife, major

Decision-Making Influence and Relative Income

FIGURE 6-4

Husband earns more

Share 28%
Wife 36%
Husband 35%

Wife earns more

Share 33%
Wife 46%
Husband 21%

*1 Percent indicated "don't know."

Source: *Women, Men, and the New Economics of Marriage* (Washington, DC: Pew Research Center, January 2010).

household financial decisions are balanced across wife-dominant, husband-dominant, and shared. However, when a wife earns more than her husband, which is an increasingly common situation, wife-dominant decisions are far more likely.

Personality is also an important determinant of family decision roles. Traits such as aggressiveness, locus of control (belief in controlling one's own situation), detachment, and compliance influence family decision power.[39] For children, age matters. Older children and teens are playing an increasingly stronger role and marketers are communicating directly to them, as with Pottery Barn and PBteen. Finally, the stage of the decision process influences decision roles. Purchase decisions evolve from the early stages of problem recognition and information search through choice and purchase. Children and teens tend to have more influence on earlier stages of the family decision process than on later stages.[40]

Conflict Resolution

Given the number of decisions families make daily, disagreements are inevitable. How they are resolved is important to marketers as well as to the health of the family unit. One study revealed six basic approaches that individuals use to resolve purchase conflicts after they have arisen (most couples generally seek to avoid open conflicts):[41]

- *Bargaining.* Trying to reach a compromise.
- *Impression management.* Misrepresenting the facts in order to win.
- *Use of authority.* Claiming superior expertise or role appropriateness (the husband/wife should make such decisions).
- *Reasoning.* Using logical argument to win.
- *Playing on emotion.* Using the silent treatment or withdrawing from the discussion.
- *Additional information.* Getting additional data or a third-party opinion.

Another study found that spouses adapt their strategies across decisions and that when they use coercive means (e.g., silent treatment) to get their way, they are satisfied with the decision *outcome* but dissatisfied with the decision *process.*[42] Although neither study included children, a study focused on how children and parents attempt to influence each other found a similar though more complex set of influence strategies.[43]

Furthermore, recent research on the conflict between mothers and adolescent daughters while shopping has revealed that leaving the store empty-handed is most likely the resolution if the daughter is younger. But for older daughters, a successful purchase is more often realized due to trust between daughter and mother and effective negotiation.[44]

MARKETING STRATEGY AND FAMILY DECISION MAKING

Formulating an effective marketing strategy for most consumer products requires a thorough understanding of the family decision-making process in the selected target markets with respect to that product. Table 6–3 provides a framework for such an analysis.

The family decision-making process often varies across market segments such as stages in the family life cycle or subculture. Therefore, a marketer must analyze family decision making *within* each of the firm's defined target markets. Within each target market, the marketer must

- Discover which family members are involved at each stage of the decision process.
- Determine what their motivations and interests are.
- Develop a marketing strategy that will meet the needs of each participant.

For example, younger children often are involved in the problem recognition stage related to breakfast. They may note a new cartoon character–based cereal or discover that their friends are eating a new cereal. They are interested in identifying with the cartoon character or being like their friends. When they request the new cereal, the parents, generally the mother, may become interested. However, she is more likely to focus on nutrition and price. Thus, a marketer needs to communicate fun, taste, and excitement to children—and nutrition, value, and taste to parents. The children can be reached on children's television programs, appropriate Internet sites, and similar media, while the mother may be more effectively communicated with through magazine ads, package information, and the Internet.

Examine the Hormel REV ad in Illustration 6–8. Use Table 6–3 to analyze this ad in terms of the family decision-making process and marketing strategy.

Segmentation analysis regarding family decision making is critical. Who is the target family member for this Hormel REV ad, and do the tactics in the ad match their motives?

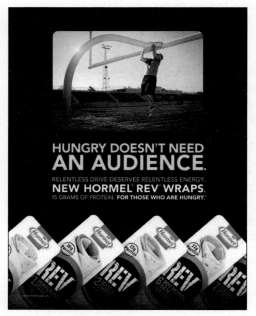

Source: Hormel Foods Corporation

Marketing Strategy Based on the Family Decision-Making Process				TABLE 6-3

Segment: _____

Stage in the Decision Process	Family Members Involved	Family Members' Motivation and Interests	Marketing Strategy and Tactics
Problem recognition			
Information search			
Alternative evaluation			
Purchase			
User/consumption			
Disposition			
Evaluation			

CONSUMER SOCIALIZATION

The family provides the basic framework in which consumer socialization occurs. **Consumer socialization** is *the process by which young people acquire skills, knowledge, and attitudes relevant to their functioning as consumers in the marketplace.*[45] We are concerned with understanding both the content of consumer socialization and the process of consumer socialization. The content of consumer socialization refers to what children learn with respect to consumption; the process refers to how they learn it. Before we address these two issues, we need to consider the ability of children of various ages to learn consumption-related skills.

LO4

The Ability of Children to Learn

Younger children have limited abilities to process certain types of information. **Piaget's stages of cognitive development** are a widely accepted set of stages of cognitive development:

Stage 1: The period of sensorimotor intelligence (0 to 2 years). During this period, behavior is primarily motor. The child does not yet "think" conceptually, though cognitive development is seen.

Stage 2: The period of preoperational thoughts (3 to 7 years). This period is characterized by the development of language and rapid conceptual development.

Stage 3: The period of concrete operations (8 to 11 years). During these years, the child develops the ability to apply logical thought to concrete problems.

Stage 4: The period of formal operations (12 to 15 years). During this period, the child's cognitive structures reach their greatest level of development, and the child becomes able to apply logic to all classes of problems.

While other approaches exist, the general pattern of less ability to deal with abstract, generalized, unfamiliar, or large amounts of information by younger children is common to all approaches.[46]

One study utilized Piaget's stages to help understand different interventions designed to improve dietary intake by children. The two stages examined were younger children (specifically the preoperational stage) and older children (specifically the concrete operational stage). The interventions were incentives (prizes), competition (against a rival school), and a personal pledge that involved signing their name to an in-class poster. Because pledges are more abstract and difficult to understand, they were less effective for the younger children.[47]

The changing capabilities of children to process information as they age present challenges to parents who are attempting to teach their children appropriate consumption behaviors.[48] As we will discuss shortly, this also poses ethical and practical issues for marketers. Children's limited learning capacity is the basis for substantial regulation of advertising to children, which we discuss in depth in Chapter 20.

The Content of Consumer Socialization

The content of consumer learning can be broken down into three categories: consumer skills, consumption-related preferences, and consumption-related attitudes.[49] **Consumer skills** are *those capabilities necessary for purchases to occur such as understanding money, budgeting, product evaluation, and so forth.* A child has to learn how to shop, how to compare similar brands, how to budget available income, and the like. The following example shows an attempt by a parent to teach her adolescent appropriate, from the parent's perspective, shopping rules:

> Son, look at this. This is just going to wash nicer, it will come through the laundry nicer, and you do a lot of the laundry yourself, and I just would rather that it's something that would wash easy, that doesn't have to be ironed, that isn't 100 percent cotton. (Mother with son, age 13)[50]

Consumption-related preferences are *the knowledge, attitudes, and values that cause people to attach differential evaluations to products, brands, and retail outlets.* For example, some parents through their comments and purchases may "teach" their children that Louis Vuitton is a prestigious brand name and that prestigious brands are desirable. This information about Louis Vuitton's prestige is not necessary to carry out the actual purchase (consumer skills), but it is extremely important in deciding to make a purchase and in deciding what to purchase (consumption-related preferences).[51]

Consumption-related attitudes are *cognitive and affective orientations toward marketplace stimuli such as advertisements, salespeople, warranties, and so forth.*[52] For example, children may learn from their parents or other family members that "you get what you pay for." This would lead them to assume a strong price–quality relationship. Or they may be taught that salespeople are not trustworthy. These attitudes will influence how they react to the various activities undertaken by marketers. What type of attitude is being formed in the following interaction?

> I'm always trying to get her to learn the relative value of things and particularly the impact of advertising and its effect on driving purchases and desires. So we try to talk about that. I point out manipulative or deceptive advertising, and give her a sense of being a critical consumer. (Father with daughter, age 13)[53]

The Process of Consumer Socialization

Consumer socialization occurs through a number of avenues, including advertising and friends. However, family is a primary source of consumer socialization. For example, a recent study of eating patterns found that children cite parents as the most important influence regarding the kinds of foods they eat. This was even true of teenagers, where parental influence was highest, and friends and advertising played a much lesser role, despite the increased advertising towards children.[54] Parents teach their children consumer skills, consumption-related preferences, and consumption-related attitudes. They do so both deliberately and casually through instrumental training, modeling, and mediation.

Instrumental training *occurs when a parent or sibling specifically and directly attempts to bring about certain responses through reasoning or reinforcement.* In other words, a parent may try directly to teach a child which snack foods should be consumed by explicitly discussing nutrition.[55] Or a parent may establish rules that limit the consumption of some snack foods and encourage the consumption of others. The following example shows an approach used with older children:

> One thing that we always talk about when we're looking at something is the price of it. "For what you're buying, is the price worth the quality of what you're buying?" (Mother with son, age 13)[56]

Parents often worry that marketing messages will simply drown out any instrumental training they try to provide. In Illustration 6–9 there is an attempt on the part of Capital One to be a partner in the socialization process.

Modeling *occurs when a child learns appropriate, or inappropriate, consumption behaviors by observing others.* Modeling generally, though not always, occurs without direct instruction from the role model and frequently without conscious thought or effort on the part of the child. Modeling is an extremely important way for children to learn relevant skills, knowledge, and attitudes. Children learn both positive and negative consumption patterns through modeling. For example, children whose parents smoke are more likely to start smoking than are children whose parents do not smoke.

Mediation *occurs when a parent alters a child's initial interpretation of, or response to, a marketing or other stimulus.* This can be seen easily in the following example from the author's personal experience:

CHILD: Can I have Skittles? If I eat them, rainbows will shoot out of my mouth! See?

PARENT: No. That's just an advertisement. Rainbows really won't shoot out of your mouth! See? They just make it look like it will so kids will buy them.

The advertisement illustrated a product attribute and triggered a desire, but the parent altered the belief in the attribute and in the believability of advertising in general. This is not to suggest that family members mediate all commercials. However, children often learn about the purchase and use of products during interactions with other family members. Thus, a firm wishing to influence children must do so in a manner consistent with the values of the rest of the family.

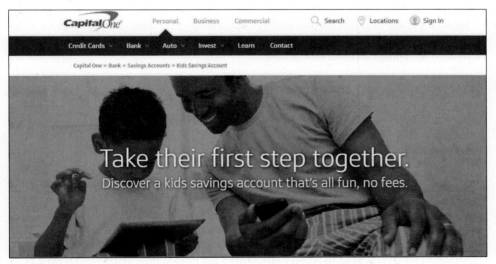

Source: Capital One

ILLUSTRATION 6-9

Capital One clearly recognizes that it can be a partner with parents in the socialization process.

The Supermarket as a Classroom

Professor James McNeal developed a five-stage model of how children learn to shop by visiting supermarkets and other retail outlets with a parent.[57]

Stage I: Observing   Parents begin taking children to the store with them at a median age of two months. During this stage, children make sensory contact with the marketplace and begin forming mental images of marketplace objects and symbols. In the early months, only sights and sounds are being processed. However, by 12 to 15 months, most children can begin to recall some of these items. This stage ends when children understand that a visit to the market may produce rewards beyond the stimulation caused by the environment.

Stage II: Making Requests   At this stage (median age is two years), children begin requesting items in the store from their parents. They use pointing and gesturing as well as statements to indicate that they want an item. Throughout most of this stage, children make requests only when the item is physically present, as they do not yet carry mental images of the products in their minds. In the latter months of stage II, they begin to make requests for items at home, particularly when they are seen on television.

Stage III: Making Selections   Actually getting an item off the shelf without assistance is the first act of an independent consumer (median age is three-and-a-half years). At its simplest level, a child's desire is triggered by an item in his or her immediate presence and this item is selected. Soon, however, children begin to remember the store location of desirable items, and they are allowed to go to those areas independently or to lead the parent there.

Stage IV: Making Assisted Purchases   Most children learn by observing (modeling) that money needs to be given to get things from a store. They learn to value money given to them by their parents and others as a means to acquire things. Soon they are allowed to select and pay for items with their own money. They are now primary consumers (median age is five-and-a-half years).

Stage V: Making Independent Purchases   Making a purchase without a parent to oversee it requires a fairly sophisticated understanding of value as well as the ability to visit a store, or a section of a store, safely without a parent. Most children remain in stage IV a long time before their parents allow them to move into stage V (median age is eight years).

McNeal's research indicates that children learn to shop, at least in part, by going shopping. Retailers are developing programs based on these learning patterns. Examples include child-sized shopping carts and kids' clubs.

MARKETING TO CHILDREN

As seen in the opening example, children are a large and growing market. Brand loyalties developed at this age may produce returns for many years. Thus, it is no surprise that marketers are aggressively pursuing these young consumers.

However, marketing to children is fraught with ethical concerns. The major source of these concerns is the limited ability of younger children to process information and to make informed purchase decisions. There are also concerns that marketing activities, particularly advertising, produce undesirable values in children, result in inappropriate diets, and cause unhealthy levels of family conflict. We will examine questionable marketing practices focused on children and the regulations designed to control them in detail in Chapter 20.

Although marketers need to be very sensitive to the limited information-processing skills of younger consumers, ethical and effective marketing campaigns can be designed to meet the needs of children and their parents. All aspects of the marketing mix must consider the capabilities of the child. Consider the following ad and the responses to the ad from children of different ages:

> The ad reads, "Inhale a lethal dose of carbon monoxide and it's called suicide. Inhale a smaller amount and it's called smoking. Believe it or not, cigarette smoke contains the same poisonous gas as automobile exhaust. So if you wouldn't consider sucking on a tailpipe, why would you want to smoke?" A picture of a smoking exhaust pipe was below the copy.
>
> **Seven- and eight-year-olds' responses:**
> "Never stand behind a bus because you could get poisonous in your face." "People sometimes get sick from exhaust."
>
> **Nine- and ten-year-olds' responses:**
> "The person who is driving is smoking." "No matter what kind of smoking it is, it can always make you sick."
>
> **Eleven-year-olds' responses:**
> "You could hurt yourself with that stuff. The same stuff in car exhaust is in cigarettes." "The tailpipe of a car is like the same as smoking and smoking could kill you . . . both of them could kill you."

Only the older children could fully engage in the analogical reasoning required to completely understand the ad. In contrast, a simpler ad that showed a dirty, grimy sock next to an ashtray full of cigarette butts with the word *gross* under the sock and *really gross* under the ashtray was understood by children of all ages (7 through 11).[58]

Reaching children used to mean advertising on Saturday morning cartoons. Now there are many more options, even for the very young. *National Geographic Kids* and *Discovery Girls* are just a few of the many magazines with strong readership among children. Children as young as three are active Internet users. Sites such as pbskids.com, Cartoonnetwork.com, and Nick.com are visited by millions of children aged 2 to 11. Direct mail can be an effective means to reach even very young children. Many firms target children or families with young children by forming "kids' clubs." Unfortunately, these clubs sometimes engage in sales techniques that are controversial if not clearly unethical. If done properly, however, they can be fun and educational for the children while delivering responsible commercial messages.

SUMMARY

LO1: Explain the concept of household types and their influence on consumption.

The household is the basic purchasing and consuming unit and is, therefore, of great importance to marketing managers of most products. The *family household* consists of two or more related persons living together in a dwelling unit. *Nonfamily households* are dwelling units occupied by one or more unrelated individuals. Family households are a primary mechanism whereby cultural and social-class values and behavior patterns are passed on to the next generation.

LO2: Summarize the household life cycle's various stages and marketing implications.

The *household life cycle* is the classification of the household into stages through which it passes over time based on the age and marital status of the adults and the presence and age of children. The household life cycle is a valuable marketing tool because members within each stage or category face similar consumption problems. Thus, they represent potential market segments.

The *HLC/occupational category matrix* is one useful way to use the HLC to develop marketing strategy. One axis is the stages in the HLC, which determine the problems the household will likely encounter; the other is a set of occupational categories, which provide a range of acceptable solutions. Each cell represents a market segment.

LO3: Understand the family decision process.

Family decision making involves consideration of questions such as who buys, who decides, and who uses. Family decision making is complex and involves emotion and interpersonal relations as well as product evaluation and acquisition. Household member participation in the decision process varies by *involvement with the specific product, role specialization, personal characteristics,* and one's *culture and subculture.* Participation also varies by stage in the decision process. Most decisions are reached by consensus. If not, a variety of conflict resolution strategies may be employed. Marketing managers must analyze the household decision process separately for each product category within each target market.

LO4: Describe the role that households play in child socialization.

Consumer socialization deals with the processes by which young people (from birth until 18 years of age) learn how to become consumers. Children's learning abilities are limited at birth, then slowly evolve with experience over time. Consumer socialization deals with the learning of consumer skills, consumption-related preferences, and consumption-related attitudes. Families influence consumer socialization through direct *instrumental training, modeling,* and *mediation.* Young consumers appear to go through five stages of learning how to shop. This learning takes place primarily in retail outlets in interaction with the parents.

LO5: Explain the sources of ethical concern associated with marketing to children.

Marketing to children is fraught with ethical issues. The main source of ethical concern is the limited ability of children to process information and make sound purchase decisions or requests. There are also concerns about the role of advertising in forming children's values, influencing their diets, and causing family conflict. However, ethical and effective marketing programs can be developed for children.

KEY TERMS

Consumer skills 208
Consumer socialization 207
Consumption-related
    attitudes 208
Consumption-related
    preferences 208
Family decision making 202

Family household 189
HLC/occupational category
    matrix 201
Household 189
Household life cycle
    (HLC) 192
Instrumental training 208

Mediation 209
Modeling 209
Nonfamily household 189
Piaget's stages of cognitive
    development 207
Step family 189
Traditional family 189

REVIEW QUESTIONS

1. The household is described as "the basic consumption unit for consumer goods." Why?

2. What is a *traditional family?* Can a single-parent family be a nuclear family?

3. How does a *nonfamily household* differ from a *family household?*

4. How has the distribution of household types in the United States been changing? What are the implications of these shifts?

5. What is meant by the *household life cycle?*

6. What is meant by the following statement? "Each stage in the household life cycle poses a series of problems that household decision makers must solve."

7. Describe the general characteristics of each of the stages in the household life cycle.

8. Describe the *HLC/occupational category matrix.* What is the logic for this matrix?

9. What is meant by *family decision making?* How can different members of the household be involved with different stages of the decision process?

10. How does family decision making differ from most organizational decision making?

11. The text states that the marketing manager must analyze the family decision-making process separately within each target market and for each product. Why?

12. What factors influence involvement of a household member in a purchase decision?

13. How do family members attempt to resolve conflict over purchase decisions?

14. What is *consumer socialization?* How is knowledge of it useful to marketing managers?

15. What are Piaget's stages of cognitive development?

16. What do we mean when we say that children learn consumer skills, consumption-related attitudes, and consumption-related preferences?

17. What processes do parents use to teach children to be consumers?

18. Describe each of the five stages children go through as they learn to shop at stores.

19. What ethical issues arise in marketing to children?

DISCUSSION QUESTIONS

20. Respond to the questions in Consumer Insight 6–1.

21. Canada has legislation giving cohabiting couples who have been living together for one year or more the same federal rights and responsibilities as married couples. Should the United States have similar legislation?

22. Rate the stages of the household life cycle in terms of their probable purchase of the following. Justify your answers.
    a. Designer jeans
    b. Trip to Cancun
    c. Diapers
    d. Breakfast bars
    e. Contribution to SPCA
    f. Golf clubs

23. Pick two stages in the household life cycle. Describe how your marketing strategy for the following would differ depending on which group was your primary target market.
    a. Minivan
    b. Razors
    c. Broadway show
    d. Casino

24. Do you think the trend toward nonfamily households will continue? Justify your response.

25. What are the primary marketing implications of Table 6–1?

26. How would the marketing strategies for the following differ by stage of the HLC? (Assume each stage is the target market.)

    a. Cell phone
    b. Scuba gear
    c. Power tools
    d. Children's toys
    e. Detergent
    f. Colleges

27. What are the marketing implications of Figure 6–4?

28. What type of the following would be best suited for each cell in Table 6–2?
    a. Hotel
    b. Television program
    c. Restaurant for the entire household
    d. Lawn mower

29. Name two products for which the horizontal axis in Table 6–2 should be the following. Justify your response.
    a. Occupational category
    b. Income
    c. Education
    d. Social class

30. How can a marketer use knowledge of how family members seek to resolve conflicts?

31. Describe a recent family purchase in which you were involved. Use this as a basis for completing Table 6–3 for a marketer attempting to influence that decision.

32. Describe four types of activities or situations in which direct *instrumental training* is likely to occur.

33. Describe four types of activities or situations in which *modeling* is likely to occur.

34. Describe four types of activities or situations in which *mediation* is likely to occur.

35. Respond to the questions in Consumer Insight 6-2.

36. Are Piaget's stages of cognitive development consistent with the five stages of learning to shop that McNeal identified?

37. Interview a middle school student and determine and describe the household decision process involved in the purchase of his or her
    a. Backpack
    b. Snack foods
    c. Bedroom furniture
    d. Cell phone
    e. Clothing

38. Interview two sporting goods salespersons from different price-level outlets. Try to ascertain which stages in the household life cycle constitute their primary markets and why this is so.

39. Interview one individual from each stage in the household life cycle. Determine and report the extent to which these individuals conform to the descriptions provided in the text.

40. Interview a family with a child under 13 at home. Interview both the parents and the child, but interview the child separately. Try to determine the influence of each family member on the following products *for the child's use.* In addition, ascertain what method(s) of conflict resolution is (are) used.
    a. Toothbrush
    b. Clothes
    c. Cereal
    d. Major toys, such as an Xbox

    e. Television viewing
    f. Fast-food restaurant

41. Interview a couple who have been married for the following periods. Ascertain and report the degree and nature of role specialization that has developed with respect to their purchase decisions. Also determine how conflicts are resolved.
    a. Less than 1 year
    b. 1–5 years
    c. 6–10 years
    d. More than 10 years

42. Pick a product and market segment of interest, and interview three households. Collect sufficient data to complete Table 6–3.

43. Pick a product of interest and, with several fellow students, complete enough interviews to fill the relevant cells in Table 6–2 using the four questions in the text. Develop an appropriate marketing strategy based on this information.

44. Interview several parents of preschool children. Determine the extent to which they agree with Piaget's four stages and McNeal's five stages.

45. Watch several hours of children's television programming (e.g., cartoons). What ethical concerns, if any, do these shows cause?

1. This opener based on E. Klinenberg, "Solo Nation," *CNN Money*, January 25, 2012, http://finance.fortune.cnn.com/2012/01/25/eric-klinenberg-going-solo/, accessed August 31, 2014; E. Klinenberg, "One's a Crowd," *New York Times Sunday Review*, February 4, 2012, www.nytimes.com/2012/02/05/opinion/sunday/living-alone-means-being-social.html?_r50, accessed August 31, 2014; G. Ifill and R. Suarez, "Why More Americans Are Living Alone," *PBS*, March 27, 2012, www.pbs.org/newshour/bb/social_issues/jan-june12/goingsolo_03-27.html, accessed August 31, 2014; M. Galante, "Why Micro Apartments Are the Next Big Trend in City Living," *Business Insider*, November 6, 2012, www.businessinsider.com/micro-apartment-trend-2012-10#ixzz2qP0bYtPC, accessed August 31,

2014; E. Klinenberg, *Going Solo* (New York: Penguin Books, 2013); J. Stanton, "A Closer Look at the Single Household," *Food Processing*, August 2013, www.foodprocessing.com/articles/2013/market-view-single-household/, accessed August 31, 2014; J. Vespa, J. Lewis, and R. Kreider, "America's Families and Living Arrangements," *2012 Population Characteristics* (Washington, DC: U.S. Census Bureau, 2013).

2. For more detailed information, see U.S. Census Bureau, "America's Families and Living Arrangements: 2007," *Population Characteristics* (September 2009); U.S. Census Bureau, America's Families and Living Arrangements: 2017, www.census.gov/data/tables/2017/demo/families/cps-2017.html.

3. Statistics in this section are drawn primarily from relevant U.S. Census Bureau reports and updates.

4. Insight based on T. Hussung, "The Evolution of American Family Structure," *Concordia St. Paul Blog & News Updates,* June 23, 2015, https://online.csp.edu/blog/family-science/the-evolution-of-american-family-structure, accessed March 28, 2018; "Parenting in America: Outlook, Worries, Aspirations Are Strongly Linked to Financial Situation," *Pew Research Center,* December 17, 2015, www.pewsocialtrends.org/2015/12/17/parenting-in-america/, accessed March 28, 2018; B. Schulte, "Unlike in the 1950s, There Is No 'Typical' U.S. Family Today," *Washington Post,* September 4, 2014, www.washingtonpost.com/news/local/wp/2014/09/04/for-the-first-time-since-the-1950s-there-is-no-typical-u-s-family/?utm_term=.f5d23b3d72b5, accessed March 28, 2018; A. Vanorman and P. Scommegna, "Changing U.S. Family Patterns Pose Policy Challenges," *Population Reference Bureau,* August 9, 2016, www.prb.org/us-bulletin-complex-families/, accessed March 28, 2018.

5. For more information, see *A Portrait of Stepfamilies* (Washington, DC: Pew Research Center, January 2011).

6. A. M. Epp and L. L. Price, "Family Identity," *Journal of Consumer Research,* June 2008, pp. 50–70.

7. See C. M. Schaninger and W. D. Danko, "A Conceptual and Empirical Comparison of Alternative Household Life Cycle Models," *Journal of Consumer Research,* March 1993, pp. 580–94; R. E. Wilkes, "Household Life-Cycle Stages, Transitions, and Product Expenditures," *Journal of Consumer Research,* June 1995, pp. 27–42; C. M. Schaninger and D. H. Lee, "A New Full-Nest Classification Approach," *Psychology & Marketing,* January 2002, pp. 25–58.

8. The U.S. Census Bureau defines "unmarried" as those who were never married, widowed, or divorced. Statistics reported in this section are drawn primarily from relevant U.S. Census Bureau reports and updates, unless otherwise noted.

9. See, e.g., N. Donthu and D. I. Gilliland, "The Single Consumer," *Journal of Advertising Research,* November–December 2002, pp. 77–84.

10. Insight based on K. Sweet, "250 Years of Consumer Habits," *Professional Remodeler,* November 1, 2004, www.proremodeler.com/250-years-consumer-habits-0, accessed August 31, 2014; *Understanding Homeowners' Renovation Decisions* (London: UK Energy Research Centre, 2013); *Homeowner Remodeling Survey* (Malvern, PA: Principia Consulting, 2013).

11. See J. Raymond, "For Richer or Poorer," *American Demographics,* July 2000, pp. 59–64.

12. Bureau of Labor Statistics, Employment Status of Mothers with Own Children under 3 Years Old by Single Year of Age of Youngest Child and Marital Status, 2015–2016 Annual Averages, April 20, 2017.

13. Estimates based on *Consumer Expenditure Survey* (Washington, DC: U.S. Bureau of Labor Statistics, 2005–2006).

14. M. Lino, K. Kuczynski, N. Rodriguez, and T. Schap, "Expenditures on Children by Families, 2015," *Miscellaneous Publication No. 1528-2015, U.S. Department of Agriculture, Center for Nutrition Policy and Promotion,* March 2017.

15. C. M. Carter, "Meet the Company Decoding How to Market to Millennial Moms," *Forbes,* May 1, 2017, www.forbes.com.

16. Examples come from corporate websites and Mintel Group, Marketing to Moms—US—September 2017, www.mintel.com, accessed March 13, 2018.

17. R. Gardyn, "Unmarried Bliss," *American Demographics,* December 2000, pp. 56–61.

18. For a discussion, including differences across groups, see www.divorcereform.org; D. Hurley, "Divorce Rate," *New York Times,* April 19, 2005, p. F7; "Marriage and Divorce: Patterns by Gender, Race, and Educational Attainment," *Bureau of Labor Statistics,* October 2013.

19. See, e.g., J. Morrow, "A Place for One," *American Demographics,* November 2003, pp. 25–29; and P. Francese, "Well Enough Alone," *American Demographics,* November 2003, pp. 32–33.

20. P. Paul, "Childless by Choice," *American Demographics,* November 2001, pp. 45–50.

21. J. Fetto, "The Baby Business," *American Demographics,* May 2003, p. 40; J. Neff, "P&G Challenges Rival K-C in Trainers Battle," *Advertising Age,* May 17, 2004, p. 10.

22. See company websites, like www.plated.com, for more information on home delivery meal kits.

23. Information from organization's website at www.singlemothersbychoice.org.

24. T. W. Bradford, "Intergenerational Gifted Asset Dispositions," *Journal of Consumer Research,* June 2009, pp. 93–111.

25. Donthu and Gilliland, "The Single Consumer."

26. For a different approach, see L. G. Pol and S. Pak, "Consumer Unit Types and Expenditures on Food Away from Home," *Journal of Consumer Affairs,* Winter 1995, pp. 403–28.

27. See J. Park, P. Tansuhaj, and E. R. Spangenberg, "An Emotion-Based Perspective of Family Purchase Decisions," in *Advances in Consumer Research,* vol. 22, ed. F. R. Kardes and M. Sujan (Provo, UT: Association for Consumer Research, 1995), pp. 723–28.

28. C. Lackman and J. M. Lanasa, "Family Decision-Making Theory," *Psychology & Marketing,* March–April 1993, pp. 81–113.

29. An exception is S. E. Beatty and S. Talpade, "Adolescent Influence in Family Decision Making," *Journal of Consumer Research,* September 1994, pp. 332–41.

30. See J. Cotte and S. L. Wood, "Families and Innovative Consumer Behavior," *Journal of Consumer Research,* June 2004, pp. 78–86; A. Shoham and V. Dalakas, "He Said, She Said . . . They Said," *Journal of Consumer Marketing* 22, no. 3 (2005), pp. 152–60; E. Bridges and R. A. Briesch, "The 'Nag Factor' and Children's Product Categories," *International Journal of Advertising* 25, no. 2 (2006), pp. 157–87; Mintel Group, "Kids as Influencers—US—February 2018," February 2018, www.mintel.com, accessed March 14, 2018.

31. See, e.g., M. A. Belch and L. A. Willis, "Family Decision at the Turn of the Century," *Journal of Consumer Behaviour* 2, no. 2 (2002), pp. 111–24; N. Razzouk, V. Seitz, and K. P. Capo, "A Comparison of Consumer Decision-Making Behavior of Married and Cohabiting Couples," *Journal of Consumer Marketing* 24, no. 5 (2007), pp. 264–74. See Carter, "Meet the Company Decoding How to Market to Millennial Moms."

32. T. Mecia, "Poll: Women, Men Disagree on How They Divide Spending," *CreditCards.com* November 29, 2016, www.creditcards.com, accessed March 14, 2018.

33. *Women Call the Shots at Home* (Washington, DC: Pew Research Center, September 2008).

34. See C.-N. Chen, M. Lai, and D. D. C. Tarn, "Feminism Orientation, Product Attributes and Husband–Wife Decision Dominance," *Journal of Global Marketing* 12, no. 3 (1999), pp. 23–39; C. Webster and M. C. Reiss, "Do Established Antecedents of Purchase Decision-Making Power Apply to Contemporary Couples?," *Psychology & Marketing,* September 2001, pp. 951–72.

35. J. B. Ford, L. E. Pelton, and J. R. Lumpkin, "Perception of Marital Roles in Purchase Decision Processes," *Journal of the Academy of Marketing Science,* Spring 1995, pp. 120–31.

36. See C. K. C. Lee and S. E. Beatty, "Family Structure and Influence in Family Decision Making," *Journal of Consumer Marketing* 19, no. 1 (2002), pp. 24–41; G. Slattery and J. Butler, "Teens Are Primary Influencer on Holiday Technology Purchases," *Business Wire,* November 23, 2004, p. 1.

37. See M. C. Reiss and C. Webster, "Relative Influence in Purchase Decision Making," in *Advances in Consumer Research,* vol. 24, ed. M. Bruck and D. J. MacInnis (Provo, UT: Association for Consumer Research, 1997), pp. 42–47; C. Webster, "The Meaning and Measurement of Marital Power," in *Advances in Consumer Research,* vol. 25, ed. J. W. Alba and J. W. Hutchinson (Provo, UT: Association for Consumer Research, 1998), pp. 395–99.

38. *Women, Men, and the New Economics of Marriage* (Washington, DC: Pew Research Center, January 2010).

39. C. Webster, "Is Spousal Decision Making a Culturally Situated Phenomenon?," *Psychology & Marketing,* December 2000, pp. 1035–58.

40. See, e.g., M. A. Belch, K. A. Krentler, and L. A. Willis-Flurry, "Teen Internet Mavens," *Journal of Business Research* 58 (2005), pp. 569–75.

41. C. Kim and H. Lee, "A Taxonomy of Couples Based on Influence Strategies," *Journal of Business Research,* June 1996, pp. 157–68.

42. C. Su, E. F. Fern, and K. Ye, "A Temporal Dynamic Model of Spousal Family Purchase-Decision Behavior," *Journal of Marketing Research,* August 2003, pp. 268–81. See also C. Su et al., "Harmonizing Conflict in Husband-Wife Purchase Decision Making," *Journal of the Academy of Marketing Science* 36 (2008), pp. 378–94.

43. K. M. Palan and R. E. Wilkes, "Adolescent–Parent Interaction in Family Decision Making," *Journal of Consumer Research,* September 1997, pp. 159–69. See also A. Aribarg, N. Arora, and H. O. Bodur, "Understanding the Role of Preference Revision and Concession in Group Decisions," *Journal of Marketing Research,* August 2002, pp. 336–49.

44. S. Gillison et al., "Mother-Adolescent Daughter Identity Interplay Processes," *Journal of Consumer Marketing* 32, no. 4 (2015), pp. 234–44.

45. For a thorough review, see D. R. John, "Consumer Socialization of Children," *Journal of Consumer Research,* December 1999, pp. 183–209. See also M. J. Dotson and E. M. Hyatt, "Major Influence Factors in Children's Consumer Socialization," *Journal of Consumer Marketing* 22, no. 1 (2005), pp. 35–42.

46. See J. Gregan-Paxton and D. R. John, "The Emergence of Adaptive Decision Making in Children," *Journal of Consumer Research,* June 1997, pp. 43–56; T. Davis, "What Children Understand about Consumption Constellations," in *Advances in Consumer Research,* vol. 27, ed. S. J. Hoch and R. J. Meyer (Provo, UT: Association for Consumer Research, 2000), pp. 72–78; E. S. Moore and R. J. Lutz, "Children, Advertising, and Product Experiences," *Journal of Consumer Research,* June 2000, pp. 31–47.

47. S. Raju, P. Rajagopal, and T. J. Gilbride, "Marketing Healthful Eating to Children," *Journal of Marketing,* May 2010, pp. 93–106.

48. Parental responses differ across cultures; see G. M. Rose, "Consumer Socialization, Parental Style, and Developmental Timetables in the United States and Japan," *Journal of Marketing,* July 1999, pp. 105–19.

49. M. Viswanathan, T. L. Childers, and E. S. Moore, "The Measurement of Intergenerational Communication and Influence on Consumption," *Journal of the Academy of Marketing Science,* Summer 2000, pp. 406–24.

50. Palan and Wilkes, "Adolescent–Parent Interaction in Family Decision Making."

51. M. F. Ji, "Children's Relationships with Brands," *Psychology & Marketing,* April 2002, pp. 369–87; E. S. Moore, W. L. Wilkie, and R. J. Lutz, "Passing the Torch," *Journal of Marketing,* April 2002, pp. 17–37.

52. See T. F. Mangleburg and T. Bristol, "Socialization and Adolescents' Skepticism toward Advertising," *Journal of Advertising,* Fall 1998, pp. 11–20; L. Carlson, R. N. Laczniak, and J. E. Keith, "Socializing Children about Television," *Journal of the Academy of Marketing Science,* Summer 2001, pp. 276–88; P. Wright, M. Friestad, and D. M. Boush, "The Development of Marketplace Persuasion Knowledge in Children, Adolescents, and Young Adults," *Journal of Public Policy and Marketing,* Fall 2005, pp. 222–33.

53. Palan and Wilkes, "Adolescent–Parent Interaction in Family Decision Making."

54. P. Dando, "Healthier Fast-Food a Reality," *Advertising Age,* March 29, 2004, p. S-7; UConn Rudd Center for Food and Policy, *Snack FACTS 2015: Evaluating Snack Food Nutrition and Marketing to Youth,* January 2016.

55. See, e.g., C. Kim, H. Lee, and M. A. Tomiuk, "Adolescents' Perceptions of Family Communication Patterns and Some Aspects of Their Consumer Socialization," *Psychology & Marketing,* October 2009, pp. 888–907.

56. Palan and Wilkes, "Adolescent–Parent Interaction in Family Decision Making."

57. J. U. McNeal, *Kids as Consumers* (New York: Lexington Books, 1992); J. U. McNeal and C. Yeh, "Born to Shop," *American Demographics,* June 1993, pp. 34–39. See also J. B. Schor, *Born to Buy* (New York: Scribner, 2004).

58. L. A. Peracchio and D. Luna, "The Development of an Advertising Campaign to Discourage Smoking Initiation among Children and Youth," *Journal of Advertising,* Fall 1998, pp. 49–56.

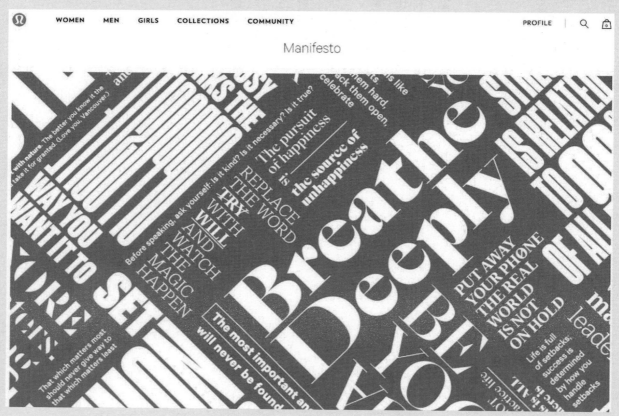

Source: lululemon

LEARNING OBJECTIVES

LO1 Explain reference groups and the criteria used to classify them.

LO2 Discuss consumption subcultures, including brand and online communities and their importance for marketing.

LO3 Summarize the types and degree of reference group influence.

LO4 Discuss within-group communications and the importance of word-of-mouth communications to marketers.

LO5 Understand opinion leaders (both online and offline) and their importance to marketers.

LO6 Discuss innovation diffusion and use an innovation analysis to develop marketing strategy.

For most products and brands, the basic purchase motivation relates to the ability of the product or service itself to meet a need of the consumer. Other purchases are fundamentally different in that consumers buy membership into a group as well. A prime example is the lululemon brand.[1] This athletic apparel retailer opened its first yoga-inspired store in Canada in 2000 and has since grown to over 400 stores worldwide. The company competes in the "athleisure" market, which sells casual comfortable clothing that can be worn both inside and outside a gym. This athletic wear is attractive to Millennials/Generation Yers, yet some competitors struggle in this market. But not lululemon. The company continues to grow, recording sales of more than $2.3 billion in 2017. It is not just the product that attracts the Millennials, but the sense of community created by the brand. Community is at the center of lululemon's vision and company manifesto, and building healthy communities is a priority. With a focus on healthy living, lululemon sells not only clothes but a lifestyle. A former executive stated: "And so when you think about lululemon and its history, it's an investment in people, giving them their best life, personal development and creating incredible product that allows them to live their life." Thus, lululemon centers on the customer, or "guest," by creating a community to which these guests want to belong. According to a top executive,

> "We have a very loyal and passionate guest and we're hyper-focused on whom we're speaking to. We're not afraid to say things that are typically on people's tongues, or maybe talk about the things that others aren't comfortable talking about and realize that actually, people really appreciate that. It's a level of authenticity. When you're focused on your muse and what you're doing, you get a following regardless of what group you're going after. We just try to be as consistent as possible to that guest and really serve him or her."

The strength of the brand can be attributed to lululemon's ability to bond with its customers and the community.

- **Company connects with its customers—** lululemon guests are immediately welcomed into the lululemon community at their first purchase. The company provides guests the opportunity to offer feedback on products while shopping by writing their suggestions on chalkboards near the fitting rooms.
- **Customers are loyal—**Although their product offerings may be seen as expensive (yoga pants can cost over $100), almost half of the company's customers would continue to shop at lululemon even if prices were to increase 5 to 10 percent. Blogs, such as www.luluaddict.com, highlight guests' passion for the brand. As one guest exclaimed, "Once you go lululemon, you never go back."
- **Shopping is an event—**Guests can shop and get a workout while at lululemon. The retailer offers free yoga and fitness classes in the store, and online for those not near a store. Interestingly, most sales are made in conjunction with these classes.

- **Brand builds community**—Community is not only built physically through the in-store classes, but also emotionally by wearing the brand's clothes. Also, in each store, a community board provides information on local yoga studios and running clubs. The store employees, or "educators," can post personal goals and aspirations on store walls for all to see.

- **Brand ambassadors expand the community**—Brand community is reinforced through the company's *brand ambassador* program. A **brand ambassador** is a person who is paid or given free products by a company in exchange for wearing or using its products and trying to encourage others to do so. lululemon's ambassador program includes "driven athletes and inspirational people who harness their passion to elevate their communities." The company enlists over 1,600 ambassadors worldwide, and they comprise local influencers, elite athletes, and outstanding yoga instructors who provide feedback on the company's product and create community. In exchange for teaching free classes, the ambassadors are given free clothing and other lululemon merchandise.

The lululemon brand has been fostering this community since the first store opened. Its members tend to be passionate, active, and devoted. They are connected to the lululemon brand, the lululemon community, and the lifestyle it represents in a very deep way that permeates their lives and helps define who they are.

As demonstrated in the opening example, even in an individualistic society like America, group memberships and identity are very important to all of us. And while we don't like to think of ourselves as conformists, most of us conform to group expectations most of the time. For example, when you decided what to wear to the last party you attended, you probably based your decision in part on the anticipated responses of the other individuals at the party. This represents a response to group influence and expectations.

TYPES OF GROUPS

LO1 The terms *group* and *reference group* need to be distinguished. A **group** is defined as *two or more individuals who share a set of norms, values, or beliefs and have certain implicitly or explicitly defined relationships to one another such that their behaviors are interdependent.* A **reference group** is *a group whose presumed perspectives or values are being used by an individual as the basis for his or her current behavior.* Thus, a reference group is simply a group that an individual uses as a guide for behavior in a specific situation.

Most of us belong to a number of different groups and perhaps would like to belong to several others. When we are actively involved with a particular group, it generally functions as a reference group. As the situation changes, we may base our behavior on an entirely different group, which then becomes our reference group. We may belong to many groups simultaneously, but we generally use only one group as our primary point of reference in any given situation. This tendency is illustrated in Figure 7–1.

Groups may be classified according to a number of variables. Four criteria are particularly useful: (1) membership, (2) strength of social tie, (3) type of contact, and (4) attraction.

The *membership* criterion is dichotomous: Either one is a member of a particular group or one is not a member of that group. Of course, some members are more secure in their membership than others are; that is, some members feel they really belong to a group, while others lack this confidence.

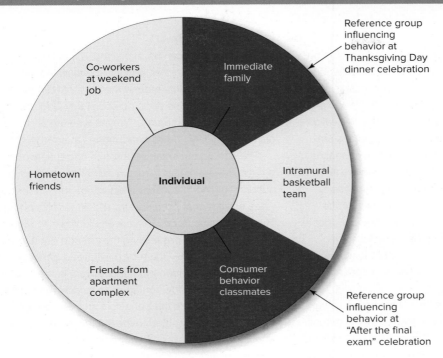

FIGURE 7-1

Reference Groups Change as the Situation Changes

Reference group influencing behavior at Thanksgiving Day dinner celebration

Co-workers at weekend job

Immediate family

Hometown friends

Individual

Intramural basketball team

Friends from apartment complex

Consumer behavior classmates

Reference group influencing behavior at "After the final exam" celebration

Strength of social tie refers to the closeness and intimacy of the group linkages. **Primary groups,** such as family and friends, involve strong ties and frequent interaction. Primary groups often wield considerable influence. **Secondary groups,** such as professional and neighborhood associations, involve weaker ties and less-frequent interaction.

Type of contact refers to whether the interaction is direct or indirect. Direct contact involves face-to-face interaction; indirect contact does not. The Internet, in particular, has increased the importance of indirect reference groups in the form of *online communities,* which are discussed in more detail later in the chapter.

Attraction refers to the desirability that membership in a given group has for the individual. This can range from negative to positive. Groups with negative desirability—**dissociative reference groups**—can influence behavior just as those with positive desirability do.[2] For example, teenagers tend to avoid clothing styles associated with older consumers. Nonmembership groups with a positive attraction—**aspiration reference groups**—also exert a strong influence. Individuals frequently purchase products thought to be used by a desired group in order to achieve actual or symbolic membership in the group.

Consumer Insight 7–1 shows the power of groups and social networks to influence attitudes and behaviors.

Consumption Subcultures

A **consumption subculture** is a distinctive subgroup of society that self-selects on the basis of a shared commitment to a particular product class, brand, or consumption activity. These groups have (1) an identifiable, hierarchical social structure; (2) a set of shared beliefs or values; and (3) unique jargon, rituals, and modes of symbolic expression.[3] Thus, they are reference groups for their members as well as those who aspire to join or avoid them.

LO2

Groups, Social Networks, and Seeding

You would probably not be surprised to learn that things like fashion and music spread through social networks. But what about things like obesity, happiness, altruism, or smoking? Research suggests these too are influenced via social networks.[4] Take weight. Research shows that people with similar body mass indices are friends. There are a number of reasonable explanations. One is similarity—people choose others who are like them (be it weight, height, etc.). Another is that social networks establish norms of behavior. The evidence supports norms as a primary explanation for why people of similar weight are friends (part of the same social network or group). Slowly over time, what is considered normal weight within a group or network increases, establishing a "new normal."

Seeding can be an effective way of marketing using the influence of group and opinion leaders within groups. For example, Rick Warren's *The Purpose Driven Life* is the best-selling hardcover book in U.S. history that has been translated into 85 languages. It is a book with Christian topics, relevant to individuals of that faith, but not so much for others who don't share that faith. It is a niche book that spread rapidly and in record numbers to evangelicals for whom the book was relevant but remained relatively unknown to people outside of this social network. *The Purpose Driven Life* was launched using "seeding," whereby free samples are given away to influential members of existing social networks. Rick Warren nurtured a group of some 1,200 pastors, provided them a free copy of the book, and encouraged them to lead their congregations through the 40-day program.

The phenomenal ability of Beats headphones to grow fivefold and reach $1 billion between 2010 and 2012, despite negative press reviews that suggested Beats headphones were overpriced and

underperforming, can be explained in part by seeding Beats headphones to celebrity influentials—locker room photos of Beats around the neck of NBA player LeBron James, Beats popping up in Lady Gaga's video "Poker Face," and rapper Lil Wayne wearing $1 million diamond-studded Beats headphones at an NBA game.

The spread of contagion through social networks is difficult to track and measure in the physical world, but data mining of consumer activity on the Internet provides estimations of the spread and impact of contagion. The firm Lotame, for example, can identify influencers in social networks possessing the desired demographics (e.g., women 25–30 years of age) and behavior (e.g., uploaded a video of their child(ren) in the last four hours), send them the contagion (e.g., a movie trailer), and count and track the behaviors and demographics of the people connected to the influencer (e.g., people who viewed the trailer partially or in its entirety).

The downside to contagion, particularly in today's open social media environment, is that it can be difficult to control what is "put out there" and linked to a specific brand and company. Employees who engage in such negative behaviors (e.g., prank and negatively toned videos involving a restaurant's products and/or facilities) can be dismissed, but correcting the damage done can be much more difficult and time-consuming.

Critical Thinking Questions

1. What is seeding, and how is it an effective tool for marketers?

2. Use group structure to explain why *The Purpose Driven Life* had little awareness outside a specific social network.

3. In what ways has the Internet enhanced marketers' ability to draw on social networks for marketing purposes?

A number of such subcultures, ranging from hip-hop to gardening to skydiving, have been examined. Each has a set of self-selecting members. They have hierarchies at the local and national levels. And they also have shared beliefs and unique jargon and rituals. Most hobbies and participation sports have consumption-based group subcultures built around them. Consumption need not be shared physically to be a shared ritual that creates and sustains a group.[5]

Note that not all, or even most, product owners or participants in an activity become members of the consumption subculture associated with it. For example, one can enjoy the *Star Trek* TV shows without becoming a member of the associated subculture. Self-selecting into a consumption subculture requires commitment, acquisition of the group's beliefs and values, participation in its activities, and use of its jargon and rituals. Consider the following excerpt regarding the consumption subculture revolving around high-end, limited-edition sneakers, where the most devoted members are called "sneakerheads":

> By 9:35 on a recent Friday night, Dominique Thomas had been camped outside the Niketown store in South Miami for two full days. Thomas, who goes by the street name DK the Line Pimp, had flown in from Denver and was the first in line to buy the $100 Cowboy Air Max 180s, which were scheduled to go on sale at 10 that night. Just 140 pairs of these limited-edition sneakers . . . were manufactured and they would be sold only at the Miami store and only that night. . . . Thomas, 21, reflected on how much getting the shoes meant to him. "Shoes run my life," he said. "Without shoes, I don't exist."[6]

As with other types of groups, members of consumption subcultures vary in their commitment to and interpretation of the group's values and norms. Consider the following quotes from sneakerheads regarding whether or not the sneakers should actually be worn:

> It's just like owning a Porsche. Every time you ride by, everyone looks at you. Well, if you have a rare, sought-after sneaker and you wear it down the street, everyone looks at you. . . . Most collectors, you can't tell they're sneakerheads. They usually wear really run-of-the-mill sneakers. Real collectors don't want to get their shoes dirty or dusty or worn. . . .[7]

Marketing and Consumption Subcultures   Consumption subcultures based on activities obviously are markets for the requirements of the activity itself, such as golf clubs for golfers. However, these groups develop rituals and modes of symbolic communication that often involve other products or services. Golf is renowned for the "uniform" that many of its adherents wear. Clothes, hats, and other items designed for golfers are based as much on providing symbolic meaning as they are for functional benefits.

While these subcultures adopt consumption patterns in large part to affirm their unique identity, the larger market often appropriates all or parts of their symbols, at least for a time. Thus, clothing initially worn by a consumption subculture, such as snowboarders or surfers, for functional or symbolic reasons may emerge as a style for a much larger group. The sneaker culture discussed earlier has given rise to a global market that puts a premium on new and cool styles. Companies like Sneakerhead and StockX provide platforms for customers to get these exclusive products. Also, the name of British shoemaker Boxfresh is a reference to hip-hop slang meaning sneakers fresh from the box, as shown in Illustration 7–1. It is attempting to appeal to this broader sneaker culture, if not directly at sneakerheads themselves.

Marketers can and should attempt to use the most respected members of a consumption subculture as a means for identifying trends and influencing consumers in the mass market. Again, the sneaker culture is instructive, as indicated by the director of Adidas's Sports Style Division:

> We have seen the sneaker culture increase over the past several years to the point where, today, bloggers [typically sneakerheads] are integral partners in helping spread the word about coming products. We're putting a lot of effort into this type of consumer, and we're spending a lot of time on them.[8]

Source: Boxfresh

Brand Communities

Consumption subcultures focus on the interactions of individuals around an activity, product category, or occasionally a brand. A **brand community** is *a nongeographically bound community, based on a structured set of social relationships among owners of a brand and the psychological relationship they have with the brand itself, the product in use, and the firm.*[9] A **community** is *characterized by consciousness of kind, shared rituals and traditions, and a sense of moral responsibility.*[10]

Athleisure apparel company lululemon has effectively created a brand community, as described at the beginning of this chapter. Brand communities are also prevalent in the auto and motorcycle industry among various manufacturers and their owner-enthusiasts, including Tesla, Jeep, Harley-Davidson, and MG (a British sports car). The following examples illustrate the nature of brand communities.[11]

Consciousness of Kind
There are several new classes of riders fouling the wind with the misapprehension that merely owning a Harley [Davidson] will transform them into a biker. This is the same type of dangerous ignorance that suggests that giving a dog an artichoke turns him into a gourmet.

Rituals and Traditions
For the past 7 years, we have sponsored a fall trip. [W]e always go the first weekend in October. [W]e . . . get on the Blue Ridge Parkway [which was] made for MGs, you know—high mountain roads, curves, and hills. We spend Friday and Saturday night in the mountains and then come back. The 1st year we had seven or eight people, last year we had 23 cars.

Moral Responsibility
A Tesla owner and enthusiast indicates a sense of dedication to help other Tesla enthusiasts. One such owner made a point of helping a terminally-ill man fulfill his dying wish of owning his own Tesla Model 3. The man was in a queue to receive delivery of the limited production car, but not likely in time, given his prognosis. The Tesla owner not only was able to get him a test drive of the car, but she also sent out a plea to Tesla to see if the man could receive his car sooner than later. He shortly did. She later posted online about the man's experience at Tesla, "private factory tour, intros around, everyone grinning to be part of this."

Marketing and Brand Communities   Brand communities can add value to the ownership of the product and build intense loyalty. A "mere" Jeep owner derives the functional and symbolic benefits associated with owning a Jeep. A member of the Jeep community derives these benefits plus increases in self-esteem from gaining skill in the off-road operation of a Jeep, the ability and confidence to use the Jeep in a wider range of situations, new friendships and social interactions, a feeling of belongingness, a positive association with FCA US LLC, and a deeper relationship with his or her Jeep.

As the Jeep example suggests, brand communities create value through sets of activities or "practices" that create brand engagement. Four categories of activities and an example of each relating to the Mini Cooper brand are shown in Table 7–1.

From the firm's perspective, building a brand community involves establishing relationships with the owner and helping owners establish relationships with each other. In addition, Table 7–1 suggests a host of activities that can be encouraged and facilitated by both the brand and brand owners to enhance brand value and loyalty. For example, Mini allows individuals to customize their cars during ordering (brand use enhancement via customization) and then track the production and delivery of their vehicle as part of the "birthing" ritual (community engagement via milestoning). The Mini website also features a Mini Owners' Lounge, which is an owners-only area where members share information about upcoming events and so on (social networking via welcoming). One such event is the Mini Getaway Tour. Brand-related events often are termed "brand fests," which are *gatherings of owners and others for the purposes of interacting with one another in the context of learning about and using the brand.*

Value Creation Activities in the Mini Brand Community	TABLE 7-1

Social Networking—Creating, enhancing, and sustaining ties among members by welcoming, empathizing, and governing.

- **Empathizing**—Lending emotional or other support to members
- **Example** (relating to members "birthing" rituals for their Mini's): Good job, Birdman! I'm like you. I watched cameras, checked tracking. . . . You'll treasure having these for your "scrap book" or should I say Minibirds's "baby book"? Jack [the car] was not on a WW ship so there were a lot less options for catching glimpses of the journey. Hang in there. Minibird is almost home!

Community Engagement—Reinforce members' escalating engagement with community by documenting, badging, milestoning, and staking.

- **Milestoning**—Noting significant events in brand ownership and consumption
- **Example** (relating to length of relationship with Mini): The odometer hit 100k miles and I loved my Mini more than ever.

Brand Use—Improving or enhancing the use of the focal brand by customizing, grooming, and commoditizing.

- **Grooming**—Caring for the brand
- **Example** (relating to washing the Mini appropriately): I try to wash at least once a week with a quick detail spray during the middle of the week to keep my Zaino shining. Newt [thread initiator] prepare yourself for an onslaught of posts suggesting that you should keep your car away from those car washes.

Impression Management—Creating positive view of brand community to nonmembers by evangelizing and justifying.

- **Evangelizing**—Sharing about the brand and inspiring others to use the brand
- **Example** (relating to the safety of the Mini): In another MINI forum that I used to visit a lot, there were a few people who had major accidents in their MINIs and I was shocked at just how tough and safe these little cars are. [T]hey weigh more than most small cars and are amazingly rigid and protective from what I've seen.

Source: Adapted from H. J. Schau, A. Muniz Jr., and E. J. Arnould, "How Brand Community Practices Create Value," *Journal of Consumer Research,* September 2009, pp. 30–51.

Online Communities and Social Networks

An **online community** is *a community that interacts over time around a topic of interest on the Internet*.[12] These interactions can take place in various forms, including online message boards and discussion groups, blogs, as well as corporate and nonprofit websites. Research indicates that online communities exist for many participants and that there is often a sense of community online, which moves beyond mere interactions to include an affective or emotional attachment to the online group. Studies have found ongoing communications among subsets of these interest groups. In addition, the patterns of communication indicate a group structure, with the more experienced members serving as experts and leaders and the newer members seeking advice and information. These groups develop unique vocabularies, netiquette, and means for dealing with behaviors deemed inappropriate.

Extent of connection can vary dramatically across members. Many members observe the group discussions without participating. Others participate but only at a limited level. Others manage and create content for the group.[13]

The ongoing evolution relating to online communities involves online social network sites. An **online social network site** is *a web-based service that allows individuals to (1) construct a public or semipublic profile within a bounded system, (2) articulate a list of other users with whom they share a connection, and (3) view and traverse their list of connections and those made by others within the system*.[14] Online social network sites take many forms, including friendship (Facebook and Instagram), media sharing (Vimeo and YouTube), corporate or brand (LEGO Ideas), business networking (LinkedIn), and micro-blogging (Twitter).

Illustration 7–2 shows how Care2, "the world's largest community for good," uses various avenues including a website and Facebook to foster an online community and further solidify brand loyalty.

Marketing and Online Communities and Social Networks   Online communities and social networks are attractive to marketers, who are spending over $15 billion on U.S. advertising on social network sites alone, which is nearly 10 percent of all online advertising.[15]

Online social network sites such as Care2, shown here, are increasingly popular for both consumers and brands as a way to foster and be connected to a community with similar lifestyles, values, and interests.

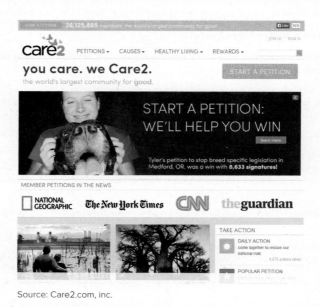

Source: Care2.com, inc.

Options range from relative standard banner and pop-up ads to more tailored approaches that maximize the specific characteristics of the venue such as sponsored Tweets, branded YouTube channels, or branded fan pages on Facebook.

Online communities and social networks are attractive for a number of reasons, including

- Consumer use is high and rising, with more than two-thirds of online adults and three-quarters of online teens saying they use social networking sites.[16]
- A majority of consumers who use social network sites use them to share information, including information about brands and products.[17]
- Customer acquisition potential seems high, with 51 percent of firms on Twitter and 68 percent of firms on Facebook indicating they have acquired a customer through these channels.[18]
- Roughly two-thirds of consumers who interact with a brand via social media are more likely to recall the brand, share information about the brand with others, feel connected to the brand, and purchase the brand.[19]

However, consumers don't just want entertainment or marketing; they want content that is relevant and useful to them. Research found that more than three-fourths of those polled prefer social media to provide incentives such as free products and coupons, and close to half want social media to provide information or solutions to their problems.[20]

While marketers are still learning about how to most effectively utilize social media, a few general guiding principles have emerged.[21] The first guiding principle is to be *transparent.* In online communities, it is critical that companies identify themselves and any posted content as such. Marketers who fail to do so risk being found out and subject to massive criticism from the community. Consider the case of Sony's PSP "Flog," or fake blog, as reported on *The Consumerist* blog:

> [T]he forces of the internet outed a marketing company working for Sony for creating fake PSP blog. The ps3do site says it's written by "Charlie" who wants to get the parents of his friend, "Jeremy," to buy "Jeremy" a PSP for Christmas. The domain name is registered to the *Zipatoni* marketing company.[22]

Indeed, not only are consumers concerned about transparency, so is the FTC, the government body tasked with regulating false and misleading advertising. When Ann Taylor offered a special gift to bloggers who posted coverage about their upcoming line, the FTC investigated. The FTC has issued new guidelines for bloggers requiring them to "clearly disclose any 'material connection' to an advertiser including payments for an endorsement or free product."[23] Consequently, transparency is important when companies interact with online groups.

The second principle is to *be a part of the community.* Online communities often expect that the company will be part of the community and not just market to it. Consider the following excerpt:

> [M]anagers tend to view social media first as a marketing tool, and indeed it is. But consumers are looking for more help, not [marketing] pitches. About two-thirds of U.S. consumers believe that companies should ramp up social media usage to "identify service/support issues and contact consumers to resolve [them]."[24]

Search Twitter for a company of interest and gauge the ratio of promotion to customer service. You are likely to find it skewed to promotion, although the better companies also will engage in product and service-failure recovery efforts. Companies such as Target and KLM Royal Dutch Airlines are reacting to customer complaints and issues delivered via Twitter and are reacting to them in real time.

The third principle is to *take advantage of the unique capabilities of each venue.* Many of the social network sites have special areas for corporate advertising and activities that extend beyond traditional banner and pop-up ads. For example, companies can have their own channel on YouTube, which they manage, monitor, and facilitate, as Jeep does. An additional example is the "like" component of Facebook. Oreo, for instance, has accumulated over 43 million likes of the cookie company's Facebook page due to its specialized, creative, and high-quality content. The company recently ran a "playwithoreo" promotion, inspiring consumers to post pictures or videos of their favorite way to eat an Oreo.[25] Caution should be heeded, though. Companies need to be aware of the limitations of Facebook and social media in altering a consumer's behavior. Recent research has shown that liking a company's Facebook page does not lead to increased purchasing:[26]

> Merely liking a page did not change behavior. Put another way, liking a company that offers flu shots does not translate into getting a flu shot.

Nevertheless, many companies like Oreo have managed Facebook in such a way that it is meaningful and engaging to customers and thus creates real value, in the form of new product ideas, for the firm.

REFERENCE GROUP INFLUENCES ON THE CONSUMPTION PROCESS

LO3

We all conform in a variety of ways to numerous groups. Sometimes we are aware of this influence, but many times we are not. Before examining the marketing implications of reference groups, we need to examine the nature of reference group influence more closely.

The Nature of Reference Group Influence

Reference group influence can take three forms: *informational, normative,* and *identification.* It is important to distinguish these types because marketing strategies depend on the type of influence involved.

Informational influence *occurs when an individual uses the behaviors and opinions of reference group members as potentially useful bits of information.* This influence is based on either the similarity of the group's members to the individual or the expertise of the influencing group member.[27] Thus, a person may notice that runners on the track team use a specific brand of nutrition bar. He or she then may decide to try that brand because these healthy and active runners use it. Use by the track team members thus provides information about the brand. The Built with Chocolate Milk ad in Illustration 7–3 shows another form of informational influence whereby a positive nonmember expert referent group endorses or recommends the brand.

Normative influence, sometimes referred to as *utilitarian* influence, *occurs when an individual fulfills group expectations to gain a direct reward or to avoid a sanction.*[28] You may purchase a particular brand of wine to win approval from a colleague. Or you may refrain

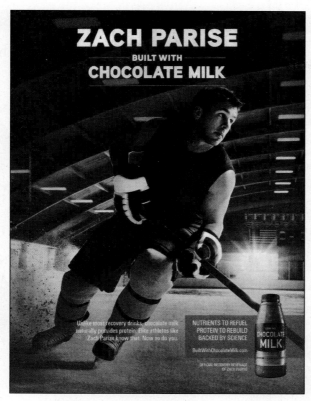

Source: MilkPEP

ILLUSTRATION 7-3

Consumers often use nonmember expert referent groups as a source of information for their purchase decisions, as shown in this Built with Chocolate Milk ad.

from wearing the latest fashion for fear of being teased by friends or to fit in with or be accepted by them. As you might expect, normative influence is strongest when individuals have strong ties to the group and the product involved is socially conspicuous.[29] Ads that promise social acceptance or approval if a product is used are relying on normative influence. Likewise, ads that suggest group disapproval if a product is not used, such as a mouthwash or deodorant, are based on normative influence.

Identification influence, also called *value-expressive* influence, *occurs when individuals have internalized the group's values and norms.* These then guide the individuals' behaviors without any thought of reference group sanctions or rewards. The individual has accepted the group's values as his or her own. The individual behaves in a manner consistent with the group's values because his or her values and the group's values are the same.

Figure 7-2 illustrates a series of consumption situations and the type of reference group influence that is operating in each case.

Degree of Reference Group Influence

Reference groups may have no influence in a given situation, or they may influence usage of the product category, the type of product used, or the brand used. Table 7-2 shows how two consumption situation characteristics—necessity/nonnecessity and visible/private consumption—combine to affect the degree of reference group influence likely to operate in a specific situation.

FIGURE 7-2   Consumption Situations and Reference Group Influence

Based on Table 7–2, the following two determinants of reference group influence emerge:

- Group influence is strongest *when the use of product or brand is visible to the group.* Products such as running shoes are highly visible. Products such as vitamins are generally not. Reference group influence typically affects only those aspects (e.g., category or brand) that are visible to the group.[30]
- Reference group influence is higher *the less of a necessity an item is.* Thus, reference groups have strong influence on the ownership of products such as designer clothes but much less influence on necessities such as a washing machine.

Two Consumption Situation Characteristics and Product/Brand Choice		**TABLE** 7-2

	Degree Needed	
	Necessity	**Nonnecessity**
Consumption	Weak reference group influence on product	Strong reference group influence on product

Visible
Strong reference group influence on brand
	Public Necessities
	Influence: Weak product and strong brand
	Examples:
	  Shoes
	  Automobiles
		Public Luxuries
		Influence: Strong product and brand
		Examples:
		  Jewelry
		  Health club

Private
Weak reference group influence on brand
	Private Necessities
	Influence: Weak product and brand
	Examples:
	  Refrigerator
	  Insurance
		Private Luxuries
		Influence: Strong product and weak brand
		Examples:
		  Hot tub
		  Home theater system

Three additional determinants of reference group influence include

- In general, *the more commitment an individual feels to a group, the more the individual will conform to the group norms.*
- *The more relevant a particular activity is to the group's functioning, the stronger the pressure to conform to the group norms concerning that activity.* Thus, style of dress may be important to a social group that frequently eats dinner together at nice restaurants and unimportant to a group that meets for basketball on Thursday nights.
- The final factor that affects the degree of reference group influence is *the individual's confidence in the purchase situation.* This can happen even if the product is not visible or important to group functioning as a result of the importance of the decision and a lack of personal decision confidence. Individual personality traits can influence confidence and thus be susceptible to reference group influence.[31]

Figure 7–3 summarizes these determinants, which marketers can use to assess the degree of group influence on their product category and brand.

MARKETING STRATEGIES BASED ON REFERENCE GROUP INFLUENCES

Marketers first must determine the degree and nature of the reference group influence that exists, *or can be created,* for the product in question. Figure 7–3 provides the starting point for this analysis.

Personal Sales Strategies

The power of groups was initially demonstrated in a classic series of studies. Eight subjects are shown four straight lines on a board—three unequal lines are grouped close together, and another appears some distance from them. The subjects are asked to determine which one of the three unequal lines is closest to the length of the fourth line shown some distance away.

FIGURE 7-3   Consumption Situation Determinants of Reference Group Influence

The subjects are to announce their judgments publicly. Seven of the subjects are working for the experimenter, and they announce incorrect matches. The order of announcement is arranged so that the naive subject responds last. The naive subject almost always agrees with the incorrect judgment of the others. This is known as the **Asch phenomenon.** Imagine how much stronger the pressures to conform are among friends or when the task is less well defined, such as preferring one brand or style to another.

Consider this direct application of the Asch phenomenon in personal selling. A group of potential customers is brought together for a sales presentation. As each design is presented, the salesperson scans the expressions of the people in the group, looking for the one who shows approval (e.g., head nodding) of the design. The salesperson then asks that person for an opinion because the opinion is certain to be favorable. The person is asked to elaborate. Meanwhile, the salesperson scans the faces of the other people, looking for more support, and then asks for an opinion of the person now showing the most approval. The salesperson continues until the person who initially showed the most disapproval is reached. In this way, by using the first person as a model, and by social group pressure on the last person, the salesperson gets all or most of the people in the group to make a positive public statement about the design. *Do you see any ethical issues in using group influences in this way?*

Advertising Strategies

Marketers often position products as appropriate for group activities. French wines gained an image of being somewhat expensive and snobbish. Many consumers viewed them as appropriate only for very special occasions. Illustration 7–4 shows an ad for DC Cool that positions itself toward a specific group activity.

Marketers use all three types of reference group influence when developing advertisements. Informational influence in advertising was shown earlier in Illustration 7–3. This type of ad uses an expert reference group (e.g., dentists, doctors, and teachers) as the information agent. Another approach is showing members of a group using a product.

The message, generally unstated, is that "these types of people find this brand to be the best; if you are like them, you will too."

Normative group influence is not portrayed in ads as much as it once was. It involves the explicit or implicit suggestion that using, or not using, the brand will result in having members of a group you belong to or wish to join rewarding or punishing you. One reason for the reduced use of this technique is the ethical questions raised by implying that a person's friends would base their reactions to the individual according to his or her purchases. Ads showing a person's friends saying negative things about the person behind his or her back because that person's coffee was not great (yes, there was such an ad campaign) were criticized for playing on people's insecurities and fears.

Identification influence is based on the fact that the individual has internalized the group's values and attitudes. The advertising task is to demonstrate that the product is consistent with the group's—and therefore the individual's—beliefs. This often involves showing the brand being used by a particular type of group, such as socially active young singles or parents of young children.

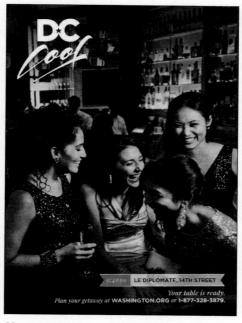

©Destination DC

COMMUNICATIONS WITHIN GROUPS AND OPINION LEADERSHIP

LO4

We learn about new products, services, and brands, as well as retail and information outlets, from our friends and other reference groups in two basic ways. First is by observing or participating with them as they use products and services. Second is by seeking or receiving advice and information from them in the form of **word-of-mouth (WOM) communications**. WOM involves *individuals sharing information with other individuals in a verbal form, including face-to-face, on the phone, and over the Internet.* As indicated in Consumer Insight 7-2, social media and the Internet continue to transform interpersonal communications and WOM.

Consumers generally trust the opinions of people (family, friends, acquaintances) more than marketing communications because, unlike marketing communications, these personal sources have no reason not to express their true opinions and feelings. As a consequence, WOM can have a critical influence on consumer decisions and business success. It is estimated that 82 percent of consumer purchases are influenced by WOM.[32] This WOM can be more effective the more explicit it is. Recent research shows that purchase intentions increase when a person recommends, as opposed to likes, the product.[33] Consumers put their faith in WOM versus advertising across a number of products and services. The information following shows the percentage of adults who put people (WOM from friends, family, or other people), as compared with advertising, at the top of their list of best sources for information.

Consumer-Generated Content: A Brand's Best Friend or Worst Enemy

The social media revolution has allowed users not only to form, join, and communicate with groups and individuals online, but also to create and distribute original content in ways not possible in the past. Such *consumer-generated content* is changing the marketing landscape, and brands are joining this online conversation with customers. Consumer-generated content (CGC), or user-generated content, is a highly effective and cost-efficient way for brands to engage with consumers, raise awareness, and increase sales. CGC encompasses all sorts of content relating to a brand, such as reviews, pictures, videos, brief comments, stories, emotional outbursts, and hashtags.[34]

Numerous studies show several extremely positive outcomes of CGC. For example, when consumers interact with CGC, revenue increased on average by 116 percent on retail sites and 101 percent on brand sites. Also, rate at which consumers perform a desired action on the brand's web page (e.g., sign up to receive e-mails), known as conversions, increased on average by 106 percent and 97 percent respectively. In a study of Facebook, CGC drove 6.9 times the level of brand engagement as brand-generated content.

Consumers invest the time and effort to create these types of content usually out of a desire to help, inform, protect, entertain, or inspire confidence in other consumers. Consumers develop an affinity to brands associated with CGC because they believe it to be quite authentic. Authenticity is considered to be of paramount importance by 87 percent of consumers, and 60 percent of consumers perceive CGC to be the most authentic form of all content (as compared to 23 percent for celebrity endorsements).

There are many examples of CGC campaigns that worked beautifully, including

- Aerie, a women's clothing company, launched a social media campaign asking consumers to post natural pictures of themselves in the company's clothing with the hashtag #AerieREAL. The goal was to bring awareness to photo retouching in the fashion industry and the impact it has on women's self-esteem. For every use of #AerieREAL, Aerie donated $1 to the National Eating Disorders Association. The company also pledged to stop retouching swimsuit photos.

	People	Advertising
Restaurants	83%	35%
Places	71	33
Prescription drugs	71	21
Hotels	63	27
Health tips	61	19
Movies	61	67
Best brands	60	33
Retirement planning	58	9
Automobiles	58	36
Clothes	50	59
Computer equipment	40	18
Websites to visit	37	12
Combined purchases: restaurant, TV, and movies	43	43

Source: Adapted from *The Influentials: One American in Ten Tells the Other Nine How to Vote, Where to Eat, and What to Buy,* by Edward Keller and Jonathan Berry. Published in 2003 by Roper ASW, LLC. CivicScience Insight Report, October 16, 2014.

- Starbucks' annual red cup CGC campaign garnered over 40,000 posts of customers' pictures of their Starbucks red holiday cups in various contexts with #RedCupsContest. The contest gave consumers the chance to express their creativity and win a large Starbucks gift card. This campaign also stimulated sales because consumers first had to make a purchase to obtain a red cup for their pictures.

However, not every CGC campaign is so successful. Here are some examples:

- McDonalds' CGC campaign that encouraged consumers to use the hashtag #McDStories was a flop. The fast-food retailer had hoped that this CGC campaign would produce positive and heartwarming posts. Instead, many consumers used this hashtag to express dissatisfaction with the brand. For example, some select tweets included "Ate McFish and vomited 1 hour later . . . The last time I got McDonalds was seriously 18 years ago in college" and "My father used to bring us to McDonalds as a reward when we were kids. Now he's horribly obese and has diabetes. Lesson learned."
- Quiznos restaurants hosted a CGC campaign in which they asked consumers to submit videos that would illustrate why Quiznos sandwiches were better than Subway sandwiches. This campaign resulted in a lawsuit from Subway that argued that Quiznos had encouraged consumers to make false negative claims about Subway sandwiches.

CGC also can involve specific requests by firms for consumer input into product design decisions. The Budweiser ad shown in Illustration 7–5 is a great example.

Consumers who generate content online are, in essence, the opinion leaders, which we discuss shortly, whose influence cannot be underestimated. Marketers are embracing these consumer conversations to help, and hopefully not hurt, their brands.

Critical Thinking Questions:

1. As mentioned, the Internet abounds with examples of CGC campaigns. Browse a social media site and find a CGC campaign. Write a brief paragraph describing your findings.
2. Reflect on and describe ways that you personally have participated in CGC. Have you created any content yourself? Do you consume CGC when shopping and/or browsing online? Please elaborate.
3. How authentic do you perceive CGC campaigns to be? What aspects of CGC campaigns would increase or decrease perceptions of authenticity?
4. Based on the examples you read in this consumer insight and your own experience with CGC, what advice would you give to a marketer who is embarking on his or her first CGC campaign?

As this information suggests, the importance of WOM is generally high, and its importance relative to advertising varies somewhat across product types. In addition, traditional mass-media advertising still plays a role, particularly at the earlier stages of the decision process, including building brand awareness.

Negative experiences are powerful motivators of WOM, a factor that must be considered by marketers because negative WOM can strongly influence recipients' attitudes and behaviors.[35] Negative experiences, which are highly emotional and memorable, motivate consumers to talk. While the number varies by situation and product, it is not at all uncommon to find that dissatisfied consumers tell twice as many people about their experience than do satisfied consumers.[36] While merely satisfying consumers (delivering what they expected) may not always motivate WOM, going beyond satisfaction to deliver more than was expected also appears to have the potential to generate substantial WOM. Thus, companies may consider strategies for "delighting" consumers or otherwise creating positive emotional experiences that consumers are motivated to pass along in the form of positive WOM (see Chapter 18).[37] Obviously, it is imperative for companies to provide both

Source: Anheuser-Busch Companies, LLC

consistent product and service quality and quick, positive responses to consumer complaints.

Moreover, it is important to note that not all personal sources are equal in value. Some folks are known in their circles as the "go-to person" for specific types of information. These individuals actively filter, interpret, or provide product- and brand-relevant information to their family, friends, and colleagues. An individual who does this is known as an **opinion leader.** The process of one person's receiving information from the mass media or other sources and passing it on to others is known as the **two-step flow of communication.** The two-step flow explains some aspects of communication within groups, but it is too simplistic to account for most communication flows. What usually happens is a multistep flow of communication. Figure 7–4 contrasts the direct flow of information from a firm to customers with the more realistic multistep flow of mass communications.

The **multistep flow of communication** involves opinion leaders for a particular product area who actively seek relevant information from the mass media as well as other sources. These opinion leaders process this information and transmit their interpretations of it to some members of their groups. These group members also receive information from the mass media as well as from group members who are not opinion leaders. Figure 7–4 also indicates that these non–opinion leaders often initiate requests for information and supply feedback to the opinion leaders. Likewise, opinion leaders receive information from their followers as well as from other opinion leaders. Note how social media facilitates this multistep flow process online.

FIGURE 7-4   Mass Communication Information Flows

Situations in Which WOM and Opinion Leadership Occur

The exchange of advice and information between group members can occur *directly* in the form of WOM when (1) one individual seeks information from another or (2) one individual volunteers information. It also can occur *indirectly* through observation as a by-product of normal group interaction.

LO5

Imagine that you are about to make a purchase in a product category with which you are not very familiar. Further imagine that the purchase is important to you—perhaps a new sound system, skis, or a bicycle. How would you go about deciding what type and brand to buy? Chances are you would, among other things, ask someone you know who you believe is knowledgeable about the product category. This person would be an opinion leader for you. Notice that we have described a *high-involvement* purchase situation in which the purchaser has limited product knowledge about an important decision. Figure 7–5 illustrates how these factors lead to varying levels of opinion leadership.[38]

In addition to *explicitly* seeking or volunteering information, group members provide information to each other through observable behaviors. Consider Clarisonic, a sonic-wave skin care device:

> One of Seattle's hottest tech startups has everything to do with making more than 2 million women so far—Lady Gaga and Oprah among them—look good and feel good about themselves. The company started on its current path by introducing the Clarisonic to highly influential skin professionals—dermatologists and spas—then branched out into luxury retail stores. Without writing checks, Oprah, Cameron Diaz, Tyra Banks, and Justin Timberlake all said publicly they were fans of Clarisonic. "Once people use it, they are our best advocates. Word of mouth is our best friend," the company president said. The product made $1.7 million in its first year and surpassed $100 million in sales five years later.[39]

The Clarisonic has succeeded mainly through observation. To illustrate, initial spa users experienced cleaner and healthier skin for others to see. Then more customers and their healthier skin were observed by others. Finally, celebrities shared their personal experiences and success with the product on social media.

Likelihood of Seeking an Opinion Leader   FIGURE 7-5

Product/purchase involvement	Product knowledge	
	High	Low
High	Moderate Likelihood	High Likelihood
Low	Low Likelihood	Moderate Likelihood

Obviously, observation and direct WOM often operate together. For example, you might be in the market for a digital camera and notice that a friend uses an Olympus. This might jump-start a conversation about digital cameras, the Olympus brand, and where to find the best deals. And while Clarisonic's success depended on observation, WOM also was involved as friends told other friends.

Characteristics of Opinion Leaders

The most salient characteristic of opinion leaders is greater long-term involvement with the product category than the non–opinion leaders in the group. This is referred to as **enduring involvement,** and it leads to enhanced knowledge about and experience with the product category or activity.[40] This knowledge and experience make opinion leadership possible.[41] Thus, an individual tends to be an opinion leader only for a specific product or activity clusters.

Opinion leadership functions primarily through interpersonal communications and observation. These activities occur most frequently among individuals with similar demographic characteristics. Thus, it is not surprising that opinion leaders are found within all demographic segments of the population and seldom differ significantly on demographic variables from the people they influence. Opinion leaders tend to be more gregarious than others are, which may explain their tendency to provide information to others. They also have higher levels of exposure to relevant media than do non–opinion leaders. And opinion leaders around the world appear to possess similar traits.[42]

Identifying and targeting opinion leaders is important. Offline, opinion leaders can be targeted through specialized media sources. For example, Adidas could assume that many subscribers to *Runner's World* serve as opinion leaders for jogging and running shoes.[43] Online, opinion leaders often can be identified in terms of their activity and influence in a given arena.[44] Matt Halfill, a sneakerhead-turned-blogger (his blog is NiceKicks), is seen as an opinion leader in the sneaker culture and companies like Adidas advertise on his blog.

Market Mavens   Opinion leaders are specialists. Their knowledge and involvement tend to be product or activity specific. Therefore, while a person might be an opinion leader for motorcycles, she or he is likely to be an opinion seeker for other products, such as cell phones. However, some individuals have information about many different kinds of products, places to shop, and other aspects of markets. They both initiate discussions with others about products and shopping, and respond to requests for market information. These generalized market influencers are **market mavens.** In essence, then, market mavens are a special type of opinion leader.

Market mavens provide significant amounts of information to others across a wide array of products, including durables and nondurables, services, and store types. They provide information on product quality, sales, usual prices, product availability, store personnel characteristics, and other features of relevance to consumers. Market mavens are extensive users of media.[45] They are also more extroverted and conscientious, which drives their tendency to share information with others.[46] Market mavens tend to be younger and have slightly higher household incomes than the overall U.S. population, but therein lies the only demographic distinction. In effect, market mavens tend to be similar demographically to those they influence.

Recent research has shown how technology and the Internet have shaped the behavior of market mavens.[47] Over 80 percent of these *influentials,* or *e-fluentials,* follow trends in technology and electronics. Also, they are more likely than the rest of the population to engage in the following behaviors:

- Seek out and write online reviews.
- Compare prices.
- Shop online.
- Purchase products that allow them to try new things.
- Exhibit brand loyalty because of product quality.
- Use multiple media devices at the same time.

Their interests and influence extend beyond technology. More than half follow trends in health and fitness, and almost half monitor trends in food and cooking, as well as music. A market maven's reach cannot be ignored by marketers, as these influencers can help a company attract new customers.

Marketing Strategy, WOM, and Opinion Leadership

Marketers are increasingly relying on WOM and influential consumers as part of their marketing strategies. Driving factors include fragmented markets that are more difficult to reach through traditional mass media, greater consumer skepticism toward advertising, and a realization that opinion leaders and online creators and critics can provide invaluable insights in the research and development process.

This is not to say that marketers have given up on traditional advertising and mass media approaches. Instead, they realize that in many cases they could make their traditional media spending go a lot further if they could tap into these influential consumers who will spread the word either indirectly through observation or directly through WOM. We examine some marketing strategies designed to generate WOM and encourage opinion leadership next.

Advertising Advertising can stimulate and simulate WOM and opinion leadership. *Stimulation* can involve themes designed to encourage current owners to talk about (tell a friend about) the brand or prospective owners to ask current owners (ask someone who owns one) for their impressions.[48] Ads can attempt to stimulate WOM by generating interest and excitement. Dove generated interest using a combination of advertising and so-called pass-it-on tools to stimulate WOM. They ran an ad offering two free bars of Dove to anyone who would recommend three friends, who also got a free bar of soap that was gift-wrapped with the name of the initiating friend on the outside. So instead of a sample from a giant company, it felt like a gift from a friend.[49]

Simulating opinion leadership involves having an acknowledged opinion leader—such as Phil Mickelson for golf equipment—endorse a brand. Illustration 7-6 is an example of this approach. Or it can involve having an apparent opinion leader recommend the product in a "slice of life" commercial. These commercials involve an "overheard" conversation between two individuals in which one person provides brand advice to the other. Finally, advertising can present the results of surveys showing that a high percentage of either knowledgeable individuals ("9 out of 10 dentists surveyed recommend . . .") or typical users recommend the brand.[50]

Product Sampling *Sampling,* sometimes called "seeding," involves getting a sample of a product into the hands of a group of potential consumers. Sampling can be a particularly potent WOM tool when it involves individuals likely to be opinion leaders. They, in turn, can serve as brand ambassadors, as in the case of lululemon described in the chapter's opener.

ILLUSTRATION 7-6

Consumers often use personal sources as primary opinion leaders. However, experts whom they don't know personally also can fill this role, as can survey results indicating that the brand is recommended by experts or typical users.

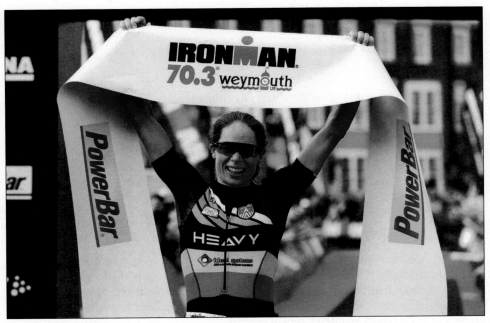

©Finnbarr Webster Editorial/Alamy

In an attempt to increase the preference for Dockers among the key 24-to-35-year-old urban market, Levi Strauss created the position of "urban networker" in key cities. The networkers identified emerging trendsetters in their cities and tied them to Dockers. This could involve noticing a new band that was beginning to catch on and providing Dockers to the members. The objective was to be associated with emerging urban "happenings" and young influentials as they evolved.[51]

BzzAgent (www.BzzAgent.com) recruits everyday people to actively spread WOM about products they like. BzzAgent is adamant that its "agents" acknowledge their association with BzzAgent and provide honest opinions. Most of the WOM occurs offline in normal conversations. Agents receive a free product sample to use and are coached on various WOM approaches. Agents report back to BzzAgent about each WOM episode and redeemable points are rewarded. Importantly, the motive of most is not the points because many don't redeem them. BzzAgent's client list is long and growing and includes Kraft Foods, Goodyear, and Wharton School Publishing. Companies hire BzzAgent to create and field a WOM campaign. Costs vary, but a 12-week campaign involving 1,000 agents can cost $100,000 or more.[52]

Retailing/Personal Selling   Numerous opportunities exist for retailers and sales personnel to use opinion leadership. Clothing stores can create "fashion advisory boards" composed of likely style leaders from their target market. An example would be a young woman in a sorority for a store like Lilly Pulitzer, trying to attract the college-aged and older Millennial.

Retailers and sales personnel can encourage their current customers to pass along information to potential new customers. When those consumers are given rewards such as discounts, it is called a referral reward program. For example, an automobile salesperson, or the dealership, might provide a free car wash or oil change to current customers who send friends in to look at a new car. Such programs are growing in popularity and companies such as United Airlines, and RE/MAX are using them. Research demonstrates that the programs are effective, particularly for encouraging positive WOM to those with whom consumers have weak rather than strong ties.[53]

Creating Buzz   **Buzz** can be defined as *the exponential expansion of WOM.* It happens when "word spreads like wildfire" with no or limited mass media advertising supporting it. Buzz drove demand for Clarisonic, as described earlier. It also made massive successes of Pokémon, Beanie Babies, the original *Blair Witch Project,* the Harry Potter books, and *Toy Story 3.*[54] Marketers create buzz by providing opinion leaders advance information and product samples, having celebrities use the product, placing the product in movies, sponsoring "in" events tied to the product, restricting supply, courting publicity, and otherwise generating excitement and mystique about the brand.

Buzz generally is not supported by large advertising budgets, but it is often created by marketing activities. In fact, creating buzz is a key aspect of *guerrilla marketing*—marketing with a limited budget using nonconventional communications strategies. Guerrilla marketing is about making an "intense connection with individuals and speed[ing] up the natural word-of-mouth process."[55] Examples of guerrilla techniques include

- Sony Ericsson hired attractive actors to pose as tourists in various metro areas. They would then hand their cell phone/digital camera to locals and ask them to take a picture in an attempt to get the camera in their hands and get them talking about it.
- Bounty, the paper towel company, installed giant "messes"—such as a spilled cup of coffee or melting ice cream—on the streets of New York City and Los Angeles. People could not help but stop to see these life-size creations and nearby signage that said "Bounty—Makes small work of BIG spills."[56]

Buzz is not just guerrilla marketing, and guerrilla tactics must be used with care. Consumer advocates are increasingly concerned about certain guerrilla tactics. There are (a) consumer, (b) ethical, and (c) legal issues with stealth or covert marketing efforts. Consider the following example:

> Gillette sponsored an unbranded website called NoScruf.org. NoScruf stands for the National Organization of Social Crusaders Repulsed by Unshaven Faces. The site was created by Porter Novelli for PR reasons on Gillette's behalf and the .org designation was to further obfuscate Gillette's role.

From a consumer standpoint, research shows that when consumers become aware of such covert marketing efforts, consumer trust, commitment, and purchase intentions are damaged. From an ethical standpoint, hiding a brand's participation in a marketing effort puts consumers at a disadvantage because, when they know, they tend to be more wary of the influence attempt. From a legal standpoint, there is movement in the direction of more stringent guidelines against such covert marketing, with one example being the FTC's new guidelines regarding bloggers and their link to marketers.[57] *Can you see additional ethical concerns surrounding "covert" or "guerrilla" marketing? How is BzzAgent's approach different from Sony Ericsson's?*

Creating buzz is often part of a larger strategy that includes significant mass media advertising. Clairol attempted to create WOM for its True Intense Color line via an online sampling program. It also launched a sweepstakes, "Be the Attraction," with a

Online Buzz, WOM, and Astroturfing

As we've seen, the Internet continues to change the nature of interpersonal communications. New avenues are rapidly evolving, and the rewards can be huge for companies that can harness the speed and ease of interconnectivity that the Internet allows. Here are a few examples:[58]

- **Viral marketing** is an online "pass-it-along" strategy. It "uses electronic communications to trigger brand messages throughout a widespread network of buyers." Viral marketing comes in many forms but often involves social media. Worldwide Breast Cancer started a Facebook campaign to create awareness of the signs and risk factors of breast cancer as well as to raise funds for the organization. The "Know Your Lemons" campaign gained over 7 million impressions on Facebook. The viral aspect kicked in when the ad was shared over 40,000 times. In addition, the campaign also raised more than $160 million for breast cancer research and awareness. Nonprofits are not the only organizations using viral techniques. Companies like Nike, Adidas, and Heineken also have enjoyed successful viral campaigns recently.

- *Snapchat* is a platform that allows users to message others privately by sending pictures or short videos that uniquely disappear a few seconds upon viewing the message. Snapchat Stories are clips that can be viewed by all of the user's Snapchat friends. These news-like feeds stay posted for 24 hours before disappearing. Snapchat is popular among Millennials, with 60 percent of users under the age of 24. Brands, especially those targeting a younger demographic, are creatively using Snapchat and its "stories" feature to connect with their customers. For example, the candy brand Sour Patch Kids attracted over 100,000 new followers with its recent "Blue Kid" Snapchat story campaign. Amazon also has used Snapchat to offer exclusive promotional deals on Black Friday.

- *Twitter* is a micro-blogging tool that allows users to communicate with others through short messages. It limits posts to 280 (formerly 140) characters. It has evolved quickly into one of the largest and fastest-growing social media outlets. For marketers there are a number of uses for Twitter. First, as we saw earlier, consumers can post complaints or information requests to

grand prize of an all-expenses-paid trip for four to the premiere of *Legally Blonde* to fuel the buzz. However, these efforts were soon supplemented with a major mass media advertising campaign.[59]

Buzz and WOM are not confined to traditional offline strategies. As discussed in Consumer Insight 7–3, marketers are leveraging increasing numbers of online strategies as well.

DIFFUSION OF INNOVATIONS

LO6

An **innovation** is *an idea, practice, or product perceived to be new by the relevant individual or group.* Whether or not a given product *is* an innovation is determined by the perceptions of the potential market, not by an objective measure of technological change. The manner by which a new product is accepted or spreads through a market is basically a group phenomenon. In this section, we will examine this process in some detail.[60]

a brand's Twitter account, to which companies can respond. Second, companies can utilize a Twitter feature called Promoted Tweets. The promotion indicator (like an advertisement) shows up on the Tweet and then the Tweet itself comes up on the search results, even of those who aren't the brand's followers on Twitter. Finally, companies like Sponsored Tweets and Opendorse are connecting brands with influential tweeters. These tweeters, often celebrities or athletes like LeBron James and Kim Kardashian who have millions of followers, get paid for tweeting about specific brands. James was recently paid $140,000 for a 140-character tweet, which amounted to $1,000 per character! For a brand to be effective on this platform, full disclosure is important.

- **Customer reviews** and review functionality on a website can be a critical marketing tool. Amazon and others allow consumers to easily post reviews of products on their sites. Given the power of WOM, this online version of WOM is a powerful decision influencer. For example, restaurant revenues have been found to increase between 5 and 9 percent if they increase their ranking on Yelp by one star. However, there are at least two factors that marketers must be concerned with regarding online reviews. First, because existing reviews are "public information," they tend to "sway" future reviews in that direction. So, if reviews trend down, that likely feeds more downward bias than if reviews were done independent of knowledge of prior reviews. Marketers can find themselves in a battle against a misguided trend, and consumers likely are not getting the best, most accurate advice. A second concern is fake reviews, where it is estimated that one in seven reviews is fake. Astroturfing is the practice whereby companies buy positive reviews of themselves and negative reviews for their competitors. The "buying" of fake reviews by one company for another is akin to false advertising. Samsung was recently fined for hiring people to criticize HTC (a competitor) products.

Clearly marketers are learning how to leverage the WOM potential of the Internet. It will be interesting to see what the future brings!

Critical Thinking Questions

1. What other Internet alternatives exist for interpersonal communication?

2. Do you trust online sources to provide accurate information? What can marketers do to increase consumer trust in online sources?

3. What do you think are typical characteristics of those who are heavy Snapchat or Twitter users?

Categories of Innovations

Try to recall new products that you have encountered in the past two or three years. As you reflect on these, it may occur to you that there are degrees of innovation. For example, wireless speakers such as Amazon's Echo are more of an innovation than is a new fat-free snack. The changes required in one's behavior, including attitudes and beliefs, or lifestyle if a person adopts the new product or service determine the degree of innovation, not the technical or functional changes in the product.

We can place any new product somewhere on a continuum ranging from no change to radical change, depending on the target market's perception of the item. This continuum is often divided into three categories or types of innovations.

Continuous Innovation Adoption of this type of innovation requires relatively minor changes in behavior or changes in behaviors that are unimportant to the consumer.

Crest 3DWhite
Whitening Therapy
toothpaste would be
considered a con-
tinuous innovation by
most.

Source: The Procter & Gamble Company

Examples include Crest 3DWhite Whitening Therapy toothpaste, Wheaties Energy Crunch cereal, and Purex 3-in-1 laundry sheets. Note that some continuous innovations require complex technological breakthroughs. However, their use requires little change in the owner's behavior or attitude. Crest 3DWhite Whitening Therapy toothpaste, shown in Illustration 7–7, is another example of a continuous innovation.

Dynamically Continuous Innovation   Adoption of this type of innovation requires a moderate change in an important behavior or a major change in a behavior of low or moderate importance to the individual. Examples include digital cameras, personal navigators, mobile apps, and Bella and Birch textured paints that are applied like wallpaper but without glue, using a special applicator. The Shout Color Catcher ad in Illustration 7–8 is a good example of a product that is a dynamically continuous innovation for most consumer groups.

Using Shout Color
Catcher would
require a major
change in an area of
moderate importance
for most individuals.
For these individuals,
it would be a dynami-
cally continuous
innovation.

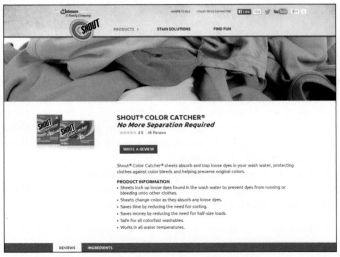

Source: S.C. Johnson & Son, Inc.

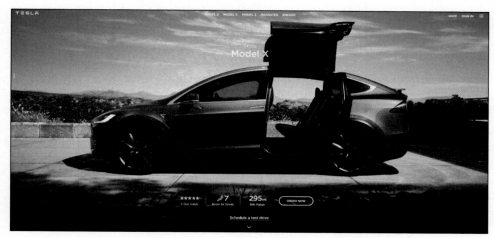

Source: Tesla

Discontinuous Innovation Adoption of this type of innovation requires major changes in behavior of significant importance to the individual or group. Examples would include the Norplant contraceptive, becoming a vegetarian, and the Tesla electric car (see Illustration 7–9).

Most of the new products or alterations introduced each year tend toward the no-change end of the continuum. Much of the theoretical and empirical research, however, has been based on discontinuous innovations. For example, individual consumers presumably go through a series of distinct steps or stages known as the **adoption process** when purchasing an innovation. These stages are shown in Figure 7–6.

Adoption Process and Extended Decision Making   **FIGURE** 7-6

Figure 7-6 also shows the steps in extended decision making, described in Chapter 1. As can be seen, the *adoption process* is basically a term used to describe extended decision making when a new product is involved. As we will discuss in detail in Chapter 14, extended decision making occurs when the consumer is *highly involved* in the purchase. High purchase involvement is likely for discontinuous innovations such as the decision to purchase a hybrid or electric car, and most studies of innovations of this nature have found that consumers use extended decision making.

However, it would be a mistake to assume that all innovations are evaluated using extended decision making (the adoption process). In fact, most continuous innovations probably trigger limited decision making. As consumers, we generally don't put a great deal of effort into deciding to purchase innovations such as Diet Coke's Ginger Lime–flavored drink or Glad microwave steaming bags.

Diffusion Process

The **diffusion process** is *the manner in which innovations spread throughout a market.* The term *spread* refers to purchase behavior in which the product is purchased with some degree of regularity.[61] The market can range from virtually the entire society (for a new soft drink, perhaps) to the students at a particular high school (for an automated fast-food and snack outlet).

For most innovations, the diffusion process appears to follow a similar pattern over time: a period of relatively slow growth, followed by a period of rapid growth, followed by a final period of slower growth. This pattern is shown in Figure 7-7. However, there are exceptions to this pattern. In particular, it appears that for continuous innovations such as new ready-to-eat cereals, the initial slow-growth stage may be skipped.

An overview of innovation studies reveals that the time involved from introduction until a given market segment is saturated (i.e., sales growth has slowed or stopped) varies from a few days or weeks to years. This leads to two interesting questions: (1) What determines how rapidly a particular innovation will spread through a given market segment? and (2) In what ways do those who purchase innovations relatively early differ from those who purchase them later?

Factors Affecting the Spread of Innovations   The rate at which an innovation is diffused is a function of the following 10 factors.

1. *Type of group.* Some groups are more accepting of change than others. In general, young, affluent, and highly educated groups accept change, including new products, readily. Thus, the target market for the innovation is an important determinant of the rate of diffusion.[62]

2. *Type of decision.* The type of decision refers to an individual versus a group decision. The fewer the individuals involved in the purchase decision, the more rapidly an innovation will spread.

3. *Marketing effort.* The rate of diffusion is heavily influenced by the extent of marketing effort involved. Thus, the rate of diffusion is not completely beyond the control of the firm.[63]

4. *Fulfillment of felt need.* The more manifest or obvious the need that the innovation satisfies, the faster the diffusion. Rogaine, a cure for some types of hair loss, gained rapid trial among those uncomfortable with thin hair or baldness.

5. *Compatibility.* The more the purchase and use of the innovation are consistent with the individual's and group's values or beliefs, the more rapid the diffusion.[64]

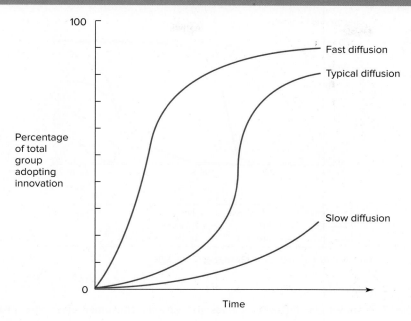

6. *Relative advantage.* The better the innovation is perceived to meet the relevant need compared with existing methods, the more rapid the diffusion. Both the performance and the cost of the product are included in relative advantage. The digital audio tape (DAT) had neither advantage compared with CDs and DVDs and thus never took off.

7. *Complexity.* The more difficult the innovation is to understand and use, the slower the diffusion. The key to this dimension is ease of use, *not* complexity of product. Specialized blogging software is making an otherwise complex task easy and fun.[65]

8. *Observability.* The more easily consumers can observe the positive effects of adopting an innovation, the more rapid its diffusion will be. Smartphones are relatively visible. Laser eye surgery, while less visible, may be a frequent topic of conversation. On the other hand, new headache remedies are less obvious and generally less likely to be discussed.

9. *Trialability.* The easier it is to have a low-cost or low-risk trial of the innovation, the more rapid is its diffusion. The diffusion of products like laser eye surgery has been hampered by the difficulty of trying out the product in a realistic manner. This is much less of a problem with low-cost items such as headache remedies, or such items as smartphones, which can be borrowed or tried at a retail outlet.

10. *Perceived risk.* The more risk associated with trying an innovation, the slower the diffusion. Risk can be financial, physical, or social. Perceived risk is a function of three dimensions: (1) *the probability that the innovation will not perform as desired;* (2) *the consequences of its not performing as desired;* and (3) *the ability (and cost) to reverse any negative consequences.*[66] Thus, many consumers may feel a need for the benefits offered by laser eye surgery and view the probability of its working successfully as being quite high. However, they perceive the consequences of failure as being extreme and irreversible and therefore do not adopt this innovation.

FIGURE 7-8   Diffusion Rates for Consumer Electronics

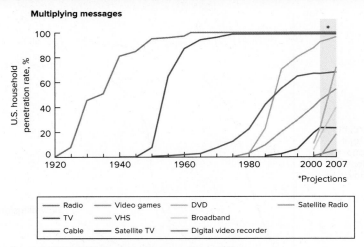

Source: *ECONOMIST* by Economist Newspaper Group, 2005.

Figure 7-8 shows the diffusion curves for various consumer electronic products. *How would you explain the differences in diffusion rates across these products in U.S. households?*

Characteristics of Individuals Who Adopt an Innovation at Varying Points in Time   The curves shown in Figures 7-7 and 7-8 are cumulative curves that illustrate the increase in the percentage of adopters over time. If we change those curves from a cumulative format to one that shows the percentage of a market that adopts the innovation at any given point in time, we will have the familiar bell-shaped curves shown in Figure 7-9.

Figure 7-9 reemphasizes the fact that a few individuals adopt an innovation very quickly, another limited group is reluctant to adopt the innovation, and the majority of the group adopts at some time in between the two extremes. Researchers have found it useful to divide the adopters of any given innovation into five groups based on the relative time at which they adopt. These groups, called **adopter categories,** are shown in Figure 7-9 and defined below:

Innovators: The first 2.5 percent to adopt an innovation.

Early adopters: The next 13.5 percent to adopt.

Early majority: The next 34 percent to adopt.

Late majority: The next 34 percent to adopt.

Laggards: The final 16 percent to adopt.

How do these groups differ? The following descriptions, though general, provide a good starting point. Clearly, however, research by product category would be necessary in fully understanding specific marketing situations.

Innovators are venturesome risk takers. They are capable of absorbing the financial and social costs of adopting an unsuccessful product. They are cosmopolitan in outlook and use other innovators rather than local peers as a reference group. They tend to be

FIGURE

Adoptions of an Innovation over Time

younger, better educated, and more socially mobile than their peers. Innovators make extensive use of commercial media, sales personnel, and professional sources in learning of new products.

Early adopters tend to be opinion leaders, like market mavens, in local reference groups. They are successful, well educated, and somewhat younger than their peers. They are willing to take a calculated risk on an innovation but are concerned with failure. Early adopters also use commercial, professional, and interpersonal information sources, and they provide information to others.

Early majority consumers tend to be cautious about innovations. They adopt sooner than most of their social group but also after the innovation has proved successful with others. They are socially active but seldom leaders. They tend to be somewhat older, less well educated, and less socially mobile than the early adopters. The early majority rely heavily on interpersonal sources of information.

Late majority members are skeptical about innovations. They often adopt more in response to social pressures or a decreased availability of the previous product than because of a positive evaluation of the innovation. They tend to be older and have less social status and mobility than those who adopt earlier.

Laggards are locally oriented and engage in limited social interaction. They tend to be relatively dogmatic and oriented toward the past. Laggards adopt innovations only with reluctance.

Marketing Strategies and the Diffusion Process

Market Segmentation   Because earlier purchasers of an innovation differ from later purchasers, firms should consider a "moving target market" approach. That is, after selecting a general target market, the firm initially should focus on those individuals within the target market most likely to be innovators and early adopters.[67] Messages to this group often can emphasize the newness and innovative characteristics of the product as well as its functional features. Because this group is frequently very involved with, and knowledgeable about, the product category, marketing communications may be able to focus on the new technical features of the product and rely on the audience to understand the benefits these features will provide.[68]

As the innovation gains acceptance, the focus of attention should shift to the early and late majority. This will frequently require different media. In addition, message themes should generally move away from a focus on radical newness. Instead, they should emphasize the acceptance the product has gained and its proven performance record.

Diffusion Enhancement Strategies   Table 7–3 provides a framework for developing strategies to enhance the market acceptance of an innovation. The critical aspect of this process is to analyze the innovation *from the target markets' perspective,* including their resistance to it.[69] This analysis will indicate potential obstacles—*diffusion inhibitors*—to rapid market acceptance. The manager's task is then to overcome these inhibitors with *diffusion enhancement strategies.* Table 7–3 lists a number of potential enhancement strategies, but many others are possible.

Consider the innovation shown in Illustration 7–10. Which factors will inhibit the dji Spark drone's diffusion, and what strategies can be used to overcome them?

TABLE 7-3	Innovation Analysis and Diffusion Enhancement Strategies	
Diffusion Determinant	**Diffusion Inhibitor**	**Diffusion Enhancement Strategies**
1. Nature of group	Conservative	Search for other markets Target innovators within group
2. Type of decision	Group	Choose media to reach all deciders Provide conflict reduction themes
3. Marketing effort	Limited	Target innovators within group Use regional rollout Leverage buzz
4. Felt need	Weak	Extensive advertising showing importance of benefits
5. Compatibility	Conflict	Stress attributes consistent with normative values
6. Relative advantage	Low	Lower price Redesign product
7. Complexity	High	Distribute through high-service outlets Use skilled sales force Use product demonstrations Extensive marketing efforts
8. Observability	Low	Use extensive advertising Target visible events when appropriate
9. Trialability	Difficult	Use free samples to early adopter types Offer special prices to rental agencies Use high-service outlets
10. Perceived risk	High	Success documentation Endorsement by credible sources Guarantees

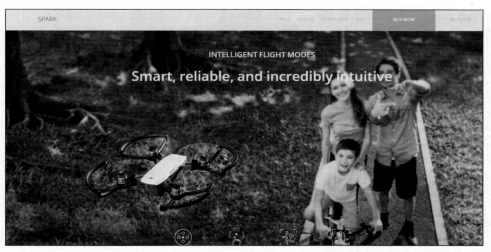

SPARK   SPECS   VIDEOS   DOWNLOADS   FAQ   **BUY NOW**   GO TO TOP

INTELLIGENT FLIGHT MODES
Smart, reliable, and incredibly intuitive

Source: DJI

ILLUSTRATION 7-10

Ten factors determine the success of innovations. How do you think the DJI Spark drone innovation will fare based on these 10 factors?

SUMMARY

LO1: Explain reference groups and the criteria used to classify them.

A *reference group* is a group whose presumed perspectives or values are being used by an individual as the basis for his or her current behavior. Thus, a reference group is simply a group that an individual uses as a guide for behavior in a specific situation. Reference groups, as with groups in general, may be classified according to a number of variables including membership, strength of social tie, type of contact, and attraction.

LO2: Discuss consumption subcultures, including brand and online communities and their importance for marketing.

A *consumption subculture* is a group that self-selects on the basis of a shared commitment to a particular product or consumption activity. These subcultures also have (1) an identifiable, hierarchical social structure; (2) a set of shared beliefs or values; and (3) unique jargon, rituals, and modes of symbolic expression.
A *brand community* is a nongeographically bound community, based on a structured set of social relationships among owners of a brand and the psychological relationship they have with the brand itself, the product in use, and the firm. Brand communities can add value to the ownership of the product and build intense loyalty.

An *online community* is a community that interacts over time around a topic of interest on the Internet. Online communities have evolved over time to include *online social network sites,* which are web-based services that allow individuals to (1) construct a public or semi-public profile within a bounded system, (2) articulate a list of other users with whom they share a connection, and (3) view and traverse their list of connections and those made by others within the system.

LO3: Summarize the types and degree of reference group influence.

Informational influence occurs when an individual uses the behaviors and opinions of reference group members as potentially useful bits of information. *Normative influence,* sometimes referred to as utilitarian influence, occurs when an individual fulfills group expectations to gain a direct reward or to avoid a sanction. *Identification influence,* also called value-expressive influence, occurs when individuals have internalized the group's values and norms.

The degree of *conformity* to a group is a function of (1) the visibility of the usage situation, (2) the level of commitment the individual feels to the group, (3) the relevance of the behavior to the functioning of the group, (4) the individual's confidence in his or her own judgment in the area, and (5) the level of necessity reflected by the nature of the product.

SMARTBOOK

LO4: Discuss within-group communications and the importance of word-of-mouth communications to marketers.

Communication within groups is a major source of information about certain products. Information is communicated within groups either directly through *word-of-mouth (WOM)* communication or indirectly through observation. WOM via personal sources such as family and friends is trusted more than marketer-based messages and therefore can have a critical influence on consumer decisions and business success. Two-thirds of all consumer product decisions are thought to be influenced by WOM. Negative experiences are a strong driver of negative WOM for all consumers.

LO5: Understand opinion leaders (both online and offline) and their importance to marketers.

Opinion leaders are highly knowledgeable about specific products or activities and are seen as the "go-to person" for specific types of information. These individuals actively filter, interpret, or provide product- and brand-relevant information to their family, friends, and colleagues. A defining characteristic of opinion leaders is their enduring involvement with the product category, which leads to their expertise and the trust people have in their opinions.

A special type of opinion leader is *market mavens*. These are individuals who are general market influencers. They have information about many different kinds of products, places to shop, and other aspects of markets. These influencers can share information both offline *(influentials)* and online *(e-fluentials)*.

Marketers attempt to identify opinion leaders primarily through their media habits and social activities. Identified opinion leaders then can be used in marketing research, product sampling, retailing/ personal selling, advertising, and buzz creation. Various offline and online strategies exist for stimulating WOM, opinion leadership, and buzz. Online strategies include viral marketing, Snapchat, and Twitter.

LO6: Discuss innovation diffusion and use an innovation analysis to develop marketing strategy.

Groups greatly affect the diffusion of innovations. *Innovations* vary in degree of behavioral change required and the rate at which they are diffused. The first purchasers of an innovative product or service are termed *innovators;* those who follow over time are known as *early adopters, early majority, late majority,* and *laggards.* Each of these groups differs in personality, age, education, and reference group membership. These characteristics help marketers identify and appeal to different classes of adopters at different stages of an innovation's diffusion.

The time it takes for an innovation to spread from innovators to laggards is affected by several factors: (1) nature of the group involved, (2) type of innovation decision required, (3) extent of marketing effort, (4) strength of felt need, (5) compatibility of the innovation with existing values, (6) relative advantage, (7) complexity of the innovation, (8) ease in observing usage of the innovation, (9) ease in trying the innovation, and (10) perceived risk in trying the innovation.

KEY TERMS

Adopter categories 248
Adoption process 245
Asch phenomenon 232
Aspiration reference groups 221
Brand ambassador 220
Brand community 224
Buzz 241
Community 224
Consumption subculture 221
Customer reviews 243
Diffusion process 246
Dissociative reference groups 221
Early adopters 249

Early majority 249
Enduring involvement 238
Group 220
Identification influence 229
Informational influence 228
Innovation 242
Innovators 248
Laggards 249
Late majority 249
Market mavens 238
Multistep flow of
   communication 236
Normative influence 228

Online community 226
Online social network
   site 226
Opinion leader 236
Primary groups 221
Reference group 220
Secondary groups 221
Two-step flow of
   communication 236
Viral marketing 242
Word-of-mouth (WOM)
   communications 233

REVIEW QUESTIONS

1. How does a *group* differ from a *reference group?*

2. What criteria are used by marketers to classify groups?

3. What is a *dissociative reference group?* In what way can dissociative reference groups influence consumer behavior?

4. What is an *aspiration reference group?* How can an aspiration reference group influence behavior?

5. What is a *consumption-based group* or a *consumption subculture?* How can marketers develop strategy based on consumption subcultures?

6. What is a *brand community?* What are the characteristics of such a group?

7. How can a marketer foster a brand community?

8. What is an *online social network site?* What are the guidelines for marketers operating in online communities and social networking sites?

9. What types of group influence exist? Why must a marketing manager be aware of these separate types of group influence?

10. What five factors determine the strength of reference group influence in a situation?

11. What is the *Asch phenomenon* and how do marketers utilize it?

12. How can a marketer use knowledge of reference group influences to develop advertising strategies?

13. What is an *opinion leader?* How does an opinion leader relate to the *multistep flow of communication?*

14. What characterizes an opinion leader?

15. What determines the likelihood that a consumer will seek information from an opinion leader?

16. How does a *market maven* differ from an *opinion leader?*

17. Explain the role of *enduring involvement* in driving opinion leadership.

18. How can marketing managers identify opinion leaders?

19. How can marketers utilize opinion leaders?

20. What is *buzz?* How can marketers create it?

21. Compare and contrast *Twitter* and *Snapchat.*

22. What is an *innovation?* Who determines whether a given product is an innovation?

23. What are the various categories of innovations? How do they differ?

24. What is the *diffusion process?* What pattern does the diffusion process appear to follow over time?

25. Describe the factors that affect the diffusion rate for an innovation. How can these factors be utilized in developing marketing strategy?

26. What are *adopter* categories? Describe each of the adopter categories.

27. How can a marketer use knowledge of adopter categories to develop marketing strategy?

DISCUSSION QUESTIONS

28. Respond to the questions in Consumer Insight 7–1.

29. Using college students as the market segment, describe the most relevant reference group(s) and indicate the probable degree of influence on decisions for each of the following:
    a. Brand of toothpaste
    b. Purchase of an electric car
    c. Purchase of breakfast cereal
    d. Becoming a vegetarian
    e. Choice of a wireless speaker such as the Amazon Echo

Answer Questions 30 to 33 using (a) shoes, (b) barbeque grill, (c) car, (d) toaster, (e) iPad, and (f) adopting a pet from a shelter.

30. How important are reference groups to the purchase of the above-mentioned products or activities? Would their influence also affect the brand or model? Would their influence be informational, normative, or identification? Justify your answers.

31. What reference groups would be relevant to the decision to purchase the product or activity (based on students on your campus)?

32. What are the norms of the social groups of which you are a member concerning the product or activity?

33. Respond to the questions in Consumer Insight 7–2.

34. Describe two groups that serve as aspiration reference groups for you. In what ways, if any, have they influenced your consumption patterns?

35. Describe two groups to which you belong. For each, give two examples of instances when the group has exerted (*a*) informational, (*b*) normative, and (*c*) identification influence on you.

36. Develop two approaches using reference group theory to reduce drug, alcohol, or cigarette consumption among teenagers.

37. What ethical concerns arise in using reference group theory to sell products?

38. Describe a consumption subculture to which you belong. How does it affect your consumption behavior? How do marketers attempt to influence your behavior with respect to this subculture?

39. Do you belong to a brand community? If so, describe the benefits you derive from this group and how it affects your consumption.

40. Do you belong to an online community or social network site? If so, describe the benefits you derive from this group and how it affects your consumption.

41. Answer the following questions for (*i*) Dyson bladeless fan, (*ii*) space flight, (*iii*) cell phone-based GPS.
    a. Is the product an innovation? Justify your answer.
    b. Using the student body on your campus as a market segment, evaluate the perceived attributes of the product.
    c. Who on your campus would serve as opinion leaders for the product?
    d. Will the early adopters of the product use the adoption process (extended decision making), or is a simpler decision process likely?

42. Describe two situations in which you have served as or sought information from an opinion leader. Are these situations consistent with the discussion in the text?

43. Are you aware of market mavens on your campus? Describe their characteristics, behaviors, and motivation.

44. Have you used Twitter recently? Why? How did it work? What marketing implications does this suggest?

45. Identify a recent (*a*) continuous innovation, (*b*) dynamically continuous innovation, and (*c*) discontinuous innovation. Justify your selections.

46. Analyze the Roomba (robotic vacuum cleaner) in terms of the determinants in Table 7–3 and suggest appropriate marketing strategies.

47. Conduct a diffusion analysis and recommend appropriate strategies for the innovation shown in Illustration 7–10.

48. Assume that you are a consultant to firms with new products. You have members of the appropriate market segments rate innovations on the 10 characteristics described in Table 7–3. Based on these ratings, you develop marketing strategies. Assume that a rating of 9 is extremely favorable (e.g., strong relative advantage or a lack of complexity) and 1 is extremely unfavorable. Suggest appropriate strategies for each of the following consumer electronic products (see table).

Attribute	A	B	C	D	E	F	G	H	I
Fulfillment of felt need	9	7	3	8	8	5	7	8	9
Compatibility	8	8	8	8	9	2	8	9	8
Relative advantage	9	2	8	9	7	8	9	8	8
Complexity	9	9	9	9	9	3	8	8	7
Observability	8	8	9	1	9	4	8	8	8
Trialability	8	9	8	9	9	2	9	2	9
Nature of group	3	8	7	8	9	9	7	7	3
Type of decision	3	7	8	8	6	7	7	3	7
Marketing effort	6	7	8	7	8	6	3	8	7
Perceived risk	3	8	7	7	3	7	8	8	5

Product

APPLICATION ACTIVITIES

49. Find two advertisements that use reference groups in an attempt to gain patronage. Describe the advertisement, the type of reference group being used, and the type of influence being used.

50. Develop an advertisement for (*i*) teeth whitening strips, (*ii*) an energy drink, (*iii*) an upscale club, (*iv*) Red Cross, (*v*) scooters, or (*vi*) vitamins using the following:
    a. An informational reference group influence
    b. A normative reference group influence
    c. An identification reference group influence

51. Interview two individuals who are strongly involved in a consumption subculture. Determine how it affects their consumption patterns and what actions marketers take toward them.

52. Interview an individual who is involved in a brand community. Describe the role the firm plays in maintaining the community, the benefits the person gets from the community, and how it affects his or her consumption behavior.

53. Identify and interview several opinion leaders on your campus for the following. To what extent do they match the profile of an opinion leader as described in the text?
    a. Local restaurants
    b. Sports equipment
    c. Music
    d. Computer equipment

54. Interview two salespersons for the following products. Determine the role that opinion leaders play in the purchase of their product and how they adjust their sales process in light of these influences.
    a. Smartphones
    b. Golf equipment
    c. Computers
    d. Art
    e. Jewelry
    f. Sunglasses

55. Follow a brand on Twitter for a week. What types of marketing strategies are they engaged in and how are they utilizing Twitter to facilitate brand awareness and solve customer problems.

REFERENCES

1. The Chapter 7 opener is based on J. H. McAlexander, J. W. Schouten, and H. F. Koenig, "Building Brand Community," *Journal of Marketing,* January 2002, pp. 38–54; H. Malcom, "Lululemon Lovers Buy into Healthy Lifestyle," *USA Today,* March 19, 2013, www.usatoday.com, accessed March 19, 2018; A. Lutz, "Lululemon's Effective Technique for Hooking Customers," *Business Insider,* May 21, 2015, www.businessinsider.com, accessed March 19, 2018; M. Newlands, "How Lululemon Made Their Brand Iconic: An Interview with SVP of Brand Programs Eric Petersen," *Forbes,* February 21, 2016, www.forbes.com, accessed March 19, 2018; M. Schlossberg, "One Sentence Sums Up Why Millennials Are Flocking to Nike, Under Armour and Lululemon," *Business Insider,* July 6, 2016, www.businessinsider.com, accessed March 19, 2018; J. Fromm, "The Lululemon Lifestyle: Millennials Seek More Than Just Comfort from Athleisure Wear," *Forbes,* July 6, 2016, www.forbes.com, accessed March 19, 2018; B. Pearson, "The Hidden Value of Thanks: 3 Ways Apple, Lululemon and Others Do It," *Forbes,* September 7, 2016, www.forbes.com, accessed March 19, 2018; C. Fernandez, "Inside Lululemon's Unconventional Influencer Network," *Fashionista,* November 2, 2016, www.fashionista.com, accessed March 19, 2018; A. Foote, "#SquadGoals: 21 Outstanding Brand Communities to Emulate," *L and T Co.,* January 12, 2017, www.landt.co,

accessed March 19, 2018; E. Bary, "Lululemon Has a Big New Fan Base," *Barron's,* March 16, 2017, www.barrons.com, accessed March 19, 2018; as well as information from various websites, including www.lululemon.com, accessed March 19, 2018; www.luluaddict.com, accessed March 19, 2018; and www.reuters.com, accessed March 19, 2018.

2. K. White and D. W. Dahl, "To Be or *Not* Be?," *Journal of Consumer Psychology* 16, no. 4 (2006), pp. 404–14.

3. J. W. Schouten and J. H. McAlexander, "Subcultures of Consumption," *Journal of Consumer Research,* June 1995, p. 43.

4. N. Christakis and J. Fowler, *CONNECTED* (New York: Little, Brown & Company, 2009); S. Clifford, "Video Prank at Domino's Taints Brand," *New York Times,* April 15, 2009, www.nytimes.com/2009/04/16/business/media/16dominos .html?_r50, accessed September 1, 2014; E. Rosen, *The Anatomy of Buzz Revisited: Real-Life Lessons in Word-of-Mouth Marketing* (New York: Random House, 2009); J. Sanburn, "How Dr. Dre Made $300 Headphones a Must-Have Accessory," *Time,* January 16, 2013, business.time. com/2013/01/16/how-dr-dre-made-300-headphones-a-must-have-accessory/, accessed September 1, 2014; D. Gilgoff, "Short Takes: Gauging the Impact of 'Purpose Driven Life,' 10 Years on," *Belief blog,* November 29, 2012, http://religion.

blogs.cnn.com/2012/11/29/short-takes-gauging-the-impact-of-purpose-driven-life-10-years-on/, accessed September 1, 2014.

5. B. Gainer, "Ritual and Relationships," *Journal of Business Research,* March 1995, pp. 253–60. See also E. J. Arnould and P. L. Price, "River Magic," *Journal of Consumer Research,* June 1993, pp. 24–45.

6. A. Hamilton and J. DeQuine, "Freaking for Sneakers," *Time,* March 13, 2006.

7. Excerpts from L. Beward, "Sneakerheads Share a Passion for Rare Soles," *McClatchy-Tribune Business News,* July 10, 2009.

8. T. Wasserman, "Sneakerheads Rule," *Adweek,* October 19, 2009, pp. 10–14.

9. Based on McAlexander, Schouten, and Koenig, "Building Brand Community."

10. A. M. Muniz Jr. and T. C. O'Guinn, "Brand Community," *Journal of Consumer Research,* March 2001, p. 413. See also R. P. Bagozzi, "On the Concept of Intentional Social Action in Consumer Behavior," *Journal of Consumer Research,* December 2000, pp. 388–96; A. M. Muniz Jr. and H. J. Schau, "Religiosity in the Abandoned Apple Newton Brand Community," *Journal of Consumer Research,* March 2005, pp. 737–47.

11. Harley-Davidson example from Schouten and McAlexander, "Subcultures of Consumption." MG example from T. W. Leigh, C. Peters, and J. Shelton, "The Consumer Quest for Authenticity: The Multiplicity of Meanings within the MG Subculture of Consumption," *Journal of the Academy of Marketing Science* 34, no. 4 (2006), pp. 481–93. Tesla example from F. Lambert, "Tesla Fulfils Bucket List of Dying Man by Delivering His Model 3 Early," *Electrek,* December 13, 2017, https://electrek.co/2017/12/13/tesla-model-3-bucket-list-dying-man/, accessed March 26, 2018; and other Tesla websites found at www.forums.tesla.com, accessed March 26, 2018; and www.teslamotorgroup.com, accessed March 26, 2018.

12. Q. Jones, "Virtual Communities, Virtual Settlements, and CyberArchaeology," *Journal of Computer-Mediated Communication* 3, no. 3 (1997), www.ascusc.org/jcmc/vol3/issue3/jones.html, accessed March 26, 2018; C. Okleshen and S. Grossbart, "Usenet Groups, Virtual Community and Consumer Behaviors," and S. Dann and S. Dann, "Cybercommuning," both in *Advances in Consumer Research,* vol. 25, ed. J. W. Alba and J. W. Hutchinson (Provo, UT: Association for Consumer Research, 1998), pp. 276–82 and 379–85, respectively; C. L. Beau, "Cracking the Niche," *American Demographics,* June 2000, pp. 38–40; P. Maclaran and M. Catterall, "Researching the Social Web," *Marketing Intelligence and Planning* 20, no. 6 (2002), pp. 319–26.

13. A. L. Blanchard and M. L. Markus, "The Experienced 'Sense' of a Virtual Community," *Database for Advances in Information Systems,* Winter 2004, pp. 65–79.

14. D. M. Boyd and N. B. Ellison, "Social Network Sites," *Journal of Computer-Mediated Communication* 13, no. 1 (2007), http://jcmc.indiana.edu, accessed June 17, 2008.

15. Statistics are estimates for 2016 from eMarketer.com.

16. A. Lenhart et al., *Teens, Social Media & Technology Overview 2015* (Washington, DC: Pew Research Center, April 9, 2015); A. Smith and M. Anderson, *Social Media Use in 2018* (Washington, DC: Pew Research Center, March 1, 2018).

17. B. Thompson, *How to Use Social Media to Improve Customer Service and Cut Costs* (Burlingame, CA: Customer Think, March 2010).

18. *State of Inbound Marketing Report* (Cambridge, MA: HubSpot, 2010).

19. *2010 Cone Consumer New Media Study Fact Sheet* (Boston, MA: Cone LLC, 2010).

20. Ibid.

21. For additional information and expertise, visit *Site Logic Marketing* at www.sitelogicmarketing.com and the online marketing blog "Marketing Logic," written by Matt Bailey, Site Logic's president.

22. Excerpt from http://consumerist.com/consumer/blogs/sonys-pspblog-flog-revealed-221384.php.

23. N. Zmuda, "Ann Taylor Investigation Shows FTC Keeping Close Eye on Blogging," *Advertising Age,* April 28, 2010.

24. B. Thompson, *Voice of Customer 2.0* (Burlingame, CA: Customer Think, March 2010).

25. J. Comm, "How Oreos Got 40 Million Likes on Facebook," *Inc.,* January 6, 2016, www.inc.com, accessed April 4, 2018; Oreo website, www.facebook.com/oreo/, accessed April 4, 2018.

26. L. K. John, D. Mochon, O. Emrich and J. Schwartz, "What's the Value of a Like?," *Harvard Business Review,* March–April 2017, pp. 108–15.

27. See T. F. Mangleburg and T. Bristol, "Socialization and Adolescents' Skepticism toward Advertising," *Journal of Advertising,* Fall 1998, pp. 11–20. See also T. F. Mangleburg, P. M. Doney, and T. Bristol, "Shopping with Friends and Teens' Susceptibility to Peer Influence," *Journal of Retailing* 80 (2004), pp. 101–16.

28. See R. J. Fisher and D. Ackerman, "The Effects of Recognition and Group Need on Volunteerism," *Journal of Consumer Research,* December 1998, pp. 262–77.

29. See K. R. Lord, M.-S. Lee, and P. Choong, "Differences in Normative and Informational Social Influence," in *Advances in Consumer Research,* vol. 28, ed. M. C. Gilly and J. Meyers-Levy (Provo, UT: Association for Consumer Research, 2001), pp. 280–85.

30. See W. Amaldoss and S. Jain, "Pricing and Conspicuous Goods," *Journal of Marketing Research,* February 2005, pp. 30–42.

31. See, e.g., M. Mourali, M. Laroche, and F. Pons, "Individualistic Orientation and Consumer Susceptibility to Interpersonal Influence," *Journal of Services Marketing* 19, no. 3 (2005), pp. 164–73.

32. T. Patton, "How Are Consumers Influenced by Referral Marketing?," *Ambassador,* March 9, 2016, www.getambassador.com, accessed April 7, 2018.

33. G. Packard and J. Berger, "How Language Shapes Word of Mouth's Impact," *Journal of Marketing Research* 54 (August 2017), pp. 572–88.

34. Insight is based on S. Bernazzani, "The 10 Best User-Generated Content Campaigns on Instagram," https://blog.hubspot.com/marketing/best-user-generated-content-campaigns, accessed March 18, 2018; D. Kirkpatrick, "Study: User-Generated Content Drives Higher Facebook Engagement Than Ads," *Marketing Dive,* February 14, 2017, www.marketingdive.com/news/study-user-generated-content-drives-higher-facebook-engagement-than-ads/436139/, accessed March 18, 2018; K. Morrison, "How Consumer-Generated Content Drives Brand Value (Report)," *Adweek,* April 25, 2016, www.adweek.com/digital/how-consumer-generated-content-drives-brand-value-report/, accessed March 18, 2018; E. Siu, "10 User Generated Content

Campaigns That Actually Worked," https://blog.hubspot.com/marketing/examples-of-user-generated-content, accessed March 18, 2018; "The 2017 Consumer Content Report: Influence in the Digital Age 2017," https://stackla.com/go/2017-consumer-content-report-influence-in-digital-age/, accessed March 18, 2018; T. Weinberg, "When User-Generated Content Goes Bad," *TNW*, June 17, 2016, https://thenextweb.com/insider/2016/06/17/user-generated-content-goes-bad/, accessed March 18, 2018; "Why Your User-Generated Content Campaign Failed," www.sitereportcard.com/1656/user-generated-content-campaign-failed/, accessed March 18, 2018; "Worst UGC Fails," https://duel.tech/worst-ugc-fails/, accessed March 18, 2018.

35. See, e.g., R. N. Laczniak, T. E. DeCarlo, and S. N. Ramaswami, "Consumers' Responses to Negative Word-of-Mouth Communication," *Journal of Consumer Psychology* 11, no. 1 (2001), pp. 57–73; A. Wilson, M. Giebelhausen, and M. Brady, "Negative Word of Mouth Can Be a Positive for Consumers Connected to the Brand," *Journal of the Academy of Marketing Science* 45 (2017), pp. 534–47.

36. E. Rosen, *The Anatomy of Buzz* (New York: Doubleday, 2000); see also D. S. Sundaram, K. Mitra, and C. Webster, "Word-of-Mouth Communications," in *Advances in Consumer Research*, vol. 25, ed. Alba and Hutchinson, pp. 527–31; A. A. Bailey, "The Interplay of Social Influence and Nature of Fulfillment," *Psychology & Marketing*, April 2004, pp. 263–78.

37. M. Johnson, G. M. Zinkhan, and G. S. Ayala, "The Impact of Outcome, Competency, and Affect on Service Referral," *Journal of Services Marketing* 5 (1998), pp. 397–415.

38. For a thorough discussion, see D. F. Duhan, S. D. Johnson, J. B. Wilcox, and G. D. Harrell, "Influences on Consumer Use of Word-of-Mouth Recommendation Sources," *Journal of the Academy of Marketing Science*, Fall 1997, pp. 283–95; C. Pornpitakpan, "Factors Associated with Opinion Seeking," *Journal of Global Marketing* 17, no. 2/3 (2004), pp. 91–113.

39. L. Timmerman, "Clarisonic Cracks Big-Time with $100M Sales, Riding Rave Reviews from Lady Gaga, Oprah," *Xconomy*, March 30, 2011, www.xconomy.com, accessed April 7, 2018; "Unpaid Celebrity Endorsements," *Celebrity Cred*, March 4, 2016, www.celebritycred.com, accessed April 7, 2018.

40. G. M. Rose, L. R. Kahle, and A. Shoham, "The Influence of Employment-Status and Personal Values on Time-Related Food Consumption Behavior and Opinion Leadership," in *Advances in Consumer Research*, vol. 22, ed. F. R. Kardes and M. Sujan (Provo, UT: Association for Consumer Research, 1995), pp. 367–72; U. M. Dholakia, "Involvement-Response Models of Joint Effects," in *Advances in Consumer Research*, vol. 25, ed. Alba and Hutchinson, pp. 499–506.

41. See M. C. Gilly, J. L. Graham, M. F. Wolfinbarger, and L. J. Yale, "A Dyadic Study of Interpersonal Information Search," *Journal of the Academy of Marketing Science*, Spring 1998, pp. 83–100.

42. R. Marshall and I. Gitosudarmo, "Variation in the Characteristics of Opinion Leaders across Borders," *Journal of International Consumer Marketing* 8, no. 1 (1995), pp. 5–22.

43. See I. M. Chaney, "Opinion Leaders as a Segment for Marketing Communications," *Marketing Intelligence and Planning* 19, no. 5 (2001), pp. 302–308.

44. Methods for understanding network influences online are still being developed. For one approach, see M. Trusov, A. V. Bodapati, and R. E. Bucklin, "Determining Influential Users in Internet Social Networks," *Journal of Marketing Research,* August 2010, pp. 643–58.

45. L. F. Feick and L. L. Price, "The Market Maven," *Journal of Marketing,* January 1987, pp. 83–97. See also R. A. Higie, L. F. Feick, and L. L. Price, "Types and Amount of Word-of-Mouth Communications about Retailers," *Journal of Retailing,* Fall 1987, pp. 260–78; K. C. Schneider and W. C. Rodgers, "Generalized Marketplace Influencers' Attitudes toward Direct Mail as a Source of Information," *Journal of Direct Marketing,* Autumn 1993, pp. 20–28; J. E. Urbany, P. R. Dickson, and R. Kalapurakal, "Price Search in the Retail Grocery Market," *Journal of Marketing,* April 1996, pp. 91–104.

46. T. A. Mooradian, "The Five Factor Model and Market Mavenism," in *Advances in Consumer Research,* vol. 23, ed. K. P. Corfman and J. G. Lynch (Provo, UT: Association for Consumer Research, 1996), pp. 260–63. For additional motivations driving mavens, see G. Walsh, K. P. Gwinner, and S. R. Swanson, "What Makes Mavens Tick?," *Journal of Consumer Marketing* 21, no. 2 (2004), pp. 109–22; "An In-Depth Look at the Market Maven Persona," *Civic Science,* February 25, 2016, https://civicscience.com, accessed April 8, 2018.

47. E. Keller and J. Berry, *The Influentials* (New York: Free Press, 2003). See also D. Godes and D. Mayzlin, "Firm-Created Word-of-Mouth Communication," *Harvard Business School Marketing Research Papers,* no. 04-03 (July 2004); I. Cakim, "E-Fluentials Expand Viral Marketing," *iMedia Connection,* October 28, 2002, www.imediaconnection.com; see also information on Burson-Marsteller's website at www.bm.com; "An In-Depth Look at the Market Maven Persona."

48. See E. Keller and B. Fay, "The Role of Advertising in Word of Mouth," *Journal of Advertising Research,* June 2009, pp. 154–58.

49. Rosen, *The Anatomy of Buzz.*

50. See C. S. Areni, M. E. Ferrell, and J. B. Wilcox, "The Persuasive Impact of Reported Group Opinions on Individuals Low vs. High in Need for Cognition," *Psychology & Marketing,* October 2000, pp. 855–75.

51. A. Z. Cuneo, "Dockers Strives for Urban Credibility," *Advertising Age,* May 25, 1998, p. 6.

52. See R. Walker, "The Hidden (in Plain Sight) Persuaders," *New York Times Magazine,* December 5, 2004; materials on BzzAgent's website at www.BzzAgent.com.

53. See E. Biyalogorsky, E. Gerstner, and B. Libai, "Customer Referral Management," *Marketing Science,* Winter 2001, pp. 82–95; G. Ryu and L. Feick, "A Penny for Your Thoughts," *Journal of Marketing,* January 2007, pp. 84–94.

54. R. Dye, "The Buzz on Buzz," *Harvard Business Review,* November 2000, p. 140; J. Lehrer, "Head Case: The Buzz on Buzz," *Wall Street Journal,* October 16, 2010, p. C12.

55. T. F. Lindeman, "More Firms Use Unique 'Guerrilla Marketing' Techniques to Garner Attention," *Knight Ridder Tribune Business News,* January 18, 2004, p. 1.

56. Ibid.; A. Zantal-Wiener, "What Is Guerrilla Marketing? 7 Examples to Inspire Your Brand," *HubSpot,* July 28, 2017, https://blog.hubspot.com/marketing/guerilla-marketing-examples, accessed April 8, 2018.

57. C. Ashley and H. A. Leonard, "Betrayed by the Buzz?," *Journal of Public Policy and Marketing,* Fall 2009, pp. 212–20.

58. A. Dobele, D. Toleman, and M. Beverland, "Controlled Infection!," *Business Horizons* 48 (2005), pp. 143–49; "7 Best

Viral Campaigns—2017," *National Positions,* January 8, 2018, https://nationalpositions.com/7-best-viral-campaigns-2017/, accessed March 24, 2018; S. Patel, "7 Brands That Are Killing It on Snapchat," *Entrepreneur,* February 6, 2017, www.entrepreneur.com, accessed March 28, 2018; J. Wertz, "Which Social Media Platforms Are Right for Your Business?," *Forbes,* February 18, 2017, www.forbes.com, accessed March 28, 2018; E. Moreau, "What Is Snapchat? An Intro to the Popular Ephemeral App," *Lifewire,* February 11, 2018, www.lifewire.com, accessed March 28, 2018; *Who Tweets?* (Washington, DC: Pew Internet, 2009); J. Van Grove, "Sponsored Tweets Launches," *Mashable,* August 3, 2009, www.mashable.com, accessed May 23, 2011; "Americans Spend 2 Hours, 12 Minutes per Month on Twitter," *Search Engine Watch,* January 26, 2011, http://blog. searchenginewatch.com, accessed March 17, 2011; "How Charlie Sheen and Other Stars Get Paid to Tweet," *Wall Street Journal Blog,* March 6, 2011, https://blogs.wsj.com, accessed May 25, 2011; "How Does Twitter Make Money?," www.buzzle.com, accessed May 23, 2011; D. Rovell, "LeBron James-sponsored Tweets Valued at $140K or $1K per character," *ESPN,* August 20, 2015, www.espn.com/nba/story/_/id/13470682/lebron-james-sponsored-tweets-232-million-followers-cost-140k, accessed March 26, 2018; D. Pogue, "Critical Mass," *Scientific American,* May 17, 2011, www.scientificamerican.com/article/critical-mass/, accessed September 1, 2014; D. Streitfeld, "In a Race to Out-Rave, 5-Star Web Reviews Go for $5," *New York Times,* August 19, 2011, www.nytimes.com/2011/08/20/technology/finding-fake-reviews-online.html, accessed September 1, 2014; D. Streitfeld, "Give Yourself 5 Stars? Online, It Might Cost You," *New York Times,* September 22, 2013, www.nytimes.com/2013/09/23/technology/give-yourself-4-stars-online-it-might-cost-you.html?_r=0, accessed September 1, 2014; C. Conner, "Online Reputation," *Forbes,* October 30, 2013, www.forbes.com/sites/cherylsnappconner/2013/10/30/online-reputation-new-methods-emerge-for-quashing-fake-defamatory-reviews/, accessed September 1, 2014.

59. K. Fitzgerald, "Bristol-Meyers Builds Buzz," *Advertising Age,* April 23, 2001, p. 18.

60. See also V. Mahajan, E. Muller, and F. M. Bass, "New Product Diffusion Models in Marketing," *Journal of Marketing,* January 1990, pp. 1–26; E. M. Rogers, *Diffusion of Innovations,* 4th ed. (New York: Free Press, 1995). For an alternative to the traditional adoption diffusion model, see C.-F. Shih and A. Venkatesh, "Beyond Adoption," *Journal of Marketing,* January 2004, pp. 59–72.

61. See M. I. Nabith, S. G. Bloem, and T. B. C. Poiesz, "Conceptual Issues in the Study of Innovation Adoption Behavior," in *Advances in Consumer Research,* vol. 24, ed. M. Bruck and D. J. MacInnis (Provo, UT: Association for Consumer Research, 1997), pp. 190–96.

62. See, e.g., S. L. Wood and J. Swait, "Psychological Indicators of Innovation Adoption," *Journal of Consumer Psychology* 12, no. 1 (2002), pp. 1–13.

63. See, e.g., E.-J. Lee, J. Lee, and D. W. Schumann, "The Influence of Communication Source and Mode on Consumer Adoption of Technological Innovations," *Journal of Consumer Affairs,* Summer 2002, pp. 1–27.

64. See N. Y.-M. Siu and M. M.-S. Cheng, "A Study of the Expected Adoption of Online Shopping," *Journal of International Consumer Marketing* 13, no. 3 (2001), pp. 87–106.

65. For a discussion of how type of innovation and consumer expertise interact, see C. P. Moreau, D. R. Lehmann, and A. B. Markman, "Entrenched Knowledge Structures and Consumer Response to New Products," *Journal of Marketing Research,* February 2001, pp. 14–29.

66. For a more complete analysis, see U. M. Dholakia, "An Investigation of the Relationship between Perceived Risk and Product Involvement," in *Advances in Consumer Research,* vol. 24, ed. Bruck and MacInnis, pp. 159–67; M. Herzenstein, S. S. Posavac, and J. J. Brakus, "Adoption of New and Really New Products," *Journal of Marketing Research,* May 2007, pp. 251–60.

67. For a discussion of when this is not appropriate, see V. Mahajan and E. Muller, "When Is It Worthwhile Targeting the Majority Instead of the Innovators in a New Product Launch?," *Journal of Marketing Research,* November 1998, pp. 488–95.

68. See, e.g., Chaney, "Opinion Leaders as a Segment for Marketing Communications."

69. M. Claudy, R. Garcia and A. O'Driscoll, "Consumer Resistance to Innovation—A Behavioral Reasoning Perspective," *Journal of the Academy of Marketing Science* 43 (2015), pp. 528–44.

Part Two CASES

IKEA is a well-known Swedish retail company that sells low-cost, stylish furniture that is purchased in a flat-packed form and usually assembled at home. It is known for a simplistic, clean-lined Scandinavian style. IKEA has large warehouse-style stores throughout the world. Although there are differences in various regions, the stores are typically set up into "rooms" that show the furniture arranged as it would be in homes so visitors can experience it. They also host kid-friendly play areas and cafeterias with Scandinavian foods, as well as some local dishes.

IKEA stores are often destination shopping centers where consumers frequently travel many miles to visit and spend the day enjoying the experience. IKEA executives believe one reason for IKEA's success is it listens to its customers' needs and wants to co-create value.

However, the exact Swedish model does not translate well directly into all cultures. So, the company takes plenty of time before entering a market to make sure it is done right. Even so, IKEA has encountered some missteps. Years often are spent conducting extensive market research and ethnography (the study of local customers and cultures), both before and after entry into a new market. IKEA researchers visit surrounding homes and talk with numerous consumers to discover local tastes, preferences, and ways of living. They also pour over market reports and perform company and consumer surveys. These practices allow IKEA to attain success in a variety of different cultures with disparate tastes and values through local adaptations. Adaptations can be found in many areas, including catalogs, products, pricing, and shopping styles. According to IKEA Chief Executive Mikael Ohlsson:

> Most people don't really know and can hardly imagine that we visit thousands of homes around every store in the world every year. We sit down in the kitchen and talk to them. That's the way we try to learn and understand. "What are you annoyed with? What are your frustrations? What would you like to have? How much can you afford? What are your alternatives?"

CATALOG ADAPTATIONS

Each year, IKEA distributes a catalog in each of the countries in which it is located. This is a massive undertaking, especially considering the vast array of lifestyles and values across the various markets. For example, in 2017, IKEA distributed 203 million copies of its 324-page catalog. There were 72 different versions specific to various regional cultures. IKEA's extensive research allows for tailoring the communication and imagery to best target consumers in a given region. There are many different types of kitchens throughout the world and the images attempt to fit the norms of the locations where consumers are viewing the catalogs. For example, in China kitchens are smaller than in the United States. IKEA modifies its catalog photos and in-store kitchen models to reflect the smaller kitchen size, as well as other important aspects appealing to Chinese consumers. Other changes are more dramatic, such as the edition for Orthodox Jews in Israel. In the Israeli version, no female models are included in the photos. Instead, all models are male and some are studying religious texts. The 2011 and 2012 versions for Saudi Arabia similarly omitted female models, or in some cases the images for the Saudi editions contain no models at all. This omission of women in these versions was meant to appeal to those male-dominated cultures. However, after consumer protests, IKEA had to issue apologies in both instances and recognize such practices are not consistent with IKEA values. This is the 2017 statement:

> We realize that people are upset about this and that the publication does not live up to what IKEA stands for and we apologize for this. We will make sure that future publications will reflect what IKEA stands for and at the same time show respect for the Haredi community.

PRODUCT ADAPTATIONS

Marketing research and talking with consumers reveal several adaptions to product offerings in the United States. IKEA quickly learned that homes are larger and Americans prefer their household furnishings to be larger as well. Curtains are made longer, sofas are made deeper, spaces in kitchen cabinetry are widened to accommodate U.S. appliances, and tableware is enlarged. Upon first entry, IKEA executives pondered why they were selling unusually high numbers of vases. It did not take long to realize that Americans were buying them as drinking glasses because the actual initial drinking glasses offered were too small for American tastes. Also, IKEA stores initially lacked large tables and serving platters to accommodate large groups of people because Thanksgiving was an unfamiliar concept. IKEA performs this type of research even within regions of the same country. Recently, IKEA felt it may have been out of touch with the large Hispanic population in California. After visiting many homes, IKEA made product adaptations such as adding more bold colors and elaborate picture frames to its offerings.

Likewise, IKEA found several differences in regional tastes, values, and preferences in India that shaped product offerings there. The market research revealed that Indian consumers prefer home furnishings with vivid colors; the family life centers around the sofa in the living room where they eat their meals, do homework, and even sleep; and Indians do not enjoy the do-it-yourself culture. In response, products offered in the Indian market are adapted to have more vivid colors, in contrast to the Scandinavian versions where white and beige color schemes are preferred. Sofas also are redesigned so that they are expandable for sleeping and entertaining and collapsible for maximizing space. Finally, delivery, assembly, and installation are highlighted ancillary products to overcome the antipathy to do-it-yourself culture.

PRICING ADAPTATIONS

In China, research shows key differences from other regions: Chinese consumers are highly price sensitive to products for domestic consumption, like household furnishings, and they view shopping as an experience more so than many other cultures. Chinese people are willing to pay a price premium for more visible Western brands, such as automobiles and Starbucks coffee. However, furniture is a much less conspicuous form of consumption. Additionally, there are many low-cost competitors of household furnishings in China. Therefore, IKEA had to reduce prices by about 50 percent before Chinese sales really took off. It was a successful strategy though, as evidenced by IKEA becoming the largest foreign commercial landowner. An average Saturday in the Bejing IKEA sees about 28,000 visitors, which approximates the weekly average in European stores.

SHOPPING STYLE ADAPTATIONS

Many Chinese visitors enjoy the shopping experience but do not make a purchase. In fact, in contrast to IKEA stores in other countries, China's IKEA stores are often filled with people sleeping in the model beds and on the sofas. It is not uncommon for whole families to pile into the bedroom displays alongside strangers to nap and then go eat in the IKEA cafeteria after awaking. Chinese IKEA management welcomes them because they will likely become customers later and by allowing visitors to spend the day in the store resting and enjoying the air-conditioning, IKEA is accommodating local culture and building brand relationships.

IKEA is committed to understanding its customers by continuously engaging in ethnography and other forms of marketing research to keep in touch with their needs, preferences, and values in regions and countries where IKEA is located and those in which it may potentially enter.

Discussion Questions

1. IKEA spends a considerable amount of time researching new markets before entering them. What are some issues that IKEA should be considering?

2. Chapter 2 discusses individual versus collective other-oriented values.
   a. China is one of the countries discussed in this case. On face value, would you expect China to have a more individual or collective orientation?
   b. The text discusses how cultural values evolve and individualism is on the rise in some Asian countries, especially among younger consumers.

What evidence do you see in this case of both individualism and collectivism?

3. Another cultural value discussed in Chapter 2 is tradition/change. In most of the cultures described in this case, it is traditional for furniture to be already assembled upon purchase, and perhaps even delivered.
   a. In which of the countries mentioned in the case would the consumers likely have the hardest time dealing with the change of purchasing furniture in a flat-packed form that needs assembly?
   b. How does IKEA overcome this discomfort?

4. IKEA's model of purchasing furniture that is flat-packed and then assembling it yourself at home is a new and different way of doing things for consumers in many countries.
   a. In terms of innovations (see Chapter 7), what type of innovation would this be considered?
   b. Does your answer for part a change if the furniture is delivered and assembled or installed by IKEA?

5. Consider the 10 factors that affect the spread of innovations discussed in Chapter 7 (see Table 7–3 for quick reference).
   a. Which of these factors would play a *positive* role in how quickly acceptance of shopping for furniture using the IKEA model would spread? Explain your answer(s).

   b. Which of these factors would play a *negative* role in how quickly acceptance of shopping for furniture using the IKEA model would spread? Explain your answer(s).

6. Perform a search on the Internet to discover the list of countries where IKEA is currently located (hint: in 2018, there are 30). Find a country that is not listed and imagine that you are an executive at IKEA. Brainstorm ideas of how you would need to adapt the products, communications, pricing, etc. to fit the culture of your chosen country.

7. Chapter 5 discusses marketing to the Hispanic subculture in America. IKEA made an effort to better understand American Hispanics in California through ethnography.
   a. What adaptations did IKEA make to better target the American Hispanic segment?
   b. Based on your knowledge of this subculture from reading the text and your personal experiences, what suggestions would you give a marketing manager at IKEA to best target this segment?

Source: A.E. Fenwick, "Smaller Kitchens in China and Photoshopped Appliances: How IKEA Adapts Its Catalogues to Suit Different Cultures around the World," *DailyMail,* August 2, 2017, www.dailymail.co.uk, accessed April 2, 2018; A. Gupta, "Is India Ready for IKEA?," *Fortune India,* March 24, 2017, www.fortuneindia.com, accessed April 2, 2018; A. Hirst, "How Ikea Became America's Furniture-Selling Powerhouse," *Curbed,* October 8, 2014, www.curbed.com; A. Ringstrom, "One Size Doesn't Fit All: IKEA Goes Local for India, China," *Reuters,* March 6, 2013, https://in.reuters.com; K. Wall, "IKEA at Last Cracks the China Market, but Success Has Meant Adapting to Local Ways," *South China Morning Post,* September 1, 2013, www.scmp.com, accessed April 2, 2018.

2-2 CVS CAREMARK DISCONTINUES THE SALE OF TOBACCO PRODUCTS

According to the American Cancer Society, smoking has resulted in $96 million in health care costs from 2000 to 2014. A well-established link exists between tobacco use and cancer. Public awareness of the dangers of smoking has led to shifting cultural norms, such that smoking is increasingly viewed as negative. While cigarette smoking has been on the decline since the 1950s, about one out of five Americans continues to smoke cigarettes, which leads to the development of cancer. The following table illustrates a breakdown of cancer incidence by sex and ethnicity.

Lung and Bronchus Cancer Incidence by Sex and Ethnicity, United States 2006–2010

	Non-Hispanic White	African American	Asian American or Pacific Islander	American Indian or Alaska Native	Hispanic/Latino
Male	82.9	94.7	48.8	70.2	45.9
Female	59.9	50.4	28.0	52.1	26.6
Total	138.6	220.0	75.0	104.1	124.2

Note: Rates are per 100,000 population

Source: American Cancer Society, Surveillance Research, 2014.

One pharmacy company is taking a stand against smoking and its negative health effects. In 2007, CVS merged with Caremark to become CVS Caremark and undertook a repositioning campaign. Beyond being a chain of drug stores, CVS Caremark is a pharmacy benefit manager that works with insurance companies and employers to control drug costs. The CVS Caremark website refers to the company as "a pharmacy innovation company helping people on their pathway to better health." In mid-September, ahead of its October 1, 2014, deadline, CVS Caremark will discontinue the sale of tobacco products in an effort to better serve its customers and society. According to the CVS Caremark CEO and president, Larry Merlo:

Ending the sale of cigarettes and tobacco products at CVS/pharmacy is simply the right thing to do for the good of our customers and our company. The sale of tobacco products is inconsistent with our purpose—helping people on their path to better health. As the delivery of health care evolves with an emphasis on better health outcomes, reducing chronic disease and controlling costs, CVS Caremark is playing an expanded role through our 26,000 pharmacists and nurse practitioners. By removing tobacco products from our retail shelves, we will better serve our patients, clients and health care providers while positioning CVS Caremark for future growth as a health care company. Cigarettes and tobacco products have no place in a setting where health care is delivered. This is the right thing to do.

An essential part of this repositioning is the introduction of a variety of basic health care services within the retail locations, from flu shots to strep throat tests. The shortage of primary care doctors and provisions in the Affordable Care Act have created an opportunity for pharmacies to play a larger role in the nation's health care. The stage is set for retail clinics to grow at a rate of 25 to 30 percent over the next few years, reaching to 2,800 in 2015, up from 1,400 in 2012. CVS Caremark already has 800 "MinuteClinics" and plans to grow that number to 1,500 by 2017. According to Larry Merlo:

We have about 26,000 pharmacists and nurse practitioners helping patients manage chronic problems like high cholesterol, high blood pressure and heart disease, all of which are linked to smoking. We came to the decision that cigarettes and providing health care just don't go together in the same setting.

There is much speculation over how this change will affect CVS Caremark, both financially and in the public perception. In order to make this change, CVS Caremark will lose $2 billion in annual revenue from tobacco products. This amount translates into 17 cents less earnings annually per share of stock. The company is planning ways to offset the impact on profits such as a smoking cessation program with the goal of helping half a million Americans quit smoking.

Aside from the financial impact, CVS Caremark is reaping benefits. In the public eye, this move is largely seen favorably. Results of a Gallup Poll of 5,550 Americans over the age of 18, the discontinuance of tobacco sales has enhanced the image of CVS Caremark in the perceptions of many consumers. Please reference the two tables for a sample of the Gallup Poll results. The first displays general reactions to CVS Caremark's decision, while the second breaks the respondents into groups based on their level of engagement with CVS Caremark. According to Larry Merlo:

The feedback has been overwhelmingly positive.

Reaction to CVS's Decision to Stop Selling Tobacco Products in Its Stores

	Strongly Disagree (1)	(2)	(3)	(4)	Strongly Agree (5)	Don't Know/ Refused
This decision helps me better understand CVS's mission and purpose.	7%	8%	19%	31%	27%	8%
This decision helps me better understand what makes CVS different from its competitors.	8%	8%	23%	29%	24%	9%

Note: Percentages may not add to 100% due to rounding.
Source: Gallup Poll 2014.

Perceptions of Consumers by Level of Engagement with CVS

	Fully Engaged	Indifferent	Actively Disengaged
Are you aware of CVS's recent decision to discontinue the sale of tobacco products (for example, cigarettes)? (% Yes)	96%	82%	80%
The decision helps me better understand CVS's mission and purpose. (% Strongly Agree)	64%	24%	16%
This decision helps me better understand what makes CVS different from its competitors. (% Strongly Agree)	61%	26%	15%
Based on CVS's decision to discontinue the sale of tobacco products, are you more or less likely to shop at CVS? (% More Likely to Shop at CVS)	47%	27%	23%

Source: Gallup Poll 2014.

Discussion Questions

1. What type of marketing strategy is CVS using?

2. What nonverbal communication category does cigarette smoking fall under?

3. Chapter 3 discusses several American cultural values. Smoking can relate to individual values from each of the three categories. Decide which of the values in each of the following categories best relates to smoking and describe that relationship.
   a. Other-oriented values
   b. Environment-oriented values
   c. Self-oriented values

4. What impact do you think CVS's decision to stop selling tobacco products will have on (a) its long-term sales and (b) smoking trends in America?

5. The case mentions that since the 1950s there has been a cultural trend away from smoking. Young people today may have different perceptions and level of exposure to the shifts in cultural norms dealing with smoking that those in other generations. Perform a brief interview with members of different generational groups to find out how perceptions may differ for different age cohorts. Compare and contrast their perceptions and stories of how smoking was normally treated in different periods of American history. Interviewees should be drawn from at least three of the following generations:
   a. Pre-Depression generation
   b. Depression generation
   c. Baby Boom generation
   d. Generation X
   e. Generation Y
   f. Generation Z

6. What type of reference group would best describe smokers today? How would your answer differ if you were referring to smokers in the early to mid-1900s?

The following questions are based on the tables provided in the case.

7. Which demographic groups have the highest incidence of lung/bronchus cancer (in terms of race and sex)? Would this group be a good target market for CVS Caremark?

8. What effect has CVS Caremark's decision had on public perceptions of the retailer?

9. Do you feel that the consumers who are fully engaged, indifferent, or actively disengaged represent the best target market for CVS Caremark? Why?

10. Based on your answers for questions 7 and 9, devise a marketing strategy for CVS Caremark to market their smoking cessation program to an ideal target market (as described by demographics and level of engagement). Make sure to consider the sections of Chapter 5 that discuss nuances of ethnic subcultures.

Source: American Cancer Society, "Tobacco: The True Cost of Smoking," July 7, 2014, www.cancer.org; CVS Caremark, "About Us," July 20, 2014, http://info.cvscaremark.com; P. Corbett, "CVS Caremark Not Quite Quitting Tobacco," *USA Today,* February 12, 2014, www.usatoday.com; N. Devorak and D. Yu, "Why CVS May Not Get Burned by Its Tobacco Decision," *GALLUP Business Journal,* March 18, 2014, http://businessjournal.gallup.com; M. Herper, "Kicking the Habit: CVS to Stop Selling Tobacco, Sacrificing $2 Billion in Sales for Public Health and Future Growth," *Forbes,* February 5, 2014, www.forbes.com; E. Landaum, "CVS Stores to Stop Selling Tobacco," *CNN,* February 5, 2014, www.cnn.com; T. Martin and M. Esterl, "CVS to Stop Selling Cigarettes," *Wall Street Journal,* February 5, 2014, http://online.wsj.com; L. Saad, "One in Five U.S. Adults Smoke, Tied for All-Time Low," *Gallup,* August 22, 2012, www.gallup.com; S. Strom, "CVS Vows to Quit Selling Tobacco Products," *New York Times,* February 5, 2014, www.nytimes.com.

2-3 BEATS BY DRE'S RISE TO THE TOP

In 2006, rapper Dr. Dre and music industry mogul James Iovine began an endeavor that would change the face of the premium headphones market. They saw an opportunity as increasing numbers of consumers listened to music primarily on mobile devices. While listening to music on cell phones and tablets has convenient mobility, most consumers were using cheap plastic earbuds that came with their devices. In addition, digital music download piracy was increasing. Together, Dr. Dre and Mr. Iovine launched a company called Beats by Dre with the purpose of dramatically enhancing the listening experience for consumers using mobile devices for music delivery. Ultimately, the goal is for the listener to have an experience likened to the sound in the record studio. According to Mr. Iovine:

> You've got to be lucky enough to identify a problem where you think you can help. . . . Apple was selling $400 iPods with $1 earbuds. Dre told me, "Man, it's one thing that people steal my music. It's another thing to destroy the feeling of what I've worked on."

After two years in development with consumer electronics manufacturer Monster, Beats by Dre introduced Beats headphones. The headphones are priced from $99 to $450, well above many of the competitors. However, Beats headphones have a unique appeal. They carry the "cool factor" of Dr. Dre and a heavy emphasis on bass. Beats headphones have been wildly popular with consumers, carrying a 70 percent market share in the premium headphones category in 2014. It is also the highest-selling brand of headphones for consumers between 17 and 35 years of age.

Consistent with the "cool factor," marketing Beats headphones has taken a grass-roots approach. According to Mr. Iovine:

> We aren't buying a lot of ads. We market it our way. We're from the music business where you never get a lot of money to market. . . . They're making a beautiful white object with all the music in the world in it. I'm going to make a beautiful black object that will play it back. Dre and I decided to market this product just like it was Tupac or U2 or Guns N' Roses. . . . We sold half a billion worth of product before we paid for one ad.

While in development, Mr. Iovine would keep various designs in his office and would ask celebrities, such as musicians Will.i.am, Gwen Stephani, and Pharrell Williams, to try them and give feedback, which spread early awareness. Co-marketing has been a favorite strategy of Beats, having partnered with many other brands, such as HP laptops, Chrysler 300s, and Radio Shack. Beats is also expanding into related product areas, including portable wireless speakers and automobile speaker systems.

Beats also sent complementary headphones to many influential celebrities in the music and sports industries, such as Lady Gaga, P. Diddy, Michael Phelps, Justin Beiber, and Ellen DeGeneres. When the public saw their favorite celebrities sporting Beats headphones, the popularity skyrocketed. *Ad Age* reports that celebrity endorsements have been shown to improve sales by as much as 20 percent. As part of an ambush marketing campaign, just before the 2008 Olympics, Beats sent customized headphones in the national colors to Lebron James. James immediately asked for 15 more and the entire U.S. Olympic basketball team arrived in Shanghai wearing Beats headphones. All this is despite the fact that Beats was not an official Olympic sponsor. As a result of these efforts, Beats headphones have become a fashion accessory in pop culture.

In early 2014, Beats began its own music streaming service called Beats Music. A streaming service helps to counteract the digital piracy issue. Not only do the musicians receive higher royalties from streaming, but they also can connect directly with the fans by controlling their profile, selling merchandise, and updating fans on upcoming events and releases. The music streaming industry is growing fast. In 2014, there were roughly 29 million subscribers of music streaming services, and many more using free streaming services like Pandora. By 2018, predictions suggest there will be around 191 million subscribers. Beats Music provides a free trial and is converting 70 percent of those consumers into subscribers. Roughly 1,000 consumers subscribed to Beats Music daily in 2014.

In the summer of 2014, Dr. Dre and Mr. Iovine sold both the electronics and music streaming businesses to Apple for $3 billion. Further, they agreed to work for Apple in an advisory role, while maintaining some equity. Analysts suggest that perhaps Dr. Dre will be able to bring the "cool" back to Apple. According to Apple CEO Tim Cook:

> Music is such an important part of all of our lives and holds a special place within our hearts at Apple. That's why we have kept investing in music and are bringing together these extraordinary teams so we can continue to create the most innovative music products and services in the world.

Mr. Iovine mirrored that sentiment:

> I've always known in my heart that Beats belonged with Apple. The idea when we started the company was inspired by Apple's unmatched ability to marry culture and technology. Apple's deep commitment to music fans, artists, songwriters and the music industry is something special.

This match has much promise; however, it remains to be seen how the corporate cultures of the two companies will align. Dr. Dre reportedly is a workaholic who disregards artificial deadlines, which might cause some friction with Apple. However, like Apple, Dr. Dre prides himself on a lack of marketing research. Apple also has historically had a market orientation, believing that consumers do not know what they want until someone shows it to them. Only time will tell how fruitful Beats and Apple will be together, but the projections show that they are poised for success.

Discussion Questions

1. Please reference the other-oriented, environment-oriented, and self-oriented values in the text. Choose a few of these values and explain how they are relevant to Beats by Dre and Beats Music.

2. Refer to the generation groups and social classes in Chapter 4 and the ethnic subcultures in Chapter 5. With all of these concepts in mind, describe an ideal target market segment for Beats Music.

3. Refer to Table 5-2 in Chapter 5, entitled, "African American Segments Identified by Yankelovich." Imagine that Beats has decided to target African Americans. Which of these segments would be the best target market for Beats? Explain your answer.

4. Refer to the three categories of innovation in Chapter 7. In which category of innovation are the following products? Justify your answer.
   a. Beats headphones
   b. Beats Music

5. Think in terms of family decision making from Chapter 6. What members of the household are likely to play each of the following roles in the purchase decision for Beats Music or Beats headphones?
   a. Initiators
   b. Information gatherers
   c. Influencers
   d. Decision makers
   e. Purchasers
   f. Users

6. Reference the section of Chapter 7 on reference group influence.
   a. Are Beats headphones a necessity or nonnecessity?
   b. Are Beats headphones visible or private?
   c. Given your answers for a and b, how has Beats by Dre capitalized on this in the past?
   d. Do you feel reference group influence will play an important role in the success of Beats? Explain your answer.

7. Review the section of Chapter 7 on marketing strategy, WOM, and opinion leadership. Which strategy or strategies of those listed has Beats by Dre used to become so popular in its market?

Source: "Beliebing in Streaming," *The Economist,* March 22, 2014, www.economist.com; M. Bush, "Beats by Dr. Dre," *Advertising Age,* November 15, 2010, www.adage.com; A. Diallo, "Beats Music to take Streaming Mass Market," *Forbes,* January 12, 2014, www.forbes.com; J. Dorris, "Beats with a Billion Eyes," *Slate,* September 11, 2013, www.slate.com; T. Fishburne, "The Power of Ambush Marketing," *Tom Fishburne: Marketoonist,* August 12, 2012, www.tomfishburne.com; B. Helm, "How Dr. Dre's Headphone Company Became a Billion-Dollar Business," *Inc.,* May 1, 2014, www.inc.com; L. Johnston, "Apple Buys Beats for $3B," *Twice,* May 28, 2014, www.twice.com; H. Karp, "Apple's New Beat: What Steve Jobs and Dr. Dre have in Common," *Wall Street Journal,* June 6, 2014, www.wsj.com; J. Sanburn, "How Dr. Dre Made $300 Headphones a Must-Have Accessory," *Time Magazine,* January 16, 2013, www.business.time.com; J. Solsman, "Beat Music Turns 7 out of 10 Free Trial Users to Paying Ones," *CNet.com,* March 20, 2014, www.cnet.com.

2-4 HOW SOCIAL MEDIA NEARLY BROUGHT DOWN UNITED AIRLINES

Online social media and social networking are growing at an exponential rate and provide a means for consumers to voice their opinions about products and services. As of January 2018, the number of active social media users (adults and children) on some of the most popular social media sites was as follows:

- Facebook—2,167 million
- YouTube—1,500 million
- Instagram—800 million
- Twitter—330 million
- LinkedIn—260 million
- Snapchat—255 million
- Pinterest—200 million

It is increasingly common for consumers to vent their dissatisfaction via one or more of these social media outlets, sometimes in the form of videos. Often these videos go viral, meaning that millions of consumers become aware of the product or service failure in a very short period of time. One iconic example is Dave Carroll, a traveling musician, whose guitar was ruined by United Airlines baggage handlers. United refused to take responsibility and Dave Carroll retaliated via social media. It all began when Carroll noticed his guitar being mishandled:

> On that first leg of the flight we were seated at the rear of the aircraft and upon landing and waiting to deplane . . . a woman sitting behind me, not aware that we were musicians cried out: "My god they're throwing guitars out there." Our bass player Mike looked out the window in time to see his bass being heaved without regard by the United baggage handlers. My $3500 710 Taylor had been thrown before his.

When Carroll got his guitar back, the neck was broken (despite having been in a protective case). He immediately notified United Airlines. He found it very difficult to find anyone who was sympathetic or would take responsibility for his damaged guitar. He was passed from employee to employee, in person and via phone and e-mail, at several airports and call centers in various U.S. states, Canada, and India. After nine months of pursuing the issue, a United Airlines customer service representative sent him an e-mail that said the airline would not be taking responsibility for the guitar (other than a rejected offer of $1,200 in flight vouchers) and would no longer communicate with him about the matter. As noted by Carroll:

> The system is designed to frustrate affected customers into giving up their claims. . . . I told [the service representative] that I would be writing three songs about United Airlines and my experience in the whole matter. I would then make videos for these songs and offer them for free download on YouTube and my own website, inviting viewers to vote on their favorite United song. My goal: to get one million hits in one year.

Carroll's first video has had over 18 million views. Within four days of Carroll's first video going online, United Airlines' stock price fell 10 percent, equaling a loss of $180 million (the cost of approximately 51,000 replacement guitars). After his videos went viral, United Airlines attempted to smooth things over with a $3,000 donation to the Thelonious Monk Institute of Jazz. However, it was too late to stop Carroll from proceeding with his video series. Since then, Carroll has been featured on *Today, CNN,* and *Jimmy Kimmel* and his "United Breaks Guitars" song has been number one on the country western download charts in iTunes in the U.K.

Clearly social media can be a means for consumers to vent negative word-of-mouth (WOM). However, it also may be a very useful and positive way for companies to communicate with and learn from their consumers. Researchers at Forrester believe that social influence can be viewed as a pyramid containing three groups. As in any target marketing scenario, companies must manage their relationships with each of these three types of influencers in unique ways to encourage them to spread positive WOM through their social networks.

- *Social Broadcasters,* the group at the top of the pyramid, are the few, most well-connected individuals who have many other users who look to them for advice. However, the other users in their network may not know these individuals personally, so they may not have a high level of trust. Other users may consider the advice of Social Broadcasters about products and services as one part of a larger information search. Social Broadcasters dislike traditional PR and want to be respected by marketers because of their broad audience. The best way to reach Social Broadcasters is through offers uniquely customized for them that reflect an appreciation for their opinions.
- *Mass Influencers,* the group in the middle of the pyramid, produce 80 percent of the influence impressions about products and services, while making up only 16 percent of the influencers. This group is less tech-savvy and motivated than the Social Broadcasters, but they influence people they know in real life as well as others. The best way to reach Mass Influencers is to give them gossip fodder. Giving them content that they cannot resist sharing with others encourages them to spread the marketer's message to a larger audience.
- *Potential Influencers,* the group at the base of the pyramid, makes up the largest group with some 80 percent of the influencers. These individuals have smaller networks that consist primarily of people they know and trust in offline. The Potential Influencers group is not very tech-savvy or as motivated as the other two groups. The best way to reach this group is to give them helpful content that is simple for them to spread to others.

Table A provides demographic information on the adult users of seven of the most popular social network sites.

Discussion Questions

1. When Dave Carroll posted his video on YouTube, it went viral. What American value do you feel motivated consumers to pass along this "video complaint" to others?

2. Of the three groups of influencers identified by Forrester, which group or groups do you think were most likely responsible for Dave Carroll's video going viral? Explain.

3. Based on your answers to 1 and 2, develop a marketing strategy for United to "recover" from its service failure. Specifically, address the following:
   a. What "message" should United be sending to the general public?
   b. What "media" outlets (traditional, online, and/or social) should it be using?

Demographics of Social Media Users: Percent of U.S. Adults Who Say They Use . . .							TABLE A
	Facebook	YouTube	Instagram	Pinterest	Snapchat	LinkedIn	Twitter
Total	68%	73%	35%	29%	27%	25%	24%
Gender							
Male	62%	75%	30%	16%	23%	25%	23%
Female	74%	72%	39%	41%	31%	25%	24%
Age							
18–24	80%	94%	71%	31%	78%	25%	45%
25–29	82%	88%	54%	39%	54%	34%	33%
30–49	78%	85%	40%	34%	26%	33%	27%
50–64	65%	68%	21%	26%	10%	24%	19%
65+	41%	40%	10%	16%	3%	9%	8%
Race/Ethnic Group							
White non-Hispanic	67%	71%	32%	32%	24%	26%	24%
Black non-Hispanic	70%	76%	43%	23%	36%	28%	26%
Hispanic	73%	78%	38%	23%	31%	13%	20%
Household Income							
$0–29,999	66%	68%	30%	20%	23%	13%	20%
$30,000–49,999	74%	78%	42%	32%	33%	20%	21%
$50,000–74,999	70%	77%	32%	34%	26%	24%	26%
$75,000+	75%	84%	42%	39%	30%	45%	32%
Education							
High school or less	60%	65%	29%	18%	24%	9%	18%
Some college	71%	74%	36%	32%	31%	22%	25%
College +	77%	85%	42%	40%	26%	50%	32%
Location							
Urban	75%	80%	42%	29%	32%	30%	29%
Suburban	67%	74%	34%	31%	26%	27%	23%
Rural	58%	59%	25%	28%	18%	13%	17%

Survey conducted January 3–10, 2018.
Source: Pew Research Center, 2018.

c. Develop a video or ad concept that United could place on social media that could help offset consumer anger over its service failure.

d. Identify which of the three Forrester groups United should focus on with its recovery campaign and defend your answer.

4. Chapter 7 defines and discusses opinion leaders. Are the individuals that create viral complaint videos opinion leaders? Why or why not?

5. Chapter 7 also discusses guiding principles that marketers should use when engaging in social media. How should United Airlines, or other companies who

have had similar issues, have operated based on these principles?

6. Several companies are using crowdsourcing as a way for customers to help solve each others' problems. How might companies harness the power of crowdsourcing to combat instances of viral negative WOM?

7. Besides being a method of communication, online social networks are also innovations that are being diffused. Are online social networks continuous, dynamically continuous, or discontinuous innovations?

8. Describe the typical user of each of the seven social networks described in Table A.

Source: C. Ayres, "Revenge Is Best Served Cold—on YouTube," *The Times,* July 22, 2009, www.timesonline.co.uk; D. Carroll, "United Breaks Guitars," DaveCarrollMusic.com, 2009, http://www.davecarrollmusic.com; "Most Famous Social Network Sites Worldwide as of January 2018, Ranked by Number of Active Users (in Millions)," *Statistica,* March 23, 2018, www.statistica.com; R. Sawhney, "Broken Guitar Has United Playing the Blues to the Tune of $180 Million," *Fast Company,* July 28, 2009, www.fastcompany.com; A. Smith and M. Anderson, "Social Media Use in 2018," *Pew Research Center,* March 1, 2018, www.pewinternet.org.

2-5 *GRACE AND FRANKIE:* THE INVISIBILITY OF BABY BOOMER WOMEN

The popular Emmy-nominated Netflix series *Grace and Frankie,* which stars nearly 80-year-old actresses Jane Fonda and Lily Tomlin, is a stark contrast to the norm of mainstream Hollywood productions in both context and content. Actresses over the age of 50 are far less likely to be featured in movies or series than their male counterparts. When major roles do exist for Baby Boomer actresses, they are frequently portrayed in a negative way. In fact, research shows that there is a negative correlation between older female parts and characteristics such as goodness, attractiveness, socioeconomic status, intelligence, and friendliness. Co-creator of *Grace and Frankie,* Howard J. Morris, explained his and co-creator Marta Kauffman's initial conversations about the show:

> Nobody was doing shows with older women. In fact, in our initial conversation, I kid you not, Marta said, "I've always wanted to do a show about older women's sexuality." This is not the show that anybody else is doing, and that really excited us.

That is exactly what Morris and Kauffman did: They deviated from the mold of Hollywood contexts by starring older actresses in a positive light and then kept going with the actual content of the show, well past what was ever covered in *Golden Girls.* The two main characters encounter various situations where they grapple with sexual issues, as well as the realities of being older women in current society. One challenge the two characters encounter is securing a 10-year loan for the marketing of their business, Vybrant, which would produce personal vibrators for senior women that are gentle on arthritic wrists. The loan officer shuts the door at the first mention of the product and then denies the loan application. The implication is that older women's sexuality is taboo and a 10-year loan is risky given their advanced ages. The characters pointed to ageism used by the loan officer as a barrier to their success. Later, after other funding is secured, a marketing team uses the two characters' images in proposed promotional materials for the Vybrant brand but edits their pictures to appear approximately 20 years younger. This move was also highly offensive to Grace and Frankie.

Another reality Grace and Frankie encounter (as well as many women of this age group) is the sense of invisibility and unwantedness. In one scene, Grace, the character played by Jane Fonda, shouts at a grocery store cashier:

> Do you not see me? Do I not exist? Do you think it's alright to ignore us?

This sentiment is reflected by a majority of Baby Boomer women. Some even have begun calling it the "Windex Effect." In a survey of Baby Boomer women, over 68 percent feel advertisers do not target them. A report from AARP found the proportion of all advertising expenditures targeting consumers over age 50 to be between five percent and eight percent. According to Marti Barletta, author of *PrimeTime Women: How to Win the Hearts, Minds, and Business of Boomer Big Spenders:*

> We are 100% invisible to marketers. That's pretty easy to establish. You only have to look at what's online, what's on television, what's on radio. We are such a pop-culture country and [that's] defined by the young because it's about novelty and it's about what's different and what's exciting.

This invisibility also is quite evident at retail events, including New York Fashion Week. Many Baby Boomer women are in attendance in various capacities, such as audience members, merchandise buyers, and company executives. However, the fashions represented are geared toward consumers aged 18 to 49 and, unsurprisingly, Baby Boomer women are not represented by any of the models. According to Judy Shapiro, author of *Why Does Fashion Ignore Post 50s?:*

> As a woman over 50, I feel like a kid whose nose is pressed up against the candy store glass. I can see the beautiful fashion confections but they remain tantalizingly out of reach.

The irony of Baby Boomer women suddenly becoming invisible to marketers after reaching a certain age is especially pointed to the consumers in this group because they were accustomed to being the darlings of marketers as they grew up and went through earlier adulthood. Baby Boomers were the largest generation at the time they came on to the scene (until they started having their own children) and thus represented huge opportunities for a variety of industries that were relevant to each of the stages of their lives. Some industry experts propose that it is not that marketers have deliberately turned their backs on Baby Boomers now. Instead, marketers have simply continued their focus on keeping their brands modern and youthful, which often translates into targeting an 18-to-34, or sometimes 18-to-49, age demographic.

No matter the reason, marketers' myopia on what age group to target fails to take some key factors into consideration. The Baby Boomer generation is still one of the largest of all generations at approximately 74.1 million people. It is also the wealthiest of all generations. Baby Boomers have around 70 percent of the country's disposable income and account for over $230 billion in consumer packaged goods sales annually.

The women of the Baby Boomer generation rack up some impressive figures on their own. They account for 70–80 percent of consumer purchasing. The net worth of women 50+ years old is $19 trillion. Baby Boomer women spend more than $55 billion per year on consumer electronics. Many of them are at the peak of their careers and are the group least impacted by the recession. Baby Boomer women average weekly salaries well above the coveted Millennial men market ($795 versus $516). That combined with the point that many of them do not

have expenses such as student loans or children living at home, and the fact that they are poised to inherit large amounts from their parents and husbands in short order, contribute to women aged 45 to 54 having the highest disposable incomes of any age/sex segment.

This state of affairs is almost mind boggling. Baby Boomer women constitute a massive market with incredible spending power. Yet, 91 percent of these women feel that marketers do not understand them. Perhaps marketers should reconsider the incredible opportunities presented by the Graces and Frankies of the world.

Discussion Questions

1. Chapter 3 discusses several values in American society.
   a. Which of those values relate to the situations described here in this case study? Why?
   b. How well do you feel the values you described in part a of this question match with the textbook's interpretation of each value's placement of current, traditional, and emerging states in Figure 3–1 in Chapter 3? Justify your response.

2. Chapter 2 examines values from a cross-cultural perspective, while Chapter 3 examines those same values from an American perspective. The value placed on aging can vary from culture to culture. This particular case is written in an American culture context, where youth is valued over age. Do you think the story would be different in another country, such as Japan, that places a greater value on age? Explain your answer.

3. The case highlights how Baby Boomer women are largely invisible and forgotten by marketers, especially at New York Fashion Week. Why do you think this once-sought-after and valuable segment of women is now virtually ignored?

4. Baby Boomers have not become invisible to all marketers and companies. Brainstorm and research an example of a company that actually is targeting Baby Boomer women. Write a brief summary of (*a*) the name and background of the company describing (*b*) the product the company makes targeting these women and (*c*) how this product is being received by Baby Boomer women.

5. Chapter 4 discusses many different generational groups.
   a. According to what you read in the case, which of these generational groups is most and which is least targeted by marketers?

b. What are some suggestions that you would give marketers on how to reach out and be more appealing to Baby Boomer women.

6. Perform primary data collection yourself to investigate this phenomenon. Assemble a small focus group of Baby Boomer women. If you have trouble locating enough participants, perform an in-depth interview with one Baby Boomer woman. Ask them/her about their/her opinion as to whether marketers are ignoring their segment. Using the *Grace and Frankie* example could be a good way to start the conversation. Ask them/her about how they/she feel(s) about being ignored (if that is the sentiment). Ask them/her what they/she would prefer marketers and advertisers do differently to better target Baby Boomer women. Write a brief summary of your findings.

Source: C. Benton, "Grace and Frankie: Turning Ageism on Its Head," *The Three Tomatoes,* July 27, 2015, http://thethreetomatoes.com; A. Brenoff, "'Grace and Frankie' Totally Nails What It Means to be Getting Older," *Huffington Post,* March 30, 2017, www.huffingtonpost.com; C. Gustke, "The Hottest Start-Up Market? Baby Boomers," *New York Times,* August 3, 2016, www.nytimes.com; L. Landers, "The Badass: Marketing to Boomer Women," *Girl Power Marketing,* May 3, 2017, https://girlpowermarketing.com; E. Mitchell, "Why Brands Need to Stop Ignoring the 'Invisible Goldmine' of Baby Boomer Women," *Adweek,* August 28, 2013, http://www.adweek.com; F. Mohammed, "How 'Grace and Frankie' Is Changing How Women View Ageing," *Girl's Globe,* August 18, 2017, www.girlsglobe.org; J. Shapiro, "Why Does Fashion Ignore Post 50s?," *Huffington Post,* September 14, 2012, www.huffingtonpost.com; S. Steimer, "Baby Boomer Women Remain Invisible to Marketers," *American Marketing Association,* September 28, 2016, www.ama.org; D. Wallis, "Selling Older Consumers Short," *AARP Real Possibilities,* March 1, 2018, www.aarp.org.

2-6 AMERICAN BEAGLE OUTFITTERS: APRIL FOOL'S JOKE TURNED REALITY

American Eagle Outfitters is a well-established retailer that often is found in mainstream shopping malls. It targets teens and young adults of both sexes with trendy clothing and accessories. American Eagle is actually one of the most popular clothing retailers in its market. A survey of teenagers revealed that American Eagle has higher "brand relevance" than its competitors, Aèropostale and Abercrombie & Fitch.

On March 24, 2014, American Eagle announced that it would be offering a new line, dog apparel to match the human clothing sold in its stores, called American Beagle Outfitters. The American Beagle website featured pictures of pooches modeling fashions for small, medium, and large dogs. It even launched a "dogumentary" on social media explaining the new line and the idea behind its creation. The dogumentary features two American Eagle employees. One cannot stand the thought of her dog wearing Halloween costumes all year long and another who believes "he's a pioneer as well as a prisoner of his own ambition." According to American Eagle's press release:

Designed to perfectly match their owner's on-trend American Eagle wardrobe, the canine collection features must-haves such as slimming doggy jeggings, fur-friendly bikinis and statement accessories, creating head-to-tail looks that complement the unique style and personality of every pooch, big and small.

Following the announcement, consumers were urged to sign up on the waiting list for access to the dog apparel and receive a 20 percent discount. Further, for a certain period, American Eagle offered a $1 donation to the ASPCA with each order. American Eagle ultimately donated $100,000.

However, with April Fool's Day just around the corner, many people speculated that the new dog apparel line was merely an April Fool's joke. This idea was supported by the fact that the company would not say when the products would be available or how they would be priced. Further, the American Eagle spokesperson refused to answer when directly asked whether this promotion was an April Fool's joke, citing a nondisclosure agreement.

When April Fool's Day arrived, American Eagle admitted that American Beagle was an April Fool's joke. But, because it was so popular among consumers, American Eagle decided to go ahead and produce the doggie fashion line. According to Michael Leedy, the chief marketing officer:

We originally felt that April Fool's Day was the perfect opportunity for us to engage with our consumers in a fun, lighthearted way, all while supporting the ASPCA. Due to the tremendous positive response and excitement from our customers for the American Beagle Outfitters line, we decided to make a limited-edition collection for Holiday 2014.

This campaign created a fair amount of publicity in many news outlets, in no small part due to the April Fool's aspect. The company also encouraged consumers to submit photos of their own dogs' style with the hashtag, #AEOStyle for a chance to be featured on the

American Beagle website. This helped to build engagement with both the American Eagle and American Beagle brands.

Pet ownership has been increasing over the last two decades. According to the National Pet Owners Survey, from the American Pet Products Association (APPA), a record 82.5 million American households owned at least one pet in 2012, which amounts to 68 percent of the households. The IBISWorld report estimates the pet ownership rate to increase by 2.2 percent each year through at least 2018.

This increase in pet ownership is due to a number of factors. While there was still growth in the pet products industry during the recession, now that there is a slow recovery taking place, consumers have more disposable income to care for pets. Please see the table "Pet Owners' Behavior during Recession" for examples of modification of consumption habits that dog owners made during a time of recession (2008) in order to provide the best care for their pets. More importantly, there is a cultural shift taking place such that consumers increasingly view dogs as members of the family, rather than companion animals or outdoor protectors. Many consumers now view themselves as "pet parents" and their dogs as "fur babies." In a survey of women, 90 percent of respondents indicated that they think of their pets as family members. According to a Consumer Products and Trends Survey, pet ownership is highest among empty-nesters, single professionals, and couples without children. These groups have more disposable income due to not having (human) children and many are looking to their dogs to fill the role of someone to care for and nurture. Please see the table "Survey of *Consumer Reports* Readers" for information on activities that pet owners engage in with dogs and cats. According to Bob Vetere, president of the American Pet Products Manufacturers Association (APPMA):

> Pets are acquiring a more significant role in the family, and with that, they are tending to be treated more in human terms. . . . People are pampering their pets more than ever . . . from interactive and innovative toys to dog walking, doggy day-care and pet-friendly hotels, restaurants and airlines.

American Eagle is not the first human apparel retailer to get into pet apparel. Americans are spending more than $1 billion on dog apparel and many retailers want a piece of the pie. High-end fashion retailers, such as Ralph Lauren, Burberry, Juicy Couture, and Kiehl's,

also offer dog apparel. There is even a Pet Fashion Week in New York City. According to Angie McKaig, CEO of PamperedPuppy.com:

> As more designers come into the marketplace with really unique designs, they catch the eye of someone who might not have bought dog clothes before, people who say to me, "I think this stuff is dumb normally."

A survey of visitors to the dog apparel and accessories site PamperedPuppy.com revealed that more than 60 percent of the visitors owned at least four pieces of clothing, four collars, and 10 toys per dog. The APPA has been tracking spending on pets for two decades. In 2013 alone, Americans spent $55.7 billion on their pets. American Pet Products Association 2013/2014 National Pet Owners Survey projects spending on pets to increase in the coming years. The booming pet industry is presenting a growing area of opportunity for American (B)Eagle Outfitters, as well as many other retailers. According to Mr. Vetere:

> The pet industry continues to see unprecedented growth. The survey reveals pet owners are willing to spend money on their pets despite a downturn in the economy.

Pet Owners' Behavior during Recession (2008)

Holiday Gifts

81% of respondents purchase gifts for their pups during the holidays.
69% spend up to $50; 24% spend $50–100; only 3% spend more than $150.
59% expect to spend the same amount on gifts for their dog as they did last year.

Trading Personal Services for Dog Services

67% would cancel their travel plans if they could not afford to pay to board their dog.
65% would regularly eat Ramen noodles before they would skimp on their dogs' high-quality food.
59% would color their own hair in the kitchen sink in order to keep groomer appointments.

Cutbacks Owners Are Willing to Make for Their Dog

Eat more meals at home (97%)
Cancel gym membership (72%)
Cancel cable or satellite service (50%)
Curb spending on new clothes (94%)
Push back plans for home remodeling (89%)
Forgo buying a new car or buy a less expensive model (88%)

Money-Saving Techniques

52% look for sales and/or clip coupons before shopping for pet products.
48% are purchasing fewer toys/treats and other nonessential dog supplies.
34% have begun buying dog food in bulk.

Source: American Kennel Club, 2008.

Survey of *Consumer Reports* Readers

	Dog Owners	Cat Owners
Fed the pet human food	63%	41%
Taught it tricks	57%	14%
Let it sleep with you	55%	75%
Gave it holiday gifts	55%	43%
Took it on vacation	45%	7%
Signed a card with its name or photo	40%	29%
Put photos of it on social media sites	32%	23%
Dressed it in outfits	18%	5%

Source: *Consumer Reports*, 2012.

Discussion Questions

1. Given the unusual circumstances of American Eagle's launch of its American Beagle line, do you feel that this April Fool's prank was genuinely a prank turned reality or do you think that it was actually a planned launch and American Eagle was testing the waters in a way that created consumer engagement and buzz in the market place? Or perhaps you have another opinion? Explain your answer.

2. As part of the launch, American Beagle allowed consumers to sign up for early sales before the dog apparel was released.
   a. Into what category of adopters discussed in the section of Chapter 7 on diffusion of innovations would the consumers that signed up early fall?
   b. What are some possible reasons behind American Beagle offering early sign ups?

3. Chapter 3 describes four consumer types with respect to their responses to cause-related marketing. Describe how each of the following groups would have a different perspective on cause-related marketing and how they would react to the American Beagle campaign partnering with ASPCA.
   a. Skeptics
   b. Balancers
   c. Attribution-oriented consumers
   d. Socially concerned consumers

4. Referring to Question 3, to which of those groups of perspectives on cause-related marketing do you personally belong? Why? Explain your answer thoroughly.

5. Chapter 4 discusses several generational groups. Which generational group do you think would serve as the best target market for American Beagle dog apparel? Would more than one be viable? Explain your answer.

6. Chapter 6 describes various stages in the household life cycle. Which of these stages would serve as the best target market for American Beagle dog apparel? Would more than one be viable? Explain your answer.

7. Please refer to the table "Pet Owners' Behavior during Recession," which shows results of a survey in the midst of the recession in 2008. Now that there has been some economic recovery, the results may differ.
   a. Perform a survey of modern-day pet owners asking the same questions. Compare and contrast your results with those from 2008.
   b. Record the generation for your respondents and perform a cross-tab analysis based on those data.
   c. Record household life-cycle stage and perform a cross-tab analysis based on those data.

Source: "American Eagle Outfitters' Canine Collection, American Beagle Outfitters, Goes from April Fool's Joke to Real-Life Dog Fashion Line," *PR Newswire*, April 1, 2014, www.prnewswire.com; C. Brough, "Pet Businesses Will Prosper: Industry Trends for 2014 and Beyond," *Multi Briefs*, 2014, www.multibriefs.com; "Current Economic Woes No Competition for Americans' Dedication to Their Dogs," *American Kennel Club*, Dec. 8, 2008; D. Hirschhorn, "Holy Shih Tzu! Americans Spend $56 Billion on Pets Last Year," *Time Magazine*, March 13, 2014, www.time.com; "How We Dote on Dogs and Cats," *Consumer Reports*, October 2012, www.consumerreports.com; P. Kennedy and M. McGarvey, "Animal-Companion Depictions in Women's Magazine Advertising," *Journal of Business Research* 61, no. 5 (May 2008), pp. 424–30; L. Lowe, "See American Eagles' New Line for Dogs: 'American Beagle Outfitters,'" *Parade*, March 26, 2014, www.parade.condenast.com; S. Maheshwari, "American Eagle Says It's Starting a Dog Brand Called American Beagle Outfitters," *Buzzfeed*, March 24, 2014, www.buzzfeed.com; S. Maheshwari, "American Eagle May Shine Brightest in the 'Post-Apocalyptic Future of Teen Retail,' Analysts Say," *Buzzfeed*, February 21, 2014, www.buzzfeed.com; N. Ogunnaike, "This Is Not a Joke: American Beagle, a Dog Clothing Line for American Eagle, to Launch in Fall," *Glamour Magazine*, April 1, 2014, www.glamour.com; "The Pet Services Industry Today," *Zoom Room*, 2014, www.zoomroomonline.com; S. Thompson, "What's Next? Pup Tents in Bryant Park?," *Advertising Age*, January 29, 2007, www.adage.com.

2-7 TIDE GOES AFTER GREEN WITH NEW PODS

Green household cleaners are gaining popularity, despite decline in the overall laundry category. In particular, the green laundry category has seen 50 percent annual growth, which, if sustained, would put sales in this category at $700 million by 2014. Despite a growing interest in the environment, consumers often use too much detergent, which has numerous negative effects on the environment, including faster equipment failure and the need to dispose of it, wasted detergent, and potential contamination of the water supply.

P&G (Procter and Gamble) has responded to the problem of excess detergent usage per load with new

Tide Pods liquid detergent tabs for the U.S. market. Premeasured tablets and sachets are popular in Europe but are just gaining popularity in the U.S. Consumers usually learn their laundry habits from their parents during their adolescence, and such habits are often difficult to change. However, P&G is spending $150 million in marketing for new Tide Pods with the goal of this innovation bringing sales growth back to a declining laundry category. Bob McDonald, P&G Chairman-CEO, said, "I think you're going to see [Tide Pods] will return market growth to the laundry category. P&G projects that liquid-filled tabs could ultimately take 30% share of the U.S. laundry market."

However, Tide Pods are quite different from what American consumers have become accustomed to in their appearance, patented design, and usage. They have a swirl pattern of orange and blue in two chambers on top of a larger white chamber within a fishbowl-style container with a flip top lid. The film that packages the detergent is water soluble. Tide Pods are twice as concentrated as Liquid Tide, but consumers do not have to worry about using too much detergent. Tide Pods use a reduced amount of water and packaging, as well as help prevent the problems associated with detergent overdosing.

In consumer tests, Tide Pods perform very well, with up to 40 percentage-point increases from pre- to post-use satisfaction. Consumers feel that Tide Pods simplify laundry by allowing consumers to spend as little time and effort as possible, while providing excellent cleansing and stain-fighting qualities. However, some consumers dislike Tide Pods, especially those who prefer to mix their own solutions of detergent, fabric softener, and/or oxy-cleaners. According to Alex Keith, VP of North American Laundry at P&G:

> There are always going to be doers of laundry who want to be that master chemist. But we know over 70% of women out there are asking for a solution that provides excellent results with minimal time and effort. So some of them are chemists because they want to be, and some of them are chemists because they think they have to be.

In addition to quantitative tests, qualitative tests of Tide Pods also are showing promise. In product tests, women who use Tide Pods show very positive reactions, and some even ask for free samples. Tide Pods will likely attract green consumers as well as consumers who were previously using Tide liquid and powder detergents. This is because Tide Pods possess environmentally friendly qualities while carrying the Tide brand name, which is known for strength and quality.

Understanding the traits of green laundry users is important in developing marketing strategies for Tide Pods. One study found the following demographic traits of mass-market green household cleaner brands:

- Families with children
- Those who work full time
- Hispanics and African Americans

Tide Pods hit stores in 2012.

Discussion Questions

1. Table 3–1 in Chapter 3 describes a green segmentation scheme of consumers that includes psychographic and demographic information. Choose four of the eight segments and describe the likely reaction that each segment will have to the introduction of Tide Pods.
2. Chapter 7 discusses diffusion of innovations.
   a. Identify whether Tide Pods is a continuous, dynamically continuous, or discontinuous innovation.
   b. Then, evaluate Tide Pods as an innovation based on Table 7-2 (use college students as the group of consumers for this example).
3. Consumer tests show that some people are reluctant to use premeasured laundry tablets because they learned to do laundry differently from their parents.
   a. How does this apprehensive attitude toward Tide Pods relate to the consumer socialization process discussed in Chapter 6?
   b. Recall and discuss examples of how your family has influenced your own consumer behaviors.
4. Chapter 7 discusses influencers.
   a. Who are likely to be the influencers for Tide Pods?
   b. How can P&G best target and utilize them?
5. How could P&G build buzz or WOM for Tide Pods?
6. Using the demographic characteristics of green cleaners listed in the case, develop a marketing campaign including (a) core theme, (b) body copy, (c) key visual aspects, and (d) media considerations for one or more target groups.

Source: "The Procter & Gamble Company," *International Directory of Company Histories*, Vol. 67, ed. J. P. Pederson (New York, NY: Saint James Press, 2005); *Green Household Cleaning Products in the U.S.* (Rockville, MD: Packaged Facts, June 2010); E. Byron, "The Great American Soap Overdose," *Wall Street Journal*, January 25, 2010, http://online.wsj.com; J. Neff, "P&G Reinvents Laundry with $150 Million Tide Pods Launch," *Advertising Age*, April 26, 2011, http://adage.com; "Tide Is Betting $150 Million That You'll Like Laundry Pods," *GoGreenZine.com*, April 27, 2011, http://gogreenezine.com; J. Neff, "Can P&G Laundry Pod Breathe Life into the Category?," *Advertising Age*, May 2, 2011, p. 5; M. Murphy, "Church & Dwight CEO Praises, Then Zings, Competitor P&G," *FoxBusiness*, May 12, 2011, http://www.foxbusiness.com; "P&G Delays Tide Pods to '12, Too Much Demand," *Business Courier*, May 27, 2011, http://assets.bizjournals.com.

2-8 HISPANIC MARKETING IN ONLINE AND MOBILE FORMATS

The Hispanic market is the fastest-growing ethnic segment and bears considerable economic importance. It is being heralded as the last true growth opportunity. From 2010 to 2050, the Hispanic population in the United States is expected to grow by 167 percent, compared to 42 percent for the total population. For many consumer packaged goods, Hispanics are expected to be the sole driver of sales growth. According to the vice president of advertising and sales of Univision, all of the growth in the beverage sales will come from Hispanics and the growth in automotive sales for Hispanics is expected to double that of non-Hispanics. According to Monica Gill, senior vice president of public affairs and government relations at Nielson:

Latinos are emerging as a powerhouse of economic influence, presenting marketers an increasingly influential consumer group that can translate into business impact. The key is to recognize that today's modern Latino is "ambicultural" with the ability to seamlessly pivot between English and Spanish languages and to embrace two distinct cultures. Understanding how to connect with this unique consumer profile will be key to successful engagement.

Each year, *Advertising Age* publishes its Hispanic Fact Pack, which provides valuable information about the sought-after demographic to marketers in many industries. The following five tables provide insights from the report as they relate to Hispanic use of social media, mobile marketing, and online purchasing.

HISPANICS AND SOCIAL NETWORKING

Tables A and B provide information about Hispanics' use of various social networking websites and how those websites affect the segment's attitudes. Table B details additional information about Hispanic attitudes relative to those of non-Hispanics.

HISPANICS AND MOBILE MARKETING

Tables C and D display information about the mobile platform preferences of Hispanics and the activities in which this segment engages. The activities in Table D are further broken down into generational groups.

	Social Networking: Largest Multiplatform Web Properties among U.S. Hispanics by Unique Visitors			**TABLE**	**A**

				Hispanic Composition	
Rank	Properties	Unique Visitors in Thousands	Percent Reach (%)	Percent (%)	Index
1	Facebook	31,463	82.1	15.9	104
2	Twitter	18,892	49.3	16.3	106
3	LinkedIn	8,577	22.4	12.5	81
4	Pinterest	7,394	19.3	12.6	82
5	Tumblr	6,480	16.9	16.5	108
6	AddThis	3,476	9.1	14.4	94
7	Yahoo Profile	2,475	6.5	14.7	96
8	Goodreads	2,149	5.6	13.7	89
9	Quizlet	1,813	4.7	17.6	115
10	Ask.fm	1,504	3.9	27.9	182
	Total Internet: Hispanic all	38,332	100	15.3	100
	Social Media–Social Networking	34,429	89.8	15.5	101

Note: Percent reach here is the percent of all Hispanic Internet users (38.3 million). Multiplatform data include both desktop and mobile platforms, and are inclusive of website, video, and app content.

Source: ComScore, May 2014, comscore.com.

Attitudes toward Social Media: TABLE B Site Users Who Agree with the Following Statements

People Who Agree	Percent Hispanic (%)	Percent Non-Hispanic (%)	Percent of All (%)
I am more likely to purchase products I see advertised on a social sharing/networking website.	10.9	8.3	8.6
I am more likely to purchase products I see used or recommended by friends on social sharing/networking websites.	18.3	17.8	17.8
I like to follow my favorite brand or companies on social sharing/networking websites.	23.5	20.2	20.6
Social sharing/networking websites are a way for me to tell people about companies and products that I like.	23.9	20.2	20.8
I sometimes post ratings or reviews online for other consumers to read.	18.2	17.8	17.9
I pay attention to ratings and reviews posted online by other consumers.	27.1	29.3	28.9
I often click on links or items posted by other people on social sharing/networking websites.	29.0	33.8	33.1
I often access social sharing/networking websites from different devices.	29.8	33.1	32.6

Mobile Platform Share among TABLE C Hispanics: Smartphone and Tablet Ownership

Smartphones			
Rank	Platform	Share (%)	Audience
1	Google (Android)	55.9	16,995
2	Apple (iOS)	38.1	11,582
3	Microsoft (Windows)	3.2	986
4	Blackberry	2.5	773
5	Symbian	0.1	38
6	Other	0.1	20
	Total	100.0	30,405

Tablets			
Rank	Platform	Share (%)	Audience
1	Google (Android)	56.4	8,414
2	Apple (iOS)	47.0	7,011
3	Microsoft (Windows)	2.8	423
4	Blackberry	0.7	101
5	HP	0.6	87
	Total	100.0	14,925

Source: ComScore, May 2014, comscore.com. Share based on three-month averages ended May 2014. Audience is in thousands.

Smartphone User Activities in the Last Week   TABLE D

Category	Percent Who Used This Function in the Last Week (%)						
	Hispanic	Non-Hispanic	Hispanic Millennials	Non-Hispanic Millennials	Hispanic 35+	Non-Hispanic 35+	All Users
Camera	51.5	51.6	54.2	53.4	48.4	50.5	51.5
Download app	66.4	61.3	66.8	62.1	65.9	60.8	62.1
E-mail	79.4	82.2	78.7	83.3	80.1	81.6	81.8
GPS	41.3	38.8	42.5	43.2	40.0	36.2	39.2
IM/chat	38.1	23.1	39.4	24.3	36.6	22.4	25.4
Listen to music	37.9	30.2	41.4	33.9	34.0	28.0	31.4
Play games	52.0	50.1	54.5	50.8	49.1	49.8	50.4
Read newspapers/periodicals	17.3	16.6	19.0	17.5	15.3	16.0	16.7
Social network/blog	74.1	69.3	77.1	73.2	70.8	67.0	70.0
Talk	91.6	92.0	91.4	92.0	91.8	92.0	91.9
Messaging	93.4	91.5	93.8	90.6	93.0	92.1	91.8
Visit websites	91.6	88.0	91.0	89.0	92.2	87.5	88.6
Watch/download/stream video	52.2	37.2	58.0	42.6	45.7	34.1	39.5

Source: Experian Marketing Services, 2014, www.experian.com/marketing-services. Data based on Experian Marketing Services' Simmons Connect Study, Fall 2013, for the dates of October 2013 through January 2014.

HISPANICS AND ONLINE PURCHASES

Finally, Table E illustrates the purchase behavior of Hispanic consumers relative to that of all American adults. This purchase behavior is further subdivided into the particular type of device.

Discussion Questions

1. What are the opportunities and challenges facing marketers that are targeting the lucrative Hispanic market through online and mobile marketing?

2. Based on the information in Tables A, B, C, D, and E, develop an overall marketing strategy for targeting the Hispanic market.

3. Based on the information in Tables A, B, C, D, and E, develop an advertising campaign including (*a*) overall positioning strategy and core theme, (*b*) key advertising copy points, (*c*) visual elements, and (*d*) key media outlets.

4. Based on the information in Tables A, B, C, D, and E, develop training materials for entry-level marketing professionals to enhance their interactions with consumers and to enhance their selection of media outlets when communicating with consumers.

Source: Crain Communications, Inc., "Advertising Age, 11th Annual Hispanic Fact Pack," *Advertising Age,* July 28, 2014; G. Llopis, "5 Steps to Capturing the Hispanic Market—The Last True Growth Opportunity," *Forbes,* September 3, 2013, www.forbes.com.

Purchases via Device by Category: Items Purchased on PC, Tablet, or Cell Phone   TABLE E

| | Percent Who Have Purchased Using a . . . (%) | | | | | |
| | Personal Computer | | Tablet | | Cell Phone | |
Category	Hispanic	All Adults	Hispanic	All Adults	Hispanic	All Adults
Apparel/accessories	54.0	59.4	52.3	47.4	36.8	29.4
Electronics	50.9	51.6	51.8	41.5	31.5	20.8
Food	22.3	22.7	32.7	23.1	15.1	11.8
Stocks/bonds/mutual funds	12.9	14.0	19.7	15.1	6.5	6.2
Tickets to movies/events	45.5	45.1	40.8	34.1	19.4	15.4
Toys/games	38.1	33.4	43.7	34.9	17.6	11.7
Travel services/reservations	52.4	58.5	40.2	32.6	17.2	10.7
Auction items	24.0	24.5	26.9	25.6	21.2	13.9
Charitable donations	17.4	16.7	18.5	16.3	16.8	11.0
Books	41.9	43.0	43.7	45.8	14.6	13.9
Music	36.3	37.5	48.0	41.6	23.8	17.0

Source: Experian Marketing Services, 2014, www.experian.com/marketing-services. Data based on Experian Marketing Services' Simmons New Media Study, for the dates of January 26, 2014, through February 2, 2014. Base of device owners for each device (e.g., 54% of Hispanics who own a computer have purchased apparel/accessories using their computer vs. 59% of all computer owners).

III

Internal Influences

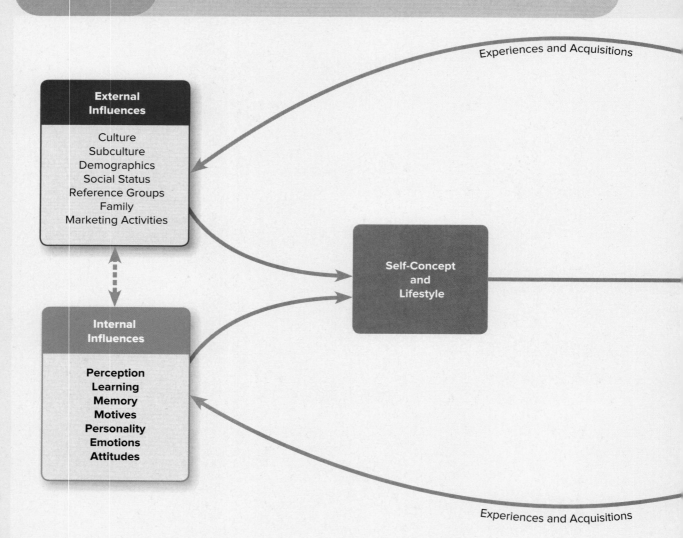

Experiences and Acquisitions

External Influences

Culture
Subculture
Demographics
Social Status
Reference Groups
Family
Marketing Activities

Internal Influences

Perception
Learning
Memory
Motives
Personality
Emotions
Attitudes

**Self-Concept
and
Lifestyle**

Experiences and Acquisitions

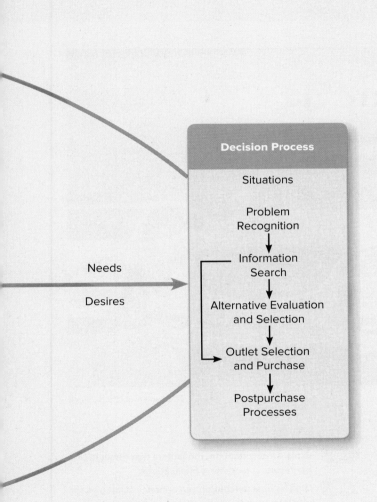

Decision Process

Situations

Problem
Recognition

Information
Search

Alternative Evaluation
and Selection

Outlet Selection
and Purchase

Postpurchase
Processes

Needs

Desires

The highlighted areas of our model, internal influences and self-concept and lifestyle, are the focal points of this part of the text. Our attention shifts from forces that are basically outside the individual to processes that occur primarily within the individual.

Part Three begins in Chapter 8, with a discussion of perception, the process by which individuals access and assign meaning to environmental stimuli. In Chapter 9, we consider learning and memory. Chapter 10 covers motivation, personality, and emotion. Chapter 11 focuses on the critical concept of attitudes and the various ways attitudes are formed and changed.

As a result of the interaction of the external influences described in the previous part of the text and the internal processes examined in this part, individuals form self-concepts and desired lifestyles, as discussed in Chapter 12. These are the hub of our model of consumer behavior. Self-concept refers to the way individuals think and feel about themselves as well as how they would like to think and feel about themselves. Their actual and desired lifestyles are the way they translate their self-concepts into daily behaviors, including consumption behaviors.

8 Perception

©Darren Brode/Shutterstock

LEARNING OBJECTIVES

LO1 Describe the nature of perception and its relationship to consumer memory and decisions.

LO2 Explain exposure, the types of exposure, and the resulting marketing implications.

LO3 Explain attention, the factors that affect it, and the resulting marketing implications.

LO4 Explain interpretation, the factors that affect it, and the resulting marketing implications.

LO5 Discuss how perception can enhance strategies for retailing, branding, advertising, and packaging.

You may have noticed that brands are showing up more and more in your favorite TV shows, movies, music videos, and video games. This is not by accident. The technique is called *product placement,* and spending on product placements in the United States is expected to surpass $11 billion in 2019. Recently, over 600 different brands were placed in prime-time TV programs, and this number is increasing. There is now a whole area of the media and PR business devoted to matching brands and shows to hit the right demographics with the right branded message. This form of promotion continues to grow, and its reach goes beyond television. Product placement is now found in movies, "streaming" or subscription video-on-demand (SVOD) services, and music videos. Below are examples in the various formats:[1]

- *Cars and TV:* Buick placed its Enclave in episodes of *black-ish,* a show that targets a multicultural and affluent audience. The goal was to encourage viewers into saying, "Wow, that's not the Buick I know!" according to Buick's marketing manager. In addition, it is expected that, by becoming part of the story line, the car is actually seen and not ignored as it likely would be in an advertisement.

- *Cars and movies:* Lexus took a risk in collaborating for two years with the *Black Panther* movie. First, as the LC 500 coupe was not yet in production during the movie shoot, engineers were reluctant to hand over prototypes to be filmed and destroyed. Second, the heavily promoted and expensive movie could fail at the box office. Not only did the movie exceed

earnings expectations in its first weekend, but online searches for Lexus and the LC 500 also increased over 10 percent.

- *Beer and streaming video services:* There is no advertising on Netflix. For companies to get their brands in front of viewers, they are placed in Netflix-original programs. Anheuser-Busch InBev placed its Stella Artois brand in the highly popular and award-winning digital series *House of Cards.* The brand fit with the show's story line. According to an executive at the beer company, "A sophisticated show for a sophisticated, beautiful beer."

- *Electronics and music videos:* Product placement in music videos has become a strategic opportunity for brands to reach a younger demographic. Beats by Dre products like headphones and speakers have appeared in Nicki Minaj and Miley Cyrus videos. The benefit to music artists is that production costs are defrayed by the product placement. To the brand, the benefit is endurance. According to one music analyst, "People will be watching the Beats Pill in Nicki Minaj's Anaconda video 5 years from now and probably still buying one as a result."

There are a number of reasons for the increase in product placements. One is the rise of the digital video recorder (DVR), which allows consumers to avoid advertising by fast-forwarding through it. Another is the increase in usage of SVOD like Netflix, attenuating the effectiveness of traditional advertising. At their best, product placements put brands into the natural flow of the storyline and thus create positive branded messages that are virtually impossible for consumers to avoid. According to Nielsen, product placements work best when there is a good "fit" between the brand and the show (think speakers in music videos). But there are limits to its usefulness. Consumers are becoming more skeptical and react negatively if the product placement is viewed as an overt sales attempt.

Perception is a process that begins with consumer exposure and attention to marketing stimuli and ends with consumer interpretation. As the opening examples suggest, exposure and attention are highly selective—meaning that consumers process only a small fraction of the available information. And as we will see, interpretation can be a highly subjective process. Thus, reality and consumer perceptions of that reality are often quite different. Marketers wishing to communicate their brand message effectively to consumers must understand the nature of perception and the many factors influencing it.

THE NATURE OF PERCEPTION

LO1

Information processing is *a series of activities by which stimuli are perceived, transformed into information, and stored.* Figure 8–1 illustrates a useful information-processing model having four major steps or stages: exposure, attention, interpretation, and memory. The first three of these constitute **perception.**

Exposure occurs when a stimulus such as a banner ad comes within range of a person's sensory receptor nerves—vision, in this example. *Attention* occurs when the stimulus (banner ad) is "seen" (the receptor nerves pass the sensations on to the brain for processing). *Interpretation* is the assignment of meaning to the received sensations. *Memory* is the short-term use of the meaning for immediate decision making or the longer-term retention of the meaning.

Figure 8–1 and the above discussion suggest a linear flow from exposure to memory. However, *these processes occur virtually simultaneously and are clearly interactive.* For example, a person's memory influences the information he or she is exposed to and attends to and the interpretations the person assigns to that information. At the same time, memory itself is being shaped by the information it is receiving.

Both perception and memory are extremely selective. Of the massive amount of information available, individuals can be exposed and attend to only a limited amount. The meaning assigned to a stimulus is as much or more a function of the individual as it is the stimulus itself. Further, much of the interpreted information will not be available to active memory when the individual makes a purchase decision.

This selectivity, sometimes referred to as **perceptual defenses,** means that *individuals are not passive recipients of marketing messages.* Rather, consumers largely determine the messages they will encounter and notice as well as the meaning they will assign them. Clearly, the marketing manager faces a challenging task when communicating with consumers.

EXPOSURE

LO2

Exposure *occurs when a stimulus is placed within a person's relevant environment and comes within range of his or her sensory receptor nerves.* Exposure provides consumers with the *opportunity* to pay attention to available information but in no way guarantees it. For example, have you ever been watching television and realized that you were not paying attention

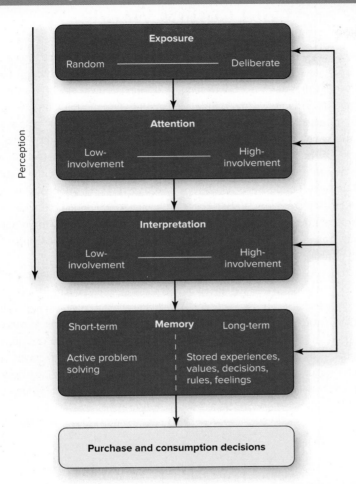

to the commercials being aired? In this case, exposure occurred, but the commercials will probably have little influence due to your lack of attention.

An individual can be exposed to only a minuscule fraction of the available stimuli. There are now hundreds of television channels, thousands of radio stations, and innumerable magazines and websites. In-store environments also are cluttered with tens of thousands of individual items and in-store advertising. Even in today's multitasking society there are limits.[2]

So what determines exposure? Is it a random process, or is it purposeful? Most of the stimuli to which individuals are exposed are "self-selected." That is, people deliberately seek out exposure to certain stimuli and avoid others. Generally, people seek *information that they think will help them achieve their goals.* An individual's goals and the types of information needed to achieve those goals are a function of that person's existing and desired lifestyle and such short-term motives as hunger or curiosity.

Of course, people also are exposed to a large number of stimuli on a more or less random basis during their daily activities. While driving, they may hear commercials, see billboards and display ads, and so on that they did not purposefully seek out.

Competing in a DVR and Cord-Cutting World

TV viewing habits are changing in the U.S., and advertisers need to take note. DVRs allow for digital recording of programs and "time-shifted" viewing. Currently over 50 percent of U.S. households have a DVR and that number is now matched by those who use SVOD, or streaming, services.[3] Furthermore, the segment of "cord cutters," those who stream exclusively, has grown to over 34 million viewers and is expected to reach 40 million in 2021. The prevalence of both DVR and SVOD sparks a major concern for marketers: increased ad avoidance. For example, DVR viewers of prerecorded content skip ads at more than twice the rate of those who view the same content live. And 50 to 90 percent of DVR users fast-forward through at least some commercials. Combined with the latest service offerings, such as Dish's AutoHop, which automatically skips over the ads for the viewer, ad avoidance is inescapable.

Nevertheless, several studies point out that most viewers who zip through DVR commercials still "notice" the ads and, in fact, will stop and view commercials they are interested in. And Inner-scope Research recently found that DVR users who fast-forwarded through TV ads were more "engaged" with the ads than those who did not.

Clearly, marketers need to think beyond traditional models as DVR technology and streaming transform how consumers watch TV. One strategy being tested is compressing ads so consumers see a shortened version of the ad, which plays in real time during fast-forwarding. With such a strategy, research suggests that the key is simplicity and having key brand information in the center of the screen, where it is most likely to be noticed. Other strategies now in use include the following:

- *Hybrid ads.* Hybrid ads mimic the show the audience is watching. These tie-ins to shows seem to be particularly effective at staving off ad skipping. Guinness used a hybrid to mimic *Mythbusters,* the show in which the ad aired. This ad yielded 41 percent higher recall than a regular Guinness ad!
- *Dynamic ad placement.* DirecTV is now using technology that allows "seamless insertion of

Selective Exposure

The highly selective nature of consumer exposure is a major concern for marketers because failure to gain exposure results in lost communication and sales opportunities. For example, consumers are highly selective in the way they shop once they enter a store. One study found that only 21 percent of U.S. shoppers visited each aisle in the store. The remainder avoided exposure to products in aisles they didn't shop. This trend continues as more shoppers visit only the fresh food sections of the store and avoid the aisles with processed foods altogether. Consumers in France, Belgium, and Holland are also highly selective shoppers, while consumers in Brazil and the United Kingdom are more likely to shop all the aisles.[4]

Media exposure is also of great concern to marketers. Media are where marketers put their commercial messages and include television, radio, magazines, direct mail, billboards, and the Internet. The impact of the active, self-selecting nature of media exposure can be seen in the zipping, zapping, and muting of television commercials. **Zipping** occurs when one fast-forwards through a commercial on a prerecorded program. **Zapping** involves switching channels when a commercial appears. **Muting** is turning the sound off during commercial breaks. Zipping, zapping, and muting are simply mechanical ways for consumers to selectively avoid exposure to advertising messages, often referred to as **ad avoidance.**

household addressable ads into both live and recorded video content from the DVR hard drive." Such micro-targeting can offer consumers ads that are much more relevant to their needs and goals, a critical factor in attitudes toward advertising in general and attention to specific ads in particular.

- *Automatic Content Recognition (ACR).* Customized ads are not exclusive to DVR technology. Roku, a streaming technology, recently developed software that makes suggestions to its viewers of other programs to watch based on what they are currently watching. Beyond that, ACR also collects information on viewers, consequently using that information to service personalized ads to viewers and measure viewership of ads.

- *"Forced" Ad Exposure:* YouTube TV, a new streaming service, provides DVR capability for programs that can be stored in the cloud. However, the DVR capability goes away when an on-demand version of the program becomes available. Viewers are then required to watch the on-demand version and the accompanying ads, even if the program was saved on DVR.

Not all is lost for advertisers. Much can be learned from these cord cutters, who connect to watch TV, and their habits. Advertisers are wise to embrace these technologies:

The data available to be unlocked by advertisers on connected TV coupled with the sheer power of television has brought us to the brink of a TV revolution—offering better experiences for all viewers and rewarding the advertisers who take part with a larger and more engaged audience pool.

Critical Thinking Questions

1. Do you think that later adopters of DVRs or SVOD services will be less interested in "ad avoidance" capabilities? Will this change as they "learn" to use these technologies?

2. Can you think of other strategies beyond those discussed that could be used to reduce consumers' tendency to skip ads?

3. Do you agree that advertisers can be rewarded by embracing these technologies and the cord cutters?

The nearly universal presence of remote controls makes zipping, zapping, and muting very simple. Indeed, existing and emerging technologies give consumers more and more control over exposure to television commercials. Two technologies are the SVOD streaming service described in the opener and the DVR offered by companies such as Dish. Consumer Insight 8–1 explores how the DVR and SVOD are reshaping the media landscape and how marketers are responding.

Avoidance of commercials is a global phenomenon that extends beyond TV to include radio, the Internet, magazines, and newspapers. Ad avoidance depends on numerous psychological and demographic factors. A study by Initiative examined ad avoidance globally and across various media. The study found that ad avoidance is increased by lifestyle (busy and hectic lifestyle), social class (higher social class), and demographics (men and younger consumers).[5]

In addition, ad avoidance appears to increase as advertising clutter increases and as consumer attitudes toward advertising become more negative. Consumers tend to dislike (and actively avoid) advertising when it is perceived to be boring, uninformative, and intrusive.[6] In China, for example, where the novelty of advertising and product variety is wearing off, ad avoidance is on the rise and feelings about advertising are becoming more negative.[7] In online settings, marketers have devised "pop-up" ads that are difficult or impossible for

ILLUSTRATION 8-1

The Delta/Tinder partnership shows how a nontraditional media approach can be used to gain exposure to firms' messages.

Source: Delta Air Lines, Inc.

Source: Tinder

viewers to eliminate. At the extreme, movie theaters air ads *prior* to the movie because the theater provides a captive audience and enhances ad recall beyond that of TV.[8] Such techniques should be used with care, however, because consumers may react very negatively to such forced exposure.[9] In fact, one study found that many online users are so turned off by pop-up ads that they use software or settings to avoid them completely![10]

As seen in the opening example, in response to ad avoidance, marketers increasingly seek to gain exposure by placing their brands within entertainment media, such as in movies and television programs, in exchange for payment or promotional or other consideration. Such **product placement** provides exposure that consumers don't try to avoid—it shows how and when to use the product and enhances the product's image. Product placement agents read scripts and meet with set designers to identify optimal placement opportunities.[11] While product placement is commonplace in the United States, it is not universally accepted. In the United Kingdom, for example, product placement was illegal until just recently. Moreover, while product placements are now allowed, they must be accompanied by a "P" logo at the beginning, end, and after ad breaks when there are "paid-for-references." The logic behind the disclosure is that it will alert consumers that the placements are essentially advertisements.[12] *What effect do you think such disclosure will have on product placement effectiveness? Do you believe that such a requirement should be enforced in the United States? What are the ethical issues involved?*

Movies and television are just some of the avenues being used. Marketers increasingly seek exposure by placing their messages in ever more unique media, such as on the side of trucks and taxis, in airplanes, at events, and in video games. Outdoor and video games are major growth areas for advertisers in this regard. Outdoor is branching out in many new ways beyond traditional billboards. As shown in Illustration 8–1, Delta, in partnership with dating app Tinder, painted interesting travel destinations on a Brooklyn wall so that singles could post selfies on their dating profiles, looking like worldly jet-setters.[13] Such outdoor efforts provide eye-catching visuals that are virtually impossible to ignore.

Video game advertising is perhaps the fastest-growing alternative media. It allows for exposure to younger males, who tend to be the gamers and avoid traditional media. As one expert notes:

Advertisers have seen that young males, specifically 18- to 24-year-olds, are increasingly turning their backs on TV and multiplexes in favor of video games and the Internet. Making the area [ads in video games] even more attractive [is] a recent study from Nielsen and game publisher Activision [which] shows that gamers not only accept brands embedded into games but can be persuaded to buy the products if the integration is relevant and authentic.[14]

As a result, the Yankee Group estimates that while ad spending in some media is growing in the 4 to 5 percent range (TV and magazines) and some is even shrinking (newspapers), ad spending in video games is growing by over 30 percent per year and is nearing the $2 billion mark.[15]

Voluntary Exposure

Although consumers often avoid commercials and other marketing stimuli, sometimes they actively seek them out for various reasons, including purchase goals, entertainment, and information. As we saw earlier, consumers actively seek out aisles containing items they want to buy.[16] And many viewers look forward to the commercials developed for the Super Bowl. Perhaps more impressive is the positive response consumers have to **infomercials**—*program-length television commercials with a toll-free number and/or web address through which to order or request additional information.* These positively affect brand attitudes and purchase intentions.[17] And they are more likely to be viewed by early adopters and opinion leaders.[18] This latter effect implicates a critical indirect influence of infomercials through word-of-mouth communications. It also highlights the role that information and relevance play in driving voluntary exposure to marketing messages.

Exposure to online messages and advertising also can be voluntary or involuntary. As we saw earlier, exposure to banner ads and pop-ups is generally *involuntary,* as consumers encounter them while seeking other information or entertainment. However, a consumer who clicks on the banner or pop-up *(click through)* is now *voluntarily* being exposed to the target site and its marketing message.

Consumers also voluntarily expose themselves to marketing messages by deliberately visiting firms' homepages and other marketer sites. For example, if you are buying a new car, you might visit manufacturer sites such as www.toyota.com and independent sites such as www.edmunds.com. You also might register online to receive coupons or regular updates or newsletters about a company's products and services. The voluntary and self-selected nature of such online offerings, where consumers "opt in" to receive e-mail-based promotions, is often referred to as **permission-based marketing.**[19] Consumers control the messages they are exposed to and, consequently, are more receptive and responsive to those messages. Permission-based marketing concepts also are being used to enhance the effectiveness of *mobile marketing* on cell phones.[20] Finally, note that online viral and buzz marketing (Chapter 7) rely heavily on consumer voluntary exposure and distribution of marketing messages.

ATTENTION

Attention *occurs when the stimulus activates one or more sensory receptor nerves, and the resulting sensations go to the brain for processing.* Attention requires consumers to allocate limited mental resources toward the processing of incoming stimuli, such as packages seen on store shelves or banner ads on the web. As we discussed earlier, the marketing environment is highly cluttered and consumers are constantly bombarded by thousands of times more stimuli than they can process. Therefore, consumer attention is selective. As one advertising agency director stated,

LO3

Every year it gets more and more important to stand out and be noticed, to be loud but simple, and to say something relevant and compelling because there is less and less opportunity to talk to consumers and you can't waste any chances.[21]

Source: The L'Oréal Group

The L'Oréal ad in Illustration 8-2 is very likely to attract attention. What factors determine and influence attention? Perhaps you are in the market for a DVD player. Once in the DVD aisle, you focus your attention on the various brands to make a purchase. However, a loud announcement briefly pulls your attention away from the display. Later, you lose concentration and begin focusing on nearby products you hadn't noticed before. These products were available all the time but were not processed until a deliberate effort was made to do so. As this example demonstrates, attention always occurs within the context of a situation. The *same individual* may devote different levels of attention to the *same stimulus* in *different situations*. Attention is determined by these three factors: the *stimulus,* the *individual,* and the *situation.*

Stimulus Factors

Stimulus factors are physical characteristics of the stimulus itself. Stimulus characteristics such as ad size and color are under the marketer's control and can attract attention independent of individual or situational characteristics. The attention garnered by stimulus factors tends to be relatively automatic. So even if you *think* you are not interested in a car (individual characteristic), a large and colorful car ad (stimulus characteristics) may be hard to ignore.

Size   Larger stimuli are more likely to be noticed than smaller ones. This is certainly the case on store shelves where shelf space is at a premium and more shelf space can translate into greater attention and sales.[22] As a consequence, consumer-products companies often pay what are called *slotting allowances* to retailers to secure shelf space. A recent report

Source: D. L. Mothersbaugh, G. R. Franke, and B. A. Huhmann 2018.

found that this fee could be as high as $1 million for a one-time placement, and that overall food and beverage companies pay grocery stores $50 billion annually to ensure products are placed on store shelves and included in the store's advertisements.[23]

Size also affects attention to advertising. Figure 8–2 indicates the relative attention-attracting ability of various sizes of magazine ads, with larger ads garnering more attention than smaller ads. Larger banner ads also attract more attention, which might help explain why banner and online ads continue to increase in size.[24]

Intensity   The *intensity* (e.g., loudness, brightness, length) of a stimulus can increase attention. For instance, the longer a scene in an advertisement is held on-screen, the more likely it is to be noticed and recalled.[25] In online contexts, one aspect of intensity is *intrusive-ness,* or the degree to which one is forced to see or interact with a banner ad or pop-up in order to see the desired content. A study in which the banner ad was the only thing on the screen for a brief period before the consumer was connected to the sought-after site produced over three times the level of noticing the ad compared with a standard banner format, and almost 25 times the click-through rate.[26] As we saw earlier, however, caution is advised in using intrusiveness because of negative attitudes and ad avoidance.

Repetition is related to intensity. It is the number of times an individual is exposed to a given stimulus, such as an ad or brand logo, over time. Attention generally decreases across repeated exposures, particularly when those exposures occur in a short period of time (intensity is high). For example, attention to multiple inserts of the same print ad within the same magazine issue has been found to drop by 50 percent from the first to the third exposure.[27]

However, the decrease in overall attention caused by repetition needs to be interpreted in view of two factors. First, consumers may shift the *focus* of their attention from one part of the ad to another across repetitions. Have you ever noticed something new about an ad after you've seen it a couple of times? This is a result of a shift in your attention as you become more familiar with the ad. One study suggests that consumers shift their attention away from the brand component of the ad (name, logo, etc.) and toward the text component.[28] This *attention reallocation* is important because many of a brand's features can be communicated through the ad's text, but convincing consumers to read is difficult. The second factor is that repetition often increases recall.[29] As we will discuss in Chapter 9, subsequent exposures, while generating less attention, appear to reinforce the learning that occurred on the first exposure.

Attractive Visuals   Individuals tend to be attracted to pleasant stimuli and repelled by unpleasant stimuli. This explains the ability of *attractive visuals,* such as mountain scenes and attractive models, to draw consumer attention to an advertisement. In fact, an ad's visual or pictorial component can have a strong influence on attention independent of other characteristics. One study found that greater graphics content directed consumers' attention and increased how much time they spent on an online retailer's website.[30] Another study of over 1,300 print ads found that the ad's picture garnered more attention than any other ad element (e.g., brand and text elements) regardless of its size. This *picture superiority* effect on attention demonstrates the importance of an ad's visual component and suggests why the heavy use of pictures in contemporary print advertising may be justified. However, because attention is limited, drawing attention to one element of an ad can detract from others. For example, increasing picture size in a print ad reduces the amount of attention consumers pay to the brand.[31]

Any factor that draws attention to itself and away from the brand and its selling points has to be used with caution. An ad's visual component represents one such factor. Attractive models represent another. One company found that putting a provocatively dressed model in its print ad drew attention away from their product and toward the model. As a consequence, consumer recall of their brand name 72 hours after exposure to the ad was reduced by 27 percent![32]

Color and Movement   Both *color* and *movement* serve to attract attention, with brightly colored and moving items being more noticeable. Certain colors and color characteristics create feelings of excitement and arousal, which are related to attention. Brighter colors are more arousing than dull. And *warm* colors, such as reds and yellows, are more arousing than *cool* colors, such as blues and grays.[33]

In store, a brightly colored package or display is more apt to receive attention. Retailers interested in encouraging impulse purchases may utilize red in their displays given its ability to attract attention and generate feelings of excitement.[34] Also, point-of-purchase displays with moving parts and signage are more likely to draw attention and increase sales. Thus, companies like Eddie Bauer are choosing dynamic digital signage over static displays.[35]

Color and movement are also important in advertising. Thus, banner ads with dynamic animation attract more attention than similar ads without dynamic animation.[36] Newspapers, such as the *Los Angeles Times,* promote the benefits of color over black-and-white advertising. Figure 8–3 shows the relative advantage of color to ad recall and purchase activities.

Illustration 8–3 shows two Konica copier ads that are identical except for the use of color. The ad with the color was noticed by significantly more readers than was the black-and-white ad.

Position   *Position* refers to the placement of an object in physical space or time. In retail stores, items that are easy to find or that stand out are more likely to attract attention.

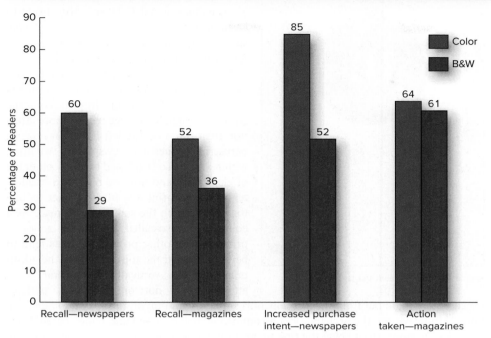

The Impact of Color versus Black and White in Advertising   FIGURE 8-3

Source: "Media Kit," *Los Angeles Times,* June 16, 2016; MPA The Association of Magazine Media, *Magazine Media Factbook 2017/18,* p. 47.

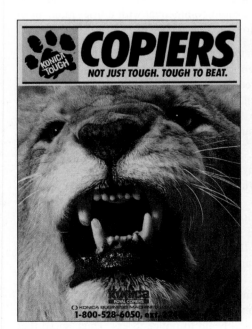

Source: Konica Business Machines, U.S.A.

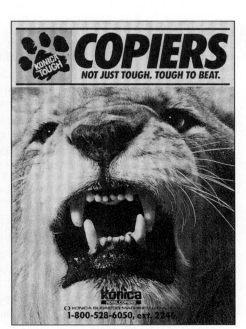

Source: Konica Business Machines, U.S.A.

ILLUSTRATION 8-3

Color can attract attention to an ad. In this case, the color Konica ad had a noted score of 62 percent, compared with 44 percent for the identical Konica black-and-white ad.

This M&M's print ad makes effective use of isolation to capture and hold attention.

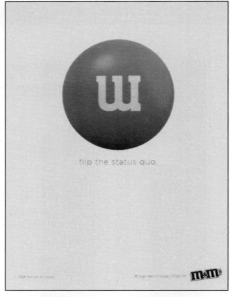

flip the status quo.

m&m's

Source: Mars, Incorporated and its Affiliates

End caps and kiosks are used for this reason. In addition, because items near the center of a consumer's visual field are more likely to be noticed than those on the periphery, consumer goods manufacturers compete fiercely for eye-level space in grocery stores.[37]

Position effects in advertising often depend on the medium and how consumers normally interact with that medium. In print contexts, ads on the right-hand page receive more attention than those on the left based on how we peruse magazines and newspapers. Attention within an ad also is affected by the positioning of elements[38] and how we read. U.S. readers tend to scan print ads from top left to bottom right, much the same way we read. As a consequence, so-called *high-impact* zones in print ads and other print documents tend to be more toward the top and left of the ad. In online contexts, vertical banners attract more attention than horizontal banners, perhaps because they stand out from the typically horizontal orientation of most print communications.[39] In television, the probability of a commercial being viewed and remembered drops sharply as it moves from being the first to air during a break to the last to air because consumers often engage in other activities during commercial breaks.[40]

Isolation   *Isolation* is separating a stimulus object from other objects. In-store, the use of stand-alone kiosks is based on this principle. In advertising, the use of "white space" (placing a brief message in the center of an otherwise blank or white advertisement) is based on this principle, as is surrounding a key part of a radio commercial with a brief moment of silence.[41] The M&M's ad in Illustration 8–4 shows an effective print ad that uses isolation.

Format   *Format* refers to the manner in which the message is presented. In general, simple, straightforward presentations receive more attention than complex presentations. Elements in the message that increase the effort required to process the message tend to decrease attention. Advertisements that lack a clear visual point of reference or have inappropriate movement (too fast, slow, or "jumpy") increase the processing effort and decrease attention. Likewise, audio messages that are difficult to understand because of foreign accents, inadequate volume, or a speech rate that is too fast[42] also reduce attention.

Contrast and Expectations   Consumers pay more attention to stimuli that *contrast* with their background than to stimuli that blend with it. Nissan's use of color ads in newspapers demonstrates an effective use of contrast.[43]

Contrast is related to the idea of expectations. Expectations drive our perceptions of contrast. Packaging, in-store displays, and ads that differ from our expectations tend to get noticed. For example, ads that differ from the type of ad consumers *expect* for a product category often motivate more attention than ads that are more typical for the product category.[44]

One concern of marketers is that once a promotion becomes familiar to consumers, it will lose its ability to attract attention. **Adaptation level theory** suggests that if a stimulus doesn't change, over time we adapt or habituate to it and begin to notice it less. Thus, an ad that

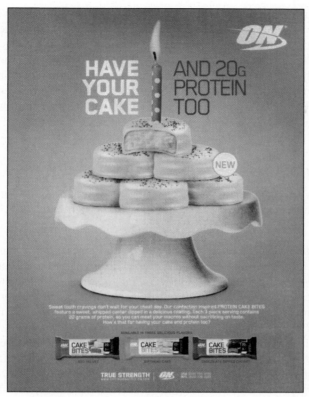

Source: Optimum Nutrition, Inc.

we initially notice when it's new may lose its ability to capture our attention as we become familiar with it. This familiarity effect is not uncommon. However, one study finds that by being original (that is, unexpected, surprising, unique), an advertisement can continue to attract attention even after consumers are familiar with it.[45] Illustration 8–5 shows an ON Cakebites ad that is unique and original, when compared with the typical ad for this product.

Interestingness What one is interested in is generally an individual characteristic. Snowboarders would be likely to attend to ads or shop in stores related to that activity, whereas nonboarders would not. However, there are characteristics of the message, store, and in-store display themselves that cause them to be of interest to a large percentage of the population. For example, in-store displays that use "tie-ins" to sporting events and movies appear to generate considerably more interest, attention, and sales than simple brand signs.[46]

In advertising, factors that increase curiosity, such as a plot, the possibility of a surprise ending, and uncertainty as to the point of the message until the end, can increase interest and the attention paid to the ad. In fact, while many DVR users skip commercials, one study found that more than 90 percent watched *certain* ads because they found them interesting.[47] Another study found that consumers were more likely to continue watching TV ads that were highly entertaining.[48]

Information Quantity Finally, *information quantity* represents the number of cues in the stimulus field. Cues can relate to the features of the brand itself, typical users of the brand, typical usage situations, and so on. This information can be provided on packaging, in displays, on websites, and in ads.

Information helps consumers make decisions. But is more information better? In advertising, the answer is that it depends on a number of factors, including the media used. In print advertising, information appears to attract attention, while in TV advertising, information appears to reduce attention. One explanation is that increases in information quantity in TV ads quickly lead to **information overload** because (unlike the situation with print ads) consumers have no control over the pace of exposure.[49] Information overload occurs when consumers are confronted with so much information that they cannot or will not attend to all of it. The result can be suboptimal decisions.[50]

Individual Factors

Individual factors are characteristics that distinguish one individual from another. Generally speaking, consumer motivation and ability are the major individual factors affecting attention.

Motivation   *Motivation* is a drive state created by consumer *interests* and *needs.* Interests are a reflection of overall lifestyle as well as a result of goals (e.g., becoming an accomplished guitar player) and needs (e.g., hunger). *Product involvement* indicates motivation or interest in a specific product category. Product involvement can be temporary or enduring. You might be temporarily involved with dishwashers if yours stops working, but involved with guitars and music your entire life. Either way, product involvement motivates attention. For example, several studies show that product involvement increases the amount of attention paid to print ads and, in particular, to the ad's body copy rather than picture.[51] So the picture superiority effect we discussed earlier may play less of a role when consumers are highly involved with the product being advertised. Another study found that consumers were more likely to click on banners for products they were involved with. *External* stimulus characteristics like animation had less influence on these consumers because they were already *internally* motivated.[52]

One way marketers have responded to consumer interests and involvement is by developing smart banners for the Internet. **Smart banners** are *banner ads that are activated based on terms used in search engines.*[53] Such *behavioral targeting* strategies are available for general websites as well, and they appear to be quite effective. For example, during one ad campaign, surfers on www.wsj.com who visited travel-related columns were targeted as potential travelers and "were 'followed' around the site and served American Airlines ads, no matter what section of wsj.com they were reading."[54] Attention was higher for these targeted ads, as was brand and message recall and trust.[55]

Ability   *Ability* refers to the capacity of individuals to attend to and process information. Ability is related to knowledge and familiarity with the product, brand, or promotion. An audiophile, for example, is more capable of attending to highly detailed product information about stereo equipment than a novice. As a consequence, experts can attend to more information, more quickly and more effectively, than novices can and tend to be less plagued by information overload. One study found that consumers with higher education and greater health-related experience were more likely to pay attention to the highly detailed technical information in "direct-to-consumer" pharmaceutical ads.[56]

Brand familiarity is an ability factor related to attention. Those with high brand familiarity may require less attention to the brand's ads because of their high existing knowledge. For example, one exposure appears to be all that is needed to capture attention and generate click-through with banner ads when brand familiarity is high. In contrast, the click-through rate is very low on the first exposure when brand familiarity is low, but increases dramatically on the fifth exposure.[57] Consumers with low brand familiarity appear to require more banner attention to yield the knowledge and trust needed to drive further attention via click-through to the site.

Situational Factors

Situational factors include stimuli in the environment other than the focal stimulus (i.e., the ad or package) and temporary characteristics of the individual that are induced by the environment, such as time pressures or a crowded store. Clutter and program involvement are two major situational factors affecting attention.

Clutter   *Clutter* represents the density of stimuli in the environment. In-store research suggests that cluttering the environment with too many point-of-purchase displays decreases the attention consumers pay to a given display. This explains why companies such as Walmart have made a concerted effort to reduce the number of displays in their stores.[58] In advertising, consumers pay less attention to a commercial in a large cluster of commercials than they do to one in a smaller set.[59] You may have noticed cable channels moving more to a single-sponsor format and actually promoting the fact that their programs will have fewer commercials!

Program Involvement   *Program involvement* refers to how interested viewers are in the program or editorial content surrounding the ads (as opposed to involvement with the ad or brand). In general, the audience is attending to the medium because of the program or editorial content, not the advertisement. So the question remains: Does involvement with the program or editorial content influence attention to the ad? The answer is clearly yes, in a positive direction, as found in recent television program research[60] and as demonstrated by Figure 8-4.

However, research shows that even when program involvement is low, marketers can increase attention by enhancing the quality of the ad itself. *Ad quality* represents how well a message is constructed in terms of being believable and appealing, and in communicating the core message effectively.[61]

Nonfocused Attention

Thus far we have been discussing a fairly high-involvement attention process in which the consumer focuses attention on some aspect of the environment as a result of stimulus, individual, or situational factors. However, stimuli may be attended to without deliberate or conscious focusing of attention. A classic example is the *cocktail party effect,* whereby an individual engaged in a conversation with a friend isn't consciously aware of other conversations at a crowded party until someone in another group says something relevant such as mentioning her name. This example suggests we are processing a host of stimuli at a subconscious level, and mechanisms in our brain evaluate this information to decide what warrants deliberate and conscious attention.[62] In fact, the idea behind *hemispheric lateralization* is that different parts of our brain are better suited for focused versus non-focused attention.

Hemispheric Lateralization   **Hemispheric lateralization** is a term applied to activities that take place on each side of the brain. The left side of the brain is primarily responsible for verbal information, symbolic representation, sequential analysis, and the ability to be conscious and report what is happening. It controls those activities we typically call *rational*

FIGURE 8-4   Involvement with a Magazine and Advertising Effectiveness

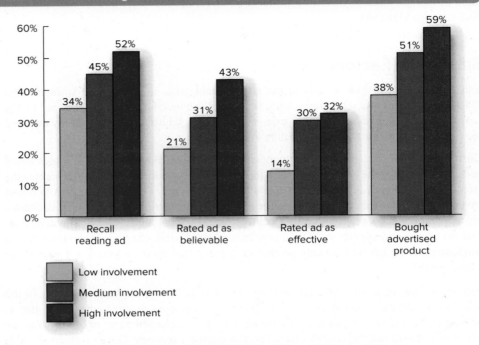

Source: *Cahners Advertising Research Report 120.1 and 120.12* (Boston: Cahners Publishing, undated).

thought. The right side of the brain deals with pictorial, geometric, timeless, and nonverbal information without the individual being able to verbally report it. It works with images and impressions.

The left brain needs fairly frequent rest. However, the right brain can easily scan large amounts of information over an extended time period. This led researcher Herbert Krugman to suggest that "it is the right brain's picture-taking ability that permits the rapid screening of the environment—to select what it is the left brain should focus on."[63] One study of banner ads found evidence of preconscious screening. Web surfers seem able to spot a banner ad without actually looking directly at it. As a consequence, direct attention to banner ads occurred only 49 percent of the time. It seems that experience with the web allows consumers to build up knowledge about banner characteristics (typical size and location) that is used to avoid direct attention.[64]

However, just because consumers don't pay direct attention to an advertisement doesn't mean it can't influence them. For example, brands contained in ads to which subjects are exposed but pay little or no attention (incidental exposure) nonetheless are more likely to be considered for purchase.[65]

Subliminal Stimuli   A message presented so fast or so softly or so masked by other messages that one is not aware of seeing or hearing it is called a **subliminal stimulus.** A subliminal ad is different from a "normal" ad in that it "hides" key persuasive information within the ad by making it so weak that it is difficult or impossible for an individual to physically detect. Normal ads present key persuasive information to consumers so that it is easily perceived.

Subliminal advertising has been the focus of intense study and public concern. It's one thing for consumers to decide not to pay attention to an ad. It's quite another for advertisers to try to bypass consumers' perceptual defenses by using subliminal stimuli.

Two books triggered public interest in masked subliminal advertising.[66] The author "documents" numerous advertisements that, once you are told where to look and what to look for, appear to contain the word *sex* in ice cubes, phalli in mixed drinks, and nude bodies in the shadows. Such masked symbols, deliberate or accidental, do not appear to affect standard measures of advertising effectiveness or influence consumption behavior. Likewise, research on messages presented too rapidly to elicit awareness indicates that such messages have little or no effect.[67] In addition, there is no evidence marketers are using subliminal messages.[68]

INTERPRETATION

Interpretation is *the assignment of meaning to sensations.* Interpretation is related to how we comprehend and make sense of incoming information based on characteristics of the stimulus, the individual, and the situation.

LO4

Several aspects of interpretation are important to consider. First, it is generally a relative process rather than absolute, often referred to as **perceptual relativity.** It is often difficult for people to make interpretations in the absence of some reference point. Consider the following actual scenario:

> An episode of QVC Network's *Extreme Shopping* program offers Muhammad Ali's boxing robe (priced at over $12,000), followed by Jane Mansfield's former mansion (almost $3.5 million), and a Volkswagen Beetle painted by Peter Max ($100,000). Then, signed and personalized Peter Max prints were offered for about $200.

In line with the notion of relativity, consumers interpreted the print price as lower when it followed the higher-priced items.[69]

A second aspect of interpretation is that it tends to be subjective and open to a host of psychological biases. The subjective nature of interpretation can be seen in the distinction between *semantic meaning,* the conventional meaning assigned to a word such as that found in the dictionary, and *psychological meaning,* the specific meaning assigned a word by a given individual or group of individuals based on their experiences, their expectations, and the context in which the term is used.

Marketers must be concerned with psychological meaning as it is the subjective experience, not objective reality, that drives consumer behavior. A firm may introduce a high-quality new brand at a lower price than competitors because the firm is more efficient. However, if consumers interpret the lower price to mean lower quality (and they often do), the new brand will not be successful regardless of the objective reality.[70]

A final aspect of interpretation is that it can be a cognitive "thinking" process or an affective "emotional" process. **Cognitive interpretation** is *a process whereby stimuli are placed into existing categories of meaning.*[71] As we saw earlier, ads are categorized as expected or unexpected, a process that can vary by culture and individual.[72] In countries like France where ads are more sexually explicit, nudity may be seen as more appropriate than in the United States. Products also are categorized. When DVD players were first introduced, most consumers probably grouped them in the same category as VCRs, but with further experience put them in separate categories. Radically "new" products (discontinuous innovation) are the most difficult to categorize, and marketers need to provide consumers with assistance to gain understanding and acceptance.[73]

ILLUSTRATION 8-6

Consumers have emotional responses to or interpretations of ads as well as cognitive ones. This Go RVing ad is likely to produce an emotional or feeling response in many members of its target audience.

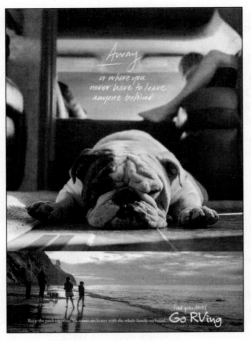

Source: Go RVing, Inc.

Affective interpretation is *the emotional or feeling response triggered by a stimulus such as an ad.* Emotional responses can range from positive (upbeat, exciting, warm) to neutral (disinterested) to negative (anger, fear, frustration). Like cognitive interpretation, there are "normal" (within-culture) emotional responses to many stimuli (e.g., most Americans experience a feeling of warmth when seeing pictures of young children with kittens). Likewise, there are also individual variations to this response (a person allergic to cats might have a negative emotional response to such a picture). Consumers confronting new products or brands often assign them to emotional as well as cognitive categories.[74] The Go RVing ad shown in Illustration 8-6 is likely to trigger an emotional interpretation as well as a cognitive one.

Consumer Insight 8-2 deals with the issue of how consumers deal with multiple cues simultaneously in interpreting a brand, service, or experience, and how marketers are tapping into the skills of specialists called *synners* to help them design appropriate multifaceted "cue sets."

Individual Characteristics

Marketing stimuli have meaning *only* as individuals interpret them.[75] Individuals are not passive interpreters of marketing and other messages but actively assign meaning based on their needs, desires, experiences, and expectations.

Traits   Inherent physiological and psychological traits, which drive our needs and desires, influence how a stimulus is interpreted. From a *physiological* standpoint, consumers differ in their sensitivity to stimuli. Some children are more sensitive to the bitter taste of certain chemicals found in green, leafy vegetables such as spinach.[76] Sweet 'N Low (an artificial sweetener containing saccharin) maintains a fiercely loyal customer base, most likely among those who (unlike most of us) don't physiologically perceive saccharin as bitter.

From a *psychological* standpoint, consumers have natural cognitive, emotional, and behavioral predispositions. As just one example, some people experience emotions more strongly than others, a trait known as *affect intensity.* A number of studies have found that consumers who are higher in affect intensity experience stronger emotional reactions to any given advertisement.[77] We discuss other personality differences in Chapter 10.

Learning and Knowledge   The meanings attached to such "natural" things as time, space, relationships, and colors are learned and vary widely across cultures, as we saw in Chapter 2. Consumers also learn about marketer-created stimuli like brands and promotions

I Smell Orange, I Taste Blue, I Feel Silver, I Hear Squiggles

The critical importance of cues—brand name, logo, sound, packaging, color, font, smell, feel, taste—to product perception, and particularly interpretation, is widely accepted by marketers. Companies spend heavily to develop the right brand names and design the right logos to communicate who they are, what they stand for, what they promise—in some cases, cleverly so, with special messages—the arrow in FedEx, the kiss in Hershey's kisses, the 31 in Baskin-Robbins 31 flavors.[78]

Microsoft's understanding of the importance of sound to its brand led it to use many musicians from around the world to compose the "inspiring, universal, optimistic, futuristic, sentimental, sexy, emotional . . ." musical notes for a new system launch. Intel's use of the four note "Intel bong" is so well known that consumers can sing it on request. Harley-Davidson deemed the sound of its HOG engine to be so important to its identity that it sought, although unsuccessfully, to trademark it.

Each cue is a part that together creates the perception of the whole product. Marketers know that the whole is more than the sum of its parts, but understanding how all the parts fit together is challenging. This is where synners, as people with synesthesia call themselves, come in. Synners have a neurological condition that crosses two or more senses—letters have colors, sounds have tastes—and puts them in a particularly good position to evaluate how the parts interact and contribute to the whole. An estimated one out of 27 people is a synner, including musician John Mayer, Nobel laureate physicist Richard Feynman, and rapper Kanye West. As a group, synners appear to have better memories and score higher on tests of creativity.

Marketers have come to appreciate synners' unique potential and have begun to incorporate their input into product planning and design. Ford Motor Co., for example, recently created the custom position *specialist in cross-sensory harmonization* for one of its engineers who is a synner. As his job title implies, he is responsible for working with the designers and engineers to coordinate the parts of the car—sound, look, feel, smell—into a harmonizing whole that Ford wants consumers to have of its cars.

Marketing attention afforded to synners reflects the increased usage of multisensory marketing to carve out brand image in a world of ever greater competition for consumer attention. This is one reason, for example, that organizations such as Zappos (e-tailer of clothing and shoes renowned for its customer care) are conducting workshops to expose their employees to an appreciation of consumer experiences with a multisensory consideration. Of course, there have been previous instances of multisensory marketing—Skittles' tagline "Taste the Rainbow"—but these were scattered. What we are witnessing now is a more focused, defined, and formal strategy that recognizes the potential of synners. Some synners are not waiting for incumbent firms to recognize their potential and have formed their own businesses such as 12.29, an olfactory branding firm founded by two synners that helps hotels, banks, and fashion runways choose the right scent.

Critical Thinking Questions

1. Did you know about the insider messages in the FedEx, Hershey's and Baskin-Robbins logos? Do you know of any others?

2. What sensory cues do you strongly associate with brands? Stores?

3. When the cues are at odds with one another, consumers get mixed messages that can lead to confusion and declines in sales (e.g., Pepsi Crystal's taste was cola, but its color was like water). What are other products that flopped because of the mismatch of cues?

Source: Browns Shoes Inc.

through their experiences with them. This experience and knowledge affect interpretations. One general finding is that consumers tend to interpret information in ways that favor their preferred brands. In one study, those higher in loyalty to a firm tended to discredit negative publicity about the firm and thus were less affected by it.[79] Similarly, another study found that consumers infer more positive motives from a company's price increase if the company has a strong reputation.[80]

The Via Spiga ad in Illustration 8–7 uses color to reinforce an interpretation that consumers have learned. *What meanings are associated with the colors in Illustration 8-7?*

Expectations   Individuals' interpretations of stimuli tend to be consistent with their *expectations,* an effect referred to as the *expectation bias.* Most consumers expect dark brown pudding to taste like chocolate, not vanilla, because dark pudding is generally chocolate flavored and vanilla pudding is generally cream colored. In a taste test, 100 percent of a sample of college students accepted dark brown *vanilla* pudding as chocolate.[81] Thus, their expectations, cued by color, led to an interpretation that was inconsistent with objective reality.

Consumers' expectations are the result of learning and can be formed very quickly, as the old saying "first impressions matter" suggests. Once established, these expectations can wield enormous influence[82] and can be hard to change. Many consumers expect, for example, that well-known brands are higher quality. As a consequence, consumers frequently evaluate the performance of a well-known brand as higher than that of an *identical* product with an unknown brand name. Many consumers also have come to expect that brands with some sort of in-store signage are on sale. As a consequence, one study found that brands with promotional signs on them in retail stores are interpreted as having reduced prices even though the signs don't indicate a price reduction and the prices aren't actually reduced.[83]

Situational Characteristics

A variety of situational characteristics have an impact on interpretation, including temporary characteristics of the individual, such as time pressure and mood,[84] and physical characteristics of the situation, such as the number and characteristics of other individuals present and the nature of the material surrounding the message in question.

Basically, the situation provides a context within which the focal stimulus is interpreted. The **contextual cues** present in the situation play a role in consumer interpretation *independent* of the actual stimulus. There are innumerable contextual cues in any given marketing context—here we examine just a few examples. *Color* can be a contextual cue. A recent study of online advertising examined various aspects of background color present during web page loads. Certain color characteristics were found to elicit feelings of relaxation (blue was more relaxing than red) and these feelings increased perceptions of faster web page loading even when actual speeds were identical.[85]

The *nature of the programming* surrounding a brand's advertisements also can be a contextual cue. Both Coca-Cola and General Foods in the past have refused to advertise some products during news broadcasts because they believe that "bad" news might affect the interpretation of their products.

The previous example expresses a concern about the impact that the content of the material surrounding an ad will have on the interpretation of the ad. As Coca-Cola suspects, it appears that ads are evaluated in a more positive light when surrounded with positive programming.[86] In addition, effects can be even more specific and have implications for marketing globally. Research finds that death-related content, which is prevalent in news programming, cues consumer thoughts of patriotism and thus increases consumer preferences for domestic versus foreign brands. Foreign brands can overcome this, however, with pro-domestic claims.[87]

Stimulus Characteristics

The stimulus is the basic entity to which an individual responds and includes the product, package, advertisement, in-store display, and so on. Consumers react to and interpret basic traits of the stimulus (size, shape, color), the way the stimulus is organized, and changes in the stimulus. As we have seen, all these processes are likely to be heavily influenced by the individual and the situation.

Traits Specific traits of the stimulus, such as size, shape, and color, affect interpretation. The meaning of many stimulus traits is learned. Color is one trait in which learning affects meaning. Canada Dry's sugar-free ginger ale sales increased dramatically when the can was changed to green and white from red. Red is interpreted as a "cola" color and thus conflicted with the taste of ginger ale.[88] White space in ads is another trait involving learned meaning. That is, over time consumers have come to believe that white space in an ad means prestige, high price, and quality. As a consequence, marketers can positively influence product perceptions by what they *don't* say in an ad![89]

Another general trait is the extent to which the stimulus is unexpected, a trait sometimes referred to as *incongruity*. Incongruity increases attention, as we saw earlier. However, it also increases liking, in part because of the pleasure consumers derive from "solving the puzzle" presented by the incongruity. As a consequence, products and ads that deviate somewhat from established norms (without going too far) are often better liked. Incongruity often requires that consumers go beyond what is directly stated or presented in order to make sense of the stimulus. These inferences, which we discuss later in the chapter, are an important part of interpretation. Rhetorical figures such as rhymes, puns, and metaphors have been shown to increase consumer attention and influence their feelings and perceptions of the brand. **Rhetorical figures** *involve the use of an unexpected twist or artful deviation in how a message is communicated either visually in the ad's picture or verbally in the ad's text or headline.*[90]

Organization   **Stimulus organization** refers to *the physical arrangement of the stimulus objects.* Organization affects consumer interpretation and categorization. For example, you likely perceive the letters that make up the words you are reading as words rather than as individual letters. This effect is enhanced by the fact that each word has letters that are close together and is separated by larger spaces, a principle called *proximity.* We discuss this and other principles next.

Proximity refers to the fact that *stimuli positioned close together are perceived as belonging to the same category.* Sometimes proximity comes from the stimulus itself. For example, when consumers read the headline "Have a safe winter. Drive Bridgestone Tires," they tend to infer from the proximity of the two statements that the ad means Bridgestone Tires will help them have a safe winter. However, the headline does not explicitly make that claim. *What ethical implications exist?*

Sometimes proximity results from the relationship of the stimulus to its context, as in ambush marketing. **Ambush marketing** involves *any communication or activity that implies, or from which one could reasonably infer, that an organization is associated with an event, when in fact it is not.* A common form of ambush marketing is to advertise heavily during the event. Proximity would lead many to believe that the company was a sponsor of the event even if it was not.[91]

Closure involves *presenting an incomplete stimulus with the goal of getting consumers to complete it and thus become more engaged and involved.* Advertisers often will use incomplete stimuli in this manner because closure is often an automatic response engaged in by consumers to interpret message meaning. Not surprisingly, increasing consumer ad involvement also increases recall, as we will discuss more in Chapter 9.[92]

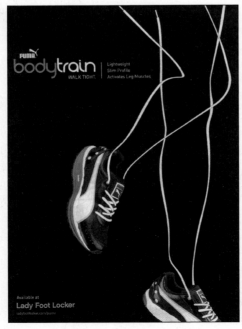

Source: PUMA

Figure–ground involves *presenting the stimulus in such a way that it is perceived as the focal object to be attended to and all other stimuli are perceived as the background.* This strategy often is used in advertising, where the goal is to make the brand stand out as the prominent focal object to which consumers will attend. Absolut, a Swedish vodka, uses figure–ground very effectively. Each ad uses the natural elements in the ad to "form" the figure of a bottle, as with Absolut Mandarin where the bottle is formed by pieces of orange peel. The Puma ad in Illustration 8-8 provides another example.

Changes   To interpret stimulus change, consumers must be able to categorize and interpret the new stimulus relative to the old. Interpreting change requires the ability to both detect change and then assign meaning to that change. Sometimes consumers won't be able to detect a change. Sometimes they can detect a change but interpret it as unimportant.

The physiological ability of an individual to distinguish between similar stimuli is called **sensory discrimination.** This involves such variables as the sound of stereo systems, the taste of food products, or the clarity of display screens. The minimum amount that one brand can differ from another (or from its previous version) with the difference still being noticed is referred to as the **just noticeable difference (j.n.d.).** The higher the initial level of an attribute, the greater that attribute must be changed before the change will be noticed. Thus, a small addition of salt to a pretzel would not likely be noticed unless that pretzel contained only a small amount of salt to begin with.

As a general rule, *individuals typically do not notice relatively small differences between brands or changes in brand attributes.* Makers of candy bars have used this principle for years. Because the price of cocoa fluctuates widely, they simply make small adjustments in the size of the candy bar rather than altering price. Because marketers want some product changes, such as reductions in the size, to go unnoticed, they may attempt to make changes that fall below the j.n.d. This strategy, sometimes referred to as *weighting out,* appears to be on the increase. However, if and when consumers do notice, the potential backlash may be quite severe, leading companies like Blue Bell ice cream to promote its packages that contain the expected amount of product (see Illustration 8–9).[93] *What is your evaluation of the ethics of this practice?*

After *noticing* a change or difference, consumers must *interpret* it. Some changes are meaningful and some are not. The relationship between change and consumers' valuation of that change tends to follow the pattern discussed for j.n.d. The higher the initial level of an attribute, the greater the attribute must change before it is seen as meaningful. For example, consumers underestimate the calories in a meal more as the portion size of the meal increases. This *mis*interpretation has important individual and societal consequences for obesity and portion control.[94]

Source: Blue Bell Creameries, L.P.

Change is often interpreted with respect to some *referent state*. The referent state might be a brand's prior model or a competitor's model. *Reference price* is also a referent state. Consumers can bring *internal* reference prices with them based on prior experience. Also, marketers can provide a reference in the form of *manufacturer's suggested retail price (MSRP)*. Consumers then are more likely to interpret the sale price with respect to the MSRP, which, if favorable, should increase perceived value of the offer and likelihood of purchase.[95]

Consumer Inferences

When it comes to marketing, "what you see is not what you get." That's because interpretation often requires consumers to make inferences. An **inference** *goes beyond what is directly stated or presented.* Consumers use available data *and* their own ideas to draw conclusions about information that is not provided.

Quality Signals   Inferences are as numerous and divergent as consumers themselves. However, some inferences related to product quality are relatively consistent across consumers. Here consumers use their own experiences and knowledge to draw inferences about product quality based on a nonquality cue.

Price-perceived quality is an inference based on the popular adage "you get what you pay for." Consumers often infer that higher-priced brands possess higher quality than do lower-priced brands.[96] Consumers sometimes take price discounts as a signal of lower quality, which is a major concern for companies such as General Motors that rely heavily on such tactics.[97]

Advertising intensity is also a quality signal. Consumers tend to infer that more heavily advertised brands are of higher quality.[98] One reason is that effort is believed to predict success, and ad spending is seen as an indicator of effort. Any factor related to advertising expense such as medium, use of color, and repetition can increase quality perceptions and choice.[99]

Warranties are another quality signal, with longer warranties generally signaling higher quality. Consumers infer that a firm wouldn't offer a longer warranty if it weren't confident in the quality of its products because honoring the warranty would be expensive.[100]

Price, advertising, and warranties are just a few quality cues. Others include *country of origin (COO),* in which consumers interpret products more positively when they are manufactured in a country they perceive positively; *brand* effects, where well-known brands are perceived as higher quality than are unknown brands; and *package size* effects, where small (versus large) packages are rated more favorably.[101]

In general, quality signals operate more strongly when consumers lack the expertise to make informed judgments on their own, when consumer motivation or interest in the decision is low, and when other quality-related information is lacking.

Interpreting Images   Consumer inferences from visual images are becoming increasingly important as advertisers increase their use of visual imagery.[102] Note how visuals dominate many print ads. For example, Clinique ran an ad that pictured a tall, clear glass of mineral water and ice cubes. A large slice of lime was positioned on the lip of the glass. In the glass with the ice cubes and mineral water were a tube of Clinique lipstick and a container of cheek base. Nothing else appeared in the ad. *What does this mean?*

Obviously, to interpret the Clinique ad, consumers must infer meaning. Until recently, pictures in ads were thought to convey reality. If so, the Clinique ad is nonsensical. Is Clinique guilty of ineffective advertising? No. All of us intuitively recognize that pictures

Source: Hyundai Motor America

do more than represent reality; they supply meaning. Thus, one interpretation of the Clinique ad is "Clinique's new summer line of makeup is as refreshing as a tall glass of soda with a twist."

The verbal translation of the meaning conveyed by images is generally incomplete and inadequate. A picture is worth a thousand words not just because it may convey reality more efficiently than words but because it may convey meanings that words cannot adequately express.

Marketers must understand the meanings their audiences assign to various images and words, and use them in combination to construct messages that will convey the desired meaning. They must be sensitive to cultural differences because interpretation is highly contingent on shared cultural experience. For example, consumers in some cultures (termed high-context cultures) tend to "read between the lines." These consumers are very sensitive to cues in the communications setting such as tone of voice. On the other hand, consumers in low-context cultures tend to ignore such cues and focus more on the message's literal or explicit meaning. One study has found that consumers in high-context cultures such as the Philippines are more likely to infer implicit meanings from ad visuals than are those in low-context cultures such as the United States.[103] The Hyundai ad in Illustration 8–10 is an example of an ad based heavily on imagery. *What does this ad mean to you? Would it mean the same to older consumers? Consumers from other cultures?*

Missing Information and Ethical Concerns   When data about an attribute are missing, consumers may assign it a value based on a presumed relationship between that attribute and one for which data are available; they may assign it the average of their assessments of the available attributes; they may assume it to be weaker than the attributes for which data are supplied; or any of a large number of other strategies may be used.[104]

Consider the following hypothetical ad copy:

- The Subaru Outback gets better gas mileage than the Toyota Camry.
- It has more cargo space than the Chevy Volt.
- It has more power than the Toyota RAV4.

Some consumers would infer from this that the Subaru gets better gas mileage than the Volt and the RAV4, has more cargo space than the Camry and the RAV4, and has more power than the Volt and the Camry.[105] These claims are not stated in the ad, making it clear that certain types of information portrayal may lead to incorrect inferences and suboptimal consumer decisions. Thus, a factually correct ad still could mislead some consumers. *Are such ads ethical?*

Consumers can be misled in a number of different ways. One way is that companies can make *direct claims* that are false. Claiming that a food or food ingredient is "mushroom in origin" when it is really a fungus or mold appears to fall into this category. This is the easiest form of deception to detect and prosecute under the law. However, other types of deception are more subtle. These fall under the broad category of *claim-belief discrepancies,* whereby a communication leads consumers to believe something about the product that is not true even though it doesn't present a direct false claim. For example, the Federal Trade Commission (FTC) felt that Kraft Foods' early ads for Kraft Cheese Singles might be misleading based on claim-belief discrepancy. That's because their ads focused on the importance of calcium and the fact that each slice was made from five ounces of milk. The FTC's concern was that reasonable consumers would infer that Kraft Cheese Singles contained the same amount of calcium as five ounces of milk even though this was not directly stated in their ads. This inference is wrong because processing milk into cheese reduces calcium content. Because parents might use Kraft Cheese Singles as a calcium source for their kids, this was of particular concern. Although more difficult from a legal standpoint, the FTC can and does hold companies responsible for claim-belief discrepancies as we see with Kraft.[106] Our understanding and regulation of deception continue to evolve as we gain a better understanding of consumer information processing. This is discussed in more detail in Chapter 20.

PERCEPTION AND MARKETING STRATEGY

LO5

Perception holds critical implications for marketing strategy in a number of areas. We turn to these next.

Retail Strategy

Retailers often use exposure very effectively. Store interiors are designed with frequently purchased items (canned goods, fresh fruits and vegetables, meats) separated so that the average consumer will travel through more of the store. This increases total exposure. High-margin items often are placed in high-traffic areas to capitalize on increased exposure.

Shelf position and amount of shelf space influence which items and brands are allocated attention. Point-of-purchase displays also attract attention and boost sales.[107] And **cross-promotions,** whereby signage in one area of the store promotes complementary products in another (milk signage in the cookie aisle), also can be effective. Recently, retailers have begun to reduce clutter by cutting out marginal, unimportant, and redundant SKUs (stock-keeping units—individual items such as brands, sizes, and versions) within a category. Consumer perceptions and sales tend to go up when the reduction in clutter does not reduce variety and choice.[108]

Another important aspect of the retail environment is *ambient scent.* Pleasant smells in a retail store can increase product evaluations by boosting emotions. In some cases this occurs even when the scent is inconsistent with the product being evaluated (e.g., pine scent and orange juice).

Brand Name and Logo Development

Shakespeare notwithstanding, marketers do not believe that "a rose by any other name would smell as sweet." Mountain Dew's marketing director ascribes part of the success of Code Red to its name: "Had it been called 'Mountain Dew Cherry' it would've done very differently."[109] Brand names can influence anything from color preference to food taste. One study found that people preferred avocado to light green even though the actual color was exactly the same. Another found that young kids liked the taste of foods such as carrots, milk, and apple juice more when they came in a McDonald's package![110] Effects such as this can be related back to expectation biases. That is, the name sets up an expectation that, in turn, biases people's perceptions of the actual experience. Given the tendency toward global brands, it is easy to imagine how complex creating an appropriate name can be.[111]

Linguistic Considerations   Sometimes brand names start out having no inherent meaning but gain associations over time as consumers gain experience with them. Ford and Toyota are examples. However, marketers increasingly tap into linguistic characteristics of words to create brand names with inherent meaning right from the start. One aspect is inherent *semantic meaning* or *morpheme.* NutraSweet took advantage of morphemes to imply nutritious and sweet. And Dodge brought back its "Hemi" engine, a name associated with high performance.[112] A second aspect is sound or *phonemes.* Sounds of letters and words can symbolize product attributes. For example, heavier sounding vowels (Frosh) might be better used to suggest richer, creamier ice cream than lighter sounding vowels (Frish).[113]

Lexicon and other naming companies such as NameLab use these concepts to create names that convey appropriate meanings. Lexicon selected the Blackberry name for Research in Motion's handheld device because *berry* suggests small, the "b" sound is associated strongly with relaxation, and the two "b" sounds at the beginning of *black* and *berry* are light and crisp, suggesting speed. Thus, a name that suggests a handheld that is small, easy to use, and fast—every consumer's dream![114]

Branding Strategies   Marketers engage in numerous strategies to leverage strong existing brand names. One is **brand extension,** where an existing brand extends to a new category with the same name such as Levi Strauss putting its Levi name on a line of upscale men's suits. Another is **co-branding,** an alliance in which two brands are put together on a single product. An example is "Intel Inside" Compaq computers. Brand extensions and co-branding can be positive or negative, as we'll discuss in Chapter 9. A key issue is *perceived fit* between the core brand and the extension or the two co-brands. Really poor fit (too much incongruity) is bad, as people find it hard to categorize and make sense of the new brand. For example, the Harley-Davidson cake decorating kit was a flop because the Harley-Davidson image of freedom, ruggedness, and adventure did not fit with baking and icing.[115]

Logo Design and Typographics   How a product or service name is presented—its *logo*—is also important.[116] Figure 8-5 shows a number of brands that have changed their logos over time.[117] *Do you think the new logos are better or worse? In what ways are they better or worse?*

Perhaps in trying to answer these questions, you realized that you don't have any criteria for making suggestions. Such criteria are hard to come by, and we are just now beginning to understand why some logos work better than others. One study provides guidance, finding that logo symbols (such as Prudential's Rock) that are natural, moderately elaborate, and

FIGURE 8-5	Recent Logo Redesigns	
Brand	**Original**	**Update**
Pizza Hut		
Olive Garden		
Marriott Hotels		
Airbnb		

Source: Pizza Hut; The Olive Garden; Marriott; Airbnb, Inc.

symmetrically balanced lead to higher levels of logo liking. *Natural* logos depict commonly experienced objects; *elaborate* logos entail complexity; *symmetrical* logos are visually balanced.

Beyond the logo symbol is also the shape and form of the letters in their name, which relates to typeface and type font. Intuitively, for example, you might think that a fancy *scripted* font signals elegance and is better suited for a fountain pen than for a mountain bike. Turns out you would be right! Different fonts do evoke different meanings and an appropriate fit between the font and product can increase choice of the brand, independent of the name.[118] *Given these various criteria, can you now assess the logo redesigns?*[119]

Media Strategy

The explosion of media alternatives makes it difficult and expensive to gain exposure to key target audiences.[120] However, the fact that the exposure process is often selective rather than random is the underlying basis for effective media strategies. Specifically, firms must

Selective Exposure to Magazines Based on Demographic Characteristics

TABLE 8-1

Demographic Characteristics	Better Homes & Gardens	Cosmopolitan	Maxim	National Geographic	Family Circle
Gender					
Male	37	29	138	107	23
Female	159	166	65	94	172
Age					
18–24	33	161	108	70	27
25–34	62	145	149	80	44
35–44	80	116	136	77	67
45–54	96	97	105	99	93
55–64	122	66	60	107	129
65+	172	45	53	148	197
Education					
College graduate	99	109	68	131	80
High school graduate	89	93	132	65	107
Household income					
Less than $25,000	110	109	135	94	142
$25,000–49,999	109	87	118	100	114
$50,000–59,999	109	92	112	97	124
$60,000–74,999	100	118	91	136	105
$75,000 or more	92	100	83	95	78

Note: 100 = Average level of use, purchase, or consumption.
Source: Simmons Research, *National Consumer Study 2018.*

determine to which media the consumers in the target market are most frequently exposed and place ad messages in those media. As one executive stated:

> We must look increasingly for matching media that will enable us best to reach carefully targeted, emerging markets. The rifle approach rather than the old shotgun.[121]

Consumer involvement can drive media exposure and strategy. For high-involvement products, ads should be placed in media outlets with content relevant to the product. Specialized media such as *Runner's World* or *Vogue* tend to attract readers who are interested in and receptive to ads for related products. In contrast, ads for low-involvement products should be placed in reputable media independent of content, as long as they are frequented by the target market.[122] In a situation such as this, the marketer must find media that the target market is interested in and place the advertising message in those media. Target markets as defined by age, ethnic group, social class, or stage in the family life cycle have differing media preferences, which then can be used to select media outlets. Table 8–1 illustrates selective exposure to several magazines based on demographic characteristics.

As we saw earlier, video game player demographics skew toward young males (for console games, average age is 26 and 68 percent are male). Companies like Burger King, who are desperate to obtain media exposure among this demographic, are moving ad dollars to in-game video ads and product placements.[123]

Technology continues to radically alter media targeting choices. Consider the impact of GPS technology on outdoor mobile ads:

While a cab travels from one end of a city to the other, an electronic billboard on top changes according to location and time of day. Thanks to a satellite feed and global positioning system, the bright, attention-getting ads on the taxi roof keep changing. As the cab passes by a college, an ad for a bookstore appears. While the cab moves through the business district at noon, an ad for a local deli fills the screen. As the cab travels through a Hispanic neighborhood, a Spanish-language ad for a snack food is shown.[124]

Advertisements

Advertisements must perform two critical tasks: capture attention and convey meaning. Unfortunately, the techniques appropriate for accomplishing one task are often counterproductive for the other.

What if you had to design a campaign to increase users for your firm's toilet bowl freshener, but research shows your target market has little inherent interest in the product. What do you do? Two strategies seem reasonable. One is to *utilize stimulus characteristics* such as bright colors or surrealism to attract attention. The second is to *tie the message to a topic in which the target market is interested.*

However, using factors unrelated to the product category to attract attention must be done with caution. First, it may detract attention away from the core brand message because stimuli compete for limited attention. That's why companies often try to use humor, sex appeal, and celebrities in ways that are relevant to the product or message. Second, it may negatively affect *interpretation.* For example, humor in an insurance ad may result in the brand's being interpreted as unreliable.

Package Design and Labeling

Packages must attract attention and convey information, and various aspects from color to shape to typography can interact in complex ways in affecting consumer perceptions.[125] Packaging has functional and perceptual components. Consider the candy coating of M&M's. It is functional because it keeps the chocolate from melting in your hands. But it is also perceptual. The bright colors are interesting and unique even though they don't taste different. One study varied the color variety (7 versus 10 colors) in a bowl of M&M's and found that as variety went up, consumers ate more![126] M&M's has refocused on color by introducing bolder colors and emphasizing color in its ads. As one executive states, "We've always had color as a unique point of difference, but we wanted to reinforce that message in a fresh, contemporary way."[127]

Bright colors, tall packages, and unusual shapes can be used to attract attention, convey meaning, and influence consumption.[128] For example, consumers tend to believe that taller, more elongated packages contain more than shorter packages of the same volume (e.g., a can of soda). As a consequence, a recent study shows that consumers of beverages buy fewer bottles than cans but perceive that the volume they buy is the same. Notice how package options such as an elongated bottle can influence perceived consumption in ways that reduce product sales and revenues.[129] Look at Illustration 8–11 of two Diet Coke cans. Which appears to contain more? If you said the one on the right, you were influenced by the elongation bias (they both contain exactly the same amount of liquid: 12 ounces).

ILLUSTRATION 8-11

Package design can strongly influence perceived volume and consumption levels. Which can do you think contains more Diet Coke?

Packages also contain product information and warnings. Ethical and legal considerations require marketers to place warning labels on a wide array of products such as cigarettes, alcoholic beverages, and many over-the-counter drugs. On the one hand, there is the desire to effectively alert users to potential risks. On the other hand, there is a desire to avoid detracting unduly from product image. The key from an ethical and legal standpoint is to not err on the side of image at the expense of the consumer. Well-designed warnings appear to be at least somewhat effective. Factors reducing their effectiveness include overly technical or complex language and a failure to indicate the positive consequences of compliance.[130]

SUMMARY

LO1: Describe the nature of perception and its relationship to consumer memory and decisions.

Perception consists of those activities by which an individual acquires and assigns meaning to stimuli. Perception occurs in three stages, namely, exposure, attention, and interpretation. If and when perception occurs, the meaning derived from a stimulus is typically transferred to memory, where it is stored and can be later retrieved when consumers are making purchase decisions.

LO2: Explain exposure, the types of exposure, and the resulting marketing implications.

Exposure occurs when a stimulus comes within range of one of an individual's primary sensory receptors. People are exposed to only a small fraction of the available stimuli. And when consumers actively avoid certain marketing stimuli, this is referred to as *selective exposure*. Selective exposure in the advertising area is termed *ad avoidance*. Marketers try to overcome avoidance by using tactics such as *product placement* and *hybrid ads.* It should be noted, however, that consumers seek out some marketing stimuli voluntarily. Examples include Super Bowl ads, ads that go viral online, and company-based e-mails that consumers choose to receive through *permission-based marketing.*

LO3: Explain attention, the factors that affect it, and the resulting marketing implications.

Attention occurs when the stimulus activates one or more of the sensory receptors and the resulting sensations go into the brain for processing. People *selectively attend* to stimuli as a function of stimulus, individual, and situational factors. *Stimulus factors* are physical characteristics of the stimulus itself, such as contrast, size, intensity, attractiveness, color, movement, position, isolation, format, and information quantity. *Individual factors* are characteristics of the individual, such as motivation and ability. *Situational factors* include stimuli in the environment other than the focal stimulus and temporary characteristics of the individual that are induced by the environment. Clutter and program involvement are situational factors of particular interest to marketers. Marketers can utilize all these factors to better develop stimuli that attract consumer attention in today's cluttered environment.

Nonfocused attention occurs when a person takes in information without deliberate effort. *Hemispheric lateralization* is a term applied to activities that take place on each side of the brain. The left side of the brain is concerned primarily with those activities typically called rational thought and the ability to be conscious and report what is happening. The right side of the brain deals with pictorial, geometric, timeless, and nonverbal information without the individual's being able to verbally report it.

A message presented so fast or so softly or so masked by other messages that one is not aware of seeing or hearing it is called a *subliminal message.* Subliminal messages have generated a great deal of interest but are not generally thought to affect brand choice or other aspects of consumer behavior in a meaningful way.

LO4: Explain interpretation, the factors that affect it, and the resulting marketing implications.

Interpretation is the assignment of meaning to stimuli that have been attended to. Interpretation tends to be relative rather than absolute (perceptual relativity) and subjective rather than objective. Two general forms of interpretation are cognitive and affective. *Cognitive interpretation* appears to involve a process whereby new stimuli are placed into existing categories of meaning. *Affective interpretation* is the emotional or feeling response triggered by the stimulus.

Interpretation is largely a function of individual traits, learning, and expectations that are triggered by the stimulus and moderated by the situation. Stimulus characteristics are critical. *Stimulus organization* is the physical arrangement of the stimulus objects and relates to the perceptual principles of *proximity, closure,* and *figure-ground.* Marketers can use these principles to design effective communication strategies. *Stimulus change* and consumer reactions to it are also of concern and have consequences in relation to such strategies as "weighting out," whereby marketers attempt to reduce the quantity offered in increments that consumers won't detect.

Interpretation often involves consumer inferences. *Inferences* go beyond what is directly stated or presented and help explain consumer use of *quality signals* (e.g., higher price means higher quality), their *interpretation of images,* and how they deal with *missing information.* Inferences also help explain how consumers can be misled by marketing messages even when those messages are *literally* true.

LO5: Discuss how perception can enhance strategies for retailing, branding, advertising, and packaging.

Marketers use their knowledge of perception to enhance strategies in a number of areas including retailing, branding, advertising, and packaging. For retailing, issues surrounding store and shelf location are important determinants of perception. For branding, issues surrounding the selection of brand names, extensions, and appropriate logos have important implications for perception. Advertising strategies and media selection are heavily influenced by considering factors that enhance exposure and attention. Packaging is a functional aspect of products, but also perceptual in that it can capture consumer attention and influence their brand interpretations.

KEY TERMS

Ad avoidance 284
Adaptation level theory 292
Affective interpretation 298
Ambush marketing 302
Attention 287
Brand extension 307
Brand familiarity 294
Closure 302
Co-branding 307
Cognitive interpretation 297
Contextual cues 301
Cross-promotions 306

Exposure 282
Figure–ground 302
Hemispheric lateralization 295
Inference 304
Infomercials 287
Information overload 294
Information processing 282
Interpretation 297
Just noticeable difference
   (j.n.d.) 303
Muting 284
Perception 282

Perceptual defenses 282
Perceptual relativity 297
Permission-based marketing 287
Product placement 286
Proximity 302
Rhetorical figures 302
Sensory discrimination 303
Smart banners 294
Stimulus organization 302
Subliminal stimulus 296
Zapping 284
Zipping 284

REVIEW QUESTIONS

1. What is *information processing?* How does it differ from *perception?*

2. What is meant by *exposure?* What determines which stimuli an individual will be exposed to? How do marketers utilize this knowledge?

3. What are *zipping, zapping,* and *muting?* Why are they a concern to marketers?

4. What are *infomercials?* How effective are they?

5. What is *ad avoidance?* How is *DVR technology* affecting it? How are marketers dealing with this phenomenon?

6. What is meant by *attention?* What determines which stimuli an individual will attend to? How do marketers utilize this?

7. What stimulus factors can be used to attract attention? What problems can arise when stimulus factors are used to attract attention?

8. What is *adaptation level theory?*

9. What is *information overload?* How should marketers deal with information overload?

10. What impact does *program involvement* have on the attention paid to commercials embedded in the program?

11. What is a *contextual cue?* Why is it of interest to marketers?

12. What is meant by *nonfocused attention?*

13. What is meant by *hemispheric lateralization?*

14. What is meant by *subliminal perception?* Is it a real phenomenon? Is it effective?

15. What is meant by *interpretation?*

16. What determines how an individual will interpret a given stimulus?

17. What is the difference between *cognitive* and *affective* interpretation?

18. What is the difference between *semantic* and *psychological* meaning?

19. What is *sensory discrimination?* What is a *just noticeable difference (j.n.d.)?*

20. What is a *consumer inference?* Why is this of interest to marketers?

21. How does a knowledge of information processing assist the manager in the following?
    a. Formulating retail strategy
    b. Developing brand names and logos
    c. Formulating media strategy
    d. Designing advertisements
    e. Designing packages and labels

22. What is *co-branding?* Is it effective?

23. What is a *cross-promotion* retail strategy? Provide two examples.

24. How can *rhetorical figures* enhance attention?
25. What is a *smart banner?* How does this relate to selective attention?
26. What is *figure-ground?*
27. What ethical concerns arise in applying knowledge of the perceptual process?
28. What is *ambush marketing?*

DISCUSSION QUESTIONS

29. Given that smoking scenes in movies increase the positive image and intention to smoke among youth, what regulations, if any, should apply to this?

30. How could a marketing manager for the following use the material in this chapter to guide the development of a national advertising campaign (choose one)? To assist local retailers or organizations in developing their promotional activities? Would the usefulness of this material be limited to advertising decisions?
    a. The Salvation Army
    b. Smartphones
    c. Qdoba Mexican Grill
    d. Lucky Jeans
    e. Belkin WiFi equipment

31. Respond to the questions in Consumer Insight 8-1.

32. Hershey created a line of upscale chocolates called "Cacao Reserve *by Hershey's.*" The company created fancy packaging, priced the product at the high end, and did little mass marketing for its new product. Initial sales were disappointingly slow even though the premium chocolate market is growing nicely, with brands like Ghirardelli faring well. As a consequence, Hershey almost immediately (within six months) dropped its prices and started mass advertising. The product ultimately flopped and was discontinued. Using concepts in this chapter, why do you think Hershey failed in its move into the premium chocolate market? Do you think the adjustments were the most appropriate, or could Hershey have taken other steps?

33. Pick three brand names that utilize a *morphemic* approach and three that utilize a *phonemic* approach. Are the morphemes and phonemes consistent with the overall positioning of these brands?

34. Develop a brand name for (*a*) a voice-activated wireless speaker, (*b*) a sports apparel store, (*c*) an Internet grocery shopping service, (*d*) a mobile app, or (*e*) a pet-walking service. Justify your name.

35. Develop a logo for (*a*) a voice-activated wireless speaker, (*b*) a sports apparel store, (*c*) an Internet grocery shopping service, (*d*) a mobile app, or (*e*) a pet-walking service. Justify your design.

36. Evaluate the in-text ads in Illustrations 8-1 through 8-10. Analyze the attention-attracting characteristics and the meaning they convey. Are they good ads? What risks are associated with each?

37. Develop three co-branded products: one that would be beneficial to both individual brands, one that would benefit one brand but not the other, and one that would benefit neither brand. Explain your logic.

38. Find an ad that you feel might mislead consumers through a *claim-belief discrepancy.* What inference processes are you assuming?

APPLICATION ACTIVITIES

39. Find and copy or describe examples of advertisements that specifically use stimulus factors to attract attention. Look for examples of each of the various factors discussed earlier in the chapter and try to find their use in a variety of promotions. For each example, evaluate the effectiveness of the stimulus factors used.

40. Repeat Question 39, but this time look for advertisements using individual factors.

41. Complete Question 34 and test your names on a sample of students. Justify your testing procedure and report your results.

42. Complete Question 35 and test your logos on a sample of students. Justify your testing procedure and report your results.

43. Find two brand names that you feel are particularly appropriate and two that you feel are not very appropriate. Explain your reasoning for each name.

44. Find and describe a logo that you feel is particularly appropriate and one that you feel is not very appropriate. Explain your reasoning.

45. Interview three students with a DVR about their behavior during television breaks when watching prerecorded programming. Do they watch any ads? Why? What do you conclude?

46. Interview three students about how they respond to banner ads and the extent to which they attend to various commercial messages on the Internet.

47. Go to a health food or alternative medicines store or section of a store. Find three products that make

health claims. Evaluate the likely effectiveness of any disclaimers that they contain.

48. Find and copy or describe an ad or other marketing message that you think makes unethical use of the perceptual process. Justify your selection.

49. Develop an ad but omit information about some key product attributes. Show the ad to five students. After they have looked at the ad, give them a questionnaire that asks about the attributes featured in the ad and about the missing attributes. If they provide answers concerning the missing attributes, ask them how they arrived at these answers. What do you conclude?

REFERENCES

1. This opener is based on T. Peterson, "Netflix Isn't Closed to Advertisers After All; Just Ask Anheuser-Busch InBev," *Advertising Age,* February 27, 2015, www.adage.com, accessed April 13, 2018; J. LaReau, "Buick Targets Affluent Viewers of 'black-ish,' 'Knife Fight,'" *Automotive News* 89 (May 2015); M. Chahal, "Is Product Placement Out of Control?," *Marketing Week* (online edition), June 23, 2015; "US Product Placement Revenues Up 13% in 1H15," *PQ Media,* June 15, 2015, www.pqmedia.com, accessed April 13, 2018; T. Hobbs, "Why Brands Need to Include Music Videos in Their Marketing Mix," *Marketing Week* (online edition), August 24, 2015; R. Plato, "Creating New Advertising Inventory Opportunities through Branded Integration Measurement," *Nielsen,* September 26, 2017, www.nielsen.com, accessed April 13, 2018; L. Muzellec, "James Bond, Dunder Mifflin, and the Future of Product Placement," *Harvard Business Review,* June 23, 2016; L. Iliff, "Lexus Basks in 'Black Panther' Glow," *Auto News,* March 4, 2018, www.autonews.com, accessed April 13, 2018.

2. For an interesting discussion, see J. J. Pilotta and D. Schultz, "Simultaneous Media Experience and Synesthesia," *Journal of Advertising Research,* March 2005, pp. 19–26.

3. Insight is based on "No More Skipping Ads?," *Los Angeles Times,* October 11, 2010; The Nielsen Company, "Milestone Marker: SVOD and DVR Penetration Are Now on Par with One Another," *Nielsen,* June 27, 2016, www.nielsen.com, accessed April 21, 2018; J. Lynch, "Cord Cutting Is Expected to Nearly Double over the Next 4 Years, Eroding the TV Ad Market," *Adweek,* September 13, 2017; R. Greenspan, "DVRs Not Necessarily Ad-Killers," *ClickZ. com,* May 24, 2004; "Jupiter: DVR Ad Skipping Threatens $8B in Advertising," *MarketingVOX.com,* May 4, 2006; "Ad Spots in the DVD Era," *Broadcast Engineering,* August 2007, p. 106; R. Dana and S. Kang, "Answer to Vexing Question: Who's Not Watching Ads," *Wall Street Journal,* October 17, 2007, p. B2; J. Mandese, "Study: DVRs 'Recapture' 96% of TV Ad Zapping," *MediaPost's Media Daily News,* May 25, 2004, www.mediapost.com; "New Age for Ads," *Cablefax Daily,* December 6, 2007, www.cablefax. com; H. Dawley, "As to Worries over Ad-Skipping, Skip It," *Media Life Research,* May 18, 2006, www.medialifemagazine.com; A.

Ambruster, "Don't Give Up on TV Ads Just Yet," *Television-Week,* July 23–30, 2007, p. 16; B. A. S. Martin, V. T. L. Nguyen, and J.-Y. Wi, "Remote Control Marketing," *Marketing Intelligence and Planning* 20, no. 1 (2002), pp. 44–48; S. A. Brasel and J. Gips, "Breaking through Fast-Forwarding," *Journal of Marketing,* November 2008, pp. 31–48; D. Kiley, "Learning to Love the Dreaded TiVo," *BusinessWeek,* April 17, 2006, p. 88; C. Limbardi, "TV Advertising's DVR Challenge," *News.com,* May 23, 2006; K. Ritchi, "Fast-Forwarding Is So Passe Advertisers Want in on DVR and Providers Are Finally Listening," *Boards,* January 2007, p. 13; B. Steinberg, "In the End, It's the Last Ad in a Pod They Recall," *Television Week,* June 11, 2007, p. 13; S. Vranica, "New Ads Take on TiVo," *Wall Street Journal,* October 5, 2007, p. B4; NDS Ltd., "DirecTV Chooses NDS Dynamic to Support Addressable Advertising," press release, March 22, 2011, www.nds.com, accessed May 27, 2011; T. Seppela, "Roku TVs Will Eavesdrop on Your Shows to Serve Up Ads," *Engadget,* April 11, 2017, www.engadget.com, accessed April 22, 2018; S. Ramachandran, "YouTube TV Will Force You to Watch Ads on Many DVR'd Shows," *Wall Street Journal,* April 10, 2017; T. Sims, "Advertisers Must Keep Up with Cord-Cutters or Else Brands Risk Creating 'Lost Generation,'" *Adweek,* February 16, 2018.

4. R. Liljenwall, "Global Trends in Point-of-Purchase Advertising," in *The Power of Point-of-Purchase Advertising,* ed. R. Liljenwall (Washington, DC: Point-of-Purchase Advertising International, 2004), ch. 10; A. LaVito, "Big Food Companies Are Trying to Reverse the Curse of the Center Aisle," *CNBC,* July 14, 2017, www.cnbc.com, accessed April 14, 2018.

5. "Ad Avoidance Highest among Key Target Groups, Says Study," *Businessline,* October 21, 2004, p. 1. See also J. Rojas-Mendez, G. Davies, and C. Madran, "Universal Differences in Advertising Avoidance Behavior," *Journal of Business Research* 62 (2009), pp. 947–54.

6. S. M. Edwards, H. Li, and J.-H. Lee, "Forced Exposure and Psychological Reactance," *Journal of Advertising,* Fall 2002, pp. 83–95; H. Li, S. M. Edwards, and J.-H. Lee, "Measuring the Intrusiveness of Advertisements," *Journal of Advertising,* Summer 2002, pp. 37–47; S. Shavitt, P. Vargas, and P. Lowrey, "Exploring

the Pole of Memory for Self-Selected Ad Experiences," *Psychology & Marketing,* December 2004, pp. 1011–32; C. H. Cho and H. J. Cheon, "Why Do People Avoid Advertising on the Internet?," *Journal of Advertising,* Winter 2004, pp. 89–97.

7. A. C. B. Tse and R. P. W. Lee, "Zapping Behavior during Commercial Breaks," *Journal of Advertising Research,* May 2001, pp. 25–28; M. Savage, "China Turning On, but Tuning Out," *Media,* May 7, 2004, p. 19.

8. P. Paul, "Coming Soon: More Ads Tailored to Your Tastes," *American Demographics,* August 2001, pp. 28–31.

9. Edwards, Li, and Lee, "Forced Exposure and Psychological Reactance."

10. "Pop-Ups—End of an Era?," *NOP World United Business Media,* September 29, 2003, www.unitedbusinessmedia.com.

11. C. A. Russell, "Investigating the Effectiveness of Product Placements in Television Shows," *Journal of Consumer Research,* December 2002, pp. 306–18; S. A. McKechnie and J. Zhou, "Product Placement in Movies," *International Journal of Advertising* 22, no. 3 (2003), pp. 349–74; M. Wiles and A. Danielova, "The Worth of Product Placement in Successful Films," *Journal of Marketing,* July 2009, pp. 44–63; P. M. Homer, "Product Placements," *Journal of Advertising,* Fall 2009, pp. 21–31. For examples when negative effects can occur, see E. Cowley and C. Barron, "When Product Placement Goes Wrong," *Journal of Advertising,* Spring 2008, pp. 89–98. Also see references related to the chapter opener.

12. E. Hall, "Nestle Breaks First Product-Placement TV Buy in U.K.," *Advertising Age,* March 3, 2011.

13. T. Nudd, "Delta Painted Exotic Locales on a Brooklyn Wall for Singles to Snap Selfies Like They're World Travelers," *Adweek,* June 7, 2017, www.adweek.com, accessed April 14, 2018.

14. T. L. Stanley, "Advergames, Content Role Juice up Marketer's Game," *Advertising Age,* February 6, 2006, p. S-3; see also L. Schneider and T. B. Cornwell, "Cashing in on Crashes via Brand Placement in Computer Games," *International Journal of Advertising* 24, no. 3 (2005), pp. 321–43.

15. P. Lehman, "Mad Ave Clicks with the Gamers," *IN,* November 2007, p. 28; "Interactive Marketing and Media Fact Pack," *Advertising Age,* 2006, p. 46; "US Online and Traditional Media Advertising Outlook, 2017–2021," *Marketing Charts,* July 10, 2017, www.marketingcharts.com, accessed April 14, 2018.

16. Liljenwall, "Global Trends in Point-of-Purchase Advertising."

17. M. Singh, S. K. Balasubramanian, and G. Chakraborty, "A Comparative Analysis of Three Communication Formats," *Journal of Advertising,* Winter 2000, pp. 59–75.

18. M. T. Elliot and P. S. Speck, "Antecedents and Consequences of Infomercials," *Journal of Direct Marketing,* Spring 1995, pp. 39–51.

19. "DoubleClick's 2004 Consumer Email Study," October 2004, www.doubleckick.com.

20. A. Z. Cuneo, "Wireless Giants Leap into Third-Screen Marketing," *Advertising Age,* September 11, 2006, p. 39.

21. S. Thompson, "Media Recipe," *Advertising Age,* October 23, 2000, p. 42.

22. K. Bouffard, "Analyst Says Grocers' Cut in Shelf Space for Orange Juice Hurts Citrus Sales," *Knight Ridder Tribune Business News,* July 22, 2004, p. 1.

23. G. Rivlin, "Rigged: Supermarket Shelves for Sale," *Center for Science in the Public Interest,* September 2016, www.cspinet.org; J. Berr, "How Grocers Wring Extra Cash Out of Shelf Space," *CBS News,* October 5, 2016, www.cbsnews.com, accessed April 15, 2018.

24. X. Drèze and F. Xavier Hussherr, "Internet Advertising," *Journal of Interactive Marketing,* Autumn 2003, pp. 8–23; "A Not-So-Banner Year," *Marketing News,* April 29, 2002, p. 3; H. Robinson, A. Wysocka, and C. Hand, "Internet Advertising Effectiveness," *International Journal of Advertising* 26, no. 4 (2007), pp. 527–41.

25. J. R. Rossiter and R. B. Silberstein, "Brain-Imaging Detection of Visual Scene Encoding in Long-Term Memory for TV Commercials," *Journal of Advertising Research,* March 2001, pp. 13–21. See also S. L. Crites Jr. and S. N. Aikman-Eckenrode, "Making Inferences Concerning Physiological Responses," *Journal of Advertising Research,* March 2001, p. 25; J. R. Rossiter et al., "So What?," *Journal of Advertising Research,* May 2001, pp. 59–61.

26. C.-H. Cho, J.-G. Lee, and M. Tharp, "Different Forced-Exposure Levels to Banner Ads," *Journal of Advertising Research,* July 2001, pp. 45–54; W. W. Moe, "A Field Experiment to Assess the Interruption Effect of Pop-Up Promotions," *Journal of Interactive Marketing,* Winter 2006, pp. 34–44.

27. R. Pieters, E. Rosbergen, and M. Wedel, "Visual Attention to Repeated Print Advertising," *Journal of Marketing Research,* November 1999, pp. 424–38.

28. R. Pieters and M. Wedel, "Attention Capture and Transfer in Advertising," *Journal of Marketing,* April 2004, pp. 36–50.

29. S. N. Singh et al., "Does Your Ad Have Too Many Pictures?," *Journal of Advertising Research,* January 2000, pp. 11–27.

30. P. J. Danaher, G. W. Mullarkey, and S. Essegaier, "Factors Affecting Web Site Visit Duration," *Journal of Marketing Research,* May 2006, pp. 182–94; B. Kahn, "Using Visual Design to Improve Customer Perceptions of Online Assortments," *Journal of Retailing* 93, no. 1 (2017), pp. 29–42.

31. Pieters and Wedel, "Attention Capture and Transfer in Advertising."

32. Telecom Research, Inc., *What the Eye Does Not See, the Mind Does Not Remember,* undated.

33. G. J. Gorn, A. Chattopadhyay, T. Yi, and D. W. Dahl, "Effects of Color as an Executional Cue in Advertising," *Management Science,* October 1997, pp. 1387–99.

34. L. Haugen and C. Weems, "P-O-P Advertising Design and Creativity," in *The Power of Point-of-Purchase Advertising,* ch. 6; H. Jagtvedt and S. A. Brasel, "Color Saturation Increases Perceived Product Size," *Journal of Consumer Research* 44 (August 2017), pp. 396–413.

35. L. Rostoks, "Sales from POP Advertising Are Measureable," *Canadian Grocer,* July–August 2001, p. 19; J. McCarthy, "Point of Purchase Last Chance to Dance," *Marketing Magazine,* March 2004, p. 33.

36. C.-H. Cho, "How Advertising Works on the WWW," *Journal of Current Issues and Research in Advertising,* Spring 1999, pp. 33–49; see also S. S. Sunder and S. Kalyanaraman, "Arousal, Memory, and Impression-Formation Effects of Animation Speed in Web Advertising," *Journal of Advertising,* Spring 2004, pp. 7–17.

37. D. Alexander, "Food Industry Giants Spend Big Money for Prime Supermarket Shelf Space," *Knight Ridder Tribune Business News,* December 14, 2003, p. 1.

38. C. Garcia, V. Ponsoda, and H. Estebaranz, "Scanning Ads," *Advances in Consumer Research,* vol. 27, ed. S. J. Hoch and R. J. Meyer (Provo, UT: Association for Consumer Research, 2000), pp. 104–109.

39. Drèze and Hussherr, "Internet Advertising."

40. D. D. McAdams, "Is Anybody Paying Attention?," *Broadcasting and Cable,* August 7, 2000, p. 38.

41. See G. D. Olsen, "Creating the Contrast," *Journal of Advertising,* Winter 1995, pp. 29–44.

42. A. Chattopadhyay, D. W. Dahl, R. J. B. Ritchie, and K. N. Shahin, "Hearing Voices," *Journal of Consumer Psychology* 13, no. 3 (2003), pp. 198–204.

43. J. Roumelis, "How to Get Noticed . . . Fast," *Marketing Magazine,* May 6, 2002, p. 26.

44. R. C. Goodstein, "Category-Based Applications and Extensions in Advertising," *Journal of Consumer Research,* June 1993, pp. 87–99; see also Y. H. Lee, "Manipulating Ad Message," *Journal of Advertising,* Summer 2000, pp. 29–43.

45. R. Pieters, L. Warlop, and M. Wedel, "Breaking through the Clutter," *Management Science,* June 2002, pp. 765–81.

46. "Signposts," *Advertising Age,* May 21, 2001, p. 3.

47. T. Elkin, "PVR Not Yet a Big Threat," *Advertising Age,* May 6, 2002, p. 55. See also L. F. Allwitt, "Effects of Interestingness on Evaluations of TV Commercials," *Journal of Current Issues and Research in Advertising,* Spring 2000, pp. 41–53; W. Friedman, "72.3% of PVR Viewers Skip Commercials," *Advertising Age,* July 2, 2002, www.adage.com.

48. J. W. Elpers, M. Wedel, and R. Pieters, "Why Do Consumers Stop Viewing Television Commercials?," *Journal of Marketing Research,* November 2003, pp. 437–53.

49. Pieters, Warlop, and Wedel, "Breaking through the Clutter"; Elpers, Wedel, and Pieters, "Why Do Consumers Stop Viewing Television Commercials?"

50. B. Lee and W. Lee, "The Effect of Information Overload on Consumer Choice Quality in an On-Line Environment," *Psychology & Marketing,* March 2004, pp. 159–83.

51. Pieters and Wedel, "Attention Capture and Transfer in Advertising"; R. Pieters and M. Wedel, "Goal Control of Attention to Advertising," *Journal of Consumer Research,* August 2007, pp. 224–33.

52. C.-H. Cho, "The Effectiveness of Banner Advertisements," *Journalism and Mass Communication Quarterly,* Autumn 2003, pp. 623–45.

53. See W. Dou, R. Linn, and S. Yang, "How Smart Are 'Smart Banners'?," *Journal of Advertising Research,* July 2001, pp. 31–43.

54. K. Oser, "Targeting Web Behavior Pays, American Airlines Study Says," *Advertising Age,* May 17, 2004, p. 8; see also L. Sherman and J. Deighton, "Banner Advertising," *Journal of Interactive Marketing,* Spring 2001, pp. 60–64.

55. A. Bleier and M. Eisenbeiss, "The Importance of Trust for Personalized Online Advertising," *Journal of Retailing* 91, no. 3 (2015), pp. 309–405.

56. A. M. Menon, A. D. Deshpande, M. Perri III, and G. M. Zinkhan, "Consumers' Attention to the Brief Summary in Print Direct-to-Consumer Advertisements," *Journal of Public Policy and Marketing,* Fall 2003, pp. 181–91.

57. M. Dahlen, "Banner Advertisements through a New Lens," *Journal of Advertising Research,* July 2001, pp. 23–30.

58. J. Spaeth, "Post-Promotion Evaluation," in *The Power of Point-of-Purchase Advertising,* ch. 6; and Liljenwall, "Global Trends in Point-of-Purchase Advertising."

59. R. G. M. Pieters and T. H. A. Bijmolt, "Consumer Memory for Television Advertising," *Journal of Consumer Research,* March 1997, pp. 362–72; see also E. Riebe and J. Dawes, "Recall of Radio Advertising in Low and High Advertising Clutter Formats," *International Journal of Advertising* 25, no. 1 (2006), pp. 71–86.

60. The Nielsen Company, *Advertising & Audiences: State of the Media,* May 2014, p. 15.

61. "The Involvement Index," *Magazine Involvement Alliance,* 2004.

62. For more detail, see T. L. Chartrand, "The Role of Conscious Awareness in Consumer Behavior," *Journal of Consumer Psychology* 15, no. 3 (2005), pp. 203–10; A. Dijksterhuis and P. K. Smith, "What Do We Do Unconsciously?," *Journal of Consumer Psychology* 15, no. 3 (2005), pp. 225–29; L. A. Peracchio and D. Luna, "The Role of Thin-Slice Judgments in Consumer Psychology," *Journal of Consumer Psychology* 16, no. 1 (2006), pp. 25–32; T. L. Chartrand et al., "Nonconscious Goals and Consumer Choice," *Journal of Consumer Research,* August 2008, pp. 189–201.

63. H. E. Krugman, "Sustained Viewing of Television," *Journal of Advertising Research,* June 1980, p. 65; H. E. Krugman, "Low Recall and High Recognition of Advertising," *Journal of Advertising Research,* February–March 1986, pp. 79–86.

64. Drèze and Hussherr, "Internet Advertising."

65. S. Shapiro, D. J. MacInnis, and S. E. Heckler, "The Effects of Incidental Ad Exposure on the Formation of Consideration Sets," *Journal of Consumer Research,* June 1997, pp. 94–104; S. Shapiro, "When an Ad's Influence Is beyond Our Conscious Control," *Journal of Consumer Research,* June 1999, pp. 16–36.

66. W. B. Key, *Subliminal Seduction* (Englewood Cliffs, NJ: Prentice Hall, 1973); W. B. Key, *Media Sexploitation* (Englewood Cliffs, NJ: Prentice Hall, 1976).

67. C. Trappey, "A Meta-Analysis of Consumer Choice and Subliminal Advertising," *Psychology & Marketing,* August 1996, pp. 517–30; S. J. Broyles, "Subliminal Advertising and the Perpetual Popularity of Playing to People's Paranoia," *Journal of Consumer Affairs* 40, no. 2 (2006), pp. 392–406. In contrast, see A. B. Aylesworth, R. C. Goodstein, and A. Kalra, "Effect of Archetypical Embeds on Feelings," *Journal of Advertising,* Fall 1999, pp. 73–81.

68. M. Rogers and C. A. Seiler, "The Answer Is No," *Journal of Advertising Research,* March 1994, pp. 36–45.

69. T. F. Stafford, "Alert or Oblivious?," *Psychology & Marketing,* September 2000, pp. 745–60.

70. See D. Grewal, K. B. Monroe, and R. Krishnan, "The Effects of Price-Comparison Advertising," *Journal of Marketing,* April 1998, pp. 46–59; D. Grewal, R. Krishnan, J. Baker, and N. Borin, "The Effects of Store Name, Brand Name, and Price Discounts," *Journal of Retailing* 3 (1998), pp. 331–52.

71. M. Viswanathan and T. L. Childers, "Understanding How Product Attributes Influence Product Categorization," *Journal of Marketing Research,* February 1999, pp. 75–94; J. Gregan-Paxton, S. Hoeffler,

and M. Zhao, "When Categorization Is Ambiguous," *Journal of Consumer Psychology* 15, no. 2 (2005), pp. 127–40.

72. Goodstein, "Category-Based Applications and Extensions in Advertising."

73. G. P. Moreau, D. R. Lehmann, and A. B. Markman, "Entrenched Knowledge Structures and Consumer Responses to New Products," *Journal of Marketing Research,* February 2001, pp. 14–29; G. Page Moreau, A. B. Markham, and D. R. Lehmann, "'What Is It?' Categorization Flexibility and Consumers' Responses to Really New Products," *Journal of Consumer Research,* March 2001, pp. 489–98.

74. J. Z. Sojka and J. L. Giese, "Thinking and/or Feeling," in *Advances in Consumer Research,* vol. 24, ed. M. Bruck and D. J. MacInnis (Provo, UT: Association for Consumer Research, 1997), pp. 438–42; J. A. Ruth, "Promoting a Brand's Emotional Benefits," *Journal of Consumer Psychology* 11, no. 2 (2001), pp. 99–113.

75. See S. Ratneshwar, "Goal-Derived Categories," *Journal of Consumer Psychology* 10, no. 3 (2001), pp. 147–57.

76. B. Turnbull and E. Matisoo-Smith, "Taste Sensitivity to 6-*n*-propylthiouracil Predicts Acceptance of Bitter-Tasting Spinach in 3-6-y-old Children," *American Journal of Clinical Nutrition* 76 (2002), pp. 1101–105.

77. For a discussion, see J. E. Escalas, M. C. Moore, and J. E. Britton, "Fishing for Feelings?," *Journal of Consumer Psychology* 14, nos. 1 & 2 (2004), pp. 105–14.

78. Insight is based on J. O'Dell, "Harley-Davidson Quits Trying to Hog Sound," *LA Times,* June 21, 2000, http://articles.latimes.com/2000/jun/21/business/fi-43145, accessed September 1, 2014; J. Rohrlich, "Who Created the Windows Start-Up Sound?," *Minyanville,* May 25, 2010, http://www.minyanville.com/businessmarkets/articles/intel-microsoft-research-in-motion-apple/5/25/2010/id/28465, accessed September 1, 2014; J. Pritchard, N. Coolbear, and J. Ward, "Enhanced Associative Memory for Colour (but Not Shape or Location) in Synaesthesia," *Cognition,* May 2013. pp. 230–34; C. Winter, "The Mind's Eye," *Bloomberg Businessweek,* January 9, 2014; W. Leung, "Synesthesia Can Be a Blessing. Just Ask Kanye West," *Globe and Mail,* February 10 2013, www.theglobeandmail.com/life/health-and-fitness/health/synesthesia-can-be-a-blessing-just-ask-kanye-west/article8414660/, accessed September 1, 2014; L. Spinney, "Synesthesia Sells," *New Scientist,* September 22, 2013, www.slate.com/articles/health_and_science/new_scientist/2013/09/cultural_synesthesia_in_marketing_tiffany_cadbury_and_corona_use_multiple.html, accessed September 1, 2014.

79. R. Ahluwalia, R. E. Burnkrant, and H. R. Unnava, "Consumer Response to Negative Publicity," *Journal of Marketing Research,* May 2000, pp. 203–14.

80. M. C. Campbell, "Perceptions of Price Unfairness," *Journal of Marketing Research,* May 1999, pp. 187–99; see also L. Xia, K. B. Monroe, and J. L. Cox, "The Price Is Unfair!," *Journal of Marketing,* October 2004, pp. 1–15.

81. G. Tom et al., "Cueing the Consumer," *Journal of Consumer Marketing,* Spring 1987, pp. 23–27. See also D. S. Kempf and R. N. Laczniak, "Advertising's Influence on Subsequent Product Trial Processing," *Journal of Advertising,* Fall 2001, pp. 27–40.

82. See K. R. Evans et al., "How First Impressions of a Customer Impact Effectiveness in an Initial Sales Encounter," *Journal of the Academy of Marketing Science,* Fall 2000, pp. 512–26.

83. J. J. Inman, L. McAlister, and W. D. Hoyer, "Promotion Signal," *Journal of Consumer Research,* June 1990, pp. 74–81.

84. See M. G. Meloy, "Mood-Driven Distortion of Product Information," *Journal of Consumer Research,* December 2000, pp. 345–58.

85. G. J. Gorn, A. Chattopadhyay, J. Sengupta, and S. Tripathi, "Waiting for the Web," *Journal of Marketing Research,* May 2004, pp. 215–25.

86. A. B. Aylesworth and S. B. MacKenzie, "Context Is Key," *Journal of Advertising,* Summer 1998, pp. 17–31; Q. Chen and W. D. Wells, "Attitude toward the Site," *Journal of Advertising Research,* September 1999, pp. 27–37; B. M. Tennis and A. B. Bakker, "Stay Tuned," *Journal of Advertising,* Fall 2001, pp. 15–25. See also S. Shapiro, D. J. MacInnis, and C.W. Park, "Understanding Program-Induced Mood Effects," *Journal of Advertising,* Winter 2002, pp. 15–26.

87. J. Liu and D. Smeesters, "Have You Seen the News Today?," *Journal of Marketing Research,* April 2010, pp. 251–62.

88. R. Alsop, "Color Grows More Important in Catching Consumers' Eyes," *Wall Street Journal,* November 29, 1989, p. B1.

89. J. W. Pracejus, G. D. Olsen, and T. C. O'Guinn, "How Nothing Became Something," *Journal of Consumer Research,* June 2006, pp. 82–90.

90. D. L. Mothersbaugh, B. A. Huhmann, and G. R. Franke, "Combinatory and Separative Effects of Rhetorical Figures on Consumers' Effort and Focus in Ad Processing," *Journal of Consumer Research,* March 2002, pp. 589–602; E. F. McQuarrie and D. Glenn Mick, "Visual and Verbal Rhetorical Figures under Directed Processing versus Incidental Exposure to Advertising," *Journal of Consumer Research,* March 2003, pp. 579–87; S. Bulmer and M. Buchanan-Oliver, "Advertising across Cultures," *Journal of Current Issues and Research in Advertising,* Spring 2006, pp. 57–71; J. Argo, M. Popa, and M. C. Smith, "The Sound of Brands," *Journal of Marketing,* July 2010, pp. 97–109.

91. T. Meenaghan, ed., "Ambush Marketing," special issue, *Psychology & Marketing,* July 1998.

92. J. Sengupta and G. J. Gorn, "Absence Makes the Mind Grow Sharper," *Journal of Marketing Research,* May 2002, pp. 186–201.

93. T. Howard, "Pay the Same, Get Less as Package Volume Falls," *USA Today,* March 17, 2003, p. 3b.

94. R. Bryant and L. Dundes, "Portion Distortion," *Journal of Consumer Affairs,* Winter 2005, pp. 399–408; P. Chandon and B. Wansink, "Is Obesity Caused by Calorie Underestimation?," *Journal of Marketing Research,* February 2007, pp. 84–99.

95. A. Krishna, R. Briesch, D. R. Lehmann, and H. Yuan, "A Meta-Analysis of the Impact of Price Presentation on Perceived Savings," *Journal of Retailing* 78 (2002), pp. 101–18; L. D. Compeau, J. Lindsey-Mullikin, D. Grewal, and R. D. Petty, "Consumers' Interpretations of the Semantic Phrases Found in Reference Price Advertisements," *Journal of Consumer Affairs,* Summer 2004, pp. 178–87; T. Mazumdar, S. P. Raj, and I. Sinha, "Reference Price Research," *Journal of Marketing,* October 2005, pp. 84–102.

96. P. Raghubir, "Free Gift with Purchase," *Journal of Consumer Psychology* 14, nos. 1 & 2 (2004), pp. 181–86.

97. S. Chatterjee, T. B. Heath, and S. Basuroy, "Failing to Suspect Collusion in Price-Matching Guarantees," *Journal of Consumer Psychology* 13, no. 3 (2003), pp. 255–67; J. Halliday, "GM

Incentive Plans Could Damage Brand," *Advertising Age,* September 27, 2004, p. 1.

98. A. Kirmani, "Advertising Repetition as a Signal of Quality," *Journal of Advertising,* Fall 1997, pp. 77–86.

99. G. L. Lohse and D. L. Rosen, "Signaling Quality and Credibility in Yellow Pages Advertising," *Journal of Advertising,* Summer 2001, pp. 73–85.

100. A. Kirmani and A. R. Rao, "No Pain, No Gain," *Journal of Marketing,* April 2000, pp. 66–79; D. Soberman, "Simultaneous Signaling and Screening with Warranties," *Journal of Marketing Research,* May 2003, pp. 176–92.

101. Z. Gurhan-Canli and D. Maheswaran, "Cultural Variations in Country of Origin Effects," *Journal of Marketing Research,* August 2000, pp. 309–17; Z. Gurhan-Canli and D. Maheswaran, "Determinants of Country-of-Origin Effects," *Journal of Consumer Research,* June 2000, pp. 96–108; P. Chao, G. Wuhrer, and T. Werani, "Celebrity and Foreign Brand Name as Moderators of Country-of-Origin Effects," *International Journal of Advertising* 24, no. 2 (2005), pp. 173–92; D. Yan, J. Sengupta, and R. Wyer, "Package Size and Perceived Quality: The Intervening Role of Unit Price Perceptions," *Journal of Consumer Psychology* 24, no. 1 (2014), pp. 4–17.

102. B. J. Phillips and E. F. McQuarrie, "The Development, Change, and Transformation of Rhetorical Style in Magazine Advertisements 1954–1999," *Journal of Advertising* 31, no. 4 (2003), pp. 1–13; L. A. Peracchio and J. Meyers-Levy, "Using Stylistic Properties of Ad Pictures to Communicate with Consumers," *Journal of Consumer Research,* June 2005, pp. 29–40; J. Z. Sojka and J. L. Giese, "Communicating through Pictures and Words," *Psychology & Marketing,* December 2006, pp. 995–1014.

103. B. J. Phillips, "The Impact of Verbal Anchoring on Consumer Response to Image Ads," *Journal of Advertising,* Spring 2000, pp. 15–24; E. F. McQuarrie and D. G. Mick, "Visual Rhetoric in Advertising," *Journal of Consumer Research,* June 1999, pp. 37–54; M. Callow and L. Schiffman, "Implicit Meaning in Visual Print Advertisements," *International Journal of Advertising* 21 (2002), pp. 259–77.

104. See R. Kivetz and I. Simonson, "The Effects of Incomplete Information on Consumer Choice," *Journal of Marketing Research,* November 2000, pp. 427–48.

105. M. J. Barone and P. J. Miniard, "How and When Factual Ad Claims Mislead Consumers," *Journal of Marketing Research,* February 1999, pp. 58–74; M. J. Barone, K. M. Palan, and P. W. Miniard, "Brand Usage and Gender as Moderators of the Potential Deception Associated with Partial Comparative Advertising," *Journal of Advertising,* Spring 2004, pp. 19–28; M. J. Barone, K. C. Manning, and P. W. Miniard, "Consumer Response to Retailers' Use of Partially Comparative Pricing," *Journal of Marketing,* July 2004, pp. 37–47.

106. For an excellent discussion, see I. L. Preston, *The Tangled Web They Weave* (Madison, WI: University of Wisconsin Press, 1994).

107. L. Petrak, "Capturing Consumer Attention," *National Provisioner,* October 2003, pp. 52–53.

108. P. Boatwright and J. C. Nunes, "Reducing Assortment," *Journal of Marketing,* July 2001, pp. 50–63. See also E. van Herpen and R. Pieters, "The Variety of an Assortment," *Marketing Science,* Summer 2002, pp. 331–41; S. J. Hoch, E. T. Bradlow, and B. Wansink, "Rejoinder to 'The Variety of an Assortment,'" *Marketing Science,* Summer 2002, pp. 342–46; A. Chernev, "When More Is Less and Less Is More," *Journal of Consumer Research,* September 2003, pp. 170–83; S. Thompson, "Kraft Vows to Kick Addiction to Extensions," *Advertising Age,* August 23, 2004, p. 1.

109. H. Chura, "Pepsi-Cola's Code Red Is White Hot," *Advertising Age,* August 27, 2001, p. 24.

110. "What's in a Name?," *Global Cosmetics Industry,* August 2002, p. 42. See also E. G. Miller and B. E. Kahn, "Shades of Meaning," *Journal of Consumer Research,* June 2005, pp. 86–92; J. L. Skorinko et al., "A Rose by Any Other Name . . . ," *Psychology and Marketing,* December 2006, pp. 975–93; "Study: Food in McDonald's Wrapper Tastes Better to Kids," *CNN.com,* accessed August 7, 2007. See also R. Raghunathan, R. W. Naylor, and W. D. Hoyer, "The Unhealthy 5 Tasty Intuition," *Journal of Marketing,* October 2006, pp. 170–84.

111. S. Zhang and B. H. Schmitt, "Creating Local Brands in Multilingual International Markets," *Journal of Marketing Research,* August 2001, pp. 313–25.

112. S. Freeman, "Revived 'Hemi' Engine Helps Chrysler Juice Up Its Sales," *Wall Street Journal,* April 30, 2004, p. B1.

113. R. R. Klink, "Creating Brand Names with Meaning," *Marketing Letters* 11, no. 1 (2000), pp. 5–20; E. Yorkston and G. Menon, "A Sound Idea," *Journal of Consumer Research,* June 2004, pp. 43–51.

114. S. Begley, "New ABCs of Branding," *Wall Street Journal,* August 26, 2002, p. B1.

115. I. P. Levin and A. M. Levin, "Modeling the Role of Brand Alliances in the Assimilation of Product Evaluations," *Journal of Consumer Psychology* 9, no. 1 (2000), pp. 43–52; K. K. Desai and K. I. Keller, "The Effects of Ingredient Branding Strategies on Host Brand Extendibility," *Journal of Marketing,* January 2002, pp. 73–93; K. Hein, "Brand Extensions Can Go Too Far," *Brandweek,* December 5, 2005, www.adweek.com, accessed April 18, 2018; www.harley-davidson.com, accessed April 18, 2018.

116. See J. Tantillo, J. D. Lorenzo-Aiss, and R. E. Mathisen, "Quantifying Perceived Differences in Type Styles," *Psychology & Marketing,* August 1995, pp. 447–57; C. Janiszewski and T. Meyvis, "Effects of Brand Logo Complexity, Repetition, and Spacing on Processing Fluency and Judgment," *Journal of Marketing Research,* June 2001, pp. 18–32; S. A. Brasel and H. Hagtvedt, "Living Brands: Consumer Responses to Animated Brand Logos," *Journal of the Academy of Marketing Science* 44 (2016), pp. 639–53.

117. V. Gendelman, "The 10 Best (and Absolute Worst) Logo Redesigns," *Company Folder,* June 9, 2015, www.companyfolder.com, accessed April 16, 2018.

118. T. L. Childers and J. Jass, "All Dressed Up with Something to Say," *Journal of Consumer Psychology* 12, no. 2 (2002), pp. 93–106; J. R. Doyle and P. A. Bottomley, "Font Appropriateness and Brand Choice," *Journal of Business Research* 57 (2004), pp. 873–80; J. R. Doyle and P. A. Bottomley, "Dressed for the Occasion," *Journal of Consumer Psychology* 16, no. 2 (2006), pp. 112–23. See also P. W. Henderson, J. L. Giese, and J. A. Cote, "Impression Management Using Typeface Design," *Journal of Marketing,* October 2004, pp. 60–72.

119. P. W. Henderson and J. A. Cote, "Guidelines for Selecting or Modifying Logos," *Journal of Marketing,* April 1998, pp. 14–30; J. T. Landry, "Making Logos Matter," *Harvard Business Review,* March–April 1998, pp. 16–17.

120. M. Peers, "Buddy, Can You Spare Some Time?," *Wall Street Journal,* January 26, 2004, p. B1; B. Frank, " 'Missing' Men Prove Prescient," *Advertising Age,* August 23, 2004, p. 16.

121. "Ford Boss Outlines Shift to 'Rifle' Media," *Advertising Age,* October 26, 1981, p. 89. See also P. J. Danaher, "Wearout Effects in Target Marketing," *Marketing Letters* 3 (1996), pp. 275–87.

122. P. N. Shamdasani, A. J. S. Stanaland, and J. Tan, "Location, Location, Location," *Journal of Advertising Research,* July 2001, pp. 7–20.

123. Lehman, "Mad Ave Clicks with the Gamers."

124. J. Guterman, "Outdoor Interactive," *American Demographics,* August 2001, p. 32.

125. O. Ampuero and N. Vila, "Consumer Perceptions of Product Packaging," *Journal of Consumer Marketing* 23, no. 2 (2006), pp. 100–112.

126. B. E. Kahn and B. Wansink, "The Influence of Assortment Structure on Perceived Variety and Consumption Quantities," *Journal of Consumer Research,* March 2004, pp. 519–33.

127. S. Thompson, "M&M's Wraps Up Promo with Color," *Advertising Age,* March 8, 2004, p. 4.

128. B. Wansink and K. Van Ittersum, "Bottoms Up!," *Journal of Consumer Research,* December 2003, pp. 455–63; V. Folkes and S. Matta, "The Effect of Package Shape on Consumers' Judgments of Product Volume," *Journal of Consumer Research,* September 2004, pp. 390–401; J. Hoegg and J. W. Alba, "Taste Perception," *Journal of Consumer Research,* March 2007, pp. 490–98.

129. S. Yang and P. Raghubir, "Can Bottles Speak Volumes?," *Journal of Retailing* 81, no. 4 (2005), pp. 269–81.

130. E. Lepkowska-White and A. L. Parsons, *Journal of Consumer Affairs,* Winter 2001, pp. 278–94; V. A. Taylor and A. B. Bower, "Improving Product Instruction Compliance," *Psychology & Marketing,* March 2004, pp. 229–45; see also J. J. Argo and K. J. Main, "Meta-Analyses of the Effectiveness of Warning Labels," *Journal of Public Policy and Marketing,* Fall 2004, pp. 193–208.

©Sparky2000/Getty Images

LEARNING OBJECTIVES

LO1 Describe the nature of learning and memory.

LO2 Explain the types of memory and memory's role in learning.

LO3 Distinguish the different processes underlying high- and low-involvement learning.

LO4 Summarize the factors affecting information retrieval from memory.

LO5 Understand the application of learning to brand positioning, equity, and leverage.

Learning and memory can be tricky things for consumers and marketers. How we learn or "come to know" something is complex and multifaceted. Once we have learned something, it is hard to "unlearn" it even when we are told or suspect that it is false. Marketers must deal with the challenge of understanding learning and memory and the implications this has for marketing messages and product design.

Some bizarre, funny, and not-so-funny examples of learning and the difficulty of unlearning include[1]

- The flies etched in urinals in men's restrooms apparently act as "targets," resulting in 80 percent less "spilling." How men "learn" to aim for the target is not well understood.
- People given large-size buckets of five-day-old stale popcorn mindlessly eat 57 percent more popcorn than people given medium-size buckets of the same popcorn. One source of such "mindless" eating could be the "clean your plate" mantra "learned" at an early age by many children in the United States.
- We "learn" from an early age that buttons get responses via video games, door bells, and so on. Interestingly, research suggests that most "crosswalk" buttons are not hooked up to anything and yet people push them endlessly in expectation of an effect.
- We have "learned" that certain noises signal successful action. Thus, while smartphones don't need a "click" for button action success (keyboard or camera), consumers often want the noise because they find it hard to "unlearn" the "noise = successful action" link.
- We have "learned" how cars should sound with combustion engines both as an operator and as pedestrians trying to stay safe. The Nissan Leaf hybrid car runs so quietly that drivers could not tell that their car was running. A synthesizer in the dashboard hooked up to speakers in the hood plays an engine sound to provide drivers with the needed feedback. To warn other people of its approach, an artificial roaring noise was added to the silent ENV hydrogen cell motorcycle.

In this chapter, we discuss the nature of learning and memory, conditioning and cognitive theories of learning, and factors affecting retrieval. Implications for marketing managers are discussed throughout, culminating with an examination of product positioning and brand equity in the final sections.

NATURE OF LEARNING AND MEMORY

LO1

Learning is essential to the consumption process. In fact, consumer behavior is largely *learned* behavior. People acquire most of their attitudes, values, tastes, behaviors, preferences, symbolic meanings, and feelings through learning. Culture, family, friends, mass media, and advertising provide learning experiences that affect the type of lifestyle people seek and the products they consume. Consider, for example, how often your movie choices are influenced by what you read online and discussions you have with friends.

Learning is *any change in the content or organization of long-term memory or behavior*[2] and is the result of information processing. In the previous chapter, we described information processing as *a series of activities by which stimuli are perceived, transformed into information, and stored.* The four activities in the series are exposure, attention, interpretation, and memory.

As Figure 9–1 indicates, different information processing systems handle different aspects of learning. The perceptual system deals with information intake through exposure and attention and, as we discussed in Chapter 8, may be conscious or unconscious. Short-term memory deals with holding information temporarily while it is interpreted and transferred into long-term memory. Long-term memory deals with storing and retrieving information to be used in decisions.

These processes are highly interrelated. For example, a consumer may notice his or her favorite brand of soda on the store shelf because of a purchase goal stored in long-term memory. The soda's current price is brought into short-term memory through the perceptual system for processing. But a reference price also may be retrieved from long-term

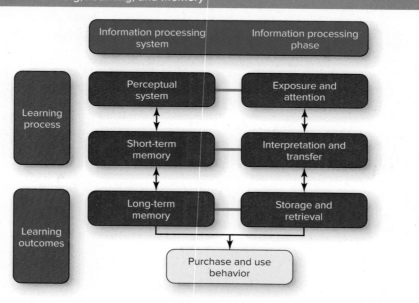

FIGURE 9-1   Information Processing, Learning, and Memory

memory as a comparison point. Finally, price perceptions associated with the consumer's favorite brand may be updated and stored in long-term memory as a consequence of the comparison process.

MEMORY'S ROLE IN LEARNING

LO2

Memory is the total accumulation of prior learning experiences. As Figure 9–1 suggests, memory is critical to learning. It consists of two interrelated components: short-term and long-term memory.[3] These are *not* distinct physiological entities. Instead, **short-term memory (STM),** or *working memory,* is that portion of total memory that is currently activated or in use. **Long-term memory (LTM)** is that portion of total memory devoted to permanent information storage.

Short-Term Memory

STM has a limited capacity to store information and sensations. In fact, it is not used for storage in the usual sense of that term. It is more like a computer file that is currently in use. Active files hold information while it is being processed. After processing is complete, the reconfigured information is printed or returned to more permanent storage such as the hard drive. A similar process occurs with STM. Individuals use STM to hold information while they analyze and interpret it. They may then transfer it to another system (write or type it), place it in LTM, or both. Thus, STM is closely analogous to what we normally call thinking. *It is an active, dynamic process, not a static structure.*

STM Is Short Lived   Information in working memory decays quickly. The memory span for prices, for example, is about 3.7 seconds.[4] The short-lived nature of STM means that consumers must constantly refresh information through **maintenance rehearsal** or it will be lost. Maintenance rehearsal is *the continual repetition of a piece of information in order to hold it in current memory for use in problem solving or transferal to LTM.* Repeating the same formula or definition several times before taking an exam is an example. Marketers frequently simulate this by repeating the brand name or a key benefit in a prominent manner several times in an ad.

STM Has Limited Capacity   The limited capacity of STM means that consumers can hold only so much information in current memory. The capacity of STM is thought to be in the range of five to nine bits of information. A bit can be an individual item or a related set of items. Organizing individual items into groups of related items that can be processed as a single unit is called *chunking.* Chunking can greatly aid in the transfer (and recall) of information from memory. A study of toll-free *vanity numbers* shows the power of chunking. Memory for completely numeric numbers was 8 percent, memory for combinations of numbers and words (800-555-HOME) was 44 percent, and memory for all words (800-NEW-HOME) was 58 percent! The number of bits goes down as the words become meaningful chunks replacing meaningless numbers.[5]

Marketers can help consumers chunk product information by organizing detailed attribute information in messages around the more general benefits that they create. Interestingly, consumers who are product experts are better able to chunk due to highly organized memory structures. As a consequence, experts are better able to learn information and avoid information overload.[6]

Elaborative Activities Occur in STM   STM is often termed working memory because that's where information is analyzed, categorized, and interpreted—that is, STM is where

Source: General Motors Holdings LLC

elaborative activities take place. Elaborative activities are *the use of previously stored experiences, values, attitudes, beliefs, and feelings to interpret and evaluate information in working memory as well as to add relevant previously stored information.* Elaborative activities serve to redefine or add new elements to memory.

Suppose your firm has developed a technology for consumers who want to communicate while driving. The voice-activated service provides drivers with hands-free calling capabilities, Internet access for directions, and the ability to receive help in case of an accident, flat tire, or car theft. How will this service be categorized? The answer depends in large part on *how* it is presented. How it is presented will influence the nature of the elaborative activities that will occur, which in turn will determine how the product is remembered. The OnStar ad in Illustration 9–1 shows how the elements of an advertisement can work together to enhance elaborative activities.

Elaborative activities can involve both concepts and imagery. **Concepts** are abstractions of reality that capture the meaning of an item in terms of other concepts. They are similar to a dictionary definition of a word. **Imagery** involves concrete sensory representations of ideas, feelings, and objects. It permits a direct recovery of aspects of past experiences. Thus, imagery processing involves the recall and mental manipulation of sensory images, including sight, smell, taste, and tactile (touch) sensations.

Pictures can increase imagery, particularly when they are *vivid,* meaning they are relatively concrete representations of reality rather than an abstraction. Pictures are not the only factor to increase imagery, however. Words and phrases in an ad also can encourage consumers to conjure up their own images (e.g., "picture it . . .," "feel it . . .," "imagine . . ."].

Marketers need to make sure that the words and pictures work together. For example, if the ad text invites consumers to engage in imagery processing but provides them with a boring picture, then consumers will be turned off to the message and less likely to buy the brand.[7]

Whether consumers are processing concepts or images, a key issue in learning and memory is the *extent of elaboration.* A major determinant of elaboration is consumer motivation or involvement. Elaboration is enhanced when consumers are more involved or interested in the brand, product, or message at hand (as we saw earlier, it also is facilitated by consumer expertise). Elaboration increases the chances that information will be transferred to LTM and retrieved at a later time by increasing the processing attention directed at that information and by establishing meaningful linkages between the new information and existing information. These linkages or associations are an important part of LTM, as discussed next.

Long-Term Memory

LTM is viewed as *an unlimited, permanent storage.* It can store numerous types of information, such as concepts, decision rules, processes, and affective (emotional) states. Marketers are particularly interested in **semantic memory,** which is *the basic knowledge and feelings an individual has about a concept.* It represents the person's understanding of an object or event at its simplest level. At this level, a brand such as Acura might be categorized as "a luxury car."

Another type of memory of interest to marketers is **episodic memory.** This is *the memory of a sequence of events in which a person participated.* These personal memories of events such as a first date, graduation, or learning to drive can be quite strong. They often elicit imagery and feelings. Marketers frequently attempt to evoke episodic memories either because their brand was involved in them or to associate the positive feelings they generate with the brand. Flashbulb memories are a special type of episodic memory. **Flashbulb memory** is *acute memory for the circumstances surrounding a surprising and novel event.*[8]

Key aspects of flashbulb memories include the following:

- They are vividly detailed and therefore highly enduring over time.
- They contain specific situational detail about location, people, activities, and felt emotions.
- They are held with a high degree of confidence.
- They are perceived as special and different from memories of ordinary or mundane experiences.

Marketers worry not only about *what* information is stored in LTM but also *how* this information is organized. Two important memory structures are schemas and scripts.

Schemas   Both concepts and episodes acquire depth of meaning by becoming associated with other concepts and episodes. A pattern of such associations around a particular concept is termed a **schema** or *schematic memory,* sometimes called a *knowledge structure.* Schematic memory is a complex web of associations. Figure 9–2 provides a simplified example of a schema by showing how one might associate various concepts with Mountain Dew to form a network of meaning for that brand. Notice that our hypothetical schema contains *product characteristics, usage situations, episodes,* and *affective reactions.* The source of some of the schema is personal experience, but other aspects may be completely or partially based on marketing activities.[9] The schematic memory of a brand is the same as the brand image, which we discuss later in the chapter. It is what the consumer thinks of and feels when the brand name is mentioned.

In the partial schema shown in Figure 9–2, concepts, events, and feelings are stored in *nodes* within memory. Thus, the concept "cool" is stored in a node, as are "music," "fun," and "Halloween." Each of these is associated either directly or indirectly with Mountain Dew. *Associative links* connect various concepts to form the complete meaning assigned to an item.

Associative links vary in terms of how strongly and how directly they are associated with a node. In our example, crisp, fun, green, and cool are directly associated with Mountain Dew. However, one or two of these may be strongly associated with the brand, as crisp and cool are shown to be by the bold lines in our example. Other nodes, such as fun and green,

FIGURE 9-2   A Partial Schematic Memory for Mountain Dew

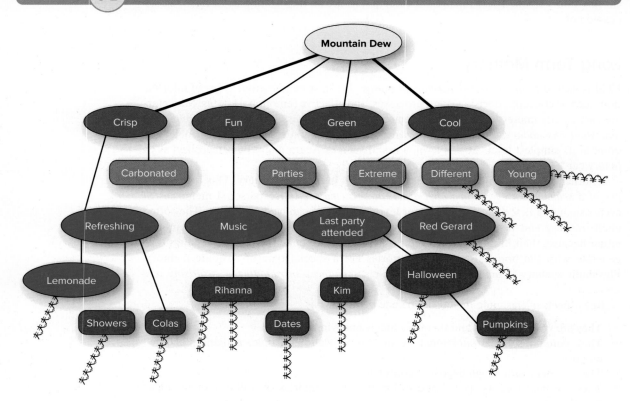

may have weaker links. Without reinforcement, the weaker links may disappear or fade over time (e.g., the Halloween party linkage). Over the longer run, so will the stronger ones (e.g., the cool linkage). Marketers spend enormous effort attempting to develop strong, easily activated links between their brands and desirable product benefits.[10] The various ways in which these linkages are established and strengthened (reinforced) are discussed in the next section, on learning.

The memory activation shown in Figure 9–2 originated with the name of a particular brand. If the activation had begun with the concept "cool," would Mountain Dew arise as a node directly linked to cool? It would depend on the total context in which the memory was being activated. In general, multiple memory nodes are activated simultaneously. Thus, a question like "What is a cool soft drink?" might quickly activate a memory schema that links Mountain Dew directly to cool. However, a more abstract question like "What is cool?" might not because of its relatively weak and indirect connection to beverages and sodas.[11] Marketers expend substantial effort to influence the schema consumers have for their brands. We will discuss this process in detail later in the chapter.

Marketers also strive to influence the schema consumers have for consumption situations. For example, consumers likely have very different beverage schemas for situations such as jogging, where thirst is a key component, than for a party, where socializing and relaxing are key components. The beverage schema for jogging might include products such as water and soda and brands such as Dasani and Pepsi. The beverage schema for a party might include products such as wine and beer and brands such as Yellow Tail and Budweiser. Brands in the schematic memory that come to mind (are recalled) for a specific problem or situation such as thirst are known as the *evoked set.*

The usage situation schema to which a brand attaches itself can have major ramifications. For example, if Canada Dry Ginger Ale associated itself strongly with a "party" situation as a mixer for cocktails, then it is much less likely to be retrieved as part of the evoked set when consumers are thinking of other usage situations, such as those involving thirst.[12] We will discuss how the evoked set influences consumer decision making in Chapter 15.

Scripts   *Memory of how an action sequence should occur,* such as purchasing and drinking a soft drink to relieve thirst, is a special type of schema known as a **script.** Scripts are necessary for consumers to shop effectively. For example, retailers who want to sell products online must first ensure their target markets learn appropriate scripts for online shopping. Also, green marketing efforts relate in part to teaching consumers appropriate scripts for disposal that include recycling.

Retrieval from LTM   The likelihood and ease with which information can be recalled from LTM is termed **accessibility.** Every time an informational node or a link between nodes is activated (accessed) in memory, it is strengthened. Thus, accessibility can be enhanced by rehearsal, repetition, and elaboration. For example, Coca-Cola might be one of the brands that always comes to mind (is retrieved) when you think of sodas because you have seen so many ads for that brand. This accessibility effect for brands is called *top-of-mind awareness.* In addition, accessibility is related to the strength and number of incoming linkages. In essence, when a concept is linked to other concepts in memory, its accessibility increases as a result of the multiple retrieval pathways. Thus, elaboration enhances retrieval by creating a rich associative network. Finally, accessibility is related to the strength and directness of links to nodes, with stronger and more direct linkages being more accessible. Thus, *cool* and *crisp* are highly accessible associations related to Mountain Dew, while *parties* and *refreshing* are less accessible. Clearly, marketers want strong and direct linkages between their brand and critical product features.

Retrieving information from LTM is not a completely objective or mechanical task. If asked to recall the sponsor of the last summer Olympics, some consumers will not remember instantly and certainly, nor accurately.[13] These individuals may *construct* a memory based on limited recall and a series of judgments or inferences. For example, many might "recall" Nike because it is a dominant firm in sports equipment and apparel. Thus, it would "make sense" for Nike to be the sponsor, which could lead some consumers to believe that Nike was indeed a sponsor of the event even if it was not.[14] Therefore, memory is sometimes shaped and changed as it is accessed.

Finally, retrieval may involve *explicit* or *implicit* memories. Traditionally, we have thought of remembering, and thus memory, as the ability to recall specific items or events. If you read this chapter and then try to answer the review questions at the end without referring back to the chapter, you are engaging in traditional memory recall. This is referred to as **explicit memory,** which is characterized by *the conscious recollection of an exposure event.* In contrast, **implicit memory** involves *the nonconscious retrieval of previously encountered stimuli.* It is a sense of familiarity, a feeling, or a set of beliefs about an item without conscious awareness of when and how they were acquired, and it has the potential to interfere with explicit memory.[15] An example of implicit memory relates to brand placements. One study found that over time, a brand's image becomes increasingly similar to the TV show in which it appears, even when consumers don't remember seeing the brand placements![16]

LEARNING UNDER HIGH AND LOW INVOLVEMENT

We have described learning as any change in the content or organization of long-term memory or behavior. In addition, we have described LTM in terms of schemas or associational networks. So how do people *learn* these associations? For example, how do consumers *learn* that Mountain Dew is cool or that Walmart has low prices?

A moment's reflection will reveal that people learn things in different ways. For example, buying a car or stereo generally involves intense, focused attention and processing. The outcome of these efforts is rewarded by better choices. However, most learning is of a much different nature. Even if they don't care for baseball, most people know who is playing in the World Series each year because they hear about it frequently. And people can identify clothes that are stylish even though they never really think much about clothing styles.

As just described, learning may occur in either a high-involvement or a low-involvement situation. Recall from Chapter 8 that information processing (and therefore learning) may be conscious and deliberate in high-involvement situations. Or it may be nonfocused and even nonconscious in low-involvement situations. A **high-involvement learning** situation is one in which *the consumer is motivated to process or learn the material.* For example, an individual reading *PC Magazine* online prior to purchasing a computer is probably highly motivated to learn relevant material dealing with the various computer brands. A **low-involvement learning** situation is one in which *the consumer has little or no motivation to process or learn the material.* A consumer whose television program is interrupted by a commercial for a product he or she doesn't currently use or feel a desire for generally has little motivation to learn the material presented in the commercial. Much, if not most, consumer learning occurs in relatively low-involvement contexts.[17]

As we will see in the following sections, the way a communication should be structured differs depending on the level of involvement the audience is expected to have. Illustration 9–2 shows the Purina ad that assumes high-involvement learning and the Keebler ad based on low-involvement learning. *Why does one ad assume a highly involved audience and the other a low-involvement audience? What differences do you notice between these two ads? Do those differences make sense?*

Figure 9–3 shows the two general situations and the five specific learning theories that we are going to consider. *Level of involvement is the primary determinant of how material is learned.* The solid lines in the figure indicate that operant conditioning and analytical reasoning are common learning processes in high-involvement situations. Classical conditioning and iconic rote learning tend to occur in low-involvement situations. And vicarious learning/modeling is common in both low- and high-involvement situations. We will discuss each of these theories in the following pages.

Conditioning

Conditioning is probably most appropriately described as a set of procedures that marketers can use to increase the chances that an association between two stimuli is formed or learned. The word *conditioning* has a negative connotation to many people and brings forth images of robot-like humans. However, the general procedure simply involves presenting two stimuli in close proximity so that eventually the two are perceived (consciously or unconsciously) to be related or associated. That is, consumers learn that the stimuli go (or do not go) together.

Source: Nestlé Group

Source: Kellogg Co.

ILLUSTRATION 9-2

An important judgment in designing an ad is the level of involvement the audience will have, as shown by the Purina and Keebler ads.

There are two basic forms of conditioned learning: classical and operant. *Classical conditioning* attempts to create an association between a stimulus (e.g., brand name) and some response (e.g., behavior or feeling). *Operant conditioning* attempts to create an association between a response (e.g., buying a brand) and some outcome (e.g., satisfaction) that serves to reinforce the response.

Classical Conditioning   Imagine that you are marketing a new brand of pen and want consumers to feel positively about that pen. How might classical conditioning help you to associate positive feelings with your unfamiliar brand? The classical conditioning procedure would have you pair the unknown brand repeatedly together with some other stimulus that you know already *automatically* elicits positive feelings or emotions, such as popular music in an ad. The goal would be that, eventually, after repeatedly pairing the brand name and the music, the brand name alone will elicit the same positive feelings produced by the music.

The process of using an established relationship between one stimulus (music) and response (pleasant feelings) to bring about the learning of the same response (pleasant feelings) to a different stimulus (the brand) is called **classical conditioning.** Figure 9–4 illustrates this type of learning. Hearing popular music (unconditioned stimulus) automatically elicits a positive emotion (unconditioned response) in many individuals. If this music is consistently paired with a particular brand of pen or other product (conditioned stimulus), the brand itself may come to elicit the same positive emotion (conditioned response).[18] In addition, some features, such as the masculine/feminine qualities of the

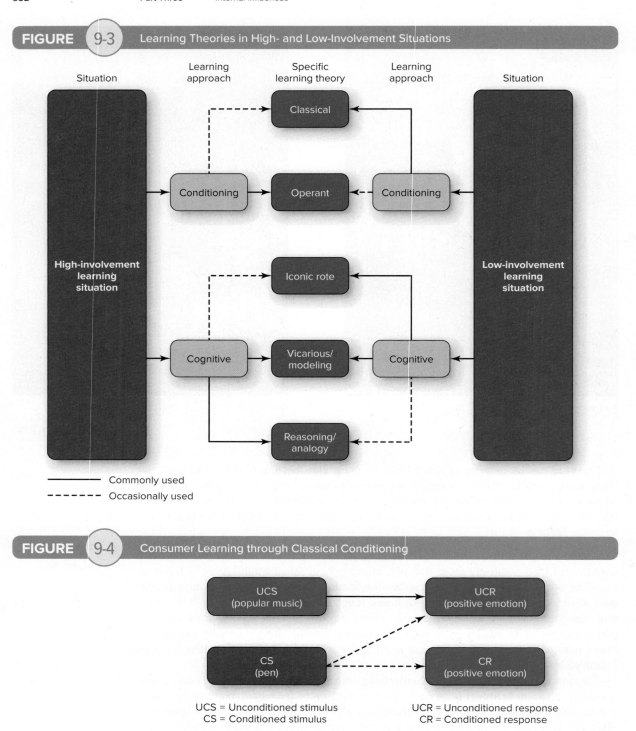

FIGURE **9-3** Learning Theories in High- and Low-Involvement Situations

FIGURE **9-4** Consumer Learning through Classical Conditioning

UCS = Unconditioned stimulus
CS = Conditioned stimulus

UCR = Unconditioned response
CR = Conditioned response

unconditioned stimulus, also may become associated with the conditioned stimulus. That is, using a scene showing males or females in an activity that elicits positive emotions may not only cause a positive emotional response to a brand consistently paired with it, but also cause the brand to have a masculine or a feminine image.[19] Thus, classical conditioning can lead to positive attitudes by influencing brand feelings and beliefs. This is important because, as we will see in later chapters, attitudes influence information search, trial, and brand choice.

Other marketing applications of classical conditioning include

- Consistently advertising a product on exciting sports programs may result in the product itself generating an excitement response.
- Christmas music played in stores may elicit emotional responses associated with giving and sharing, which in turn may increase the propensity to purchase.

Learning via classical conditioning is most common in low-involvement situations, where relatively low levels of processing effort and awareness are involved.[20] However, after a sufficient number of low-involvement "scannings" or "glances at" the advertisement, the association may be formed or learned.

Operant Conditioning   **Operant conditioning** (or instrumental learning) involves rewarding desirable behaviors such as brand purchases with a positive outcome that serves to reinforce the behavior.[21] The more often a response is reinforced, the more likely it will be repeated in the future as consumers *learn* that the response is associated with a positive outcome.

Imagine that you are marketing the snack Pirate Booty's Baked Rice and Corn Puffs. You believe your product has a light, crisp taste that consumers will like. But how can you influence them to learn to consume your brand? One option, based on the operant conditioning procedure, would be to distribute a large number of free samples through the mail, at shopping malls, or in stores. Many consumers would try the free sample (desired response). To the extent that the taste of these baked puffs is indeed pleasant (a positive outcome that serves as a reinforcement), the probability of continued consumption is increased. This is shown graphically in Figure 9–5.

Unlike the relatively automatic associations created by classical conditioning, operant conditioning requires that consumers first engage in a deliberate behavior and come to understand its power in predicting positive outcomes that serve as reinforcement. As suggested in Figure 9–3, such learning is common under conditions of higher involvement.

Operant conditioning often involves influencing consumers to purchase a specific brand or product (desired response). Thus, a great deal of marketing strategy is aimed at securing an initial trial. Free samples (at home or in the store), special price discounts on new products, and contests all represent rewards offered to consumers to try a particular product or brand. If they try the brand under these conditions and like it (reinforcement), they are likely to take the next step and purchase it in the future. This process of encouraging partial responses leading to the final desired response (consume

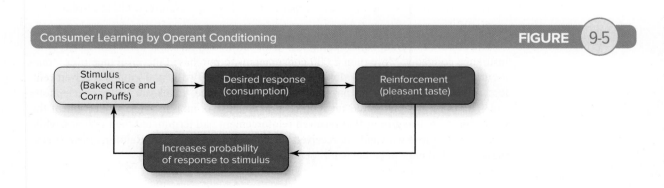

Consumer Learning by Operant Conditioning   **FIGURE** 9-5

Stimulus (Baked Rice and Corn Puffs) → Desired response (consumption) → Reinforcement (pleasant taste)

Increases probability of response to stimulus

FIGURE   9-6   The Process of Shaping in Purchase Behavior

Consume a free sample of Baked Rice and Corn Puffs that was sent to your home

Purchase a second package using the discount coupon that accompanied the free sample

Repurchase the product at full price

a free sample, buy at a discount, buy at full price) is known as **shaping** and is illustrated in Figure 9–6.

In one study, 84 percent of those given a free sample of a chocolate while in a candy store made a purchase, whereas only 59 percent of those not provided a sample made a purchase. Thus, shaping can be very effective. Illustration 9–3 shows an ad for Ciba Vision Dailies lenses. This ad is designed to induce trial, the first step in shaping.

While reinforcement increases the likelihood of behavior such as a purchase being repeated, a negative consequence (punishment) has exactly the opposite effect. Thus, the purchase of a brand that does not function properly greatly reduces the chances of future purchases of that brand. This underscores the critical importance of consistent product quality.

Operant conditioning is used widely by marketers. The most common application is to offer consistent-quality products so that the use of the product to meet a consumer need is reinforcing. Other applications include

- Congratulating the purchaser after a sale, with an e-mail or personal contact, for making a wise purchase (reinforcing).
- Giving free product samples or introductory coupons to encourage product trial (shaping).
- Making store interiors, shopping malls, or downtown areas pleasant places to shop (reinforcing) by providing entertainment, controlled temperature, exciting displays, and so forth.

The power of operant conditioning was demonstrated by an experiment conducted by an insurance company. More than 2,000 consumers who purchased life insurance over a one-month period were randomly divided into three groups. Two of the groups received reinforcement after each monthly payment in the form of a nice "thank-you" letter or telephone call. The third group received no such reinforcement. Six months later, 10 percent of the members of the two groups that received reinforcement had terminated their policies, while 23 percent of those who had not received reinforcement had done so! Reinforcement (being thanked) led to continued behavior (sending in the monthly premium).[22]

Cognitive Learning

Cognitive learning encompasses all the mental activities of humans as they work to solve problems or cope with situations. It involves learning ideas, concepts, attitudes, and facts that contribute to our ability to reason, solve problems, and learn relationships without direct experience or reinforcement. Cognitive learning can range from very simple information acquisition (as in iconic rote learning) to complex, creative problem solving (as in analytical reasoning). Three types of cognitive learning are important to marketers.

Iconic Rote Learning Learning *a concept or the association between two or more concepts in the absence of conditioning* is known as **iconic rote learning.** For example, one may see an ad that states, "Ketoprofen is a headache remedy," and associate the new concept "ketoprofen" with the existing concept "headache remedy." Notice the distinction from conditioning in that there is neither an unconditioned stimulus (classical) nor a direct reward or reinforcement (operant) involved.

Source: Novartis AG

Also, it is important to point out that unlike more complex forms of cognitive learning, iconic rote learning generally involves considerably less cognitive effort and elaboration.[23] A substantial amount of low-involvement learning involves iconic rote learning. Numerous repetitions of a simple message that occur as the consumer scans the environment may result in the essence of the message being learned. Through iconic rote learning, consumers may form beliefs about the characteristics or attributes of products without being aware of the source of the information. When the need arises, a purchase may be made based on those beliefs.[24]

Vicarious Learning or Modeling It is not necessary for consumers to directly experience a reward or punishment to learn. Instead, they can observe the outcomes of others' behaviors and adjust their own accordingly.[25] Similarly, they can use imagery to anticipate the outcome of various courses of action. This is known as **vicarious learning** or **modeling.**

This type of learning is common in both low- and high-involvement situations. In a high-involvement situation, such as purchasing a new suit shortly after taking a job, a consumer may deliberately observe the styles worn by others at work or by role models from other environments, including advertisements. Many ads encourage consumers to imagine the feelings and experience of using a product.[26] Such images not only enhance learning about the product, but may even influence how the product is evaluated after an actual trial.

A substantial amount of modeling also occurs in low-involvement situations. Throughout the course of their lives, people observe others using products and behaving in a great variety of situations. Most of the time they pay little attention to these behaviors. However, over time they learn that certain behaviors, and products, are appropriate in some situations and others are not.

Courtesy of iRobot Corp. Produced by BPL Marketing, London. Photography by Chris Biggs, London

Analytical Reasoning The most complex form of cognitive learning is **analytical reasoning.** In reasoning, individuals engage in creative thinking to restructure and recombine existing information as well as new information to form new associations and concepts. Information from a credible source that contradicts or challenges one's existing beliefs often will trigger reasoning.[27] The ad in Illustration 9–4 challenges implicit consumer beliefs.

One form of analytical reasoning is the use of analogy. **Analogical reasoning** is *an inference process that allows consumers to use an existing knowledge base to understand a new situation or object.* That is, it allows consumers to use knowledge about something they are familiar with to help them understand something they are not familiar with. For example, if you have not tried or adopted an e-reader such as the Kindle or Kobo, you may learn about it by

relating it to your laptop computer and Word documents. Your computer allows for digital storage and downloading of documents which you "open" and "read" on a screen. You might reason that this is much like downloading, opening, and reading any digital content on any digital device. Given the similarities, you might correctly infer that digital readers allow for convenient and mobile access to your online books and magazines. You may also incorrectly infer that flipping through pages and finding your place will be difficult and that reading in such a format will be "hard on your eyes." Thus, from the analogical comparison you could come away with a relatively complete (though in some areas perhaps inaccurate) set of beliefs about the digital reader based on its similarity to your laptop computer and the Word documents you already use.[28]

Learning to Generalize and Differentiate

Regardless of which approach to learning is applicable in a given situation, consumers' ability to differentiate and generalize from one stimulus to another (for example, one brand to another) is critical to marketers.

Stimulus discrimination or differentiation refers to the *process of learning to respond differently to similar but distinct stimuli.* This process is critical for marketers who want consumers to perceive their brands as possessing unique and important features compared with other brands. For example, the management of Bayer aspirin feels that consumers should not see its aspirin as being the same as other brands. In order to obtain a premium price or a large market share, Bayer must teach consumers that its aspirin is distinct from other brands. Stimulus discrimination is an important consideration in brand image and product positioning, discussed later in the chapter.[29]

Stimulus discrimination is critical when brand scandals erupt. Scandals don't always hurt just the scandalized brand but can damage competitors in that industry, especially similar competitors, an effect termed *spillover.* One of the best ways for competitors to protect against spillover from scandals is to be highly differentiated from the scandalized brand.[30]

Summary of Learning Theories with Examples of Involvement Level			TABLE 9-1
Theory	**Description**	**High-Involvement Example**	**Low-Involvement Example**
Classical conditioning	A response elicited by one object is elicited by a second object if both objects frequently occur together.	The favorable emotional response elicited by the word *America* comes to be elicited by a car brand after repeated exposure to its *Made in America* campaign. This response is in addition to any cognitive learning that may have occurred.	The favorable emotional response elicited by a song in an ad for a new breath mint comes to be elicited by that brand after repeated pairing with the song even though the consumer pays little attention to the ad.
Operant conditioning	A response that is reinforced is more likely to be repeated when the same (or similar) situation arises in the future.	A suit is purchased after extensive thought and the consumer finds that it is comfortable and doesn't wrinkle. A sport coat made by the same firm is later purchased because of the positive experience with its suits.	A familiar brand of peas is purchased without much thought due to the low importance of the decision. The peas taste "fresh" so the consumer continues to purchase this brand.
Iconic rote learning	A concept or the association between two concepts is learned without conditioning.	A consumer with little expertise about Blu-ray players tries hard to learn brand information by examining it carefully several times. Learning is limited, however, because his or her lack of expertise inhibits elaboration.	A consumer learns a company's most recent jingle because it is catchy and can't stop replaying it in his or her head.
Vicarious learning or modeling	Behaviors are learned by watching the outcomes of others' behaviors or by imagining the outcome of a potential behavior.	A consumer carefully watches the reactions that other co-workers have to her friend's new briefcase before deciding to buy one.	A child learns that people dress up for special occasions without really ever thinking about it.
Analytical reasoning	Individuals use thinking to restructure and recombine existing and new information to form new associations and concepts.	A consumer buying a car carefully processes information about a new gas/electric hybrid car by using the analogy of homes powered by solar energy.	When a store is out of black pepper, a consumer buys white pepper instead based on the quick reasoning that "pepper is pepper."

Stimulus generalization, often referred to as the *rub-off effect, occurs when a response to one stimulus is elicited by a similar but distinct stimulus.*[31] Thus, a consumer who learns that Oreo cookies taste good and therefore assumes that the Oreo pie crust also will taste good has engaged in stimulus generalization. Stimulus generalization is common and provides a major source of brand equity and opportunities for brand extensions, which are discussed later in the chapter.

Summary of Learning Theories

Theories of learning help us understand how consumers learn across a variety of situations. We have examined five specific learning theories: classical conditioning, operant conditioning, iconic rote learning, vicarious learning/modeling, and analytical reasoning. Each of these learning theories can operate in a high- or a low-involvement situation, although some are more common in one type of situation than another. Table 9–1 summarizes these theories and provides examples from both high- and low-involvement contexts.

LEARNING, MEMORY, AND RETRIEVAL

Joe's Crab Shack's growth slowed considerably in the late 2010s,[32] as did Chrysler's and Gillette's in the 2000s,[33] Saturn's in the early 1990s,[34] and L&M cigarettes' in the 1980s.[35] In each case, at least some of the decline in growth was attributed to sharply reduced advertising. As one executive stated,

LO4

Some time after the company moved away from advertising and marketing, it became clear that people would quickly forget about our products if we didn't support them in the marketplace.[36]

These examples emphasize that marketers want consumers to learn *and* remember positive features, feelings, and behaviors associated with their brands. However, consumers forget. In conditioned learning, forgetting is often referred to as **extinction** because the desired response (e.g., pleasant feelings or brand purchase) decays or dies out if learning is not repeated and reinforced. In cognitive learning, forgetting is often referred to as a **retrieval failure** because information that is available in LTM cannot be accessed, that is, retrieved from LTM into STM.

Two aspects of forgetting that are of concern to marketers are the *likelihood of forgetting* in any given situation and the *rate of forgetting*. Figure 9–7 illustrates a commonly found rate of forgetting for advertising. In this study, aided and unaided recall of four advertisements from *American Machinist* magazine were measured. As can be seen, the probability of ad recall (likelihood) dropped rapidly over the first five days and then stabilized (rate).[37]

At times, marketers or regulatory groups desire to accelerate forgetting or extinction. For example, the American Cancer Society and other organizations offer programs designed to help individuals "unlearn" smoking behavior. Manufacturers want consumers to forget unfavorable publicity or outdated product images. *Corrective advertising,* a government

| FIGURE | 9-7 | Forgetting over Time: Magazine Advertisement |

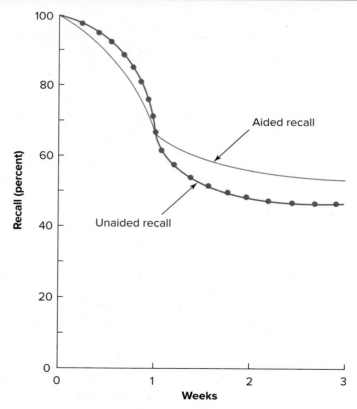

Source: LAP Report #5260.1 (New York: Weeks McGraw-Hill, undated).

requirement that firms remove inaccurate learning caused by past advertising, is described in Chapter 20.

Consumers forget brands, brand associations, and other information for a variety of reasons. First, learning may be weak to begin with. Second, information from competing brands and ads may cause memory interference. Third, the response environment (e.g., the retail store) may not be set up to encourage retrieval of previously learned information (e.g., from advertising). We turn to these issues next.

Strength of Learning

How can the HIV Alliance teach you to minimize your AIDS risk so that you will not forget? Or how can Neutrogena teach you about its line of sunless tanning products so you remember key features when shopping at CVS? That is, what is required to bring about a long-lasting learned response?

One factor is strength of learning. The stronger the original learning (e.g., of nodes and links between nodes), the more likely relevant information will be retrieved when required. *Strength of learning* is enhanced by six factors: *importance, message involvement, mood, reinforcement, repetition,* and *dual coding.*

Importance Importance refers to the value that consumers place on the information to be learned. Importance might be driven by inherent interest in the product or brand, or by the need to make a decision in the near future. The more important it is for the individual to learn a particular behavior or piece of information, the more effective and efficient he or she becomes in the learning process. This is largely due to the greater elaborative activities involved in fully processing and categorizing the material.

One emerging area of interest to marketers is how bilingual consumers process and recall second-language ads. For example, if Hispanic consumers process an ad in English, will it still be as effective as when they process the same ad in Spanish? Generally speaking, processing an ad in a second language is more difficult. This tends to reduce learning and recall for ads in a consumer's second language. Does this mean that second-language ads can never be effective? The answer appears to depend on importance. When importance is high, bilingual consumers expend more processing effort to understand the second-language ad, leading to greater learning and recall.[38]

Importance is one dimension that separates high-involvement learning situations from low-involvement situations. Therefore, high-involvement learning tends to be more complete than low-involvement learning.[39] Unfortunately, marketers are most often confronted with consumers in low-involvement learning situations.

Message Involvement When a consumer is not motivated to learn the material, processing can be increased by causing the person to become involved *with the message itself.* For example, playing an instrumental version of a popular song with lyrics related to product attributes ("Like a rock" in classic Chevrolet pickup ads) may cause people to "sing along," either out loud or mentally. This deepened involvement with the message, relative to merely listening to the lyrics being sung, increases the extent of processing of the message and memory of the associated features or theme.[40]

In Chapter 8 we discussed various strategies for increasing consumer attention including incongruity, rhetoric, incomplete messages, and interesting ads with plots and surprise endings. These strategies also tend to enhance message involvement and thus lead to stronger learning and memory.[41]

Several issues regarding message involvement are important to consider. First, there is evidence that scent may be important to memory. One study found that positive scents present during exposure to an ad increased attention to the ad and resulted in higher brand recall.

Not surprisingly, marketers are currently developing technologies that will allow for "scent-emitting" technologies for Internet applications and in-store kiosks![42]

A second issue is the role of suspense. Sometimes marketers wait until the very end of a message to reveal the brand name in an attempt to attract interest and attention. However, this strategy must be used with caution because waiting until the end of an ad to reveal the brand gives consumers little opportunity to integrate new information into their existing brand schemas. As a result, the associative linkages are weaker and memory is reduced. These results suggest that marketers should strongly consider mentioning the brand relatively early in any marketing message.[43]

A final issue regards message strategies that highlight a brand's personal relevance to the consumer. One such strategy is self-referencing. **Self-referencing** indicates that consumers are relating brand information to themselves. The "self" is a powerful memory schema, and integrating brand information into this schema enhances learning and memory. Self-referencing can be encouraged in ads by using nostalgia appeals, which encourage consumers to remember past personal experiences.[44] It also can be encouraged by using language such as "you" and "your" (second-person pronoun).

Mood   Get happy, learn more? Research indicates that this is indeed true. A positive mood during the presentation of information such as brand names enhances learning. A positive mood during the reception of information appears to enhance its relational elaboration—it is compared with and evaluated against more categories. This produces a more complete and stronger set of linkages among a variety of other brands and concepts, which in turn enhances retrieval (access to the information).[45]

Learning enhancement caused by a positive mood suggests the types of programs that marketers attempting to encourage consumer learning should advertise on. Likewise, it suggests that those commercials that enhance one's mood also would increase learning.[46]

Reinforcement   Anything that increases the likelihood that a given response will be repeated in the future is considered **reinforcement.** While learning frequently occurs in the absence of reinforcement, reinforcement has a significant impact on the speed at which learning occurs and the duration of its effect.

Source: Nestlé Group

A *positive reinforcement* is a pleasant or desired consequence. A couple who like Mexican food see an ad for a new Chipotle Mexican Grill in their area and decide to try it. They enjoy the food, service, and atmosphere. They are now more likely to select the Chipotle Mexican Grill the next time they dine out.

A *negative reinforcement* involves the removal or the avoidance of an unpleasant consequence. Vicks ads promise to relieve sinus pain and pressure. If they convince a consumer to try the sinus formula and it performs well, this consumer is likely to purchase and use it again in the future and, based on stimulus generalization, perhaps try other Vicks products as well.

Illustration 9-5 is an ad for CoffeeMate that provides an additional example of reinforcement in that it suggests the positive outcomes of using its brand.

Earworms—Music That Gets Stuck in Our Heads

Through repetitive exposure, consumers unintentionally, inattentively, unknowingly learn the jingles, and songs, that lie dormant for days, months, years, even decades in the consumers' memory that on occasion can be triggered and brought to awareness by a fragrance, a few musical notes, a flash of a picture. Such recall may be accompanied by the feeling of surprise—the unearthing of buried information—and nostalgia—memories tied to the music. Soon, however, the tune returns to its state of dormancy.[49]

However, some jingles and songs in memory refuse to be "turned off" and play in an endless, repetitive loop in our heads for hours, days, and, for a small minority, even weeks or months. They pop up and demand to be sung or hummed repeatedly. They are called *earworms*. Some 98 percent of people have experienced this annoying condition. In a recent study, the top four earworms were

- Chili's "Baby Back Ribs" jingle.
- "Who Let the Dogs Out" by Baha Men.
- "We Will Rock You" by Queen.
- Kit Kat candy-bar jingle ("Gimme a Break . . .").

Music most likely to cause an earworm is simple, upbeat, and repetitive and has an element of the unexpected—like a rhythmic variation, a shifting time signature, or an extra beat.

Music is a ubiquitous component of commercials. Sometimes the music is created specifically for the product—Chili's "Baby Back Ribs," Dr. Pepper's "I'm a Pepper." Sometimes the music is a piece of popular music specially culled to appeal to the target market (e.g., Apple's use of U-2's "Vertigo") and sometimes music is selected for its ability to enhance the features of the product—Rolling Stone's "Start Me Up" for a new Windows release.

As annoying as earworms can be, they do prove that music serves as a hook of sorts for brands. A better understanding of earworms may be key to a better understanding of the automaticity of music and memory.

Critical Thinking Questions

1. Have you experienced earworms? What song got stuck in your head? How long did it last?

2. What is your opinion of musicians licensing their music to advertisements? Is this "selling out" or is it a smart way for a win-win for marketers and musicians?

3. What are the (dis)advantages of using popular music in advertisements? Original music?

Punishment is the opposite of reinforcement. It is any consequence that decreases the likelihood that a given response will be repeated in the future. If the couple who tried the Chipotle Mexican Grill described earlier thought that the service was bad or that the food was poorly prepared, they would be unlikely to patronize it in the future.

Obviously, it is critical for marketers to determine precisely what reinforces consumer purchases so they can design promotional messages and products that encourage initial and repeat purchases.

Repetition   Repetition enhances learning and memory by increasing the accessibility of information in memory or by strengthening the associative linkages between concepts.[47] Quite simply, the more times people are exposed to information or engage in a behavior, the more likely they are to learn and remember it. For example, compared with one showing of a Miller Lite beer commercial, three showings during a championship baseball game produced two-and-one-third times the recall.[48] For reasons that are not completely clear, certain music "motivates" automatic self-repetition on the part of the consumer, which creates stronger learning and brand associations, as discussed in Consumer Insight 9–1.

The effects of repetition depend, of course, on importance and reinforcement. Less repetition of an advertising message is necessary for someone to learn the message if the subject matter is important or if there is a great deal of relevant reinforcement. Because many advertisements do not contain information of current importance to consumers or direct rewards for learning, repetition plays a critical role in the promotion process for many products.[50] As we saw earlier, classical conditioning and iconic rote learning (low-involvement learning) rely heavily on repetition.

Figure 9–8 shows how ad repetition affects recall for low- and high-awareness brands. High repetition works better than low and the gains in recall are more pronounced the longer the campaign runs and for low-awareness brands.[51]

Both the number of times a message is repeated and the timing of those repetitions affect the extent and duration of learning and memory.[52] Figure 9–9 illustrates the relationship between repetition timing and product recall for a food product. One group of homemakers,

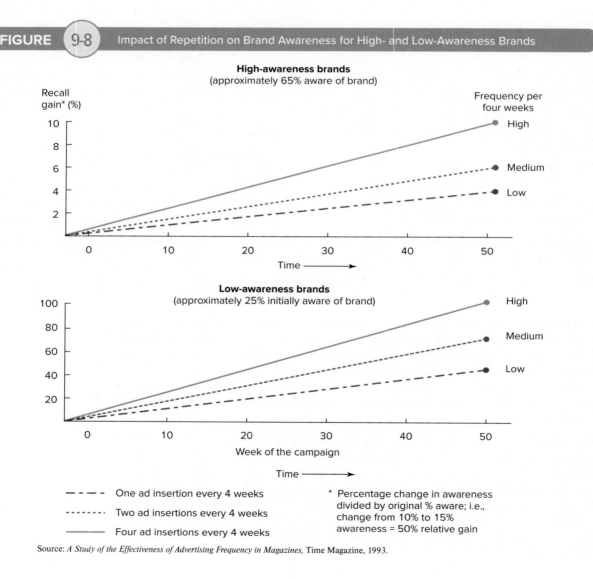

FIGURE 9-8 Impact of Repetition on Brand Awareness for High- and Low-Awareness Brands

Source: *A Study of the Effectiveness of Advertising Frequency in Magazines,* Time Magazine, 1993.

represented by the curved line in the figure, was exposed to a food product advertisement once a week for 13 consecutive weeks. For this group, product recall increased rapidly and reached its highest level during the 13th week. Forgetting occurred rapidly when advertising stopped, and recall was virtually zero by the end of the year.

A second group of homemakers was exposed to the same 13 direct-mail advertisements. However, they received one ad every four weeks. The zigzag line in the figure shows the recall pattern for this group. In this case, learning increased throughout the year, but substantial forgetting occurred between message exposures.

Given a finite budget, how should a firm allocate its advertising across a budget cycle—should it concentrate it all at once or spread it out over time? The answer depends on the task. Any time it is important to produce widespread knowledge of the product rapidly, such as during a new-product introduction, frequent (close together) repetitions should be used. This is referred to as **pulsing.** Thus, political candidates frequently hold back a significant proportion of their media budgets until shortly before the election and then use a media blitz to ensure widespread knowledge of their desirable attributes. More long-range programs, such as store or brand image development, should use more widely spaced repetitions.[53]

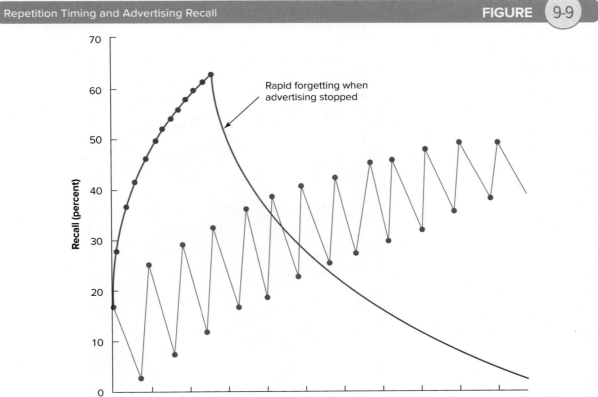

Repetition Timing and Advertising Recall   **FIGURE 9-9**

Source: Reprinted from H. J. Zielski, "The Remembering and Forgetting of Advertising," *Journal of Marketing*, The American Marketing Association, January 1959, p. 240, with permission from Journal of Marketing Research, published by the American Marketing Association. The actual data and a refined analysis were presented in J. L. Simon, "What Do Zielski's Data Really Show about Pulsing?," *Journal of Marketing Research*, August 1979, pp. 415–20.

Marketers must walk a fine line in terms of repetition. Too much repetition can cause consumers to actively shut out the message, evaluate it negatively, or disregard it, an effect called **advertising wearout**.[54] One strategy for avoiding wearout is to utilize variations on a common theme.[55] For example, ads for Target continually emphasize core brand themes and the "red dot" symbol. However, they have done so over time in different and interesting ways, including roaming animated spokes characters, a white dog with a red dot around one eye, and so on. Cross-cultural research suggests that a consistent theme with a varied execution is an effective strategy for avoiding advertising wearout in Southeast Asia as well.[56]

Dual Coding   Consumers can store (code) information in different ways. Storing the same information in different ways (dual coding) results in more internal pathways (associative links) for retrieving information. This in turn can increase learning and memory.

One example of dual coding is when consumers learn information in two different contexts—for example, a consumer sees two ads for the same brand of dandruff shampoo, one with an office theme and one with a social theme. The varied theme (context) provides multiple paths to the brand and therefore enhances recall later on. Illustration 9-6 shows one theme that Clorox uses for its disinfectant products. It has other themes as well. By using multiple themes for its disinfectant products, Clorox can enhance consumer memory beyond its traditional bleach products.

Another example of dual coding relates to information being stored in different memory modes, such as verbal versus visual.[57] Dual coding helps explain why *imagery* enhances memory.

ILLUSTRATION 9-6

Using varied themes across ads can aid dual coding and enhance memory. Note the differences between this Clorox ad and others you may have seen.

Source: The Clorox Company

High-imagery stimuli leave a dual code because they are stored in memory on both verbal and pictorial dimensions, whereas low-imagery stimuli are coded only verbally. As a consequence, high-imagery brand names such as Apple and Mustang are substantially easier to learn and remember than low-imagery names.

Echoic memory—memory of sounds, including words—is another memory mode that appears to have characteristics distinct from visual and verbal memory.[58] This provides the opportunity for dual coding when the sound component of a message (e.g., background music) conveys similar meanings to that being conveyed by the verbal message.[59]

Learning and memory appear to be enhanced when the key ideas communicated through one mode are consistent with those communicated through other modes.[60] For example, one study finds that having the picture (visual) and text (verbal) convey consistent ideas makes it easier for bilingual consumers to process an ad in their second language. The result is greater learning and memory of the second-language ad.[61]

Memory Interference

Sometimes consumers have difficulty retrieving a specific piece of information because other related information in memory gets in the way. This effect is referred to as **memory interference.** A common form of interference in marketing is due to competitive advertising. For example, seeing an ad for Canada Dry Ginger Ale might interfere with your memory of Mountain Dew. Competitive advertising makes it harder for consumers to recall any given advertisement and its contents. And even if they can recall the contents of a specific ad, they often will have a hard time associating that ad with a specific brand. As a consequence, competitive advertising can either reduce memory for the brand claims made in a specific advertisement or lead to brand-claim confusion across advertisements for competing brands.[62]

Competitive advertising interference increases as the number of competing ads within the same product category increases and as the similarity of those ads to each other increases. Given the high levels of advertising clutter, it should not be surprising that this is an area of concern for marketers and advertisers. The major question is, *What can marketers do to decrease competitive interference?* A number of strategies exist, many related to the learning and memory concepts we discussed earlier.

Avoid Competing Advertising   One strategy is to avoid having your ad appear in the same set of ads (same pod in a TV format) as your competitors'. Some companies actually pay a premium to ensure this exclusivity. Another strategy, called *recency planning,* involves trying to plan advertising exposures so that they occur as close in time to a consumer purchase occasion as possible. The idea behind this concept is that reducing the time to purchase reduces the chances that an ad for a competing brand will be seen prior to purchase.[63]

Strengthen Initial Learning   Another strategy is to increase the strength of the initial learning because stronger learning is less subject to memory interference. Evidence for the value of this strategy comes from the fact that memory interference is less pronounced in high-involvement contexts and for highly familiar brands. This is not surprising when you consider that high-involvement learning should result in stronger brand schemas and that brand schemas for familiar brands are stronger than those for unfamiliar brands.[64]

Additional evidence for the role of learning comes from advertising strategies that encourage dual coding. Specifically, brands can reduce competitive interference by showing different ad versions for the same brand (shampoo ad in office context and social context) or by varying the modality across exposures (radio ad followed by a print ad).[65]

Interestingly, while strong initial learning of a brand's key attributes can yield positive memory effects, it also can make it harder for the brand to add or change attributes. That is, the strong initial learning interferes with consumer learning and memory for new brand information.[66] This can make brand *repositioning* a challenging task. Repositioning is discussed later in the chapter.

Reduce Similarity to Competing Ads   Ads within the same product class (e.g., ads for different brands of cell phone) have been shown to increase interference, as have ads that are similar to competing ads. Similarity can be in terms of ad claims, emotional valence, and ad execution elements such as background music or pictures. Interestingly, similarity between ad execution elements can lead to memory interference even when the ads are for brands in different product categories (print ads for bleach and soda each picturing mountain scenes). Just as unique ads can break through advertising clutter to garner greater attention, unique ads are also more resistant to competitive memory interference.[67]

Provide External Retrieval Cues   Retrieval cues provide an external pathway to information that is stored in memory.[68] The reason that brand names are so important is because they can serve as a retrieval cue. Seeing a brand name can trigger recall of brand information stored in memory, as well as retrieval of images and emotions associated with prior advertisements for the brand.

However, brand name is not always enough to trigger recall of prior advertising for the brand. For example, seeing the brand on a store shelf may not be sufficient to cue consumers' memory for prior advertising. This is of major consequence for marketers because failure to recall prior advertising information and emotion during purchase reduces advertising effectiveness. In this case, marketers can use point-of-purchase displays or package cues that link directly back to the advertisements for that brand.[69] For example, during the classic "Got Milk?" campaign, in-store signage with the "Got Milk?" slogan was used to remind consumers about the TV ads that emphasized how awful it feels to run out of milk. This enhanced the ability of consumers to recall both affect and information from the commercial and was very successful.

Response Environment

Retrieval also is affected by the similarity of the retrieval (response) environment to the original learning environment and type of learning.[70] Thus, the more the retrieval situation offers cues similar to the cues present during learning, the more likely effective retrieval is to occur. One strategy is to configure the retrieval environment to resemble the original learning environment. The "Got Milk?" example discussed earlier represents attempts by marketers to match the in-store retrieval environment to the learning environment by providing retrieval cues.

Another strategy is to configure the learning environment to resemble the most likely retrieval environment. Suppose a chewing gum brand knows that its retrieval environment will be in retail stores. In this case, conditioning a positive feeling to the *brand and package* by consistently pairing a visual image of the package with pleasant music would likely be most appropriate. This is because the response environment (the store shelf) visually presents consumers with brand packages. And because learning was conditioned to a visual of the brand's package (learning environment configured to match the retrieval environment), seeing the package on the shelf will likely elicit the learned response.

BRAND IMAGE AND PRODUCT POSITIONING

Brand Image

Brand image refers to *the schematic memory of a brand.* It contains the target market's interpretation of the product's attributes, benefits, usage situations, users, and manufacturer/marketer characteristics. It is what people think of and feel when they hear or see a brand name. It is, in essence, the set of associations consumers have *learned* about the brand.[71] *Company image* and *store image* are similar except that they apply to companies and stores rather than brands.

LO5

The importance of branding and brand image can be seen in the fact that products that have traditionally been unbranded such as water, apples, and meat are increasingly being branded. Consider the meat industry. It must deal with a number of issues, not the least of which is that many consumers see meat as difficult and time-consuming to prepare. As one industry expert said:

> A lot of consumers don't have the time and expertise to take a raw roast and cook it for six to eight hours, so what we have to do in this industry is understand that and do something about it.[72]

Tyson has responded by offering a line of fully cooked chicken, pork, and beef meals that are fast, easy, and safe to prepare. This move builds nicely on Tyson's strong reputation for quality fresh meat products and its prepackaged lunch meats. Given today's consumers' dual concerns over convenience and food safety, Tyson is well positioned with a strong and consistent image that consumers trust and can relate to. The ability to benefit from a brand image is called *brand equity,* which we discuss in the next section.

Brand image is a major concern of both industrial and consumer goods marketers. Consider the following headlines from recent marketing publications:

Buick Leads GM's Efforts at Reinvention

How Microsoft Got Hip

Pepsi Max Drops the Diet, Aims to Rekindle Cola War

How powerful are brand images? Think of Nike, McDonald's, Kate Spade, Hershey's, Coke, Discovery Channel, Amazon.com, and Goodyear. For many consumers, each of these names conjures up a rich pattern of meanings and feelings. These meanings and imagery are powerful drivers of consumer decision making, which explains why strong brands also tend to be market leaders in terms of sales and profits. Examine Illustration 9–7. *What meanings and imagery are elicited by the Garmin brand? Does this brand have a strong image?*

Brand images can hinder as well as help products.[73] Lilly Pulitzer recently introduced a clothing line for Target. Lilly dresses, which can cost over $300 in store, were sold for no more than $44 at Target. This upscale

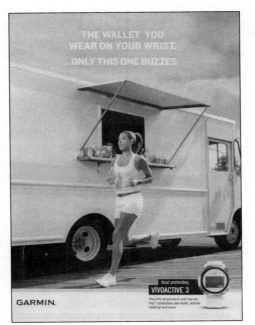

Source: Garmin Ltd. or its subsidiaries

ILLUSTRATION 9-7

Brand names such as Garmin provide an anchor to which consumers can attach meaning. This allows marketers to invest in product improvements and communications with a reasonable possibility of benefiting from those investments.

brand–discount store collaboration received backlash. According to one brand consultant, "The more popular it is at Target, the worse it is for Lilly Pulitzer the brand." Lilly has a strong image. However, making the product accessible at lower prices hurt Lilly's image of exclusivity. In this case, Lilly Pulitzer may have been better off using a *new brand strategy* with no ties to the Lilly Pulitzer name.[74] We discuss this strategy later in the chapter.

Product Positioning

Product positioning is a *decision by a marketer to try to achieve a defined brand image relative to competition within a market segment.* That is, marketers decide that they want the members of a market segment to think and feel in a certain way about a brand relative to competing brands. The term *product positioning* is most commonly applied to decisions concerning brands, but it also is used to describe the same decisions for stores, companies, and product categories.

Product positioning has a major impact on the long-term success of the brand, presuming the firm can create the desired position in the minds of consumers. A key issue in positioning relates to the need for brands to create product positions that differentiate them from competitors in ways that are meaningful to consumers.[75] A brand that fails to differentiate itself from competitors (stimulus discrimination) will generally find it difficult to generate consumer interest and sales.

Consider Saturn. Its original positioning emphasized customer service and the retail experience. This differentiated Saturn from the competition and resulted in strong sales. However, its ads stopped focusing on customer service in 2002 and after that sales slumped. As a result, it switched advertising agencies with the hopes of *repositioning* its brand in the minds of customers by focusing back on customer service.[76] These efforts ultimately failed, and the Saturn line was discontinued.

An important component of brand image is the appropriate usage situations for the product or brand. Often marketers have the opportunity to influence the usage situations for which a product or brand is seen as appropriate. What do you think of when you think of cranberry sauce? Odds are that Thanksgiving and perhaps Christmas are part of your image of cranberry sauce. In fact, these are probably the only usage situations that came to mind. However, in one study, sales for cranberry sauce increased almost 150 percent over a three-month period after consumers saw advertisements promoting nontraditional uses. Thus, expanding the usage situation component of cranberry sauce's product position could dramatically increase its sales.[77]

The terms *product position* and *brand image* often are used interchangeably. In general, however, product position involves an explicit reference to a brand's image relative to another brand or the overall industry. It is characterized by statements such as "HP printers are the most reliable printers available." Brand image generally considers the firm's image without a direct comparison to a competitor. It is characterized by statements such as "HP printers are extremely reliable."

Once a marketer decides on an appropriate product position, the marketing mix is manipulated in a manner designed to achieve that position in the target market.[78] For example, Sunkist Growers offers a fruit jelly candy called Sunkist Fruit Gems that comes in various fruit flavors. It is positioned as a "healthful, natural" snack for adults and children. From a product standpoint, the candy is made from pectin (a natural ingredient from citrus peels) and contains no preservatives and less sugar than most fruit jelly candies. Thus, the product itself communicates the desired position.

However, other aspects of the marketing mix also can contribute. For example, Sunkist could distribute the candy through the produce departments of supermarkets. Notice how distribution then supports the desired product position or image. A consumer receiving a message that this is a healthful, natural product should be more receptive when the product is found near other healthful, natural products such as apples and oranges.

Marketing managers frequently fail to achieve the type of product image or position they desire because they fail to anticipate or test for consumer reactions. Toro's initial lightweight snowthrower was not successful. Why? It was named the Snowpup, and consumers interpreted this to mean that it was a toy or lacked sufficient power. Sales success came only after a more macho, power-based name was utilized—first Snowmaster and later Toro.

Perceptual mapping offers marketing managers a useful technique for measuring and developing a product's position. Perceptual mapping takes consumers' perceptions of how similar various brands or products are to each other and relates these perceptions to product attributes. Figure 9–10 is a perceptual map for various chocolate candy brands. This perceptual map also provides the ideal points for five market segments—I_1, I_2, I_3, I_4, I_5. The size of the circle around the ideal point represents the relative size of the segment, with segment 4 (I_4) being the largest and segment 5 (I_5) being the smallest. These ideal points represent the image or characteristics each segment desires in a chocolate candy. If the chocolate candies in this map were all that existed, it would indicate that segment 2 consumers are not being

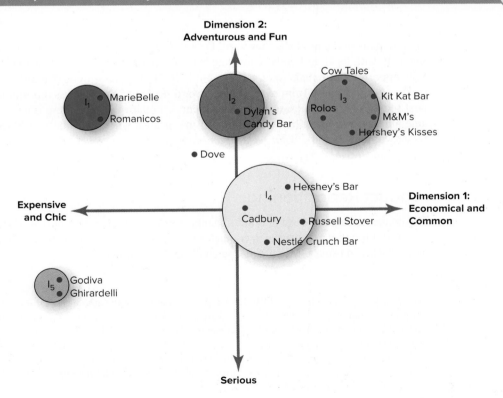

FIGURE 9-10

Perceptual Map for Chocolate Candy

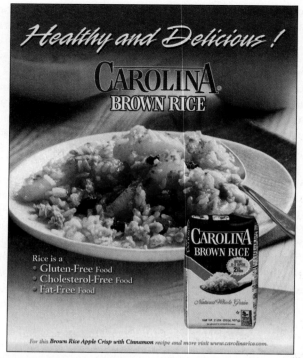

Courtesy of Riviana Foods, Inc.

offered many of the products they want. Dylan's Candy Bar positions its brand to target this segment, with its "Fun Foods" chocolate bars (flavors include "bacon" and "potato chip"). Still, opportunities remain to target segment 2. Is Dove well positioned? It appears not; that is, Dove would benefit from *repositioning* toward segment 2. We discuss repositioning in the next section. Notice that even though segment 3 is relatively large, there is also a considerable amount of competition, something of importance when deciding which segments to target with new brands. *What segment and competitor factors would make it more difficult to enter segment 5 than segment 2?*

Product Repositioning

The images consumers have of brands change over time as a function of their own changing needs, as a function of changes in competitors, and as a function of changes initiated by the brand itself. Consider GM's efforts and challenges with Buick:

General Motor's launch of the 2010 Buick LaCrosse was one of the automaker's most critical post-bankruptcy initiatives, as the company sought to attract younger consumers with a more sophisticated car design and image overhaul to match. The 2010 model drew good reviews, *but targeted consumers* [between 46 and 55 years old—about 10 years younger than current Buick buyers] were disinclined to even visit Buick showrooms given the brand's association with plush, easy-driving sedans favored by retirees. As one executive stated, "We have a huge challenge with Buick because many people don't know what the brand stands for."[79]

The lack of clarity of the Buick image and the lack of fit between target market *perceptions* of the brand and what they want in an automobile mean that successful *repositioning* of Buick is critical for its long-term success. **Product repositioning** refers to *a deliberate decision to significantly alter the way the market views a product.* This could involve its level of performance, the feelings it evokes, the situations in which it should be used, or even who uses it.[80]

Illustration 9–8 shows a firm's efforts to reposition its brand in the minds of its target customers. Other recent repositioning efforts include the following:

- Old Spice is moving from an uninteresting deodorant for older generations to a brand that is "sexy, surprising, fun and youthful."[81]
- Pabst Blue Ribbon, an American beer known for being cheap and consumed by college students, is seen as a high-end alcoholic drink of choice in China, selling for $44.
- Hyundai is attempting to move from a low-price image to one that is "refined and elegant."[82]

Repositioning can be very difficult and costly, requiring consumers to *unlearn* old associations and replace them with new ones.[83] This can take years to accomplish. In the auto industry, it is estimated that repositioning can take up to 10 years. According to one industry expert, "People's perceptions change very slowly."[84]

Repositioning also may require drastic action. For example, Hardee's was able to reverse plummeting sales only after completely walking away from the thin patties common in fast-food hamburgers and focusing exclusively on its now signature Thickburger made from Black Angus beef.[85] Sometimes companies will even change their brand name to allow a fresh start. For example, when Bell Atlantic and GTE Wireless merged, they changed their name to Verizon.

BRAND EQUITY AND BRAND LEVERAGE

Brand equity is *the value consumers assign to a brand above and beyond the functional characteristics of the product.*[86] For example, many people pay a significant premium for Bayer aspirin relative to store brands of aspirin although they are chemically identical.

Brand equity is nearly synonymous with the reputation of the brand. However, the term *equity* implies economic value.[87] Thus, brands with "good" reputations have the potential for high levels of brand equity, whereas unknown brands or brands with weak or negative reputations do not. The outcomes of brand equity include increased market share, decreased consumer price sensitivity, and enhanced marketing efficiency.[88]

Brand equity is based on the product position of the brand. A consumer who believes that a brand delivers superior performance is exciting to use, and is produced by a company with appropriate social values is likely to be willing to pay a premium for the brand, to go to extra trouble to locate and buy it, to recommend it to others, to forgive a mistake or product flaw, or to otherwise engage in behaviors that benefit the firm that markets the brand. Thus, one source of economic value from a positive brand image results from consumers' behaviors toward existing items with that brand name.[89]

Another source of value for a brand image is that consumers may assume that the favorable aspects of the image associated with an existing product will apply to a new product with the same brand name. This is based on the principle of stimulus generalization described earlier in this chapter. **Brand leverage,** often termed *family branding, brand extensions,* or *umbrella branding,* refers to *marketers capitalizing on brand equity by using an existing brand name for new products.*[90] If done correctly, consumers will assign some of the characteristics of the existing brand to the new product carrying that name.

Relatively recent brand extensions include Starbucks ice cream, Listerine breath strips, and Campbell's tomato juice.

However, stimulus generalization does not occur just because two products have the same brand name. There must be a connection between the products. Pace is finally leveraging its brand equity beyond salsas by extending its name into related products such as refried beans, taco sauces, and bean dip. According to Pace's brand manager:

> We feel we have the ability to expand into Mexican meals, it's just now about choosing the right products and aligning with what consumers are making.[91]

In contrast, Campbell's was not able to introduce a spaghetti sauce under the Campbell's name (it used Prego instead). Consumer research found that

> Campbell's, to consumers, says it isn't authentic Italian. Consumers figured it would be orangy and runny like our tomato soup.[92]

Successful brand leverage generally requires that the original brand have a strong positive image and that the new product fit with the original product on at least one of four dimensions:[93]

1. *Complement.* The two products are used together.
2. *Substitute.* The new product can be used instead of the original.
3. *Transfer.* Consumers see the new product as requiring the same manufacturing skills as the original.
4. *Image.* The new product shares a key image component with the original.

It is important for marketers to understand what the key "fit" criteria are for consumers. For example, one study found that consumers would prefer Fruit Loops lollipops over Fruit Loops hot cereal. Apparently, the key fit criterion of concern was not the *transfer* of manufacturing capability, but rather the *image* component of taste.[94]

It is also important for marketers to realize that the more the new product category is a "stretch" for the brand, the more their advertising messages must help to explain how the products fit together.[95] For example, Revlon tried to launch its own vitamins with the expression "Now, Revlon beauty begins from the inside-out." Notice how the slogan associates cosmetics and vitamins in terms of beauty.

Finally, it is important for marketers to realize that the way in which they advertise a brand can enhance perceptions of fit and make a brand more extendable into a broader set of product categories. Examples of successful and unsuccessful brand extensions include the following:

- Harley-Davidson has applied its name successfully to a wide variety of products, but its Harley-Davidson wine coolers and cake decorating kit (as mentioned in Chapter 8) were not successful.
- Evian failed in its attempt to market its Evian water bra.
- The Tide To Go pen is successful in large part because of the equity of the Tide laundry detergent.
- Coleman successfully expanded from camping stoves and lanterns into a complete line of camping equipment.

Illustration 9–9 shows ads for two different product offerings that demonstrate the concept of brand extension. Which of the two, McCafé coffees or Oprah's O That's Good, is closest to its existing products?

Source: McDonald's

Source: Mealtime Stories, LLC

ILLUSTRATION 9-9

Brand extensions are most likely to succeed when the new product is closer to existing products, as with McCafé. However, the greatest rewards are sometimes associated with extensions into more distinct product categories, as with Oprah's O That's Good side dishes.

Sometimes brand extensions are not feasible. When marketers want to target distinct market segments with an image distinct from the original brand, they generally need to create a new brand rather than extend the existing one. Toyota did this when moving into the luxury automobile market with the new brand Lexus, as did Honda with the new brand Acura. These new brands have images that are distinct from the original brand. Using unique brand names for this purpose avoids diluting or confusing the original brand image.

Brand extensions also can involve risks, one being that a failure of any product with a brand name can hurt all the products with the same brand name (consumers generalize both good and bad outcomes).[96] Another risk is diluting the original brand image, or equity.[97]

A brand's strong equity is valuable and needs to be protected. Consumer Insight 9–2 is a cautionary tale of how changes to brand messaging, through brand name and logo, that do not resonate with the target audience can do much to quickly erode brand equity.

A strong image is generally focused on a fairly narrow set of characteristics. Each additional product added to that product name alters the image somewhat. If too many or too dissimilar products are added to the brand name, the brand image may become diffuse or confused.[98] For instance, were Porsche to offer a ski boat that competed on price rather than performance, it could damage its core image, particularly among existing owners.[99] Some observers feel that Nike is in danger of such a brand dilution as it attaches its name to an ever-wider array of products.

Perhaps Jane Walker Should Just Keep on Walking

In March 2018, Diageo—the liquor company that produces Johnnie Walker Black Label Scotch whiskey—launched a promotional version of its product called *Jane Walker* in recognition of International Women's Day and Women's History Month. This limited-edition promotional version, in which 250,000 bottles were produced, simply changed Johnnie to Jane in the brand name and replaced the iconic logo on the packaging of the walking man in a top hat and tuxedo with a long-haired woman in the same outfit and posture. It appears that the long-term goal of this short-term promotional effort was to reposition the J. W. brand to more effectively attract the female market segment.[100]

Repositioning the brand to attract female consumers seemed to make sense, given the increasing number of U.S. women drinking whiskey. According to Nielsen Research, the percentage of U.S. whiskey drinkers who are female reached almost 30 percent in 2016. Diageo identified this segment as a potential growth opportunity. The launch for Jane Walker was tied to women's empowerment events—namely International Women's Day and Women's History Month. According to Stephanie Jacoby, Vice President of Johnnie Walker:

> Important conversations about gender continue to be at the forefront of culture and we strongly believe there is no better time than now to introduce our Jane Walker icon and contribute to pioneering organizations that share our mission. . . . We are proud to toast the many achievements of women and everyone on the journey towards progress in gender equality. . . . Scotch as a category is seen as particularly intimidating by women. It's a really exciting opportunity to invite women into the brand.

Some media outlets applauded the launch of Jane Walker. However, many more media outlets, organizations, and the general public took a much dimmer view. There was a lot of negative buzz in both social and traditional media. There seemed to be no shortage of reasons that people found Jane Walker to be offensive.

- The suggestion by the VP of Johnnie Walker that the whiskey product category itself is intimidating and scary to women effectively alienated many women. It also insulted many women who already drink whiskey.

- Diageo appeared to be motivated to launch this campaign purely to boost sales to women because the company was doing nothing visible to change gender dynamics, power asymmetries, or any other type of inequality to women.

- Many people felt the timing of the launch being attached to International Women's Day and Women's History Month was questionable at best and was labeled as patronizing, pandering, and even appropriation of women's empowerment issues.

The launch of Jane Walker highlights the challenges involved in repositioning. It appears to have alienated the very group it was designed to attract—female whiskey drinkers. In fact, it treads dangerous ground to potentially being offensive. According to Akshar Peerbhoy, COO of an advertising and branding agency:

> Firstly, you could end up isolating potential consumers, which is a loss of precious potential revenues. Secondly, the brand could annoy the group they are targeting because they don't want to be stereotyped. Thus a brand could actually end up losing market share, instead of gaining it. With social media, the backlash could be worse.

Clearly, repositioning is sometimes necessary and desirable. However, as this example shows, missteps can lead to erosion of brand equity and this must be handled carefully.

Critical Thinking Questions:

1. Please evaluate how Jane Walker helps or hurts the brand equity of Johnnie Walker.

2. Explain the failure of the Jane Walker promotion in terms of "lack of fit" of the promotional effort to (*a*) the target segment and (*b*) the core brand and its image and history.

3. What advice would you have given marketers at Johnnie Walker to improve this campaign?

SUMMARY

SMARTBOOK

LO1: Describe the nature of learning and memory.

Learning is any change in the content or organization of long-term memory or behavior and is the result of information processing. Information processing is a series of activities by which stimuli are perceived, transformed into information, and stored. The four activities in the series are exposure, attention, interpretation, and memory. Thus, memory is both an outcome of learning and a part of the process of learning. For example, when interpreting the price of a brand, consumers may retrieve information about competitor prices (prior learning) and once the comparison is made, store their price perception about the new brand in memory (new learning).

LO2: Explain the types of memory and memory's role in learning.

Memory is the result of learning, which involves information processing. Most commonly, information goes directly into *short-term memory* (STM) for processing, where two basic activities occur: maintenance rehearsal and elaborative activities. *Maintenance rehearsal* is the continual repetition of a piece of information in order to hold it in current memory. *Elaborative activities* are the use of stored experiences, values, attitudes, and feelings to interpret and evaluate information in current memory.

Long-term memory (LTM) is information from previous information processing that has been stored for future use. LTM undergoes continual restructuring as new information is acquired. Information is stored in LTM in associative networks, or schemas. Consumers often organize information in LTM around brands in the form of *brand schemas.* These schemas represent the brand's image in terms of key attributes, feelings, experiences, and so on.

LO3: Distinguish the different processes underlying high- and low-involvement learning.

Consumers learn in various ways, which can be broadly classified into high- versus low-involvement learning. *High-involvement learning* occurs when an individual is motivated to acquire the information. *Low-involvement learning* occurs when an individual is paying only limited or indirect attention to an advertisement or other message. Low-involvement learning tends to be limited as a result of a lack of elaborative activities.

Learning also can be classified as either conditioned or cognitive. There are two forms of conditioned learning: classical and operant. *Classical conditioning* attempts to create an association between a stimulus (e.g., brand name) and some response (e.g., behavior or feeling) and is generally low involvement in nature. *Operant conditioning* attempts to create an association between a response (e.g., buying a brand) and some outcome (e.g., satisfaction) that serves to reinforce the response and is generally high involvement in nature.

The *cognitive* approach to learning encompasses the mental activities of humans as they work to solve problems, cope with complex situations, or function effectively in their environment. Cognitive learning includes *iconic rote learning* (generally low involvement), *vicarious learning/modeling* (low or high involvement), and *analytical reasoning* (generally high involvement).

Stimulus generalization is one way of transferring learning by generalizing from one stimulus situation to other, similar ones. *Stimulus discrimination* refers to the opposite process of learning—responding differently to somewhat similar stimuli. The ability of consumers to differentiate and generalize is critical for successful brand positioning and leverage.

LO4: Summarize the factors affecting information retrieval from memory.

Once learned, information is *retrieved* from LTM for use in evaluations and decisions. *Retrieval failures* or *extinction* of a learned response represents a reduction in marketing effectiveness. Retrieval depends on strength of initial learning, memory interference, and the response environment. *Strength of learning* depends on six basic factors: importance, message involvement, reinforcement, mood, repetition, and dual coding. *Importance* refers to the value that the consumer places on the information to be learned—greater importance increases learning and retrieval. *Message involvement* is the degree to which the consumer is interested in the message itself—the greater the message involvement, the greater the learning and retrieval. *Reinforcement* is anything that increases the likelihood that a response will be repeated in the future—the greater the reinforcement, the greater the learning and retrieval. *Mood* is the temporary mental state or feeling of the consumer. Learning and memory appear to be greater in positive mood conditions. *Repetition* refers to the number of times that we are exposed to the information or that we engage in a behavior. Repetition increases learning and memory but can also lead to *wearout. Dual coding* involves creating multiple complementary pathways to a concept in LTM. Dual coding increases learning and retrieval.

Memory interference occurs when consumers have difficulty retrieving a specific piece of information because other related information in memory gets in the way. A common form of memory interference is due to competitive advertising. Competitive interference increases with increased advertising clutter. But it can be reduced by avoiding competitive clutter, strengthening learning, reducing similarity to competitor ads, and providing retrieval cues.

The *response environment* also can be critical to retrieval. Matching the response environment to the learning environment, or matching the learning environment to the response environment, can enhance the ease and likelihood of retrieval.

LO5: Understand the application of learning to brand positioning, equity, and leverage.

Brand image, a market segment or individual consumer's schematic memory of a brand, is a major focus of marketing activity. *Product positioning* is a decision by a marketer to attempt to attain a defined and differentiated brand image, generally in relation to specific competitors. A brand image that matches a target market's needs and desires will be valued by that market segment. Such a brand is said to have *brand equity* because consumers respond favorably toward it in the market. In addition, these consumers may be willing to assume that other products with the same brand name will have some of the same features, which relates to how consumers learn to generalize from one stimulus to another. Introducing new products under the same name as an existing product is referred to as *brand leverage* or *brand extension.*

KEY TERMS

Accessibility 329
Advertising wearout 344
Analogical reasoning 336
Analytical reasoning 336
Brand equity 351
Brand image 347
Brand leverage 351
Classical conditioning 331
Cognitive learning 335
Concepts 326
Conditioning 330
Elaborative activities 326
Episodic memory 327
Explicit memory 329
Extinction 338

Flashbulb memory 327
High-involvement
  learning 330
Iconic rote learning 335
Imagery 326
Implicit memory 329
Learning 324
Long-term memory
  (LTM) 325
Low-involvement learning 330
Maintenance rehearsal 325
Memory interference 345
Modeling 335
Operant conditioning 333
Perceptual mapping 349

Product positioning 348
Product repositioning 351
Pulsing 343
Punishment 341
Reinforcement 340
Retrieval failure 338
Schema 327
Script 329
Self-referencing 340
Semantic memory 327
Shaping 334
Short-term memory (STM) 325
Stimulus discrimination 336
Stimulus generalization 337
Vicarious learning 335

REVIEW QUESTIONS

1. What is *learning?*
2. What is *memory?*
3. Define *short-term memory* and *long-term memory.*
4. Discuss the nature of *short-term memory* in terms of its endurance and capacity.
5. What is *maintenance rehearsal?*
6. What is meant by *elaborative activities?*

7. What is meant by *imagery* in working memory?
8. What is *semantic memory?*
9. How does a *schema* differ from a *script?*
10. What is *episodic memory* and how does it relate to *flashbulb memory?*
11. Describe *low-involvement learning.* How does it differ from *high-involvement learning?*

12. What do we mean by *cognitive learning* and how does it differ from the *conditioning theory* approach to learning?

13. Distinguish between learning via *classical conditioning* and learning that occurs via *operant conditioning.*

14. What is *iconic rote learning?* How does it differ from classical conditioning? Operant conditioning?

15. Define *modeling.*

16. What is meant by learning by *analytical reasoning?*

17. Describe *analogical reasoning.*

18. What is meant by *stimulus generalization?* When do marketers use it?

19. Define *stimulus discrimination.* Why is it important?

20. Explain *extinction* and *retrieval failure* and why marketing managers are interested in them.

21. What factors affect the *strength of learning?*

22. How does *self-referencing* relate to *strength of learning* and retrieval?

23. What is *memory interference* and what strategies can marketers use to deal with it?

24. Why is it useful to match the retrieval and learning environments?

25. What is a *brand image?* Why is it important?

26. What is *product positioning? Repositioning?*

27. What is *perceptual mapping?*

28. What is *brand equity?*

29. What does *leveraging brand equity* mean?

DISCUSSION QUESTIONS

30. How would you determine the best product position for the following?
    a. A brand of tablet computer
    b. A cell phone targeting children
    c. A local animal shelter
    d. A line of power tools targeting women
    e. A brand of toothpaste

31. Is low-involvement learning really widespread? Which products are most affected by low-involvement learning?

32. Almex and Company introduced a new coffee-flavored liqueur in direct competition with Hiram Walker's tremendously successful Kahlua brand. Almex named its new entry Kamora and packaged it in a bottle similar to that of Kahlua, using a pre-Columbian label design. The ad copy for Kamora reads, "If you like coffee—you'll love Kamora." Explain Almex's marketing strategy in terms of learning theory.

33. Describe the brand images the following brands have among students on your campus.
    a. Samsung Galaxy smartphone
    b. Your student government
    c. Coke Zero
    d. Toyota Prius Hybrid
    e. The United Way
    f. Chevy Volt

34. In what ways, if any, would the brand images you described in response to the previous question differ with different groups, such as (*a*) middle-aged professionals, (*b*) young blue-collar workers, (*c*) high school students, and (*d*) retired couples?

35. What role does *dual coding* play in the learning process?

36. Respond to the questions in Consumer Insight 9–1.

37. Evaluate Illustrations 9–1 through 9–5 in light of their apparent objectives and target market.

38. Respond to the questions in Consumer Insight 9–2.

APPLICATION ACTIVITIES

39. Fulfill the requirements of Question 33 by interviewing three male and three female students.

40. Answer Question 34 based on interviews with five individuals from each group.

41. Pick a consumer convenience product, perhaps a personal care product such as suntan lotion or toothpaste, and create advertising copy stressing (*a*) a positive reinforcement, (*b*) a negative reinforcement, and (*c*) a punishment.

42. Find and describe three advertisements, one based on cognitive learning, another based on operant conditioning, and the third based on

classical conditioning. Discuss the nature of each advertisement and how it utilizes that type of learning.

43. Find and describe three advertisements that you believe are based on low-involvement learning and three that are based on high-involvement learning. Justify your selection.

44. Select a product and develop an advertisement based on low-involvement learning and one on high-involvement learning. When should each be used (be specific)?

45. Find two advertisements for competing brands that you feel do a good job of avoiding competitive advertising interference and two that you think do not. Justify your selection.

46. Visit a grocery store and examine product packages or point-of-purchase information that could serve as retrieval cues for a brand's ongoing advertising campaign. Write a brief report of your findings and describe the nature and effectiveness of the retrieval cues utilized. Could they have been better? Explain.

47. Select a product that you feel has a good product position and one that has a weak position. Justify your selection. Describe an ad or package for each product and indicate how it affects the product's position.

48. Select a product, store, or service of relevance to students on your campus. Using a sample of students, measure its brand image. Develop a marketing strategy to improve its image.

49. Develop a campaign to reduce the risk of STDs (sexually transmitted diseases) for students on your campus by teaching them the value of
    a. Abstinence from sex outside of marriage
    b. Safe sex

50. Find a recent brand extension that you feel will be successful and one that you feel will fail. Explain each of your choices.

REFERENCES

1. This opener is based on R. Krulwich, "There's a Fly in My Urinal," *NPR,* December 18, 2009, www.npr.org/templates/story/story.php?storyId=121310977, accessed September 1, 2014; B. Wansink, *Mindless Eating* (New York: Bantam, 2010); "Placebo Buttons," *ABC New* video, May 23, 2010, http://abcnews.go.com/GMA/video/placebo-buttons-pushing-10722406, accessed September 1, 2014; M. Wright, "5 Fake Sounds Designed to Help Humans," *Sharp Company Blog,* June 20, 2011, www.humansinvent.com/#!/889/5-fake-sounds-designed-to-help-humans/, accessed September 1, 2014.

2. A. A. Mitchell, "Cognitive Processes Initiated by Exposure to Advertising," in *Information Processing Research in Advertising,* ed. R. Harris (New York: Erlbaum, 1983), pp. 13–42.

3. For differing views, see A. J. Malter, "An Introduction to Embodied Cognition," in *Advances in Consumer Research,* vol. 23, ed. K. P. Corfman and J. G. Lynch (Provo, UT: Association for Consumer Research, 1996), pp. 272–76; M. E. Hill, R. Radtke, and M. King, "A Transfer Appropriate Processing View of Consumer Memory," *Journal of Current Issues and Research in Advertising,* Spring 1997, pp. 1–21.

4. M. Vanhuele, G. Laurent, and X. Drèze, "Consumers' Immediate Memory for Prices," *Journal of Consumer Research,* September 2006, pp. 163–72.

5. J. Fetto, "Call Me Vain," *American Demographics,* November 2002, p. 15.

6. See K. Mason, T. Jensen, S. Burton, and D. Roach, "The Accuracy of Brand and Attribute Judgments," *Journal of the Academy of Marketing Science,* Summer 2001, pp. 307–17; S. Putrevu, J. Tan, and K. R. Lord, "Consumer Responses to Complex Advertisements," *Journal of Current Issues and Research in Advertising,* Spring 2004, pp. 9–24.

7. P. K. Petrova and R. B. Cialdini, "Fluency of Consumption Imagery and the Backfire Effects of Imagery Appeals," *Journal of Consumer Research,* December 2005, pp. 442–52.

8. G. Wolters and J. J. Goodsmit, "Flashbulb and Event Memory of September 11, 2001," *Psychological Reports,* June 2005, pp. 605–19; H. A. Roehm Jr. and M. L. Roehm, "Can Brand Encounters Inspire Flashbulb Memories?," *Psychology & Marketing,* January 2007, pp. 25–40; A. Bohn and D. Bernsten, "Pleasantness Bias in Flashbulb Memories," *Memory and Cognition,* April 2007, pp. 565–77. See also H. Ahn, M. W. Liu, and D. Soman, "Memory Markers," *Journal of Consumer Psychology* 19 (2009), pp. 508–16.

9. K. A. Braun, "Postexperience Advertising Effects on Consumer Memory," *Journal of Consumer Research,* March 1999, pp. 319–34; M. Supphellen, O. Eismann, and L. E. Hem, "Can Advertisements for Brand Extensions Revitalize Flagship Products?," *International Journal of Advertising* 23 (2004), pp. 173–96.

10. M. Morrin, J. Lee, and G. M. Allenby, "Determinants of Trademark Dilution," *Journal of Consumer Research,* September 2006, pp. 248–57.

11. See E. J. Cowley, "Recovering Forgotten Information," in *Advances in Consumer Research,* vol. 21, ed. C. T. Allen and D. R. John (Provo, UT: Association for Consumer Research, 1994), pp. 58–63.

12. K. K. Desai and W. Hoyer, "Descriptive Characteristics of Memory-Based Consideration Sets," *Journal of Consumer Research,* December 2000, pp. 309–23. See also P. Nedungadi, A. Chattopadyay, and A. V. Muthukrishnan, "Category Structure, Brand Recall, and Choice," *International Journal of Research in Marketing* 18 (2001), pp. 191–202; E. Cowley and A. A. Mitchell, "The Moderating Effect of Product Knowledge on the Learning

and Organization of Product Information," *Journal of Consumer Research,* December 2003, pp. 443–54.

13. E. Macdonald, H. Wilson, and U. Konus, "Better Customer Insight—in Real Time," *Harvard Business Review,* September 2012, pp. 102–108.

14. G. Venkataramani and M. T. Pham, "Relatedness, Prominence, and Constructive Sponsor Identification," *Journal of Marketing Research,* August 1999, pp. 299–312.

15. E. Kyung, M. Thomas, and A. Krishna, "When Bigger Is Better (and When It Is Not): Implicit Bias in Numeric Judgments," *Journal of Consumer Research* 44, no. 1 (2017), pp. 62–79.

16. K. B. Monroe and A. Y. Lee, "Remembering versus Knowing," *Journal of the Academy of Marketing Science,* Spring 1999, pp. 207–25; E. A. van Reijmersdal, P. C. Neijens, and E. G. Smit, "Effects of Television Brand Placement on Brand Image," *Psychology & Marketing,* May 2007, pp. 403–20.

17. S. A. Hawkins, S. J. Hoch, and J. Meyers-Levy, "Low-Involvement Learning," *Journal of Consumer Psychology* 11, no. 1 (2001), pp. 1–11.

18. See R. P. Grossman and B. D. Till, "The Persistence of Classically Conditioned Brand Attitudes," *Journal of Advertising,* Spring 1998, pp. 23–31; J. Kim, J.-S. Lim, and M. Bhargava, "The Role of Affect in Attitude Formation," *Journal of the Academy of Marketing Science,* Spring 1998, pp. 143–52; W. E. Baker, "When Can Affective Conditioning and Mere Exposure Directly Influence Brand Choice?," *Journal of Advertising,* Winter 1999, pp. 31–46; B. D. Till and R. L. Priluck, "Stimulus Generalization in Classical Conditioning," *Psychology & Marketing,* January 2000, pp. 55–72; B. D. Till, S. M. Stanley, and R. Priluck, "Classical Conditioning and Celebrity Endorsers," *Psychology and Marketing,* February 2008, pp. 179–96.

19. B. D. Till and R. L. Priluck, "Conditioning of Meaning in Advertising," *Journal of Current Issues and Research in Advertising,* Fall 2001, pp. 1–8.

20. For discussions of the role of awareness in classical conditioning, see C. Janiszewski and L. Warlop, "The Influence of Classical Conditioning Procedures on Subsequent Attention to the Conditioned Brand," *Journal of Consumer Research,* September 1993, pp. 171–89; R. Priluck and B. D. Till, "The Role of Contingency Awareness, Involvement, and Need for Cognition in Attitude Formation," *Journal of the Academy of Marketing Science* 32, no. 3 (2004), pp. 329–44; I. Kirsch et al., "The Role of Cognition in Classical and Operant Conditioning," *Journal of Clinical Psychology,* April 2004, pp. 369–92.

21. See, e.g., W. H. Motes and A. G. Woodside, "Purchase Experiments of Extra-ordinary and Regular Influence Strategies Using Artificial and Real Brands," *Journal of Business Research* 53 (2001), pp. 15–35; Kirsch et al., "The Role of Cognition in Classical and Operant Conditioning."

22. B. J. Bergiel and C. Trosclair, "Instrumental Learning," *Journal of Consumer Marketing,* Fall 1985, pp. 23–28. See also W. Gaidis and J. Cross, "Behavior Modification as a Framework for Sales Promotion Management," *Journal of Consumer Marketing,* Spring 1987, pp. 65–74.

23. E. Heit, J. Briggs, and L. Bott, "Modeling the Effects of Prior Knowledge on Learning Incongruent Features of Category Members," *Journal of Experimental Psychology: Learning, Memory, and Cognition,* September 2004, pp. 1065–81.

24. See J. W. Pracejus, "Is More Always Better?," in *Advances in Consumer Research,* vol. 22, ed. F. R. Kardes and M. Sujan (Provo, UT: Association for Consumer Research, 1995), pp. 319–22; K. P. Gwinner and J. Eaton, "Building Brand Image through Event Sponsorship," *Journal of Advertising,* Winter 1999, pp. 47–57.

25. T. P. Ballinger, M. G. Palumbo, and N. T. Wilcox, "Precautionary Saving and Social Learning across Generations," *The Economic Journal,* October 2003, pp. 920–47.

26. For a way to measure such images, see L. A. Babin and A. C. Burns, "A Modified Scale for the Measurement of Communication-Evoked Mental Imagery," *Psychology & Marketing* 15, no. 3 (May 1998), pp. 261–78.

27. S. P. Jain and D. Maheswaran, "Motivated Reasoning," *Journal of Consumer Research,* March 2000, pp. 358–71.

28. J. Gregan-Paxton, J. D. Hibbard, F. F. Brunel, and P. Azar, "So That's What That Is," *Psychology & Marketing,* June 2002, pp. 533–50; J. Gregan-Paxton and P. Moreau, "How Do Consumers Transfer Existing Knowledge?," *Journal of Consumer Psychology* 13, no. 4 (2003), pp. 422–30. See also M. R. Goode, D. W. Dahl, and C. P. Moreau, "The Effect of Experiential Analogies on Consumer Perceptions and Attitudes," *Journal of Marketing Research,* April 2010, pp. 274–86.

29. For an application to trademark infringement, see C. Pullig, C. J. Simmons, and R. G. Netemeyer, "Brand Dilution," *Journal of Marketing,* April 2006, pp. 52–66.

30. R. Trump and K. Newman, "When Do Unethical Brand Perceptions Spill Over to Competitors?," *Marketing Letters,* June 2017, pp. 219–30; M. L. Roehm and A. M. Tybout, "When Will a Brand Scandal Spill Over, and How Should Competitors Respond?," *Journal of Marketing Research,* August 2006, pp. 366–73.

31. See Till and Priluck, "Stimulus Generalization in Classical Conditioning."

32. R. Ruggless, "Sales Decline Steeply at Joe's Crab Shack and Brick House," *Nation's Restaurant News,* May 17, 2017, www .nrn.com, accessed May 2, 2018; "Ignite Restaurant Group/ Advertising," *eMarketer Inc.,* https://retail-index.emarketer.com/ company/data/53fb4e4eddb53b4f60ebede7/53fb4efbddb53d57 b8093b77/lfy/false/ignite-restaurant-group-advertising, accessed May 2, 2018.

33. M. Maremont, "Gillette Chief Says Cost-Cutting Plan Will Take Time," *Wall Street Journal,* June 7, 2001, p. B2; J. Halliday, "Chrysler Hikes Spending to 'Re-establish' Three Brands," *Advertising Age,* November 9, 2009, p. 4.

34. "Behind Saturn's Stumble," *Advertising Age,* January 24, 1994, p. 22.

35. "L&M Lights Up Again," *Marketing & Media Decisions,* February 1984, p. 69.

36. Ibid.

37. An additional study by Nielsen reports similar results: D. Brandt, "Understanding Memory in Advertising," *Nielsen,* February 22, 2017, www.nielsen.com, accessed May 4, 2018.

38. D. Luna and L. A. Peracchio, "Where There Is a Will . . .," *Psychology & Marketing,* July–August 2002, pp. 573–93; see also R. S. Wyer Jr., "Language and Advertising Effectiveness," *Psychology & Marketing,* July–August 2002, pp. 693–712.

39. See R. G. M. Pieters, E. Rosbergen, and M. Hartog, "Visual Attention to Advertising," in *Advances in Consumer Research*, vol. 23, ed. Corfman and Lynch, pp. 242–48; S. M. Leong, S. H. Ang, and L. L. Tham, "Increasing Brand Name Recall in Print Advertising among Asian Consumers," *Journal of Advertising*, Summer 1996, pp. 65–81.

40. M. L. Roehm, "Instrumental vs. Vocal Versions of Popular Music in Advertising," *Journal of Advertising Research*, May 2001, pp. 49–58. See also W. E. Baker and R. J. Lutz, "An Empirical Test of an Updated Relevance–Accessibility Model," *Journal of Advertising*, Spring 2000, pp. 1–13; C. Stutz, "How Hit Songs in Commercials Might Be Making You Shop More," *Billboard*, January 10, 2018, www.billboard.com, accessed May 2, 2018.

41. See, e.g., M. Wedel and R. Pieters, "Eye Fixations on Advertisements and Memory for Brands," *Marketing Science*, Fall 2000, pp. 297–312.

42. M. Morrin and S. Ratneshwar, "Does It Make Sense to Use Scents to Enhance Brand Memory?," *Journal of Marketing Research*, February 2003, pp. 10–25.

43. W. E. Baker, H. Honea, and C. A. Russell, "Do Not Wait to Reveal the Brand Name," *Journal of Advertising*, Fall 2004, pp. 77–85; see also W. E. Baker, "Does Brand Name Imprinting in Memory Increase Brand Information Retention?," *Psychology & Marketing*, December 2003, pp. 1119–35.

44. See R. E. Burnkrant and H. R. Unnava, "Effects of Self-Referencing on Persuasion," *Journal of Consumer Research*, June 1995, pp. 17–26; P. Krishnamurthy and M. Sujan, "Retrospection versus Anticipation," *Journal of Consumer Research*, June 1999, pp. 55–69.

45. K. R. Lord, R. E. Burnkrant, and H. R. Unnava, "The Effects of Program-Induced Mood States on Memory for Commercial Information," *Journal of Current Issues and Research in Advertising*, Spring 2001, pp. 1–14; S. J. Newell, K. V. Henderson, and B. T. Wu, "The Effects of Pleasure and Arousal on Recall of Advertisements during the Super Bowl," *Psychology & Marketing*, November 2001, pp. 1135–53.

46. T. Ambler and T. Burne, "The Impact of Affect on Memory of Advertising," *Journal of Advertising Research*, March 1999, pp. 25–39; S. Youn et al., "Commercial Liking and Memory," *Journal of Advertising Research*, May 2001, pp. 7–13.

47. See P. Malaviya, J. Meyers-Levy, and B. Sternthal, "Ad Repetition in a Cluttered Environment," *Psychology & Marketing*, March 1999, pp. 99–118.

48. J. O. Eastlack Jr., "How to Get More Bang from Your Television Bucks," *Journal of Consumer Marketing*, Third Quarter 1984, pp. 25–34. See also L. W. Turley and J. R. Shannon, "The Impact and Effectiveness of Advertisements in a Sports Arena," *Journal of Services Marketing* 14, no. 4 (2000), pp. 323–36.

49. Insight is based on J. Kellaris, "Dissecting Earworms," in *Proceedings of the Society for Consumer Psychology Winter 2003 Conference*, ed. C. Page and S. Posavac (New Orleans, LA: American Psychological Society, 2003), pp. 220–22; K. Bruno, "Best-Ever Advertising Jingles," *Forbes*, June 30, 2010, www .forbes.com/2010/06/30/advertising-jingles-coca-cola-cmo-network-jingles_slide_7.html, accessed September 1, 2014; A. Scott, "How Bill Gates and Mick Jagger Struck Deal on Windows 95 Launch," *Business Journals*, June 28, 2011, www.bizjournals. com, accessed September 1, 2014; T. Faulkner, "How Commercial Jingles Work," *howstuffworks*, http://money.howstuffworks.com/ commercial-jingle2.htm, accessed September 1, 2014; S. Watson, "Why Do Songs Get Stuck in My Head?," *howstuffworks*, http:// science.howstuffworks.com/life/songs-stuck-in-head1.htm, accessed September 1, 2014.

50. See Hawkins, Hoch, and Meyers-Levy, "Low-Involvement Learning."

51. See also J. P. Jones, "Single-Source Research Begins to Fulfill Its Promise," *Journal of Advertising Research*, May 1995, pp. 9–16.

52. See S. N. Singh, S. Mishra, N. Bendapudi, and D. Linville, "Enhancing Memory of Television Commercials through Message Spacing," *Journal of Marketing Research*, August 1994, pp. 384–92; E. Ephron, "More Weeks, Less Weight," *Journal of Advertising Research*, May 1995, pp. 18–23; H. Noel, "The Spacing Effect," *Journal of Consumer Psychology* 16, no. 3 (2006), pp. 306–20.

53. For more on spacing effects, see C. Janiszewski, H. Noel, and A. G. Sawyer, "A Meta-Analysis of the Spacing Effect in Verbal Learning," *Journal of Consumer Research*, June 2003, pp. 138–49; S. L. Appleton-Knapp, R. A. Bjork, and T. D. Wickens, "Examining the Spacing Effect in Advertising," *Journal of Consumer Research*, September 2005, pp. 266–76; A. G. Sawyer, H. Noel, and C. Janiszewski, "The Spacing Effects of Multiple Exposures on Memory," *Journal of Advertising Research*, June 2009, pp. 193–97.

54. See M. H. Blair and M. J. Rabuck, "Advertising Wearin and Wearout," *Journal of Advertising Research*, September 1998, pp. 7–25; D. W. Stewart, "Advertising Wearout," *Journal of Advertising Research*, September 1999, pp. 39–42; M. C. Campbell and K. L. Keller, "Brand Familiarity and Advertising Repetition Effects," *Journal of Consumer Research*, September 2003, pp. 292–304.

55. D. Schumann, R. E. Petty, and D. S. Clemons, "Predicting the Effectiveness of Different Strategies of Advertising Variation," *Journal of Consumer Research*, September 1990, pp. 192–202.

56. C. Yoo, H. Bang, and Y. Kim, "The Effects of a Consistent Ad Series on Consumer Evaluations," *International Journal of Advertising* 28, no. 1 (2008), pp. 105–23.

57. W. J. Bryce and R. F. Yalch, "Hearing versus Seeing," *Journal of Current Issues and Research in Advertising*, Spring 1993, pp. 1–20; A. C. Burns, A. Biswas, and L. A. Babin, "The Operation of Visual Imagery as a Mediator of Advertising Effects," *Journal of Advertising*, June 1993, pp. 71–85.

58. T. Clark, "Echoic Memory Explored and Applied," *Journal of Consumer Marketing*, Winter 1987, pp. 39–46. See also C. E. Young and M. Robinson, "Video Rhythms and Recall," *Journal of Advertising Research*, July 1989, pp. 22–25.

59. J. J. Kellaris, A. D. Cox, and D. Cox, "The Effect of Background Music on Ad Processing," *Journal of Marketing*, October 1993, pp. 114–25. See also M. Hahn and I. Hwang, "Effects of Tempo and Familiarity of Background Music on Message Processing in TV Advertising," *Psychology & Marketing*, December 1999, pp. 659–75.

60. K. R. Lord and S. Putrevu, "Communicating in Print," *Journal of Current Issues and Research in Advertising*, Fall 1998, pp. 1–18.

61. D. Luna and L. A. Peracchio, "Moderators of Language Effects in Advertising to Bilinguals," *Journal of Consumer Research*, September 2001, pp. 284–95.

62. See R. D. Jewell and H. R. Unnava, "When Competitive Interference Can Be Beneficial," *Journal of Consumer Research,* September 2003, pp. 283–91; A. Kumar and S. Krishnan, "Memory Interference in Advertising," *Journal of Consumer Research,* March 2004, pp. 602–11.

63. See M. Dahlen and J. Nordfalt, "Interference Effects of a Purchase on Subsequent Advertising within the Category," *Journal of Current Issues and Research in Advertising,* Spring 2004, pp. 1–8.

64. R. J. Kent and C. T. Allen, "Competitive Interference Effects in Consumer Memory for Advertising," *Journal of Marketing,* July 1994, pp. 97–105; A. Kumar, "Interference Effects of Contextual Cues in Advertisements on Memory for Ad Content," *Journal of Consumer Psychology* 9, no. 3 (2000), pp. 155–66; S. Law, "Can Repeating a Brand Claim Lead to Memory Confusion?," *Journal of Marketing Research,* August 2002, pp. 366–78; K. A. Braun-LaTour and M. S. LaTour, "Assessing the Long-Term Impact of a Consistent Advertising Campaign on Consumer Memory," *Journal of Advertising,* Summer 2004, pp. 49–61; M. Laroche, M. Cleveland, and I. Maravelakis, "Competitive Advertising Interference and Ad Repetition Effects," *International Journal of Advertising* 25, no. 3 (2006), pp. 271–307.

65. H. R. Unnava and D. Sirdeshmukh, "Reducing Competitive Ad Interference," *Journal of Marketing Research,* August 1994, pp. 403–11.

66. Jewell and Unnava, "When Competitive Interference Can Be Beneficial"; K. L. Keller, S. E. Heckler, and M. J. Houston, "The Effects of Brand Name Suggestiveness on Advertising Recall," *Journal of Marketing,* January 1998, pp. 48–57.

67. Kumar, "Interference Effects of Contextual Cues in Advertisements on Memory for Ad Content."

68. D. Fernandes, S. Puntoni, S. van Osselaer, and E. Cowley, "When and Why We Forget to Buy," *Journal of Consumer Psychology* 26, no. 3 (2016), pp. 363–80.

69. M. C. Macklin, "The Effects of an Advertising Retrieval Cue on Young Children's Memory and Brand Evaluations," *Psychology & Marketing,* May 1994, pp. 291–311; Keller, Heckler, and Houston, "The Effects of Brand Name Suggestiveness on Advertising Recall"; N. T. Tavassoli and Y. H. Lee, "The Differential Interaction of Auditory and Visual Advertising Elements with Chinese and English," *Journal of Marketing Research,* November 2003, pp. 468–80.

70. See J. W. Park, "Memory-Based Product Judgments," and E. J. Cowley, "Altering Retrieval Sets," both in *Advances in Consumer Research,* vol. 22, ed. Kardes and Sujan, pp. 159–64 and 323–27, respectively; M. E. Hill and M. King, "Comparative vs. Noncomparative Advertising," *Journal of Current Issues and Research in Advertising,* Fall 2001, pp. 33–52.

71. S. M. J. Van Osselaer and J. W. Alba, "Consumer Learning and Brand Equity," *Journal of Consumer Research,* June 2000, pp. 1–16; W. R. Dillon et al., "Understanding What's in a Brand Rating," *Journal of Marketing Research,* November 2001, pp. 415–29; K. L. Keller, "Brand Synthesis," *Journal of Consumer Research,* March 2003, pp. 595–600.

72. S. Thompson, "Meat Gets Branded," *Advertising Age,* September 24, 2001, p. 6.

73. S. M. J. Van Osselear and J. W. Alba, "Locus of Equity and Brand Extension," *Journal of Consumer Research,* March 2003, pp. 539–50.

74. N. Zipkin, "What Brands Can Learn from Lilly Pulitzer and Target's Sold-Out Collection," *Entrepreneur,* April 20, 2015, www.entrepreneur.com/article/245290, accessed May 4, 2018; M. Garber, "Why Do People Hate Lilly Pulitzer?," *Atlantic,* April 22, 2015, www.lillypultizer.com, accessed May 4, 2018.

75. For a discussion of perceived differences generated by trivial attributes, see S. M. Broniarczyk and A. D. Gershoff, "The Reciprocal Effects of Brand Equity and Trivial Attributes," *Journal of Marketing Research,* May 2003, pp. 161–75.

76. J. Halliday, "Losing Its Brand Soul," *Advertising Age,* February 5, 2007, pp. 4, 35.

77. B. Wansink, "Making Old Brands New," *American Demographics,* December 1998, pp. 53–58.

78. See, e.g., C. Young, "Brain Waves, Picture Sorts®, and Branding Moments," *Journal of Advertising Research,* August 2002, pp. 42–53; E. Maoz and A. M. Tybout, "The Moderating Role of Involvement and Differentiation in the Evaluation of Brand Extensions," *Journal of Consumer Psychology* 12, no. 2 (2002), pp. 119–31; F. Völckner and H. Sattler, "Drivers of Brand Extension Success," *Journal of Marketing,* April 2006, pp. 18–34; H. Mao and H. S. Krishnan, "Effects of Prototype and Exemplar Fit on Brand Extension Evaluations," *Journal of Consumer Research,* June 2006, pp. 41–49.

79. N. O'Leary, "Buick Leads GM's Efforts at Reinvention," *Adweek,* July 20, 2009, p. 4.

80. See V. Gerson, "Showing Customers Your Best Face," *Bank Marketing,* January 1999, pp. 26–30; D. James, "Image Makeovers Require Gentle Touch," *Marketing News,* July 2, 2001, p. 4.

81. J. DeMers, "5 Examples of Rebranding Done Right," *Forbes,* July 7, 2016, accessed May 4, 2018.

82. J. Halliday, "Hyundai and Kia Head Upscale via Different Routes," *Advertising Age,* November 1, 2004, p. 12.

83. Jewell and Unnava, "When Competitive Interference Can Be Beneficial"; K. K. Desai and S. Ratneshwar, "Consumer Perceptions of Product Variants Positioned on Atypical Attributes," *Journal of the Academy of Marketing Science,* Winter 2003, pp. 22–35.

84. J. Halliday, "Little Else Matters," *Advertising Age,* August 16, 2004, p. 6.

85. K. Macarthur, "Hardee's," *Advertising Age,* November 1, 2004, p. S-18.

86. M. Supphellen, "Understanding Core Brand Equity," *International Journal of Marketing Research* 42, no. 3 (2000), pp. 319–38; M. M. Mackay, "Application of Brand Equity Service Measures in Service Markets," *Journal of Services Marketing* 15, no. 3 (2001), pp. 21–29; D. A. Aaker and R. Jacobson, "The Value of Brand Attitude in High-Technology Markets," *Journal of Marketing Research,* November 2001, pp. 485–93; S. Brown, R. V. Kozinets, and J. F. Sherry Jr., "Teaching Old Brands New Tricks," *Journal of Marketing,* July 2003, pp. 19–33.

87. A. Chaudhuri, "How Brand Reputation Affects the Advertising-Brand Equity Link," *Journal of Advertising Research,* June 2002, pp. 33–43.

88. P. Chandon, B. Wansink, and G. Laurent, "A Benefit Congruency Framework of Sales Promotion Effectiveness," *Journal of Marketing,* October 2000, pp. 65–81.

89. N. Dawar and M. M. Pillutla, "Impact of Product-Harm Crises on Brand Equity," *Journal of Marketing Research,* May 2000, pp. 215–26; H. Kim, W. G. Kim, and J. A. An, "The Effect of Consumer-Based Brand Equity on Firms' Financial Performance," *Journal of Consumer Marketing* 20, no. 4 (2003), pp. 335–51; D. DelVecchio and D. C. Smith, "Brand-Extension Price Premiums," *Journal of the Academy of Marketing Science,* Spring 2005, pp. 184–96.

90. See T. Erdem and B. Sun, "An Empirical Investigation of the Spillover Effects of Advertising and Sales Promotions in Umbrella Branding," *Journal of Marketing Research,* November 2002, pp. 408–20; J. H. Washburn, B. D. Till, and R. Priluck, "Brand Alliance and Customer-Based Brand-Equity Effects," *Psychology & Marketing,* July 2004, pp. 487–508.

91. S. Thompson, "Campbell Extends Pace beyond Salsa," *Advertising Age,* August 30, 2004, p. 10.

92. H. Schlossberg, "Slashing through Market Clutter," *Marketing News,* March 5, 1990, p. 6.

93. Maoz and Tybout, "The Moderating Role of Involvement and Differentiation in the Evaluation of Brand Extensions"; H. Chun, C. W Park, A. Eisingerich, and D. MacInnis, "Strategic Benefits of Low Fit Brand Extensions: When and Why?," *Journal of Consumer Psychology* 25, no. 4 (2015), pp. 577–95.

94. S. M. Broniarczyk and J. W. Alba, "The Importance of the Brand in Brand Extension," *Journal of Marketing Research,* May 1994, pp. 214–28; see also T. Meyvis and C. Janiszewski, "When Are Broader Brands Stronger Brands?," *Journal of Consumer Research,* September 2004, pp. 346–57.

95. S. Bridges, K. L. Keller, and S. Sood, "Communication Strategies for Brand Extensions," *Journal of Advertising,* Winter 2000, pp. 1–12; R. Klink and D. C. Smith, "Threats to the External Validity of Brand Extension Research," *Journal of Marketing Research,* August 2001, pp. 326–35. See also Völckner and Sattler, "Drivers of Brand Extension Success"; C. Blankson and S. P. Kalafatis,

"Congruence between Positioning and Brand Advertising," *Journal of Advertising Research,* March 2007, pp. 79–94.

96. V. Swaminathan, R. J. Fox, and S. K. Reddy, "The Impact of Brand Extension Introduction on Choice," *Journal of Marketing,* October 2001, pp. 1–15.

97. Effects can be negative or positive. See, e.g., D. R. John, B. Loken, and C. Joiner, "The Negative Impact of Extensions," *Journal of Marketing,* January 1998, pp. 19–32; Z. Gurhan-Canli and D. Maheswaran, "The Effects of Extensions on Brand Name Dilution and Enhancement," *Journal of Marketing Research,* November 1998, pp. 464–73; S. Balachander and S. Ghose, "Reciprocal Spillover Effects," *Journal of Marketing,* January 2003, pp. 4–13.

98. For exceptions, see Meyvis and Janiszewski, "When Are Broader Brands Stronger Brands?"

99. A. Kirmani, S. Sood, and S. Bridges, "The Ownership Effect in Consumer Response to Brand Line Stretches," *Journal of Marketing,* January 1999, pp. 88–101.

100. Insight based on Global Data Consumer, "Can a Whiskey Brand Extension Just for Women Cut It in a #MeToo World?," *Drinks Insight,* March 6, 2018, www.drinks-insight-network.com/comment/can-whiskey-brand-extension-just-women-cut-metoo-world/, accessed April 24, 2018; P. Golikeri, "Can Jane Walk Like Johnnie?," *DNA,* April 4, 2018, www.dnaindia.com/business/report-can-jane-walk-like-johnnie-2600726, accessed April 24, 2018; S. Gunelius, "The Problem with Johnnie Walker's Jane Walker Scotch Was Perception," *Entrepreneur,* March 7, 2018, www.entrepreneur.com/article/309990, accessed April 24, 2018; N. Linou, " 'Jane Walker': Appropriating Women's Rights to Sell More Booze," *United Nations Development Programme,* April 5, 2018, www.undp.org/content/undp/en/home/blog/2018/Jane_Walker_Appropriating_womens_rights_to_sell_more_booze.html, accessed April 24, 2018; K. Lutz, "Jane Walker by Johnny Walker," *Total Prestige Magazine,* www.totalprestigemagazine.com/jane-walker-by-johnny-walker/, accessed April 24, 2018.

chapter

10 Motivation, Personality, and Emotion

©Andriy Blokhin/Shutterstock

LEARNING OBJECTIVES

LO1 Define motivation and summarize the motivation sets put forth by Maslow and McGuire.

LO2 Articulate motivation's role in consumer behavior and marketing strategy.

LO3 Define personality and the various theories of personality.

LO4 Discuss how brand personality can be used in developing marketing strategies.

LO5 Define emotions and list the major emotional dimensions.

LO6 Discuss how emotions can be used in developing marketing strategies.

364

Brands, like people, have personalities. Brand personality, as we will see later in the chapter, is a set of human characteristics that become associated with a brand. These characteristics contribute to a brand's image. Personality traits and other brand associations can be affected in positive and negative ways by numerous factors including advertising, word-of-mouth, direct product experience, and so on. Gap Inc. owns a portfolio of brands—including Gap, Banana Republic, Old Navy, and Athleta—each with its own brand personality. While two of these brands are enjoying success, the other two are not. Recently Gap Inc. announced the closure of 200 Gap and Banana Republic stores. A lack of brand identity, or image, has been a contributing factor.[1]

Gap is "boring": The flagship brand, Gap, which has enjoyed success in the past, has found itself struggling with brand image. It is undergoing an identity crisis from once being considered "effortlessly cool," to being viewed now as "basic" and "boring." Known for its "uniform" of khaki pants, white shirts, and denim, Gap is not meeting the needs of its target market, the Millennials, who crave unique style at a lower price point. But Gap's fast-fashion competitors H&M, Forever 21, and Uniqlo are.

Banana Republic is "forgettable": Banana Republic also is facing an identity crisis as fallout from Gap's struggling image. This chain, once positioned as a luxury, upscale brand, has lost its originality over the years.

Consequently, it is losing in a crowded market to competitors like White House Black Market and Ann Taylor.

Old Navy is "joyful": On the other hand, Old Navy is helping keep the Gap brand portfolio afloat. With low prices and colorful clothes, the brand is bringing "joy" to its target market. With its recent campaign of "Hi, Fashion," Old Navy has solidified its strong identity.

Athleta is "welcoming": Athleta, like Old Navy, is serving Gap Inc. well. This athleisure apparel company has performed well against competitors like lululemon with its "welcoming" and "inclusive" image. The brand appeals to real women and remains true to its 35-to-55-year-old female customer base.

Gap Inc. maintains its belief in the power of the brand. Hence, it is trying to fix its "image" problem overall and with its struggling brands. To do so, the company is leveraging its strong brands—Old Navy and Athleta—and focusing on the customer. Nevertheless, Gap Inc. still has work to do to help restore the identity of Gap and Banana Republic. As stated by an Athleta executive,

When Gap is its best, it's always in the center of the cultural conversation. They are building a team right now and will be fine-tuning their reason for being, and they're going to connect differently with customers. But the most important thing is that we're actually stronger as a portfolio and an enterprise together with these brands because we can learn from each other.

As the opening example suggests, brand personality is critical to brand image and consumer behavior. It is also part of three interrelated aspects of consumer behavior, namely, motivation, personality, and emotions. *Motivation* is the energizing force that activates behavior and provides purpose and direction to that behavior. It helps answer the question of "why" consumers engage in specific behaviors. *Personality* reflects the relatively stable behavioral tendencies that individuals display across a variety of situations. It helps answer the question of "what" behaviors consumers choose to engage in to achieve their goals. *Emotions* are strong, relatively uncontrollable feelings that affect our behavior. Emotions are triggered by a complex interplay between motives, personality, and external factors. Indeed, the three concepts are closely interrelated and are frequently difficult to separate.

THE NATURE OF MOTIVATION

LO1

Motivation is the reason for behavior. A **motive** is a construct representing an unobservable inner force that stimulates and compels a behavioral response and provides specific direction to that response. A motive is why an individual does something. The terms *need* and *motivation* often are used interchangeably. This is because when a consumer feels a gap between a desired state and his or her actual current state, a need is recognized and experienced as a drive state referred to as motivation. Needs and motives influence what consumers perceive as relevant and also influence their feelings and emotions. For example, a consumer who feels hungry is motivated to satisfy that need, will view food and ads for food as personally relevant, and will experience negative emotions prior to eating and positive emotions after eating.

There are numerous theories of motivation. This section describes two particularly useful approaches. The first approach, *Maslow's need hierarchy,* is a macro theory designed to account for most human behavior in general terms. The second approach, based on McGuire's work, uses a fairly detailed set of motives to account for specific aspects of consumer behavior.

Maslow's Hierarchy of Needs

Maslow's hierarchy of needs is based on four premises:[2]

1. All humans acquire a similar set of motives through genetic endowment and social interaction.
2. Some motives are more basic or critical than others.
3. The more basic motives must be satisfied to a minimum level before other motives are activated.
4. As the basic motives become satisfied, more advanced motives come into play.

Thus, Maslow proposed a need hierarchy shared by all. Table 10–1 illustrates this hierarchy, briefly describes each level, and provides marketing examples.

Maslow's theory is a good guide to general behavior. It is not an ironclad rule, however. Numerous examples exist of individuals who sacrificed their lives for friends or ideas, or who gave up food and shelter to seek self-actualization. However, we do tend to regard such behavior as exceptional, which indicates the general validity of Maslow's overall approach.[3] It is important to remember that any given consumption behavior can satisfy more than

Marketing Strategies and Maslow's Need Hierarchy

Marketing Strategies and Maslow's Need Hierarchy   **TABLE 10-1**

I. Physiological: Food, water, sleep, and, to an extent, sex, are physiological motives.

Products   Health foods, medicines, sports drinks, low-cholesterol foods, and exercise equipment.

Themes   Advil: "Relief That's Fast. Strength That Lasts."

Cheerios: "Can Help Lower Cholesterol"

Peloton: "We use technology to bring group exercise—benefits and energy included—right to your home."

II. Safety: Seeking physical safety and security, stability, familiar surroundings, and so forth are manifestations of safety needs.

Products   Smoke detectors, preventive medicines, insurance, retirement investments, seat belts, burglar alarms, and sunscreen.

Themes   First Alert: "First Alert test kits and home safety products allow you to gain peace of mind in your home."

Coppertone Sunscreen: "Summer fun shouldn't include sunburns."

Janus Henderson Investors: "Knowledge. Shared."

III. Belongingness: Belongingness motives are reflected in a desire for love, friendship, affiliation, and group acceptance.

Products   Personal grooming, foods, entertainment, clothing, and many others.

Themes   Olive Garden Restaurants: "We're All Family Here."

Tums: "You are important. You are loved. You should take your calcium."

Grand Marnier: "Add flavor to good company."

IV. Esteem: Desires for status, superiority, self-respect, and prestige are examples of esteem needs. These needs relate to the individual's feelings of usefulness and accomplishment.

Products   Clothing, furniture, liquors, hobbies, stores, cars, and many others.

Themes   L'Oréal: "Because I'm Worth It."

Tiffany and Co.: "There's Only One"

BMW: "The Ultimate Driving Machine."

V. Self-Actualization: This involves the desire for self-fulfillment, to become all that one is capable of becoming.

Products   Education, hobbies, sports, some vacations, gourmet foods, museums.

Themes   U.S. Navy: "Forged by the Sea."

Nike: "Just Do It."

Culinary Institute of America: "Food Is Life. Create and Savor Yours."

one need. Likewise, the same consumption behavior can satisfy different needs at different times. For example, a number of motives could cause one to take up the sport of golf. The First Tee ad in Illustration 10–1 appeals to self-actualization.

McGuire's Psychological Motives

Maslow presented a hierarchical set of five basic motives, and other researchers have proposed hundreds of additional, very specific motives. McGuire developed a classification system that organizes these various theories into 16 categories.[4] This system helps marketers isolate motives likely to be involved in various consumption situations. McGuire first divides motivation into four main categories using two criteria:

1. Is the mode of motivation cognitive or affective?
2. Is the motive focused on preservation of the status quo or on growth?

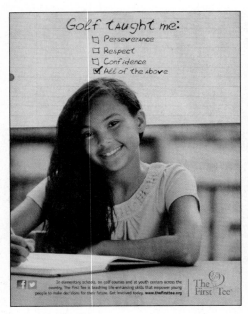

Source: The First Tee

ILLUSTRATION 10-1

Appeals to self-actualization focus on individuals challenging themselves and reaching their full potential, as shown in this The First Tee ad.

Cognitive motives focus on the person's need for being adaptively oriented toward the environment and achieving a sense of meaning. *Affective* motives deal with the need to reach satisfying feeling states and to obtain personal goals. *Preservation-oriented* motives emphasize the individual as striving to maintain equilibrium, while *growth* motives emphasize development. These four main categories are then further subdivided on the bases of source and objective of the motive:

3.   Is this behavior actively initiated or in response to the environment?
4.   Does this behavior help the individual achieve a new internal or a new external relationship to the environment?

The third criterion distinguishes between motives that are actively or internally aroused versus those that are a more passive response to circumstances. The final criterion is used to categorize outcomes that are internal to the individual and those focused on a relationship with the environment.

McGuire's 16 motives and their implications for marketing are briefly described in the following sections.

Cognitive Preservation Motives   *Need for Consistency (active, internal)*   A basic desire is to have all facets of oneself consistent with each other.[5] These facets include attitudes, behaviors, opinions, self-images, views of others, and so forth. *Cognitive dissonance* is a common motive of this type. For example, making a major purchase is not consistent with the need to save money. This inconsistency motivates the individual to reduce it (see Chapter 18).

Understanding the need for consistency is also important for structuring advertising messages relating to attitude change. A need for internal consistency means consumers are reluctant to accept information that disagrees with existing beliefs. Thus, marketers wishing to change attitudes must use highly credible sources or other techniques to overcome this (see Chapter 11).

Need for Attribution (active, external)   This set of motives deals with our need to determine who or what causes the things that happen to us and relates to an area of research called **attribution theory**.[6] Do we attribute the cause of a favorable or unfavorable outcome to ourselves or to some outside force?

Need for attribution is extremely relevant to consumer reactions to promotional messages (in terms of credibility). Because consumers do not passively receive messages but rather attribute "selling" motives and tactics to ads and the advice of sales personnel, they do not believe or they discount many sales messages.[7] Marketers use a variety of means to overcome this. One approach is to use a credible spokesperson, as seen in the Pistachios ad in Illustration 10–2. This technique is discussed in depth in Chapter 11.

Need to Categorize (passive, internal)   People have a need to categorize and organize the vast array of information and experiences they encounter in a meaningful yet manageable way,[8] so they establish categories or mental partitions to help them do so. Prices are often categorized such that different prices connote different categories of goods. Automobiles over $25,000 and automobiles under $25,000 may elicit two different meanings because

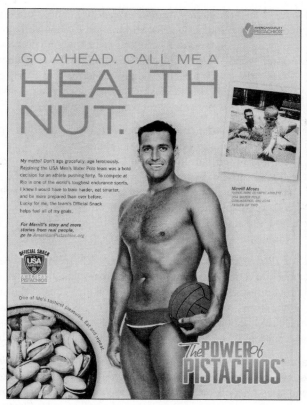

Source: American Pistachio Growers

of information categorized on the basis of price level. Many firms price items at $9.95, $19.95, $49.95, and so forth. One reason is to avoid being categorized in the over $10, $20, or $50 group.

Need for Objectification (passive, external)   These motives reflect needs for observable cues or symbols that enable people to infer what they feel and know. Impressions, feelings, and attitudes are subtly established by viewing one's own behavior and that of others and drawing inferences as to what one feels and thinks. In many instances, clothing plays an important role in presenting the subtle meaning of a desired image and consumer lifestyle. Brands play a role in this, as shown in Figure 10-1 later in this chapter.

Cognitive Growth Motives   ***Need for Autonomy (active, internal)***   The need for independence and individuality is a characteristic of the American culture, as described in Chapter 2. All individuals in all cultures have this need at some level. Americans are taught that it is proper and even essential to express and fulfill this need (in contrast to Eastern countries such as Japan, which value affiliation).

Owning or using products and services that are unique is one way consumers express their autonomy.[9] Marketers have responded to this motive by developing limited editions of products and providing wide variety and customization options. In addition, many products are advertised and positioned with independence, uniqueness, or individuality themes, as shown in the Kiton ad in Illustration 10-3.

Source: Kiton

Need for Stimulation (active, external) People often seek variety and difference out of a need for stimulation.[10] Such variety-seeking behavior may be a prime reason for brand switching and some so-called impulse purchasing.[11] The need for stimulation is curvilinear and changes over time.[12] That is, individuals experiencing rapid change generally become satiated and desire stability, whereas individuals in stable environments become bored and desire change.

Teleological Need (passive, internal) Consumers are pattern matchers who have images of desired outcomes or end states with which they compare their current situation. Behaviors are changed and the results are monitored in terms of movement toward the desired end state. This motive propels people to prefer mass media such as movies, television programs, and books with outcomes that match their view of how the world should work (e.g., the good guys win). This has obvious implications for advertising messages.

Utilitarian Need (passive, external) These theories view the consumer as a problem solver who approaches situations as opportunities to acquire useful information or new skills. Thus, a consumer watching a situation comedy on television not only is being entertained but is learning clothing styles, lifestyle options, and so forth. Likewise, consumers may approach ads and salespeople as a source of learning for future decisions as well as for the current one.

Affective Preservation Motives *Need for Tension Reduction (active, internal)* People encounter situations in their daily lives that create uncomfortable levels of stress. To effectively manage tension and stress, people are motivated to seek ways to reduce arousal. A variety of products and activities often are promoted in terms of tension relief. Illustration 10–4 shows how Secret's "Don't pit out when you stress out" ad is focused on this need.

Need for Expression (active, external) This motive deals with the need to express one's identity to others. People feel the need to let others know who and what they are by their actions, which include the purchase and use of goods. The purchase of many products, such as clothing and automobiles, allows consumers to express an identity to others because the products have symbolic meanings. For example, fashion-oriented watches such as Fossil satisfy more than the functional need to tell time—they allow consumers to express who they are.

Need for Ego Defense (passive, internal) The need to defend one's identity or ego is another important motive. When one's identity is threatened, the person is motivated to protect his or her self-concept and utilize defensive behaviors and attitudes. Many products can provide ego defense. A consumer who feels insecure may rely on well-known brands for socially visible products to avoid any chance of making a socially incorrect purchase.

Need for Reinforcement (passive, external) People often are motivated to act in certain ways because they were rewarded for behaving that way in similar situations in the past.[13] This is the basis for operant learning. Products designed to be used in public situations (clothing, furniture, and artwork) frequently are sold on the basis of the amount and type of reinforcement that will be received. Keepsake Diamonds has exploited this motive with an ad that states, "Enter a room and you are immediately surrounded by friends sharing your excitement."

ILLUSTRATION 10-4

Today's hurried life-styles often produce uncomfortable levels of tension. Products such as Secret help deal with the effects of stress and fulfill a fundamental need.

Source: The Procter & Gamble Company

Affective Growth Motives   *Need for Assertion (active, internal)*   Many people are competitive achievers who seek success, admiration, and dominance. Important to them are power, accomplishment, and esteem. As the fuel ad in Illustration 10–5 shows, the need for assertion underlies numerous ads.

Need for Affiliation (active, external)   Affiliation refers to the need to develop mutually helpful and satisfying relationships with others. It relates to altruism and seeking acceptance and affection in interpersonal relations. As we saw in Chapter 7, group membership is a critical part of most consumers' lives, and many consumer decisions are based on the need to maintain satisfying relationships with others. Marketers frequently use such affiliation-based themes such as "Your kids will love you for it" in advertisements.[14]

Need for Identification (passive, internal)   The need for identification results in the consumer's playing various roles. A person may play the role of college student, sorority member, bookstore employee, fiancée, and many others. One gains pleasure from adding new, satisfying roles and by increasing the significance of roles already adopted. Marketers encourage consumers to assume new roles (become a skateboarder) and position products as critical for certain roles ("No working mother should be without one").

Consumer need for assertion underlies the strategy for this fuel ad.

Source: Ball Corporation

Need for Modeling (passive, external)   The need for modeling reflects a tendency to base behavior on that of others. Modeling is a major means by which children learn to become consumers. The tendency to model explains some of the conformity that occurs within reference groups. Marketers use this motive by showing desirable types of individuals using their brands. Tag Heuer, for example, has used Tom Brady and Cara Delevingne in its "Don't Crack Under Pressure" campaign.

MOTIVATION THEORY AND MARKETING STRATEGY

LO2

Consumers do not buy products; instead, they buy motive satisfaction or problem solutions. For example, a study of Porsche buyers in the United States found that some were motivated by power and status (need for assertion), others by excitement and adventure (need for stimulation), and others by escapism (need for tension reduction). Such motives are not constrained to the United States. A study of car buyers in India found fairly similar motives. For example, they found a "Potency" buyer group interested in power (need for assertion), a "Utility" buyer group interested in basic transportation (utilitarian need), an "Adventure" buyer group interested in fun (need for stimulation), and a "Liberation" buyer group interested in freedom (need for autonomy).[15] Thus, firms must discover the motives that their products and brands can satisfy and develop marketing mixes around these motives.

An important question that often arises is, "Do marketers create needs?" The answer depends in part on what is meant by the term *need*. If it is used to refer to the basic motives described in this chapter, it is clear that marketers seldom if ever *create* a need. Human genetics and experience basically determine motives. Long before marketing or advertising appeared, individuals used perfumes, clothing, and other items to gain acceptance, display status, and so forth. However, marketers do create demand. **Demand** is *the willingness to buy a particular product or service.* It is caused by a need or motive, but it is not the motive. For example, a mouthwash ad might use a theme suggesting that without mouthwash people will not like you because you have bad breath. This message ties mouthwash to an existing need for affiliation in hopes of creating demand for the brand.

The following sections examine how motives, which drive consumption,[16] relate to various aspects of marketing strategy.

Discovering Purchase Motives

Suppose a marketing researcher asked a consumer why he or she wears J. Crew clothes (or owns a mountain bike, or uses cologne, or whatever). Odds are the consumer would offer several reasons, such as "They're in style," "My friends wear them," "I like the way they fit," or "They look good on me." However, there may be other reasons that the consumer is reluctant to admit or perhaps is not even aware of: "They show that I have money," "They make me sexually desirable," or "They show I'm trendy and urbane." All or any combination of the above motives could influence the purchase of clothes or many other items.

The first group of motives mentioned above were known to the consumer and admitted to the researcher. Motives that are known and freely admitted are called **manifest motives.** Any of the motives we have discussed can be manifest; however, motives that conform to a society's prevailing value system are more likely to be manifest than are those in conflict with such values.

The second group of motives described above either were unknown to the consumer or were such that he or she was reluctant to admit them. Such motives are **latent motives.** Figure 10–1 illustrates how the two types of motives might influence a purchase.

The first task of the marketing manager is to determine the combination of motives influencing the target market. Manifest motives are relatively easy to determine. Direct questions (Why do you purchase J. Crew clothing?) generally will produce reasonably accurate assessments of manifest motives.

FIGURE 10-1 Latent and Manifest Motives in a Purchase Situation

Manifest Motives	Consumption Behavior	Latent Motives
Their clothes are stylish and come in a variety of sizes and colors		It will show that I'm sophisticated and trendy
Their clothes are high quality and comfortable	Purchase J. Crew clothes	
A number of my friends wear J. Crew clothes		It's an upscale and urbane brand that will help make me powerful and popular

⟵——— The linkage between behavior and motives that are known and freely admitted

◀- - - - - - - The linkage between behavior and motives that either are unknown or are such that the consumer is reluctant to admit or reveal them

Determining latent motives is substantially more complex. Motivation research or **projective techniques** are designed to provide information on latent motives. One example is the third-person technique whereby consumers provide reasons why "other people" might buy a certain brand. Oreo used projective techniques and was surprised to find that "many regarded Oreo as almost 'magical.'" As a result, "Unlocking the Magic of Oreo" became a campaign theme.[17] For more details on projective techniques, see Appendix A and Table A-1.

Beyond projective techniques, a popular tool for identifying motives is **laddering,** or constructing a **means–end** or **benefit chain.**[18] A product or brand is shown to a consumer, who names all the benefits that product might provide. For each of these benefits, the respondent is then asked to identify further benefits. This is repeated until no additional benefits are identified.

For example, a respondent might mention "fewer colds" as a benefit of taking a daily vitamin. When asked the benefit of fewer colds, one respondent might identify "more efficient at work" and "more energy." Another might name "more skiing" and "looking better." Both use the vitamin to reduce colds but as a means to different ultimate benefits. *How should vitamin ads aimed at each of these two consumers differ?*

Marketing Strategies Based on Multiple Motives

Once a manager has isolated the combination of motives influencing the target market, the next task is to design the marketing strategy around the appropriate set of motives. This involves everything from product design to marketing communications. The nature of these decisions is most apparent in the communications area. Suppose the motives shown in Figure 10–1 are an accurate reflection of a desired target market. *What communications strategy should the manager use?*

One consideration is the extent to which more than one motive is important. If multiple motives are important, the product and ads must provide and communicate them, respectively. A second consideration is whether the motive is manifest or latent. Communicating manifest benefits is relatively easy. For example, J. Crew's website provides hundreds of thumbnails of its many different products by category so that consumers can visually evaluate its products in terms of style, color, and quality. This is a *direct appeal* to manifest motives. However, because latent motives often are less than completely socially desirable, *indirect appeals* frequently are used. So, J. Crew's website uses font, white space, designer collections, and so forth, to *indirectly suggest* its upscale and trendy nature.

Any given ad may focus on only one or a few purchasing motives. However, the campaign needs to cover all the important purchase motives of the target market to position the product in their schematic memory in a manner that corresponds to their manifest and latent motives for the product. *To what motives does the ChapStick ad shown in Illustration 10-6 appeal?*

ILLUSTRATION 10-6

Most ads like this ad for *ChapStick* would appeal to multiple motives and desires. Both the picture and the text should be based on the set of motives associated with acquiring and using the brand.

For naturally delicious lips just swipe.

INTRODUCING
ChapStick 100% Natural Lip Butter
made from 100% naturally sourced oils
and butters for softer, healthier-looking lips.
shopchapstick.com

ChapStick
PUT YOUR LIPS FIRST

Source: Pfizer Inc.

Motivation and Consumer Involvement

As we have seen in previous chapters, involvement is an important determinant of how consumers process information and learn. We also will see in future chapters that involvement is an important determinant of how consumers form attitudes and make purchase decisions. **Involvement** is a motivational state caused by consumer perceptions that a product, brand, or advertisement is relevant or interesting.[19] Needs play a strong role in determining what is relevant or interesting to consumers. For example, watches may be involving because they tell time (utilitarian need), because they allow for self-expression (expressive need), or because they provide a way to fit in (affiliation need).[20] In addition, the situation itself may influence involvement. For example, some consumers may be involved with computers on an ongoing basis (enduring involvement), while others may be involved only in specific situations such as an upcoming purchase (situational involvement).

Involvement is important to marketers because it affects numerous consumer behaviors. For example, consumer involvement increases attention, analytical processing, information search, and word-of-mouth.[21] Involvement is also important to marketers because it affects marketing strategies. For example, high-involvement consumers tend to be product experts and are more persuaded by ads that include detailed product information. On the other hand, low-involvement consumers lack product expertise and are more persuaded by images, emotion, and message source. As a consequence, you often will find highly informational ads for automobiles in magazines such as *Car and Driver* that are targeted at high-involvement consumers. Alternatively, image and emotional approaches are often the norm in general-interest magazines, where involvement is likely moderate to low.

Marketing Strategies Based on Motivation Conflict

With the many motives consumers have, there are frequent conflicts between motives. Resolution of a motivational conflict often affects consumption patterns. For example, recent research has shown that consumers with perceived conflicting goals are more likely to pay more for products and services that save time, such as express shipping.[22] Hence, in many instances, the marketer can analyze situations that are likely to result in a motivational conflict, provide a solution to the conflict, and thus encourage purchase of its brand. We address the three key types of motivation conflict next.

Approach–Approach Motivational Conflict   A consumer who must choose between two attractive alternatives faces **approach–approach conflict.** The more equal the attractions, the greater the conflict. A consumer who recently received a large cash gift for graduation (situational variable) might be torn between a trip to Hawaii (perhaps powered by a need for stimulation) and a new mountain bike (perhaps driven by the need for assertion). This conflict could be resolved by a timely ad designed to encourage one or the other action. Or a price modification, such as "buy now, pay later," could result in a resolution whereby both alternatives are selected.

Approach–Avoidance Motivational Conflict   A consumer facing a purchase choice with both positive and negative consequences confronts **approach–avoidance conflict.** Consumers who want a tan but don't want to risk the skin damage and health risks associated with extended sun exposure face this situation. Lancôme's Flash Bronze sunless tanner resolves this problem by allowing consumers the aesthetic and social benefits of having a tan (approach) without the risk of skin cancer (avoidance).

Avoidance–Avoidance Motivational Conflict   A choice involving only undesirable outcomes produces **avoidance–avoidance conflict.** When a consumer's old washing machine fails, this conflict may occur. The person may not want to spend money on a new washing machine, or pay to have the old one repaired, or go without one. The availability of credit is one way of reducing this motivational conflict. Advertisements emphasizing the importance of regular maintenance for cars, such as oil filter changes, also use this type of motive conflict: "Pay me now, or pay me (more) later."

Marketing Strategies Based on Regulatory Focus

Consumers are often strategic in terms of the behaviors they choose to attain a desired outcome. Some of this, we will see later, is a function of personality. Some of this relates to the particular set of motives that happen to be salient or important when consumers are reacting to stimuli and making decisions. The salience of particular sets of motives triggers consumers to regulate their behavior in different ways to achieve desired outcomes. Two prominent sets of motives are termed promotion and prevention. **Promotion-focused motives** revolve around a desire for growth and development and are related to consumers' hopes and aspirations. **Prevention-focused motives** revolve around a desire for safety and security and are related to consumers' sense of duties and obligations.[23]

Regulatory focus theory suggests that consumers will react differently depending on which broad set of motives is most salient. When promotion-focused motives are more salient, consumers seek to gain positive outcomes, think in more abstract terms, make decisions based more on affect and emotion, and prefer speed versus accuracy in their decision making. When prevention-focused motives are more salient, consumers seek to avoid negative outcomes, think in more concrete terms, make decisions based more on factual substantive information, and prefer accuracy over speed in their decision making. In essence, when promotion-focused motives are most salient, consumers are "eager," more risk-seeking decision makers looking for ways to maximize the possibility that they will attain the most positive possible outcomes. When prevention-focused motives are most salient, consumers are "vigilant," more risk-averse decision makers looking for ways to minimize the chances that they will experience negative outcomes and attempt to avoid making mistakes.

Considerable insight has been gained into the motives, characteristics, and decision-making styles that distinguish a promotion focus from a prevention focus. These differences have important marketing consequences, some of which we already have addressed, and some of which will be addressed in later chapters. Table 10–2 describes differences and the marketing-related dimensions to which they relate.

Whether promotion or prevention motives are most salient depends both on the individual and on the situation. Both prevention and promotion motives reside in each person simultaneously. However, as a result of early childhood experiences, one or the other tends to dominate in each person. This aspect is called *chronic accessibility.* That is, these aspects have been a key focus for so long for these consumers that they tend to be brought to mind when stimuli and decisions are encountered. One aspect of this that has important implications for marketers and market segmentation is the fact that promotion-focused individuals tend to possess more independent self-concepts while prevention-focused individuals tend to possess more interdependent self-concepts. As we saw in Chapter 2, such differences relate to global differences across Western (individualistic) and Eastern (interdependent) cultures. Thus, marketers in Asia should expect that, on average, consumers will be more naturally prevention focused than those in the United States and Western Europe and would benefit from adapting their strategies accordingly. For example, it appears that ads that "frame" the message in terms of acquiring positive outcomes work better in the United States than in China, whereas ads that frame the message in terms of avoiding losses work better in China than in the United States.

Differences in Regulatory Focus		TABLE 10-2

Dimension	Promotion-Focused	Prevention-Focused
Motives	Hopes, wishes, aspirations	Obligations, responsibilities
	Regulate nurturance needs	Regulate security needs
	Growth and development	Status quo
Characteristics		
• Time	Long-term focus	Short-term focus
• Mental imagery	Abstract	Concrete
• Desired steady state	Change	Stability
• Desired feelings	Fun and enjoyment	Safety and security
• Failure emotions	Dejection	Agitation
• Desired self trait	Creativity	Self-control
• Self-concept	Independent	Interdependent
Decision Making		
• Style	Eager style to maximize gains	Vigilant style to minimize losses
• Meta-goals	Speed over accuracy	Accuracy over speed
• Ad cue effects	Affect and emotion	Product facts
• Choice of compromise brand	Lower probability	Higher as compromise brand is less extreme and thus less risky
• Importance of "fit" in brand extensions	Less important	More important as fit reduces risk

Situational factors, such as characteristics of the decision, the environment, and so on, also can *temporarily* make one orientation more prominent. Examples that marketers can use include

- *Ad theme:* achievement (promotion) versus avoidance (prevention).
- *Message frame:* benefits to be gained (promotion) versus losses to be avoided (prevention).
- *Advertising context:* ad placement in shows, magazines, or websites that are likely to elicit a promotion focus (e.g., *O Magazine,* which focuses on ideals and aspirations) versus those likely to elicit a prevention focus (e.g., *The Evening News,* which tends to focus on negative events).

Consumer Insight 10–1 examines one situational component related to regulatory focus.

PERSONALITY

LO3

While motivations are the energizing and directing force that makes consumer behavior purposeful and goal directed, the personality of the consumer helps guide and further direct the behaviors chosen to accomplish goals in different situations. **Personality** is *an individual's characteristic response tendencies across similar situations.* Thus, two consumers might have equal needs for tension reduction but differ in their level of extroversion and, as a consequence, engage in very different behaviors designed to satisfy that need.

While there are many theories of personality, those found to be most useful in a marketing context are called *trait theories.* Trait theories examine personality as an individual difference and thus allow marketers to segment consumers as a function of their personality differences. Trait theories assume that (1) all individuals have internal characteristics or traits related to action tendencies and (2) there are consistent and measurable differences between individuals on those characteristics. To demonstrate, imagine how you might respond if you were asked to describe the personality of a friend. You might say that one of your friends is aggressive, competitive, and outgoing. What you have described are the behavioral tendencies or *traits* your friend has exhibited over time across a variety of situations. Most trait theories state that traits are inherited or formed at an early age and are relatively unchanging over the years. Differences between personality theories center on which traits or characteristics are the most important.

When Consumers Wait Until the Last Minute to Buy

Sometimes consumers put off purchase decisions until the last minute. Think about the Last-Minute Shopper segment discussed in Consumer Insight 1–1: Have you ever still been shopping on Christmas Eve? Or have you ever waited until right before a vacation to book a flight and hotel? Well, you are not alone, and the consequences are significant. A recent study examined how people react to different advertising themes when they were either booking a last-minute summer vacation or planning for a winter-break vacation many months away. Two ad themes for an online travel service were created, with differing taglines, as follows:[24]

- Prevention-focused ad: *Don't get stuck at home! Don't get ripped off!*
- Promotion-focused ad: *Give yourself a memorable vacation! Get the best deals!*

After viewing the ads, consumers were asked how much they would pay for a ticket from the service. The results may surprise you because scaring people sometimes led to a willingness to pay more, but not always. *Can you predict when the prevention-focused ad worked better and when the promotion-focused ad worked better?* Here are the results:

- Last-minute summer vacation (how much would you pay for a ticket?)
  - Prevention-focused ad: $672
  - Promotion-focused ad: $494
- Future winter-break vacation (how much would you pay for a ticket?)
  - Prevention-focused ad: $415
  - Promotion-focused ad: $581

This may seem odd until you consider the fact that when consumers are shopping at the last minute (last-minute summer vacation in the example above), their goals are prevention-focused such as minimizing losses and mistakes. The prevention-focused ad worked best in this situation because it played into consumer fears about those losses. Alternatively, when consumers are shopping well in advance (future winter-break vacation in the example above), their goals are promotion-focused goals such as personal growth and aspirations. The promotion-focused ad worked best in this situation because it played into those consumer desires and aspirations.

According to Jennifer Aaker, an expert in this area: [It's] about how people are motivated by hope and optimism on one hand and by fear on the other.

For holiday marketers, the results seem clear: Utilize positive (promotion-focused) messages early on and negative (prevention-focused) messages close to the holiday. Last-minute shoppers beware!

Critical Thinking Questions

1. Why is it that fear-based appeals are not always the most effective?
2. How might airlines and hotels be able to determine and utilize decision timing in their online marketing efforts?
3. Do you see any ethical issues associated with applying knowledge of decision timing to decisions about promotional themes? Explain.

Multitrait Approach

Some trait research attempts to examine a consumer's entire personality profile across a set of relatively exhaustive dimensions. Specifically, *multitrait personality theory* identifies several traits that in combination capture a substantial portion of the personality of the individual. The multitrait theory used most commonly by marketers is the **Five-Factor Model.**[25] This theory identifies five basic traits formed by genetics and early learning. These core traits interact and manifest themselves in behaviors triggered by situations. Table 10–3 lists the five traits and some of their manifestations.

Core Trait	Manifestation
Extroversion	Prefers to be in a large group rather than alone Talkative when with others Bold
Instability	Moody Temperamental Touchy
Agreeableness	Sympathetic Kind to others Polite with others
Openness to experience	Imaginative Appreciative of art Finds novel solutions
Conscientiousness	Careful Precise Efficient

The Five-Factor Model has proven useful in such areas as understanding bargaining and complaining behavior[26] and compulsive shopping.[27] There is evidence that it may have validity across cultures.[28] The advantage of a multitrait approach such as this is the broad picture it allows of the determinants of behavior. For example, suppose research focused on the single dimension of extroversion and found that those who complained about a dissatisfactory purchase tended to be extroverts. *What insights does this provide for training those who deal with consumer complaints? What training insights are added if we also learn such people are conscientious?* Clearly, the more we know, the better we can satisfy these customers.

Single-Trait Approach

Single-trait theories emphasize one personality trait as being particularly relevant to understanding a particular set of behaviors. They do not suggest that other traits are nonexistent or unimportant. Rather, they study a single trait for its relevance to a set of behaviors, in our case, consumption-related behaviors. Three such consumer traits are described next. We emphasize that given the strong interrelationship between motivation and personality, it is not uncommon for personality traits to evidence motivational aspects.[29] Traits labeled as "needs" often reflect these motivational bases.

Consumer Ethnocentrism   **Consumer ethnocentrism** *reflects an individual difference in consumers' propensity to be biased against the purchase of foreign products.*[30] Consumers low in ethnocentrism tend to be more open to other cultures, less conservative, and more open to purchasing foreign-made products. Consumers high in ethnocentrism tend to be less open to other cultures, more conservative, and more likely to reject foreign-made products in favor of domestics. Consequently, Banana Republic, perhaps in a bid to help its struggling image, as discussed in the chapter opener, is promoting sophisticated, American-made accessories in its "The Company We Keep" collection.[31] Consumer ethnocentrism is a global phenomenon, thus also affecting perceptions of American brands doing business in other countries.[32]

Need for Cognition   *Need for cognition (NFC)* reflects an individual difference in consumers' propensity to engage in and enjoy thinking.[33] Compared with low-NFC individuals, those high in NFC engage in more effortful processing of persuasive communications, prefer verbal to visual information, and are less swayed by the opinions of others. NFC has obvious implications for marketing communications. In addition, research linking NFC to demographic characteristics such as gender (e.g., women are generally higher in NFC) helps to make this personality factor more actionable in terms of media targeting.[34]

Consumers' Need for Uniqueness   *Consumers' need for uniqueness* reflects an individual difference in consumers' propensity to pursue differentness relative to others through the acquisition, utilization, and disposition of consumer goods.[35] It affects what consumers own and value, why they own it, and how they use it. The concept fits with the increasingly common marketing practice of deliberate scarcity—producing less of an item than the predicted demand. Such a strategy helps preserve the uniqueness of the product and enhances the distinctiveness and status of those who own it.

THE USE OF PERSONALITY IN MARKETING PRACTICE

LO4

Sometimes consumers choose products that fit their personality. For example, a timid person might forgo a flashy car because "it's just not me." Other times, consumers use products to bolster an area of their personality where they feel weak. Thus, a timid person who wants to feel more assertive might drive a powerful, flashy sports car. Clearly, products and brands help consumers express their personality.

Brand image is what people think of and feel when they hear or see a brand name (Chapter 9). A particular type of image that some brands acquire is a **brand personality.** Brand personality is *a set of human characteristics that become associated with a brand.* Consumers perceive brand personalities in terms of five basic dimensions, each with several facets, as shown in Figure 10–2. A scale has been developed to measure brand personality in the United States and, with adaptations, in countries such as Russia and Chile.[36]

Researchers have drawn the following conclusions about brand personality:[37]

- Consumers readily assign human characteristics to brands.
- Brand personalities create expectations about key brand characteristics.
- Brand personalities are often the basis for a long-term relationship with the brand.

Not surprisingly, marketers are paying increasing attention to brand personality. Jaguar, Reebok, and Sprite are just a few of the many companies that have attempted to enhance their brand personalities to better target key customer groups. Jaguar has tried to be less "aloof"; Reebok, to be "hip and aggressive"; and Sprite, to have more "street cred."[38]

The ability of a brand's personality to affect customer relationships is critical, and one study provides key insights. Specifically, consumer relationships with "sincere" brands were found to deepen over time along the lines of a "friendship." Alternatively, consumer relationships with "exciting" brands were found to weaken over time along the lines of a "short-lived fling." This advantage for sincere brands required, however, that the brand consistently deliver high quality.[39]

Nonprofits also can benefit from understanding and managing brand personality. One study shows that nonprofits (compared to for-profits) are generally seen as warmer but less competent. Warmth is related to the sincerity dimension of Figure 10-2. Competence is related to reliability and effectiveness, as shown in Figure 10-2. The perceived lack of competence hinders consumer willingness to buy from (or donate to) a nonprofit despite perceptions of the organization's good intentions. However, cues that enhance credibility, such as an endorsement from a credible source, can bridge this gap and therefore increase purchase/donation intentions for the nonprofit firm.[40]

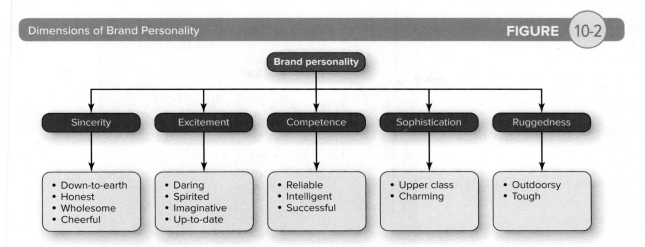

FIGURE 10-2

Dimensions of Brand Personality

Communicating Brand Personality

Because brand personality can serve as a way to target specific market segments, marketers need to manage and communicate brand personality. Bourjois, a French cosmetics company, created unique makeup sets that communicate distinctive personalities. It used "various cocktails, holiday destinations, [and] fashion statements that have different personality attributes" on its packaging. One set, for example, used the martini and the name *Fabulous Flirtini*. According to its branding company Dragon Rouge, the strategy was to

> [offer] several different color stories with the same theme to capture as many consumers as possible and to promote a range of personalities to connect with a range of consumers. At the same time the sets reflected the core attributes of Bourjois: profusion of color, joie de vivre, whimsy, sassy and fun.[41]

As you can see, numerous elements can be used to communicate brand personality. Three important advertising tactics are celebrity endorsers, user imagery, and executional factors.[42]

Celebrity Endorsers   Celebrity endorsers are often a useful way to personify a brand because the characteristics and meanings of the celebrity can be transferred to the brand, especially if the personalities of the brand and celebrity are seen as congruent.[43] Examples include[44]

- Nike and Serena Williams—edgy, individualistic brand.
- Infiniti and Stephen Curry—high-performing, innovative brand.

User Imagery   User imagery involves showing a typical user along with images of the types of activities he or she engages in while using the brand. User imagery helps define who the typical user is in terms of his or her traits, activities, and emotions. The emotion and tone of the activities also can transfer to the brand. Examples include[45]

- Mountain Dew—features young, active users engaged in fun and exciting activities.
- Dansko—features "real women" on their feet all day such as medical professionals and chefs.

Executional Factors   Executional factors go beyond the core message to include "how" it is communicated. The "tone" of the ad (serious vs. quirky), the appeal used (fear vs. humor), the logo and typeface characteristics (*scripted font* may signal sophistication),

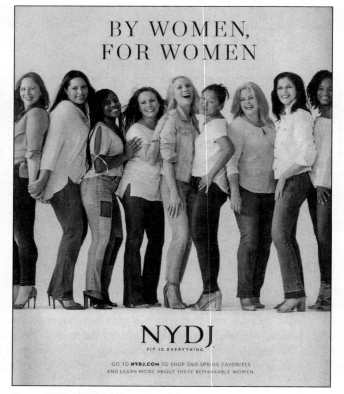

Source: NYDJ APPAREL, LLC

the pace of the ad, and even the media outlet chosen all can communicate a brand's personality. Examples include[46]

- *Tone.* Listerine in Canada wanted a way to be both lighthearted and powerful, so it leveraged an action-hero theme from a popular movie. Listerine went from "old-fashioned and serious" to "powerful and larger than life."
- *Media.* Keds placed ads in fashion magazines such as *Glamour* and *Cosmo* to establish a more hip, fashionable personality.
- *Pace.* Molson in Canada wanted a "spirited, adventurous and slightly naughty" personality, so it created TV ads in which "a festive Latin beat is punctuated with fast-moving, sexually charged party scenes."
- *Logo.* Kate Spade has an understated logo—a tiny "spade" stamp with the brand name—that resonates with Millennials, who increasingly prefer brands without logos. As such, competitor Michael Kors has changed the look of its handbags to include fewer "MK" logos on the bags.

What type of brand personality is created by the NYDJ ad in Illustration 10–7? What advertising elements are being used?

EMOTION

LO5

Emotions are strong, relatively uncontrolled feelings that affect behavior.[47] Emotions are strongly linked to needs, motivation, and personality. Unmet needs create motivation that is related to the arousal component of emotion. Unmet needs generally yield negative emotions, while met needs generally yield positive emotions. As a result, products and brands that generate positive consumption emotions increase consumer satisfaction and loyalty.[48]

Personality also plays a role. For example, some people are more emotional than others, a consumer trait termed *affect intensity*. Consumers higher in affect intensity experience stronger emotions and are more influenced by emotional appeals.[49]

All emotional experiences tend to have several common elements. First, emotions often are triggered by environmental events (e.g., viewing an ad, consuming a product that meets a need). However, they also can be initiated by internal processes such as imagery. As we have seen, advertisers frequently use imagery to evoke specific emotional responses.

Second, emotions are accompanied by *physiological changes* such as (1) eye pupil dilation, (2) increased perspiration, (3) more rapid breathing, (4) increased heart rate and blood pressure, and (5) enhanced blood sugar level. Third, emotions generally, though not necessarily, are accompanied by *cognitive thought*.[50] The types of thoughts and our ability to think rationally vary with the type and degree of emotion.[51]

A fourth characteristic is that emotions have associated *behaviors*. While the behaviors vary across individuals and within individuals across time and situations, there are unique behaviors characteristically associated with different emotions: fear triggers fleeing (avoidance) responses, anger triggers striking out (approach), grief triggers crying, and so forth.[52]

Finally, emotions involve *subjective feelings*. In fact, it is the feeling component we generally refer to when we think of emotions. Grief, joy, anger, and fear feel very different. These subjectively determined feelings are the essence of emotion. These feelings have a specific component we label as the emotion, such as sad or happy. In addition, emotions carry an evaluative, or a like–dislike, component.

We use *emotion* to refer to the identifiable, specific feeling, and *affect* to refer to the liking–disliking aspect of the specific feeling. Emotions are generally evaluated (liked and disliked) in a consistent manner across individuals and within individuals over time, but there are cultural, individual, and situational variations.[53] For example, few of us generally want to be sad or afraid, yet we occasionally enjoy a movie or book that scares or saddens us.

Figure 10–3 reflects current thinking on the nature of emotions.

Types of Emotions

If asked, you could doubtless name numerous emotions. Thus, it is not surprising that researchers have attempted to categorize emotions into manageable clusters. Some researchers have suggested that three basic dimensions—pleasure, arousal, and dominance (PAD)—underlie all emotions. Specific emotions reflect various combinations and levels of these

TABLE 10-4 Emotional Dimensions, Emotions, and Emotional Indicators

Dimension	Emotion	Indicator/Feeling
Pleasure	Duty	Moral, virtuous, dutiful
	Faith	Reverent, worshipful, spiritual
	Pride	Proud, superior, worthy
	Affection	Loving, affectionate, friendly
	Innocence	Innocent, pure, blameless
	Gratitude	Grateful, thankful, appreciative
	Serenity	Restful, serene, comfortable, soothed
	Desire	Desirous, wishful, craving, hopeful
	Joy	Joyful, happy, delighted, pleased
	Competence	Confident, in control, competent
Arousal	Interest	Attentive, curious
	Hypoactivation	Bored, drowsy, sluggish
	Activation	Aroused, active, excited
	Surprise	Surprised, annoyed, astonished
	Déjà vu	Unimpressed, uninformed, unexcited
	Involvement	Involved, informed, enlightened, benefited
	Distraction	Distracted, preoccupied, inattentive
	Surgency	Playful, entertained, lighthearted
	Contempt	Scornful, contemptuous, disdainful
Dominance	Conflict	Tense, frustrated, conflictful
	Guilt	Guilty, remorseful, regretful
	Helplessness	Powerless, helpless, dominated
	Sadness	Sad, distressed, sorrowful, dejected
	Fear	Fearful, afraid, anxious
	Shame	Ashamed, embarrassed, humiliated
	Anger	Angry, agitated, enraged, mad
	Hyperactivation	Panicked, confused, overstimulated
	Disgust	Disgusted, revolted, annoyed, full of loathing
	Skepticism	Skeptical, suspicious, distrustful

Source: Adapted from M. B. Holbrook and R. Batra, "Assessing the Role of Emotions on Consumer Responses to Advertising," *Journal of Consumer Research*, December 1987, pp. 404–20.

three dimensions. Table 10–4 lists the three primary PAD dimensions, a variety of emotions or emotional categories associated with each dimension, and indicators or items that can be used to measure each emotion.

EMOTIONS AND MARKETING STRATEGY

LO6

Emotions play a role in a wide range of marketing situations relating to products, retailing, consumer coping, and advertising. We examine each of these in the following sections.

Emotion Arousal as a Product and Retail Benefit

Emotions are characterized by positive or negative evaluations. Consumers actively seek products whose primary or secondary benefit is emotion arousal.[54] Movies, books, and music are obvious examples,[55] as are resort destinations such as Las Vegas and adventure travel programs. Recent Super Bowl advertisements designed to fuel consumer emotion and excitement about brands include Budweiser's "Born The Hard Way" and Audi's "Daughter." Beyond products and brands, retailers also feature events and environments that arouse emotions such as excitement. For example, websites using avatars are perceived as more social, which enhances pleasure, arousal, perceived hedonic value, and purchase intentions.[56]

One specific emotion that is getting increased attention in terms of relationship marketing is **gratitude**. Gratitude in a consumer context is *the emotional appreciation for benefits received.* Firms can invest in relationship improvements in many ways, including time, effort, investments in equipment specific to the customer, and so on. Research shows that these relationship marketing efforts on the part of the firm lead to the following outcomes:

- Increased consumer gratitude.
- Increased consumer trust in the firm.
- Increased customer purchases.
- Increased "gratitude-based reciprocity" behaviors.

Gratitude-based reciprocity behaviors include (a) buying products based on gratitude for the relationship marketing efforts, (b) giving more business to the firm due to feelings of "owing" them, and (c) buying a broader set of products from the firm as a "payback" for its prior relationship marketing efforts and positive word-of-mouth. Gratitude, it turns out, is a powerful emotion. It causes consumers to want to reward firms for their relationship marketing efforts in ways that lead to greater sales and positive word-of-mouth.[57]

Although consumers seek positive emotions, the majority of the time, this is not always the case, as when we enjoy a sad movie. Additionally, products can arouse negative emotions such as the frustration and anger we feel when high-tech gadgets are difficult to use.[58]

Emotion Reduction as a Product and Retail Benefit

Few people like to feel sad, powerless, humiliated, or disgusted. Responding to this, marketers design or position many products to prevent or reduce the arousal of unpleasant emotions. The most obvious of these products are the various over-the-counter medications designed to deal with anxiety or depression. Food and alcohol are consumed, often harmfully, to reduce stress. Flowers are heavily promoted as an antidote to sadness. Weight-loss products and other self-improvement products are frequently positioned primarily in terms of guilt-, helplessness-, shame-, or disgust-reduction benefits. Personal grooming products often emphasize anxiety reduction as a major benefit. Charities frequently stress guilt reduction or avoidance as a reason for contributing.[59]

Consumer Coping in Product and Service Encounters

Consumers must cope with the negative emotions they experience in various marketing situations. **Coping** *involves consumer thoughts and behaviors in reaction to a stress-inducing situation designed to reduce stress and achieve more desired positive emotions.*[60] Avoidance is a common mechanism. For example, when a decision involves a trade-off that evokes strong negative emotions (e.g., price versus safety), consumers often will delay the purchase to avoid making a decision.[61] In retail settings, consumers in a bad mood attempt to cope by avoiding salespeople they perceive as happy. However, if they are forced to deal with a happy salesperson, it makes them feel worse, which reduces salesperson effectiveness.[62] *What marketing and training aspects relating to service personnel does this suggest?*

One typology of coping strategies categorizes three broad types in response to negative emotions emanating from stressful events such as bad customer service or product failure. The three types are[63]

- *Active coping.* Thinking of ways to solve the problem, engaging in restraint to avoid rash behavior, and making the best of the situation.
- *Expressive support seeking.* Venting emotions and seeking emotional and problem-focused assistance from others.
- *Avoidance.* Avoiding the retailer mentally or physically or engaging in complete self-denial of the event.

Each strategy can have positive and negative marketing consequences. Active coping may involve working with the company to resolve the situation or switching from the firm altogether. Likewise, consumers may vent to the company (expressive support seeking), which is desirable, or they may vent to friends (negative WOM), which is damaging. Finally, denial (avoidance) may result in customer retention, but physical avoidance of the retailer will result in lost sales. As you can see, proper training of service personnel to handle product and service failures as well as the careful design of retail and service facilities to reduce stressors is critical.

Consumer ability to *effectively* cope with stressful situations relates to the concept of **consumer emotional intelligence,** which is defined as *a person's ability to skillfully use emotional information to achieve a desirable consumer outcome.* It is an ability variable rather than a personality trait. Consumers higher in emotional intelligence are better at perceiving, facilitating, understanding, and managing emotional information. For example, a consumer with higher emotional intelligence may understand better how to channel his or her feelings of anger over a service failure to obtain a solution that is desirable to the consumer.[64] A failure to appropriately channel such feelings can result in "rage episodes," which appear to be on the increase in the United States. In response, firms need to better understand what triggers rage episodes and train their employees so they can (a) engage in behaviors to minimize their likelihood and (b) train their employees to effectively and safely handle such rage episodes when they do occur.[65]

Emotion in Advertising

Emotion arousal is often used in advertising regardless of whether it is specifically relevant to the brand's performance. Consider the following headlines:

- Under Armour taps raw emotion.
- Kleenex for Men to play on emotion in TV return.
- P&G's Emotional new "Thank you, Mom" tugs at the heartstrings.

The ASICS ad shown in Illustration 10–8 provides an example of the effective use of emotion to attract attention to an ad and to position a brand.

Emotions can play a variety of roles in advertising. Emotional content in ads *enhances their attention, attraction, and maintenance capabilities.* Advertising messages that trigger the emotional reactions of joy, warmth, and suspense[66] are more likely to be attended to than are more neutral ads. As we saw in Chapter 8, attention is a critical early step in the perception process.

Emotions are characterized by a state of heightened physiological arousal. Individuals become more alert and active when aroused. Given this enhanced level of arousal, *emotional*

ILLUSTRATION 10-8

Emotional appeals, such as in this ASICS ad, can play a powerful role in developing a brand image.

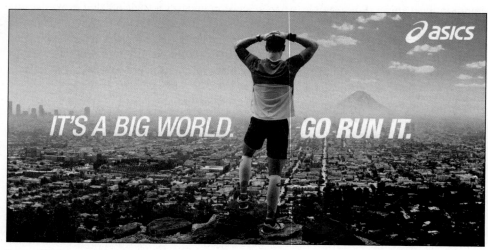

IT'S A BIG WORLD.   GO RUN IT.

asics

Source: ASICS America Corporation

Source: Edgewell Personal Care

messages may be processed more thoroughly than neutral messages. More effort and increased elaboration activities may occur in response to the emotional state.[67] As a consequence of this greater attention and processing, emotional ads *may be remembered better than neutral ads.*[68]

Emotional advertisements that *trigger a positively evaluated emotion will enhance liking of the ad itself.*[69] For example, warmth is a positively valued emotion that is triggered by experiencing directly or vicariously a love, family, or friendship relationship. Ads high in warmth are liked more than neutral ads. Liking an ad has a positive impact on liking the product and purchase intentions.[70] As you might suspect, ads that irritate or disgust consumers can create negative reactions to the advertised brand.[71]

Repeated exposure to positive emotion-eliciting ads *may increase brand preference through classical conditioning.*[72] Repeated pairings of positive emotion (unconditioned response) with the brand name (conditioned stimulus) may result in the positive affect occurring when the brand name is presented. *Brand preference also may occur in a direct, high-involvement way.* A person having a single or few exposures to an emotional ad may simply decide he or she likes the product. This is a much more conscious process than implied by classical conditioning. Such a process seems more likely for hedonic products involving high levels of emotional value rather than utilitarian products. For hedonic products, ad-evoked emotion is a relevant cue on which to base a product evaluation.[73]

Advertising using emotional appeals continues to be popular. For example, P&G continues to employ its successful "Thank you, Mom" campaign during the Olympics. The most recent series of emotion-based ads, showing scenes with athletes, such as a speed skater of the Muslim faith, end with the tagline, "Imagine if the world could see what a mom does." This long-running campaign has been effective, as "emotional connections drive viewer engagement," according to an advertising analytics executive.[74] Illustration 10-9 shows how Edge taps into emotions through the use of humor.

LO1: Define motivation and summarize the motivation sets put forth by Maslow and McGuire.

Consumer motivations are energizing forces that activate behavior and provide purpose and direction to that behavior. There are numerous motivation theories. Maslow's need hierarchy states that basic motives must be minimally satisfied before more advanced motives are activated. It proposes five levels of motivation: physiological, safety, belongingness, esteem, and self-actualization.

McGuire developed a more detailed set of motives—the needs for consistency, attribution, categorization, objectification, autonomy, stimulation, desired outcomes (teleological), utility, tension reduction, expression, ego defense, reinforcement, assertion, affiliation, identification, and modeling.

LO2: Articulate motivation's role in consumer behavior and marketing strategy.

Consumers often are aware of and will admit to the motives causing their behavior. These are *manifest motives.* They can be discovered by standard marketing research techniques such as direct questioning. Direct advertising appeals can be made to these motives. At other times, consumers are unable or unwilling to admit to the motives that are influencing them. These are *latent motives.* They can be determined by motivation research techniques such as word association, sentence completion, and picture response (see Appendix Table A–1). Although direct advertising appeals can be used, indirect appeals are often necessary. Both manifest and latent motives are operative in many purchase situations.

Involvement is a motivational state caused by consumer perceptions that a product, brand, or advertisement is relevant or interesting. Consumer needs play a strong role in shaping involvement, and marketers must adapt their strategies depending on the level (high versus low) and type (enduring versus situational) of involvement exhibited by their target audience.

Because of the large number of motives and the many different situations that consumers face, motivational conflict can occur. In an *approach–approach conflict,* the consumer faces a choice between two attractive alternatives. In an *approach–avoidance conflict,* the consumer faces both positive and negative consequences in the purchase of a particular product. And finally, in an *avoidance–avoidance conflict,* the consumer faces two undesirable alternatives.

Regulatory focus theory suggests that consumers react differently depending on whether promotion-focused

or prevention-focused motives are more salient. When promotion-focused motives are more salient, consumers seek to gain positive outcomes, think in more abstract terms, make decisions based more on affect and emotion, and prefer speed versus accuracy in their decision making. When prevention-focused motives are more salient, consumers seek to avoid negative outcomes, think in more concrete terms, make decisions based more on factual substantive information, and prefer accuracy over speed in their decision making. Which motive set is more salient can depend on individual and situational factors and has numerous marketing implications.

LO3: Define personality and the various theories of personality.

The *personality* of a consumer guides and directs the behavior chosen to accomplish goals in different situations. Trait theories of personality assume that (1) all individuals have internal characteristics or traits related to action tendencies and (2) there are consistent and measurable differences between individuals on those characteristics. Most of these theories assume that traits are formed at an early age and are relatively unchanging over the years.

Multitrait theories attempt to capture a significant portion of a consumer's total personality using a set of personality attributes. The Five-Factor Model of personality is the most widely used multitrait approach. Single-trait theories focus on one aspect of personality in an attempt to understand a limited part of consumer behavior. Various traits related specifically to consumer behavior include consumer ethnocentricity, need for cognition, and consumers' need for uniqueness.

LO4: Discuss how brand personality can be used in developing marketing strategies.

Brands, like individuals, have personalities, and consumers tend to prefer products with brand personalities that are pleasing to them. Consumers also prefer advertising messages that portray their own or a desired personality. Brand personality can be communicated in a number of ways, including celebrity endorsers, user imagery, and executional ad elements such as tone and pace.

LO5: Define emotions and list the major emotional dimensions.

Emotions are strong, relatively uncontrollable feelings that affect our behavior. Emotions occur when environmental events or our mental processes trigger physiological changes such as increased heart rate. These changes are interpreted as specific emotions resulting from the situation. They affect consumers' thoughts and behaviors. The major dimensions of emotion are pleasure, arousal, and dominance. Each of these major dimensions has specific emotions and feelings associated with it.

LO6: Discuss how emotions can be used in developing marketing strategies.

Marketers design and position products to both arouse and reduce emotions. In addition, consumers must cope with stressful marketing situations such as service and product failures. The various coping mechanisms can be beneficial or detrimental to the firm depending on various factors and require that marketers consider not only their responses to failure but also service-setting design to reduce consumer stressors. Advertisements include emotion-arousing material to increase attention, degree of processing, remembering, and brand preference through classical conditioning or direct evaluation.

KEY TERMS

Approach–approach conflict 375
Approach–avoidance conflict 375
Attribution theory 368
Avoidance–avoidance conflict 375
Benefit chain 374
Brand personality 380
Consumer emotional
    intelligence 386
Consumer ethnocentrism 379

Coping 385
Demand 372
Emotion 382
Five-Factor Model 378
Gratitude 384
Involvement 375
Laddering 374
Latent motives 373
Manifest motives 373

Maslow's hierarchy of needs 366
Means–end chain 374
Motivation 366
Motive 366
Personality 377
Prevention-focused motives 376
Projective techniques 374
Promotion-focused motives 376
Regulatory focus theory 376

REVIEW QUESTIONS

1. What is a *motive?*
2. What is meant by a *motive hierarchy?* How does Maslow's hierarchy of needs function?
3. Describe each level of Maslow's hierarchy of needs.
4. Describe each of McGuire's motives.
5. Describe *attribution theory.*
6. What is meant by *motivational conflict* and what relevance does it have for marketing managers?
7. What is a *manifest motive?* A *latent motive?* How is each measured?
8. How do you appeal to manifest motives? Latent motives?
9. Describe the following motivation research techniques (see Appendix A and Appendix Table A–1 for details):
    a. Association
    b. Completion
    c. Construction

10. What is the relationship between *involvement* and *motivation?*
11. Describe *regulatory focus theory.*
12. What is *personality?*
13. What is *consumer ethnocentrism,* and why is it important to global marketers?
14. How can knowledge of personality be used to develop marketing strategy?
15. What is an *emotion?* What are the basic dimensions of emotion?
16. What physiological changes accompany emotional arousal?
17. What factors characterize emotions?
18. What is consumer *gratitude* and what outcomes are associated with this emotion?
19. How do marketers use emotions in product design and advertising?
20. What is *coping* and what are the general types of coping mechanisms used by consumers?

DISCUSSION QUESTIONS

21. How could Maslow's motive hierarchy be used to develop marketing strategy for the following?
    a. American Bird Conservancy
    b. Redken shampoo
    c. Purell hand sanitizer
    d. Chipotle Mexican Grill
    e. BlackBerry
    f. Crest Whitestrips

22. Which of McGuire's motives would be useful in developing a promotional campaign for the following? Why?
    a. Cadillac CTS
    b. Supercuts (hair salon chain)
    c. Nokia Android smartphones
    d. Just for Men hair coloring
    e. Twitter
    f. Habitat for Humanity

23. Describe how motivational conflict might arise in purchasing, patronizing, or giving to the following:
    a. Greenpeace
    b. Chevy Volt
    c. Walmart
    d. Red Bull energy drink
    e. Taco Bell restaurant
    f. ADT home security system

24. Describe the manifest and latent motives that might arise in purchasing, shopping at, or giving to the following:
    a. Yukon hybrid
    b. Saks Fifth Avenue
    c. Bose sound system
    d. A kitten
    e. Mercedes-Benz convertible
    f. iPhone

25. Do marketers create needs? Do they create demand? What ethical issues are relevant?

26. Respond to the questions in Consumer Insight 10–1.

27. How might knowledge of personality be used to develop an advertising campaign for the following?
    a. Rainforest Action Network (an environmental group)
    b. Smartphones
    c. American Express travel services
    d. Ready-to-drink iced tea
    e. J. Crew women's shoes
    f. Clinique cosmetics

28. Using Table 10–3, discuss how you would use one of the core personality source traits in developing a package design for an organic, shade-grown coffee.

29. How would the media preferences of those on each end of the consumer need-for-uniqueness continuum differ?

30. How would the shopping behaviors of those on each end of the ethnocentrism continuum differ?

31. How would you use emotion to develop a marketing strategy for each of the following?
    a. Visa card use
    b. Skydiving
    c. Orthodontist
    d. Silk (soy milk)
    e. Honda Civic Hybrid
    f. Iceland

32. List all the emotions you can think of. Which ones are not explicitly mentioned in Table 10–4? Where would you place them in this table?

APPLICATION ACTIVITIES

33. Develop an advertisement for one of the items in Question 21 based on relevant motives from McGuire's set.

34. Repeat Question 33 using Maslow's need hierarchy.

35. Repeat Question 33 using emotions.

36. Find and copy or describe two advertisements that appeal to each level of Maslow's hierarchy. Explain why the ads appeal to the particular levels, and speculate on why the firm decided to appeal to these levels.

37. Find and copy or describe an ad that contains direct appeals to manifest motives and indirect appeals to latent motives. Explain how and why the ad is using each approach.

38. Select a product of interest and use motivation research techniques to determine the latent purchase motives for five consumers (see Appendix A and Appendix Table A–1 for details).

39. Have five students describe the personality of the following. To what extent are their descriptions similar? Why are there differences?

    a. Fossil watches

    b. Prada sunglasses

    c. Toyota

    d. Dell computer

    e. Cheesecake Factory restaurant

    f. The university bookstore

40. Find and copy an ad that you feel communicates a strong brand personality. Describe that personality in terms of the dimensions in Figure 10-2. Describe the various techniques used in the ad (e.g., celebrity endorser, user imagery, and executional factors) and how that links to the personality they are communicating.

41. Find and copy an ad with strong emotional appeals and another ad from the same product category with limited emotional appeals. Why do the companies use different appeals?

    a. Have 10 students rank or rate the ads in terms of their preferences and then explain their rankings or ratings.

    b. Have 10 different students talk about their reactions to each ad as they view it. What do you conclude?

42. Ask two students to describe the coping mechanisms they use when dealing with product or service failures. Identify factors that cause their coping to be beneficial (e.g., complaining to the company) rather than detrimental (e.g., negative WOM) to the firm.

REFERENCES

1. This chapter opener based on L. Monllos, "The Gap's Biggest Problem Is That It Lost Its Brand Identity," *Adweek*, June 17, 2015, www.adweek.com, accessed May 28, 2018; L. Bever, "How Millennial Shoppers Have Made Gap's Uniform Look Obsolete," *Washington Post*, June 16, 2015; S. Li, "Does Gap Have an Identity Problem?," *Los Angeles Times*, May 18, 2016; E. Adams, "Has Gap Finally Figured Out What Its Customers Want?," *Racked*, September 8, 2016, www.racked.com, accessed May 25, 2018; A. Pasquarelli, "Gap Seeks New Grip on Shoppers," *Advertising Age*, July 18, 2016; A. Pasquarelli, "Old Navy Succeeds by Saying Bye to Celebs and Hi to Fashion," *Advertising Age*, July 27, 2017; C. Lieber, "Athleta Doesn't Ignore Older Women and That's Why It's Successful," *Racked*, September 7, 2017, www.racked.com, accessed May 25, 2018; V. Craig, "Banana Republic on the Brink: Can Gap's Struggling Brand be Saved?," *Fox Business*, January 30, 2017, www.foxbusiness.com, accessed May 27, 2018; D. Forte, "How Gap Is Reimagining Itself as a Customer-Centric Organization," *Multichannel Merchant*, March 1, 2018, www.multichannelmerchant.com, accessed May 25, 2018.

2. A. H. Maslow, *Motivation and Personality*, 2nd ed. (New York: Harper & Row, 1970).

3. See R. Yalch and F. Brunel, "Need Hierarchies in Consumer Judgments of Product Designs," in *Advances in Consumer Research*, vol. 23, ed. K. P. Corfman and J. G. Lynch (Provo, UT: Association for Consumer Research, 1996), pp. 405–10.

4. W. J. McGuire, "Psychological Motives and Communication Gratification," in *The Uses of Mass Communications*, ed. J. G. Blumler and C. Katz (Newbury Park, CA: Sage, 1974), pp. 167–96; W. J. McGuire, "Some Internal Psychological Factors Influencing Consumer Choice," *Journal of Consumer Research*, March 1976, pp. 302–19.

5. See A. G. Woodside and J.-C. Chebat, "Updating Heider's Balance Theory in Consumer Behavior," *Psychology & Marketing*, May 2001, pp. 475–95.

6. M. C. Campbell and A. Kirmani, "Consumers' Use of Persuasion Knowledge," *Journal of Consumer Research*, June 2000, pp. 69–83; R. N. Laczniak, T. E. DeCarlo, and S. N. Ramaswami, "Consumers' Responses to Negative Word-of-Mouth Communication," *Journal of Consumer Psychology* 11, no. 31 (2001), pp. 57–73.

7. See M. Friestad and P. Wright, "Persuasion Knowledge," *Journal of Consumer Research*, June 1995, pp. 62–74.

8. See B. H. Schmit and S. Zhang, "Language Structure and Categorization," *Journal of Consumer Research*, September 1998, pp. 108–22; J. A. Rosa and J. F. Porac, "Categorization Bases and Their Influence on Product Category Knowledge Structures," *Psychology & Marketing*, June 2002, pp. 503–32.

9. M. Lynn and J. Harris, "The Desire for Unique Consumer Products," *Psychology & Marketing*, September 1997, pp. 601–16.

10. R. K. Ratner, B. E. Kahn, and D. Kahneman, "Choosing Less-Preferred Experiences for the Sake of Variety," *Journal of Consumer Research*, June 1999, pp. 1–15; R. K. Ratner and B. E. Kahn, "The Impact of Private versus Public Consumption on Variety-Seeking Behavior," *Journal of Consumer Research*, September 2002, pp. 246–57.

11. M. Trivedi, "Using Variety-Seeking-Based Segmentation to Study Promotional Response," *Journal of the Academy of Marketing Science*, Winter 1999, pp. 37–49; M. Trivedi and M. S. Morgan, "Promotional Evaluation and Response among Variety Seeking Segments," *Journal of Product and Brand Management* 12, no. 6 (2003), pp. 408–25; J. Chen and S. Paliwoda, "The Influence of Company Name in Consumer Variety Seeking," *Brand Management*, February 2004, pp. 219–31.

12. See D. Goldman, "Pain? It's a Pleasure," *American Demographics*, January 2000, pp. 60–61; J. J. Inman, "The Role of Sensory-Specific Satiety in Attribute-Level Variety Seeking," *Journal of Consumer Research*, June 2001, pp. 105–19.

13. C. Hsee, Y. Yang, and B. Ruan, "The Mere-Reaction Effect: Even Nonpositive and Noninformative Reactions Can Reinforce Actions," *Journal of Consumer Research* 42 (October 2015), pp. 420–34.

14. See G. M. Zinkhan, J. W. Hong, and R. Lawson, "Achievement and Affiliation Motivation," *Journal of Business Research,* March 1990, pp. 135–43.

15. Porsche example from A. Taylor III, "Porsche Slices Up Its Buyers," *Fortune,* January 6, 1995, p. 24. Indian car example from "New Car Buyers in India Seek Emotive Needs," *India Television,* December 21, 2004, www.indiatelevision.com, accessed June 7, 2011.

16. I. Barbopoulos and L.-O. Johansson, "The Consumer Motivation Scale: Development of a Multi-Dimensional and Context-Sensitive Measure of Consumption Goals," *Journal of Business Research* 76 (2017), pp. 119–26.

17. C. Rubel, "Three Firms Show That Good Research Makes Good Ads," *Marketing News,* March 13, 1995, p. 18.

18. T. J. Reynolds and J. C. Olson, *Understanding Consumer Decision Making* (Mahwah, NJ: Erlbaum, 2001); G. S. Mort and T. Rose, "The Effect of Product Type on Value Linkages in the Means-End Chain," *Journal of Consumer Behaviour,* March 2004, pp. 221–34; F. Huber, S. C. Beckmann, and A. Herrmann, "Means-End Analysis," *Psychology & Marketing,* September 2004, pp. 715–37.

19. See J. L. Zaichkowsky, "The Personal Involvement Inventory," *Journal of Advertising,* December 1994, pp. 59–70.

20. See P. Quester and A. L. Lim, "Product Involvement/Brand Loyalty," *Journal of Product and Brand Management* 12, no. 1 (2003), pp. 22–38.

21. See U. M. Dholakia, "A Motivational Process Model of Product Involvement and Consumer Risk Perception," *European Journal of Marketing* 35, no. 11/12 (2001), pp. 1340–60; C.-W. Park and B.-J. Moon, "The Relationship between Product Involvement and Product Knowledge," *Psychology & Marketing,* November 2003, pp. 977–97.

22. J. Etkin, I. Evangelidis, and J. Aaker, "Pressed for Time? Goal Conflict Shapes How Time Is Perceived, Spent and Valued," *Journal of Marketing Research* 52 (June 2015), pp. 394–406.

23. This section on regulatory focus, including Table 10-2, is based on the following: E. T. Higgins, "Beyond Pleasure and Pain," *American Psychologist,* December 1997, pp. 1280–300; J. L. Aaker and A. Y. Lee, "'I' Seek Pleasures and 'We' Avoid Pains," *Journal of Consumer Research,* June 2001, pp. 33–49; A. Chernev, "Goal-Attribute Compatibility in Consumer Choice," *Journal of Consumer Psychology* 14, nos. 1 & 2 (2004), pp. 141–50; M. T. Pham and T. Avnet, "Ideals and Oughts and the Reliance on Affect versus Substance in Persuasion," *Journal of Consumer Research,* March 2004, pp. 503–18; A. Bosmans and H. Baumgartner, "Goal-Relevant Emotional Information," *Journal of Consumer Research,* December 2005, pp. 424–34; J. L. Aaker and A. Y. Lee, "Understanding Regulatory Fit," *Journal of Marketing Research,* February 2006, pp. 15–19; T. Avnet and E. T. Higgins, "How Regulatory Fit Affects Value in Consumer Choices and Opinions," *Journal of Marketing Research,* February 2006, pp. 1–10; Y.-J. Kim, "The Role of Regulatory Focus in Message Framing in Antismoking Advertisements for Adolescents," *Journal of Advertising,* Spring 2006, pp. 143–51; J. Yeo and J. Park, "Effects of Parent-Extension Similarity and Self Regulatory Focus on Evaluations of Brand Extensions," *Journal of Consumer Psychology* 16, no. 3 (2006), pp. 272–82; M. Mourali, U. Bockenholt, and M. Laroche, "Compromise and Attraction Effects under Prevention and Promotion Motivations," *Journal of Consumer Research,* August 2007, pp. 234–47; A. Y. Lee, P. A. Keller, and B. Sternthal, "Value from Regulatory Construal Fit," *Journal of Consumer Research,* February 2010, pp. 735–47.

24. Insight based on "No Time before Valentine's Day?," *Science Daily,* January 27, 2008; C. Mogilner, J. L. Aaker, and G. L. Pennington, "Time Will Tell," *Journal of Consumer Research,* February 2008, pp. 670–81; S. Vedantam, "Care to Know the Motivation behind That Gift, Love?," *Washington Post,* February 11, 2008, p A3.

25. See J. S. Wiggins, *The Five-Factor Model of Personality* (New York: Guilford Press, 1996).

26. E. G. Harris and J. C. Mowen, "The Influence of Cardinal-, Central-, and Surface-Level Personality Traits on Consumers' Bargaining and Complaint Behaviors," *Psychology & Marketing,* November 2001, pp. 1155–85.

27. J. C. Mowen and N. Spears, "Understanding Compulsive Buying among College Students," *Journal of Consumer Psychology* 8, no. 4 (1999), pp. 407–30.

28. W. Na and R. Marshall, "Validation of the 'Big Five' Personality Traits in Korea," *Journal of International Consumer Marketing* 12, no. 1 (1999), pp. 5–19.

29. See N. Brody and H. Ehrlichman, *Personality Psychology* (Englewood Cliffs, NJ: Prentice Hall, 1998); A. Deponte, "Linking Motivation to Personality," *European Journal of Personality* 18 (2004), pp. 31–44.

30. See S. Sharma, T. A. Shimp, and J. Shin, "Consumer Ethnocentrism," *Journal of the Academy of Marketing Science,* Winter 1995, pp. 26–37; G. Balabanis and A. Diamantopoulos, "Domestic Country Bias, Country-of-Origin Effects, and Consumer Ethnocentrism," *Journal of the Academy of Marketing Science,* Winter 2004, pp. 80–95.

31. T. Tucker, "Banana Republic Is Promoting Made in America Labels in a Special Collection," *American Manufacturing,* April 21, 2017, www.americanmanufacturing.org, accessed June 1, 2018; company website, accessed June 1, 2018.

32. M. Supphellen and K. Gronhaug, "Building Foreign Brand Personalities in Russia," *International Journal of Advertising* 22, no. 2 (2003), pp. 203–26; H. Kwak, A. Jaju, and T. Larsen, "Consumer Ethnocentrism Offline and Online," *Journal of the Academy of Marketing Science,* Summer 2006, pp. 367–85.

33. C. S. Areni, M. E. Ferrell, and J. B. Wilcox, "The Persuasive Impact of Reported Group Opinions on Individuals Low vs. High in Need for Cognition," *Psychology & Marketing,* October 2000, pp. 855–75; J. Z. Sojka and J. L. Giese, "The Influence of Personality Traits on the Processing of Visual and Verbal Information," *Marketing Letters,* February 2001, pp. 91–106.

34. See, e.g., L. K. Waters and T. D. Zakrajsek, "Correlates of Need for Cognition Total and Subscale Scores," *Educational and Psychological Measurement,* Spring 1990, pp. 213–17.

35. K. T. Tian, W. O. Bearden, and G. L. Hunter, "Consumers' Need for Uniqueness," *Journal of Consumer Research,* June 2001, pp. 50–66. See also K. T. Tian and K. McKenzie, "The Long-Term Predictive Validity of the Consumers' Need for Uniqueness Scale," *Journal of Consumer Psychology* 10, no. 3 (2001), pp. 171–93.

36. J. L. Aaker, "Dimensions of Brand Personality," *Journal of Marketing Research,* August 1997, pp. 347–56. For international adaptations, see Supphellen and Gronhaug, "Building Foreign Brand Personalities in Russia"; J. I. Rojas-Mendez, I. Erenchun-Podlech, and E. Silva-Olave, "The Ford Brand Personality in Chile," *Corporate Reputation Review,* Fall 2004, pp. 232–51; Y. Sung and S. F. Tinkham, "Brand Personality Structures in the United States and Korea," *Journal of Consumer Psychology* 15, no. 4 (2005), pp. 334–50.

37. Aaker, "Dimensions of Brand Personality." Also see T. Triplett, "Brand Personality Must Be Managed or It Will Assume a Life of Its Own," *Marketing News,* May 9, 1994, p. 9; D. MacInnis and V. Folkes, "Humanizing Brands: When Brands Seem to Be Like Me, Part of Me, and in a Relationship with Me," *Journal of Consumer Psychology* 27, no. 3 (2017), pp. 355–74.

38. K. Greenberg, "Levinson: Jaguar Ads to Stress Quality, Youth, a Bit of Humor," *Brandweek,* April 26, 2004, p. 32; B. Russak, "Calling the Shots," *Footwear News,* October 25, 2004, p. 42; K. MacArthur and J. Neff, "Sprite Shifts Gears in Quest for Street Cred," *Advertising Age,* January 26, 2004, p. 1.

39. J. Aaker, S. Fournier, and S. A. Brasel, "When Good Brands Do Bad," *Journal of Consumer Research,* June 2004, pp. 1–16.

40. J. Aaker, K. D. Vohs, and C. Mogilner, "Nonprofits Are Seen as Warm and For-Profits as Competent," *Journal of Consumer Research,* August 2010, pp. 224–37.

41. From http://dragonrouge-usa.com/, accessed February 24, 2008.

42. For a detailed discussion, see D. A. Aaker, R. Batra, and J. G. Meyers, *Advertising Management,* 4th ed. (Englewood Cliffs, NJ: Prentice Hall, 1992), ch. 8. See also T. T. Wee, "Extending Human Personality to Brands," *Brand Management,* April 2004, pp. 317–30.

43. A. Mishra, S. Roy and A. Bailey, "Exploring Brand Personality-Celebrity Endorser Personality Congruence in Celebrity Endorsements in the Indian Context," *Psychology and Marketing* 32 (December 2015), pp. 1158–74.

44. S. Kang, "Nike, Serena Williams Partner Up," *Wall Street Journal,* December 12, 2003, p. B2; Nissan, "INFINITI and Stephen Curry Announce Global Partnership," press release, June 28, 2017, www.nissannews.com, accessed June 1, 2018.

45. B. Schneider-Levy, "Why These Major Comfort Shoe Brands Are Casting Regular Women as Models," *Footwear News,* February 9, 2018, www.footwearnews.com, accessed June 1, 2018.

46. Russak, "Calling the Shots"; "Listerine Mouthwash and PocketPaks," *Marketing Magazine,* November 18, 2002, p. C9; M. Warren, "Molson Debuts a Saucy Brazilian," *Marketing Magazine,* March 24, 2003, p. 2; A. Lutz, "Millennials Are Rejecting a Strategy Coach, Abercrombie & Fitch, and Michael Kors Have Relied on for Years," *Business Insider,* December 12, 2015, www.businessinsider.com, accessed June 1, 2018; L. Faw, "Keds Proclaims 'Ladies First' with Celeb-Backed Campaign," *Media Post,* February 26, 2016, www.mediapost.com, accessed June 1, 2018.

47. For a thorough discussion, see R. P. Bagozzi, M. Gopinath, and P. U. Nyer, "The Role of Emotions in Marketing," *Journal of the Academy of Marketing Science,* Spring 1999, pp. 184–207. See also M. E. Hill et al., "The Conjoining Influences of Affect and Arousal on Attitude Formation," *Research in Consumer Behavior* 9 (2000), pp. 129–46.

48. See, e.g., D. M. Phillips and H. Baumgartner, "The Role of Consumption Emotions in the Satisfaction Response," *Journal of Consumer Psychology* 12, no. 3 (2002), pp. 243–52; D. Martin et al., "The Role of Emotion in Explaining Consumer Satisfaction and Future Behavioural Intention," *Journal of Services Marketing* 22, no. 3 (2008), pp. 224–36.

49. See, e.g., D. J. Moore and P. M. Homer, "Dimensions of Temperament," *Journal of Consumer Psychology* 9, no. 4 (2000), pp. 231–42.

50. J. A. Ruth, F. F. Brunel, and C. C. Otnes, "Linking Thoughts to Feelings," *Journal of the Academy of Marketing Science,* Winter 2002, pp. 44–58.

51. See B. J. Babin, J. S. Boles, and W. R. Darden, "Salesperson Stereotypes, Consumer Emotions, and Their Impact on Information Processing," *Journal of the Academy of Marketing Science,* Spring 1995, pp. 94–105.

52. For a discussion of coping strategies, see S. Yi and H. Baumgartner, "Coping with Negative Emotions in Purchase-Related Situations," *Journal of Consumer Psychology* 14, no. 3 (2004), pp. 303–17.

53. See L. Dube and M. S. Morgan, "Trend Effects and Gender Differences in Retrospective Judgments of Consumption Emotions," *Journal of Consumer Research,* September 1996, pp. 156–62; J. L. Aaker and P. Williams, "Empathy versus Pride," *Journal of Consumer Research,* December 1998, pp. 241–61; M. Geuens and P. D. Pelsmacker, "Affect Intensity Revisited," *Psychology & Marketing,* May 1999, pp. 195–209.

54. J. A. Ruth, "Promoting a Brand's Emotion Benefits," *Journal of Consumer Psychology* 11, no. 2 (2001), pp. 99–113.

55. See K. T. Lacher and R. Mizerski, "An Exploratory Study of the Responses and Relationships Involved in the Evaluation of, and in the Intention to Purchase, New Rock Music," *Journal of Consumer Research,* September 1994, pp. 366–80.

56. L. C. Wang et al., "Can a Retail Web Site Be Social?," *Journal of Marketing,* July 2007, pp. 143–57.

57. I. Soscia, "Gratitude, Delight, or Guilt," *Psychology and Marketing,* October 2007, pp. 871–94; R. W. Palmatier et al., "The Role of Customer Gratitude in Relationship Marketing," *Journal of Marketing,* September 2009, pp. 1–18.

58. S. L. Wood and C. Page Moreau, "From Fear to Loathing?," *Journal of Marketing,* July 2006, pp. 44–57.

59. B. A. Huhmann and T. P. Brotherton, "A Content Analysis of Guilt Appeals in Popular Magazine Advertisements," *Journal of Advertising,* Summer 1997, pp. 35–45. Guilt appeals also are used by environmental groups, such as in T. Baek and S. Yoon, "Guilt and Shame: Environmental Message Framing Effects," *Journal of Advertising* 46, no. 3 (2017), pp. 440–53.

60. Based on A. Duhachek, "Coping," *Journal of Consumer Research,* June 2005, pp. 41–53.

61. M. F. Luce, "Choosing to Avoid," *Journal of Consumer Research,* March 1998, pp. 409–33.

62. N. M. Puccinelli, "Putting Your Best Face Forward," *Journal of Consumer Psychology* 16, no. 2 (2006), pp. 156–62.

63. Duhachek, "Coping."

64. B. Kidwell, D. M. Hardesty, and T. L. Childers, "Consumer Emotional Intelligence," *Journal of Consumer Research,* June 2008, pp. 154–66.

65. J. R. McColl-Kennedy et al., "Consumer Rage Episodes," *Journal of Retailing* 85, no. 2 (2009), pp. 222–37.

66. See L. F. Alwitt, "Suspense and Advertising Responses," *Journal of Consumer Psychology* 12, no. 1 (2002), pp. 35–49.

67. H. Mano, "Affect and Persuasion," *Psychology & Marketing,* July 1997, pp. 315–35; A. M. Isen, "An Influence of Positive Affect on Decision Making in Complex Situations," *Journal of Consumer Psychology* 11, no. 2 (2001), pp. 75–85.

68. A. Y. Lee and B. Sternthal, "The Effects of Positive Mood on Memory," *Journal of Consumer Research,* September 1999, pp. 115–27; K. R. Lord, R. E. Burnkrant, and H. R. Unnava, "The Effects of Program-Induced Mood States on Memory for Commercial Information," *Journal of Current Issues and Research in Advertising,* Spring 2001, pp. 1–14; S. J. Newell, K. V. Henderson, and B. T. Wu, "The Effects of Pleasure and Arousal on Recall of Advertisements during the Super Bowl," *Psychology & Marketing,* November 2001, pp. 1135–53.

69. M. Royo-Vela, "Emotional and Informational Content in Commercials," *Journal of Current Issues and Research in Advertising,* Fall 2005, pp. 13–38; C. Chang, "Context-Induced and Ad-Induced Affect," *Psychology & Marketing,* September 2006, pp. 757–82.

70. W. Janssens and P. De Pelsmacker, "Emotional or Informative?," *International Journal of Advertising* 24, no. 3 (2005), pp. 373–94; J. Kim and J. D. Morris, "The Power of Affective Response and Cognitive Structure in Product-Trial Attitude Formation," *Journal of Advertising,* Spring 2007, pp. 95–106.

71. B. M. Fennis and A. B. Bakker, "Stay Tuned—We Will Be Right Back after These Messages," *Journal of Advertising,* Fall 2001, pp. 15–25; J. D. Morris et al., "The Power of Affect," *Journal of Advertising Research,* May–June 2002, pp. 7–17; T. A. Shimp and E. W. Stuart, "The Role of Disgust as an Emotional Mediator of Advertising Effects," *Journal of Advertising,* Spring 2004, pp. 43–53.

72. E. Walther and S. Grigoriadis, "Why Sad People Like Shoes Better," *Psychology & Marketing,* October 2004, pp. 755–73; P. R. Darke, A. Chattapadhyay, and L. Ashworth, "The Importance and Functional Significance of Affective Cues in Consumer Choice," *Journal of Consumer Research,* December 2006, pp. 322–28.

73. See R. Adaval, "Sometimes It Just Feels Right," *Journal of Consumer Research,* June 2001, pp. 1–17.

74. B. Brunsman, "P&G Declared Winner of Olympic Advertising," *Cincinnati Business Courier,* August 24, 2016; J. Neff, "P&G Tackles Bias in New 'Proud Sponsor of Moms' Work," *Ad Age,* November 1, 2017, www.adage.com, accessed June 1, 2018.

chapter

11

Attitudes and Influencing Attitudes

©Pixtal/age fotostock

©Purestock/Getty Images

LEARNING OBJECTIVES

LO1 Define attitude and its role in consumer behavior.

LO2 Summarize the three components of attitudes.

LO3 Discuss attitude change strategies associated with each attitude component.

LO4 Describe the elaboration likelihood model of persuasion.

LO5 Describe the role of message source, appeal, and structure on attitudes.

LO6 Discuss segmentation and product development applications of attitudes.

Avocados today can be found everywhere, from grocery stores to trendy brunch places, and in everything, from guacamole to smoothies. But this fruit has not always enjoyed such popularity in the United States. Early 20th century Americans did not like this buttery green produce because its original name, *ahuacate,* translated to "testicle." It was too erotic by American standards and the name eventually became "avocado." Furthermore, avocados were sold as a luxury good, and prices were close to $24 in today's dollar for one avocado.[1]

What changed? Rudolph Hass, a postman, turned one tree into the patented Hass avocado tree. This tree produced large quantities of high-quality fruit and was adopted quickly by other avocado growers. Production soared, and prices fell, making it available to a larger audience. Sales of the fruit also rose with the influx of Latin American immigrants. But price, availability, and immigration were not the only reasons for the increase in popularity. Attitudes also have changed.

As we will discuss later in the chapter, brands and organizations can influence consumer behavior by changing attitudes. With avocados, existing beliefs were changed, and new beliefs added. By changing the name, the fruit was no longer negatively considered an aphrodisiac, as folklore once claimed. Also, with year-round production of avocados, the fruit was no longer seen as a rare treat to be consumed by those living where the fresh fruit is grown.

In recent years, marketers have promoted new beliefs about avocados. Besides encouraging weight loss, the avocado's health benefits are staggering, from fighting heart disease and diabetes, to helping prevent depression. Also, new usage occasions for consuming avocados are being emphasized. Avocados are no longer just for guacamole to be served with chips at parties. Avocados are now used as a condiment in avocado-oil mayonnaise or as a burger topping, an ingredient in ice cream, and a breakfast/brunch menu item like avocado toast. In fact, a recent Super Bowl advertisement by "Avocados of Mexico" used humor to emphasize this very point. According to one nutrition expert,

> Avocados truly deserve superfood status. . . . Avocado blends well with both sweet and savory ingredients, and provides the satisfaction factor that makes dishes decadent.

With these changed attitudes, avocado consumption in the U.S. has increased over 250 percent since 2002, with the average American eating seven pounds a year. Restaurants, including fast-food outlets like Wendy's and Subway, promote avocados on their menus to attract customers. Once unenthusiastically viewed as "Green Gold" and the "aristocrat of salad fruits," the avocado has solidified its overwhelming acceptance in today's American diet.

LO1

As the chapter's opening example indicates, brands and organizations attempt to influence consumer attitudes and their resulting consumption behaviors.

An **attitude** is *an enduring organization of motivational, emotional, perceptual, and cognitive processes with respect to some aspect of our environment.* It is a learned predisposition to respond in a consistently favorable or unfavorable manner with respect to a given object. Thus, an attitude is the way one thinks, feels, and acts toward some aspect of his or her environment, such as a retail store, television program, or product.[2] Attitudes are formed as the result of all the factors we have discussed in previous chapters, and they represent an important influence on an individual's lifestyle. In this chapter, we examine attitude components, general attitude change strategies, and the effect of marketing communications on attitudes.

ATTITUDE COMPONENTS

LO2

As Figure 11–1 illustrates, it is useful to consider attitudes as having three components: cognitive (beliefs), affective (feelings), and behavioral (response tendencies). Each of these attitude components is discussed in more detail below.

Cognitive Component

The **cognitive component** consists of *a consumer's beliefs about an object.* For most attitude objects, people have a number of beliefs. For example, an individual may believe that AMP beverages

- Are popular with younger consumers.
- Provide consumers with lots of energy.
- Contain a lot of vitamins.
- Are priced competitively with other energy drinks.
- Are made by a sports-oriented company.

FIGURE 11-1   Attitude Components and Manifestations

Initiator	Component	Component manifestation	Attitude
Stimuli: Products, situations, retail outlets, sales personnel, advertisements, and other attitude objects	Affective	Emotions or feelings about specific attributes or overall object	Overall orientation toward object
	Cognitive	Beliefs about specific attributes or overall object	
	Behavioral	Behavioral intentions with respect to specific attributes or overall object	

The total configuration of beliefs about this beverage brand represents the cognitive component of an attitude toward AMP. Beliefs can be about the emotional benefits of owning or using a product (one can believe it would be exciting to own or drive a convertible) as well as about objective features.[3] Many beliefs about attributes are evaluative in nature; for example, high gas mileage, attractive styling, and reliable performance are generally viewed as positive beliefs. This brings up the distinction between a *feature* and a *benefit,* both of which are beliefs. A product may have five milligrams of sodium per serving (a nonevaluative *feature* belief), which means that it is low in sodium and better for your health (both evaluative *benefit* beliefs). Marketers must promote benefits rather than features, especially for less-knowledgeable consumers and for complex products. Otherwise consumers will not know how to evaluate and respond to the claims.[4] For example, Quaker Oats helps consumers interpret the nutritional information on its package with statements such as "the soluble fiber in oatmeal can help reduce cholesterol."

The more positive beliefs associated with a brand, the more positive each belief is, and the easier it is for the individual to recall the beliefs, the more favorable the overall cognitive component is presumed to be.[5] And because all the components of an attitude are generally consistent, the overall attitude is more favorable. This logic underlies what is known as the **multiattribute attitude model.**

Multiattribute Attitude Model   There are several versions of this model. The simplest is

$$A_b = \sum_{i-1}^{n} X_{ib}$$

where

A_b = Consumer's attitude toward a particular brand b

X_{ib} = Consumer's belief about brand b's performance on attribute i

n = Number of attributes considered

This version assumes that all attributes are equally important in determining our overall evaluation. However, a moment's reflection suggests that frequently a few attributes, such as price, quality, or style, are more important than others. Thus, it is often necessary to add an importance weight for each attribute:

$$A_b = \sum_{i=1}^{n} W_i X_{ib}$$

where

W_i = The importance the consumer attaches to attribute i

This version of the model is useful in a variety of situations. However, it assumes that more (or less) is always better. This is frequently the case. More miles to the gallon is always better than fewer miles to the gallon, all other things being equal. This version is completely adequate for such situations.

For some attributes, more (or less) is good up to a point, but then further increases (decreases) become bad. For example, adding salt to a saltless pretzel generally will improve the consumer's attitude toward the pretzel up to a point. After that point, additional amounts of salt will decrease the attitude. Thus, we need to introduce an *ideal point* into the multiattribute attitude model:

$$A_b = \sum_{i=1}^{n} W_i |I_i - X_{ib}|$$

where

I_i = Consumer's ideal level of performance on attribute i

Because multiattribute attitude models are used widely by marketing researchers and managers, we will work through an example using the weighted, ideal point model. The simpler models would work in a similar manner.

Imagine that Coca-Cola gathers data on a set of beliefs about Diet Coke from a segment of consumers (more details on measuring the various attitude components can be found in Appendix A and Appendix Table A–3). These consumers perceive Diet Coke to have the following levels of performance (the Xs) and desired performance (the Is) on four attributes:

	(1)	(2)	(3)	(4)	(5)	(6)	(7)	
Low price			I	X				High price
Sweet taste		I				X		Bitter taste
High status			I		X			Low status
Low calories	IX							High calories

This segment of consumers believes (the Xs) that Diet Coke is average priced, very bitter in taste, somewhat low in status, and extremely low in calories. Their ideal soda (the Is) would be slightly low priced, very sweet in taste, somewhat high in status, and extremely low in calories. Because these attributes are not equally important to consumers, they are assigned weights based on the relative importance a segment of consumers attaches to each.

A popular way of measuring importance weights is with a 100-point *constant-sum scale*. For example, the importance weights shown below express the relative importance of the four soft-drink attributes such that the total adds up to 100 points.

Attribute	Importance
Price	10
Taste	30
Status	20
Calories	40
	100 points

In this case, calories are considered the most important attribute, with taste slightly less important. Price is given little importance.

From this information, we can index this segment's attitude toward Diet Coke as follows:

$$A_{\text{Diet Coke}} = (10)(|3 - 4|) + (30)(|2 - 6|) + (20)(|3 - 5|) + (40)(|1 - 1|)$$
$$= (10)(1) + (30)(4) + (20)(2) + (40)(0)$$
$$= 170$$

This involves taking the absolute difference between the consumer's ideal soft-drink attributes and beliefs about Diet Coke's attributes and multiplying these differences by the importance attached to each attribute. In this case, the attitude index is computed as 170. Is this good or bad? Because an attitude index is relative, to fully evaluate it, we must compare it with the segment's attitudes toward competing brands. However, if Diet Coke were perceived as the ideal soft drink, an attitude index of zero would result. Thus, the closer to zero an attitude index calculated in this manner is, the better. It is important to note that, in general, the multiattribute attitude model merely *represents* a process that is much less precise and structured than implied by the model.

Affective Component

Feelings or *emotional reactions to an object* represent the **affective component** of an attitude. A consumer who states, "I like Diet Coke" or "Diet Coke is a terrible soda," is expressing the results of an emotional or affective evaluation of the product. This overall evaluation may be simply a vague, general feeling developed without cognitive information or beliefs about the product. Or it may be the result of several evaluations of the product's performance on each of several attributes. Thus, the statements "Diet Coke tastes bad" and "Diet Coke is not good for your health" imply a negative affective reaction to specific aspects of the product that, in combination with feelings about other attributes, will determine the overall reaction to the brand.

DESIGNED WITH PURPOSE

MARVIN

Source: Marvin Windows and Doors

Marketers are increasingly turning their attention to the affective or "feeling" component of attitudes to provide a richer understanding of attitudes than that based solely on the cognitive or "thinking" component. As a consequence, marketers now commonly distinguish *utilitarian* or functional benefits and attitudes from *hedonic* or emotional benefits and attitudes.[6] For example, one study found that consumer acceptance of handheld Internet devices was influenced by both utilitarian benefits such as usefulness and hedonic aspects such as fun to use.[7] Another study found that in some cases hedonic aspects of giving blood such as fear and joy were stronger determinants of overall attitude toward blood donation than utilitarian beliefs.[8]

In addition, marketers are beginning to consider both form *and* function in product designs and focus considerable attention on the aesthetic aspects of design (appearance, sensory experience). The iPhone and iPad are examples of products with high **aesthetic appeal** that tap consumers' affective reactions by going beyond the cognitive associations of functionality.[9] The Marvin Windows ad in Illustration 11-1 shows a product high in aesthetic appeal.

Affective reactions to a specific product or benefit can vary by situation and individual. For example, a consumer's belief that Diet Coke has caffeine may result in positive feelings if he or she needs to stay awake to work late but negative feelings if he or she wants to get to sleep quickly. The Swanson ad in Illustration 11-2 is an example of an affective ad that likely will bring about emotional reactions to a number of the captions, such as "giving thanks."

Marketers sometimes measure the affective component on verbal scales much like those used to measure the cognitive component (for more detail, see Appendix A and Appendix Table A-3). So, consumers might be asked to rate Diet Coke overall (or specific attributes such as taste) on the following dimensions by placing an X in the appropriate space:

	(1)	(2)	(3)	(4)	(5)	(6)	(7)	
Good								Bad
Like								Dislike
Happy								Sad
Pleasant								Unpleasant

Individuals differ in their affective reactions to product characteristics. Likewise, the same individual will react differently to the same attribute in different situations. Would you enjoy an experience that induced the following, as shown within this Swanson ad?

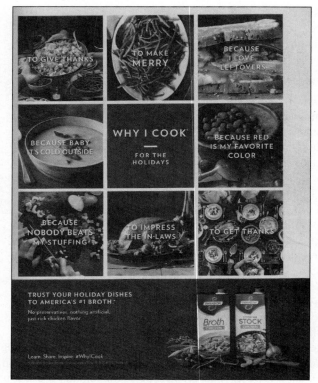

Source: CSC Brands, L.P.

SAM and AdSAM®   However, sometimes marketers want to tap feelings and emotions more directly and bypass the cognitive processing that often goes along with verbal scales. One such measure is SAM based on the three dimensions of emotion called pleasure-arousal-dominance (PAD) and AdSAM® where the same dimensions are referred to as Appeal, Engagement and Empowerment. Emotional approaches in advertising are discussed in Chapter 10.

The AdSAM® measurement system, termed the Attitude Self-Assessment Manikin, provides 199 descriptive adjectives of which the most relevant are selected by the AdSAM® model and included in the AdSAM® output. This system is designed to be most useful in advertising and marketing communication planning and evaluation. The AdSAM® graphical character directly taps into an individual's emotional response and has been shown to be highly predictive of intended behavior and recall of messages. From a global standpoint, AdSAM® is effective across different cultures and languages because the pictorial representations don't require translation or alteration.[10] AdSAM® as shown for each dimension on the following page as follows: top panel—Appeal; middle—Engagement; bottom—Empowerment. An interactive sample survey can be found at www.adsam.com

Behavioral Component

The **behavioral component** of an attitude is *one's tendency to respond in a certain manner toward an object or activity.* A series of decisions to purchase or not purchase Diet Coke or to recommend it or other brands to friends would reflect the behavioral component. Brand interest, as represented by tendencies to seek out the brand on store shelves or search for brand information, also reflects the behavioral component. The behavioral component provides response tendencies or behavioral intentions. *Actual behaviors reflect these intentions as they are modified by the situation in which the behavior will occur.*

Source: Copyright 2000 AdSAM Marketing LLC.

Direct versus Indirect Approach   Actual behaviors and response tendencies are most often measured by fairly direct questioning (for more detail, see Appendix A and Appendix Table A-3). For example, consumers might be asked about their intentions to buy Diet Coke, as follows:

How likely is it that you will buy Diet Coke the next time you purchase a soft drink (put an X in the appropriate space)?

Definitely Will	Probably Will	Might	Probably Will Not	Definitely Will Not
___	___	___	___	___

Such direct questioning may work well for most consumption, but not so well for sensitive topics such as alcohol, pornography, and eating patterns where consumers may understate negative behaviors or intentions. In these cases, asking *indirect* questions such as estimating the behaviors of other people similar to themselves (neighbors, those with similar jobs, etc.) may help reduce the bias.

Component Consistency

Figure 11-2 illustrates a critical aspect of attitudes: *All three attitude components tend to be consistent.*[11] This means that a change in one attitude component tends to produce related changes in the other components. This tendency is the basis for a substantial amount of marketing strategy.

FIGURE 11-2   Attitude Component Consistency

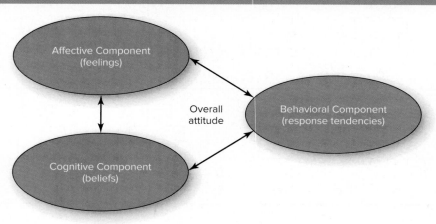

Marketing managers ultimately are concerned with influencing behavior. But it is often difficult to influence behavior directly. Marketers generally are unable to directly cause consumers to buy, use, or recommend their products. However, consumers often will listen to sales personnel, attend to advertisements, or examine packages. Marketers, therefore, can indirectly influence behavior by providing information, music, or other stimuli that influence a belief or feeling about the product if the three components are indeed consistent with each other.

Some research has found only a limited relationship among the three components.[12] Let's examine the sources of this inconsistency by considering an example. Suppose an individual reports positive beliefs and affect toward the iPhone but does not own an iPhone or purchases another brand. At least six factors may account for inconsistencies between *measures* of beliefs and feelings and *observations* of behavior.

1. *Lack of need.* A favorable attitude requires a need or motive before it can be translated into action. Thus, the consumer may not feel a need for a smartphone or might already own an acceptable, though less-preferred, brand.
2. *Lack of ability.* Translating favorable beliefs and feelings into ownership requires ability. The consumer might not have sufficient funds to purchase an iPhone; thus, she might purchase a less-expensive brand.
3. *Relative attitudes.* In the prior example, only attitudes toward the iPhone were considered. However, purchases often involve trade-offs across competing brands. Thus, a consumer may have a relatively high attitude toward the iPhone but a slightly higher attitude toward a competing brand. In a choice situation, relative attitudes are a stronger predictor of behavior.
4. *Attitude ambivalence.* While consumers often strive to hold consistent beliefs, feelings, and intentions toward a specific attitude object, this is not always the case. Sometimes a consumer has an **ambivalent attitude,** which involves *holding mixed beliefs and/or feelings about an attitude object.* Think of seafood. A consumer with an ambivalent attitude toward seafood would agree that "Sometimes I feel seafood tastes good, but other times I feel it tastes bad." Ambivalent attitudes are less stable over time and less predictive of behavior. Firms should avoid ambivalent attitudes by creating consistent messages and experiences over time. Firms also may attempt to gain market share by creating ambivalence among customers of competing brands.[13]

5. *Weak beliefs and affect.* If the cognitive and affective components are weakly held, and if the consumer obtains additional information while shopping, then the initial attitudes may give way to new ones. Specifically, stronger attitudes or those attitudes held with more confidence tend to be stronger predictors of behavior. Attitudes can be weak because of ambivalence. However, they also can be weak because of a general lack of experience with the brand. Thus, direct (and consistently positive) experience tends to yield attitudes that are more strongly and confidently held.[14] As a consequence, companies often spend enormous amounts of money on coupons and free samples to generate direct product experience.

In addition to direct experience, factors related to strength of learning such as importance, message involvement, reinforcement, and repetition (see Chapter 9) also are related to attitude strength because attitudes are generally learned.

6. *Interpersonal and situational influences.* An individual's attitudes were measured above. However, many purchase decisions involve others directly or indirectly. Thus, an office manager may purchase something other than an iPhone to better meet the needs of the entire staff. Situation and other consumers' expectations in those situations also can play a role. For example, it may be seen by some as more desirable to purchase and use an iPhone in front of friends (even though they themselves like another brand better) because their friends think the iPhone is the coolest brand.

In summary, attitude components—cognitive, affective, and behavioral—tend to be consistent. However, as we see, the degree of apparent consistency can be reduced by a variety of factors. Marketers must incorporate these factors when developing persuasive messages and strategies.

ATTITUDE CHANGE STRATEGIES

Marketers often attempt to influence consumer behavior by changing one or more of the underlying attitude components. Such influence can be positive, as we saw in the chapter's opening vignette. However, social, ethical, and regulatory concerns arise when companies attempt to promote potentially harmful consumption behaviors or when persuasion attempts are deemed deceptive.

Change the Cognitive Component

A common and effective approach to changing attitudes is to focus on the cognitive component.[15] Four basic marketing strategies—change beliefs, shift importance, add beliefs, and change ideal—are used for altering the cognitive structure of a consumer's attitude.

Change Beliefs This strategy involves shifting beliefs about the performance of the brand on one or more attributes.[16] The Morning Star Farms ad in Illustration 11-3 is a great example. Another example is Target, which is repositioning itself as a sleeker, more boutique-like retailer. Building on its "Tar-zhay" foundation, Target is trying to change existing merchandise by partnering with brands like Hunter (rain boots) and Magnolia (home décor). The company also is trying to improve perceptions of its grocery department. According to the CEO,

> It will be subtle changes. It may not be something we shout about, but we know the changes we're making in assortment and presentation and service. . . . They don't jump out at you, but we know what we've done and the guest responds well to it.[17]

The Morning Star Farms ad shows how marketers attempt to alter the cognitive component of an attitude by changing current beliefs, adding new beliefs, shifting the importance of beliefs, or changing the beliefs about the ideal product.

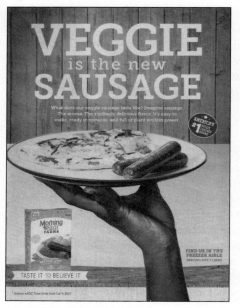

Source: Kellogg Co.

Attempts to change beliefs generally involve providing facts or statements about performance. It is important to realize that some beliefs are strongly held and thus hard to change. As a consequence, marketers may have more success changing overall brand attitudes by targeting weaker brand beliefs that are more vulnerable to persuasion attempts.[18]

Shift Importance   Most consumers consider some product attributes to be more important than others. Marketers often try to convince consumers that those attributes on which their brands are relatively strong are the most important. For example, General Motors uses detailed narratives of drivers in distress to emphasize the importance of instant communications and emergency assistance, which its OnStar system provides.

Sometimes evaluative factors that otherwise would not be prominent to consumers can be enhanced by cues in the ad. One study created ads with references to Asian culture (e.g., picture of the Great Wall of China) to enhance "ethnic self-awareness." When ethnic self-awareness was enhanced, Asian consumers reacted more positively to ads containing an Asian spokesperson.[19]

Add Beliefs   Another approach to changing the cognitive component of an attitude is to add new beliefs to the consumer's belief structure, as illustrated in the chapter opener. For example, similar to the avocado industry, the California Pomegranate Council wants consumers to know that beyond possessing vitamins and minerals (already known), new research shows that pomegranates contain "powerful antioxidants [that] help retard aging and can neutralize almost twice as many free radicals as red wine and seven times as many as green tea."[20]

Change Ideal   The final strategy for changing the cognitive component is to change the perceptions of the ideal brand or situation. Thus, many conservation organizations strive to influence our beliefs about the ideal product in terms of minimal packaging, nonpolluting manufacturing, extensive use of recycled materials, and nonpolluting disposition after its useful life.

Change the Affective Component

Firms increasingly attempt to influence consumers' liking of their brands without directly influencing either beliefs or behavior. If the firm is successful, increased liking will tend to lead to increased positive beliefs,[21] which could lead to purchase behavior should a need for the product arise. Or, perhaps more common, increased liking will lead to a tendency to purchase the brand should a need arise,[22] with purchase and use leading to increased positive beliefs. Marketers use three basic approaches to directly increase affect: classical conditioning, affect toward the ad itself, and mere exposure.

Classical Conditioning   One way of directly influencing the affective component is through classical conditioning (see Chapter 9). In this approach, a stimulus the audience likes, such as music, is consistently paired with the brand name. Over time, some of the positive affect associated with the music will transfer to the brand.[23] Other liked stimuli, such as pictures, frequently are used for this reason.

Affect toward the Ad or Website   As we saw in Chapter 10, liking the advertisement (attitude toward the ad, or Aad) generally increases the tendency to like the brand (attitude toward the brand, or Abr).[24] Somewhat similar results are associated with liking the website on which an ad appears (Aweb).[25] Using humor, celebrities, or emotional appeals increases Aad and Aweb. For example, vivid websites with rich sensory content that appeal to multiple senses produce more positive Aweb than do less-vivid sites.[26] The Sherwin Williams ad in Illustration 11–4 contains an ad that relies on positive affect.

Ads that arouse negative affect or emotions such as fear, guilt, or sorrow also can enhance attitude change. For example, an ad for a charity assisting refugees could show pictures that would elicit a variety of unpleasant emotions such as disgust or anger and still be effective.[27]

Mere Exposure   While controversial, there is evidence that affect or brand preference also may be increased by **mere exposure**.[28] That is, simply presenting a brand to an individual on a large number of occasions might make the individual's attitude toward the brand more positive. A common explanation of the mere exposure effect is that "familiarity breeds liking." Thus, the repetition of advertisements for low-involvement products may well increase liking (through enhanced familiarity) and subsequent purchase of the advertised

Source: The Sherwin-Williams Company

ILLUSTRATION 11-4

Ads can change the affective component of an attitude toward a brand without altering the belief structure if the ad itself elicits a positive response (is liked). Ads that are primarily pictorial, such as this Sherwin Williams ad, often are used for this purpose, though the pictures themselves convey cognitive as well as emotional meanings.

brands without altering the initial belief structure. Mere exposure effects underlie the use of simple reminder ads as well as product placements.[29]

Classical conditioning, Aad, and mere exposure can alter affect directly and, by altering affect, alter purchase behavior without first changing beliefs. This has a number of important implications:

- Ads designed to alter affect need not contain any cognitive (factual or attribute) information.
- Classical conditioning principles should guide such campaigns.
- Aad and ad-evoked affect are critical for this type of campaign unless mere exposure is being used.
- Repetition is critical for affect-based campaigns.
- Cognitively based measures may be inappropriate to assess advertising effectiveness.

As these guidelines suggest, classical conditioning, Aad, and mere exposure tend to occur in low-involvement situations (see Chapter 9). There is at least one major exception, however. When emotions and feelings are important product performance dimensions, then such feelings and emotions are relevant to the evaluation. In these situations, Aad can readily influence Abr under high involvement. As we discussed earlier in the chapter, hedonic (versus utilitarian) products are those for which affect and emotion are relevant performance criteria. Not surprisingly, hedonic products are those for which affect, emotions, and Aad can play a role in more conscious, high-involvement settings.[30]

Change the Behavioral Component

Behavior, specifically purchase or use behavior, may precede the development of cognition and affect. Or it may occur in contrast to the cognitive and affective components. For example, a consumer may dislike the taste of diet soft drinks and believe that artificial sweeteners are unhealthy. However, rather than appear rude, the same consumer may accept a diet drink when offered one by a friend due to social norms. Drinking the beverage may alter her perceptions of its taste and lead to liking; this in turn may lead to increased learning, which changes the cognitive component.

Behavior can lead directly to affect, to cognitions, or to both simultaneously.[31] Consumers frequently try new brands or types of low-cost items in the absence of prior knowledge or affect. Such purchases are as much for information (Will I like this brand?) as for satisfaction of some underlying need such as hunger.

Internet marketers have been particularly concerned about their ability to simulate direct experiences for products in a virtual context. One research study finds that for experiential products such as sunglasses, creating a *virtual direct experience* (in this case, a video that simulated viewing the content with and without the sunglasses) led to more positive beliefs, affect, and purchase intentions.[32] The ability to simulate experiences with products in an online context relates to the issue of "touch," which is a major online purchasing factor discussed in Chapter 17.

Changing behavior prior to changing affect or cognition is based primarily on operant conditioning (see Chapter 9). Thus, the key marketing task is to induce people to purchase or consume the product while ensuring that the purchase or consumption will indeed be rewarding.[33] Coupons, free samples, point-of-purchase displays, tie-in purchases, and price reductions are common techniques for inducing trial behavior. Because behavior often leads to strong positive attitudes toward the consumed brand, a sound distribution system (limited stockouts) is important to prevent current customers from trying competing brands.

INDIVIDUAL AND SITUATIONAL CHARACTERISTICS THAT INFLUENCE ATTITUDE CHANGE

LO4

Attitude change is determined by individual and situational factors as well as marketing activities.[34] Individual factors include gender, need for cognition, consumer knowledge, ethnicity, and, as we saw in Chapter 10, regulatory focus. Situational factors include program context, level of viewer distraction, and buying occasion.

Marketers continue to focus considerable attention on consumer involvement, which has both individual (intrinsic interest) and situational (current need to make a purchase decision) components. Consumer involvement is an important motivational factor that influences elaborative processing, learning, and attitudes. The **elaboration likelihood model (ELM)** is a theory about how attitudes are formed and changed under varying conditions of involvement. Thus, the ELM integrates select individual, situational, and marketing factors to understand attitudes.[35]

The ELM suggests that involvement is a key determinant of how information is processed and attitudes are changed. High involvement results in a *central route* to attitude change by which consumers deliberately and consciously process those message elements that they believe are relevant to a meaningful and logical evaluation of the brand (see Figure 11-3). These elements are elaborated on and combined into an overall evaluation. The multiattribute attitude model represents a high-involvement view of attitude change.

In contrast, low involvement results in a *peripheral route* to attitude change in which consumers form impressions of the brand based on exposure to readily available cues in the message regardless of their relevance to the brand or decision. Attitudes formed through the peripheral route are based on little or no elaborative processing. Classical conditioning, Aad, and mere exposure represent low-involvement views of attitude change.

The ELM suggests that vastly different communications strategies are required to communicate effectively with high- versus low-involvement consumers. In general, detailed factual information (central cues) is effective in high-involvement, central-route situations. Low-involvement, peripheral-route situations generally require limited information and instead rely on simple affective and cognitive cues such as pictures, music, and characteristics of people in the ad (peripheral cues). *Which persuasion route is most likely being used in Illustration 11-4?*

Cue Relevance and Competitive Situation

Generally speaking, compared with attitudes formed under the peripheral route, attitudes formed under the central route tend to be stronger, more resistant to counterpersuasion attempts, more accessible from memory, and more predictive of behavior.[36]

However, it is important to realize that central route processing involves extensive processing of *decision-relevant* information or cues. And what consumers find relevant can vary by product and situation. For example, an attractive picture can be peripheral or central. In an ad for orange soda, a picture of cute puppies would be a peripheral cue (and influence attitudes under low involvement), while a picture of fresh, juicy orange slices would be a central cue (and influence attitudes under high involvement).[37] Similarly, emotions likely represent a central cue for hedonic products and thus influence attitudes under high involvement.

In addition, the competitive situation also can work to enhance the role of peripheral cues even under high involvement. For example, if competing brands are comparable in terms of their product features (central cues), highly involved consumers prefer the brand with the strongest peripheral cues in its advertising.[38] The basic idea is that relative attitudes

FIGURE 11-3   The Elaboration Likelihood Model

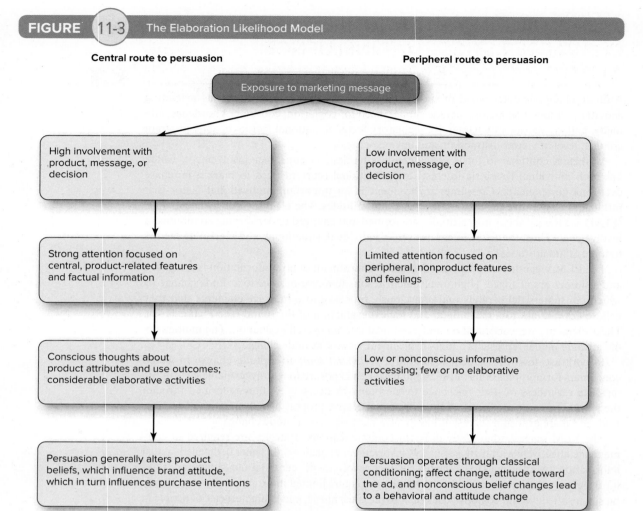

Central route to persuasion   **Peripheral route to persuasion**

Exposure to marketing message

High involvement with product, message, or decision

Low involvement with product, message, or decision

Strong attention focused on central, product-related features and factual information

Limited attention focused on peripheral, nonproduct features and feelings

Conscious thoughts about product attributes and use outcomes; considerable elaborative activities

Low or nonconscious information processing; few or no elaborative activities

Persuasion generally alters product beliefs, which influence brand attitude, which in turn influences purchase intentions

Persuasion operates through classical conditioning; affect change, attitude toward the ad, and nonconscious belief changes lead to a behavioral and attitude change

are critical in competitive settings and peripheral cues become the tiebreaker between otherwise equivalent (parity) brands. As you can see, the role of peripheral cues can extend beyond low-involvement settings in certain competitive situations.

Consumer Resistance to Persuasion

Consumers are not passive to persuasion attempts. Instead, consumers are often skeptical (an individual characteristic) and resist persuasion.[39] Also, consumers frequently infer an advertiser's intent and respond in light of that presumed selling intent.[40] For example, a recent ad for the American Pistachio Growers stated, "All snacks go with beer. Only one goes with a six pack." A consumer could respond to the ad as follows: "Of course they're going to tell me pistachios will make me healthy. They're trying to sell more pistachios. I'm still not convinced." To help reduce the likelihood of such responses, the ad makes use of the American Heart Association and scientific research to bolster its health claims.

Strongly held attitudes are harder to change than weakly held attitudes. Think of something you feel strongly about—perhaps your school or your favorite sports team. What would be required to change your attitude? Clearly, it would be difficult. Consumers tend to avoid messages that are counter to their attitudes (e.g., committed smokers tend to avoid anti-smoking ads). And if they do encounter such messages, they tend to (a) discredit the source as unreliable, (b) discount the importance of the issue or attribute at hand, and (c) if all else fails, "contain" the negative information so it doesn't "spill over" to the entire brand.[41] These behaviors are particularly likely for loyal customers of a brand—thus, it is possible to see why loyal customers can be so valuable to firms.

COMMUNICATION CHARACTERISTICS THAT INFLUENCE ATTITUDE FORMATION AND CHANGE

LO5

In this section, we describe communication techniques that can be used to form and change attitudes. Obviously, as with all aspects of consumer behavior, individual and situational characteristics interact with the communication features to determine effectiveness.

Source Characteristics

The source of a communication represents "who" delivers the message. Sources include people (celebrities, typical consumers), animated spokescharacters (Jolly Green Giant, Mr. Peanut), and organizations (the company, a third-party endorser). The source of a message is important because consumers respond differently to the same message delivered by different sources.

Source Credibility   Persuasion is easier when the target market views the message source as highly credible. **Source credibility** consists of *trustworthiness* and *expertise*. A source that has no ulterior motive to provide anything other than complete and accurate information generally would be considered trustworthy. However, product knowledge is required for a source to have expertise. Thus, a friend might be trustworthy but lack expertise. Alternatively, salespeople and advertisers may have ample knowledge but be viewed with skepticism by consumers.

Individuals who are recognized experts and who have no apparent motive to mislead can be powerful sources because of their ability to reduce risk.[42] An example is 1-800-PetMeds®, with its TV advertisements in which a veterinarian discusses pain management options for your pet. Relatively unknown individuals similar to those in the target market can be effective spokespersons as well, but for different reasons. In a **testimonial ad,** *a person, generally a typical member of the target market, recounts his or her successful use of the product, service, or idea.*[43] Testimonials are important on the web as well. Amazon and other online marketers offer customer reviews, which appear to be important determinants of attitudes and purchase behavior.[44] Similarity of the source enhances the believability and relevance of these testimonials.

Independent *third-party endorsements* by organizations such as the American Dental Association (ADA) are widely viewed as both trustworthy and expert by consumers and are actively sought by marketers. Such endorsements appear to be used by consumers as brand-quality cues.[45] The remarkable success of Crest toothpaste is largely attributable to the ADA endorsement. Other examples include

- The American Heart Association—Quaker Oats and Subway.
- J.D. Power and Associates—Edward Jones.
- Good Housekeeping Seal of Approval—LiftMaster garage doors.

Of course, the company itself is the most obvious source of most marketing messages. This means developing a corporate reputation or image for trustworthiness can greatly enhance the impact of the firm's marketing messages.[46] Furthermore, where the company places those messages can enhance believability, such as on the package versus in an advertisement.[47]

Source credibility can influence persuasion in various situations. First, a credible source can enhance attitudes when consumers lack the ability or motivation to form direct judgments of the product's performance.[48] This is more of a low-involvement process. Second, a credible source can enhance message processing and acceptance. In fact, expert sources can increase attitudes in some high-involvement settings as a result of their perceived decision relevance.[49]

Cultural differences also can play a role. For example, Thai consumers are more influenced by expert sources than are Canadian consumers. Thai consumers are more risk averse and more likely to defer to authority, thus making them more prone to external sources of influence.[50]

One factor that can diminish the credibility of any source is if consumers believe that the firm is paying the source for his or her endorsement.[51] This is especially relevant for celebrities and athletes who are paid large sums for their endorsements.

Celebrity Sources   Celebrities are widely used in advertising. Marketers are increasingly using culturally diverse celebrities to reach an ethnically diverse U.S. population. Halle Berry (Revlon), LeBron James (Nike), Sofia Vergara (Rooms To Go), and Apolo Ohno (Hershey's) are just a few such celebrities with endorsement contracts or their own product lines.

A visible use of celebrity endorsers has been the decades-long mustache campaign for milk. The L'Oréal ad in Illustration 11–5 clearly targets the growing ethnic market in the United States.

Celebrity sources are effective for a variety of reasons:[52]

Source: The L'Oréal Group

- *Attention.* Celebrities may attract attention to the advertisement. Consumers tend to be curious about celebrities and are drawn to ads in which they appear.
- *Attitude toward the ad.* A celebrity's likeability and popularity often translate into higher Aad, which can enhance brand attitudes.
- *Trustworthiness.* Despite being paid for their endorsements, celebrities often develop strong and credible public personas that consumers trust—and this trust translates into purchases. Even a genuine smile also can increase purchase intentions.[53] One study finds that private actions are just as important as professional achievements for many consumers, which explains why personal scandals can lead to a company firing an endorser, such as Kellogg's dropping Michael Phelps.[54]

- *Expertise.* Some celebrities are also experts. This occurs frequently in areas such as music and sports. Sabian's partnership with Neil Peart is an example in music. Nike's partnership with Tiger Woods in golf apparel is an example in sports.
- *Aspirational aspects.* Consumers may identify with or desire to emulate the celebrity. As a consequence, they may imitate the behavior and style of a celebrity through purchases of similar brands and styles. For example, popular actresses often lead the way in terms of clothing and hair styles for young women.
- *Meaning transfer.* Consumers may associate known characteristics of the celebrity with attributes of the product that coincide with their own needs or desires. For example, with a loyal and strong fan base including over 100 million Instagram followers, Selena Gomez is seen as a powerful icon. Coach partnered with Gomez to design fashion accessories for the "authentic, honest woman . . . and Selena possesses that ease and that romantic charm and that cool confident attitude."[55]

As the last point suggests, effectiveness of a celebrity endorser can generally be improved by matching the image of the celebrity with the personality of the product and the actual or desired self-concept of the target market.

When the three components shown in Figure 11–4 are well matched, effective attitude formation or change can result.[56] For example, Rihanna "has captured the fashion world with her fearless approach and experimental attitude" with her Fenty x Puma clothing and shoes line. Her recently launched Savage x Fenty reflects her edgy yet empowering attitude: "I want women to own their beauty."[57] In this case, there should be a strong match between the celebrity, the clothing line, and the female consumers who want to emulate the singer's style and personality. Sometimes images don't mesh and should be avoided. For example, Burger King canceled talks with Paris Hilton when it decided her racy image might be too extreme for the franchise.[58] A recent study also supports the importance of match-up in sports marketing in China.[59]

Using a celebrity as a company spokesperson creates special risks. One risk is overexposure. If a celebrity endorses many products, consumers' reactions may become less positive. Thus, marketers might consider limiting the number of products "their" celebrities endorse.[60] An additional risk is that negative behavior involving the spokesperson will affect the individual's credibility and, in turn, damage the firm's image.[61] Rawlings and Nike terminated their deals with Michael Vick after his indictment for dog fighting. And to protect

Matching Endorser with Product and Target Audience   **FIGURE** 11-4

its family image, NASCAR was quick to penalize Dale Earnhardt Jr. for using profanity in an interview. And PLBS, a Pittsburgh company that made Big Ben Beef Jerky, terminated its contract with Ben Roethlisberger after several off-field scandals, citing their "morals clause."

Rather than use celebrities, many firms, as discussed in Chapter 7, are turning to brand ambassadors or social media influencers ("influentials") to promote their brands. In addition, many firms are creating **spokescharacters.**[62] Tony the Tiger and the Green Giant are perhaps the most famous, although Geico's gecko and Aflac's duck have quickly become household names. Spokescharacters can be animated animals, people, products, or other objects. A major advantage of spokescharacters is complete image control. This eliminates many of the problems associated with real celebrities. Such characters come to symbolize the brand and give it an identity that competitors cannot easily duplicate. Illustration 11–6 shows how M&M's uses spokescharacters as product symbols.

Sponsorship   **Sponsorship,** *a company providing financial support for an event* such as the Olympics or a concert, is one of the most rapidly growing marketing activities and a multibillion-dollar industry.[63] Sponsorships in North America continue to grow and total spending exceeds $23 billion per year.[64] One high-profile example is Monster Energy's replacement of Sprint as NASCAR's title sponsor.[65] Another example is Coke's sponsorship of the FIFA World Cup.[66] The potential to generate goodwill in sports sponsorships is particularly high among rabid fans.[67] These fans may react along these lines: "Adidias supports my team, so I'm going to support Adidas."

Sponsorships often work in much the same manner as using a celebrity endorser, and the matchup described in Figure 11–4 is important (where the sponsor replaces the endorser

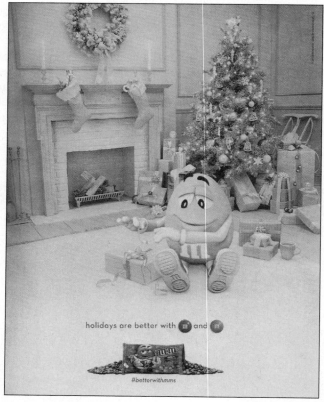

Source: Mars, Incorporated and its Affiliates

in Figure 11–4). Mismatches can generate consumer backlash such as the negative reactions over an Ohio hospital's plan to name its children's emergency and trauma center after Abercrombie & Fitch, a company that advocacy groups see as engaging in "not-exactly-child-friendly advertising."[68] Sponsor match-up is important in countries such as France and Australia as well.[69]

Finally, it is important to remember that sponsorships should be promoted through offline, online, and social media to maximize awareness and effectiveness.

Appeal Characteristics

As you would expect, the nature of the appeal, or "how" a message is communicated, affects attitude formation and change.

Fear Appeals

The picture at the top of an ad is a snapshot of a young couple sitting together on their back deck. The headline reads: "I woke up in the hospital. Patti never woke up." The copy describes how carbon monoxide poisoning caused the tragedy. The ad, one of a series of similar ads, is for First Alert carbon monoxide detector.

Fear appeals use *the threat of negative (unpleasant) consequences if attitudes or behaviors are not altered.* Fear appeals have been studied primarily in terms of physical fear (physical harm from smoking, unsafe driving, and eating genetically modified foods), but social fears (disapproval of one's peers for incorrect clothing, bad breath, or smoking) also are used in advertising.[70]

There is some evidence that individuals avoid or distort extremely threatening messages. At the same time, fear appeals tend to be more effective as higher levels of fear are aroused. Thus, those using fear appeals want to maximize the level of fear aroused while not presenting a threat so intense as to cause the consumer to distort, reject, or avoid the message. This task is difficult because individuals respond differently to threats. Thus, the same "threatening" advertisement may arouse no fear in one individual or group and a high level of fear in another.[71] To further complicate matters, creating fear may not be enough. Recent research suggests that making people feel *accountable* to act by playing on guilt or regret emotions (e.g., ad for heart attack prevention medicine showing what the family goes through if you fail to act and die from a heart attack) also may be necessary to induce desired behaviors.[72] Consumer Insight 11–1 provides an example of both the tripartite attitude approach and fear appeals in the efforts to decrease cigarette consumption in the United States.

Examine Illustration 11–7. *Is this U.S. Department of Transportation ad an effective use of a fear appeal?*

Fear appeals are frequently criticized as unethical. Frequent targets of such criticisms are fear appeals based on social anxieties about bad breath, body odor, dandruff, or soiled clothes. The thrust of these complaints is that these appeals raise anxieties unnecessarily; that is, the injury or harm that they suggest will occur is unlikely to occur or is not really harmful. Fear appeals used to produce socially desirable behaviors such as avoiding drug use or avoiding acknowledged physical risks such as carbon monoxide poisoning are subject to much less criticism.[73]

Humorous Appeals   At almost the opposite end of the spectrum from fear appeals are **humorous appeals.**[74] Ads built around humor appear to increase attention to and liking of the ad, particularly for those individuals high in *need for humor.*[75] It also increases attitude toward

Scare You Smokeless

Prior to the 1970s, cigarette smoking was a "perceived and promoted" healthy habit recommended by doctors, Santa Claus, and infants.[76] Cigarettes were packed with the c-rations provided to soldiers during WWII. Celebrities, including lovable cartoon characters Fred Flintstone and Barney Rubble of the long-running TV series *The Flintstones,* promoted the enjoyment of smoking cigarettes.

Today smoking cigarettes is understood to be an unhealthy habit. The three pronged effort—affective, behavioral, cognitive—to decimate cigarette consumption, along with antismoking advertisements and the increase in cigarette prices, has been credited with the decline of smoking in the United States. To decrease consumer top-of-the-mind awareness (cognitive component), cigarette advertising was banned from TV and radio (1971). To make it harder to engage in smoking behavior, 38 states have some form of ban on smoking in enclosed public areas—restaurants, offices, theaters (behavioral component). To induce fear as a deterrent (affective component), cigarette packages were required to carry warning labels proclaiming its health hazard (1984).

In recent years, the suggestion for the United States to follow in the footsteps of 40 other countries—for example, Thailand, England, Canada—to include graphics, such as photos of diseased lungs and rotting teeth, on the health warning labels has been championed as a technique to aid efforts to prevent, decrease, and eliminate the consumption of tobacco. It is a more severe form of the fear appeal discussed previously and designed to operate directly via the affective component of attitudes (though it also likely indirectly operates via cascading effects on thoughts and behaviors). Research in other countries where the effort has been ongoing finds that consumers report that the graphic images help them to decrease cigarette consumption and prevent initial use. Whether or not the enactment of such a requirement in the United States would lead to similar results will remain moot. The courts have recently ruled that requiring cigarette

manufacturers to include graphics is a violation of the First Amendment right of free speech.

Cigarette manufacturers and governmental regulation bodies now will have to contend with the recent arrival of e-cigarettes. A battery-powered device that looks like a cigarette, e-cigarettes or electronic cigarettes vaporize a liquid solution that can deliver nicotine or non-nicotine flavorings smoke free. Too new to be a real commercial threat, but growing too fast to be ignored, cigarette manufacturers are hedging their bets by buying e-cigarette companies (in 2012, Lorillard bought e-cigarette company Blu for $135 million; in 2014 Altria announced it was buying e-cigarette company Green Smoke for $110 million) and developing their own e-cigarette brands, MarkTen (Altria) and Vuse (Reynolds). With insufficient information to know whether e-cigarettes will act as a deterrent or as a gateway to smoking conventional cigarettes and whether its long-term effect is less threatening to health than traditional cigarettes, governmental regulating bodies have waded tepidly into the regulation waters.

E-cigarettes are an interesting case study in attitude formation for new products. Companies are marketing the products as safe (cognitive component) and the users as sophisticated and individualistic (affective component), which will likely drive adoption in the future by consumers. Government regulating bodies are finding it hard to form "attitudes" towards this new nicotine delivery device due to the lack of information and research with which to form those attitudes. As we can see, attitudes are important for consumers, marketers, and government regulators.

Critical Thinking Questions

1. Describe each attitude component used in deterring cigarette smoking in the U.S.

2. Using what you know about fear appeals, do you think the graphic approach will work better than verbal warnings?

3. Find and evaluate an advertisement for e-cigarettes using the information from this chapter.

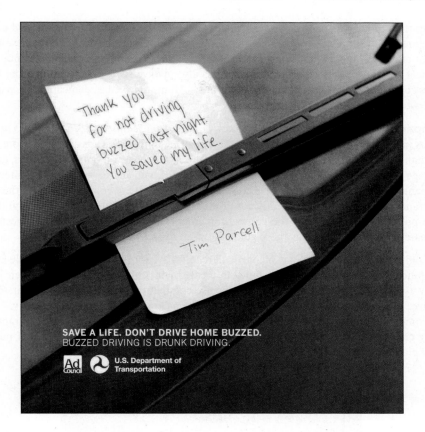

the brand.[77] The overall effectiveness of humor is generally increased when the humor relates to the product or brand in a meaningful way and is viewed as appropriate for the product by the target audience.[78] Illustration 11–8 shows an ad for Barilla that makes effective use of humor.

Here is another effective use of humor:

> Snickers' "You're just not you when you're hungry" featured Betty White whining during a touch football game, before eating a Snickers bar offered by a friend, and then turning back into himself. This ad aired during the Super Bowl and won *USA Today*'s ad meter award.[79] The humor points to how being hungry makes one grumpy and that Snickers satisfies that hunger. This campaign is still effective today. The Betty White ad was classic and started the Snickers campaign that is still in play.

While it is generally recommended that humor be relevant, companies have been successful using humor that is only loosely

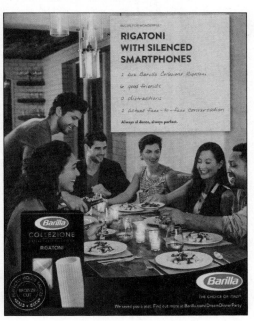

tied to the product (e.g., Geico's gecko ads in which the confusion between the two creates the humor, even though the gecko has nothing to do with auto insurance). In these cases, humor attracts attention, and the positive emotional response may transfer to the brand via classical conditioning or Aad.[80] Humorous ads also involve risk. What is considered funny varies across individuals, cultures, and situations.[81] Humor viewed as demeaning or insulting can cost a company image and sales.

Comparative Ads   Comparative ads *directly compare the features or benefits of two or more brands* (as shown in the Blue ad in Illustration 11–9). Comparative ads are often more effective than noncomparative ads in generating attention, message and brand awareness, greater message processing, favorable sponsor brand attitudes, and increased purchase intentions and behaviors. However, comparative ads also can have negative consequences for the sponsor brand such as lower believability, lower attitude toward the ad and sponsor brand, and more positive attitude toward the competitor brand(s).[82] Available evidence suggests that comparative ads should follow these guidelines:[83]

- Comparative advertising may be particularly effective for promoting new or little-known brands with strong product attributes to create their position or to upgrade their image by association. When established brands use comparative ads, they may appear "defensive." This may be particularly true if comparisons are seen as overly derogatory.
- Comparative advertising is likely to be more effective if its claims are substantiated by credible sources. Also, research should be used to determine the optimal number of claims.

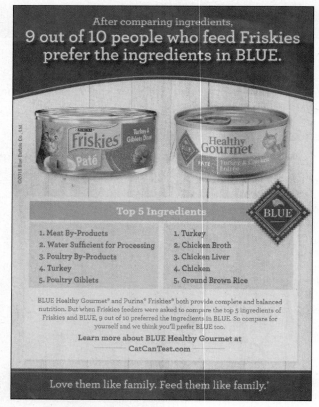

Source: Blue Pet Products, Inc

- Audience characteristics, especially brand loyalty associated with the sponsoring brand, are important. Users of the named competitor brands appear to resist comparative claims.
- Because comparative ads are more interesting than noncomparatives (and more offensive), they may be effective in stagnant categories where noncomparative ads have ceased to be effective.
- Print media appear to be better vehicles for comparative advertisements because print lends itself to more thorough comparisons.
- Care must be used with *partially* comparative ads because of their misleading potential. A partially comparative ad contains comparative and noncomparative information and may lead consumers to believe the sponsor brand is superior on all attributes, not just the compared attributes.

Emotional Appeals   Emotional or feeling ads are being used with increasing frequency. **Emotional ads** are *designed primarily to elicit a positive affective response rather than to provide information or arguments.* Emotional ads such as those that arouse feelings of warmth trigger physiological reactions (see Chapter 10). Emotional advertisements may enhance persuasion by increasing[84]

- Attention and processing of the ad and, therefore, ad recall.
- Liking of the ad.
- Product liking through classical conditioning.
- Product liking through high-involvement processes.

As we discussed previously, whether emotional ads operate through classical conditioning and Aad (low involvement) or through more analytical high-involvement processes depends on the relevance of the emotion to evaluating key aspects of the product.

In addition, emotional ads appear to work better than rational or informational ads for heavy (versus light) users of a brand and more established (versus new) brands in a market. This effect may be due to the fact that heavy users and established brands already have an established knowledge base for attribute information, making emotions a more compelling differentiating feature.[85] The "Don't Wait. Communicate." ad by FEMA in Illustration 11–10 is designed to elicit emotional responses. Furthermore, a recent study uncovered "contagious" consequences of emotional messages. Positive emotions evoked by one brand's message may transfer and, subsequently, benefit a proximately close but unrelated product.[86]

Value-Expressive versus Utilitarian Appeals
Value-expressive appeals attempt to build a personality for the product or create an image of the product user. **Utilitarian appeals** involve informing the consumer of one or more functional benefits that are important to the target market. Which is better under what conditions?

Both theory and some empirical evidence indicate that *utilitarian* appeals are most effective for functional products and *value-expressive* appeals are most effective for products designed to enhance self-image or provide other intangible benefits.[87]

ILLUSTRATION 11-10

Ads such as FEMA's "Don't Wait. Communicate." ad evoke powerful emotional responses in some individuals. These emotional responses often facilitate attitude change.

Source: Department of Homeland Security

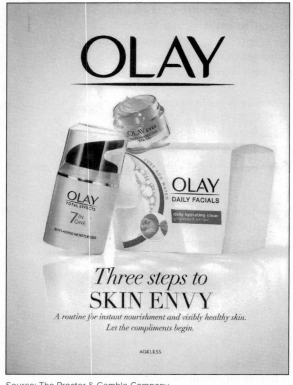

Source: The Procter & Gamble Company

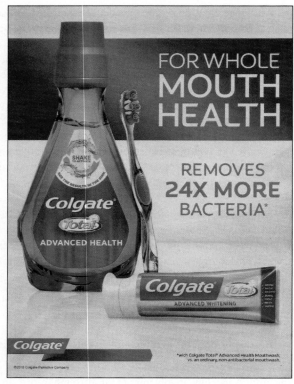

Source: Colgate-Palmolive Company

ILLUSTRATION 11-11

Utilitarian appeals such as the Colgate ad generally work best with functional products; value-expressive appeals such as the Olay ad work best with products designed to enhance one's image or provide other intangible benefits.

Which to use can be difficult when, as in the case of automobiles, many consider the product primarily utilitarian while many others consider it primarily value-expressive. Some marketers hedge their bets in such situations by appealing to both aspects simultaneously. Illustration 11–11 contains an example of each approach. Which appeal is primarily being used in the Olay ad versus the Colgate ad?

Research also indicates that banner ads on websites should differ for the two types of products. For utilitarian products, banner ads serve primarily to transport consumers to the more detailed target ads or sites. For value-expressive products, banner ads should influence attitudes on the basis of exposure to the banner ad itself, not on clickthrough to the target ad.[88]

Message Structure Characteristics

One-Sided versus Two-Sided Messages   In advertisements and sales presentations, marketers generally present only the benefits of their product without mentioning any negative characteristics it might possess or any advantages a competitor might have. These are **one-sided messages** because only one point of view is expressed. The idea of a **two-sided message,** presenting both good and bad points, is counterintuitive, and most marketers are reluctant to try such an approach. However, two-sided messages are generally more effective than one-sided messages in changing a strongly held attitude. One reason is because they are unexpected and increase consumer trust in the advertiser. They are particularly effective with highly educated consumers. One-sided messages are most effective at reinforcing existing attitudes. However, product type, situational variables, and advertisement format influence the relative effectiveness of the two approaches.[89]

Positive versus Negative Framing   **Message framing** refers to presenting one of two equivalent value outcomes either in positive or gain terms (positive framing) or in negative or loss terms (negative framing). There are various *types* of message frames, and the type of frame influences whether positive or negative framing is better.[90] The simplest form appears to be **attribute framing,** where only a single attribute is the focus of the frame. A classic example is describing ground beef as either 80 percent fat free (positive frame) or 20 percent fat (negative frame). In attribute framing situations, positive framing yields the most positive evaluations because it emphasizes the desirable aspects of the specific attribute.

Goal framing is where "the message stresses either the positive consequences of performing an act or the negative consequences of not performing the act."[91] The act could be purchasing a specific brand, having a yearly mammogram, and so on. In each case the act is beneficial. However, in the positive frame, the benefits of the act are emphasized (e.g., increased chance of finding a tumor), while in the negative frame, the risks of not engaging in the act are emphasized (e.g., decreased chance of finding a tumor). In goal-framing situations, the *negative* frame is generally more effective. This is likely due to the risk-averse nature of consumers coupled with the risk-enhancing nature of the negative goal frame.

Framing effects can vary across products, consumers, and situations. Thus, decisions to use positive or negative framing ultimately should be based on research for the specific product and market.[92]

Nonverbal Components   In Chapter 9, we discussed how pictures enhance imagery and facilitate learning. Pictures, music, surrealism, and other nonverbal cues are also effective in attitude change. Emotional ads, described earlier, often rely primarily or exclusively on nonverbal content to arouse an emotional response. Nonverbal ad content also can affect cognitions about a product. For example, an ad showing a person drinking a new beverage after exercise provides information about appropriate usage situations without stating "good to use after exercise." Thus, nonverbal components can influence attitudes through affect, cognition, or both.

MARKET SEGMENTATION AND PRODUCT DEVELOPMENT STRATEGIES BASED ON ATTITUDES

`LO6`

Market Segmentation

Identifying market segments is a key aspect of marketing. Properly designed marketing programs should be built around the unique needs of each market segment. The importance of various attributes is one way of defining customer needs for a given product. *Segmenting consumers on the basis of their most important attribute or attributes* is called **benefit segmentation.**[93]

To define benefit segments, a marketer needs to know the importance that consumers attach to various product or service features. This allows consumers who seek the same benefits to be grouped into segments. Additional information about consumers within each segment then can be obtained to develop a more complete picture of each segment. Based on this information, separate marketing programs can be developed for each of the selected target segments.

Product Development

While the importance consumers attach to key attributes provides a meaningful way to understand needs and form benefit segments, the ideal levels of performance indicate the consumers' desired level of performance in satisfying those needs. These ideal levels of

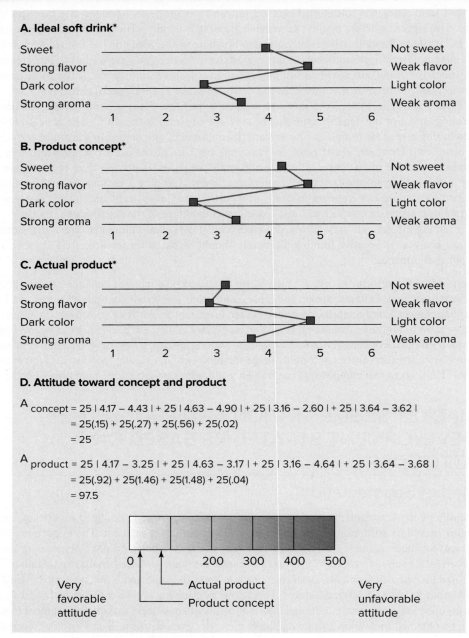

TABLE 11-1 Using the Multiattribute Attitude Model in the Product Development Process

A. Ideal soft drink*

	1	2	3	4	5	6	
Sweet							Not sweet
Strong flavor							Weak flavor
Dark color							Light color
Strong aroma							Weak aroma

B. Product concept*

	1	2	3	4	5	6	
Sweet							Not sweet
Strong flavor							Weak flavor
Dark color							Light color
Strong aroma							Weak aroma

C. Actual product*

	1	2	3	4	5	6	
Sweet							Not sweet
Strong flavor							Weak flavor
Dark color							Light color
Strong aroma							Weak aroma

D. Attitude toward concept and product

$$A_{concept} = 25 \mid 4.17 - 4.43 \mid + 25 \mid 4.63 - 4.90 \mid + 25 \mid 3.16 - 2.60 \mid + 25 \mid 3.64 - 3.62 \mid$$
$$= 25(.15) + 25(.27) + 25(.56) + 25(.02)$$
$$= 25$$

$$A_{product} = 25 \mid 4.17 - 3.25 \mid + 25 \mid 4.63 - 3.17 \mid + 25 \mid 3.16 - 4.64 \mid + 25 \mid 3.64 - 3.68 \mid$$
$$= 25(.92) + 25(1.46) + 25(1.48) + 25(.04)$$
$$= 97.5$$

0 — 200 — 300 — 400 — 500

Very favorable attitude

Actual product
Product concept

Very unfavorable attitude

*Measured on a six-point semantic differential scale.

performance can provide valuable guidelines in developing a new product or reformulating an existing one.

Table 11-1 describes how Coca-Cola used this approach in developing a new soft drink.[94] The first step is constructing a profile of a consumer segment's ideal level of performance on key soft-drink attributes. As shown in Table 11-1, four attributes were identified for a particular type of soft drink, and ideal performance was obtained from consumer ratings as shown in section A.

A second step is creating a product concept that closely matches the ideal profile. The concept could be a written description, picture, or actual prototype. As section B in Table 11–1 shows, consumers evaluated the product concept developed by Coca-Cola as being fairly close to their ideal on each of the four attributes. Only color appears to be off target slightly by being a little too dark.

The next step is translating the concept into an actual product. When Coca-Cola did this and presented the product to the consumers, they did not perceive it to be similar to either the product concept or their ideal (see section C in Table 11–1). Although the actual product achieved a reasonable attitude rating, the product concept scored higher (section D, Table 11–1). Thus, the product could benefit from further improvements to better align it with the ideal profile. This same basic procedure can be used to help design ads, packages, or retail outlets.

SUMMARY

LO1: Define attitude and its role in consumer behavior.

Attitudes can be defined as the way people think, feel, and act toward some aspect of their environment. As a result of all the factors discussed so far in the text, attitudes influence, as well as reflect, the lifestyle individuals pursue.

LO2: Summarize the three components of attitudes.

Attitudes have three components: cognitive, affective, and behavioral. The *cognitive component* consists of the individual's beliefs or knowledge about the object. It generally is assessed by using a version of the multiattribute attitude model. Feelings or emotional reactions to an object represent the *affective component* of the attitude and can be assessed in various ways including AdSAM®. The *behavioral component* reflects overt actions and statements of behavioral intentions with respect to specific attributes of the object or the overall object. In general, all three components tend to be consistent with each other. However, a number of factors can create inconsistencies and marketers must understand and incorporate these in their marketing research and communications strategies.

LO3: Discuss attitude change strategies associated with each attitude component.

Attitude change strategies can focus on affect, behavior, cognition, or some combination. Attempts to change affect generally rely on classical conditioning. Change strategies focusing on behavior rely more on operant conditioning. Changing cognitions usually involves information processing and cognitive learning. It can involve changing beliefs about such things as a brand's attribute levels, shifting the importance of a given attribute, adding beliefs about new attributes, or changing the perceived ideal point for a specific attribute or for the brand concept overall.

LO4: Describe the elaboration likelihood model of persuasion.

The *elaboration likelihood model (ELM)* is a theory about how attitudes are formed and changed under varying conditions of involvement. The ELM suggests different communications strategies depending on involvement. In general, detailed factual information (central cues) is effective in high-involvement, central route situations. Low-involvement, peripheral route situations generally require limited information and instead rely on simple affective and cognitive cues such as pictures, music, and characteristics of people in the ad (peripheral cues). The ELM has found general support. However, what is perceived as relevant can depend on the situation (e.g., attractive model and hair may be "central" in shampoo ad but "peripheral" in car ad), and the nature of competition can bolster the role of peripheral cues even under high involvement.

LO5: Describe the role of message source, appeal, and structure on attitudes.

Three communication characteristics are important to attitudes: source characteristics, message appeal characteristics, and message structure characteristics.

In terms of source characteristics, *source credibility* is composed of two dimensions: trustworthiness and expertise. Persuasion is much easier when the message source is viewed as highly credible. Celebrities are widely used as product or company spokespersons. They are most effective when their image matches the personality of the product and the actual or desired self-concept of the target market.

In terms of message appeals, the appeals used to change attitudes are important and are varied. *Fear appeals* use threat of negative consequences if attitudes or behaviors are not altered. *Humorous appeals* also can be effective in influencing attitudes. However, the humorous message must remain focused on the brand or main selling point to be maximally effective. *Comparative ads* produce mixed results. They are most effective for unknown brands having a strong functional advantage. The decision to use a *value-expressive* or *utilitarian appeal* depends on whether the brand fills value-expressive or utilitarian needs. However, this is complicated when the brand fills both types of needs. *Emotional appeals* have been found to have a strong effect on attitudes toward both the ad and the product.

Message structure has three facets. *Two-sided* (versus *one-sided*) *messages* can increase trust and message acceptance, but effects depend on characteristics of the individual and situation. *Message framing* effects—presenting equivalent value outcomes either in positive (positive framing) or negative (negative framing) terms—depend on type of frame. Positive *attribute framing* tends to work best whereas negative *goal framing* tends to work best. *Nonverbal* aspects of the ad, such as pictures, surrealism, and music, also affect attitudes.

LO6: Discuss segmentation and product development applications of attitudes.

Consumer evaluations, feelings, and beliefs about specific product features form the basis for market segmentation strategies, such as *benefit segmentation,* and for new-product development strategies.

KEY TERMS

Aesthetic appeal 401
Affective component 401
Ambivalent attitude 404
Attitude 398
Attribute framing 421
Behavioral component 402
Benefit segmentation 421
Cognitive component 398
Comparative ads 418

Elaboration likelihood
  model (ELM) 409
Emotional ads 419
Fear appeals 415
Goal framing 421
Humorous appeals 415
Mere exposure 407
Message framing 421
Multiattribute attitude model 398

One-sided messages 420
Source credibility 411
Spokescharacters 414
Sponsorship 414
Testimonial ad 411
Two-sided message 420
Utilitarian appeals 419
Value-expressive appeals 419

REVIEW QUESTIONS

1. What is an *attitude?*
2. What are the components of an attitude?
3. Are the components of an attitude consistent? What factors reduce the apparent consistency among attitude components?
4. What is the *multiattribute attitude model?*
5. What is *attitude ambivalence?*
6. What strategies can be used to change the following components of an attitude?
   a. Affective
   b. Behavioral
   c. Cognitive

7. What is meant by *mere exposure?*
8. What is the *elaboration likelihood model?*
9. What strategies can consumers use to resist persuasion? Which consumers are most likely to do so?
10. What are the two characteristics of the source of a message that influence its ability to change attitudes? Describe each.
11. What is *source credibility?* What causes it?
12. Why are celebrity sources sometimes effective? What risks are associated with using a celebrity source?

13. Name five possible characteristics of an appeal that would influence or change attitudes. Describe each.

14. Are *fear appeals* always effective in changing attitudes? Why?

15. What characteristics should *humorous ads* have?

16. Are *emotional appeals* effective? Why?

17. Are *comparative appeals* effective? Why?

18. What is a *value-expressive appeal?* A *utilitarian appeal?* When should each be used?

19. What are the three characteristics of the message structure that influence its ability to change attitudes? Describe each.

20. What is meant by *positive message framing* and *negative message framing?* How does the effectiveness of a positive versus negative frame vary depending on whether it's a *goal frame* or *attribute frame?*

21. What are the nonverbal components of an ad? What impact do they have on attitudes?

22. When is a *two-sided message* likely to be more effective than a *one-sided message?*

23. How can attitudes guide new-product development?

24. What is a *benefit segment?*

DISCUSSION QUESTIONS

25. Which version of the multiattribute attitude model and which attributes would you use to assess student attitudes toward the following? Justify your answer.
    a. Student health system
    b. Target store
    c. Hybrid automobiles
    d. Cats as pets
    e. Energy drinks

26. Respond to the questions in Consumer Insight 11-1.

27. Assume you wanted to improve or create favorable attitudes among college students toward the following. Would you focus primarily on the affective, cognitive, or behavioral component? Why?
    a. ASPCA
    b. BMW motorcycles
    c. Organic (cage-free) eggs
    d. Skydiving
    e. Not driving after drinking
    f. Using the bus for most local trips
    g. Oreo cookies
    h. Volunteering for Habitat for Humanity

28. Suppose you used the multiattribute attitude model and developed a fruit-based carbonated drink that was successful in the United States. Could you use the same model in the following countries? If not, how would it have to change?
    a. India
    b. Chile
    c. Qatar

29. Suppose you wanted to form highly negative attitudes toward smoking among college students.
    a. Which attitude component would you focus on? Why?
    b. Which message characteristic would you use? Why?
    c. What type of appeal would you use? Why?

30. What communications characteristics would you use in an attempt to improve college students' attitudes toward the following?
    a. Buick
    b. Levis
    c. Volunteering at a local shelter
    d. Yahoo!
    e. MADD
    f. White-water rafting

31. Is it ethical to use fear appeals to increase demand for the following?
    a. Complexion medication among teenagers
    b. Dandruff-control shampoos among adults
    c. Emergency response devices among elderly consumers
    d. Weight-loss supplements for young women

32. Name two appropriate and two inappropriate celebrity spokespersons for each of the products or causes in Question 27. Justify your selection.

33. What benefit segments do you think exist for the following?
    a. Crossroads Guitar Festival
    b. NASCAR
    c. Major art museums
    d. Jazz concert

APPLICATION ACTIVITIES

34. Find and copy two magazine or newspaper advertisements, one based on the affective component and the other on the cognitive component. Discuss the approach of each ad in terms of its copy and illustration and what effect it creates in terms of attitude. Also discuss why the marketer might have taken that approach in each advertisement.

35. Repeat Activity 34 for utilitarian and value-expressive appeals.

36. Identify a television commercial that uses a humorous appeal. Then interview five individuals not enrolled in your class and measure their
    a. Awareness of this commercial
    b. Recall of the brand advertised
    c. Recall of relevant information
    d. Liking of the commercial
    e. Preference for the brand advertised

    Evaluate your results and assess the level of communication that has taken place in terms of these five consumers' exposure, attention, interpretation, and preferences for this product and commercial.

37. Describe a magazine, Internet, or television advertisement, or a package that uses the following. Evaluate the effectiveness of the ad or package.
    a. Aesthetic appeal
    b. Source credibility
    c. Celebrity source
    d. Testimonial
    e. Fear appeal
    f. Humorous appeal
    g. Emotional appeal
    h. Comparative approach
    i. Extensive nonverbal elements
    j. A two-sided appeal
    k. Positive message framing
    l. Negative message framing

38. Measure another student's ideal beliefs and belief importance for the following. Examine these ideal beliefs and importance weights and then develop a verbal description (i.e., concept) of a new brand for these items that would satisfy this student's needs. Next, measure that student's attitude toward the concept you have developed in your verbal description.
    a. Sunglasses
    b. Spa
    c. Automobile
    d. Credit card
    e. Dietary supplements
    f. Charity

39. Use the multiattribute attitude model to assess 10 students' attitudes toward several brands in the following product categories. Measure the students' behavior with respect to these brands. Are they consistent? Explain any inconsistencies.
    a. Television news program
    b. Sports drinks
    c. Healthy dinners
    d. Fast-food restaurants
    e. Exercise
    f. Coffee shops

40. Develop two advertisements for the following with college students as the target. One ad should focus on the cognitive component and the other on the affective component.
    a. Timex sport watches
    b. Toyota Prius
    c. Red Bull energy drink
    d. Reducing smoking
    e. Increasing exercise
    f. Adidas athletic shoes

41. Repeat Activity 40 using utilitarian and value-expressive appeals.

42. Develop a positively framed and an equivalent negatively framed message about a product attribute. Have five students react to these messages. What do you conclude?

REFERENCES

1. This opener is based on R. Ferdman, "The Rise of The Avocado, America's New Favorite Fruit," *Washington Post,* January 22, 2015; A. MacMillan, "Why You Should Eat More Avocado," *Time,* April 13, 2017, www.time.com, accessed June 5, 2018; E. Rude, "Americans Are Totally Obsessed with Avocados Thanks to This Man," *Time,* June 27, 2017, www.time.com, accessed June 5, 2018; Mintel, "Seasonal Dining Trends—US—January 2018," January 2018, www.mintel.com, accessed June 5, 2018;

E. Brady, "Ad Meter 2018: Avocados from Mexico Aims to Leave Football Fans Laughing Again," *USA Today,* February 2, 2018, www.usatoday.com, accessed June 5, 2018; E. Bernstein, "The Food That Helps Battle Depression," *Wall Street Journal,* April 2, 2018, www.wsj.com, accessed June 5, 2018; M. Hemmes, "Since 2002, U.S. Avocado Consumption Has Grown 250 Percent," *Fresh Plaza,* April 23, 2018, www.freshplaza.com, accessed June 5, 2018; restaurant websites www.menu.wendys.com and www.subway.com, accessed June 5, 2018.

2. See R. E. Petty, D. T. Wegener, and L. R. Fabriger, "Attitudes and Attitude Change," *Annual Review of Psychology* 48 (1997), pp. 609–38.

3. J. A. Ruth, "Promoting a Brand's Emotional Benefits," *Journal of Consumer Psychology* 11, no. 2 (2001), pp. 99–113.

4. B. Wansink and M. M. Cheney, "Leveraging FDA Health Claims," *Journal of Consumer Affairs* 39, no. 2 (2005), pp. 386–98.

5. See M. Wanke, G. Bohner, and A. Jurkowitsch, "There Are Many Reasons to Drive a BMW," *Journal of Consumer Research,* September 1997, pp. 170–77.

6. K. E. Voss, E. R. Spangenberg, and B. Grohmann, "Measuring the Hedonic and Utilitarian Dimensions of Consumer Attitude," *Journal of Marketing Research,* August 2003, pp. 310–20; T. Lageat, S. Czellar, and G. Laurent, "Engineering Hedonic Attributes to Generate Perceptions of Luxury," *Marketing Letters,* July 2003, pp. 97–109; R. Chitturi, R. Raghunathan, and V. Mahajan, "Delight by Design," *Journal of Marketing,* May 2008, pp. 48–63.

7. G. C. Bruner II and A. Kumar, "Explaining Consumer Acceptance of Handheld Internet Devices," *Journal of Business Research* 58 (2005), pp. 553–58.

8. C. T. Allen et al., "A Place for Emotion in Attitude Models," *Journal of Business Research* 58 (2005), pp. 494–99.

9. C. Page and P. M. Herr, "An Investigation of the Processes by Which Product Design and Brand Strength Interact to Determine Initial Affect and Quality Judgments," *Journal of Consumer Psychology* 12, no. 2 (2002), pp. 133–47; H. Hagtvedt and V. M. Patrick, "Art Infusion," *Journal of Marketing Research,* June 2008, pp. 379–89.

10. J. D. Morris et al., "The Power of Affect," *Journal of Advertising Research,* May–June 2002, pp. 7–17; J. D. Morris, "Observations: SAM," *Journal of Advertising Research,* November–December 1995, pp. 63–68.

11. For an excellent review, see P. A. Dabholkar, "Incorporating Choice into an Attitudinal Framework," *Journal of Consumer Research,* June 1994, pp. 100–18. See also Morris et al., "The Power of Affect"; P. E. Grimm, "A_b Components' Impact on Brand Preference," *Journal of Business Research* 58 (2005), pp. 508–17; P. M. Homer, "Relationships among Ad-Induced Affect, Beliefs, and Attitudes," *Journal of Advertising,* Spring 2006, pp. 35–51.

12. R. E. Petty and J. A. Krosnick, *Attitude Strength* (Mahwah, NJ: Erlbaum, 1995); S. J. Kraus, "Attitudes and the Prediction of Behavior," *Personality and Social Psychology Bulletin* 21 (1995), pp. 58–75; R. Madrigal, "Social Identity Effects in a Belief-Attitude-Intentions Hierarchy," *Psychology & Marketing,* February 2001, pp. 145–65; W. E. Baker, "The Diagnosticity of Advertising Generated Brand Attitudes in Brand Choice Contexts," *Journal of Consumer Psychology* 11, no. 2 (2001), pp. 129–39.

13. S. O. Olsen, J. Wilcox, and U. Olsson, "Consequences of Ambivalence on Satisfaction and Loyalty," *Psychology & Marketing,*

March 2005, pp. 247–69; C. Homburg, N. Koschate, and W. D. Hoyer, "The Role of Cognition and Affect in the Formation of Customer Satisfaction," *Journal of Marketing,* July 2006, pp. 21–31. See also C. A. Roster and M. L. Richins, "Ambivalence and Attitudes in Consumer Replacement Decisions," *Journal of Consumer Psychology* 19 (2009), pp. 48–61.

14. See, e.g., J. R. Priester et al., "The A^2SC^2 Model: The Influence of Attitudes and Attitude Strength on Consideration and Choice," *Journal of Consumer Research,* March 2004, pp. 574–87; B. Johnson, "Consumers Cite Past Experience as the No. 1 Influencer When Buying," *Advertising Age,* November 20, 2006, p. 21.

15. See S. A. Hawkins, S. J. Hoch, and J. Meyers-Levy, "Low-Involvement Learning," *Journal of Consumer Psychology* 11, no. 31 (2001), pp. 1–11.

16. For guidelines on structuring message arguments to enhance beliefs, see C. S. Areni, "The Proposition–Probability Model of Argument Structure and Message Acceptance," *Journal of Consumer Research,* September 2002, pp. 168–87.

17. K. Kumar, "CEO Brian Cornell Says Target Is Speeding Up Change to Compete in Today's Retail World," *Star Tribune,* March 3, 2018, www.startribune.com, accessed June 8, 2018.

18. See A. Drolet and J. Aaker, "Off-Target?," *Journal of Consumer Psychology* 12, no. 1 (2002), pp. 59–68; A. H. Tangari et al., "How Do Antitobacco Campaign Advertising and Smoking Status Affect Beliefs and Intentions?," *Journal of Public Policy and Marketing,* Spring 2007, pp. 60–74.

19. M. R. Forehand and R. Deshpande, "What We See Makes Us Who We Are," *Journal of Marketing Research,* August 2001, pp. 336–48. See also J. K. Maher and M. Hu, "The Priming of Material Values on Consumer Information Processing of Print Advertisements," *Journal of Current Issues and Research in Advertising,* Fall 2003, pp. 21–30.

20. From website at www.pomegranates.org/techinfo.html, accessed June 10, 2011.

21. For a discussion of program-induced affect and extremity of beliefs, see R. Adaval, "How Good Gets Better and Bad Gets Worse," *Journal of Consumer Research,* December 2003, pp. 352–67.

22. See M. J. J. M. Candel and J. M. E. Pennings, "Attitude-Based Models for Binary Choices," *Journal of Economic Psychology* 20 (1999), pp. 547–69; H.-P. Erb, A. Bioy, and D. J. Hilton, "Choice Preferences without Inferences," *Journal of Behavioral Decision Making,* July 2002, pp. 251–62.

23. See, e.g., W. E. Baker, "When Can Affective Conditioning and Mere Exposure Directly Influence Brand Choice?," *Journal of Advertising,* Winter 1999, pp. 31–46; B. D. Till and R. L. Priluck, "Stimulus Generalization in Classical Conditioning," *Psychology & Marketing,* January 2000, pp. 55–72.

24. See, e.g., R. E. Goldsmith, B. A. Lafferty, and S. J. Newell, "The Impact of Corporate Credibility and Celebrity Credibility on Consumer Reaction to Advertisements and Brands," *Journal of Advertising,* Fall 2000, pp. 43–54; K. S. Coulter, "An Examination of Qualitative vs. Quantitative Elaboration Likelihood Effects," *Psychology & Marketing,* January 2005, pp. 31–49.

25. J. S. Stevenson, G. C. Bruner II, and A. Kumard, "Webpage Background and Viewer Attitudes," *Journal of Advertising Research,*

January 2000, pp. 29–34; G. C. Bruner II and A. Kumard, "Web Commercials and Advertising Hierarchy-of-Effects," *Journal of Advertising Research,* January 2000, pp. 35–43. See also L. Dailey, "Navigational Web Atmospherics," *Journal of Business Research* 57 (2004), pp. 795–803; V. Landers, S. Beatty, S. Wang, and D. Mothersbaugh, "The Effect of Online versus Offline Retailer-Based Image Incongruity on the Flow Experience," *Journal of Marketing Theory and Practice* 23, no. 4 (Fall 2015), pp. 370–87.

26. J. R. Coyle and E. Thorson, "The Effects of Progressive Levels of Interactivity and Vividness in Web Marketing Sites," *Journal of Advertising,* Fall 2001, pp. 65–77.

27. See M.-H. Huang, "Is Negative Affect in Advertising General or Specific?," *Psychology Marketing,* May 1997, pp. 223–40. See also P. S. Ellen and P. F. Bone, "Does It Matter if It Smells?," *Journal of Advertising,* Winter 1998, pp. 29–39.

28. A. Rindfleisch and J. J. Inman, "Explaining the Familiarity-Liking Relationship," *Marketing Letters* 9, no. 1 (1998), pp. 5–19; E. L. Olson and H. M. Thjomoe, "The Effects of Peripheral Exposure to Information on Brand Preference," *European Journal of Marketing* 37, no. 1/2 (2003), pp. 243–55; G. Menon and P. Raghubir, "Ease-of-Retrieval as an Automatic Input in Judgments," *Journal of Consumer Research,* September 2003, pp. 230–43.

29. S. Auty and C. Lewis, "Exploring Children's Choice," *Psychology & Marketing,* September 2004, pp. 697–713.

30. See Ruth, "Promoting a Brand's Emotional Benefits"; R. Adaval, "Sometimes It Just Feels Right," *Journal of Consumer Research,* June 2001, pp. 1–17; M. T. Pham et al., "Affect Monitoring and the Primacy of Feelings in Judgment," *Journal of Consumer Research,* September 2001, pp. 167–88; C. W. M. Yeung and R. S. Wyer Jr., "Affect, Appraisal, and Consumer Judgment," *Journal of Consumer Research,* September 2004, pp. 412–24.

31. See D. S. Kempf, "Attitude Formation from Product Trial," *Psychology & Marketing,* January 1999, pp. 35–50.

32. D. A. Griffith and Q. Chen, "The Influence of Virtual Direct Experience (VDE) on On-line Ad Message Effectiveness," *Journal of Advertising,* Spring 2004, pp. 55–68.

33. See G. J. Gaeth et al., "Consumers' Attitude Change across Sequences of Successful and Unsuccessful Product Usage," *Marketing Letters* 8, no. 1 (1997), pp. 41–53; L. A. Brannon and T. C. Brock, "Limiting Time for Response Enhances Behavior Corresponding to the Merits of Compliance Appeals," *Journal of Consumer Psychology* 10, no. 3 (2001), pp. 135–46.

34. See, e.g., M. L. Roehm and B. Sternthal, "The Moderating Effect of Knowledge and Resources on the Persuasive Impact of Analogies," *Journal of Consumer Research,* September 2001, pp. 257–72; M. Moorman, P. C. Neijens, and E. G. Smit, "The Effects of Magazine-Induced Psychological Responses and Thematic Congruence on Memory and Attitude toward the Ad in a Real-Life Setting," *Journal of Advertising,* Winter 2002, pp. 27–40; S. Putrevu, J. Tan, and K. R. Lord, "Consumer Responses to Complex Advertisements," *Journal of Current Issues and Research in Advertising,* Spring 2004, pp. 9–24.

35. See R. E. Petty, J. T. Cacioppo, and D. Schumann, "Central and Peripheral Routes to Advertising Effectiveness," *Journal of Consumer Research,* September 1993, pp. 135–46; J. Meyers-Levy and P. Malaviya, "Consumers' Processing of Persuasive Advertisements," *Journal of Marketing* 63 (1999), pp. 45–60; C. S. Areni, "The Effects of Structural and Grammatical Variables on Persuasion," *Psychology & Marketing,* April 2003, pp. 349–75; D. D. Rucker and R. E. Petty, "Increasing the Effectiveness of Communications to Consumers," *Journal of Public Policy and Marketing,* Spring 2006, pp. 39–52. For additional perspectives, see T. P. Novak and D. L. Hoffman, "The Fit of Thinking Style and Situation," *Journal of Consumer Research,* June 2009, pp. 56–72; M. L. Cronley, S. P. Mantel, and F. R. Kardes, "Effects of Accuracy Motivation and Need to Evaluate on Mode of Attitude Formation and Attitude-Behavior Consistency," *Journal of Consumer Psychology* 20 (2010), pp. 274–81.

36. See, e.g., Petty and Krosnick, *Attitude Strength.* For a discussion of attitude persistence under low involvement, see J. Sengupta, R. C. Goodstein, and D. S. Boninger, "All Cues Are Not Created Equal," *Journal of Consumer Research,* March 1997, pp. 351–61.

37. P. W. Miniard et al., "Picture-Based Persuasion Processes and the Moderating Role of Involvement," *Journal of Consumer Research,* June 1991, pp. 92–107.

38. P. W. Miniard, D. Sirdeshmukh, and D. E. Innis, "Peripheral Persuasion and Brand Choice," *Journal of Consumer Research,* September 1992, pp. 226–39; T. B. Heath, M. S. McCarthy, and D. L. Mothersbaugh, "Spokesperson Fame and Vividness Effects in the Context of Issue-Relevant Thinking," *Journal of Consumer Research,* March 1994, pp. 520–34. See also B. Yoo and R. Mandhachitara, "Estimating Advertising Effects on Sales in a Competitive Setting," *Journal of Advertising Research,* September 2003, pp. 310–21; S. S. Posavac et al., "The Brand Positivity Effect," *Journal of Consumer Research,* December 2004, pp. 643–51.

39. T. F. Mangleburg and T. Bristol, "Socialization and Adolescents' Skepticism toward Advertising," *Journal of Advertising,* Fall 1998, pp. 11–21; C. Obermiller and E. R. Spangenberg, "On the Origin and Distinctiveness of Skepticism toward Advertising," *Marketing Letters* 11, no. 4 (November 2000), pp. 311–22; D. M. Hardesty, J. P. Carlson, and W. O. Bearden, "Brand Familiarity and Invoice Price Effects on Consumer Evaluations," *Journal of Advertising,* Summer 2002, pp. 1–15.

40. M. C. Campbell and A. Kirmani, "Consumers' Use of Persuasion Knowledge," *Journal of Consumer Research,* June 2000, pp. 69–83; R. Ahluwalia and R. E. Burnkrant, "Answering Questions about Questions," *Journal of Consumer Research,* June 2004, pp. 26–42; D. M. Hardesty, W. O. Bearden, and J. P. Carlson, "Persuasion Knowledge and Consumer Reactions to Pricing Tactics," *Journal of Retailing* 83, no. 2 (2007), pp. 199–210; M. Isaac and K. Grayson, "Beyond Skepticism: Can Accessing Persuasion Knowledge Bolster Credibility?," *Journal of Consumer Research* 43, no. 6 (April 2017), pp. 895–912.

41. R. Ahlusalia, "Examination of Psychological Processes Underlying Resistance to Persuasion," *Journal of Consumer Research,* September 2000, pp. 217–32.

42. A. Wang, "The Effects of Expert and Consumer Endorsements on Audience Response," *Journal of Advertising Research,* December 2005, pp. 402–12; R. Arora, C. Stoner, and A. Arora, "Using Framing and Credibility to Incorporate Exercise and Fitness in Individual's Lifestyle," *Journal of Consumer Marketing* 23, no. 4 (2006), pp. 199–207; D. Biswas, A. Biswas, and N. Das, "The Differential Effects of Celebrity and Expert Endorsements on

Consumer Risk Perceptions," *Journal of Advertising,* Summer 2006, pp. 17-31.

43. R. D. Reinartz, "Testimonial Ads," *Bank Marketing,* March 1996, pp. 25-30; J. Nicholson, "Testimonial Ads Defend Client Turf," *Editor & Publisher,* October 23, 1999, p. 33; O. Appiah, "The Effectiveness of 'Typical-User' Testimonial Advertisements on Black and White Browsers' Evaluations of Products on Commercial Websites," *Journal of Advertising Research,* March 2007, pp. 14-27.

44. Wang, "The Effects of Expert and Consumer Endorsements on Audience Response."

45. D. H. Dean, "Brand Endorsement, Popularity, and Event Sponsorship as Advertising Cues Affecting Pre-Purchase Attitudes," *Journal of Advertising,* Fall 1999, pp. 1-11; D. H. Dean and A. Biswas, "Third-Party Organization Endorsement of Products," *Journal of Advertising,* Winter 2001, pp. 41-57.

46. Goldsmith, Lafferty, and Newell, "The Impact of Corporate Credibility and Celebrity Credibility on Consumer Reaction to Advertisements and Brands"; B. A. Lafferty, R. E. Goldsmith, and S. J. Newell, "The Dual Credibility Model," *Journal of Marketing Theory and Practice,* Summer 2002, pp. 1-12; Z. Gurhan-Canli and R. Batra, "When Corporate Image Affects Product Evaluations," *Journal of Marketing Research,* May 2004, pp. 197-205.

47. T. Fajardo and C. Townsend, "Where You Say It Matters: Why Packages Are a More Believable Source of Product Claims Than Advertisements," *Journal of Consumer Psychology* 26, no. 3 (2016), pp. 426-34.

48. S. P. Jain and S. S. Posavac, "Prepurchase Attribute Verifiability, Source Credibility, and Persuasion," *Journal of Consumer Psychology* 11, no. 3 (2001), pp. 169-80.

49. See P. M. Homer and L. R. Kahle, "Source Expertise, Time of Source Identification, and Involvement in Persuasion," *Journal of Advertising* 19, no. 1 (1990), pp. 30-39.

50. C. Pornpitakpan and J. N. P. Francis, "The Effect of Cultural Differences, Source Expertise, and Argument Strength on Persuasion," *Journal of International Consumer Marketing* 13, no. 1 (2001), pp. 77-101.

51. D. J. Moore, J. C. Mowen, and R. Reardon, "Multiple Sources in Advertising Appeals," *Journal of the Academy of Marketing Science,* Summer 1994, pp. 234-43. See also N. Artz and A. M. Tybout, "The Moderating Impact of Quantitative Information on the Relationship between Source Credibility and Persuasion," *Marketing Letters* 10, no. 1 (1999), pp. 51-62.

52. Sengupta, Goodstein, and Boninger, "All Cues Are Not Created Equal"; B. Z. Erdogan, M. J. Baker, and S. Tagg, "Selecting Celebrity Endorsers," *Journal of Advertising Research,* May-June 2001, pp. 39-48; M. R. Stafford, N. E. Spears, and C.-K. Hsu, "Celebrity Images in Magazine Advertisements," *Journal of Current Issues and Research in Advertising,* Fall 2003, pp. 13-20; A. J. Bush, C. A. Martin, and V. D. Bush, "Sports Celebrity Influence on the Behavioral Intentions of Generation Y," *Journal of Advertising Research,* March 2004, pp. 108-18.

53. J. Ilicic, A. Kulczynski, and S. Baxter, "How a Smile Can Make a Difference: Enhancing the Persuasive Appeal of Celebrity Endorsers," *Journal of Advertising Research* 58, no. 1 (March 2018), pp. 51-68.

54. Knowledge Networks, "Michael Jordan Trumps Tiger, Lance in Influence on Purchase Consideration," press release, October 27, 2003, www.knowledgenetworks.com; E. York, "Phelps Brand, Endorsements Take a Hit," *Advertising Age,* February 9, 2009, www.adage.com.

55. M. Schneier, "Coach Confirms Its Partnership with Selena Gomez," *New York Times,* December 16, 2016.

56. B. D. Till and M. Busler, "The Match-Up Hypothesis," *Journal of Advertising,* Fall 2000, pp. 1-13; Erdogan, Baker, and Tagg, "Selecting Celebrity Endorsers"; A. B. Bower and S. Landreth, "Is Beauty Best?," *Journal of Advertising,* Spring 2001, pp. 1-12; R. Batra and P. M. Homer, "The Situational Impact of Brand Image Beliefs," *Journal of Consumer Psychology* 14, no. 3 (2004), pp. 318-30.

57. N. Pike, "Rihanna's Fashion Forays," *British Vogue,* April 7, 2017; S. Honeycutt, "Good Girl Gone Mogul: A Guide to Rihanna's Growing Business Empire," *Billboard,* May 14, 2018, www.billboard.com, accessed June 8, 2018.

58. K. Macarthur, "BK and Paris," *Advertising Age,* August 30, 2004, p. 6.

59. M. T. Liu, Y. Huang, and J. Minghua, "Relations among Attractiveness of Endorsers, Match-up, and Purchase Intention in Sport Marketing in China," *Journal of Consumer Marketing* 24, no. 6 (2007), pp. 358-65.

60. C. Tripp, T. D. Jensen, and L. Carlson, "The Effects of Multiple Product Endorsements by Celebrities on Consumers' Attitudes and Intentions," *Journal of Consumer Research,* March 1994, pp. 535-47; J. R. Priester and R. E. Petty, "The Influence of Spokesperson Trustworthiness on Message Elaboration, Attitude Strength, and Advertising Effectiveness," *Journal of Consumer Psychology* 13, no. 4 (2003), pp. 408-21.

61. B. D. Till and T. A. Shimp, "Endorsers in Advertising," *Journal of Advertising,* Spring 1998, pp. 67-82; T. A. Louie, R. L. Kulik, and R. Jacobson, "When Bad Things Happen to the Endorsers of Good Products," *Marketing Letters* 12, no. 1 (February 2001), pp. 13-23.

62. J. A. Garretson and R. W. Niedrich, "Spokes-Characters," *Journal of Advertising,* Summer 2004, pp. 25-36; J. A. Garretson and S. Burton, "The Role of Spokescharacters as Advertisement and Package Cues in Integrated Marketing Communications," *Journal of Marketing,* October 2005, pp. 118-32.

63. For an excellent overview, see T. Meenaghan, "Understanding Sponsorship Effects," *Psychology & Marketing,* February 2001, pp. 95-122; see also B. Walliser, "An International Review of Sponsorship Research," *International Journal of Advertising* 22 (2003), pp. 5-40.

64. "Global Sponsorship Spending by Region 2009-2018," www.statista.com, accessed June 8, 2018.

65. D. Long, "Monster Energy Extends Title Sponsorship of NASCAR Cup Series to 2019 Only," *NBC Sports,* April 10, 2018, www.nbcsports.com, accessed June 8, 2018.

66. R. Thomaselli, "Offical Sponsors Score with World Cup," *Advertising Age,* July 26, 2010, p. C-3.

67. R. Madrigal, "The Influence of Social Alliances with Sports Teams on Intentions to Purchase Corporate Sponsors' Products," *Journal of Advertising,* Winter 2000, pp. 13-24.

68. N. Zmuda, "Children's Hospital in Hot Water over Corporate Sponsorships," *Advertising Age,* March 12, 2008, www.adage.com.

69. S. R. McDaniel, "An Investigation of Match-Up Effects in Sport Sponsorship Advertising," *Psychology & Marketing,* March 1999, pp. 163–84; N. J. Rifon et al., "Congruence Effects in Sponsorships," *Journal of Advertising,* Spring 2004, pp. 29–42; T. B. Cornwell, S. W. Pruitt, and J. M. Clark, "The Relationship between Major-League Sports' Official Sponsorship Announcements and the Stock Prices of Sponsoring Firms," *Journal of the Academy of Marketing Science* 33, no. 4 (2005), pp. 401–12; N. D. Fleck and P. Quester, "Birds of a Feather Flock Together," *Psychology & Marketing,* November 2007, pp. 975–1000.

70. C. Pechmann et al., "What to Convey in Antismoking Advertisements for Adolescents," *Journal of Marketing,* April 2003, pp. 1–18; M. S. LaTour and J. F. Tanner Jr., "Randon," *Psychology & Marketing,* May 2003, pp. 377–94; J. P. Dillard and J. W. Anderson, "The Role of Fear in Persuasion," *Psychology & Marketing,* November 2004, pp. 909–26; I. Vermeir, T. De Bock and P. Van Kenhove, "The Effectiveness of Fear Appeals Featuring Fines versus Social Disapproval in Preventing Shoplifting among Adolescents," *Psychology & Marketing* 34, no. 3 (March 2017), pp. 264–74.

71. P. A. Keller and L. G. Block, "Increasing the Persuasiveness of Fear Appeals," *Journal of Consumer Research,* March 1996, pp. 448–60; M. S. LaTour and H. J. Rotfeld, "There Are Threats and (Maybe) Fear-Caused Arousal," *Journal of Advertising,* Fall 1997, pp. 45–59; M. Laroche et al., "A Cross-Cultural Study of the Persuasive Effect of Fear Appeal Messages in Cigarette Advertising: China and Canada," *International Journal of Advertising* 20, no. 3 (2001), pp. 297–318.

72. K. Passyn and M. Sujan, "Self-Accountability Emotions in Fear Appeals," *Journal of Consumer Research,* March 2006, pp. 583–89.

73. See M. S. LaTour, R. L. Snipes, and S. J. Bliss, "Don't Be Afraid to Use Fear Appeals," *Journal of Advertising Research,* March 1996, pp. 59–66.

74. D. L. Alden, A. Mukherjee, and W. D. Hoyer, "The Effects of Incongruity, Surprise and Positive Moderators and Perceived Humor in Television Advertising," *Journal of Advertising,* Summer 2000, pp. 1–14; K. Flaherty, M. G. Weinberger, and C. S. Gulas, "The Impact of Perceived Humor, Product Type, and Humor Style in Radio Advertising," *Journal of Current Issues and Research in Advertising,* Spring 2004, pp. 25–36; J. Elpers, A. Mukherjee, and W. D. Hoyer, "Humor in Television Advertising," *Journal of Consumer Research,* December 2004, pp. 592–98.

75. T. W. Cline, M. B. Altsech, and J. J. Kellaris, "When Does Humor Enhance or Inhibit Ad Responses?," *Journal of Advertising,* Fall 2003, pp. 31–45.

76. Insight based on M. N. Gardner and A. M. Brandt, "The Physician in US Cigarette Advertisements, 1930–1953," *American Journal of Public Health,* February 2006, pp. 222–32; R. R. Vernellia, *The History of Tobacco* (Boston University Medical Center, Community Outreach Health Information System, 1999), http://academic.udayton.edu/health/syllabi/tobacco/history.htm, accessed August 27, 2014; "Hanna-Barbera Production Flintstones–Winston Compilation (1960)," UCSF Tobacco Industry videos, https://archive.org/details/tobacco_djq03d00, accessed August 27, 2014; S. Egan, "Why Smoking Rates Are at New Lows," *New York Times,* June 25, 2013, http://well.

blogs.nytimes.com/2013/06/25/why-smoking-rates-are-at-new-lows/, accessed August 27, 2014; 15 U.S.C. § 1335, "Unlawful Advertisements on Medium of Electronic Communication" (Legal Information Institute, Cornell University Law School), www.law.cornell.edu/uscode/text/15/1335, accessed August 27, 2014; "U.S. Smoking Bans, State by State," *Huffington Post,* May 25, 2011, www.huffingtonpost.com/2011/02/23/smoking-bans-state-by-sta_n_826672.html#s244139title=Alabama, accessed August 27, 2014; Centers for Disease Control and Prevention, "Highlights: Warning Labels," www.cdc.gov/tobacco/data_statistics/sgr/2000/highlights/labels/, accessed August 27, 2014; G. T. Fong, D. Hammond, and S. C. Hitchman, "The Impact of Pictures on the Effectiveness of Tobacco Warnings," *Bulletin of the World Health Organization,* August 2009, pp. 640–43; A. C. Villanti et al., "Perceptions and Perceived Impact of Graphic Cigarette Health Warning Labels on Smoking Behavior among U.S. Young Adults," *Nicotine & Tobacco Research,* March 14, 2014, pp. 469–77; S. Almasy, "FDA Changes Course on Graphic Warning Labels for Cigarettes," *CNN,* March 20, 2013, www.cnn.com/2013/03/19/health/fda-graphic-tobacco-warnings/, accessed August 27, 2014; M. McArdle, "E-Cigarettes: A $1.5 Billion Industry Braces for FDA Regulation," *Businessweek,* February 06, 2014, www.businessweek.com/articles/2014-02-06/e-cigarettes-fda-regulation-looms-for-1-dot-5-billion-industry#p1, accessed August 27, 2014.

77. M. Eisend, "A Meta-Analysis of Humor in Advertising," *Journal of the Academy of Marketing Science* 37 (2009), pp. 191–203.

78. See, e.g., H. S. Krishnan and D. Chakravarti, "A Process Analysis of the Effects of Humorous Advertising Executions on Brand Claims Memory," *Journal of Consumer Psychology* 13, no. 3 (2003), pp. 230–45.

79. E. B. York, "Snickers Uses Humor to Satisfy Generations of Hunger," *Advertising Age,* March 29, 2010, p. 22.

80. H. Chung and X. Zhao, "Humour Effect on Memory and Attitude," *International Journal of Advertising* 22 (2003), pp. 117–44; Y. Zhang and G. M. Zinkhan, "Responses to Humorous Ads," *Journal of Advertising,* Winter 2006, pp. 113–27.

81. D. L. Fugate, J. B. Gotlieb, and D. Bolton, "Humorous Services Advertising," *Journal of Professional Services Marketing* 21, no. 1 (2000), pp. 9–22; M. F. Toncar, "The Use of Humour in Television Advertising," *International Journal of Advertising* 20 (2001), pp. 521–39; K. Macarthur, "Subway Cans Schtick to Focus on Food in Its Creative," *Advertising Age,* March 1, 2004, p. 4.

82. D. Grewal et al., "Comparative versus Noncomparative Advertising," *Journal of Marketing,* October 1998, pp. 1–15; M. E. Hill and M. King, "Comparative vs. Noncomparative Advertising," *Journal of Current Issues and Research in Advertising,* Fall 2001, pp. 33–52; K. C. Manning et al., "Understanding the Mental Representations Created by Comparative Advertising," *Journal of Advertising,* Summer 2001, pp. 27–39; L. D. Compeau, D. Grewal, and R. Chandrashekaran, "Bits, Briefs, and Applications," *Journal of Consumer Affairs,* Winter 2002, pp. 284–94; J. R. Priester et al., "Brand Congruity and Comparative Advertising," *Journal of Consumer Psychology* 14, no. 1/2 (2004), pp. 115–23.

83. A. Chattopadhyay, "When Does Comparative Advertising Influence Brand Attitude?," *Psychology & Marketing,* August 1998, pp. 461–75; M. J. Barone and P. W. Miniard, "How and When Factual Ad Claims Mislead Consumers," *Journal of Marketing*

Research, February 1999, pp. 58–74; S. V. Auken and A. J. Adams, "Across- versus Within-Class Comparative Advertising," *Psychology & Marketing,* August 1999, pp. 429–50; A. B. Sorescu and B. D. Gelb, "Negative Comparative Advertising," *Journal of Advertising,* Winter 2000, pp. 25–40; S. P. Jain, B. Buchanan, and D. Maheswaran, "Comparative versus Non-comparative Advertising," *Journal of Consumer Psychology* 9, no. 4 (2000), pp. 201–11; A. V. Muthukrishnan, L. Warlop, and J. W. Alba, "The Piecemeal Approach to Comparative Advertising," *Marketing Letters* 12, no. 1 (2001), pp. 63–73; S. P. Jain and S. S. Posavac, "Valenced Comparisons," *Journal of Marketing Research,* February 2004, pp. 46–58; M. J. Barone, K. M. Palan, and P. W. Miniard, "Brand Usage and Gender as Moderators of the Potential Deception Associated with Partial Comparative Advertising," *Journal of Advertising,* Spring 2004, pp. 19–28.

84. See, e.g., M. E. Hill et al., "The Conjoining Influences of Affect and Arousal on Attitude Formation," *Research in Consumer Behavior* 9 (2000), pp. 129–46; J. D. Morris et al., "The Power of Affect," *Journal of Advertising Research,* May–June 2002, pp. 7–17; M.-H. Huang, "Romantic Love and Sex," *Psychology & Marketing,* January 2004, pp. 53–73; D. J. MacInnis and G. E. de Mello, "The Concept of Hope and Its Relevance to Product Evaluation and Choice," *Journal of Marketing,* January 2005, pp. 1–14.

85. R. K. Chandy et al., "What to Say When," *Journal of Marketing Research,* November 2001, pp. 399–414; R. D. Jewell and H. R. Unnava, "Exploring Differences in Attitudes between Light and Heavy Brand Users," *Journal of Consumer Psychology* 14, no. 1/2 (2004), pp. 75–80.

86. J. Hasford, D. Hardesty and B. Kidwell, "More Than a Feeling: Emotional Contagion Effects in Persuasive Communication," *Journal of Marketing Research* 52 (December 2015), pp. 836–47.

87. J. S. Johar and M. J. Sirgy, "Value-Expressive versus Utilitarian Advertising Appeals," *Journal of Advertising,* September 1991, pp. 23–33; S. Shavitt, "Evidence for Predicting the Effectiveness of Value-Expressive versus Utilitarian Appeals," *Journal of Advertising,* June 1992, pp. 47–51; M. E. Slama and R. B. Singley, "Self-Monitoring and Value-Expressive vs. Utilitarian Ad Effectiveness," *Journal of Current Issues and Research in Advertising,* Fall 1996, pp. 39–49; L. Dube, A. Chattopadhyay, and A. Letarte, "Should Advertising Appeals Match the Basis of Consumers' Attitudes?,"

Journal of Advertising Research, November 1996, pp. 82–89; J.-S. Chiou, "The Effectiveness of Different Advertising Message Appeals in the Eastern Emerging Society," *International Journal of Advertising* 21 (2002), pp. 217–36.

88. M. Dahlen and J. Bergendahl, "Informing and Transforming on the Web," *International Journal of Advertising* 20, no. 2 (2001), pp. 189–205.

89. A. E. Crowley and W. D. Hoyer, "An Integrative Framework for Understanding Two-Sided Persuasion," *Journal of Consumer Research,* March 1994, pp. 561–74; G. Bohner et al., "When Small Means Comfortable," *Journal of Consumer Psychology* 13, no. 4 (2003), pp. 454–63; M. Eisend, "Understanding Two-Sided Persuasion," *Psychology & Marketing,* July 2007, pp. 615–40.

90. I. P. Levin, S. L. Schneider, and G. J. Gaeth, "All Frames Are Not Created Equal," *Organizational Behavior and Human Decision Processes,* November 1998, pp. 149–88.

91. Ibid.

92. P. A. Keller, I. M. Lipkus, and B. K. Rimer, "Affect, Framing, and Persuasion," *Journal of Marketing Research,* February 2003, pp. 54–64; J. Meyers-Levy and D. Maheswaran, "Exploring Message Framing Outcomes When Systematic, Heuristic, or Both Types of Processing Occur," *Journal of Consumer Psychology* 14, no. 1/2 (2004), pp. 159–67; B. Shiv, J. A. E. Britton, and J. W. Payne, "Does Elaboration Increase or Decrease the Effectiveness of Negatively versus Positively Framed Messages?," *Journal of Consumer Research,* June 2004, pp. 199–208; S. Putrevu, "Effects of Mood and Elaboration on Processing and Evaluation of Goal-Framed Appeals," *Psychology & Marketing* 31, no. 2 (February 2014), pp. 134–46; A. Nagpal, J. Lei, and A. Khare, "To Choose or to Reject: The Effect of Decision Frame on Food Customization Decisions," *Journal of Retailing* 91, no. 3 (2015), pp. 422–35.

93. See, e.g., J. W. Peltier and J. A. Schribrowsky, "The Use of Need-Based Segmentation for Developing Segment-Specific Direct Marketing Strategies," *Journal of Direct Marketing,* Fall 1997, pp. 53–62; R. Ahmad, "Benefit Segmentation," *International Journal of Marketing Research* 45 (2003), pp. 373–88.

94. H. E. Bloom, "Match the Concept and the Product," *Journal of Advertising Research,* October 1977, pp. 25–27.

12 Self-Concept and Lifestyle

©Flamingo Images/Shutterstock

LEARNING OBJECTIVES

LO1 Describe self-concept, how it is measured, and how it is used to position products.

LO2 Define lifestyle and its relationship to the self-concept and to psychographics.

LO3 Explain specific lifestyle typologies and summarize those for luxury sports cars and technology.

LO4 Explain general lifestyle typologies and summarize those for VALS™ and PRIZM®.

LO5 Discuss international lifestyles and one existing segmentation scheme.

In Chapter 6, we identified how meal kits have gained popularity among families with younger children as these kits simplify meal preparation at home. The meal kit industry, which recorded $1.5 billion in sales in 2016, continues to grow, and not just among this group of consumers. Meal kits also have piqued the curiosity of those consumers who enjoy cooking. In a recent Mintel study of cooking lifestyles, 16 percent of this group have tried a meal kit (and plan to use one again) and close to a third are interested in trying one.[1]

Consumers who enjoy cooking, or Cooking Enthusiasts, comprise the largest of five cooking lifestyle groups identified by Mintel. The breakdown is as follows:

Segment	Percent of U.S. Adults
Cooking Enthusiasts	46%
Conflicted Cooks	19
Infrequent Cooks	12
Unenthusiastic Cooks	18
Non-Cooks	6

Note: Percentages may not add to 100 percent due to rounding.

Interestingly, the consumers within the Cooking Enthusiasts segment are not defined by demographics, but by lifestyle. In general, cooking for these enthusiasts is characterized by

- *Pleasure and proficiency:* These consumers are "eager to cook" and "either like or love cooking." The majority choose to cook at home because of a desire to do so, as opposed to having to do so. For more than three-fourths, cooking is viewed as a favorite hobby. Being good at cooking may contribute to their enjoyment. More than three-quarters would rate their skills at least at the intermediate level.
- *Community and well-being:* They cook to spend time with their families. It is also a way to connect family members with their heritage. Many cook out of a desire for a healthy lifestyle.
- *Process:* They enjoy grocery shopping. They like to try new recipes, and recipes that require the use of multiple appliances appeal to this group. They can show off their skills and be creative. Furthermore, almost half cook a meal from scratch at least three times a week. Cooking to have leftovers is a benefit for 75 percent of Cooking Enthusiasts.

Appreciating the attitudes and motivations of Cooking Enthusiasts has implications for food delivery programs and kitchen appliance brands. For example, meal kits allow these cooks to spend time with family while cooking creative and healthy meals. Also, high-tech kitchen gadgets, such as sous vide machines, smart slow cookers, and Google Home, appeal to the process and proficiency of cooking. As such, marketing to Cooking Enthusiasts means understanding who they are according to their lifestyle as opposed to their demographics, like age or gender.

In this chapter, we will discuss the meaning of lifestyle and the role it plays in developing marketing strategies. Lifestyle is, in many ways, an outward expression of one's self-concept. That is, the way an individual chooses to live, given the constraints of income and ability, is heavily influenced by that person's current and desired self-concept. Therefore, we begin the chapter with an analysis of the self-concept. We then describe lifestyles, the ways lifestyle is measured, and examples of how lifestyle is being used to develop marketing programs.

SELF-CONCEPT

LO1

Self-concept is defined as *the totality of the individual's thoughts and feelings having reference to himself or herself as an object.* It is an individual's perception of and feelings toward him- or herself. In other words, your self-concept is composed of the attitudes you hold toward yourself.

The self-concept can be divided into four basic parts, as shown in Table 12–1: actual versus ideal, and private versus social. The actual–ideal distinction refers to the individual's perception of *who I am now* (**actual self-concept**) and *who I would like to be* (**ideal self-concept**). The private self refers to *how I am or would like to be to myself* (**private self-concept**), and the social self is *how I am seen by others or how I would like to be seen by others* (**social self-concept**).

Interdependent/Independent Self-Concepts

The self-concept is important in all cultures. However, those aspects of the self that are most valued and most influence consumption and other behaviors vary across cultures. Researchers have found it useful to categorize self-concepts into two types: independent and interdependent, also referred to as one's separateness and connectedness.[2]

An independent construal of the self is based on the predominant Western cultural belief that individuals are inherently separate. The **independent self-concept** *emphasizes personal goals, characteristics, achievements, and desires.* Individuals with an independent self-concept tend to be individualistic, egocentric, autonomous, self-reliant, and self-contained. They define themselves in terms of what they have done, what they have, and their personal characteristics.[3]

An interdependent construal of the self is based more on the common Asian cultural belief in the fundamental connectedness of human beings. The **interdependent self-concept** *emphasizes family, cultural, professional, and social relationships.* Individuals with an interdependent self-concept tend to be obedient, sociocentric, holistic, connected, and relation oriented. They define themselves in terms of social roles, family relationships, and commonalities with other members of their groups.

Independent and interdependent self-concepts are not discrete categories; rather, they are constructs used to describe the opposite ends of a continuum along which most cultures lie.

TABLE 12-1 Dimensions of a Consumer's Self-Concept

Dimensions of Self-Concept	Actual Self-Concept	Ideal Self-Concept
Private self	How I actually see myself	How I would like to see myself
Social self	How others actually see me	How I would like others to see me

However, as we emphasized in Chapter 2, most cultures are heterogeneous. Therefore, within a given culture, subcultures and other groups will vary on this dimension, as will individuals.[4] For example, women across cultures tend to have more of an *interdependent* self-concept than do men.[5]

Variation in the degree to which an individual or culture is characterized by an independent versus an interdependent self-concept has been found to influence message preferences, consumption of luxury goods, and the types of products preferred. For example, ads emphasizing acting alone and autonomy tend to be effective with consumers with independent self-concepts, whereas ads emphasizing group membership work better with consumers with interdependent self-concepts.[6] The Yeti ad in Illustration 12–1 should be effective with individuals whose independent self-concept is dominant.

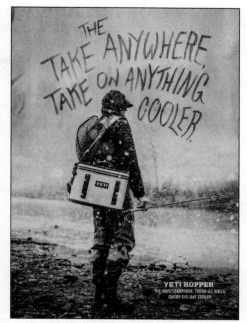

Source: Yeti Coolers, LLC

However, it is also important to note that ads themselves can cue self-concepts and make them more salient at least for some consumers. In a study of Gen X Chinese consumers, individualistic ads made the independent self-concept more salient, while collectivist ads made the interdependent self-concept more salient. This makes sense if you view these consumers as younger and bicultural in that they are navigating between traditional and emerging value sets. Ads, therefore, can influence the weight placed on a given value set.[7]

Possessions and the Extended Self

Some products acquire substantial meaning to an individual or are used to signal particularly important aspects of that person's self to others. Belk developed a theory called the *extended self* to explain this.[8] The **extended self** consists of *the self plus possessions;* that is, people tend to define themselves in part by their possessions. Thus, some possessions are not just a manifestation of a person's self-concept; they are an integral part of that person's self-identity. People are, to some extent, what they possess. If one were to lose key possessions, he or she would be a somewhat different individual.[9]

While these key possessions might be major items, such as one's home or automobile, they are equally likely to be smaller items with unique meanings, such as a souvenir, a photograph, a pet, or a favorite cooking pan. Such objects have meaning to the individual beyond their market value. Consider these statements from consumers who lost their possessions in natural disasters and who had ample insurance to replace them:

Yea, we got better stuff, but it doesn't mean anything to us. It's just stuff.

You can't put back or replace what you had. It was too personal—it was customized.[10]

Products become part of one's extended self for a variety of reasons. Souvenirs often become part of the extended self as representations of memories and feelings:

> You can't really tell what Paris is like . . . you know, a lot of it is just feelings; feelings you can't put into words; or [that] pictures cannot capture. . . . They [a hat and blouse] are just reminders.
>
> I had a really wonderful trip and really sort of discovered myself; you know, I learned to be independent on my own. I really didn't have the money to buy this [necklace and boomerang charm], but I decided I wanted something really permanent. . . . The boomerang is a symbol of going back there sometime.[11]

Gifts often take on important meanings as representations of relationships:

> That gift was my grandfather's ring. . . . Even now when I look at it, I think about its past with him and the journeys it took around the world in the Navy back in World War II.
>
> The key chain is special because every so often, when I think about who gave it to me, it brings back old thoughts and feelings. It is a symbol of friendship between us, and it keeps us in touch.[12]

Some products become embedded with meaning, memories, and value as they are used over time, as with an old baseball glove. At other times, a single peak experience with a product such as a mountain bike can propel the product into the extended self. A **peak experience** is *an experience that surpasses the usual level of intensity, meaningfulness, and richness and produces feelings of joy and self-fulfillment.*[13] Finally, products that are acquired or used to help consumers with major life transitions (e.g., leaving home, first job, marriage) are also likely to be or become part of the extended self.[14]

Extended self also can relate to nonproduct entities such as activities (golfing), other people (my best friend), TV shows (*Star Trek*), and sports teams (Green Bay Packers).

A scale has been developed to measure the extent to which an item has been incorporated into the extended self.[15] It is a Likert scale (see Appendix A) in which consumers express levels of agreement (from strongly agree to strongly disagree on a seven-point scale) to the following statements:

- My _____ helps me achieve the identity I want to have.
- My _____ helps me narrow the gap between what I am and what I try to be.
- My _____ is central to my identity.
- My _____ is part of who I am.
- If my _____ is stolen from me, I will feel as if my identity has been snatched from me.
- I derive some of my identity from my _____.

Owning a product affects a person even if it does not become an important part of the person's extended self. The **mere ownership effect,** or the *endowment effect,* is *the tendency of an owner to evaluate an object more favorably than a nonowner.* This occurs almost immediately upon acquiring an object and increases with time of ownership. Thus, people tend to value an object more after acquiring it than before. People also tend to value objects they own more highly than they value similar objects owned by others.[16]

The extent to which brands become part of the extended self appears to be affected by individual differences in **brand engagement.** Brand engagement *refers to the extent to which an individual includes important brands as part of his or her self-concept.* Sample items used to measure brand engagement include "I have a special bond with the brands that I like," "I often feel a personal connection between my brands and me," and "Part of me is defined by important brands in my life."[17] Research shows that the strongest predictor of brand engagement is materialism. It also shows that consumers with higher brand engagement like products better when the brand logo is prominently displayed on the product. *Would you consider Cooking Enthusiasts from the opener to be high in brand engagement and materialism? If so, what design aspects relating to logo for kitchen appliances would be important to this group? Explain.*

The concept of the extended self and the mere ownership effect have numerous implications for marketing strategy. One is that communications that cause potential consumers to *visualize product ownership* may result in enhanced product evaluations. Product sampling or other trial programs may have similar results.

Measuring Self-Concept

Using the self-concept in marketing requires that it be measurable. The most common measurement approach is the semantic differential (see Appendix A). Malhotra has developed a set of 15 pairs of adjectives, shown in Table 12–2. These have proven effective in describing the ideal, actual, and social self-concepts of individuals as well as the images of automobiles and celebrities. *Using this scale, determine your actual and desired private and social self-concepts.*

This instrument can be used to ensure a match between the self-concept (actual or ideal) of a target market, the image of a brand, and the characteristics of an advertising spokesperson. For example, in its decision to sign Serena Williams to a multiyear endorsement contract, Nike undoubtedly saw a match between the desired self-concept of young women, the desired image for Nike's women's athletic apparel line, and the image of Serena Williams.[18]

Measurement Scales for Self-Concepts, Person Concepts, and Product Concepts   **TABLE 12-2**

1. Rugged	___	___	___	___	___	___	___	Delicate
2. Excitable	___	___	___	___	___	___	___	Calm
3. Uncomfortable	___	___	___	___	___	___	___	Comfortable
4. Dominating	___	___	___	___	___	___	___	Submissive
5. Thrifty	___	___	___	___	___	___	___	Indulgent
6. Pleasant	___	___	___	___	___	___	___	Unpleasant
7. Contemporary	___	___	___	___	___	___	___	Noncontemporary
8. Organized	___	___	___	___	___	___	___	Unorganized
9. Rational	___	___	___	___	___	___	___	Emotional
10. Youthful	___	___	___	___	___	___	___	Mature
11. Formal	___	___	___	___	___	___	___	Informal
12. Orthodox	___	___	___	___	___	___	___	Liberal
13. Complex	___	___	___	___	___	___	___	Simple
14. Colorless	___	___	___	___	___	___	___	Colorful
15. Modest	___	___	___	___	___	___	___	Vain

Source: N. K. Malhotra, "A Scale to Measure Self-Concepts, Person Concepts, and Product Concepts," *Journal of Marketing Research,* November 1981, p. 462. Reprinted with permission from Journal of Marketing Research, published by the American Marketing Association.

Using Self-Concept to Position Products

People's attempts to obtain their ideal self-concept, or maintain their actual self-concept, often involve the purchase and consumption of products, services, and media.[19] This process is described in Figure 12–1. While this figure implies a rather conscious and deliberate process, many times that is not the case. For example, a person may drink diet colas because his desired self-concept includes a trim figure, but he is unlikely to think about the purchase in these terms. However, as the following statement illustrates, sometimes people do think in these terms:

> And I feel if you present yourself in the right way, people will start to notice. But this leads back to image and self-worth, which can be achieved through having the right clothes and a good hair-cut. . . . [H]aving a good portrait of yourself on the outside can eventually lead to an emotionally stable inside.[20]

All this suggests that marketers should strive to develop product images that are consistent with the self-concepts of their target markets.[21] While everyone's self-concept is unique, there is also significant overlap across individuals and groups, which is one basis for market segmentation. For example, many consumers see themselves as environmentalists. Companies and products that create an image of being concerned about or good for the environment are likely to be supported by these consumers.

Consumers maintain and enhance their self-concepts not only by what they consume, but by what they avoid.[22] Some consumers make a point of avoiding certain product categories, such as red meat, or certain brands, such as Nike, as part of maintaining "who they are."

In general, consumers prefer brands that match their self-concepts. However, it is important to realize that the degree to which such "self-image congruity" influences brand preference and choice depends on a number of product, situational, and individual factors. First, self-image congruity is likely to matter more for products such as perfume where value-expressive *symbolism* is critical than for more utilitarian products such as a garage door opener. Second, self-image congruity (especially ideal social self) is likely to matter more when the situation involves *public* or *conspicuous consumption* (e.g., having a beer with friends at a bar) than when consumption is private (e.g., having a beer at home).[23]

FIGURE 12-1   The Relationship between Self-Concept and Brand Image Influence

Finally, self-image congruity is likely to matter more for consumers who place heavy weight on the opinions and feelings of others (called *high self-monitors*) than for consumers who do not (called *low self-monitors*), particularly in public situations where consumption behaviors can be observed by others.[24]

Look at Illustration 12–2 and the various aspects of self-concept listed in Table 12–2. *To which aspect(s) of self-concept does this Michael Kors ad appeal?*

Marketing Ethics and the Self-Concept

The self-concept has many dimensions. Marketers have been criticized for focusing too much attention on the importance of being beautiful, with *beautiful* being defined as young and slim with a fairly narrow range of facial features.

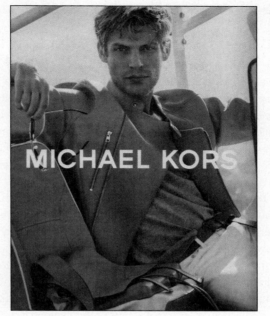

ILLUSTRATION 12-2

Ads that position products to match the self-concept of the target market are generally successful. Ads, such as this Michael Kors ad, can appeal to the consumer's actual or ideal, private or social self.

Source: Michael Kors

Virtually all societies appear to define and desire beauty, but the intense exposure to products and advertisements focused on beauty in America today is unique. Critics argue that this concern leads individuals to develop self-concepts that are heavily dependent on their physical appearance rather than other equally or more important attributes.

Consider the following statements from two young women:

> I never felt that I looked right. Like I can see outfits that I'd love to wear, but I know that I could never wear them. I probably could wear them and get away with it, but I'd be so self-conscious walking around that I'd be like, "oh, my God." Like I always try to look thinner and I guess everybody does.
>
> I am pretty content with my hair because I have good hair. I have good eyesight (laughs) so I don't have to wear glasses or anything that would make my face look different from what it is. In terms of bad points, well there is a lot. I got a lot of my father's features. I wish I had more of my mother's. My hands are pretty square. I have a kind of a big butt. Then, I don't have that great of a stomach.[25]

These young women have self-concepts that are partly negative as a result of their perceptions of their beauty relative to the standard portrayed in the media. Critics of advertising claim that most individuals, but particularly young women, acquire negative components to their self-concepts because very few can achieve the standards of beauty presented in advertising. Recent research indicates that similar negative self-evaluations occur in males as a result of idealized images of both physical attractiveness and financial success.[26]

The ethical question is complex. No one ad or company has this type of impact. It is the cumulative effect of many ads across many companies reinforced by the content of the mass media that presumably causes some to be overly focused on their physical beauty. And, as stated earlier, concern with beauty existed long before advertising.

Consumer Insight 12–1 delves deeper into the Dove campaigns and the complex issues involved.

Mind the Gap—The Real You and the Ideal You

The consumers' actual self is how they see themselves. The consumers' ideal self is how they would like to see themselves. A gap, sometimes small, sometimes big, may exist between the ideal self and the actual self, as discussed earlier in this chapter.

In 2004 Unilever, the parent company of Dove, conducted a survey of 3,200 women in 10 countries (U.S., Japan, Canada, Argentina, Netherlands, Great Britain, France, Portugal, Italy, Brazil) to understand what beauty means to women. The study revealed that only 2 percent of women saw themselves as beautiful. For 98 percent of women, their perception of their actual beauty fell short of their ideal. The study had identified a gap between women's ideal self-concept and actual self-concept.[27]

Following on the heels of the study, Dove launched the Dove Campaign for Real Beauty to zero in on the gap. The campaign sought to broaden the definition of beauty beyond the stereotypic narrow confines. The campaign included billboard, print, TV, video, and digital. The billboards featured a woman and two tick box options such as "Fat or Fit?" or "Withered or Wonderful?" and invited passersby to visit a website to cast their votes. The print ads, "featuring six real women with real bodies and real curves," were "created to debunk the stereotype that only thin is beautiful." The enormously successful campaign was showered with media attention and recognized with awards. It also received criticism: The models "are still head-turners, with straight white teeth, no visible pores, and not a cell of cellulite . . . they represent a beauty standard still idealized and, for the overwhelming majority of consumers, still pretty damn unattainable."

The next phase of The Dove Real Beauty campaign, Dove Real Beauty Sketch, was launched in 2013 as three- and seven-minute, web-only commercials. A forensic artist sketched two portraits of the person, one as she described herself concealed behind a screen out of the artist's sight—the real self—and another sketch as a stranger described her. The two sketches revealed that strangers saw these women as more attractive than women saw themselves. The video, capturing the heartfelt emotional response by the women—tears, surprise—when they saw the two portraits of themselves went viral and generated substantial buzz. This campaign, like the previous ones, received both support—"a real expression of the insecurity of so many women who tend to sell themselves short"—and criticism—"pandering, soft-focus fake empowerment ads."

Dove is in the beauty business. Its Dove Campaign for Real Beauty focused on acceptance of real beauty beyond the stereotypical beauty ideal. Its Dove Sketch campaign showed women that they are more beautiful than they see themselves. Both campaigns have received accolades for bringing to light the overemphasis of the importance of physical beauty to women's self-concept. Both campaigns have been criticized for its focus on women's beauty and their underlying message of the importance of physical beauty. Hate it or love it, authentic or fake, the campaigns have sold a lot of Dove products.

Critical Thinking Questions

1. Are you aware of the Dove Campaign for Real Beauty? Dove Sketch campaign? What was your initial reaction? Has your reaction changed over time?

2. Dove's parent company Unilever owns Axe and owned, at the time the campaigns launched, Slimfast. Does this make the Dove Real Beauty and Dove Sketch campaigns a sham? Or can the campaigns still be authentic?

3. The 2004 TV, print, billboard Dove campaign and the 2013 web-only Dove campaign illustrate the increasing power of social media and viral marketing. What are other social media–driven successful advertising campaigns?

THE NATURE OF LIFESTYLE

As Figure 12–2 indicates, **lifestyle** is basically *how a person lives*. It is how a person enacts her or his self-concept and is determined by past experiences, innate characteristics, and current situation. One's lifestyle influences all aspects of consumption behavior and is a function of inherent individual characteristics that have been shaped and formed through social interaction as the person has evolved through the life cycle.

The relationship between *lifestyle* and *self-concept* was demonstrated in a study comparing various lifestyle-related activities, interests, and behaviors across those with independent versus interdependent self-concepts. *Independents* were more likely to seek adventure and excitement through travel, sports, and entertainment; to be opinion leaders; and to prefer magazines over TV. *Interdependents* were more likely to engage in home and domestic-related activities and entertainment, including cooking at home and from scratch. Interdependents were also more likely to engage in social activities revolving around family and the community.[28]

Individuals and households both have lifestyles. Although household lifestyles are determined in part by the individual lifestyles of the household members, the reverse is also true.

Individuals' *desired* lifestyles influence their needs and desires and thus their purchase and use behaviors. Desired lifestyle determines many of a person's consumption decisions, which in turn reinforce or alter that person's lifestyle.

Marketers can use lifestyle to segment and target specific markets. As the chapter's opening vignette illustrates, kitchen appliance brands need to adjust their approach to the cooking lifestyle segments. Similarly, those who live the extreme sports lifestyle have a specific pattern of attitudes, behaviors, and purchase patterns that marketers must be aware of and adapt to. Illustration 12–3 shows an ad for Reebok targeting the extreme sports enthusiast.

Consumers are seldom explicitly aware of the role lifestyle plays in their purchase decisions. For example, few consumers would think, "I'll have a Starbucks coffee at a Starbucks outlet to maintain my lifestyle." However, individuals pursuing an active, social lifestyle might purchase Starbucks in part because of its convenience, its "in" status, and the presence

Lifestyle and Consumption Process   **FIGURE** 12-2

Lifestyle determinants	Lifestyle	Impact on behavior
• Demographics	How we live	Purchases
• Subculture		• How
• Social class	• Activities	• When
• Motives	• Interests	• Where
• Personality	• Likes/dislikes	• What
• Emotions	• Attitudes	• With whom
• Values	• Consumption	
• Household life cycle	• Expectations	Consumption
• Culture	• Feelings	• Where
• Past experiences		• With whom
		• How
		• When
		• What

This Reebok ad targets the lifestyle of extreme sports enthusiasts.

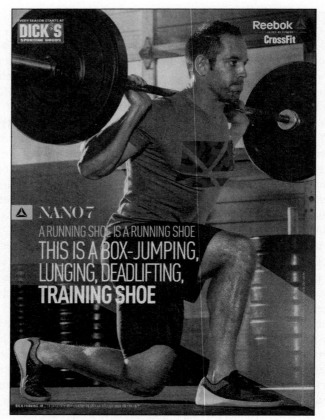

Source: Reebok International

of others at Starbucks outlets. Thus, lifestyle frequently provides the basic motivation and guidelines for purchases, although it generally does so in an indirect, subtle manner.

Measurement of Lifestyle

Attempts to develop quantitative measures of lifestyle were initially referred to as **psychographics.**[29] In fact, the terms *psychographics* and *lifestyle* are frequently used interchangeably. Psychographics or lifestyle studies typically include the following:

- *Attitudes*—evaluative statements about other people, places, ideas, products, and so forth.
- *Values*—widely held beliefs about what is acceptable or desirable.
- *Activities and interests*—nonoccupational behaviors to which consumers devote time and effort, such as hobbies, sports, public service, and church.
- *Demographics*—age, education, income, occupation, family structure, ethnic background, gender, and geographic location.
- *Media patterns*—the specific media the consumers utilize.
- *Usage rates*—measurements of consumption within a specified product category; often consumers are categorized as heavy, medium, or light users or as nonusers.

A large number of individuals, often 500 or more, provide the above information. Statistical techniques are used to place them into groups whose members have similar response patterns. Most studies use the first two or three dimensions described above to group individuals. The other dimensions are used to provide fuller descriptions of each group. Other studies include demographics as part of the grouping process.[30]

General versus Specific Lifestyle Schemes

Lifestyle measurements can be constructed with varying degrees of specificity. At one extreme, marketers can study the general lifestyle patterns of a population. These general lifestyle approaches are not specific to any one product or activity, so they have broad applicability in developing marketing strategies for a wide range of products and brands. General approaches include VALS™ and PRIZM®, which are discussed in later sections of this chapter.

At the other extreme, firms can conduct very specific lifestyle studies focused on those aspects of individual or household lifestyles most relevant to their product or service. For these studies, lifestyle measurement is product or activity specific. Let's take an in-depth look at two specific lifestyle schemes.

Luxury Sports Cars   Porsche examined the lifestyles of its buyers. What it found surprised it a bit because although key demographics (e.g., high education and income) were similar across its buyers, their lifestyles and motivations were quite different. The segments and their descriptions are listed below:[31]

- *Top Guns* (27 percent). Ambitious and driven, this group values power and control and expects to be noticed.
- *Elitists* (24 percent). These old-family-money "blue-bloods" don't see a car as an extension of their personality. Cars are cars no matter what the price tag.
- *Proud Patrons* (23 percent). This group purchases a car to satisfy themselves, not to impress others. A car is a reward for their hard work.
- *Bon Vivants* (17 percent). These thrill seekers and "jet-setters" see cars as enhancing their already exciting lives.
- *Fantasists* (9 percent). This group uses their car as an escape, not as a means to impress others. In fact, they feel a bit of guilt for owning a Porsche.

How would Porsche's marketing approach need to be changed across these different lifestyle segments?

Technology   How technology is used by consumers is of critical importance to marketers. Numerous technology and Internet lifestyle profiles exist such as the Technographics segmentation scheme by Forrester Research.[32] Experian Information Systems provides another typology, based on an extensive analysis of attitudes, lifestyle, and adoption and usage patterns related to technology. The segments and their descriptions are listed below:[33]

- *Wizards* (31 percent). Characterized by the statement "Technology is life." Enthusiastic and adventurous users of new technology. Driven by desire for new technology as a means for improving all aspects of life. Demographics: Young adults and students (youngest group with mean age of 42); household income, at $79k, is slightly below average; 31 percent nonwhite; trend single and male. Tech lifestyle: First to buy new electronic equipment, likely to purchase products advertised on cell phone, high use for gaming and social aspects. Latest technology includes iPhone, Blu-ray, and smart TV.
- *Journeymen* (13 percent). Characterized by the statement "Technology is an important part of my life." A notch down from wizards on enthusiasm, this group nonetheless is knowledgeable and confident in their use of new technology. Demographics: Young and

ILLUSTRATION 12-4

Experian Information Systems has identified four lifestyle segments related to technology. To which segment(s) will this Joule ad most appeal?

Source: ChefSteps

established adults (average age is 43); household income, at $104k, is above average; 27 percent nonwhite; trend married with kids. Tech lifestyle: Shop online, e-mail a key influence on shopping, technology a big changer of how they work and spend leisure time. Latest technology includes smartphone and DVR.

- *Apprentices* (31 percent). Characterized by the statement "Technology is changing my life." Take advantage of new technology, but there is room to grow, and they are willing to grow and learn. Affordability is the key barrier, not attitudes. Demographics: Established and middle-aged (average age is 48); household income, at $95k, is slightly above average; 17 percent nonwhite; trend married and female. Tech lifestyle: Technology is used to search and has changed how they gather information. Technology is a major source of information and shopping. Latest technology includes DVD drive on computer, LCD TV, and satellite radio.

- *Novices* (25 percent). Characterized by the statement "Technology has a limited impact on my life." This group is disconnected from emerging technology and resistant to change. Want simple and easy-to-use devices. Attitudinally not engaged. Demographics: Mature adults and retirees (average age is 55); household income, at $61k, is below average; 18 percent nonwhite; trend grandparents. Tech lifestyle: Confused by technology, use cell phone only for calling. E-mail is one of the few online activities. Latest technology includes DVD player and DVR in satellite box.

To which of these groups will the Joule ad in Illustration 12-4 appeal?

While specific lifestyle studies are useful, many firms have found general lifestyle studies to be of great value also. Two popular general systems are described next.[34]

THE VALS™ SYSTEM

LO4

By far the most popular application of psychographic research by marketing managers is Strategic Business Insights' (SBI) VALS™ program. **VALS** provides a systematic classification of American adults into eight distinct consumer segments.[35]

VALS is based on enduring psychological characteristics that correlate with purchase patterns. Respondents are classified according to their *primary motivation,* which serves as one of VALS's two dimensions. As we saw in Chapter 10, motives are critical determinants of behavior. Motives have strong linkages to personality and self-concept. Indeed, a core premise behind VALS is that "People buy products and services and seek experiences that fulfill characteristic motives and give shape, substance, and satisfaction to their lives." Three primary motivations underlie VALS:

- *Ideals motivation.* These consumers are guided in their choices by their beliefs and principles rather than by feelings or desire for social approval. They purchase functionality and reliability.
- *Achievement motivation.* These consumers strive for a clear social position and are strongly influenced by the actions, approval, and opinions of others. They purchase status symbols.
- *Self-expression motivation.* These action-oriented consumers strive to express their individuality through their choices. They purchase experiences.

These three orientations determine the types of goals and behaviors that individuals will pursue. Table 12–3 provides more detailed descriptions of the goals, motivations, and behavioral tendencies of each motivational group.

The second dimension, termed *resources,* reflects the ability of individuals to pursue their dominant self-orientation. It refers to the full range of psychological, physical, demographic, and material means on which consumers can draw. Resources generally increase from adolescence through middle age and then remain relatively stable until they begin to decline with older age. Resources are an important part of VALS because they can aid or inhibit a consumer's ability to act on his or her primary motivation.

On the basis of these two concepts, SBI has identified eight general psychographic segments, as shown in Figure 12–3. Table 12–4 provides selected characteristics for each segment. Each of these segments is described briefly next.

TABLE 12-3 Underlying Differences Across VALS™ Motivational Types

	Primary Motivation		
	Ideals	**Achievement**	**Self-Expression**
They are	Information seeking	Goal oriented	Spontaneous
They make	Choices based on principles	Choices to enhance position	Choices to have emotional impact
They buy	Functionality and reliability	Success symbols	Experiences
They seek	Understanding	Social approval	Adventure, excitement, novelty
They pursue	Self-development	Self-improvement	Self-reliance
They resist	Impulse	Risk	Authority
They ask	What "should" I do?	What are others like me doing?	What do I feel like doing?

Source: Strategic Business Insights (SBI), www.strategicbusinessinsights.com/vals.

FIGURE 12-3 US VALS™ Framework

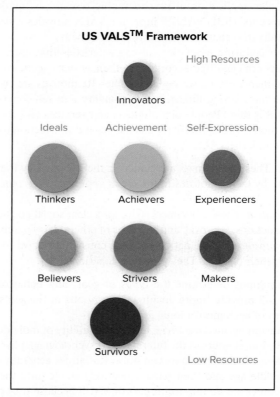

©2015 by Strategic Business Insights. All rights reserved. www.strategicbusinessinsights.com/vals.

TABLE 12-4 VALS Segments: Selected Characteristics

	Innovators	Thinkers	Believers	Achievers	Strivers	Experiencers	Makers	Survivors
Percent of U.S. Adults	8	15	13	14	12	12	11	15
Mean income (household)	$133,000	$121,000	$69,000	$118,000	$42,000	$85,000	$65,000	$29,000
Mean age (in years)	43	60	51	38	35	28	46	65
Female	50	52	77	50	40	47	31	60
Married	43	78	60	82	26	21	73	37
Employed full time	63	49	48	72	40	48	59	12
Have children under 18	30	26	40	60	48	n/a	48	15
Used Facebook in past 30 days	77	60	64	79	70	80	63	32
Own smartphone and tablet	47	41	32	51	26	38	25	7
Pray daily	15	40	49	34	27	35	36	51
Traveled out of country in last 3 years	51	40	17	30	14	23	17	10

Note: Except for income and age, numbers represent percent of each group that possesses the characteristic.

Source: Strategic Business Insights (SBI), www.strategicbusinessinsights.com/vals.

Source: BMW AG

The VALS™ Segments

Innovators are successful, sophisticated, take-charge people with high self-esteem. They are change leaders and are the most receptive to new ideas and technologies. Their purchases reflect cultivated tastes for upscale, niche products and services, as demonstrated by the BMW ad focusing on personal positioning as shown in Illustration 12–5.

Thinkers are mature, satisfied, comfortable, and reflective. They tend to be well educated and actively seek out information in the decision-making process. They favor durability, functionality, and value in products.

Believers are strongly traditional and respect rules and authority. Because they are fundamentally conservative, they are slow to change and technology averse. They choose familiar products and "me-too" established brands.

Achievers have goal-oriented lifestyles that center on family and career. They avoid situations that encourage a high degree of stimulation or change. They prefer premium products that demonstrate success to their peers as shown in the Movado ad Illustration 12–6.

Strivers are trendy and fun loving. They have little discretionary income and tend to have narrow interests. They favor stylish products that emulate the purchases of people with greater material wealth. Many Strivers believe that life isn't fair.

Experiencers appreciate the unconventional. They are active and impulsive, seeking stimulation from the new, offbeat, and risky (see the Utah ad in Illustration 12–7). They spend a comparatively high proportion of their income on fashion, socializing, and entertainment.

Makers value practicality and self-sufficiency. They choose hands-on constructive activities and spend leisure time with family and close friends. Because they prefer value to luxury, they buy basic products. Makers prefer to "buy American." The Ram's Vikings ad in Illustration 12–8 is designed to appeal to Makers who look for tough and rugged products that will stand up to hard use.

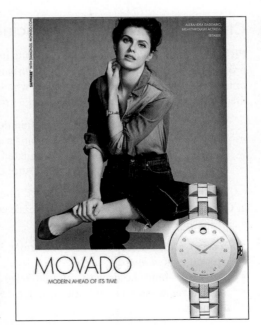

Source: Movado Group, Inc.

Experiencers are impulsive and social. They like places where they can be independent and experience new challenges such as this terrain in Utah.

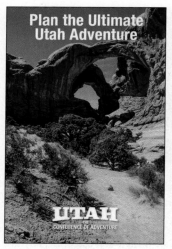

Plan the Ultimate Utah Adventure

UTAH
THE CONFLUENCE OF ADVENTURE

Source: OARS Companies Inc.

Survivors lead narrowly focused lives. Because they have the fewest resources, they do not exhibit a primary motivation and often feel powerless. They are primarily concerned about safety and security, so they tend to be brand loyal and buy discounted merchandise. As described in Chapter 4, meeting the needs of these consumers is a challenge for both marketers and public policymakers.

GEO-LIFESTYLE ANALYSIS (CLARITAS PRIZM®)

PRIZM® is a state-of-the-art geo-demographic classification system from Claritas that merges U.S. Census data with extensive data on product consumption and media usage patterns. The output is a set of 68 lifestyle segments. Each household in the United States can be profiled in terms of these lifestyle groups. The logic of **geo-demographic analysis** is as follows:

People with similar cultural backgrounds, means and perspectives naturally gravitate toward one another. They choose to live amongst their peers in neighborhoods offering affordable advantages and compatible lifestyles. Once settled in, people naturally emulate their neighbors. They adopt similar social values, tastes and expectations. They exhibit shared patterns of consumer behavior toward products, services, media and promotions.[36]

Claritas PRIZM Premier: Social and Lifestage Groups

PRIZM organizes its 68 individual segments into broader social and lifestage groups.[37] The broadest social groupings are based on "urbanization." For Claritas urbanization is determined by population density, relates to where people live, and is strongly related to the lifestyles people lead. The four major social groups are

- *Urban*—major cities with high population density.
- *Suburban*—moderately dense "suburban" areas surrounding metropolitan areas.
- *Second city*—smaller, less densely populated cities or satellites to major cities.
- *Town & rural*—low-density towns and rural communities.

The broadest lifestage groups are based on age and the presence of children. As we saw in Chapter 6, these factors strongly influence consumption patterns and lifestyle. The three major lifestage groups are

- *Younger years*—singles and couples; under 35 years of age without kids, or middle aged without kids *at home.*
- *Family life*—households with children *living at home.*
- *Mature years*—singles and couples; age 55 and over, or age 45–64 without children *at home.*

Source: Dodge Ram, FCA US LLC

PRIZM gets even finer-grained detail by further dividing each social and lifestage group by level of affluence (e.g., income and wealth) because affluence is a strong demographic determinant of activities, consumption patterns, and lifestyle. When possible, Nielsen (Claritas' data partner) also merges the general **PRIZM** information with clients' customer databases as a way to further enhance precision.

Sample PRIZM Segments

We briefly describe six specific segments and use them in demonstrating how **PRIZM** can be used in developing a successful marketing strategy (for all segments, visit www .mybestsegments.com).

- *Networked Neighbors* (Suburban/Family—**PRIZM** segment 02). This is a family portrait of suburban wealth: a place of million-dollar homes and manicured lawns, high-end cars, and exclusive private clubs. The nation's second-wealthiest lifestyle is characterized by married couples with children, graduate degrees, high technology use, and six-figure incomes earned by business executives, managers, and professionals. They play tennis, use LinkedIn, and drive an Acura.

- *Young Digerati* (Urban/Younger Years—**PRIZM** segment 04). The Young Digerati are tech-savvy and live in fashionable neighborhoods on the urban fringe. Affluent and highly educated, Young Digerati communities are typically filled with trendy apartments and condos, fitness clubs and clothing boutiques, casual restaurants, and all types of bars—from juice to coffee to microbrew. Many have chosen to start families while remaining in an urban environment. They hike and backpack, drive Audis, and use Uber.

- *Big Fish, Small Pond* (Town/Mature—**PRIZM** segment 09). Older, upper-class, college-educated professionals, the members of Big Fish, Small Pond are often among the leading citizens of their small-town communities. These upscale, empty-nesting couples enjoy the trappings of success, including belonging to country clubs, maintaining large investment portfolios, and spending freely on computer technology. They watch Fox Business on TV and drive a Lexus.

- *Pools & Patios* (Suburban/Family—**PRIZM** segment 30). Pools & Patios is a segment of middle-aged suburban families. In these stable neighborhoods graced with backyard pools and patios, residents work as white-collar managers and professionals, and are now at the top of their careers. They are above-average technology users, often researching products and shopping online. They play soccer and own a Nissan.

- *Golden Ponds* (Town/Mature—PRIZM segment 58). Golden Ponds is mostly a retirement lifestyle, dominated by downscale singles and couples over 50 years old. Found in small bucolic towns around the country, these high-school-educated seniors live in small apartments on less than $30,000 a year. Daily life is often a succession of sedentary activities such as reading, watching TV, playing bingo, and doing craft projects. They watch The Weather Channel and drive Buicks.
- *Young & Rustic* (Town/Younger Years—PRIZM segment 65). Young & Rustic is composed of restless singles and young families in the nation's rural areas. They enjoy the outdoors on their ATVs but are also big video gamers and follow NASCAR and monster trucks. They shop at Walmart, listen to country music, and drive a Chevrolet.

An Application of PRIZM

Marketing a Las Vegas Casino   One Las Vegas casino used PRIZM to identify its core consumers and markets and identify opportunities for future growth. It merged its own customer database with the PRIZM system in order to categorize each customer in its database into one of the 68 segments. With these data, it was able to find out which segments represented its core customers. These segments included *Young Digerati; Big Fish, Small Pond;* and *Pools & Patios.* While consumers in these segments differ in various ways, they are all highly educated, affluent professionals who like to travel.

The casino also looked at which segments were least attractive for its business. These included the *Young and Rustics* and *Golden Ponds.* Given the casino's core customer, these results make sense because both of these segments are less-educated, lower-income consumers who tend to engage in sedentary activities or activities close to home.

Finally, the casino searched for attractive segments that held opportunity but were currently being underleveraged. One such segment was the *Networked Neighbors* (formerly known as *Blue Blood Estates*), which holds key similarities to the casino's core customers in terms of education, income, and travel.

Having identified high-opportunity segments, the casino realigned and refocused its marketing efforts to specifically target those groups while also staying true to its core. By understanding its core customers, and where households that looked like its core customers existed in target markets, it was successful in attracting new and profitable customers in a cost-effective manner.

INTERNATIONAL LIFESTYLES

LO5

The VALS and PRIZM systems presented in this chapter are oriented to the United States. In addition, VALS has systems for China, Dominican Republic, Japan, Nigeria, the United Kingdom, and Venezuela. As we saw in Chapter 2, marketing is increasingly a global activity. If there are discernible lifestyle segments that cut across cultures, marketers can develop cross-cultural strategies around these segments. Although language and other differences would exist, individuals pursuing similar lifestyles in different cultures should be responsive to similar product features and communication themes.

Not surprisingly, a number of attempts have been made to develop such systems.[38] Large international advertising agencies and marketing research firms are leading the way. Experian Information Services' Mosaic™ Global evaluated roughly 380 million households across 25 countries in Asia, Europe, and North America. Its goal was a global segmentation scheme based on core underlying similarities in demographics, lifestyles, and behavior regardless of where the households are located in the world.[39] According to one executive,

> We're looking for the bedrock values, the fundamental stable things in people's lives that determine who they are, to understand the underlying motivations that drive their attitudes as well as their behavior.[40]

Their analysis uncovered 10 global lifestyle segments along dimensions of affluence, or wealth, and where they live, from urban to rural. The segments are described in Table 12–5, overlaying PRIZM's urbanization terminology. While these segments exist in all the countries studied, the percentage of the population in each group varied by country. For example, the United Kingdom has a high proportion of Bourgeois Prosperity. Found in a British magazine, the Sharps ad in Illustration 12–9 has a global appeal to the Bourgeois Prosperity segment. This type of ad often is used by marketers to target similar lifestyle groups across different cultures, allowing for a relatively standardized ad theme.

Global Lifestyle Segments Identified by Mosaic™ Global	TABLE 12-5

Sophisticated Singles (8 percent). Urban and wealthy; young and social people, mostly single and well educated, who enjoy life in large cities, are international in their outlook, and innovative in their lifestyle and purchases. More common in European countries, such as Finland and France.

Bourgeois Prosperity (9 percent). Suburban and wealthy; middle to late middle-aged people, who are well educated, married and with older children, and living in big houses in traditional, quiet suburban locations. Many have worked their way up to leadership positions in their companies. More common in Australia and the U.K.

Career and Family (9 percent). Second City and wealthy; younger people, married and with young children, enjoying good careers in technology, and living in new, modern-decorated private estates from which they commute to work. Family members are early adopters of technology and latest consumer products. More common in Hong Kong, Norway, and the U.S.

Comfortable Retirement (3 percent). Rural and wealthy; people who are retired or close to retirement, with a significant nest egg, living in communities with others in similar lifestage but often away from their grown children. Leisure activities include gardening and supporting the arts. More common across Europeans, especially from The Netherlands.

Routine Service Workers (9 percent). Suburban with average wealth; people at various stages in their life cycle, living in older houses, and working in white-collar service jobs. They are relatively well informed about social trends but not quick to innovate. Asians and the Irish more represented for this group.

Hard Working Blue Collar (11 percent). Suburban with average to low income/wealth; people with families, employed in craft or manual skill positions. Leisure time spent on home improvement and outdoor activities. More common in New Zealand for this group.

Metropolitan Strugglers (19 percent). Urban with low income; people who live in rental units in transient areas with high levels of crime and drug addiction, are employed in low-skill jobs, and have limited to no access to a car or consumer credit. Retail options are limited to discount stores. Hong Kong, Sweden, and the U.S. are more common in this group.

Low Income Elders (6 percent). Urban to suburban with low income; people who are retired or close to retirement, rely on the government for their income, rent small houses or apartments, and live modest lifestyles. They enjoy watching TV and visiting their grown children. More common in Spain and other European countries.

Post Industrial Survivors (12 percent). Town & Rural with low income; people living in older, single-family houses in towns traditionally dependent on coal, steel, and chemicals, and working as manual laborers. They are slow to adopt innovative products and take few vacations. More common in European countries.

Rural Inheritance (15 percent). Rural with average to low income; people who live far away from big cities, are self-employed, and work in agriculture and tourism. They do not regularly eat in restaurants, have their clothes dry cleaned, or their children tutored. Greece and Ireland are more common in this group.

Note: Percentages may not add to 100 percent due to rounding.

Source: ©Mosaic Global E-Handbook, Experian Information Services, undated.

This Sharps ad would have strong appeal to Bourgeois Prosperity.

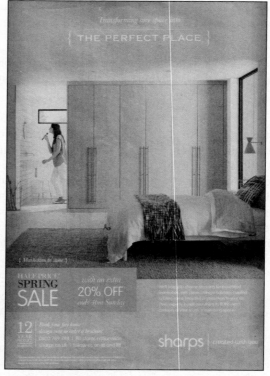

Source: Sharps Bedrooms Limited

SUMMARY

LO1: Describe self-concept, how it is measured, and how it is used to position products.

The *self-concept* is one's beliefs and feelings about oneself. There are four types of self-concept: *actual self-concept, social self-concept, private self-concept,* and *ideal self-concept.* The self-concept is important to marketers because consumers purchase and use products to express, maintain, and enhance their self-concepts. Marketers, particularly those in international marketing, have found it useful to characterize individuals and cultures by whether they have a predominantly *independent self-concept* (the individual is the critical component) or an *interdependent self-concept* (relationships are of primary importance).

An individual's self-concept, the way one defines oneself, typically includes some of the person's possessions. The self-concept including the possessions one uses to define oneself is termed the *extended self.* Marketers can position products and brands as a means to enhance an individual's self-concept in terms of the

extended self. Sometimes products and brands can be positioned to help maintain the self-concept, as when the ideal and actual self-concepts are consistent. At other times, products and brands can be positioned to enhance the self-concept, as when the actual self-concept is lower than the ideal.

LO2: Define lifestyle and its relationship to the self-concept and to psychographics.

Lifestyle can be defined simply as how one lives. It is a function of a person's inherent individual characteristics that have been shaped through social interaction as the person moves through his or her life cycle. It is how an individual expresses his or her self-concept through actions.

Psychographics is the primary way that lifestyle is made operationally useful to marketing managers. This is a way of describing the psychological makeup or lifestyle of consumers by assessing such lifestyle dimensions as activities, interests, opinions, values, and demographics. Lifestyle measures can be macro and reflect how individuals live in general, or micro and describe their attitudes and behaviors with respect to a specific product category or activity.

LO3: Explain specific lifestyle typologies and summarize those for luxury sports cars and technology.

Lifestyle measurements can be constructed with varying degrees of specificity. At one extreme, firms can conduct very specific lifestyle studies focused on those aspects of individual or household lifestyles most relevant to their product or service. For these studies, lifestyle measurement is product or activity specific. Porsche conducted a lifestyle segmentation study for its brand and found various segments with very different purchase motives. Experian examined technology users and found very different groups in terms of their attitudes, usage, and adoption of emerging technologies.

LO4: Explain general lifestyle typologies and summarize those for VALS™ and PRIZM®.

At the other extreme, marketers can study the general lifestyle patterns of a population. These general lifestyle approaches are not specific to any one product or activity, so they have broad applicability in developing marketing strategies for a wide range of products and brands. General approaches include VALS and PRIZM.

The *VALS* system divides the United States into eight groups: Innovators, Thinkers, Believers, Achievers, Strivers, Experiencers, Makers, and Survivors. These groups were derived on the basis of two dimensions. The first, *primary motivation,* has three categories: *ideals* (those guided by their basic beliefs and values), *achievement* (those striving for a clear social position and influenced by others), and *self-expression* (those who seek self-expression, physical activity, variety, and excitement). The second dimension is the physical, mental, and material *resources* to pursue one's dominant motivation.

Geo-demographic analysis is based on the premise that individuals with similar lifestyles tend to live near each other. PRIZM is a system that examines demographic and consumption data down to the individual household with 68 lifestyle segments organized around social groupings and lifestage.

LO5: Discuss international lifestyles and one existing segmentation scheme.

In response to the rapid expansion of international marketing, a number of attempts have been made to develop lifestyle measures applicable across cultures. Experian's Mosaic™ Global analyzed hundreds of millions of households across the world and found 10 global lifestyle segments based on core similarities in demographics, lifestyle, and behavior.

KEY TERMS

Actual self-concept 434
Brand engagement 436
Extended self 435
Geo-demographic analysis 448
Ideal self-concept 434
Independent self-concept 434

Interdependent self-concept 434
Lifestyle 441
Mere ownership effect 436
Peak experience 436
Private self-concept 434
PRIZM 448

Psychographics 442
Self-concept 434
Social self-concept 434
VALS 444

REVIEW QUESTIONS

1. What is a *self-concept?* What are the four types of self-concept?
2. How do marketers use insights about the self-concept?
3. How can one measure the self-concept?
4. How does an *interdependent self-concept* differ from an *independent self-concept?*
5. What is the *extended self?*

6. What is a *brand engagement?*
7. What ethical issues arise in using the self-concept in marketing?
8. What do we mean by *lifestyle?* What factors determine and influence lifestyle?
9. What is *psychographics?*
10. When is a product- or activity-specific psychographic instrument superior to a general one?

11. What are the dimensions on which VALS is based? Describe each.

12. Describe the VALS system and each segment in it.

13. What is *geo-demographic analysis?*

14. Describe the PRIZM system.

15. Describe the global lifestyle segments identified by Experian's Mosaic Global.

DISCUSSION QUESTIONS

16. Use Table 12–2 to measure your four self-concepts. To what extent are they similar? What causes the differences? To what extent do you think they influence your purchase behavior?

17. Use Table 12–2 to measure your self-concept (you choose which self-concept and justify your choice). Also measure the images of three celebrities you admire. What do you conclude?

18. Respond to the questions in Consumer Insight 12–1.

19. What possessions are part of your extended self? Why?

20. Is your self-concept predominantly independent or interdependent? Why?

21. What ethical concerns are associated with ads that portray a standardized ideal image of beauty?

22. For each of the following products, develop one ad that would appeal to a target market characterized by predominantly independent self-concepts and another ad for a target market characterized by predominantly interdependent self-concepts.
    a. Amazon.com
    b. Mini Cooper automobile
    c. Timex watch
    d. Tommy Hilfiger clothing

23. Use the self-concept theory to develop marketing strategies for the following products:
    a. The National Alzheimer Association contributions
    b. BMW
    c. Army ROTC recruitment
    d. A&W root beer
    e. Purell
    f. Disney Cruiseline

24. Does VALS make sense to you? What do you like or dislike about it?

25. How would one use VALS to develop a marketing strategy?

26. Develop a marketing strategy based on VALS for
    a. Starbucks
    b. Grand Canyon kayak vacation

    c. SiriusXM satellite radio
    d. Kawasaki jet ski
    e. Triumph motorcycles
    f. NBA

27. Develop a marketing strategy for each of the eight VALS segments for
    a. Verizon wireless
    b. Vacation package
    c. DaVinci Gourmet coffee syrups
    d. CNN
    e. Facial cleansers
    f. Walmart

28. Does PRIZM make sense to you? What do you like or dislike about it? Is it really a measure of lifestyle?

29. How would one use PRIZM to develop a marketing strategy?

30. Develop a marketing strategy for each of the Mosaic Global lifestyle segments for the products in Question 26. What challenges do you face in trying to market these products to global market segments?

31. The following quote is from Paul Casi, president of Glenmore distilleries: "Selling cordials is a lot different from selling liquor. Cordials are like the perfume of our industry. You're really talking high fashion and you're talking generally to a different audience—I don't mean male versus female—I'm talking about lifestyle."
    a. In what ways do you think the lifestyle of cordial drinkers would differ from that of those who drink liquor but not cordials?
    b. How would you determine the nature of any such differences?
    c. Of what use would knowledge of such lifestyle differences be to a marketing manager introducing a new cordial?

32. How is one likely to change one's lifestyle at different stages of the household life cycle? Over one's life, is one likely to assume more than one of the VALS lifestyle profiles described?

33. To which VALS category do you belong? To which do your parents belong? Which will you belong to when you are your parents' age?

34. Generalizing from the global fashion lifestyles in the opener, develop a marketing strategy for

   a. A spa
   b. Makeup
   c. Jewelry
   d. Shoes
   e. Clothes

APPLICATION ACTIVITIES

35. Develop an instrument to measure the interdependent versus independent self-concept.

36. Use the instrument you developed in Activity 35 to measure the self-concepts of 10 male and 10 female students, all of the same nationality. What do you conclude?

37. Develop your own psychographic instrument (set of relevant questions) that measures the lifestyles of college students.

38. Using the psychographic instrument developed in Activity 37, interview 10 students (using the

questionnaire instrument). On the basis of their responses, categorize them into lifestyle segments.

39. Find and copy or describe ads that would appeal to each of the eight VALS segments.

40. Find and copy or describe ads that would appeal to each of the PRIZM segments discussed in the text.

41. Repeat Activity 40 for the Mosaic Global lifestyle segments.

42. Repeat Activity 40 for the Experian Technology segments.

REFERENCES

1. Opening example based on A. Khan, "5 High-Tech Cooking Gadgets," *U.S. News & World Report,* July 3, 2014, www.usnews.com, accessed June 14, 2018; N. Cole, "The Healthy Meal Kit Service Industry Is Worth $1.5 Billion (Here's What the Future of Food Looks Like)," *Inc.,* February 17, 2017, www.inc.com, accessed June 14, 2018; Mintel, "Cooking Enthusiasts—US—November 2017," November 2017, www.mintel.com, accessed June 14, 2018; B. Chen, "To Invade Homes, Tech Is Trying to Get in Your Kitchen," *New York Times,* March 25, 2018.

2. N. Y. Wong and A. C. Ahuvia, "Personal Taste and Family Face," *Psychology & Marketing,* August 1998, pp. 423–41; T. Sun, M. Horn, and D. Merrit, "Values and Lifestyles of Individualists and Collectivists," *Journal of Consumer Marketing* 21, no. 5 (2004), pp. 318–31.

3. See, e.g., E. C. Hirschman, "Men, Dogs, Guns, and Cars: The Semiotics of Rugged Individualism," *Journal of Advertising,* Spring 2003, pp. 9–22.

4. C. L. Wang and J. C. Mowen, "The Separateness–Connectedness Self-Schema," *Psychology & Marketing,* March 1997, pp. 185–207.

5. C. L. Wang et al., "Alternative Modes of Self-Construal," *Journal of Consumer Psychology* 9, no. 2 (2000), pp. 107–15.

6. See A. Reed II, "Activating the Self-Importance of Consumer Selves," *Journal of Consumer Research,* September 2004, pp. 286–95; Sun, Horn, and Merrit, "Values and Lifestyles of Individualists and Collectivists"; N. Agrawal and D. Maheswaran, "The Effects of Self-Construal and Commitment on Persuasion,"

Journal of Consumer Research, March 2005, pp. 841–49; C. J. Torelli, "Individuality or Conformity?," *Journal of Consumer Psychology* 16, no. 3 (2006), pp. 240–48; J. H. Leigh and Y. Choi, "The Impact of Attributions about Life Events on Perceptions of Foreign Products," *Psychology & Marketing,* January 2007, pp. 41–68; A. B. Monga and L. Lau-Gesk, "Blending Cobrand Personalities," *Journal of Marketing Research,* August 2007, pp. 389–400.

7. M. Zhang, "The Effect of Advertising Appeals in Activating Self-Construals," *Journal of Advertising,* Spring 2009, pp. 63–81.

8. R. W. Belk, "Possessions and the Extended Self," *Journal of Consumer Research,* September 1988, pp. 139–68; R. Belk, "Extended Self and Extending Paradigmatic Perspective," *Journal of Consumer Research,* June 1989, pp. 129–32. See also M. L. Richins, "Valuing Things," *Journal of Consumer Research,* December 1994, pp. 504–21; M. L. Richins, "Special Possessions and the Expression of Material Values," *Journal of Consumer Research,* December 1994, pp. 522–31; A. C. Ahuvia, "Beyond the Extended Self," *Journal of Consumer Research,* June 2005, pp. 171–84.

9. See S. S. Kleine, R. E. Kleine III, and C. T. Allen, "How Is a Possession 'Me' or 'Not Me'?," *Journal of Consumer Research,* December 1995, pp. 327–43.

10. S. Sayre and D. Horne, "I Shop, Therefore I Am," *Advances in Consumer Research,* vol. 23, ed. K. P. Corfman and J. G. Lynch (Provo, UT: Association for Consumer Research, 1996), pp. 323–28.

11. See L. L. Love and P. S. Sheldon, "Souvenirs," *Advances in Consumer Research,* vol. 25, ed. J. W. Alba and J. W. Hutchinson (Provo, UT: Association for Consumer Research, 1998), pp. 170–74.

12. C. S. Areni, P. Kiecker, and K. M. Palan, "Is It Better to Give Than to Receive?," *Psychology & Marketing,* January 1998, pp. 81–109. See also C. F. Curasi, L. L. Price, and E. J. Arnould, "How Individuals' Cherished Possessions Become Families' Inalienable Wealth," *Journal of Consumer Research,* December 2004, pp. 609–22.

13. K. J. Dodson, "Peak Experiences and Mountain Biking," in *Advances in Consumer Research,* vol. 23, ed. Corfman and Lynch, pp. 317–22.

14. C. H. Noble and B. A. Walker, "Exploring the Relationships among Liminal Transitions, Symbolic Consumption, and the Extended Self," *Psychology & Marketing,* January 1997, pp. 29–47.

15. E. Sivadas and K. A. Machleit, "A Scale to Determine the Extent of Object Incorporation in the Extended Self," in *Marketing Theory and Applications,* vol. 5, ed. C. W. Park and D. C. Smith (Chicago: American Marketing Association, 1994).

16. S. Sen and E. J. Johnson, "Mere-Possession Effects without Possession in Consumer Choice," *Journal of Consumer Research,* June 1997, pp. 105–17; M. A. Strahilevitz and G. Loewenstein, "The Effect of Ownership History of the Valuation of Objects," *Journal of Consumer Research,* December 1998, pp. 276–89; K. P. Nesselroade Jr., J. K. Beggan, and S. T. Allison, "Possession Enhancement in an Interpersonal Context," *Psychology & Marketing,* January 1999, pp. 21–34.

17. D. Sprott, S. Czellar, and E. Spangenberg, "The Importance of a General Measure of Brand Engagement," *Journal of Marketing Research,* February 2009, pp. 92–104. The full set of eight measurement items can be found on page 93 of their article.

18. S. Kang, "Nike, Serena Williams Partner Up," *Wall Street Journal,* December 12, 2003, p. B2.

19. J. G. Helgeson and M. Supphellen, "A Conceptual and Measurement Comparison of Self-Congruity and Brand Personality," *International Journal of Market Research* 46, no. 2 (2004), pp. 205–33; L. N. Chaplin and D. R. John, "The Development of Self-Brand Connections in Children and Adolescents," *Journal of Consumer Research,* June 2005, pp. 119–29; J. E. Escalas and J. R. Bettman, "Self-Construal, Reference Groups, and Brand Meaning," *Journal of Consumer Research,* December 2005, pp. 378–89; C. Yim, K. Chan, and K. Hung, "Multiple Reference Effects in Service Evaluations," *Journal of Retailing* 83, no. 1 (2007), pp. 147–57; V. Swaminathan, K. L. Page, and Z. Gurhan-Canli, "'My' Brand or 'Our' Brand," *Journal of Consumer Research,* October 2007, pp. 248–59; S. Kim and D. Gal, "From Compensatory Consumption to Adaptive Consumption: The Role of Self-Acceptance in Resolving Self-Deficits," *Journal of Consumer Research* 41 (August 2014), pp. 526–42; S. Chu, K. Windels, and S. Kamal, "The Influence of Self-Construal and Materialism on Social Media Intensity: A Study of China and the United States," *International Journal of Advertising* 35, no. 3 (May 2016), pp. 569–88.

20. S. J. Gould, "An Interpretive Study of Purposeful, Mood Self-Regulating Consumption," *Psychology & Marketing,* July 1997, pp. 395–426.

21. See J. W. Hong and G. M. Zinkhan, "Self-Concept and Advertising Effectiveness," *Psychology & Marketing,* January 1995, pp. 53–77; A. Mehta, "Using Self-Concept to Assess Advertising Effectiveness," *Journal of Advertising Research,* January 1999, pp. 81–89; M. J. Barone, T. A. Shimp, and D. E. Sprott, "Product Ownership as a Moderator of Self-Congruity Effects," *Marketing Letters,* February 1999, pp. 75–85.

22. E. N. Banister and M. K. Hogg, "Mapping the Negative Self," and A. M. Muniz and L. O. Hamer, "Us versus Them," both in *Advances in Consumer Research,* vol. 28, ed. M. C. Gilly and J. Meyers-Levy (Provo, UT: Association for Consumer Research, 2001), pp. 242–48 and 355–61, respectively.

23. For a broader discussion of situational factors, see T. R. Graeff, "Consumption Situations and the Effects of Brand Image on Consumers' Brand Evaluations," *Psychology & Marketing,* January 1997, pp. 49–70.

24. M. K. Hogg, A. J. Cox, and K. Keeling, "The Impact of Self-Monitoring on Image Congruence and Product/Brand Evaluation," *European Journal of Marketing* 34, no. 5/6 (2000), pp. 641–66.

25. J. Meyers-Levy and L. A. Peracchio, "Understanding the Socialized Body," *Journal of Consumer Research,* September 1995, p. 147.

26. C. S. Gulas and K. McKeage, "Extending Social Comparison," *Journal of Advertising,* Summer 2000, pp. 17–28; D. Smeesters and N. Mandel, "Positive and Negative Media Image Effects on the Self," *Journal of Consumer Research,* March 2006, pp. 576–82.

27. Insight based on N. Etcoff, S. Orbach, J. Scott, and H. D'Agostino, "Findings of the Global Study on Women, Beauty and Well-Being," *Unilever White Paper,* September 2004, www.clubofamsterdam.com/contentarticles/52%20Beauty/dove_white_paper_final.pdf; "The Dove® Campaign for Real Beauty," *Dove,* www.dove.us/social-mission/campaign-for-real-beauty.aspx, accessed August 28, 2014; J. Neff, "Ten Years In, Dove's 'Real Beauty' Seems to Be Aging Well," *Advertising Age,* January 22, 2014, http://adage.com/article/news/ten-years-dove-s-real-beauty-aging/291216/, accessed August 28, 2014; N. Bahadur, "Dove 'Real Beauty' Campaign Turns 10: How a Brand Tried to Change the Conversation About Female Beauty," *Huffington Post,* February 6, 2014, www.huffingtonpost.com/2014/01/21/dove-real-beauty-campaign-turns-10_n_4575940.html, accessed August 28, 2014; B. Garfield, "Women May Be 'Real' but Product Is Baloney," *Advertising Age,* July 25, 2005, p. 53; E. Spitznagel, "How Those Dove 'Real Beauty Sketch' Ads Went Viral," *Businessweek,* April 26, 2013, www.businessweek.com/articles/2013-04-26/how-those-dove-real-beauty-sketch-ads-went-viral#p1, accessed August 28, 2014; J. Grose, "The Story Behind Dove's Mega Viral 'Real Beauty Sketches' Campaign," *Fast Company,* April 19, 2013, www.fastcocreate.com/1682823/the-story-behind-doves-mega-viral-real-beauty-sketches-campaign, accessed August 28, 2014.

28. M. J. Dutta-Bergman and W. D. Wells, "The Values and Lifestyles of Idiocentrics and Allocentrics in an Individualistic Culture," *Journal of Consumer Psychology* 12, no. 3 (2002), pp. 231–42.

29. See E. H. Demby, "Psychographics Revisited," *Marketing Research,* Spring 1994, pp. 26–30.

30. See F. W. Gilbert and W. E. Warren, "Psychographic Constructs and Demographic Segments," *Psychology & Marketing,* May 1995, pp. 223–37.

31. Based on A. Taylor III, "Porsche Slices Up Its Buyers," *Fortune*, January 16, 1995, p. 24.

32. Based on a Forrester Research report by J. Kolko, "Why Techno-Graphics *Still* Works," December 14, 2004. Used by permission of Forrester Research.

33. Segment descriptions from *2010 Technology Adoption Consumer Report* (Costa Mesa, CA: Experian, Spring 2010).

34. For a critical review and alternative approach, see D. B. Holt, "Poststructuralist Lifestyle Analysis," *Journal of Consumer Research*, March 1997, pp. 326–50. Alternative lifestyle systems also are described in C. Walker and E. Moses, "The Age of Self-Navigation," *American Demographics*, September 1996, pp. 36–42; P. H. Ray, "The Emerging Culture," *American Demographics*, February 1997, pp. 29–56.

35. Based on material provided by Strategic Business Insights.

36. *How to Use PRIZM* (Claritas Inc., 1986), p. 1.

37. Information regarding PRIZM is based on *Prizm$_{NE}$: The New Evolution Segment Snapshots* (Claritas Inc., 2003); other information from Claritas Inc., 2005: www.claritas.com/MyBestSegments/tutorials/Nielsen_PRIZM/engage.html, accessed June 11, 2011, and www.claritas.com/MyBestSegments, accessed June 11, 2011; information from segmentationsolutions.nielsen.com/mybestsegments/, accessed June 16, 2018; information from www.claritas360.claritas.com/mybestsegments/#, accessed June 16, 2018.

38. For example, see M. T. Ewing, "Affluent Asia," *Journal of International Consumer Marketing* 12, no. 2 (1999), pp. 25–37.

39. Experian, "Mosaic Global Factsheet Final," October 2007, www.experian.co.uk, accessed June 16, 2018.

40. S. Elliott, "Research Finds Consumers Worldwide Belong to Six Basic Groups That Cross National Lines," *New York Times*, June 25, 1998, p. D8.

Part Three CASES

3-1 PATAGONIA'S ECO-FASHION PUSH

Concerns about the environment continue to grow. Consumers are becoming more educated about environmental friendliness with over one-third of consumers believing that it is important for companies to be environmentally conscious. Not surprisingly, green household products had the highest adoption rate of all consumer goods categories in six out of the eight countries that were included in a recent survey.

While automobiles often garner the lion's share of media attention regarding the environment, consumers also voice concerns about the impact of the products that they eat and wear. According to one expert:

> Early in the study, we asked consumers what green products they were looking for, and they were looking for products that were closer to them—that they put in their body or on their body.

In terms of what consumers are putting on their bodies, environmentally friendly apparel, also called *eco-fashion,* is becoming increasingly popular. Consumers favor natural fibers in their clothing over synthetic materials. A survey from Cotton Incorporated found that 83 percent of consumers believe that clothing made from 100 percent natural fibers is better for the environment than other clothing materials. However, consumers also consider their awareness of a brand's corporate actions, values, recycling and packaging efforts, sustainability, and supply chain decisions when making decisions about environmentally friendly apparel.

Patagonia is an apparel company that shares the environmentally conscious values of many consumers. Since 1985, Patagonia has donated at least one percent of annual sales to environmental charities. Patagonia's One Percent for the Planet program has influenced other companies to follow its lead. Patagonia is continuously looking for new ways to be more environmentally friendly. According to Patagonia's founder, Yvon Chouinard:

> We're switching all our nylon to something called Nylon 6, which can be recycled infinitely. We're recycling cotton; we're recycling wool. We send polyester back to Japan, where it gets melted down into its original polymer. Of course, the best thing to do is make clothing so it never wears out, right?

Patagonia's 2011 fall collection continued the theme of environmental responsibility. The fabrics used are environmentally friendly. Thirty-six percent of their fabrics are Bluesign approved. Bluesign is an independent auditor that requires members to establish management systems to improve environmental performance as follows:

> Bluesign® members agree at the outset to establish management systems for improving environmental performance in five key areas of the production process—resource productivity, consumer safety, water emissions, air emissions, and occupational health and safety. Members regularly report their progress and must meet improvement goals to maintain their status; bluesign® technologies performs regular audits.

In addition, all styles currently being released are eligible for the Common Threads Recycling Initiative. In this program, consumers are encouraged to reduce clothing consumption, repair worn clothing when possible, reuse clothing by donating it to others, and recycle worn clothing when beyond repair.

Patagonia's designs are popular among everyday consumers and celebrities. Brad Pitt has been seen sporting Patagonia clothing, which may have had something to do with him being named one of Hollywood's "Greenest Stars."

In 2010, Cotton Incorporated conducted a Consumer Environment Survey to study consumers' attitudes about environmental friendliness in the apparel industry. They segmented consumers into five groups based on their attitudes and behaviors regarding environmentally friendly apparel, as shown in Table A.

Attitudes and Behaviors of Green Apparel Consumers			TABLE A

Consumer segment	%	Attitudes and Behaviors
Dark green	7	Very likely to seek out environmentally friendly apparel; would be extremely bothered and complain if company engaged in practices that were not environmentally friendly.
Green	9	Very likely to seek out environmentally friendly apparel.
Light green	54	Somewhat or moderately likely to seek out environmentally friendly apparel.
Pale green	14	Do not seek out environmentally friendly apparel.
Non-green	16	Do not seek out environmentally friendly apparel; would not be bothered if firm engaged in practices that were not environmentally friendly.

Source: Cotton Incorporated's 2010 *Consumer Environment Survey.*

Further, the researchers at Cotton Incorporated profiled each of these five green consumer segments based on the characteristics of apparel that played the most important role in their apparel purchases. A summary of each segment's profile is available in Table B.

Finally, Cotton Incorporated's researchers profiled each of the green consumer segments with demographic information shown in Table C.

Discussion Questions

1. Using the information provided in the tables, which of the five green segments identified by Cotton International would you target if you were marketing a clothing line in each of the following situations. Explain your choices.
   a. Well-known brand name that is moderately environmentally friendly but has the potential for mass appeal.
   b. Well-known brand name with a track record of environmental friendliness and a high natural-fiber content.
   c. Moderately well-known brand name, with low prices, that has been cited in the past for behaving in ways that are not environmentally friendly.
2. The green segmentation scheme presented in this case is particular to green apparel. Compare and contrast the green apparel segments with the green segments described in Table 3–1 of the text.
3. The case mentions that Brad Pitt has been spotted in the media wearing Patagonia clothing. In what ways is this potentially positive for the brand?
4. Consider that Patagonia was going to sign a celebrity endorser to its brand.
   a. What factors should Patagonia consider when choosing a celebrity endorser?
   b. What celebrity would be a good endorser for Patagonia? Justify your answer.

Purchase Drivers for the Green Apparel Segments					TABLE B

% of consumers citing the factor as important in apparel purchases	Dark green (%)	Green (%)	Light green (%)	Pale green (%)	Non-green (%)
Fit	99	99	97	99	96
Color	96	92	86	86	85
Style	96	93	90	88	84
Price	96	94	94	93	93
Environmental friendliness	93	84	55	27	12
Fiber content	91	82	67	51	44
Laundering instructions	87	79	66	57	47
Brand name	76	74	51	39	34

Source: Cotton Incorporated's 2010 *Consumer Environment Survey.*

5. Chapter 12 outlines the VALS lifestyle segments. Which of these lifestyle segments is the most likely target market for Patagonia products? Could more than one group be a good target market? Justify your answer.

6. In terms of Cotton Incorporated's five green consumer segments for apparel, their purchase motivations, and their demographics, describe a target market for Patagonia.

Source: J. Pearson, "Hollywood Goes Green!," *Star Magazine,* 2007, www.starmagazine.com; S. Casey, "Patagonia: Blueprint for Green Business," *Fortune,* May 29, 2007, money.cnn.com; T. Foster, "Patagonia's Founder on Why There's 'No Such Thing as Sustainability,'" *Fast Company,* July, 1, 2009, www.fastcompany.com; "Shades of the Green Consumer," *Cotton Incorporated Supply Chain Insights,* 2010, E. Grady; "Patagonia Launches Common Threads Initiative to Curb Clothing Consumption," *Treehugger,* November, 15, 2010, www.treehugger.com; "Introducing the Common Threads Initiative," *Patagonia,* 2011, www.patagonia.com; "Seventh Gen and Whole Foods Top Green Brands Ranking," *Environmental Leader,* June 10, 2011, www.environmentalleader.com; E. Grady, "Patagonia Steps Up Sustainability in New Fall 2011 Styles," *Treehugger,* June 12, 2011, www.treehugger.com; "Survey: People Getting Smarter About Going Green," *Ad Age Blogs,* June 13, 2011, adage.com.

TABLE C   Demographics of Green Consumers

	Dark green (%)	Green (%)	Light green (%)	Pale green (%)	Non-green (%)
Gender					
Male	51	46	39	31	45
Female	49	54	62	69	55
Age					
Average age (years)	39	36	38	38	38
14 to 24	12	20	20	20	21
25 to 34	23	23	17	13	15
35 to 44	30	27	25	26	26
45 to 54	36	30	39	41	39
Income					
Average annual (000)	70	64	61	58	63
Ethnicity					
Caucasian	57	63	64	67	67
African American	16	10	12	13	15
Hispanic	14	16	17	14	12
Asian	8	8	5	1	3
Other	6	3	3	4	2
Education Level					
Less than high school diploma	6	15	10	15	13
High school graduate	27	34	34	36	33
Some college	21	18	26	30	26
College degree or higher	46	34	30	19	29
Children in the Household					
Yes	59	60	51	47	50
No	41	40	49	53	50
Region					
South	35	45	35	33	40
West	26	19	25	26	18
Midwest	20	21	20	25	26
Northeast	19	15	20	18	15

Source: Cotton Incorporated's 2010 *Consumer Environment Survey.*

3-2 REPOSITIONING MCDONALD'S

McDonald's is a ubiquitous part of life in both American and global culture. Traditionally, McDonald's restaurants were largely standardized and consumers knew what to expect when they entered any one of its restaurants: They would walk up to the counter to order fast food from an employee. Then, if they stayed in the restaurant to eat, they would expect a brightly colored and well-lit environment where they could sit in hard plastic chairs, perhaps near a playground. This was fine for decades, but now the competitive environment has changed with the likes of Chipotle and Panera Bread entering the marketspace.

Not all of that scene is changing, but quite a bit is. McDonald's is gradually reimaging its stores in an effort to improve consumer perceptions of quality by repositioning the brand as a modern, progressive burger company. According to CEO Steve Easterbrook, who has successfully turned around McDonald's downward slip:

> As customers' expectations increased, McDonald's simply didn't keep pace with them. Making meaningful improvements in quality, convenience, and value will win back some of McDonald's best customers.

Many adjustments have been made as part of this repositioning effort in many areas, including changes to the (1) interior design, (2) menu and ingredients, (3) packaging, and (4) use of technology.

Franchise locations are in the process of updating the interior designs to one of several new modernized styles. The colors of the new styles are more muted than the former bright primary colors. Individual franchisees can select the style they prefer from style books that provide a catalog of options of tabletops, wall patterns, and lighting fixtures. The idea is not for a standardized dining room for every store, but for there to be a cohesive theme with individual differences that best suit the particular space. The expectation is that these design changes will create a more welcoming environment and have a positive effect on sales. According to Max Carmona, McDonald's senior director of U.S. restaurant design:

> We've moved away from a cafeteria feel to a more comfortable and, in some ways, more intimate restaurant. . . . At any point in time we'll have 8 to 10 designs in our portfolio, and how they're applied to different building types, they end up manifesting themselves a little bit differently based on size and restaurant configuration.

Under Easterbrook's leadership, several changes were made to the menu and the ingredients. The changes were largely based on customer feedback and dietary trends. The McCafé beverages and signature crafted sandwiches were welcome additions to the menu. Another very popular change that began in 2015 was all-day breakfast. According to Easterbrook:

> Customers have been asking for this for years. We challenged ourselves to move past legacy barriers to deliver, and we did.

Several of the changes made involved the quality of the input ingredients. For example, the quarter pounders are made with fresh versus frozen beef and butter is being used rather than margarine. Artificial preservatives are no longer in Chicken McNuggets, artificial growth hormones are no longer in milk, and high-fructose corn syrup is no longer used in the buns. One change that is especially appealing to socially conscious consumers is that McDonald's has begun using cage-free eggs and has committed to using only cage-free eggs by 2025.

In 2016, McDonald's redesigned the packaging of its bags, cups, and sandwich containers. The design was meant to be a modern font and simplified feel to stand out in a landscape of distractions. This was the first packaging redesign since 2013. The package redesign also brought McDonald's closer to its commitment to using 100 percent fiber-based packaging from recycled or certified sustainable sources by 2020.

McDonald's also has made some radical changes from its traditional model in terms of technology. According to Stephen Dutton, Consumer Foodservice Analyst for Euromonitor International:

> Going digital is McDonald's most recent push to lure customers back to its stores. Digital engagement is an increasingly important aspect of the modern foodservice experience and it enhances the level of convenience that consumers want and expect from a quick-service chain.

McDonald's is increasingly implementing the "Experience of the Future" at its restaurant locations. In these restaurants, rather than ordering food from an employee at the counter, customers can skip the counter all together. Instead, they approach a digital video kiosk with a touchscreen to select and customize their food order.

A "guest experience leader" is nearby to assist customers with any issues. Then, customers proceed to their table, where their food is delivered. Another new development is the McDonald's app with the mobile order and pay function, where customers can purchase their order from the app and then have it delivered to their car on the curb-side of a McDonald's restaurant. Finally, McDonald's has partnered with UberEATS to provide delivery in many markets. By the end of 2017, the mobile order and pay function was available in 20,000 U.S. stores and the digital kiosks were in 2,500 locations. By 2020, the vast majority of McDonald's restaurants are planned to be updated to the "Experience of the Future."

McDonald's various efforts to reimage its stores and reposition its brand appear to be effective so far. In 2017 and 2018, both customer traffic and sales were up after dropping in the several years prior. This performance is outpacing competitors such as Burger King and Taco Bell, during the same time period. Further, measures of customer perceptions and satisfaction illustrate an increase in regard to service, taste, and quality.

Discussion Questions

1. Chapter 8 talks about package design and labeling. One of the changes McDonald's made as part of its reimaging was changing the packaging of the bags and containers. How might these changes influence consumer perceptions?

2. Chapter 9 discusses brand image, positioning, and repositioning. Reflect on McDonald's brand image prior to and after its repositioning efforts.
   a. Make a list of several of McDonald's competitors.
   b. Construct a perceptual map that includes McDonald's prior to repositioning versus its competitors.
   c. Construct another perceptual map that includes McDonald's after repositioning versus its competitors.

   d. Compare and contrast the two perceptual maps and write a brief description summarizing your findings.

3. Chapter 9 tells us that repositioning of a brand or product is a deliberate decision to significantly alter the way the market views the brand or product. In your opinion, are these changes enough to consti-tute a significant change in public perceptions of McDonald's? Justify your response.

4. What difficulties may McDonald's face when reposi-tioning its brand image?

5. Chapter 7 discusses different types of innovations (continuous, discontinuous, and dynamically con-tinuous). McDonald's is incorporating several new technologies as part of the repositioning effort. What types of innovations are the following? Why?
   a. Mobile app
   b. Kiosks
   c. UberEATS delivery

6. Chapter 10 discusses brand personality.
   a. Describe McDonald's traditional brand personality.
   b. Describe McDonald's new brand personality based on its repositioning efforts.
   c. What recommendations would you give McDonald's in terms of communicating its new brand personality?

Source: N. Berg, "McDonald's 2.0: How Fast-Food Chains Are Using Design to Go Local," *Curbed,* April 11, 2018, www.curbed.com, accessed April 24, 2018; S. Bomkamp, "McDonald's Goes for Graphic Punch in New Packaging," *Chicago Tribune,* January 7, 2016, www.chicagotribune.com, accessed April 24, 2018; A. Dixon, "McDonald's Unveils Its Plan for the Future," *QSR Magazine,* March 2, 2017, www.qsrmagazine.com, accessed April 24, 2018; T. Dua, "Anatomy of a Comeback: How McDonald's Got Its Groove Back," *Digiday,* January 14, 2016, www.digiday.com, accessed April 24, 2018; M. Fleming, "McDonald's Sees Brand Perception Boost as Customer Experience Focus Pays Off," *Marketing Week,* January 30, 2018, www.marketingweek.com, accessed April 24, 2018; D. Klein, "Why 2018 Could Be McDonald's Best Year Ever," *QSR Magazine,* December 2017, www.qsrmagazine.com, accessed April 24, 2018; V. Wong, "After 60 Years, McDonald's Is Getting Rid of Its 'Cafeteria Look,'" *Buzzfeed,* January 10, 2016, www.buzzfeed.com, accessed April 24, 2018; V. Wong, "McDonald's Will Shift to Cage-Free Eggs by 2025," *Buzzfeed,* September 9, 2015, www.buzzfeed.com; V. Wong, "America, Meet McDonald's Self-Service Kiosks," *Buzzfeed,* July 18, 2015, www.buzzfeed.com, accessed April 24, 2018.

3-3 *LET'S MOVE!* CAMPAIGN CELEBRITIES ENDORSING SODA?!

In February 2010, First Lady Michelle Obama launched her *Let's Move!* Campaign to improve the lives of young Americans through healthier diets and more active life-styles. This effort was especially needed at a time when childhood obesity had become a problem of epic pro-portions in the United States. The key to making prog-ress within *Let's Move!* was developing collaborative partnerships with various stakeholders, including families, schools, food companies, legislators, and even celebrities.

In the years since the launch of the campaign, child obesity remains a problem in the United States, but some headway has been made in several states, such as New York, Mississippi, and Pennsylvania (Philadelphia). In March 2014, Partnership for a Healthier America published a report that extolled its members for putting more grocers in poor areas and healthier foods in restaurants. Sixteen member food manufacturer partners pledged to cut 1.5 trillion calories from their products by 2015. Also, the American Beverage Association, participated by placing calorie labels on the front of beverages. While the progress is yet modest, a fundamental shift in the lifestyles of America's youth is something that takes time to evolve.

One major method Mrs. Obama utilized to popularize the *Let's Move!* Campaign among young people was partnering with celebrities. Celebrity endorsements are a well-established strategy in marketing that can lend credibility to brands. Several celebrities and athletes have participated in and endorsed the *Let's Move!* Campaign in various ways. Even Mrs. Obama used her own celebrity to endorse companies that partnered with the *Let's Move!* Campaign. Subway restaurants joined the initiative by pledging to offer nutritious foods on its kid's menu and to meet the same federal restrictions that are placed on school lunches. In a show of appreciation, Mrs. Obama held a news conference at a Washington, D.C., Subway restaurant, where she ate lunch with athletes who endorsed Subway, along with a group of school children and parents. According to Sam Kass, the executive director of *Let's Move!:*

> Having celebrities and athletes of great presence really helps us get the message out. They're cultural icons who have real powerful voices in our communities and particularly for young people—they really respond to messages and their leadership.

Unfortunately, not all of the celebrities who have partnered with *Let's Move!* have delivered consistent messages to the young people they influence. While the campaign does not have official spokespeople, the celebrities have an informal obligation to serve as role models of the messages they are promoting. An organization called Center for Science in the Public Interest (CSPI) has been monitoring the behavior of the *Let's Move!* celebrity partners. Unfortunately, a high number of the celebrity partners also have promoted junk food. According to executive director Michael Jacobson:

> The message is completely inconsistent with *Let's Move!*. Kids are especially influenced by celebrities. They think if they consume their product, a little of that glamour or athletic prowess will rub off on them.

Three celebrities in particular who partnered with the *Let's Move!* Campaign have drawn the ire of critics for their endorsement of sodas: Michelle Kwan, Beyoncé, and Shaquille O'Neal. Each of these celebrities went on to endorse sugar-laden, unhealthy drinks after lending their celebrity to the *Let's Move!* Campaign. The *Let's Move!* Campaign specifically speaks out against sodas and encourages young Americans to consume water or unsweetened beverages instead, so these moves in favor of sodas are very contradictory and erode the credibility of both the celebrities themselves and the campaign.

Michelle Kwan is a U.S. Olympic figure skater who hosted the kick-off event for the 2014 *Let's Read! Let's Move!* summer program, which encouraged children to be active, eat healthy food, and read during the summer. Ms. Kwan is also a member of the President's Council on Fitness, Sports, and Nutrition. The conflict arose when Ms. Kwan also became one of Coca-Cola's "Four Pack" of athletes promoting its soda during the Sochi winter games. The fact that both campaigns would want Ms. Kwan as an endorser is logical considering their similar target markets. However, their messages on soda are very different. The President's Council on Fitness suggests that consumers drink water, unsweetened beverages, or heavily dilute fruit juices. Meanwhile, Coca-Cola prefers a message more focused on "balance" between consuming calories and physical activity to maintain an energy balance.

Beyoncé is a popular singer among young people. She participated in the *Let's Move!* Campaign by creating a music video called "Move Your Body" that featured her dancing in a school cafeteria with children and eating an apple. Only two years later, critics noticed that she partnered with Pepsi in a $50 million promotional deal. The CSPI issued an open letter to Beyoncé criticizing this move. Neither Beyoncé nor her representatives answered CSPI.

> Your image is one of success, health, talent, fitness, and glamour. But by lending your name and image to PepsiCo, you are associating those positive attributes with a product that is quite literally sickening Americans.

Another celebrity that is drawing fire for soda associations is retired NBA star Shaquille O'Neal. He joined Mrs. Obama at an elementary school to lead children in aerobic exercises. He was officially there in the capacity of a Reebok representative but was still involved with the *Let's Move!* Campaign. Not long after, Mr. O'Neal launched his own line of sodas, Soda Shaq Cream Soda drinks with AriZona Beverages. The sodas, which contain 270 calories each, even feature Mr. O'Neal's face prominently on the packaging. According to Mr. Jacobson at CSPI:

> Clearly, Shaq knows better. He has said he avoids soda himself, and worries about obesity and diabetes. But he's now using his name, face and reputation to make those health problems even bigger. It's shameful hypocrisy, presumably motivated by money.

Other athletes that have participated in the *Let's Move!* Campaign also have endorsed other nonsoda, unhealthy food choices. For example, Eli Manning endorsed Double Stuff Oreos and Dunkin' Donuts and David Beckham promoted Burger King.

Experts warn that in order to avoid criticisms of hypocrisy, celebrities should endorse products and ideas they actually believe in and use in reality. In fact, China has proposed regulations to encourage truth in advertising that would prohibit celebrities from endorsing products they do not use themselves. Denise Lamberston, the founder/partner of the LMS agency who specializes in celebrity partnerships, advises that due to the transparency of the Internet and social media, celebrities who do not actually consume the products they endorse are quickly identified as inauthentic, thus weakening those celebrities' credibility.

Before partnering with a celebrity to endorse a product, there are several legal measures organizations can have in place to reduce the risk. First, the arrangement should not legally violate any previous agreements with third parties and the celebrity should agree that he or she will not enter into any subsequent agreements with other competing organizations for a period of time. Second, there should be a morals clause that would allow the agreement to be terminated for criminal or morally reprehensible behavior. The wording of this clause should be very specific in order to avoid any ambiguity or post facto disagreement between celebrities and organizations about what behaviors qualify. Finally, the agreement should ensure that celebrity endorsements on social media are compliant with federal regulations. For example, endorsement tweets should use hashtags that clearly identify them as sponsored content, such as #ad or #sponsored.

Ultimately, an ongoing debate exists as to whether celebrity endorsements are even effective. A study by Experian Marketing Services showed that 43 percent of viewers are less likely to buy products that have celebrity endorsements, unless the celebrity is an expert in the area. Ace Metrix, an advertising analytics agency, reported that television ads that contain celebrities have poorer performance than those without celebrities. The worst-performing advertisements were those in which a celebrity endorsed a product that was perceived as unlikely for the celebrity to actually use. Finally, a 2014 article in the *Social Influence* journal reported that celebrity endorsements are a risk that often does not pay off. What is worse is that if a celebrity were to have a personal scandal, then that negative publicity also rubs off on the brand.

A 2012 article in the *Journal of Advertising Research* reported that athlete celebrity endorsements are effective for increasing sales both in an absolute sense and relative to competitors. Further, each time the athlete has an achievement, the sales and stock returns jump. A Nielsen study found that consumers are five times more likely to purchase products that are endorsed by credible, third-party sources, which indicates that celebrity endorsements are effective provided that the celebrity is a credible expert in the product category. This is where it is important for the celebrity's actual use of the product to be believable. Please see Table A for a listing of several celebrity endorsements that may have varying levels of believability in terms of the celebrity's use of the product. Conversely, a Harris Interactive study showed that 53 percent of adults believe celebrity endorsements of political and social causes are very effective. There is also some evidence that celebrity endorsements are more effective on children than adults. According to Andrew Cheyne, a researcher of advertising that targets children at Berkeley Media Studies Group, children's admiration for celebrities is consistent no matter what product they are endorsing and does not simply turn off if the object of their admiration promotes an unhealthy product.

Discussion Questions

1. Chapter 11 discusses source characteristics and celebrity endorsements. Three constructs that influence the effectiveness of a celebrity endorser are expertise, aspirational aspects, and meaning transfer. Think in the context of the *Let's Move!* Campaign.

Celebrity Endorsers and Sponsors

TABLE **A**

Celebrity	Sponsor
Melissa Joan Hart	Disney Paint
Justin Bieber	OPI
David Hasselhoff	Lean Pockets
Lisa Rinna	Depends
Bill Wyman	Signature Metal Detector
Mr. T	FlavorWave Oven Turbo
Eva Longoria	Lay's Potato Chips
Shannen Doherty	Education Connection
Snoop Dogg	Norton Anti-Virus Software
Kiss	Kiss Kasket
Brooke Shields	La-Z-Boy
Bruce Willis	"Die Hard" Cologne
John Cena	Fruity Pebbles
Sylvester Stallone	Protein Pudding
Nelly	"Pimp Juice"
Lil' Romeo	"Rap Snacks"
Jeff Foxworthy	Beef Jerky
Hulk Hogan	"Hulkster" Cheeseburger
Danny DeVito	Limoncello

   a. Evaluate Michelle Kwan on these three aspects relative to the *Let's Move!* Campaign.
   b. Evaluate Beyoncé on these three aspects relative to the *Let's Move!* Campaign.
   c. Evaluate Shaquille O'Neal on these three aspects relative to the *Let's Move!* Campaign.

2. Chapter 11 also discusses fit between a celebrity endorser and the product that he or she endorses. Do you feel that there is a better fit between the *Let's Move!* Campaign and each of the following celebrities or between their endorsed soda brand and each of the following celebrities. Justify your answer.
   a. Michelle Kwan
   b. Beyoncé
   c. Shaquille O'Neal

3. Review the celebrity endorsements listed in the table.
   a. Choose three celebrity/product pairs that you feel are the best in terms of fit. Justify your selection.
   b. Choose three celebrity/product pairs that you feel are the worst in terms of fit. Justify your selection.
   c. Compare and contrast your choices from part a and part b.

4. Chapter 8 discusses consumer inferences. Reflect on what you read about the *Let's Move!* promotions and the celebrity endorsers' subsequent behavior.
   a. What aspect of consumer inferences in Chapter 8 is related to this situation?
   b. How might that aspect affect the inferences that consumers draw about the *Let's Move!* Campaign and endorsements in the case?

5. Chapter 9 discusses schemas, which also are known as schematic memories and knowledge structures. Construct a schema diagram for each of the following celebrities as brands.
   a. Michelle Kwan
   b. Beyoncé
   c. Shaquille O'Neal

6. Chapter 10 discusses Maslow's hierarchy of needs. Which of the needs in Maslow's hierarchy of needs does the *Let's Move!* Campaign hope to activate in young consumers by encouraging them to make healthy food and exercise choices? (Hint: Multiple needs could be correct.)

7. Chapter 4 discusses several generational groups.
   a. Which of the generational groups is the target market for the *Let's Move!* Campaign?
   b. Based on what you know about the generations listed in Chapter 4, make suggestions about how the *Let's Move!* Campaign might better communicate with the generation you selected in part a.

Source: M. Bittman, "Why Do Stars Think It Is OK to Sell Sodas?," *New York Times,* January 5, 2013, http://opinionator.blogs.nytimes.com; S. Brewster, "'Let's Read! Let's Move!': Michelle Kwan Kicks Off Education Department Program," *Huffington Post,* July 10, 2013, www.huffingtonpost.com; A. Elberse and J. Verluen, "The Economic Value of Celebrity Endorsements," *Journal of Advertising Research,* June 2012, pp. 149–65; K. Harrington, "Save Your Money: Celebrity Endorsements Not Worth the Cost," *Forbes,* January 31, 2014, www.forbes.com; "Health Group Questions Michelle Kwan's Dual Roles as Both Member of the President's Council on Fitness and Coke Ambassador," *Center for Science in the Public Interest,* February 18, 2014, www.cspinet.org; M. Jacobson, "Kwan Should Stop Spinning for Coke," *Huffington Post,* March 25, 2014, www.huffingtonpost.com/; P. Kaur, "Does Celebrity Endorsement Actually Work?," *Marketing Interactive,* February 24, 2013, www.marketing-interactive.com; L. Kornowski, "No One Cares About Celebrity Endorsements, Says Study Likely to Freak Kim Kardashian Out," *Huffington Post,* April 25, 2014, www.huffingtonpost.com; "Accomplishments," *Let's Move!,* September 2014, www.letsmove.gov/; "Let's Move Slowly!," *Economist,* March 9, 2013, www.economist.com; R. Lynch, "13 Celebrity Endorsement Deals That Backfired," *Los Angeles Times,* February 26, 2014, www.latimes.com; R. Mann, "China Cracks Down on Laughable Celebrity Endorsements: New Law Requires Celebs to Actually

Use the Products They Pitch," *Ad Week*, September 2, 2014, www.adweek.com; C. May, "Health Group Upset Shaq Promoting 'Let's Move!' with First Lady While Selling Soda," *Daily Caller*, September 5, 2013, http://dailycaller.com; K. McQuade, "Strangest Celebrity Partnerships Like David Hasselhoff and Frozen Food," *Huffington Post*, July 18, 2013, www.huffingtonpost.com; M. Salup, "The Evolution of Celebrity Endorsements," *Huffington Post*, February 24, 2014, www.huffingtonpost.com; A. Sifferlin, "Let's Move: But Not with Shaq and Beyonce," *Time*, September 16, 2013, http://healthland.time.com; K. Thompson, "Michelle Obama Touts Subway's Kids Menu," *Washington Post*, January 23, 2014, www.washingtonpost.com; J. Thomas, "Want a Celebrity Endorsement on Twitter? 3 Legal Precautions to Know," *Entrepreneur*, March 25, 2014, www.entrepreneur.com.

3-4 ATTENTION, MILLENNIALS! AUTOMOBILE MANUFACTURERS ADAPT FOR YOU

The Millennial generation is the largest generation since their parents constituted the previous largest generation: the Baby Boomers. The Millennial generation encompasses a fairly wide range of ages, but the oldest of the group are now in their early thirties and are living very grown-up lives, complete with major consumer purchases. This generation is very attractive to marketers because of its sheer size and purchasing power. Yet, the Millennials think about brands and make purchases differently and are much more in tune with digital communication than any other generation.

Not long ago, parents struggled to keep their children from watching too much television. Now, as those children are coming of age, television advertisers have the opposite problem as they compete for the attention of Millennials. Young people are still consuming media at very high rates, but now they are in many new places other than television, like social media and mobile devices. To illustrate, in 1983, 100 million Americans watched the finale of *Mash* on television, compared to a mere 10 million who watched the finale of *Breaking Bad* on live television. Meanwhile, advertising on small mobile screens does not carry the same effect as advertising in traditional media once did.

Consumers are increasingly ignoring and disregarding advertising. This lack of attention to advertising is compounded by Americans engaging in other activities while viewing traditional media. (See Tables A and B for statistics regarding these factors for various demographic groups, including Millennials.)

According to the CEO of Starcom MediaVest, one of the largest advertising buying agencies:

> I am nervous about us all being out of a job a year from now if Reed Hastings [chief executive of Netflix] takes over the world.

Millennials in particular are the subject of many marketing research companies. Various recent surveys show that this generation spends more time on social media,

TABLE A — Types of Advertisements Most Ignored and Disregarded

	Total	Gender		Age				Education		
		Male	Female	18–34	35–44	45–54	55+	H.S. or less	Some college	College grad+
	%	%	%	%	%	%	%	%	%	%
Any (NET)	91	90	92	90	92	88	93	89	92	94
Internet banner ads	43	42	45	42	47	43	43	40	46	46
Internet search engine ads	20	20	21	21	21	19	20	17	22	23
Television ads	14	15	13	9	13	14	20	17	12	12
Radio ads	7	7	8	11	7	5	6	8	7	7
Newspaper ads	6	6	5	7	4	7	5	6	5	6
None of these	9	10	8	10	8	12	7	11	8	6

Base: American adults

Source: Harris Interactive Poll.

Activities Done While Watching Television — TABLE B

	Total	Gender			Age				Education		
		Male	Female	18–34	35–44	45–54	55+	H.S. or less	Some college	College grad+
	%	%	%	%	%	%	%	%	%	%
Surf the Internet using a computer	56	53	59	68	59	55	45	52	57	62
Read a book, magazine, or newspaper	44	37	51	42	41	44	47	35	50	51
Go on a social networking site (e.g., Facebook, Twitter)	40	34	45	57	47	36	21	33	44	46
Text on my mobile phone	37	35	39	57	46	38	14	28	41	47
Shop online	29	27	31	40	33	27	19	22	31	39
Surf the Internet using my mobile phone	18	20	16	30	23	15	6	10	19	29
Read a book on an e-reader device (e.g., Kindle, Nook)	7	6	9	6	8	9	7	5	10	9
Surf the Internet on a tablet computer (e.g., iPad, Xoom)	7	8	6	7	13	4	5	6	5	11
Something else	30	26	33	32	26	28	30	26	33	32
None	14	18	11	8	12	16	20	19	12	10
Not applicable	3	4	2	5	3	2	2	3	2	4

Base: American adults
Source: Harris Interactive Poll.

particularly on mobile devices, than any other group. Millennials spend 14.5 hours per week on average on mobile devices. However, while it is less than Generation X and Baby Boomers, they still spend 25 hours per week on average watching television. In response, advertisers are expected to spend $17.7 billion on mobile advertising in 2014, which is double the amount spent in 2013. Thirty-six percent of Millennials say that digital advertising is the most influential media for brand decisions, while 19 percent of Millennials say the same for television advertising. Meanwhile, 44 percent of Millennials want to have an open dialogue with brands using social channels. A full 55 percent of Millennials feel that a recommendation from a friend is the strongest influence of brand choice. Often, these recommendations are created sharing branded content on social media.

Automobile manufacturers are particularly attracted to Millennials and many of them are having to learn new ways to appeal as they focus their efforts on this group. They are trying new approaches to the product offerings, like flashy colors. Also, many automobile manufacturers are attempting to garner the attention of Millennials through nontraditional tactics involving consumer engagement and entertaining, quirky content on social media. Volkswagen, Ford, Toyota, and Mini Cooper have had some success through advertising on Buzzfeed, an entertaining website known for viral content that targets Millennials. Jonathan Perelman, vice president of agency strategy and industry development at Buzzfeed, states:

The power for auto brands, really any brand, but really for automotive brands is you can tell a really compelling, sometimes funny story that's adding value to the consumer so that they're not only going to want to engage with that ad, but also share it with their friends. There's an implied endorsement that you as my friend understand what I like. You're going to have a significant lift in your feelings toward the brand. That's the power today in social content marketing. Being able to be in the conversation, adding value to the consumer and tapping into the networks where people are already communicating.

According to Chris Travell, vice president of strategic consulting for Maritz Research:

> Millennials are an important group of buyers in the industry today, and not just in terms of sheer size. They are also helping to refine the vehicle shopping and ownership experience. These younger buyers are much more connected than previous car buyers. The manufacturer that develops a strategy that resonates with millennial buyers will increase the likelihood of consideration the next time that customer is in the market. In turn, this will increase the likelihood of selling a car to that customer.

However, there is a wide disparity among Millennials' responses to automobile manufacturers' efforts. Fiat failed miserably with its campaign "Endless Fun," which featured seven-year-old memes and .gifs featuring bizarre images of things like people dancing around a Fiat in horse masks. Honda chose an unconventional method by mocking how other advertisers focus on Millennial stereotypes in its #UnBuenFit campaign.

Ford is one automobile manufacturer that seems to have tapped into ways of communicating with Millennials that has been very effective. Ford has been the number one brand in purchase consideration for Millennials for the past several years. According to Sheryl Connelly, global consumer trends and futuring manager at Ford:

> This group of consumers is an incredible market opportunity, but the way that millennials interact with brands is totally different from earlier generations. Understanding their priorities helps us market to them, so that we're giving a message that is relevant to them.

Ford has discovered a formula that turns Millennial consumers into brand ambassadors, and it appears to be working. Amy Marentic, Ford's global car and crossover marketing manager, explains Ford's approach to Millennials:

> We're turning a 108-year-old brand over to consumers. I'm very serious about that. Our market share with Millennials has increased significantly. . . . We're now the top selling brand to all Millennials . . . don't be afraid to turn your brand over to others.

Ford points to several techniques that have led to its success. The first is to get Millennials talking to each other about the brand. When Ford was preparing to launch its Fiesta model in the U.S., it gave 100 of the vehicles to influential, web-savvy Millennials, who were dubbed as "Fiesta Agents." Ms. Marentic said:

> We gave them a Fiesta for six months, and gave them gas and insurance, and they had to do monthly missions for us and then put the results online. If I tell them how great the new Ford Fiesta is, they won't notice, but when their friends and family tell them, they'll pay attention.

Second, Ford appeals to Millennials' love of technology through new technology called MyFord Touch. MyFord Touch performs many tasks while consumers are driving, including syncing their phones, reading their texts, adjusting the temperature, and making dinner suggestions.

> [Millennials] are always on and they want their experience in the car to be always on. It understands 10,000 voice commands.

Finally, Ms. Marentic suggests that Ford's success with Millennials comes from being edgy and entertaining. For example, in order to improve the formerly stuffy image of the Ford Focus, Ford created a spokescharacter named Doug that is only present on social media such as Twitter and YouTube. Doug is a rude-mannered and irreverent orange sock puppet. For example, when Doug is informed by a Ford marketing executive that the Focus has double French stitching on the seats, Doug replies:

> How many times have I sat in single-French-stitched seats and said, 'I might as well be at the town dump sitting on garbage cans'?

This is precisely the untraditional type of content that Ford has used to successfully capture the attention of Millennials that remains so elusive for other automobile manufacturers and brands.

Discussion Questions

1. Chapter 8 discusses factors that affect consumer attention. How do the following situational factors play a role in Millennials' attention to Ford's promotions?
   a. Clutter
   b. Program involvement

2. Chapter 11 discusses appeal characteristics in advertising. Use Google Videos or Google Images to find examples of the advertisements for the Ford Fiesta advertising campaigns. Evaluate those advertisements based on

   a. Appeal characteristics

   b. Message structure characteristics

3. Chapter 8 discusses stimulus factors in advertising. Use Google Videos or Google Images to find examples of the advertisements for Ford Fiesta's advertising campaigns. Evaluate those advertisements based on the following stimulus factors:

   a. Size

   b. Intensity

   c. Attractive visuals

   d. Color and movement

   e. Position

   f. Isolation

   g. Format

   h. Contrast and expectations

   i. Interestingness

   j. Information quantity

4. Evaluate the information displayed in Tables A and B. Imagine you are a marketing manager for an automobile manufacturer that is targeting Millennials. Your goal is to gain the attention of your target market. Use that information to answer the following questions.

   a. According to the Table A, which types of media are least likely to be ignored by Millennials?

   b. How do the media that are least likely to be ignored compare with what media other surveys show Millennials prefer?

   c. Assume that television advertising is a part of your promotional mix. How would you handle the fact that a large part of your target market is multitasking while watching television?

   d. Imagine that your target market is a different demographic. How would your answers to the previous parts of this question change?

5. Chapter 9 discusses strength of learning. Ford is hoping that Millennials learn that Ford is focused on their needs and wants. So far, it appears to be working. Strength of learning is enhanced by the following six factors. Evaluate Ford's marketing to Millennials on these factors.

   a. Importance

   b. Message involvement

   c. Mood

   d. Reinforcement

   e. Repetition

   f. Dual coding

6. Chapter 9 also discusses brand image and product positioning. Think about Ford and other automobile manufacturers' brand images. Then, construct a perceptual map that includes several automobile manufacturers that are targeting Millennials.

7. Chapter 10 discusses Maslow's hierarchy of needs. Which of those needs does Ford attempt to cater to when marketing to Millennials? (Hint: More than one answer is correct.)

Sources: "Are Advertisers Wasting Their Money?," *Harris Interactive: A Nielsen Company,* December 3, 2010, www.harrisinteractive.com; C. Arreola, "Honda Targets Latino Millennials in Unconventional Way," *Latina,* July 18, 2014, www.latina.com; V. Bond, "How Car Marketers Harness the Viral Power of Buzzfeed to Reach Millennials," *Automotive News,* December 1, 2013, www.autonews.com; "Distracted TV Viewers," *Harris Interactive: A Nielsen Company,* June 15, 2011, www.harrisinteractive.com; D. Fenn, "4 Tips from Ford on Marketing to Millennials," *CBS Money Watch,* June 22, 2011, www.cbsnews.com; "Ford Now Leads Sales Consideration with Millennials," *Ford Motor Company,* August 19, 2014, http://corporate.ford.com; J. Fromm, "Ford Recognizes Millennial Consumer Marketing Trends," *Future Cast Millennial Marketing Insights,* 2014, http://millennialmarketing.com; J. Gapper, "Advertisers Have Lost the Attention of a Generation," *Financial Times,* June 18, 2014, www.ft.com; "Millennials: The New Age of Brand Loyalty," *Adroit Digital,* 2014, www.adroit.digital.com; J. Perez, "Fiat Tries to Target Millennials with New Ads, Fails Miserably," *Yahoo! Auto,* June 18, 2014, https://autos.yahoo.com; I. Slutsky, "Ford and Twitter Talk Keys to Marketing to Millennials," *Advertising Age,* August 19, 2011, http://adage.com; "Traditional or Digital Ads? Millennials Show Mixed Feelings," *EMarketer,* April 15, 2014, www.emarketer.com; B. Tuttle, "Selling Cars to Millennials: Quirky Models, Flashy Colors Aim to Get Gen Y Out of Neutral," *Time,* November 20, 2012, http://business.time.com; S. Vranica, "Millennials Spend 14.5 Hours per Week on Smartphones," *Wall Street Journal,* July 2, 2014, http://blogs.wsj.com.

3-5 MEAL KITS ARE SHIFTING HOW CONSUMERS SHOP FOR FOOD

Meal kits are a relatively recent innovation in the way consumers shop for food. The kits are designed to be all-inclusive meals. The packages arrive with premeasured, high-quality ingredients along with recipe instructions for consumers to cook meals in their own homes. As meal kits have become increasingly popular, there is a proliferation of niches to suit various tastes, preferences, and diets. Here are some examples: Blue Apron focuses on sustainable farming, direct shipping, and less food waste; Purple Carrot offers vegan meals; Green Blender provides healthy smoothies; Peach Dish focuses on Southern-inspired dishes; Hello Fresh allows consumers to customize their selections; Chef'd offers recipes from famous celebrity chefs; Green Chef only offers organic ingredients; and so on. Meal kits initially were intro-duced to the U.S. through digital mail-order service, but more recently have been made available at many brick-and-mortar retailers as well. For example, Albertson's grocery stores acquired Plated and other retailers, such as Kroger and Walmart, are beginning to offer their own meal kits.

Meal kits do come at a premium cost when compared to shopping for groceries in bulk at a traditional grocery store. However, they provide the additional value of the convenience of forgoing the shopping trip, search-ing for recipes, meal planning, and even chopping and measuring ingredients in many cases. This convenience is appealing to many Americans as it eases the pressures experienced by people leading busy lives and working long hours, especially as more women are choosing to join the workforce rather than maintain a domestic lifestyle.

According to Nielsen Research, at the end of 2017, 9 percent of Americans, or 10.5 million households, had purchased a meal kit within the last six months. Further, 25 percent of consumers, or 30 million households, say they would try a meal kit within the next six months. Meal kits are seeing three times the growth of tradi-tional food shopping options, such as restaurants and traditional grocery stores. Robert Jones, senior VP of Business Development of Chef'd, says some predict the market could reach $35 billion by 2025:

> I think there's definitely an experiential component of meal kits that differentiates itself from traditional grocery or restaurants. You're educating, it's a family experience and you're interested in food and making new foods in an entirely different way and breaking out of the traditional 10 to 15 meals that families usually cook at home. It allows you to step outside those normal dinner-time options and try something new.

Despite their popularity, consumers are finding some negatives in their meal kit experiences: (1) excessive packaging and (2) uncertainty as to whether it is truly cooking.

Many consumers have complained and several have canceled their subscriptions based on the large amount of cardboard, plastic, and ice packs that are used to ship small amounts of ingredients in the meal kits. Meal kit companies counter that because they know their exact demand, they reduce food waste that is less visible to consumers in the supply chain, such as traditional grocery stores throwing out spoiled produce. Some

meal kit companies, such as Plated, are taking steps to become carbon neutral by using recycled and renewable packaging.

Some consumers also question whether they are actually cooking the meals in the meal kits or if they are merely assembling them. It depends on whether consumers find the planning of the meal and recipe, shopping for and choosing the particular ingredients, and measuring and cutting up the ingredients to be essential parts of the cooking equation in their minds. This concern echoes back to the 1950s when marketers introduced cake mixes in boxes that only required the addition of water. Consumers did not feel connected to the cooking process or an ownership of the final product. The solution to that dilemma was marketers' changing the formula so that consumers had to add an egg or possibly cooking oil, and then consumers were happy. Meal kit companies point to this as being just another step in the gradual trend of removing the labor involved in putting dinners on the table that we have seen over the last 50 years as women entered the workforce, no different than TV dinners and take-out food. Nick Taranto, co-CEO and cofounder of Plated, says:

> Part of why this is such a big idea is because we're con-necting our aspiration to cook and share food to the reality of a busy modern life. We have this primal desire to eat food together. But a lot of people in our parents' generation did not learn how to cook, so many of us did not have the opportunity to learn from them. In some ways, the family dinner stopped with our grandparents.

In fact, meal kits are providing a cooking education of sorts for many consumers who did not learn to cook from their parents or grandparents. This education has the potential to ultimately cannibalize the industry to some degree as consumers develop skills to cook on their own terms and possibly become more interested in shopping at traditional grocery stores that provide a wider variety of ingredients at more value pricing than the single-serving portions found in meal kits.

The early adopters of meal kits were Millennial urban-ites. This market placed a higher premium on convenience due to living in major metro areas where grocery stores are less accessible and cost of living is higher, which made the higher cost per meal of meal kits more comparable to what they already paid for food. However, as there has been a proliferation of meal kit companies to service various niches of the population, meal kits are gaining more mass appeal among other market segments as well. A Nielsen

Research study of global health and wellness shows that 60 percent of Americans actively make food shopping decisions to prevent negative health conditions, such as obesity, diabetes, and high cholesterol. Also, 81 percent of consumers believe that meal kits are healthier than prepared foods in traditional grocery stores. So, the stage is set for growth. Please see Table A for the demographics of consumers with the highest indices for meal kits in 2017.

As part of a larger study, called *Merging Tables & Aisles: Understanding Shifts in U.S. Total Food and Beverage Demand,* Nielsen develops four distinct, data-driven consumer segments that illustrate new ways Americans are purchasing and consuming food based on spending and preferences for channel, occasion, and location. They are Traditionalist Food Shoppers, Restaurant Occasion Lovers, Digital Adopters, and Multi-Channel Adapters.

- *Traditionalist Food Shoppers.* These are older consumers who generally are retired without children in the household. They spend most of their food dollars in traditional grocery outlets and value convenience. They are the least likely of all consumers to use a smartphone or digital device in their food shopping. They are not drivers of growth or demand shifts.

Demographic Characteristics of Fresh Meal Kit Delivery Service Subscribers, 2017 (Index*) TABLE A	
Male	152
Age 25–34	261
Age 35–44	219
Married or partnered	135
Children in household	237
Age of children in household: 6–11	114
Employed full time	174
Master's degree or doctorate	240
White non-Hispanic	115
Hispanic	113
Urban resident	191
Household income: $75,000–$99,999	131
Household income: $100,000+	197
Region: Northeast	123
Region: West	143

*Index of 100 = Average of all U.S. adults
Source: Packaged Facts, 2017.

- *Restaurant Occasion Lovers.* This group is younger and more diverse in terms of age and ethnicity than Traditionalist Food Shoppers. They are primarily suburban and have older children or teens, if any kids are at home. Taste is their highest value and they tend to eat out relatively often. However, they do not use much digital technology when making food-shopping decisions.
- *Digital Adopters.* This group is mostly composed of younger, urban parents who are highly educated and have high incomes. They spend a large proportion of their food dollars on food innovations, such as online retailers, digital order and delivery, in-store apps, and meal kit providers. Their most important value is taste. They are the most likely group to use digital promotions and experiment with digital tools of all varieties and are at the forefront of food innovations that are influenced by technology.
- *Multi-Channel Adapters.* This group is the most likely to spread its spending across various channels for different occasions, typically using each for its traditional purpose (i.e., grocery stores for eating at home and restaurants for eating out). They value convenience and speed in formats such as convenience stores and fast-food restaurants, but good taste is more important when eating in more typical restaurants. They do use some innovations and digital delivery but prefer to have a personal endorsement from a family or friend.

Please see Table B for more detailed information on each of these four segments.

Discussion Questions

1. Chapter 8 talks about co-branding. Which of the meal kit companies mentioned in the case uses co-branding and how?
2. Chapter 9 discusses schemas, schematic memory, and schematic diagrams. See Figure 9–2 for an example.
   a. Draw a schematic diagram for meal kits in general.
   b. Choose a brand of meal kit with which you are familiar. If you are not familiar with any, then choose one, do a brief Internet search, and become familiar. Then, draw a schematic diagram for that particular brand of meal kit.
   c. Write a brief description of how the schematic diagram for the generic meal kits is similar and different from the schematic diagram for a particular brand of meal kit.

TABLE B   Nielsen Food Shopper Segments

	Traditionalist Food Shoppers	Restaurant Occasion Lovers	Digital Adopters	Multi-Channel Adapters
Percent of shoppers	37%	31%	9%	23%
Percent of food spend	28%	31%	17%	24%
Average monthly food spend	$310	$405	$705	$415
Average household size	< 3	< 3	> 3	< 3
Channel skews (Index > = 120)	• Convenience and small format • Club • Drug store • Grocery • Mass	• Digital order and delivery • Fast food • Casual dine • Fine dine • Meal kit providers • Online-only	• Digital order and delivery • Meal kit providers • Online-only • Food trucks	• Food trucks
Occasion skews (Index > = 120)	• Snacks from digital order and delivery	• Breakfast from fast-food/casual dine, and convenience and small format	• Breakfast from food trucks, fine dine, casual dine, drug store, convenience and small format, meal kits and online-only	• Lunch from food trucks
	• Dinner from drug store	• Lunch from drug store, fine dine, and online-only	• Lunch from online-only, fine dine, meal kits, and drug store	• Dinner from meal kits and digital order and delivery
		• Dinner from online-only	• Dinner from convenience and small format and online-only	
		• Snacks from drug store and online-only	• Snacks from non-FMCG retailers	
Location skews (Index > = 120)	• Food trucks at home • Digital order and delivery at work or school	• Food trucks on-site • Digital order and delivery at home • Convenience and small format and online-only at work or school	• Traditional FMCG and food trucks at store or on-site • Food trucks, casual and fine dine at home • Traditional FMCG, food trucks, restaurants, and meal kits at work or school • Club, grocery, casual dine, fine dine, and digital order and delivery on-the-go	• Digital order and delivery at home • Food trucks and online-only at work or school • Club and drug store on-the-go
Priorities (ranked #1–5)	• Convenient location • Food tastes good • Can get in and out quickly • Good value • Products are fresh	• Food tastes good • Convenient location • Good value • Can get in and out quickly • High-quality offerings	• Food tastes good • Good value • Can order online • Someone will deliver to my home • High-quality offerings, wide selection of specialty/ethnic items	• Convenient location • Food tastes good • Can get in and out quickly • Good value • Products are fresh

Source: The Nielsen Company, 2018. The Harris Poll Share of Stomach survey was conducted online, in English, within the United States between June 16 and 20, 2017, among 2,075 adults aged 18+.

3. Chapter 9 discusses conditioning as a form of learning. Several brands of meal kits offer free trials before consumers commit to a subscription. What type of conditioning are meal kit marketers using when they do this? Why?

4. Chapter 10 discusses Maslow's hierarchy of needs. Which of the needs could be satisfied with subscribing to a meal kit plan? Why? (Hint: There is more than one correct answer.)

5. Chapter 12 discusses the VALS psychographic segmentation scheme. Which of the VALS segments are most likely to subscribe to meal kit plans? Which of the VALS segments is least likely to subscribe to meal kit plans? Justify your responses.

6. Chapter 10 discusses using projective techniques, such as laddering, to discover latent and manifest motives. Assemble a small group of consumers who have used meal kits and conduct a focus group about their perceptions and motivations for purchasing meal kits. If you cannot find enough people for a focus group, a depth interview with one person also would work. Why did they purchase or subscribe to a meal kit? What were their feelings and experiences? Which one(s) did they try? Why? Would they try the same brand or another brand again? Why or why not? These are some sample questions to start moderating the focus group, but there are many more you could ask to facilitate a conversation. Write a brief description of your process and findings.

7. Chapter 7 discusses diffusion of innovations. What type of innovation is the meal kit concept?

8. Imagine you were going to launch a meal kit business. The case mentions several meal kit companies that serve market niches, such as vegan and Southern-inspired cuisines. Brainstorm an idea for a meal kit plan. Then, using the information in the tables, information from the text, and your own knowledge, describe a target market that would be a good fit with the market niche your meal kit plan would best satisfy.

Source: "Getting to Know Today's Meal Kit Shoppers," *Nielsen,* April 13, 2017, www.nielsen.com, accessed April 24, 2018; K. Hardy, "What's Driving the Meal-Kit Movement: At-Home Delivery Meal Kits Have Disrupted the Entire Spectrum of the American Food Market," *QSR Magazine,* August 17, 2017, www.qsrmagazine.com, accessed April 24, 2018; M. Lappe, "The Best Meal-Kit Delivery Services to Try in 2018," *Self,* January 1, 2018, www.self.com, accessed April 24, 2018; M. Leonhardt, "Who Buys Meal Kit Services," *Time,* July 20, 2017, www.time.com, accessed April 24, 2018; "Meal Kit Mania: Innovation for Foodies," *Nielsen,* March 5, 2018, www.nielsen.com, accessed April 24, 2018; Z. Meyer, "Walmart Goes Gourmet, Taking Its Meal Kits Nationwide," *USA Today,* March 5, 2018. www .usatoday.com, accessed April 24, 2018; N. Miller, "17% of Adults Receive Meal Kit Delivery," *Packaged Facts,* July 13, 2017, www.packagedfacts.com, accessed April 24, 2018; E. Segran, "The $5 Billion Battle for the American Dinner Plate," *Fast Company,* June 8, 2015, www.fastcompany.com, accessed April 24, 2018; The Nielsen Company, *Merging Tables & Aisles: Understanding Shifts in U.S. Total Food and Beverage Demand* (2018); "Understanding Today's Food Shoppers," *Nielsen,* January 8, 2018, www.nielsen.com, accessed April 24, 2018; "Why Brick and Mortar Is Key for Meal Kits," *Cheddar,* April 13, 2018, www.cheddar.com, accessed April 24, 2018.

3-6 HELLO KITTY MANIA

Hello Kitty is a Japanese cartoon character that has maintained global popularity since 1974. Hello Kitty is a very cute cat with rounded features and no mouth. Sanrio, the makers of Hello Kitty, have produced and disseminated a huge assortment of Hello Kitty–themed merchandise. In doing so, some have even claimed that Hello Kitty "conquered the world." Hello Kitty has become a national icon of sorts for Japan, as she has served as an ambassador for UNICEF for both Japan and the United States and even has played a role as a Japanese diplomatic envoy to China.

Hello Kitty has become a brand phenomenon throughout the globe for generations of consumers. Hello Kitty originally targeted young girls and preteens in the 1970s. After its popularity began to wane in the 1980s, Sanrio repositioned Hello Kitty as retro in the 1990s to appeal to a much wider range of female consumers. Hello Kitty products were marketed to the adult women who were familiar with Hello Kitty from their childhoods. In the early 2000s, popularity waned again but was revived by partnerships with luxury products and jewelry. Hello Kitty's image graces over 50,000 products, which are sold in over 70 countries. Over the last 40 years, the product line has grown into a brand worth $7 billion and generates over $789 million in revenue annually.

The Hello Kitty brand is heavily licensed and has been used in co-branding campaigns with a wide variety of retail brands. Forbes recently named it one of the best-selling license entertainment products. Numerous brands have collaborated with Hello Kitty, including Target, Sephora, McDonald's, Walmart, Forever 21, Tervis, Fender, Uglydoll, Kidrobot, the NFL, the MLB, Minnetonka, Vans, Swarovski, and many more. Hello Kitty has gotten into the transportation business as well. Eva Air is flying Hello Kitty airplanes out of Taiwan. Star Cruises is sailing Hello Kitty cruises in Singapore and Malaysia. In 2014, Hello Kitty reached a 40-year milestone, without any shortage of limited-edition products to commemorate the date. The Japanese American National Museum in Los Angeles also honored Hello Kitty's 40th anniversary.

Hello Kitty's popularity among so many consumers of various ages in countries all over the world is a much-discussed topic among many Hello Kitty enthusiasts to the executives at Sanrio. In part, the answer lies in Japanese popular culture and the Japanese love for *kawaii*. *Kawaii* means cuteness, and it pervades Japanese society. The use of cute cartoon characters with rounded features and pastel colors is extremely prevalent in Japanese culture and branding. *Kawaii* is much more than a style or trend. It is embedded in social and gender roles of young Japanese women and even dictates their behavior. For example, *kawaii* young women often act silly and speak in squeaky voices.

Japanese companies like Sanrio have successfully exported *kawaii* culture to the rest of world. The cuteness serves as a comfort of sorts for people living in congested urban lifestyles. Japanese companies take care to cultivate and protect their *kawaii* image. According to Yauko Nakamura, the president of a Tokyo-based marketing company:

> Japanese products are made to be *kawaii* so that they are liked by women. In Japan, women hold the spending power. Even for things that women don't purchase themselves, such as a car, they have a strong say in the final decision.

Several experts in Japanese culture give similar responses. Hello Kitty can be anything for anyone. The appeal of Hello Kitty comes from her reflections of each consumer's unique projections. According to the author of *Japanamerica: How Japanese Pop Culture Has Invaded the US:*

> Kitty's appeal is that she's an emotional blank slate. As one of her designers told me: "Kitty feels like you do. We project upon that mouth-less, expressionless kitten, making her the perfectly interactive toy or doll or marketing tool in an age where interactivity is not only desired, it's expected."

Sanrio's public relations manager Kazuo Tohmatsu said:

> Hello Kitty represents the deep desire among all people, regardless of nationality or race, to feel joy and happiness, without having to qualify it at any deep intellectual level. Hello Kitty doesn't judge. She lets you feel how you feel without forcing you to question why.

David Marchi, senior manager of brand management and marketing at Sanrio, views Hello Kitty in a similar way:

> She is not graphically portrayed with a visual mouth, and it lends to her appeal. When you look at her she can be everything and anything. She can appeal to a little girl, an alternative teen, an executive. She can be for anyone.

Still, others focus on Hello Kitty's symbolization of desirable virtues. For example, Helen McCarthy, an author and expert on Japanese animation and comics, said:

> Hello Kitty stands for the innocence and sincerity of childhood and the simplicity of the world. Women and girls all over the world are happy to buy in to the image of the trusting, loving childhood in a safe neighborhood that Hello Kitty represents. They don't want to let go of that image, so as they grow up, they hang onto Hello Kitty out of nostalgic longing—as if by keeping a symbolic object, they can somehow keep hold of a fragment of their childhood self.

Finally, according to Nick Currie, an Osaka-based musician and cultural commentator:

> Hello Kitty symbolizes some essential Japanese virtues: agreeableness, harmony, commerce, cuteness, nature, fertility, affluence and the avoidance of aggression. She [also] represents the irresistible idiocy of consumer culture, hardwired to our neurological system. We shop with almost the same reflexes that make us stretch out to stroke a big-eyed, fluffy kitten. That may be a universal impulse.

Consumers of a wide range of ages adore the brand and often begin to incorporate Hello Kitty into their self-concepts. Many customers have adopted the habit of collecting Hello Kitty items. This practice is especially encouraged by many releases of special limited-edition collector items. However, some fans' passion for collecting Hello Kitty merchandise develops into an obsession as they go to what many people would call extremes.

Meet Natasha Goldsworth, one of the world's most avid collectors of Hello Kitty memorabilia. For her, Hello Kitty is more than a hobby; it is a lifestyle and a huge part of her identity. At 29 years of age, she has been collecting for over 15 years and has filled every room of her apartment with Hello Kitty with all manner of items including jewelry, handbags, furniture, clothing, appliances, décor, doll houses, and over 4,000 plush Hello Kitty toys. She also edits and maintains a website devoted to Hello Kitty called hellokitty4u.com. According to Ms. Goldsworth:

> I live in my little pink lagoon with all my kitties, they cheer me up and I like having them around me. Before people come over I do have to warn them about my kitty kingdom because some people just can't handle it. . . . I'm actually thinking about moving into a bigger place. There just isn't enough room for all of my kitties.

Ms. Goldsworth is currently seeking a romantic partner and would like to be married, but her obsessive collecting of Hello Kitty paraphernalia has become an obstacle to her previous romantic pursuits. When it comes to a decision between a potential romantic partner and her Hello Kitty collection, Hello Kitty is victorious. Ms. Goldsworth says:

> Boyfriends in the past have tried to make me give her up, so I got rid of them. It's part of who I am and I'm not changing for anybody. . . . Others have asked me to sell my collection and I've had to tell them no. If a man doesn't like my kitty kingdom and can't accept me for who I am then I'm not interested in them.

Ms. Goldsworth estimates she has spent near $80,000 on her Hello Kitty collection. However, she makes other financial sacrifices to support her habit, such as sacrificing vacations and eating out for years. Her most valuable Hello Kitty possession is a limited-edition cuddly Hello Kitty wearing a handmade Hanita wedding dress. Once she finds her future husband who is supportive of her Hello Kitty–centric lifestyle, she plans to wear a human-sized replica of that same dress.

> When I get married I want to wear the same Hanita dress. My dad's already agreed to wear a pink tie and I want to have Hello Kitty on top of the wedding cake.

To Ms. Goldsworth and other extreme Hello Kitty enthusiasts, collecting Hello Kitty merchandise is a way of life. This lifestyle is known as collection obsession, and the object of collection (Hello Kitty in this case) becomes engrained in the collector's identity. It is important to note that obsessive collecting is distinct from hoarding. Hoarders keep almost everything. They have a very anxious time organizing and throwing anything away because of a belief that they will use the items again. Several television programs have featured examples of extreme hoarders. Obsessive collectors, on the other hand, accumulate only particular objects, are meticulously organized, know exactly how many items are in the collection and where they are located, and enjoy proudly displaying their collections. According to Julie Pike, a clinical psychologist from the Anxiety Disorder Treatment Center in Durham, N.C:

> With hoarding, we look at three main behaviors: one acquiring too many possessions; second, having great difficulty discarding something; and three difficulty organizing. . . .
>
> Unlike hoarders, collectors are proud, not ashamed, of their possessions. More likely, collectors have an obsession or preoccupation. Most of us have a degree of that rather than the ends of a continuum. But if collectors get in a place where they are spending so much money that they can't pay their mortgage, that's a problem. Or if they are spending so much time at it that they can't go to their job or leave their house.

Discussion Questions

1. Chapter 8 discusses branding strategies. One of the ways that the Hello Kitty brand became disseminated so widely is by using a co-branding strategy with many other brands.
   a. What are some of the brands mentioned in the case that partnered with Hello Kitty?
   b. Discuss the perceived fit between each of those brands and Hello Kitty.
   c. Discuss the target market for each of those co-branded offerings. Are the target markets the same? If not, how do they differ?

d. Perform an Internet search to discover more brands with which Hello Kitty is currently partnering.

e. Repeat the analysis in parts b and c for the new brands that you uncovered in your Internet search.

f. What characteristics of Hello Kitty make it able to be a successful co-branding partner with so many other types of brands?

2. Chapter 9 discusses brand image and product positioning. Reflect on Hello Kitty as a brand and then answer the following:

a. Describe Hello Kitty's brand image.

b. Based on your answers from the question about co-branding, select a product category from the co-branded Hello Kitty products and brainstorm a short list of competitors in the market for that product category.

c. Construct a perceptual map that includes a Hello Kitty co-branded product and your list of brainstormed products in that category.

d. Write a short narrative describing the process you used to develop the perceptual map and your interpretation of the content of the perceptual map.

3. Chapter 10 covers McGuire's psychological motives. Review the cognitive preservation motives, cognitive growth motives, affective preservation motives, and affective growth motives. Which of these motives could describe why Hello Kitty enthusiasts, such as Ms. Goldsworth, accumulate such large Hello Kitty collections?

4. Chapter 11 discusses spokescharacters, a communication characteristic that influences attitudes. The case describes how Hello Kitty served as a spokescharacter for UNICEF for many years, as well as a diplomatic tool for Japanese–Chinese diplomacy. Some characteristics that influence the success of celebrity sources include their expertise, aspirational aspects, and meaning transfer. How do these characteristics apply to Hello Kitty as a spokescharacter?

5. Chapter 12 discusses self-concept and lifestyle. Think about Ms. Goldsworth as an example of an obsessive Hello Kitty collector.

a. Do you feel that her Hello Kitty possessions have become part of Ms. Goldsworth's extended self? Explain your rationale.

b. Think about the concepts of actual self-concept, ideal self-concept, private self-concept, and social self-concept. Using her quotes in the case, interpret how these self-concepts may differ for Ms. Goldsworth.

6. Review the VALS segments discussed in Chapter 12. Which of these segments do you think obsessive collectors (who are able to fund the purchases required for large collections) would best fit?

Source: Z. Bissonnette, "Hobbies: When Collection Becomes Compulsion, Think 'Sell,'" *CNBC*, July 15, 2013, www.cnbc.com; T. Borchard, "10 Things You Should Know About Compulsive Hoarding," *Psych Central*, 2016, http://psychcentral.com, accessed April 24, 2018; B. Bremner, "In Japan, Cute Conquers All," *Bloomberg Businessweek*, June 24, 2002, http://www.businessweek.com; D. Dana, "Japan Grows Its Soft Power through the Export of Kawaii," *Investoralist*, January 19, 2010, www.investoralist.com; M. Fitzpatrick, "Hello Kitty at 40: The Cat That Conquered the World," *BBC*, August 18, 2014, www.bbc.com; S. Harwin, "Forever 21 and Sanrio Team Up for Hello Kitty Forever Collection," *Catster*, November 21, 2012, www.catster.com; J. Howenstine, "Hello Kitty x Vans 2014 Collection," *Nice Kicks*, June 16, 2014, www.nicekicks.com; S. James, "'My Collection Obsession': One Man's Collector Is Another's Hoarder," *ABC News*, August 17, 2011, http://abcnews.go.com; M. Keane, "The Cutesy Hello Kitty Character Came to Be Popular with Everyone from Small Children to Motorcycle Gangs," *Wall Street Journal*, April 12, 2013, http://online.wsj.com; R. Lamb, "Swarovski Flaunts Hello Kitty Collection with Facebook-First Approach," *Luxury Daily*, July 7, 2011, www.luxurydaily.com; B. London, "'If a Man Doesn't Like My Kitty Kingdom, Then I'm Not Interested': 29-Yr-Old Woman Has Spent over £50,000 on Her Hello Kitty Obsession . . . and Yes, She Is Still Single," *Mail Online*, June 11, 2014, www.dailymail.co.uk; "Minnetonka for Hello Kitty Collaboration Debuts for Fall 2014," *Hello Kitty Junkie*, July 30, 2014, www.hellokittyjunkie.com; J. Osterheldt, "At 40, Hello Kitty Is Timeless," *Kansas City Star*, June 25, 2014, www.kansascity.com; S. Parsons, "'Kawaii' Culture," *Japan in Perspective*, May 16, 2013, www.japaninperspective.com; J. Sholl, "What Is the Difference between Compulsive Hoarding and Collecting?," *Psychology Today*, December 17, 2010, www.psychologytoday.com; P. St. Michel, "The Rise of Japan's Creepy-Cute Craze," *Atlantic*, April 14, 2014, www.theatlantic.com; "Tervis Introduces New Hello Kitty Collection," *Gift Shop*, August 13, 2012, www.giftshopmag.com; E. Walker, "Top Cat: How 'Hello Kitty' Conquered the World," *Independent*, May 21, 2008, www.independent.co.uk; K. Webley, "Hoarding: How Collecting Stuff Can Destroy Your Life," *Time*, April 26, 2010, http://content.time.com.

3-7 XEROX'S ONGOING BATTLE TO REPOSITION

Xerox is a fantastic example of brand positioning. So fantastic, in fact, that its name has become synonymous with the photocopier industry and often is used as a verb. Xerox has very strong global brand recognition and historically has been a leader in its industry. However, this well-known brand position actually may be a hindrance to the company as Xerox attempts to reposition itself in consumers' minds in an evolving competitive landscape. In an age of digital media and cloud computing, businesses have much less need for copier and fax machines. Xerox has moved into several other areas of business but continues to struggle to shift consumer perceptions along with it.

Xerox has experienced multiple failed brand reposition attempts. In the early 1970s, Xerox wanted consumers to think of the brand as a leader in the information systems and data processing business, but Xerox Data Systems was abandoned after spending millions of dollars. Likewise, Xerox later failed with its Telecopier, XTEN network, and Team Xerox attempts to reposition the company. These previous repositioning failures have not deterred Xerox from trying to reposition again.

After decades, Xerox's most recent attempts to reposition the brand began in 2008 when the company introduced a new corporate logo. This change extended to product design, product naming, and building signage. According to Richard Wergan, the Xerox director of worldwide branding:

> We are a very different company today than we were when our current brand architecture was developed. The new logo is meant to disrupt the mental model of Xerox as just a copier company.

Research at the time showed that the old corporate logo (called a wordmark) had become too familiar and consumers did not pay it much attention. The new logo included a red sphere that is representative of a globe and worldwide connections, was encircled by intersecting graphic ribbons, and used FS Albert font with curved edges. Internal documents at Xerox described the logo as

> I am FS Albert. I am a modern and approachable font. My rounded corners make me more human and less technical.

In 2010, Xerox acquired a company called Affiliated Computer Services, or ACS, a well-established business processing company that aids its clients with digital documents like credit card applications, medical billing, mass-transit ticketing systems, and municipal paperwork. With this acquisition, just over half of Xerox's revenue came from business solution services, rather than sales of copier and fax equipment. Xerox launched its most expensive advertising campaign to date in an effort to shift the company's image to that of a business solutions services provider. Ursula Burns, Xerox CEO, said that

> [this campaign] aimed at disrupting old perceptions of the Xerox brand and positioning the new Xerox as the world's leading enterprise for business process and document management.

The advertisements in this campaign focused on Xerox's business solutions relationships with several well-known clients, such as Procter & Gamble, Target, Ducati, the New York Mets, the University of Notre Dame, and Marriot International. These organizations happily allowed their brand names to be used in the campaign. In each advertisement, employees or spokescharacters were shown dealing with back-office functions that were interfering with their core purpose. For example, one including P&G portrayed Mr. Clean attempting to scan documents with one hand while cleaning a table with another hand. The advertisements targeted businesspeople with decision-making power. In order to reach this target, ads were placed in airports, in business publications like *The Wall Street Journal,* and on business news channels like CNBC.

Unfortunately, the 2010 advertising campaign did not have the intended effect. Rather, Xerox's client companies garnered more benefits from the ads, while Xerox continued to be viewed as a copier company. However, CEO Ursula Burns still had heart and knew that repositioning the Xerox brand and a business services brand would not happen overnight. She said:

> We need to expand even further into business process outsourcing and IT outsourcing. It's a $500 billion industry and so we have a long way to go before we tap that market. We're showing proof points as we go along. But you can't be confused about the reality. It's all about managing this transition, so that you don't fall in love too much with the future to the point where you hate the past.

Determined to reposition the brand to thrive in the digital services marketplace and compete with the likes of IBM and Accenture, Xerox pushed on. Another approach that Xerox used was to change perceptions through content in social media marketing. Xerox partnered with *Forbes* and *The Week* to create Xerox-branded pages that post content on topics like analyzing big data and managing the Millennial generation. According to Jay Bartlett, Xerox vice president of global social marketing:

> Everything across our social media channels and content we're developing is very much about driving thought leadership in these spaces you'd never expect to see our name. This is really the notion that content and social go hand in glove. We married the two, and we think that's a recipe to help us utilize word-of-mouth marketing to help with our repositioning.

In 2013, Xerox launched a new advertising campaign that recognized that the enduring perception among consumers was that Xerox was in the business of copy machines and leveraged that fact to highlight its business services in a humorous way. Chista Carone, Xerox's chief marketing officer at the time, describes the rationale and a spot from that campaign:

> It became clear that we needed to draw the connection between who we were and who we are. We needed to get back to the basics of explaining our purpose and giving people a reason to believe that the copier company could stand for so much more than copies. That's why our latest campaign, which broke in February, acknowledges our past, even embraces it, while helping people connect the dots to today's Xerox. It's a no-nonsense, straight-talk effort. One 30-second spot from Young & Rubicam opens with a woman standing in front of—yes!—a copying machine. "When I say Xerox, I know what you're thinking," she says, then prints an image of a transit map. "Transit fares, as in the 37 billion transit fares we help collect each year." Another commercial features the same woman proclaiming that revolutionizing an industry is a hard act to follow, and then explaining some of the breadth and scale of services offered by Xerox.

That year marked the 75th anniversary of the first xerographic image. Xerox did not let this occasion pass unnoticed or uncelebrated. According to CEO Ursula Burns:

> Now is the time when many companies would look back, and we certainly will, but only for a moment. The real focus of our celebration will be the future and how Xerox will continue to simplify how work gets done.

"Simplifying how work gets done" is a message and position that Xerox hopes will resonate with business-people. This theme is present in its press releases and throughout the content in its own website and sponsored pages. For example, each of Xerox's seven outsourcing services incorporates the message on the web page. Please see the table for examples of this.

Outsourcing Service	Simplifying Message
Human Resources	Did you know Xerox is the 2nd largest benefits and pensions administrator globally? It's just one of the **surprising ways Xerox is helping companies simplify how work gets done.** . . .
Customer Care	Did you know Xerox has 175 customer care centers globally, staffed with over 46,000 agents? It's just one of the **surprising ways Xerox is helping companies simplify how work gets done.** . . .
Finance & Accounting	Did you know Xerox has over 24,000 professionals operating in over 90 global service centers? It's just one of the **surprising ways Xerox is helping companies simplify how work gets done.** . . .
Document Management	Did you know Gartner positions Xerox as a leader in the 2013 Gartner Magic Quadrant for managed print services? It's because Xerox finds **surprising ways to help simplify how work gets done.** . . .
Health care	Did you know Xerox offers services that touch two out of every three insured lives in the U.S.? It's because Xerox has surprising ways to help every area of the health care industry **simplify how work gets done.** . . .
Transportation	Did you know Xerox ranks #1 as a provider of worldwide transportation services to governments? It's because Xerox has proven solutions to help **simplify the way the world moves.** . . .

Will Xerox's latest efforts successfully reposition the brand to consumers as a business services company? Or will Xerox forever be relegated to the position as a photocopier giant? Xerox appears to be making the right moves, but only time will tell.

Discussion Questions

1. Chapter 9 discusses schemas, which also are known as schematic memories and knowledge structures. Construct a schema diagram for Xerox.
2. Chapter 9 also discusses product positioning, repositioning, and perceptual mapping.
   a. Construct a perceptual map that includes the Xerox brand before 2008 (before recent repositioning efforts).
   b. Construct a perceptual map that includes the Xerox brand in current times.
   c. Discuss how Xerox's position differs (or does not differ) between the two perceptual maps from part a and part b.
3. Chapter 9 further discusses brand equity and brand leverage. Xerox has strong brand equity because it has been a well-known and established brand for many years.

a. According to the chapter, successful brand leverage requires that the original brand have a strong positive image and that the new product fit with the original product on at least one of what four dimensions?

b. Which of these four dimensions does the business services solutions "product" fit with the original Xerox brand?

4. Chapter 11 discusses appeal characteristics in advertising. Use Google Videos or Google Images to find examples of the advertisements for either Xerox's 2010 or 2013 advertising campaign. Evaluate those advertisements based on

a. Appeal characteristics

b. Message structure characteristics

5. Chapter 8 discusses stimulus factors in advertising. Use Google Videos or Google Images to find examples of the advertisements for either Xerox's 2010 or 2013 advertising campaign. Evaluate those advertisements based on the following stimulus factors:

a. Size

b. Intensity

c. Attractive visuals

d. Color and movement

e. Position

f. Isolation

g. Format

h. Contrast and expectations

i. Interestingness

j. Information quantity

6. Chapter 10 discusses McGuire's psychological motives. Which of the motives does Xerox communicate to business customers could be fulfilled by using its business services?

Source: L. Abinanti, "Xerox Gets Positioning Right," *Messages That Matter,* April 15, 2014, www.messagesthatmatter.com; C. Carone, "Xerox's Brand Repositioning Challenge," *Advertising Age,* March 12, 2013, http://adage.com; Fast Company Staff, "Fresh Copy: How Ursula Burns Reinvented Xerox," *Fast Company,* November 19, 2011, www.fastcompany.com; D. Kiley, "Xerox Gets a Brand Makeover," *Business Week,* January 7, 2008, www.businessweek.com; D. Maggiore, "Xerox Stretches Its Brand Positioning," *Innis Maggiore Ad Agency,* September 17, 2010, www.innismaggiore.com; D. Mattoli, "Xerox Touts Its Business-Services Side," *Wall Street Journal,* September 2, 2010, http://online.wsj.com; E. Schwartz, "CEO Strategy: Charting 'Dual Transformation' at Xerox and Barnes & Noble," *Innosight* 10, no. 4 (December 2012), www.innosight.com; J. Sternberg, "How Content Drives Xerox's Transformation," *Digiday,* June 21, 2013, http://digiday.com; Street Authority, "Climb Aboard the Xerox Transformation," *MSN Money,* June 27, 2013, http://money.msn.com; "Xerox Celebrates 75th Anniversary of the Creation of Xerography," *PIWorld,* October 17, 2013, www.piworld.com.

3-8 THE TALE OF TWO EMOTIONAL ADS

The use of emotion in advertising is a long-tested, tried-and-true technique used by many marketers. In fact, there is a sizeable amount of research that demonstrates its effectiveness. According to Nielsen Consumer Neuroscience, emotional engagement is one of the three dimensions on which very successful ads often score well (along with attention and conversion to long-term memory). The Institute of Practitioners in Advertising compared the profitability of advertising campaigns with emotional appeals to those with rational appeals and found that emotional content performs twice as well as rational content (31 percent to 16 percent). When compared to those with a mix of emotional and rational content, emotional ad campaigns are still the top performers (31 percent to 26 percent). Studies using functional magnetic resonance imaging (fMRI) research reveal that consumers primarily use emotions over information to evaluate brands. Ultimately, emotions are the driving factor in why consumers choose to spend more on brand name products over cheaper, equivalent-quality generic versions that logic would support. According to Dan Hill, the author of *Emotionomics: Leveraging Emotions for Business Success:*

> Emotions process sensory input in only one-fifth the time our conscious, cognitive brain takes to assimilate that same input. Emotions, rather than cognitive thinking, have a more profound impact on our actions; create lasting, instinctual impressions.

While it is well-established that emotional advertising can be highly successful, achieving that success is not as straightforward as simply evoking some consumer emotional response. Various emotional campaigns have been true home runs with consumers, while others simply strike out or, even worse, damage the brand. According to Randall Beard, president of Nielsen Expanded Verticals:

> Best-in-class ads share several characteristics: they're relatable, follow an upbeat and simple story line, use novel and striking imagery and make an emotional connection. These characteristics provide a strong foundation for creative development, but there's no "one-size-fits-all" formula.

Take the case in point of two ads from the 2015 Super Bowl that cost upwards of $4.5 million per 30 seconds of airtime: Budweiser's "Lost Dog" and Nationwide's "Make Safe Happen."

Budweiser had a very successful ad, named "Puppy Love," in the 2014 Super Bowl that featured a Labrador puppy. In 2015, Budweiser created a sequel, called "Lost Dog," in which the puppy gets lost in an attempt to ride along in a horse trailer with the famous Budweiser Clydesdales. The puppy makes his way almost home through various adversities but encounters an angry wolf. The Clydesdales break free from the stables to come rescue the puppy from the wolf and the best friends are reunited and make their way back home to the farm together.

"Lost Dog" was an immediate sensation as consumers took to social media, using hashtags #BudweiserPuppy and #BestBuds to make positive comments. There were over 2.1 million posts about this ad on Twitter alone. Several of the posts came from celebrities, which brought even more attention to the ad and Budweiser brand. A Houston Texans' cheerleader with 15,000 followers tweeted, "And @Budweiser commercial made me cry like a baby for like the third year in a row. #bestbuds." Ryan Seacrest tweeted, "The @Budweiser commercial farmer should be the next #Bachelor. . .#SuperBowl." The friendship between the Budweiser puppy and Clydesdales and the positive heartstrings it pulled among viewers led to "Lost Puppy" being voted as the top of 61 advertisements for the 2015 Super Bowl in *USA Today*'s Ad Meter's consumer panel of 6,703 voters.

In a stark contrast, Nationwide Insurance demonstrated a far less successful use of emotion in its ad, called "Make Safe Happen." In this advertisement, a boy talks about all sorts of things he will never get to do, such as fly or get married, all because he died from an accident. The ad goes on to show various scenes of accidents that could kill small children, such as drowning in a bathtub, ingesting poisons from household cleaners, or being crushed by a television.

Like the Budweiser ad, Nationwide's "Make Safe Happen" also elicited an almost immediate response from consumers and celebrities via social media. However, the valence of the consumers' posts was very different. Judd Apatow tweeted, "Exciting game but that Damn Nationwide commercial haunts my dreams and my waking life!" and Ken Jennings (*Jeopardy!* champion) tweeted, "The Seahawks haven't completed a

pass but on the plus side I haven't killed any of my kids, Nationwide." Nationwide pulled the spot from the airwaves within hours, but the damage had been done. The chief marketing officer at Nationwide who was responsible for the spot tried to defend it by saying that the ad was intended to raise awareness of preventive choices consumers could make to keep their children safe. He ultimately ended up stepping down from his position a few months later. The following year, Nationwide did not even advertise at all in the 2016 Super Bowl, despite one of its most prominent pitchmen being a starting quarterback.

Both of these ads elicited the emotion of heartache, yet they produced very disparate results. Sadness, grief, and other negative emotions can be very useful in emotional advertising. However, those that are best received generally have some sort of positive resolution instead of leaving consumers wallowing in their negative feelings. According to Graeme Newell, marketing consultant, speaker, and founder of 602 Communications:

> One key component to successful emotional advertising is to find and capitalize on the core value of the brand, not just reach blindly for an emotional reaction. Otherwise, companies risk mocking an audience's emotional intelligence. In this example, Nationwide blindsided audiences with emotion just for effect, which came across as manufactured and heavy-handed.

Discussion Questions

1. Chapter 10 discusses the use of emotion in advertising. The three primary emotional dimensions are pleasure, arousal, and dominance, but there are many other various emotions under each category. Review Table 10–4 and determine which emotions each of the two advertisements mentioned in this case elicits.

2. Chapter 8 discusses several stimulus factors in advertising that can increase attention to ads. Look up "Lost Dog" and "Make Safe Happen" and view them online. Evaluate and compare these two ads based on the stimulus factors in the text.

3. Chapter 8 discusses exposure, in terms of selective exposure and voluntary exposure. What type of exposure do you think most consumers who viewed the two ads discussed in this case experienced? Explain your reasoning.

4. Chapter 9 discusses schemas, schematic memory, and schematic diagrams. See Figure 9–2 for an example.

   a. Draw a schematic diagram for Budweiser with "Lost Dog" in mind.

   b. Draw a schematic diagram for Nationwide with "Make Safe Happen" in mind.

   c. Write a brief description comparing and contrasting your schematic diagrams for part a and part b.

5. Chapter 11 discusses communication characteristics that influence attitude formation and change. Discuss "Lost Dog" and "Make Safe Happen" in terms of

   a. Appeal characteristics

   b. Message structure characteristics

6. Chapter 7 discusses WOM communications and opinion leadership. How did these concepts play a role in the respective success and failure of "Lost Dog" and "Make Safe Happen"?

Source: "Ads with Impact: What Messaging Themes Speak Loudest to Customers?," *Nielsen,* October 15, 2015, www.nielsen.com; R. Dooley, "Emotional Ads Work Best," *NeuroMarketing with Roger Dooley et al.,* www.neurosciencemarketing.com; J. Durando, "Why Nationwide Aired Upsetting Super Bowl Ad," *USA Today,* February 2, 2015, www.usatoday.com; B. Horovitz, "Budweiser 'Lost Dog' Finds Way to Top of Super Bowl Ad Meter," *USA Today,* February 1, 2015, www.usatoday.com; C. Miller, "The Dangerous Power of Emotional Advertising," *Contently,* April 14, 2016, www.contently.com, accessed April 24, 2018; P. Murray, "How Emotions Influence What We Buy: The Emotional Core of Consumer Decision-Making," *Psychology Today,* February 26, 2013, www.psychologytoday.com; A. Rodriguez, "Nationwide CMO Exits in Wake of 'Dead Boy' Super Bowl Ad," *Advertising Age,* May 6, 2015, www.adage.com; D. Rucker, "Emotion in Advertising: The Difference between a Spark and a Backfire," *Forbes,* October 5, 2017, www.forbes.com, accessed April 24, 2018; M. Tanier, "Super Bowl Ad Lessons Learned, a Year after Commercial That Went Way Wrong," *Bleache Report,* February 3, 2016, www.bleachereport.com, accessed April 24, 2018; The Nielsen Company, *Global Trust in Advertising Winning Strategies for an Evolving Media Landscape,* September 2015; N. Zipkin, "The 10 Most Talked-About Super Bowl Commercials of 2015," *Entrepreneur,* February 2, 2015, www.entrepreneur.com.

3-9 THE WORLD SHARES A COKE

The "Share a Coke" campaign has been one of Coca-Cola's most successful marketing campaigns of all time and has revitalized consumer enthusiasm for the Coca-Cola brand across the globe. Its beginnings were a humble 151-word abstract in Australia that resulted in 250 of the most common first names for teens and Millennials being printed on labels of soda bottles with the imperative for consumers to "share" a coke with someone with those names. Before this campaign, 50 percent of the young people in Australia had never even tasted a Coke. As Lucie Austin, a Coca-Cola brand executive said:

> We gave consumers an opportunity to express themselves through a bottle of Coke, and to share the experience with someone else. The campaign capitalized on the global trend of self-expression and sharing, but in an emotional way.

This small 2011 Australian campaign was hugely successful and ultimately ended up being an excellent test market for the "Share a Coke" concept. Since then, Coca-Cola has expanded it to over 70 countries.

The campaign came to the United States in the summer of 2014 with a limited release of the 500 most common Millennial first names. It was not long before consumers were scouring convenience stores and groceries for their own names and those of their friends and loved ones. The U.S. campaign was an amazing success and resulted in an increase in sales of Coca-Cola products for the first time in a 10-year period, while sales of competitor brands Pepsi and Dr Pepper Snapple remained negative.

Since then, the "Share a Coke" campaign has expanded in the U.S. each subsequent year. In 2015, 1,000 names were made available. Eventually, Coca-Cola provided a website where consumers could order personalized Coca-Cola products with certain hard-to-find names. In 2016, "Share a Coke" was back, but with the twist of printing popular song lyrics on the bottles. In 2017, Coca-Cola expanded the "Share a Coke" campaign in multiple ways. The personalized products were expanded to Coke Life and Cherry Coke, in addition to the previously offered Coca-Cola Classic, Coke Zero, and Diet Coke. The list was further expanded to include more than 77 percent of the first names of Americans between the ages of 13 and 34. Also, in line with the musical theme from the previous year, Coca-Cola produced over 1,000 personalized jingles, from 25 different musical tracks and nine different singers. Consumers could find jingles for names like Johnny and Megan on the Coca-Cola website. The jingles covered a wide range of musical genres from country western to reggae. Another innovation was printing the names of vacation hot spots including Hawaii, Bali, Ibiza, and Miami. Consumers could enter a code from their Coca-Cola products in a dedicated website to win trips to those locations.

Coca-Cola has made various adaptations to best fit local and cultural preferences in different countries. According to Ajay Bathija, Marketing Director of Coca-Cola India:

> We did not want to copy/paste the global campaign and decided to add an Indian flavour to it. Our consumer research showed that relationships in the country are becoming more informal than before and we wanted to highlight it. Our study also showed that many teenagers in India perceive their relationships differently; for example, the word "Dad" means not just an ATM but also their champ to them. This campaign is talking about the changing relationships of young India.

Therefore, in India, some labels included local slang for parents, such as Papa, Didi, and Bhai, along with popular names across 11 different languages spoken in India.

In South Africa, consumers were having trouble finding their names due to such a wide variety of local tribes within the country. As a solution, Coca-Cola introduced voice-activated vending machines that allowed consumers to print their own names on 200 ml cans. These innovative machines caught on and produced cans at a rate of about six cans per minute, roughly double the international standard of three cans per minute.

Launched in Vietnam and spread to markets throughout ASEAN countries, with a wide variety of languages, a focus was put on using emoticons on the bottles in a variation of the campaign called "Share a Feeling." Emoticons were thought to be a universal language that young people can use to express themselves. According to Pratik Thakar, head of Creative Content & Design Excellence, ASEAN & APAC:

> Emoticons have become a perfect sharing platform, sharing of human feelings. It transcends language barriers and has pretty much become a part of popular culture across most ASEAN markets.

In each country, Coca-Cola has used a quiet launch, which actually leads to more word-of-mouth (WOM) sharing because consumers are more likely to spread information they perceive to have discovered on their own before others. Promotional samples are sent to local opinion leaders, including celebrities like American actress Emma Roberts, and Bollywood actor Tahir Raj Bhasin, to create buzz. The name of the campaign itself,

"*Share* a Coke," is a powerful call to action itself. The hashtag #ShareaCoke boosted the spreadability of the campaign as consumers would often post selfies with the bottles with their names on the label. For example, 25 million new followers liked Coca-Cola on Facebook in the first year of the campaign. By 2016, over 600,000 pictures were shared on Instagram with the hashtag #ShareaCoke.

With such great success of the "Share a Coke" campaigns, Coca-Cola gives no indication that the campaign expansions will slow or stop any time soon. This will be an interesting case to watch unfold into the future.

Discussion Questions

1. Chapter 10 discusses Maslow's hierarchy of needs. Which of the needs does the "Share a Coke" campaign satisfy? Explain your answer.

2. Likewise, Chapter 10 discusses McGuire's psychological motives. Which of these motives might lead consumers to be influenced by the "Share a Coke" campaign? Explain your answer.

3. Chapter 11 discusses the three components of attitude (cognitive, affective, and behavioral). Which of these components does Coca-Cola focus on in the "Share a Coke" campaign? Does your response change based on the context of the country in which the campaign is being used? For example, before the initial Australian 2011 campaign, roughly half of the young people had never tried Coca-Cola, whereas most people in the U.S. had tried Coca-Cola many times before the campaign was launched there. Explain.

4. Chapter 11 discusses sources characteristics, and particularly celebrity sources.
   a. How did Coca-Cola use celebrity sources?
   b. Why would these celebrity endorsers be effective?

5. Chapter 12 discusses possessions and the extended self. Discuss how the "Share a Coke" campaign incorporated the concept of self to encourage sales of its products.

6. Chapter 4 discusses generational groups. Which of these segments is Coca-Cola targeting with "Share a Coke" and why?

7. Coca-Cola appears to have no plans to discontinue the "Share a Coke" expansions in the near future. What recommendations would you have for future iterations?

Source: "3 Marketing Lessons from the 'Share a Coke' Campaign," *MayeCreate Design,* May 7, 2016, www.mayecreate.com, accessed April 24, 2018; "#ShareACokeZA," *OLC Experiential,* www.offlimit.co.za, accessed October 19, 2018; M. Bright, " 'Share a Coke' Is Back This Summer—with a Twist," *Refinery29,* June 1, 2017, www.refinery29.com, accessed April 24, 2018; "Coca-Cola's 'Share a Coke' Returns with Emoticon Campaign 'Share a Feeling,'" *Isobar,* April 8, 2015, www.isobar.com, accessed April 24, 2018; S. Dikshit, "Coca-Cola Launches Its 'Share a Coke' Campaign in the Indian Market," *Afaqs!,* April 4, 2018, www.afaqs.com, accessed April 24, 2018; M. Esterl, " 'Share a Coke' Credited with a Pop in Sales," *Wall Street Journal,* September 25, 2014, www.wsj.com; L. Handley, "Coca-Cola Puts Vacation Destinations on Labels in Update of 'Share a Coke' Names on Bottles Campaign," *CNBC,* April 19, 2017, www.cnbc.com, accessed April 24, 2018; T. McQuilken, " 'Share a Coke' Campaign Grows Sales for First Time in 10 Years, WSJ Reports," *Adweek,* September 26, 2014, www.adweek.com; E. Schultz, "Coke Made 1,000 Songs Featuring People's Names," *Advertising Age,* July 10, 2017, www.adage.com, accessed April 24, 2018; M. Schneider, "Coke Creates 1,000-Plus Songs for Its 'Share a Coke' Campaign," *Billboard,* July 10, 2017, www.billboard.com, accessed April 24, 2018; E. Tarver, "What Makes the 'Share a Coke' Campaign So Successful? (KO) 2015," *Investopedia,* October 7, 2015, www.investopedia.com; S. Tewari, "Coca-Cola Goes Desi with Regional Language Packaging Under 'Share a Coke' Campaign," *LiveMint,* April 6, 2018, accessed April 24, 2018; www.livemint.com; K. Windle, "Share a Coke and a Word: How Coca-Cola Captured Millennials through Word of Mouth Marketing," *Medium,* May 19, 2016, www.medium.com, accessed April 24, 2018.

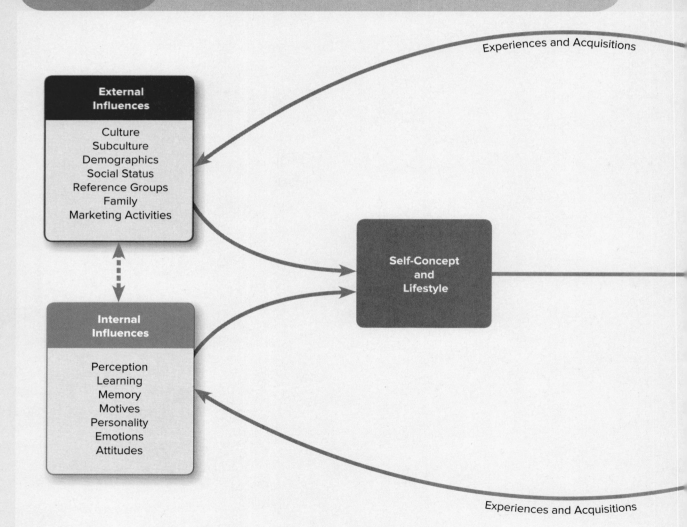

Experiences and Acquisitions

External Influences

Culture
Subculture
Demographics
Social Status
Reference Groups
Family
Marketing Activities

Internal Influences

Perception
Learning
Memory
Motives
Personality
Emotions
Attitudes

Self-Concept and Lifestyle

Experiences and Acquisitions

Up to now, we have focused on various sociological and psychological factors that contribute to different patterns of consumer behavior. Though these various influences play a significant role in behavior, all behavior takes place within the context of a situation. Chapter 13 provides a discussion of the impact situational variables have on consumer behavior.

Of particular importance to marketers is how situations and internal and external sources of influence affect the purchase decision process. The extended consumer decision process, shown on this page, is composed of a sequence of activities: problem recognition, information search, brand evaluation and selection, outlet choice and purchase, and postpurchase processes. However, extended decision making occurs only in those relatively rare situations when the consumer is highly involved in the purchase. Lower levels of purchase involvement produce limited or nominal decision making. Chapter 14 describes those various types of decisions and their relationship to involvement. It also analyzes the first stage of the process—problem recognition.

Information search, in various forms including online, mobile, and offline, constitutes the second stage of the consumer decision process and is discussed in Chapter 15. Chapter 16 examines the alternative evaluation and selection process. Chapter 17 deals with outlet selection and the in-store and online influences that often determine final brand choice. The final stage of the consumer decision process, presented in Chapter 18, involves behaviors after the purchase. These include postpurchase dissonance, product use and disposition, and satisfaction and loyalty. Both cognitive (thinking) and emotional (feeling) processes are important at each stage of the decision process.

Decision Process

Situations

Problem Recognition

Information Search

Alternative Evaluation and Selection

Outlet Selection and Purchase

Postpurchase Processes

Needs

Desires

chapter

13 Situational Influences

Source: Yum! Brands RSC

LEARNING OBJECTIVES

LO1 Define situational influence.

LO2 Explain the four types of situations and their relevance to marketing strategy.

LO3 Summarize the five characteristics of situations and their influence on consumption.

LO4 Discuss ritual situations and their importance to consumers and marketers.

LO5 Describe the use of situational influence in developing marketing strategy.

Springtime in the United States signals blooming flowers, baseball season, and, for the typical high school teenager, prom. The annual prom ritual began in the late 1800s as a college graduation event and has morphed into a $4 billion industry. A recent study by Visa found that teens and their families spend an average of $919 on "all things prom." The costs included items directly associated with the event (e.g., the dance ticket, clothing, flowers, food, and transportation), as well as associated activities such as pre-prom get-togethers, professional photographers, and post-prom parties. For some, no expense is spared. Some have been known to involve yachts and camels![1]

The prom ritual understandably attracts florists' attention. And in a recent twist, KFC joined with a local Louisville florist to create and promote a *chicken corsage* during the prom season. The corsage "kit" cost $20, which included a fresh flower corsage from the florist and a $5 KFC gift card. Although the corsage kit was initially offered locally, demand spread nationally.

A new complementary ritual to prom that has sparked marketers' interest: the "promposal." Today, how one asks a date to prom appears to be as important as the prom itself—and flowers may no longer be enough. Promposals now include private plane rentals, sky diving, and lavish jewelry. In its same study, Visa estimated the average promposal cost at $324.

The prom ritual has a powerful pull on the American psyche and as such appears to be impervious to such aspects as economic downturns. Part of this may be a function of the relative cost of prom compared to the other (more significant) costs of raising a child. The Prom Price Index, based on 10 prom-related items found in the Consumer Price Index (CPI), has risen 23 percent from 1998 to 2017, whereas the CPI has increased 50 percent in that timeframe. This appears to have given parents the "license" to spend more on prom. As one expert says:

> A middle-income couple will spend about $234,000 to raise a child from birth through age 17, according to the U.S. Agricultural Department. But as college and other costs hit the stratosphere, at least the prom can be had for a song.

Beyond such functional explanations, however, is the powerful emotional aspect surrounding prom. According to one merchandiser, such considerations appear to make the demand for prom dresses "recession-proof":

> Despite financial struggles in the recession, families pulled it together to make it happen. It's such an important event. People save their money for this, and if everything else is going bad, this is the one thing they want to make sure is perfect for their daughter's life.

Prom, the annual spring ritual of high school teens, has become a thriving industry. For many families, there appears to be no limit to what they will spend on this "big, dress-up, transition-to-adulthood event" to make it the perfect life experience for their child. Marketers are taking note.

As the model we have used to organize this text indicates, the purchase decision and consumption process always occur in the context of a specific situation. Therefore, before examining the decision process, we first must develop an understanding of situations. In this chapter, we will examine the situations in which consumption occurs, the way situations influence consumption behaviors, key characteristics of situations, the nature of ritual situations, and situation-based marketing strategies.

THE NATURE OF SITUATIONAL INFLUENCE

LO1
Consumers do not respond to stimuli such as advertisements and products presented by marketers in isolation; instead, they respond to marketing influences and the situation simultaneously. To understand a consumer's behavior, we must know about the *consumer;* about the primary *stimulus* object, such as a product or advertisement to which the consumer is responding; and about the *situation* in which the response is occurring.[2]

We define **situational influence** as *all those factors particular to a time and place that do not follow from a knowledge of the stable attributes of the consumer and the stimulus and that have an effect on current behavior.*[3] Thus, with one exception, the situation stands apart from the consumer and the stimulus. The exception is in the case of *temporary* (as opposed to stable) characteristics of a consumer or stimulus that are specific to the situation and sometimes even caused by it. For example, a consumer may generally be upbeat (stable trait), but just prior to viewing a firm's ad sees a disturbing news flash that puts her in a bad mood. This bad mood is a transient state (situational factor) caused by the surrounding media context in which the focal ad appears. Other such temporary conditions include illness and time pressure. Consumer involvement also includes a situation-specific component. That is, some consumers are involved only when they have to make a purchase.

A key marketing finding is that consumers often react and behave very differently depending on the situation. We discussed some of these effects in earlier chapters. For example, an ad or in-store display that might otherwise attract consumer attention may not do so in a cluttered environment (Chapter 8). Or an ad that might be persuasive in a nonpurchase situation may be much less persuasive in a purchase situation where consumers are in the market to buy (Chapter 11). The interplay between situation, marketing, and the individual is shown in Figure 13–1.

Consumer behavior occurs within four broad categories or types of situations: the communications situation, the purchase situation, the usage situation, and the disposition situation.

The Communications Situation

LO2
The situation in which consumers receive information has an impact on their behavior. Whether one is alone or in a group, in a good mood or bad, in a hurry or not influences the degree to which one sees and listens to marketing communications. Is it better to advertise on a happy or sad television program? A calm or exciting program? These are some of the questions managers must answer with respect to the **communications situation.**[4] Marketers often attempt to place their ads in appropriate media contexts to enhance their effectiveness. Some even go so far as to mandate that their ads be "pulled" when programming content negative to their company or industry will appear. Recent examples include AT&T and State Farm. *What are the ethical implications of such policies?*[5]

A marketer is able to deliver an effective message to consumers who are interested in the product and are in a receptive communications situation. However, finding high-interest potential buyers in receptive communications situations is a difficult challenge.

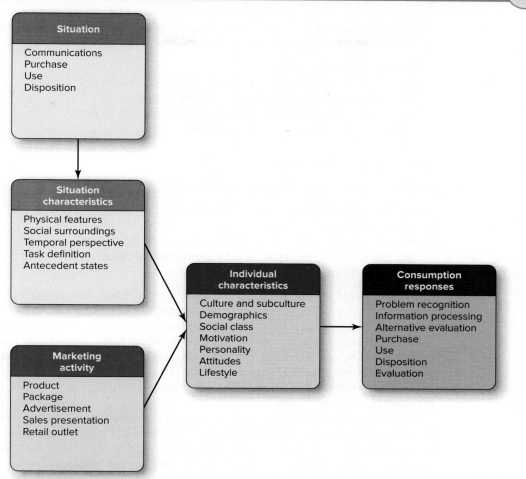

The Situation Interacts with the Marketing Activity and the Individual to Determine Behavior FIGURE 13-1

For example, consider the difficulty a marketer would have in communicating to you in the following communications situations:

- Your favorite team just lost the most important game of the year.
- Final exams begin tomorrow.
- Your roommates watch only comedy programs.
- You have the flu.
- You are driving home on a cold night, and your car heater doesn't work.

The Purchase Situation

The situation in which a purchase is made can influence consumer behavior. Mothers shopping with children are more apt to be influenced by the product preferences of their children than when shopping without them. A shortage of time, such as trying to make a purchase between classes, can affect the store-choice decision, the number of brands considered, and the price the shopper is willing to pay. At an even more basic level, whether or not a consumer is in a "purchase mode" influences a whole host of behaviors from advertising responses to shopping. Consider, for example, how differently you might behave at Best Buy if you were there only to browse versus being there to replace a broken Blu-ray player.

Marketers must understand how **purchase situations** influence consumers in order to develop marketing strategies that enhance the purchase of their products. For example, how would you alter your decision to purchase a beverage in the following purchase situations?

- You are in a very bad mood.
- A good friend says, "That stuff is bad for you!"
- The store you visit does not carry your favorite brand.
- There is a long line at the checkout counter as you enter the store.
- You are with someone you want to impress.

The Usage Situation

What beverage would you prefer to consume in each of the following usage situations?

- On Friday afternoon after your last final exam.
- With your parents for lunch.
- After dinner on a cold, stormy evening.
- At a dinner with a friend you have not seen in several years.
- When you are feeling sad or homesick.

Marketers need to understand the **usage situations** for which their products are, or may become, appropriate. Using this knowledge, marketers can communicate how their products create consumer satisfaction in each relevant usage situation. For example, a recent study found that consuming two 1.5-cup servings of oat-based cereal a day could lower cholesterol. How could General Mills take advantage of this finding to increase sales of its oat-based cereal Cheerios? A recent ad depicts a dad coming home late from work and having Cheerios for dinner. When asked why by his young daughter, he replies, "Because they taste just as good at night."

Research indicates that *expanded usage situation* strategies can produce major sales gains for established products.[6] Coach went away from the traditional two-occasion (everyday and dressy) approach to handbags and moved toward what it calls a "usage voids" approach. Now Coach offers a wide range of products, including weekend bags, coin purses, clutches, and wristlets in a variety of colors and fabrics. The goal is to get consumers more attuned to the various usage situations available in which to accessorize and then create bags to fit the situations.[7] Dunkin' Donuts found that over half of donut consumption was for breakfast, but roughly 34 percent was for nonbreakfast snacks. In response, the company has

created simple yet imaginative make-at-home snack and dessert recipes, such as Cocoa Donut and Strawberry Grilled Cheese, to encourage consumers to think of and use the company's products in new ways. [They are also tapping the specialty occasions market with] limited-time offers, such as the heart-shaped Valentine's "Cupid's Choice."[8]

The Daisy sour cream ad in Illustration 13–1 provides another example of a company trying to expand the usage situations for its brand.

The Disposition Situation

Consumers frequently must dispose of products or product packages after or before product use. As we will examine in detail in Chapter 18, decisions made by consumers regarding the **disposition situation** can create significant social problems as well as opportunities for marketers.

Some consumers consider ease of disposition an important product attribute. These people may purchase only items that can be easily recycled. Often disposition of an existing product must occur before or simultaneously with the acquisition of the new product. For example, most consumers must remove their existing bed before using a new one. Marketers need to understand how situational influences affect disposition decisions in order to develop more effective and ethical products and marketing programs. Government and environmental organizations need the same knowledge in order to encourage socially responsible disposition decisions.

How would your disposition decision differ in these situations?

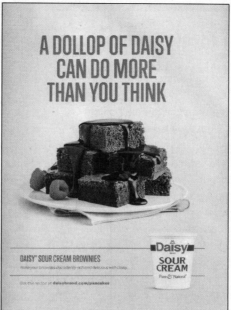

A DOLLOP OF DAISY CAN DO MORE THAN YOU THINK

DAISY® SOUR CREAM BROWNIES

≡Daisy≡ SOUR CREAM

Source: Daisy Brand LLC

- You have finished a soft drink in a can at a mall. There is a trashcan nearby, but there is no sign of a recycling container.
- You have finished reading the newspaper after class, and you note that you are running late for a basketball game.
- You and two friends have finished soft drinks. Both your friends toss the recyclable cans into a nearby garbage container.
- A local charity will accept old refrigerators if they are delivered to the charity. Your garbage service will haul one to the dump for $15. You just bought a new refrigerator. You don't know anyone (or you do know someone) with a pickup or van.

SITUATIONAL CHARACTERISTICS AND CONSUMPTION BEHAVIOR

The situations discussed above can be described on a number of dimensions that determine their influence on consumer behavior. The five key dimensions or characteristics are physical surroundings, social surroundings, temporal perspectives, task definition, and antecedent states.[9] These characteristics have been studied primarily in the United States. While the same characteristics of the situation exist across cultures, a marketer should not assume that the response to these characteristics would be the same. For example, a crowded store might cause a different emotional reaction among American consumers than among consumers in India.[10]

Physical Surroundings

Physical surroundings include decor, sounds, aromas, lighting, weather, and configurations of merchandise or other materials surrounding the stimulus object. Physical surroundings are a widely used type of situational influence, particularly for retail applications. Consumer Insight 13–1 sheds further light onto one aspect of the physical retail environment, namely mannequins.

Mannequins, More Than Just Store Dummies

Perhaps equally as true as the statement "the clothes make the man" is the statement "the mannequin makes the clothes." Forty-two percent of consumers polled in a recent study stated that what they saw displayed on a mannequin influenced their purchase decision.[11]

With the forecast that "[a]ll department stores will become museums, and all museums will become department stores," threatening to become ever more real with online retail encroachment into their sales, brick-and-mortar stores are fighting back with an army of mannequins. The plain white faceless, sometimes headless, torso mannequin that quietly blended unnoticed into the background has been replaced with a new breed of mannequins that scream with attention-arresting poses and astoundingly realistic physical features.

To be more than the colorless, uniform clothes-hanger mannequins of yesteryear, mannequins today are being created to personalize the brand. For example, Nike mannequins come alive in action poses to communicate the energy and dynamism of athleticism, and the runway model poses of Guess mannequins exemplify fashion sophistication and confidence.

Mannequins have long been the silent salespersons, ranking third, after friends and family, in influencing purchasing behavior. It turns out that realistic, larger-sized mannequins are better salespeople. Recent research shows that women are three times more likely to buy clothes when they see them on a mannequin related to their size. Macy's, Nordstrom, and the British Debenhams department stores are using or report plans to use more realistic, full-bodied mannequins. Developed after an extensive study that involved scanning thousands of women's bodies to arrive at a better understanding of women's proportions, the mannequins in David's Bridal,

the largest chain of bridal stores in the United States, have thicker waists and realistic imperfections.

Another trend in mannequin realism centers not so much on creating more realistic body types, but on providing mannequins with realistic details including pierced ears, tattoos, movable limbs to better display clothes, and articulated fingers to better show off rings. Mannequins have progressed beyond being the silent salesperson. Some mannequins are also data collectors. EyeSee Mannequins are traditional-looking mannequins, except they have eyes fitted with a camera lens that captures data on passersby. The data are fed to facial recognition software; mined for shoppers' age, gender, and ethnicity; and used in forecasting models to develop marketing campaigns and store displays. Mindful of consumer privacy, EyeSee mannequins do not record or send data of a sensitive nature such as biometric data.

Much more than just store dummies, mannequins contribute to the brick-and-mortar shopping experience, exuding appeal to entice consumers to visit stores, poising provocatively to capture consumer attention, sized and detailed to motivate consumers to make purchases. Mannequins serve as store ambassadors, evangelizing brand image and selling clothes.

Critical Thinking Questions

1. Have you noticed the new mannequins in stores where you shop for clothes? What is your reaction?

2. The new types of mannequins have centered more on women than men. Would men be more likely to buy clothes displayed on mannequins related to their size?

3. Digital mannequins collect data from passersby who are unaware that they are being recorded. Is this ethical?

External retail factors such as the architecture, arrangement, and assortment of retailers are an important influence on consumer shopping experiences. In addition, store interiors often are designed to create specific feelings in shoppers that can have an important cueing or reinforcing effect on purchase. All physical aspects of the store, including lighting,

©Purestock/SuperStock   ©Purestock/SuperStock

layout, presentation of merchandise, fixtures, floor coverings, colors, sounds, odors, and dress and behavior of sales personnel, combine to produce these feelings, which in turn influence purchase tendencies.[12] A retail clothing store specializing in extremely stylish, modern clothing would want its fixtures, furnishings, and colors to reflect an overall mood of style, flair, and newness (see Illustration 13-2). In addition, the store personnel should carry this theme in terms of their own appearance and apparel. Compare this with the interior of a so-called discount retailer, also shown in the illustration. It is important to note that one is not superior to the other. Each attempts to create an appropriate atmosphere for its target audience.

The sum of all the physical features of a retail environment is referred to as the **store atmosphere** or environment (see Chapter 17). Store atmosphere influences consumer judgments of store quality and image. It also has been shown to influence shoppers' moods and their willingness to visit and linger. **Atmospherics** is *the process managers use to manipulate the physical retail environment to create specific mood responses in shoppers.*[13] Atmospherics is also important online and is receiving increasing attention from marketers.[14]

Atmosphere is referred to as **servicescape** when describing a service business such as a hospital, bank, or restaurant.[15] Figure 13-2 classifies services according to the reason the customer is using the service and the length of time the service will be used. The consumption purpose is categorized along a continuum from strictly utilitarian, such as dry cleaning, to completely hedonic, such as a massage. The time can range from a few minutes to days or weeks. Physical characteristics and the feelings and image they create become increasingly important as hedonic motives and the time involved with the service increase. Thus, the physical characteristics of a vacation resort may be as important as or more important than the intangible services provided.

It is important that Figure 13-2 be interpreted correctly. It indicates that the physical environment at Starbucks is more important to the service experience than the physical features of dry cleaners are. *This does not mean that the physical aspects of dry cleaners are not important.* Indeed, an organized, professional-appearing dry cleaning establishment is likely to produce more satisfied customers than one with the opposite characteristics. What the

FIGURE 13-2   Typology of Service Environments

Time Spent in Facility	Consumption Purpose		
Utilitarian -- _Hedonic_			
Short [minutes]	Dry cleaner Bank	Fast food Hair salon	Facial Coffee at Starbucks
Moderate [hour(s)]	Medical appointment Legal consultation	Business dinner Exercise class	Theater Sporting event
Extended [day(s)]	Hospital Trade show	Conference hotel Training center	Cruise Resort

figure does indicate is that the relative importance of tangible physical features increases as one moves to extended, hedonic consumption experiences.

Having established the importance of the physical environment, we will now examine some of its components.

Colors As we saw in Chapter 8, certain colors and color characteristics create feelings of excitement and arousal that are related to attention. Bright colors are more arousing than dull colors. And _warm_ colors, such as reds and yellows, are more arousing than _cool_ colors, such as blues and greys.[16] Which color would be best for store interiors? The answer is, it depends. For the dominant interior color, cool colors (e.g., blue) should probably be used because they increase sales and customer satisfaction.[17] However, the attention-getting nature of warm colors should not be overlooked and can be used effectively as an accent color in areas where the retailer wants to attract attention and drive impulse purchases.[18] Cool colors also appear to be capable of reducing wait time perceptions by inducing feelings of relaxation.[19]

As we saw in Chapter 2, the meaning of colors varies across cultures. Therefore, this and all other aspects of the physical environment should be designed specifically for the cultures involved.

Aromas There is increasing evidence that odors can affect consumer shopping.[20] One study found that a scented environment produced a greater intent to revisit the store, higher purchase intention for some items, and a reduced sense of time spent shopping.[21] Another study found that one aroma, but not another, increased slot machine usage in a Las Vegas casino.[22] A third study found that the presence of a certain aroma in a retail setting increased pleasure, arousal, time spent, and money spent at the retailer.[23] A fourth study found that a pleasantly scented environment enhanced brand recall and evaluations, particularly for unfamiliar brands. The pleasant scent increased the time spent evaluating the brands (attention), which, in turn, increased memory.[24]

Given these results, it is not surprising that a billion-dollar _environmental fragrancing_ industry has developed around the use of ambient scents.[25] However, marketers still have a lot to learn about if, when, and how scents can be used effectively in a retail environment.[26] In addition, scent preferences are highly individualized; a pleasant scent to one individual

The Impact of Background Music on Restaurant Patrons		TABLE 13-1

Variables	Slow Music	Fast Music
Service time	29 min	27 min
Customer time at table	56 min	45 min
Customer groups leaving before seated	10.5%	12.0%
Amount of food purchased	$55.81	$55.12
Amount of bar purchases	$30.47	$21.62
Estimated gross margin	$55.82	$48.62

Source: R. E. Milliman, "The Influence of Background Music on the Behavior of Restaurant Patrons," *Journal of Consumer Research,* September 1986, p. 289. Copyright © 1986 by the University of Chicago. Used by permission.

may be repulsive to another. Moreover, some shoppers object to anything being deliberately added to the air they breathe, and others worry about allergic reactions.[27]

Music   Music influences consumers' moods, which influence a variety of consumption behaviors both in traditional retailer settings and in online settings.[28] Is slow-tempo or fast-tempo background music better for a restaurant? Table 13–1 indicates that slow music increased gross margin for one restaurant by almost 15 percent per customer group compared with fast music. However, before concluding that all restaurants should play slow music, examine the table carefully. Slow music appears to have relaxed and slowed down the customers, resulting in more time in the restaurant and substantially more purchases from the bar. Restaurants that rely on rapid customer turnover might be better off with fast-tempo music.

Other aspects of music besides tempo are also important. For example, research suggests that matching music to the musical preferences of the target audience is critical to positive retail outcomes such as satisfaction and enjoyment, browsing time, spending, perceived service quality, and positive word-of-mouth. In addition, research suggests that music that creates moderate levels of arousal (versus extremely low or high) yields the most positive retail outcomes.[29]

Because of the impact that music can have on shopping behavior, firms exist to develop music programs to meet the unique needs of specific retailers. An emerging trend is having music more in the foreground so it becomes part of the shopping experience and drives store image. AEI, a major supplier of foreground music, does intense research on the demographics and psychographics of each client store's customers. The age mix, buying patterns, and traffic flows of each part of the day are analyzed. AEI characterizes its approach as

[creating] environments where sounds, video, lighting and architecture blend together to give a brand a voice, creating emotional attachments that encourage consumers to shop longer, increase spending and return often.[30]

Firms such as Abercrombie & Fitch, Banana Republic, Bath & Body Works, and Eddie Bauer use companies like AEI to create appropriate and consistent shopping environments throughout their chains.

Crowding   Crowding generally produces negative outcomes for both the retail outlet and the consumer.[31] As more people enter a store or as more of the space of the store is filled with merchandise, an increasing percentage of the shoppers will experience a feeling of being crowded, confined, or claustrophobic. Most consumers find these feelings to be unpleasant and will take steps to change them. The primary means of doing so is to spend less time in the store by buying less, making faster decisions, and using less of the available information. This in turn tends to produce less satisfactory purchases, an unpleasant shopping trip, and a reduced likelihood of returning to the store.

Marketers should design their outlets in ways that will help reduce consumers' perceptions of crowding. This is difficult because retail shopping tends to occur at specific times, such as holiday weekends. Retailers must balance the expense of having a larger store than required most of the time against the cost of having dissatisfied customers during key shopping periods. Using extra personnel, opening additional checkout lines, and implementing similar measures can enhance the flow of consumers through a store during peak periods and reduce the crowding sensation. In addition, recent research shows that music tempo can be important. Specifically, music with a slow tempo offsets the negative emotions experienced as a result of crowding. Because music tempo adjustments are less expensive than store expansion or new personnel, this is an important finding for retail strategy.[32]

Marketers need to be sensitive to cross-cultural differences because personal space and resulting crowding perceptions can vary from culture to culture. For example, one study found that when the activity is for fun, such as an amusement park or concert, Middle East consumers perceive less crowding and appreciate crowding more than North American consumers.[33]

Social Surroundings

Social surroundings are *the other individuals present in the particular situation.* People's actions are frequently influenced by those around them. What would you wear in each of the following situations?

- Studying alone for a final.
- Meeting at the library with a date to study for a final.
- Going to a nice restaurant with a date.
- Meeting a prospective employer for lunch.

Illustration 13–3 shows how Wrangler is positioning its brand for casual rather than formal social settings.

Social influence is a significant force acting on our behavior because individuals tend to comply with group expectations, particularly when the behavior is visible (see Chapter 7). Thus, shopping, a highly visible activity, and the use of many publicly consumed brands are subject to social influences.[34] This is particularly true of those who are highly susceptible to interpersonal influence, a stable personality trait. As just one example, a recent study finds that consumers are more likely to engage in variety-seeking behavior in public (versus private) consumption situations even if it means consuming products they like less. The reason is that consumers feel that others view them more positively (more fun, interesting, exciting) if their purchases show more variety. This tendency is stronger for those more susceptible to interpersonal influence.[35]

Marketers have recently begun to examine the role of social influence on embarrassment. **Embarrassment** is *a negative emotion influenced by both the product and the situation.* Certain products are more embarrassing than others (condoms, hearing aids, etc.), and embarrassment is driven by the presence of others in the purchase or usage situation. Because embarrassment can deter purchases, this is an important area for marketers. One finding is that familiarity with purchasing the product reduces embarrassment, so marketers might

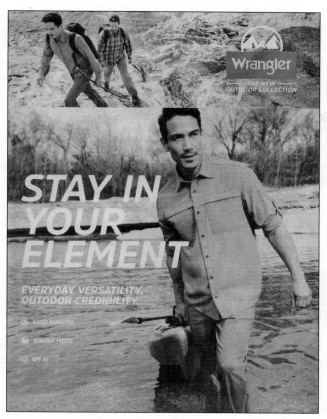

Source: Wrangler, A VF Company

try advertisements that show the purchase of a potentially embarrassing product in which no awkwardness or embarrassment occurs. For extremely sensitive products (e.g., adult diapers), strategies might include home delivery options with discreet labeling to completely avoid the social component.[36]

Shopping can provide a social experience outside the home for making new acquaintances, meeting existing friends, or just being near other people. Some people seek status and authority in shopping because the salesperson's job is to wait on the customer. This allows these individuals a measure of respect or prestige that may otherwise be lacking in their lives. Thus, consumers, on occasion, shop *for* social situations rather than, or in addition to, products. The presence of others *during* the shopping trip also can influence impulse buying. Results show that compared with shopping alone, shopping with close friends increased impulse buying, while shopping with close family members decreased impulse buying. It seems that consumers believe that norms differ such that their friends view impulse buying as more acceptable than does family.[37]

Frequently, marketing managers will not have any control over social characteristics of a situation. For example, when a television advertisement is sent into the home, the advertising manager cannot control whom the viewer is with at the time of reception. However, the manager can use the knowledge that some programs are generally viewed alone (weekday, daytime programs), some are viewed by the entire family (prime-time family comedies), and others are viewed by groups of friends (Super Bowl). The message presented can be structured to these viewing situations. Marketers also can use social consumption themes in

In the United States and other countries, dual-career and single-parent families have caused consumers to feel time starved. Online shopping provides many such consumers both time savings and control over when they shop. This Instacart ad would appeal to this consumer.

Source: Maplebear Inc.

their ads to enhance the likelihood that consumers will consider the social component in their decisions. For example, one study found that brand personality (fun and sophistication) conveyed by a celebrity endorser in an ad only enhanced purchase intentions when a social context was evoked.[38]

Temporal Perspectives

Temporal perspectives are *situational characteristics that deal with the effect of time on consumer behavior.* Time as a situational factor can manifest itself in a number of ways.[39] The amount of time available for the purchase has a substantial impact on the consumer decision process. In general, the less time there is available (i.e., increased time pressure), the shorter will be the information search, the less available information will be used, and the more suboptimal purchases will be made.[40] In addition, research suggests that time pressure decreases perceptions of retailer service quality.[41]

Limited purchase time also can result in a smaller number of product alternatives being considered. The increased time pressure experienced by many dual-career couples and single parents tends to increase the incidence of brand loyalty, particularly for nationally branded products. The obvious implication is that these consumers feel safer with nationally branded or "known" products, particularly when they do not have the time to engage in extensive comparison shopping.

Time as a situational influence affects consumers' choice of stores and behaviors in those stores.[42] A number of retail firms have taken advantage of the temporal perspective factor. Perhaps the most successful of these is the 7-Eleven chain, which caters almost exclusively to individuals who either are in a hurry or want to make a purchase after regular shopping hours.

Online shopping is growing rapidly in part as a result of the time pressures felt by many dual-career and single-parent households. Shopping online has two important time-related dimensions. First, it has the potential to reduce the amount of time required to make a specific purchase. Second, it provides the consumer with almost total control over *when* the purchase is made (see Chapter 17). These features are among the major reasons for the rapid growth in online outlets and sales (see the Instacart ad in Illustration 13–4).

Task Definition

Task definition is *the reason the consumption activity is occurring.* The major task dichotomy used by marketers is between purchases for self-use versus gift giving.

Gift Giving Consumers use different shopping strategies and purchase criteria when shopping for gifts versus shopping for the same item for self-use.[43] Consumers give gifts for many reasons. Social expectations and ritualized consumption situations such as birthdays often require gift giving independent of the giver's actual desires.[44] Gifts also are given to elicit return favors in the form of either gifts or actions. And, of course, gifts are given as an expression of love and caring.[45]

The type of gift given and desired varies by occasion and gender.[46] One study found that wedding gifts tend to be *utilitarian,* while birthday gifts tend to be *fun.* Thus, both the general task definition (gift giving) and the specific task definition (gift-giving occasion) influence purchase behavior, as does the relationship between the giver and the recipient.

Gift giving produces anxieties on the part of both givers and receivers.[47] Gifts communicate symbolic meaning on several levels. The gift item itself generally has a known, or knowable, price that can be interpreted as a measure of the esteem the giver has for the receiver. The image and functionality of the gift implies the giver's impression of the image and personality of the receiver. It also reflects on the image and thoughtfulness of the giver.

The nature of a gift can signify the type of relationship the giver has or desires with the receiver.[48] Consider the following:

> The biggest moment of revelation, the moment I knew he was "serious" about me, was when he showed up with a gift for my daughter. Other men had shown the typical false affection for her in order to get on my good side, but he was only civil and polite to her, never gushy. One day, however, he showed up with a very nice skateboard for my daughter. . . . The gift marked a turning point in our relationship. I think for him it marked the time that he decided it would be OK to get serious about a woman with a child.[49]

As the example above indicates, the act of giving/receiving a gift can alter the relationship between the giver and the receiver. In addition, items received as gifts often take on meaning associated with the relationship or the giver. For example, a gift may be cherished and protected because it symbolizes an important friendship.[50]

Of course, gift giving is culture specific (see Chapter 2).[51] For example, in characterizing gift giving in Korea (collectivist) compared with the United States (individualistic), one expert summarized:

> Koreans reported more gift-giving occasions, a wider exchange network, more frequent giving of practical gift items, especially cash gifts, strong face-saving and group conformity motivations, more social pressure to reciprocate, higher gift budget, and frequent workplace giving.[52]

Antecedent States

Features of the individual person that are not lasting characteristics, such as momentary moods or conditions, are called **antecedent states.** For example, most people experience states of depression or excitement from time to time that are not normally part of their individual makeup.

Moods   Moods are *transient feeling states that are generally not tied to a specific event or object.*[53] They tend to be less intense than emotions and may operate without the individual's awareness. Although moods may affect all aspects of a person's behavior, they generally do not completely interrupt ongoing behavior as an emotion might. Individuals use such terms as *happy, cheerful, peaceful, sad, blue,* and *depressed* to describe their moods.

Moods both affect and are affected by the consumption process.[54] Moods influence decision processes, the purchase and consumption of various products, and perceptions of service.[55] Positive moods appear to be associated with increased browsing and impulse purchasing. Negative moods also increase impulse and compulsive purchasing in some

Consumers' moods vary over the course of time. This Yoplait ad shows how astute firms develop products and services relevant to the various moods consumers experience or want to experience.

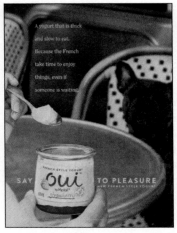

Source: General Mills, Inc.

consumers. One explanation is that some shopping behaviors play both a mood maintenance (positive moods) and mood enhancement (negative moods) role.[56]

Mood also can play an important role in the communications situation. Such effects are often called *program context effects* and relate to the nature of the programming surrounding the focal ad (see Chapter 8). The television, radio, and magazine content viewed just prior to the focal ad can influence consumers' moods and arousal levels, which, in turn, influence their information-processing activities.[57] A basic finding is that ad and brand attitudes often are influenced in a mood-congruent manner. Thus, a TV show that puts a consumer in a positive mood (elicits positive affective reactions) should improve ad and brand attitudes compared with one that puts the consumer in a negative mood. However, in cases where so-called negative programming also is liked by the viewer (a sad movie that a viewer loves), then program liking still can provide a positive boost in ad and brand attitudes.[58] Given such complexities, marketers must pretest their ads in contexts as close to their expected programming environment as possible.

Consumers actively manage their mood states (see the Yoplait ad in Illustration 13-5).[59] That is, consumers often seek situations, activities, or objects that will alleviate negative moods or enhance positive ones. Products and services are one means consumers use to manage their mood states. Thus, a person feeling bored, sad, or down might view a situation comedy on television, go to a cheerful movie, visit a fun store, eat at an upbeat restaurant, or purchase a new Blu-ray disc, shirt, or other fun product.[60] Consumers may engage in such mood-regulating behavior both at a nonconscious level and also at a deliberate, conscious level:

> [T]here are certain products that I purchase specifically to make me feel better. For instance, occasionally, I enjoy smoking a cigar. Certainly the cigar serves no other purpose than to make me feel good.
>
> While other cosmetics, perfumes and nice clothes can make me feel good, they seldom have the same power to transform my temperament like a manicure and pedicure can.[61]

Marketers attempt to influence moods and to time marketing activities with positive mood-inducing events.[62] Many companies prefer to advertise during light television programs because viewers tend to be in a good mood while watching these shows. Restaurants, bars, shopping malls, and many other retail outlets are designed to induce positive moods in patrons. As discussed earlier, music often is played for this reason. Finally, marketers can position their products and services in terms of mood enhancement.

Momentary Conditions   Whereas moods reflect states of mind, *momentary conditions reflect temporary states of being,* such as being tired, being ill, having extra money, being broke, and so forth. However, for conditions, as for moods, to fit under the definition of antecedent states, they must be momentary and not constantly with the individual. Hence, an individual who is short of cash only momentarily will act differently from someone who is always short of cash.[63]

As with moods, individuals attempt to manage their momentary conditions, often through the purchase or consumption of products and services. For example, individuals feeling tired or sleepy during the day may drink a cup of coffee or a soft drink or eat a candy bar. Massages are consumed to relieve sore muscles. A variety of medications are sold to relieve

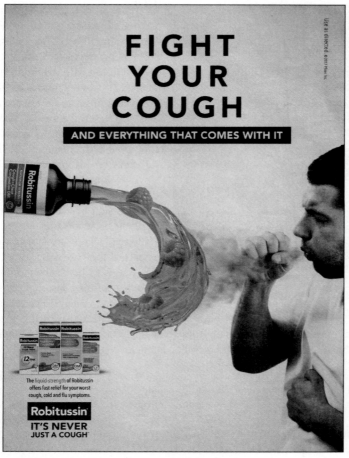

Source: Pfizer Inc.

physical discomfort associated with overexertion, colds, allergies, and so forth. Pawnshops provide cash for individuals temporarily needing funds, as do banks and other financial institutions. Thus, a great deal of marketing activity is directed toward momentary conditions. Illustration 13–6 shows an ad for Robitussin designed to relieve a momentary condition.

RITUAL SITUATIONS

Rituals are receiving increasing attention by marketing scholars and practitioners. A **ritual situation** can be described as *a socially defined occasion that triggers a set of interrelated behaviors that occur in a structured format and that have symbolic meaning.*[64] Ritual situations can range from completely private to completely public. A completely private ritual situation would be an individual's decision to drink a private toast or say a private prayer on the anniversary of an event with special meaning to the individual. A couple who celebrate their first date by returning to the same restaurant every year are involved in a more public ritual. Weddings and proms (as described in the chapter opener) tend to be even more public. Finally, national and global holidays present very public ritual situations.

Ritual situations are of major importance to marketers because they often involve prescribed consumption behaviors. Every major American holiday (ritual situation) has consumption rituals associated with it. For example, more than 60 percent of the toy industry's sales occur at Christmas.

ILLUSTRATION 13-7

Ritual situations generally have consumption patterns associated with them. This Smithfield ad is tapping into ritual situations.

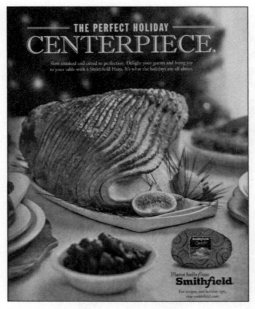

Source: Smithfield Foods, Inc

While there is significant variation across individuals and households, there is enough shared behavior that marketers can develop products and promotions around the common ritual situations that arise each year. For example, candy marketers produce and promote a wide array of candies for Valentine's Day and Halloween. Illustration 13–7 shows how Smithfield is capitalizing on consumption rituals.

Marketers also attempt to change or create consumption patterns associated with ritual situations.[65] Mother's Day is a $10 billion occasion in which card giving is largely a ritual behavior created by marketers.[66] Halloween cards are now being promoted as part of the Halloween ritual.[67] And many firms seek to make their products and services part of the consumption pattern associated with "coming of age." These occasions often are marked with religious ceremonies and after-ceremony parties. Traditionally, these events have tended to focus on religious aspects and responsibility to family and community. For example:

In Latin America, the quinceañera, a celebration dating back to the Aztecs that commemorates the spiritual and physical coming of age of a 15-year-old girl, is typically observed with a ceremony in the Catholic church and a backyard party for family members.[68]

The "after-ceremony" celebrations range from simple and inexpensive to elaborate and costly. However, the trend is definitely toward more elaborate and costly parties with modern themes, expensive catering and entertainment, and interactive activities to entertain hundreds of guests. For example:

One Hispanic family spent $30,000 to celebrate their daughter's quinceañera with "a horse drawn, pumpkin-shaped crystal carriage with liveried servants in powdered wigs, a silver tulle gown and a gala at which 260 guests danced until dawn in the shadow of Sleeping Beauty's castle at Disneyland."[69]

Ritual situations also can result in injurious consumption. Binge or excessive drinking is a serious health and social problem on many college campuses, though its incidence appears to be on the decline. Recent research suggests that this can be understood as a ritual behavior in that it is triggered by social occasions (e.g., birthdays), involves a set of interrelated behaviors and routines (e.g., start drinking on game days at a specific time), and results in special meaning and rewards for participants (e.g., fun, acceptance by group). When approached from this perspective, more effective strategies for minimizing such behaviors may result.

SITUATIONAL INFLUENCES AND MARKETING STRATEGY

LO5

In the previous sections, we described a variety of marketing strategies based on situational influences. Here we will focus more specifically on the process by which such strategies can be developed.

It is important to note that individuals do not encounter situations randomly. Instead, most people "create" many of the situations they face. Thus, individuals who choose to engage in physically demanding sports such as jogging, tennis, or racquetball are indirectly choosing to expose themselves to the situation of "being tired" or "being thirsty." This allows marketers to develop products, advertising, and segmentation strategies based on the situations that individuals selecting various lifestyles are likely to encounter.

After identifying the different situations that might involve the consumption of a product, marketers must determine which products or brands are most likely to be purchased or consumed across those situations. One method of approaching this is to jointly scale situations and products. An example is shown in Figure 13–3. Here, *use situations* that ranged from "private consumption at home" to "consumption away from home where there is a concern for other people's reaction to you" were scaled in terms of their similarity and relationship to products appropriate for that situation.

For use situation I, "to clean my mouth upon rising in the morning," toothpaste and mouthwash are viewed as most appropriate (see Figure 13–3). However, use situation II, "before an important business meeting late in the afternoon," involves both consumption away from home and a concern for the response from others. As a result, mint-flavored gums or candies are preferred. *Where do you think a product like Listerine Oral Care Strips would be located on this map?*

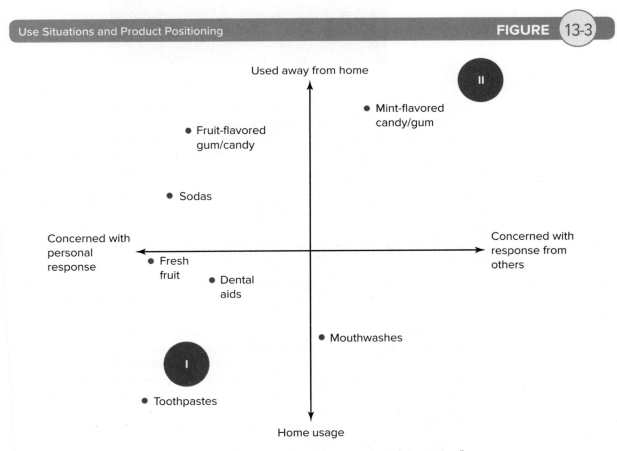

Use Situations and Product Positioning   **FIGURE 13-3**

I = Use situation: "To clean my mouth upon rising in the morning."
II = Use situation: "Before an important business meeting late in the afternoon."

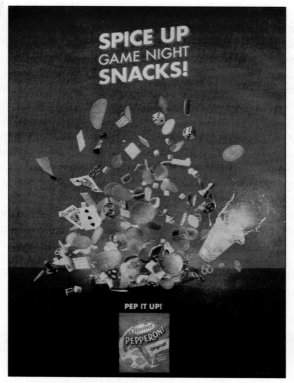

Source: Hormel Foods Corporation

Determining how products are *currently used* across situations can help the marketer develop appropriate advertising and positioning strategies. In our example, Wrigley's might advertise its Spearmint Gum as having breath-freshening capabilities that make it appropriate for use in social situations away from home. Or a marketer may try to change the situations for which a product is used. In Figure 13-3, mouthwash is not seen as appropriate for consumption away from home. What if a version of Scope was developed that one swallowed after use? Could it successfully be promoted for use away from home? Would it be able to compete against breath strips? Illustration 13-8 promotes a new usage situation for Hormel pepperoni in its "Spice Up Game Night Snacks" campaign.

Another approach for developing situation-based marketing strategies is to follow these five steps:[70]

1. Use observational studies, focus group discussions, depth interviews, and secondary data to discover the various usage situations that influence the consumption of the product.
2. Survey a larger sample of consumers to better understand and quantify how the product is used and the benefits sought in the usage situation by the market segment.
3. Construct a person–situation segmentation matrix. The rows are the major usage situations and the columns are groups of users with unique needs or desires. Each cell contains the key benefits sought. (Table 13-2 illustrates such a matrix for suntan lotion, including sunscreen.) Then:
4. Evaluate each cell in terms of potential (sales volume, price level, cost to serve, competitor strength, and so forth).
5. Develop and implement a marketing strategy for those cells that offer sufficient profit potential given your capabilities.

Person–Situation Segments for Suntan Lotions   TABLE 13-2

Suntan Lotion Use Situation	Potential Users of Suntan Lotion				
	Young Children	Teenagers	Adult Women	Adult Men	General Situation Benefits
Beach/boat activities	Prevent sunburn/skin damage	Prevent sunburn while tanning	Prevent sunburn/ skin change/ dry skin	Prevent sunburn	Container floats
Home/pools sunbathing	Prevent sunburn/skin damage	Tanning without sunburn	Tanning without skin damage or dry skin	Tanning without sunburn/skin damage	Lotion won't stain clothes or furniture
Tanning booth		Tanning	Tanning with moisturizer	Tanning	Designed for sunlamps
Snow skiing		Prevent sunburn	Prevent sunburn/ skin damage/ dry skin	Prevent sunburn	Antifreeze formula
Person benefits	Protection	Tanning	Protection and tanning with soft skin	Protection and tanning	

Source: Adapted from P. Dickson, "Person–Situation: Segmentation's Missing Link," *Journal of Marketing Research,* Fall 1982, pp. 56–64. Reprinted with permission from *Journal of Marketing Research,* published by the American Marketing Association.

SUMMARY

SMARTBOOK™

LO1: Define *situational influence.*

Situational influence is all those factors particular to a time and place that do not follow from a knowledge of the stable attributes of the consumer and the stimulus and that have an effect on current behavior.

LO2: Explain the four types of situations and their relevance to marketing strategy.

Four categories of situations are communications, purchase, usage, and disposition situations. The situation in which consumers receive information is the communications situation. The situation in which a purchase is made is the purchase situation. The situation in which the product or service is used is the usage situation. The situation in which a product or product package is disposed of either after or before product use is the disposition situation. Each type of situation has marketing implications such as within what programming to advertise (communications situation), the effect of other people on an individual's shopping behavior in-store (buying situation),

the ability to expand beyond traditional uses for a given product (usage situation), and the factors contributing to recycling behavior (disposition situation).

LO3: Summarize the five characteristics of situations and their influence on consumption.

Five characteristics of situations have been identified. *Physical surroundings* include geographical and institutional location, decor, sound, aromas, lighting, weather, and displays of merchandise or other material surrounding the product. Retailers are particularly concerned with the effects of physical surroundings. The sum of all the physical features of a retail environment is referred to as the *store atmosphere* or environment. *Atmospherics* is the process managers use to manipulate the physical retail environment to create specific mood responses in shoppers. Atmosphere is referred to as *servicescape* when describing a service business such as a hospital, bank, or restaurant.

Social surroundings deal with other persons present who could have an impact on the individual consumer's behavior. The characteristics of the other persons present, their roles, and their interpersonal interactions are potentially important social situational influences.

Temporal perspectives relate to the effect of time on consumer behavior, such as effects of time of day, time since last purchase, time since or until meals or payday, and time constraints imposed by commitments. Convenience stores have evolved and been successful by taking advantage of the temporal perspective factor.

Task definition reflects the purpose or reason for engaging in the consumption behavior. The task may reflect different buyer and user roles anticipated by the individual. For example, a person shopping for dishes to be given as a wedding present is in a different situation from a person buying dishes for personal use.

Antecedent states are features of the individual person that are not lasting or relatively enduring characteristics. *Moods* are temporary states of depression or high excitement, and so on, which all people experience. *Momentary conditions* are such things as being tired, being ill, having a great deal of money (or none at all), and so forth.

LO4: Discuss ritual situations and their importance to consumers and marketers.

A *ritual situation* can be described as a set of interrelated behaviors that occur in a structured format, that have symbolic meaning to consumers, and that occur in response to socially defined occasions. Ritual situations can range from completely private to completely public. They are of major importance to marketers because they often involve prescribed consumption behaviors.

LO5: Describe the use of situational influence in developing marketing strategy.

Situational influences may have direct influences, but they also interact with product and individual characteristics to influence behavior. In some cases, the situation will have no influence whatsoever because the individual's characteristics or choices are so intense that they override everything else. But the situation is always potentially important and therefore of concern to marketing managers.

KEY TERMS

Antecedent states 499
Atmospherics 493
Communications situation 488
Disposition situation 491
Embarrassment 496
Moods 499

Physical surroundings 491
Purchase situations 490
Ritual situation 501
Servicescape 493
Situational influence 488
Social surroundings 496

Store atmosphere 493
Task definition 498
Temporal perspectives 498
Usage situations 490

REVIEW QUESTIONS

1. What is meant by the term *situation?* Why is it important for a marketing manager to understand situational influences on purchasing behavior?

2. What are *physical surroundings* (as a situational variable)? Give an example of how they can influence the consumption process.

3. How does crowding affect shopping behavior?

4. What is *store atmosphere?*

5. What is *atmospherics?*

6. What is a *servicescape?*

7. What are *social surroundings* (as a situational variable)? Give an example of how they can influence the consumption process.

8. What is *temporal perspective* (as a situational variable)? Give an example of how it can influence the consumption process.

9. What is *task definition* (as a situational variable)? Give an example of how it can influence the consumption process.

10. Why do people give gifts?

11. How might the receipt of a gift affect the relationship between the giver and the receiver?

12. What are *antecedent conditions* (as a situational variable)? Give an example of how they can influence the consumption process.

13. What is a *mood?* How does it differ from an *emotion?* How do moods influence consumption behavior?

14. How do people manage their moods?

15. How do moods differ from *momentary conditions?*

16. What is meant by the statement, "Situational variables may interact with product or personal characteristics"?

17. Are individuals randomly exposed to situational influences? Why or why not?

18. What are *ritual situations?* Why are they important?

19. Describe a process for developing a situation-based marketing strategy.

DISCUSSION QUESTIONS

20. Discuss the potential importance of each type of situational influence in developing a marketing strategy to promote the purchase of (gifts to/shopping at):
    a. National Audubon Society
    b. Subway
    c. iPhone
    d. Coca-Cola Zero
    e. 7-Eleven
    f. Ray-Ban eyewear

21. What product categories seem most susceptible to situational influences? Why?

22. Flowers are appropriate gifts for women for many situations but seem to be appropriate for men only when they are ill. Why is this so? How might 1-800-FLOWERS change this?

23. How could the store atmosphere at the following be improved?
    a. The main library on campus
    b. The bank lobby near campus
    c. A diner near campus
    d. A convenience store near campus
    e. The student career services office

24. Speculate on what a matrix like the one shown in Table 13–2 would look like for the following:
    a. Tablet computer
    b. Eyewear

    c. Ice cream
    d. Shoes
    e. Motor scooter
    f. Coffee

25. Does Table 13–1 have implications for outlets other than restaurants? If yes, which ones and why?

26. Do your shopping behavior and purchase criteria differ between purchases made for yourself and purchases made as gifts? How?

27. Describe a situation in which a mood (good or bad) caused you to make an unusual purchase.

28. Describe a relatively private ritual that you or someone you know has. What, if any, consumption pattern is associated with it?

29. Describe the consumption rituals your family has associated with the following ritual situations:
    a. Family birthdays
    b. Summer vacations
    c. Thanksgiving
    d. Halloween
    e. Mother's Day
    f. Father's Day
    g. New Year's Eve

30. Respond to the questions in Consumer Insight 13–1.

APPLICATION ACTIVITIES

31. Interview five people who have recently purchased the following. Determine the role, if any, played by situational factors.
    a. Cell phone
    b. Jewelry
    c. Motorcycle
    d. A fast-food restaurant meal
    e. A cup of coffee
    f. Health insurance

32. Interview a salesperson for the following. Determine the role, if any, this individual feels situational variables play in his or her sales.
    a. Renter's insurance
    b. BMX bikes
    c. Fine chocolates
    d. Flowers

33. Conduct a study using a small (five or so) sample of your friends in which you attempt to isolate the situational factors that influence the type, brand, or amount of the following purchased or used.
    a. Health club
    b. Clothing
    c. Movie attendance
    d. Volunteer work
    e. TV dinners
    f. Car tires

34. Create a list of 10 to 20 use situations relevant to campus area restaurants. Then interview 10 students and have them indicate which of these situations they have encountered, and ask them to rank these situations in terms of how likely they are to occur. Discuss how a restaurant could use this information in trying to appeal to the student market.

35. Visit three stores selling the same product line. Describe how the atmosphere differs across the stores. Why do you think these differences exist?

36. Visit three local coffee shops. Describe how the servicescapes differ across the shops. Why do you think these differences exist?

37. What kind of online atmosphere does each of the following have? How would you improve it?
    a. Toyota.com
    b. Harley-Davidson.com
    c. Nike.com
    d. Charities.org
    e. Cabelas.com
    f. Cheerios.com

38. Copy or describe an advertisement that is clearly based on a situational appeal. Indicate
    a. Which situational variable is involved.
    b. Why the company would use this variable.
    c. Your evaluation of the effectiveness of this approach.

39. Create graduation gift, anniversary gift, and self-use ads for the following. Explain the differences across the ads:
    a. Trip abroad
    b. Gourmet coffee maker
    c. Magazine subscription
    d. Set of dishes
    e. Blender
    f. Watch

40. Interview five students and determine instances where their mood affected their purchases. What do you conclude?

41. Interview five students and determine the consumption rituals they have with respect to the following. What do you conclude?
    a. New Year's Day
    b. Spring break
    c. Memorial Day
    d. Valentine's Day
    e. Mother's Day
    f. Father's Day

REFERENCES

1. This opener is based on *Week* Staff, "The $4 Billion Prom Industry: By the Numbers," *Week,* May 26, 2011; L. Grisham, "KFC Sells Chicken Corsage Just in Time for Prom," *USA Today,* April 14, 2014, www.usatoday.com; Visa Inc., "Cost of High School 'Promposals' Hits $324," *Visa,* March 31, 2015, www.visa.com, accessed June 19, 2018; R. Schatz, "Crazy Prom Spending: Why the Bubble May Be Ready to Burst," *Fortune,* May 15, 2015, www.fortune.com, accessed June 19, 2018; J. Chang, M. McAfee, and L. Effron, "Teens Stage Elaborate 'Promposals' to Score Dates, Social Media 'Likes,'" *ABC News,* May 3, 2016, www.abcnews.com, accessed June 19, 2018; J. McGinty, "The Prom Is Becoming a Cheap(er) Date," *Wall Street Journal,* April 20, 2018,

www.wsj.com, accessed June 19, 2018; J. Glum, "Teens Are Spending Way More on Prom Than Their Parents Did. Here's Where the Money Goes," *Time,* May 2, 2018, www.time.com, accessed June 19, 2018.

2. See K. S. Lim and M. A. Razzaque, "Brand Loyalty and Situational Effects," *Journal of International Consumer Marketing* 4 (1997), pp. 95–115.

3. R. W. Belk, "Situational Variables and Consumer Behavior," *Journal of Consumer Research,* December 1975, p. 158.

4. See K. R. Lord, R. E. Burnkrant, and H. R. Unnava, "The Effects of Program-Induced Mood States on Memory for Commercial Information," *Journal of Current Issues and Research in Advertising,* Spring 2001, pp. 1–14; S. Shapiro, D. J. MacInnis, and C. W. Park, "Understanding Program-Induced Mood Effects," *Journal of Advertising,* Winter 2002, pp. 15–26; P. De Pelsmacker, M. Geuens, and P. Anckaert, "Media Context and Advertising Effectiveness," *Journal of Advertising,* Summer 2002, pp. 49–61; S. Jun et al., "The Influence of Editorial Context on Consumer Response to Advertisements in a Specialty Magazine," *Journal of Current Issues and Research in Advertising,* Fall 2003, pp. 1–11; C. Yoon, M. P. Lee, and S. Danziger, "The Effects of Optimal Time of Day on Persuasion Processes in Older Adults," *Psychology and Marketing,* May 2007, pp. 475–95.

5. L. Sanders and J. Halliday, "BP Institutes 'Ad-Pull' Policy for Print Publications," *Advertising Age,* May 24, 2005, www.adage.com.

6. B. Wansink, "Making Old Brands New," *American Demographics,* December 1997, pp. 53–58.

7. E. Byron, "Case by Case," *Wall Street Journal,* November 17, 2004, p. A1.

8. "Glazed Still Tops among Donuts," *Baking Management,* May 23, 2011.

9. I. Sinha, "A Conceptual Model of Situation Type on Consumer Choice Behavior and Consideration Sets," in *Advances in Consumer Research,* vol. 21, ed. C. T. Allen and D. R. John (Provo, UT: Association for Consumer Research, 1994), pp. 477–82. See also Byron, "Case by Case."

10. See J. A. F. Nicholls et al., "Situational Influences on Shoppers," *Journal of International Consumer Marketing* 9, no. 2 (1996), pp. 21–39; J. A. F. Nicholls, T. Li, and S. Roslow, "Oceans Apart," *Journal of International Consumer Marketing* 12, no. 1 (1999), pp. 57–72.

11. Insight based on Mark Twain quote from Brainy Quotes, www.brainyquote.com/quotes/quotes/m/marktwain104599.html, accessed August 28, 2014; A. D'Innocenzio, "Mannequin Makeovers Include Back Fat, Tattoos, Pubic Hair and Bigger Waists," *National Post,* January 28, 2014, http://life.nationalpost.com/2014/01/28/mannequin-makeovers-include-back-fat-tattoos-pubic-hair-and-bigger-waists/, accessed August 28, 2014; R. Walker, "Museum Quality," *New York Times Magazine,* January 9, 2005, www.nytimes.com/2005/01/09/magazine/09CONSUMED.html, accessed August 28, 2014; S. Clifford, "Stores Demand Mannequins with Personality (Heads Optional)," *New York Times,* June 15, 2011, www.nytimes.com/2011/06/16/business/16mannequin.html, accessed August 28, 2014; K. Bishop, "Store Uses Plus-Size Mannequins to Reflect True Shape of Shoppers," *NBC News,* November 6, 2013, www.nbcnews.com/business/consumer/store-uses-plus-size-mannequins-reflect-true-shape-shoppers-f8C11542388, accessed August 28, 2014; J.

Stern, "Department Store Mannequins Are Watching You. No, Really," *ABC News,* November 26, 2012, http://abcnews.go.com/Technology/department-store-mannequins-watch-eyesee-analyzes-shoppers-webcams/story?id=17813441, accessed August 28, 2014; N. Anitha and C. Selvaraj, "The Effects of Mannequins on Consumers' Perception and Shopping Attitude," in *Information Processing and Management, BAIP 2010,* pp. 641–47.

12. See E. Sherman, A. Mathur, and R. B. Smith, "Store Environment and Consumer Purchase Behavior," *Psychology & Marketing,* July 1997, pp. 361–78; J. Baker et al., "The Influence of Multiple Design Cues on Perceived Merchandise Value and Patronage Intentions," *Journal of Marketing,* April 2002, pp. 120–41; R. Reynolds-McIlnay, M. Morrin, and J. Nordfalt, "How Product-Environment Brightness Contrast and Product Disarray Impact Consumer Choice in Retail Environments," *Journal of Retailing* 93, no. 3 (2017), pp. 266–82.

13. For an extensive review, see L. W. Turley and R. E. Milliman, "Atmospheric Effects on Shopping Behavior," *Journal of Business Research* 49 (2000), pp. 193–211. See also A. d'Astous, "Irritating Aspects of the Shopping Environment," *Journal of Business Research* 49 (2000), pp. 149–56; A. Sharma and T. F. Stafford, "The Effect of Retail Atmospherics on Customers' Perceptions of Salespeople and Customer Persuasion," *Journal of Business Research* 49 (2000), pp. 183–91.

14. P. Sautter, M. R. Hyman, and V. Lukosius, "E-Tail Atmospherics," *Journal of Electronic Commerce Research* 5, no. 1 (2004), pp. 14–24; E. E. Manganari, G. J. Siomkos, and A. P. Vrechopoulos, "Store Atmosphere in Web Retailing," *European Journal of Marketing* 43, no. 9/10 (2009), pp. 1140–53.

15. M. J. Bitner, "Servicescapes," *Journal of Marketing,* April 1992, pp. 57–71. See also K. D. Hoffman, S. W. Kelley, and B. C. Chung, "A CIT Investigation of Servicescape Failures and Associated Recovery Strategies," *Journal of Services Marketing* 17, no. 4/5 (2003), pp. 322–40.

16. G. J. Gorn, A. Chattopadhyay, T. Yi, and D. W. Dahl, "Effects of Color as an Executional Cue in Advertising," *Management Science,* October 1997, pp. 1387–99.

17. See J. A. Bellizzi and R. E. Hite, "Environmental Color, Consumer Feelings, and Purchase Likelihood," *Psychology & Marketing,* September 1992, pp. 347–63.

18. B. E. Kahn and L. McAlister, *Grocery Revolution* (Reading, MA: Addison-Wesley, 1997).

19. G. J. Gorn, A. Chattopadhyay, J. Sengupta, and S. Tripathi, "Waiting for the Web," *Journal of Marketing Research,* May 2004, pp. 215–25.

20. D. J. Mitchell, B. E. Kahn, and S. C. Knasko, "There's Something in the Air," *Journal of Consumer Research,* September 1995, pp. 229–38; A. Madzharov, L. Block, and M. Morrin, "The Cool Scent of Power: Effects of Ambient Scent on Consumer Preferences and Choice Behavior," *Journal of Marketing,* January 2015, pp. 83–96.

21. E. R. Spangenberg, A. E. Crowley, and P. W. Henderson, "Improving the Store Environment," *Journal of Marketing,* April 1996, pp. 67–80.

22. A. R. Hirsch, "Effects of Ambient Odors on Slot-Machine Usage in a Las Vegas Casino," *Psychology & Marketing,* October 1995, pp. 585–94.

23. M. Morrison et al., "In-Store Music and Aroma Influences on Shopper Behavior and Satisfaction," *Journal of Business Research* 64 (2011), pp. 558-64.

24. M. Morrin and S. Ratneshwar, "The Impact of Ambient Scent on Evaluation, Attention, and Memory for Familiar and Unfamiliar Brands," *Journal of Business Research* 49 (2000), pp. 157-65.

25. See, e.g., "Environmental Fragrancing,"*Laboratory News,* May 26, 2011, www.labnews.co.uk, accessed June 15, 2011.

26. P. F. Bone and P. S. Ellen, "Scents in the Marketplace," *Journal of Retailing* 75, no. 2 (1999), pp. 243-62.

27. P. Sloan, "Smelling Trouble," *Advertising Age,* September 11, 1995, p. 1.

28. See S. Oakes, "The Influence of the Musicscape within Service Environments," *Journal of Services Marketing* 4, no. 7 (2000), pp. 539-56; Morrison et al., "In-Store Music and Aroma Influences on Shopper Behavior and Satisfaction"; S. Morin, L. Dube, and J. C. Chebat, "The Role of Pleasant Music in Servicescapes," *Journal of Business Research* 83, no. 1 (2007), pp. 115-30.

29. J. C. Sweeney and F. Wyber, "The Role of Cognitions and Emotions in the Music-Approach-Avoidance Behavior Relationship," *Journal of Services Marketing* 16, no. 1 (2002), pp. 51-69; C. Caldwell and S. A. Hibbert, "The Influence of Music Tempo and Musical Preference on Restaurant Patrons' Behavior," *Psychology & Marketing,* November 2002, pp. 895-917.

30. B. Zimmers, "Business Deals Put AEI Music CEO in Good Mood," *Puget Sound Business Journal,* June 23, 2000, p. 44; see also C. A. Olson, "Shopping to the Music Made Easy," *Billboard,* July 31, 1999, pp. 73-74.

31. See K. A. Machleit, S. A. Eroglu, and S. P. Mantel, "Perceived Retail Crowding and Shopping Satisfaction," *Journal of Consumer Psychology* 9, no. 1 (2000), pp. 29-42. For an exception, see F. Pons, M. Laroche, and M. Mourali, "Consumer Reactions to Crowded Retail Settings," *Psychology & Marketing,* July 2006, pp. 555-72.

32. S. A. Eroglu, K. A. Machleit, and J. C. Chebat, "The Interaction of Retail Density and Music Tempo," *Psychology & Marketing,* July 2005, pp. 577-89.

33. Pons, Laroche, and Mourali, "Consumer Reactions to Crowded Retail Settings."

34. T. R. Graeth, "Consumption Situations and the Effects of Brand Image on Consumers' Brand Evaluations," *Psychology & Marketing,* January 1997, pp. 49-70. See also S. Ramanathan and A. L. McGill, "Consuming with Others," *Journal of Consumer Research,* December 2007, pp. 506-24; Y. Huh, J. Vosgerau and C. Morewedge, "Social Defaults: Observed Choices Become Choice Defaults," *Journal of Consumer Research* 41, no. 3 (2014), pp. 746-60.

35. R. K. Ratner and B. E. Kahn, "The Impact of Private versus Public Consumption on Variety-Seeking Behavior," *Journal of Consumer Research,* September 2002, pp. 246-57.

36. See, e.g., D. W. Dahl, R. V. Manchanda, and J. J. Argo, "Embarrassment in Consumer Purchase," *Journal of Consumer Research,* December 2001, pp. 473-81. See also D. Grace, "How Embarrassing!," *Journal of Service Research,* February 2007, pp. 271-84.

37. X. Luo, "How Does Shopping with Others Influence Impulsive Purchasing?," *Journal of Consumer Psychology* 15, no. 4 (2005), pp. 288-94.

38. R. Batra and P. M. Homer, "The Situational Impact of Brand Image Beliefs," *Journal of Consumer Psychology* 14, no. 3 (2004), pp. 318-30.

39. L. A. Brannon and T. C. Brock, "Limiting Time for Responding Enhances Behavior Corresponding to the Merits of Compliance Appeals," *Journal of Consumer Psychology* 10, no. 3 (2001), pp. 135-46; R. Suri and K. B. Monroe, "The Effects of Time Constraints on Consumers' Judgments of Prices and Products," *Journal of Consumer Research,* June 2003, pp. 92-104.

40. S. M. Nowlis, "The Effect of Time Pressure on the Choice of Brands That Differ in Quality, Price, and Product Features," *Marketing Letters,* October 1995, pp. 287-96; R. Dhar and S. M. Nowlis, "The Effect of Time Pressure on Consumer Choice Deferral," *Journal of Consumer Research,* March 1999, pp. 369-84; R. Pieters and L. Warlop, "Visual Attention during Brand Choice," *International Journal of Research in Marketing,* February 1999, pp. 1-16.

41. S. D. Strombeck and K. L. Wakefield, "Situational Influences on Service Quality Evaluations," *Journal of Services Marketing* 22, no. 5 (2008), pp. 409-19.

42. P. Van Kenhove, K. De Wulf, and W. Van Waterschoot, "The Impact of Task Definition on Store-Attribute Saliences and Store Choice," *Journal of Retailing* 75, no. 1 (1999), pp. 125-37; P. Van Kenhove and K. De Wulf, "Income and Time Pressure," *International Review of Retail, Distribution and Consumer Research,* April 2000, pp. 149-66.

43. See B. H. Schmitt and C. J. Shultz II, "Situational Effects on Brand Preferences for Image Products," *Psychology & Marketing,* August 1995, pp. 433-46.

44. T. M. Lowrey, C. C. Otnes, and J. A. Ruth, "Social Influences on Dyadic Giving over Time," *Journal of Consumer Research,* March 2004, pp. 547-58.

45. For a review and framework, see D. Larsen and J. J. Watson, "A Guide Map to the Terrain of Gift Value," *Psychology & Marketing,* August 2001, pp. 889-906; see also G. Saad and T. Gill, "An Evolutionary Psychology Perspective on Gift Giving among Young Adults," *Psychology & Marketing,* September 2003, pp. 765-84.

46. M. A. McGrath, "Gender Differences in Gift Exchanges," *Psychology & Marketing,* August 1995, pp. 371-93; K. M. Palan, C. S. Areni, and P. Kiecker, "Gender Role Incongruency and Memorable Gift Exchange Experiences," and J. F. Durgee and T. Sego, "Gift-Giving as a Metaphor for Understanding New Products That Delight," both in *Advances in Consumer Research,* vol. 28, ed. M. C. Gilly and J. Meyers-Levy (Provo, UT: Association for Consumer Research, 2001), pp. 51-57 and 64-69, respectively.

47. D. B. Wooten, "Qualitative Steps toward an Expanded Model of Anxiety in Gift-Giving," *Journal of Consumer Research,* June 2000, pp. 84-95.

48. See, e.g., J. A. Ruth, C. C. Otnes, and F. F. Brunel, "Gift Receipt and the Reformulation of Interpersonal Relationships," *Journal of Consumer Research,* March 1999, pp. 385-402.

49. R. W. Belk and G. S. Coon, "Gift Giving as Agapic Love," *Journal of Consumer Research,* December 1993, pp. 404–405. See also J. A. Ruth, F. F. Brunel, and C. C. Otnes, "An Investigation of the Power of Emotions in Relationship Realignment," *Psychology & Marketing,* January 2004, pp. 29–52.

50. C. S. Areni, P. Kiecker, and K. M. Palan, "Is It Better to Give Than to Receive?," *Psychology & Marketing,* January 1998, pp. 81–109.

51. A. Joy, "Gift Giving in Hong Kong and the Continuum of Social Ties," *Journal of Consumer Research,* September 2001, pp. 239–55; S. L. Lotz, S. Shim, and K. C. Gehrt, "A Study of Japanese Consumers' Cognitive Hierarchies in Formal and Informal Gift-Giving Situations," *Psychology & Marketing,* January 2003, pp. 59–85.

52. S.-Y. Park, "A Comparison of Korean and American Gift-Giving Behaviors," *Psychology & Marketing,* September 1998, pp. 577–93.

53. See R. P. Bagozzi, M. Gopinath, and P. U. Nyer, "The Role of Emotion in Marketing," *Journal of the Academy of Marketing Science,* Spring 1999, pp. 184–206; H. T. Luomala and M. Laaksonen, "Contributions from Mood Research," *Psychology & Marketing,* March 2000, pp. 195–233.

54. M. B. Holbrook and M. P. Gardner, "Illustrating a Dynamic Model of the Mood-Updating Process in Consumer Behavior," *Psychology & Marketing,* March 2000, pp. 165–94.

55. J. P. Forgas and J. Ciarrochi, "On Being Happy and Possessive," *Psychology & Marketing,* March 2001, pp. 239–60; R. Adaval, "Sometimes It Just Feels Right," *Journal of Consumer Research,* June 2001, pp. 1–17.

56. D. W. Rook and M. P. Gardner, "In the Mood," *Research in Consumer Behavior* 6 (1993), pp. 1–28; W. R. Swinyard, "The Effects of Mood, Involvement, and Quality of Store Experience on Shopping Intentions," *Journal of Consumer Research,* September 1993, pp. 271–80; R. J. Faber and G. A. Christenson, "In the Mood to Buy," *Psychology & Marketing,* December 1996, pp. 803–19. See also N. Garg, B. Wansink, and J. J. Inman, "The Influence of Incidental Affect on Consumers' Food Intake," *Journal of Marketing,* January 2007, pp. 194–206, for an application of mood to food choice.

57. See Reference 4.

58. See, e.g., K. S. Coulter, "The Effects of Affective Responses to Media Context on Advertising Evaluations," *Journal of Advertising,* Winter 1998, pp. 41–51.

59. H. T. Luomala and M. Laaksonen, "A Qualitative Exploration of Mood-Regulatory Self-Gift Behaviors," *Journal of Economic Psychology* 20 (1999), pp. 147–82.

60. H. Mano, "The Influence of Pre-Existing Negative Affect on Store Purchase Intentions," *Journal of Retailing* 75, no. 2 (1999), pp. 149–73.

61. S. J. Gould, "An Interpretive Study of Purposeful, Mood Self-Regulating Consumption," *Psychology & Marketing,* July 1997, pp. 395–426.

62. See M. G. Meloy, "Mood-Driven Distortion of Product Information," *Journal of Consumer Research,* December 2000, pp. 345–58.

63. See P. A. Walsh and S. Spiggle, "Consumer Spending Patterns," in *Advances in Consumer Research,* vol. 21, ed. Allen and John, pp. 35–40; N. Karlsson, T. Garling, and M. Selart, "Explanations of Prior Income Changes on Buying Decisions," *Journal of Economic Psychology* 20 (1999), pp. 449–63.

64. See B. Gainer, "Ritual and Relationships," *Journal of Business Research,* March 1995, pp. 253–60.

65. See C. C. Otnes and L. M. Scott, "Something Old, Something New," *Journal of Advertising,* Spring 1996, pp. 33–50.

66. "$10 Billion for Mom," *CNN Money,* April 21, 2004, http://money.cnn.com/.

67. A. Z. Cuneo, "Using Halloween to Scare Up Sales," *Advertising Age,* October 8, 2001, p. 4.

68. A. Chozick, "Fairy-Tale Fifteenths," *Wall Street Journal,* October 15, 2004, p. B1.

69. Ibid.

70. For a similar approach, see R. Brodie, "Segmentation and Market Structure When Both Consumer and Situational Characteristics Are Explanatory," *Psychology & Marketing,* September 1992, pp. 395–408.

14

Consumer Decision Process and Problem Recognition

Source: The Procter & Gamble Company

LEARNING OBJECTIVES

LO1 Describe the impact of purchase involvement on the decision process.

LO2 Explain problem recognition and how it fits into the consumer decision process.

LO3 Summarize the uncontrollable determinants of problem recognition.

LO4 Discuss the role of consumer problems and problem recognition in marketing strategy.

The plug to the lamp is one of the eight cords in the power strip, but which one? You are going to have to trace the cord from the lamp to the power strip, which is underneath the desk. You rummage through your desk drawer looking for a rubber band. You know you have rubber bands somewhere among the scattering of paper clips, pens, ties, and odds and ends. It's a mess. These are a few examples of common problems we all have. They are a bit irritating and annoying, but not really of any great importance and not likely to occur with frequency. So we just work around them. These *work-around problems* fall in the category of "nominal decision making," a type of decision making that in effect involves no decision per se.

Prior to social media, the doyenne of solutions to work-around problems was Heloise, who offered her Helpful Hints.[1] Now with social media as part of our daily lives, and most notably with the popularity of Pinterest, Heloise-like "life hacks" have sprung up, offering help for problems you never knew you had, like using recycled bread tags to label and identify cords in the power strip and using old tins to organize your messy desk drawers. These enthusiastically, freely offered solutions parallel the product strategy to increase sales by suggesting other ways to use the products besides the obvious. For example, Arm & Hammer Baking Soda offers many other versatile uses of its baking soda besides baking—as a deodorizer for rugs and refrigerators and as an ingredient to build a model of an active volcano.

For consumers engaged in nominal decision making, store signage and display may remind them to make purchases that they might otherwise forget. Some stores print coupons of the consumer's previously purchased products on the back of the customer's receipts to serve as reminders.

It's very likely that most households in the United States have cleaning products—detergents, dishwashing liquids, cleanser, bleach—that clean "well enough." Consumers are likely not actively involved in looking for alternatives. However, if you are Procter & Gamble, faced with increasingly shorter product life cycles, you are forced to innovate and continuously improve solutions currently on the market. Enter P&G's Swiffer line of cleaning products that promises to make sweeping, dusting, and vacuuming better and easier. Vacuum cleaners are a common household appliance that perform well enough and are infrequently replaced. Then Dyson introduced improvements—bagless vacuum cleaners with "cyclone" efficiency, wheels that eliminated annoying run-ins with furniture—solving problems that you didn't know you had.

With the rise of crowdsourcing—Quirky, Kickstarter—the ability to develop and market solutions to "problems you didn't know you had" now can extend beyond the Procter & Gambles of the world to individual consumers. Examples include Quirky Bandits, rubber bands with hooks to "keep pens and drawing supplies together, fasten sunglasses to the rearview mirror," and Cordies, to organize cords on desks by "reining in all these loose chords to reduce tangling."

The consumer decision process begins with problem recognition. Nominal problems are those that involve little to no thought. For nominal problems, consumers follow habit and buy the same brand.

They perform the same behavior to *work around* the problem. But solutions offered may be so clever that they knock consumers into awareness of the existence of problems they didn't know they had.

This chapter examines the nature of the consumer decision process and analyzes the first step in that process: problem recognition. Within problem recognition, we focus on (1) the process of problem recognition, (2) the uncontrollable determinants of problem recognition, and (3) marketing strategies based on the problem recognition process.

TYPES OF CONSUMER DECISIONS

LO1

The term *consumer decision* produces an image of an individual carefully evaluating the attributes of a set of products, brands, or services and rationally selecting the one that solves a clearly recognized need for the least cost. It has a rational, functional connotation. Consumers do make many decisions in this manner; however, many other decisions involve little conscious effort. Further, many consumer decisions focus not on brand attributes but rather on the feelings or emotions associated with acquiring or using the brand or with the situation in which the product is purchased or used. Thus, a brand may be selected not because of an attribute (price, style, functional characteristics) but because "it makes me feel good" or "my friends will like it."[2]

Although purchases and related consumption behavior driven by emotional or situational needs have characteristics distinct from the traditional attribute-based model, the decision-process model provides useful insights into all types of consumer purchases. As we describe the process of consumer decision making in this and the next four chapters, we will indicate how it helps us understand emotion-, situation-, and attribute-based decisions.

Consumer decisions are frequently the result of a single problem, for example, running low on gasoline. At other times, they result from the convergence of several problems, such as an aging automobile and a growing feeling of inadequacy or low self-esteem. Furthermore, once the decision process begins, it may evolve and become more complex with multiple goals. A consumer noticing a simple need for gas may want to minimize the price paid, avoid one or more brands because of their environmental record, and decide to find a station with food service attached. This consumer may wind up choosing between a station with a lower price and its own food service or another station with a higher price but with a preferred food outlet such as Taco Bell attached, or perhaps spending the extra time to buy gas at one and food at the other.[3]

As Figure 14–1 indicates, there are various types of consumer decision processes.[4] As the consumer moves from a very low level of involvement *with the purchase* to a high level of involvement, decision making becomes increasingly complex. While purchase involvement is a continuum, it is useful to consider nominal, limited, and extended decision making as general descriptions of the types of processes that occur along various points on the continuum. Keep in mind that the types of decision processes are not distinct but rather blend into each other.

Before describing each type of decision process, we must clarify the concept of purchase involvement. We define **purchase involvement** as *the level of concern for, or interest in,*

FIGURE 14-1

Involvement and Types of Decision Making

Low-involvement purchase → High-involvement purchase

Nominal decision making

Problem recognition
Selective

↓

Information search
Limited internal

↓

Purchase

↓

Postpurchase
No dissonance
Very limited evaluation

Limited decision making

Problem recognition
Generic

↓

Information search
Internal
Limited external

↓

Alternative evaluation
Few attributes
Simple decision rules
Few alternatives

↓

Purchase

↓

Postpurchase
No dissonance
Limited evaluation

Extended decision making

Problem recognition
Generic

↓

Information search
Internal
External

↓

Alternative evaluation
Many attributes
Complex decision rules
Many alternatives

↓

Purchase

↓

Postpurchase
Dissonance
Complex evaluation

the purchase process triggered by the need to consider a particular purchase. Thus, purchase involvement is a *temporary state* of an individual or household. It is influenced by the inter-action of individual, product, and situational characteristics.

Note that purchase involvement is *not* the same as **product involvement** or enduring involvement. A consumer may be very involved with a brand (Starbucks or Dodge) or a product category (coffee or cars) and yet have a very low level of involvement with a particular purchase of that product because of brand loyalty, time pressures, or other reasons. For example, think of your favorite brand of soft drink or other beverage. You may be quite loyal to that brand, think it is superior to other brands, and have strong, favorable feelings about it. However, when you want a soft drink, you probably just buy your preferred brand without much thought.

Or a consumer may have a rather low level of involvement with a product (school supplies or automobile tires) but have a high level of purchase involvement because he or she desires to set an example for a child, impress a friend who is on the shopping trip, or save money.

The following sections provide a brief description of how the purchasing process changes as purchase involvement increases.

Nominal Decision Making

Nominal decision making, sometimes referred to as *habitual decision making,* in effect *involves no decision per se.* As Figure 14–1 indicates, a problem is recognized, internal search (long-term memory) provides a single preferred solution (brand), that brand is purchased, and an evaluation occurs only if the brand fails to perform as expected. Nominal decisions occur when there is very low involvement with the purchase.

A completely nominal decision does not even include consideration of the "do not purchase" alternative. For example, you might notice that you are nearly out of Colgate toothpaste and resolve to purchase some the next time you are at the store. You don't even consider not replacing the toothpaste or purchasing another brand. At the store, you scan the shelf for Colgate and pick it up without considering alternative brands, its price, or other potentially relevant factors.

Nominal decisions can be broken into two distinct categories: brand loyal decisions and repeat purchase decisions. These two categories are described briefly below and examined in detail in Chapter 18.

Brand Loyal Purchases   At one time, you may have been highly involved in selecting a brand of toothpaste and, in response, used an extensive decision-making process. Having selected Colgate as a result of this process, you now may purchase it without further consideration, even though using the best available toothpaste is still important to you. Thus, you are committed to Colgate because you believe it best meets your overall needs and you have formed an emotional attachment to it (you like it). You are brand loyal. It will be very difficult for a competitor to gain your patronage.

In this example, you have a fairly high degree of product involvement but a low degree of purchase involvement because of your brand loyalty. Should you encounter a challenge to the superiority of Colgate, perhaps through a news article, you most likely would engage in a high-involvement decision process before changing brands.

Repeat Purchases   In contrast, you may believe that all ketchup is about the same and you may not attach much importance to the product category or purchase. Having tried Del Monte and found it satisfactory, you now purchase it whenever you need ketchup. Thus, you are a repeat purchaser of Del Monte ketchup, but you are not committed to it.

Should you encounter a challenge to the wisdom of buying Del Monte the next time you need ketchup, perhaps because of a point-of-sale price discount, you would probably engage in only a limited decision process before deciding on which brand to purchase.

Limited Decision Making

Limited decision making involves internal and limited external search, few alternatives, simple decision rules on a few attributes, and little postpurchase evaluation. It covers the middle ground between nominal decision making and extended decision making. In its simplest form (lowest level of purchase involvement), limited decision making is similar to nominal decision making. For example, while in a store you may notice a point-of-purchase display for Jell-O and pick up two boxes without seeking information beyond your memory that

"Jell-O tastes good" or "Gee, I haven't had Jell-O in a long time." In addition, you may have considered no other alternative except possibly a very limited examination of a "do not buy" option. Or you may have a decision rule that you buy the cheapest brand of instant coffee available. When you run low on coffee (problem recognition), you simply examine coffee prices the next time you are in the store and select the cheapest brand.

Limited decision making also occurs in response to some emotional or situational needs. For example, you may decide to purchase a new brand or product because you are bored with the current, otherwise satisfactory, brand. This decision might involve evaluating only the newness or novelty of the available alternatives.[5] Or you might evaluate a purchase in terms of the actual or anticipated behavior of others. For example, you might order or refrain from ordering wine with a meal depending on the observed or expected orders of your dinner companions.

In general, limited decision making involves recognizing a problem for which there are several possible solutions. There is internal and a limited amount of external search. A few alternatives are evaluated on a few dimensions using simple selection rules. The purchase and use of the product are given very little evaluation afterward, unless there is a service problem or product failure.

Extended Decision Making

As Figure 14–1 indicates, **extended decision making** involves an extensive internal and external information search followed by a complex evaluation of multiple alternatives and significant postpurchase evaluation. It is the response to a high level of purchase involvement. After the purchase, doubt about its correctness is likely and a thorough evaluation of the purchase takes place. Relatively few consumer decisions reach this level of complexity. However, products such as homes, personal computers, and complex recreational items such as home theatre systems frequently are purchased via extended decision making.

Even decisions that are heavily emotional may involve substantial cognitive effort. For example, a consumer may agonize over a decision to take a ski trip or visit parents even though the needs being met and the criteria being evaluated are largely emotions or feelings rather than attributes per se, and are therefore typically fewer in number with less external information available.

As Figure 14–1 illustrates, problem recognition is the first stage of the decision process. We will describe this stage and discuss the marketing applications associated with it in the remainder of this chapter. We devote the next four chapters to the remaining four stages of the consumer decision process and discuss the relevant marketing applications in those chapters.

Our discussion of the decision process is based primarily on studies conducted in America. Where appropriate throughout this section of the text, we will point out some of the similarities and differences in decision making across cultures. As just one example relating to family decision making (Chapter 6), researchers found that in China, the more patriarchal social structure leads to more husband-dominated decisions and fewer joint husband-wife decisions than in the United States.[6] Given shifting values, particularly among the youth in Southeast Asia as discussed in Chapter 2, this result is likely also to be a function of the age of the couples in question.

THE PROCESS OF PROBLEM RECOGNITION

LO2

A day rarely passes in which a person does not face multiple problems that are resolved by consuming products and services. Routine problems of depletion, such as the need to get gasoline as the gauge approaches empty or the need to replace a frequently used food item, are readily recognized, defined, and resolved. The unexpected breakdown of a major

Source: Nestlé Group

appliance such as a refrigerator creates an unplanned problem that also is easily recognized but is often more difficult to resolve. Recognition of other problems, such as the need for a smartphone or a GPS system in the car, may take longer, as they may be subtle and evolve slowly over time.

Feelings, such as boredom, anxiety, or the "blues," may arise quickly or slowly over time. Such feelings often are recognized as problems subject to solution by purchasing behavior (I'm sad; I think I'll go to the mall/to a movie/to a restaurant). At other times, such feelings may trigger consumption behaviors without deliberate decision making. A person feeling restless may eat snack food without really thinking about it. In this case, the problem remains unrecognized (at the conscious level) and the solutions tried are often inappropriate (eating may not reduce restlessness).

Marketers develop products to help consumers solve problems. They also attempt to help consumers recognize problems, sometimes well in advance of their occurrence (see the Purina Tidy Cats ad in Illustration 14–1).

The Nature of Problem Recognition

Problem recognition is the first stage in the consumer decision process. **Problem recognition** is the result of a discrepancy between a desired state and an actual state that is sufficient to arouse and activate the decision process.[7] An **actual state** is *the way an individual perceives his or her feelings and situation to be at the present time.* A **desired state** is *the way an individual* wants *to feel or be at the present time.* For example, you probably don't want to be bored on Friday night. If you find yourself alone and becoming bored, you would treat this as a problem because your actual state (being bored) and your desired state (being pleasantly occupied) are different. You then could choose to watch a television program, play a video game, call a friend, go out, or take a wide array of other actions.

The kind of action taken by consumers in response to a recognized problem relates directly to the problem's importance to the consumer, the situation, and the dissatisfaction or inconvenience created by the problem.

Without recognition of a problem, there is no need for a decision. This condition is shown in Figure 14–2, when there is no discrepancy between the consumer's desired state (what the consumer would like) and the actual state (what the consumer perceives as already existing). Thus, if Friday night arrives and you find yourself engrossed in a novel, your desire to be pleasantly occupied (desired state) and your condition of enjoying a novel would be consistent, and you would have no reason to search for other activities.

On the other hand, when there is a discrepancy between a consumer desire and the perceived actual state, recognition of a problem occurs. Figure 14–2 indicates that any time the desired state is perceived as being greater than or less than the actual state, a problem exists. For example, being pleasantly occupied (desired state) would generally exceed being bored (actual state) and result in problem recognition. However, if your roommate suddenly

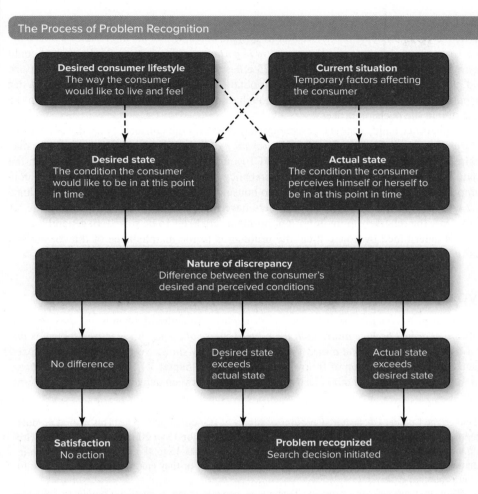

The Process of Problem Recognition

FIGURE 14-2

Desired consumer lifestyle
The way the consumer would like to live and feel

Current situation
Temporary factors affecting the consumer

Desired state
The condition the consumer would like to be in at this point in time

Actual state
The condition the consumer perceives himself or herself to be in at this point in time

Nature of discrepancy
Difference between the consumer's desired and perceived conditions

No difference

Desired state exceeds actual state

Actual state exceeds desired state

Satisfaction
No action

Problem recognized
Search decision initiated

showed up with a rowdy party, you might find yourself with more stimulation (actual state) than the medium level you actually desire. This too would result in problem recognition.

In Figure 14–2, consumer desires are shown to be the result of the desired lifestyle of the consumer (as described in Chapter 12) and the current situation (time pressures, physical surroundings, and so forth, as described in Chapter 13). Thus, a consumer whose self-concept and desired lifestyle focus on outdoor activities will desire frequent participation in such activities. A current situation of new snow in the mountains or warm weather at the beach would tend to increase that person's desire to be engaged in outdoor sports.

Perceptions of the actual state also are determined by a consumer's lifestyle and current situation. Consumers' lifestyles are a major determinant of their actual state because that is how they choose to live given the constraints imposed by their resources. Thus, a consumer who has chosen to raise a family, have significant material possessions, and pursue a demanding career is likely to have little free time for outdoor activities (actual state). The current situation—a day off work, a big project due, or a sick child—also has a major impact on how consumers perceive the actual situation.

It is important to note that it is the consumer's *perception* of the actual state that drives problem recognition, not some objective reality. Consumers who smoke cigars may believe that this activity is not harming their health because they do not inhale. These consumers do not recognize a problem with this behavior despite the reality that it is harmful.

The Desire to Resolve Recognized Problems   The level of one's desire to resolve a particular problem depends on two factors: (1) *the magnitude of the discrepancy between the desired and actual states* and (2) *the relative importance of the problem.* An individual could desire to have a car that averages at least 25 miles per gallon while still meeting certain size and power desires. If his or her current car obtains an average of 22 miles per gallon, a discrepancy exists, but it may not be large enough to motivate the consumer to proceed to the next step in the decision process.

On the other hand, a large discrepancy may exist and the consumer may not proceed to information search because the *relative importance* of the problem is small. A consumer may desire a new Honda and own a 15-year-old Toyota. The discrepancy is large. However, the relative importance of this particular discrepancy may be small compared with other consumption problems such as those related to housing, utilities, and food. Relative importance is a critical concept because all consumers have budget constraints, time constraints, or both. Only the relatively more important problems are likely to be solved. In general, importance is determined by how critical the problem is to the maintenance of the consumer's desired lifestyle.

Types of Consumer Problems

Consumer problems may be either active or inactive. An **active problem** is *one the consumer is aware of or will become aware of in the normal course of events.* An **inactive problem** is *one of which the consumer is not aware.* (This concept is very similar to the concept of felt need discussed in the "Diffusion of Innovations" section of Chapter 7.) The following is a *classic marketing example* that should clarify the distinction between active and inactive problems.

Timberlane Lumber Co. acquired a source of supply of Honduran pitch pine. This natural product lights at the touch of a match even when damp and burns for 15 to 20 minutes. It will not flare up and is therefore relatively safe. It can be procured in sticks 15 to 18 inches long and 1 inch in diameter. These sticks can be used to ignite fireplace fires, or they can be shredded and used to ignite charcoal grills.

Prior to marketing the product, Timberlane commissioned a marketing study to estimate demand and guide in developing marketing strategy. Two large samples of potential consumers were interviewed. The first sample was asked how they lit their fireplace fires and what problems they had with this procedure. Almost all the respondents used newspaper, kindling, or both, and very few experienced any problems. The new product was then described, and the respondents were asked to express the likelihood that they would purchase such a product. Only a small percentage expressed any interest. However, a sample of consumers that were paid to use the new product for several weeks felt it was a substantial improvement over existing methods and expressed a strong desire to continue using the product. Thus, the problem was there (because the new product was strongly preferred over the old by those who tried it), but most consumers were not aware of it. This is an *inactive problem.* Before the product can be successfully sold, the firm must activate problem recognition.

In contrast, a substantial percentage of those interviewed about lighting charcoal fires expressed a strong concern about the safety of liquid charcoal lighter. These individuals expressed great interest in purchasing a safer product. This is an *active problem.* Timberlane need not worry about problem recognition in this case. Instead, it can concentrate on illustrating how its product solves the problem that the consumers already know exists.

As this example indicates, active and inactive problems require different marketing strategies. Active problems require the marketer only to convince consumers that its

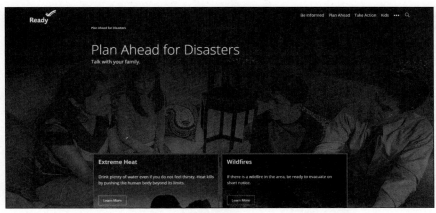

Source: Department of Homeland Security

Source: The Procter & Gamble Company

brand is the superior solution. Consumers are already aware of the problem. In contrast, inactive problems require the marketer to convince consumers that they *have* the problem *and* that the marketer's brand is a superior solution to the problem. This is a much more difficult task.

Illustration 14–2 shows two ads, one for Febreze relating to an active problem and one for Ready.gov pertaining to an inactive problem. The ad on the left first must make consumers aware of a problem (inactive) they likely didn't know of. The ad on the right assumes consumers are aware of the problem (active) and simply focuses on its unique ability to solve it.

UNCONTROLLABLE DETERMINANTS OF PROBLEM RECOGNITION

A discrepancy between what is desired by a consumer and what the consumer has is the necessary condition for problem recognition. A discrepancy can be the result of a variety of factors that influence consumer desires, perceptions of the existing state, or both. These factors are often beyond the direct influence of the marketing manager, such as a change in family composition. Figure 14–3 summarizes the major nonmarketing factors that influence problem recognition. The marketing factors influencing problem recognition are discussed in the next section of this chapter.

Most of the nonmarketing factors that affect problem recognition are fairly obvious and logical. Most were described in some detail in prior chapters. For example, as we discussed in Chapter 2, a person's culture affects almost all aspects of his or her desired state. Thus, the desire to be recognized as an independent, unique person with distinctive behaviors and possessions differs sharply between American and Japanese consumers because of cultural influences.

Previous decisions and individual development were not discussed in earlier chapters. A previous decision to buy a bike or skis could lead to a current desire to have a car rack to carry them. A decision to become a homeowner may trigger desires for numerous home and garden items. Past decisions also may deplete purchasing power with the result that fewer problems are recognized or are assigned sufficient importance to trigger action.[8] Prior decisions can influence future decisions even within the same category. One study finds that consumers get tired of food items such as cereal and pretzels, not because they don't like the

---

ILLUSTRATION 14-2

Often, marketers need to trigger problem recognition in market segments, as with Ready.gov relating to disaster planning. However, at other times, the market is well aware of the problem and the communication can focus on the brand's ability to solve the problem, as with Febreze.

LO3

FIGURE 14-3 Nonmarketing Factors Affecting Problem Recognition

brand, but because, from a sensory (taste) standpoint, they become bored. Consumers solve this "problem" by variety seeking—that is, they switch to other products. The good news for marketers is that the boredom relates to taste and not the brand itself. So if the brand can offer variety to consumers, they will switch to different *options* but stay loyal to the *brand.* Kellogg's and other food marketers offer huge variety to accommodate this uncontrollable element. Just a few of Kellogg's cereals, for example, are their Corn Flakes, Froot Loops, and Special K.[9]

Individual development causes many changes in desired and actual states. For example, as individuals gain skills, their desires related to those skills change. Beginning skiers, musicians, and gardeners typically desire products and capabilities that will no longer be appropriate as their skills increase. Emotional and psychological development (or lack thereof) also can be related to the need to trigger problem recognition. Concerns over cyber bullying have led Facebook, along with Secret deodorant, to develop a campaign called "mean stinks" in an effort to get young girls to realize the seriousness of hateful words about others on social media.

Government agencies and various consumer groups also actively attempt to trigger problem recognition, often in relation to the consumption of various products. Warning labels on alcohol and cigarettes are two examples of these types of efforts, as are antismoking campaigns and campaigns that stress the dangers of drinking and driving. The HPV.com ad is geared toward triggering problem recognition, illustrating the negative effects of not being vaccinated, as shown in Illustration 14-3.

MARKETING STRATEGY AND PROBLEM RECOGNITION

LO4

Marketing managers have four concerns related to problem recognition. First, they need to know the problems consumers are facing. Second, they must know how to develop the marketing mix to solve consumer problems. Third, managers occasionally want to cause consumers to recognize problems. Finally, there are times when they desire to suppress problem recognition among consumers. The remainder of this chapter discusses these issues.

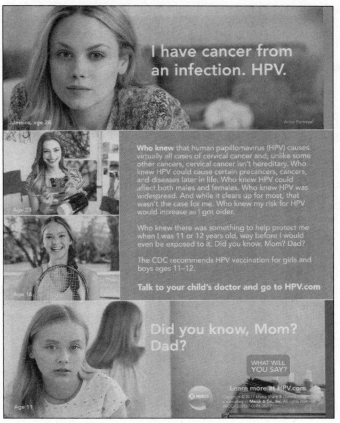

Source: Merck & Co., Inc

Discovering Consumer Problems

Simple *intuition* is perhaps the most common approach to discovering consumer problems. Its benefits are that it is relatively inexpensive, fast, and easy. Its drawbacks are that the intuition, because it tends to be generated by an individual, may be wrong or not apply to a wide range of consumers, thus increasing the likelihood of failure for new product introductions. Thus, marketing research is often conducted as a substitute for, or as a complement to, intuition as a means for increasing the success rate of new products. Numerous research approaches exist for uncovering consumer problems. A number of the relatively well-established approaches are discussed next. In addition, Consumer Insight 14–1 discusses a new online approach based on monitoring consumer online and social media.

Activity and Product Analysis   *Activity analysis* focuses on a particular activity, such as preparing dinner, maintaining the lawn, or swimming. Then, surveys or focus groups (see Appendix A) attempt to determine what problems consumers encounter during the performance of the activity. For example, a shampoo company could use such an approach to develop products specifically for the hair-related problems associated with swimming in chlorinated pools. *Product analysis* is similar to activity analysis but

Identifying Consumer Problems Using Online and Social Media

Traditional methods of discovering consumer problems have tended toward direct questioning of consumers. Today's online environment, however, can be seen as a potential goldmine for identifying consumer problems at both the category and brand levels by monitoring the "conversations" happening online. Sometimes those conversations will be happening on a brand's own online and social media outlets, as when a consumer tweets a company about a recent product failure. Sometimes these conversations will be happening in the broader social media environment, as when bloggers discuss product failures or general needs in a specific product area. Consider the following statements from Radian6, a leader in the field of social media measurement:[10]

> Problems, needs, and wish lists from your potential customers or your competitor's customers are being tossed out to the social web all the time. From product reviews to casual statements about what's not working right, consumers are giving you loads of intelligence about what problems they need you to solve.

Tracking is not enough—responding to problems and concerns is a critical part of the whole package. That is, it is not enough to know, via postings on your brand's Facebook Fan Page, that there are problems with your newest software release. It is critical that those problems be solved in a timely and appropriate manner. Radian6's comments are informative here as well:

> [It's] about understanding how your business solves problems for people, and then connecting with them in a meaningful, helpful way when they need you most. It's not about a sales pitch. It's about creating a solution for someone that they're asking for.

Sounds simple, right? Think again. Online and social media outlets (both the company's and general) are extensive. Imagine trying to monitor all of the conversations or "chatter" happening in cyberspace at any given time and filtering that down to usable information. One study by Forrester Research notes numerous such venues including customer forums, blogs, Facebook, and Twitter. And that's before you consider the company's website and e-mail. These options are a growing source of potential consumer feedback and input. The challenge is how to track, consolidate, interpret, and react to all of the online chatter. The interpretation part can be difficult particularly for non-brand-specific problems. It's easy to know when a customer is complaining that your software has a specific flaw; it's much harder to recognize those broader consumer needs that lead to truly breakthrough innovations. Though tracking specific types of key words can help, the interpretation process is still difficult and as yet not well understood. Platforms such as Radian6—part of Salesforce marketing cloud (salesforce.com)—offer proprietary solutions to help companies through these and the many challenges associated with this form of consumer problem discovery.

Critical Thinking Questions

1. What are some advantages of online and social media tracking compared to traditional methods?

2. In what ways might the viral nature of a given topic be important to marketers in assessing the importance of a given problem?

3. Do you see any ethical concerns related to this approach? Explain.

examines the purchase or use of a particular product or brand. Thus, consumers may be asked about problems associated with using their mountain bikes or laptop computers.

Problem Analysis Problem analysis is different in that it *starts* with a problem and asks respondents to indicate which activities, products, or brands are associated with (or perhaps could eliminate) those problems. For example, a study dealing with packaging problems could include questions such as:

_____ packages are hard to open.

Packages of _____ are hard to reseal.

Packages of _____ don't fit on the shelf.

Packages of _____ waste too many resources.

Human Factors Research Human factors research attempts to determine human capabilities in areas such as vision, strength, response time, flexibility, and fatigue and the effect on these capabilities of lighting, temperature, and sound. Many methods can be employed in human factors research. However, observational techniques such as slow-motion and time-lapse photography, video recording, and event recorders are particularly useful. This type of research sometimes can identify functional problems that consumers are unaware of. For example, it can be used in the design of such products as lawn mowers, kitchen utensils, smartphone keyboards, and computers to minimize user fatigue.

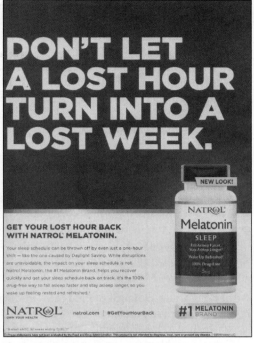

Source: Aurobindo Pharma

Emotion Research Marketers are increasingly conducting research on the role of emotions in problem recognition and resolution. Common approaches are surveys, focus group research, and personal interviews that examine the emotions associated with certain problems (see Table 10-4 for specific survey measures for emotions). For example, researchers are beginning to examine how consumers cope with the negative emotions associated with product or service failures. Findings suggest that certain emotions (e.g., anger) are associated with certain coping strategies (e.g., confrontation). This type of research is critical to marketers in helping them anticipate consumer reactions to problems and train their customer service personnel to respond appropriately.[11] For subtle or sensitive problems and emotions, projective techniques (see Appendix A, Table A-1) may be necessary.[12]

Responding to Consumer Problems

Once a consumer problem is identified, the manager may structure the marketing mix to solve the problem. This can involve developing a new product or altering an existing one, modifying channels of distribution, changing pricing policy, or revising advertising strategy. For example, in Illustration 14-4 the Natrol ad is being positioned as a unique solution to a problem (trouble sleeping).

As you approach graduation, you will be presented with opportunities to purchase insurance, acquire credit cards, and solve other problems associated with the onset of financial independence and a major change in lifestyle. These opportunities reflect various firms' knowledge that many individuals in your situation face problems that their products will help solve.

Weekend and night store hours and, in part, the rapid growth of online stores are a response of retailers to the consumer problem of limited weekday shopping opportunities. Solving this problem has become particularly important to families with both spouses employed.

The examples described above represent only a small sample of the ways marketers react to consumer problem recognition. Each firm must be aware of the consumer problems it can solve, which consumers have these problems, and the situations in which the problems arise.

Helping Consumers Recognize Problems

There are occasions when the manager will want to cause problem recognition rather than react to it. In the earlier example, Timberlane faced having to activate problem recognition in order to sell its product as a fireplace starter. Toy marketers are attempting to reduce their dependence on the Christmas season by activating problem recognition at other times of the year. For example, Fisher-Price has had "rainy day" and "sunny day" promotions in the spring and summer months. Illustrations 14–1 and 14–2, presented earlier, show attempts to activate problem recognition.

Generic versus Selective Problem Recognition   Two basic approaches to causing problem recognition are *generic problem recognition* and *selective problem recognition*. These are analogous to the economic concepts of generic and selective demand.

Generic problem recognition involves a *discrepancy that a variety of brands within a product category can reduce.* Generally, a firm will attempt to influence generic problem recognition when the problem is latent or of low importance and one of the following conditions exists:

* It is early in the product life cycle.
* The firm has a high percentage of the market.
* External search after problem recognition is apt to be limited.
* It is an industry-wide cooperative effort.

Telephone sales programs often attempt to arouse problem recognition, in part because the salesperson can then limit external search to one brand. Advertising for food-related cooperatives such as milk, beef, and produce frequently focuses on generic problem recognition. The California Walnuts ad shown in Illustration 14–5 is an example of a current campaign of this type. Note that the ad does not promote a specific brand.

Firms with large market shares in a product category often focus on generic problem recognition because any sales increase will probably come to their brands. However, a smaller firm that generates generic problem recognition for its product category may be generating more sales for its competitors than for itself. But even firms with large market share can lose share if generic problem recognition campaigns are not done carefully. In the early 1990s, Borden increased marketing efforts for its popular Creamette pasta brand substantially and promoted recipes using pasta. Its sales increased only 1.6 percent, compared with the industry's growth of 5.5 percent.[13] Its efforts apparently helped the sales of its competitors more than its own sales.

Selective problem recognition involves *a discrepancy that only one brand can solve.* The Sleep Number ad shown in Illustration 14–6 is focused on creating selective problem recognition. Firms attempt to cause selective problem recognition to gain or maintain market share, whereas increasing generic problem recognition generally results in an expansion of the total market.

Source: California Walnuts

Approaches to Activating Problem Recognition How can a firm influence problem recognition? Recall that problem recognition is a function of the (1) *importance* and (2) *magnitude* of a discrepancy between the desired state and an existing state. Thus, a firm can attempt to influence the size of the discrepancy by altering the desired state or perceptions of the existing state. Or the firm can attempt to influence perceptions of the importance of an existing discrepancy.

Many marketing efforts attempt to *influence the desired state;* that is, marketers often advertise the benefits their products will provide, hoping that these benefits will become desired by consumers. The Maui Jim ad in Illustration 14–7 attempts to influence the desired state by showing how well the product works. Do you feel Maui Jim is

Source: Sleep Number Corporation

This Maui Jim ad attempts to influence the desired state by showing the optimal outcomes that are possible.

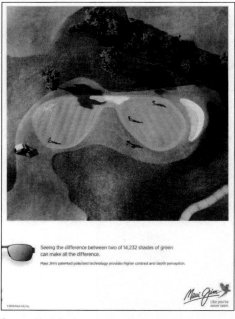

Source: Maui Jim, Inc

effective in influencing consumers to buy its products?

It is also possible to *influence perceptions of the existing state* through advertisements. Many personal care and social products take this approach. "Even your best friend won't tell you . . ." or "Kim is a great worker, but this coffee . . ." are examples of messages designed to generate concern about an existing state. The desired states are assumed to be fresh breath and good coffee. These messages are designed to cause individuals to question if their existing state coincides with this desired state.

The Tylenol ad in Illustration 14–8 is designed to target an undesirable actual state that the product is designed to correct. In this case, if your child has the flu and is in bed, taking Tylenol can help the child get out of bed and have fun outdoors.

Focusing on the actual state is a way to activate problem recognition and ultimately change behaviors, as shown in this Tylenol ad.

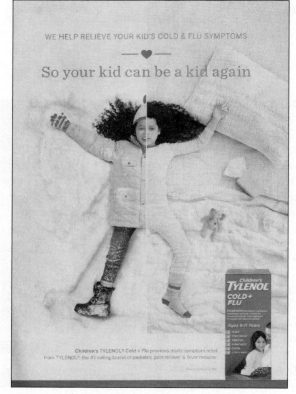

Source: Johnson & Johnson Consumer Inc

Critics frequently question the ethics of activating problem recognition. This is particularly true for problems related to status or social acceptance. This debate is generally discussed in terms of marketers' "creating needs," which we discussed in Chapter 10.

The Timing of Problem Recognition   Consumers often recognize problems at times when purchasing a solution is difficult or impossible, as the following examples demonstrate:

- We decide we need snow chains when caught in a blizzard.
- We become aware of a need for insurance *after* an accident.
- We desire a flower bed full of tulips in the spring but forgot to plant bulbs in the fall.
- We want cold medicine when we are sick but don't feel like driving to the store.

In some instances, marketers attempt to help consumers solve such problems after they arise. For example, some pharmacies will make home deliveries. However, the more common strategy is to trigger problem recognition in advance of the actual problem (see Illustration 14–1). That is, it is often to the consumer's and marketer's advantage for the consumer to recognize and solve potential problems *before* they become actual problems.

Some companies, particularly insurance companies, attempt to initiate problem recognition through mass media advertising; others rely more on point-of-purchase displays and other in-store influences (see Chapter 17). Retailers, as well as manufacturers, are involved in this activity. For example, prior to snow season, the following sign was placed on a large rack of snow shovels in the main aisle of a large hardware store:

> REMEMBER LAST WINTER
> WHEN YOU *NEEDED*
> A SNOW SHOVEL?
> THIS YEAR BE PREPARED!

Suppressing Problem Recognition

As we have seen, competition, consumer organizations, and governmental agencies occasionally introduce information in the marketplace that triggers problem recognition that particular marketers would prefer to avoid. The American tobacco industry has made strenuous attempts to minimize consumer recognition of the health problems associated with cigarette smoking. For example, a Newport cigarette advertisement showed a happy, laughing couple under the headline "Alive with pleasure." This could easily be interpreted as an attempt to minimize any problem recognition caused by the mandatory warning at the bottom of the advertisement: "Warning: The Surgeon General has determined that cigarette smoking is dangerous to your health."

Obviously, marketers do not want their current customers to recognize problems with their brands. Effective quality control and distribution (limited out-of-stock situations) are important in this effort. Packages and package inserts that assure the consumer of the wisdom of his or her purchase are also common.

SUMMARY

LO1: Describe the impact of purchase involvement on the decision process.

Consumer decision making becomes more extensive and complex as *purchase involvement* increases. The lowest level of purchase involvement is represented by *nominal decisions:* A problem is recognized, long-term memory provides a single preferred brand, that brand is purchased, and only limited postpurchase evaluation occurs. As one moves from *limited decision making* toward *extended decision making,* information search increases, alternative evaluation becomes more extensive and complex, and postpurchase evaluation becomes more thorough.

LO2: Explain problem recognition and how it fits into the consumer decision process.

Problem recognition involves the existence of a discrepancy between the consumer's desired state (what the consumer would like) and the actual state (what the consumer perceives as already existing). Both the desired state and the actual state are influenced by the consumer's lifestyle and current situation. If the discrepancy between these two states is sufficiently large and important, the consumer will begin to search for a solution to the problem.

LO3: Summarize the uncontrollable determinants of problem recognition.

A number of factors beyond the control of the marketing manager can affect problem recognition. The desired state is commonly influenced by (1) culture/subculture, (2) social status, (3) reference groups, (4) household characteristics, (5) financial status/expectations, (6) previous decisions, (7) individual development, (8) emotions, (9) motives, and (10) the current situation. The actual state is influenced by (1) past decisions, (2) normal depletion, (3) product/brand performance, (4) individual development, (5) emotions,

(6) government/consumer groups, (7) availability of products, and (8) the current situation.

LO4: Discuss the role of consumer problems and problem recognition in marketing strategy.

Before marketing managers can respond to problem recognition generated by outside factors, they must be able to *identify* consumer problems. Surveys and focus groups using *activity, product,* or *problem analysis* are commonly used. *Human factors research* approaches the same task from an observational perspective. *Emotion research* focuses on the role of emotions in problem recognition and resolution. And, as Consumer Insight 14–1 points out, tracking of online and social media is proving to be an increasingly powerful tool as well.

Once managers are aware of problem recognition patterns among their target market, they can react by designing the marketing mix to solve the recognized problem. This may involve product development or repositioning, a change in store hours, a different price, or a host of other marketing strategies.

Marketing managers often want to influence problem recognition rather than react to it. They may desire to generate *generic problem recognition,* a discrepancy that a variety of brands within a product category can reduce, or to induce *selective problem recognition,* a discrepancy that only one brand in the product category can solve.

Attempts to *activate problem recognition* generally do so by focusing on the desired state. However, attempts to make consumers aware of negative aspects of the existing state are also common. In addition, marketers attempt to influence the timing of problem recognition by making consumers aware of potential problems before they arise.

Finally, managers may attempt to minimize or suppress problem recognition by current users of their brands.

KEY TERMS

Active problem 520
Actual state 518
Desired state 518
Extended decision making 517

Generic problem recognition 526
Inactive problem 520
Limited decision making 516
Nominal decision making 516

Problem recognition 518
Product involvement 515
Purchase involvement 514
Selective problem recognition 526

SMARTBOOK

REVIEW QUESTIONS

1. What is meant by *purchase involvement?* How does it differ from product involvement?
2. How does consumer decision making change as purchase involvement increases?
3. What is the role of *emotion* in the consumer decision process?
4. How do *nominal, limited,* and *extended decision making* differ? How do the two types of nominal decision making differ?
5. What is *problem recognition?*
6. What influences the motivation to resolve a recognized problem?
7. What is the difference between an *active* and an *inactive problem?* Why is this distinction important?
8. How does lifestyle relate to problem recognition?
9. What are the main uncontrollable factors that influence the *desired* state?
10. What are the main uncontrollable factors that influence the *existing* state?
11. How can you measure problem recognition?
12. In what ways can marketers react to problem recognition? Give several examples.
13. How does *generic problem recognition* differ from *selective problem recognition?* Under what conditions would a firm attempt to influence generic problem recognition? Why?
14. How can a firm cause problem recognition? Give examples.
15. How can a firm suppress problem recognition?

DISCUSSION QUESTIONS

16. What products do you think *generally* are associated with nominal, limited, and extended decision making? Under what conditions, if any, would these products be associated with a different form of decision making?
17. What products do you think *generally* are purchased or used for emotional reasons? How would the decision process differ for an emotion-driven purchase compared to a more functional purchase?
18. What products do you think *generally* are associated with brand-loyal decision making and which with repeat-purchase decision making? Justify your response.
19. Describe a purchase you made using nominal decision making, one using limited decision making, and one using extended decision making. What caused you to use each type of decision process?
20. Describe two recent purchases you have made. What uncontrollable factors, if any, triggered problem recognition? Did they affect the desired state, the actual state, or both?
21. How would you measure consumer problems among the following?

    a. College students
    b. Children aged 2 to 4
    c. Internet shoppers
    d. New residents in a town
    e. Vegans
    f. Newly married couples

22. How would you determine the existence of consumer problems of relevance to a marketer of the following?

    a. Women's spa
    b. Internet retail outlets
    c. Online health food store
    d. Public library
    e. Hawaiian vacation resort
    f. Mountain bikes

23. Discuss the types of products that resolve specific problems that occur for most consumers at different stages of their household life cycle.
24. How would you activate problem recognition among college students for the following?

    a. Volunteering time at the Salvation Army
    b. Student recreation center
    c. A vegan diet
    d. Rooms To Go
    e. Using a designated driver if drinking
    f. Laundry service

25. How would you influence the time of problem recognition for the following?
    a. Fire alarm battery replacement
    b. Gift basket
    c. Car tune-up
    d. Air conditioner filters
    e. Health insurance
    f. Vitamins

26. Respond to the questions in Consumer Insight 14–1.

APPLICATION ACTIVITIES

27. Interview five students and identify three consumer problems they have recognized recently. For each problem, determine
    a. The relative importance of the problem.
    b. How the problem occurred.
    c. What caused the problem (i.e., change in desired or actual states).
    d. What action they have taken.
    e. What action is planned to resolve each problem.

28. Track a brand's Twitter account for a week. Write a report on the role that Twitter and other social media can play in identifying consumer problems. As part of the report, discuss whether or not you believe that some venues are better than others at providing insights for general versus brand-specific problems.

29. Interview three students and identify recent instances when they engaged in nominal, limited, and extended decision making (a total of nine decisions). What specific factors appear to be associated with each type of decision?

30. Interview three students and identify five products that each buys using a nominal decision process. Identify those that are based on brand loyalty and those that are merely repeat purchases. What characteristics, if any, distinguish the brand-loyal products from the repeat products?

31. Find and describe an advertisement that is attempting to activate problem recognition. Analyze the advertisement in terms of the type of problem and the action the ad is suggesting. Also, discuss any changes you would recommend to improve the effectiveness of the ad in terms of activating problem recognition.

32. Using two consumers from a relevant market segment, conduct an activity analysis for an activity that interests you. Prepare a report on the marketing opportunities suggested by your analysis.

33. Using two consumers from a relevant market segment, conduct a product analysis for a product that interests you. Prepare a report on the marketing opportunities suggested by your analysis.

34. Conduct a problem analysis, using a sample of five college freshmen. Prepare a report on the marketing opportunities suggested by your analysis.

35. Interview five tobacco smokers and ascertain what problems they see associated with smoking.

36. Interview someone from the local office of the American Cancer Society concerning its attempts to generate problem recognition among smokers.

REFERENCES

1. This opener is based on S. McNamara, "25 Clever Ideas to Make Life Easier," November 1, 2011, *Mum's Grapevine,* http://mumsgrapevine.com.au/2011/11/25-clever-ideas_household-tips_storage-ideas/, accessed August 28, 2014; L. Deal, "Solutions to Problems That I Didn't Know That I Had," *Pinterest,* www.pinterest.com/lindsayfayedeal/solutions-to-problems-that-i-didn-t-know-that-i-ha/, accessed August 28, 2014; information from Arm and Hammer Company website, www.armandhammer.com/solutions.aspx, accessed August 28, 2014; T. Luna, "Long CVS Receipts Spark Social Media Sensation," *Boston Globe,* August 31, 2013, www.bostonglobe.com/business/2013/08/30/long-cvs-receipts-spark-social-media-sensation/VzQeVzNmBB3ECqy6vQtj1N/story.html, accessed August 28, 2014; information from Swiffer company website, www.swiffer.com/, accessed August 28, 2014; information from Dyson company website, www.dyson.com/, accessed August 28, 2014; information from Quirky company website, www.quirky.com/, accessed August 28, 2014.

2. See B. Shiv and J. Huber, "The Impact of Anticipating Satisfaction on Consumer Choice," *Journal of Consumer Research,* September 2000, pp. 202–16; M. T. Pham et al., "Affect Monitoring and the Primacy of Feelings in Judgment," *Journal of Consumer Research,* September 2001, pp. 167–88.

3. See J. R. Bettman, M. F. Luce, and J. W. Payne, "Constructive Consumer Choice," *Journal of Consumer Research,* December 1998, pp. 187–217.

4. For more complex but valuable approaches, see ibid.; R. Lawson, "Consumer Decision Making within a Goal-Driven Framework," *Psychology & Marketing,* August 1997, pp. 427–49.

5. M. Trivedi, F. M. Bass, and R. C. Rao, "A Model of Stochastic Variety-Seeking," *Marketing Science,* Summer 1994, pp. 274–97; S. Menon and B. E. Kahn, "The Impact of Context on Variety Seeking in Product Choice," *Journal of Consumer Research,* December 1995, pp. 285–95; R. K. Ratner, B. E. Kahn, and D. Kahneman, "Choosing Less-Preferred Experiences for the Sake of Variety," *Journal of Consumer Research,* June 1999, pp. 1–15.

6. J. B. Ford, M.S. LaTour, and T. L. Henthorne, "Perception of Marital Roles in Purchase Decision Processes," *Journal of the Academy of Marketing Science* 23, no. 2 (1995), pp. 120–31.

7. See C. J. Hill, "The Nature of Problem Recognition and Search in the Extended Health Care Decision," *Journal of Services Marketing* 15, no. 6 (2001), pp. 454–79.

8. D. Soman, "Effects of Payment Mechanism on Spending Behavior," *Journal of Consumer Research,* March 2001, pp. 460–74.

9. See H. C. M. Van Trijp, W. D. Hoyer, and J. J. Inman, "Why Switch? Product Category-Level Explanations for True Variety-Seeking Behavior," *Journal of Marketing Research,* August 1996, pp. 281–92; J. J. Inman, "The Role of Sensory-Specific Satiety in Attribute-Level Variety Seeking," *Journal of Consumer Research,* June 2001, pp. 105–20.

10. Insight based on D. Alston, "Social Media Monitoring—Top 10 Reasons for Monitoring Brands," *TopRank,* May 2008, www.toprankblog.com, accessed June 16, 2011; *CMOs Must Connect the Dots of the Online Brand* (Cambridge, MA: Forrester Research, Inc., June 27, 2010); *Brands Cannot Ignore Offline Conversations* (Cambridge, MA: Forrester Research, Inc., September 3, 2010); information found at Radian6's websites: www.radian6.com, accessed June 16, 2011, and www.salesforce.com/products/marketing-cloud/social-media-marketing/?mc=radian6, accessed June 25, 2018.

11. S. Yi and H. Baumgartner, "Coping with Negative Emotions in Purchase-Related Situations," *Journal of Consumer Psychology* 14, no. 3 (2004), pp. 303–17.

12. See, e.g., G. Zaltman, "Metaphorically Speaking," *Marketing Research,* Summer 1996, pp. 13–20; C. B. Raffel, "Vague Notions," *Marketing Research,* Summer 1996, pp. 21–23.

13. E. Lesly, "Why Things Are So Sour at Borden," *BusinessWeek,* November 22, 1993, p. 84.

15

Information Search

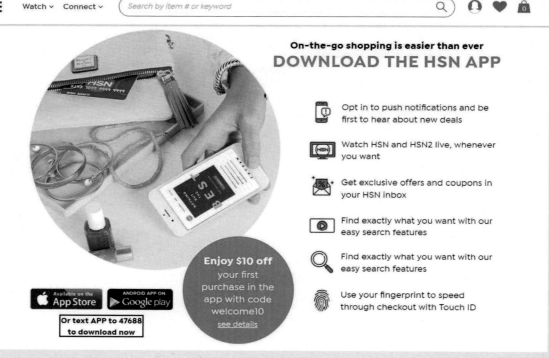

Source: HSN Interactive LLC

LEARNING OBJECTIVES

LO1 Discuss internal and external information search and their role in different decision types.

LO2 Summarize the types of information consumers search for.

LO3 Describe the categories of decision alternatives relating to the evoked set.

LO4 Discuss available information sources and the role of Internet and mobile search.

LO5 Discuss the major cost–benefit factors driving the amount of external search.

LO6 Summarize the marketing strategies based on information search patterns.

Consumers still watch TV and lots of it. And TV (in particular TV ads) can be a valuable information source for some products and services. The difference is that now there is a growing trend for consumers (70 percent of adults) to watch TV with a second screen—cell phone or tablet—in hand.[1] The second screen allows marketers to extend the reach of their commercials and to provide consumers with additional routes for information search. Advertisers in recent Super Bowls have embraced the second screen for this purpose. Budweiser, a perennial favorite, combined a Twitter campaign with one of its spots, encouraging viewers to tweet a prespecified hashtag. In return, Budweiser donated money to safe-driving programs. Furthermore, companies like Abercrombie & Fitch have developed advertisements that play across both TV and social media platforms.

Apps also have been developed to coordinate the dual-screen experiences. Take the HSN and QVC apps. These apps synchronize the shopping networks' shows with the consumer's smartphone to combine TV watching and searching/shopping—or so-called couch commerce. The time lapse between advertising exposures to search to purchase is very short in many cases due to the nominal or limited decision-machining context involved (see Chapter 14) and the ease and convenience of searching and shopping using these apps. As stated on HSN's website about its app, "Easily find your favorites using our new shop and search features."

Shazam is an app that enables consumers to identify a song from just a few bars of music and is so well known it has become a verb. Hold up your cell phone or tablet to the TV (or radio or other broadcast device) while a tune is playing and Shazam will identify it. Not only will the name of the song and the artist surface (in a sense, automated information search), but Shazam will even take you to a website to purchase the music. Recently, Shazam has moved beyond music to partner with marketers to integrate TV programs and ads with the consumer's second-screen experience. So, for example, viewers who Shazammed a Toyota ad aired during a recent Super Bowl could enter a contest to win a Camry car.

Today's TV viewing consumers have more power at their disposal related to information search and purchase through the second screen. The increasing trend for consumers to watch TV with a device in hand provides marketers with opportunities to engage consumers watching TV programs. A major current challenge is that the majority of consumers are not using their second screens to engage in activities related to the TV program (instead surfing unrelated materials while TV commercials are airing) because they find second-screen content lacking.

Nevertheless, Budweiser and Abercrombie & Fitch, as discussed at the beginning of this chapter opener, are examples of how, moving forward, marketers know they must enhance the value of the consumer search experience and interface via the second screen.

This chapter examines the information search stage of the decision process that occurs after problem recognition. Within information search, we focus on (1) the amount and type of search, (2) categories of decision alternatives relating to the evoked set, (3) sources and channels of information including the Internet and mobile, (4) the cost–benefit factors driving external search, and (5) marketing strategies based on information search patterns.

THE NATURE OF INFORMATION SEARCH

LO1

Once a problem is recognized, relevant information from long-term memory is used to determine such things as (1) whether a satisfactory solution is known, (2) what the characteristics of potential solutions are, and (3) what appropriate ways exist to compare solutions. This is **internal search.** If a resolution is not reached through internal search, then the search process is focused on external information relevant to solving the problem. This is **external search,** which can involve independent sources, personal sources, marketer-based information, and product experience.[2] It is important to note that even in extended decision making with extensive external search, the initial internal search generally produces a set of guides (e.g., must-have attributes) or decision constraints (e.g., maximum price that can be paid) that limit and guide external search. Search has benefits such as finding a lower price or getting higher quality. However, search has costs that tend to limit the amount of search even for very important decisions. That is, information search involves mental as well as physical activities that consumers must perform that take time, energy, and money.

As discussed in Chapter 14, the amount of search depends on purchase involvement, which is a major determinant of the type of decision process consumers engage in. Purchase involvement, and the amount of external search, increases as consumers move from nominal decision making to extended decision making. Internal information tends to dominate in nominal decision making, where typically a consumer recalls a single satisfactory solution and purchases it without further search or evaluation. External search tends to dominate in extended decision making, where typically a consumer examines and evaluates numerous alternatives across numerous criteria using information from many sources. For limited decision making, external search can play a moderate role in some instances, particularly when the consumer is aware of several possible alternative solutions to his or her problem and therefore must search and evaluate on a limited basis to make a choice.[3]

Search after problem recognition also can be limited by prior search and learning. That is, deliberate external search also occurs in the absence of problem recognition. **Ongoing search** is done both *to acquire information for possible later use and because the process itself is pleasurable.* For example, individuals highly involved with an activity, such as tennis, are apt to seek information about tennis-related products on an ongoing basis without a recognized problem with their existing tennis equipment (recall that enduring involvement is characteristic of opinion leaders). In addition, consumers acquire a substantial amount of relevant information on an ongoing basis without deliberate search—through low-involvement learning (see Chapter 9).

TYPES OF INFORMATION SOUGHT

LO2

A consumer decision requires information on the following:[4]

1. The appropriate evaluative criteria for the solution of a problem.
2. The existence of various alternative solutions.
3. The performance level or characteristic of each alternative solution on each evaluative criterion.

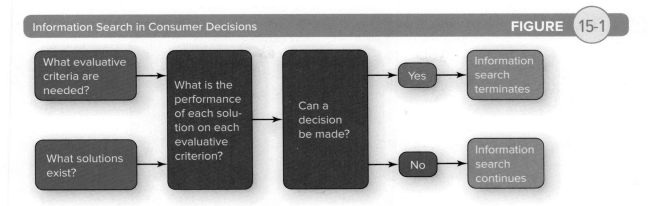

FIGURE 15-1

Information Search in Consumer Decisions

Information search, then, seeks each of these three types of information, as shown in Figure 15-1.

Evaluative Criteria

Suppose you are provided with money to purchase a laptop computer, perhaps as a graduation present. Assuming you have not been in the market for a computer recently, your first thought would probably be, "What features do I want in a computer?" You would then engage in internal search to determine the features or characteristics required to meet your needs. These desired characteristics are your *evaluative criteria*. If you have had limited experience with computers, you also might engage in external search to learn which characteristics a good computer should have. You could check with friends, read reviews in *PC Magazine* online, talk with sales personnel, visit computer websites, post questions on an online discussion board, or personally inspect several computers. The Vionic ad in Illustration 15-1 is an example of how a company tries to focus consumers toward an attribute on which it excels but that consumers may not automatically have in mind when selecting a brand.

A detailed discussion of evaluative criteria appears in Chapter 16.

Appropriate Alternatives

After and while searching for appropriate evaluative criteria, you would probably seek *appropriate alternatives*—in this case, brands or, possibly, stores. In general, there are five groupings of alternatives. First is the set of all possible alternatives that could solve a consumer problem. Within this set there are four categories of decision alternatives. The **awareness set** is composed of *those brands consumers are aware of.* The **inert set** is composed of *those brands consumers are aware of and view in a neutral manner.* These are brands that might be seen as acceptable by consumers if their favorite alternative is not available. These are also brands for which consumers will be open to positive information although they will not be actively seeking it out. The **inept set** is composed of *those brands consumers are aware of and view negatively.* These brands are ones for which consumers will generally not process or accept positive information even if readily available.

The **evoked set** (also called the **consideration set**) is composed of *those brands or products one will evaluate for the solution of a particular consumer problem.*[5] Note that while evoked sets are frequently composed of brands from a single product category (brands of cereals

L03

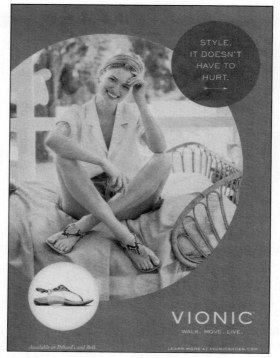

Source: Vionic Group LLC

or computers), this need not be the case because substitute products also can play a role.[6] For example, one landscaping company found that consumers often view landscaping as a "home improvement decision." As a consequence, their landscaping services often compete with other home improvement products such as interior decorating instead of, or in addition to, other landscaping services.

In addition, the evoked set or consideration set often varies with the usage situation. For example, pancakes may only be in a consumer's consideration set for weekend breakfast situations because they are too inconvenient for busy weekday mornings. Companies often will try to expand the usage situations for their products in various ways, as we saw in Chapter 13. In this example, premade frozen pancakes that are toaster-ready may be a way to get pancakes into the weekday breakfast consideration set.[7]

Finally, note that if a consumer does not have an evoked set or lacks confidence that his or her evoked set is adequate, that consumer will probably engage in external search to learn about additional alternatives. In addition, consumers also may learn about additional acceptable brands as an incidental aspect of moving through the decision process. Thus, an important outcome of information search is the development of a *complete* evoked set.

Figure 15-2 illustrates the general relationships among these classes of alternatives. A similar process operates with respect to retail outlet selection.[8]

One study examined the awareness and evoked sets across numerous product categories. Several results and strategic implications of this study are worth noting.

- The awareness set was always larger than the evoked set. That is, consumers know about more brands than they will seriously consider. And because awareness does not equal consideration and because consideration is necessary for a chance at being chosen, marketers are very concerned (once they have built sufficient awareness) about moving their

Categories of Decision Alternatives   FIGURE 15-2

brands into consumer evoked sets and must engage in persuasive messaging and other strategies to do so.

- The evoked set for some categories—for example, mouthwash and toothpaste—were basically one brand. This means that for categories, nominal decision making (choosing one brand repeatedly over time) is the norm. Later in the chapter we will discuss the use of disruption strategies for brands in this situation that are not in a consumer's evoked set.
- The evoked sets for some categories were somewhat large, but that may be due to variety seeking. For example, the evoked set for fast food was five brands. However, one can imagine that consumers are loyal to brands of fast-food restaurants *within* type, but they variety seek or otherwise switch across situations. So, McDonald's may be the hamburger alternative, KFC the chicken alternative, Pizza Hut the pizza alternative, Taco Bell the Mexican alternative, and so on.

Now let's apply Figure 15-2 to our laptop example. Again, you would start with an internal search. You might say to yourself, "Lenovo, Microsoft, Toshiba, Apple, Dell, Samsung, Acer, and HP all make notebook computers. After my brother's experience, I'd never buy Toshiba. I've heard good things about Lenovo, Apple, and Samsung. I think I'll check them out." Thus, the eight brands you thought of as potential solutions are your awareness set, and Figure 15-3 shows how these break out into the other three categories of decision alternatives.

FIGURE 15-3 Example of Decision Alternatives for Laptop Computers

Alternative Characteristics

To choose among the brands in the evoked set, the consumer compares them on relevant evaluative criteria. This process requires the consumer *to gather information about each brand on each pertinent evaluative criterion.* In our example of a computer purchase, you might collect information on the price, memory, processor, weight, screen clarity, and software package for each brand you are considering. In addition, emotional considerations relating to comfort, styling, and ease of use may factor in as well.

SOURCES OF INFORMATION

LO4

Refer again to our laptop computer example. We suggested that you might recall what you know about computers, check with friends and an online discussion board, consult *Consumer Reports* and read reviews in *PC Magazine* online, talk with sales personnel, or personally inspect several computers to collect relevant information. The following represent the five primary sources of information available to consumers:

- *Memory* of past searches, personal experiences, and low-involvement learning.
- *Personal sources,* such as friends, family, and others.
- *Independent sources,* such as magazines, consumer groups, and government agencies.
- *Marketing sources,* such as sales personnel, websites, and advertising.
- *Experiential sources,* such as inspection or product trial.

These sources are shown in Figure 15–4. Each of these sources has an offline, online, and mobile component.[9] As just one example, offline marketing sources such as TV advertising and brochures correspond to online banner ads and corporate websites, and mobile ads.

Internal information is the primary source used by most consumers most of the time (nominal and limited decision making). However, note that information in long-term memory was *initially* obtained from external sources. Thus, a consumer may resolve a consumption problem using only or mainly stored information. At some point, however, the individual acquired that information from an external source, such as direct product experience, friends, or low-involvement learning.

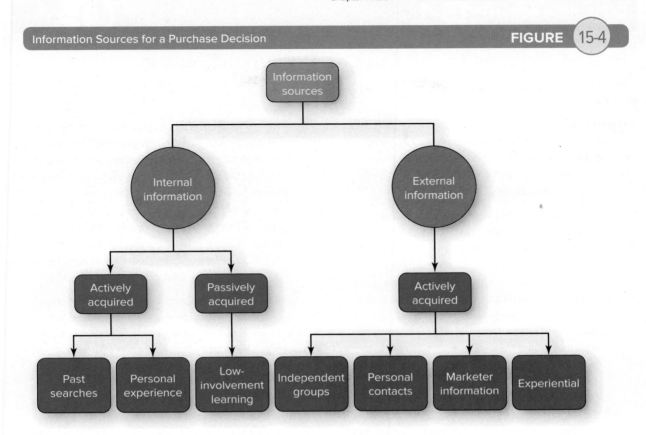

Information Sources for a Purchase Decision   FIGURE 15-4

Marketing-originated messages are only one of five potential information sources, and they are frequently reported to be of limited *direct* value in consumer decisions.[10] However, marketing activities influence all five sources. Thus, the characteristics of the product, the distribution of the product, and the promotional messages about the product provide the underlying or basic information available in the market. An independent source such as *Consumer Reports* bases its evaluation on the functional characteristics of the product, as do personal sources such as friends. Marketers are continually looking for ways to get their information channeled through nonmarketing sources. As we discussed in Chapter 7, product sampling to influencers (with appropriate disclosure) is just one means of getting the word out through nonmarketing channels.

In addition, although consumers may not use (or believe they use) advertising or other marketer-provided data as immediate input into many purchase decisions, there is no doubt that continual exposure to advertising frequently influences the perceived need for the product, the composition of the awareness and evoked sets, the evaluative criteria used, and beliefs about the performance levels of each brand.[11] As a consequence, the long-term *total* influence of advertising and other marketer-provided information on consumer decision making and sales can be substantial.

Internet Search

The Internet gives consumers unprecedented access to information. Global Internet usage continues to grow rapidly, and more than four billion people are online around the world. Asia (2 billion), Europe (705 million), Africa (453 million), and Latin America/Carribean (437 million) have the highest number of Internet users. North America has 346 million

From Stadiums to the Couch—Personalizing the Search Experience

The Internet has dramatically expanded the ability of consumers to search for information. Today, most companies go well beyond simple and *generic* product information by providing highly personalized information and information search experiences. Consider the following:[12]

- *Sports and Concert Venues.* Trying to find a seat for a concert or football game can be stressful, especially when searching for a ticket online. "Will I be able to see the performer from my seat? Or see my team score a touchdown?" are questions often asked by consumers, but not easily answered with the generic overhead stadium view found online. Consequently, consumers may abandon the search and not commit to the purchase. A highly customized search experience is now possible thanks to virtual seating technology used by many stadiums as well as Ticketmaster. IOMedia's Virtual Venue and Ballena Technologies' Seats3D, for example, allow sports and music fans to search for tickets at a specific venue and experience a three-dimensional view from any seat. With Virtual Venue, Ticketmaster's customers are more efficient in their search and ultimately make quicker purchases. And according to one college sports marketer, "The Seats3D tools have significantly increased our online customer service, helped brand our football facility as fan-friendly and increased ticket revenue."
- *Netflix.* Relaxing on the couch and watching Netflix may not be very relaxing if the consumer does not know what to choose from a catalog of over 5,500 titles. Netflix realizes that customers can be overwhelmed by so many options and has helped the search process through a personalization algorithm.

Netflix customizes the recommendations daily for each individual user with options like "because you watched this." Also, those who want to search beyond the 50 to 100 personalized recommendations now have access to Flixable, a user-friendly website that acts as a "Netflix search engine." Flixable's site is designed to help users easily search Netflix's extensive collection by genre, actor, or title. Users also can sort and filter alphabetically, by release date, or when added to the catalog.

Note how the technologies allow for search beyond *generic* product information by personalizing information to each customer. In the case of Ticketmaster, each consumer can "search" for just the right ticket via its interactive virtual seating tool, resulting in faster decisions and more sales. In the case of Netflix, recommendations are customized, and search through the extensive catalog, using Flixable, is now manageable. Personalizing information search is critical to a more positive and engaging information search experience. According to a Netflix executive,

"The biggest challenge for Netflix is: if you're tired and it's the end of the day, you could read a book or a magazine, you could go on Facebook, watch linear TV or watch Netflix. We want to make Netflix so engaging you keep choosing it."

Critical Thinking Questions

1. What is the difference between generic information and personalized information?
2. How does personalized information create greater customer engagement?
3. In general, what influence might online search have on the role of salespeople?

---

users, with 95 percent of the population online. Since 2000, growth was strongest for regions such as Africa, Middle East, Latin America, and Asia, where Internet usage as a percent of the total population is still relatively low. Asia overshadows other regions of the world in terms of current users and potential growth, in view of its population size (4.2 billion), growing middle class, and increased access to low-cost technology.[13] Consumer Insight 15–1 shows some of the various ways in which companies use the Internet to create an information search "experience" that is more engaging, easier, and faster, and extends the search environment to include virtual trial and interactive tools.

Nearly 90 percent of U.S. adults have used the Internet, and growth of new users has slowed considerably. Early on, Internet users were predominantly young, educated, white males. Today, the demographic characteristics of Internet users look much more like those of the population in general. The demographic factors with any real remaining influence are age (Internet usage decreases with age), education, and income (Internet usage increases with both education and income).[14] Perhaps not surprisingly, given this demographic information, seven of the top 10 reasons for nonuse of the Internet are related (directly and indirectly) to age, income, and educa-

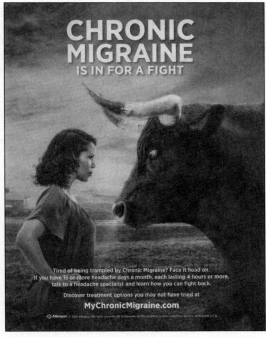

Source: Allergan

tion. These reasons, in order of importance, are (1) not interested, (2) no computer, (3) too difficult, (4) don't know how, (5) too old to learn, (6) don't have access, and (7) too expensive.[15]

The Internet is a major and often preferred avenue through which consumers search for information.[16] Consider the following:[17]

- *Online information is expected.* Most Internet users *expect* to find information about a product or brand of interest to them on a company's website.
- *Online information boosts offline sales.* Internet users are more likely to purchase a company's product offline if its website provides product-related information.
- *Online sources are viewed as valuable.* Corporate and third-party websites match or beat traditional TV and print advertising as an information source in many categories.
- *Online sources reduce the salesperson's role.* Internet users tend to require considerably less purchase assistance from a salesperson.

Not surprisingly, an important activity online, consuming over 20 minutes on average a day, is *using a search engine to find information.*[18] And seven of the top 20 activities on the Internet are tied to information search or purchase, as follows:[19]

Use search engine to find information	87%
Look for health-related information	83
Look for information about a hobby or interest	83
Research a product/service before buying it	78
Buy a product	66
Buy or make a travel reservation	66
Use an online classified ad or site	53

Source: Pew Internet & American Life Project, www.pewinternet.org.

It is important to note, however, that traditional media can be effective at guiding consumers' information search activities to company websites, as shown in the Allergan ad in Illustration 15-2.

Search engines such as Google, Yahoo, and Bing are important search tools for consumers. Online search prior to purchase is the norm for most Internet users. In fact, search engines are the number-one online shopping tool, followed by coupon sites, retailer e-mails, online reviews, and shopping comparison sites. Notice that all the tools listed are sources of some form of information and thus play a role in the information search and acquisition process. The influence of online search cannot be overestimated because[20]

- Ninety-four percent of online purchases are preceded by online search.
- Seventy-four percent of offline purchases are likely to be preceded by online search.
- Consumers who "pre-search" and are exposed to online ads spend 41 percent more in-store.

The nature of search terms used by consumers is critical for marketers to understand so that they can build these into their search marketing strategies. One study categorized search terms into *brand only* (retailer's brand), *generic* (general product-related terms), and *brand-item* (brand plus generic). As shown in Figure 15–5, most of the search leading up to the purchase was generic—that is, general product-related terms that did not include any of the retailers being tracked in the study. As you might expect, generic search dominated early in the search process (3 to 12 weeks out), while branded search dominated just prior to purchase.[21] *What strategic implications do these results hold for online marketers?*

Economic considerations are a major motivator of online search.[22] For example, car buyers who used the Internet were able to make decisions faster and get a better buy—on average by $741.[23] And coupon sites, which are increasingly popular, help consumers get better deals with ease. However, *information overload* (see Chapter 8) is a challenge on the Internet. General search engines are useful. However, more specialized services and tools

FIGURE 15-5   The Nature of Search Using Online Search Engines

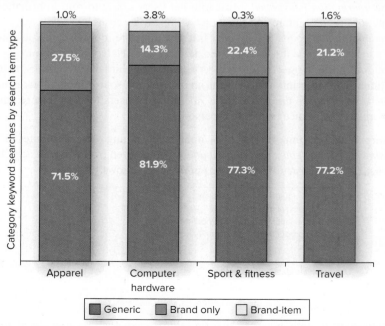

Source: "The Nature of Search Using Online Search Engines," *Search Before the Purchase* (New York: DoubleClick, February 2005), p. 2.

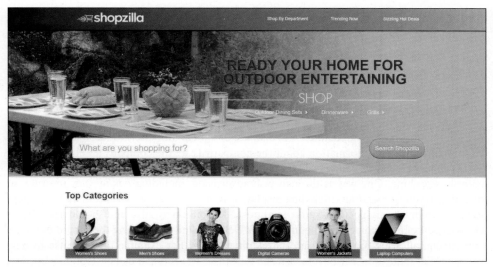

Source: Connexity, Inc

ILLUSTRATION 15-3

Online shopping services, such as Shopzilla, are increasingly popular as a way for consumers to deal with the enormous amount of information on the Internet.

continue to evolve to aid consumers more specifically in their search and decision making. Comparison shopping sites are a popular version of these services. Comparison sites often focus on price but can be designed to filter brands based on a broader set of evaluative criteria set by the consumer (see the Shopzilla site shown in Illustration 15-3). These services use **bots,** or software "robots," that do the shopping/searching for users, and are therefore often referred to as *shopping bots.*[24] Examples include BizRate.com, pricegrabber.com, and NexTag.com.

In addition to marketer-based information, the Internet contains personal sources of information in online communities as well as in the brand review features of many shopping services.[25] One study finds that consumer reviews are utilized heavily (72 percent) by consumers during online search for performance information.[26] As discussed in Chapter 7, WOM and personal sources are influential because of consumer trust in these sources.

Marketing Strategy and Information Search on the Internet   As the online population increasingly mirrors the general population, segmentation and target marketing are increasingly critical to online success. Consider the following:

> Where higher education marketing is different is the complexity of the audiences. A college . . . in particular has to please—if you are talking about the institutional website—alumni, donors, current students, prospective students, parents (and) the media. It's daunting sometimes.

Furman University decided that its general website was inadequate for admissions. So the university created a separate website to target high school students interested in the institution. The site was designed to target this tech-savvy group specifically, with virtual tours, message boards, and online student journals (with no editing by administration!).[27]

Obviously, universities are not the only ones who must deal with diverse consumer needs and characteristics. For example, consumers of various ethnicities in the United States often prefer and primarily use ethnic (versus mainstream) websites.[28] Global marketers must adapt as well. One study finds that Japanese websites use less individualistic approaches than do U.S. websites.[29]

More specifically, with respect to the Internet's role in information search and decision making, marketers have at least three major strategic issues to deal with:

1. How can they drive their information to consumers?
2. How can they drive consumers to their information?
3. How (if at all) can online selling be utilized or integrated with existing channels?

The first two issues are addressed in this section. The third is covered in Chapter 17. The first two issues are highly interrelated in that many of the strategies companies use to drive information to consumers (e.g., banner ads) also are designed, ultimately, to drive consumers to additional sources of information about the company (e.g., the company's website).

Driving a firm's information to consumers is important because consumers are not always actively searching. One way is through web advertising, including *banner ads.* Internet, or digital, marketing spending (including display, search, and behavioral placement) continues to grow rapidly. It is expected to grow to almost $120 billion by 2021 and should account for close to half of all media spending in the U.S.[30] Broadband is changing the nature of online advertising, allowing for more use of streaming media. For example, in response to data showing that many new car buyers visit the web prior to visiting a dealer, Honda placed its national TV ads for the Odyssey minivan on numerous websites. Viewers could click on the video or view it and ask for additional information. This goes beyond the traditional banner ad approach, and yet both drive the brand and information to the consumer.[31]

E-mail is also an important tool for pushing information to consumers. Many consumers see e-mail as a replacement for direct mail. However, spam (unsolicited e-mails) is not well received by consumers. Thus, *permission-based e-mail* (PBE), in which the consumer "opts in" to receive e-mail, is the norm for most reputable marketers. Even with PBE, marketers need to be careful—too many e-mails that lack relevance still may be viewed as spam.[32]

As we saw earlier, social media such as Facebook and Twitter can be used to drive a firm's information to consumers in a number of ways. Facebook allows for the delivery of ads to its members. Twitter has an ad option called promoted tweets, where a promotion code shows up on the tweet and then the tweet comes up in search results (see Chapter 7).[33]

Driving consumers to a firm's information is a daunting and important task given the explosion in the amount and sources of information on the web. Companies have websites to which they want consumers to go and return frequently.[34] Various strategies are possible. Offline media are one avenue for calling attention to a website. In fact, given that many younger consumers watch TV and surf the web simultaneously (see opener), research is demonstrating "upticks" in search volume on search engines such as Google *in real time,* based on traditional TV ads that attract consumer interest. That is, consumers see a TV ad for a product of interest, then use Google to search for more information. This behavioral outcome of traditional advertising online is an important step in driving consumers to a company's information and to the next stage in the decision process.[35]

Banner ads are another way to drive traffic to websites. While *click-through rates* (percentage who click through to the corporate website) are generally low, marketers are looking beyond immediate click-through to measures that include brand awareness, brand attitudes, and purchase intentions. A recent study found that these mobile advertising campaigns can increase favorable consumer attitudes and purchase intentions for high-involvement, utilitarian products.[36] And so the idea is that boosting awareness and attitudes will drive *long-term* website visits and purchases.

Website visits that occur as a result of *exposure* to an online ad but that do not occur at the time of exposure have been termed *view-throughs.* It is estimated that "half or more of the ad-related visits in a campaign are attributed to the view-through effect as opposed to direct clicks." And, beyond view-through, as online ads become more interactive, other metrics are possible. Mini Cooper used an interactive banner that allowed viewers to see various owner profiles. Useful metrics here would be the interaction rate (percent that interacted in some way with the ad such as paging through the owner profiles) and time spent with the ad.[37]

As you might expect, appropriate or targeted ad placement is helpful in increasing online ad performance across various outcomes including click-through rates. For example, Dolby ran interactive banners relating to thunder and the outdoors. The campaign did well overall but did markedly better (e.g., 60 percent higher click-through rate) when placed on the National Geographic site because of the higher relevance of these themes to the site's viewers.[38]

Social networking sites are also getting into the act. Facebook has ad-targeting features and can target based on the "Fan" status of a member, whereby ads are only delivered to Facebook members who have "liked" a given brand.[39] Given that relevance is a key driver of attention, interest, and engagement as measured by processing and click-throughs (Chapter 8), such personalized targeting can be extremely effective. Levi's used interactive videos placed in social media in China to tap the self-expression needs of urban youth. The interactive videos allowed users to tailor the experience through different destinations and plots, and were designed ultimately to "drive users" to key Levi's product information and images.[40]

Behavioral targeting is another form of targeting that is based not on what people say but what they actually do online. Specifically, **behavioral targeting** *involves tracking consumer click patterns on a website and using that information to decide on banner ad placement.*[41] Pepsi used behavioral targeting to promote Aquafina to consumers interested in healthy lifestyles. Online behavioral tracking helped them determine which consumers were the "healthy lifestyles" consumers, and then ads for Aquafina were delivered to those consumers across over 4,000 websites. The result was a 300 percent greater click-through rate for the targeted Aquafina campaign compared to their previous nontargeted campaigns. Again, the perceived relevance of the message to the target audience is a key factor to the success of behavioral targeting.[42] Concerns over privacy and transparency are driving efforts at industry self-regulation, which could or already do include "no-tracking lists" and privacy browsing features.

As we saw earlier, online consumers are heavy users of search engines. Not surprisingly, spending on search-related marketing efforts (including ads and search optimization activities discussed shortly) is the largest single category of digital marketing, and represents over 40 percent of all digital marketing spending.[43] Because search results are ordered and consumers often don't *drill down* beyond the first page of listings, keyword selection and other techniques relating to search engine optimization are critical for the firm in terms of getting its website the highest-priority listing for the most appropriate search terms. **Search engine optimization (SEO)** *involves techniques designed to ensure that a company's web pages "are accessible to search engines and focused in ways that help improve the chances they will be found."*[44]

SEO strategies are critical to Internet search success. One estimate is that the top five spots on a Google search can be worth $50 to $100 million per year depending on the industry and company. A recent report found that searching for the generic keyword "home repair" did not get The Home Depot in the top 10 listings. Rather, it came in at number 16 (and on page 2) behind such brands as Lowe's and This Old House. The problem, according to one expert, is that The Home Depot failed to place key "category-defining keywords [such as 'home repair'] in the URLs."[45] This is in line with our earlier discussion of the critical nature of generic terms in the consumer Internet search process. SEO relates to what is termed "organic" or natural search results. Paid or "sponsored" listings are also available through programs such as Google's Ads (formerly "Adwords") program, in which companies pay for "sponsored" listings for specific search terms.

Website design is also critical. While we will discuss this issue more in Chapter 17, it is clear that driving *ongoing and repeat* traffic to a website requires such factors as relevant and frequently updated content. Techniques can include product-related news features, user-related discussion forums, updates on new products and features, and so on. RSS (really simple syndication) feeds that pull information on an ongoing basis from various online sources can be used to keep sites relevant and current. Marketers also can offer opt-in e-mail updates, which can trigger site visits.[46]

Mobile Search

Mobile search and marketing appears to be the next major growth arena for firms. Roughly 95 percent of U.S. adults have a mobile phone, and 77 percent have a smartphone.[47] Not surprising, U.S. mobile advertising spending (including display, search, and messaging-based ads) has increased dramatically in the last decade and is estimated at $70 billion.[48] This growth can be attributed to the increased penetration of smartphones and to users' becoming more comfortable operating and using smartphones as an information, decision, and buying tool. A recent study of smartphone users by Experian highlighted seven segments, as follows:[49]

- *Prodigies* (5 percent) are constantly connected, mobile-centric tech trendsetters. They are 10 times more likely than the average smartphone owner to be interested in receiving ads on the phones, and seven times more likely to say they would buy the products in those ads.
- *Tribals* (13 percent) are hyperconnected, often with multiple devices, and strong influencers of others through social media.
- *Personals* (11 percent) are mobile-savvy and love their phone. They prefer connecting with friends through direct messaging than social media. Sixty percent are more likely than the average smartphone owner to actually purchase products advertised on their phone.
- *Pragmatists* (18 percent) are mobile professionals who manage home and work with their phone. They are less likely than average to purchase items they see advertised on their phone.
- *Browsers* (24 percent) are still learning to use their smartphone. They are more comfortable accessing online content through their mobile browser than through apps.
- *Occasionals* (11 percent) use their phone mostly to make calls, but they do play games or check the news and weather. They are more receptive to digital advertising on their personal computer.
- *Talkers* (13 percent) exhibit fairly light mobile use, using their phone mainly for verbal conversations and the occasional video call. Digital and mobile advertising is most effective to supplement campaigns run in traditional media.

Clearly these segments and their characteristics are important to marketers in relation to information search and product purchasing. In particular, the Prodigies and Personals are key users of search and buying features of cell phones and are open to mobile "push" marketing in the form of advertisements. Tribals seem to be worth pursuing because of their presence on social media and commanding influence.

One area of particular importance to marketers is local mobile search. **Local mobile search** is defined as *searches for information from a mobile device pertaining to the current (or future planned) geographic location of a consumer.* Google provides a useful illustration of this type of search and marketing efforts related to it. Punch the key words "Italian restaurant" into Google on your mobile phone and what you will get will be heavily skewed to "local" search results. That is, Google knows your location based on your phone's location and will deliver results that not only list Italian restaurants close to you, but also provide a map of how to get there, the phone number for each restaurant, and so on. You also could select alternate locations as when you are planning to go on a vacation and want to search for restaurants ahead of time. Google also can deliver relevant mobile banner ads to you through Google's Ads location-based targeting program.[50]

You may have noticed from the smartphone segment descriptions that some consumers are much more likely to use their phones for local mobile search. Pew Research finds that two of the top eight local search categories include search for (1) local restaurants and businesses and (2) local coupons and discounts. Clearly, "apps" for local information are a key strategic point that we will also return to later. Roughly 74 percent of U.S. adults access local information via their mobile devices including local mobile apps. As with Internet usage, the major demographic differences in local mobile search and app usage are age, education, and income, with local mobile search/app usage decreasing with age and increasing with education and income.[51]

Marketing Strategy and Mobile Search

Mobile browsers and apps appear to be a critical part of local mobile search strategies. Examine Figure 15-6. Notice how local mobile search is changing how consumers find stores and brands, and also how they search for information. Consumers historically have

FIGURE 15-6

Mobile Local Search and Marketing Strategy

Mobile Users Engage in the Following:

Retail App Strategies

Locate a store nearby to purchase a specific product

Look up information online about product while shopping in a store

Compare store and online prices while shopping in a store

Find or redeem a coupon or coupon code

"Location Finder" Apps (e.g., Google maps)

"Streamlined" Search Functionality (e.g., barcode scanner)

Mobile "Loyalty Card" or App (e.g., purchase tracker)

searched for information that was available "within" a store while they were at the store and searched for information "outside" of the store either prior to or after their store search. No longer is that the case, with many mobile users searching for information "outside" the store while shopping in the store. This gives retailers and in-store sales personnel somewhat less control over the shopping experience and puts the consumer more in the driver's seat. Clearly, however, retailers must figure out how to be a part of this increasing search pattern and design or participate in apps and programs that resonate with consumers. Walmart was reluctant to share prices with price-matching apps at first, but has relented.

Many useful search and shopping apps exist. Consider Skyscanner, which provides mobile search for inexpensive flights via an app. According to its website:

> Skyscanner is a metasearch engine, meaning that we search hundreds of airlines, hotel, car rental and travel agency websites to bring all the options in one place. In other words, we're a comparison website. We think this makes booking your travel easier, because it helps you find the best deal for you. We know that everyone is different, and every trip is different, too. Sometimes we want the cheapest flight, sometimes the fastest; sometimes we book a minivan to Orlando and sometimes a convertible along the California coast. Filters, quality ratings, reviews . . . we develop features with you, the traveler, in mind.[52]

Such functionality, ease, and possible search benefits make it clear why this and other apps are becoming increasingly popular with travelers, and shoppers. Why go from store to store to make sure you are getting the lowest price when Shopsavvy will conduct the search for you while you are in the store from your mobile phone?[53] Figure 15–6 provides additional directions for thinking about the kinds of local mobile apps that consumers may want.

Consumer Insight 15-2 examines additional strategic considerations in the mobile marketing arena.

AMOUNT OF EXTERNAL INFORMATION SEARCH

LO5

Marketers are particularly interested in external information search, as this provides them with direct access to the consumer. How much external information search do consumers actually undertake? Nominal and limited decision making (e.g., convenience goods such as soft drinks) involve little or no external search by definition. Therefore, this section focuses on major purchases such as appliances, professional services, and automobiles where we might expect substantial amounts of direct external search prior to purchases. However, across various measures (stores visited, brands considered, sources utilized, total overall search), one observation emerges: *external information search is skewed toward limited search, with the greatest proportion of consumers performing little external search immediately prior to purchase.* Consider the following results:

- Surveys of *shopping behavior* have shown a significant percentage of all durable purchases are made after the consumer has visited only one store.[54]
- Although the *number of alternative brands or models considered* tends to increase as the price of the product increases, various studies show small consideration sets as follows: (1) nearly half of watch purchasers considered only one brand *and* one model; (2) 27 percent of major appliance buyers considered only one brand;[55] and (3) while Internet use increased automobile search, online searchers still only examined three models.[56]

Push and Pull Strategies in Mobile Marketing

Mobile marketing strategies can be viewed similarly to those on the Internet—that is, driving information to consumers (push strategies) and driving consumers to information (pull strategies).[57]

Mobile Push. Driving information to consumers on mobile devices can involve a variety of strategies. One strategy that will continue to grow as more consumers use mobile Internet is ads placed on mobile web pages. As with computer-based approaches, mobile ads can be targeted to be most relevant to the specific mobile content being viewed. Another strategy is permission-based or opt-in text messaging promotions. According to a media consulting group, the best text message programs involve

- Building an "opt-in" database—this can be done through traditional and e-mail marketing in which consumers are asked to text in or register at a specific website.
- Developing the text-message "ad"—this should include (a) a hook relating to why the individual is being contacted; (b) a call to action, such as entering a code to get a discount; and (c) an "opt-out" option.
- Rolling out the campaign—this involves delivering the text promotion to those on the opt-in list.

Adidas used a variation of this approach as sponsor for the NBA All-Star week. It had game information, store events, athlete appearances, and shoe releases as part of its promotions. Consumers opted in and then could access all the promotional materials at any time during the week by texting "originals."

Mobile Pull. Driving consumers to information on mobile devices also can involve a number of strategies. One is to use traditional media to build awareness about a mobile site or promotional event. AT&T held a mobile contest on U.S. college campuses for a free Dave Matthews Band concert to the school that could generate the most "invitations" sent through text messaging for the band to play at their school. To generate awareness and drive students to its mobile space, AT&T blanketed college campuses with posters telling students to "Text DMB to 959" or "visit ATTBLUEROOM.COM to enter." As we have seen, mobile search is another important option. Mobile Internet use is increasing rapidly and the functionality and geo-targeting capabilities of providers such as Google and Yahoo allow marketers to drive traffic not only to traditional websites and mobile content, but also to local restaurants and retailers.

Critical Thinking Questions

1. With cell or smartphones even less easily controlled and monitored than home computers, what ethical and regulatory issues are raised regarding mobile marketing to children?

2. Beyond the approaches discussed above, what other mobile marketing approaches are emerging? Are they effective? Explain.

3. What challenges do marketers face as they have to create campaigns that span mobile, Internet, and traditional media?

- In terms of *total overall search,* the following classification scheme can be used: (1) nonsearchers—little or no search, (2) limited-information searchers—low to moderate search, and (3) extended-information searchers—high search. Eight separate studies spanning almost 50 years (1955 to 2003), multiple products and services (appliances, automobiles, and professional services), and two countries (America and Australia) show remarkable consistency in terms of the total external information search undertaken—namely, extended searchers only account for between seven and 20 percent of buyers.[58]

The following section tries to explain why, even for high-involvement products and services, external search immediately prior to purchases is often low.

COSTS VERSUS BENEFITS OF EXTERNAL SEARCH

Buyers appear to weigh the benefits of search against the costs they incur. Search benefits include such aspects as lower price, higher quality, greater comfort with purchase, and so on. Search costs include time; money; hassle; the opportunity costs of other, more enjoyable forgone activities; and so on. All else equal, greater perceived benefits increase search, while greater perceived costs reduce search. When buyers perceive that the next brand (or store, or bit of information) will cost them more than it will benefit them, they stop searching. On the benefits side, given ongoing search and incidental learning, as discussed earlier, the amount of accumulated knowledge can be substantial for many consumers and thus lower the benefits of search *just prior to purchase.* On the costs side, the Internet can greatly lower search costs. When it does, it increases search and leads to better consumer decisions and a more enjoyable shopping experience.[59]

In this section, we examine four basic types of factors that influence the expected benefits and perceived costs of search both online and offline: *market characteristics, product characteristics, consumer characteristics,* and *situation characteristics* (see Table 15-1).[60]

Market Characteristics

Market characteristics (or, more accurately, consumer perceptions of them) include the number of alternatives, price range, store distribution, and information availability.[61] Obviously, the greater the *number of alternatives* (products, stores, brands) available to resolve a particular problem, the more external search there is likely to be. At the extreme, there is no need to search for information in the face of a complete monopoly such as utilities or driver's licenses. However, too many brands or too many noncomparable models across stores can frustrate consumer search efforts and lead to lower search or search within one store. Some marketers strategically develop a large number of models so that key accounts can have exclusive models and avoid direct price competition with other retailers on those exact models.[62] *What ethical concerns are raised by this practice?*

The *perceived range of prices* among equivalent brands in a product class is a major factor in stimulating external search. For example, shopping 36 retail stores in Tucson for five popular-branded toys produced a total low cost of $51.27 and a total high cost of $105.95. Clearly, efficient shopping for those products in that market would provide a significant financial gain. Pricing strategies such as price matching can affect consumer price perceptions. One study suggests that consumers interpret such policies as signaling lower prices, which, under high search costs, yields less search.[63] It appears that the percentage savings available from shopping may be as important as the dollar amount. The chance to save $50 when purchasing a $200 item appears to motivate more search than is the case when purchasing a $5,000 item.[64] This relates to the perceptual relativity discussed in Chapter 8.

Store distribution—the number, location, and distances between retail stores in the market—affects the number of store visits a consumer will make before purchase. Because store visits take time, energy, and, in many cases, money, a close proximity of stores often will increase this aspect of external search.[65]

In general, *information availability,* including format, is directly related to information use.[66] However, too much information can cause information overload and the use of less information. In addition, readily available information tends to produce learning over time, which may reduce the need for additional external information immediately prior to a purchase.[67]

Factors Affecting External Search Immediately Prior to Purchase	TABLE 15-1

Influencing Factor	Increasing the Influencing Factor Causes External Search to:
I Market Characteristics	
A. Number of alternatives	Increase
B. Price range	Increase
C. Store concentration	Increase
D. Information availability	Increase
1. Advertising	
2. Point-of-purchase	
3. Websites	
4. Sales personnel	
5. Packaging	
6. Experienced customers	
7. Independent sources	
II. Product characteristics	
A. Price	Increase
B. Differentiation	Increase
C. Positive products	Increase
III. Consumer characteristics	
A. Learning and experience	Decrease
B. Shopping orientation	Mixed
C. Social status	Increase
D. Age and household life cycle	Mixed
E. Product involvement	Mixed
F. Perceived risk	Increase
IV. Situation characteristics	
A. Time availability	Increase
B. Purchase for self	Decrease
C. Pleasant surroundings	Increase
D. Social surroundings	Mixed
E. Physical/mental energy	Increase

Product Characteristics

Perceived product *differentiation*—feature and quality variation across brands—is associated with increased external search.

In addition, consumers appear to enjoy shopping for *positive products*—those whose acquisition results in positive reinforcement (e.g., flowers, sports equipment). In contrast, shopping for *negative products*—those whose primary benefit is negative reinforcement, or the removal of an unpleasant condition (e.g., life insurance, auto repairs)—is viewed as less pleasant. All else equal, consumers engage in more external search for positive products.[68]

Consumer Characteristics

A variety of consumer characteristics affect perceptions of expected benefits, search costs, and the need to carry out a particular level of external information search.[69] As described earlier, the first step a consumer normally takes in response to a problem or opportunity is a search of memory for an appropriate solution. If the consumer finds a solution that he or she is confident is satisfactory, external search is unlikely.[70] However, overconfidence can lead to inadequate search and poor choices. It also can make it harder for companies to reposition their brands when consumers wrongly assume they "know" about the brand.[71]

A satisfying *experience* with a particular brand is a positive reinforcing process. It increases the probability of a repeat purchase of that brand and decreases the likelihood of external search.[72] However, at least some familiarity with a product class is necessary for external search to occur. For example, external search prior to purchasing a new automobile is high for consumers who have a high level of *general knowledge about cars* and low for those who have a substantial level of knowledge about existing brands.[73] Thus, consumers facing a completely unfamiliar product category may lack sufficient general knowledge to conduct an external search.

Consumers tend to form general approaches or patterns of external search. These general approaches are termed *shopping orientations*.[74] For example, some individuals engage in extensive ongoing information search because they are market mavens, as described in Chapter 7. This orientation would generally reduce the need to search *just prior to a purchase* as adequate existing knowledge would exist. Other orientations would have different effects.

External search tends to increase with various measures of *social status* (education, occupation, and income), though middle-income individuals search more than those at higher or lower levels. *Age* of the shopper is inversely related to information search. External search appears to decrease as the age of the shopper increases. This may be explained in part by increased learning and product familiarity gained with age. New households and individuals moving into new stages of the *household life cycle* have a greater need for external information than established households.

Consumers who are *highly involved with a product category* generally seek information relevant to the product category on an ongoing basis.[75] This ongoing search and the knowledge base it produces may reduce their need for external search immediately before a purchase, although variety-seeking needs can override this effect.[76]

The *perceived risk* associated with unsatisfactory product performance, either instrumental or symbolic, increases information search prior to purchase.[77] Higher perceived risk is associated with increased search and greater reliance on personal sources of information and personal experiences. Perceived risk can be situational, such as the higher risk felt when buying wine for a dinner party versus for personal consumption at home. Risk also can be perceived as high when a consumer has little prior purchase experience in the product category, in which case information search may help reduce perceived risk.[78] We will discuss perceived risk further in Chapter 17.

Situation Characteristics

As indicated in Chapter 13, situational variables can have a major impact on search behavior. For example, recall that one of the primary reactions of consumers to crowded store conditions is to minimize external information search. *Temporal perspective* is probably the most important situational variable with respect to search behavior. As the time available to solve a particular consumer problem decreases, so does the amount of external information search.[79]

Gift-giving situations *(task definition)* tend to increase perceived risk, which, as we have seen, increases external search. Likewise, multiple-item purchase tasks such as buying a bike and a bike rack or several items for a meal produce increased levels of information search.[80] Shoppers with limited physical or emotional energy *(antecedent state)* will search for less information than others. Pleasant *physical surroundings* increase the tendency to search for information, at least *within* that outlet. *Social surroundings* can increase or decrease search, depending on the nature of the social setting (see Chapter 13 for a more complete discussion).

MARKETING STRATEGIES BASED ON INFORMATION SEARCH PATTERNS

Sound marketing strategies take into account the nature of information search engaged in by the target market prior to purchase. Two dimensions of search are particularly appropriate: the type of decision influences on the level of search and the nature of the evoked set influences on the direction of the search. Table 15–2 illustrates a strategy matrix based on these two dimensions. This matrix suggests the six marketing strategies discussed in the following sections. As you will see, although there is considerable overlap between the strategies, each has a unique thrust.

LO6

Maintenance Strategy

If the brand is purchased habitually by the target market, the marketer's strategy is to maintain that behavior. This requires consistent attention to product quality, distribution (avoiding out-of-stock situations), and a reinforcement advertising strategy. In addition, the marketer must defend against the disruptive tactics of competitors. Thus, it needs to maintain product development and improvements and to counter short-term competitive strategies, such as coupons, point-of-purchase displays, or rebates.

Morton salt and Del Monte canned vegetables have large repeat purchaser segments that they have successfully maintained. Budweiser, Marlboro, and Crest have large brand-loyal purchaser segments. They have successfully defended their market positions against assaults by major competitors in recent years. In contrast, tobacco company Liggett & Myers lost 80 percent of its market share when it failed to engage in maintenance advertising.[81] Quality-control problems caused Schlitz beer to lose substantial market share.

The Purina ONE ad in Illustration 15–4 shows the use of a maintenance strategy against the challenge of competitors. Note that the ad stresses the improvements to the product.

Disrupt Strategy

If the brand is not part of the evoked set and the target market engages in nominal decision making, the marketer's first task is to *disrupt* the existing decision pattern. This is a difficult task because the consumer does not seek external information or even consider alternative brands before a purchase. Low-involvement learning over time could generate a positive product position for the brand, but this alone would be unlikely to shift behavior.

In the long run, a major product improvement accompanied by attention-attracting advertising could shift the target market into a more extensive form of decision making. In the short run, attention-attracting advertising aimed specifically at breaking habitual decision making can be successful. This advertising might be targeted via online and social media

Marketing Strategies Based on Information Search Patterns			TABLE 15-2
	Target Market Decision-Making Pattern		
Position	**Nominal Decision Making (no search)**	**Limited Decision Making (limited search)**	**Extended Decision Making (extensive search)**
Brand in evoked set	Maintenance strategy	Capture strategy	Preference strategy
Brand not in evoked set	Disrupt strategy	Intercept strategy	Acceptance strategy

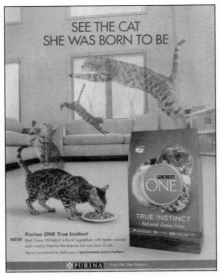

Source: Nestlé Group

as well with a strong but simple benefits-based approach. Free samples, coupons, rebates, and tie-in sales are common approaches to disrupting nominal decision making. Thus, participation in local mobile coupon app programs could be helpful. Likewise, striking package designs and point-of-purchase displays may disrupt a habitual purchase sequence.[82] Comparative advertising also is often used for this purpose.

The Neutrogena ad in Illustration 15–5 is an example of a disrupt strategy. The ad tries to convince consumers to change to the advertised brand based on several key benefits.

Capture Strategy

Limited decision making generally involves a few brands that are evaluated on only a few criteria, such as price or availability. Much of the information search occurs at the point of purchase or in readily available media prior to purchase. If the brand is one given this type of consideration by the target market, the marketer's objective is to capture as large a share of the purchases as practical.

Because these consumers engage in limited search, the marketer needs to know where they search and what information they are looking for. In general, the marketer will want to supply information, often on price and availability, on its website, on mobile apps, in local media including efforts related to local mobile search, and at the point of purchase through

Source: Johnson & Johnson Consumer Inc

displays and adequate shelf space. The marketer also will be concerned with maintaining consistent product quality and adequate distribution.

Intercept Strategy

If the target market engages in limited decision making and the brand is not part of the evoked set, the objective will be to intercept the consumer during the search for information on the brands in the evoked set or during general search for related information. Again, the emphasis will be on local media with cooperative advertising and at the point of purchase with displays, shelf space, package design, and so forth. Coupons also can be effective. The marketer will have to place considerable emphasis on attracting the consumers' attention because they will not be seeking information on the brand. The behavioral targeting strategy used by Snapple on a women's online community website is a great example of an online intercept strategy. As one ad executive stated:

> The big trick with this product was changing [the audience's perception] of Snapple-a-Day from an on-the-go, quirky product to something that has real health benefits for women and that has to be more of a planned purchase.[83]

The promotion shown in the Scrubbing Bubbles ad in Illustration 15–6 would be effective as part of a capture or intercept strategy.

In addition to the strategies mentioned above, low-involvement learning, product improvements, and free samples can be used to move the brand into the target market's evoked set.

Preference Strategy

Extended decision making with the brand in the evoked set requires a preference strategy. Because extended decision making generally involves several brands, many attributes, and a number of information sources, a simple capture strategy may not be adequate. Instead, the marketer needs to structure an information campaign that will result in the brand being preferred by members of the target market.

The first step is a strong position on those attributes important to the target market.[84] This will be discussed in considerable detail in Chapter 16. Next, information must be provided in all the appropriate sources. This may require extensive advertising to groups or influential online participants (e.g., bloggers) who will recommend it to others (e.g., druggists for over-the-counter drugs, veterinarians, and county agents for agricultural products). Independent groups should be encouraged to test the brand, and sales personnel should be

Source: S.C. Johnson & Son, Inc.

ILLUSTRATION 15-6

The Scrubbing Bubbles ad shown here reflects an intercept strategy in that it gives consumers an immediate incentive to purchase its brand.

Source: Honda Motor Co., Ltd.

provided detailed information on the brand's attributes. In addition, it may be wise to provide the sales personnel with extra motivation (e.g., extra commissions paid by the manufacturer) to recommend the product. Point-of-purchase displays and pamphlets also should be available. A well-designed website is essential.

Illustration 15–7 shows Honda's website is part of an effective preference strategy. It assumes an involved search, provides detailed information relative to multiple product attributes, and so on.

Acceptance Strategy

Acceptance strategy is similar to preference strategy. However, it is complicated by the fact that the target market is not seeking information about the brand. Therefore, in addition to the activities involved in the preference strategy described above, the marketer must attract the consumers' attention or otherwise motivate them to learn about the brand. This can be difficult, but various automakers over the years have gone as far as to pay customers to test drive their cars (Chrysler) or loan their cars to opinion leaders (Ford) in an effort to move their brand into consumer consideration sets by encouraging trial and/or positive WOM.

The Internet can play an important role in an acceptance strategy. Because keyword searches prior to a purchase tend to be generic, this opens up important opportunities for companies that are not in the evoked set to engage in search engine optimization strategies to give their brand exposure to the consumer during the decision process—hopefully to the point of moving the brand into consumers' evoked sets. Obviously, a well-designed website is a critical part of this strategy.

Long-term advertising designed to enhance low-involvement learning is another useful technique for gaining acceptance. Extensive advertising with strong emphasis on attracting attention also can be effective. The primary objective of these two approaches is not to sell the brand; rather, the objective is to move the brand into the evoked set. Then, when a purchase situation arises, the consumer will seek additional information on this brand.

SUMMARY

SMARTBOOK

LO1: Discuss internal and external information search and their role in different decision types.

Following problem recognition, consumers typically engage in some form and amount of search. *Internal search* is accessing relevant information from long-term memory to be used to determine if a satisfactory solution is known, what the characteristics of potential solutions are, what the appropriate ways to compare solutions are, and so forth. If a resolution is not reached through internal search, then the search process is focused on external information relevant to solving the problem. This is *external search,* which can involve independent sources, personal sources, marketer-based information, and product experience. Internal information tends to dominate in nominal decision making, whereas external search tends to dominate in extended decision making. For limited decision making, external search can play a moderate role in some instances.

LO2: Summarize the types of information consumers search for.

Information may be sought on (1) the appropriate *evaluative criteria* for the solution of the problem, (2) the existence of various *alternative solutions,* and (3) the *performance* of each alternative solution on each evaluative criterion.

LO3: Describe the categories of decision alternatives relating to the evoked set.

From the set of all possible alternatives that could solve a consumer problem, the following are the categories of decision alternatives: alternatives that consumers are aware of *(awareness set),* alternatives that consumers are aware of and view in a neutral manner *(inert set),* alternatives that consumers are aware of and view negatively *(inept set),* and alternatives that consumers are aware of and view positively *(evoked set).* The evoked set (also called the *consideration set*) represents the alternatives that the consumer seeks additional information on during the remaining internal and external search process. Therefore, marketers are first concerned with making sure their brand is in the awareness set. But, because awareness does not equal consideration and because

consideration is necessary for a chance at being chosen, marketers are also very concerned about moving their brands into consumer evoked sets and must engage in persuasive messaging and other strategies to do so.

LO4: Discuss available information sources and the role of Internet and mobile search.

Consumer internal information (information stored in memory) may have been actively acquired in previous searches and personal experiences, or it may have been passively acquired through low-involvement learning. In addition to their own *memory,* consumers can seek information from the following four major types of external sources: (1) *personal sources,* such as friends and family; (2) *independent sources,* such as consumer groups, paid professionals, and government agencies; (3) *marketing sources,* such as sales personnel and advertising; and (4) *experiential sources,* such as direct product inspection or trial. Each of these sources of information can be accessed through the Internet or mobile devices. Internet and mobile search options are dramatically changing the way in which consumers search for information prior to a purchase and provide marketers with many unique opportunities and challenges.

LO5: Discuss the major cost–benefit factors driving the amount of external search.

Explicit external information search *after* problem recognition is often limited. It is often suggested that consumers generally should engage in relatively extensive external search prior to purchasing an item in order to reap higher benefits of the purchase such as higher brand quality or lower price. However, this view ignores the fact that information search is not free. It takes time, energy, and money and often can require giving up more desirable activities. Therefore, consumers should engage in external search only to the extent that the expected benefits, such as a lower price or a more satisfactory purchase, outweigh the expected costs. Numerous aspects affect the perceived costs and/or benefits of search. They can be *market characteristics* (e.g., number of brands), *product characteristics* (e.g., price), *consumer characteristics* (e.g., prior search and learning), and *situational characteristics* (e.g., time availability).

LO6: Summarize the marketing strategies based on information search patterns.

Sound marketing strategy takes into account the nature of information search engaged in by the target market. The level of search and the brand's position in or out of the evoked set are two key dimensions. Based on these two dimensions, the following six potential information strategies are suggested: (1) *maintenance,* (2) *disrupt,* (3) *capture,* (4) *intercept,* (5) *preference,* and (6) *acceptance.*

KEY TERMS

Awareness set 537
Behavioral targeting 547
Bots 545
Consideration set 537
Evoked set 537

External search 536
Inept set 537
Inert set 537
Internal search 536
Local mobile search 548

Ongoing search 536
Search engine optimization
   (SEO) 547

REVIEW QUESTIONS

1. When does *information search* occur? What is the difference between internal and external information search?

2. What kind of information is sought in an external search for information?

3. What are *evaluative criteria* and how do they relate to information search?

4. How does a consumer's *awareness set* influence information search?

5. What roles do the *evoked set, inert set,* and *inept set* play in a consumer's information search?

6. What are the primary sources of information available to consumers?

7. What is *behavioral targeting?*

8. What is *search engine optimization?*

9. What is *local mobile search?*

10. How do nonsearchers, limited-information searchers, and extended-information searchers differ in their search for information?

11. What factors might influence the search effort of consumers who are essentially one-stop shoppers? How do these factors differ in terms of how they influence limited-information searchers and extended-information searchers?

12. What factors have to be considered in the total cost of the information search? How might these factors be different for different consumers?

13. Explain how different *market characteristics* affect information search.

14. How do different *consumer characteristics* influence a consumer's information search effort?

15. How do *product characteristics* influence a consumer's information search effort?

16. How do *situational characteristics* influence a consumer's information search effort?

17. Describe the information search characteristics that should lead to each of the following strategies:
   a. Maintenance
   b. Disrupt
   c. Capture
   d. Intercept
   e. Preference
   f. Acceptance

18. Describe each of the strategies listed in Question 17.

DISCUSSION QUESTIONS

19. Pick a product/brand that you believe would require each strategy in Table 15–2 (six products in total). Justify your selection. Develop a specific marketing strategy for each (six strategies in total).

20. Which product classes are most likely to have evoked sets of one? Relate this to the type of decision process.

21. Use a shopping service such as NexTag to help you choose a brand of coffeemaker. In what way does it help you form your evoked or consideration set? Is information overload a problem? Explain.

22. Do you have a local mobile search app? If so, what is your evaluation of it? If no, why not?

23. What information sources do you think students on your campus use when acquiring the items listed below? Consider the various sources listed in Figure 15–4 in developing your answer. Do you think there will be individual differences? Why?
    a. Movies
    b. Restaurants
    c. Apartment
    d. Computer
    e. Fitness equipment
    f. A charity contribution
    g. Dress clothes
    h. Smartphones

24. What factors contribute to the size of the awareness set, evoked set, inert set, and inept set?

25. Discuss factors that may contribute to external information search and factors that act to reduce external search for information before purchase or adoption of the following:
    a. Car insurance
    b. International travel
    c. Exercise club
    d. Formal wear
    e. Eye wear
    f. Counseling services

26. Is it ever in the best interest of a marketer to encourage potential customers to carry out an extended prepurchase search? Why or why not?

27. What implications for marketing strategy does Figure 15–2 suggest?

28. What implications for online marketing strategy does Figure 15–5 suggest?

29. What role, if any, should the government play in ensuring that consumers have easy access to relevant product information? How should it accomplish this?

30. Respond to the questions in Consumer Insight 15–1.

31. Describe a recent purchase in which you engaged in extensive search and one in which you did little prepurchase search. What factors caused the difference?

32. What is your awareness set, evoked set, inert set, and inept set for the following? In what ways, if any, do you think your sets will differ from those of the average member of your class? Why?
    a. Automobiles
    b. Energy drinks
    c. Car insurance providers
    d. Jewelry stores
    e. Book stores
    f. Laptop computers
    g. Restaurants

APPLICATION ACTIVITIES

33. Develop an appropriate questionnaire and complete Question 23 using information from five students not in your class. Prepare a report discussing the marketing implications of your findings.

34. For the same products listed in Question 32, ask five students to list all the brands they are aware of in each product category. Then have them indicate which ones they might buy (evoked set), which ones they are indifferent toward (inert set), and which brands they strongly dislike and would not purchase (inept set). What are the marketing implications of your results?

35. Develop a short questionnaire designed to measure the information search consumers engage in prior to purchasing an expensive recreational or entertainment item or service. Your questionnaire should include measures of types of information sought, as well as sources that provide this information. Also include measures of the relevant consumer characteristics that might influence information search, as well as some measure of past experience with the products. Then interview two recent purchasers of each product, using the questionnaire you have developed. Analyze each consumer's response and classify each consumer

in terms of information search. What are the marketing implications of your results?

36. For each strategy in Table 15-2, find one brand that appears to be following that strategy. Describe in detail how it is implementing the strategy.

37. Develop a questionnaire to determine which products college students view as positive and which they view as negative. Measure the shopping effort associated with each type. Explain your overall results and any individual differences you find.

REFERENCES

1. The opener is based on G. Hayes, "Rebooting 2nd Screen & Social TV: Interactive TV 3.0," *Personalizemedia,* May 29, 2013, www.personalizemedia.com/rebooting-2nd-screen-social-tv-interactive-tv-3-0/, accessed August 29, 2014; A. A. Newman, "Like That Vase on the TV? Click Your Phone to Buy It," *New York Times,* March 17, 2014, www.nytimes.com/2014/03/18/business/media/like-that-vase-on-the-tv-click-your-phone-to-buy-it.html?_r50, accessed August 29, 2014; A. Satariano, "Shazam's TV Strategy," *Bloomberg Businessweek,* July 5, 2012, www.businessweek.com/articles/2012-07-05/shazams-tv-strategy, accessed August 29, 2014; M. Ballve, "Chart of the Day: The Beginnings of Second Screen Commerce," *Business Insider,* February 11, 2013, www.businessinsider.com/chart-of-the-day-mobile-activity-2013-2, accessed August 29, 2014; T. Spangler, "TV Viewers Aren't Thrilled with Second-Screen Synchronized Content, Study Finds," *Variety,* January 9, 2014, http://variety.com/2014/digital/news/tv-viewers-arent-thrilled-with-second-screen-synchronized-content-study-finds-1201040757/, accessed August 29, 2014; C. Thompson, "10 Super Bowl Ads That Rocked the Second Screen Experience," *Invoca,* February 10, 2016, https://blog.invoca.com/10-super-bowl-ads-that-rocked-second-screen-experience/, accessed July 9, 2018; B. Ho, "The Long and Short of Second Screen Marketing Opportunities," *Criteo,* November 14, 2017, www.criteo.com/insights/second-screen-marketing-opportunities/, accessed July 9, 2018; J. Langdon, "The 'Second Screen' Is Actually First: The Challenge for TV Advertisers," *Brand Quarterly,* February 8, 2018, www.brandquarterly.com/second-screen-actually-first-challenge-tv-advertisers, accessed July 9, 2018; company websites for HSN and QVC.

2. G. Punji and R. Brookes, "Decision Constraints and Consideration-Set Formation in Consumer Durables," *Psychology & Marketing,* August 2001, pp. 843–63.

3. An outstanding discussion of the trade-off consumers make between memory-based decisions (internal search) and external search is in J. R. Bettman, M. F. Luce, and J. W. Payne, "Constructive Consumer Choice Processes," *Journal of Consumer Research,* December 1998, pp. 187–217.

4. See, e.g., R. Smith and B. Deppa, "Two Dimensions of Attribute Importance," *Journal of Consumer Marketing* 26, no. 1 (2009), pp. 28–38.

5. S. S. Posavac, D. M. Sanbonmatsu, and E. A. Ho, "The Effects of the Selective Consideration of Alternatives on Consumer Choice and Attitude-Decision Consistency," *Journal of Consumer Psychology* 12, no. 3 (2002), pp. 203–13; T. Erdem and J. Swait, "Brand Credibility, Brand Consideration, and Choice," *Journal of Consumer Research,* June 2004, pp. 191–98; M. Paulssen and

R. P. Bagozzi, "A Self-Regulatory Model of Consideration Set Formation," *Psychology & Marketing,* October 2005, pp. 785–812; J. R. Hauser et al., "Disjunctions of Conjunctions, Cognitive Simplicity, and Consideration Sets," *Journal of Marketing Research,* June 2010, pp. 485–96.

6. E. M. Felcher, P. Malaviya, and A. L. McGill, "The Role of Taxonomic and Goal-Derived Product Categorization in, within, and across Category Judgments," *Psychology & Marketing,* August 2001, pp. 865–87.

7. P. Aurier, S. Jean, and J. L. Zaichkowsky, "Consideration Set Size and Familiarity with Usage Context," in *Advances in Consumer Research,* vol. 27, ed. S. J. Hoch and R. J. Meyer (Provo, UT: Association for Consumer Research, 2000), pp. 307–13; K. K. Desai and W. D. Hoyer, "Descriptive Characteristics of Memory-Based Consideration Sets," *Journal of Consumer Research,* December 2000, pp. 309–23.

8. R. R. Brand and J. J. Cronin, "Consumer-Specific Determinants of the Size of Retail Choice Sets," *Journal of Services Marketing* 11, no. 1 (1997), pp. 19–38.

9. L. R. Klein and G. T. Ford, "Consumer Search for Information in the Digital Age," *Journal of Interactive Marketing,* Summer 2003, pp. 29–49; B. T. Ratchford, M.-S. Lee, and D. Talukdar, "The Impact of the Internet on Information Search for Automobiles," *Journal of Marketing Research,* May 2003, pp. 193–209; H. Li, T. Daugherty, and F. Biocca, "The Role of Virtual Experience in Consumer Learning," *Journal of Consumer Psychology* 13, no. 4 (2003), pp. 395–407; A. E. Schlosser, "Experience Products in the Virtual World," *Journal of Consumer Research,* September 2003, pp. 184–98; D. A. Griffith and Q. Chen, "The Influence of Virtual Direct Experience (VDE) on On-line Ad Message Effectiveness," *Journal of Advertising,* Spring 2004, pp. 55–68.

10. For a review and conflicting evidence, see A. A. Wright and J. G. Lynch Jr., "Communications Effects of Advertising versus Direct Experience When Both Search and Experience Attributes Are Present," *Journal of Consumer Research,* March 1995, pp. 108–18.

11. See C. F. Mela, S. Gupta, and D. R. Lehmann, "The Long-Term Impact of Promotion and Advertising on Consumer Brand Choice," *Journal of Marketing Research,* May 1997, pp. 248–61; M. J. Sirgy et al., "Does Television Viewership Play a Role in the Perception of Quality of Life?," *Journal of Advertising,* Spring 1998, pp. 125–42.

12. Insight is based on M. Singleton, "Ticketmaster Can Now Show You the View from Your Seat before You Purchase a Ticket," *The Verge,* May 10, 2017, www.theverge.com, accessed June 28, 2018; L. O'Reilly, "Netflix Lifted the Lid on How the Algorithm

That Recommends You Titles to Watch Actually Works," *Business Insider,* February 26, 2016, www.businessinsider.com, accessed June 28, 2018; M. Mercado, "'Flixable,' a Netflix Search Engine, Is a Much More Intuitive Way to Find a Movie for Your Next Night in," *Bustle,* January 25, 2018, www.bustle.com, accessed June 28, 2018; information found on the various corporate websites.

13. *World Internet Users Statistics and World Population Stats,* www .internetworldstats.com, Copyright © 2018, Miniwatts Marketing Group, accessed June 27, 2018.

14. *The Web at 25 in the U.S.* (Washington, DC: Pew Internet & American Life Project, February 2014).

15. K. Zickhuhr, "Who's Not Online and Why," *Pew Research Center,* September 25, 2013, www.pewinternet.org.

16. S. Hays, "Has Online Advertising Finally Grown Up?," *Advertising Age,* April 1, 2002, p. C1.

17. "Counting on the Internet," *Pew Internet & American Life Project,* December 29, 2002, www.pewinternet.org; Klein and Ford, "Consumer Search for Information in the Digital Age"; Ratchford, Lee, and Talukdar, "The Impact of the Internet on Information Search for Automobiles"; *DoubleClick's Touch-points II,* DoubleClick research report, March 2004, www.doubleclick.com; *Double-Click's Touch-points III,* DoubleClick research report, July 2005, www.doubleclick.com; B. T. Ratchford, D. Talukdar, and M. Lee, "The Impact of the Internet on Consumers' Use of Information Sources for Automobiles," *Journal of Consumer Research,* June 2007, pp. 111-19.

18. B. Fitzgerald, "Data Point: Yes, Email Still Eats Up a Good Chunk of Your Day," *Wall Street Journal,* May 20, 2014, www.blogs.wsj.com, accessed June 28, 2018.

19. "Internet Activities," *Pew Internet & American Life Project,* www.pewinternet.org, accessed June 18, 2011.

20. comScore, "Yahoo! and comScore Study Finds Online Consumers Who Pre-Shop on the Web Spend More In-Store," press release, July 30, 2007, www.comscore.com, accessed June 19, 2011; *State of the U.S. Online Retail Economy through Q1 2009* (Reston, VA: comScore, 2009); D. M. Arbesman, "Online Shopper Intelligence Study Released," *compete pulse,* February 22, 2010, http://blog.compete.com, accessed June 15, 2011; "Study Shows Online Shoppers Are Doing Their Homework," *e-commerce news,* February 26, 2010, http://ecommercejunkie. com, accessed June 15, 2011.

21. *Search before the Purchase,* DoubleClick research report, February 2005, www.doubleclick.com.

22. J. L. Joines, C. W. Scherer, and D. A. Scheufele, "Exploring Motivations for Consumer Web Use and Their Implications for E-commerce," *Journal of Consumer Marketing* 20, no. 2 (2003), pp. 90-108.

23. Ratchford, Lee, and Talukdar, "The Impact of the Internet on Information Search for Automobiles."

24. L. Gentry and R. Calantone, "A Comparison of Three Models to Explain Shop-Bot Use on the Web," *Psychology & Marketing,* November 2002, pp. 945-56; Y. Xu and H. Kim, "Order Effect and Vendor Inspection in Online Comparison Shopping," *Journal of Retailing* 84, no. 4 (2008), pp. 477-86.

25. B. Bickart and R. M. Schindler, "Internet Forums as Influential Sources of Consumer Information," *Journal of Interactive Marketing,* Summer 2001, pp. 31-40; P. Chatterjee, "Online Reviews," in *Advances in Consumer Research,* vol. 28, ed. M. C. Gilly and J. Meyers-Levy (Provo, UT: Association for Consumer Research, 2001), pp. 129-33.

26. J. Loechner, "Online Research a Significant Part of Consumer Buying," *MediaPost,* February 22, 2011, www.mediapost.com, accessed June 15, 2011.

27. A. Parmar, "Student e-union," *Marketing News,* April 1, 2004, pp. 14-15.

28. "Ethnic Groups Online," *eMarketer,* June 20, 2005.

29. N. Singh and H. Matsuo, "Measuring Cultural Adaptation on the Web," in *Advances in Consumer Research,* vol. 30, ed. P. A. Keller and D. W. Rook (Provo, UT: Association for Consumer Research, 2003), pp. 271-72.

30. S. VanBoskirk, "US Digital Marketing Spend Will Near $120 Billion by 2021," *Forbes,* January 26, 2017, www.forbes.com, accessed June 28, 2018.

31. J. Halliday, "Half Hit Web before Showrooms," *Advertising Age,* October 4, 2004, p. 76.

32. E-mail material based on *DoubleClick's 2004 Consumer E-mail Study,* DoubleClick, October 2004, www.doubleclick.com.

33. *Who Tweets?* (Washington, DC: Pew Internet, 2009); J. Van Grove, "Sponsored Tweets Launches," *Mashable,* August 3, 2009, https://mashable.com, accessed May 23, 2011; "How Does Twitter Make Money," Buzzle.com, accessed May 23, 2011.

34. J. S. Ilfeld and R. S. Winer, "Generating Web Traffic," *Journal of Advertising Research,* October 2002, pp. 49-61; R. Bhargave, A. Mantonakis, and K. White, "The Cue-of-the-Cloud Effect: When Reminders of Online Information Availability Increase Purchase Intentions and Choice," *Journal of Marketing Research* 53 (October 2016), pp. 699-711.

35. D. Zigmond and H. Stipp, "Assessing a New Advertising Effect," *Journal of Advertising Research,* June 2010, pp. 162-68.

36. Y. Bart, A. Stephen, and M. Sarvary, "Which Products Are Best Suited to Mobile Advertising? A Field Study of Mobile Display Advertising Effects on Consumer Attitudes and Intentions," *Journal of Marketing Research* 51 (June 2014), pp. 270-85.

37. R. E. Bruner and M. Gluck, *Best Practices for Optimizing Web Advertising Effectiveness,* DoubleClick, May 2006, www .doubleclick.com.

38. Ibid.

39. J. Smith, "10 Powerful Ways to Target Facebook Ads Every Performance Advertiser Should Know," *Inside Facebook,* July 27, 2009, www.insidefacebook.com, accessed June 19, 2011; D. Mochon, K. Johnson, J. Schwartz, and D. Areily, "What Are Likes Worth? A Facebook Page Field Experiment," *Journal of Marketing Research* 54 (April 2017), pp. 306-17.

40. N. Madden, "Levi's Partners with Tudou for Interactive Video Campaign," *Advertising Age,* December 22, 2010.

41. W. Dou, R. Linn, and S. Yang, "How Smart Are 'Smart Banners'?," *Journal of Advertising Research* 41, no. 4 (2001), pp. 31-43.

42. E. Steel, "How Marketers Hone Their Aim Online," *Wall Street Journal,* June 19, 2007.

43. Statista, "Digital Marketing Spending in the United States from 2014-2019, by Segment," 2018, www.statista.com, accessed June 28, 2018.

44. D. Sullivan, "Intro to Search Engine Optimization," *Search Engine Watch,* October 14, 2002, https://searchenginewatch.com.

45. B. S. Bulik, "Meet the Brands Hiding on Google," *Advertising Age,* April 27, 2010.

46. See, e.g., T. P. Novak, D. L. Hoffman, and Y.-F. Yung, "Measuring the Customer Experience in Online Environments," *Marketing Science,* Winter 2000, pp. 22-42; J. R. Coyle and E. Thorson, "The Effects of Progressive Levels of Interactivity and Vividness in Web Marketing Sites," *Journal of Advertising,* Fall 2001, pp. 65-77.

47. "Mobile Fact Sheet," *Pew Research Center,* February 5, 2018, www.pewinternet.org, accessed June 29, 2018.

48. J. Koetsier, "Mobile Advertising Will Drive 75% of All Digital Ad Spend in 2018," *Forbes,* February 23, 2018, www.forbes.com, accessed June 29, 2018; estimates from *eMarketer.* This and related information available at www.emarketer.com, accessed June 29, 2018; /reports.

49. Cross-Channel Marketing Team, "Meet Today's New Smartphone Consumers: Marketing across Channels," *Experian,* April 3, 2014, www.experian.com, accessed June 29, 2018.

50. R. Aronauer, "Going Mobile to Market," *Sales & Marketing Management,* June 2007; "Search Marketing Fact Pack 2008," *Advertising Age,* November 3, 2008.

51. *Location-Based Services* (Washington, DC: Pew Internet & American Life Project, September 12, 2014).

52. L. Danguillecourt, "What Is Skyscanner?," *Skyscanner,* March 23, 2018, www.skyscanner.com/tips-and-inspiration/who-is-skyscanner, accessed June 29, 2018.

53. N. Zmuda, "Yes, There's an App for That Too," *Advertising Age,* March 1, 2010, p. 8.

54. R. A. Westbrook and C. Farnell, "Patterns of Information Source Usage among Durable Goods Buyers," *Journal of Marketing Research,* August 1979, pp. 303-12; J. E. Urbany, P. R. Dickson, and W. L. Wilkie, "Buyer Uncertainty and Information Search," *Journal of Consumer Research,* September 1989, pp. 208-15.

55. Urbany, Dickson, and Wilkie, "Buyer Uncertainty and Information Search"; *Warranties Rule Consumer Follow-Up* (Washington, DC: Federal Trade Commission, 1984), p. 26.

56. Ratchford, Lee, and Talukdar, "The Impact of the Internet on Information Search for Automobiles."

57. Insight is based on M. Kamvar and S. Baluja, "A Large Scale Study of Wireless Search Behavior," in *Proceedings of SIGCHI Conference on Human Factors in Computing Systems,* ed. R. Ginter et al. (Montreal: Conference on Human Factors in Computing Systems, 2006), pp. 701-709; "Search Marketing," in *Advertising Age Fact Pack 2007* (New York: Crain Communications, November 5, 2007); *Best Practices: A Blueprint for Building a Retail Mobile Marketing Program* (Irvine, CA: SmartReply, 2007); "Case Studies," *MobileMarketing Magazine,* November 19, 2007, p. 22; "Special Report: Interactive Marketing," *promomagazine.com,* accessed April 15, 2008.

58. G. Katona and E. Mueller, "A Study of Purchase Decisions," in *Consumer Behavior: The Dynamics of Consumer Reaction,* ed. L. Clark (New York: New York University Press, 1955), pp. 30-87; J. Newman and R. Staelin, "Prepurchase Information Seeking for New Cars and Major Household Appliances," *Journal of Marketing Research,* August 1972, pp. 249-57; J. Claxton, J. Fry, and B. Portis, "A Taxonomy of Prepurchase Information Gathering Patterns," *Journal of Consumer Research,* December 1974, pp. 35-42; G. C. Kiel and R. A. Layton, "Dimensions of Consumer Information Seeking Behavior," *Journal of Marketing Research,* May 1981, pp. 233-39; J. B. Freiden and R. E. Goldsmith, "Prepurchase Information-Seeking for Professional Services," *Journal of Services Marketing,* Winter 1989, pp. 45-55; Urbany, Dickson, and Wilkie, "Buyer Uncertainty and Information Search"; G. N. Souter and M. M. McNeil, *Journal of Professional Services Marketing* 11, no. 2 (1995), pp. 45-60; Klein and Ford, "Consumer Search for Information in the Digital Age."

59. J. G. Lynch Jr. and D. Ariely, "Wine Online," *Marketing Science,* Winter 2000, pp. 83-103; D. Ariely, "Controlling the Information Flow," *Journal of Consumer Research,* September 2000, pp. 233-48; Ratchford, Lee, and Talukdar, "The Impact of the Internet on Information Search for Automobiles."

60. For a similar model of online search, see S. Kulviwat, C. Guo, and N. Engchanil, "Determinants of Online Search," *Internet Research* 14, no. 3 (2004), pp. 245-53; A. L. Jepsen, "Factors Affecting Consumer Use of the Internet for Information Search," *Journal of Interactive Marketing,* Summer 2007, pp. 21-34.

61. D. R. Lichtenstein, N. M. Ridgway, and R. G. Netemeyer, "Price Perceptions and Consumer Shopping Behavior," *Journal of Marketing Research,* May 1993, pp. 234-45.

62. M. N. Bergen, S. Dutta, and S. M. Shugan, "Branded Variants," *Journal of Marketing Research,* February 1996, pp. 9-19.

63. J. Srivastava and N. Lurie, "A Consumer Perspective on Price-Matching Refund Policies," *Journal of Consumer Research,* September 2001, pp. 296-307.

64. D. Grewal and H. Marmorstein, "Market Price Variation, Perceived Price Variation, and Consumers' Price Search Decisions for Durable Goods," *Journal of Consumer Research,* December 1994, pp. 453-60.

65. See B. G. C. Dellaert, "Investigating Consumers' Tendency to Combine Multiple Shopping Purposes and Destinations," *Journal of Marketing Research,* May 1998, pp. 177-89.

66. See C. Moorman, "Market-Level Effects of Information," *Journal of Marketing Research,* February 1998, pp. 82-98; A. D. Miyazaki, D. E. Sprott, and K. C. Manning, "Unit Prices on Retail Shelf Labels," *Journal of Retailing* 76, no. 1 (2000), pp. 93-112.

67. See C. M. Fisher and C. J. Anderson, "The Relationship between Consumer Attitudes and Frequency of Advertising in Newspapers for Hospitals," *Journal of Hospital Marketing* 7, no. 2 (1993), pp. 139-56.

68. S. Widrick and E. Fram, "Identifying Negative Products," *Journal of Consumer Marketing* no. 2 (1983), pp. 59-66.

69. See D. D'Rozario and S. P. Douglas, "Effect of Assimilation on Prepurchase Information-Search Tendencies," *Journal of Consumer Psychology* 8, no. 2 (1999), pp. 187-209; C. Merrill, "Where the Cars Are Caliente," *American Demographics,* January 2000, pp. 56-59.

70. J. Lee and J. Cho, "Consumers' Use of Information Intermediaries and the Impact on Their Information Search Behavior in the Financial Market," *Journal of Consumer Affairs* 39, no. 1 (2005), pp. 95-120.

71. J. W. Alba and J. W. Hutchinson, "Knowledge Calibration," *Journal of Consumer Research,* September 2000, pp. 123–49.

72. C. M. Heilman, D. Bowman, and G. P. Wright, "The Evolution of Brand Preferences and Choice Behaviors of Consumers New to a Market," *Journal of Marketing Research,* May 2000, pp. 139–55. See also D. Mazursky, "The Effects of Invalidating Information on Consumers' Subsequent Search Patterns," *Journal of Economic Psychology,* April 1998, pp. 261–77.

73. See J. A. Barrick and B. C. Spilker, "The Relations between Knowledge, Search Strategy, and Performance in Unaided and Aided Information Search," *Organizational Behavior and Human Decision Processes* 90 (2003), pp. 1–18.

74. See T. Williams, M. Slama, and J. Rogers, "Behavioral Characteristics of the Recreational Shopper," *Journal of Academy of Marketing Science,* Summer 1985, pp. 307–16; J. R. Lumpkin, J. M. Hawes, and W. R. Darden, "Shopping Patterns of the Rural Consumer," *Journal of Business Research,* February 1986, pp. 63–81; W. W. Moe, "Buying, Searching, or Browsing," *Journal of Consumer Psychology* 13, no. 1/2 (2003), pp. 29–39.

75. See U. M. Dholakia, "Involvement-Response Models of Joint Effects," in *Advances in Consumer Research,* vol. 25, ed. J. W. Alba and J. W. Hutchinson (Provo, UT: Association for Consumer Research, 1998), pp. 499–506.

76. T. H. Dodd, B. E. Pinkleton, and A. W. Gustafson, *Psychology & Marketing,* May 1996, pp. 291–304. See also J. R. McColl-Kennedy and R. E. Fetter Jr., "An Empirical Examination of the Involvement to External Search Relationship," *Journal of Services Marketing* 15, no. 2 (2001), pp. 82–98.

77. G. R. Dowling and R. Staelin, "A Model of Perceived Risk and Intended Risk-Handling Activity," *Journal of Consumer Research,* June 1994, pp. 119–34. See also J. B. Smith and J. M. Bristor, "Uncertainty Orientation," *Psychology & Marketing,* November 1994, pp. 587–607.

78. A. Chaudhuri, "Product Class Effects on Perceived Risk," *International Journal of Research in Marketing,* May 1998, pp. 157–68; K. Mitra, M. C. Reiss, and L. M. Capella, "An Examination of Perceived Risk, Informational Search, and Behavioral Intentions," *Journal of Services Marketing* 13, no. 3 (1999), pp. 208–28.

79. See, e.g., M. W. H. Weenig and M. Maarleveld, "The Impact of Time Constraint on Information Search Strategies in Complex Choice Tasks," *Journal of Economic Psychology* 23 (2002), pp. 689–702. For an exception, see C. J. Hill, "The Nature of Problem Recognition and Search in the Extended Health Care Decision," *Journal of Services Marketing* 15, no. 6 (2001), pp. 454–79.

80. A. G. Abdul-Muhmin, "Contingent Decision Behavior," *Journal of Consumer Psychology* 8, no. 1 (1999), pp. 91–111.

81. "L&M Lights Up Again," *Marketing and Media Decisions,* February 1984, p. 69.

82. L. L. Garber, "The Package Appearance in Choice," in *Advances in Consumer Research,* vol. 22, ed. F. R. Kardes and M. Sujan (Provo, UT: Association for Consumer Research, 1995), pp. 653–60.

83. K. Oser, "Snapple Effort Finds Women as They Browse," *Advertising Age,* May 3, 2004.

84. See, e.g., Erdem and Swait, "Brand Credibility, Brand Consideration, and Choice."

How Stitch Fix Works

Curious about how our service works? Here are the basics: We match you with a personal stylist who hand-selects clothing & accessories just for you based on your size, style and budget.

GET STARTED →

Source: Stitch Fix, Inc

LEARNING OBJECTIVES

LO1 Discuss how actual consumer choice often differs from rational choice theory.

LO2 Summarize the types of choice processes consumers engage in.

LO3 Explain evaluative criteria and their measurement.

LO4 Describe the role of evaluative criteria in consumer judgment and marketing strategy.

LO5 Summarize the five decision rules for attribute-based choice and their strategic relevance.

One goal of consumer decision making is to make the best decision possible; another goal is to have (the freedom of) many alternatives from which to choose. These two goals clash when the consumer has too many alternatives and feels overwhelmed. This is choice overload. It is more likely to occur when the choice is one with which the consumer lacks expertise and familiarity, one that is important to the consumer, and one that offers numerous alternatives, each possessing numerous, varied, nonoverlapping features. A consumer faced with the decision of choosing the best health insurance from the list of dozens of alternatives on the government health exchange is more likely to experience choice overload and describe the situation as a nightmare, while the consumer who is choosing an ice cream from 32 flavors is likely to describe the situation as a fun experience. In choice-overload situations, consumers are likely to make poorer choices and feel greater dissatisfaction with their choice, for which they blame themselves.[1]

Faced with choice overload, consumers may exhibit choice paralysis, choosing to make no decision, which, of course, can hurt consumers and marketers alike. The "decision" to not choose has been shown to be equally likely in relatively trivial decisions such as choosing not to buy a jar of jam when presented 30 alternatives, as it is with more important decisions such as (not) enrolling in 40l(k) retirement plans. Fortunately, consumers can use heuristics to simplify decisions and thus avoid possible negative consequences of not choosing. These are rules of thumb or mental shortcuts, such as "buy the most popular brand" or "buy the lowest price," that consumers use to aid the decision process. Heuristics serve the practical purpose of helping consumers make "satisficing" choices that, while not "maximally best," are still good enough.

The proliferation of brands and line extensions both online and offline increases the likelihood of choice overload. Supermarkets, for example, carry something like 40,000 brands—15 types of Thomas's English Muffins, 27 versions of Crest toothpaste. However, instead of more, Costco, the giant warehouse retailer, has adopted a practice of carrying fewer selections. This practice may be as much a contributor to Costco's success as its discount pricing practice. Research shows that people buy more with limited offerings and are more satisfied with their choices.

Online retailers, facing no space barrier, may offer consumers so many alternatives that consumers suffer choice overload, a situation that may contribute to consumer abandonment of their merchandise-filled shopping carts. E-tailers like Stitch Fix, Fancy, Birch Box, and Kiwi Crate are attempting to address the problem of choice overload by eliminating consumer choice altogether. Stitch Fix, a "personal stylist for women," begins the shopping process by having customers fill out a survey on their preferences. This helps the consumer think through what he or she wants. The data form the basis of an algorithm that generates recommendations for the customer. The shopper also can provide a link to her Pinterest, which provides more granular information that the shopper's personal stylist can use to handpick items. For the $20 styling fee, the shopper receives a five-item box or "fix" of clothing and accessories, each averaging $55. Items the shopper doesn't want can be returned at no cost to the shopper.

Choice overload is a reality, and yet most consumers like to feel they have adequate options to choose from. The task for marketers is to hit the sweet spot and offer enough, but not so much that it triggers choice overload. To that end, marketing strategies include product assortment optimization—determining an appropriate number of alternatives, with meaningful differentiation—and strategies to ease the consumer decision-making process—structuring the decision process and lessening perceived risk.

As the opening examples suggest, consumers make decisions in a variety of ways, with a variety of overarching goals, and the decisions they make range from simple to complex. The decision stage after problem recognition and information search is alternative evaluation and selection. Alternative selection also is referred to as consumer choice and, in reality, consumers often are evaluating alternatives for choice even during the search process. Consumer evaluation and choice of alternatives are the focus of this chapter.

CONSUMER CHOICE AND TYPES OF CHOICE PROCESS

LO1

Marketers sometimes assume that the process underlying consumer choice follows *rational choice theory*. Rational choice theory implicitly or explicitly assumes a number of things about consumer choice that often are not true. These assumptions are discussed next.

- *Assumption 1:* Consumers seek one optimal solution to a problem and choose on that basis.

    However, increasingly, marketers are coming to understand that these conditions don't always describe consumer choice. First, consumers don't always have the goal of finding the "optimal brand" for them. Instead, there are alternative metagoals, where a **metagoal** refers to *the general nature of the outcome being sought*. In addition to selecting the optimal alternative, metagoals include minimizing decision effort or maximizing the extent to which a decision is justifiable to others.[2] Consider nominal decision making from Chapter 14. Consumers who are low in purchase involvement may engage in little or no external search because they can recall from memory a brand that is at least satisfactory. In this case, consumers usually will choose this brand with no further search or decision effort, even though it may not be the optimal brand for them. This is because, given low purchase involvement, other goals come into play such as minimizing search and decision effort.

- *Assumption 2:* Consumers have the skill and motivation to find the optimal solution.

    However, marketers are increasingly aware that consumers often don't have the ability or the motivation to engage in the highly demanding task of finding the optimal solution. For example, consumers are subject to **bounded rationality**—*a limited capacity for processing information.*[3] Moreover, as suggested in Chapter 14, most decisions do not generate enough purchase involvement to motivate consumers to seek the optimal solution through extended decision making. As the opening example suggests, many websites in the United States are attempting to help consumers deal with the information overload that accompanies too many choices.

    In the United Kingdom, choice overload was the motivation behind a site called Just Buy This One, which recommends only one brand within a product category and price range with three reasons why it's the best choice. According to a company executive:

We knew that 25% of people are overwhelmed by the choice on price comparison sites and we decided to create something utterly simple and extremely useful. Online shopping used to be the simple solution, but it's gotten too crowded.[4]

- *Assumption 3:* The optimal solution does not change as a function of situational factors such as time pressure, task definition, or competitive context.

    However, marketers are increasingly aware that preferences can and do shift as a function of the situation (Chapter 13), or context, or how the consumer processes the information.[5] For example, limited decision making is more likely when we are tired or hurried. In addition, when decision complexity is enhanced or new brands are added to the competitive set, it can alter consumer choices, as we discuss later in the chapter.[6]

Thus, as you read this chapter, it is important to keep in mind that consumer decisions (a) are often not rational in the sense of finding the optimal solution, (b) are not optimal due to the cognitive and time limits of consumers, and (c) are malleable in that they change based on the situation. In addition, it is important to keep in mind that consumer decisions are much more circular, emotional, and incomplete than our formal examination here might suggest.

Types of Consumer Choice Processes

Let's begin by examining the three general types of decision processes that consumers can engage in. You will notice that some are not even based on a comparison of brands and their features, which is often a major (and sometimes incorrect) assumption made by marketing managers. The three choice processes are affective choice, attitude-based choice, and attribute-based choice. While we describe them separately for simplicity, it is important to keep in mind that these are not mutually exclusive, and combinations may be used in a single decision. First, let's look at three decision scenarios involving a digital camera:

LO2

Scenario 1 (Affective Choice). As a consumer shops at a local store, one camera catches her eye: She examines it, looking at the lines and overall look. She thinks the camera looks sleek, modern, and cool. She examines another camera but thinks it looks too serious and boring. After a few more minutes of contemplation about what a great impression she would make using the first camera to take pictures at parties and weddings, she decides to buy the first camera.

Scenario 2 (Attitude-Based Choice). The consumer remembers that her friend's Canon PowerShot worked well and looked "good"; her parents had a Nikon Coolpix that also worked well but was rather large and bulky; and her old Sony Cyber-shot had not performed as well as she had expected. At her local electronics store, she sees that the Canon and Nikon models are about the same price and decides to buy the Canon PowerShot.

Scenario 3 (Attribute-Based Choice). After consulting the Internet to determine what features she is most interested in, the consumer then goes to her local electronics store and compares the various brands on the features most important to her—namely, camera size, zoom, automatic features, and storage size. She mentally ranks each model on these attributes and her general impression of each model's quality. On the basis of these evaluations, she chooses the Canon PowerShot.

These three scenarios relate to different choice processes. The first scenario represents affective choice.[7] **Affective choice** tends to be more holistic in nature. The brand is not decomposed into distinct components, each of which is evaluated separately from the whole. The evaluation of such products is generally focused on the way they will make the user feel as they are used. The evaluation itself often is based exclusively or primarily on the immediate emotional response to the product or service.[8] Decisions based on affect use the "How do I feel about it" heuristic or decision rule.[9] Consumers imagine or picture using the product or service and evaluate the feeling that this use will produce.[10]

Consumer use of the affective choice process is affected by underlying purchase motives. Affective choice is most likely when the underlying motive is consummatory rather than instrumental. **Consummatory motives** *underlie behaviors that are intrinsically rewarding to the individual involved.* **Instrumental motives** *activate behaviors designed to achieve a second goal.* For example, the consumer in Scenario 1 is clearly motivated primarily by the emotional rewards involved in having and using a camera that makes her look trendy and fashionable (consummatory motive), whereas other consumers may be motivated by having a camera that takes high-quality pictures that can be enjoyed later (instrumental motive).[11] Illustration 16–1 shows ads appealing to each of these motives. How do the Bermuda and Emergen-C ads differ in motive appeals?

Marketers continue to learn more about affect-based decisions.[12] It is clear that such decisions require different strategies than the more cognitive decisions generally considered in marketing. For those decisions that are likely to be affective in nature (largely triggered by consummatory motives), marketers should design products and services that will provide the appropriate emotional responses.[13] They also should help consumers visualize how they will feel during and after the consumption experience.[14] This is particularly important for new brands or products and services. Consumers who have experience with a product or brand have a basis for imagining the affective response it will produce. Those who do not may incorrectly predict the feelings the experience will produce. For example, individuals imagining a white-water rafting trip may conclude that it would produce feelings of terror rather than exhilaration. Illustration 16–2 shows an ad for the Big Green Egg that helps consumers envision the positive experiences and accompanying feelings they would have if they owned the product.

The second scenario represents attitude-based choice. **Attitude-based choice** *involves the use of general attitudes, summary impressions, intuitions, or heuristics; no attribute-by-attribute comparisons are made at the time of choice.*[15] It is important to note that many

ILLUSTRATION 16-1

The Bermuda ad on the left appeals to a consummatory motive by showing that the product or consumption is rewarding in and of itself. The Emergen-C ad on the right appeals to an instrumental motive by showing that the product is a means to an end.

Source: Bermuda Tourism Authority

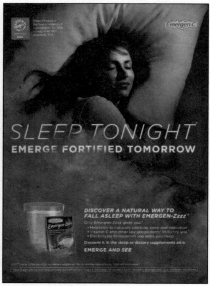

Source: Pfizer Inc.

decisions, even for important products, appear to be attitude-based. Recall from Chapters 14 and 15 that most individuals collect very little product information from external sources immediately before a purchase. They are most likely making attitude-based decisions.

Motivation, information availability, and situational factors interact to determine the likelihood that attitude-based choices are made. As one would suspect, the lower the motivation to make an optimal decision, the more likely an attitude-based choice will be made. This relates to purchase involvement and nominal and limited decision making in Chapter 14, which are likely to be heavily skewed toward attitude-based choice. When information is difficult to find or access, or when consumers face time pressures, attitude-based choices are more likely. Notice how time pressures increase the perceived cost of search and make attitude-based choices from memory appear much more attractive.

Source: Big Green Egg

The third scenario represents attribute-based choice. **Attribute-based choice** *requires the knowledge of specific attributes at the time the choice is made, and it involves attribute-by-attribute comparisons across brands.* This is a much more effortful and time-consuming process than the global comparisons made when affective and attitude-based choices are involved. It also tends to produce a more nearly optimal decision. Again, motivation, information availability, and situational factors interact to determine the likelihood that attitude-based choices are made.

Consumers with high purchase involvement or motivation are more likely to make attribute-based choices, which most resemble the extended decision-making approach we discussed in Chapter 14. More accessible brand and attribute information increases, the likelihood that attribute-based choices are made. This can be used by marketers of brands that have important attribute-based advantages but that lack strong reputations or images in the target market. The approach would be to provide attribute-based comparisons in an easy-to-process format, such as a brand-by-attribute matrix. Such a matrix could be presented in ads, on packages, in point-of-purchase displays, on the brand's website, and so on. An appropriate comparison format and structure is critical to making the firm's brand the focal point of comparison.[16] This could be done by listing the brand first, perhaps in bold or colored type.

The ads in Illustration 16-3 show the differences between attribute-based and attitude-based choice strategies. The Muscletech ad on the left focuses on specific features of the brand and would be consistent with an attribute-based choice. The Jockey ad on the right focuses on the brand and an overall impression of the product and its users and would be consistent with an attitude-based choice.

It is important to note that these three processes are not always used in isolation. For example, affective or emotional criteria can be considered along with functional criteria. Sometimes consumers are more driven by emotions and end up choosing functionally inferior brands.[17] Such trade-offs between hedonic and utilitarian attributes are important for marketers to consider in developing products and promotional campaigns. In addition, sometimes affective and attitude-based processes can be used by consumers to establish

Source: Xiwang Foodstuffs Co Ltd

Source: Jockey International, Inc

ILLUSTRATION 16-3

The Muscletech ad on the left encourages attribute-based choice with primacy given to its key product features. Ads such as this Jockey ad on the right assume or encourage attitude-based choice by focusing on brand, overall performance, and image rather than specific product features.

LO3

or narrow their consideration sets. This type of *phased* decision making is common, and understanding the role of affect and attitudes in the formation of the evoked set is critical for marketers.

Given the nature, complexity, and importance of attribute-based choice to both consumers and marketers, the focus of the remainder of the chapter is on issues related to attribute-based choice. Figure 16–1 provides an overview of the stages of the attribute-based choice process.

EVALUATIVE CRITERIA

Attribute-based choices rely heavily on a comparison of brands on one or more attributes. These attributes are called evaluative criteria because they are the dimensions on which the brands are evaluated. **Evaluative criteria** are *the various dimensions, features, or benefits a consumer looks for in response to a specific problem.* While functional attributes are common, evaluative criteria also can be emotions (the pleasure associated with eating chocolate cake) and the reactions of important reference group members (for socially consumed products). Before purchasing a computer, you might be concerned with cost, speed, memory, operating system, display, and warranty. These would be your evaluative criteria. Someone else could approach the same purchase with an entirely different set of evaluative criteria.

Alternative Evaluation and Selection for Attribute-Based Choice

FIGURE 16-1

Evaluative criteria are perceived and utilized by consumers in a number of ways including extremes (lower price or more miles per gallon are better), limits (it must not cost more than $100; it must get more than 25 miles per gallon), or ranges (any price between $85 and $99 is acceptable).[18] For new product categories, consumers often must first determine which levels of various criteria are desirable. For example, a consumer who buys a barbecue grill for the first time and has limited experience with grills may have to determine if he prefers gas to charcoal, domed or traditional shape, and so forth. After purchase and use, these preference levels become more firmly established and stable.[19]

Nature of Evaluative Criteria

Evaluative criteria are typically associated with desired benefits. Thus, consumers want fluoride (evaluative criteria) in their toothpaste to reduce cavities (benefit). It is often more persuasive for marketers to communicate brand benefits rather than (or in addition to) evaluative criteria because the benefits are what consumers specifically desire. The James Trussart ad in Illustration 16–4 focuses primarily on product benefits rather than technical features.

Evaluative criteria can differ in type, number, and importance. The *type of evaluative criteria* a consumer uses in a decision varies from *tangible* cost and performance features to *intangible* factors such as style, taste, prestige, feelings generated, and brand image.[20] Illustration 16–5 shows how two similar products stress different types of evaluative criteria. The BLUE Freedom ad on the left stresses tangible attributes and technical performance. The Milk Bone ad on the right focuses more on intangible attributes and feelings.

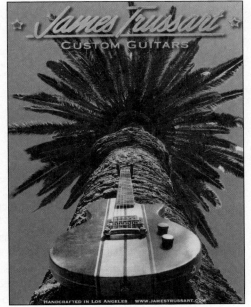

Source: James Trussart Custom Guitars

ILLUSTRATION 16-4

Consumers are generally interested in product features only in relation to the benefits those features provide. This James Trussart ad emphasizes core benefits (custom guitars) rather than the technical characteristics that generate those benefits.

Source: Blue Pet Products, Inc

Source: The J.M. Smucker Company

For fairly simple products such as toothpaste, soap, or facial tissue, consumers use relatively few evaluative criteria. On the other hand, the purchase of an automobile, smartphone, or house may involve numerous criteria. Individual characteristics such as product familiarity and age and situational characteristics such as time pressure also affect the number of evaluative criteria considered.[21] For example, time pressure tends to reduce the number of attributes examined.[22]

The *importance* that consumers assign to each evaluative criterion is of great interest to marketers. Three consumers could use the same six evaluative criteria shown in the following table when considering a laptop computer. However, if the importance rank they assigned each criterion varied as shown, they would likely purchase different brands.

| | Importance Rank for | | |
Criterion	Consumer A	Consumer B	Consumer C
Price	**1**	6	3
Processor	5	**1**	4
Display quality	3	3	**1**
Memory	6	**2**	5
Weight	4	4	**2**
After-sale support	**2**	5	6

Consumer A is concerned primarily with cost and support services. Consumer B wants computing speed and power (as represented by processor and memory). Consumer C is concerned primarily with ease of use (as represented by display and weight). If each of these three consumers represented a larger group of consumers, we would have three distinct market segments based on the importance assigned to the same criteria.

Evaluative criteria and their importance affect which brands consumers select. They also influence if and when a problem will be recognized. For example, consumers who attach more importance to automobile styling relative to cost buy new cars *more frequently* than do those with the opposite importance rankings.[23] Thus, marketers want to understand which criteria consumers use to evaluate their brands so they can develop and communicate appropriate brand features to the target market. Also, marketers sometimes want to change the evaluative criteria that consumers utilize in ways that benefit their brands.[24] Thus, measuring evaluative criteria is an important marketing activity.

Measurement of Evaluative Criteria

Before a marketing manager or a public policy decision maker can develop a sound strategy to affect consumer decisions, he or she must determine

- Which evaluative criteria are used by the consumer.
- How the consumer perceives the various alternatives on each criterion.
- The relative importance of each criterion.

Therefore, it is often difficult to determine which criteria consumers are using in a particular brand-choice decision, particularly if emotions or feelings are involved. This is even more of a problem when trying to determine the relative importance they attach to each evaluative criterion.

Determination of Which Evaluative Criteria Are Used   To determine which criteria are used by consumers in a specific product decision, the marketing researcher can use either direct or indirect methods of measurement.

Direct methods include asking consumers what criteria they use in a particular purchase or, in a focus group setting, noting what consumers say about products and their attributes. However, consumers sometimes will not or cannot verbalize their evaluative criteria for a product, particularly if emotions or feelings are involved. For example, Hanes Corporation suffered substantial losses ($30 million) on its L'erin cosmetics line when, *in response to consumer interviews,* it positioned it as a functional rather than a romantic or emotional product. Eventually, the brand was successfully repositioned as glamorous and exotic, although consumers did not *express* these as desired attributes.[25]

Thus, *indirect* measurement techniques such as **projective techniques** (Appendix A and Appendix Table A–1), which allow the respondent to indicate the criteria someone else might use, are often helpful. The "someone else" will likely be a *projection* of the respondent, of course—thus, the marketer can indirectly determine the evaluative criteria that would be used.

Perceptual mapping is another useful indirect technique for determining evaluative criteria. First, consumers judge the similarity of alternative brands. This generally involves having the consumer look at possible pairs of brands and indicate which pair is most similar, which is second most similar, and so forth until all pairs are ranked. These similarity judgments are processed via a computer to derive a perceptual map of the brands. No evaluative criteria are specified by the consumer. The consumer simply ranks the similarity between all pairs of alternatives, and a perceptual configuration is derived in which the consumer's still-unnamed evaluative criteria are the dimensions of the configuration.

For example, consider the perceptual map of beers shown in Figure 16–2. This configuration was derived from a consumer's evaluation of the relative similarity of these brands of beer. The horizontal axis is characterized by physical characteristics such as taste, calories, and fullness. The vertical axis is characterized by price, quality, and status. Naming each axis, and thus each evaluative criterion, is done using judgment. This procedure allows marketers to understand consumers' perceptions and the evaluative criteria they use to differentiate brands.

FIGURE 16-2   Perceptual Mapping of Beer Brand Perceptions

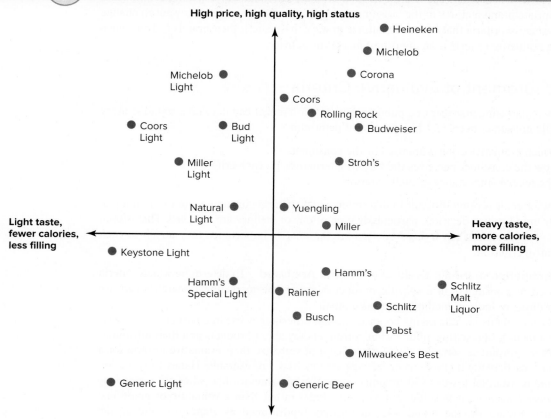

Determination of Consumers' Judgments of Brand Performance on Specific Evaluative Criteria   A variety of methods are available for measuring consumers' judgments of brand performance on specific attributes. These include *rank ordering scales, semantic differential scales,* and *Likert scales* (see Appendix A and Appendix Table A–3). The semantic differential scale is probably the most widely used technique.

None of these techniques is very effective at measuring emotional responses to products or brands. Projective techniques can provide some insights. SAM, the graphical approach designed to tap more directly into the pleasure–arousal–dominance dimensions of emotions (see Chapter 11), is also a useful option.

Determination of the Relative Importance of Evaluative Criteria   The importance assigned to evaluative criteria can be measured either by direct or by indirect methods. No matter which technique is used, the usage situation should be specified because attribute importance often changes with the situation. The *constant sum scale* is the most common method of direct measurement (see Chapter 11).

The most popular indirect measurement approach is **conjoint analysis.** In conjoint analysis, the consumer is presented with a set of products or product descriptions in which the evaluative criteria vary. For example, the consumer may be presented with the description of 24 different laptop computers that vary on four criteria. Two might be as follows:

Intel Core i7 processor	Intel Core i5 processor
Energy Star certified (yes)	Energy Star certified (no)
5.7 pounds	4.2 pounds
$1,200	$825

The consumer ranks all 24 such descriptions in terms of his or her preference for those combinations of features. Using these preference ranks, sophisticated computer programs derive the relative importance consumers assign to each level of each attribute tested (see Appendix A and Appendix Figure A–1 for details).

Conjoint analysis was used by Sunbeam in reformulating its food processor line for various segments. Sunbeam tested 12 different attributes: price, motor power, number of blades, bowl shape, and so forth. Various segments emerged *based on the relative importance of these attributes.* In order of importance, the key attributes for two segments were as follows. These results helped Sunbeam develop models specifically for each of these segments and that better met their needs on important evaluative criteria.

Cheap/Large Segment	Multispeed/Multiuse Segment
$49.99 price	$99.99 price
4-quart bowl	2-quart bowl
Two speeds	Seven speeds
Seven blades	Functions as blender and mixer
Heavy-duty motor	Cylindrical bowl
Cylindrical bowl	Pouring spout

INDIVIDUAL JUDGMENT AND EVALUATIVE CRITERIA

LO4

If you were buying a laptop computer, you would probably make direct comparisons across brands on features such as price, weight, and display clarity. These comparative judgments might not be completely accurate. For example, the display that is the easiest to read in a five-minute trial might not be the easiest to read over a two-hour work session. For other attributes, such as quality, you might not be able to make direct comparisons. Instead, you might rely on brand name or price to indicate quality. In addition, consumer perceptions of the importance of product features are influenced by various external factors. The accuracy of direct judgments, the use of one attribute to indicate performance on another (surrogate indicator), and variations in attribute importance are critical issues for marketers.

Accuracy of Individual Judgments

The average consumer is not adequately trained to judge the performance of competing brands on complex evaluative criteria such as quality or durability. For more straightforward criteria, however, most consumers can and do make such judgments. Prices generally can be judged and compared directly. However, even this can be complex. Is a six-pack of 7.5-ounce cans of Coca-Cola selling for $2.49 a better buy than a two-liter bottle priced at $1.67 each? Consumer groups have pushed for unit pricing (pricing by common measurements such as cost per ounce) to make such comparisons simpler. The federal Truth In Lending Act was passed to facilitate direct price comparisons among alternative lenders.

The ability of an individual to distinguish between similar stimuli is called **sensory discrimination** (see Chapter 8). This could involve such variables as the sound of stereo

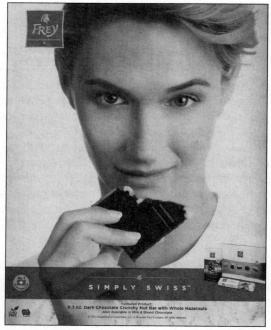

Source: Migros

systems, the taste of food products, or the clarity of display screens. The minimum amount that one brand can differ from another, with the difference still being noticed, is referred to as the *just noticeable difference (j.n.d.).* As we saw in Chapter 8, this ability is not well developed in most consumers. In general, research indicates that *individuals typically do not notice relatively small differences between brands or changes in brand attributes.* In addition, the complexity of many products and services as well as the fact that some aspects of performance can be judged only after extensive use makes accurate brand comparisons difficult.[26]

The inability of consumers to accurately evaluate many products can result in inappropriate purchases (buying a lower-quality product at a higher price than necessary).[27] This is a major concern of regulatory agencies and consumer groups as well as for marketers of high-value brands.

Use of Surrogate Indicators

Consumers frequently use an observable attribute of a product to indicate the performance of the product on a less-observable attribute.[28] For example, a consumer might infer that because a product has a relatively high price, it also must be of high quality. *An attribute used to stand for or indicate another attribute* is known as a **surrogate indicator.** As discussed in Chapter 8, consumers often use such factors as price, advertising intensity, warranties, brand, and country of origin as surrogate indicators of quality—what we termed quality signals. Illustration 16–6 shows an ad for Frey chocolate. This ad is attempting to take advantage of a surrogate indicator of quality.

In general, surrogate indicators operate more strongly when consumers lack the expertise to make informed judgments on their own, when consumer motivation or interest in the decision is low, and when other quality-related information is lacking. Unfortunately, the relationship between surrogate indicators and functional measures of quality is often modest at best.[29] Obviously, when consumers rely on surrogates that have little relationship to actual quality, they are likely to make suboptimal decisions.

Surrogate indicators are based on consumers' beliefs that two features such as price level and quality level generally go together. Consumers also form beliefs that certain variables do not go together—such as *lightweight* and *strong; rich taste* and *low calories;* and *high fiber* and *high protein.*[30] Marketers attempting to promote the presence of two or more variables that many consumers believe to be mutually exclusive have a high risk of failure unless very convincing messages are used. Thus, it is important for marketers to fully understand consumers' beliefs about the feasible relationships of attributes related to their products.

The Relative Importance and Influence of Evaluative Criteria

The importance of evaluative criteria varies among individuals and also within the same individual over time. That is, although consumers often have a general sense of how important various criteria are, this can be influenced by a number of factors. These include the following:

- *Usage situation.* The situation in which a product or service is used (Chapter 13) can have important influences on the criteria used to make a choice. For example, speed of service and convenient location may be very important in selecting a restaurant over a lunch break but relatively unimportant when selecting a restaurant for a special occasion.[31]
- *Competitive context.* Generally speaking, the lower the variance across competing brands on a given evaluative criterion, the less influence it is likely to have in the decision process.[32] For example, you might think that the weight of a notebook computer is important. However, if all the brands you are considering weigh between 4 and 5 pounds, this attribute suddenly may become less of a factor in your decision.
- *Advertising effects.* Advertising can affect the importance of evaluative criteria in a number of ways. For example, an ad that increases attention and elaborative processing of an attribute can increase its perceived importance and/or influence in the decision.[33] As we saw in Chapters 8 and 9, contrast, prominence, and imagery are just a few of the tactics that can be used to enhance attention and elaboration.

Evaluative Criteria, Individual Judgments, and Marketing Strategy

Obviously, marketers must understand the evaluative criteria consumers use relative to their products and develop products that excel on those features. All aspects of the marketing communications mix then must communicate this excellence.

Marketers also must recognize and react to the ability of individuals to judge evaluative criteria, as well as to their tendency to use surrogate indicators. For example, most new consumer products are initially tested against competitors in blind tests. A **blind test** is one in which *the consumer is not aware of the product's brand name.* Such tests enable the marketer to evaluate the functional characteristics of the product and to determine if an advantage over a particular competitor has been obtained without the contaminating, or halo, effects of the brand name or the firm's reputation. *Can you see any drawbacks to only using blind tests in evaluating the market potential of products?*

Marketers also make direct use of surrogate indicators. Hyundai's 10-year, 100,000-mile warranty was a milestone in the industry when introduced two decades ago. The goal was to overcome low-quality perceptions related to another surrogate—namely, country of origin. That is, consumers in the United States were unsure of the quality of Korean-made automobiles at the time, and the warranty was designed to overcome this.

For image products such as fine wines, imported beers, and so forth, higher prices tend to signal higher quality. Therefore, although, for most products, higher prices lead to lower quantity demanded, for such image-based products, higher prices generally drive higher demand due to the quality that is inferred based on the higher price.

Brand names are also a strong surrogate for quality. Elmer's glue emphasized the well-established reputation of its brand in promoting its new super glue: Ads for Elmer's Wonder Bond said, "Stick with a name you can trust." Firms with a limited reputation sometimes can form *brand alliances* (as discussed in Chapter 8) with a reputable firm and gain from the quality associated with the known brand. Thus, a new brand of ice cream that used a branded ingredient such as M&Ms would gain from M&Ms' quality image.[34] Country-of-origin themes such as "Made in America," "Italian Styling," or "German Engineering" are also common.

Marketers also must understand the factors that influence consumer perceptions of the importance of evaluative criteria. Understanding that attributes may be important but wield little influence on decisions because of similarity across competitors is a critical insight. It speaks to the need for marketers to examine critical *points of differentiation* on which the brand can be positioned. Advertising themes that emphasize specific usage occasions for which the brand is particularly appropriate can be effective, as can strategies such as imagery that draw attention to attributes on which the firm's brand excels.

DECISION RULES FOR ATTRIBUTE-BASED CHOICES

LO5

As we describe some of the choice rules consumers use to select among alternatives, remember that these rules are representations of imprecise and often nonconscious or low-effort mental processes. The following example is a good representation of a consumer using a complex choice rule (compensatory with one attribute weighted heavily):

> I really liked the Ford [minivan] a lot, but it had the back tailgate that lifted up instead of the doors that opened. I suspect that if that had been available we might have gone with the Ford instead because it was real close between the Ford and the GM. The liftgate in the back was the main difference, and we went with the General Motors because we liked the doors opening the way they did. I loved the way the Ford was designed on the inside. I loved the way it drove. I loved the way it felt and everything, but you are there manipulating all these kids and groceries and things and you have got to lift this thing, and it was very awkward. It was hard to lift, and if you are holding something you have got to steer all the kids back, or whack them in the head. So that was a big thing. You know it was a lot cheaper than the GM. It was between $1,000 and $2,000 less than General Motors, and because money was a factor, we did go ahead and actually at one point talk money with a [Ford] dealer. But we couldn't get the price difference down to where I was willing to deal with that tailgate is what it comes down to.[35]

Despite the fact that the choice rules we describe are not precise representations of consumer decisions, they do enhance our understanding of how consumers make decisions and provide guidance for marketing strategy.

Suppose you have six laptop computers in your evoked set and you have assessed them based on six evaluative criteria: price, weight, processor, battery life, after-sale support, and display quality. Further, suppose that each brand excels on one attribute but falls short on one or more of the remaining attributes, as shown in Table 16–1.

Which brand would you select? The answer would depend on the decision rule you utilize. Consumers commonly use five decision rules: conjunctive, disjunctive, elimination-by-aspects, lexicographic, and compensatory. More than one rule may be used in any given decision. The most common instance of this is using a relatively simple rule to reduce the number of alternatives considered and then to apply a more complex rule to choose among the remaining options.[36] An example would be eliminating from consideration all those

	Consumer Perceptions*					
Evaluative Criteria	Acer	HP	Samsung	Dell	Lenovo	Toshiba
Price	5	3	3	4	2	1
Weight	3	4	5	4	3	4
Processor	5	5	5	2	5	5
Battery life	1	3	1	3	1	5
After-sale support	3	3	4	3	5	3
Display quality	3	3	3	5	3	3

Performance Levels on the Evaluative Criteria for Six Laptop Computers — **TABLE 16-1**

*1 = Very poor; 5 = Very good.

apartments that are too far from campus or that rent for more than $700 per month (conjunctive decision rule). The choice from among the remaining apartments might involve carefully trading off among features such as convenience of location, price, presence of a pool, and size of rooms (compensatory rule). Note that some online shopping services such as PriceGrabber complete the first phase in this process by filtering out all brands that don't meet the consumer's criteria.

The first four rules we will describe are *noncompensatory* rules. This means that a high level of one attribute cannot offset a low level of another. In the apartment example, the consumer would not consider an apartment that was right next to campus if it costs more than $700 per month. An excellent location could not compensate for an inappropriate price. In contrast, the last rule we will describe is a *compensatory* rule in which consumers average across attribute levels. This allows a high level of one value to offset a low value of another.

Finally, note that the conjunctive and disjunctive decision rules may produce a set of acceptable alternatives, whereas the remaining rules generally produce a single "best" alternative.

Conjunctive Decision Rule

The **conjunctive decision rule** establishes minimum required performance standards for each evaluative criterion and selects the first or all brands that meet or exceed these minimum standards. Thus, in making the decision on the computer, you would say, "I'll consider all (or I'll buy the first) brands that are acceptable on the attributes I think are important." For example, assume that the following represent your minimum standards:

Price	3
Weight	4
Processor	3
Battery life	1
After-sale support	2
Display quality	3

Any brand of computer falling below any of these minimum standards (cutoff points) would be eliminated from further consideration. Referring to Table 16-1, we can see that four computers are eliminated—Lenovo, Acer, Dell, and Toshiba. These are the computers that failed to meet all the minimum standards. Under these circumstances, the two remaining brands may be equally satisfying. Or you might use another decision rule to select a single brand from these two alternatives.

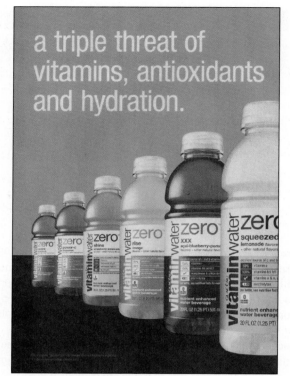

Source: The Coca-Cola Company

Because individuals have limited ability to process information, the conjunctive rule is frequently used to reduce the size of the information processing task to some manageable level. This often is done in the purchase of such products as homes, computers, and bicycles; in the rental of apartments; or in the selection of vacation options. A conjunctive rule is used to eliminate alternatives that are out of a consumer's price range, are outside the location preferred, or do not offer other desired features. After eliminating those alternatives not providing these features, the consumer may use another decision rule to make a brand choice among those remaining alternatives that satisfy these minimum standards.

The conjunctive decision rule is commonly used in many low-involvement purchases as well. In such a purchase, the consumer generally evaluates a set of brands one at a time and selects the first brand that meets all the minimum requirements.

If the conjunctive decision rule is used by a target market, it is critical to meet or surpass the consumers' minimum requirement on each criterion. For low-involvement purchases, consumers often purchase the first brand that does so. For such products, extensive distribution and dominant shelf space are important. It is also necessary to understand how consumers "break ties" if the first satisfactory option is not chosen. The Zero Vitamin Water ad in Illustration 16–7 tries to assure consumers that its brand has every feature they might need.

Disjunctive Decision Rule

The **disjunctive decision rule** *establishes a minimum level of performance for each important attribute* (often a fairly high level, which sets the performance standard very high and makes it hard for a brand to attain). All brands that meet or exceed the performance level for *any* key attribute are considered acceptable. Using this rule, you would say, "I'll consider all (or buy the first) brands that perform really well on any attribute I consider important." Assume that you are using a disjunctive decision rule and the attribute cutoff points shown below:

Price	5
Weight	5
Processor	Not critical
Battery life	Not critical
After-sale support	Not critical
Display quality	5

You would find Acer (price), Samsung (weight), and Dell (display quality) to warrant further consideration (see Table 16–1). As with the conjunctive decision rule, you might purchase the first brand you find acceptable, use another decision rule to choose among the three, or add additional criteria to your list.

When the disjunctive decision rule is used by a target market, it is critical to meet or surpass the consumers' requirements on at least one of the key criteria. This should be emphasized in advertising messages and on the product package. Because consumers often purchase the first brand that meets or exceeds one of the requirements, extensive distribution and dominant shelf space are important. Again, it is also necessary to understand how consumers break ties if the first satisfactory option is not chosen. The Escort Radar ad in Illustration 16–8 stresses one important attribute and would be appropriate for consumers who placed a high importance on this attribute and used a disjunctive decision rule.

Elimination-by-Aspects Decision Rule

The **elimination-by-aspects decision rule** requires the consumer to rank the evaluative criteria in terms of their importance and to establish a cutoff point for each criterion. All brands are first considered on the most important criterion. Those that do not meet or exceed the cutoff point are dropped (eliminated) from further consideration. If more than one brand remains in the set after this first elimination phase, the process is repeated on those brands for the second most important criterion. This continues until only one brand remains. Thus, the consumer's logic is, "I want to buy the brand that has a high level of an important attribute that other brands do not have."

Consider the rank order and cutoff points shown below. What would you choose using the elimination-by-aspects rule?

	Rank	Cutoff Point
Price	1	3
Weight	2	4
Display quality	3	4
Processor	4	3
After-sale support	5	3
Battery life	6	3

Price would eliminate Lenovo and Toshiba (see Table 16–1). Of those remaining, Samsung, HP, and Dell meet or exceed the weight hurdle (Acer is eliminated). Notice that Toshiba also meets the minimum weight requirement but would not be considered because it had been eliminated in the initial consideration of price. Only Dell meets or exceeds the third requirement, display quality.

Source: Cedar Electronics Holdings Corp

Using the elimination-by-aspects rule, you end up with a choice that has all the desired features of all the other alternatives, plus one more.

For a target market using the elimination-by-aspects rule, it is critical to meet or surpass the consumers' requirements on one more (in order) of the criteria used than the competition. This competitive superiority should be emphasized in advertising messages and on the product package. Firms also can attempt to alter the relative importance that consumers assign to the evaluative criteria. The Domenica Fiore ad in Illustration 16–9 is consistent with this rule. It indicates that the brand has desirable features other competitors do not have (100 percent traceable organic farming).

Lexicographic Decision Rule

The **lexicographic decision rule** *requires the consumer to rank the criteria in order of importance.* The consumer then selects the brand that performs *best* on the most important attribute. If two or more brands tie on this attribute, they are evaluated on the second most important attribute. This continues through the attributes until one brand outperforms the others. The consumer's thinking is something like this: "I want to get the brand that does best on the attribute of most importance to me. If there is a tie, I'll break it by choosing the one that does best on my second most important criterion."

The lexicographic decision rule is similar to the elimination-by-aspects rule. The difference is that the lexicographic rule seeks maximum performance at each stage, whereas the elimination-by-aspects seeks satisfactory performance at each stage. Thus, using the lexicographic rule and the data from the elimination-by-aspects example above would result in the selection of Acer because it has the best performance on the most important attribute.

ILLUSTRATION 16-9

Elimination-by-aspects choices seek a brand that has a high level of an attribute that other brands do not have, as shown in this Domenica Fiore ad.

Source: Domenica Fiore

Had Acer been rated a 4 on price, it would be tied with Dell. Then, Dell would be chosen based on its superior weight rating.

When this rule is being used by a target market, the firm should try to be superior to the competition on *the* key attribute. This competitive superiority should be emphasized in advertising. It is essential that the product at least equal the performance of all other competitors on the most important criterion. Outstanding performance on lesser criteria will not matter if a competitor is superior on the most important attribute. If a competitive advantage is not possible on the most important feature, attention should be shifted to the second most important (assuming equal performance on the most important one). If it is not possible to meet or beat the competition on the key attribute, the firm must attempt to make another attribute more important.

The Stouffer's ad shown in Illustration 16–10 emphasizes one key feature, presumably the most important to its target market. To the extent that its customers use a lexicographic rule, this ad should be effective in driving choice of this brand.

Compensatory Decision Rule

The four previous rules are *noncompensatory* decision rules because very good performance on one evaluative criterion cannot compensate for poor performance on another evaluative criterion. On occasion, consumers may wish to average out some very good features with some less attractive features of a product in determining overall brand preference. That appears to be the case with the new mini package craze being used by companies such as Frito-Lay, Nabisco, and Keebler. Some consumers have complained that the prices are high on a per-serving basis. Frito-Lay and others are counting on the fact that the convenience and calorie-control elements of their new 100-calorie packets will offset price in the minds

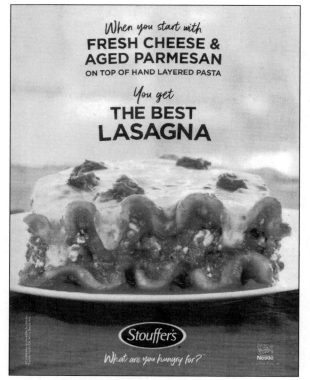

Source: Nestlé Group

of their target consumer. That is, they assume the target market will use a compensatory decision rule for this product. It appears this is the case, as explained by one customer who balked at the notion of buying in bulk and then measuring out 100-calorie servings into plastic bags:

> If you want to mess with those baggies, that's fine. But for those of us in the real world, we'll take the 100 cal packs. Sure, we might pay a few more pennies per ounce, but we also can't sneak any extra in while refilling.[37]

The **compensatory decision rule** states that *the brand that rates highest on the sum of the consumer's judgments of the relevant evaluative criteria will be chosen.* This can be illustrated as

$$R_b = \sum_{i=1}^{n} W_i B_{ib}$$

where

R_b = overall rating of brand b

W_i = importance or weight attached to evaluative criterion i

B_{ib} = evaluation of brand b on evaluative criterion i

n = number of evaluative criteria considered relevant

This is the same as the multiattribute attitude model described in Chapter 11. If you used the relative importance scores shown below, which brand would you choose using the compensatory rule?

	Importance Score
Price	30
Weight	25
Processor	10
Battery life	05
After-sale support	10
Display quality	20
Total	100

Using this rule, you would choose Dell because it has the highest preference (see Table 16–1). The calculations for Dell are as follows:

$$R_{Dell} = 30(4) + 25(4) + 10(2) + 5(3) + 10(3) + 20(5)$$
$$= 120 + 100 + 20 + 15 + 30 + 100$$
$$= 385$$

Products and services targeting consumers likely to use a compensatory rule can offset low performance on some features with relatively high performance on others. However, it is important to have a performance level at or near the competition's on the more important features because they receive more weight in the decision than do other attributes. Recall the description of the minivan purchase from the beginning of this section. This customer preferred most of the features of the Ford but bought the GM because Ford was very weak on one key attribute. However, the consumer did express a willingness to change the decision had the price differential been greater. Thus, for compensatory decisions, the total mix of the relevant attributes must be considered to be superior to those of the competition.

The compensatory rule tends to be the most time-consuming and mentally taxing. Also, consumers often find it difficult to consider more than a few attributes at a time in the trade-off process. In addition, as competitors enter the market, they can change the attractiveness of existing alternatives. This situational influence is discussed in Consumer Insight 16–1.

Summary of Decision Rules

As shown below, each decision rule yields a somewhat different choice. Therefore, marketers must understand which decision rules are being used by target consumers in order to position a product within this decision framework.

Decision Rule	Brand Choice
Conjunctive	HP, Samsung
Disjunctive	Dell, Samsung, Acer
Elimination-by-aspects	Dell
Lexicographic	Acer
Compensatory	Dell

Context Effects on Consumer Choice

Rational choice theory suggests that consumer choices and preferences should be independent of the context. As a simple example, it is assumed that consumers will evaluate a $5 discount the same way regardless of context. However, this is not the case. Consumers tend to perceive the value of the $5 discount as higher when it is on a product originally priced at $10 and lower on a product originally priced at $100. The reason goes back to Chapter 8 and relative preferences. Consumers appear to evaluate the $5 savings *in the context of* or *relative to* the original price of the product.

In a similar way, consumers are affected by the competitive context in which they make choices, or what we referred to in Chapter 13 as the purchase situation. There are numerous context effects on consumer choice. Here we will discuss two, the center-stage and decoy effects. These effects may occur when a consumer faces a choice from three alternatives.[38]

Center-stage effect: Where a product is *physically* located has an influence on preference for that product. If choosing among three options, we tend to prefer, and choose, the one that is physically positioned in the middle. This center-stage effect has been shown to occur in many and varied situations including seating (71 percent choose to sit in the middle of three chairs), as well as with the purchase of chewing gum (50 percent choose the middle of three packs). One reason this may occur is that we tend to choose what we visually attend to, and it appears that we tend to look first/most at items in the center. Gas stations have applied the center-stage effect to increase sales of premium (the most expensive) gas by placing this option in the middle of the two

lower-priced options on the gas pump. Note how with the gasoline choice situation, the center-stage effect is independent of attribute levels (e.g., quality, price) or the weights consumers might attach to them but is, rather, a function of a completely other attribute (physical location of the pump), which is irrelevant to the characteristics of gasoline, which therefore violates rational choice theory.

Decoy effect: The decoy effect involves placing a third and clearly inferior brand into the choice set to influence choice outcomes. We begin with Decoy Effect: Choice Context 1 (left graph), in which there are two apartments (A and B) evaluated on two attributes (distance from campus in miles and quality on a 1–100 scale where 100 is best). As the graph on the left shows, option A is further from campus (a negative) but of higher quality (a positive), while option B is nearer to campus (a positive) but of lower quality (a negative). In addition, because some consumers care about quality more than distance and some are just the opposite, assume that the choice percentages between A and B are split equally (50 percent choose A and 50 percent choose B).

Now consider Decoy Effect: Choice Context 2 (right graph). Here an apartment option is added (Apartment C) that is clearly inferior to Apartment A (that is, Apartment A is said to dominate C). An important point here is that Apartments A and B have not changed at all. Only the context of choice has changed because a third option was added that is obviously inferior to Apartment A and not obviously better than Apartment B. Rational choice theory would say that an irrelevant choice option should not change a consumer's original choice. In this case, Apartment C should be irrelevant. Those who chose A

Research clearly indicates that people do use these decision rules.[39] Low-involvement purchases generally involve relatively simple decision rules (conjunctive, disjunctive, elimination-by-aspects, or lexicographic) because consumers will attempt to minimize the mental cost of such decisions.[40] High-involvement decisions and purchases involving considerable perceived risk tend to increase evaluation efforts and often may involve not

Decoy Effect: Choice Context 1

Quality

Apartment A
(better quality; farther away)
50% choice

Apartment B
(lower quality; closer)
50% choice

Distance (lower is better)

Decoy Effect: Choice Context 2

Quality

Apartment A
(better quality; farther away)
60% choice

Apartment C
(as far away as A but of lower quality)
0% choice

Apartment B
(lower quality; closer)
40% choice

Distance (lower is better)

Source: Charts based on K. Hendricks, "The Decoy Effect: Why You Make Irrational Choices Every Day (Without Even Knowing It)," blog entry, February 12, 2018, www.kenthendricks.com, accessed July 5, 2018.

previously should never choose C because C is clearly inferior (same distance as A but of lower quality). Those who chose B previously should still prefer B because it is better than C on their more preferred attribute, namely distance. However, this is not what happens. Instead, the addition of the decoy (Apartment C) appears to make it easier for consumers to see how A is better than C, but it does not make it obvious that B is better than C. As a consequence, adding the "irrelevant" option of Apartment C triggers Apartment A's choice or market share to increase by pulling market share from Apartment B. In a sense, the decoy "attracts" consumers to Apartment A, and it does so even if no one chooses the decoy, as shown in the figure.

Marketers can utilize these and other "contextual" factors to influence consumer choices and can do so in such a way to move consumers "toward" the options they most want consumers to select and "away" from options they might otherwise select. You might wonder how it is possible that choice context can matter so much. One explanation, according to consumer choice expert Dan Ariely, is that "we [as consumers] actually don't know our preferences that well, and because we don't know our preferences that well, we're susceptible to all the influences from external forces."

Critical Thinking Questions

1. Why do the center-stage and decoy effects contradict rational choice theory?

2. Besides typically looking first at the center of the screen, can you think of other reasons why consumers prefer middle options on websites?

3. Do you see any ethical issues related to strategies designed to position brands against decoy alternatives? Explain.

only more complex rules (compensatory) but also stages of decision making, with different attributes being evaluated using different rules at each stage.[41] Of course, individual, product, and situational characteristics also influence the type of decision rule used.[42]

A marketing manager must first determine which rule or combination of rules the target consumers will most likely use in a particular purchase situation and then develop the appropriate marketing strategy.

LO1: Discuss how actual consumer choice often differs from rational choice theory.

Rational choice theory assumes that (1) consumers seek one optimal solution to a problem and choose on that basis, (2) consumers have the skill and motivation to find the optimal solution, and (3) the optimal choice does not change as a function of the situation. However, all of these assumptions have been shown to be incorrect for at least some consumer decisions. Reasons include that consumers have alternative *metagoals,* consumers are subject to *bounded rationality,* and situations actually influence consumer perceptions of the optimal choice.

LO2: Summarize the types of choice processes consumers engage in.

Affective choice tends to be more holistic in nature. The brand is not decomposed into distinct components, each of which is evaluated separately from the whole. Decisions based on affect use the "How do I feel about it" heuristic or decision rule and tend to occur in response to *consummatory motives.*

Attitude-based choice involves the use of general attitudes, summary impressions, intuitions, or heuristics; no attribute-by-attribute comparisons are made at the time of choice. Lower purchase involvement, scarce information, and certain situational factors such as time pressure increase the likelihood of attitude-based choice.

Attribute-based choice requires the knowledge of specific attributes at the time the choice is made, and it involves attribute-by-attribute comparisons across brands. This is a much more effortful and time-consuming process than the global comparisons made when affective and attitude-based choices are involved. It also tends to produce a more nearly optimal decision. Higher purchase involvement, easily accessible brand-attribute information, and situational factors such as lower time pressure increase the likelihood of attribute-based choice.

LO3: Explain evaluative criteria and their measurement.

Evaluative criteria are the various features or benefits a consumer looks for in response to a specific problem. They are the performance levels or characteristics consumers use to compare different brands in view of their particular consumption problem.

The measurement of (1) which evaluative criteria are used by the consumer, (2) how the consumer perceives the various alternatives on each criterion, and (3) the relative importance of each criterion is a critical first step in utilizing evaluative criteria to develop marketing strategy. The measurement task is not easy, although a number of techniques are available including *perceptual mapping,* the *constant-sum scale,* and *conjoint analysis.*

LO4: Describe the role of evaluative criteria in consumer judgment and marketing strategy.

The ability of an individual to distinguish between similar stimuli is called *sensory discrimination.* Some evaluative criteria such as price, size, and color can be judged easily and accurately by consumers. Other criteria, such as quality, durability, and health benefits, are much more difficult to judge. In general, research indicates that *individuals typically do not notice relatively small differences between brands or changes in brand attributes.* In addition, the complexity of many products and services and the fact that some aspects of performance can be judged only after extensive use make accurate brand comparisons difficult. In such cases, consumers often use price, brand name, or some other variable as a *surrogate indicator* of quality. Marketers can use surrogate cues as a means to affect consumer choice in situations where consumers find it difficult to make accurate assessments of alternatives. Marketers also can attempt to influence the relative importance of attributes in such a way as to favor their brands through advertising as well as position in regards to specific usage occasions.

LO5: Summarize the five decision rules for attribute-based choice and their strategic relevance.

When consumers judge alternative brands on several evaluative criteria, they must have some method to select one brand from the various choices. Decision rules serve this function. A decision rule specifies how a consumer compares two or more brands. Five commonly used decision rules are *disjunctive, conjunctive, lexicographic, elimination-by-aspects,* and *compensatory.* The decision rules work best with functional products and cognitive decisions. Marketing managers must be aware of the decision rule(s) used by the target market because different decision rules require different marketing strategies.

SMARTBOOK

KEY TERMS

Affective choice 569
Attitude-based choice 570
Attribute-based choice 571
Blind tests 579
Bounded rationality 568
Compensatory decision rule 586
Conjoint analysis 576

Conjunctive decision rule 581
Consummatory motives 570
Disjunctive decision rule 582
Elimination-by-aspects decision
   rule 583
Evaluative criteria 572
Instrumental motives 570

Lexicographic decision rule 584
Metagoal 568
Perceptual mapping 575
Projective techniques 575
Sensory discrimination 577
Surrogate indicator 578

REVIEW QUESTIONS

1. What is *rational choice* theory?
2. What is meant by *bounded rationality?*
3. What is a *metagoal?*
4. What are three common metagoals for consumer decisions?
5. What is *affective choice,* and when is it most likely to occur?
6. What is the difference between *consummatory motives* and *instrumental motives?*
7. How does *attribute-based choice* differ from *attitude-based choice?* When is each most likely?
8. What are *evaluative criteria,* and on what characteristics can they vary?
9. How can you determine which evaluative criteria consumers use?
10. What methods are available for measuring consumers' judgments of brand performance on specific attributes?
11. How can the importance assigned to evaluative criteria be assessed?

12. What is *sensory discrimination,* and what role does it play in the evaluation of products? What is meant by a *just noticeable difference?*
13. What are *surrogate indicators?* How are they used in the consumer evaluation process?
14. What factors influence the *importance* of evaluative criteria?
15. What is the *conjunctive decision rule?*
16. What is the *disjunctive decision rule?*
17. What is the *elimination-by-aspects decision rule?*
18. What is the *lexicographic decision rule?*
19. What is the *compensatory decision rule?*
20. How can knowledge of consumers' evaluative criteria and criteria importance be used in developing marketing strategy?
21. How can knowledge of the decision rules consumers might use in a certain purchase assist a firm in developing marketing strategy?

DISCUSSION QUESTIONS

22. Respond to the questions in Consumer Insight 16–1.
23. Would you use an attribute-based or an attitude-based decision approach to purchasing (or renting or giving to) the following? Which, if any, situational factors would change your approach?
    a. Adopting a pet from a shelter
    b. A movie
    c. An e-reader
    d. A BBQ grill
    e. A personal trainer

   f. Athletic shoes
   g. A new shampoo
   h. An apartment
   i. A smartphone
   j. Habitat for Humanity

24. Repeat Question 23 but speculate on how your instructor would answer. In what ways might his or her answer differ from yours? Why?
25. For which, if any, of the options in Question 23 would you make an affective decision? What role would situational factors play?

26. What metagoals might you have, and what would be their relative importance to you, in purchasing (or renting or giving to) the options in Question 23?

27. List the evaluative criteria and the importance of each that you would use in purchasing (or renting or giving to) the options in Question 23. Would situational factors change the criteria? The importance weights? Why?

28. Repeat Question 27 but speculate on how your instructor would answer. In what ways might his or her answer differ from yours? Why?

29. Describe a purchase decision for which you used affective choice, one for which you used attitude-based choice, and one for which you used attribute-based choice. Why did the type of decision process you used vary?

30. Identify five products for which surrogate indicators may be used as evaluative criteria in a brand-choice decision. Why are the indicators used, and how might a firm enhance their use (i.e., strengthen their importance)?

31. The table below represents a particular consumer's evaluative criteria, criteria importance, acceptable level of performance, and judgments of performance with respect to several brands of motor scooters. Discuss the brand choice this consumer would make when using the lexicographic, compensatory, and conjunctive decision rules.

Evaluative Criteria	Criteria Importance	Minimum Acceptable Performance	Alternative Brands					
			Aprilia	Vespa	Honda	Piaggio	BMW	Kymco
Price	30	4	2	4	2	4	2	4
Horsepower	15	3	4	2	5	5	4	5
Weight	5	2	3	3	3	3	3	3
Gas economy	35	3	4	4	3	2	4	5
Color selection	10	3	4	4	3	2	5	2
Frame	5	2	4	2	3	3	3	3

Note: 1 = Very poor; 2 = Poor; 3 = Fair; 4 = Good; and 5 = Very good.

32. Describe the decision rule(s) you used or would use in buying (or renting or giving to) the options listed in Question 23. Would you use different rules in different situations? Which ones? Why? Would any of these involve an affective choice?

33. Describe your last two major and your last two minor purchases. What role did emotions or feelings play? How did they differ? What evaluative criteria and decision rules did you use for each? Why?

34. Discuss surrogate indicators that could be used to evaluate the perceived quality of the products or activities listed in Question 23.

APPLICATION ACTIVITIES

35. Present 10 students with the choice set from the left panel of Consumer Insight 16–1 and present a different set of 10 students with the choice set from the right panel. Do you observe the decoy effect (choice share of option A goes up with the addition of the inferior option C)? Have the students who chose the decoy explain their choice—what reasons do they provide?

36. Conduct an extensive interview with two students who recently made a major purchase. Have them describe the process they went through. Report your results. If each represented a market segment, what are the strategy implications?

37. Develop a list of evaluative criteria that students might use in evaluating alternative apartments they might rent. After listing these criteria, go to the local or student newspaper or local online apartment locator, select several apartments, and list them in a table similar to the one in Question 31. Then have five other students evaluate this information and have each indicate the apartment he or she would rent if given only those alternatives. Next,

ask them to express the importance they attach to each evaluative criterion, using a 100-point constant-sum scale. Finally, provide them with a series of statements that describe different decision rules and ask them to indicate the one that best describes the way they made their choice. Calculate the choice they should have made given their importance ratings and stated decision rules. Have them explain any inconsistent choices. Report your results.

38. Develop a short questionnaire to elicit the evaluative criteria consumers might use in selecting the following. Also, have each respondent indicate the relative importance he or she attaches to each of the evaluative criteria. Then, working with several other students, combine your information and develop a segmentation strategy based on consumer evaluative criteria and criteria importance. Finally, develop an advertisement for each market segment to indicate that their needs would be served by your brand.
    a. Wrist watch
    b. Running shoes
    c. Movie
    d. Fast-food restaurant
    e. Credit card
    f. Charity
    g. Home theater system
    h. Health club

39. Set up a taste test experiment to determine if volunteer taste testers can perceive a just noticeable difference between three different brands of the following. To set up the experiment, store each test brand in a separate but identical container and label the containers L, M, and N. Provide volunteer taste testers with an adequate opportunity to evaluate each brand before asking them to state their identification of the actual brands represented

as L, M, and N. Evaluate the results and discuss the marketing implications of these results.
    a. Colas
    b. Diet colas
    c. Lemon-lime drinks
    d. Carbonated waters
    e. Tortilla chips
    f. Orange juices

40. For a product considered high in social status, develop a questionnaire that measures the evaluative criteria of that product, using both a *direct* and an *indirect* method of measurement. Compare the results and discuss their similarities and differences and which evaluative criteria are most likely to be used in brand choice.

41. Find and copy or describe an ad that uses a surrogate indicator. Is it effective? Why? Why do you think the firm uses this approach?

42. Find and copy or describe an ad that attempts to change the importance consumers assign to product class evaluative criteria. Is it effective? Why? Why do you think the firm uses this approach?

43. Find and copy or describe two ads that are based on affective choice. Why do you think the firm uses this approach? Are the ads effective? Why?

44. Interview a salesperson for one of the following products. Ascertain the evaluative criteria, importance weights, decision rules, and surrogate indicators that he or she believes consumers use when purchasing this product. What marketing implications are suggested if their beliefs are accurate for large segments?
    a. Luxury cars
    b. Kitchen furniture
    c. Air purification systems
    d. Cosmetics
    e. Ski clothes

REFERENCES

1. This chapter opener is based on A. M. Tybout and B. J. Calder, eds., *Kellogg on Marketing,* 2nd ed. (New York: John Wiley & Sons, 2010), pp. 351–52; S. S. Iyengar and M. R. Lepper, "When Choice Is Demotivating: Can One Desire Too Much of a Good Thing?," *Journal of Personality and Social Psychology* 79, no. 6 (2001), pp. 995–1006; R. H. Thaler and C. R. Sustein, *Nudge: Improving Decisions about Health, Wealth, and Happiness* (New Haven: Yale University Press, 2008), pp. 109–10; P. M. Todd and G. Gigerenzer, "Simple Heuristics That Make Us Smart," *Behavioral and Brain Sciences* 23, no. 5 (2000), pp. 727–41; A. E.

Weiss, "Keep It Simple: Avoid Giving Your Customers Decision Overload," *Guardian,* March 13, 2014, www.theguardian.com/small-business-network/2014/mar/13/avoid-giving-customers-decision-overload, accessed August 29, 2014; "Supermarket Choice Overload: Consumer Reports," *Local SYR,* February 4, 2014, www.localsyr.com/story/d/story/supermarket-choice-overload-consumer-reports/25371/xybHtf6gOEeL5YJD12lpJA, accessed August 29, 2014; M. Little, "Costco's Strategy for Avoiding the Bullwhip," blog post on *Supply Chain Management,* September 10, 2013, http://cmuscm.blogspot.com/2013/09/

costcos-strategy-for-avoiding-bullwhip.html, accessed August 29, 2014; P. Boatwright and J. C. Nunes, "Reducing Assortment: An Attribute-Based Approach," *Journal of Marketing,* July 2001, pp. 50–63; N. LaPorte, "The Anti-Zappos Subscription Shopping Finds Its Niche," *Fast Company,* March 2014, pp. 44, 46; A. Chernev and R. Hamilton, "Assortment Size and Option Attractiveness in Consumer Choice among Retailers," *Journal of Marketing Research,* June 2009, pp. 410–20; www.stitchfix.com, accessed July 5, 2018.

2. See, for example, J. R. Bettman, M. F. Luce, and J. W. Payne, "Constructive Consumer Choice Processes," *Journal of Consumer Research,* December 1998, pp. 187–217; C. L. Brown and G. S. Carpenter, "Why Is the Trivial Important?," *Journal of Consumer Research,* March 2000, pp. 372–85; J. Swait and W. Adamowicz, "The Influence of Task Complexity on Consumer Choice," *Journal of Consumer Research,* June 2001, pp. 135–48; M. Heitmann, D. R. Lehmann, and A. Herrmann, "Choice Goal Attainment and Decision and Consumption Satisfaction," *Journal of Marketing Research,* May 2007, pp. 234–50. See also O. Amir and D. Ariely, "Decisions by Rules," *Journal of Marketing Research,* February 2007, pp. 142–52.

3. For a discussion and related research, see G. A. Haynes, "Testing Boundaries of the Choice Overload Phenomenon," *Psychology and Marketing,* March 2009, pp. 204–12.

4. E. Hall, "Overwhelmed U.K. Online Shoppers Can Justbuythisone," *Advertising Age,* December 16, 2010.

5. See recent examples such as T. Ghosal, E. Yorkston, J. Nunes, and P. Boatwright, "Multiple Reference Points in Sequential Hedonic Evaluation: An Empirical Analysis," *Journal of Marketing Research* 52 (October 2014), pp. 563–77; L. Lee et al., "Money, Time and the Stability of Consumer Preferences," *Journal of Marketing Research* 52 (April 2015), pp. 184–99.

6. S. Yang and M. Lynn, "More Evidence Challenging the Robustness and Usefulness of the Attraction Effect," *Journal of Marketing Research* 51 (August 2014), pp. 508–13; K. Lee, K. Weaver, and S. Garcia, "I'll Have Fries with That: Increasing Choice Complexity Promotes Indulgent Food Choices," *Psychology & Marketing* 33, no. 7 (July 2016), pp. 505–15.

7. B. Mittal, "A Study of the Concept of Affective Choice Mode for Consumer Decisions," in *Advances in Consumer Research,* vol. 21, ed. C. T. Allen and D. R. John (Provo, UT: Association for Consumer Research, 1994), p. 256.

8. J. F. Durgee and G. C. O'Connor, "Why Some Products 'Just Feel Right,'" in *Advances in Consumer Research,* vol. 22, ed. F. R. Kardes and M. Sujan (Provo, UT: Association for Consumer Research, 1995), p. 652.

9. See M. T. Pham et al., "Affect Monitoring and the Primacy of Feelings in Judgment," *Journal of Consumer Research,* September 2001, pp. 167–87. See also P. R. Darke, A. Chattopadhyay, and L. Ashworth, "The Importance and Functional Significance of Affective Cues in Consumer Choice," *Journal of Consumer Research,* December 2006, pp. 322–28.

10. M. T. Pham, "Representativeness, Relevance, and the Use of Feelings in Decision Making," *Journal of Consumer Research,* September 1998, pp. 144–59. For a more elaborate model of affective appraisal and its influence on subsequent judgment, see C. W. M. Yeung and R. S. Wyer Jr., "Affect, Appraisal, and Consumer Judgment," *Journal of Consumer Research,* September 2004, pp. 412–24.

11. See also R. Dhar and K. Wertenbroch, "Consumer Choice between Hedonic and Utilitarian Goods," *Journal of Marketing Research,* February 2000, pp. 60–71.

12. See B. Shiv and A. Fedorikhin, "Heart and Mind in Conflict," *Journal of Consumer Research,* December 1999, pp. 278–91.

13. J. A. Ruth, "Promoting a Brand's Emotional Benefits," *Journal of Consumer Psychology* 11, no. 2 (2001), pp. 99–113; J. C. Sweeney and G. N. Soutar, "Consumer Perceived Value," *Journal of Retailing* 77 (2001), pp. 203–20.

14. See P. Krishnamurthy and M. Sujan, "Retrospection versus Anticipation," *Journal of Consumer Research,* June 1999, pp. 55–69. See also B. Shiv and J. Huber, "The Impact of Anticipating Satisfaction on Consumer Choice," *Journal of Consumer Research,* September 2000, pp. 202–16; C. P. S. Fong and R. S. Wyer Jr., "Cultural, Social, and Emotional Determinants of Decisions under Uncertainty," *Organizational Behavior and Human Decision Processes* 90 (2003), pp. 304–22.

15. This section is based on S. P. Mantell and F. R. Kardes, "The Role of Direction of Comparison, Attribute-Based Processing, and Attitude-Based Processing in Consumer Preference," *Journal of Consumer Research,* March 1999, pp. 335–52. For a discussion of the specific role of advertising-based attitudes, see W. E. Baker, "The Diagnosticity of Advertising Generated Brand Attitudes in Brand Choice Contexts," *Journal of Consumer Psychology* 11, no. 2 (2001), pp. 129–39.

16. See R. Dhar, S. M. Nowlis, and S. J. Sherman, "Comparison Effects on Preference Construction," *Journal of Consumer Research,* December 1999, pp. 293–306.

17. C. Qui, Y. H. Lee, and C. W. M. Yeung, "Suppressing Feelings," *Journal of Consumer Psychology* 19 (2009), pp. 427–39.

18. G. Kalyanaram and J. D. C. Little, "An Empirical Analysis of Latitude of Price Acceptance in Consumer Package Goods," *Journal of Consumer Research,* December 1994, pp. 408–18.

19. See S. Hoeffler and D. Ariely, "Constructing Stable Preferences," *Journal of Consumer Psychology* 8, no. 2 (1999), pp. 113–39; A. V. Muthukrishnan and F. R. Kardes, "Persistent Preferences for Product Attributes," *Journal of Consumer Research,* June 2001, pp. 89–102.

20. P. H. Bloch, "Seeking the Ideal Form," *Journal of Marketing,* July 1995, pp. 16–29; Dhar and Wertenbroch, "Consumer Choice between Hedonic and Utilitarian Goods." See also D. Horsky, P. Nelson, and S. S. Posavac, "Stating Preference for the Ethereal but Choosing the Concrete," *Journal of Consumer Psychology* 14, no. 1/2 (2004), pp. 132–40.

21. D. J. Mitchell, B. E. Kahn, and S. C. Knasko, "There's Something in the Air," *Journal of Consumer Research,* September 1995, pp. 229–38; D. R. Lichtenstein, R. G. Netemeyer, and S. Burton, "Assessing the Domain Specificity of Deal Proneness," *Journal of Consumer Research,* December 1995, pp. 314–26; D. R. Lichtenstein, S. Burton, and R. G. Netemeyer, "An Examination of Deal Proneness across Sales Promotion Types," *Journal of Retailing* 2 (1997), pp. 283–97; V. Ramaswamy and S. S. Srinivasan, "Coupon Characteristics and Redemption Intentions," *Psychology & Marketing,* January 1998, pp. 50–80.

22. See, e.g., R. Pieters and L. Warlop, "Visual Attention during Brand Choice," *International Journal of Research in Marketing* 16 (1999), pp. 1–16.

23. B. L. Bagus, "The Consumer Durable Replacement Buyer," *Journal of Marketing,* January 1991, pp. 42-51.

24. A. Kirmani and P. Wright, "Procedural Learning, Consumer Decision Making, and Marketing Choice," *Marketing Letters* 4, no. 1 (1993), pp. 39-48; G. S. Carpenter, R. Glazer, and K. Nakamoto, "Meaningful Brands from Meaningless Differentiation," *Journal of Marketing Research,* August 1994, pp. 339-50; S. M. Broniarczyk and A. D. Gershoff, "Meaningless Differentiation Revisited," in *Advances in Consumer Research,* vol. 24, ed. M. Bruck and D. J. MacInnis (Provo, UT: Association for Consumer Research, 1997), pp. 223-28.

25. B. Abrams, "Hanes Finds L'eggs Methods Don't Work with Cosmetics," *Wall Street Journal,* February 3, 1983, p. 33.

26. See S. H. Ang, G. J. Gorn, and C. B. Weinberg, "The Evaluation of Time-Dependent Attributes," *Psychology & Marketing,* January 1996, pp. 19-35.

27. P. M. Parker, "Sweet Lemons," *Journal of Marketing Research,* August 1995, pp. 291-307; S. Shapiro and M. T. Spence, "Factors Affecting Encoding, Retrieval, and Alignment of Sensory Attributes in a Memory-Based Brand Choice Task," *Journal of Consumer Research,* March 2002, pp. 603-17; B.-K. Lee and W.-N. Lee, "The Effect of Information Overload on Consumer Choice Quality in an On-Line Environment," *Psychology & Marketing,* March 2004, pp. 159-83.

28. See A. Kirmani and A. R. Rao, "No Pain, No Gain," *Journal of Marketing,* April 2000, pp. 66-79.

29. See, e.g., V. P. Norris, "The Economic Effects of Advertising," *Current Issues and Research in Advertising,* 1984, pp. 39-134; S. Burton and D. R. Lichtenstein, "Assessing the Relationship between Perceived and Objective Price-Quality," in *Advances in Consumer Research,* vol. 27, ed. M. E. Goldberg, G. Gorn, and R. W. Pollay (Provo, UT: Association for Consumer Research, 1990), pp. 715-22; D. J. Faulds, O. Grunewald, and D. Johnson, "A Cross-National Investigation of the Relationship between the Price and Quality of Consumer Products," *Journal of Global Marketing* 8, no. 1 (1994), pp. 7-25.

30. K. M. Elliott and D. W. Roach, "Are Consumers Evaluating Your Products the Way You Think and Hope They Are?," *Journal of Consumer Marketing,* Spring 1991, pp. 5-14; J. Baumgartner, "On the Utility of Consumers' Theories in Judgments of Covariation," *Journal of Consumer Research,* March 1995, pp. 634-43.

31. See S. Ratneshwar et al., "Benefit Salience and Consumers' Selective Attention to Product Features," *International Journal of Research in Marketing* 14 (1997), pp. 245-59; R. Dhar and I. Simonson, "Making Complementary Choices in Consumption Episodes," *Journal of Marketing Research,* February 1999, pp. 29-44; J. K. H. Lee and J. H. Steckel, "Consumer Strategies for Purchasing Assortments within a Single Product Class," *Journal of Retailing* 75, no. 3 (1999), pp. 387-403.

32. See, e.g., P. W. J. Verlegh, H. N. J. Schifferstein, and D. R. Wittink, "Range and Number-of-Levels Effects in Derived and Stated Measures of Attribute Importance," *Marketing Letters* 13, no. 1 (2002), pp. 41-52.

33. M. P. Gardner, "Advertising Effects on Attributes Recalled and Criteria Used for Brand Evaluations," *Journal of Consumer Research,* December 1983, pp. 310-18; S. B. MacKenzie, "The Role of Attention in Mediating the Effect of Advertising on Attribute Importance," *Journal of Consumer Research,* September 1986, pp. 174-95; G. D. Olsen, "Creating the Contrast," *Journal of Advertising,* Winter 1995, pp. 29-44.

34. A. R. Rao, L. Qu, and R. W. Ruekert, "Signaling Unobservable Product Quality through a Brand Ally," *Journal of Marketing Research,* May 1999, pp. 258-68; C. Janiszewski and S. M. J. van Osselaer, "A Connectionist Model of Brand-Quality Associations," *Journal of Marketing Research,* August 2000, pp. 331-50.

35. C. J. Thompson, "Interpreting Consumers," *Journal of Marketing Research,* November 1997, p. 443. Published by the American Marketing Association; reprinted with permission.

36. See G. Haubl and V. Trifts, "Consumer Decision Making in Online Shopping Environments," *Marketing Science,* Winter 2000, pp. 2-21.

37. S. Thompson, "Food Marketers Count on Snacks," *Advertising Age,* April 24, 2006, p. 4.

38. Insight based on J. Huber, J. Payne and C. Puto, "Adding Asymmetrically Dominated Alternatives: Violations of Regularity and Similarity Hypothesis," *Journal of Consumer Research* 9 (June 1982), pp. 90-98; P. Rodway, A. Schepman, and J. Lambert, "Preferring the One in the Middle: Further Evidence for the Centre-Stage Effect," *Applied Cognitive Psychology* 26 (2012), pp. 215-22; N. Patel, "Psychological Hacks That Will Make Your Pricing Page Irresistible," *Marketing Land,* May 18, 2015, www.marketingland.com, accessed July 5, 2018; K. Hendricks, "The Decoy Effect: Why You Make Irrational Choices Every Day (Without Even Knowing It)," blog entry, February 12, 2018, www.kenthendricks.com, accessed July 5, 2018; K. Hendricks, "The Center-Stage Effect: This Is Why You Choose the Product in the Middle (Even if It Is Bad)," blog entry, March 2, 2018, www.kenthendricks.com, accessed July 5, 2018.

39. M. L. Ursic and J. G. Helgeson, "The Impact of Choice and Task Complexity on Consumer Decision Making," *Journal of Business Research,* August 1990, pp. 69-86; P. L. A. Dabholkar, "Incorporating Choice into an Attitudinal Framework," *Journal of Consumer Research,* June 1994, pp. 100-18; T. Elrod, R. D. Johnson, and J. White, "A New Integrated Model of Non-compensatory and Compensatory Decision Strategies," *Organizational Behavior and Human Decision Processes* 95 (2004), pp. 1-19.

40. See E. Coupey, "Restructuring," *Journal of Consumer Research,* June 1994, pp. 83-99.

41. See D. L. Alden, D. M. Stayman, and W. D. Hoyer, "Evaluation Strategies of American and Thai Consumers," *Psychology & Marketing,* March 1994, pp. 145-61; J. E. Russo and F. Lecleric, "An Eye-Fixation Analysis of Choice Processes for Consumer Nondurables," *Journal of Consumer Research,* September 1994, pp. 274-90.

42. See J. G. Helgeson and M. L. Ursic, "Information Load, Cost/Benefit Assessment and Decision Strategy Variability," *Journal of the Academy of Marketing Science,* Winter 1993, pp. 13-20; W. J. McDonald, "The Roles of Demographics, Purchase Histories, and Shopper Decision-Making Styles in Predicting Consumer Catalog Loyalty," *Journal of Direct Marketing,* Summer 1993, pp. 55-65; M. S. Yadav, "How Buyers Evaluate Product Bundles," *Journal of Consumer Research,* September 1994, pp. 342-53; A. V. Muthukrishnan, "Decision Ambiguity and Incumbent Brand Advantage," *Journal of Consumer Research,* June 1995, pp. 98-109; D. E. Hansen and J. G. Helgeson, "Consumer Response to Decision Conflict from Negatively Correlated Attributes," *Journal of Consumer Psychology* 10, no. 3 (2001), pp. 150-69.

17 Outlet Selection and Purchase

©Iain Masterton/Alamy

LEARNING OBJECTIVES

LO1 Describe how retailing is evolving.

LO2 Discuss the relationship among retail outlets as part of omni-channel shopping.

LO3 Explain the retail and consumer attributes that affect outlet selection.

LO4 Summarize the in-store and online influences on brand choice.

LO5 Understand how purchase plays a role in the shopping process.

Brick-and-mortar stores are fighting for their survival using technology—the very thing that in many ways threatens its existence—to do so.[1] Here are some examples:

Window Displays. It isn't that consumers are going to the mall any less; it's that they are visiting fewer stores. Having shopped online, they have narrowed their selection of alternatives and have less need to visit as many stores as they had in the past. This creates a greater challenge for window displays purposed to convert passersby to shoppers. With the help of technology, the staid, flat, static window displays can be transformed into visual hooks that hijack consumer attention, encourage consumer interaction, and drive foot traffic into stores. For example, using (Kinect technology) sensors, the Nike Hyperdunk1shoes window display lets you measure how high you can jump (to dunk a basketball) as follows:

. . . you stand on a street-side blue dot and jump as high as you can. Then, the system asks if you'd like to save your score—you respond by touching a "yes" or "no" decal on the window, which makes the entire plate glass window feel like a touch screen (though really, the camera is just tracking the movement of your hand). You can compare yourself, Strava-style, to others on a web ranking site.

For its "Merry Kissmass" holiday window display, retailer Ted Baker created a giant digital Mistletoe atop the entrance of its New York City store. Consumers were invited "to take 'selfies' kissing in front of a digital backdrop and tag them (hashtag) KissTed on Instagram or Twitter. The photos, displayed on another screen, were entered into a contest to win a romantic getaway."

Shoppertainment. Brick-and-mortar stores have the opportunity to create "shoppertainment" experiences for consumers using technology to help design environments that are emotionally engaging, entertaining, and memorable. A showcase example is the 44,000-square-foot Burberry flagship store on Regent Street in London. Housed in the remodeled 1820 Prince Regent building, the Burberry store is theatrical and technologically integrated throughout. Upon entering the store, consumers see the world's tallest indoor retail screen (over 22 feet), self-supporting stone staircases, and well-placed scatterings of "bespoke blackened bronze lanterns, furniture, plasterwork, timber paneling and flooring, traditional glass signage," all of which provide the intended effect—giving customers the feeling that they have arrived at Burberry World Live, the Burberry web landing page. Mirrors instantly transform into screens to show "runway footage and exclusive video and satellite technology-enabled live streaming of events." At set times throughout the day, "disruptive digital takeovers" occur and all 500 speakers and 100 screens are synchronized to show the same thing. RFID (radio-frequency identification)-tagged merchandise trigger mirrors in the store and in the fitting rooms to turn into video screens that provide the consumer with product information they would not otherwise have—design, stitching, history—and in the process create touch points for consumers to form deep engagement with the brand. To make purchasing web-easy, iPad-armed Burberry personnel not only can answer questions about inventory and place orders, but also can take payment on the spot, eliminating the need for customers to carry merchandise to cashiers and wait in line to pay for products. The store is designed to provide a website user experience in a brick-and-mortar store.

Inventory. The advantage of web stores for unlimited inventory can be matched by brick-and-mortar stores that extend their physical inventory with virtual inventory displayed on large-screen kiosks, touch-screen order points, and online kiosks. One example is the virtual footwear wall piloted by Adidas, the global athletic retailer. The wall, which includes LCD touch screens that allow consumers to create shoes and see them rendered in 3-D, has led to substantial increase in sales.

Tracking Consumers. Web stores can track consumer wanderings on the Internet by following the trail of cookies (bits of software code). Now a number of firms (RetailNext, Euclid, ShopperTrak, Brickstream, Shopperception) are using technology—smartphones' unique Wi-Fi address, heat maps, sensors that track radio signals from mobile phones—to allow brick-and-mortar stores to do the same in the physical world. Brick-and-mortar stores can capture data—consumer wanderings in the store, the amount of time they spent at various locations, the items they considered, the number of passersby who entered the store, the length of time of their stay, whether or not they return—that can be analyzed to provide information vital for planning staffing needs, merchandise decisions, store layouts, and window displays to attract customers and influence shoppers. In addition, with knowledge of consumer in-store location, retailers can send information and offers—coupons, discounts—about merchandise to the consumer's smartphone (Shopperception and Shopkick) when consumers are in the vicinity of the merchandise.

Clearly, retailing is an exciting area of marketing. *What's next on the retail horizon?*

Before, during, or after searching for information and selecting a brand, consumers select a retail outlet from which to make a purchase. Brands are critical to retail outlets because brands are a major determinant of at which outlets consumers will shop. Retail outlets are critical to brands because retailers provide brands with the access to the consumers they desire. The TheraBreath ad in Illustration 17-1 provides an example of the importance of retail outlets and brands to each other as the brand and several retailers are advertised simultaneously.

Our focus in this chapter is to describe the evolving retail landscape, the factors affecting outlet selection, and the in-store (and online) determinants of brand choice.

ILLUSTRATION 17-1

This TheraBreath ad shows how marketers often use advertising to create brand demand and to direct consumers to appropriate outlets.

Source: Dr. Harold Katz, LLC

THE EVOLVING RETAIL SCENE

LO1

As the opening examples illustrate, retailing is changing dramatically, particularly as a function of technology. We use *retail outlet* to refer to any source of products or services for consumers. This has moved well beyond physical stores and catalogs to include the Internet, interactive TV ads, and mobile shopping apps. Roughly 25 years ago, the following description of the future of retailing by Bill Gates, founder of Microsoft, seemed far-fetched. However, much if not all of what he predicted already has happened or is happening now, along with a few things he didn't predict. Consider his statement:

You're watching "Seinfeld" on TV, and you like the jacket he's wearing. You click on it with your remote control. The show pauses and a Windows-style dropdown menu appears at the top of the screen, asking if you want to buy it. You click "yes." The next menu offers you a choice of colors; you click on black. Another menu lists your credit cards asking which one you'll use for this purchase. Click on MasterCard or whatever. Which address should the jacket go to, your office or your home or your cabin? Click on one address and you're done—the menus disappear and "Seinfeld" picks up where it left off.

Just as you'll already have taught the computer about your credit cards and addresses, you will have had your body measured by a 3-D version of supermarket scanners, so the system will know your exact size. And it will send the data electronically to a factory, where robots will custom tailor the jacket to your measurements. An overnight courier service will deliver it to your door the next morning.[2]

Today, computers can learn and recall consumer information and preferences in a number of ways including behavioral tracking, full-body scanners exist that allow for custom-fitted apparel, and many TV service providers display interactive TV ads that allow users to get more information about products in the ads and even, as in the case of Reebok, purchase them.[3] Beyond interactive TV ads is the concept of interactive TV shows in which brands within the shows can be searched and bought using the TV remote (see Chapter 8). If you think this seems far-fetched, a wide range of brands, from charities to cars to cosmetics, are now using interactive videos to engage viewers with the expectation of converting them to buyers.[4]

Our main focus in the current chapter is on store (bricks-and-mortar) and Internet (online) retailing with additional discussion on mobile retailing, including the increasing role of mobile apps in terms of their influence on how consumers shop both online and in store. Also, other forms of nonstore retailing such as catalogs, telemarketing, direct mail, and TV (referred to as **in-home shopping**) continue to be important. A number of these are discussed as well, as appropriate. The integration of the Internet and mobile with stores has given rise to an additional issue that we discuss, namely, omni-channel marketing and consumers.

Online Retailing

As indicated in Chapter 15, the Internet is a major information source. It is also a major retail channel and one aspect of in-home shopping. The following table shows the current size of online retailing.[5]

Current Size of Online Retailing in the United States	
U.S. Internet users (millions)	289
Total U.S. retail sales online (billions)	$452
Total U.S. retail sales (billions)	$5,080
Online spending as a percent of all retail spending	8.9%

Several aspects of this table specifically, and online shopping more generally, are worth noting. First, annual growth in the number of Internet users has stabilized. This is because most of the U.S. adult population—about 90 percent—are already online (see Chapter 15). Second, the percentage of online sales to total retail sales continues to rise, with an estimate for 2021 more than doubling 2014's 6.5 percent.[6] Third, estimates indicate that between 66 and 88 percent of Internet users have purchased a product online at some point. Thus, future growth in online sales will continue to come more from increasing the amount of online spending from *existing* buyers than from increasing the number of Internet users. And there is still substantial room to grow, across product categories, from online grocery sales, which have very low Internet penetration at 3 percent, to online clothing sales, which are still only 18 percent of retail sales.[7] Finally, the Internet has a major influence on in-store sales, which further increases its importance as a retail channel. Such "cross-channel" effects are discussed later in the chapter.

The top five categories of online purchases in the U.S. include (1) apparel (including accessories and footwear), (2) electronics and appliances, (3) personal care products, (4) beauty items, and (5) home furnishings. Recent reports indicate that Amazon accounts for over 40 percent of U.S. online retail sales.[8] According to Mintel, consumers shop online for various reasons, with price and convenience topping the list, as follows:[9]

Reason to Buy Online	Percent
Better prices	60
More convenient	59
No shipping fees	42
Only available online	26
Option to pick up in store	17
Customer service is just as good	12
Same-day delivery	9
Ability to buy directly from social media platform	4
Online tools help me virtually try it out first	3

Percentages sum to more than 100 because many consumers listed several reasons for buying online.

Source: Lightspeed/Mintel, "Online Shopping, U.S., May 2018," www.mintel.com.

In the past, consumers shopped with catalogs for similar reasons as shopping online. Until recently, though, many industry experts predicted the demise of catalogs. Despite a substantial drop in the number mailed to consumers, catalogs still capture consumers' attention (23 percent of consumers) and motivate shopping (one-third of consumers). According to one retail expert, catalogs are an opportunity to "differentiate brands and sustain existing customer relationships." Catalogs and the Internet appear to work in a complementary fashion, as part of an omni-channel strategy to be discussed later in the chapter.[10]

There are consumers who may be attracted to the ease of buying online and the ability to get good deals and may not mind if Internet shopping is functional—but not all consumers view the Internet in this way. Clearly, for online buying to continue growing, marketers must overcome barriers that suppress online buying. This is not a simple proposition. There are consumers who enjoy shopping and the "fun" factor in shopping. Many probably enjoy the social aspect of shopping with others that the Internet generally lacks. Other barriers are discussed next.

Barriers to Online Shopping   For some products, people, and situations, the Internet offers a better combination of selection, convenience, price, and other attributes than do catalogs, traditional stores, or other outlets. However, in many cases, consumers prefer traditional retail stores. Indeed, traditional offline stores are still the top-ranked *purchasing* channel for most consumers in most categories.[11] An obvious barrier to Internet shopping is online access, although, as we've seen in Chapter 15, this is diminishing rapidly. For those who are online, other barriers exist for U.S. shoppers, as listed below:[12]

Reason *Not* to Buy Online	Percent
I buy it in-store instead	54
Prefer to see it in person	49
Don't want to pay shipping fees	27
Don't want to wait on delivery	22
Prices are too high online	13
Prefer to talk to salesperson in person	10
Inadequate product descriptions	8
Poor product images	6

Percentages sum to more than 100 because many consumers listed several reasons for NOT buying online.

Source: Lightspeed/Mintel, "Online Shopping, U.S., May 2018," www.mintel.com.

These and other barriers relate to the issue of converting browsers to buyers, a major concern to Internet marketers looking to enhance online sales. One barrier in particular, the issue of wanting "to see it in person" or inability to "touch," is being addressed by marketers. Innovative technology now helps simulate the experience for online shoppers (see Chapter 11) with expectations of converting them to online buyers. For example, 3-D software allows consumers to envision their view from any seat in a stadium before buying tickets for a sporting event (see Chapter 15), thereby alleviating a fan's concern of not being able to "touch" or, in this case, "see" the game.

Mobile Retailing

With more than three-fourths of U.S. adults owning a smartphone, mobile phones, and apps are increasingly playing a role in how consumers shop. Currently, mobile retailing (or m-commerce) accounts for roughly 34 percent of all online retail, or e-commerce, sales, and is projected to exceed 50 percent by 2021.[13] Mobile is becoming a separate yet important shopping and buying channel for retailers. One study found that as consumers become more comfortable with shopping on their phones, they order and spend more.[14] Furthermore, a recent survey reported the following behaviors of smartphone shoppers:[15]

- The top two categories shopped for in the prior month are clothing, shoes, and accessories (70 percent) and electronics (51 percent).
- Of those that use their phone for shopping, almost two-thirds shop weekly on their phone.
- More than half have at least three shopping apps on their phone.

Smartphone users can access the retailer's mobile website or download a mobile app to shop and make purchases. The apps are downloaded for several reasons, as identified below. But to be used, the advantages must be clear to shoppers. Shopping apps that are easy to navigate, offer big discounts, and have a wide range of products are valued most by mobile shoppers. Retailers want their apps to be downloaded. Research has found that the retailer will retain twice as many customers if those shoppers make a purchase on the retailer's app within seven weeks of download.[16]

Reasons to Download Shopping Apps	Percent
To access discounts or offers	49
To complete a purchase	37
Got a specific reward for downloading the app	34
To make a specific activity/task easier	32
Recommended by others	32
Past experience with a similar app	20
Activity unavailable on the mobile website	12

Percentages sum to more than 100 because many consumers listed several reasons to download shopping apps.

Source: Google, "How People Shop on Their Phones," *Think with Google,* October 2016.

Mobile retailing also influences how consumers shop *in the store.* Beyond price comparison and discounts, mobile websites and apps allow consumers to search for brands, prices, and deals while standing in a physical store. In no small way, mobile and mobile apps have become an in-store influence and can interact with other in-store elements to influence shopping in numerous ways that were historically not possible.

Smartphone Activities Done In-Store	Percent
Compared prices	51
Browsed or looked for products	43
Looked for discounts or offers	42
Read reviews of a product	35
Took a picture of a product	27
Tried on/used a product	21
Spoke with a sales representative	15
Shared a product with friends/family	12

Percentages sum to more than 100 because many consumers listed several reasons for smartphone activities done in-store.

Note: Activities done in the past 30 days

Source: Google, "How People Shop on Their Phones," *Think with Google,* October 2016.

As highlighted in the table above, smartphone technology enhances the consumer's in-store shopping experience with the ability to share pictures of products with others or gain knowledge about the product from experts outside the store environment. Consumer Insight 17–1 discusses additional technological advancements in mobile retailing. But as with online retailing, there are limitations to mobile retailing to be discussed later in the chapter.

Store-Based Retailing

The majority of retail sales take place in physical stores, and this will remain true for the foreseeable future. A recent study reported that 50 percent of Gen Yers typically shop, and prefer to do so, at brick-and-mortar locations.[17] However, traditional store-based retailing is certainly vulnerable in ways that play into the hands of online retailers, as stated earlier in the chapter. Department stores such as Sears and Macy's are closing stores, and other brick-and-mortar retailers like Toys 'R' Us and Radio Shack have closed their operations permanently.[18] Why are consumers abandoning physical stores? Consider the results of a Roper survey asking consumers why they don't like shopping in stores:[19]

Reason Not to Shop In-Store	Percent
Salespeople are poorly informed	74
Waiting in long lines	73
Hard time finding things	64
Parking and traffic	64
Dealing with crowds	58
Hard to get someone to wait on you	54
The time it takes to shop	38
Don't like shopping	34

Percentages sum to more than 100 because many consumers listed several reasons NOT to shop in-store.

Source: From Roper Reports Telephone Survey, August 2003.

Obviously, for many people, in-store shopping is perceived as neither fun nor an efficient use of time. However, retailers are fighting back with different formats.[20] Lifestyle centers that mimic small-town retailing of the past with sidewalks, restaurants, and parks, in an outdoor setting, are emerging to generate excitement and adapt to the changing shopping habits of consumers. Brand stores are emerging as major sales volume outlets as well

Mobile Retailing: The Next Technological Frontier

The next technological development in the modern shopping experience is the incorporation of mobile retailing. The time has come for retailers to embrace mobile retailing as they did online retailing. Some brick-and-mortar and online retailers have begun to supplement existing shopping experiences with mobile apps. For instance, Kroger's app allows customers to find information and discounts on products available for purchase while shopping in-store. In some cases, retailers are selling to consumers exclusively through mobile apps, similar to online-only retailers. For example, an app called Myntra sells thousands of fashion brands of clothing, shoes, and household décor directly to consumers.[21]

This shift toward mobile retailing is taking place in many innovative ways to enhance the consumer shopping experience. Several emerging trends in mobile retailing are listed below:

- **Push-Based Apps.** Initially, most retailing apps were pull-based, whereby consumers would have to initiate an interaction with an app, such as requesting information or putting something in a shopping cart. Now, more and more apps are push-based. The apps anticipate user needs and provide related information through automatic updates. For example, Saks Fifth Avenue uses push notifications to invite consumers to livestream their holiday window unveiling. Consumers who opted in to the push notifications also receive a variety of tailored alerts, ranging from the availability of Saks' holiday gift-giving guide to promotional gift card giveaways.

- **In-Store Beacons and Mobile Ads.** Many retailers place Bluetooth devices throughout their brick-and-mortar stores to alert mobile customers (within the signal's range) of product information, sales, and customized ads. Target uses this technology to let shoppers know, via push notifications, of nearby deals as they walk throughout the store. Target's app even includes indoor mapping that provides walking directions to the aisle location of desired products—and indicates whether those products are on sale.

- **One-Click Mobile Payments.** Mobile payments through apps are not uncommon; however, prior to 2017, Amazon had exclusive rights to the "one-click" payments technology. When Amazon's patent expired, this enabled many more retailers to begin using one-click mobile payments—because they no longer had to pay a licensing fee to Amazon. One example is TGI Fridays restaurants. Once a customer's payment information is stored

as promotional devices for brands, such as Levi's, Nike, and Reebok. Stores within stores also are being tried. Walmart has eyeglasses, banks, and restaurants all under one roof. Major retailers like Walmart and Nordstrom are experimenting with smaller versions of its larger stores.[22]

Apart from different formats, traditional department stores have tried to create "destination areas" within their stores that enhance their overall image and drive ongoing store traffic. For example, Macy's has bridal salons in select locations, and Target offers designer collections, such as Lilly Pulitzer (see Chapter 9), to draw consumers in.[23] In fact, Target's use of designer fashion collections has created a trendier image than that created by Walmart and others.

More and more, retailers are trying to enhance the experiential component of their stores through layout, music, personal shoppers, and so on. Some stores are targeted at the in the TGI Fridays mobile app, ordering food and drinks is more streamlined. Patrons can reorder drinks to their table without requesting a server, or they can order takeout to be picked up from any restaurant location, all with a click of one button.

- **Augmented Reality (AR).** Some retailers are experimenting with AR to allow consumers to visualize a product in their homes, on their bodies, or in other contexts. For example, Anthropologie has an app that gives consumers detailed 3-D views of their furniture superimposed over images of the rooms in the consumers' own homes. The app also allows consumers to view furniture from different angles, in various degrees of lighting and shadows. Anthropologie's AR technology helps alleviate consumers' perceived risks, discussed later in the chapter, associated with buying furniture.

- **Artificial Intelligence (AI).** Retailers are using artificial intelligence technology to interact with consumers in various ways. For example, apps with AI can learn consumers' preferences and subsequently make personalized suggestions. One such AI tool is the "chatbot." H&M uses a chatbot to engage its consumers by first asking a few questions about their preferences. Based on the consumers' responses, the chatbot then follows up with various suggestions of products available for purchase through the app. More generally, retailers use "chatbots" to manage customer service and facilitate the purchasing process for their customers.

As new technological trends continue to emerge, and consumers become increasingly familiar with them, it will become increasingly more important for retailers to remain current to provide optimal shopping experiences for their consumers.

Critical Thinking Questions

1. Consider the new mobile retailing technologies discussed in the insight. Do you feel these technologies enhance the customer's shopping experience? Why or why not?

2. Consider your own previous experiences with mobile retailing as a consumer. Answer the following questions and be prepared to share with others.
    a. As a consumer, have you experienced any of the new mobile retailing trends?
    b. If so, which, and how would you describe your experience?
    c. Are there any of these emerging trends in mobile retailing that you would prefer not to engage with as a consumer? Why or why not?

3. Some consumers have ethical issues with mobile retailing. What potential negatives could you see with these emerging technologies and how might you recommend that retailers address them?

experiential component. American Girl stores don't just sell dolls; they also offer experiences such as dining and parties! Part of this appears to play off of the socialization of children to the shopping experience as well as mother–daughter and father–daughter shopping experiences (see Chapter 6). Similarly, Bass Pro Shops sell products, but also have aquariums to showcase fish, a shooting range, a restaurant, and so on. To attract the experience-driven Millennial, or Gen Y, shopper, The Home Depot offers in-store classes on topics such as ceiling fan installation or drywall repair, and sells the corresponding materials for these projects.[24]

As you can see, as the functionality of the web has made competing on that dimension more difficult for traditional retailers, they are focusing on becoming giant entertainment centers, an emphasis on the social element. For example, the Mall of America near Minneapolis is built around an amusement park. It also has a miniature golf course,

The Place for fun.

MALL OF AMERICA® & DESTINATION BLOOMINGTON
VISITORS GUIDE

Source: The Bloomington Convention and Visitors Bureau/Home of Mall of America

nightclubs, theme restaurants, and an aquarium (see Illustration 17-2). More than 1 million people from nearby Chicago visit the Mall of America each year. According to a senior manager, "They can get anything you can get here in Chicago, except the experience."[25] Retailing is clearly an exciting, competitive area. Those retailers who best understand their consumers will be the ones to prosper in the future.

Omni-Channel Retailing for the Omni-Channel Shopper

LO2

As described earlier, technology has enabled consumers to more easily access the retailer through various channels, including online or in-store. Because consumers access many channels, and often simultaneously, most retailers are engaging in multi- or omni-channel marketing to reach their customers. Various channels include physical stores, the Internet and mobile, catalogs, and so on. This cross-channel approach can take many forms and can be successful for a number of reasons. For example, regional in-store retailers such as Tyler's, shown in Illustration 17-3, can use the Internet to instantly become national and international in scope. On the flip side, the Internet allows traditional retailers such as Nordstrom and Saks Fifth Avenue to reach smaller communities where they could not otherwise operate economically.

The need for omni-channel marketing reflects shifts in consumer shopping. Consumers are increasingly likely to be **omni-channel shoppers**—that is, *consumers who browse and/or purchase using multiple channels.*[26] That is, they might use a mobile app that looks for deals and coupons at that store. Or they might search the Internet at home to get more information

Source: Tyler's

ILLUSTRATION 17-3

An online sales site, such as this Tyler's site, instantly converts a local or regional firm into a national and even international one.

about the product and then buy it at a store. Or they may order the product online and pick it up in the store. Research on omni-channel shoppers suggests that[27]

- Roughly 73 percent of shoppers utilize two or more channels to browse and buy.
- Omni-channel shoppers have higher incomes and spend an average of 4 percent more with an in-store retailer and 10 percent more online than single-channel shoppers.
- The more channels used, the more money an omni-channel shopper spends in-store.

The need for omni-channel shopping arises because no retailing format is optimal on all dimensions. Retail channels tend to be complementary. Thus, the Internet can be used to overcome a lack of informed salespeople or the inconvenience of researching products in-store, while in-store can provide "touch" and immediacy of purchasing.[28]

Omni-Channel Shopping Behaviors   As previously mentioned, omni-channel shoppers can use the various retail channels in many ways while searching for and purchasing a product. These *shoppers who search online and ultimately buy a product at a physical store* engage in **webrooming. Showrooming** is the opposite. As discussed in Chapter 4, showrooming is common among Gen Yers who go to the brick-and-mortar store to touch, try out, or try on a product and then buy it online. Showrooming has gained momentum among consumers looking for a deal. The Internet facilitates price comparisons (see Chapter 15), and often the cheapest price is found online, not in-store. Nevertheless, webrooming is more common (69 percent of consumers) than is showrooming (46 percent).[29] The barriers to online shopping mentioned earlier in the chapter contribute to the preference for webrooming.

Figure 17–1 illustrates omni-channel shopping across the three channels discussed in the chapter, highlighting the showrooming and webrooming behaviors. Using the digital camera purchase example from Chapter 16, a consumer engaging in webrooming will research cameras online at home before visiting her local Best Buy to examine the actual cameras she identified in her online search. While at Best Buy, she physically inspects the relevant cameras and ultimately purchases the Canon PowerShot. Instead of doing online research at home before going to the store, the webrooming consumer may do her research while in store using her phone, researching cameras through either Best Buy's app or other mobile websites. She again examines the actual products identified from her search while at the physical Best Buy location and purchases the Canon PowerShot in-store. The showrooming consumer follows the path in reverse. With the camera purchase, the consumer starts her process at her local Best Buy. While in the store, she examines the various cameras and decides which brand she wants to purchase (the Canon PowerShot). But instead of buying the product at the store, she goes home and searches the Internet for the best price on the PowerShot and buys it through a different online retailer. Or she may use a price comparison app while in Best Buy and make the purchase from Amazon or another online retailer

FIGURE 17-1   Omni-Channel Shoppers Search and Purchase in Multiple Channels: Showrooming and Webrooming

offering a lower price before leaving the store. *Would you classify yourself as someone who engages in webrooming or showrooming?*

The Omni-Channel Retailing Strategy   As illustrated above, omni-channel shoppers are savvy consumers. Given their heavy reliance on mobile and mobile shopping apps, these shoppers tend to be younger Gen Yers as well as upscale and tech-savvy Gen X and older Gen Yers. Understanding the value omni-channel shoppers can provide has motivated retailers to develop a well-coordinated channel system for these customers. Consider the following statement by a Macy's executive:

> We talk a lot at Macy's about "omnichannel" retailing. Our customer is multi-dimensional. She is busy at work and out with friends. She always has her mobile device in her hand. She's active on Facebook and Twitter and YouTube and a dozen other social media sites. We want that customer to be able to interact with Macy's no matter where she is or how she shops. It makes no difference to us whether she buys something in our store or online, or whether she is shopping from her desktop computer or her Droid or her iPad. Macy's best customers are those who shop us in-stores and online. We have a whole series of strategies in place to drive our store customers to the Web, and our online customer to the stores. Today's customer is not monolithic. And that's the way we are approaching our customer.[30]

Marketing across channels, though rewarding in terms of consumer spending, is quite challenging. Consider the major task of coordinating a seamless look and feel across channels, while making sure to be plugged into the appropriate mobile apps and optimized for the major search engines. It may not be surprising then that around 25 percent of companies have not yet developed an omni-channel strategy.[31] An effective omni-channel approach can take advantage of the same technology consumers use to shop to help combat showrooming and bring customers back in the store. Several courses of action within an omni-channel system include[32]

- *Design the physical store to look like a "showroom."* With this layout, stores will not carry inventory in-store, but consumers can try on, feel, and see the product, and then order it online in-store. Having the purchase shipped home, the consumer no longer has to be concerned with out-of-stock items or carrying shopping bags.
- *Educate employees.* As stated earlier, consumers avoid shopping in stores due to ineffective sales associates. To keep shoppers in-store, employees should be properly trained to have up-to-date knowledge of the store's products. Furthermore, sales associates clutching mobile devices can better help consumers with ordering or product assistance throughout the store.
- *Provide in-aisle checkout service.* By bringing the "sales register" to the customer, the challenge that consumers may abandon their purchase when seeing a long line at checkout may be avoided.
- *Provide price comparisons in-store.* Deal-seeking showroomers may leave one retailer's store to buy online from a competitor. Giving these consumers an opportunity to compare prices in-store and match competitors' prices keeps the shopper's purchase not only in the store but also with the retailer overall.

Illustration 17–4 shows how retailers such as Nordstrom can appeal to the omni-channel shopper. Some companies have started to see the benefits of omni-channel retailing.

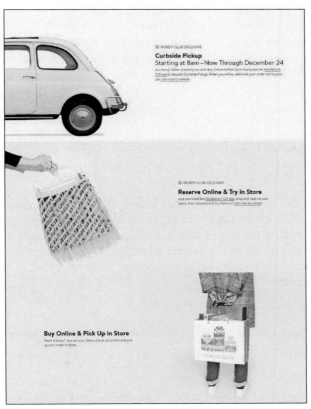

Source: Nordstrom, Inc

ILLUSTRATION 17-4

A retailer's website, such as this for Nordstrom, highlights various services provided in-store to appeal to the omni-channel shopper.

Omni-Channel Shopping

IKEA, the giant Swedish retailer of all things for your home, has giant brick-and-mortar showroom stores well known for its meandering pathways that encourage wanderings throughout the store—the better for consumers to see and buy things. IKEA also has an easy-to-navigate website from which consumers can order goods. Plus, it mails a catalog to consumers' homes. Even with this "triple threat," IKEA still had not solved the consumer's problem of determining how things—sofas, chairs, table—will look in their homes. That was until IKEA introduced its augmented reality app. This is how it works. A consumer flipping through the IKEA catalog sees something she likes—say, a sofa. She scans the page with her smartphone or tablet. Then she places the catalog where she would likely place the sofa—say, against the wall and in front of the window. Using her smart device, she can see how the sofa would look in her home. The virtual reality app, available for 100 of the 300 products in the IKEA catalog, is likely to be helpful to the 14 percent of IKEA customers who buy the wrong size furniture and the 70 percent of IKEA customers who don't know the size of their homes.[33]

Retailers who started out as pure play web stores have discovered the value and benefits of adding brick-and-mortar stores. Warby Parker, the purveyor of stylish, boutique eyewear, is a case in point. Introduced in 2010, it successfully disrupted the eyewear industry with the implementation of its e-commerce model, selling eyewear directly to consumers. It was able to offer prices below industry standards by vertically integrating the design and manufacturing of eyewear, thereby eliminating the practice of paying (exorbitant) brand licensing fees. Taking a page out of Apple's retail store, its newly opened Soho New York brick-and-mortar store is designed with the focus on the consumer experience. The 20-foot-wide store has the feel of an old library—terrazzo floor, brass library lamps, rolling ladders, (meticulously selected) musty books (that consumers can buy). Rather than locked behind glass cases, eyewear is out in the open for consumers to try. Consumers can view themselves in one of the mirrors that surround the store or take a photo of themselves in a custom photobooth—an experience more novel than a selfie taken with a cell phone. To complete the offering, an in-house optometrist is available seven days a week to provide $50 eye exams booked online.

E-tailers can use their webstore data—customer characteristics and location, sales volume—to guide

Integrating shopping technology into their stores, Timberland displays "Touchwalls," an inventory system, on store walls. Crate&Barrel stores provide shoppers with "Mobile Totes" to scan product bar codes with a tablet and learn more about those products. Crate&Barrel's sales increased 10 percent when testing this technology. The importance of adapting to the consumer's use of technology when shopping is summarized by a Crate&Barrel executive:[34]

> More and more, people are actually expecting that we know their shopping preferences. They are expecting us to be smarter and smarter.

Consumer Insight 17–2 explores additional examples and approaches to omni-channel consumers and marketing.

decisions for their physical store—store location, store size, merchandise. For example, analysis of its web shoppers guided webstore Bonobos, the purveyor of upscale men's clothing, to open its physical stores, Guideshop, to solve the problem of customers' desire to try on clothes before they buy them online. Customers make appointments (usually lasting 45 minutes) to visit a Guideshop store for fittings. Guideshops are smaller stores (700 square feet) that carry sufficient inventory—khaki chinos in all 11 waist sizes and 4 inseam lengths—for store personnel to fit and size customers. Customers can then purchase clothing from the Bonobos website during their visit or at a later time of their choosing.

Analysis of webstore data may suggest that rather than a flagship store, the e-tailer is better served with a less expensive pop-up store in a high-foot-traffic area for a short amount of time (a few days to several months). This is an option that Etsy, seller of handmade products, and even eBay, the online auction house, have used. Like an old-fashioned craft fair, Etsy's pop-up stores provided a physical space for its sellers to showcase their handmade products. Sellers used laptops to show their inventory and used smart devices to transact sales using Paypal and Square. E-bay's first physical store, its Christmas emporium in London, was housed in a container box. Opened for four days of holiday shopping, it attracted 2,500 customers. The store's virtual inventory consisted of 350 top-rated products projected onto walls, each accompanied by social media recommendations and bearing a QR (quick response) code that consumers could scan with mobile devices to pay eBay. By establishing an offline presence, these online retailers are doubling down benefits from the interaction of their physical and web markets. Physical stores showcase selected merchandise that consumers can touch and feel while relying on their e-stores' virtual merchandise for their backroom inventory. The physical store can attract new customers while simultaneously creating buzz for its web market customers.

Critical Thinking Questions

1. What products are currently marketed web-only that, in your opinion, should remain web-only versus those that should consider establishing a (permanent, pop-up) physical store?

2. Some traditional retailers (Macy's, Nordstrom, Walmart) have made themselves omni-channel. They have established web stores, allowing customers the convenience of buying online and returning in-store. Has this convenience encouraged you to buy products that you otherwise wouldn't have?

3. Would you consider yourself an omni-channel shopper? What is the value of this approach to you as a consumer?

ATTRIBUTES AFFECTING RETAIL OUTLET SELECTION

LO3

The selection of a specific retail outlet involves a comparison of the alternative outlets on the consumer's evaluative criteria. This section considers a number of evaluative criteria commonly used by consumers to select retail outlets. While much of the research on outlet selection relates to choosing among retail stores (e.g., JCPenney versus Sears), when applicable we also draw linkages to choosing among online retailers (e.g., barnesandnoble.com versus Amazon.com) based on emerging evidence.

Outlet Image

A given consumer's or target market's perception of all the attributes associated with a retail outlet is generally referred to as the **store image**. This is the same as the concept of *brand image* discussed in Chapter 9. One study found the following nine dimensions and

23 components of these nine dimensions of store image.[35] Notice that the store atmosphere component is primarily affective, or feeling in nature.

Store Image	
Dimension	**Components**
Merchandise	Quality, selection, style, price
Service	Layaway plan, sales personnel, easy return, credit, delivery
Clientele	Customers
Physical facilities	Cleanliness, store layout, shopping ease, attractiveness
Convenience	Location, parking
Promotion	Advertising
Store atmosphere	Congeniality, fun, excitement, comfort
Institutional	Store reputation
Posttransaction	Satisfaction

Source: J. D. Lindquist, "Meaning of Image," *Journal of Retailing,* Winter 1974, pp. 29–38.

This study focused on stores; the components and, probably, the dimensions will require adjusting for use with other types of retail outlets. For example, a study of *online retailer image* found the following seven dimensions and related components that influenced online outlet selection.[36] *Which dimensions and components of store image translate the most to an online context and which the least?*

Online Retailer Image	
Dimension	**Components**
Usefulness	Good product offers and information, value, aligned with interests
Enjoyment	Fun, attractive, pleasant to browse
Ease of use	Easy to use and navigate, flexible site
Trustworthiness	Reputation, information safety and security
Style	Helpful, friendly, knowledgeable, calm
Familiarity	Advertising online and offline, general familiarity
Settlement	Fast and flexible delivery and transactions

Source: Reprinted from H. van der Heijden and T. Verhage, "Online Store Image," *Information and Management* 41 (2004), pp. 609–17.

As these studies suggest, overall retailer image (both Internet and store-based) relates to both functional and affective dimensions. The importance of the affective component cannot be overstated.

Marketers make extensive use of image data in formulating retail strategies.[37] First, marketers control many of the elements that determine an outlet's image. Second, differing groups of consumers desire different things from various types of retail outlets. Thus, a focused, managed image that matches the target market's desires on both affective and functional elements is essential for most retailers. For example, fashion retailers build affective image by relying on designer collections to enhance their high-end, fashion-forward appeal, as shown in Dillard's ad in Illustration 17–5.

Other outlets focus on more functional attributes. For example, online retailers Amazon.com and Rakuten.com focus heavily on breadth of merchandise and price. And brick-and-mortar stores like 7-Eleven focus almost exclusively on convenience (easy access, extended hours, and quick service) for consumers in those situations where convenience is the key attribute. Interestingly, convenience stores such as upstart Choice Market are expanding their offerings to include fresh

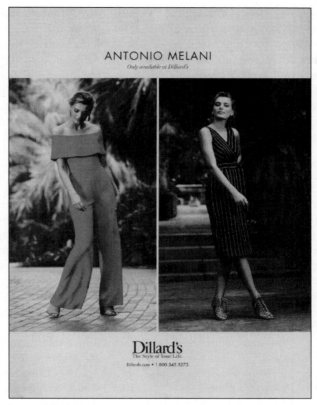

Source: Dillard's

ILLUSTRATION 17-5

Designer collections are one way retailers can enhance their image and position their stores appropriately for their target customers, as shown in this Dillard's ad.

foods and online ordering to meet demands of consumers who want more breadth in selection with convenience. From Choice's website:

> So we decided to do things a little differently. You shouldn't have to choose between quality ingredients, accommodating hours, and instant access when you're shopping for food. At Choice, you can have it all—fresh, local, and on-demand. We combined quick service, fresh quality food from local vendors, and the latest technology into a new kind of convenience store: Choice, a Denver market open 24×7. Buy your groceries, customize a meal, grab a snack on the go, and pick up whatever necessities you may have forgotten—all at the same place, and all within a few minutes. Can't get to the store? Order online, on our app, or through Postmates. Choice is at your fingertips.[38]

Retailer Brands

Closely related to store image are **store brands.** At the extreme, the store or outlet is the brand. The Gap, Victoria's Secret, and lululemon are examples. All the items carried in the store are the store's own brand. Traditionally, retailers carried only manufacturers' brands, and only a few, such as Sears, developed their own house or store brands. In the 1970s, many stores began to develop store brands as low-price alternatives to national brands, and many continue with this approach.[39]

Increasingly, however, retailers such as Walmart and Target are developing and promoting high-quality brands with either the store's name or an independent name. Such brands not only provide attractive margins for these outlets; if they are developed appropriately, they also become an important attribute of the outlet. That is, they are another reason for the consumer to shop that store.[40] And importantly, no other outlet can carry this brand. The key to success of store brands seems clear—high quality at a reasonable price. The traditional pattern of providing reasonable quality at a low price is no longer necessarily optimal.[41] In fact, emphasizing quality over price may be particularly beneficial if the brand carries the store's name or will become associated with the store. In fact, a recent study finds that, at least up to a point, increased consumer use of retailer brands (e.g., Target's Archer Farms) leads to increased loyalty to that retailer (Target).[42]

Retail Advertising

Retailers use advertising to communicate their attributes, particularly sale prices, to consumers. It is clear that price advertising (traditional, online, and mobile) can attract people to stores. Revealing results were obtained in a major study involving newspaper ads in seven cities for a range of product categories (motor oil, sheets, digital watches, pants, suits, coffee makers, dresses, and mattresses). The impact of the retail advertisements varied widely by product category. For example, 88 percent of those who came to the store in response to the advertisement for motor oil purchased the advertised item, compared with only 16 percent of those responding to the dress ad. Approximately 50 percent of the shoppers overall purchased the advertised item that attracted them to the store.

As Figure 17–2 illustrates, purchases of the advertised item understate the total impact of the ad. *Sales of additional items to customers who came to purchase an advertised item* are referred to as **spillover sales.** Spillover sales in this study equaled sales of the advertised items; that is, for every $1 spent on the sale item by people who came to the store in response to the advertising, another $1 was spent on some other item(s) in the store.[43]

Another study produced the results shown below:[44]

	Reason for Visiting Store	
Action	Purchase Promoted Item	Other Reason
Dollars spent on promoted items	$11.30	$ 3.27
Dollars spent on regular items	18.48	21.90
Total	$29.78	$25.17
Store profit	$ 5.64	$ 5.77

Retailers evaluating the benefits of price or other promotions must consider the impact on overall store sales and profits, not just those of the advertised item. And while a large percentage of retail advertising stresses price, particularly sales price, studies continue to show that price is frequently not the prime reason consumers select a retail outlet.[45] Thus, many retailers could benefit by emphasizing service, selection, or the affective benefits of their outlets, especially in appealing to the omni-channel shopper. Affective benefits may be particularly effective for hedonic rather than utilitarian products.[46]

Online retailers advertise in mass media both to attract consumers to their sites and to build an image. Price and value are clearly important attributes for online shoppers,[47] and many sites promote this feature. In addition, research suggests that customization of online promotions such as e-mail to better match the characteristics and needs of target customers can dramatically increase online store traffic.[48]

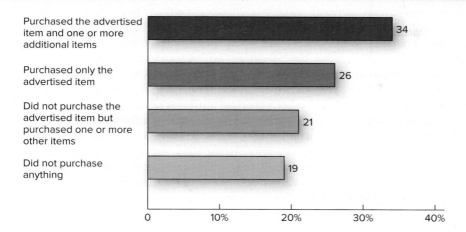

Expenditures of Individuals Drawn to a Store by an Advertised Item   FIGURE 17-2

Price Advertising Decisions   Retailers face three decisions when they consider using price advertising:

1.   How large a price discount should be used?
2.   Should comparison or reference prices be used?
3.   What verbal statements should accompany the price information?

Consumers tend to assume that any advertised price represents a price reduction or sale price. Showing a comparison price increases the perceived savings significantly. However, the strength of the perception varies with the manner in which the comparison or reference price is presented. A **reference price** is *a price with which other prices are compared.* In the claim, "Regularly $9.95, now only $6.95," $9.95 is the reference price. An **external reference price** is *a price presented by a marketer for the consumer to use to compare with the current price.* An **internal reference price** is *a price or price range*[49] *that a consumer retrieves from memory to compare with a price in the market.*[50]

Although there are situational influences and individual differences,[51] most consumers understand external reference prices and are influenced by them but do not completely believe them.[52] The reason for the lack of belief is the practice of some retailers of using inflated reference prices. These inflated prices could be "suggested list prices" in markets where virtually all sales are at a lower level. Or they may reflect prices that the store set for the merchandise originally that were too high and produced few sales. The price reduction being shown then merely corrects an earlier pricing error but does not provide meaningful benefit to the consumer. Because price and sale advertising have a strong impact on consumer purchases, the FTC and many states have special guidelines and regulations controlling their use.[53]

The best approach for retailers seems to be to present the sale price and (1) the dollar amount saved if it is large, (2) the percentage saved when it is large, and (3) both if both are large. Thus, $10 savings on a $200 item should show the dollar savings but not the percentage savings. A $10 saving on a $20 item could emphasize both the dollar and the percentage savings. A $1 saving on a $3 item should focus on the percentage savings.[54] The regular price could be shown in any of these conditions.[55] The regular price (the price on which the savings are calculated) should be the price at which the store normally sells a reasonable volume of the brand being discounted.

Such words or phrases as "now only," "compare at," or "special" appear to enhance the perceived value of a sale. However, this varies by situation, initial price level and discount size, consumer group, and retail outlet.[56] Is "50 percent off" or "buy one, get one free" likely to be perceived as a better value? It depends in large part on the nature of the item being promoted. For stock-up items such as detergent, they are viewed as equivalent. However, for perishable items such as bread, the "50 percent off" is seen as a better value.[57]

Retailers need to use caution in how they use price advertising. Such advertising signals not only the price of the advertised items but also the price level of the store.[58] And because price level, quality, service, and other important attributes often are linked in the consumer's mind, inappropriate price advertising can have a negative effect on the store's image.[59]

The Target circular ad in Illustration 17–6 places primary emphasis on the dollar savings but not the reference price or the sale price. To the extent that the target audience "knows" that the regular price for this item is high, they will use this internal reference price or range in making a judgment. And because the dollar savings are relatively large, the research we have reviewed suggests that presenting the dollar savings is sound strategy.

Outlet Location and Size

Location plays an important role in consumer store choice. If all other things are approximately equal, the consumer generally will select the closest store.[60] Likewise, the size of an outlet is an important factor. Unless the customer is particularly interested in fast service or convenience, he or she would tend to prefer larger outlets over smaller outlets, all other things being equal.[61] Interestingly, some of the major online players are "superstores" such as Amazon.com. Thus, retailer size appears to play a role online as well.

This Target circular ad focuses primarily on the dollar savings. Should the percentage savings also be stressed?

Source: Target Corporation

The **retail attraction model,** also called the **retail gravitation model,** is used to calculate the level of store attraction based on store size and distance from the consumer. In the retail gravitation model, store size is measured in square footage and assumed to be a measure of breadth of merchandise. The distance or travel time to a store is assumed to be a measure of the effort, both physical and psychological, to reach a given retail area.

The effect of distance or travel time varies by product.[62] For a convenience item or minor shopping good, distance is important because shoppers are unwilling to travel very far for such items. However, major high-involvement purchases such as automobiles or specialty items such as wedding dresses generate greater willingness to travel.

Willingness to travel also varies with the size of the shopping list for that trip.[63] Thus, a consumer who would not be willing to travel very far to purchase three or four convenience items may willingly go much farther if 20 or 30 such items are to be purchased on the same trip.

Consumers often combine shopping trips and purposes.[64] Thus, a consumer may visit a health club, have lunch with a friend, pick up the laundry, shop for food for the next few days, and pick up a prescription on one trip. Thus, retail patronage is in part a function of an outlet's location in relation to other outlets and consumers' travel patterns. Combining outlets or adding departments in response to such shopping patterns can produce value for customers and increased revenue for the firm.[65] For example, many supermarkets also have pharmacies.

CONSUMER CHARACTERISTICS AND OUTLET CHOICE

The preceding discussion by and large has focused on store attributes independently of the specific characteristics of the consumers in the target market. However, different consumers have vastly differing desires and reasons for shopping and must be considered in relation to outlet features. If, for example, location is the only factor guiding outlet selection, today's shopper should always choose mobile stores given their proximity—the consumer's hand. Yet, as discussed earlier, the majority of retail sales take place in brick-and-mortar stores. Consumers may be willing to sacrifice distance to try on a business suit or talk with a salesperson about different brands of laptops. This section of the chapter examines two consumer characteristics that are particularly relevant to store choice: perceived risk and shopper orientation.

Perceived Risk

The purchase of products involves the risk (see Chapter 15) that they may not perform as expected. Such a failure may result in a high

- *Social cost* (e.g., a hairstyle that is not appreciated by one's peers).
- *Financial cost* (e.g., an expensive pair of shoes that become too uncomfortable to wear).
- *Time cost* (e.g., a television repair that requires the set to be taken to the shop, left, and then picked up later).
- *Effort cost* (e.g., a USB flash drive that is loaded with several hours of work before it fails).
- *Physical cost* (e.g., a new medicine that produces a harmful side effect).

The first of these is generally termed *social risk;* the next three are often considered to be *economic risk.* Product categories vary in the level and type of risk generally associated with them.[66] Table 17–1 shows that socks and gasoline are low in economic and social

TABLE 17-1 The Economic and Social Risk of Various Types of Products

Social Risk	Economic Risk	
	Low	**High**
Low	Wine (personal use) Socks Kitchen supplies Pens/pencils Gasoline	Laptop Auto repairs Clothes washer Insurance Doctor/lawyer
High	Fashion accessories Hairstyles Gifts (inexpensive) Wine (entertaining) Deodorant	Business suits Living room furniture Automobile Snowboard Ski suit

risk, while hairstyles and small gifts are low in economic risk but high in social risk. Other products, such as laptops and auto repairs, are low in social risk but high in economic risk. Finally, automobiles and living room furniture are high in both economic and social risk.[67] Table 17–1 also indicates the role of the situation in perceived risk. Wine is shown as low in both social and economic risk when used for personal consumption but high in social risk when served while entertaining.

The perception of these risks differs among consumers, depending in part on their past experiences and lifestyles. For this reason, **perceived risk** is considered a consumer characteristic as well as a product characteristic.[68] For example, while many individuals would feel no social risk associated with the brand of car owned, others would.

Like product categories, retail outlets are perceived as having varying degrees of risk. Traditional outlets are perceived as low in risk, whereas more innovative outlets such as online are viewed as higher risk.[69]

The above findings lead to a number of insights into retailing strategy,[70] including the following:

- Nontraditional outlets need to minimize the perceived risk of shopping, particularly if they sell items with either high economic or social risk. Lands' End attempts to reduce perceived risk by emphasizing toll-free, 24-hour ordering and customer service by phone; online ordering and live-chat customer service; and a 100 percent satisfaction guarantee. Word-of-mouth from satisfied customers reinforces these advertised policies.
- Nontraditional outlets need brand-name merchandise in those product categories with high perceived risk. Most online retailers feature such items.
- Traditional outlets, websites, and mobile apps of well-known retailers have a major advantage with high-perceived-risk product lines. These lines should generally be their primary strategy focus. Low-risk items can be used to round out the overall assortment.
- Economic risks can be reduced through warranties, reasonable return policies, security verification systems, and so forth. Such factors are critical to online shopping where financial security concerns are often high. Social risk is harder to reduce. A skilled sales force, known brands, and satisfaction guarantees can help reduce this type of risk.

Illustration 17–7 shows how Lands' End reduces perceived risk by providing a product guarantee.

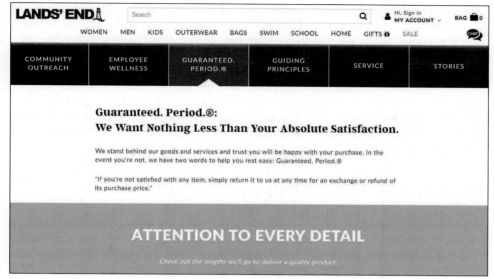

Source: Land's End

ILLUSTRATION 17-7

Guaranteeing complete satisfaction no matter what can greatly reduce the perceived risk of a purchase, particularly one made online, as shown by Lands' End.

Shopping Orientation

Individuals go shopping for more complex reasons than simply acquiring a product or set of products. Diversion from routine activities, exercise, sensory stimulation, social interactions, learning about new trends, and even acquiring interpersonal power ("bossing" clerks) are nonpurchase reasons for shopping.[71] Of course, the relative importance of these motives varies both across individuals and within individuals over time as the situation changes.[72] See again Illustration 17-2, which shows how malls can provide an inviting environment for activities in addition to shopping.

A shopping style that puts particular emphasis on certain activities or shopping motivations is called a **shopping orientation.** Shopping orientations are closely related to general lifestyle and are subject to similar influences. A recent study examined the shopper motivations of U.S. adult consumers across brick-and-mortar and digital (including mobile) retail outlets and found six shopping orientation segments, identified in the table below:[73]

Orientation	Percent	Characteristics
Bargain Hunter	22	These "precision shoppers" stick to a strict budget and often put their family's needs ahead of their own.
Knowledge Seeker	21	These "ratings and review junkies" do their homework online before making a purchase and may or may not buy it in store.
Practical Player	17	These "no-nonsense shoppers" tend to buy the basics, keep within their means, and want a fast, easy, and convenient shopping experience.
Store Reassurer	16	These consumers prefer to shop at a store rather than online. They can touch and feel the product and be more confident they are buying the right thing.
Brand Desirer	16	These shoppers choose brands that reflect their status and values and like to buy the very latest, often being the first to discover and try new things. Quality is a priority over price for this group.
Mobile Warrior	9	For these consumers, the smartphone is the most important weapon in their shopping arsenal, whether it's used to store coupons, research alternative products, or make purchases.

Note: Due to rounding, numbers add to over 100 percent.

Source: Y&R BAVLabs, "Shopperstates™: Six Dimensions of the New American Shopper," December 2015. Copyright 2015.

Webrooming likely appeals to *Store Reassurers* and those *Knowledge Seekers* who do purchase in-store, whereas *Mobile Warriors* are likely to engage in showrooming. Retailers seeking to entice *Mobile Warriors* to the store may pursue omni-channel tactics described earlier in the chapter, including in-store technology integration similar to Crate&Barrel's Mobile Totes. *Brand Desirers* may seek out boutique shops to find their brand-name products. However, they may shop at Target and other discounters who have added designer labels to their lineup. *Bargain Hunters* may not be the appropriate target for all retail stores, but large discount retailers such as Walmart are able to cater to the needs of this segment. And *Practical Players* are being offered the convenience of such service-oriented retailers as LensCrafters and Supercuts.

IN-STORE AND ONLINE INFLUENCES ON BRAND CHOICES

LO4

It is not uncommon to enter a retail outlet with the intention of purchasing a particular brand but to leave with a different brand or additional items. Influences operating within the retail outlet induce additional information processing and subsequently affect the final purchase decision. This portion of the chapter examines seven variables that singularly and in combination influence brand decisions inside a retail outlet (either a store or website): *point-of-purchase materials, price reductions, outlet atmosphere, stockout situations, website design, mobile and mobile apps,* and *sales personnel.* We begin by examining the extent and nature of unplanned purchases.

The Nature of Unplanned Purchases

The fact that consumers often purchase brands different from or in addition to those planned has led to an interest in unplanned purchases. **Unplanned purchases** are defined as *purchases made in a retail outlet that are different from those the consumer planned to make prior to entering that retail outlet.* While the term *unplanned purchase* implies a lack of rationality or alternative evaluation, this is not necessarily true. For example, the decision to purchase Del Monte rather than Green Giant peas because Del Monte is on sale is certainly not illogical.

Viewing most in-store and online purchase decisions as the result of additional information processing within the retail outlet leads to more useful marketing strategies than does viewing such purchases as random or illogical.[74] This approach allows the marketer to utilize knowledge of the target market, its motives, and the perception process to increase sales of specific items. Point-of-Purchase Advertising International (POPAI) uses the following definitions regarding in-store purchases:

- *Specifically planned.* A specific brand or item decided on before visiting the store and purchased as planned.
- *Generally planned.* A prestore decision to purchase a product category such as vegetables but not the specific item.
- *Substitute.* A change from a specifically or generally planned item to a functional substitute.
- *Unplanned.* An item bought that the shopper did not have in mind on entering the store.
- *In-store decisions.* The sum of generally planned, substitute, and unplanned purchases.

Unplanned purchases as defined above can be further subdivided into two categories: reminder purchases and impulse purchases. A *reminder purchase* would occur when a

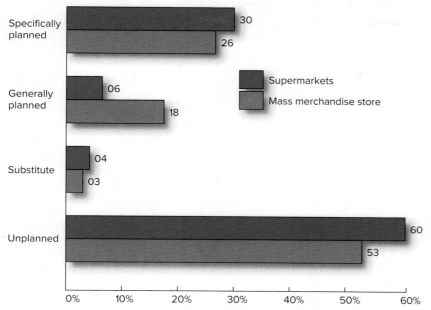

FIGURE 17-3

Supermarket Decisions: Two-Thirds Are Made In-Store

Source: *1995 POPAI Consumer Buying Habits Study* (Washington, DC: Point-of-Purchase Advertising Institute, 1995), p. 18, www.popai.com.

consumer notices Band-Aids in a store and remembers that she is almost out at home.[75] An **impulse purchase** would occur when a consumer sees a candy bar in the store and purchases it with little or no deliberation as the result of a sudden, powerful urge to have it.[76]

Figure 17–3 and Table 17–2 illustrate the extent of purchasing (in the United States and Canada) that is not specifically planned. It reveals that consumers make most item or brand decisions *after* entering the store. Interestingly, high levels of in-store decision making also have been found in the United Kingdom (76 percent), France (76 percent), Belgium (69 percent), Holland (80 percent), Australia (70 percent), and Brazil (88 percent).[77] *Can you explain differences in terms of cultural values?*

The research by POPAI regarding in-store decision rates was confirmed by a more recent OgilvyAction study of "six retail channels in the U.S." based on nearly 7,000 shopper intercept interviews. From this, they concluded that "72.4 percent of shoppers make in-store purchase decisions at the category, brand or quantity level."[78]

However, overall statistics can hide the fact that the rate of in-store and unplanned purchasing varies by product, consumer, and situation.

- *Product.* You may have noticed in Table 17–2 that some grocery items such as fresh fruits and vegetables, soft drinks, coffee, and antacids have relatively higher specifically planned rates. The rates of planning look even higher if you include generally planned. Interestingly, a recent grocery shopping study found that "94 percent of U.S. households prepare a written shopping list prior to grocery shopping, and 72 percent of shoppers never or only occasionally buy items not on the list."[79] It should be noted that grocery lists often include what POPAI would term "generally planned" and thus still would fall under "in-store" decisions. That's because as long as consumers must make some sort of decision, be it product type, brand, or size, then there is a chance for the retailer to have influence in the store.

TABLE 17-2	In-Store Purchase Behavior				
Product	Specifically Planned	Generally Planned +	Substituted +	Unplanned =	In-Store Decisions
Total study average*	30%	6%	4%	60%	70%
Hair care*	23	4	5	68	77
Magazines/newspapers*	11	3	1	84	89
Oral hygiene products*	30	5	5	61	71
Automotive oil*	21	–	–	79	79
Tobacco products*	32	6	–	61	68
Coffee*	42	5	6	47	58
First-aid products*	7	10	–	83	93
Cereal*	33	9	6	52	67
Soft drinks*	40	3	5	51	60
Mixers	23	6	4	68	77
Fresh fruits, vegetables*	67	7	1	25	33
Cold remedies†	28	35	19	18	72
Toothpaste/toothbrushes†	38	31	16	15	62
Antacids/laxatives†	39	37	12	12	61
Facial cosmetics†	40	34	11	15	60

Sources: *1995 POPAI Consumer Buying Habits Study (Englewood, NJ: Point-of-Purchase Advertising Institute, 1995);
†1992 POPAI/Horner Canadian Drug Store Study (Englewood, NJ: Point-of-Purchase Advertising Institute, 1992).

- **Consumer.** While overall POPAI estimates in-store decisions are made 70 percent of the time, this is higher in China (88 percent) and much lower in Germany (38 percent).[80] Considering the cultural, historical, and value-related factors that drive such differences, it is critical for marketers to understand on a country-by-country basis.
- **Situation.** When consumers choose a retailer for its lower prices and are only shopping one store during their outing (e.g., a trip to Walmart to shop for groceries for the week), unplanned purchases are higher.[81]

In conclusion, while the rate and nature of consumer in-store decisions vary as a function of numerous factors, consumers still make a substantial number of decisions "in-store." Thus, marketing efforts to influence in-store decisions are substantial as well. Such efforts are discussed next.

Point-of-Purchase Materials

Point-of-purchase (P-O-P) materials are common in the retailing of many products, and the impact these materials have on brand sales can be substantial. Research by POPAI examined the sales increase or "lift" generated by the addition of various types of P-O-P materials in supermarkets.[82] They examined both store-shelf and product-display materials. Shelf-based materials are placed in the main shelf for the product category and include price signage, coupon dispensers, shelf talkers, and dangling signage. Product display materials are those

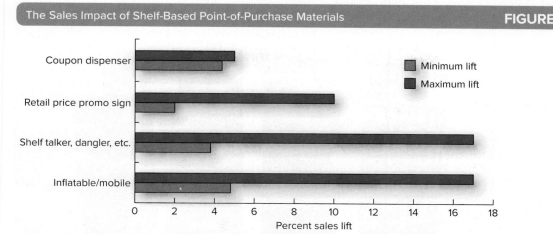

FIGURE 17-4

The Sales Impact of Shelf-Based Point-of-Purchase Materials

Source: *2001 POPAI P-O-PMeasure UP: Learnings from the Supermarket Class of Trade Study* (Washington, DC: POPAI, 2001), www.popai.com.

included with product displays located at the ends of aisles (end caps), on the store floor, and so on. Figure 17–4 provides a visual representation of the lift provided by four different shelf-based P-O-P materials.

This figure demonstrates that the effectiveness of P-O-P materials can vary substantially. Effectiveness also can vary across brands and products. Factors such as frequency of promotion, brand familiarity, prevalence of certain types of P-O-P, and extent of P-O-P change can influence effectiveness. Many of these factors relate to the ability to capture consumer attention (Chapter 8). Consider the following comment from a POPAI report:

> When consumers visit the main shelf and the same types of P-O-P advertisements are presented from week to week and brand-to-brand, they appear to be less receptive to the message.[83]

Thus, the relative prevalence of price promotion signs and coupon dispensers may help to explain why they provide less lift than do other approaches. Despite variability across type, category, and brand, P-O-P materials and mobile in-store advertising are an important and increasingly measurable in-store influence.[84] P-O-P materials are important globally, as shown by the Nestlé displays in Illustration 17–8.

Price Reductions and Promotional Deals

Price reductions and promotional deals (coupons, multiple-item discounts, and gifts) are generally accompanied by the use of some point-of-purchase materials. Therefore, the relative impact of each is sometimes not clear.[85] Nonetheless, there is ample evidence that in-store price reductions affect decision making and choice.[86] The general pattern, observed in the United States, the United Kingdom, Japan, and Germany, is a sharp increase in sales when the price is first reduced, followed by a return to near-normal sales over time or after the price reduction ends.[87]

Sales increases in response to price reductions come from four sources:[88]

1. Current brand users may buy ahead of their anticipated needs (stockpiling). Stockpiling often leads to increased consumption of the brand because it is readily available.

Point-of-purchase displays such as these Nestlé displays, are effective across cultures.

Source: Nestlé Group

2. Users of competing brands may switch to the reduced-price brand. These new brand buyers may or may not become repeat buyers of the brand.
3. Nonproduct category buyers may buy the brand because it is now a superior value to the substitute product or to "doing without."
4. Consumers who do not normally shop at the store may come to the store to buy the brand.

High-quality brands tend to benefit more than brands from lower-quality tiers when prices are reduced, and they suffer less when prices are raised.[89]

As discussed earlier under price advertising, consumers judge store quality and image in part on the basis of the number and nature of reduced-price items in the store.[90] Therefore, retailers need to carefully consider their sale price policies in view of both the sales of the discounted items and the impact these discounts will have on the store image. In addition, shoppers who purchase a large number of items at one time prefer stores with "everyday low prices"—all items in the store have relatively low prices, but few are reduced beyond that level ("on sale")—to stores with somewhat higher standard prices but many sale items.[91] Is a shirt from an Internet retailer priced at $24.95 plus $5.00 shipping and handling a better or worse deal than the same shirt priced at $29.95 with shipping and handling free? Consumers tend to perceive the former to be a better deal than the latter. Research has shown that *partitioned prices* (the first scenario above) produced greater demand and a lower recalled total cost than the combined price (the second scenario).[92]

Outlet Atmosphere

Store atmosphere is influenced by such attributes as lighting, layout, presentation of merchandise, fixtures, floor coverings, colors, sounds, odors, and the dress and behavior of sales and service personnel (see Chapter 13).

Atmosphere is referred to as **servicescape** when describing a service business such as a hospital, bank, or restaurant.[93] **Atmospherics** is the process managers use to manipulate the physical retail or service environment to create specific mood responses in shoppers. Internet retailers also have *online atmospheres* that are determined by graphics, colors, layout, content, entertainment features, interactivity, tone, and so forth.[94] *What type of atmosphere is portrayed in the Montague Bookmill site shown in Illustration 17-9?*

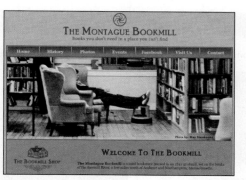

Source: The Montague Bookmill

ILLUSTRATION 17-9

Retail website designs such as that shown in the Montague Bookmill website should create an appropriate atmosphere or feelings as well as provide content and functionality.

A store's atmosphere affects the shopper's mood/emotions and willingness to visit and linger. It also influences the consumer's judgments of the quality of the store and the store's image.[95] Similarly, research shows that online atmospherics influence shopping behavior. For example, one study found that designing a website to elicit affective responses such as pleasure and arousal leads to increased willingness to browse.[96] Another study found that when a website offers restricted navigation, negative emotions (due to consumers' felt loss of control) occur, which lead to website avoidance.[97] Perhaps more important, positive mood/emotion induced while in the store or on the website increases satisfaction with the store or website, which can produce repeat visits and store loyalty.[98]

A major component of store atmosphere is the *number, characteristics, and behavior of other customers.*[99] Crowding must be considered because it can generate negative emotions and reduce browsing. And training staff how to appropriately deal with unruly customers is critical because the behaviors of other customers can influence the overall atmosphere.[100]

Music can have a major impact on the store environment (see Chapter 13). It can influence the time spent in the store or restaurant, the mood of the consumer, and the overall impression of the outlet.[101] However, it is important to match the music to the target audience. As shown below, baby boomers responded positively to classic rock music in a supermarket setting, but older adults did not:[102]

	Baby Boomers			Older Adults		
	Classic Rock	Big Band	Top 40	Classic Rock	Big Band	Top 40
Items purchased	31	11	15	4	12	14
Dollars spent	34	21	21	16	17	24
Shopping minutes	27	16	29	21	30	28

Marketers also are beginning to investigate the impact of *odors* on shopping behaviors (see Chapter 13).[103] Early studies suggest that odors can have a positive effect on the shopping experience, particularly if they are consistent with other aspects of the atmosphere such as the music being played.[104] However, like music, odor preference varies across customers, so caution must be used to ensure that the aroma is not offensive to target customers.[105]

Figure 17–5 illustrates the way store atmosphere influences shopper behavior. Several aspects in this figure are noteworthy. First, the physical environment interacts with individual characteristics. Thus, an atmosphere that would produce a favorable response in teenagers might produce a negative response in older shoppers. Second, store atmosphere influences sales personnel and customers, whose interactions then influence each other.

FIGURE 17-5   Store Atmosphere and Shopper Behavior

Source: "Framework for Understanding Environment-User Relationships in Service Organizations," Figure 2 in M. J. Bitner, "Servicescapes: The Impact of Physical Surroundings on Customers and Employees," from the April 1992 issue of the *Journal of Marketing.* Used by permission.

Finally, while this model focuses on store-based retailing, emerging research will continue to advance our understanding of online atmospherics.

Stockouts

Stockouts, *the store being temporarily out of a particular brand,* obviously affect a consumer's purchase decision. The consumer must then decide whether to (a) buy the same brand but at another store, (b) switch brands, (c) delay the purchase and buy the desired brand later at the same store, or (d) forgo the purchase altogether. Stockouts also can produce negative attitudes and/or word-of-mouth concerning the original store or positive attitudes and/or word-of-mouth concerning the substitute store or brand.

Three types of perceived costs affect the likely response of a consumer to a stockout.[106] *Substitution costs* refer to the reduction in satisfaction the consumer believes a replacement size, brand, or product will provide. This is a function of the consumer's commitment or loyalty to the preferred brand and the perceived similarity of potential substitutes.[107]

Transaction costs refer to the mental, physical, time, and financial costs of purchasing a substitute product or brand. *Opportunity costs* are the reduction in satisfaction associated with forgoing or reducing consumption of the product.[108]

Website Functioning and Requirements

Research suggests that roughly 7 in 10 online shopping carts are started but abandoned prior to purchase. This means billions in potential lost sales. The top five reasons for shopping cart abandonment are as follows:[109]

Shipping and handling costs too high	44%
Not ready to make the purchase	41
Wanted to compare prices on other sites	27
Product price higher than willing to pay	25
Wanted to save products in cart for later consideration	24

Clearly, there are many areas in which the design and functioning of retail websites can be improved. Obviously, managing shipping charges is important and companies are responding. Amazon.com offers Amazon Prime, a member-based program where consumers pay a fixed annual fee for free second-day shipping and reduced-rate overnight. Some retargeting efforts toward abandoned carts utilize e-mail marketing campaigns focused in part on some sort of promotional deal, in part because price and delivery charges are important online components. Complexity of the online buying process is also a problem. As a consequence, online retailers are simplifying and streamlining the online checkout process.[110] Some companies, such as Lands' End mentioned earlier, are offering live chat, which connects consumers to a customer service representative at any point in the checkout process to answer questions and offer help. Online privacy and security are ongoing concerns. **Online privacy concerns** *relate to consumer fears regarding how personal information about them that is gathered online might be used.* These concerns are a top online buying deterrent and represent billions in lost sales. To overcome them, various website strategies are possible, such as the use of security verification systems like VeriSign.[111] In addition, credit card companies are getting into the game with *single-use numbers.* Consumers who were offered and adopted this controlled payment option increased their online purchases between 50 and 200 percent.[112]

A study by ATG asked consumers how the online shopping experience could be improved.[113] Many of the factors that consumers suggested appear to be capable of increasing online purchase rates. Some of the major factors are shown in Table 17–3.

Clearly consumers who abandoned carts because they were not ready (second highest reason) may have been unprepared due to their perception that they didn't have good enough information to make a choice. Thus, more detailed information and easier-to-access information (via search and navigation) should increase online purchases. Personalized offerings tend to motivate purchases because they are more directly relevant to consumer problems.

Mobile and Mobile Apps

Mobile retailing is on the rise. And as Figure 17–1 illustrates, mobile phones and apps are undoubtedly influencing how consumers shop both inside and outside the store environment. Retailers, even powerful ones like Walmart, don't want to get left behind, as omni-channel shoppers generate more sales. Walmart always has been reluctant to provide pricing information publicly, but since the advent of price-comparison mobile apps, they

TABLE 17-3	Improving Website Functionality

Website Factor	Percent
More detailed product information	45
Better search capabilities	36
Live help options	29
Better navigation	26
Make it easier to contact store	25
Improve the checkout process	22
More offers tailored to my interests or needs	16
Provide better access via mobile and social media	8

Source: *Consumer Shopping Experiences, Preferences, and Behaviors* (Cambridge, MA: ATG, October 2010).

have decided to do so to avoid being excluded from this important source of shopping influence. Despite their strong presence in retailing, mobile apps do have limitations such as requiring too much memory on the user's phone, or not being useful. Shoppers may drop the app, as a result. To bring users back to the app, retailers should focus on those features that make apps appealing in the first place: security, storage of preferences for future shopping, and personalization, among others. And given that many mobile app users are deal-prone, retailers who offer an exclusive or bonus deal, or discount on future purchases, may be able to reconnect with these customers.[114] *Beyond what has been suggested in this chapter, can you think of interesting ways that marketers could allow for mobile phones to interact with elements of the store and store shelf that would positively influence retail sales?*

Sales Personnel

For most low-involvement purchases in the United States, self-service is predominant. As purchase involvement increases, the likelihood of interaction with a salesperson also increases. Thus, most studies of effectiveness in sales interactions have focused on high-involvement purchases such as insurance, automobiles, or industrial products. There is no simple explanation for effective sales interactions. Instead, the effectiveness of sales efforts is influenced by the interactions of[115]

- The salesperson's knowledge, friendliness, skill, and authority.
- The nature of the customer's buying task.
- The customer–salesperson relationship.

Thus, specific research is required for each target market and product category to determine the optimal personnel selling strategy.

Consider the following shopping experience:

I also had lousy service in the store. The sales guy seemed to be trying to sell me the cheaper shoe to get me out the door. . . . The thing that irritated me was that I thought I was a fairly knowledgeable shopper and I thought that they should understand some of these things. . . . They weren't very knowledgeable. . . . I got the impression they didn't like their jobs.[116]

Is this consumer likely to return to this outlet? Will he recommend it to his friends? It is clear that knowledgeable, helpful salespeople enhance the shopping experience, while those who are not have the opposite effect.

In the online context, online sales clerks interact with customers as they shop on the marketer's website. These online sales clerks are called *avatars* and can be defined as "virtual characters that can be used as company representatives." One study found that avatars increased store attitude, product attitude, and purchase likelihood. It also found that for high-involvement products, expert avatars were more influential because of their increased credibility, while for lower-involvement products, attractive-looking avatars were more effective as a result of their likeability.[117]

PURCHASE

Once the consumer has selected the brand and retail outlet, he or she must complete the transaction. This involves what is normally called *purchasing* or *renting* the product. In traditional retail environments, this was straightforward and did not generally stop or delay purchases, with the possible exception of major and more complex purchases such as a home or car. However, as we saw earlier, many consumers starting to make an online purchase quit without making one for a variety of reasons. Making online purchasing itself easier is clearly an important factor. Streamlining the mobile purchase process, as well as the emerging purchase format on social media, is also important.

Credit plays a major role in consumer purchases, and new technologies are being tested on an ongoing basis. And research indicates that the ability to pay by credit card rather than cash substantially increases consumers' willingness to pay and the amount they purchase.[118] Thus, it may be to the retailer's advantage to encourage credit card use even though it must pay a percentage of these sales to the credit card companies.

Businesses need to simplify the actual purchase as much as possible. This involves strategies as straightforward as managing the time spent in line at the checkout register to more complex operations, such as computerized credit checks to minimize credit authorization time. In an omni-channel system, this simplification could extend to providing one-click payment options on the mobile app or in-aisle checkout capability at the store. Many businesses appear to overlook the fact that the actual purchase act is generally the last contact the consumer will have with the store on that trip. Although first impressions are important, so are final ones. Store personnel need to be not only efficient at this activity but also helpful and personable. And online retailers need to minimize the complexity, hassle, and stress involved.

LO5

SUMMARY

SMARTBOOK

LO1: Describe how retailing is evolving.

Retail outlet refers to any source of products or services for consumers. Retailing has moved well beyond traditional physical stores and catalogs to include the Internet, interactive TV ads, and mobile shopping apps. Computers learn and recall consumer information and preferences; full-body scanners allow for custom-fit apparel; and interactive TV ads and shows do or will allow for product information search and purchase from the ad or show. The Internet and mobile phones and apps are changing the way consumers shop both prior to and during a store visit in unprecedented ways that are influencing the stores and brands that consumers choose.

LO2: Discuss the relationship among retail outlets as part of omni-channel shopping.

While store-based retailing continues to dominate in terms of overall sales, online and mobile retailing as well as other forms of in-home retailing including catalogs are increasingly important retail outlets to shoppers. Consequently, most retailers are engaging in multi- or omni-channel marketing to reach their customers. The need for omni-channel marketing reflects shifts in consumer shopping. Consumers are increasingly likely to be *omni-channel shoppers*—that is, consumers who browse and/or purchase using multiple channels. Omni-channel shoppers can use the various retail channels in many ways while searching for and purchasing a product. Omni-channel shoppers who search online and ultimately buy a product at a physical store engage in *webrooming*. *Showrooming* is the opposite. Omni-channel shoppers have higher incomes and spend more than single-channel shoppers. Retailers like Crate&Barrel are implementing omni-channel strategies to court these customers.

LO3: Explain the retail and consumer attributes that affect outlet selection.

The decision process used by consumers to select a retail outlet is the same as the process described for selecting a brand. The only difference is in the nature of the evaluative criteria used. Retail outlet *image* is an important evaluative criterion. Store-based image and online retailer image are both important, although the dimensions consumers use to judge them vary. *Store brands* can both capitalize on a store's image and enhance, or detract from, it. *Outlet location and size* are important, with closer and larger outlets generally

being preferred over more distant and smaller ones. Consumer characteristics such as *perceived risk* and *shopping orientation* are also important determinants of outlet choice.

LO4: Summarize the in-store and online influences on brand choice.

While in a retail outlet, consumers often purchase a brand or product that differs from their plans before entering. Such purchases are referred to as *unplanned purchases.* Most of these decisions are the result of additional information processing induced by in-store or online stimuli. However, some are impulse purchases made with little or no deliberation in response to a sudden, powerful urge to buy or consume the product. Such variables as *point-of-purchase displays, price reductions, outlet atmosphere, website design, mobile and mobile apps, sales personnel,* and brand or product *stockouts* can have a major impact on sales patterns.

LO5: Understand how purchase plays a role in the shopping process.

Once the outlet and brand have been selected, the consumer must acquire the rights to the item. This often involves credit. Whether purchasing is in-store, online, or via mobile or on social media, the retailer's job is to simplify the process because it will enhance the likelihood of purchase and enhance its image.

KEY TERMS

Atmospherics 625
External reference price 615
Impulse purchase 621
In-home shopping 600
Internal reference price 615
Omni-channel shoppers 606
Online privacy concerns 627

Perceived risk 618
Reference price 615
Retail attraction (gravitation) model 617
Servicescape 625
Shopping orientation 619
Showrooming 607

Spillover sales 614
Stockouts 626
Store atmosphere 624
Store brands 613
Store image 611
Unplanned purchases 620
Webrooming 607

REVIEW QUESTIONS

1. The consumer faces the problems of both what to buy and where to buy it. How do these two types of decisions differ?
2. How is the retail environment changing?
3. Describe online retailing.

4. Describe mobile retailing.
5. What are concerns for consumers in using online retailing and mobile apps?
6. What is *omni-channel shopping,* and what implications does it hold for retailer strategy?

7. What are meant by *showrooming* and *webrooming?* Why are they important issues for retailers?

8. What is a *store image,* and what are its dimensions and components?

9. Describe *online retailer image,* and compare/ contrast it with *store image.*

10. What is a *store brand?* How do retailers use store brands?

11. What key decisions do retailers make with respect to retail price advertising?

12. What is meant by the term *spillover sales?* Why is it important?

13. How does the size of and distance to a retail outlet affect store selection and purchase behavior?

14. How is store choice affected by the *perceived risk* of a purchase?

15. What is meant by *social risk?* How does it differ from *economic risk?*

16. What is a *shopping orientation?*

17. Describe six motivation-based shopping orientations across retail type.

18. What is meant by an *in-store purchase decision?* Why is it important?

19. What is meant by an *impulse purchase?* Why is it important?

20. Once in a particular retail outlet, what in-store and/ or online characteristics can influence brand and product choice? Give an example of each.

21. Describe the impact of point-of-purchase displays on retail sales.

22. Describe the impact of price reductions and deals on retail sales.

23. What is meant by *store atmosphere? Online atmosphere?* How do they affect consumer behavior?

24. What is a *servicescape?*

25. Why do consumers planning to make a purchase at an online outlet often fail to do so?

26. What are frequent problems consumers encounter while shopping online?

27. What can happen in response to a *stockout?*

DISCUSSION QUESTIONS

28. Name two mobile apps that affect the choice of brands in the store?

29. Does the image of a retail outlet affect the image of the brands it carries? Do the brands carried affect the image of the retail outlet?

30. What challenges face omni-channel retailers in managing their image across channels?

31. Respond to the questions in Consumer Insight 17–1.

32. How are social and economic risks associated with the following products likely to affect the outlet choice behavior of consumers? How would the perception of these risks differ by consumer? Situation?
    a. Sports car
    b. Athletic shoes (for running)
    c. Wine (as a gift)
    d. Hairdresser
    e. Mountain bike
    f. Mouthwash
    g. Smartphone
    h. Movie for a date

33. Describe an appropriate strategy for an online store such as Target for each of the motivation-based shopping orientations described in the text.

34. Describe an appropriate strategy for a mobile app of a retailer such as Starbucks for each of the motivation-based shopping orientations described in the text.

35. Suggest other methods for developing motivation-based shopping orientations.

36. How should retailer strategies to encourage unplanned purchases differ depending on the type of unplanned purchase generally associated with the product category?

37. What in-store characteristics could traditional retailers use to enhance the probability of purchase among individuals who visit a store? Describe each factor in terms of how it should be used, and describe its intended effect on the consumer for the following products:
    a. Perfume
    b. Ice cream
    c. Coffee after a meal
    d. Flowers from a supermarket

e. B_{12} drinkable shots

f. Motor oil

38. What website characteristics could online retailers use to enhance the probability of purchase among individuals who visit their websites? Describe each factor in terms of how it should be used, and describe its intended effect on the consumer for the following products:

a. Dorm furniture from Target.com

b. Electronics from Amazon.com

c. Laptop from HP.com

d. Backpack from REI.com

e. Apparel from JCPenney.com

f. Cosmetics from Macys.com

g. Tools from Sears.com

39. What type of store atmosphere is most appropriate for each of the following retailer types? Why?

a. Bookstore serving college students

b. Cosmetic section of Sears

c. Auto dealership service department

d. Consumer electronics

e. Mercedes automobiles

f. Inexpensive furniture

g. Thai food restaurant

40. Repeat Question 39 (except for *c* and *g*) for online retailers.

41. How would you respond to a stockout of your preferred brand (or model) of the following? What factors other than product category would influence your response?

a. SUV

b. Cereal

c. Deodorant

d. Dress shirt/blouse

e. Perfume/aftershave lotion

f. Soft drink

APPLICATION ACTIVITIES

42. Describe the current state of online retailing and mobile retailing.

43. Pick a residential area in your town and develop a gravitational model for (*a*) nearby supermarkets or (*b*) shopping malls. Conduct telephone surveys to test the accuracy of your model.

44. Develop a questionnaire to measure the image of the following. Have 10 other students complete these questionnaires. Discuss the marketing implications of your results.

a. Target

b. Americangirl.com

c. Subway

d. Local coffee shop

e. BMW.com

f. Walmart

g. Saks Fifth Avenue

45. Have 10 students on your campus describe their shopping orientations in terms of animals as follows: "Think about an animal that best describes you as a shopper and explain what it is about your shopping behavior that makes this animal an appropriate metaphor." Combine your descriptions with those of two other students. Do any patterns emerge? What are the retailing implications?

46. For several of the products listed in Table 17–2, interview several students not enrolled in your class and ask them to classify their last purchase as specially planned, generally planned, substitute, or unplanned. Then combine your results with those of your classmates to obtain an estimate of student behavior. Compare student behavior with the behavior shown in Table 17–2 and discuss any similarities or differences.

47. Arrange with a local retailer (convenience store, drugstore, or whatever) to temporarily install a point-of-purchase display. Then set up a procedure to unobtrusively observe the frequency of evaluation and selection of the brand before and while the display is up. Describe your findings.

48. Visit two retail stores selling the same type of merchandise and prepare a report on their use of P-O-P materials. Explain any differences.

49. Interview the manager of a drug, department, or grocery store on his or her views of P-O-P materials and price advertising.

50. Develop an appropriate questionnaire and construct a new version of Table 17–2 using products relevant to college students. What are the marketing implications of this table?

51. Determine, through interviews, the general shopping orientations of students on your campus. What are the marketing implications of your findings?

52. Interview 10 students on your campus and determine their attitudes toward and use of the Internet and online shopping. Place each into one of the six shopper segments described in the text. Do they fit into these segments? Combine your results with those of four other students. What do you conclude?

REFERENCES

1. This chapter opener is based on J. Reingold, "Is Brick-and-Mortar Retail in a Death Spiral?," *Fortune,* November 26, 2013, http://features.blogs.fortune.cnn.com/2013/11/26/is-brick-and-mortar-retail-in-a-death-spiral/, accessed August 29, 2014; C. Phillips, "Expert Predictions: The Demise of Bricks and Mortar Retail," *Power Retail,* February 6, 2013, www.powerretail.com.au/hot-topics/demise-of-bricks-and-mortar-retail/, accessed August 29, 2014; J. Wang, "Retailers Entice Shoppers with a Visual Hook," *Orange County Register,* January 21, 2014, www.heraldonline.com/2014/01/29/5618838/retailers-entice-shoppers-with.html, accessed August 29, 2014; K. Campbell-Dollaghan, "Nike's Kinect-Powered Window Displays Are Watching You," *Fast Company,* March 26, 2013, www.fastcodesign.com/1672213/nikes-kinect-powered-window-displays-are-watching-you, accessed August 29, 2014; "Ted Baker 'Merry Kissmas' Interactive Christmas Window Display," *BWD,* http://thebwd.com/ted-baker-merry-kissmas-interactive-christmas-window-display/, accessed August 29, 2014; C. W. Smith, "Burberry Regent Street," *Retail Innovation,* http://retail-innovation.com/burberry-regent-street/, accessed August 29, 2014; E. Williams, "Heritage Meets Digital in New Flagship Burberry Store," *Creative Review,* September 14, 2012, www.creativereview.co.uk/cr-blog/2012/september/burberry-mixes-heritage-with-digital-high-tech-in-new-london-store, accessed August 29, 2014; Burberry, "Burberry Regent Street Fact Sheet," press release, September 2012, www.emtecnica.com/burberry-regent-street-fact-sheet.pdf, accessed August 29, 2014; B. Andersen and W. Eckstein, "What's in Store—How Technology Is Transforming the Retail Industry," *KPMG,* June 2013, www.kpmg.com/US/en/services/Advisory/management-consulting/management-consulting-by-function/Documents/kpmg-retail-brick-and-mortar.pdf, accessed August 29, 2014; B. Johns, "Adidas' Digital Signage Boosts Sales by 40%," *Integrated Solutions for Retailers,* February 2013, www.retailsolutionsonline.com/doc/adidas-boosts-sales-with-digital-signage-0001?sectionCode5Spotlight&templateCode5Enhanced Standard&user51863032&source5nl:36447, accessed August 29, 2014; S. Kessler, "Here's What Brick-and-Mortar Stores See When They Track You," *Fast Company,* August 1, 2013, www.fastcompany.com/3015060/heres-what-brick-and-mortar-stores-see-when-they-track-you, accessed August 29, 2014; O. Kharif, "Retailers Enlist the Smartphone to Encourage Shopping," *Bloomberg Businessweek,* April 4, 2013, www.businessweek.com/articles/2013-04-04/retailers-enlist-the-smartphone-to-encourage-shopping, accessed August 29, 2014; A. Flaherty, "New Technology Helps Stores Track Your Every Move This Season," *Huffington Post,* November 30, 2013, www.huffingtonpost.com/2013/11/30/stores-track-you_n_4363811.html, accessed August 29, 2014.

2. S. Sherman, "Will the Information Superhighway Be the Death of Retailing?," *Fortune,* April 18, 1994, p. 17.

3. L. Petrecca, "Interactive TV Ads Are Clicking with Viewers," *USA Today,* July 11, 2008, www.usatoday.com, accessed June 24, 2011.

4. N. Gilliland, "Five Examples of Brands Using Interactive Video," *Econsultancy,* May 17, 2017, https://econsultancy.com/blog/69094-five-examples-of-brands-using-interactive-video, accessed July 12, 2018.

5. Information in table based on "Internet Users and 2017 Population in North America," *Internet World Stats,* June 2017, www.internetworldstats.com, accessed July 9, 2018; Statista, "E-Commerce Share of Total Retail Sales in United States from 2013–2021," 2018, www.statista.com, accessed July 9, 2018; U.S. Census Bureau, "Quarterly Retail E-Commerce Sales," May 17, 2018.

6. See "E-Commerce Share of Total Retail Sales in United States from 2013–2021."

7. J. Nicholson, "New Insights on Retail E-Commerce," *U.S. Department of Commerce,* July 26, 2017, www.esa.doc.gov, accessed July 9, 2018.

8. L. Thomas, "Amazon Grabbed 4 Percent of All US Retail Sales in 2017, New Study Says," *CNBC,* January 3, 2018, www.cnbc.com, accessed July 10, 2018.

9. Mintel Group, Ltd., "Online Shopping, U.S., May 2018," www.mintel.com, accessed July 9, 2018.

10. R. White, "The Old-Fashioned Mail-Order Catalog Is Making a Comeback," *Los Angeles Times,* November 23, 2017.

11. See, e.g., *US eCommerce Forecast: 2008 to 2012* (Cambridge, MA: Forrester Research, Inc., January 18, 2008).

12. *See* Mintel Group, "Online Shopping, U.S., May 2018."

13. Statista, "U.S. Mobile Retail Commerce Sales as a Percentage of Retail E-Commerce Sales from 2017 to 2021," 2018, www.statista.com/statistics/249863/us-mobile-retail-commerce-sales-as-percentage-of-e-commerce-sales/, accessed July 10, 2018.

14. R. Wang, E. Malthouse, and L. Krishnamurthi, "On the Go: How Mobile Shopping Affects Customer Purchase Behavior," *Journal of Retailing* 91, no. 2 (2015), pp. 217–34.

15. Google, "How People Shop on Their Phones," *Think with Google,* October 2016, www.thinkwithgoogle.com/advertising-channels/apps/app-marketing-mobile-shopping/, accessed July 10, 2018; Forthea, "Google 'Mobile First' Index Shift Is Coming: Get Ready for a Faster 2017," *Forthea,* October 21, 2016, www.forthea.com/google-mobile-first-index-announced-2017/, accessed July 10, 2018.

16. P. Robles, "Mobile Retail Apps Are Beating Out Mobile Websites," *EConsultancy,* March 19, 2018, https://econsultancy.com/blog/69877-mobile-retail-apps-are-beating-out-mobile-websites, accessed July 10, 2018.

17. R. Klara, "Contrary to Popular Belief, Millennial Shoppers Actually Like Going to Brick-and-Mortar Stores," *Ad Week,* August 22, 2017, www.adweek.com.

18. J. Sanburn, "Why the Death of Malls Is About More Than Shopping," *Time,* July 20, 2017; T. Rucinski, "Toys 'R' Us Plans to Close All U.S. Stores; 33,000 Jobs at Risk: Source," *Reuters,* March 14, 2018, www.reuters.com, accessed July 12, 2018.

19. From Roper Reports Telephone Survey, August 2003.

20. See A. Z. Cuneo, "What's in Store?," *Advertising Age,* February 25, 2002, p. 1; R. V. Kozinets et al., "Themed Flagship Brand Stores in the New Millennium," *Journal of Retailing* 78 (2002), pp. 17–29.

21. Insight is based on "Beacons Are Beckoning: How Mobile Technology Is Changing Retail," *Business.com,* February 22, 2017, www.business.com/articles/how-mobile-technology-is-changing-retail/, accessed June 15, 2018; B. Lawlor, "5 Mobile Trends Changing the Retail Industry," *Mobile Business Insights,* November 1, 2017, https://mobilebusinessinsights.com/2017/11/5-mobile-trends-changing-the-retail-industry/, accessed June 15, 2018; U. Lawlor, "5 Retail Brands Who Excel in the Art of Push Notifications," *XtremePush,* https://xtremepush.com/5-retail-brands-who-excel-in-the-art-of-push-notifications/, accessed July 12, 2018; B. Lawrence, "7 Mobile Retail Trends to Watch in 2018," *Inviqa,* February 27, 2018, https://inviqa.com/blog/7-mobile-retail-trends-watch-2018, accessed June 15, 2018; N. Luna, "Tech Tracker: TGI Fridays Taps AI Tech to Build Guest Engagement," *Nation's Restaurant News,* June 18, 2018, www.nrn.com/technology/tech-tracker-tgi-fridays-taps-ai-tech-build-guest-engagement, accessed July 12, 2018; S. Perez, "Target Rolls Out Bluetooth Beacon Technology in Stores to Power New Indoor Maps in Its App," *TechCrunch,* September 20, 2017, https://techcrunch.com/2017/09/20/target-rolls-out-bluetooth-beacon-technology-in-stores-to-power-new-indoor-maps-in-its-app/, accessed July 12, 2018; A. Sheehan, "How These Retailers Use Augmented Reality to Enhance the Customer Experience," *Shopify,* February 21, 2018, www.shopify.com/retail/how-these-retailers-are-using-augmented-reality-to-enhance-the-customer-experience, accessed July 12, 2018.

22. S. M. Pardy, "For Retailers, Best Things That Come in Small Packages Include Stores," *CoStar,* May 16, 2007, www.costar.com, accessed June 25, 2011; S. Kapner, "Nordstrom Tries on a New Look: Stores without Merchandise," *Wall Street Journal,* September 10, 2017.

23. A. Z. Cuneo, "On Target," *Advertising Age,* December 11, 2000, p. 1.

24. E. Byron, "America's Retailers Have a New Target Customer: The 26-Year-Old Millennial," *Wall Street Journal,* October 9, 2017.

25. D. Rushe, "Big, Bold . . . and Broken: Is the US Shopping Mall in a Fatal Decline?," *Guardian,* July 23, 2017, accessed July 12, 2018.

26. E. Sopadjieva, U. Dholakia, and B. Benjamin, "A Study of 46,000 Shoppers Show That Omnichannel Retailing Works," *Harvard Business Review,* January 3, 2017.

27. The section on omni-channel marketing is based on U. Konus, P. C. Verhoef, and S. A. Neslin, "Multichannel Shopper Segments and Covariates," *Journal of Retailing* 84, no. 4 (2008), pp. 398–413; W. Kwon and S. J. Lennon, "Reciprocal Effects between Multichannel Retailers' Offline and Online Brand Images," *Journal of Retailing* 82, no. 3 (2009), pp. 376–90; "Have You Met the Omni-Channel Shoppers?," *BizReport,* October 23, 2009, www.bizreport.com, accessed June 25, 2011; *Cross-Channel Shopping Behaviors* (Cambridge, MA: Forrester Research Inc., 2010); *Perfect Storm* (San Mateo, CA: Coremetrics, 2010); *Fuel Your Marketing Efforts* (San Mateo, CA: Coremetrics, 2010); *Cross-Channel Commerce* (Cambridge, MA: ATG, March 2010); *Understanding Consumer Patterns and Preferences in Multi-Channel Retailing* (Somers, NY: IBM, 2011); Sopadjieva, Dholakia, and Benjamin, "A Study of 46,000 Shoppers Show That Omnichannel Retailing Works."

28. See also K. C. Gehrt and R.-N. Yan, "Situational, Consumer, and Retailer Factors Affecting Internet, Catalog, and Store Shopping," *International Journal of Retail and Distribution Management* 32, no. 1 (2004), pp. 5–18.

29. For discussion on showrooming and webrooming, see, e.g., H. Khan, "Consumers Are Showrooming and Webrooming Your Business, Here's What That Means and What You Can Do About It," *Shopify,* June 7, 2018, www.shopify.com, accessed July 9, 2018.

30. B. Kilcourse, "Gaming Google," *Retail Systems Research,* March 1, 2011.

31. D. Virgillito, "10 Examples of Outstanding Omni-Channel Brands," *Shopify,* October 2, 2017, www.shopify.com/enterprise/10-examples-of-outstanding-omnichannel-brands, accessed July 12, 2018.

32. B. Pearson, "Whatever Happened to Showrooming? How Big Retail Is Taking Back the Shopping Trip," *Forbes,* August 16, 2017, accessed July 10, 2018; Khan, "Consumers Are Showrooming and Webrooming Your Business, Here's What That Means and What You Can Do About It."

33. M. Wilson, "Ikea's New Catalog Magically Transforms into Furniture," *Fast Company,* August 2, 2013, www.fastcodesign.com/1673164/ikeas-new-catalog-magically-transforms-into-your-furniture, accessed August 29, 2014; L. Stinson, "So Smart: New Ikea App Places Virtual Furniture in Your Home," *Wired Magazine,* August 20, 2013, www.wired.com/design/2013/08/a-new-ikea-app-lets-you-place-3d-furniture-in-your-home/, accessed August 29, 2014; R. Empson, "Warby Parker Opens Retail Store in NYC, with Boston Up Next, Beats Google & Amazon to the Offline Punch," *Techcrunch,* April 4, 2013, http://techcrunch.com/2013/04/13/warby-parker-opens-retail-store-in-nyc-with-boston-up-next-beats-google-amazon-to-the-offline-punch/, accessed August 29, 2014; C. Chaey, "Take a Look Inside Warby Parker's New NYC Flagship Store," *Fast Company,* April 12, 1013, www.fastcompany.com/3008182/where-are-they-now/take-look-inside-warby-parkers-new-nyc-flagship-store, accessed August 29, 2014; S. Clifford, "Once Proudly Web Only, Shopping Sites Hang Out Real Shingles," *New York Times,* December 18, 2012, www.nytimes.com/2012/12/19/business/shopping-sites-open-brick-and-mortar-stores.html?_r=0, accessed August 29, 2014; O. St. John, "Bonobos Opens Stores That Don't Sell Anything," *USA Today,* March 12, 2013, www.usatoday.com/story/money/business/2013/03/12/savvy-small-business-bonobs-ants/1916885/, accessed August 29, 2014; L. Bustos, "Why

Online Pure Plays Are Opening Physical Shops," *Get Elastic ecommerce,* February 4, 2013, www.getelastic.com/why-online-pure-plays-are-opening-physical-shops/, accessed August 29, 2014; P. Marsden, "e-Bay's London Pop-Up Shop: A Vision of Social Commerce Tomorrow?," *Digital Intelligence Today,* December 4, 2012, http://digitalintelligencetoday.com/EBAYS-LONDON-POP-UP-SHOP-A-VISION-OF-SOCIAL-COMMERCE-TOMORROW/, accessed August 29, 2014.

34. Virgillito, "10 Examples of Outstanding Omni-Channel Brands."

35. J. D. Lindquist, "Meaning of Image," *Journal of Retailing,* Winter 1974, pp. 29–38; see also M. R. Zimmer and L. L. Golden, "Impressions of Retail Stores," *Journal of Retailing,* Fall 1988, pp. 265–93.

36. H. van der Heijden and T. Verhagen, "Online Store Image," *Information and Management* 41 (2004), pp. 609–17. See also J. R. Coyle and E. Thorson, "The Effects of Progressive Levels of Interactivity and Vividness in Web Marketing Sites," *Journal of Advertising,* Fall 2001, pp. 65–77; C. Page and E. Lepkowska-White, "Web Equity," *Journal of Consumer Marketing* 19, no. 3 (2002), pp. 231–48; E. J. Johnson, S. Bellman, and G. L. Lohse, "Cognitive Lock-In and the Power Law of Practice," *Journal of Marketing,* April 2003, pp. 62–75; P. Katerattanakul and K. Siau, "Creating a Virtual Store Image," *Communications in ACM,* December 2003, pp. 226–32. See also B. B. Holloway and S. E. Beatty, "Satisfiers and Dissatisfiers in the Online Environment," *Journal of Service Research,* May 2008, pp. 347–64.

37. See N. Sirohi, E. W. McLaughlin, and D. R. Witink, "A Model of Consumer Perceptions and Store Loyalty Intentions for a Supermarket Retailer," *Journal of Retailing* 2 (1998), pp. 223–45; K. Macarthur, "What's in a Name?," *Advertising Age,* April 17, 2006, p. 43.

38. J. Black, "Welcome to the New Convenience Store," *Wall Street Journal,* April 28–29, 2018; Choice Market company website, https://choicemarket.co/about/, accessed July 14, 2018.

39. See S. Burton, D. R. Lichtenstein, R. G. Netemeyer, and J. A. Garretson, "A Scale for Measuring Attitude toward Private Label Products," *Journal of the Academy of Marketing Science,* Fall 1998, pp. 293–306.

40. See M. Corstjens and R. Lal, "Building Store Loyalty through Store Brands," *Journal of Marketing Research,* August 2000, pp. 281–91.

41. P. S. Richardson, A. K. Jain, and A. Dick, "Household Store Brand Proneness," *Journal of Retailing* 2 (1996), pp. 159–85; S. C. Choi and A. T. Coughlan, "Private Label Positioning," *Journal of Retailing* 82, no. 2 (2006), pp. 79–93. For a conflicting view, see K. L. Ailawadi, S. A. Neslin, and K. Gegdenk, "Pursuing the Value-Conscious Consumer," *Journal of Marketing,* January 2001, pp. 71–89.

42. K. L. Ailawadi, K. Pauwels, and J. E. M. Steenkamp, "Private-Label Use and Store Loyalty," *Journal of Marketing,* November 2008, pp. 19–30.

43. *The Double Dividend* (New York: Newspaper Advertising Bureau Inc., February 1977).

44. F. J. Mulhern and D. T. Padgett, "The Relationship between Retail Price Promotions and Regular Price Purchases," *Journal of Marketing,* October 1995, pp. 83–90. For similar results, see S. Burton, D. R. Lichtenstein, and R. G. Netemeyer, "Exposure to Sales Flyers and Increased Purchases in Retail Supermarkets," *Journal of Advertising Research,* September 1999, pp. 7–14.

45. See, e.g., V. Severin, J. J. Louviere, and A. Finn, "The Stability of Retail Shopping Choices over Time and across Countries," *Journal of Retailing* 77 (2001), pp. 185–202.

46. See, e.g., P. Chandon, B. Wansink, and G. Laurent, "A Benefit Congruency Framework of Sales Promotion Effectiveness," *Journal of Marketing,* October 2000, pp. 65–81.

47. See, e.g., van der Heijden and Verhagen, "Online Store Image."

48. A. Ansari and C. F. Mela, "E-Customization," *Journal of Marketing Research,* May 2003, pp. 131–45.

49. See C. Janiszewski and D. R. Lichtenstein, "A Range Theory of Price Perception," *Journal of Consumer Research,* March 1999, pp. 353–68.

50. See R. A. Briesch, L. Krishnamurthi, and T. Mazumdar, "A Comparative Analysis of Reference Price Models," *Journal of Consumer Research,* September 1997, pp. 202–14; R. W. Niedrich, S. Sharma, and D. H. Wedell, "Reference Price and Price Perceptions," *Journal of Consumer Research,* December 2001, pp. 339–54; P. K. Kopalle and J. Lindsey-Mullikin, "The Impact of External Reference Price on Consumer Price Expectations," *Journal of Retailing* 79 (2003), pp. 225–36. For a different approach, see K. B. Monroe and A. Y. Lee, "Remembering versus Knowing," *Journal of the Academy of Marketing Science,* Spring 1999, pp. 207–25.

51. See V. Kumar, K. Karande, and W. J. Reinartz, "The Impact of Internal and External Reference Prices on Brand Choice," *Journal of Retailing* 3 (1998), pp. 401–26.

52. T. A. Suter and S. Burton, "Reliability and Consumer Perceptions of Implausible Reference Prices in Retail Prices," *Psychology & Marketing,* January 1996, pp. 37–54; M. S. Yadav and K. Seiders, "Is the Price Right? Understanding Contingent Processing in Reference Price Formation," *Journal of Retailing* 74, no. 3 (1998), pp. 311–29; L. D. Compeau and D. Grewal, "Comparative Price Advertising," *Journal of Public Policy & Marketing,* Fall 1998, pp. 257–73. See also M. J. Barone, K. C. Manning, and P. W. Miniard, "Consumer Response to Retailers' Use of Partially Comparative Pricing," *Journal of Marketing,* July 2004, pp. 37–47.

53. See A. Biswas et al., "Consumer Evaluation of Reference Price Advertisements," *Journal of Public Policy & Marketing,* Spring 1999, pp. 52–65.

54. T. B. Heath, S. Chatterjee, and K. R. France, "Mental Accounting and Changes in Price," *Journal of Consumer Research,* June 1995, pp. 90–97.

55. See S.-F. S. Chen, K. B. Monroe, and Y.-C. Lou, "The Effects of Framing Price Promotion Messages on Consumers' Perceptions and Purchase Intentions," *Journal of Retailing* 3 (1998), pp. 353–72; M. R. Stafford and T. F. Stafford, "The Effectiveness of Tensile Pricing Tactics in the Advertising of Services," *Journal of Advertising,* Summer 2000, pp. 45–60.

56. See A. Biswas and S. Burton, "Consumer Perceptions of Tensile Price Claims in Advertisements," *Journal of the Academy of Marketing Science,* Summer 1993, pp. 217–30; K. N. Rajendran and G.-J. Tellis, "Contextual and Temporal Components of Reference Price," *Journal of Marketing,* January 1994, pp. 22–39; D. Grewal, H. Marmorstein, and A. Sharma, "Communicating

Price Information through Semantic Cues," *Journal of Consumer Research,* September 1996, pp. 148–55.

57. I. Sinha and M. F. Smith, "Consumers' Perceptions of Promotional Framing of Price," *Psychology & Marketing,* March 2000, pp. 257–75.

58. See D. Simester, "Signaling Price Image Using Advertised Prices," *Marketing Science* 14, no. 2 (1995), pp. 166–88; J. Srivastave and N. Lurie, "A Consumer Perspective on Price-Matching Refund Policies," *Journal of Consumer Research,* September 2001, pp. 296–307.

59. G. S. Bobinski Jr., D. Cox, and A. Cox, "Retail 'Sale' Advertising, Perceived Retailer Credibility, and Price Rationale," *Journal of Retailing* 3 (1996), pp. 291–306.

60. See, e.g., Severin, Louviere, and Finn, "The Stability of Retail Shopping Choices over Time and across Countries."

61. See I. Simonson, "The Effect of Product Assortment on Buyer Preferences," *Journal of Retailing* 75, no. 3 (1999), pp. 347–70; R. E. Stassen, J. D. Mittelstaedt, and R. A. Mittelstaedt, "Assortment Overlap," *Journal of Retailing* 75, no. 3 (1999), pp. 371–86.

62. C. S. Craig, A. Ghosh, and S. McLafferty, "Models of the Retail Location Process: A Review," *Journal of Retailing,* Spring 1984, pp. 5–33.

63. See D. R. Bell, T.-H. Ho, and C. S. Tang, "Determining Where to Shop," *Journal of Marketing Research,* August 1998, pp. 352–69.

64. See B. G. C. Dellaert et al., "Investigating Consumers' Tendency to Combine Multiple Shopping Purposes and Destinations," *Journal of Marketing Research,* May 1998, pp. 177–88.

65. See P. R. Messinger and C. Narasimhan, "A Model of Retail Formats Based on Consumers' Economizing on Shopping Time," *Marketing Science* 1 (1997), pp. 1–23.

66. A. Chaudhuri, "Product Class Effects on Perceived Risk," *International Journal of Research in Marketing,* May 1998, pp. 157–68; R. Batra and I. Sinha, "Consumer-Level Factors Moderating the Success of Private Label Brands," *Journal of Retailing* 76, no. 2 (2000), pp. 175–91.

67. Based on V. Prasad, "Socioeconomic Product Risk and Patronage Preferences of Retail Shoppers," *Journal of Marketing,* July 1975, p. 44.

68. G. R. Dowling and R. Staelin, "A Model of Perceived Risk and Intended Risk-Handling Activity," *Journal of Consumer Research,* June 1994, pp. 119–34; L. W. Turley and R. P. LeBlanc, "An Exploratory Investigation of Consumer Decision Making in the Service Sector," *Journal of Services Marketing* 7, no. 4 (1993), pp. 11–18; J. B. Smith and J. M. Bristor, "Uncertainty Orientation," *Psychology & Marketing,* November 1994, pp. 587–607.

69. R. B. Settle, P. L. Alreck, and D. E. McCorkle, "Consumer Perceptions of Mail/Phone Order Shopping Media," *Journal of Direct Marketing,* Summer 1994, pp. 30–45; C. R. Jasper and S. J. Ouellette, "Consumers' Perception of Risk and the Purchase of Apparel from Catalogs," *Journal of Direct Marketing,* Spring 1994, pp. 23–36; D. Biswas and A. Biswas, "The Diagnostic Role of Signals in the Context of Perceived Risks in Online Shopping," *Journal of Interactive Marketing,* Summer 2004, pp. 30–45.

70. See also J. C. Sweeney, G. N. Soutar, and L. W. Johnson, "The Role of Perceived Risk in the Quality–Value Relationship," *Journal of Retailing* 75, no. 1 (1999), pp. 75–105.

71. See K. L. Wakefield and J. Baker, "Excitement at the Mall," *Journal of Retailing* 74, no. 4 (1998), pp. 515–39; H. McDonald, P. Darbyshire, and C. Jevons, "Shop Often, Buy Little," *Journal of Global Marketing* 13, no. 4 (2000), pp. 53–71; J. A. F. Nicholls et al., "Inter-American Perspectives from Mall Shoppers," *Journal of Global Marketing* 15, no. 1 (2001), pp. 87–103; B. Jin and J.-O. Kim, "Discount Store Retailing in Korea," *Journal of Global Marketing* 15, no. 2 (2001), pp. 81–107; J. L. Joines, C. W. Scherer, and D. A. Scheufele, "Exploring Motivations for Consumer Web Use and Their Implications for E-commerce," *Journal of Consumer Marketing* 20, no. 2 (2003), pp. 90–108.

72. See M. A. Eastlick and R. A. Feinberg, "Gender Differences in Mail-Catalog Patronage Motives," *Journal of Direct Marketing,* Spring 1994, pp. 37–44; "The Call of the Mall," *EDK Forecast,* October 1994, pp. 1–3; "Black, Hip, and Primed to Shop," *American Demographics,* September 1996, pp. 52–58; J. A. F. Nicholls et al., "The Seven Year Itch?," *Journal of Consumer Marketing* 19, no. 2 (2002), pp. 149–65.

73. These segments and how retailers are targeting them are based on Y&R BAV Labs, "Shopperstates™: Six Dimensions of the New American Shopper," *Young & Rubicam,* December 15, 2015, www.slideshare.net/YRGlobal/shopperstates-six-dimension-of-the-new-american-shopper?from_action=save, accessed July 13, 2018; K. Richards, "Infographic: 6 Types of Shoppers and the Brands They'll Pay More For," *Adweek,* December 21, 2015, www.adweek.com/brand-marketing/infographic-6-types-shoppers-and-brands-theyll-pay-more-168697/, accessed July 13, 2018.

74. See J. E. Russo and F. Lecleric, "An Eye Fixation Analysis of Choice Processes for Consumer Nondurables," *Journal of Consumer Research,* September 1994, pp. 274–90.

75. See L. G. Block and V. G. Morwitz, "Shopping Lists as an External Memory Aid for Grocery Shopping," *Journal of Consumer Psychology* 8, no. 4 (1999), pp. 343–75.

76. See D. W. Rook and R. J. Fisher, "Normative Influences on Impulsive Buying Behaviors," *Journal of Consumer Research,* December 1995, pp. 305–13; R. Puri, "Measuring and Modifying Consumer Impulsive Buying Behavior," *Journal of Consumer Psychology* 5, no. 2 (1996), pp. 87–113; U. M. Dholakia, "Temptation and Resistance," *Psychology & Marketing,* November 2000, pp. 955–82; R. F. Baumeister, "Yielding to Temptation," *Journal of Consumer Research,* March 2002, pp. 670–76.

77. R. Liljenwall, "Global Trends in Point-of-Purchase Advertising," in *The Power of Point-of-Purchase Advertising,* ed. R. Liljenwall (Washington, DC: Point-of-Purchase Advertising International, 2004), p. 191.

78. "Shopping Decisions Made In-Store," *Archibald Container Corporation,* October 2, 2008.

79. B. Hurst, "Shopping Impulses Hit 'Before the Store,'" *RetailWire,* January 19, 2011, www.retailwire.com, accessed January 21, 2011.

80. "Shopper Decisions Made In-Store," *WPP,* www.wpp.com, accessed June 13, 2011.

81. D. R. Bell, D. Corsten, and G. Knox, "From Point of Purchase to Path to Purchase," *Journal of Marketing,* January 2011, pp. 31–45.

82. *P-O-P Measures Up* (Washington, DC: Point-of-Purchase Advertising Institute, 2001).

83. Ibid.

84. See *POPAI/Horner Drug Store Study* (Englewood, NJ: Point-of-Purchase Advertising Institute, 1992); A. J. Greco and L. E. Swayne, "Sales Response of Elderly Consumers to P-O-P Advertising," *Journal of Advertising Research,* September 1992, pp. 43–53; *POPAI/Kmart/Procter & Gamble Study of P-O-P Effectiveness* (Englewood, NJ: Point-of-Purchase Advertising Institute, 1993); *P-O-P Measures Up;* T. Lee, "Experts Say Point-of-Purchase Advertising Can Influence Shoppers' Choices," *Knight Ridder Tribune Business News,* January 19, 2002. For exceptions, see C. S. Areni, D. F. Duhan, and P. Kiekeer, "Point-of-Purchase Displays, Product Organization, and Brand Purchase Likelihoods," *Journal of the Academy of Marketing Science,* Fall 1999, pp. 428–41; M. Bues, M. Steiner, M. Stafflage, and M. Krafft, "How Mobile In-Store Advertising Influences Purchase Intention: Value Drivers and Mediating Effects from a Consumer Perspective," *Psychology & Marketing* 34, no. 2 (February 2017), pp. 157–74.

85. See E. T. Anderson and D. I. Simester, "The Role of Sale Signs," *Marketing Science* 2 (1998), pp. 139–55.

86. See, e.g., G. A. Taylor, "Coupon Response in Services," *Journal of Retailing* 77 (2001), pp. 139–51; C. M. Heilman, K. Nakamoto, and A. G. Rao, "Pleasant Surprises," *Journal of Marketing Research,* May 2002, pp. 242–52; D. M. Hardesty and W. O. Bearden, "Consumer Evaluations of Different Promotion Types and Price Presentations," *Journal of Retailing* 79 (2003), pp. 17–25.

87. A. S. C. Ehrenberg, K. Hammond, and G. J. Goodhardt, "The After-Effects of Price-Related Consumer Promotions," *Journal of Advertising Research,* July 1994, pp. 11–21; P. Papatla and L. Krishnamurthi, "Measuring the Dynamic Effects of Promotions on Brand Choice," *Journal of Marketing Research,* February 1996, pp. 20–36.

88. See C. F. Mela, K. Jedidi, and D. Bowman, "The Long-Term Impact of Promotions on Consumer Stockpiling Behavior," *Journal of Marketing Research,* May 1998, pp. 250–62; J. E. Urbany, P. R. Dickson, and A. G. Sawyer, "Insights into Cross- and Within-Store Price Search," *Journal of Retailing* 76, no. 2 (2000), pp. 243–58. See also M. Zeelenberg and M. van Putten, "The Dark Side of Discounts," *Psychology & Marketing,* August 2005, pp. 611–22, for the negative effects of postpromotion when loyal customers miss a discount opportunity.

89. K. Sivakumar and S. P. Raj, "Quality Tier Competition," *Journal of Marketing,* July 1997, pp. 71–84; S. M. Nowlis and I. Simonson, "Sales Promotions and the Choice Context as Competing Influences on Consumer Decision Making," *Journal of Consumer Psychology* 9, no. 1 (2000), pp. 1–16.

90. D. Grewal, R. Krishnan, J. Baker, and N. Borin, "The Effect of Store Name, Brand Name, and Price Discounts on Consumers' Evaluations and Purchase Intentions," *Journal of Retailing* 3 (1998), pp. 331–52.

91. D. R. Bell and J. M. Lattin, "Shopping Behavior and Consumer Preference for Store Price Format," *Marketing Science* 17, no. 1 (1998), pp. 66–88. See also R. Lal and R. Rao, "Supermarket Competition," *Marketing Science* 16, no. 1 (1997), pp. 60–80.

92. V. G. Morwitz, E. A. Greenleaf, and E. J. Johnson, "Divide and Prosper," *Journal of Consumer Research,* November 1998, pp. 453–63.

93. K. L. Wakefield and J. G. Blodgett, "The Effect of the Servicescape on Customers' Behavioral Intentions in Leisure Service Settings," *Journal of Services Marketing* 10, no. 6 (1996), pp. 45–61; K. L. Wakefield and J. G. Blodgett, "Customer Response to Intangible and Tangible Service Factors," *Psychology & Marketing,* January 1999, pp. 51–68; B. D. Keillor, G. T. M. Hult, and D. Kandemir, "A Study of the Service Encounter in Eight Countries," *Journal of International Marketing* 12, no. 1 (2004), pp. 9–35.

94. See C. Mathwick, N. Malhotra, and E. Rigdon, "Experiential Value," *Journal of Retailing* 77 (2001), pp. 39–56; P. D. Lynch, R. J. Kent, and S. S. Srinivasan, "The Global Internet Shopper," *Journal of Advertising Research,* May 2001, pp. 15–23; T. P. Novak, D. L. Hoffman, and A. Duhachek, "The Influence of Goal-Directed and Experiential Activities on Online Flow Experiences," *Journal of Consumer Psychology* 13, no. 1/2 (2003), pp. 3–16; A. P. Vrechopoulos et al., "Virtual Store Layout," *Journal of Retailing* 80, no. 1 (2004), pp. 13–22; J. H. Song and G. M. Zinkhan, "Determinants of Perceived Web Site Interactivity," *Journal of Marketing,* March 2008, pp. 99–113.

95. E. Sherman, A. Mathur, and R. B. Smith, "Store Environment and Consumer Purchase Behavior," *Psychology & Marketing,* July 1997, pp. 361–78; J. Baker et al., "The Influence of Multiple Store Environment Cues on Perceived Merchandise Value and Patronage Intentions," *Journal of Marketing,* April 2002, pp. 120–41; E. D. Brocato, J. Baker, and C. Voorhees, "Creating Consumer Attachment to Retail Service Firms through Sense of Place," *Journal of the Academy of Marketing Science* 43 (2015), pp. 200–20; J. Sevilla and C. Townsend, "The Space-to-Product Ratio Effect: How Interstitial Space Influences Product Aesthetic Appeal, Store Perceptions, and Product Preference," *Journal of Marketing Research* 52 (October 2016), pp. 665–81.

96. S. A. Eroglu, K. A. Machleit, and L. M. Davis, "Empirical Testing of a Model of Online Store Atmospherics and Shopper Responses," *Psychology & Marketing,* February 2003, pp. 139–50. See also S. Menon and B. Kahn, "Cross-Category Effects of Induced Arousal and Pleasure on the Internet Shopping Experience," *Journal of Retailing* 78 (2002), pp. 31–40.

97. L. Dailey, "Navigational Web Atmospherics," *Journal of Business Research* 57 (2004), pp. 795–803.

98. B. Babin and W. R. Darden, "Good and Bad Shopping Vibes," *Journal of Business Research,* March 1996, pp. 210–60; K. Chang, "The Impact of Perceived Physical Environments on Customers' Satisfaction and Return Intentions," *Journal of Professional Services Marketing* 21, no. 2 (2000), pp. 75–85; D. Grewal et al., "The Effects of Wait Expectations and Store Atmosphere Evaluations on Patronage Intentions in Service-Intensive Retail Stores," *Journal of Retailing* 79 (2003), pp. 259–68; Menon and Kahn, "Cross-Category Effects of Induced Arousal and Pleasure on the Internet Shopping Experience"; Eroglu, Machleit, and Davis, "Empirical Testing of a Model of Online Store Atmospherics and Shopper Responses."

99. See K. A. Machleit, S. A. Eroglu, and S. P. Mantel, "Perceived Retail Crowding and Shopping Satisfaction," *Journal of Consumer Psychology* 9, no. 1 (2000), pp. 29–42; K. Harris and S. Baron, "Consumer-to-Consumer Conversations in Service Settings," *Journal of Service Research,* February 2004, pp. 287–303; J. J. Argo, D. W. Dahl, and R. V. Manchanda, "The Influence of Mere Social Presence in a Retail Context," *Journal of Consumer Research,* September 2005, pp. 207–12; K. Zhang, S. E. Beatty, and D. L. Mothersbaugh, "A CIT Investigation of Other Customers' Influence in Services," *Journal of Services Marketing* 24, no. 5 (2010), pp. 389–99.

100. S. J. Grove and R. P. Fisk, "The Impact of Other Customers' Service Experiences," *Journal of Retailing* 1 (1997), pp. 63–85.

101. See, e.g., S. Oakes, "The Influence of Musicscape within Service Environments," *Journal of Services Marketing* 4, no. 7 (2000), pp. 539–56; J. C. Sweeney and F. Wyber, "The Role of Cognitions and Emotions in the Music-Approach-Avoidance Behavior Relationship," *Journal of Services Marketing* 16, no. 1 (2002), pp. 51–69; C. Caldwell and S. A. Hibbert, "The Influence of Music Tempo and Musical Preference on Restaurant Patrons' Behavior," *Psychology & Marketing,* November 2002, pp. 895–917; S. Morin, L. Dube, and J. C. Chebat, "The Role of Pleasant Music in Servicescapes," *Journal of Retailing* 83, no. 1 (2007), pp. 115–30.

102. C. S. Gulas and C. D. Schewe, "Atmospheric Segmentation," in *Enhancing Knowledge Development in Marketing,* ed. R. Achrol and A. Mitchell (Chicago: American Marketing Association, 1994), pp. 325–30. Similar results are in J. D. Herrington and L. M. Capella, "Effects of Music in Service Environments," *Journal of Services Marketing* 2 (1996), pp. 26–41.

103. D. J. Mitchell, B. E. Kahn, and S. C. Knasko, "There's Something in the Air," *Journal of Consumer Research,* September 1995, pp. 229–38; A. R. Hirsch, "Effects of Ambient Odors on Slot-Machine Usage in a Las Vegas Casino," *Psychology & Marketing,* October 1995, pp. 585–94; M. Wilkie, "Scent of a Market," *American Demographics,* August 1995, pp. 40–49; P. Sloan, "Smelling Trouble," *Advertising Age,* September 11, 1995, p. 1; E. R. Spangenberg, A. E. Crowley, and P. W. Henderson, "Improving the Store Environment," *Journal of Marketing,* April 1996, pp. 67–80; P. F. Bone and P. S. Ellen, "Scents in the Marketplace," *Journal of Retailing* 75, no. 2 (1999), pp. 243–62.

104. A. S. Mattila and J. Wirtz, "Congruency of Scent and Music as a Driver of In-Store Evaluations and Behavior," *Journal of Retailing* 77, no. 2 (2001), pp. 273–89.

105. See A. M. Fiore, X. Yah, and E. Yoh, "Effects of Product Display and Environmental Fragrancing on Approach Responses and Pleasurable Experiences," *Psychology & Marketing,* January 2000, pp. 27–54.

106. K. Campo, E. Gijsbrechts, and P. Nisol, "Towards Understanding Consumer Response to Stock-Outs," *Journal of Retailing* 76, no. 2 (2000), pp. 219–42.

107. G. J. Fitzsimons, "Consumer Response to Stockouts," *Journal of Consumer Research,* September 2000, pp. 249–67.

108. See, e.g., L. M. Sloot, P. C. Verhoef, and P. H. Franses, "The Impact of Brand Equity and the Hedonic Level of Products on Consumer Stock-Out Reactions," *Journal of Retailing* 81, no. 1 (2005), pp. 15–34.

109. "Reasons Why Website Visitors Abandoned Their Shopping Carts," *See Why,* June 3, 2010, http://seewhy.com/blog, accessed June 13, 2011.

110. M. Prince, "Online Retailers Turn to New Shopping Carts to Drive Sales," *Wall Street Journal Online,* November 10, 2004.

111. See, e.g., A. D. Miyazaki and A. Fernandez, "Consumer Perceptions of Privacy and Security Risks for Online Shopping," *Journal of Consumer Affairs* 35, no. 1 (2001), pp. 27–44; E. B. Andrade, V. Kaltcheva, and B. Weitz, "Self-Disclosure on the Web," in *Advances in Consumer Research,* vol. 29, ed. S. M. Broniarczyk and K. Nakamoto (Provo, UT: Association for Consumer Research, 2002), pp. 350–53; A. D. Miyazaki and S. Krishnamurthy, "Internet Seals of Approval," *Journal of Consumer Affairs* 36, no. 1 (2002), pp. 28–49; G. R. Milne and M. J. Culnan, "Strategies for Reducing Online Privacy Risks," *Journal of Interactive Marketing,* Summer 2004, pp. 15–29; T. B. White, "Consumer Disclosure and Disclosure Avoidance," *Journal of Consumer Psychology* 14, no. 1/2 (2004), pp. 41–51.

112. "Single-Use Numbers Increase Confidence, Boost Online Spending, Study Says," *InternetRetailer.com,* February 3, 2005.

113. *Consumer Shopping Experiences, Preferences, and Behaviors* (Cambridge, MA: ATG, October 2010).

114. Google, "How People Shop on Their Phones."

115. See, e.g., R. Lacey, J. Suh, and R. M. Morgan, "Differential Effects of Preferential Treatment on Relational Outcomes," *Journal of Service Research,* February 2007, pp. 241–56; R. Di Mascio, "The Service Models of Frontline Employees," *Journal of Marketing,* July 2010, pp. 63–80; J. Paul, K. Sankaranarayanan, and N. Mekoth, "Consumer Satisfaction in Retail Stores: Theory and Implications," *International Journal of Consumer Studies* 40 (2016), pp. 635–42.

116. B. B. Stern, G. J. Thompson, and E. J. Arnould, "Narrative Analysis of a Marketing Relationship," *Psychology & Marketing* 3 (1998), pp. 195–214.

117. M. Holzwarth, C. Janiszewski, and M. M. Neumann, "The Influence of Avatars on Online Consumer Shopping Behavior," *Journal of Marketing,* October 2006, pp. 19–36.

118. D. Prelec and D. Simester, "Always Leave Home without It," *Marketing Letters,* February 2001, pp. 5–12; D. Soman, "Effects of Payment Mechanism on Spending Behavior," *Journal of Consumer Research,* March 2001, pp. 460–74.

Source: Inter IKEA Systems B.V.

LEARNING OBJECTIVES

LO1 Describe the various postpurchase processes engaged in by consumers.

LO2 Define and discuss postpurchase dissonance.

LO3 Discuss the issues surrounding product use and nonuse and their importance to marketers.

LO4 Summarize disposition options and their relevance to marketers and public policy.

LO5 Explain the determinants and outcomes of satisfaction and dissatisfaction.

LO6 Describe the relationship between satisfaction, repeat purchase, and customer commitment.

Once consumers have purchased a product or service, postpurchase issues of usage, disposition, and postpurchase valuation and satisfaction kick in. Just as we have found biases in perception and decision making "prepurchase," such biases exist "postpurchase" as well. The following are just a few examples:

- *Product use.* Consumers given larger-sized containers of popcorn eat (53 percent) more than consumers given medium-sized containers. Consumers given larger ice cream scoopers served themselves more ice cream than consumers given smaller ice cream scoopers. In "mindless" eating, people are unaware that their eating behavior is influenced by seemingly irrelevant environmental factors—size of container, serving utensil.[1]

- *Product value based on consumer effort.* Consumers who purchase products that must be assembled value them more than those that come assembled (sometimes termed the *IKEA effect*). The IKEA effect is *retroactive,* occurring after *successful* completion of the necessary assembly. The IKEA effect suggests that products sold "with some assembly required" may be adding labor-infused value to the products.

- *Product value based on ownership.* Consumers who own a product will, on average, require a significantly higher price to sell it than the average price consumers shopping for the product are willing to pay. This increased valuation of the product bestowed by "mere" ownership is known as the *endowment effect* and has been repeatedly demonstrated with a wide range of goods—candy bars, pens, mugs, hats, tee shirts—and might explain why consumers keep old products rather than sell or donate them even after a replacement has been found and purchased.

How we use and value products and services is subject to a host of influences, postpurchase. Postpurchase and the various processes and influences involved are the focus of this chapter.

FIGURE 18-1 Postpurchase Consumer Behavior

Purchase is followed by a number of processes including use, evaluation, and, in some cases, satisfaction, and consumer responses related to satisfaction include repurchase, positive word-of-mouth, and loyalty. Evaluation also can lead to dissatisfaction, which is sometimes associated with complaining, as well as erosion of loyalty, brand switching, and negative word-of-mouth. Appropriate responses to product and service failure are critical, including putting in processes to track potential problems such as call centers and the social media options discussed in Chapter 7. Once a problem is recognized, appropriate action is important as a way to try to reverse or eliminate the negative outcomes of dissatisfaction. Effective CRM programs and high-quality service, as discussed in the opener, are often important aspects of marketing strategy designed to either deliver high satisfaction or deal effectively with dissatisfaction when it occurs.

LO1   Figure 18–1 shows the relationships among these various processes, which are the focus of this chapter. It also indicates that immediately following a purchase, and often prior to usage, consumers may feel doubt or anxiety, known as postpurchase dissonance.

POSTPURCHASE DISSONANCE

LO2   I still like it [a dining room set] a whole lot better than what we used to have. But I think if we had taken longer we would have gotten more precisely what we wanted. I mean we got a great deal. You couldn't get that for that price, so I am happy with the money part of it, but some days I wish we had spent more and gotten something a bit different.[2]

This is a common consumer reaction after making a difficult, relatively permanent decision. Doubt or anxiety of this type is referred to as **postpurchase dissonance**.[3] Some, but not all, consumer purchase decisions are followed by postpurchase dissonance. The probability and magnitude of such dissonance are a function of

- *The degree of commitment or irrevocability of the decision.* The easier it is to alter the decision, the less likely the consumer is to experience dissonance.
- *The importance of the decision to the consumer.* The more important the decision, the more likely dissonance will result.
- *The difficulty of choosing among the alternatives.* The more difficult it is to select from among the alternatives, the more likely the experience and magnitude of dissonance. Decision difficulty is a function of the number of alternatives considered, the number of relevant attributes associated with each alternative, and the extent to which each alternative offers attributes not available with the other alternatives.
- *The individual's tendency to experience anxiety.* Some individuals have a higher tendency to experience anxiety than do others. The higher the tendency to experience anxiety, the more likely the individual will experience postpurchase dissonance.

Dissonance does not generally occur for low-involvement nominal and limited decision making. These decisions are relatively easy and unimportant. Dissonance is most common in high-involvement extended decision making, where trade-offs among desirable attributes create conflict (as in the price–quality trade-off made in the dining room decision above). Such trade-offs create negative emotions and decision delay.[4] Thus, when such trade-offs exist, salespeople and ads could attempt to refocus consumer attention on the positive aspects of the decision or provide incentives to make a purchase even in the face of the difficult trade-off.

After the purchase, consumers may use one or more of the following approaches to reevaluate or alter the decision to reduce dissonance:

- Increase the desirability of the brand purchased.
- Decrease the desirability of rejected alternatives.
- Decrease the importance of the purchase decision.
- Reverse the purchase decision (return the product before use).

Advertising and follow-up sales efforts can have a huge effect on postpurchase dissonance because consumers, in their reevaluation process, often search for and are receptive to information that confirms the wisdom of their purchase. Direct mailers like a postcard, follow-up calls, and e-mails all can be effective. Johnston & Murphy sends follow-up e-mails thanking customers for their recent purchase, pointing them to its website, and soliciting feedback. Dick's Sporting Goods sends an incentive for a future purchase along with a thank-you e-mail to customers. Such communications can go a long way in reducing dissonance and increasing satisfaction. The Doctors of Osteopathic Medicine ad in Illustration 18–1 provides an additional example of the reinforcement potential of advertising in the postpurchase process.

A concept very similar to postpurchase dissonance is **consumption guilt.** Consumption guilt occurs when *negative emotions or guilt feelings are aroused by the use of a product or a service.* A person driving a large car may experience some negative feelings due to concern over resource utilization and pollution. The example below illustrates consumption guilt quite clearly:

I have to count calories much more than I did before. I still buy a sundae once in a while but the joy of eating ice cream will probably forever be connected with guilt over eating something so unhealthy. When I think about it, I realize that most products make me feel good and bad at the same time.[5]

Marketers of products whose target markets might experience consumption guilt need to focus on validating the consumption of the product. They need to find ways to give the consumer permission or a rationale for indulging in that consumption act.[6]

Advertisements for high-involvement purchase items, such as the use of Doctors of Osteopathic Medicine shown here, can serve to confirm the wisdom of a purchase as well as influence new purchasers.

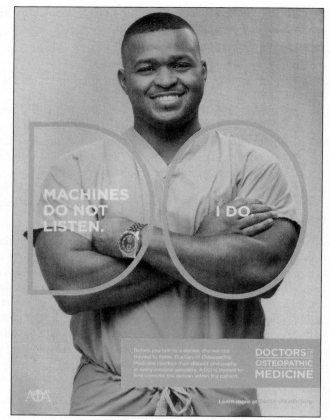

Source: American Osteopathic Association

PRODUCT USE AND NONUSE

Product Use

LO3

Most consumer purchases involve nominal or limited decision making and therefore arouse little or no postpurchase dissonance. Instead, the purchaser or some other member of the household uses the product without first worrying about the wisdom of the purchase. And as Figure 18–1 shows, even when postpurchase dissonance occurs, it is still generally followed by product use.

Marketers need to understand how consumers use their products for a variety of reasons. Understanding both the functional and symbolic ways in which a product is used can lead to more effective product designs and marketing campaigns. For example, the existence of the sneakerhead consumption subculture (Chapter 7) has influenced many aspects of sneaker design and marketing, including the creation of expensive, limited-edition designs that are targeted specifically to the sneakerhead collector.

Use innovativeness refers to *a consumer using a product in a new way.*[7] Marketers who discover new uses for their products can greatly expand sales.

- Arm & Hammer discovered that consumers were using its baking soda for a variety of noncooking uses, such as deodorizing refrigerators. It now advertises such uses and has developed product packaging, such as its Fridge Fresh Air Filters, specific to such uses. It also has a section on its website where consumers can submit their own "solutions" to common household problems using Arm & Hammer baking soda.

- WD-40, a lubricant, is renowned for the wide array of applications that consumers suggest for it, including as an additive to fish bait and for removing gum from a carpet.
- The manufacturer of Mentos mints benefited from a televised "misuse" of the candy. During a late-night television program, a chemistry teacher demonstrated the making of a soft drink geyser by dropping Mentos into Diet Coke. Mentos's sales increased roughly 20 percent as a result.

Just as the Internet can be used as a way to observe and track consumer problems, it also can be used as a means for tracking innovative product uses. And web-based submission options on a brand's website make direct collection of such ideas easier than ever.[8]

Marketers frequently can take advantage of the fact that the use of one product may require, be enhanced by, or suggest the use of other products. The Dove DermaSeries ad in Illustration 18–2 provides a great example of the concept. Dove is promoting the use of its body lotion, body wash, and face cream together "to make peace with dry skin." Consider houseplants and fertilizer; bikes and helmets; dresses and shoes. Retailers can promote such items jointly, display them together, or train their sales personnel to make relevant complementary sales.

Stringent product liability laws and aggressive civil suits also are forcing marketing managers to examine how consumers use their products. These laws have made firms responsible for harm caused by products *not only when the product is used as specified by the manufacturer but in any reasonably foreseeable use of the product.* Thus, the manufacturer must design products with both the primary purpose *and* other potential uses in mind. This requires substantial research into how consumers actually use products.

When marketers discover confusion about the proper way to use a product, it is often to their advantage to teach consumers how to use it and engage in marketing communications that increase the chances of proper use. After all, how many consumers blame themselves when a product failure occurs as a result of their own failure to follow usage instructions?[9] At other times, a firm can gain a competitive advantage by redesigning the product so that it is easier to use properly.

Source: Unilever

Product Nonuse

As Figure 18–1 indicates, not all purchases are followed by use. **Product nonuse** occurs when a consumer actively acquires a product that is not used or used only sparingly relative to potential use.[10]

For many products and most services, the decisions to purchase and to consume are made simultaneously. A person who orders a meal in a restaurant also is deciding to eat the meal at that time. However, a decision to purchase food at a supermarket requires a second decision to prepare and consume the food. The second decision occurs at a different point in time and in a different environment from the first. Thus, nonuse can occur because the situation or the purchaser changes between the purchase and the potential usage occasion. For example, a

Source: The Cholula Food Company

point-of-purchase display featuring a new food item shown as part of an appealing entrée might cause a consumer to imagine an appropriate usage situation and to purchase the product. However, without the stimulus of the display, the consumer may not remember the intended use or may just never get around to it. Nonuse situations such as the following are common:[11]

Wok. "I wanted to try and cook stirfry, but I didn't take time out to use it."

Skirt. "My ingenious idea was that I'd lose a few pounds and fit into the size 4 rather than gain a few and fit into the size 6. Obviously, I never lost the weight, so the skirt was snug."

Gym membership. "Couldn't get in the groove to lift."

In such cases, the consumer has wasted money and the marketer is unlikely to get repeat sales or positive referrals. Many such purchases are difficult for the marketer to correct after the purchase. In other cases, consumers would have used the product if reminded or motivated at the proper time. In the last example above, good records would indicate that this member was not using the gym. A personal letter, e-mail, text, or telephone invitation to come in might be enough to get this person started.

Some products are known to be kept on hand by consumers; that is, they stock up on certain items. In this case, a major goal of advertising should be to encourage people to consume the product at the next appropriate occasion and perhaps even suggest situations that would be appropriate. Because consumers have the product available, the task is not to encourage purchase but to motivate near-term consumption such as including Cholula hot sauce into consumers' regular breakfast routines, as suggested in Illustration 18–3.

The division between the initial purchase decision and the decision to consume is particularly strong with online, as well as catalog, purchases. In effect, two decisions are involved in these purchases: the initial decision to order the product and a second decision to keep or return the item when it is received. Not only is it likely that several days will have passed between the two decisions, but substantially different information is available at the "keep or return" decision point. In particular, consumers can physically touch, try on, or otherwise experience the item.

Obviously, online, and even catalog, retailers want to maximize the percentage of items kept rather than returned. Intuitively, one might think that a strict return policy would accomplish this. However, such a policy also might reduce the number of initial orders. In fact, a liberal return policy appears to maximize initial orders and also may minimize returns. Such a policy reduces perceived risk and signals higher quality (surrogate indicator), which increases initial orders. Consumers also tend to perceive items ordered under liberal return policies as having higher quality after receiving them, which reduces returns.[12] One study found that half of consumers check a retailer's return policy before making a purchase, and companies like Zappos and Nordstrom offer "hassle-free" return policies in response to this important postpurchase feature.[13] In addition to return policies, online tools that can better represent products so that a maximal fit to consumer needs is attained can help. Scanner-based, full-body measurement technology that also makes recommendations about sizes, styles, and brands (Chapter 17) should dramatically increase how well clothing fits even if it is ordered online without first trying it on. This should reduce returns and company costs and increase customer satisfaction.

DISPOSITION

Disposition of the product or the product's container may occur before, during, or after product use. Or for products that are completely consumed, such as an ice cream cone, no disposition may be involved.

LO4

The United States produces several hundred million tons of refuse a year.[14] Packaging is an important component. Millions of pounds of product packages are disposed of every day. These containers are thrown away as garbage or litter, used in some capacity by the consumer, or recycled. Creating packages that utilize a minimal amount of resources is important for economic reasons as well as being a matter of social responsibility. Many firms are responding to this issue, as the examples below illustrate:

- Crate & Barrel stopped using white bleached board in its famous black and white boxes and switched to more renewable fiber that contains postconsumer recyclable material.
- Zappos launched the #imnotabox campaign to inspire consumers to reuse their packaging in creative ways, such as children's toys or household containers like a planter.[15]

Beyond packaging is the physical product that continues to exist even though it may no longer meet a consumer's needs either in an instrumental (no longer works) or symbolic (no longer the latest trend) way. Either situation requires disposition. For some consumers, recycling is more prominent than others (see Chapter 3 on green marketing), and companies and government organizations are working to encourage recycling and make it more convenient. Still, only about a third of solid waste (trash) is recycled.[16]

Exploding demand and short product lifespans for high-tech gadgets such as cell phones, personal computers, and various other personal electronics devices are creating growing concerns over **e-waste.** Both instrumental and symbolic considerations can drive e-waste. Consumer and corporate solutions are necessary and evolving, although one recent estimate is that only one in four computers is recycled![17] Examples of efforts to reduce e-waste include the following:

- Mobile phone manufacturers, including Apple and Samsung, offer easy recycling programs for old phones. For some of its newer models, Apple will give the consumer a gift card towards the purchase of a new Apple product.[18]

Source: The L'Oréal Group

- Sony has developed a recycling plan whereby it will offset pound-for-pound that amount of materials recycled for new products produced. To date, over 200,000 tons of electronics scrap has been collected through the program. Sony is partnering with a recycling company and banking on the project's paying for itself as a result of the value of such ingredients as copper typically found in e-waste. Big issues are consumer awareness and convenience.[19]
- Companies such as HP and Office Depot are engaged in ongoing efforts related to print cartridges. HP provides a self-addressed, postage-paid envelope in which you can return used ink cartridges to its recycling center. Office Depot offers discounts through its customer rewards program for those who return used cartridges.

Figure 18-2 illustrates the various alternatives for disposing of a product or package. Unfortunately, while "throw it away" is only one of many disposition alternatives, it is by far the most widely used by many consumers. Environmental groups work hard to change these behaviors, as do some firms and other organizations (as shown in the Kiehl's ad in Illustration 18-4). Other firms, however, continue to use unnecessary or hard-to-recycle packaging and product components.

Product Disposition and Marketing Strategy

Why should a marketing manager be concerned about the disposition of a used product? Perhaps the best reason is the cumulative effect that these decisions have on the quality of the environment and the lives of current and future generations. However, there are also short-term economic reasons for concern. Disposition decisions affect the purchase decisions of both the individual making the disposition and other individuals in the market for that product category.

There are five major ways in which disposition decisions can affect a firm's marketing strategy. First, for most durable goods, consumers are reluctant to purchase a new item until they have "gotten their money's worth" from the old one. These consumers mentally depreciate the value of a durable item over time. If the item is not fully mentally depreciated, they are reluctant to write it off by disposing of it to acquire a new one. Allowing old items to be traded in is one way to overcome this reluctance.[20]

Second, disposition sometimes must occur before acquisition of a replacement because of space or financial limitations. For example, because of a lack of storage space, a family living in an apartment may find it necessary to dispose of an existing bedroom set before acquiring a new one. Or someone may need to sell his current bicycle to raise supplemental funds to pay for a new bicycle. Thus, it is to the manufacturer's and retailer's advantage to assist the consumer in the disposition process.

Third, frequent decisions by consumers to sell, trade, or give away used products may result in a large used-product market that can reduce the market for new products. A **consumer-to-consumer sale** occurs when *one consumer sells a product directly to another with or without the assistance of a commercial intermediary.* Garage sales, flea markets, classified ads, and online outlets such as eBay and craigslist exist as a result of consumer demand to buy and sell used items. In addition, consumers may give or sell their used items to resellers. Thrift and consignment stores, featuring used clothing, appliances, and furniture, run by both commercial and nonprofit groups, are an important part of the economy.

Disposition Alternatives

FIGURE 18-2

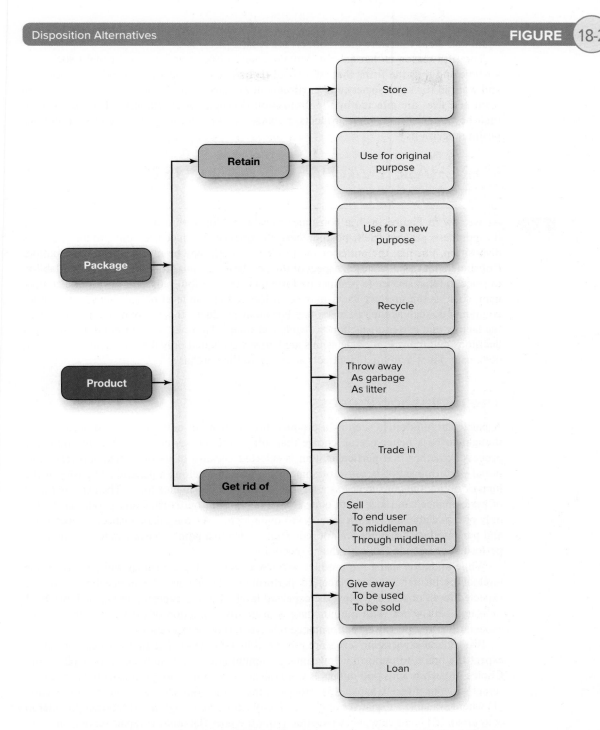

A fourth reason for concern with product disposition is that the United States is not completely a throwaway society. Many Americans continue to be very concerned with waste and how their purchase decisions affect waste.[21] Such individuals might be willing to purchase, for example, a new vacuum cleaner if they were confident that the old one would be rebuilt and resold. However, they might be reluctant to throw their old vacuums away or to go to the effort of reselling the machines themselves. Thus, manufacturers and retailers could take steps to ensure that products are reused.

The fifth reason is that environmentally sound disposition decisions benefit society as a whole and thus the firms that are part of that society. Firms' owners and employees live and work in the same society and environment as many of their consumers. Their environment and lives are affected by the disposition decisions of consumers. Therefore, it is in their best interest to develop products, packages, and programs that encourage proper disposition decisions.

PURCHASE EVALUATION AND CUSTOMER SATISFACTION

LO5

As we saw in Figure 18-1, a consumer's evaluation of a purchase can be influenced by the purchase process itself, postpurchase dissonance, product use, and product/package disposition. Further, the outlet or the product or both may be involved in the evaluation. Consumers may evaluate each aspect of the purchase, ranging from information availability to price to retail service to product performance. In addition, satisfaction with one component, such as the product itself, may be influenced by the level of satisfaction with other components, such as the salesperson.[22] For many products, this is a dynamic process, with the factors that drive satisfaction evolving over time.[23] However, keep in mind that nominal decisions and many limited decisions are actively evaluated only if some factor, such as an obvious product malfunction, directs attention to the purchase.[24]

The Evaluation Process

A particular alternative such as a product, brand, or retail outlet is selected because it is thought to be a better overall choice than other alternatives considered in the purchase process. Whether that particular item is selected because of its presumed superior functional performance or because of some other reason, such as a generalized liking of the item or outlet, the consumer has a level of expected performance for it. The expected level of performance can range from quite low (this brand or outlet isn't very good, but it's the only one available and I'm in a hurry) to quite high.[25] As you might suspect, expectations and perceived performance are not independent. Up to a point, consumers tend to perceive performance to be in line with their expectations.[26]

While and after using the product, service, or outlet, the consumer will perceive some level of performance. This perceived performance level could be noticeably above the expected level, noticeably below the expected level, or at the expected level. As Table 18-1 indicates, satisfaction with the purchase is primarily a function of the initial performance expectations and perceived performance relative to those expectations.[27]

Two general expectation levels are presented in Table 18-1. The first is when consumers expect the brand to perform below some minimum level and requires a bit of explanation. Choice of such brands and outlets is not typical because they would normally be in a consumer's inept set (see Chapter 15). However, three situations will drive choice in this case: (1) where available alternatives don't exist (AT&T is the only high-speed Internet provider in your area), (2) in an emergency situation (your tire goes flat and the repair service only carries a brand you find undesirable), or (3) when family decisions result in a suboptimal choice for some family members (the child is thrilled with Chuck E. Cheese; the parents are not).

Table 18-1 shows that an outlet or brand whose performance confirms a low-performance expectation generally will result in neither satisfaction nor dissatisfaction but rather with

Expectations, Performance, and Satisfaction			TABLE 18-1
	Expectation Level		
Perceived Performance Relative to Expectation	**Below Minimum Desired Performance**	**Above Minimum Desired Performance**	
Better	Satisfaction*	Satisfaction/Commitment	
Same	Nonsatisfaction	Satisfaction	
Worse	Dissatisfaction	Dissatisfaction	

*Assuming the perceived performance surpasses the minimum desired level.

what can be termed *nonsatisfaction*. That is, the consumer is not likely to feel disappointment or engage in complaint behavior. However, this purchase will not reduce the likelihood that the consumer will search for a better alternative the next time the problem arises.

A brand whose perceived performance falls below expectations generally produces dissatisfaction. If the discrepancy between performance and expectation is sufficiently large, or if initial expectations were low, the consumer may restart the entire decision process. Most likely, he or she will place an item performing below expectations in the inept set and no longer consider it. In addition, the consumer may complain or initiate negative word-of-mouth communications.

When perceptions of product performance match expectations that are at or above the minimum desired performance level, satisfaction generally results. Likewise, performance above the minimum desired level that exceeds a lower expectation tends to produce satisfaction. Satisfaction reduces the level of decision making the next time the problem is recognized; that is, a satisfactory purchase is rewarding and encourages one to repeat the same behavior in the future (nominal decision making). Satisfied customers are also likely to engage in positive word-of-mouth communications about the brand, which can lead to the acquisition of new customers.

Product performance that exceeds expected performance generally will result in satisfaction and sometimes in commitment. Commitment, discussed in depth in the next section, means that the consumer is enthusiastic about a particular brand and is somewhat immune to actions by competitors.

The need to develop realistic consumer expectations poses a difficult problem for the marketing manager. For a brand or outlet to be selected, the consumer must view it as superior on the relevant combination of attributes. Therefore, the marketing manager naturally wants to emphasize its positive aspects. If such an emphasis creates expectations in the consumer that the item cannot fulfill, a negative evaluation may occur. Negative evaluations can produce brand switching, unfavorable word-of-mouth communications, and complaint behavior. Thus, the marketing manager must balance enthusiasm for the product with a realistic view of the product's attributes.

Determinants of Satisfaction and Dissatisfaction   Because performance expectations and actual performance are major factors in the evaluation process, we need to understand the dimensions of product and service performance. A major study of the reasons customers switch service providers found competitor actions to be a relatively minor cause. Most customers did not switch from a satisfactory provider to a better provider. Instead, they switched because of perceived problems with their current service provider. The nature of these problems and the percentage listing each as a reason they changed providers follow (the percentages sum to more than 100 because many customers listed several reasons that caused them to switch):[28]

- *Core service failure* (44 percent): Mistakes (no record of hotel reservation), billing errors, and service catastrophes that harm the customer ("the dry cleaners ruined my wedding dress").
- *Service encounter failures* (34 percent): Service employees were uncaring, impolite, unresponsive, or unknowledgeable.
- *Pricing* (30 percent): High prices, price increases, unfair pricing practices, and deceptive pricing.
- *Inconvenience* (21 percent): Inconvenient location, hours of operation, waiting time for service or appointments.
- *Responses to service failures* (17 percent): Reluctant responses, failure to respond, and negative responses ("it's your fault").
- *Attraction by competitors* (10 percent): More personable, more reliable, higher quality, and better value.
- *Ethical problems* (7 percent): Dishonest behavior, intimidating behavior, unsafe or unhealthy practices, or conflicts of interest.
- *Involuntary switching* (6 percent): Service provider or customer moves, or a third-party payer such as an insurance company requires a change.

Other studies have found that waiting time has a major impact on evaluations of service. Consumers have particularly negative reactions to delays over which they believe the service provider has control and during which they have little to occupy their time.[29] The impact can be staggering. Recent reports indicate U.S. consumers who switch providers due to poor customer service cost companies over $60 billion a year.[30] *What are the marketing strategy implications of these results?*

Failure on a given product or service characteristic often has a stronger effect on consumers than success on that same characteristic, something referred to as the *negativity bias.*[31] Thus, depending on the attributes and decision rule involved (see Chapter 16), this could mean first meeting expectations across all relevant features before maximizing performance on a few.

Firms are using technology as a way to deliver more convenient service both online and in the store. Price check scanners in the store or mobile local price apps, as well as self-checkout lanes, can make the in-store experience more satisfying. And website functionality such as avatars and text and video chat with customer representatives can be critical to customer satisfaction online. When technology fails or is complicated to use, consumers typically experience dissatisfaction. In the case of online checkout, such factors can result in lost sales as consumers abandon their shopping carts (see Chapter 17).

For many products, there are two dimensions to performance: instrumental and expressive, or symbolic. **Instrumental performance** relates *to the physical functioning of the product.* **Symbolic performance** relates to *aesthetic or image-enhancement performance.* For example, the durability of a blazer is an aspect of instrumental performance, whereas styling represents symbolic performance. Complete satisfaction requires adequate performance on both dimensions. However, for at least some product categories such as clothing, "[d]issatisfaction is caused by a failure of instrumental performance, while complete satisfaction also requires the symbolic functions to perform at or above the expected levels."[32]

In addition to symbolic and instrumental performance, products also provide affective performance. **Affective performance** is *the emotional response that owning or using the product or outlet provides.*[33] It may arise from the instrumental or symbolic performance or from the product itself; for example, a suit that produces admiring glances or compliments may produce a positive affective response. Or the affective performance may be the primary product benefit, such as for an emotional movie or novel.

Research regarding online satisfiers and dissatisfiers finds the following four dimensions to be important:[34]

- *Website Design and Interaction:* Includes factors such as information quality, navigation, price, merchandise availability, purchase process, and order tracking.
- *Security and Privacy:* Includes factors related to security such as fraud and identity theft and privacy related to unwanted marketing efforts.
- *Fulfillment and Reliability:* Includes factors such as timely delivery, order accuracy, billing accuracy, and the quality of the merchandise.
- *Customer Service:* Includes factors relating to service level such as customer support, ability and ease of communication, as well as factors relating to returns such as clear and fair return policies.

A study of German consumers finds similar drivers of satisfaction with online retailers.[35] Finally, research suggests that in multi- or omni-channel contexts involving the Internet, the issue of integration is critical in that content, processes, image, and so on should be consistent to the extent possible and appropriate across different channels within a company or brand.[36]

DISSATISFACTION RESPONSES

Figure 18–3 illustrates the major options available to a dissatisfied consumer. The first decision is whether or not to take any external action. By taking no action, the consumer decides to live with the unsatisfactory situation. This decision is a function of the importance of the purchase to the consumer, the ease of taking action, the consumer's existing level of overall satisfaction with the brand or outlet, and the characteristics of the consumer involved. It is

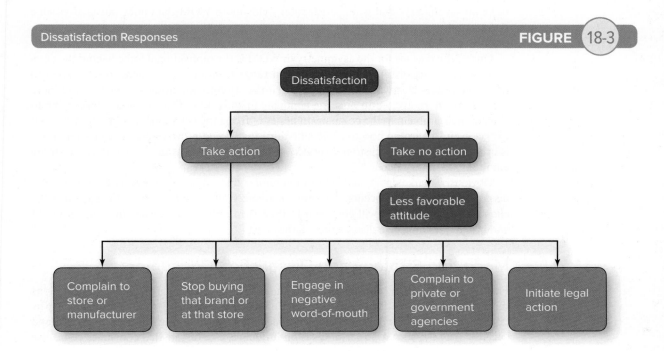

Dissatisfaction Responses   FIGURE 18-3

important to note that even when no external action is taken, the consumer is likely to have a less favorable attitude toward the store or brand.[37]

Consumers who take action in response to dissatisfaction generally pursue one or more of five alternatives. As Figure 18–3 indicates, the most favorable of these alternatives from a company's standpoint is for consumers to complain to it. This at least gives the company a chance to resolve the problem. Many times, however, consumers do not complain to the company, but instead take actions such as switching brands or engaging in negative word-of-mouth (WOM).

Consumers are satisfied with the vast majority of their purchases. Still, because of the large number of purchases they make each year, most individuals experience dissatisfaction with some of their purchases. For example, one study asked 540 consumers if they could recall a case in which one or more of the grocery products they normally purchase were defective. They recalled 1,307 separate unsatisfactory purchases.

These purchases produced the following actions (the study did not measure negative word-of-mouth actions such as warning friends):

- 25 percent of these unsatisfactory purchases resulted in brand switching.
- 19 percent caused the shopper to stop buying the products.
- 13 percent led to an in-store inspection of future purchases.
- 3 percent produced complaints to the manufacturer.
- 5 percent produced complaints to the retailer.
- 35 percent resulted in the items being returned.

In a similar study of durable goods, 54 percent of the dissatisfied customers said they would not purchase the brand again (brand switching) and 45 percent warned their friends (negative WOM) about the product.[38]

As we discussed in Chapter 7, WOM is a critical factor in consumer behavior. Consumers trust WOM more than many other sources and, therefore, tend to rely on it heavily when making decisions. Unfortunately for companies, when it comes to WOM, there appears to be an asymmetry—that is, dissatisfaction yields more WOM than does satisfaction. One estimate puts the ratio at two to one, with consumers telling twice as many people about a negative product or service experience than a positive one.[39]

One of the reasons for the asymmetry in WOM is the motivational force behind the emotions surrounding dissatisfaction, which can range from disappointment to frustration to rage. The results clearly point to the fact that the stronger the negative emotion, the more consumers are motivated to hurt the company in some way. That is, rather than trying to explain their problem to the company in hopes of fixing the situation, angry customers want to "get even." Learning how to avoid situations that would provoke such negative emotions is critical, as is training customer service employees to identify and deal with these strong emotions when they occur.[40]

Obviously, marketers should strive to minimize dissatisfaction *and* to effectively resolve dissatisfaction when it occurs. However, marketers also need to strive to maximize the chances that consumers will complain to their firm rather than engage in negative WOM and brand switching. We discuss these issues next.

Marketing Strategy and Dissatisfied Consumers

Firms need to satisfy consumer expectations by (1) creating reasonable expectations through promotional efforts and (2) maintaining consistent quality so the reasonable expectations are fulfilled. Because dissatisfied consumers tend to engage in negative WOM and because WOM is such a powerful decision influence, one dissatisfied consumer can cause a ripple or multiplier effect in terms of discouraging future sales.[41] Both offline and online WOM are important to consider.

> I feel mad. I put it in my Christmas letter to 62 people across the country. I mean, I told everybody don't buy one of these things because the transmission is bad.[42]

The above example is a marketer's nightmare. Yet the rise of social media has created challenges in this arena that make the above example seem like a minor nuisance. One Comcast customer, in trying to cancel his service, received aggressive treatment from the customer service representative. The customer's response was to post a recording of the call online. The recording has received millions of "plays" as a result, and Comcast quickly apologized.[43] Another such incident, with serious financial consequences to the company, involved Dave Carroll and United Airlines:

> Dave Carroll is a musician and was travelling with his $3,500 710 Taylor acoustic guitar. From his seat he saw baggage handlers throwing his guitar without regard to its safety. When he reached his destination, he found that the guitar was ruined. United did not take responsibility even though Carroll complained to the company numerous times in numerous ways. So, being a musician, Dave made a music video about this experience and posted it on YouTube. This video has had over 10 million views and within days of being posted, United's stock fell 10 percent![44]

When a consumer is dissatisfied, the most favorable consequence is for the person to communicate this dissatisfaction to the firm but to no one else. In the above example, Dave Carroll made numerous attempts that United did not heed. This is unfortunate because such complaining can alert the firm to problems, enable it to make amends where necessary, and minimize negative word-of-mouth communications. Many firms have discovered that customers whose complaints are resolved to their satisfaction are sometimes even more satisfied than are those who did not experience a problem in the first place, particularly if the problem is minor and not repeated.[45]

Unlike Dave Carroll, consumers often do not complain for a variety of reasons.[46] These include

- *Demographics.* Lack of resources such as income and education.
- *Personality.* Traits such as introversion and agreeableness.
- *Company.* Makes complaining process difficult and uncomfortable.

A lack of consumer complaining is always a problem, but when the firm contributes to it, it does so at the risk of damaging its reputation and its bottom line. Consider United's stock price drop worth $180 million.

Handling negative consumer comments and complaints generated via online social media can be particularly challenging. AT&T is one company that has gotten serious about dealing with bad press online based on issues with its network, particularly as it was the only option for iPhone users initially. Consider the following:

> On a normal day, AT&T has 10,000 mentions on social networks, but during stressful moments . . . they rise precipitously. The marketer is out to calm those twit storms by staffing up its social-media customer-care corps. The team began with five people dedicated to responding to customer dissatisfaction on Twitter and YouTube and has since moved to Facebook and grown to 19 people. To date, 47% of people reached on social media respond to the social team, which results in 32,000 service tickets per month.[47]

Such efforts by AT&T and others are designed to (a) recognize customer problems and utilize their input in the new era of social media, (b) act on the consumer input, and (c) influence the "narrative" by contributing to the conversation (see Consumer Insight 14–1 for more detail on such strategies).

Acting on complaints in a timely and effective manner is a key to customer satisfaction and subsequent buying.[48] Most consumers who complain want a tangible result. Further, the results desired vary by customer type and the nature of the problem, requiring customized response capabilities.[49] Failure to deal effectively with this expectation can produce increased dissatisfaction. Therefore, firms need to resolve the cause of consumer complaints, not just give the consumers the opportunity to complain.[50]

In fact, for many firms, retaining customers by encouraging and responding effectively to complaints is more economical than attracting new customers through advertising or other promotional activities. It has been estimated that it costs only one-fifth as much to retain an old customer as to obtain a new one.[51] Training in-store and online *front-line employees* who deal directly with customers to use appropriate communication styles and empowering them to resolve problems as they arise are two ways firms can increase customer evaluations, satisfaction, and retention (see also Chapter 17).[52]

Unfortunately, many corporations are not organized to effectively resolve and learn from consumer complaints. This area represents a major opportunity for many businesses.[53] Consider the following about Dollar Shave Club:

> Customer service is a regular budget item for Dollar Shave Club. Company leaders say the time a customer service representative speaks to members is the only chance to pamper them and make them feel like they belong to an exclusive club. When [a] customer complained of the difficulty shaving her legs because she was pregnant with twins and couldn't see her toes, a customer service agent mailed a free pedicure set and a collection of baby books.[54]
>
> Dollar Shave ensures that it has a rich understanding of its members—so that it can deliver an outstanding customer experience. "We don't respond to situations; we respond to people," is the philosophy that drives the company's member engagement.[55]

Dollar Shave Club's approach yielded dividends. The razor and personal grooming company has doubled its membership with a happy and engaged customer base.[56] Illustration 18–5 shows how Marriott is aligning its processes to proactively deal with customer issues and the customer experience.

ILLUSTRATION 18-5

Marriott is aligning its internal processes toward proactively responding to consumer issues and needs.

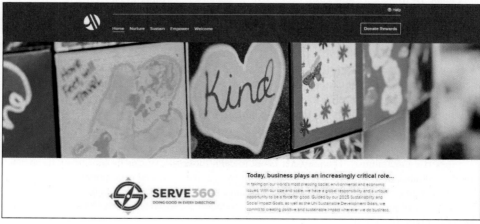

Source: Marriott

CUSTOMER SATISFACTION, REPEAT PURCHASES, AND CUSTOMER COMMITMENT

Satisfaction is an important driver of customer loyalty, and many organizations are investing in programs to enhance customer satisfaction, as shown by the following excerpt about New York–Presbyterian Hospital (NYP):

LO6

> NYP has looked very carefully at best practices for improving patient satisfaction across the country. To improve the patient experience, NYP implemented the Commitment to Care philosophy. Commitment to Care is a set of service expectations for all staff to follow in their work and interaction with patients, families, and colleagues. The expectations are based on feedback that comes directly from patients and address their key priorities and needs. It was created to give employees clarity about what is expected of them and a clear set of standards by which to evaluate and recognize staff for issues related to service. Metrics [on key service dimensions] are an important tool for both the hospital and for our patients.[57]

Given increasingly sophisticated and value-conscious consumers and multiple brands that perform at satisfactory levels, producing satisfied customers is necessary but not sufficient for many marketers. Instead, the objective is to produce committed or brand-loyal customers.

Figure 18–4 illustrates the composition of the buyers of a particular brand at any point in time. Of the total buyers, some percentage will be satisfied with the purchase. As we have seen, marketers are spending considerable effort to make this percentage as high as possible. The reason is that, while many satisfied customers will switch brands,[58] satisfied customers are much more likely to become or remain repeat purchasers than are dissatisfied customers, particularly when satisfaction perceptions are strong and held with confidence.[59] **Repeat purchasers** continue to buy the same brand though they do not have an emotional attachment to it. They may do so out of habit or because they don't see viable options to their current choice.

Creating Committed Customers Is Increasingly the Focus of Marketing Strategy	**FIGURE** 18-4

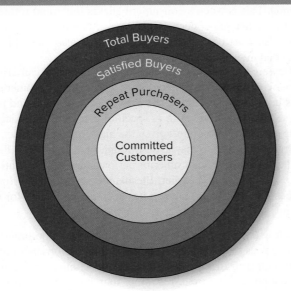

As we saw earlier, some dissatisfied customers also may become or remain repeat purchasers. These individuals perceive the **switching costs**—*the costs of finding, evaluating, and adopting another solution*—to be too high.[60] However, they may engage in negative word-of-mouth and are vulnerable to competitors' actions.

Repeat purchasers are desirable, but *mere* repeat purchasers are vulnerable to competitor actions. That is, they are buying the brand out of habit or because it is readily available where they shop, or because it has the lowest price, or for similar superficial reasons. These customers have no commitment to the brand. They are not brand loyal. **Brand loyalty** is defined as

> a biased (i.e., nonrandom) behavioral response (i.e., purchase/recommend) expressed over time by a decision-making unit with respect to one or more alternative brands out of a set of such brands that is a function of psychological (decision-making, evaluative) processes.[61]

Service and store loyalty are generally defined in the same or a similar manner.[62] Thus, a consumer loyal to a brand (store or service), or a **committed customer,** has an emotional attachment to the brand or firm. The customer likes the brand in a manner somewhat similar to friendship. Consumers use expressions such as "I trust this brand," "I like this outlet," and "I believe in this firm" to describe their commitment, as in the following customer quote:

> I tried it myself one time and eventually adopted a taste for it. Now I drink it all the time. I have it every morning after I come in from my run. I drink it after I clean the house. I always have a glass of it in my hand. That's me. I am very loyal to Gatorade. I would say that I am very loyal to that. I know they have other brands of that now, I see coupons all the time, but I have never even picked up a bottle of them. Never even tried them. Because I like Gatorade a lot. I really do.[63]

In a higher involvement context, NYP Hospital, discussed earlier, goes well beyond having, measuring, and reporting on key metrics to high-touch efforts that deliver personalized and humane service to its patients and treat patients and family with compassion and respect. The same can be said for Dollar Shave Club and its customer service efforts with members. Such efforts go well beyond mere satisfaction toward building a committed, loyal customer base.

Brand loyalty can arise through a number of processes, including

- *Brand identification.* This is when a consumer believes the brand reflects and reinforces some aspect of his or her self-concept. This type of commitment is most common for symbolic products such as beer and automobiles. It is also likely in service situations that involve extended interpersonal encounters.[64]
- *Brand comfort.* Research in services also has found that loyalty can arise from *consumer comfort.* Consumer comfort is "a psychological state wherein a customer's anxiety concerning a service has been eased, and he or she enjoys peace of mind and is calm and worry free concerning service encounters with [a specific] provider."[65] Service employees likely play a strong role in developing comfort given the high-contact nature of many services.
- *Brand delight.* Brand loyalty also may arise through performance so far above expected that it delights the customer.[66] Such superior performance can be related to the product, the firm itself, or, as mentioned earlier, the manner in which the firm responds to a complaint or a customer problem. Delight has been demonstrated for high-involvement services as well as for more mundane customer website visits.[67]

Given the above, it is obvious that it is more difficult to develop brand-loyal consumers for some product categories than for others. Indeed, for low-involvement product categories with few opportunities for truly distinct performance or customer service, most firms should focus on creating satisfied repeat purchasers rather than loyal or committed customers.[68]

Committed customers are unlikely to consider additional information when making a purchase. They are also resistant to competitors' marketing efforts—for example, coupons. Even when loyal customers do buy a different brand to take advantage of a promotional deal, they generally return to their original brand for their next purchase.[69] Committed customers are more receptive to line extensions and other new products offered by the same firm. They are also more likely to forgive an occasional product or service failure.[70]

Finally, committed customers are likely to be a source of positive word-of-mouth communications. This is extremely valuable to a firm. Positive WOM communications from a committed customer increase the probability of the recipient's both becoming a customer and sharing the positive comments with other people.[71] Consumer Insight 18-1 shows how some marketers are utilizing a WOM measure to capture customer satisfaction and loyalty and predict future growth.

It is no surprise, therefore, that many marketers attempt to create satisfied customers and then try to convert them to committed customers. Committed customers are much more profitable to the firm than mere repeat purchasers, who in turn are more profitable than occasional buyers.[72]

Repeat Purchasers, Committed Customers, and Profits

Churn is a term used to refer to *turnover in a firm's customer base.* If a firm has a base of 100 customers and 20 leave each year and 20 new ones become customers, it has a churn rate of 20 percent. Churn at Amica, an insurance company dedicated to loyalty, is at an amazingly low 2 percent per year![73] Recent churn rates for select industries include big-box electronics (16 percent), telecom/wireless (20 percent), online retail (21 percent), retail (27 percent), and cable (31 percent).[74] Reducing churn is a major objective of many firms today. Why? It typically costs more to obtain a new customer than to retain an existing one, and new customers generally are not as profitable as longer-term customers. Consider the profits generated by one credit card firm's customers over time:[75]

Year	Profits
Acquisition cost	($51)
Year 1	$30
Year 2	$42
Year 3	$44
Year 4	$49
Year 5	$55

Acquisition costs include such expenses as advertising, establishing the account, mailing the card, and so forth. First-year profits are low because many new customers are acquired as a result of a promotional deal of some type. In addition, their initial usage rate tends to be low and they don't use all the features. This is a common pattern for both consumer and industrial products. Auto service profits per customer increased from $25 the first year to $88 in the fifth year, and an industrial laundry found they went from $144 to $258.

Figure 18-5 shows the sources of the growth of profit per customer over time. *Price premium* refers to the fact that repeat and particularly committed customers tend to buy the brand consistently rather than waiting for a sale or continually negotiating price. *Referrals* refers to profits generated by new customers acquired as a result of recommendations from existing customers. *Lower costs* occur because both the firm and the customer learn how to interact more efficiently over time. Finally, customers tend to use a wider array of a firm's products and services over time.[76]

Do You Know Your Net Promoter Score?

Companies are always looking for better ways to measure true attitudinal loyalty. One approach that has garnered considerable interest is called the Net Promoter Score (NPS). It might surprise you to find that NPS does not measure attitudinal loyalty through satisfaction scores or through some direct loyalty measure.[77] Instead, it is an *indirect* measure based on word-of-mouth (WOM). The technique is based on the following question:

"How likely is it that you would recommend (company X) to a friend or colleague?"

0-----1-----2-----3-----4-----5-----6-----7-----8-----9-----10

| Not at All Likely | Neutral | Extremely Likely |

Three categories of consumers are created based on their answers to this question as follows:

Promoters: score 9 or 10
Passives: score 7 or 8
Detractors: score 0 to 6

NPS is then calculated by subtracting the proportion of a firm's customers who are detractors from the proportion who are promoters. Passives, or passively satisfied customers, are seen as essentially neutral in a way that makes them unlikely to engage in any proactive behavior regarding the company, either positive or negative. So, a company with 60 percent promoters, 30 percent passives, and 10 percent detractors would have an NPS of (60% promoters − 10% detractors), or NPS = 50. Thus, the **Net Promoter Score** *measures the percentage of a firm's customer base left after subtracting out the firm's detractors*. A recent study reported that NPS scores vary by customer age, with the lowest scores given by young adults and the highest given by consumers 65 years and older. Perhaps not surprisingly given its customer service issues discussed earlier in the chapter, Comcast received the lowest NPS score, for the third year in a row, across all companies evaluated. Several points about NPS are worth noting.

1. Higher NPS scores, in many industries, are strongly related to positive firm growth. That is, if a firm's NPS score is going up (growth in promoters relative to detractors), then future growth in revenues is likely.

FIGURE (18-5) Sources of Increased Customer Profitability over Time

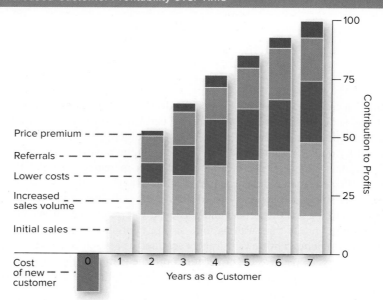

Source: F. F. Reichheld and W. E. Sasser Jr., "Zero Defections: Quality Comes to Services," *Harvard Business Review*, September-October 1990.

This makes sense when you consider how powerful and trusted WOM is as a source of consumer information and as a basis for consumer choice.

2. NPS, although based on a WOM question, appears to tap into attitudinal loyalty because recommending to a friend or colleague involves social risk and requires proactive behavior on the part of the firm. Such risk taking and effort on behalf of a brand would seem most likely for a consumer who is highly *committed* to that brand.

3. NPS is very simple compared to many satisfaction and loyalty questionnaires that can involve dozens of questions.

NPS is not perfect (doesn't work well in all industries) and is not the only measure out there (other measures exist that are highly correlated with a firm's financial performance). However, the simplicity of NPS and its strong relationship with growth have made it popular with companies such as GE, Intuit, and American Express. The simplicity of NPS also can be a weakness when used inappropriately, and care in its use is important. NPS is a barometer of what's going on with the company. Measuring NPS is useless unless it aids change management at all levels of the organization to align firm and employee actions with customer feedback. As one expert notes:

> If we're going to act, we need more than a number. [Consumer] comments are essential, with driver analysis the next step. What do [consumers] comment about? What leads to being a promoter? To a detractor? And what will get passives off the fence?

Therefore, companies who use NPS often recommend supplementing the "recommend" question with questions that get at underlying reasons for the score. One company follows the "recommend" question with an open-end question that asks, "What is your primary reason for your rating [on the recommend question]?" Such an approach is still quite simple and yet provides the basis for marketing strategies to convert passively satisfied and detractor customers into promoters.

Critical Thinking Questions

1. Why do you think NPS is strongly related to firm growth?
2. Do you think NPS also is related to firm profits?
3. When might NPS not be a good predictor of firm growth?

Although committed customers are most valuable to a firm, reducing churn can have a major impact on profit even if the retained customers are primarily repeat purchasers. Reducing the number of customers who leave a firm in a year increases the average life of the firm's customer base.[78] As we saw earlier, the longer a customer is with a firm, the more profits the firm derives from that customer. Thus, a stable customer base tends to be highly profitable per customer. Reducing the number of customers who leave various types of firms each year by 5 percent has been found to increase the average profits per customer as follows:[79]

Firm Type	Percent Increase in Average Profits per Customer
Auto service	30%
Branch banks	85
Credit card	75
Credit insurance	25
Insurance brokerage	50
Industrial laundry	45

The motivation for marketers to retain customers, or to try to bring back a customer who has left, is obvious.[80] Phil Bressler, the co-owner of five Domino's Pizza outlets in Maryland, found that a regular customer was worth more than $5,000 over the 10-year life of the franchise agreement. He makes sure that every employee in every store is constantly aware of that number. Poor service or a bad attitude may cost the outlet several thousands of dollars, not just the $10 or $15 that might be lost on the single transaction![81]

However, retaining some customers is more profitable than others. For example, at a typical commercial bank, the top 20 percent of customers generate six times more revenue than they cost. In contrast, the bottom 20 percent generate three to four times more costs than they do revenue. Firms increasingly understand the need to either strip out value-added services, raise prices to the point where unprofitable customers become profitable (or leave because they don't perceive enough value for the price), or gently encourage unprofitable customers to leave. Consider the following:

- One electric utility serves its top 350 business clients with six customer service representatives. The next 700 are served by six more, and the remaining 30,000 are served by two. The 300,000 residential customers must deal with an automated 800 number.
- One financial institution codes its credit card customers with colors that appear when their accounts appear on a service rep's screen. Green (profitable) customers are granted waivers and otherwise given white-glove treatment. Red (unprofitable) customers have no bargaining power. Yellow (marginal profit) customers are given a moderate level of accommodation.

Sprint went so far as to "fire" customers that contacted customer service very frequently. Sprint sent letters to these high-cost, or unprofitable, customers that read in part:

> The number of inquiries you have made to us during this time has led us to determine that we are unable to meet your current wireless needs. Therefore after careful consideration, the decision has been made to terminate your wireless service agreement.[82]

Sprint did receive negative publicity for firing over 1,000 customers, but the company's reason was to provide better service for the remaining 53 million customers.[83]

Firing customers is tricky business. It can keep costs down and profits up, but it also can alienate former customers and create negative emotions (abandonment, anger, rage), and thus negative WOM.[84] Therefore, marketers are trying to understand the best ways to "fire" customers. Clearly, a gentle, humane, and fair approach can help. For example, some companies go so far as to offer suggestions about where the customer might find a better "fit" with his or her needs.

Repeat Purchasers, Committed Customers, and Marketing Strategy

An important step in developing a marketing strategy for a particular segment is to specify the objectives being pursued. Several distinct possibilities exist:

1. Attract new users to the product category.
2. Capture competitors' current customers.
3. Encourage current customers to use more.
4. Encourage current customers to become repeat purchasers.
5. Encourage current customers to become committed customers.

Each of the objectives listed above will require different strategies and marketing mixes. The first two objectives require the marketer to convince potential customers that the marketer's brand will provide superior value to not using the product or to using another brand. Advertisements promising superior benefits, coupons, free trials, and similar strategies are

Customer Satisfaction Outcomes   FIGURE 18-6

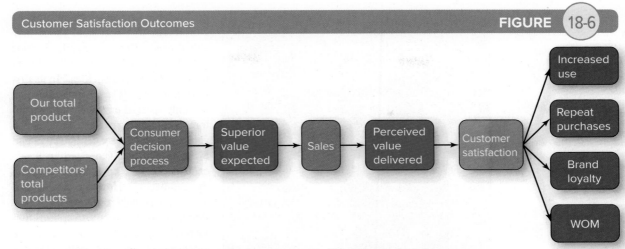

common approaches. While some firms are content to consider the sale the last step, smart firms now realize the critical importance of retaining customers after the initial sale. This is true even for infrequently purchased items—rather than repeat sales, the marketer wants positive, or at least neutral, word-of-mouth communications.

The last three objectives, listed earlier, focus on marketing to the firm's current customers. All require customer satisfaction as a necessary precondition. As Figure 18-6 indicates, this requires that the firm deliver the value expected by the customer. Techniques for creating satisfied customers were described earlier. Marketing efforts focused on a firm's current customers are generally termed *relationship marketing*.

Relationship Marketing   *An attempt to develop an ongoing, expanding exchange relationship with a firm's customers* is called **relationship marketing**.[85] In many ways, it seeks to mimic the relationships that existed between neighborhood stores and their customers many years ago. In those relationships, the store owner knew the customers not only as customers but also as friends and neighbors. The owner could anticipate their needs and provide help and advice when needed. Relationship marketing attempts to accomplish the same results, but because of the large scale of most operations, the firm must use databases, customized mass communications, and advanced employee training and motivation.[86]

Consider the following example:

> Lees Supermarkets, a family-owned and -operated company, started a Shoppers Club that records the purchases of members. Frequent or heavy shoppers are offered special incentives and deals. These offers can be customized on the basis of past purchasing patterns. In addition, last Thanksgiving, 600 regular, high-volume members were rewarded with free turkeys. Such an unexpected reward can produce delight and loyalty among key customers.[87]

Relationship marketing has five key elements:[88]

1. Developing a core service or product around which to build a customer relationship.
2. Customizing the relationship to the individual customer.
3. Augmenting the core service or product with extra benefits.
4. Pricing in a manner to encourage loyalty.
5. Marketing to employees so that they will perform well for customers.

This list of elements makes it clear that relationship marketing is centered on understanding consumer needs at the individual consumer level.[89] Companies engage in *crowdsourcing,*

Successful customer loyalty programs such as Capital One's Venture Card are based on understanding the needs of key customers (in this case travelers) and providing benefits of value to them.

Source: Capital One

in which the firm solicits input from its consumers, to understand those individual needs. Recent examples include Frito-Lay's "Do Us a Flavor" and Starbucks's "My Starbucks Idea." In its first year, the "Do Us a Flavor" campaign not only sparked enthusiasm from customers submitting close to 4 million flavor ideas like Cheesy Garlic Bread and Sriracha, but also generated an 8 percent increase in Lay's sales following the campaign.[90] However, not all customers are equally receptive to relationship marketing efforts. Perceptions that such relationships with the firm will be inconvenient and not yield adequate benefits and concerns over privacy are several factors that reduce consumer propensity to engage with relationship marketing efforts.[91]

A substantial amount of effort is currently being focused on **customer loyalty programs.** In addition to frequent-flier programs offered by most major airlines, programs designed to generate repeat purchases include the following:

- Pizza Hut recently launched Hut Rewards. This loyalty program allows customers to earn points for each dollar spent on mobile orders. Points, however, cannot be earned from phone or in-person orders. Pizza Hut uses the participants' data gathered through the online program to personalize offers and promotions for these mobile customers.[92]
- Sports franchises use card-based reward programs where members earn points for attending events and can redeem those points for team memorabilia, food, and drinks. Teams also can use the member data to create personalized communications and offerings, including season-ticket packages to their most attractive members.[93]

However, it is important to distinguish between programs that simply generate repeat purchases and those that generate committed and loyal customers.[94] Committed customers have a reasonably strong emotional attachment to the product or firm. Generating committed customers requires that the firm consistently meet or exceed customer expectations. Further, customers must believe that the firm is treating them fairly and is, to some extent at least, concerned about their well-being. Thus, *generating committed customers requires a customer-focused attitude in the firm.* It also requires that this attitude be translated into actions that meet customers' needs.[95]

Loyalty programs can be effective in generating committed customers if they understand and fulfill key customer needs (e.g., promotional awards on a favored brand), as shown by the Capital One ad in Illustration 18–6.

Research continues to investigate online, or e-, loyalty. While differences in type of site and purpose of visit (buying versus browsing) are likely to exist, evidence supports Figure 18–6 in suggesting that perceived value and satisfaction are important determinants of online loyalty just as they are for products, services, and traditional retail outlets.[96] In addition, research has identified factors unique to online settings that drive e-loyalty. For example, one study finds security and privacy to be critical.[97] Other research identifies customization and personalization, interactivity, convenience, and online community as factors that drive e-loyalty, WOM, and willingness to pay.[98]

SUMMARY

LO1: Describe the various postpurchase processes engaged in by consumers.

Purchase is followed by a number of processes including use, evaluation, and, in some cases, satisfaction, and consumer responses related to satisfaction including repurchase, positive word-of-mouth, and loyalty. Evaluation also can lead to dissatisfaction, which is sometimes associated with complaining, as well as erosion of loyalty, brand switching, and negative word-of-mouth.

LO2: Define and discuss postpurchase dissonance.

Following some purchases, consumers experience doubts or anxiety about the wisdom of the purchase. This is known as *postpurchase dissonance.* It is most likely to occur (1) among individuals with a tendency to experience anxiety, (2) after an irrevocable purchase, (3) when the purchase was important to the consumer, and (4) when it involved a difficult choice between two or more alternatives.

LO3: Discuss the issues surrounding product use and nonuse and their importance to marketers.

Whether or not the consumer experiences dissonance, most purchases are followed by product use. This use may be by the purchaser or by some other member of the purchasing unit. Monitoring product usage can indicate new uses for existing products, needed product modifications, appropriate advertising themes, and opportunities for new products. Product liability laws have made it increasingly important for marketing managers to be aware of all potential uses of their products.

Product nonuse is also a concern. Both marketers and consumers suffer when consumers buy products that they do not use or use less than they intended.

Thus, marketers frequently attempt to influence the decision to use the product as well as the decision to purchase the product.

LO4: Summarize disposition options and their relevance to marketers and public policy.

Disposition of the product or its package may occur before, during, or after product use. Understanding disposition behavior is important to marketing managers because of the ecological concerns of many consumers (and resulting green marketing efforts, see Chapter 3), the costs and scarcity of raw materials, and the activities of federal and state legislatures and regulatory agencies. *E-waste* is an emerging area of concern related to disposition.

LO5: Explain the determinants and outcomes of satisfaction and dissatisfaction.

Consumer perceptions regarding satisfaction and dissatisfaction are a function of a comparison process between consumer expectations of performance and their perceptions of actual performance. When expectations are met or exceeded, satisfaction is likely to result, and in some cases commitment or loyalty is developed. When expectations are not met, dissatisfaction is the likely result. Service is a major determinant of customer satisfaction even when the core purchase involves a physical product. Service and product failures, failure to adequately address product and service problems, and bad pricing are key factors that lead to dissatisfaction.

Dissatisfaction can lead to many undesirable responses from the perspective of the firm, including erosion of loyalty, negative word-of-mouth, and switching brands. One positive response for the firm is customer complaining, although customers often are reluctant to complain and companies are often not well prepared to act on those complaints when they do occur.

LO6: Describe the relationship between satisfaction, repeat purchase, and customer commitment.

Satisfaction results in a number of positive outcomes including repeat purchases, positive word-of-mouth, and, in some cases, loyalty. Not all satisfied customers are loyal. Simply meeting expectations (passive satisfaction in the language of Consumer Insight 18–1) is typically not enough to generate the psychological commitment that is associated with loyalty. *Repeat purchasers* are also not necessarily loyal customers. Repeat purchasing can occur out of habit (it's what I always buy) or

necessity (it is the only option out there) and not out of a commitment to the brand. Repeat purchasers who are not *committed customers* are vulnerable to competitor attempts to steal them away. Thus, *brand loyalty* or customer commitment, defined as a willingness to repurchase coupled with a psychological commitment to the brand, is critical to marketers. As online retailing continues to grow, marketers are examining ways in which e-satisfaction and e-loyalty can be bolstered. *Relationship marketing* and loyalty programs are strategic efforts on the part of the firm that can be used to bolster satisfaction, repeat purchases, and, in some cases, loyalty.

KEY TERMS

Affective performance 652
Brand loyalty 658
Churn 659
Committed customer 658
Consumer-to-consumer sale 648
Consumption guilt 643

Customer loyalty programs 664
E-waste 647
Instrumental performance 652
Net Promoter Score 660
Postpurchase dissonance 642
Product nonuse 645

Relationship marketing 663
Repeat purchasers 657
Switching costs 658
Symbolic performance 652
Use innovativeness 644

REVIEW QUESTIONS

1. What are the major postpurchase processes engaged in by consumers?

2. How does the type of decision process affect the postpurchase processes?

3. What is *postpurchase dissonance?*

4. What characteristics of a purchase situation are likely to contribute to postpurchase dissonance?

5. In what ways can a consumer reduce postpurchase dissonance?

6. What is *consumption guilt?*

7. What is *use innovativeness?*

8. What is a *reasonably foreseeable use of a product* and why is it important to companies?

9. What are effective ways for a company to get at innovative product uses by customers?

10. What is meant by *product nonuse,* and why is it a concern of marketers?

11. What is meant by the disposition of products and product packaging, and why does it interest governmental regulatory agencies and marketers?

12. What is *e-waste,* and why is it a growing concern?

13. What factors influence consumer satisfaction? In what way do they influence consumer satisfaction?

14. What is the difference between *instrumental* and *symbolic performance,* and how does each contribute to consumer satisfaction?

15. What is *affective performance?*

16. What courses of action can a consumer take in response to dissatisfaction? Which are used most often?

17. What determines satisfaction for online retailers?

18. What would marketers like consumers to do when dissatisfied? How can marketers encourage this?

19. What is *churn?* How does it affect profits?
20. What are the sources of increased profits from longer-term customers?
21. What is the relationship between customer satisfaction, repeat purchases, and committed customers?
22. What is the difference between *repeat purchasers* and *committed customers?*
23. What are *switching costs?*
24. Why are marketers interested in having committed customers?
25. What is the *Net Promoter Score?*
26. What is *relationship marketing?* What strategies are involved?
27. What are *loyalty programs?* What do most of them actually do?
28. What factors influence e-loyalty?

DISCUSSION QUESTIONS

29. How should retailers deal with consumers immediately after purchase to reduce postpurchase dissonance? What specific action would you recommend, and what effect would you intend it to have on the recent purchaser of (gift of) the following?
    a. PBS donation
    b. A condominium
    c. Dance lessons
    d. A hybrid automobile
    e. Microwave oven
    f. Tropical fish
30. What type of database should your university maintain on its students? In general, what ethical concerns surround the use of such databases by institutions and companies?
31. How should manufacturers deal with consumers immediately after purchase to reduce postpurchase dissonance? What specific action would you recommend and what effect would you intend it to have on the recent purchaser of the following?
    a. Cell phone
    b. Expensive watch
    c. Tablet computer
    d. Corrective eye surgery
32. How do some companies capitalize on the concept of use innovativeness?
33. Discuss how you could determine how consumers actually use the following. How could this information be used to develop marketing strategy?
    a. Microwave
    b. Wrist watches
    c. Online banking services
    d. Movies on demand
    e. Hair color
    f. Hotel reward points
34. How would you go about measuring consumer satisfaction among purchasers of the following? What questions would you ask, what additional information would you collect, and why? How could this information be used for evaluating and planning marketing programs?
    a. Cell phone service
    b. Walmart.com
    c. Car insurance
    d. Six Flags theme parks
    e. Health care services
    f. Exercise bike
35. What level of product dissatisfaction should a marketer be content with in attempting to serve a particular target market? What characteristics contribute to dissatisfaction, regardless of the marketer's efforts?
36. Describe the last time you were dissatisfied with a purchase. What action did you take? Why?
37. Are you a *mere* repeat purchaser of any brand, service, or outlet? Why are you not a committed customer? What, if anything, would make you a committed customer?
38. Respond to the questions in Consumer Insight 18–1.
39. What are some of the possible negative consequences of "firing" customers?

40. Are you a committed customer to any brand, service, or outlet? Why?

41. Design a customer loyalty program for the following:

a. High-end hotel chain
b. Grocery store chain
c. Cosmetics line
d. Catering service

APPLICATION ACTIVITIES

42. Develop a brief questionnaire to determine product nonuse among college students and the reasons for it. With four other classmates, interview 50 students. What do you conclude?

43. Develop a questionnaire designed to measure consumer satisfaction of a clothing purchase of $100 or more. Include in your questionnaire items that measure the product's instrumental, symbolic, and affective dimensions of performance, as well as what the consumer wanted on these dimensions. Then interview several consumers to obtain information on actual performance, expected performance, and satisfaction. Using this information, determine if consumers received what they expected (i.e., evaluation of performance) and relate any difference to consumer expressions of satisfaction. What are the marketing implications of your results?

44. Develop a survey to measure student dissatisfaction with service purchases. For purchases they were dissatisfied with, determine what action they took to resolve this dissatisfaction and what the end result of their efforts were. What are the marketing implications of your findings?

45. Develop a questionnaire to measure repeat purchase behavior and brand loyalty. Measure the repeat purchase behavior and brand loyalty of 10 students with respect to the following. Determine why the brand-loyal students are brand loyal.
a. Batteries
b. Spaghetti sauce

c. Coffee
d. Paper towels
e. Clothing stores
f. Online stores

46. With the cooperation of a durables retailer, assist the retailer in sending a postpurchase letter of thanks to every other customer immediately after purchase. Then, approximately two weeks after purchase, contact the same customers (both those who received the letter and those who did not) and measure their purchase satisfaction. Evaluate the results.

47. Interview a grocery store manager, a department store manager, and a restaurant manager. Determine the types of products their customers are most likely to complain about and the nature of those complaints.

48. Measure 10 students' disposition behaviors with respect to the following. Determine why they use the alternatives they do.
a. Laptop computer
b. Cell phones
c. Mattress
d. Televisions
e. Plastic items

49. Interview 20 students to determine which, if any, customer loyalty programs they belong to, what they like and dislike about them, and the impact they have on their attitudes and behaviors. What opportunities do your results suggest?

REFERENCES

1. This chapter opener is based on B. Wansink, *Mindless Eating: Why We Eat More Than We Think* (New York: Bantam Books, 2006); D. M. Mochon, M. I. Norton, and D. Ariely, "Bolstering and Restoring Feelings of Competence Via the IKEA Effect," *International Journal of Research in Marketing,* December 2012, pp. 363–69; D. Kahneman, J. L. Knetsch, and R. H. Thaler, "Anomalies: The Endowment Effect, Loss Aversion, and Status Quo Bias," *Journal of Economic Perspectives,* Winter 1991, pp. 193–206.

2. G. J. Thompson, "Interpreting Consumers," *Journal of Marketing Research,* November 1997, p. 444. Published by the American Marketing Association; reprinted with permission.

3. See J. C. Sweeney, D. Hausknecht, and G. N. Soutar, "Cognitive Dissonance after Purchase," *Psychology & Marketing,* May 2000, pp. 369–85.

4. M. F. Luce, "Choosing to Avoid," *Journal of Consumer Research,* March 1998, pp. 409–33.

5. S. J. Gould, "An Interpretative Study of Purposeful, Mood Self-Regulating Consumption," *Psychology & Marketing,* July 1997, pp. 395–426.

6. See, e.g., R. Kivetz and I. Simonson, "Self-Control for the Righteous," *Journal of Consumer Research,* September 2002, pp. 199–217; J. Xu and N. Schwarz, "Do We Really Need a Reason to Indulge?," *Journal of Marketing Research,* February 2009, pp. 25–36.

7. See S. Ram and H.-S. Jung, "Innovativeness in Product Usage," *Psychology & Marketing,* January 1994, pp. 57–69; N. M. Ridgway and L. L. Price, "Exploration in Product Usage," *Psychology & Marketing,* January 1994, pp. 70–84; K. Park and C. L. Dyer, "Consumer Use Innovative Behavior," in *Advances in Consumer Research,* vol. 22, ed. F. R. Kardes and M. Sujan (Provo, UT: Association for Consumer Research, 1995), pp. 566–72; K. Lyytinen and M. Fisher, "Unintended Consequences: How Consumer Misuse Can Boost Sales," *Entrepreneur,* April 8, 2014, www.entrepreneur.com, accessed July 17, 2018.

8. M. B. Kemp, *CMOs Must Connect the Dots of the Online Brand* (Cambridge, MA: Forrester Research, Inc., July 27, 2010).

9. V. A. Taylor and A. B. Bower, "Improving Product Instruction Compliance," *Psychology & Marketing,* March 2004, pp. 229–45; D. Bowman, C. M. Heilman, and P. B. Seetharaman, "Determinants of Product-Use Compliance Behavior," *Journal of Marketing Research,* August 2004, pp. 324–38.

10. A. B. Bower and D. E. Sprott, "The Case of the Dusty Stair-Climber," in *Advances in Consumer Research,* vol. 22, ed. Kardes and Sujan, pp. 582–87. See also B. Wansink and R. Deshpande, *Marketing Letters* 5, no. 1 (1994), pp. 91–100.

11. Bower and Sprott, "The Case of the Dusty Stair-Climber," p. 585.

12. S. L. Wood, "Remote Purchase Environments," *Journal of Marketing Research,* May 2001, pp. 157–69.

13. S. Hyken, "How Zappos and Nordstrom Use Convenience to Create Confidence," *Forbes,* February 11, 2018, www.forbes.com/sites/shephyken/2018/02/11/how-zappos-and-nordstrom-use-convenience-to-create-confidence/#19ebe0535794, accessed July 17, 2018.

14. For detailed statistics, visit the U.S. Environmental Protection Agency website at www.epa.gov, accessed July 17, 2018.

15. T. Nudd, "Zappos' Cool New Shoebox Can Be Cut Up and Repurposed in a Bunch of Unique Ways," *Adweek,* May 23, 2016, www.adweek.com/creativity/zappos-cool-new-shoebox-can-be-cut-and-repurposed-bunch-unique-ways-171637/, accessed June 24, 2018; www.imnotabox.com/blog, accessed July 17, 2018.

16. L. Williams, "Current United States Recycling Statistics," *Green Living,* www.greenliving.lovetoknow.com, accessed June 30, 2011.

17. K. Y. Larkin, "Computer Recycling Statistics," *Green Living,* www.greenliving.lovetoknow.com, accessed June 30, 2011.

18. D. Nield, "How to Recycle Your Phone No Matter Where You Live," *Popular Science,* March 7, 2017, www.popsci.com/recycle-your-phone, accessed July 17, 2018; Apple GiveBack, www.apple.com/shop/trade-in?afid=p238%7Cs00BQdc5f-dc_mtid_1870765e38482_pcrid_276100614169_&cid=aos-us-kwgo-brand–slid–product-, accessed July 17, 2018.

19. K. Hall, "Sony Likes the Yield from Its Junk," *BusinessWeek,* September 17, 2007, p. 40; Sony, "Recycling Activities in North America," August 23, 2017, www.sony.net/SonyInfo/csr_report/environment/recycle/northamerica.html, accessed July 17, 2018.

20. E. M. Okada, "Trade-ins, Mental Accounting, and Product Replacement Decisions," *Journal of Consumer Research,* March 2001, pp. 433–66.

21. A. Biswas, "The Recycling Cycle," *Journal of Public Policy & Marketing,* Spring 2000, pp. 93–105.

22. See B. G. Goff, J. S. Boles, D. N. Bellenger, and C. Stojack, "The Influence of Salesperson Selling Behaviors on Customer Satisfaction with Products," *Journal of Retailing* 2 (1997), pp. 171–83.

23. V. Mittal, P. Kumar, and M. Tsiros, "Attribute-Level Performance, Satisfaction, and Behavioral Intentions over Time," *Journal of Marketing,* April 1999, pp. 88–101; R. J. Slote-Graff and J. J. Inman, "Longitudinal Shifts in the Drivers of Satisfaction with Product Quality," *Journal of Marketing Research,* August 2004, pp. 269–80.

24. See, e.g., A. S. Mattila, "The Impact of Cognitive Inertia on Post-Consumption Evaluation Processes," *Journal of the Academy of Marketing Science* 31, no. 3 (2003), pp. 287–99.

25. See, e.g., K. E. Clow, D. L. Kurtz, J. Ozment, and B. S. Ong, "The Antecedents of Consumer Expectations of Services," *Journal of Services Marketing* 11, no. 4 (1997), pp. 230–48.

26. See J. Ozment and E. A. Morash, "The Augmented Service Offering for Perceived and Actual Service Quality," *Journal of the Academy of Marketing Science,* Fall 1994, pp. 352–663; G. B. Voss, A. Parasuraman, and D. Grewal, "The Roles of Price, Performance, and Expectations in Determining Satisfaction in Service Exchanges," *Journal of Marketing,* October 1998, pp. 48–61.

27. See, e.g., C. P. Bebko, "Service Intangibility and Its Impact on Customer Expectations," *Journal of Services Marketing* 14, no. 1 (2000), pp. 9–26; B. Bickart and N. Schwartz, "Service Experiences and Satisfaction Judgments," *Journal of Consumer Psychology* 11, no. 1 (2001), pp. 29–41; D. M. Szymanski and D. H. Henard, "Customer Satisfaction," *Journal of the Academy of Marketing Science,* Winter 2001, pp. 16–35; J. C. Sweeney and G. N. Soutar, "Consumer Perceived Value," *Journal of Retailing* 77 (2001), pp. 203–20; P. K. Kopalle and D. R. Lehmann, "Strategic Management of Expectations," *Journal of Marketing Research,* August 2001, pp. 386–94; J. Wirtz and A. Mattila, "Exploring the Role of Alternative Perceived Performance Measures and Needs-Congruency in the Customer Satisfaction Process," *Journal of Consumer Psychology* 11, no. 3 (2001), pp. 181–92; E. Garbarino and M. S. Johnson, "Effects of Consumer Goals on Attribute Weighting, Overall Satisfaction, and Product Usage," *Psychology & Marketing,* September 2001, pp. 929–49; M. Heitmann, D. R. Lehmann, and A. Herrmann, "Choice Goal Attainment and Decision Consumption Satisfaction," *Journal of Marketing Research,* May 2007, pp. 234–50.

28. S. M. Keaveney, "Customer Switching Behavior in Service Industries," *Journal of Marketing,* April 1995, pp. 71–82. See also D. Grace and A. O'Cass, "Attributions of Service Switching," *Journal of Services Marketing* 14, no. 4 (2001), pp. 300–21; V. Mittal, J. M. Katrichis, and P. Kumar, "Attribute Performance and Customer Satisfaction over Time," *Journal of Services Marketing* 15, no. 5 (2001), pp. 343–56; C. de Matos, J. Henrique, and C. Rossi, "Service Recovery Paradox," *Journal of Service Research,* August 2007, pp. 66–77; S. Anderson, L. K. Pearo, and S. K. Widener, "Drivers of Service Satisfaction," *Journal of Service Research,* May 2008, pp. 365–81.

29. See, e.g., S. Taylor, "The Effects of Filled Waiting Time and Service Provider Control over the Delay on Evaluations of Service," *Journal of the Academy of Marketing Science,* Winter 1995, pp. 38–48; M. K. Hui, M. V. Thakor, and R. Gill, "The Effect of Delay Type and Service Stage on Consumers' Reactions to Waiting," *Journal of Consumer Research,* March 1998, pp. 469–79; "Customer Service Pain Points Still Driving Consumers Away," January 27, 2015, www.marketingcharts.com/industries/retail-and-e-commerce-50772, accessed July 18, 2018.

30. S. Hyken, "Bad Customer Service Costs Businesses Billions of Dollars," *Forbes,* August 27, 2016, www.forbes.com/sites/shephyken/2016/08/27/bad-customer-service-costs-businesses-billions-of-dollars/#7ef9d59e5152, accessed July 18, 2018.

31. V. Mittal, W. T. Ross Jr., and P. M. Baldsare, "The Asymmetric Impact of Negative and Positive Attribute-Level Performance on Overall Satisfaction and Repurchase Levels," *Journal of Marketing,* January 1998, pp. 33–47. See also G. J. Gaeth et al., "Consumers' Attitude Change across Sequences of Successful and Unsuccessful Product Usage," *Marketing Letters* 8, no. 1 (1997), pp. 41–53.

32. I. E. Swan and L. J. Combs, "Product Performance and Consumer Satisfaction: A New Concept," *Journal of Marketing,* April 1976, pp. 25–33.

33. See H. Mano and R. L. Oliver, "Assessing the Dimensionality and Structure of the Consumption Experience," *Journal of Consumer Research,* December 1993, pp. 451–66; L. W. Turley and D. L. Bolton, "Measuring the Affective Evaluations of Retail Service Environments," *Journal of Professional Services Marketing* 19, no. 1 (1999), pp. 31–44. See also S. M. Nowlis, N. Mandel, and D. B. McCabe, "The Effect of a Delay between Choice and Consumption on Consumption Enjoyment," *Journal of Consumer Research,* December 2004, pp. 502–10; R. D. Raggio, and J. Folse, "Gratitude Works," *Journal of the Academy of Marketing Science* 37 (2009), pp. 455–69.

34. B. B. Holloway and S. E. Beatty, "Satisfiers and Dissatisfiers in the Online Environment," *Journal of Service Research* 10, no. 4 (2008), pp. 347–64.

35. H. Evanschitzky et al., "E-satisfaction," *Journal of Retailing* 80 (2004), pp. 239–47.

36. R. Sousa and C. A. Voss, "Service Quality in Multichannel Services Employing Virtual Channels," *Journal of Service Research,* May 2006, pp. 356–71.

37. See, e.g., J. Singh, "A Typology of Consumer Dissatisfaction Response Styles," *Journal of Retailing,* Spring 1990, pp. 57–97; J. Singh, "Voice, Exit, and Negative Word-of-Mouth Behaviors," *Journal of the Academy of Marketing Science,* Winter 1990, pp. 1–15; K. Gronhaug and O. Kvitastein, "Purchases and Complaints," *Psychology & Marketing,* Spring 1991, pp. 21–35; S. W. Kelley and M. A. Davis, "Antecedents to Customer Expectations for Service Recovery," *Journal of the Academy of Marketing Science,* Winter 1994, pp. 52–61; M. A. Jones, D. L. Mothersbaugh, and S. E. Beatty, "Switching Barriers and Repurchase Intentions in Services," *Journal of Retailing* 76, no. 2 (2000), pp. 259–74; M. A. Jones and J. Suh, "Transaction-Specific Satisfaction and Overall Satisfaction," *Journal of Services Marketing* 14, no. 2 (2000), pp. 147–59; J. Lee, J. Lee, and L. Feick, "The Impact of Switching Costs on the Customer Satisfaction-Loyalty Link,"

Journal of Services Marketing 15, no. 1 (2001), pp. 35–48; I. Roos, B. Edvardsson, and A. Gustafsson, "Customer Switching Patterns in Competitive and Noncompetitive Service Industries," *Journal of Service Research,* February 2004, pp. 256–71.

38. See also S. P. Brown and R. F. Beltramini, "Consumer Complaining and Word-of-Mouth Activities," in *Advances in Consumer Research,* vol. 16, ed. T. K. Srull (Provo, UT: Association for Consumer Research, 1989), pp. 9–11; J. E. Swan and R. L. Oliver, "Postpurchase Communications by Consumers," *Journal of Retailing,* Winter 1989, pp. 516–33.

39. J. Goodman and S. Newman, "Understanding Customer Behavior and Complaints," *Quality Progress,* January 2003, pp. 51–55. Statistics have been provided by former government agencies such as the White House Office of Consumer Affairs; see, for example, www.helpscout.net or www.customerservicemanager.com.

40. See, e.g., A. K. Smith and R. N. Bolton, "The Effect of Consumers' Emotional Responses to Service Failures on Their Recovery Effort Evaluations and Satisfaction Judgments," *Journal of the Academy of Marketing Science,* Winter 2002, pp. 5–23; N. N. Bechwati and M. Morrin, "Outraged Consumers," *Journal of Consumer Psychology* 13, no. 4 (2003), pp. 440–53; R. Bougie, R. Pieters, and M. Zeelenberg, "Angry Customers Don't Come Back, They Get Back," *Journal of the Academy of Marketing Science,* Fall 2003, pp. 377–93.

41. I. M. Wetzer, M. Zeelenberg, and R. Pieters, "'Never Eat in That Restaurant, I Did!,'" *Psychology & Marketing,* August 2007, pp. 661–80.

42. Thompson, "Interpreting Consumers."

43. E. Hu, "Comcast 'Embarrassed' by the Service Call Making Internet Rounds," *NPR,* July 15, 2014, www.npr.org/sections/alltechconsidered/2014/07/15/331681041/comcast-embarrassed-by-the-service-call-making-internet-rounds, accessed July 18, 2018.

44. See, e.g., C. Ayres, "Revenge Is Best Served Cold—on YouTube," *Times,* July 22, 2009; R. Sawhney, "Broken Guitar Has United Playing the Blues to the Tune of $180 Million," *Fast Company,* July 28, 2009.

45. See R. A. Spreng, G. D. Harrell, and R. D. Mackoy, "Service Recovery," *Journal of Services Marketing* 9, no. 1 (1995), pp. 15–23; L. Dube and M. F. Maute, "Defensive Strategies for Managing Satisfaction and Loyalty in the Service Industry," *Psychology & Marketing,* December 1998, pp. 775–91. For an alternative view, see T. W. Andreassen, "From Disgust to Delight," *Journal of Service Research,* August 2001, pp. 39–49; G. Maxham II and R. G. Netemeyer, "A Longitudinal Study of Complaining Customers' Evaluations of Multiple Service Failures and Recovery Efforts," *Journal of Marketing,* October 2002, pp. 57–71; S. Weun, S. E. Beatty, and M. A. Jones, "The Impact of Service Failure Severity on Service Recovery Evaluations and Post-Recovery Relationships," *Journal of Services Marketing* 18, no. 2 (2004), pp. 133–46.

46. A literature review and model are in N. Stephens and K. P. Gwinner, "Why Don't Some People Complain?," *Journal of the Academy of Marketing Science,* Summer 1998, pp. 172–89. See also A. L. Dolinsky et al., "The Role of Psychographic Characteristics as Determinants of Complaint Behavior," *Journal of Hospital Marketing* 2 (1998), pp. 27–51; E. G. Harris and J. C. Mowen, "The Influence of Cardinal-, Central-, and Surface-Level Personality Traits on Consumers' Bargaining and Complaining

Behavior," *Psychology & Marketing,* November 2001, pp. 1115–85; C. Kim et al., "The Effect of Attitude and Perception on Consumer Complaint Intentions," *Journal of Consumer Marketing* 20, no. 4 (2003), pp. 352–71; J. C. Chebat, M. Davidow, and I. Codjovi, "Silent Voices," *Journal of Service Research,* May 2005, pp. 328–42; K. Bodey and D. Grace, "Contrasting 'Complainers' with 'Non-complainers' on Attitude Toward Complaining, Propensity to Complain, and Key Personality Characteristics," *Psychology & Marketing,* July 2007, pp. 579–94; C. Orsingher, S. Valentini, and M. de Angelis, "A Meta-Analysis of Satisfaction with Complaint Handling in Services," *Journal of the Academy of Marketing Science* 38 (2010), pp. 169–86.

47. K. Patel, "How AT&T Plans to Lift Its Image Via Social Media," *Advertising Age,* June 21, 2010.

48. J. Strauss and D. J. Hill, "Consumer Complaints by E-Mail," *Journal of Interactive Marketing,* Winter 2001, pp. 63–73. See also A. S. Mattila and J. Wirtz, "Consumer Complaining to Firms," *Journal of Services Marketing* 18, no. 2 (2004), pp. 147–55; G. Knox and R. van Oest, "Customer Complaints and Recovery Effectiveness: A Customer Base Approach," *Journal of Marketing* 78, no. 5 (September 2014), pp. 42–57.

49. See A. K. Smith, R. N. Bolton, and J. Wagner, "A Model of Customer Satisfaction with Service Encounters Involving Failure and Recovery," *Journal of Marketing Research,* August 1999, pp. 356–72; A. Palmer, R. Beggs, and C. Keown-McMullan, "Equity and Repurchase Intention Following Service Failure," *Journal of Services Marketing* 14, no. 6 (2000), pp. 513–28; A. S. Mattila, "The Effectiveness of Service Recovery in a Multi-Industry Setting," *Journal of Services Marketing* 15, no. 7 (2001), pp. 583–96; J. G. Maxham III and R. G. Netemeyer, "Modeling Customer Perceptions of Complaint Handling over Time," *Journal of Retailing* 78 (2002), pp. 239–52; M. Davidow, "Organizational Responses to Customer Complaints," *Journal of Service Research,* February 2003, pp. 225–50; C. Homburg and A. Furst, "How Organizational Complaint Handling Drives Customer Loyalty," *Journal of Marketing,* July 2005, pp. 95–114; J. Cambra-Fierro, I. Melero, and F. Sese, "Managing Complaints to Improve Customer Profitability," *Journal of Retailing* 91, no. 1 (2015), pp. 109–24.

50. See C. Goodwin and I. Ross, "Consumer Evaluations of Response to Complaints," *Journal of Consumer Marketing,* Spring 1990, pp. 39–47; J. G. Blodgett, D. J. Hill, and S. S. Tax, "The Effects of Distributive, Procedural, and Interactional Justice on Postcomplaint Behavior," *Journal of Retailing* 2 (1997), pp. 185–210; C. M. Voorhees, M. K. Brady, and D. M. Horowitz, "A Voice from the Silent Masses," *Journal of the Academy of Marketing Science* 34, no. 4 (2006), pp. 514–27.

51. P. Sellers, "What Customers Really Want," *Fortune,* June 4, 1990, pp. 58–62.

52. B. A. Sparks, G. L. Bradley, and V. J. Callan, "The Impact of Staff Empowerment and Communication Style on Customer Evaluations," *Psychology & Marketing,* August 1997, pp. 475–93; M. Giebelhausen, S. Robinson, N. Sirianni, and M. Brady, "Touch versus Tech: When Technology Functions as a Barrier or a Benefit to Service Encounters," *Journal of Marketing* 78 (July 2014), pp. 113–24.

53. See F. F. Reichheld, "Learning from Customer Defections," *Harvard Business Review,* March 1996, pp. 56–69. See also H. Estelami, "The Profit Impact of Consumer Complaint Solicitation across

Market Conditions," *Journal of Professional Services Marketing* 20, no. 1 (1999), pp. 165–95; N. A. Morgan, E. W. Anderson, and V. Mittal, "Understanding Firms' Customer Satisfaction Information Usage," *Journal of Marketing,* July 2005, pp. 131–51.

54. D. Pierson, "Why Dollar Shave Club Invests in Unscripted Customer Service," *Los Angeles Times,* September 26, 2015, www.latimes.com, accessed July 18, 2018.

55. J. Pigato, "How 9 Successful Companies Keep Their Customers," *Entrepreneur,* April 3, 2015, www.entrepreneur.com/article/243764, accessed July 18, 2018.

56. Ibid.; Pierson, "Why Dollar Shave Club Invests in Unscripted Customer Service."

57. R. Liebowitz, "Putting Patients First," *Healthcare Executive,* July–August 2008, pp. 42–44.

58. T. O. Jones and W. E. Sasser Jr., "Why Satisfied Customers Defect," *Harvard Business Review,* November 1995, pp. 88–95; P. T. L. P. Leszczyc and H. J. P. Timmermans, "Store-Switching Behavior," *Marketing Letters* 8, no. 2 (1997), pp. 193–204; B. Mittal and W. M. Lassar, "Why Do Customers Switch?," *Journal of Services Marketing* 12, no. 3 (1998), pp. 177–94; C. Homburg and A. Giering, "Personal Characteristics as Moderators of the Relationship between Customer Satisfaction and Loyalty," *Psychology & Marketing,* January 2001, pp. 43–66.

59. See V. Mittal and W. Kamakura, "Satisfaction, Repurchase Intent, and Repurchase Behavior," *Journal of Marketing Research,* February 2001, pp. 131–42; M. Chandrashekaran et al., "Satisfaction Strength and Customer Loyalty," *Journal of Marketing Research,* February 2007, pp. 153–63.

60. For a discussion of switching costs and repurchase intentions, see Jones, Mothersbaugh, and Beatty, "Switching Barriers and Repurchase Intentions in Services"; P. G. Patterson and T. Smith, "A Cross-Cultural Study of Switching Barriers and Propensity to Stay with Service Providers," *Journal of Retailing* 79 (2003), pp. 107–20; T. A. Burnham, J. K. Frels, and V. Mahajan, "Consumer Switching Costs," *Journal of the Academy of Marketing Science,* Spring 2003, pp. 109–26; M. A. Jones et al., "The Positive and Negative Effects of Switching Costs on Relational Outcomes," *Journal of Service Research,* May 2007, pp. 335–55.

61. J. Jacoby and D. B. Kyner, "Brand Loyalty versus Repeat Purchasing Behavior," *Journal of Marketing Research,* February 1973, pp. 1–9. See also S. Rundle-Thiele and M. M. Mackay, "Assessing the Performance of Brand Loyalty Measures," *Journal of Services Marketing* 15, no. 7 (2001), pp. 529–46; A. Chaudhuri and M. B. Holbrook, "The Chain of Effects from Brand Trust and Brand Affect to Brand Performance," *Journal of Marketing,* April 2001, pp. 81–93; C. F. Curasi and K. N. Kennedy, "From Prisoners to Apostles," *Journal of Services Marketing* 16, no. 4 (2002), pp. 322–41; V. Liljander and I. Roos, "Customer-Relationship Levels," *Journal of Services Marketing* 16, no. 7 (2002), pp. 593–614.

62. See, e.g., R. R. G. Javalgi and C. R. Moberg, "Service Loyalty," *Journal of Services Marketing* 11, no. 3 (1997), pp. 165–79.

63. S. Fournier, "Consumers and Their Brands," *Journal of Consumer Research,* March 1998, p. 355.

64. See E. Garbarino and M. S. Johnson, "The Different Roles of Satisfaction, Trust, and Commitment in Customer Relationships," *Journal of Marketing,* April 1999, pp. 70–87; J. Singh and

D. Sirdeshmukh, "Agency and Trust Mechanisms in Consumer Satisfaction and Loyalty Judgments," *Journal of the Academy of Marketing Science,* Winter 2000, pp. 150–67; D. Sirdeshmukh, J. Singh, and B. Sabol, "Consumer Trust, Value, and Loyalty in Relational Exchanges," *Journal of Marketing,* January 2002, pp. 15–37; C. B. Battacharya and S. Sen, "Consumer–Company Identification," *Journal of Marketing,* April 2003, pp. 76–88.

65. D. F. Spake et al., "Consumer Comfort in Service Relationships," *Journal of Service Research,* May 2003, pp. 316–32.

66. R. L. Oliver, R. T. Rust, and S. Varki, "Customer Delight," *Journal of Retailing* 73, no. 3 (1997), pp. 311–36; R. T. Rust and R. L. Oliver, "Should We Delight the Customer?," *Journal of the Academy of Marketing Science,* Winter 2000, pp. 86–94.

67. A. Finn, "Reassessing the Foundations of Customer Delight," *Journal of Service Research,* November 2005, pp. 103–16.

68. R. L. Oliver, "Whence Consumer Loyalty," *Journal of Marketing,* Special Issue 1999, pp. 33–44.

69. See J. Deighton, C. M. Henderson, and S. A. Neslin, "The Effects of Advertising on Brand Switching and Repeat Purchasing," *Journal of Marketing Research,* February 1994, pp. 28–43.

70. See D. Bejou and A. Palmer, "Service Failure and Loyalty," *Journal of Services Marketing* 12, no. 1 (1998), pp. 7–22; R. L. Hess Jr., S. Ganesan, and N. M. Klein, "Service Failure and Recovery," *Journal of the Academy of Marketing Science,* Spring 2003, pp. 127–45.

71. M. Johnson, G. M. Zinkhan, and G. S. Ayala, "The Impact of Outcome, Competency, and Affect on Service Referral," *Journal of Services Marketing* 12, no. 5 (1998), pp. 397–415.

72. E. W. Anderson, C. Fornell, and R. T. Rust, "Customer Satisfaction, Productivity, and Profitability," *Marketing Science* 16, no. 2 (1997), pp. 129–45.

73. J. McGregor, "Customer Service Champs," *Bloomberg Businessweek,* February 18, 2010.

74. Statista, "Customer Churn Rate in the United States in 2017, by Industry," 2018, www.statista.com/statistics/816735/customer-churn-rate-by-industry-us/, accessed July 18, 2018.

75. F. F. Reichheld and W. E. Sasser Jr., "Zero Defections," *Harvard Business Review,* September 1990, pp. 105–11; R. Jacob, "Why Some Customers Are More Equal Than Others," *Fortune,* September 19, 1994, pp. 215–24. See also V. A. Zeithaml, "Service Quality, Profitability, and the Economic Worth of Customers," *Journal of the Academy of Marketing Science,* Winter 2000, pp. 67–85.

76. For additional research examining these various outcomes, see T. Hennig-Thurau, K. P. Gwinner, and D. D. Gremler, "Understanding Relationship Marketing Outcomes," *Journal of Service Research,* February 2002, pp. 230–47; P. C. Verhoef, P. H. Franses, and J. C. Hoekstra, "The Effect of Relational Constructs on Customer Referrals and Number of Services Purchased from a Multiservice Provider," *Journal of the Academy of Marketing Science* 30, no. 3 (2002), pp. 202–16; H. S. Bansal, P. G. Irving, and S. F. Taylor, "A Three-Component Model of Customer Commitment to Service Providers," *Journal of the Academy of Marketing Science* 32, no. 3 (2004), pp. 234–50; C. Homburg, N. Koschate, and W. D. Hoyer, "Do Satisfied Customers Really Pay More?," *Journal of Marketing,* April 2005, pp. 84–96; K. Seiders, G. B. Voss, D. Grewal, and A. L. Godfrey, "Do Satisfied Customers Buy More?," *Journal of Marketing,* October 2005, pp. 26–43; S. Sunder, V. Kumar, and Y. Zhao, "Measuring the Lifetime Value of a Customer in the Consumer Packaged Goods Industry," *Journal of Marketing Research* 53 (December 2016), pp. 901–21.

77. Insight based on F. F. Reichheld, "The One Number You Need to Grow," *Harvard Business Review,* December 2003, pp. 46–54; M. Anstead, "What's Missing When It Comes to Net Promoter," *Credit Union Journal,* March 30, 2009, p. 8; M. Creamer, "Do You Know Your Score?," *Advertising Age,* July 23, 2006, p. 1, 24; T. L. Keiningham et al., "A Longitudinal Examination of Net Promoter and Firm Revenue Growth," *Journal of Marketing,* July 2007, pp. 39–51; A. Gigliotto et al., "NPS Not the Only Way," *Marketing News,* September 15, 2007, pp. 48–52; C. Pasquale, "Closing the Customer Feedback Loop," *Harvard Business Review,* December 2009, pp. 43–47; Tempkin Group, "Net Promoter Score Benchmark Study, 2017," October 2017, https://temkingroup.com/product/net-promoter-score-benchmark-study-2017/, accessed July 19, 2018; Bain & Company, *Net Promoter System,* www.netpromotersystem.com, accessed July 19, 2018.

78. See S. Li, "Survival Analysis," *Marketing Research,* Fall 1995, pp. 17–23.

79. Reichheld and Sasser, "Zero Defections," p. 110.

80. For a discussion on bringing back customers to the company, see, for example, V. Kumar, Y. Bhagwat, and X. Zhang, "Regaining 'Lost' Customers: The Predictive Power of First-Lifetime Behavior, the Reason for Defection, and the Nature of the Win-Back Offer," *Journal of Marketing* 79, no. 4 (July 2015), pp. 34–55; E. Ascarza, R. Iyengar, and M. Schleicher, "The Perils of Proactive Churn Prevention Using Plan Recommendations: Evidence from a Field Experiment," *Journal of Marketing Research* 53 (February 2016), pp. 46–60; D. Pick, J. S. Thomas, S. Tillmanns, and M. Krafft, "Customer Win-Back: The Role of Attributions and Perceptions in Customers' Willingness to Return," *Journal of the Academy of Marketing Science* 44, no. 2 (2016), pp. 218–40.

81. See also S. Lingle, "How Much Is a Customer Worth?," *Bank Marketing,* August 1995, pp. 13–16.

82. J. Shin and K. Sudhir, "Should You Punish or Reward Current Customers?," *MIT Sloan Management Review* 55 (Fall 2013), pp. 58–64.

83. A. Cuneo, "Was Sprint's Sacking of 1,200 Customers Sound Business?," *Advertising Age,* July 12, 2007.

84. See, e.g., T. Wagner, T. Hennig-Thurau, and T. Rudolph, "Does Customer Demotion Jeopardize Loyalty?," *Journal of Marketing,* May 2009, pp. 69–85.

85. See G. S. Day, "Managing Market Relationships," *Journal of the Academy of Marketing Science,* Winter 2000, pp. 24–30.

86. See the special issue on relationship marketing, *Journal of the Academy of Marketing Science,* Fall 1995; G. E. Gengler and P. P. Leszczyc, "Using Customer Satisfaction Research for Relationship Marketing," *Journal of Direct Marketing,* Winter 1997, pp. 23–29.

87. L. Freeman, "Marketing the Market," *Marketing News,* March 2, 1998, p. 1. Other examples are in G. B. Voss and Z. G. Voss, "Implementing a Relationship Marketing Program," *Journal of Services Marketing* 11, no. 4 (1997), pp. 278–98; B. G. Yovovich,

"Scanners Reshape the Grocery Business," *Marketing News,* February 16, 1998, p. 1; and G. Brewer, "The Customer Stops Here," *Sales & Marketing Management,* March 1998, pp. 31–36.

88. L. L. Berry, "Relationship Marketing of Services," *Journal of the Academy of Marketing Science,* Fall 1995, pp. 236–45.

89. See N. Bendapudi and L. L. Berry, "Customers' Motivations for Maintaining Relationships with Service Providers," *Journal of Retailing* 73, no. 1 (1997), pp. 15–37.

90. E. Mitchell, "Lay's 'Do Us a Flavor' Contest: Customers Vote for Their Favorite Chips," *Ad Week,* February 19, 2013, www .adweek.com/digital/lays-do-us-a-flavor-contest-customers-vote-for-their-favorite-chips/, accessed July 19, 2018; BrandIndex, "Crowd-sourcing Campaign Appears to Boost Brand Perception for Lay's," *Forbes,* October 11, 2014, www.forbes.com/sites/brandindex/2014/10/11/crowdsourcing-campaign-appears-to-boost-brand-perception-for-lays/#5e19a470571d, accessed July 19, 2018; Starbucks, https://ideas.starbucks.com/, accessed July 19, 2018.

91. C. Ashley et al., "Why Consumers Won't Relate," *Journal of Business Research,* July 2011, pp. 749–56.

92. B. Tuttle, "Pizza Hut Just Launched a Rewards Program. Here's How Easy It Is to Get a Free Pizza," *Time,* August 1, 2017, http://time.com/money/4882438/pizza-hut-rewards-program-free-pizza/, accessed July 19, 2018; Staff, "Pizza Hut Introduces Rewards," *Strategy Online,* March 28, 2018, http://strategyonline.ca/2018/03/28/pizza-hut-introduces-hut-rewards/, accessed July 19, 2018.

93. J. Raymond, "Home Field Advantage," *American Demographics,* April 2001, pp. 34–36.

94. See G. Levin, "Marketers Flock to Loyalty Offers," *Advertising Age,* May 24, 1993, p. 13; C. Miller, "Rewards for the Best Customers," *Marketing News,* July 5, 1993, p. 1; J. Fulkerson, "It's in the Cards," *American Demographics,* July 1996, pp. 38–43; J. Passingham, "Grocery Retailing and the Loyalty Card," *Journal of the Market Research Society,* January 1998, pp. 55–63. See also L. O'Brien and C. Jones, "Do Rewards Really Create Loyalty?," *Harvard Business Review,* May 1995, pp. 75–82; R. N. Bolton, P. K. Kannan, and M. D. Bramlett, "Implications of Loyalty Programs Membership and Service Experiences for Customer Retention and Value," *Journal of the Academy of Marketing Science,* Winter 2000, pp. 95–108; A. W. Magi, "Share of Wallet in Retailing," *Journal of Retailing* 79 (2003), pp. 97–106.

95. See F. Rice, "The New Rules of Superlative Services," *Fortune,* Autumn–Winter 1993, pp. 50–53; P. Sellers, "Keeping the Buyers," *Fortune,* Autumn–Winter 1993, pp. 56–58; G. A. Conrad, G. Brown, and H. A. Harmon, "Customer Satisfaction and Corporate Culture," *Psychology & Marketing,* October 1997, pp. 663–74.

96. J. Holland and S. M. Baker, "Customer Participation in Creating Site Brand Loyalty," *Journal of Interactive Marketing,* Autumn 2001, pp. 34–45; R. E. Anderson and S. S. Srinivasan, "E-Satisfaction and E-Loyalty," *Psychology & Marketing,* February 2003, pp. 123–38; L. C. Harris and M. M. H. Goode, "The Four Levels of Loyalty and the Pivotal Role of Trust," *Journal of Retailing* 80 (2004), pp. 139–58.

97. J. Gummerus et al., "Customer Loyalty to Content-Based Web Sites," *Journal of Services Marketing* 18, no. 3 (2004), pp. 175–86.

98. S. S. Srinivasan, R. Anderson, and K. Ponnavolu, "Customer Loyalty in E-commerce," *Journal of Retailing* 78 (2002), pp. 41–50.

4-1 SCENT MARKETING REACHES CONSUMERS' EMOTIONS

Scent Marketing, which also is known as ambient marketing, is known to marketers as branding's final frontier. Some marketers call it the "business of emotional transportation." Retailers have long been manipulating atmospheric variables, like music, color, and physical layouts. However, scent has received much less attention until recent times. Studies have shown that the power of scent can have tremendous effects on consumers' emotions and subsequent behavior. Scent is able to lift consumers' moods, influence them to linger within retail stores, and increase purchases. According to Professor Eric Spangenberg:

> We've shown that scent can increase the customer's positive shopping behavior. . . . It keeps people in the store longer, they enjoy it more and they express more positive intentions to return.

Retailers using scent marketing can be divided roughly into two groups: those using natural scents and those using technology to implement artificial scents. Consumers are widely aware of the first group, especially with retailers that sell baked goods. Cinnabon and Panera Bread are two examples of retailers that rely heavily on scent to promote their goods. Cinnabon intentionally locates its stores in indoor shopping areas, such as malls and airports, so that smells can linger in the walkways and lure consumers. Cinnabon places its ovens near the front of the stores so the scent of warm cinnamon rolls will carry even further. A test location that had the oven in the back of the store had significantly lowered sales. The cinnamon treats are baked every half hour so the smell does not dissipate. Franchisees are instructed to use the weakest oven hood that is allowed so that the maximum amount of aroma possible will infiltrate the surrounding areas. Likewise, Panera Bread reassigned bakers from night shifts to day shifts so that consumers would have more exposure to the scent of baking bread. Both of these retailers also carefully craft their menu of savory items so the scents do not clash with the smell of baked goods, steering away from ingredients like garlic.

The benefits of scent marketing are not limited to food retailers. Many other types of retail locations also have joined the scent marketing trend. Many retailers are investing in developing their own custom "brand scent." According to Andrew Kindfuller, chief executive officer of ScentAir, a prominent manufacturer of scent diffusers:

> Brands realize now that this is a part of doing business. We're implementing these systems in many different environments—not just hotels and retail, but funeral homes, retirement villages, and medical and dental and law offices.

Singapore Airlines, Westin Hotels, Ritz Carlton, Victoria Secret, Juicy Couture, Bloomingdale's SonyStyle electronics stores, Select Comfort bedding stores, casinos, cruise lines, banks, and even Goodwill Industries are just some of the examples of businesses cited in popular media as using scent marketing. These companies use scent diffusion systems to consistently and evenly pump their custom aromas through the air.

Arriving at a brand scent is no simple task. Retailers pay anywhere from $5,000 to $50,000 to formulate a signature scent that consumers come to identify with a brand and that will keep the customers in stores longer to drive up sales. The technology has come a long way, from simple fans to cold air diffusion and dry air evaporation that incorporate HVAC systems in the stores. According to Jennifer Dublino, chief operating officer of the Scent Marketing Institute:

> In the old days, they used these cartridges with some sort of material soaked in scented oil and a fan would blow it out. The scent would be really intense at first, but then it would wane.

Back then, merchandise in the store would be coated in a fine film of oil. Recent advances solved that issue. According to Ed Burke, marketing director of ScentAir:

> The mist is so fine you can't even see it coming out of the atomizer. You don't have to worry about residue, and you can control the intensity.

Scent marketing works so well because consumers' sense of smell is directly linked to their emotions, more so than any of the other senses. Smells send signals from consumers' odor receptors in their noses directly to the amygdala, which is the emotion processing area of the brain. According to Pam Ellen, a marketing professor at Georgia State University:

> All of the other senses, you think before you respond, but with scent, your brain responds before you think.

According to Steven Semoff, co-president of the Scent Marketing Institute:

> In retail spaces, you're saturated with visual and audio to the point where you've learned to turn them off, but olfactory is a different kettle of fish. Sight and hearing senses go to the left brain, but smell is hardwired to the right brain's limbic system, which is your emotional core. It triggers an emotional response, and the customer builds an emotional connection with the brand.

Unfortunately for retailers, there are some pitfalls associated with scent marketing. Not all consumers respond to various scents in similar ways. Certain scents can trigger allergic reactions and asthmatic episodes in a small proportion of consumers. Also, many consumers may find smells to be offensive, especially if the odor is too strong or they have prior associations between a particular scent and a negative experience. Further, if there is a mismatch between the setting and the scent, then it could have deleterious effects. According to Ladd Smith, the president of the Research Institute for Fragrance Materials:

> One man's pleasure is another's pollution. Involuntary exposure drives us crazy.

Even worse, many people have ethical concerns about the use of scent marketing, particularly when consumers are unaware that it is being used. The Federal Communications Commission says that transmitting information below the consumer's threshold of awareness is unethical. Martin Linstrom, the author of *Brand Sense,* discusses scent marketing in the context of real estate:

> "People will make quicker decisions, be willing to pay more for the property and most likely be so emotionally engaged that they are removed from the rational part of their behavior," Lindstrom says. "I don't need to tell you that this is on the ethical line in my opinion, but from a pure behavioral point of view, that is most likely going to happen."

Kevin Bradford, a marketing professor at the University of Notre Dame, echoes this sentiment:

> Scent affects mood and scent affects emotion. It works without you having the opportunity to filter it. To me, that is extremely unethical. . . . Scent could be introduced to the environment at a level lower than what consumers could possibly detect, and it would still affect their emotions. Consumers should be able to detect the things that are influencing them.

Yet, others disagree. For example, Alex Hiller, of Nottingham Business Schools, says:

> Yes, changing smells is manipulative—this is the whole point. But it is mild, and I would argue that consumers realize and accept that in all artificial, and especially retail, environments, some mild form of manipulation does take place and it in no way constrains anyone's freedom, autonomy or well-being.

The founder of Nose Knows Design, Tracy Pepe, argues that it is no different than manipulating lighting to create a more pleasant retail environment. She says:

> Scent is very similar to great lighting. Great lighting—as opposed to just a lightbulb—can change the mood. It can warm you up. It can invite your guests. Smell is the same thing. . . . We, as a society, are kind of dead, visually. We're on our phones, we are constantly looking at screens. So there's this hole. And what scent does is that it propels you back in time so you remember what it felt like. If you're walking in a mall, for example, and you smell crayons, you're going right to that emotional connection of peeling the paper off. And all of a sudden there's a human aspect to it.

In any case, scent marketing is becoming increasingly prevalent among all types of retailers. Whether ethical or not, it is effective and does not appear to be going anywhere. According to the executive director of marketing at the National Retail Federation, Mike Gatti:

> It is fairly widespread here. . . . A lot of retail companies use it, and its purpose really is to keep customers in your store, to create this welcoming environment—and it works; it does keep people in your store longer. It helps people feel better in their shopping, and in a lot of cases causes them to spend more money.

Discussion Questions

1. Chapter 13 discusses aromas as a situational characteristic that influences consumer behavior. Assemble a small group of consumers and perform a focus group about their impressions of scent marketing. Also, investigate what effects consumers believe these scents have with their behavior. Compare and contrast these conscious reactions with what behavioral effects we know that scents have based on existing research.

2. Chapter 14 discusses the nature of problem recognition. Discuss the role that scent marketing might play in problem recognition in terms of actual state and desired state.

3. Chapter 16 discusses consumer choice processes. Does scent marketing most impact affective choice, attitude-based choice, or attribute-based choice? Justify your answer.

4. Chapter 16 also discusses bounded rationality, which is consumers' limited capacity for processing information. Many retailers who use scent diffusers use such small amounts of scent that consumers may not realize that the retailer's scent is playing a role. Discuss the ethical implications.

5. When it comes to the ethical implications of scent marketing, do you feel that there is a difference in retailers that use natural scents (like food retailers baking in the retail space) versus retailers that use artificially manufactured scents?

6. Brainstorm a short list of brands, make sure that some are typically involved with nominal decision making and others are typically associated with extensive decision making. Then, imagine you are a marketer for those brands, and describe the types of aromas that would match with each brand.

7. Visit a local shopping mall and the lobbies of several major hotel chains. Pay attention to the smells that you encounter while in each retail establishment. Prepare a short report that compares and contrasts the scents that you encounter in each location.

Source: J. Caplan, "Scents and Sensibility," *Time,* October 8, 2006, http://content.time.com; M. Hague, "A Sense of Occasion: How Luxury Hotels and Condos Seduce You with Signature Scents," *Globe and Mail,* September 10, 2014, www.theglobeandmail.com; A. Kadet, "The New Muzak: Scent Marketing," *Market Watch,* May 15, 2012, www.marketwatch.com; R. Klara, "In a Growing Trend, Retailers Are Perfuming Stores with Near-Subliminal Scents," *Adweek,* March 5, 2012, www.adweek.com; C. Lewis, "When Scent Crosses the Ethical Line," *Globe and Mail,* September 10, 2014, www.theglobeandmail.com; D. Montaldo, "Retailers Tap into Consumer's Response to Smell," *About.com,* http://couponing.about.com; S. Naussaur, "Using Scent as a Marketing Tool, Stores Hope It—and Shoppers—Will Linger," *Wall Street Journal,* May 20, 2014, http://online.wsj.com; "N.Y. Grocery Turns to Scent Marketing," *CBS News,* July 18, 2011, www.cbsnews.com; J. Smialek, "Retailers Mix Holiday Tunes, Scents to Spur Christmas Sales," *Round Table,* December 19, 2012, www.mhsroundtable.com; J. Sutton, "Scent Makers Sweeten the Smell of Commerce," *Reuters,* December 19, 2011, www.reuters.com; "The Smell of Commerce: How Companies Use Scents to Sell Their Products," *Independent,* August 11, 2011, www.independent.co.uk; J. Vlahos, "Scents and Sensitivity," *New York Times,* September 9, 2007, www.nytimes.com; C. Winter, "What Should a Bank Smell Like?," *Business Week,* January 9, 2014, www.businessweek.com.

4-2 AMAZON PRIME AIR PREPARES FOR TAKEOFF

In 2013, Amazon's CEO Jeff Bezos introduced his company's plans to revolutionize the way that packages are delivered to consumers on a *60 Minutes* interview. The new service, called Amazon Prime Air, will consist of a fleet of drones that will deliver small packages directly to consumers' doorsteps within a half hour of making a purchase on Amazon.com. According to Mr. Bezos:

> It could be a 10-mile radius from a fulfillment center. So, in urban areas, you could actually cover very significant portions of the population. And so, it won't work for everything; you know, we're not gonna deliver kayaks or table saws this way. These are electric motors, so this is all electric; it's very green, it's better than driving trucks around. This is . . . this is all an R&D project.

Since its inception, Amazon has had a reputation for innovation, and its future plans are no different. The online retail giant began with digital media, such as books and music, and evolved to offer a huge variety of products, such as clothing, furniture, toys, electronics, and more, as consumers became increasingly comfortable with online shopping. One consumer barrier for online shopping was shipping costs, so Amazon introduced its subscription-based Amazon Prime program that included free shipping and other consumer benefits. Now, as many other online retailers have followed suit and started to offer free shipping, Amazon's competitive advantage has eroded.

With Amazon Prime Air, Amazon would again offer innovative benefits that would set it apart from its competitors. Also, being able to offer such quick delivery would allow Amazon to better compete with brick-and-mortar retailers that offer consumers more immediate gratification of possessing products at the time of purchase, rather than waiting a number of days for delivery. With Amazon Prime Air, consumers will be able to enjoy their purchases very quickly, while still enjoying the convenience and comfort of shopping in their own homes. According to Mr. Bezos:

> I would define Amazon by our big ideas, which are customer centricity, putting the customer at the center of everything we do, invention. We like to pioneer, we like to explore, we like to go down dark alleys and see what's on the other side. . . . You gotta earn your keep in this world. When you invent something new, if customers come to the party, it's disruptive to the old way.

The public's reception of Amazon's announcement was mixed. Many consumers were excited at the prospect of Amazon Prime Air services. However, others felt that it was simply a cheap publicity stunt to draw headlines on the day before Cyber Monday. Others who resided near Amazon fulfillment centers were concerned about the noise that a fleet of drones would cause while flying overhead 24 hours a day. Some consumers even announced plans to shoot the drones out of the sky, either because they dislike the idea of drones or because they want the packages that they would carry.

Likewise, the business community had mixed perceptions. Many of Amazon's competitors, as well as logistics companies, scoffed at the idea of Amazon Prime Air. The CEO of FedEx called the idea "almost amusing," and the CEO of eBay called it a "long term fantasy"; Groupon answered the announcement with a satirical proposal of its own innovative delivery system, a catapult. Meanwhile, Google announced its own plan, called Project Wing, to utilize drones for other purposes, including delivering disaster relief.

While Amazon's research and development speeds forward, the biggest barrier to launching Amazon Prime Air is legal regulation from the Federal Aviation Administration (FAA). According to Mr. Bezos

> The hardest challenge in making this happen is going to be demonstrating this to the standards of the FAA that this is a safe thing to do. . . . I know it can't be before 2015, because that's the earliest we could get the rules from the FAA. My guess is that's, that's probably a little optimistic. But could it be, you know, four, five years? I think so. It will work, and it will happen, and it's gonna be a lot of fun.

Amazon has joined a coalition of firms, including 3-D Robotics, Parrot, and DJI Innovations, whose purpose is to advocate for the legalization of drone use for commercial purposes and educate the public on the safety and benefits of their use. The coalition has the support of Congress, as the FAA Modernization and Reform Act of 2012 mandated that the FAA open United States national airspace to civilian and commercial small drone traffic. However, FAA regulations have not yet been revised. In 2014, Amazon petitioned the FAA for an exemption to its rules that restrict the commercial use of drones and for permission for the company to begin to test its drones in an outdoor setting. So far, the FAA has not approved Amazon's request. In order to continue its research and development on the drones, Amazon plans to carry on by taking its outdoor testing to India, where there is a much more lenient regulatory environment. It is imperative that the research and development continues so that once the regulations in the United States are revised to allow commercial drones, Amazon will be prepared to launch its program.

Discussion Questions

1. Chapter 15 discusses information search. If Amazon is successful with its launching of Amazon Prime Air, how could this change the information search in the consumer decision process, and could it result in more online purchases?

2. Chapter 16 discusses evaluative criteria and Chapter 18 discusses postpurchase cognitive dissonance. What are some things that Amazon could do to aid consumers in making decisions about a product and the evaluative criteria for the product they are considering purchasing? Could this help make consumers feel more comfortable about purchasing a product online and reduce postpurchase guilt and dissonance?

3. Chapter 17 discusses perceived risks. What perceived risk is Amazon reducing? How?

4. Chapter 17 also discusses characteristics of online shoppers and provides a typology of online shopping segments. Justify your response. (Hint: Multiple segments could be correct depending on your justification.)

   a. Which of these segments would be most likely to adopt Amazon Prime Air?

   b. Which of these segments would be least likely to adopt Amazon Prime Air?

5. Chapter 13 discusses situational characteristics. Which situational characteristics might play a role in a consumer's decision to purchase with Amazon Prime Air? Explain.

6. Chapter 7 discusses types of innovation. Is Amazon Prime Air best described as a continuous, dynamically continuous, or discontinuous innovation?

Source: C. Dillow, "Amazon Aims for Drone Delivery," *Fortune,* December 12, 2013, http://fortune.com; J. Freed, "FedEx CEO Finds Delivery Drones 'Almost Amusing,'" *Huffington Post,* December 18, 2013, www.huffingtonpost.com; D. Gross, "Amazon's Drone Delivery: How Would It Work?," *CNN,* December 2, 2013, www.cnn.com; "Groupon Unveils Their Answer to Amazon's Drone Delivery: Catapults," *Huffington Post,* December 11, 2013, www.huffingtonpost.com; A. Kleinman, "eBay CEO Calls Amazon Drones a 'Long-Term Fantasy,'" *Huffington Post,* www.huffingtonpost.com; D. Kravets, "FAA Grounds Amazon's Drone Delivery Plans," *Arts Technica,* June 24, 2014, http://arstechnica.com; L. Lorrenzetti, "Amazon May Be Flying to India to Test Drone Deliveries," *Fortune,* August 20, 2014, http://fortune.com; E. Mack, "Beware! 8 Sinister Consequences of Google and Amazon Drones," *Cnet,* September 2, 2014, www.cnet.com; G. McNeal, "Six Things You Should Know About Amazon's Drones," *Forbes,* July 11, 2014, www.forbes.com; T. Mogg, "Bezos Maintains He's Serious About Amazon's Drone Delivery Service, Currently Testing Tech," *Digital Trends,* April 14, 2014, www.digitaltrends.com; D. Nicks, "Amazon's Drone Strike," *Time,* December 2, 2013, http://business.time.com; C. Rose, "Amazon's Jeff Bezos Looks to the Future," *CBS News,* December 1, 2013, www.cbsnews.com; M. Snider, "Amazon Looks to Gain Liftoff for Drone Delivery Testing," *USA Today,* August 17, 2014, www.usatoday.com.

4-3 NISSAN GOES AFTER THE DOG LOVER NICHE

Nissan identified a sizeable market segment consisting of consumers who are dog lovers and who consider their pets to be part of their families. As such, they often consider their canine family members in the consumer decision-making process, even when it comes to large purchases, such as vehicles. Nissan used market research from The Kennel Club that surveyed over 1,300 dog owners. The study showed the following about dog owners:

- 99.9 percent consider their pet as part of the family.
- 90.5 percent take their dog(s) on car trips lasting 10+ minutes.
- 88.7 percent take their dog(s) in the car at least once a week.
- 88.9 percent consider dog-friendly features when buying a car.

According to Brian Moody, the executive editor at Autotrader:

> Car shoppers need to take every aspect of their lifestyle into account when searching for their perfect ride. Dogs have their own unique needs on the road, just like humans, so take those into account if you find yourself chauffeuring your pup often. Some dealerships allow dogs on test drives, so don't be afraid to ask if you can take your pet along to see how easy it is for your dog to get in and out of the vehicle and ride safely.

In response, Nissan recently introduced its concept car, the Nissan X-Trail 4Dogs, specifically to cater to the needs and wants of this niche group. According to Ryan Gains, Chief Marketing Manager of X-Trail:

> It's clear from the research that for dog owners, dogs are a key part of the family. Ensuring their pet's needs are catered for is often just as important as making sure the children are comfortable and happy. The Nissan X-Trail is a car that's built for family adventures, and the X-Trail 4Dogs concept takes that to the next level.

Many consumers drive their dogs to parks, hiking trails, or just around town on errands. The Nissan X-Trail 4Dogs has many features, as shown below, making it the perfect vehicle for owners to take their dogs along, with added safety and comfort during transit.

Nissan X-Trail 4Dogs Features

Outside Features:

- Pull-out ramp for easy loading in/out of cargo area
- Pull-out 360-degree shower (and blow dryer!)

Inside Features:

- Two-way cameras in cargo & front seat areas (so owner and pet can see each other)
- Padded leather upholstery (for easy cleaning and comfort)
- No-spill water bowl
- Smart device dog treat dispenser

Dog lovers were thrilled with the idea when Nissan released the concept. However, it was still yet to go into production as of 2018.

Nissan did, however, incorporate several of the features from the X-Trail 4Dogs concept into an optional expansion kit for the existing X-Trail SUV, called the Paw Pack. This kit costs less than $1,000 and includes features such as the ramp, dog bed, and no-spill water bowl. Instead of the padded leather, there is a plastic liner insert to avoid spills and messes. The two-way cameras, automated treat dispenser, and shower with blow dryer did not make it from the concept car to the Paw Pack, but dog owners are still hopeful the X-Trail 4Dogs model will be produced in the future.

A recent study by the American Pet Products Association (APPA) showed that 84.6 million households in the United States have pets, with 48 percent of households having at least one dog.

Table A provides demographic information regarding who owns what types of pets. This survey is the first

Pet Ownership by Generational Group (%)			TABLE A	
	Gen Y	Gen X	Baby Boomers	Depression Era
Pet owners	35	27	32	6
Dog	38	26	31	5
Cat	35	27	32	6
Bird	46	24	28	2
Reptile	53	26	19	2
Horse	49	21	26	4

Source: The 2017–2018 APPA National Pet Owners Survey.

to reveal that Millennials (or Gen Yers) have overtaken Baby Boomers in pet ownership.

Table B provides information regarding specific behaviors and attitudes of dog owners.

Dog Owner Behaviors and Attitudes TABLE B	
Behaviors	
Percent of Dog Owners Who . . .	
Have health insurance for their dog	10
Use calming products for their dog	21
Use an electronic tracking device on their dog	43
Give their dog vitamins	9
Give their dog treats	95
Purchase gifts for their dog	78
Hold holiday or birthday parties for their dog	11
Bought pet-themed merchandise	25
Make provisions for their pet in their will	49
Attitudes	
Percent of Dog Owners Who Feel . . .	
Pets are a good source of affection	85
Exercising with a pet is more enjoyable than exercising alone	68
The health benefits of pet ownership are very important to me	69
People should only have a pet if committed to spending time with it	85
Owning a pet can be beneficial to my health	82
Buying BPA-free pet products is important to me	45
Buying pet products made in the USA is important to me	64

Source: The 2017–2018 APPA National Pet Owners Survey.

Understandably, the U.S. pet market is big business and shows no signs of slowing down!

Discussion Questions

1. Chapter 14 discusses the nature of problem recognition. Imagine you are a marketing manager for Nissan X-Trail 4Dogs and designing a marketing strategy to stimulate problem recognition:
   a. Would you focus on the actual state or the desired state? Why?
   b. Describe a sample advertisement or promotional communication that you might use in a campaign based on your answer for part a.
2. Chapter 14 also discusses different approaches for discovering consumer problems. Which of these approaches do you think Nissan used when creating the concept for the X-Trail 4Dogs? Justify your response.
3. Chapter 15 discusses marketing strategies based on information patterns. Which strategy would you recommend that marketers of the Nissan X-Trail 4Dogs use?
4. Chapter 16 discusses different types of consumer choice processes. Which choice process would the consumer likely use when making a car purchasing decision?
5. Chapter 6 discusses family decision making and the household life cycle. Many dog owners consider their dog or dogs to be part of their family and consider them when making purchases. Which of the family purchase roles could a dog play in the decision-making process for a family vehicle?
6. Using the information you learned from the textbook and this case, describe some demographics and psychographics of a consumer that you feel would be a member of the ideal target market for the Nissan X-Trail 4Dogs.

Source: M. Allen, "Nissan Sets Tails Wagging with Dog-Friendly Paw Pack," *iNews Essential Daily Briefing,* September 7, 2017, www.inews.co.uk, accessed May 8, 2018; J. Perez, "Nissan X-Trail Adds 'Paw Pack' in U.K. for Canine Adventures," *Motor1.com,* September 5, 2017, www.motor1.com, accessed May 8, 2018; "Pets by the Numbers," *Animal Sheltering,* May 1, 2018, www.animalsheltering.org, accessed May 8, 2018; D. Phillips-Donaldson, "Baby Boomers, Step Aside: Millennials Now Own More Pets," *Pet Food Industry,* April 1, 2015, www.petfoodindustry.com; L. Walford, "National Dog Day—Dogs Love to Ride in Cars Almost as Much as People," *Auto Connected Car News,* August 26, 2016, www.autoconnectedcar.com, accessed May 8, 2018; E. Wieseman, "Nissan Built a Car for Dogs—We Find Out What They Really Think," *Telegraph,* March 11, 2017, www.telegraph.co.uk, accessed May 8, 2018; R. Yarrow and S. McLennan, "Nissan X-Trail 4Dogs—The 'Pawfect' Car for Family Adventures," *Nissan Motor Corporation Global Newsroom,* March 1, 2017, www.newsroom.nissan-global.com, accessed May 8, 2018.

4-4 WAWA DOMINATES WITH ITS MOBILE APP

Wawa, Inc., is a Pennsylvania-based chain of over 750 convenience stores along the East Coast. Wawa started from humble beginnings as a dairy delivery service in the early 1800s and eventually became a food market in the 1960s, as consumer demands shifted. Wawa has been able to avoid the negative stereotypes of gas station food because it was first a food retailer. In 2015, a Market Force Information study of consumers named Wawa "America's Most Beloved Convenience Store." The results of a 2018 Market Force consumer survey showed Wawa as a top choice for sandwiches in the quick service restaurant (QSR) category—beating the likes of Jersey Mike's, Jimmy John's, and Jason's Deli. This is the first time in history that a convenience store won the QSR category!

The two studies also highlight the rapid increase in mobile ordering using an app. Over a three-year period, usage rose from 11 percent (2015) to 39 percent (2018). Wawa had a 67 percent mobile app awareness, the highest of any of its competitors within the sandwich QSR category. This is due to its app features with relatively novel benefits. Consumers can pay in-store with the app through registered gift cards, engage in the Wawa Rewards program, check hours of operation, find directions to the nearest Wawa, check real-time fuel prices, and view nutritional information. However, perhaps the most popular feature of Wawa's mobile app is that it offers the capability of mobile ordering. Consumers on road trips or routine commutes can order and pay for their sandwiches and coffees from their smartphones and have their orders freshly made and waiting for them when they arrive at the store. According to Jim Morey, Wawa's executive vice president:

> At Wawa, we exist to go beyond filling customer orders, to fulfill customers' lives every day. This new mobile ordering enhancement takes that commitment to the next level. We recognize that our customers are increasingly busy and constantly on-the-go, and by offering mobile ordering, we will be able to offer a convenience that allows our customers to order wherever they are, at any time they want. . . . Ten minutes is an unimportant amount of time until someone is running late, hungry and out of gas all at once. We can't stop those mornings from happening; we can make those mornings a lot more manageable.

To use the mobile ordering feature, customers must join the Wawa Rewards loyalty program and load a refillable gift card to their app for payment. Once a customer has completed the initial setup, he or she is more likely to repurchase within the next 60 days than an in-person customer due to the convenience and ease of accessibility. According to Marcus Higgins, VP of sales at EatStreet (an online ordering provider):

> The reason consumers prefer online versus traditional (phone or in-person) orders is because it offers instant gratification. It's all about being able to have the convenience to go online, look at a menu, look at the items you want and not have to wait for someone.

The use of the mobile app enables Wawa to track customer information, such as demographics, buying behavior, and preferences to provide a better experience through targeted marketing strategies. Providing direct communication with customers is used to develop brand loyalty, offer promotions, and integrate Wawa into consumers' routines. For example, the Wawa app can send a notification with a coupon to a customer based on previous order history (e.g., for someone who typically buys a breakfast sandwich around 7:15 a.m., a scheduled reminder with a coupon for a breakfast sandwich will be sent via the app as an incentive to place a mobile order for pickup on the way to work). Research has shown that deals and promotions in digital and mobile ordering make consumers more than twice as likely to place an order.

As shown, Wawa is on the right track to continue to satisfy customers and encourage loyalty. Mobile ordering is rapidly growing in popularity as an industry trend. A milestone was reached in 2016 when, for the first time, the number of digital orders at restaurants surpassed the number of orders made over the phone. Between 2016 and 2017 alone, digital ordering through mobile apps, text messages, and the Internet at restaurants grew by 18 percent to 1.9 billion food service visits. In 2018, one out of every 10 apps on consumers' mobile phones was a restaurant app and 58 percent of consumers had placed a food order through either a website or a digital app in the previous 12 months. By 2020, mobile ordering is projected to be a $38 billion industry.

Restaurants that have not started integrating mobile ordering capabilities are already behind the curve and will be grappling to keep up in the future.

Discussion Questions

1. Chapter 13 discusses the nature of situational influences in terms of communication, purchase, use, and disposition situations. How might a consumer's experience with mobile ordering with the Wawa app be impacted by situational influences?

2. Chapter 14 discusses the types of consumer decisions.
   a. Which type(s) of decision making would purchasing a sandwich from a quick service restaurant (QSR) be?
   b. Which type of decision making are marketers at Wawa hoping that the mobile app will encourage consumers purchasing a sandwich from a QSR to be?
   c. Assume that purchasing a sandwich from a QSR is categorized as nominal decision making in a given situation. Which of the two categories of this type of decision making is purchasing a sandwich from a QSR most likely to be? Why?

3. Chapter 17 discusses unplanned purchases and impulse purchases. Convenience stores like Wawa earn a substantial portion of revenue from unplanned and impulse purchases from customers in stores.
   a. What effect could mobile ordering have on unplanned and impulse purchasing by Wawa consumers?
   b. What could Wawa do to combat any reduction in impulse purchasing?

4. Chapter 17 discusses how mobile apps are often used in omni-channel shopping. Brainstorm some ideas about how the Wawa app could be used to encourage more in-store purchases, as well as those made on mobile ordering from other places?

5. Chapter 18 discusses repeat purchasing and loyalty programs. The chapter tells us that there is a difference in loyalty programs that simply generate repeat purchases and those that generate committed and loyal customers. The case mentions that Wawa uses a loyalty program called Wawa Rewards.
   a. What does the chapter suggest makes the difference for a loyalty program to generate committed and loyal customers?
   b. Do you feel that Wawa Rewards is generating repeat purchases or committed and loyal customers? Explain your answer.

6. Chapter 3 discusses American cultural values and illustrates the traditional, emerging, and current states of those values. Which of the values relates to this case and do you feel the representation in Figure 3–1 fits with the information in this case?

Source: B. Castiglia, "Food Ordering Forecast," *Modern Restaurant Management,* December 13, 2017, www.modernrestaurantmanagement.com, accessed May 8, 2018; "Digital Foodservice Ordering Continues Double-Digit Growth in U.S. and Now Accounts for 1.9 Billion Foodservice Visits," *NPD,* March 6, 2017, www.npd.com, accessed May 8, 2018; J. Kell, "Digital Foodservice Ordering Continues Double-Digit Growth in U.S. and Now Accounts for 1.9 Billion Foodservice Visits," *Fortune,* June 9, 2017, www.fortune.com, accessed May 8, 2018; A. Kelso, "The Top Online Ordering Trends Restaurants Can't Ignore," *QSR Web,* June 9, 2017, www.qsrweb.com, accessed May 8, 2018; "New Study from Market Force Information Reveals America's Favorite Quick-Service Restaurants," *Market Force Information,* April 25, 2018, www.marketforce.com, accessed May 8, 2018; M. Pomranz, "This Convenience Store Chain Is America's Favorite Sandwich Shop," *Food + Wine,* April 18, 2018, www.foodandwine.com, accessed May 8, 2018; K. Taylor, "The Biggest Change in Fast Food Isn't About Food—and It Should Terrify Chains That Can't Keep Up," *Business Insider,* May 1, 2016, www.businessinsider.com, accessed May 8, 2018; "Wawa Announces Mobile Ordering Option for All Wawa Rewards Members through the Wawa App," *Globe Newswire,* May 16, 2017, www.globenewswire.com, accessed May 8, 2018; "Why Wawa Went to Mobile Order Ahead," *PYMNTS.com,* May 25, 2017, www.pymnts.com, accessed May 8, 2018.

4-5 MACY'S EMBRACES BEACON TECHNOLOGY

Since the advent of online retailing, there has been an inherent tension between it and brick-and-mortar retailers. Consumers are increasingly making their purchases in an online setting as the breadth of options has proliferated and consumers have become less apprehensive about entering financial information on websites. A consumer survey by SmartFocus, a digital marketing company, showed that the majority of consumers still prefer to shop and purchase in brick-and-mortar stores, but nearly 60 percent of consumers are increasing their online shopping activities. According to the CEO of SmartFocus, Rob Mullen:

The US shopper survey shows that consumers are becoming more sophisticated about digital shopping. Using mobile phones and tablets to find bargains is becoming the norm rather than the exception.

Millennials are more likely to shop online than any other generation and are more receptive to sharing their data with online advertisers in exchange for more personalized shopping experiences. Mr. Mullen said:

In today's digital world, it's about reaching out to shoppers with their preferred technology—their mobile phone—and offering them relevant deals. The survey reinforces the fact that shoppers know the value of their personal data—and are willing to trade some of that for access to discounted offers. Besides the sale in question, shoppers will also benefit when marketers are able to analyze their data. Data analysis enables discovery of previously unrecognized patterns of behavior and allows merchants to put together more relevant offers.

Another concern for brick-and-mortar stores is showrooming. This is the practice of consumers shopping in brick-and-mortar stores in order to inspect products physically, but then actually purchasing the products from online retailers. The SmartFocus survey showed that about 60 percent of consumers engage in showrooming, with the primary motivation of seeking lower prices. Showrooming demonstrates that there is an inherent value of shopping within the physical store and actually coming in contact with products that interest consumers. This is especially true in the apparel context, where consumers gain much more product information from handling clothing and trying it on than from viewing pictures and descriptions online. According to Arnie Gullov-Singh, chief revenue officer for a women's fashion website:

Women especially still want to try something on. The future for brick-and-mortar is about that instant gratification and solving for that problem, and less about solving for fulfilling demand for things.

Some retailers are finding productive ways to work with digital media to turn showrooming to their advantage. Thomas Husson, a mobile analyst at Forrester Research, said:

Instead of fearing showrooming, I think retailers can leverage mobile as a bridge between offline and online worlds.

Macy's is partnering with technology companies Apple and Shopkick to engage consumers through their mobile devices during the time while they are shopping in the stores. Macy's recently conducted a pilot test of location-based marketing, called shopBeacon, in its flagship stores in Manhattan and San Francisco. Shopkick installed Apple's iBeacon transmitters throughout the stores that would allow the retailer to track consumers' movements as they shopped different locations throughout the stores. This location-based technology operates through the Bluetooth technology in shoppers' smartphones. As the consumers entered the stores, the Shopkick app would send alerts to the consumers' mobile devices to welcome them. Then, as they walked near certain locations within the stores, more alerts would offer various promotions, such as personalized department-level deals, discounts, recommendations, and rewards, for the products in their immediate vicinity. In order to be tracked, shoppers need to download the Shopkick app. Also, the app could tie shoppers' online browsing with the store visits, reminding them of items they liked online when they enter the store. According to Holly Thomas, vice president of national media relations and cause marketing at Macy's, New York:

[Shopkick] presented a great opportunity to pilot a location-based effort that would allow us to communicate with our customer via the one thing she always has on her—her mobile phone. Once a customer downloads the Shopkick app to her iPhone, we are able to give her special offers, information and rewards just for walking in a Macy's store. We think this is a dynamic and exciting addition to our mobile and digital efforts.

The pilot test was so successful that Macy's expanded the shopBeacon technology to all the Macy's retail locations in 2014. At 4,000 new devices, this was the largest-scale expansion of in-store location-based technology by a major retailer to date. In a press release, Macy's chairman and chief executive officer said:

Macy's and Bloomingdale's remain committed to operating at the forefront of innovation, as well as fostering a locally relevant shopping experience in every store. We will continue to test, to learn, and to proceed aggressively with new ideas that excite our customers and that make shopping more convenient and fun. Our goal remains to help our customers shop whenever, wherever and however they prefer, and to use the entire inventory of the company to satisfy demand. We are a multi-faceted retailer with stores, technology, Internet capability and mobile access that come together for our customers. They are at the center of all our decisions, and our ongoing research and development will continue to help us understand how to personally engage with them.

The largest challenge to making shopBeacons in Macy's stores a success is consumer acceptance. Consumers need to proactively download an app to engage with this in-store location-based technology. However, the allure of highly personalized promotions that would enhance their shopping experiences is a motivation for many to download an app and share their personal data, especially if they are already engaged with the retailer.

Discussion Questions

1. Would this shopBeacon technology be best targeted to individuals engaged in the nominal, limited, or extended decision-making process (or more than one)? Justify your response.

2. Chapter 17 discusses omni-channel shoppers. Do you think the benefits of this technology will outweigh the possible nuisance of push notifications as they move through the store and simultaneously receive information on their smartphones?

3. Chapter 15 discusses mobile search and details five segments of mobile phone users. Which of these segments do you feel will be most accepting of shopBeacon technology? Which would be least accepting? Why?

4. Chapter 15 also discusses marketing strategies based on information search patterns. Which of these strategies is best complimented by location-based technology? (Hint: More than one could be correct with a logical explanation.) Explain your answer.

5. Chapter 17 discusses the nature of unplanned purchases. How would Macy's shopBeacon program affect

   a. Planned purchases

   b. Unplanned purchases

6. Assemble a small group of consumers and conduct a focus group on their perceptions of location-based technology like shopBeacon. Would they download the app to engage with it? Would they opt in for some retailers and not others? Why? Would it play a role in their selection of retailers to patronize?

7. Chapter 9 discusses brand image and product positioning. Think about Macy's and other department stores' brand images. One axis should be high versus low technology adoption. The other axis could be any bipolar set of adjectives of your choosing. Then, construct a perceptual map that includes several department stores.

8. Chapter 7 discusses types of innovation. Is shopBeacon best described as a continuous, dynamically continuous, or discontinuous innovation?

Source: R. Borison, "Macy's, Shopkick up the Ante for Personalized Shopping," *Mobile Commerce Daily,* November 21, 2013, www.mobilecommercedaily.com; H. Bray, "How Location-Based Apps Will Shape the Future of Shopping," *Discover,* April 30, 2014, http://blogs.discovermagazine.com; D. Butcher, "Macy's Exec: Location-Based Mobile Rewards Key Tactic to Drive Foot Traffic," *Mobile Commerce Daily,* August 19, 2010, www.mobilecommercedaily.com; H. Clancy, "Apple's iBeacon Signals Turning Point for Mobile Engagement," *Fortune,* February 28, 2014, http://fortune.com; S. Cole, "Macy's Begins Pilot Test of Apple's iBeacon in Flagship New York, San Francisco Stores," *Apple Insider,* November 20, 2013, http://appleinsider.com; T. Danova, "Beacons: What They Are, How They Work, and Why Apple's iBeacon Technology Is Ahead of the Pack," *Business Insider,* September 13, 2014, www.businessinsider.com; A. Fiorletta, "Macy's Invests in New Omnichannel Strategies," *Retail Touchpoints,* September 16, 2014, www.retailtouchpoints.com; N. Gagliordi, "Macy's Rolls Out Retail's Largest Beacon Installation," *ZD Net,* September 15, 2014, www.zdnet.com; E. Griffith, "Consumers Hate In-Store Tracking (but Retailers, Startups and Investors Love it)," *Fortune,* March 24, 2014, http://tech.fortune.cnn.com; A. Guesenhues, "Macy's Takes iBeacon Technology Nationwide, Installing More Than 4,000 Devices," *Marketing Land,* September 16, 2014, http://marketingland.com; C. Kern, "New Survey Reveals Brick-and-Mortar Shopping Still Thrives, but Online Shopping Is Growing," *Integrated Solutions for Retailers,* September 17, 2014, www.retailsolutionsonline.com; J. McDermott, "WTF Are In-Store Beacons?," *DigiDay,* January 17, 2014, http://digiday.com; S. Perlberg, "Retailers Look for Digital Magic as In-Store Sales Decline," *Wall Street Journal,* September 10, 2014, http://blogs.wsj.com.

4-6 TESLA'S NOVEL AND ENVIRONMENTAL APPROACH DRIVES AMAZING BRAND LOYALTY

Tesla Motors, Inc., is a Palo Alto, California–based automotive company that is shifting paradigms in terms of automotive vehicles themselves and the way they are marketed. Teslas are priced as luxury vehicles, starting in the range of $70,000 to $120,000 depending on the model. Tesla produces fully electronic vehicles that are powered by 7,000 battery cells that are linked to an electric motor. They can drive roughly 250 miles on a single charge, which restricts their use for long road trips. However, Tesla is in the process of building charging stations on the route between New York City and Los Angeles that will be solar-powered. According to the founder of Tesla, Elon Musk:

> You can drive for free, forever, on pure sunlight. That's the, you know, message we're trying to convey. So even if, like, there's a zombie apocalypse and the grid breaks down, you'll still be able to charge your car.

While Tesla is still a young company, it has been wildly successful, even during times of economic recession. The sales per square foot of Tesla showrooms double that of Apple. Tesla's order backlog is roughly 30 weeks long, at a value of over $226 million, while the production rate by the end of 2015 is expected to be 100,000 vehicles per year. Several states, including

California, Nevada, Arizona, New Mexico, and Texas, competed for Tesla's new $5 billion Gigafactory that will produce lithium ion batteries and employ up to 6,500 people.

Tesla's customers are extremely loyal to the Tesla brand. Critics draw parallels between the level of fanaticism of Tesla customers and that of Apple customers. In *Consumer Reports'* 2013 annual survey, Tesla Motors received the highest owner satisfaction score: 99 out of 100. Tesla customers evangelize the brand to almost anyone who will listen, which is one way that its popularity has spread organically. Tesla meet-up events for brand enthusiasts are quite common and even featured on Tesla's website. Tesla's extreme brand loyalty can be attributed to several factors, including its revolutionary approach that challenges the traditional automotive industry, an emotional connection, and a culture of transparency.

To its customers, Tesla stands for revolution of the automotive industry in terms of new technology and a new way of conducting business that is at odds with the established automotive industry. Tesla eschews traditional advertising and the franchise dealership model that is common among established automotive brands. Instead, Tesla takes a direct marketing approach with very little mainstream advertising and nonnegotiable pricing. Tesla primarily sells directly to consumers through its website and operates comparatively tiny retail showrooms that often house a single vehicle. These showrooms often are found within high-end indoor shopping malls where there is much more foot traffic than traditional automobile dealerships enjoy. Much of the awareness of the brand is spread through free positive publicity. According to Jeremy Anwyl, the vice president of Edmunds.com:

> They're selling very few cars when you think about it—but they are getting an awful lot of buzz. You have to credit [Musk], who's very Steve Jobs–like in how he deals with the media. A lot of the attention is not generated through what we consider traditional advertising. It's really through social media.

This direct-to-consumers approach has made enemies out of auto dealership associations, which have filed a series of lawsuits against Tesla in various states in order to halt direct sales, claiming that laws requiring consumers to purchase vehicles from franchises encourage healthy price competition. Tesla owners have turned out in droves to protest these lawsuits both online and in places like Missouri and Texas. This controversy only serves to further reinforce brand loyalty and a sense of a bond among Tesla's customers, as it gives them a common enemy to rail against: the mainstream institution of the traditional combustion engine automotive manufacturers.

Another reason behind Tesla's brand loyalty is that Tesla has succeeded in establishing an emotional connection with its customers as well. Tesla's fully electric technology stands for an effort to solve energy problems in environmentally friendly ways. Saving the environment is a cause for which many consumers hold a deep passion. For example, one Tesla enthusiast said:

> That's how cool this car is. You feel like you're part of something bigger, a new age of motor vehicles. . . . Elon Musk is my hero.

Finally, Tesla's culture of transparency is another incredibly attractive feature to consumers. Tesla establishes a relationship of open communication with its customers through social media and its blog. Whenever there has been any negative publicity, the chief executive officer, Elon Musk, has addressed it publicly through Twitter and published internal e-mail correspondences on its website. Recently, in an effort to develop increasingly environmentally friendly technology, Tesla made its designs open source so that they could be improved more quickly with the help of the public. According to Mr. Musk:

> It is impossible for Tesla to build electric cars fast enough to address the carbon crisis.

In sum, Tesla's revolutionary approach disrupts the competitive status quo of the automotive industry and pushes the standards of environmental friendliness. This style, coupled with intense emotional connection and a standard of transparency, has proven to drive a very high level of brand loyalty among consumers and enthusiasm among investors. This is an innovative brand from which the public can expect great things to come.

Discussion Questions

1. Chapter 9 discusses schemas, which also are known as schematic memories and knowledge structures. Construct a schema diagram for Tesla.

2. Describe at least two segments of the market for Tesla electronic vehicles. List the different needs,

demographics, and psychographics for owning a Tesla for each of these segments.

3. Based on your analysis in the previous question, develop ads for each segment. Be sure to include key positioning statements, key copy points, visuals, and so forth for each and defend your decisions.

4. Evaluate Tesla's website (www.teslamotors.com).

5. In this age of $3-per-gallon gasoline and concerns about carbon emission, discuss how Tesla can be both a utilitarian decision and a value-expressive decision.

6. In general, how do gas prices or fuel costs factor into the decision-making process for consumers in terms of influencing the consideration set and decision-making rule used in selecting a transportation option? In the context of Tesla's high sticker price, does your answer change? If so, how? Detail and explain. (Hint: Consider the marketing strategies based on information search patterns in Chapter 15.)

7. To which of the eight "Shades of Green" segments discussed in Chapter 3 does Tesla appeal most? Explain your answer.

8. Chapter 7 discusses types of innovation. Is a Tesla best described as a continuous, dynamically continuous, or discontinuous innovation? Explain your answer.

Source: P. D'Arcy, "Tesla Marketing Strategy," *Science of Revenue*, January 20, 2014, http://scienceofrevenue.com; S. Dechert, "Tesla Scores Again with 'Interactive' Marketing," *Clean Technica*, August 21, 2014, http://cleantechnica.com; M. McCarthy, "Tesla Generates Small Sales, Big Buzz without Paid Ads," *Advertising Age*, June 10, 2013, http://adage.com; M. Niquette, "Consumer Advocates Support Tesla Direct Sales in Dispute," *Bloomberg*, March 20, 2014, www.bloomberg.com; J. Owyang, "Tesla Lets Go, to Gain the Market," *Web-Strategist.com*, June 14, 2014, www.web-strategist.com; S. Pelley, "Tesla and SpaceX: Elon Musk's Industrial Empire," *CBS News*, March 30, 2014, www.cbsnews.com; S. Reynolds, "Why You Should Copy Tesla's Way of Marketing," *Forbes*, September 1, 2013, www.forbes.com; D. Smith, "How GoPro and Tesla Hacked Digital Marketing," *The Next Web*, May 7, 2014, http://thenextweb.com; A. Taylor, "Is Tesla the Ultimate Momentum Stock?," *Fortune*, August 15, 2014, http://fortune.com; T. Walsh, "The Cult of Tesla Motors Inc: Why This Automaker Has the Most Loyal Customers," *The Motley Fool*, September 2, 2014, www.fool.com.

4-7 GILT GROUPE'S INNOVATIVE APPROACH TO LOYALTY PROGRAMS

Gilt Groupe is an online fashion retailer that offers luxury fashion brands at substantial discounts. Consumers must become members to view the content and be allowed access to Gilt's frequent flash sales. Gilt Groupe has become wildly popular, as over 6 million members have joined since its inception in 2007. However, as flash sales sites are becoming so popular, the number of such sites is naturally increasing. IBIS World predicts that by 2018 there would be around 150 flash sales sites, which would be a sharp increase from the roughly 90 sites in 2014. Thus, Gilt Groupe is innovating in ways to stand out and keep its customers engaged.

Gilt Groupe has launched a loyalty program called Gilt Insider Program, which takes a novel approach to loyalty programs. Unlike many traditional loyalty programs that only award points to members when they make purchases, Gilt Insider Program awards points, called Insider points, to members for a variety of activities that engage them with the brand. Members still earn points by purchasing products, but they also can earn points through referring friends, visiting flash sales, connecting with the brand through social media, and browsing the website. Gilt Groupe studied its customers' behavior and aligned the program with actions that customers are already doing to reinforce engagement with the brand.

According to Elizabeth Francis, chief marketing officer at Gilt Groupe:

> We wanted to create a loyalty program that rewards our members not just for their purchasing but for all the ways they interact with our brand. Gilt Insider perks are a collection of our member's most requested asks—from having early sale access to a brand they love, to deeper discounts, to the opportunity to attend exclusive events. The rewards program is designed to provide Gilt members with a platform to pick and choose from the rewards they love the most.

The reward structure is somewhat unique, but it fits well with Gilt Groupe's business model. Insider points can be redeemed for a variety of rewards, including early access to flash sales, access to exclusive events, additional discounts, and free shipping. Because the Gilt Groupe business model revolves around exclusive access to flash sales of limited quantities of luxury items, early access is incredibly valuable to its customers. Gilt Groupe has used the knowledge of what its customers value most and have formulated the Gilt Insider Program to incentivize consumer engagement. Ms. Francis said:

> It's expensive from a technology perspective. We communicate frequently with our customers. We knew what our members wanted. This is a great way for us to engage.

According to a 2013 global Nielsen survey of Internet users, these incentives should appeal to many consumers. Eighty-four percent of respondents said they are more likely to patronize retailers with loyalty programs. Seventy-five percent of respondents report that discounted and free products are the most appealing reward. Enhanced customer service is an important reward for 44 percent of respondents and free shipping was important to 42 percent of respondents. According to Julie Currie, the senior vice president of global loyalty at Nielsen:

> Savvy retailers are mining the data and looking for new and innovative ways to achieve the benefits most important to their customers. . . . In markets where loyalty programs are long established, customers tend to be savvy about copy-cat promotional offerings that don't offer unique advantages. New and innovative concepts, especially in the online space, that connect with how consumers want to shop are proving to be most effective.

While it is possible for members to accumulate points through many types of engagement other than making purchases, it would take a very long time to earn enough points without purchasing to earn rewards. For example, members earn 25 points for referring a friend and 100 points for visiting the site for five consecutive days. However, lower-level rewards like free shipping start at 3,500 points. In order to reach the lowest denomination of voucher discount ($80) without making a purchase, a member would need to browse a Gilt Groupe sale every weekday for 250 weeks. Purchases, which earn five points per dollar spent, accumulate at a much higher rate.

As members of the Gilt Insider Program accumulate points, they achieve access to three tiers of program status: Select, Premier, and Noir. These tiers are accessible at the 5,000-, 10,000-, and 25,000-point thresholds. With advancement to each additional tier, members are offered additional perks, such as waitlist priority and exclusive VIP customer service lines. For wealthier customers, which are a target market for Gilt Groupe, holding exclusive status with special privileges is more of a motivation than discounts. According to Ms. Francis:

> To make it fair we crafted a program that rewarded engagement, i.e., site visitation and social interaction, in addition to purchasing, so that members could advance up tiers as they earned points.

Tiered loyalty programs, which are modeled after airlines' loyalty programs, are a growing trend that is meant to entice consumers in an environment where traditional loyalty programs have become so common that they often are expected and overlooked. According to Jeff Berry, the senior director of knowledge development for LoyaltyOne, a global provider of loyalty programs for retailers:

> When pretty much every retailer is offering a program with points per purchase, tiers offer that extra incentive to choose one over another. It almost has become the overall scorecard for customers, so they understand where they are relative to where they could be.

While the Gilt Insider Program is an innovative way to stand out from other flash sales sites and the proliferation of loyalty programs among retailers, whether it is a sustainable advantage is yet to be seen. The average North American consumer belongs to between 8 and 12 loyalty programs. According to Niraj Dawar, the author of *Tilt: Shifting Your Strategy from Products to Consumers:*

> From a brand manager's perspective, the question is what is a consumer loyal to, are they loyal to the brand that you're selling or are they loyal to the points? If they're loyal to the points the moment you stop those points your product will stop selling. Or the moment a competitor offers an equivalent amount of points on a slightly different program, the consumer will switch.

Customer Insight Group, Inc., a consulting group that specializes in loyalty program marketing, offers the following 10 tips for successful loyalty programs, many of which the Gilt Insider Program incorporates:

- Only require and gather customer information that you plan on using.
- Make sure your employees know the benefits of your loyalty program and that they don't keep it a secret.
- Enrollment in your loyalty program lagging? Create an employee contest to see who can enroll the most new customers.
- One easy way to entice more customers to join your program is offer them an incentive at enrollment.
- Don't just focus on adding members. To get results, you need member participation.
- Make it easy for your staff to talk about the benefits of the loyalty program by giving them a script.

- Secret shop your loyalty program to see if there are training issues.
- Consider implementing a minimum loyalty program enrollment requirement for employees and make it a component of their employee evaluation.
- Customers will carry your loyalty card if your customers see value in the program and if they are engaged in your brand.
- Tier your loyalty program so customers have a reason to give you a greater share of wallet and loyalty.

Discussion Questions

1. Define *loyalty* as you understand it from the text. Do you think the Gilt Insider Program at Gilt Groupe helps create loyalty? Explain.

2. Conduct a small focus group of consumers who you think may fit the Gilt Groupe target market. Ask the participants about their perceptions of the Gilt Insider Program. How effective do they think this loyalty program will be in generating engagement and loyalty? What is their opinion of the rewards that are offered as part of the program? Then, repeat this exercise with another group of consumers who you think would not be part of the Gilt Groupe target market.

3. This loyalty program was designed to achieve two goals, namely, increasing consumer engagement with Gilt Groupe and increasing sales from Gilt Groupe.
   a. How well do you think that the Gilt Insider Program will meet each of these goals?
   b. Which of the goals do you think will be best achieved by this loyalty program?

c. This program was launched in 2013. Because some time has passed since then, perform an Internet search to discover any reports on the Gilt Insider Program's progress. How well did your predictions from part a and part b perform?

4. Many Gilt Groupe members will likely log in to Gilt.com to browse the flash sales daily in order to accumulate points in the Gilt Insider Program. This engagement will expose them to sales, and many are likely to make unplanned purchases. Chapter 13 discusses situational influences. What situational characteristics are likely to play a role in these purchase decisions? (Hint: More than one category could apply.)

5. Chapter 17 discusses Internet retailing and provides a typology of online shopping segments.
   a. Which segments are very likely to enroll in the Gilt Insider Program? Why?
   b. Which segments are very unlikely to enroll in the Gilt Insider Program? Why?

6. Chapter 9 discusses schemas, which also are known as schematic memories and knowledge structures. Construct a schema diagram for Gilt Groupe.

Source: A. Bosanac, "Customer Loyalty Programs Turn Shameless Amid Intense Competition," *Huffington Post,* August 11, 2014, www.huffingtonpost.com; S. Burnett, "Customer Loyalty Programs: Stats, Facts and Tips for 2014," *Customer Insight Group, Inc.,* February 14, 2014, www.customerinsightgroup.com; C. Gallarello, "Gilt.com Unveils Gilt Insider Program," *Gilt.com,* July 18, 2013, www.gilt.com; Gilt, "Gilt.com Unveils Gilt Insider Program," *PR Newswire,* July 18, 2013, www.prnewswire.com; K. Grant, "Retail Loyalty Programs Add Tiers to Reward Big Spenders," *CNBC,* August 28, 2013, www.cnbc.com; "Nielsen Survey: 84 Percent of Global Respondents More Likely to Visit Retailers That Offer a Loyalty Program," *Nielsen,* November 12, 2013, www.nielsen.com; T. Novellino, "Taking a Nooner with Gilt.Com Now Pays Points," *Upstart Business Journal,* July 18, 2013, http://upstart.bizjournals.com; H. Ongley, "Seems Like Gilt Wants You to Hack Their New Loyalty Program," *Styleite,* July 18, 2013, www.styleite.com.

4-8 ALBERTSONS DITCHES SELF-CHECKOUT IN FAVOR OF HUMAN CONTACT

Albertsons, a major national grocery store chain, is eliminating self-checkout stations in many of its stores to promote more human contact with customers. One hundred Albertsons locations, owned by the independent company Albertsons LLC, are phasing out self-checkout lines and replacing them with more traditional lanes with cashiers. This move is only the start of an effort to increase the employee interaction with customers. Albertsons' executives feel shoppers are not getting enough human interaction and there is a lack of relationship-building during the shopping experience:

> We just want the opportunity to talk to customers more . . . that's the driving motivation. . . . Our customers are our highest priority, and we want to provide them with an excellent experience from the time they park their car to when they leave.

After the announcement, there was some public concern because many consumers preferred self-service checkout options and were upset at the prospect of losing them. Albertsons representatives quickly reassured customers that this change is only affecting some of the independently owned Albertsons. In particular, SUPERVALU, which operates 460 Albertsons in the Pacific Northwest, California, and Nevada, made swift moves to let their shoppers know that this publicized change would not be affecting their stores. According to another Albertsons spokesperson, Lilia Rodriguez:

> Despite many incorrect reports, Albertsons stores owned by SUPERVALU will continue to operate self check-out lanes. Since this story broke last week, our customers have called us and we learned first-hand that they want and appreciate the convenience of self check-out lanes.

As evidenced by the conflicting quotes, there is some disagreement as to how beneficial self-service checkout is for customers. Self-service checkout lanes were originally introduced as a way to reduce retailers' labor costs and speed up shoppers' checkout times. They have quickly spread in popularity. For example, in 1999 only six percent of grocery stores offered self-service checkouts. By 2007, 69 percent of stores offered the stations. Many consumers feel the machines provide them with valuable convenience. Others feel they are actually less convenient, given that the self-service machines often have error messages that require a cashier to come help anyway. According to David Livingston of DJL Research, whether it is more beneficial to have a human cashier or a self-service checkout may depend on the quality of the employees in terms of customer service.

> I advised many clients not to [install self-checkouts] because they have such excellent cashiers and customer service. The cashiers were friendly, attractive and much faster than self-checkouts. Encountering a friendly cashier was part of the shopping experience. For large sterile retailers, there is no doubt that self checkouts will be better received by customers. How often must we encounter some inept, hideous-looking, slow cashier chewing gum? If this is the best certain retailers can hire, then of course, offer self-checkouts.

Tables A, B, and C provide further information about consumers' perceptions and behaviors in relation to self-service checkout options.

TABLE A — Importance of Self-Checkout When Selecting Primary Grocery Store

Not at all important	31%
Not too important	32%
Somewhat important	26%
Very important	14%

Source: Food Marketing Institute, "U.S. Grocery Shopper Trends," 2007 report.

TABLE B — Consumer Insights into Self-Checkout: "I Like Self-Checkout . . ."

When I'm only buying a few items	66%
Because I believe it's faster than regular lanes	53%
Because it provides greater privacy	41%
Because I like to bag my own groceries	34%
No matter how many items I buy	32%
As I don't believe a cashier adds customer service to the checkout process	24%

Source: Food Marketing Institute, "U.S. Grocery Shopper Trends," 2007 report.

TABLE C — What Percentage of Transactions Did You Conduct Using Self-Service Devices This Past Week?

Location	Average	100%	75%	50%	25%	None
Bank	73	36	21	16	9	18
Grocery store	38	8	11	19	20	42
Retail store	33	6	10	17	24	43
Airline	29	15	8	6	5	66
Hotel/motel	21	8	5	8	8	71
Restaurant	18	4	5	9	13	70
Hospital/clinic/ doctor's office	10	2	2	6	9	81
Other location	19	5	5	9	12	68

Source: NRC Corporation, 2008 Self-Service Consumer Survey for North America, "The Self-Service Revolution Is Real."

Discussion Questions

1. The presence of self-service checkout lanes and/ or service employees is part of the physical surroundings in Albertsons' store atmosphere, or environment.

   a. Using the Typology of Service Environments in Figure 13–2, describe where Albertsons would be positioned within the grid.

   b. Does having more human contact and less self-checkout lanes influence Albertsons' position?

2. Chapter 17 discusses the relationship between involvement, sales personnel, and the likelihood of self-service. Cashiers are a basic form of sales personnel. Describe Albertsons' service environment in terms of involvement and the appropriateness of sales personnel versus self-service.

3. Interpret the information in Tables A, B, and C.

   a. What are the primary needs that self-service checkouts satisfy for those customers who prefer them?

   b. What other industries present the best opportunities for the self-service checkout industry to grow?

4. Chapter 10 discusses Maslow's hierarchy of needs. What need is Albertsons attempting to fulfill by increasing its human contact with its customers? Explain.

5. Chapter 7 discusses categories of innovations. What type of innovation is self-service checkout technology?

Source: "The Self-Service 'Buy-and-Pay' Market," *Packaged Facts,* June 2008; A. Anand, "Major Grocer Getting Rid of Self-Checkout Lanes," *MSNBC,* July 10, 2011, http://msnbc.msn.com; "Supervalu-Owned Albertsons Stores Maintain Self Check-out Lanes," *Business Wire,* July 11, 2011, www.marketwatch.com; A. Gasparro, "US Supermarkets Look beyond Standard Self-Checkout Service," *Wall Street Journal,* July 11, 2011, http://online.wsj.com; C. Moran, "Some Albertsons Ditching Self-Checkout Lanes in Favor of Humans," *Consumerist. com,* July 11, 2011, http://consumerist.com; A. Turano, "Why Self-Checkout Lanes Are Increasingly Getting Checked-off," *Retail Customer Experience,* July 11, 2011, http://retailcustomerexperience.com.

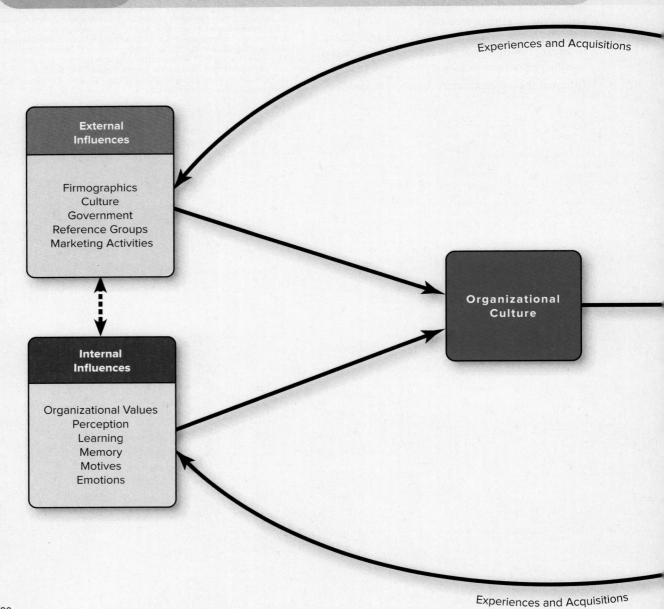

Experiences and Acquisitions

External Influences

Firmographics
Culture
Government
Reference Groups
Marketing Activities

Internal Influences

Organizational Values
Perception
Learning
Memory
Motives
Emotions

Organizational Culture

Experiences and Acquisitions

Decision Process

Situations

Problem Recognition

↓

Information Search

↓

Alternative Evaluation and Selection

↓

Outlet Selection and Purchase

↓

Postpurchase Processes

Needs/ Desires

The stereotype of organizational buying behavior is one of a cold, efficient, economically rational process. Computers rather than humans could easily, and perhaps preferably, fulfill this function. In reality, nothing could be further from the truth. In fact, organizational consumer behavior is as human as individual and household consumer behavior.

Organizations pay price premiums for well-known brands and for prestige brands. They avoid risk and fail to properly evaluate products and brands both before and after purchase. Individual members of organizations use the purchasing and consumption process as a political arena and attempt to increase their personal, departmental, or functional power through purchasing. Marketing communications are perceived and misperceived by organization members. Likewise, organizations learn correct and incorrect information about the world in which they operate.

Organizational purchase decisions take place in situations with varying degrees of time pressure, importance, and newness. They typically involve more people and criteria than do individual or household decisions. Thus, the study of organizational buying behavior is a rich and fun-filled activity.

On this and the facing page is a version of our model of consumer behavior modified for organizational buying. Chapter 19 explains these modifications.

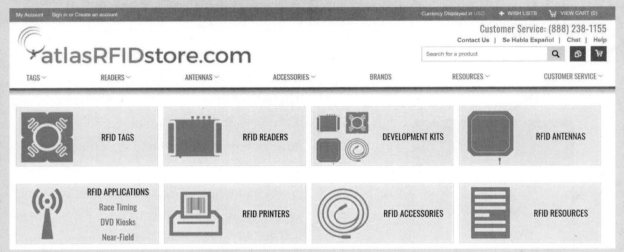

Source: atlasRFIDstore

LEARNING OBJECTIVES

LO1 Describe the organizational purchase process.

LO2 Summarize the external factors that influence organizational culture.

LO3 Summarize the internal factors that influence organizational culture.

LO4 Explain the influence of organizational buyer segments on marketing strategy.

It may sound funny to say it this way, but businesses are consumers too! They have needs and wants, are influenced by internal factors like values, and are influenced by external factors like reference groups. Relationships matter, as do efforts to build and foster brand image. Technology also plays a central role in those relationships and the purchase process. Business e-commerce, like its consumer counterpart, is growing and expected to surpass $1 trillion in the U.S. by 2021. Consider the following trends:[1]

Personalization and customer experience still matter. Almost half of today's business buyers are Gen Yers. This tech-savvy group has come to expect an easy, self-service purchase process available 24/7 online. But business-to-business (B2B) sellers shouldn't be fooled into thinking self-service means no service. These buyers count on an effective and personal, online customer experience. For example, sellers use pricing, a key factor in business purchase decisions, to personalize the buyer's online experience. Specialized software exists to help sellers customize prices for buyers based on factors like how much they buy and the length of their business relationships. Technology enhancements also can provide a more intuitive and interactive search and buying process. AtlasRFID, a seller of localized tracking technology products to buyers including Boeing and Procter & Gamble, has an online system that categorizes the countless items into "buckets." Customers click through buckets and filter options based on their own preferences. In the end, customers can easily compare multiple items side-by-side.

Mobile is here to stay. Mobile buying is growing among businesses (B2B) like it is with consumers (B2C). Over 40 percent of business customers use mobile devices in the buying process—from product research and price comparisons, to the purchase itself. The convenience of mobile buying for consumer purchases is now expected by buyers in the professional realm. B2B sellers are embracing m-commerce and benefiting from their efforts. For example, 4imprint—a customized promotional products firm—enjoyed a 38 percent increase in mobile revenue by enhancing the mobile experience for customers and increasing its mobile marketing efforts. More generally, a recent Google and Boston Consulting Group study finds:

> Mobile increases loyalty. Our study shows that a positive mobile experience increases repurchase rate and builds customer loyalty. More than 90% of B2B buyers reporting a superior mobile experience say they are likely to buy again from the same vendor compared with only about 50% of those reporting a poor mobile experience.

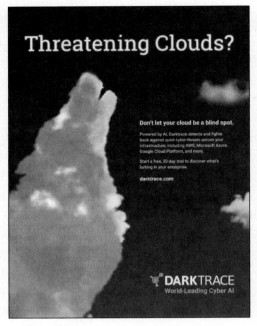

Source: Darktrace

Appreciating what drives businesses, and the people who run them, is critical to marketing success. Purchase decisions by businesses often are described as "rational" or "economic." However, as the chapter opener suggests, various factors beyond functional utility influence organizational decisions, especially online. This is not so surprising when you consider that businesses and other organizations are made up of individuals, and that these individuals, not "the organization," make the purchase decisions.

Understanding organizational purchasing requires many of the same concepts used to understand individual consumer or household needs. The DarkTrace ad in Illustration 19-1 is a great example. Although larger and often more complex than individual consumers and households, organizations too develop preferences, memories, and behaviors through perceptions, information processing, and experience. Likewise, organizations develop cultures that create relatively stable patterns of behaviors over time and across situations.

Like households, organizations make different types of buying decisions. In some instances, these buying decisions are routine replacement decisions for a frequently purchased commodity product or service such as paper or pens. At the other end of the continuum, organizations face new, complex purchase decisions that require careful problem definition, extensive information search, a long and often technical evaluation process, perhaps a negotiated purchase, and a long period of use and postpurchase evaluation.

Because there are many similarities between analyzing consumer behavior and analyzing organizational buyer behavior, our basic conceptual model of buyer behavior still holds. However, organizations are not just a collection of individuals. Organizations do develop unique rules and cultures that influence the behavior of their members. Thus, it is important that we understand the unique characteristics of organizations that relate to their purchasing behavior.

Figure 19-1 shows our basic model of buyer behavior modified to be applicable to an organizational buying context. We will begin our discussion by examining the organization decision process. Then we will examine the internal and external factors that determine organizational culture, the organizational equivalent of household lifestyle.

ORGANIZATIONAL PURCHASE PROCESS

Decision-Making Unit

LO1

Decision-making units (DMUs) are the individuals (representing functional areas and management) within an organization who participate in making a given purchase decision.[2] These often function as **buying centers** when they consist of individuals from various areas of the firm, such as accounting, engineering, manufacturing, and marketing, who meet specifically to make a purchase decision. They are often relatively permanent for recurring

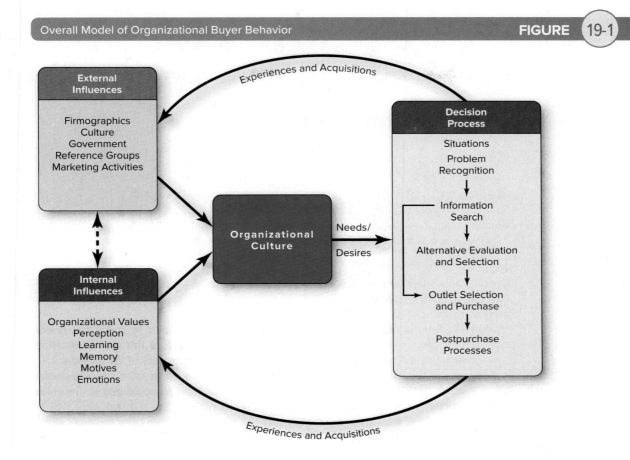

FIGURE 19-1

Overall Model of Organizational Buyer Behavior

decisions and ad hoc for nonroutine ones. Large, highly structured organizations ordinarily involve more individuals in a purchase decision than do smaller, less-formal organizations. Important decisions are likely to involve individuals from a wider variety of functional areas and organizational levels than are less important purchase decisions.

The following describes a Hewlett-Packard salesperson's view of the DMU and the buying process for very expensive imaging systems for large hospitals:

Selling in the hospital market is a two-stage process and the buying cycle ranges from 3 to 12 months. In the first stage, I deal with medical professionals. They are most concerned with image quality, product reliability, and service. I must establish relationships and awareness of our products' functionality and reliability with a number of people, and the product demonstration is critical.

The second stage is negotiations with administrators, who are more driven by price and cost issues. But much depends on the hospital's situation. For example, if a hospital is renowned for cancer treatment, they want the best available systems in that area and are more price sensitive with other equipment.[3]

In Table 19-1, we see that buyers in retail and wholesale firms assign different priorities to the performance of suppliers than do the operations people in those same firms.

TABLE 19-1   Service Attribute Importance for Retail and Wholesale Buyers and Operations Personnel

Attribute*	Buyer Rating	Operations Rating
Ordering ease	H	M
Product availability	H	M
Delivers on time	H	M
Delivered sorted	M	H
Palletizing capability	M	H
Master package quality	M	H

*H = high importance; M = modest importance.

Source: M. B. Cooper, C. Droge, and P. J. Daugherty, "How Buyers and Operations Personnel Evaluate Service," *Industrial Marketing Management,* no. 20 (1991), p. 83.

Organizations marketing to these firms must meet the needs of each group and communicate that to each group. Note that focusing only on the buyers, a common strategy, is not likely to be successful.

How the final purchase decision is made is determined in part by individual power, expertise, the degree of influence each functional area possesses in this type of decision, how the organization resolves group decision conflicts, and the nature of the decision.[4]

Members of the decision-making unit play various roles, such as information gatherer, key influencer, decision maker, purchaser, or user. A plant manager could play all five roles, while corporate engineers may simply be sources of information.

Decision-making units are likely to vary over the product life cycle (new products versus older ones). Consider the changes in the DMU that took place in the purchase of microprocessors by an original equipment manufacturer (OEM) over the stages of the microprocessor's product life cycle. Early stages in the life of the new microprocessor presented a difficult, important decision that required a large DMU. As the product grew in its utilization, a simpler decision evolved, as did a change in the structure of the DMU. Finally, as the microprocessor moved into a mature stage, it became a routine low-priority decision involving primarily the purchasing function. These changes are illustrated below:

Stage of Product Life Cycle	Size of DMU	Key Functions Influencing the Purchase Decision
Introduction	Large	Engineering and R&D
Growth	Medium	Production and top management
Maturity	Small	Purchasing

Purchase Situation

The buying process is influenced by the importance of the purchase and the complexity and difficulty of the choice. Simple, low-risk, routine decisions are generally made by an individual or even an automated process without extensive effort. At the other extreme are decisions that are complex and have major organizational implications. A continuum of purchase situations lies between these two extremes. A useful categorization of organizational purchase situations is provided in Table 19–2 and described in the following paragraphs.[5]

	Straight Rebuy	Modified Rebuy	New Task
Organizational Purchase Situations and Buying Responses		**TABLE 19-2**	
Situational characteristics			
Purchase importance	Low	Moderate	High
Choice complexity	Low	Moderate	High
Purchasing characteristics			
Size of DMU	Very small	Medium	Large, evolving
Level of DMU	Low	Mid-level	Top of organization
Time to decision	Very brief	Moderate	Long
Information search	None/very limited	Moderate	Extensive
Analysis techniques	None/price comparisons	Several	Extensive, complex
Strategic focus	None	Limited	Dominates

Note that this is similar to the purchase involvement construct discussed in Chapter 14. For consumers, we divided the purchase involvement continuum into three categories: nominal, limited, and extended. These correspond closely to the straight rebuy, modified rebuy, and new task purchase situations shown in Table 19–2.

Straight Rebuy   This situation occurs when the purchase is of minor importance and is not complex. This is generally the case when reordering basic supplies and component parts. In such cases, the reordering process may be completely automated or done routinely by clerical personnel. Such purchases often are handled under a contract that is reviewed and perhaps rebid periodically. Price or reliability tends to be the dominant evaluative criterion. No consideration is given to strategic issues.

Modified Rebuy   This strategy is used when the purchase is moderately important to the firm or the choice is more complex. This typically involves a product or service that the organization is accustomed to purchasing, but the product or the firm's needs have changed. Or because the product is important to the firm (it is simple, but the firm uses a lot of it or it is an important component of the firm's output), the firm may periodically reevaluate brands or suppliers. The DMU is likely to include several representatives, including some midlevel managers. More information is gathered and more evaluative criteria are analyzed. Strategic issues also begin to play a role.

New Task   This approach tends to occur when the buying decision is very important and the choice is quite complex. This would involve decisions on such things as an initial sales automation system or a new advertising agency. The buying organization typically will have had little experience with the decision and perhaps with the product or service. The DMU is likely to be large and evolve over time. Top management will be involved in the decision, and strategic issues will be of prime importance. The time involved is frequently quite long, ranging from many months to a year or more.

Clearly, the marketing strategy and tactics for one particular type of purchase situation would be inappropriate for others. Thus, marketers must understand the purchase task confronting their organizational consumers and develop appropriate marketing strategies.

Steps in the Organizational Decision Process

Because organizational decisions typically involve more individuals in more complex decision tasks than do individual or household decisions, marketing efforts to affect this process are much more complex.[6] Shown in Table 19–3 are the likely stages in the decision process and sources of influence at each stage in a large company's decision to acquire a new customer relationship management (CRM) system. Obviously, such decisions won't be made the same way for every organization. However, the key here is recognizing that this is a new task buy situation in which the DMU will involve many sources of influence, with varying criteria, varying levels of power, and varying media habits. The company trying to sell the CRM system must provide relevant information to each source of influence in order to be successful. This is no easy task in such a complex and large DMU.

Problem Recognition   In Table 19–3, the sales manager and director of operations play the key roles in recognizing the need. Triggers for this problem recognition could be numerous, including conflicts between field sales agents and sales assistants, as well as ongoing customer service problems identified by field sales agents or customers themselves and passed on to the sales manager.

TABLE 19-3 Decision Process in Purchasing a New CRM System

Stages of the Purchase Decision Process	Key Influences within Decision-Making Unit	Influences outside the Decision-Making Unit
Problem recognition	Director of operations Sales manager	Field sales agents Administrative staff Sales assistants CRM sales representative
Information search	Data/CRM specialist Director of Operations Purchasing manager	Operations personnel CRM sales representative Other corporate users Office systems consultant
Alternative evaluation	Vice President of Sales Data/CRM specialist Director of Operations Sales manager Purchasing manager	Office systems consultant CRM sales representative
Purchase decision	General management Vice President of Sales Purchasing manager	
Product usage	Director of Operations Sales manager	Field sales agents Administrative staff Sales assistants CRM sales representative
Evaluation	Director of Operations Sales manager Vice President of Sales General management	Field sales agents Administrative staff Sales assistants

Group Involvement in the Decision Process in High-Tech Organizations   TABLE 19-4

Stages of Decision Process	Board of Directors	Top Management	Head of Department	Lab Technician or Operator	Purchasing Manager or Buyer	Finance Manager Accountant
Recognizing the need to purchase	L	M	H	M	L	L
Determining product specifications	L	M	H	M	L	L
Deciding which suppliers to consider	L	M	H	L	L	L
Obtaining quotations and proposals	L	M	H	L	M	L
Evaluating quotations and proposals	L	H	H	L	L	M
Final product or supplier selection	M	H	H	L	L	L

Level of Involvement in Each Stage of Decision Process

Note: L = low; M = moderate; H = high.

Source: Reprinted from R. Abratt, "Industrial Buying in Hi-Tech Markets," *Industrial Marketing Management* 15 (1986), p. 295. Copyright 1986; reprinted with permission from Elsevier Science.

Table 19–4 shows that in high-tech markets, the head of a department is most likely to recognize a problem or need to purchase. Perhaps more important is that purchasing managers are not a source of problem recognition. This points out the danger of salespeople calling on purchasing agents only. As shown in Table 19–4, problem recognition and determining specifications often occur without much involvement of purchasing personnel.

Information Search   Information search can be both formal and informal.[7] Site visits to evaluate a potential vendor, laboratory tests of a new product or prototype, and investigation of possible product specifications are part of formal information search. Informal information search can occur during discussions with sales representatives, while attending trade shows, or when reading industry-specific journals. Industrial buyers search for information both to help make the best decision and to support their actions and recommendations within the organization.[8]

For complex technology products, organizational buyers often hire consultants both to provide information and to help evaluate alternatives. Consider the role played by consultants in the purchase of sales automation (SA) systems:

> The second step in the buying cycle was to evaluate the potential to automate existing processes. . . . Customers were usually not equipped to do this in-house. It was common for SA consultants to help them. Their deep understanding of the industry, and their skills and experience, made them the best option for this step.
>
> In the third step, the customer decided how the different functions to be automated were related, and determined how data was to be collected, stored, and analyzed. This again was usually done by SA consultants with the support of the customer's information systems department.
>
> The customer decided the type of SA software and hardware to be purchased. . . . Here again, the customer relied heavily on the consultant.[9]

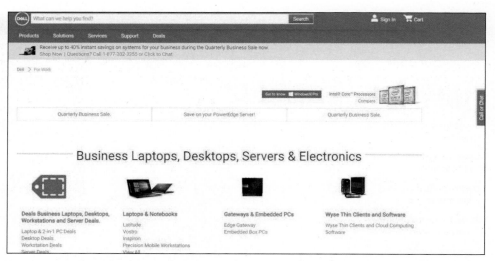

Source: Dell Technologies

Organizational buyers often search for product and price information on the Internet. The Dell Computer site shown in Illustration 19-2 provides detailed information online to help businesses assess which products are the right fit for the right price.

Evaluation and Selection   The evaluation of possible vendors and selection of a given vendor often follow a **two-stage decision process**.[10] The first stage is making the buyer's approved vendor list. A conjunctive decision process is very common. In this manner, the organization can screen out potential vendors that do not meet all its minimum criteria. In a government missile purchase, 41 potential manufacturers of a given missile electronics system were first identified. After site visits to inspect manufacturing capability and resources, the organization pared this list of 41 down to 11 that met the government's minimum criteria.

A second stage of organizational decision making could involve other decision rules, such as disjunctive, lexicographic, compensatory, or elimination-by-aspects. For the government purchase discussed above, a lexicographic decision process was used next, with the most important criterion being price. Using this decision rule, the organization selected two vendors.

The process of evaluation and selection is further complicated by the fact that different members of the decision-making unit have differing evaluative criteria.[11] Recall the difference in criteria for imaging systems between hospital administrators and medical professionals described earlier. Table 19-5 shows that purchasing, management, engineering, and operations use differing sets of performance criteria. For example, purchasing is more concerned with pricing policies, terms and conditions, and order status; engineers are more concerned with product knowledge, product operations, and applications knowledge. A salesperson calling on these accounts would need to understand and respond to the unique as well as the shared criteria of these purchase influencers. A recent study in South Africa similarly found that different criteria were important for different members of the DMU for indoor industrial circuit panels.[12] The SAP ad shown in Illustration 19-3 focuses on several key performance criteria of organizational buyers. *To which function or level of the organization is this ad targeted?*

It generally is assumed that business purchases are strictly economic, with the goal of maximizing the profits of the purchasing organization.[13] However, power, prestige, security, and similar noneconomic criteria also play important roles in business purchase decisions.[14] Research finds that there are organizations that buy "green," similar to the "green

| Evaluative Criteria and Organizational Role | | | | TABLE 19-5 |

Evaluative Criteria Used in Purchase Decision	Functional Role in Organization			
	Purchasing	Management	Engineering	Operations
Vendor offers broad line	X	X		
Many product options available	X	X		
Ease of maintenance of equipment			X	X
Competence of service techniques		X	X	X
Overall quality of service		X	X	
Product warranty	X	X	X	X
Delivery (lead time)				X
Time needed to install equipment	X			X
Construction costs	X		X	X
Vendor has lowest price	X	X	X	
Financial stability of vendor	X		X	X
Vendor willing to negotiate price	X			
Vendor reputation for quality	X	X	X	
Salesperson competence		X	X	X
Compatibility with equipment	X	X		
Available computer interface	X			

Source: Adapted from D. H. McQuiston and R. G. Walters, "The Evaluative Criteria of Industrial Buyers: Implications for Sales Training," *The Journal of Business and Industrial Marketing,* Summer–Fall 1989, p. 74.

consumers" described in Chapter 3. These organizations have policies or individual champions for socially responsible buying behavior by the organization.[15] Firms wishing to do business with these organizations must meet their requirements for products produced in an environmentally sound manner.

Brand image and equity also play roles in the evaluation process for organizations. Obviously, brand can be a surrogate indicator of quality (see Chapter 16). And research suggests that while brand may not always be the most important consideration, it can result in organizational buyers paying a price premium.[16]

Purchase and Decision Implementation   Once the decision to buy from a particular organization has been made, the method of purchase must be determined. From the seller's point of view, this means how and when it will get paid. In many purchases, payment is not made until delivery. Others involve progress payments. For a firm working on the construction of a building or highway or developing a new military aircraft that will take several years, payment timing is critical.

On an international basis, purchase implementation and method of payment are even more critical. Some countries prohibit the removal of capital from their country without an offsetting purchase. This led Caterpillar Tractor Company to sell earthmoving equipment in South America in exchange for raw materials, such as copper, that it could sell or use in its manufacturing operations.

ILLUSTRATION 19-3

Organizations buy for many reasons. The SAP ad attempts to persuade based on several key evaluative criteria.

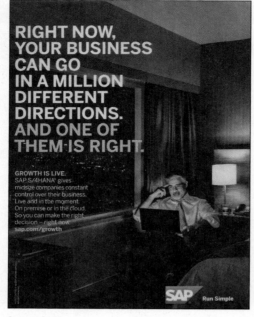

Source: SAP

Terms and conditions—payments, warranties, delivery dates, and so forth—are both complex and critical in business-to-business markets. One U.S. manufacturer of steam turbines lost a large order to a foreign manufacturer because its warranty was written too much to the advantage of the seller.

Firms marketing to organizations such as ADM Logistics increasingly use the Internet to sell their products directly to customers or through online wholesalers (see Illustration 19-4).[17] They also use it to generate leads for telephone or direct sales calls and to solicit orders either online or via a toll-free number.

Usage and Postpurchase Evaluation
After-purchase evaluations of products are typically more formal for organizational purchases than are household evaluations of purchases. In mining applications, for example, a product's life is broken down into different components such that total life-cycle cost can be assessed. Many mines will operate different brands of equipment side by side to determine the life-cycle costs of each before repurchasing one in larger quantities.

A major component of postpurchase evaluation is the service the seller provides during and after the sale.[18] Table 19-6 indicates the importance that one group of customers and managers assigned to different aspects of after-sales service. Notice that the managers did not have a very good understanding of what was important to its customers. Clearly, this firm needs a better understanding of its customers' needs.

ILLUSTRATION 19-4

ADM Logistics clearly understands that the Internet is a major source of supply for many organizational buyers.

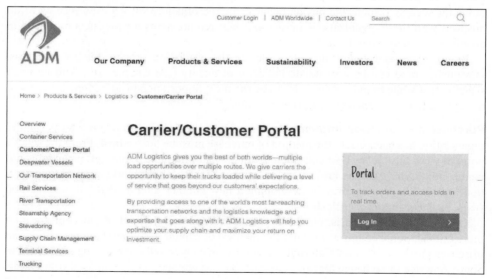

Source: Archer Daniels Midland Company

After-Sales Services "GAPS"						TABLE 19-6
	Importance of Service Item			Ratings of Service		
After-Sales Service Item	Customers	Managers	Gap	Customers	Managers	Gap
Attitude and behavior of technician	H	M	+	M	M	0
Availability of technical service staff	H	M	+	M	H	−
Repair time when service needed	M	H	−	M	H	−
Dispatch of breakdown call	H	M	+	M	H	−
Availability of spare parts during call	M	M	0	H	H	0
Service contract options	M	H	−	M	H	−
Price-performance ratio for services rendered	M	H	−	M	H	−
Response time when service needed	M	H	−	M	H	−

Note: H = high rating; M = moderate rating. Gap is positive (manager lower than customer), negative (manager higher than customer), or zero (manager and customer are the same).

Source: Adapted from H. Kasper and J. Lemmink. "After-Sales Service Quality: Views between Industrial Customers and Service Managers," *Industrial Marketing Management* 18 (1989), p. 203, with permission from Elsevier.

Similar to households, dissatisfied organizational buyers may switch suppliers or engage in negative word-of-mouth communications.[19] Firms marketing to organizations pursue strategies similar to those followed by consumer marketers in dealing with dissatisfied customers. They seek to minimize dissatisfaction and encourage those who become dissatisfied to complain to them and to no one else.[20]

Otis Elevator uses customer problems and a sophisticated database not only to increase customer satisfaction but to improve the design and functioning of its elevators. The following is an excerpt regarding their OTISLINE service center:

Imagine you are a building maintenance supervisor. It is 5 o'clock in the morning. You awaken and prepare to go to work. Unbeknownst to you, one of the elevators in your building has had a malfunction. If ignored, it could cause a bigger problem, delaying thousands of people on their way to their office suite. As you make your coffee, the monitoring system on the elevator detects the problem and makes a service call. Even before you get on the road to the office, a mechanic has arrived with the part and fixed the glitch. You enter, board the same elevator and know nothing about the problem until you pass the Otis mechanic on his way out the door.

The preceding scenario could be a true story written by Otis Elevator, thanks to the OTISLINE system. Simply put, OTISLINE is a communications service center for customers. Operators work 24 hours a day, handling emergency calls, dispatching mechanics and entering and updating information on the elevators. Close to 1.35 million elevators are handled by Otis call centers at 325 locations around the globe.[21]

The Role of the Internet and Mobile in the Organizational Decision Process

Just as the Internet has become a major force in consumer decisions, so too is it an important tool in organizations, as discussed in the opener. Business-to-business (B2B) e-commerce is currently estimated at roughly $900 billion in the United States, and over $7.5 trillion worldwide. E-commerce represents an increasing proportion of all B2B sales, currently estimated at 11 percent in the U.S.[22] As we have seen, the Internet and mobile can play a variety of roles in the decision process from lead generation, to information provision, to efficient and automated order fulfillment.[23]

As in business-to-consumer (B2C), search is a major influence in B2B buying. Consider the following statistics:[24]

- Search or search engines are involved in over 90 percent of B2B decisions.
- 71 percent of B2B searches start with a generic, as opposed to a brand- or company-specific, search.
- On average, 12 searches are made before a brand's specific website is accessed.
- Online B2B videos, talking about product features, for example, are watched by 70 percent of B2B potential buyers as part of the research process.
- Almost 50 percent of B2B potential buyers engage in product research on their mobile devices.
- Over 50 percent of B2B potential buyers use social media for search.

In terms of relative influence of different sources, the following statistics suggest that search and search engines dominate at each stage of the decision process:[25]

- Research stage—search used 30 percent more than B2B trade publications.
- Consideration stage—search used 21 percent more than B2B trade publications.
- Choice stage—search used 62 percent more than traditional media.

Perhaps not surprisingly, two-thirds of B2B sellers use search engine marketing, with more than one quarter of total marketing budgets dedicated to paid search.[26] From a strategic point of view, the increased availability of information from the Internet means there has been a need to change the role of salespeople. Salespeople are a dominant part of marketing strategy for B2B, much more so than in B2C. Historically, there was a clear informational role for salespeople. However, given the informational role of the web in today's B2B environment, salespeople have needed to adopt the role of solution provider rather than information provider.[27]

In terms of website design, recent research suggests that site organization (ease of navigation), customization, privacy/security, information value, and personalization are important drivers of B2B website effectiveness.[28] These characteristics are similar to those found to be important in B2C contexts (see Chapter 17). The same connection can be made for B2B mobile effectiveness. B2B buyers use their smartphones for work purchases as they do in a personal situation. For example, visiting a vendor's site for product information and comparing prices and products are the top two search activities on a smartphone.[29] Likewise, the impact of social media on purchase decisions and customer satisfaction cannot be ignored.[30]

Having examined organizational purchasing behavior in some detail, let us now apply the remainder of our revised model to further our understanding of organizations as consumers.

ORGANIZATIONAL CULTURE

L02

At the hub of our consumer model of buyer behavior are self-concept and lifestyle. Organizations also have a type of self-concept in the beliefs and attitudes the organization members have about the organization and how it operates. Likewise, organizations have a type of lifestyle in that they have distinct ways of operating. We characterize these two aspects of an organization as its **organizational culture** (see Figure 19-1). Organizational culture is much like lifestyle in that organizations vary dramatically in how they make decisions and how they approach problems involving risk, innovation, and change.[31] The term **corporate culture** is often used to refer to the organizational culture of a business firm.

Organizational culture reflects and shapes organizational needs and desires, which in turn influence how organizations make decisions. For example, the Environmental Protection Agency, the Red Cross, and IBM are three large organizations. Each has a different organizational culture that influences how it gathers information, processes information, and makes decisions.

EXTERNAL FACTORS INFLUENCING ORGANIZATIONAL CULTURE

Firmographics

We discussed earlier the important role of consumer demographics in understanding consumer behavior. Firmographics are equally important. **Firmographics** involve both *organization characteristics*—for example, size, activities, objectives, location, and industry category—*and characteristics of the composition of the organization*—for example, gender, age, education, and income distribution of employees.

Size   Large organizations are more likely to have a variety of specialists who attend to purchasing, finance, marketing, and general management; in smaller organizations, one or two individuals may have these same responsibilities. Larger organizations are generally more complex because more individuals participate in managing the organization's operations. That there are often multiple individuals involved in the purchase decision in a large organization means advertising and sales force efforts must be targeted at various functions in the firm. Each message might need to emphasize issues of concern only to that function. The same purchase decision in a smaller firm might involve only the owner or manager. Different media would be required to reach this person, and one message would need to address all the key purchase issues.

Activities and Objectives   The activities and objectives of organizations influence their style and behavior. For example, the Navy, in procuring an avionics system for a new fighter plane, operates differently than Boeing does in purchasing a similar system for a commercial aircraft. The Navy is a government organization carrying out a public objective, whereas Boeing seeks a commercial objective at a profit.

Table 19-7 is a matrix that provides examples of the interface between broad organizational objectives and activities. Organizational objectives can be categorized as commercial, governmental, nonprofit, and cooperative. The general nature of organizational activity is

Organizational Activities Based on Organizational Objective and Nature of Activity			**TABLE 19-7**
General Organizational Objective	**Nature of Organizational Activity**		
	Routine	**Complex**	**Technical**
Commercial	Office management	Human resource management	New-product development
Governmental	Highway maintenance	Tax collection	Space exploration
Nonprofit	Fund-raising	Increase number of national parks	Organ donor program
Cooperative	Compile industry statistics	Establish industry standards	Applied research

described as routine, complex, or technical. For example, a government organization purchasing highway maintenance services would operate differently from a government organization procuring missiles. Likewise, a cooperative wholesale organization set up as a buying cooperative for several retailers would have a different organizational culture from a cooperative research institute set up by firms in the semiconductor industry. And a nonprofit organization involved in organ donations is likely to differ from one organized to gather industry statistics.

Commercial firms can be usefully divided into public firms (stock is widely traded) and private firms (one or a few individuals own a controlling share of the firm). In public firms, management is generally expected to operate the firm in a manner that will maximize the economic gains of the shareholders. These organizations face consistent pressures to make economically sound, if not optimal, decisions.

However, a substantial percentage of business purchases involve privately held firms whose CEO is often the controlling shareholder. In this situation, the firm can and frequently does pursue objectives other than profit maximization. One study found that the following motives drive the management of such firms:[32]

- Building a place for the entire family to work and be involved.
- Having complete, autocratic control over an environment.
- Building a lasting "empire."
- Becoming wealthy.
- Doing what the family expects.
- Avoiding corporations or working for others.
- Obtaining status.
- Improving the world or the environment.

Segmenting these firms according to the motives of the owners is a useful approach for developing sales messages. For example, Micron Technology targeted the owners and managers of smaller, entrepreneurial firms. Its ads positioned it as understanding and caring about the needs and concerns of these individuals more than the larger firms do. One ad stated, "They wouldn't give you the time of day. They said you weren't a player. . . . They're holding on line three." Merrill Lynch, shown in Illustration 19–5, is also clearly targeting this group with an ad designed to appeal to concerns regarding long-term wealth management.

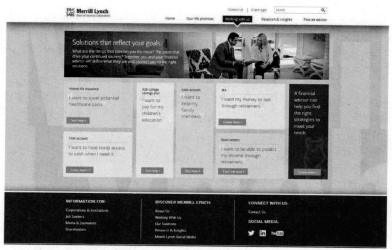

Source: Bank of America Corporation

Location   As we saw in Chapter 5, there are a number of regional subcultures in the United States. These subcultures influence organizational cultures as well as individual life-styles. For example, firms on the West Coast tend to be more informal in their operations than those on the East Coast. Dress is more casual, relationships are less formalized, and business is on more of a personal level in the West than elsewhere in the country. The Midwest and South also have unique business styles. Marketing communications and sales force training need to reflect these differences.

Location-based differences are magnified when doing business in foreign cultures. Firms that open branches outside their home countries frequently experience some difficulties managing the workforce and operating within the local community. Global B2B selling is as difficult as global B2C selling. Chinese relationships were discussed in Chapter 2, using the term *guanxi*. Recall that *guanxi* is personal connections/relationships on which an individual can draw to secure resources or advantages when doing business such as supply chain management, as well as in the course of social life.[33] However, firms must be careful to fully understand this and other culturally bound concepts. One Chinese informant indicated that Americans overdo the stereotypical "wine and dine" aspect, which is looked at with suspicion by the Chinese. Consider the following:

> I find that some foreigners come and they try too hard to overly respect Chinese local cultures and China in general. It comes across as almost a bit fake. Chinese sides pick up on that. They will use it. Chinese are good at looking for weakness that they can exploit. Some foreigners come here and are overly respectful. I explain to them that that is not respectful in Chinese cultures.[34]

It appears that the "over-the-top" or "trying too hard" aspect is a problem. Americans react the same way to overeager efforts by marketers in that they see it as a sign of desperation and not genuine or real. Nuance and true understanding are keys to successful ventures cross-culturally.

Industry Category   Two firms can be similar in terms of size (large), location (Illinois), activity (manufacturing), objective (profit), and ownership (public) and still have sharply differing cultures due in part to being in differing industries. If one of the two firms described above manufactured heavy equipment and the other, computers, we would expect differing cultures to exist.

Organization Composition   Organization cultures influence the behaviors and values of those who work in the organizations. However, the types of individuals who work in the organization also heavily influence organization cultures. An organization composed primarily of young, highly educated, technically oriented people (say, a software engineering firm) will have a different culture from an organization composed primarily of older, highly educated, nontechnical individuals (say, an insurance firm). While the culture of most organizations is influenced more by the characteristics of the founder and top managers, the overall composition of the organizational membership is also important.[35]

Macrosegmentation   Organizations with distinguishing firmographics can be grouped into market segments through a process called **macrosegmentation.** These segments, based on differences in needs due to firmographics, are called *macrosegments.*[36] For example, using size to segment its customers, IBM developed a program called IBM Express, which offers flexible and reasonably priced products and services tailored to customers with fewer than 1,000 employees.[37] Also, one corporate bank stated:

> We've tried too long to be everything to everyone. We're in the process of rolling out a strategy in all our branches where we segment customers and tailor our marketing campaigns to those segments.

Two of the macrosegments the bank is targeting are midsized and small businesses. Each segment will have a marketing team that focuses on that segment.[38]

Culture/Government

Variations in values and behaviors across cultures affect organizations as well as individuals.[39] For example, in most American firms, shareholder or owner wealth is a dominant decision criterion. Corporate downsizing has resulted in hundreds of thousands of workers and managers losing their jobs in order to enhance profitability. These actions have been acceptable in American society. Similar corporate behavior would not be accepted in much of Europe or Japan. In these societies, worker welfare is often on a par with or above concern about corporate profit. Plant closure laws, layoff regulations, and worker benefits tend to be much higher than in America.

In America, Japan, and most of Europe, bribery and similar approaches for making sales are not acceptable, and these governments enforce a wide array of laws prohibiting such behaviors. In America, both the legal and social constraints against bribery are strong enough to make corporate gift giving from a supplier to a buyer difficult or impossible.[40] In other parts of the world, "bribes" are an expected part of many business transactions. This poses a difficult ethical dilemma for firms doing business in these regions. Ignoring any legal constraints imposed by the American government, *should an American firm provide an expensive "gift" to the purchasing agent in a foreign country where it is common knowledge that such gifts are essential to do business with the country's firms?*

In many parts of the world, businesses and governments are partners or at least work closely together. In the United States, an arm's-length or even adversarial relationship is more common. One example of this is the antitrust investigation launched by the U.S. government against Google. *How do you think this might affect Google's culture over time?*

Reference Groups

Reference groups influence organizational behavior and purchasing decisions. Perhaps the most powerful type of reference group in industrial markets is that of lead users. **Lead users** are *innovative organizations that derive a great deal of their success from leading change.* As a result, their adoption of a new product, service, technology, or manufacturing process is watched and often emulated by the majority.[41] This statement from a Hewlett-Packard salesperson illustrates their role:

> Another aspect of hospital buying behavior is the role of key accounts. A pyramid of influence operates in this market, with smaller and medium-sized hospitals often relying on larger research and teaching hospitals for technology cues. Therefore, maintaining a strong position in influential hospitals is critical.[42]

Other reference groups such as trade associations, financial analysts, and dealer organizations also influence an organization's decision to buy or not buy a given product, or to buy or not buy from a given supplier. **Reference group infrastructure** refers to *the flow of purchase influence within an industry.* As an example, the success of a new technology product depends on how the firm influences the reference groups located along the continuum separating it from its market. The more the firm gains positive endorsement or use throughout this infrastructure, the greater its chances of customers treating it as a preferred source of supply.

If we combine the concept of lead users with reference group infrastructure, as shown in Figure 19–2, we have a more comprehensive picture of organizational reference group systems.

Combining Lead-User and Infrastructure Reference Groups

FIGURE 19-2

User reference groups

Infrastructure reference groups

Followers
Early adopters
Lead user
Business press
Trade press
Financial analysts
Industry analysts
Intermediaries
Supportive products
Firm

Market push
Lead users accelerate market adoption

Market pull
Lead users accelerate diffusion of information through infrastructure

Source: R. Best and R. Angelihard, "Strategies for Leveraging a Technology Advantage," *Handbook of Business Strategy,* 1988.

Because the lead users play such a critical role, their adoption of a product, technology, or vendor can influence the overall infrastructure in two powerful ways. First, a lead user's decision to adopt a given supplier's innovative product adds credibility to the product and supplier. This in turn has a strong positive impact on the infrastructure that stands between the firm and its remaining target customers. Second, a lead-user decision to purchase will have a direct impact on firms inclined to follow market trends.

The strategy implication of this is clear. Marketers of new industrial products, particularly technology products, should focus initial efforts on securing sales to visible lead users.

INTERNAL FACTORS INFLUENCING ORGANIZATIONAL CULTURE

Organizational Values

Hewlett-Packard (HP) and Apple Computer both manufacture and market computers. However, each organization has a distinct organizational culture. HP is corporate and formal and takes itself seriously. Apple is less formal, is creative, and promotes a more open organizational culture. Marketing managers must understand these differences in order to best serve the respective organizational needs.

LO3

As you examine the following eight common business values, think of how HP might differ from Apple, Macy's from Target, Amazon.com from Rakuten.com, or FedEx from the U.S. Postal Service. Each is a large organization, but each has a unique set of values that

Tips for Building a Positive Organizational Culture: Examples from Business

Organizational culture plays a critical role in shaping an organization, the lives of its employees, and the relationships with vendors and customers that surround it within its supply chain. A recent research report stated that 95 percent of human resource leaders believe culture drives business results. Increases in employee satisfaction, teamwork, engagement, and retention are just a few of the internal rewards that are to be reaped.[43]

However, external benefits dealing with developing relationships in the supply chain that ultimately lead to revenue generation are also extensive. As more Millennials have joined the organizational ranks, increased emphasis has been placed on the organization's culture. Studies show that Millennials place greater importance on a positive culture than on their own compensation. This sentiment applies to both the organizations they work for, as well as those with which they do business. One study finds that 80 percent of Millennial B2B buyers consider the organizational culture of its vendors to be an important factor, particularly relating to values such as trust, transparency, the environment,

society, and philanthropic issues. These buyers strongly consider a fit between the two organizational cultures when forging and maintaining lasting B2B relationships.

While there is no formula to create and replicate the "ideal" organizational culture, observation of companies that have successfully built positive organizational cultures can provide fruitful lessons and set examples for others to emulate. The following are current examples of such companies and key elements important to their cultures:

- **Larger common goal.** Southwest Airlines does an excellent job of sharing its goals and vision with its employees, as well as giving them license to take initiative in providing extra effort and service to others in fulfilling that vision. Instilling shared values encourages a sense of excitement among employees and being part of a larger common purpose.
- **Sense of safety and well-being.** Chevron established a positive organizational culture by showing employees "the Chevron way" of caring about their personal health and safety. This value really sets Chevron apart in an industry

underlies its organizational culture. To the degree that organizations differ on these values, a firm marketing to them will have to adapt its marketing approach.

1. Risk taking is admired and rewarded.
2. Competition is more important than cooperation.
3. Hard work comes first, leisure second.
4. Individual efforts take precedence over collective efforts.
5. Any problem can be solved.
6. Active decision making is essential.
7. Change is positive and is actively sought.
8. Performance is more important than rank or status.

The values as stated above are representative of an innovative organization that seeks change, views problems as opportunities, and rewards individual efforts.[44] It is hard to imagine the U.S. Postal Service or many other bureaucratic organizations encouraging such values. On the other hand, these values underlie many high-technology start-up organizations.

where competitors sometimes have a negative reputation for safety. Chevron provides health and fitness centers as well as health-oriented programs like massages and personal trainers for its employees.

- **Evolution of culture.** Google has a reputation for its extremely positive organizational culture with benefits such as free meals, employee trips and parties, gyms, and dog-friendly environments—and has been the model for many other small startup companies that followed. As Google grew and expanded to different locations, its positive organizational culture evolved with it, while keeping its focus on core values (work–life balance in this case).
- **Display of trust.** Adobe is a company that is known for its creative products. To encourage this creativity within the organization, Adobe gives its employees challenging projects along with the freedom and support needed to succeed. Managers deliberately do not micromanage employees because that implies a lack of trust. Instead, managers act as coaches. Risk taking is promoted among employees without fear of penalty. In this way, employees feel a sense of trust, independence, and freedom to experiment and create the solutions possible.

Having a positive organizational culture is not only important to Millennial employees but can also provide a competitive advantage over others. Each company discussed here has clearly invested heavily on building a desired culture based on values shared by its employees, vendors, and customers.

Critical Thinking Questions

1. Research the companies discussed in these examples. How have firmographics played a role in the development of each organizational culture discussed in this insight?

2. Research the organizational values of one of the companies discussed in the insight and one of its competitors. Compare and contrast the values, and comment on how those values shaped the organizational culture of each of the two companies.

3. Consider the organizational culture of organizations where you have been employed. Reflect on how each of these cultural elements discussed above were reflected (or not) in those organizations. How do you feel that they may have impacted the organizational culture?

Consumer Insight 19–1 provides a look into how organizations try to build positive cultures through shared values.

The BCLP Law ad in Illustration 19–6 would appeal to organizations and individuals with an orientation toward efficiency and active problem solving.

Perception

To process information, a firm must go through the same sequential stages of exposure, attention, and interpretation as consumers. Of course, given the more complex nature of organizations, the processes involved are also more complex.[45] A business customer develops certain images of seller organizations from their products, people, and organizational activities. Like people, organizations have memories and base their decisions on images or memories they have developed. Once an image is formed by an organization, it is very difficult to change. Therefore, it is important for an organization to develop a sound communications strategy to build and reinforce a desired image or brand position.[46]

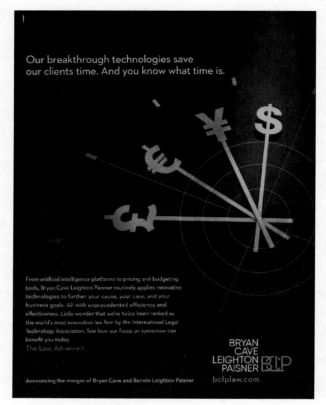

Source: Bryan Cave Leighton Paisner LLP

The Comcast Business ad in Illustration 19–7 provides a great example of how industrial ads can be designed to work across cultures.[47]

Ad size and repetition have a positive effect on awareness and action. One major study found a 20 percent gain in awareness when two or more ads are placed in the same issue of a specialized business magazine compared with only one.[48] The size of the advertisement also affects action in the form of inquiries generated by the advertisement. Research examining B2B magazine advertisements shows that full-page ads are much more effective at generating inquiries than smaller ads. However, print advertising was recently reported to be slightly less effective than traditional online banner ads.[49]

While advertising (online and traditional) plays an important role in communicating to organizations, direct sales calls are the most important persuasive element of the communications mix in most industrial markets. This is the case despite the high cost of such calls, which is thought to be in the range of $300 per call. One reason for the significant role of salespeople is that businesses are not just economic entities. Business buyers prefer to do business with firms they know, like, and trust. Those relationships are most often formed between members of the firms involved, with sales personnel being the most common representative of the selling organization. As one successful salesperson stated:

You have to have a great product but you also have to make the customer like you as a salesperson.[50]

Source: Comcast Corporation

Learning

Like individuals, organizations learn through their experiences and perceptions.[51] Positive experiences with vendors are rewarding and tend to be repeated. Purchasing processes and procedures that prove effective tend to be institutionalized in rules and policies. Likewise, negative experiences with vendors produce learning and avoidance behavior, and purchasing procedures that don't work are generally discarded. Developing the capacity to learn efficiently is increasingly a key to organizational success.[52]

Motives and Emotions

Organizational decisions tend to be less emotional than many consumer purchase decisions. However, because humans with psychological needs and emotions influence these decisions, this aspect of marketing to an organizational customer cannot be overlooked or underestimated.

Quite often there is considerable personal or career risk in organizational purchase decisions. The risk of making a bad purchase decision can elicit feelings of self-doubt or psychological discomfort. These are personal emotions that will influence purchase decisions. FedEx appeals to risk avoidance with ads that ask, in essence:

How do you explain to your boss that the important papers didn't arrive but you saved the company $5 by using a less expensive overnight mail service?

ORGANIZATIONAL BUYER SEGMENTS AND MARKETING STRATEGY

LO4

Each of the factors discussed in this chapter is important for marketing strategy because each contributes to the type of buyer that an organization faces. There are many different ways to characterize or segment organizational buyers. One important way is in terms of transactional versus relational exchanges. Some buyers, due to size, their market position and strategies, and culture, are more transactional in their approach to buying, while others are more relational. **Transactional exchanges** *involve single transactions, are short lived, involve few investments by the buyer and seller in the relationship, and involve low loyalty.* Alternatively, **relational exchanges** *involve multiple events, occur over an extended period of time, involve significant investments by the buyer and seller, and involve higher levels of loyalty.*[53] The following excerpt from an industry analyst puts it this way:

> There are two types of buyers: transactional and relational. The transactional buyer, as implied by the name, is focused only on the transaction. What's the cheapest, the best, the fastest for the money. If a distributor [seller] wins one transaction, he earns no loyalty from the transactional customer, only the opportunity to compete again in the next transaction. A relational customer, on the other hand, is focused on finding a distributor he can trust and depend upon. Money [price] is a factor, but the relational customer believes that if he builds a relationship with a trustworthy distributor, he'll be treated fairly on price.[54]

Research suggests that many of the factors we have discussed in this chapter influence whether the relationship will be transactional or relational. These factors are:[55]

- *Industry structure.* When there are only a few buyers, then buyers have power over sellers. In many cases, because the seller threat is reduced, buyers may prefer more relational exchanges to facilitate value creation activities of the partnership.
- *Decision-making culture.* When buying decisions are relegated to the procurement department, a short-term and price-focused decision-making culture is more likely and such buyers should tend to prefer transactional exchanges.
- *Decision-making structure.* When the DMU is larger and cross-functional, this reflects a more complex decision process and buyers facing such a structure should tend to prefer relational exchanges.
- *Risk tolerance.* Buyers with lower risk tolerance should prefer relational exchanges because such an approach reduces uncertainty over access to and quality of the inputs they buy.
- *Nature of the purchase.* Buyers engaged in complex purchases (e.g., new task buy) that require substantial education and after-sale support should tend to prefer relational exchanges that deliver on these important aspects.

The notion of relational exchange relates to *relationship marketing,* which we discussed in Chapter 18. Relationship marketing is at least as important in industrial marketing as it is in consumer marketing.[56] The basic idea at the organizational level is for the seller to work closely with the buyer over time with the objective of enhancing the buyer's profits or operations while also making a profit. Relationships are formed to create value that otherwise wouldn't be possible. That is, a buyer and suppler working together may be able to pool resources, technology, and patents to develop a new product faster and cheaper than either could have done alone.

Healthy business relationships depend on a number of value dimensions.[57] These are:

- *Legitimacy and compatibility.* This dimension deals with actual delivered quality, perceived quality as represented by brand reputation, as well as trust and reliability.
- *Social relations.* This dimension deals with friendship, closeness, and the extent of buyer–seller communication.
- *Economic and shared values.* This dimension deals with the extent to which buyer and seller are integrated through joint manufacturing, information technology, and values.
- *Learning bonds.* This dimension deals with the extent to which buyer and seller cooperate in learning through joint research and development, staff exchanges, and training.

There are often gaps between buyers' and sellers' perceptions of relationship quality, with sellers overrating quality, particularly early in the relationship.

Relationship Length	Buyer	Seller
Short Term		
Legitimacy/compatibility	4.9	5.7*
Social	4.7	5.2*
Economic/shared values	4.5	4.8
Learning	2.8	3.1
Medium Term		
Legitimacy/compatibility	4.9	5.4*
Social	4.8	4.9
Economic/shared values	4.5	4.7
Learning	3.3	2.9
Long Term		
Legitimacy/compatibility	5.4	5.3
Social	5.2	5.4
Economic/shared values	5.1	5.0
Learning	3.8	3.4

Note: Higher numbers mean higher perceived performance. Asterisk means significant difference.

Source: Adapted from B. R. Barnes, P. Naude, and P. Mitchell, "Perceptual Gaps and Similarities in Buyer–Seller Dyadic Relationships," *Industrial Marketing Management* 36 (2007), p. 667.

Relationships are dynamic, and the strategies employed to maintain those relationships may need to be adapted over time.[58] Clearly, the long-term success of a relationship depends on buyers perceiving high value from the relationship. This is less likely earlier in the relationship and sellers tend to be biased toward more positive perceptions. Such *mis*-perceptions are clearly important to examine, and the buyer–seller gaps must be eliminated or substantially reduced for the relationship to remain healthy. This can involve periodic assessments by both parties using so-called relationship performance scorecards and the development of strategies to reduce any value gaps.[59]

Some businesses make the mistake of assuming all buyers are worth developing relational exchanges with. As in the consumer domain (B2C), in the organizational domain (B2B) this is not always true. Some customers are worth having strong relationships with, some should be managed as transactional clients, and some should be terminated. Consumer Insight 19-2 provides insights into these strategic issues and decisions.

Loyalty and Relationship Marketing Strategies

Not all relationships are created equal and not all buyers are worth a relational investment. Buyers who want and are willing to pay for value-added services and who desire positive relationship outcomes such as enhanced performance and lower costs of transactions are worth investing in and having relationships with. Those that see the world through a strict price lens and don't want, or won't pay for, value-added services need to be treated in a different manner.[60]

It begins by understanding two things about a buyer:

1. How much does it cost to serve them? This relates to the profitability of a buyer and also how much of an investment in value-added services can be made while still being profitable.

2. Where is the buyer on the "loyalty ladder." Buyers at higher levels of loyalty want to make relationship-specific investments in your firm, want to collaborate on new ventures, are willing to pay premiums, and so on.

Combining these two factors leads to four different organizational buyer segments:

- **Commodity Buyers** (Low Cost/Low Loyalty). These customers don't want value-added services and don't want to pay for them. They simply want the basic product (commodity) at the lowest price. These customers, if they are profitable due to their low cost, should be served as a transactional customer.

- **Underperforming Buyers** (High Cost/Low Loyalty). Unless the firm can cut costs to make them a profitable commodity buyer, or convince them to pay for the value-added services to make them a profitable partner, they generally should be terminated. While not easy, it actually can be more profitable to NOT sell to a buyer.

- **Partner Buyers** (High Cost/High Loyalty). Although expensive to serve, these customers generally are loyal and thus tend to be willing to pay for the value-added services provided. These customers should be managed in a relational manner, with an eye toward increasing the efficiencies of the relationship to lower costs and increase profits.

- **Most Valuable Customers** (Low Cost/High Loyalty). These buyers are most profitable because they demand and pay for value-added services but are lower in cost to serve due to economies of scale, experience, and so on. These customers, like partners, should be managed in a relational manner.

Many businesses market and manage to their buyers in the same way. The buyer segments listed above, however, show that some buyers are worth having a relationship with and others are not. One expert estimates that fewer than 10 percent of buyers fall into the Most Valuable Customer category. Because relational or relationship marketing is expensive in terms of both time and effort, only some buyer segments are worthy of having a relationship with.

Critical Thinking Questions

1. What makes some customers more valuable than others?

2. How might you move an underperformer to partner status?

3. Why are commodity buyers worth holding onto?

SMARTBOOK

LO1: Describe the organizational purchase process.

Like households, organizations make many buying decisions. In some instances, these buying decisions are routine replacement decisions; at other times, they involve new, complex purchase decisions. Three purchase situations are common to organizational buying: *straight rebuy, modified rebuy,* and *new task.* Each of these purchase situations will elicit different organizational behaviors.

The organizational decision process involves problem recognition, information search, evaluation and selection, purchase implementation, and postpurchase evaluation. While functional attributes such as price and quality certainly play a critical role, brand image also can be important, in some cases even increasing the prices that organizational buyers are willing to pay.

Purchase implementation is more complex, and the terms and conditions more important than in household decisions. How payment is made is of major importance. Finally, use and postpurchase evaluation are often quite formal. Many organizations will conduct detailed in-use tests to determine the life-cycle costs of competing products or spend considerable time evaluating a new product before placing large orders. Satisfaction depends on a variety of criteria and on the opinions of many different people. To achieve customer satisfaction, each of these individuals has to be satisfied with the criteria important to him or her.

LO2: Summarize the external factors that influence organizational culture.

Organizations have a style or manner of operating that we characterize as organizational culture. *Firmographics* (organization characteristics such as size, activities, objectives, location, and industry category, and characteristics of the composition of the organization such as the gender, age, education, and income distribution of employees) have a major influence on organizational culture. The process of grouping buyer organizations into market segments on the basis of similar firmographics is called *macrosegmentation.*

Reference groups play a key role in business-to-business (B2B) markets. *Reference group infrastructures* exist in most organizational markets. These reference groups often include third-party suppliers, distributors, industry experts, trade publications, financial analysts, and key customers. *Lead users* have been shown to be a key reference group that influences both the reference group infrastructure and other potential users.

Other external influences on organizational culture include the local culture in which the organization operates and the type of government it confronts.

LO3: Summarize the internal factors that influence organizational culture.

Internal factors affecting organizational culture include organizational values, perception, learning, memory, motives, and emotions. Organizations hold values that influence the organization's style. Individuals in the organization also hold these values in varying degrees. Organizations also develop images, have motives, and learn. Seller organizations can affect how they are perceived through a variety of communication alternatives. Print advertising, direct mail, sales calls, and online are common. Whereas organizations have rational motives, their decisions are influenced and made by people with emotions. A seller organization has to understand and satisfy both to be successful.

LO4: Explain the influence of organizational buyer segments on marketing strategy.

Each of the factors discussed in this chapter is important for marketing strategy because each contributes to the type of buyer that an organization faces. One important way to segment organizational buyers is in terms of transactional versus relational exchanges. *Transactional exchanges* involve single transactions, are short lived, involve few investments by the buyer and seller in the relationship, and involve low loyalty. Alternatively, *relational exchanges* involve multiple events, occur over an extended period of time, involve significant investments by the buyer and seller, and involve higher levels of loyalty. Factors such as industry structure, decision-making culture and structure, risk tolerance, and the nature of the purchase influence whether a buyer takes a relational or transactional approach. Marketers must adjust their strategies, particularly as they regard relationship marketing, depending on the type of buyer they face. Periodic audits can be helpful in ensuring that buyers are getting the value they desire from a relationship.

KEY TERMS

Buying centers 694
Corporate culture 705
Decision-making units
 (DMUs) 694
Firmographics 705

Lead users 708
Macrosegmentation 707
Organizational culture 704
Reference group infrastructure 708
Relational exchanges 714

Terms and conditions 702
Transactional exchanges 714
Two-stage decision process 700

REVIEW QUESTIONS

1. How can an organization have a culture? What factors contribute to different organizational cultures?

2. How would different organizational activities and objectives affect organizational culture?

3. What are *organizational values?* How do they differ from personal values?

4. What are *firmographics,* and how do they influence organizational culture?

5. Define *macrosegmentation* and describe the variables used to create a macrosegmentation of an organizational market.

6. What types of reference groups exist in organizational markets?

7. What are *lead users,* and how do they influence word-of-mouth communication and the sales of a new product?

8. What is a *decision-making unit?* How does it vary by purchase situation?

9. How can a seller organization influence perceptions of a buyer organization?

10. What are *organizational motives?*

11. What is a *two-stage decision process?*

12. What is the distinction between relational and transactional exchanges?

13. What are the three purchase situations commonly encountered by organizations? How do organizations typically respond to each situation?

14. In what ways does the Internet play a role in the organizational decision process?

DISCUSSION QUESTIONS

15. Describe three organizations with distinctly different organizational cultures. Explain why they have different organizational cultures and the factors that have helped shape the style of each.

16. Respond to the questions in Consumer Insight 19–1.

17. Describe how Hewlett-Packard might vary in its organizational culture from the following. Justify your response.
    a. Dell Computer
    b. Lenovo
    c. Apple

18. Discuss how the following pairs differ from each other in terms of organizational activities and objectives. Discuss how these differences influence organizational cultures.
    a. Walmart, Target
    b. FedEx, the U.S. Postal Service
    c. Amazon.com, Banana Republic
    d. Mercedes-Benz, Kraft Foods

19. What role does brand/brand image play in the organizational decision process?

20. Discuss how Acer might use a macrosegmentation strategy to sell computers to businesses.

21. Discuss how a small biotechnology firm could influence the reference group infrastructure and the lead users to accelerate adoption of its products in the market.

22. "Industrial purchases, unlike consumer purchases, do not have an emotional component." Comment.

23. For each of the three purchase situations described in the chapter (Table 19–2), describe a typical purchase for the following:
    a. Wendy's
    b. Mercedes-Benz
    c. Target
    d. Your university
    e. Publix

24. Respond to the questions in Consumer Insight 19–2.

APPLICATION ACTIVITIES

25. Interview an appropriate person at a large and at a small organization, and ask each to identify purchase situations that could be described as straight rebuy, modified rebuy, and new task. For each organization and purchase situation, determine the following:
    a. Size and functional representation of the decision-making unit
    b. The number of choice criteria considered
    c. Length of the decision process
    d. Number of vendors or suppliers considered

26. Review two issues of a magazine targeting organization buyers or purchase influencers. What percent of the ads contain emotional or other noneconomic appeals?

27. Interview a representative from a commercial, a governmental, and a nonprofit organization. For each, determine its firmographics, activities, and objectives. Then relate these differences to differences in the organizational cultures of the organizations.

28. Interview a person responsible for purchasing for a business or government agency. Have that person describe and evaluate any attempts at relationship marketing by its suppliers. What do you conclude?

29. For a given organization, identify its reference groups. Create a hierarchical diagram, as shown in Figure 19-2, and discuss how this organization could influence groups that would in turn create favorable communication concerning this organization.

30. Interview a manager at a business or government agency who has recently been involved in an important purchase decision (e.g., a capital equipment acquisition). Have the manager describe the key influences at each phase of the decision process as shown in Table 19-3. Discuss how this information might be used in developing a marketing strategy for this industry.

REFERENCES

1. This opener based on "B2B End-User Buyers Are Human, Too," *eMarketer,* October 29, 2014, www.emarketer.com/Article/B2B-End-User-Buyers-Human-Too/1011423, accessed July 22, 2018; K. Snyder and P. Hilal, "The Changing Face of B2B Marketing," *Think with Google,* March 2015, www.thinkwithgoogle.com/consumer-insights/the-changing-face-b2b-marketing/, accessed July 22, 2018; J. Spero, "How Mobile Is Reshaping the B2B Landscape for Growth," *Think with Google,* October 2017, www.thinkwithgoogle.com/marketing-resources/experience-design/b2b-marketing-reshaping-growth/, accessed July 22, 2018; R. Archacki, K. Protextor, G. Barrios, and N. De Bellefonds, "Mobile Marketing and the New B2B Buyer," *Boston Consulting Group,* September 29, 2017, www.bcg.com/publications/2017/marketing-sales-digital-go-to-market-transformation-mobile-marketing-new-b2b-buyer.aspx, accessed July 22, 2018; J. Carter, "B2B E-Commerce Trends to Take Notice of in 2018," *Forbes,* February 15, 2018, www.forbes.com/sites/theyec/2018/02/15/b2b-e-commerce-trends-to-take-notice-of-in-2018/#ff8f6ca7339e, accessed July 22, 2018; R. Genson, "The B2B Ecommerce Trends Report: Millennial Buyers, Payment Options and a Maturing Market," *Big Commerce,* July 19, 2018, www.bigcommerce.com/blog/b2b-ecommerce-trends/, accessed July 22, 2018; various company websites.

2. See e.g., T. V. Bonoma, "Major Sales" *Harvard Business Review,* July–August 2006, pp. 2–13.

3. F. V. Cespedes, "Hewlett-Packard Imaging Systems Division," Harvard Business School case 9-593-080, September 6, 1994, p. 4.

4. R. Ventakesh, A. K. Kohli, and G. Zaltman, "Influence Strategies in Buying Centers," *Journal of Marketing,* October 1995, pp. 71–82; M. A. Farrell and B. Schroder, "Influence Strategies in Organizational Buying Decisions," *Industrial Marketing Management* 25 (1996), pp. 393–403.

5. See W. J. Johnson and J. E. Lewin, "Organizational Buying Behavior," *Journal of Business Research,* January 1996, pp. 1–15; E. J. Wilson, R. C. McMurrian, and A. G. Woodside, "How Buyers Frame Problems," *Psychology & Marketing,* June 2001, pp. 617–55. See also L. C. Leonidou, "Industrial Buyers' Influence Strategies," *Journal of Business and Industrial Marketing* 21, no. 1 (2005), pp. 33–42.

6. S. J. Puri and C. M. Sashi, "Anatomy of a Complex Computer Purchase," *Industrial Marketing Management,* January 1994, pp. 17–27; E. Day and J. C. Barksdale Jr., "Organizational Purchasing of Professional Services," *Journal of Business and Industrial Marketing* 9, no. 3 (1994), pp. 44–51; D. Narayandas, "Building Loyalty in Business Markets," *Harvard Business Review,* September 2005, pp. 1–9.

7. See A. M. Weiss and J. B. Heide, "The Nature of Organizational Search in High-Technology Markets," *Journal of Marketing Research,* May 1993, pp. 220–33.

8. P. M. Doney and G. M. Armstrong, "Effects of Accountability on Symbolic Information Search and Information Analysis by Organizational Buyers," *Journal of the Academy of Marketing Science,* Winter 1996, pp. 57–65; P. L. Dawes, D. Y. Lee, and D. Midgley, "Organizational Learning in High-Technology Purchasing Situations," *Industrial Marketing Management* 36 (2007), pp. 285–99.

9. D. Narayandas, "SalesSoft, Inc.," Harvard Business School case 9-596-112, March 24, 1998.

10. For a discussion of organizational decision making, see J. B. Heide and W. M. Weiss, "Vendor Consideration and Switching Behavior for Buyers in High-Technology Markets," *Journal of Marketing,* July 1995, pp. 30–43; W. E. Patton III, "Use of Human Judgment Models in Industrial Buyers' Vendor Selection Decisions," *Industrial Marketing Management* 25 (1996), pp. 135–49; J. Yu

and C. Tsai, "A Decision Framework for Supplier Rating and Purchase Allocation," *Computers & Industrial Engineering* 55 (2008), pp. 634–46.

11. J. E. Stoddard and E. F. Fern, "Buying Group Choice," *Psychology & Marketing,* January 2002, pp. 59–90.

12. M. Bendixen, K. A. Bukasa, and R. Abratt, "Brand Equity in the Business-to-Business Market," *Industrial Marketing Management* 33 (2004), pp. 371–80.

13. See K. N. Thompson, B. J. Coe, and J. R. Lewis, "Gauging the Value of Suppliers' Products," *Journal of Business and Industrial Marketing* 9, no. 2 (1994), pp. 29–40.

14. See e.g., A. Kumar and D. B. Grisaffe, "Effects of Extrinsic Attributes on Perceived Quality, Customer Value, and Behavioral Intentions in B2B Settings," *Journal of Business-to-Business Marketing* 11, no. 4 (2004), pp. 43–63.

15. M. E. Drumwright, "Socially Responsible Organizational Buying," *Journal of Marketing,* July 1994, pp. 1–19. See also D. Pujari, K. Peattie, and G. Wright, "Organizational Antecedents of Environmental Responsiveness in Industrial New Product Development," *Industrial Marketing Management* 33 (2004), pp. 381–91.

16. M. Bendixen et al., "Brand Equity in the Business-to-Business Market," *Industrial Marketing Management* 33 (2004), pp. 371–80. See also P. Michell, J. King, and J. Reast, "Brand Values Related to Industrial Products," *Industrial Marketing Management* 30 (2001), pp. 415–25; H. Hansen, B. M. Samuelsen, and P. R. Silseth, "Customer Perceived Value in B-t-B Service Relationships," *Industrial Marketing Management,* April 2008, pp. 206–17.

17. See e.g., G. S. Lynn et al., "Factors Impacting the Adoption and Effectiveness of the World Wide Web in Marketing," *Industrial Marketing Management* 31 (2002), pp. 35–49; H. Min and W. P. Galle, "E-Purchasing," *Industrial Marketing Management* 32 (2003), pp. 227–33.

18. K. Smith, "Service Aspects of Industrial Products," *Industrial Marketing Management* 27 (1998), pp. 83–93.

19. S. Y. Lam et al., "Customer Value, Satisfaction, Loyalty, and Switching Costs," *Journal of the Academy of Marketing Science* 32, no. 3 (2004), pp. 293–311; R. E. Plank and S. J. Newell, "The Effect of Social Conflict on Relationship Loyalty in Business Markets," *Industrial Marketing Management* 36 (2007), pp. 59–67; C. Jayawardhena, "Outcomes of Service Encounter Quality in a Business-to-Business Context," *Industrial Marketing Management* 36 (2007), pp. 575–88.

20. S. W. Hansen, J. E. Swan, and T. L. Powers, "Encouraging 'Friendly' Complaint Behavior in Industrial Markets," *Industrial Marketing Management* 25 (1996), pp. 271–81.

21. United Technologies, "UTC Products at a Glance: OTISLINE," press release, http://utc.com, accessed July 28, 2008.

22. P. Demery, "U.S. B2B E-Commerce Is on Course to Hit $1.18 Trillion by 2021," *Digital Commerce,* June 5, 2017, www.digitalcommerce360.com/2017/06/05/u-s-b2b-e-commerce-course-hit-1-18-trillion-2021/, accessed July 22, 2018; A. Orendorff, "Global Ecommerce: Statistics and International Growth Trends," *Shopify,* September 1, 2017, www.shopify.com/enterprise/global-ecommerce-statistics, accessed July 22, 2018; Statista, "E-commerce Share of Total B2B Sales in the United States from 2015-2021," 2018, www.statista.com/statistics/273104/us-b2b-e-commerce-share/, accessed July 22, 2018.

23. H. H. Bauer, M. Grether, and M. Leach, "Building Customer Relations over the Internet," *Industrial Marketing Management* 31 (2002),

pp. 155–63; J. B. MacDonald and K. Smith, "The Effects of Technology-Mediated Communication on Industrial Buyer Behavior," *Industrial Marketing Management* 33 (2004), pp. 107–16; G. Easton and L. Araujo, "Evaluating the Impact of B2B E-commerce," *Industrial Marketing Management* 32 (2003), pp. 431–39; L. M. Hunter et al., "A Classification of Business-to-Business Buying Decisions," *Industrial Marketing Management* 33 (2004), pp. 145–54.

24. G. Hotchkiss et al., *The Role of Search in Business to Business Buying Decisions* (Kelowna, BC, Canada: Enquiro, October 27, 2004); P. Bruemmer, "Search Plays Key Role in B2B Sales," *Search Engine Guide,* June 2005, www.searchengineguide.com, accessed July 1, 2011; Snyder and Hilal, "The Changing Face of B2B Marketing"; K. Lee, "Most B2B Buyers Use Social Media in Their Research," *Fronetics,* July 26, 2016, www.fronetics.com/most-b2b-buyers-use-social-media-research/, accessed July 23, 2018.

25. Bruemmer, "Search Plays Key Role in B2B Sales."

26. "Google It: Here's Why 66% of B2B Marketers Use Search Engine Marketing," *IZEA,* September 26, 2016, https://izea.com/2016/09/26/b2b-marketers-search-engine-marketing/, accessed July 23, 2018; "B2B Content Marketing 2017 Benchmark, Budgets and Trends—North America," *Content Marketing Institute,* September 2017, https://contentmarketinginstitute.com/wp-content/uploads/2016/09/2017_B2B_Research_FINAL.pdf, accessed July 23, 2018.

27. C. Klein, "Death of the Dark Side of Sales," *Sales Bloggers Union,* February 15, 2010, www.salesbloggers.com, accessed July 1, 2011.

28. G. Chakraborty, V. Lala, and D. Warren, "What Do Customers Consider Important in B2B Web Sites?," *Journal of Advertising Research,* March 2003, pp. 50–61; G. Chakraborty, P. Srivastava, and D. L. Warren, "Understanding Corporate B2B Web Sites' Effectiveness from North American and European Perspective," *Industrial Marketing Management* 34 (2005), pp. 420–29.

29. "B2B End-User Buyers Are Human, Too."

30. R. Agnihotri, R. Dingus, M. Hu, and M. Krush, "Social Media: Influencing Customer Satisfaction in B2B Sales," *Industrial Marketing Management* 53 (February 2016), pp. 172–80.

31. See S. Kitchell, "Corporate Culture, Environmental Adaptation, and Innovation Adoption," *Journal of the Academy of Marketing Science,* Summer 1995, pp. 195–205; P. Berthon, L. F. Pitt, and M. T. Ewing, "Corollaries of the Collective," *Journal of the Academy of Marketing Science,* Spring 2001, pp. 135–50.

32. K. M. File and R. A. Prince, "A Psychographic Segmentation of Industrial Family Businesses," *Industrial Marketing Management,* May 1996, pp. 223–34.

33. M. Ewing, A. Caruana, and H. Wong, "Some Consequences of *Guanxi,*" *Journal of International Consumer Marketing* 4 (2000), p. 77. See also F. Balfour, "You Say *Guanxi,* I Say Schmoozing," *BusinessWeek,* November 19, 2007, pp. 84–85; J. Luo, E. Ngai, and M. Liu, "Green Supply Chain Collaboration Implementation in China: The Mediating Role of Guanxi," *Transportation Research Part E: Logistics and Transportation Review* 74 (February 2015), pp. 37–49 (reprint).

34. H. Gao, D. Ballantyne, and J. G. Knight, "Paradoxes and Guanxi Dilemmas in Emerging Chinese-Western Intercultural Relationships," *Industrial Marketing Management,* February 2010, pp. 264–72.

35. See J. E. Stoddard and E. F. Fern, "Risk-Taking Propensity in Supplier Choice," *Psychology & Marketing,* October 1999, pp. 563–82.

36. See R. L. Griffith and L. G. Pol, "Segmenting Industrial Markets," *Industrial Marketing Management,* January 1994, pp. 39–46.

37. J. Gilbert, "Small but Mighty," *Sales & Marketing Management,* January 2004, pp. 30–35.

38. G. Brewer, "Selling an Intangible," *Sales & Marketing Management,* January 1998, pp. 52–58. See also S. P. Kalafatis and V. Cheston, "Normative Models and Practical Applications of Segmentation in Business Markets," *Industrial Marketing Management* 26 (1997), pp. 519–30.

39. See e.g., C. Nakata and K. Sivakumar, "Instituting the Marketing Concept in a Multinational Setting," *Journal of the Academy of Marketing Science* 29, no. 3 (2001), pp. 255–75.

40. See F. Gibb, "To Give or Not to Give," *Sales & Marketing Management,* September 1994, pp. 136–39.

41. A. N. Link and J. Neufeld, "Innovation vs. Imitation: Investigating Alternative R&D Strategies," *Applied Economics* 18 (1986), pp. 1359–63.

42. Cespedes, "Hewlett-Packard Imaging Systems Division."

43. Insight is based on E. Almquist, "How Digital Natives Are Changing B2B Purchasing," *Harvard Business Review,* March 14, 2018, https://hbr.org/2018/03/how-digital-natives-are-changing-b2b-purchasing, accessed July 24, 2018; R. Baiorunos, "Why Organizational Culture Is the Most Powerful, Practical Tool for Impact and What to Do About It," *Forbes,* June 6, 2017, www.forbes.com/sites/forbesnonprofitcouncil/2017/06/06/why-organizational-culture-is-the-most-powerful-practical-tool-for-impact-and-what-to-do-about-it/#47a27c1e2907, accessed July 15, 2018; M. Daimler, "Why Great Employees Leave 'Great Cultures,'" *Harvard Business Review,* May 11, 2018, https://hbr.org/2018/05/why-great-employees-leave-great-cultures, accessed July 15, 2018; "Organizational Culture: What Is Corporate Culture?," *Virgin Pulse,* www.virginpulse.com/organizational-culture/, accessed July 15, 2018; A. Fridman, "Why Culture Is the Key to Trust in B2B Customer Relationships," *Oracle,* November 17, 2017, https://blogs.oracle.com/smb/why-culture-is-the-key-to-trust-in-b2b-customer-relationships, accessed July 24, 2018; S. Patel, "10 Examples of Companies with Fantastic Cultures," *Entrepreneur,* August 6, 2015, https://www.entrepreneur.com/article/249174, accessed July 15, 2018; D. Smith, "How to Define and Build a Great Organizational Culture in 2018," *Medium,* December 18, 2017, https://medium.com/the-mission/how-to-define-and-build-a-great-organizational-culture-in-2018-f8b972e433b6, accessed July 15, 2018.

44. For a discussion of innovativeness, see G. T. M. Hult, R. F. Hurley, and G. A. Knight, "Innovativeness," *Industrial Marketing Management* 33 (2004), pp. 429–38.

45. D. I. Gilliland and W. J. Johnston, "Toward a Model of Business-to-Business Marketing Communications Effects," *Industrial Marketing Management* 26 (1997), pp. 15–29.

46. See S. M. Mudambi, P. Doyle, and V. Wong, "An Exploration of Branding in Industrial Markets," *Industrial Marketing Management* 26 (1997), pp. 433–46; J. Lapierre, "The Role of Corporate Image in the Evaluation of Business-to-Business Professional Services," *Journal of Professional Services Marketing* 16 (1998), pp. 21–41; D. H. McQuiston, "Successful Branding of a Commodity Product," *Industrial Marketing Management* 33 (2004), pp. 345–54.

47. L. Hochwald, "It's the Sizzle That Sells," *Sales & Marketing Management,* April 1997, p. 51.

48. *CARR Report No. 120.3* (Boston: Cahners Publishing Co., undated).

49. "B2B Content Marketing 2017 Benchmark, Budgets and Trends—North America."

50. G. Conlon, "A Day in the Life of Sales," *Sales & Marketing Management,* September 1997, pp. 42–63.

51. See J. M. Sinkula, "Market Information Processing and Organizational Learning," *Journal of Marketing,* January 1994, pp. 35–45; G. T. M. Hult and E. L. Nichols Jr., "The Organizational Buyer Behavior Learning Organization," *Industrial Marketing Management,* May 1996, pp. 197–207; S. J. Bell, G. J. Whitwell, and B. A. Lukas, "Schools of Thought in Organizational Learning," *Journal of the Academy of Marketing Science,* Winter 2002, pp. 70–86.

52. D. A. Garvin, "Building a Learning Organization," *Harvard Business Review,* July 1993, pp. 78–91; S. F. Slater and J. C. Narver, "Market Orientation and the Learning Organization," *Journal of Marketing,* July 1995, pp. 63–74; G. T. M. Hult, "Cultural Competitiveness in Global Sourcing," *Industrial Marketing Management* 31 (2002), pp. 25–34; C. Lai et al., "The Effects of Market Orientation on Relationship Learning and Relationship Performance in Industrial Marketing," *Industrial Marketing Management,* February 2009, pp. 166–72.

53. J. N. Sheth and R. H. Shah, "Till Death Do Us Part . . . but Not Always," *Industrial Marketing Management* 23 (2003), pp. 627–31.

54. M. Dandridge, "Seven Myths Busted," *Electrical Wholesaling,* March 2010.

55. Sheth and Shah, "Till Death Do Us Part . . . but Not Always."

56. See e.g., A. Walter et al., "Functions of Industrial Supplier Relationships and Their Impact on Relationship Quality," *Industrial Marketing Management* 32 (2003), pp. 159–69; Sheth and Shah, "Till Death Do Us Part . . . but Not Always"; T. L. Keiningham, T. Perkins-Munn, and H. Evans, "The Impact of Customer Satisfaction on Share-of-Wallet in a Business-to-Business Environment," *Journal of Service Research,* August 2003, pp. 37–50.

57. B. R. Barnes, P. Naude, and P. Mitchell, "Perceptual Gaps and Similarities in Buyer–Seller Dyadic Relationships," *Industrial Marketing Management* 36 (2007), pp. 662–75. See also C. Steinman, R. Deshpande, and J. U. Farley, "Beyond Market Orientation," *Journal of the Academy of Marketing Science* 28, no. 1 (2000), pp. 109–19; P. H. Andersen and R. Kumar, "Emotions, Trust and Relationship Development in Business Relationships," *Industrial Marketing Management* 35 (2006), pp. 522–35.

58. J. Zhang, G. Watson IV, R. Palmatier, and R. Dant, "Dynamic Relationship Marketing," *Journal of Marketing* 80 (September 2016), pp. 53–75.

59. S. Janda, J. B. Murray, and S. Burton, "Manufacturer–Supplier Relationships," *Industrial Marketing Management* 31 (2002), pp. 411–20; L. F. Lages, A. Lancastre, and C. Lages, "The B2B-RELPERF Scale and Scorecard," *Industrial Marketing Management,* August 2008, pp. 686–97; J. M. Whipple, D. F. Lynch, and G. N. Nyaga, "A Buyer's Perspective on Collaborative versus Transactional Relationships," *Industrial Marketing Management* 39 (2010), pp. 507–18.

60. Insight based primarily on D. Narayandas, "Building Loyalty in Business Markets," *Harvard Business Review,* September 2005, pp. 1–9. See also K. A. Richards and E. Jones, "Customer Relationship Management," *Industrial Marketing Management,* April 2008, pp. 120–30; S. F. King and T. F. Burgess, "Understanding Success and Failure in Customer Relationship Management," *Industrial Marketing Management,* June 2008, pp. 421–31.

5-1 CUTIES: HOW COMMODITY FRUITS BECAME A BRANDED SENSATION

For many years in the United States, navel oranges reigned supreme in citrus. There weren't any particularly well-known brands of navel oranges or any other citrus for that matter; there were just various varieties of breeds of citrus that were supplied to retailers as commodity products. Retailers would remove the fruit from shipping packaging that sometimes had a supplier company brand and offer them in grocery displays devoid of any brand at all. However, around the turn of the twenty-first century, shifting consumer tastes and savvy marketers changed the entire face of the citrus industry in the United States.

Grocers began noticing an uptick in consumer demand for Spanish clementines and mandarins over navel oranges. This shift was driven in large part by consumers valuing the convenience of easy peeling and dislike of the presence of seeds in fruit. Citrus farmers in California began noticing this change and in turn began uprooting navel, lemon, and grapefruit groves and replacing them with clementines and mandarins.

Sun Pacific and Paramount Citrus, two huge citrus farming operations in California that also were aware of these shifting consumer tastes, joined forces and planted massive acreage of clementines to meet this demand. But more importantly, these two companies successfully branded their produce as Cuties. Within a few years, the Cuties group produced more than three-quarters of the seedless mandarins in the United States. The companies parted ways a number of years later, and Sun Pacific retained the Cuties brand, while Paramount Citrus created a different brand, Wonderful Halos, for the same fruit grown in the groves that they retained. According to Sun Pacific Vice President of Business Development Howard Nager:

> There are very few brands in the produce industry that a three-year-old can recognize without a label on it and say "that's a Cutie." A lot of work has been done. We were the first to come to market here and the category has just exploded. It has really driven the citrus category.

The Cuties brand is actually three different types of fruit depending on the season of the year. From the California groves, Cuties are clementines in mid-October through early January, but from January through May, they are murcotts and tangos. Sun Pacific describes all the fruits under the umbrella of mandarins. By branding all of these fruits as Cuties, Sun Pacific is able to supply retailers throughout a longer period of the year to keep up with consumer demand. Moreover, they have outsourced production to countries such as Chile and Peru for greater supply and a longer availability window for consumers.

It is important to note that Sun Pacific is dealing with two types of buyers, namely the business-to-business (B2B) customer such as retailers as well as business-to-consumer (B2C) end consumers such as individuals and households. Both are important since retailers (B2B) must stock Cuties for consumers to be able to purchase them and consumers (B2C) must want the product for it to sell. Promotions targeted at the end consumer (B2C) are called "pull strategies" because they create demand at the end of the supply chain that pulls the product through the chain. Promotions targeted at the retailer (B2B) customer are called "push strategies" because they focus on getting products on store shelves and thus pushing product through the chain. This push and pull for Cuties is shown in Figure A.

Businesses such as Sun Pacific that "sell through" the supply chain to get to the end consumer must utilize both push and pull strategies. However, the relative focus can vary, and Sun Pacific has taken a very heavy-up pull strategy approach. Sun Pacific took a citrus commodity and developed it into a household name through using a pull strategy. Although its buyers in the supply chain are retailers, the retailers' customers are consumers. By promoting Cuties to consumers directly, Sun Pacific was able to stimulate consumer demand at the end of the supply chain, which in turn stimulates the retailers' demand for Cuties to sell to consumers and pulls the brand through the supply chain.

Push versus Pull Supply Chain Strategies

FIGURE A

Push Supply Chain Strategy

Producer (Sun Pacific) → B2B Buyer (Retailer) → B2C Buyer (End Consumer)

Pull Supply Chain Strategy

Producer (Sun Pacific) ← B2B Buyer (Retailer) ← B2C Buyer (End Consumer)

The primary consumer target of Cuties promotions is Millennial and Generation X parents. For example, Cuties' 2017 "100 Days of Summer" campaign featured celebrity endorsers who were popular with Millennial and Generation X parents, a crowdsourcing contest from Snapchat to design new stickers for Cuties, and tie-ins with iHeartRadio stations. The efforts appear to be working as Cuties were named the preferred produce brand among parents in the 2017 Brand Love study by a youth research firm, Smarty Pants. According to Howard Nager:

> The Brand Love study is great affirmation that our approach to creating strong relationships with parents—especially Millennials, who are now the largest generation—is working. Millennials represent immense purchasing power now and in the future. It's why we spend a great deal of time learning about what's important to them, and use those insights to guide our marketing efforts. . . . The positivity of our brand and family-friendly focus resonates with parents. Our goal this season was to nurture deep, long-lasting relationships with parents to increase engagement, brand preference and drive customers to our retail partners.

As mentioned above, the customers of Sun Pacific are industrial buyers. For several years after the introduction of Cuties, retailers, such as grocery stores and wholesale clubs that sell to end consumers, primarily made up that group of customers. However, Cuties experienced a boost in distribution and consumer awareness in 2014, when Sun Pacific struck a deal with McDonald's to include Cuties as an option in Happy Meals and for sale à la carte. The vast majority of Cuties (83 percent) are sold as part of Happy Meals rather than à la carte, which reflects the success of the consumer promotions geared toward Millennial and Generation X parents.

This co-branding agreement with McDonald's was originally a limited-time promotion lasting from December 2014 through March 2015, but it was highly successful. It was so successful that McDonald's brought Cuties back again in 2016 and thereafter. The incorporation of Cuties into Happy Meals is part of McDonald's larger efforts to offer various healthier options in Happy Meals. This is a very significant move for health advocates, such as The Alliance for Healthier Generation, which partners with McDonald's to improve healthy nutrition for children, because it marked the first time that McDonald's offered a whole fruit option. By June 2018, McDonald's made a transition to healthier Happy Meals at all McDonald's retail locations in the U.S.—and made a commitment to have similar changes implemented in half of its locations globally, within the 120 countries where McDonald's stores are located, by 2022. Between 2014 and 2017 alone, McDonald's sold 78 million Cuties to consumers, which translates to roughly 180 Cuties per minute.

The branding of Cuties has been so successful that Sun Pacific is not stopping there. The company is expanding the branding efforts to other commodity produce and experiencing good results so far. The newest relatives of Cuties mandarins are Mighties kiwi fruits and Sunnies grapes. Other produce companies are following suit and branding their own citrus products as well.

Discussion Questions

1. Chapter 19 describes various purchase situations.
   a. When McDonald's originally made the agreement with Sun Pacific to incorporate Cuties in Happy Meals in 2014, what type of purchase situation was that? Explain.
   b. In 2016, when McDonald's reincorporated Cuties into Happy Meals, what type of purchase situation was that? Explain.

2. Chapter 19 discusses the organizational decision process. Consider the various stages of the decision-making process that may have taken place within McDonald's to arrive at the choice to incorporate Cuties into the Happy Meals and the à la carte menu. While it is impossible to know the proprietary information on exactly how this decision was made, you could speculate as to some aspects of how it may have taken place.
   a. What factors likely may have led to the problem recognition?
   b. What other alternatives might McDonald's have considered in the alternative evaluation?
   c. Why do you think Cuties were eventually selected as the purchase decision?

3. Chapter 19 discusses the differences between transactional exchanges versus relational exchanges and various factors that influence whether business relationships would be more likely to be one or the other (industry structure, decision-making culture, decision-making structure, risk tolerance, and nature of purchase).
   a. Do you think grocery retailers are engaged in transactional or relational exchanges with Sun Pacific? Explain your reasoning relative to the factors listed in the text and case.

   b. Do you think McDonald's is engaged in transactional or relational exchanges with Sun Pacific? Explain your reasoning relative to the factors listed in the text and case.

4. Are buyers of Cuties just "paying more for the name," or is it due to the economic benefits associated with the name? What, if any, economic benefits accrue to buyers of Cuties?

5. The case distinguishes push and pull strategies. The case mentions that Sun Pacific heavily uses a pull strategy because the promotions target the end consumers of the supply chain. However, they also would have to promote to the retailers (B2B) customers as well to ensure they stock the product on their stores and outlets. Design promotional materials, including key selling points, that Sun Pacific could use to "sell" its product successfully to its B2B customers.

6. Executives of Sun Pacific explicitly state that advertising and promotions are targeting Millennials as part of the pull strategy. In what ways do the promotions for Cuties, as well as the product itself, appeal to this generation?

Source: C. Carter, "Best of 2017: Inside McDonald's 'Fresh' Evolution: From Burgers and Fries to Cuties, Smoothies and Salads," *Southeast Produce Weekly,* May 18, 2017, https://southeastproduceweekly.com, accessed May 13, 2018, C. Collen, "Cuties Prominent in Healthy Snack Study," *America Fruit,* October 10, 2017, www.fruitnet.com, accessed May 13, 2018; E. Crawford, "McDonald's Raises the Bar for Children's Food with New Nutritional Standards for Happy Meals," *Food Navigator USA,* May 14, 2018, www.foodnavigator-usa.com, accessed May 13, 2018; "Cuties Mandarins & Clementines," *Sun Pacific,* May 15, 2018, https://sunpacific.com, accessed May 13, 2018; A. Ferree, "Cuties Season Is Here! The Latest on Our Work with McDonald's," March 30, 2017, https://medium.com, accessed May 13, 2018; M. Jordan, "The Big War over a Small Fruit," *Wall Street Journal,* July 13, 2012, www.wsj.com; T. Karst, "Chile Expects Bump Up in Clementine Exports," *Packer,* May 21, 2018, https://www.thepacker.com, accessed May 13, 2018; M. Khuraibet, "McDonald's Revamps Happy Meal with Nutritious Options," *El Paisano Online,* February 22, 2018, https://elpaisanoonline.com, accessed May 13, 2018; "McDonald's Is Bringing Cuties Back," *QSR Magazine,* January 22, 2016, www.qsrmagazine.com, accessed May 13, 2018; K. O'Brien, "Cuties Marks '100 Days of Sunshine' in New Campaign for Favored Citrus Brand," *Drum,* November 6, 2017, www.thedrum.com, accessed May 13, 2018; S. Rich, "The Shape of Fruits to Come," *Smithsonian,* March 16, 2012, www.smithsonianmag.com; "U.S.: Sun Pacific 'Always Looking for More' Mandarins," *FreshFruitPortal.com,* October 26, 2017, www.freshfruitportal.com, accessed May 13, 2018; "U.S.: Cuties Continues to Shine with Millennial and Gen X Parents," *FreshFruitPortal.com,* April 23, 2018, https://www.freshfruitportal.com, accessed May 13, 2018.

5-2 FARMERS' BRAND LOYALTY FOR HEAVY FARM EQUIPMENT MACHINERY

Farmers are traditionally known to be quite brand loyal when it comes to heavy farm equipment machinery. Commonly heard phrases in the farming community are, "if it's not red, it should be left in the shed," or "bleed green and run like a Deere." Dealerships often play into the brand rivalries with signs displaying slogans like, "Friends don't let friends drive red tractors."

Farming operations, which are commonly businesses that are handed down through families, are fiercely protective of "their" brand of tractors and other machinery. The chosen brand is often a point of identification or rivalry with other regional farming businesses. According to Barry Nelson, manager of media relations for John Deere:

> The number one thing people think of when they hear John Deere is the color green. But some people, like in the urban areas, don't understand the strength of the color green or red. Farm families grow up with these different brands and the color is important. It's what they identify with.

Take for instance two brothers from Mount Horeb, Wisconsin, Shawn and Mark Farrell, who are the fifth generation of farmers in their family farming operation, and the third generation of loyal John Deere customers. While in the market for a new tractor for the farm, the brothers broke tradition and bought a New Holland tractor that had a comparable engine and transmission to their other John Deere tractors but cost $40,000 less. However, instead of being satisfied with their purchase, both brothers disliked the New Holland tractor, opted for their hired workers to use it rather than using it themselves, and bought a John Deere version shortly thereafter.

Once every three years, *Farm Equipment* magazine conducts a survey on brand loyalty of farmers across the 12 states of the Corn Belt, Lake States, and Northern Plains regions of the United States. Specifically, this survey provides a longitudinal view of how farmers perceive their own brand loyalty in heavy farm equipment machinery and what might influence shifts in that loyalty. The survey data look at farmers' responses overall, as well as break them down by the loyal customers of the top four preferred brands: AGCO, Case IH, John Deere, and New Holland (see the following tables for selected insights from this study). Table A shows the percentages of farmers who consider themselves to be brand loyal (overall and by major brand for the last three surveys). Table B shows the percentages of farmers who begin the purchase decision process with the desire to purchase their primary brand (overall and by major brand for the last three surveys). Table C shows what percentage of farmers are willing to consider a nonpreferred brand due to a changing market environment with decreasing commodity prices (overall and by major brand). The information in Table C was collected beginning in 2017, so data from the previous years are unavailable. Finally, Table D shows a

TABLE A — Percentage of Farmers Who Consider Themselves to Be Brand Loyal

Equipment Brand	2017	2014	2011
Industry/all farmers	75	69	63
AGCO farmers	60	33	25
Case IH farmers	80	74	35
John Deere farmers	77	71	73
New Holland farmers	63	63	44

Source: *Farm Equipment* Survey, 2017.

TABLE B — Percentage of Farmers Who Begin Purchase Decision Process with Desire to Purchase Same Brand

Equipment Brand	2017	2014	2011
Industry/all farmers	78	67	67
AGCO farmers	65	50	75
Case IH farmers	76	66	53
John Deere farmers	84	71	79
New Holland farmers	69	63	56

Source: *Farm Equipment* Survey, 2017.

TABLE C — Percentage of Farmers Willing to Consider a Nonpreferred Brand Due to Declines in Commodity Prices

Equipment Brand	2017
Industry/all farmers	49
AGCO farmers	63
Case IH farmers	40
John Deere farmers	50
New Holland farmers	50

Source: *Farm Equipment* Survey, 2017.

ranking of which factors would lead farmers to break their brand loyalty and switch to a different heavy farm equipment machinery brand.

Factors That Could Cause Farmers to Switch Heavy Farming Machinery Brands   TABLE D

Factor	2017 Rank	% VI + SI	2014 Rank	% VI + SI	2011 Rank	% VI + SI
Better product engineering	1	98.5%	3	98.2%	2	99.0%
Better parts availability	2	98.2%	1	99.0%	1	100.0%
Better dealer repair/service	3	97.5%	2	99.0%	3	98.0%
Product specialist at dealership	4	95.3%	4	97.1%	4	96.0%
Lower equipment invoice price	5	94.7%	6	90.8%	6	92.9%
Better manufacturer warranty	6	92.3%	5	92.4%	5	94.8%
Equipment uptime guarantees/ loaner programs	7	87.9%	8	84.1%	7	91.8%
Bad experience with current dealership	8	85.5%	7	85.6%	8	79.6%
Bad experience with current brand	9	80.3%	9	81.9%	10	78.6%
More attractive equipment financing	10	78.4%	12	58.5%	11	72.2%
Change in ownership of current dealership or dealer location	11	69.4%	10	72.6%	9	79.6%
Ability to consolidate buyer to one dealer	12	68.1%	11	65.7%	12	72.2%

Note: Ranking calculated by adding percentage of farmers indicating factor is "very important" + "somewhat important."
Source: *Farm Equipment* Survey, 2017.

The survey results show that the majority of farmers feel a great sense of brand loyalty to "their" brand, whichever one it is, and think of that particular brand first when beginning the purchase decision process. Although family tradition is not measured in this survey, it also anecdotally appears to play a large role in brand loyalty within the heavy farm equipment machinery context. However, the survey results show that this staunch brand loyalty can be called into question for nearly half of the farmers when prices in commodity markets drop. Because the products that farmers manufacture and supply to other buyers down their supply chains are commodities, drops in commodity prices can create a serious economic influence in decision making. However, the lower equipment invoice price factor is interestingly only the fifth-ranked factor that might lead farmers to switch from their preferred brand.

The survey results, as well as industry specialists and anecdotal evidence, indicate that other factors may be more important in maintaining brand loyalty. Three of the top four highest-rated factors in the survey are related to service quality offered by heavy farm equipment machinery dealerships (parts availability, dealer repair/service, product specialist at a dealership). While the order of the ranking fluctuates over the years, these three dealership service quality factors, along with product engineering, have remained the top four factors that might lead farmers to abandon their brand loyalty.

The Farrell brothers said that their relationship with sales, service, and parts employees at their local dealership helps solidify their brand loyalty to John Deere. Industry specialist and consultant Scott Deming echoes this sentiment:

As a dealer, you need to figure out a way to get farmers not to remember what they bought, but who they bought it from. If you put the right price on it, anybody can sell anything to anybody once. That doesn't create loyalty. All it does is tell the customer he got a great deal. When [farmers] say "better parts availability," what that means is I don't have to worry, which means I can sleep at night, which means that when I call you, I trust in my heart and soul that you're going to be there.

Discussion Questions

1. Define brand loyalty as you understand it from the text. How does John Deere (or any of the other three major brands) create loyalty? Explain.

2. Chapter 19 describes various purchase situations (straight rebuy, modified rebuy, and new task).
   a. What type of purchase situation did the Farrell brothers engage in when they bought their New Holland tractor? Explain.
   b. What type of purchase situation did the Farrell brothers and their preceding two generations of farmers engage in when they bought their John Deer tractor? Explain.
   c. What type of purchase situation would someone who just purchased a farming operation as a new venture and has had no prior farming experience engage in when that person seeks to purchase a tractor? Explain.

3. Using all possible sources of information including the case, the Internet, and direct contact with heavy farm equipment machinery dealers, develop what you think the decision-making unit looks like for a heavy farm equipment machinery purchase, such as a tractor. Does its size depend on the size of the company or other factors? Explain.

4. Explain the role of reference groups for heavy farm equipment machinery brands, such as John Deere.

5. Chapter 19 discusses the difference in transactional exchanges and relational exchanges. Which of these types do you think is most common in the heavy farm equipment machinery industry and why?

6. Chapter 15 discusses marketing strategies based on information search patterns and makes recommendations of preferable strategies based on decision-making patterns and the position of a brand (whether it is in the evoked set).
   a. Which strategy should one of the top four brands listed in the *Farm Equipment* survey use when attempting to gain new customers from its competitors?
   b. Which strategy should one of the top four brands listed in the *Farm Equipment* survey use when attempting to retain its existing brand loyal customers?
   c. Which strategy should a brand that is NOT listed in the *Farm Equipment* survey use when attempting to gain new customers?

Source: J. Elftman, "Building Customer Loyalty through Quality Service, Not Low Prices," *Farm Equipment,* April 6, 2016, http://farm-equipment. com, accessed May 13, 2018; D. Kanicki, "Most Farmers Still Loyal to 'Their' Brand," *Farm Equipment,* September 2, 2017, http://farm-equipment.com, accessed May 13, 2018; D. Kanicki, "To the Point: Customer Loyalty Is the Secret," *Farm Equipment,* September 12, 2017, http://farm-equipment.com, accessed May 13, 2018; J. Petersen, "Customer Experience Larger Than Brand Loyalty," *AgriSync,* May 18, 2018, www.agrisync.com, accessed May 13, 2018; R. Schultz, "For Farmers, Brand Loyalty a Part of Their Identity," *Wisconsin State Journal,* November 24, 2012, http://host.madison.com.

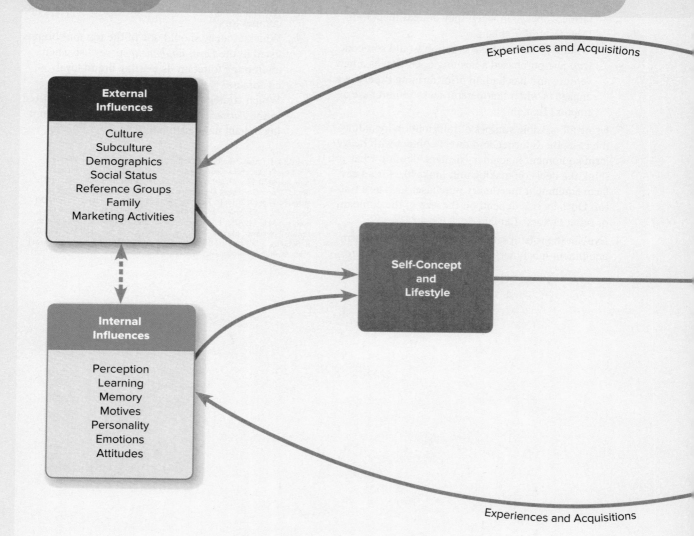

External Influences

Culture
Subculture
Demographics
Social Status
Reference Groups
Family
Marketing Activities

Internal Influences

Perception
Learning
Memory
Motives
Personality
Emotions
Attitudes

Self-Concept and Lifestyle

Experiences and Acquisitions

Experiences and Acquisitions

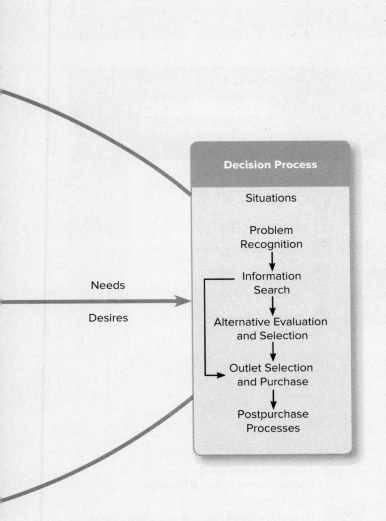

Decision Process

Situations

Problem
Recognition

Information
Search

Alternative Evaluation
and Selection

Outlet Selection
and Purchase

Postpurchase
Processes

Needs

Desires

Throughout the text, we have emphasized that knowledge of consumer behavior is as important to those who would regulate consumer behavior as it is to those who engage in marketing activities. Government officials, consumer advocates, and citizens all need to understand consumer behavior to develop, enact, and enforce appropriate rules and regulations for marketing activities. Consumers in particular need to understand their own behaviors and how their purchase and consumption behaviors help determine the type of marketplace and society we have.

In this section, we will analyze the role of consumer behavior principles in regulating marketing practices.

We will pay particular attention to the regulation of marketing activities focused on children. We also discuss regulations covering advertising, product, and pricing practices aimed at adults.

20 Marketing Regulation and Consumer Behavior

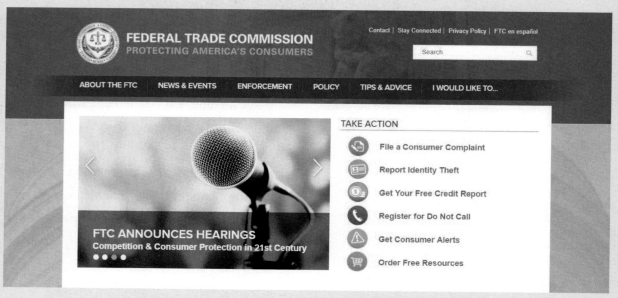

Source: United States Federal Trade Commission, www.ftc.gov

LEARNING OBJECTIVES

LO1 Explain the two major concerns in marketing to children that CARU deals with.

LO2 Describe the various marketing activities aimed at children that are controversial.

LO3 Discuss new guidelines by the FTC regarding online privacy protection for adults.

LO4 Explain marketing communication issues related to adults including deceptive advertising.

LO5 Discuss regulation concerns when marketing to adults as they relate to product and price.

Agencies such as the FTC, FDA, USDA, and FCC likely spring to mind in relation to government regulation. News media are populated with stories of the need for government regulatory bodies to protect consumers from the hidden dangers in the marketplace. In 2014 Toyota was fined $1.2 billion, the largest payment by an automaker in U.S. history, for safety issues of sudden acceleration from sticky pedals and floor mat entrapment, linked to 37 deaths.[1] Sharing the news space with Toyota was another car maker accused of corporate misconduct. GM must explain its failure to ask for a recall for its Chevy Cobalts and Saturn Ions with defective ignition switches that shut off. The problem, resulting in at least 12 deaths, is one that GM knew of as early as 2001. Two months into 2014, Nestlé, USA, issued a massive recall of its Hot Pockets product out of concern that it was made with USDA-recalled "diseased and unsound" beef. In 2012 the nation was shocked by news stories of a nationwide outbreak of fungal meningitis carried in steroid medication produced by New England Compounding Center that killed 64 people and left at least 751 people with lingering and, in some cases, debilitating symptoms. And in 2015, Blue Bell Creameries recalled its products after three consumers died from listeria-infected ice cream.

Consumers have no way to test the safety of cars they are driving, the foods they are eating, or the medications they are taking, and must rely on government regulatory bodies for this assurance. From this perspective, governmental regulatory bodies are cast in a mediating role to protect consumers from the actions of companies. The FTC's website shown at the beginning of this chapter prominently displays its purpose of protecting America's consumers.

Another perspective that may not come as quickly to mind is the need for government regulating bodies to protect companies from consumers, as in the case of counterfeit products. Imitation is not always the sincerest form of flattery. Sometimes it's just counterfeit. Media alerts of the arrest of major producers of fake health and beauty products—Vicks Vaporub, Vaseline, Chapstick, Johnson's Baby Oil—are reminders of the harm that may come to consumers who unknowingly buy counterfeit.

But what about the situation when consumers knowingly seek out and buy counterfeit goods. Consumer demand for counterfeit goods is strong, with an estimated worldwide underground economy that rivals illicit drugs and surpasses that of weapons smuggling and human trafficking. Consumer demand for counterfeits includes not only fake innocuous items that have low performance risk like fashion items—Dr. Dre Beats headphones, Mont Blanc pens, Rolex watches, Gucci purses— but also fakes that have high performance risk—fake alcohol, fake drugs—items that hold the potential to threaten consumer health, safety, and welfare. Consumers knowingly buy fakes with their concomitant lower quality as a means to own brand-image items beyond their economic reach. Ownership of fake goods also may serve as a means to help consumers create or bolster a desired identity.

Interestingly, unbeknownst to consumers, part of the identity derived from buying counterfeit goods may be its impact on consumers to engage in subsequent unethical behavior such as cheating.

Consumer complicity is a major reason not only for the strength of counterfeiting, but also for the strength of piracy, a consumer behavior related to counterfeiting. With media—music, movies, e-books, TV programs, video games—now readily available on demand, wait time has been reduced to zero. With the effortless click of a mouse or a swipe across the screen, the media are instantly available for consumption and can be had just as easily whether consumers pay for them or not. Piracy occurs when consumers opt not to pay for them. Anti-piracy efforts, including the "Six Strike Anti-Piracy Scheme," do not seem to have created a noteworthy drop in piracy behavior, but a concomitant rise in anonymity services that hide the identity and location of the user seems to indicate that users would rather hide than quit this behavior.

Government regulation is one leg of a three-legged stool—consumers, business, and government. Each leg is needed to balance the whole.

Marketing is a highly visible, important activity. It affects the lives of individuals, the success of nonprofit groups, and the profits of businesses. As indicated throughout the text, there are many issues where the appropriate ethical action for marketers is not clear-cut. As a marketing manager, you will face many such situations in your career. However, society has declared that some marketing actions are clearly inappropriate. It has done so by enacting laws and regulations that prohibit or require specific marketing actions. In this chapter, we examine the regulation of marketing practices. Regulating marketing activities requires the same level of understanding of consumer behavior as does managing marketing programs. Our consideration of the regulation of marketing practices will separate regulations designed to protect children from those designed to protect adults.

A KEY CAVEAT about the material in this chapter is that consumer regulation is an ongoing and dynamic endeavor, particularly as it relates to technology, e-commerce, and marketing to children. Thus, what may be accurate at one point in time may become incomplete or obsolete at a later time. This is true of the material in this chapter and also true of any organization's knowledge and information and policies relating to various areas of regulation. Thus, it is the responsibility of all involved to ensure that up-to-the-minute information is sought prior to decision making and action in this arena. As you will see, the breadth, complexity, and evolution of the issues involved make regulation, compliance, and enforcement a highly demanding set of activities for both firms and government regulators.

REGULATION AND MARKETING TO CHILDREN

LO1   The regulation of marketing activities aimed at children focuses primarily on product safety, advertising and promotions, and privacy protection. Product safety issues focus on appropriate product design and materials. We will concentrate on privacy protection and advertising and other promotional activities[2] targeting children as consumers. The regulation of these activities rests heavily on theories of children's consumer behavior, particularly their information-processing skills.

There are a variety of state, federal, and voluntary guidelines and rules governing marketing to children. Despite these rules, many feel that some marketers continue to take advantage of children and that the overall marketing system, particularly advertising, is socializing children to value things (products) rather than intangibles such as relationships and integrity.

One basis for the concern over marketing to children is based on *Piaget's stages of cognitive development* (Chapter 6), which indicates that children lack the ability to fully process and understand information, including marketing messages, until around 12 years of age.[3] This and related theories are the basis for most regulation of advertising aimed at children and, according to critics, for some marketing programs that deliberately exploit children.

Concerns about the Ability of Children to Comprehend Commercial Messages

The American advertising industry's primary self-regulatory body, the National Advertising Division (NAD) of the Council of Better Business Bureaus, maintains a special unit to review advertising aimed at children—the **Children's Advertising Review Unit (CARU).** Four of the eight principles that underlie CARU's guidelines for advertising directed to children relate to their ability to comprehend commercial messages:[4]

1. Advertisers have special responsibilities when advertising to children or collecting data from children online. They should take into account the limited knowledge, experience, sophistication, and maturity of the audience to which the message is directed. They should recognize that younger children have a limited capacity to evaluate the credibility of information, may not understand the persuasive intent of advertising, and may not even understand that they are being subjected to advertising.
2. Advertising should be neither deceptive nor unfair, as these terms are applied under the Federal Trade Commission Act, to the children to whom it is directed.
3. Advertisers should have adequate substantiation for objective advertising claims, as those claims are reasonably interpreted by the children to whom they are directed.
4. Advertising should not stimulate children's unreasonable expectations about product quality or performance.

Some of the specific guidelines relating to information processing that guide CARU's policing of children's advertising are shown in Table 20–1.

Information Processing–Related Guidelines of CARU	TABLE 20-1

1. Whether an advertisement leaves a misleading impression should be determined by assessing how reasonable children in the intended audience would interpret the message, taking into account their level of experience, sophistication, and maturity; limits on their cognitive abilities; and their ability to evaluate the advertising claims.
2. Claims should not unduly exploit a child's imagination. While fantasy, using techniques such as animation and computer-generated imagery, is appropriate for both younger and older children, it should not create unattainable performance expectations nor exploit the younger child's difficulty in distinguishing between the real and the fanciful.
3. Advertisements should demonstrate the performance and use of the product in a way that can be duplicated by a child for whom the product is intended.
4. All disclosures and disclaimers material to children should be understandable to the children in the intended audience, taking into account their limited vocabularies and level of language skills. For young audiences, simple words should be chosen, e.g., "You have to put it together." Because children rely more on information presented in pictures than in words, demonstrative disclosures are encouraged.
5. Program personalities, live or animated, should not be used to advertise products, premiums, or services in or adjacent to a television program primarily directed to children under 12 years of age in which the same personality or character appears.

Source: *Self-Regulatory Program for Children's Advertising* (New York: Children's Advertising Review Unit, Council of Better Business Bureaus, 2014).

CARU and others are interested in the impact that the *content* of children's advertising has, as well as the ability of children to process advertising messages. However, our current focus is limited to children's abilities to *comprehend* advertising messages. There are two main components to this concern: (1) Do children understand the selling intent of commercials? and (2) Can children understand specific aspects of commercials, such as comparisons?

Do Children Understand the Selling Intent of Commercials?   Research suggests that younger children have at least some difficulty understanding the selling intent of commercials.[5] Currently, the advertising industry strives to separate children's commercials from the programs by prohibiting overlapping characters and by using *separators,* such as, "We will return after these messages."

This problem is growing in intensity, as children's products are often the "stars" of animated children's films and television programs. Increasingly, product lines and television programs (and movies) are being designed jointly with the primary objective being sales of the toy line. Parents have expressed concerns ranging from the effects that toy-based programming has on their children's behaviors and emotional development to the fear that such programming may replace other more creative and child-oriented programs.[6]

This concern has led to a variety of proposals to restrict or eliminate such programs. These proposals have produced an ongoing debate about who controls the television set. One argument is that it is the parent's responsibility to monitor and regulate their children's viewing behaviors. If a sufficient number of parents find such programs inappropriate and refuse to let their children watch them, advertisers will quit sponsoring them and they will no longer be available. Another argument is that today's time-pressured parents do not have time to screen all the shows their children watch. Furthermore, tremendous peer pressure can develop for children to watch a particular show or own the products associated with it. Denying a child the right to watch such a show then causes arguments and resentment. Therefore, society should set appropriate standards within which broadcasters should operate. *Which, if either, of these views matches your own?*

Can Children Understand the Words and Phrases in Commercials?   The second aspect of comprehension involves specific words or types of commercials that children might misunderstand. For example, research indicates that disclaimers such as "Part of a nutritious breakfast," "Each sold separately," and "Batteries not included" are ineffective with preschool children.[7] Not only do young children have a difficult time understanding these phrases, the problem is compounded when such disclaimers are presented in a manner that does not meet the Federal Trade Commission's "Clear and Conspicuous" requirements for such disclaimers.[8] For example, consider the following toy ad disclaimer:

> The disclaimer noted that "TV Teddy comes with one tape. Other tapes sold separately." However, it appeared near the bottom of the screen in lettering that measured only 3.5 percent of the screen height against a multicolor background. It was not repeated by an announcer and appeared for less than three seconds. A child would have to read at 200 words per minute to read the message!

In relation to words and phrases, CARU recommends wording and language that are age appropriate (such as simple words for young audiences) and prohibits price minimizations such as "only" and "just." It also suggests specific phrasing for certain situations, such as "you have to put it together," rather than "assembly required." Several recent cases involving CARU and the information-processing skills of children include the following:

- LEGO agreed to change future advertising for its Lord of the Rings Pirate Ship Ambush playset to clearly identify what items were part of the initial purchase. CARU was concerned that the advertisement could mislead children into thinking that the playset came with additional mini-figurines, which were actually not included with the purchase. Without disclosure of what was contained in the set, CARU found "that a child could reasonably believe that all of the product shown is included with the playset."[9]

- Dave & Buster's agreed to stop its "Free Video Game Play" commercials, which aired on Cartoon Network. The advertisements opened with "Free Video Game Play" written in large bold letters on the screen. But as the commercial progressed, voiceovers and words, written in smaller font size at the bottom of the screen, provided the terms for free play: The offer excluded certain games, was valid only for certain days and times, and required the purchase of a $50 power card. CARU argued the card purchase and exclusions were "not adequately disclosed to the child audience."[10]

Concerns about the Effects of the Content of Commercial Messages on Children

Even if children accurately comprehend television ads, there are concerns about the effects the content of these messages has on children. These concerns stem in part from the substantial amount of time American children spend viewing television. The large amount of time children devote to watching television, including commercials, gives rise to two major areas of concern:

- The impact of commercial messages on children's values.
- The impact of commercial messages on children's health and safety.

The remaining four of the eight basic principles that underline CARU's guidelines for advertising directed at children focus on these concerns (the other four, as we saw, are concerned with children's information-processing capabilities). They are[11]

1. Products and content inappropriate for children should not be advertised directly to them.
2. Advertisers should avoid social stereotyping and appeals to prejudice, and are encouraged to incorporate minority and other groups in advertisements and to present positive role models whenever possible.
3. Advertisers are encouraged to capitalize on the potential of advertising to serve an educational role and influence positive personal qualities and behaviors in children, e.g., being honest and respectful of others, taking safety precautions, engaging in physical activity.
4. Although there are many influences that affect a child's personal and social development, it remains the prime responsibility of the parents to provide guidance for children. Advertisers should contribute to this parent–child relationship in a constructive manner.

Several of the specific guidelines derived from these principles are provided in Table 20–2.

Health and Safety   CARU recently challenged a television commercial for Kraft's Capri Sun. In the spot, children were participating in "imaginative but mildly risky play," including jumping on concrete walls, balancing on surfboards, and playing in a swimming pool. However, there was no adult supervision of the pool play in the ad. According to CARU, this violates the third guideline in Table 20–2. CARU acknowledged that the advertisement portrayed children "engaged in healthy physical activity in a fun and fast-paced advertisement," yet ultimately decided an activity not promoted safely should not be promoted at all. Kraft disagreed with CARU's position on adult supervision but chose to remove the pool scene from the commercial.[12] *What do you think? Was CARU correct or was Kraft?*

In many instances, children and teenagers are exposed to advertising directed at adults. For example, CARU found that Proactiv Solution cleansing system, which is labeled as

TABLE 20-2   Examples of Specific Guidelines of the Children's Advertising Review Unit

1. Advertising should not urge children to ask parents or others to buy products. It should not suggest that a parent or adult who purchases a product or service for a child is better, more intelligent, or more generous than one who does not.
2. Advertisers should not convey to children that the possession of a product will result in greater acceptance by peers or lack of a product will result in less acceptance by peers.
3. Advertisements should not portray adults or children in unsafe situations, or in acts harmful to themselves or others. For example, when activities (such as bicycle riding or skateboarding) are shown, proper precautions and safety equipment should be depicted; when an activity would be unsafe without adult supervision, supervision should be depicted.
4. Advertising should not portray or encourage behavior inappropriate for children (e.g., violence or sexuality) or include material that could unduly frighten or provoke anxiety in children; nor should advertisers targeting children display or knowingly link to pages of a website that portray such behaviors or materials.

Source: *Self-Regulatory Program for Children's Advertising* (New York: Children's Advertising Review Unit, Council of Better Business Bureaus, 2014).

"keep out of reach of children," was being advertised in time slots and locations likely to involve children's programming and viewership. The company responded by removing the ad from those time slots and locations.[13]

Even ads clearly not targeting children can have potentially harmful consequences:

A television commercial for Calgonite automatic dishwasher detergent showed a woman inside an automatic dishwasher. The commercial was withdrawn voluntarily after CARU received a complaint that a three-year-old child had climbed into a dishwasher shortly after viewing the commercial.[14]

The problem caused by the Calgonite commercial illustrates the difficulty marketers face. This commercial was not aimed at children nor shown during a children's program. The fact that children watch prime-time television extensively places an additional responsibility on marketers.[15]

Ensuring that advertisements portray only safe uses of products is sometimes difficult, but it is not a controversial area. Advertising of health-related products, particularly snack foods and cereals, is much more controversial.

Values   Advertising is frequently criticized as fostering overly materialistic, self-focused, and short-term values in children:

We cannot afford to raise a generation of children that measures its own value by the insignia on their clothes—not by the compassion in their hearts or the knowledge in their minds.[16]

One reason is the magnitude of advertising focused on kids. One estimate is that marketers spend $15 billion per year marketing to children, with a growing proportion allocated to digital ads.[17] In addition, estimates of the number of TV ads that children are exposed to ranges from 18,000 to 40,000 per year.[18] Many are concerned that this consistent pressure to buy and own things is producing negative values in children.

Numerous cosmetics companies and day spas are now targeting children at increasingly younger ages with both products and advertisements. Most position the products in terms of fun rather than sensuality. For example, Disney's products are packaged in boxes with pictures of Tinkerbell, Winnie the Pooh, and similar characters.[19] According to an industry expert, girls 8 to 12 are now wearing platform (high) heels and "low-rise jeans, tight miniskirts and midriff-baring T-shirts."[20]

There is also an increase in concern about looking thin and in eating disorders in children, both girls and boys, as young as five or six.[21] Many find this apparent shortening of childhood and the related body image problems inappropriate. They assign a large part of the blame to the marketing of products such as cosmetics and the media, in general. For example, a recent study reported that 87 percent of female characters, aged 10 to 17, on TV are below average in weight.[22] One teenager summed up the concern:

> It's crazy how we're so inundated with these images of perfection and . . . we're teaching young girls that that's normal. It's setting us up to fail because we're not perfect. We're not Photoshopped in real life.[23]

Summary of Advertising and Children   Available evidence suggests that the vast majority of ads meet CARU guidelines.[24] CARU reviews thousands of ads every year and has over a 95 percent success rate in resolving issues related to children's advertising.[25] However, given the enormous amount of time children spend with all forms of media, most will see many ads that are in violation of these guidelines. Clearly, CARU does not cover all aspects of advertising. For example, it does not, nor could it, oppose generating desires for products that many families cannot afford. Nonetheless, CARU has greatly enhanced the level of responsibility in advertising aimed at children. Many consumer advocates would like it to expand the areas it covers and increase the stringency of its rules.

Controversial Marketing Activities Aimed at Children

LO2

There are a number of marketing activities targeted at children in addition to television advertising that are controversial and for which various regulatory proposals are being considered. For example, violent entertainment products (movies, videos, and music) labeled for those 17 and older were, until recently, routinely marketed to kids. Highly publicized acts of violence by teenagers produced threats of regulation and improved self-regulation by the industries.[26] However, it remains a problem.

Three additional issues are described in this section, namely, online marketing, mobile and social media marketing, and commercialization of schools.

Online Marketing and Children   Children are major users of the Internet. Not surprisingly, marketers use the Internet to communicate with kids. Two major concerns have emerged: invading children's privacy and exploitation of children through manipulative sales techniques. We will consider the online privacy issue in the next section.

Concern regarding manipulative Internet practices often revolves around the creation of sites that blur the line between entertainment and advertising. This goes back to concerns touched on earlier in terms of difficulties that children have in discerning selling intent and their ability to distinguish commercial from noncommercial content. Adver-games are just one area of concern. These customized games, which are placed on a company's website, prominently feature or integrate the company's brands and products as part of the game itself. HappyMeal.com is one example. Consider the following excerpt to parents about this McDonald's online game site:

> At HappyMeal.com we offer engaging screen time that is fun for kids and sparks imagination and creativity. It also promotes active lifestyles and balanced eating choices, such as apple slices and low-fat dairy with awesome music videos, games and other activities.[27]

Along with this message to parents, the game's homepage states, "Hey kids, this is advertising." Nevertheless, this game site has McDonald's products placed throughout. And as we saw earlier, young children have a difficult time understanding the difference between "content" and "advertising." Adver-games are a little of both and, in that sense, make it even tougher for younger children, especially, to recognize selling intent.

Mobile and Social Media Marketing and Children   Sometimes referred to as the "third screen," mobile devices, including tablets, are an increasingly integral part of our lives. And marketers see younger children as the next big-growth market. A considerable proportion of those in their teen years and younger have cell phones. In the U.S., almost half of 10- to 12-year-olds have a smartphone, and in South Korea 72 percent of those 11 to 12 years old have smartphones.[28] And a recent estimate indicates 42 percent of U.S. children 8 years old and younger have their own tablets.[29]

Various types of promotional efforts are being used, including ringtones, mobile games, text-in contests, and mobile advertising. Other subtle, yet still promotional, efforts are making their way to social media, such as celebrity "tweets" about products they like (see Chapter 7). Also, texts with an update from a favorite TV program may include ads of products that have paid to access the information of those receiving the texts.[30] The ability of marketers to infiltrate yet another media domain with promotions and materials that are seen as further blurring the line between advertising and entertainment has many parents and consumer advocate groups worried. Some years back when Disney announced that it would, in a partnership with Sprint, offer cellular phone service targeted specifically at children in the 8- to 12-year range, concerns grew even stronger. Consider an excerpt from a letter to Congress by Commercial Alert, a nonprofit consumer advocate group:

> If Disney Corporation and the others just wanted to give children a way to contact parents in emergencies, that would be one thing. The telecommunications companies—to parents at least—are playing up this angle. Telecommunications lobbyists in Washington will harp on it as well. But despite the industry's rhetoric, Disney and the telecommunications companies really want to use children as conduits to their parents' wallets. And marketers want another way to bypass parents and speak directly to the nation's children.
>
> *Advertising Age* reported on July 11th that many corporations, including McDonald's, Coca-Cola, and Timex, are moving "from small [mobile phone advertising] tests to all-out campaign[s]." Children already are bombarded with too much advertising. They don't need more advertising through their mobile phones, whether it is telemarketing, text message marketing, adver-games, or any other type of commercial messages.[31]

Concerns also have been raised for products targeted for adults but advertised online and on social media. For example, teenage use of JUUL, an e-cigarette for adults, is escalating. This vaping device is promoted on social media sites like Snapchat, Twitter, and Instagram, and these messages are easily accessed and seen by children. Furthermore, these sites discuss accessories including stickers or wraps to disguise the device, with themes that appeal to children. Despite the surge in underage usage of JUUL, the manufacturer doesn't market these wraps or sell its devices to anyone under 21 years old on its website and has an explicit social media and marketing policy "directed to existing adult smokers."[32] Obviously, the battle lines are being drawn. *Which side of this debate do you come down on more—that of the marketers or of the consumer advocates? Does your answer depend on the age of the children and the nature of the tactics utilized?*

Commercialization of Schools   There have been ongoing concerns and controversy around the commercialization of elementary and high schools. Schools are often motivated by money as budgets continue to be tight. The issue of commercialization covers a broad sphere of activities. Consumers Union has the following classification system:[33]

- *In-school ads.* Ads in such places as school buses, scoreboards, and bulletin boards, as well as coupons and free samples. For example, Sonic Drive-in launched Sonic Invasion, which included in-school ads and e-mail blasts designed to get students to go to a website and vote for their school. Although the call to action wasn't buying burgers, the exposure for Sonic clearly was a positive aspect of the campaign for the company. Other aspects might include schools' selling naming rights to companies and covering lockers with ads.

- *Ads in classroom.* Ads in classroom magazines and television programs. This also includes ads in magazines distributed in school libraries. Channel One has created substantial controversy in this area. It provides 12 minutes of news to participating schools but contains two minutes of commercials. Research indicates that the commercials have an impact on students.
- *Corporate-sponsored educational materials and programs.* Also called sponsored educational materials, or SEMs. SEMs are teaching materials provided by corporations, usually for free. They come in various forms, including posters, activity sheets, and multimedia teaching aids. While many criteria can be used to evaluate these materials, one of the main criteria is the level of commercialism. Highly commercialized SEMs that are thinly veiled ads with little educational value draw the most scrutiny.
- *Corporate-sponsored contests and incentive programs.* When companies gain access through various contests and incentives, including prizes such as travel and free pizza.

Another area of great concern includes direct sales, usually by food products companies. The major food and beverage companies are working to develop and comply with voluntary guidelines designed to deal with this issue.

Children's Online Privacy Issues

Online privacy relates to the collection and use of information from websites. Collecting information from children is a sensitive issue, as well it should be, given all we know about their information-processing deficits relative to those of adults. Concern over the invasion of children's privacy prompted Congress to pass the **Children's Online Privacy Protection Act (COPPA)** in October 1998. It authorizes the FTC to develop specific rules to implement the provisions of the act. In 1999, the FTC issued the *Children's Online Privacy Protection Rule,* also referred to as The Rule. Key provisions of The Rule under COPPA are detailed in Table 20–3.

The Rules became effective in April 2000 and were last revised in 2013 to address technology and Internet changes and children's increased usage of mobile devices. The amended rules cover children's privacy online, including websites, social media, and apps.[34] The Rules appear to be working, although, clearly, ongoing diligence on the part of the FTC and commercial entities is required.

CARU adopted similar but more detailed rules. Privacy is now a major CARU issue:

- CARU was concerned that Pottermore.com, a website featuring stories and characters from the Harry Potter book series, did not properly receive verifiable parental consent before collecting personally identifiable information from children, nor did it prevent children from changing their age in order to register on the site. The website operator worked to get its site into compliance.[35]
- "Age-gating" mechanisms are used to determine if parental consent is needed for users of online services including apps. The educational mobile app Friendzy asked a skill-based math question, with multiple-choice answers, to verify age. CARU decided that this method was insufficient for gaining parental consent. The app maker agreed to make changes according to CARU's recommendations.[36]

The importance of consumer education also plays a prominent role in the FTC's approach. This can be seen in the fact that it has created an online learning tool on its website dedicated toward helping kids learn to be smarter consumers as part of its fight against online privacy invasion among children (see the OnGuardOnline.gov site shown in Illustration 20–1).

TABLE 20-3   Key Provisions of The Rule under COPPA

The primary goal of COPPA is to place parents in control over what information is collected from their young children online.

The Rule applies to operators of commercial websites and online services (including mobile apps) directed to children under 13 that collect, use, or disclose personal information from children, and operators of general audience websites or online services with actual knowledge that they are collecting, using, or disclosing personal information from children under 13. The Rule also applies to websites or online services that have actual knowledge that they are collecting personal information directly from users of another website or online service directed to children. Nonprofits are not covered.

Privacy Policy—Post a clear and comprehensive online privacy policy describing their information practices for personal information collected online from children.

Parental Notice—Provide direct notice to parents and obtain verifiable parental consent, with limited exceptions, before collecting personal information online from children.

Parental Consent—Give parents the choice of consenting to the operator's collection and internal use of a child's information, but prohibit the operator from disclosing that information to third parties (unless disclosure is integral to the site or service, in which case, this must be made clear to parents).

Parental Access—Provide parents access to their child's personal information to review and/or have the information deleted.

Parental Prevention—Give parents the opportunity to prevent further use or online collection of a child's personal information.

Confidentiality—Maintain the confidentiality, security, and integrity of information it collects from children, including by taking reasonable steps to release such information only to parties capable of maintaining its confidentiality and security.

Data Retention and Deletion—Retain personal information collected online from a child for only as long as is necessary to fulfill the purpose for which it was collected and delete the information using reasonable measures to protect against its unauthorized access or use.

Source: *Complying with COPPA: Frequently Asked Questions* (Washington, DC: Federal Trade Commission, 2013).

ILLUSTRATION 20-1

Education is an important aspect of the FTC's fight against online privacy invasion among children. OnGuardOnline.gov is designed to help parents protect their children's privacy.

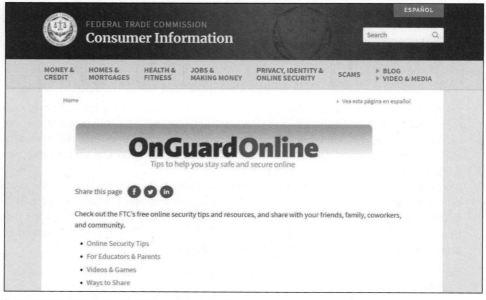

Source: United States Federal Trade Commission, www.ftc.gov

REGULATION AND MARKETING TO ADULTS

Regulation of marketing activities aimed at adults focuses on numerous issues including privacy, marketing communications, product features, and pricing practices. We deal with each of these in this section.

Consumer Privacy

There is increasing demand for regulation to protect the privacy of adults. Historically, concern was focused on offline issues such as the selling of subscription and customer lists, and the combination of that information with publicly available information to create powerful marketing databases. Today, the major focus of adult online privacy issues relates to the Internet as well as social media and the way in which those earlier problems and issues are magnified given the speed, amount, and ease of information gathering and combination that is now possible.[37] Companies argue that data collection and mining in order to offer a more targeted offering are beneficial to consumers. Consumer advocates often argue that such procedures are invasive. *Which side do you most agree with and why? Does it depend on what types of information are collected?*

With adult privacy issues, the FTC has been hesitant to craft specific legislation. Instead, it offered guidelines under a "notice and choice" approach, indicating that consumer-oriented commercial websites that collect personal identifying information from or about consumers should comply with four standards: (1) notice—of information collection and sharing practices, (2) choice—as to how personally identifying information (PII) is used, (3) access—to their information and to correct or delete information, and (4) security—firms should ensure that the collected information is secure.

However, in response to the rapidly changing online environment, and in particular in response to the increased use of "covert" behavioral tracking and targeting of consumers online, the FTC has put forth a framework and guidelines, as detailed in Table 20-4.

FTC Privacy Protection Framework	TABLE 20-4

Part 1: Privacy by Design: Companies should promote consumer privacy throughout their organizations and at every stage of the development of their products and services.

- Companies should incorporate substantive privacy protections into their practices, such as data security, reasonable collection limits, sound retention and disposal practices, and data accuracy.
- Companies should maintain comprehensive data management procedures throughout the life cycle of their products and services.

Part 2: Simplified Consumer Choice: Companies should simplify consumer choice.

- Companies do not need to provide choice before collecting and using consumer data for practices that are consistent with the context of the transaction or the company's relationship with the consumer, or are required or specifically authorized by law.
- For practices requiring choice, companies should offer the choice at a time and in a context in which the consumer is making a decision about his or her data. Companies should obtain affirmative express consent before (1) using consumer data in a materially different manner than claimed when the data was collected; or (2) collecting sensitive data for certain purposes.

Part 3: Transparency: Companies should increase the transparency of their data practices.

- Privacy notices should be clearer, shorter, and more standardized to enable better comprehension and comparison of privacy practices.
- Companies should provide reasonable access to the consumer data they maintain; the extent of access should be proportionate to the sensitivity of the data and the nature of its use.
- All stakeholders should expand their efforts to educate consumers about commercial data privacy practices.

Source: *Protecting Consumer Privacy in an Era of Rapid Change: Recommendations for Businesses and Policymakers* (Washington, DC: The Federal Trade Commission, March 2012).

A major aspect of privacy relates to consumer choice to have their online searching and browsing behavior tracked. This is dealt with in Part 2 of the FTC's guidelines. In more specific language, the FTC offered the following comments:

> Most of us at the Commission believe that it's time for a Do Not Track mechanism with respect to third-party ads; that is, consumers should be able to choose whether or not to allow the collection of data about online searching and browsing.[38]

The FTC's framework and guidelines are currently voluntary. However, the FTC chair made clear the need for companies to be proactive in their approach to this issue, stating:

> Some in the industry support what we're doing, but we know that others will claim that we are going too far. To those highly-paid professional naysayers, I have only one question: What are you for? Because it can't be the status quo on privacy.[39]

Marketing Communications

LO4

There are three major concerns focused on the information that marketers provide to consumers, generally in the form of advertisements: the accuracy of the information provided, the adequacy of the information provided, and the cumulative impact of marketing information on society's values. We will look briefly at advertising's impact on society's values before focusing on the accuracy and adequacy of consumer information.

Advertising and Values   We discussed the impact of advertising on values in the previous section on advertising to children. The concern is the same for advertising directed at adults—the long-term effect of a constant flow of messages emphasizing materialistic or narcissistic values may be negative for both individuals and society. Many feel that the ads for Axe body products for men objectify young women. Indeed, major controversy erupted when it was discovered that Dove, the brand that is actively promoting realistic body images and offering resources to women to feel better about their physical appearance, is owned by Unilever, the same company that owns and markets Axe. The contradiction is readily apparent. Bloggers had a field day and even developed an ad that spoofed the original Dove ad in ways that played off the contradiction.[40]

Most ads for women's cosmetics and clothing emphasize beauty or sex appeal as major benefits. Each individual ad is probably harmless. However, critics charge that when people see such themes repeated thousands of times for hundreds of products, they learn to consider a person's looks to be more important than other attributes.[41] This can lead to injurious consumption patterns such as excessive tanning or inappropriate dieting despite knowledge of the associated health hazard.[42] These harmful effects may be most severe in younger women, as discussed earlier.[43] Further, those who cannot afford such products or who are not "good looking" suffer. Others argue that individuals have been concerned with their looks and possessions in virtually all cultures and times. They argue that advertising does not cause a society's values; it merely reflects them.

Portrayals of beauty and casual attitudes toward sex are not the only ways advertisements are argued to influence values. The portrayal of women in the mass media in general and in advertising in particular often has been limited to stereotypical roles or as decoration.[44] This in turn can influence the concepts girls develop of themselves and their role choices. Of course, many firms now portray females in a more positive, realistic fashion, as shown in the Riders by Lee ad in Illustration 20–2.

A Nike campaign generated a positive response from many women as well as advertising critics. A television ad in the campaign combined quick camera takes and slow-motion shots

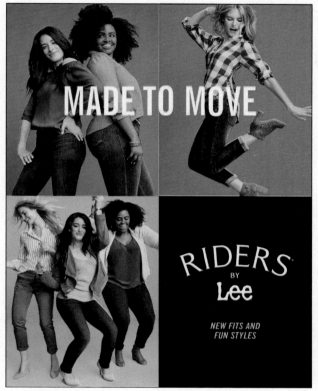

ILLUSTRATION 20-2

Many firms now portray females in a more positive, realistic fashion, as shown in this Riders by Lee ad.

of teenage girls on a playground, with images of girls playing on swing sets and monkey bars. The sound portion is a variety of girls' voices describing the long-term benefits of female participation in sports:

> I will like myself more; I will have more self-confidence if you let me play sports. If you let me play, I will be 60 percent less likely to get breast cancer. I will suffer less depression if you let me play sports.
> I will be more likely to leave a man who beats me. If you let me play, I will be less likely to get pregnant before I want to; I will learn what it means to be strong.[45]

The manner in which ethnic groups, the elderly, and other social groups are portrayed in ads and the mass media can affect the way members of these groups view themselves as well as the way others see them.[46] Marketers need to ensure that their ads reflect the diversity of the American society in a manner that is realistic and positive for all the many groups involved. These portrayals should involve both the content of the ads and the shows sponsored by the ads.[47] For example, the relative absence of Hispanic roles and actors on network television has been an ongoing concern among Hispanics, although evidence suggests that this is changing.[48]

Consumer Information Accuracy   The salesperson tells you, "My brand is the best there is." Does he or she need scientific proof to make such a statement? At what point does permissible puffery become misleading and illegal? Does it vary by the situation? The consumer group involved?[49]

Pragmatic Implications: A Psychological View of Deception

The FTC Act requires, among other things, that an advertisement must be truthful and nondeceptive, and advertisers must have evidence to back up their claims. It can be very difficult to understand when a marketing message is deceptive. One way to get a better handle on it is to understand that the FTC doesn't view only what is directly stated by an advertiser, but also what could be reasonably inferred by consumers in the given situation.[50] Specifically, there are direct claims and two types of implications that can be inferred from a claim. We illustrate with examples:

- *Direct claim:* Royal makes tires for the Jeep Cherokee. If you have a Jeep Cherokee and find that Royal doesn't make tires for the Jeep Cherokee, this is a false claim.
- *Logical implication:* Royal makes tires for all SUVs. Because the Jeep Cherokee is an SUV, if Royal doesn't make tires for the Jeep Cherokee, this is again a false claim.

Direct claims and logical implications are relatively straightforward. If the evidence does not support the claim, the claim is said to be false.

However, another category of implications exists called pragmatic implications. **Pragmatic implications** *are the implied meanings (that are neither directly stated nor logically implied) that consumers derive when interpreting language in a "practical" way.* For example, if a friend tells you, when asked, that he "can" come right over to help you with a project, you might *infer* that this means he *will* come to help. Notice, however, that the friend didn't actually (directly) say he would help, only that he could. Your inference that he *would* help is called a pragmatic implication. Inferences are part of the perceptual process (Chapter 8). Let's go back to the Royal tires example one more time.

- *Pragmatic implication:* Need new tires for your Jeep Cherokee? Royal can help.

Many consumers would *infer* from this claim that what Royal meant to say was that it has tires to fit the Jeep Cherokee. But again, notice that it never directly made a claim to that effect. The question is, can Royal be held liable for deceptive advertising in this situation? The answer is yes if it doesn't indeed have tires to fit the Jeep Cherokee because the FTC, when judging

An ad shows a pair of attractive female legs. The headline reads, "Her legs are insured for $1,000,000. Her policy came with one minor stipulation. Schick Silk Effects." Schick Silk Effects is a women's razor. How do you interpret this ad? Many would assume that the insurance company insisted on her using only this brand as a condition of the policy. This suggests that the insurance company considers this razor to be very good at protecting women's legs while they shave. However, in exceedingly fine print at the very bottom of the ad is this disclaimer: "Policy condition included by insurer at the request of Warner-Lambert Co." Warner-Lambert was the firm marketing Silk Effects at the time of the ad. In other words, the firm that owns the razor had the requirement that this razor be used in the insurance policy. This leads to a very different interpretation of the ad. *Should this ad be illegal? Is it unethical?*

These consumer accuracy worries have spilled over to the Internet. *Native advertising,* paid advertising to look like the media format in which it appears such as an article for an online news publication, is on the rise. Over 40 percent of brands use this method, which is expected to account for 74 percent of ad revenue in 2021. Native ads look like articles, for example, instead of a typical online banner ad, and flow with the rest of the content on the web page. What distinguishes them from an article is that they say "sponsored by" or "recommended by" a brand. But half of a group of consumers recently surveyed did not deception, looks not only at what is directly stated, but also what a reasonable consumer might infer.

A few categories of pragmatic implications are

- *Hedge words:* These are words that pragmatically imply something not literally stated. An example would be "Weedex fights weeds." Many consumers seeing this statement would likely believe that what is being claimed is that Weedex "kills" weeds. Because Weedex never directly claimed this, one might be tempted to say that it did not deceive consumers. But, if the FTC judged that, among other things, a consumer acting reasonably would infer that the claim meant "kill" and that in fact Weedex does not kill weeds (or Weedex doesn't have sufficient evidence to support that claim), it could deem the statement as deceptive advertising.
- *Juxtaposed imperatives:* This is a fancy way of saying that you put two unrelated statements together in a manner that makes them seem related and changes their meaning. Consider the following: "Have a safe winter. Drive on Royal tires." Many consumers seeing this claim would likely infer something to the effect that "using Royal tires will help me drive safer in the winter."

However, what was directly stated was simply, "Have a safe winter. . . ." and "Drive on Royal tires. . . ." Again, even though the claim was not directly made, the fact that it was indirectly made (through a pragmatic implication) means it could be judged as deceptive.

If this sounds complicated, it is. In some industries, like insurance, there are literally whole units dedicated to "policing" what their marketing materials say in order to ensure compliance in terms of the FTC Act and other state and federal laws that might apply. The bottom line in marketing communication is that "just because you don't state something directly doesn't mean you didn't state it at all." And the law provides recourse for both false direct claims as well as false implied claims.

Critical Thinking Questions

1. In what way does understanding consumer perception help marketers avoid deceptive advertising?
2. Can you think of other techniques or methods that might generate pragmatic implications and thus put a marketer in danger of deceptive advertising?
3. What effects do you think occur when it is revealed via an FTC settlement that a firm was engaged in deception?

understand what "sponsored" meant. It is not surprising, then, that the FTC is concerned that native ads may be misleading.

The delivery of relevant messages and cultivating user engagement are important goals, of course. That is the point of advertising, after all. But it's equally important that advertising not mislead consumers. By presenting ads that resemble editorial content, an advertiser risks implying, deceptively, that the information comes from a nonbiased source.[51]

Because of such problems, various businesses, consumer groups, and regulatory agencies are deeply concerned with the interpretation of marketing messages and deceptive advertising. However, determining the exact meaning of a marketing message is not a simple process, nor is judging whether an ad is deceptive or not. Consumer Insight 20–1 tries to shed light on consumer deception by using a psychological framework.

Obtaining accurate assignments of meaning is made even more difficult by the variation in information-processing skills and motivations among different population groups.[52] For example, this warning was ruled inadequate in a product liability case involving a worker who was injured while inflating a truck tire:

Always inflate tire in safety cage or use a portable lock ring guard. Use a clip-on type air chuck with remote valve so that operator can stand clear during tire inflation.

The court held that (1) "there is a duty to warn *foreseeable* users of all hidden dangers" and (2) "in view of the unskilled or semiskilled nature of the work and the existence of many in the workforce who do not read English, warnings *in the form of symbols* might have been appropriate since the employee's ability to take care of himself was limited."[53] Thus, marketers often must go to considerable lengths to provide messages that the relevant audience will interpret correctly.

Regulating the verbal content of ads is difficult. Regulating the more subtle meanings implied by the visual content of ads is much more difficult.[54] For example, some are critical of beer advertisements that portray active young adults in groups having fun and consuming beer. These critics contend that the visual message of these ads is that alcohol consumption is the appropriate way for young adults to be popular and have fun.

Both government and business self-regulatory groups have begun regulating visual communications.[55]

- The FTC challenged ads for Beck's beer that featured young adults drinking on a sailing ship. It charged that the ads promoted unsafe marine conduct.
- The NAD required Balance Bar to drop all claims referring to clinical studies and *visuals of physicians* in its advertising after ruling that its formula was not proved to be "clinically effective for the general population."

But issues regarding visual aspects can go even deeper. As discussed in Chapter 8, consumers do not notice relatively small differences between brands or changes in brand attributes, and that applies to packaging. For example, brands have become creative with their packages to offset higher production costs and avoid price increases. Jif peanut butter, as an illustration, maintained the dimensions of its 18-ounce jar but inserted a dimple in the base so that the jar would hold only 16 ounces. The package looks the same and is sold for the same price, but consumers get less peanut butter. Thus, less product disguised in a larger package can be sold at the same price.[56] In addition, private label, or store, brands have been known to imitate national brands' packaging to benefit from the national brand's image. This often creates confusion in the mind of the consumer.[57] Illustration 20–3 shows French's, a national brand, and Target's Market Pantry, a store brand, with similar packages. *Are consumers misled by such packages, in either situation?*

Corrective advertising is advertising run by a firm to cause consumers to unlearn inaccurate information they acquired as a result of the firm's earlier advertising. Three examples of corrective advertising messages follow:

- "Do you recall some of our past messages saying that Domino sugar gives you strength, energy, and stamina? Actually, Domino is not a special or unique source of strength, energy, and stamina. No sugar is, because what you need is a balanced diet and plenty of rest and exercise."
- "If you've wondered what some of our earlier advertising meant when we said Ocean Spray cranberry juice cocktail has more food energy than orange juice or tomato juice, let us make it clear: we didn't mean vitamins and minerals. Food energy means calories. Nothing more."

   "Food energy is important at breakfast since many of us may not get enough calories, or food energy, to get off to a good start. Ocean Spray cranberry juice cocktail helps because it contains more food energy than most other breakfast drinks."

©Sheila Fitzgerald/Shutterstock   Source: Target Corporation

"And Ocean Spray cranberry juice cocktail gives you and your family vitamin C plus a great wake-up taste. It's . . . the other breakfast drink."

- Sugar Information, Inc.: "Do you recall the messages we brought you in the past about sugar? How something with sugar in it before meals could help you curb your appetite? We hope you didn't get the idea that our little diet tip was any magic formula for losing weight. Because there are no tricks or shortcuts; the whole diet subject is very complicated. Research hasn't established that consuming sugar before meals will contribute to weight reduction or even keep you from gaining weight."

Although the effectiveness of corrective advertising has been debated, the FTC considers it a useful tool in protecting the public. Likewise, firms injured by the false claims of competitors often request it as a remedy. Indeed, the threat of lawsuits by competitors can serve as a strong deterrent of comparative advertising. For example, Procter & Gamble has revisited its aggressive advertising strategy across its various brands in light of all the substantial litigation it has created (e.g., lawsuits by Playtex, J&J-Merck, Kimberly-Clark, and Georgia Pacific).[58]

Adequacy of Consumer Information   It is important that consumers have not only accurate information but adequate information as well. To ensure information adequacy, a number of laws have been passed, such as the federal truth-in-lending legislation.

Nutritional labeling has been required for years and was significantly revised in 1990 with the Nutrition Labeling and Education Act (NLEA). Research findings on the impact of such labels are mixed, but the labels do provide valuable information to many consumers. A consistent stream of consumer behavior research since these rules were enacted has uncovered a number of potential improvements in the manner in which the information should be presented. Unfortunately, as with many such programs, those who are relatively disadvantaged in terms of education and income are least able to use this type of information.[59]

Over the years, the FDA has mandated changes to nutrition labels on packaged foods, such as the inclusion of trans fats and, most recently, added sugars. Furthermore, the label's new look is more obvious in its presentation of calories and serving size. The logic behind this change, which involves costs to companies in terms of label redesign, is "to reflect new

The FDA's label rules require packaging adaptations by companies and serve as a way for certain brands, such as in this Kind ad, to differentiate themselves from the competition on an attribute of importance to consumers.

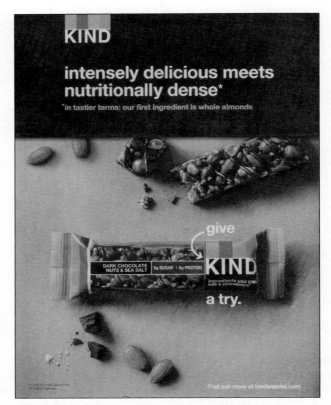

Source: Kind LLC

scientific information, including the link between diet and chronic diseases such as obesity and heart disease . . . and make it easier for consumers to make better informed food choices."[60]

Obviously, this ruling provides opportunities for some food marketers and challenges for others. Campbell Soup, for example, welcomed the label change because "transparency is the single most important ingredient." But the new label requirements could signal difficulties for brands that use added sugar, such as sodas, cereals, or snack foods.[61] Given consumer health concerns, marketers of products such as Kind (Illustration 20–4) can use natural ingredients as a point of differentiation in prominent locations on the package.

Marketers, consumer groups, and public officials would like consumers to have all the information they need to make sound choices. One approach is to provide all potentially relevant information. This approach is frequently recommended by regulatory agencies and is required for some product categories such as drugs.

Problems with this approach can arise, however. The assumption behind full disclosure is that each consumer will utilize those specific information items required for the particular decision. Unfortunately, consumers frequently do not react in this manner. This is true particularly for low-involvement purchases, but it also can be true of higher-involvement purchases as well. Instead, consumers may experience *information overload* (Chapter 8) and ignore all or most of the available data. The Braun ad shown in Illustration 20–5 was designed to chunk information to help reduce information overload.

In the drug category, relatively simple print ads require attached disclosures, usually printed in small type, telling of dosage, precautions, and warnings in order to comply with federal full-disclosure regulations. Many marketers claim that such ads add to the costs of advertising and therefore reduce the available consumer information without an offset in

Source: The Procter & Gamble Company

consumer benefit.[62] Many consumer advocates agree that the current approach is not meeting the needs of consumers.

In the area of online privacy policies, which appear to be increasing in length, there is considerable variation in format that can affect consumer information overload and comprehension.[63] The FTC has made this a part of its framework (see Table 20-4).

A current issue confronting marketers and regulators is disclosure in online advertising. Disclosure involves providing relevant qualifiers to advertising claims such as "limited to stock on hand" or "available at participating outlets only." The FTC requires disclosures to be "clear and conspicuous," and this standard has been translated into clear guidelines for print, television, and radio ads. The FTC provides the following general guidelines to online marketers. *Are these general guidelines enough?*

- Place the disclosure near the claim it is qualifying.
- Make the disclosure prominent.
- Avoid having other aspects distract from the disclosure.
- Repeat the disclosure if ad length warrants it.
- Make sure disclosures are adequate in volume, size, and duration.
- Make the language of the disclosure understandable to the intended audience.

Product Issues

Consumer groups have two major concerns with products: *Are they safe?* and *Are they environmentally sound?* A variety of federal and state agencies are involved in ensuring that products are safe to use. The most important are the Food and Drug Administration and the

LO5

Consumer Product Safety Commission. Product safety is generally not a controversial issue. However, it is impossible to remove all risk from products.

Should tricycles be banned? Accidents involving tricycles are a major cause of injury to young children. Manufacturers, consumer groups, and individuals differ on where the line should be drawn and who should draw it. Some feel that tricycles should indeed be banned. Others feel that parents should decide if their children should ride tricycles. However, both would agree that information on both the risks of tricycle riding and ways of reducing the risk should be made available to purchasers, though there is disagreement on who should make the information available and how it should be made available. Of course, tricycles represent only one of many products subject to such a debate.

Procter & Gamble's Tide laundry detergent has faced this very challenge. When Tide Pods were first launched in 2012, small children ingested the laundry soap, thinking the packets were candy. Procter & Gamble changed the pods' packaging, added a bitter taste, and marketed warnings to parents to keep the product out of their young child's reach. Recently, the manufacturer has battled the "Tide Pod Challenge." In this risky game, which has been perpetuated on social media, teenagers record themselves eating the pods and post the video online. To stop this misuse, Procter & Gamble has enlisted the help of advocacy groups and social media companies to stop the spread of these videos, and ultimately the game.[64]

We examined consumers' desires for environmentally sound products in some detail in Chapter 3. As indicated there, many consumers want products whose production, use, and disposition produce minimal environmental harm. Many marketers are striving to produce such products. Nonetheless, consumer groups continue to push for more stringent regulation in this area.

Potentially injurious products such as guns, tobacco products, and alcoholic beverages are subject to a wide variety of regulations at the federal, state, and even city levels. The FDA's latest package designs for cigarettes require half of the package to be covered by a verbal warning accompanied by a visual "warning" such as a picture of damaged teeth or lungs.[65] Recently, by court order, tobacco companies have engaged in corrective advertising on television and in print to counter prior claims that tobacco is not addictive. However, one expert is concerned that these ads will be not be seen by possible future smokers: "There's not many young people that watch prime-time television or read an actual newspaper, and the tobacco industry knows that too."[66] *How effective do you think warnings and advertisements are in stopping consumption of these potentially injurious products?*

Pricing Issues

Consumer groups want prices that are fair (generally defined as competitively determined) and accurately stated (contain no hidden charges). The FTC is the primary federal agency involved in regulating pricing activities.

Perhaps the most controversial pricing area today is the use of reference prices. An **external reference price** is *a price provided by the manufacturer or retailer in addition to the actual current price of the product.* Such terms as "compare at $X," "usually $X," "suggested retail price $Y—our price only $X" are common ways of presenting reference prices (see Chapter 17). The concern arises when the reference price is one at which no or few sales actually occur. Most states and the federal government have regulations concerning the use of reference prices, but they are difficult to enforce. Given the history of abuse of reference prices, it is not surprising that many consumers are skeptical of them.

SMARTBOOK

LO1: Explain the two major concerns in marketing to children that CARU deals with.

Marketing to children is a major concern to regulators and consumer groups. One major reason for this concern is evidence based on Piaget's theory of cognitive development that children are not able to fully comprehend commercial messages. Comprehension here has two dimensions. The first is that children often don't understand the persuasive intent of commercials. The second is that children often don't comprehend specific words and phrases. A second reason for concern over marketing to children is the potential effects it has on their safety and values. *CARU (Children's Advertising Review Unit of the Better Business Bureau)* has specific voluntary guidelines by which it evaluates advertisements targeted at children.

LO2: Describe the various marketing activities aimed at children that are controversial.

There are a number of marketing activities aimed at children other than television advertising that cause concerns. Marketing to children through mobile devices is an emerging concern. Corporate programs that place strong sales messages in "educational" materials supplied to schools also have come under attack. Children's advocates are now particularly concerned about marketing to children on the Internet. The federal government has passed legislation to protect children's online privacy called *COPPA (Children's Online Privacy Protection Act).* CARU also has guidelines on this topic.

LO3: Discuss new guidelines by the FTC regarding online privacy protection for adults.

With adult privacy issues, the FTC has been hesitant to craft specific legislation. However, in response to the rapidly changing online environment, and in particular in response to the increased use of "covert" behavioral tracking and targeting of consumers online, the FTC has put

forth a framework and guidelines that deal with designing privacy into organizations, simplifying consumer choice in the area of privacy, and offering greater transparency and simplicity to privacy practices and statements.

A major aspect of privacy relates to consumer choice to have their online searching and browsing behavior tracked. The FTC is supportive of a Do Not Track approach to this issue, which would allow consumers to opt out if they wish.

LO4: Explain marketing communication issues related to adults including deceptive advertising.

There is concern about the cumulative effect of advertising on adult values just as there is with children. In addition, regulators and businesses alike are concerned that adults receive accurate and adequate information about products. Accuracy of information relates to deceptive advertising, and it is important to keep in mind that the FTC examines ads in terms of the truthfulness of both direct claims and implications. *Pragmatic implications* are one form of implication and *are the implied meanings (that are neither directly stated nor logically implied) that consumers derive when interpreting language in a "practical" way.*

Regulation also is focused on the amount of information provided. The assumption that appears to underlie much of this legislation is that more or full information is desirable. However, intuition and research suggest that too much information can lead to overload and suboptimal consumer outcomes.

LO5: Discuss regulation concerns when marketing to adults as they relate to product and price.

The focus of consumer concern and regulation of products is twofold: (1) Are they safe? and (2) Are they environmentally sound? Concern with pricing is that prices be fair and accurately presented in a manner that allows comparison across brands.

Children's Advertising Review
  Unit (CARU) 733
Children's Online Privacy
  Protection Act (COPPA) 739

Corrective advertising 746
External reference price 750

Pragmatic implications 744

REVIEW QUESTIONS

1. What are the major concerns in marketing to children?
2. What are the main issues concerning children's ability to comprehend advertising messages?
3. What is *CARU?* What does it do? What are some of its rules?
4. What are the major concerns about the *content* of commercial messages targeting children?
5. What are the issues concerning the impact of advertising on children's health and safety?
6. What are the issues concerning the impact of advertising on children's values?
7. Why are consumer advocates worried about online marketing to kids?
8. What are the concerns associated with mobile and social media marketing to children?
9. What is meant by "commercialization of schools"? What are the various areas in which commercialization can occur, and what are the major concerns?
10. Describe the key provisions of The Rules under *COPPA.*
11. How would you go about deciding if COPPA has been effective?
12. What are the major concerns with marketing communications targeting adults?
13. What are the issues concerning the impact of advertising on adults' *values?*
14. What is a pragmatic implication, and how does it relate to information accuracy and deception?
15. What are the concerns with *consumer information adequacy?*
16. What is *information overload?*
17. What is *corrective advertising?*
18. What are the FTC's general guidelines for "clear and conspicuous" *disclosure* in an online setting?
19. What are the major regulatory issues with respect to products?
20. What are the major regulatory issues with respect to prices?
21. What is a *reference price?* What is the concern with reference prices?

DISCUSSION QUESTIONS

22. A television advertisement for General Mills' Total cereal made the following claim: "It would take 16 ounces of the leading natural cereal to equal the vitamins in 1 ounce of fortified Total." The Center for Science in the Public Interest filed a petition against General Mills claiming that the advertisement is deceptive. It was the center's position that the claim overstated Total's nutritional benefits because the cereal is not 16 times higher in other factors important to nutrition.
    a. Is the claim misleading? Justify your answer.
    b. How should the FTC proceed in cases such as this?
    c. What are the implications of cases such as this for marketing management?

23. Turkey ham looks like ham and tastes like ham, but it contains no pork; it is all turkey. A nationwide survey of consumers showed that most believed the meat product contained both turkey and ham. The USDA approved this label based on a dictionary definition for the term *ham:* the thigh cut of meat from the hind leg of any animal. Discuss how consumers processed information concerning this product and used this information in purchasing this product. (One court ruled the label to be misleading but was overruled by a higher court.)
    a. Is the label misleading?
    b. How should the FTC proceed in such cases?

24. How much and what type of (if any) advertising should be allowed on television programs aimed at children of the following ages?
    a. Under 6
    b. 6 to 9
    c. 10 to 12

25. Are the self-regulatory attempts by the food and beverage industry enough in regard to regulating food marketing to children? What, if any, additional actions would you propose? Explain.

26. Does advertising influence children's values? What can the FTC or CARU do to ensure that positive values are promoted? Be precise in your response.

27. What rules, if any, should govern mobile marketing to children? What about social media marketing?

28. What rules, if any, should govern online marketing to kids?

29. What rules, if any, should govern advertising and promotional messages presented in the classroom?

30. Does advertising influence or reflect a society's values?

31. Do you agree that beer advertisements portraying groups of active young adults having fun while consuming beer teach people that the way to be popular and have fun is to consume alcohol?

32. Respond to the questions in Consumer Insight 20-1.

33. Do you think corrective advertising works? Evaluate the three corrective messages described in the text.

34. "Because riding tricycles is a major cause of accidental injury to young children, the product should be banned." State and defend your position on this issue (the first part of the statement is true).

35. To what extent, if at all, do you use nutrition labels to guide your purchases? Why?

36. Do you believe reference prices generally reflect prices at which substantial amounts of the product are normally sold? Does this vary by store, season, or other circumstances?

APPLICATION ACTIVITIES

37. Watch two hours of Saturday morning children's programming on a commercial channel (not public broadcasting). Note how many commercials are run. What products are involved? What are the major themes? Would hundreds of hours of viewing these commercials over the course of several years have any impact on children's values or behaviors?

38. With parental consent, interview a child 2 to 4 years of age, one between 5 and 7, and one between 8 and 10. Determine their understanding of the selling intent and techniques of television commercials.

39. Interview two grade-school teachers and get their responses to material provided by corporations and the level of educational versus commercial content.

40. Repeat Question 37 for prime-time television and adults.

41. Find and copy or describe an ad that you feel is misleading. Explain why.

42. Visit a large supermarket. Considering both cost and nutrition, identify the best and worst breakfast cereals focused on children. What do you conclude?

REFERENCES

1. This opener is based on J. Hyde, "Toyota's $1.2 Billion Fine, GM Recall Highlight Defects in U.S. Auto Safety," *Motoramic,* March 19, 2014, http://autos.yahoo.com/blogs/motoramic/toyota-s-1-2-billion-fine--gm-recall-highlight-defects-in-u-s--auto-safety-164518294.html, accessed August 29, 2014; J. Aleccia, "Hot Pockets Included in Massive Meat Recall," *NBC News,* February 18, 2014, www.nbcnews.com/health/health-news/hot-pockets-included-massive-meat-recall-n33241, accessed August 29, 2014; T. W. Martin, "Dangers from Compounding Pharmacies Persist," *Wall Street Journal,* September 9, 2013, http://online.wsj.com/news/articles/SB10001424127887324324404579041001254487312, accessed August 29, 2014; A. Zulueta, "Massive Fake Health and Beauty Supplies Ring Busted," *CNN,* March 9, 2014, www.cnn.com/2014/03/08/justice/new-york-counterfeit-beauty-supplies/, accessed August 29, 2014; S. Hargreaves, "Counterfeit Goods Becoming More Dangerous," *CNN,* September 27, 2012, http://money.cnn.com/2012/09/27/news/economy/counterfeit-goods/, accessed August 29, 2014; G. McCraken, "Culture and Consumption: A Theoretical Account of the Structure and Movement of the Cultural Meaning of Consumer Goods," *Journal of Consumer Research,* 1986, pp. 71–84; F. Gino, M. I. Norton, and D. Ariely, "The Counterfeit Self: The Deceptive Costs of Faking It," *Psychological Science* 21 (2010), pp. 712–20; Ernesto, "Six Strikes Anti-Piracy Scheme Turns One Year, but Does It Work?," *TorrentFreak,* February 25, 2014, http://torrentfreak.com/six-strikes-anti-piracy-scheme-turns-one-year-140225/, accessed August 29, 2014; J. Axelrod and E. Rand, "How Investigators Cracked the Blue Bell Listeria Outbreak Case," *CBS News,* October 13, 2015, www.cbsnews.com/news/how-investigators-cracked-blue-bell-listeria-outbreak-case/, accessed July 25, 2018.

2. For an overview of this area, see S. Bandyopadhyay, G. Kindra, and L. Sharp, "Is Television Advertising Good for Children?," *International Journal of Advertising* 20, no. 1 (2001), pp. 89–116.

3. See D. R. John, "Consumer Socialization of Children," *Journal of Consumer Research,* December 1999, pp. 183–209.

4. *Self-Regulatory Program for Children's Advertising* (New York: Children's Advertising Review Unit (CARU), Council of Better Business Bureaus, 2014).

5. See M. C. Martin, "Children's Understanding of the Intent of Advertising," *Journal of Public Policy & Marketing,* Fall 1997, pp. 205–16.

6. L. Carlson, R. N. Laczniak, and D. D. Muehling, "Understanding Parental Concern about Toy-Based Programming," *Journal of Current Issues and Research in Advertising,* Fall 1994, pp. 59–72.

7. M. A. Stutts and G. G. Hunnicutt, "Can Young Children Understand Disclaimers?," *Journal of Advertising* 16, no. 1 (1987), pp. 41–46.

8. R. H. Kolbe and D. D. Muehling, "An Investigation of the Fine Print in Children's Television Advertising," *Journal of Current Issues and Research in Advertising,* Fall 1995, pp. 77–95; D. D. Muehling and R. H. Kolbe, "A Comparison of Children's and Prime-Time Fine-Print Advertising Disclosure Practices," *Journal of Advertising,* Fall 1998, pp. 37–47.

9. ASRC, "CARU Recommends LEGO Modify Future Advertising for 'Pirate Ship Ambush' to Better Disclose What Comes with Initial Purchase," press release, December 5, 2013, www.asrcreviews.org/caru-recommends-lego-modify-future-advertising-for-pirate-ship-ambush-to-better-disclose-what-comes-with-initial-purchas/, accessed July 26, 2018.

10. ASRC, "CARU Refers Dave & Buster's to FTC after Company Declines to Participate in CARU Process," press release, October 25, 2017, www.asrcreviews.org/caru-refers-dave-busters-to-ftc-after-company-declines-to-participate-in-caru-process/, accessed July 26, 2018; Federal Trade Commission, "Response to CARU Referral" (letter), December 12, 2017, www.ftc.gov/public-statements/2017/12/dave-busters, accessed July 26, 2018.

11. *Self-Regulatory Program for Children's Advertising.*

12. ASRC, "CARU Recommends Kraft Modify TV Ad That Doesn't Adequately Depict Adult Supervision; Company Agrees to Do So," press release, December 17, 2015, www.asrcreviews.org/caru-recommends-kraft-modify-tv-ad-that-doesnt-adequately-depict-adult-supervision-company-agrees-to-do-so/, accessed July 26, 2018.

13. CARU, Council of Better Business Bureaus, "CARU Recommends Guthy-Renker Discontinue Advertising Proactiv to Children," press release, June 9, 2008.

14. "B-M Drops Spots after Query by NAD," *Advertising Age,* April 20, 1981, p. 10.

15. See C. Preston, "The Unintended Effects of Advertising upon Children," *International Journal of Advertising* 18, no. 3 (1999), pp. 363–76.

16. H. Clinton, "FTC Action," *Advertising Age,* October 9, 2000, p. 58. For an opposing view, see R. Bergler, "The Effects of Commercial Advertising on Children," *International Journal of Advertising* 18, no. 4 (1999), pp. 411–25.

17. "Advertising Strategies to Target Kids Raise Questions," *10News.com,* July 11, 2005; S. Loeb, "Digital Ad Spend on Kids Expected to Double by 2019," *VatorNews,* September 11, 2017, http://vator.tv/news/2017-09-11-digital-ad-spend-on-kids-expected-to-double-by-2019, accessed August 2, 2018; Statista, "Spending on Advertising to Children Worldwide from 2012–2019, by Format," 2018, www.statista.com/statistics/750865/kids-advertising-spending-worldwide, accessed July 26, 2018.

18. See, e.g., *The Role of Media in Childhood Obesity* (Washington, DC: Kaiser Family Foundation, 2004); P. M. Ippolito, *TV Advertising to Children 1977 v. 2004* (Washington, DC: Bureau of Economics, FTC, Research Presentation, July 14, 2005); L. Moses, "A Look at Kids' Exposure to Ads," *Adweek,* March 11, 2014, www.adweek.com/digital/look-kids-exposure-ads-156191/, accessed July 26, 2018.

19. M. M. Cardona, "Young Girls Targeted by Makeup Companies," *Advertising Age,* November 27, 2000, p. 15.

20. M. Scott, "Girls Clamoring for Grown-up Shoe Styles," *Marketing News,* November 19, 2001, p. 25.

21. M. Irvine, "More Young Children Fret over Body Image," *Eugene Register Guard,* July 23, 2001, p. 1; K. Wallace, "Kids as Young as 5 Concerned About Body Image," *CNN,* February 13, 2015, www.cnn.com/2015/02/13/living/feat-body-image-kids-younger-ages/index.html, accessed July 26, 2018.

22. "Children, Teens, Media, and Body Image: A Common Sense Research Brief," *Common Sense Media,* January 21, 2015, www.commonsensemedia.org/research/children-teens-media-and-body-image, accessed July 26, 2018.

23. Wallace, "Kids as Young as 5 Concerned About Body Image."

24. S. W. Colford, "Top Kid TV Offender: Premiums," *Advertising Age,* April 29, 1991, p. 52.

25. *Guidance for Food Advertising Self-Regulation* (New York: National Advertising Review Council, White Paper, May 28, 2004).

26. See K. Anders, "Marketing and Policy Considerations for Violent Video Games," *Journal of Public Policy & Marketing,* Fall 1999, pp. 270–73; I. Teinowitz, "FTC Report Refuels Debate on Violent Entertainment," *Advertising Age,* April 30, 2001, p. 4; I. Teinowitz, "Violence Revisited," *Advertising Age,* December 3, 2001, p. 3; I. Teinowitz, "Entertainment Gets a Pass," *Advertising Age,* December 10, 2001, p. 16.

27. "For Parents," www.happymeal.com/#legal, accessed July 26, 2018.

28. Y. Noguchi, "Connecting with Kids, Wirelessly," *Washington Post,* July 7, 2005, p. A1; J. Howard, "When Kids Get Their First Cell Phones around the World," *CNN,* December 11, 2017, www.cnn.com/2017/12/11/health/cell-phones-for-kids-parenting-without-borders-explainer-intl/index.html, accessed July 26, 2018.

29. Howard, "When Kids Get Their First Cell Phones around the World."

30. C. Knorr, "Sneaky Ways Advertisers Target Kids," *Common Sense Media,* February 7, 2014, www.commonsensemedia.org/blog/sneaky-ways-advertisers-target-kids, accessed July 27, 2018.

31. Commercial Alert, "Children's Advocates Ask Congress to Investigate Marketing of Mobile Phones to Kids," press release, July 26, 2005, www.commercialalert.org.

32. L. Pawlak, "What Parents Need to Know About JUULing, the Disturbing New Vaping Trend," *Working Mother,* April 2, 2018, www.workingmother.com/what-parents-need-to-know-about-juuling-latest-vaping-trend, accessed July 27, 2018; "JUUL Marketing and Social Media Code," www.juul.com/our-responsibility#marketing-code, accessed July 27, 2018.

33. Classification scheme and descriptions come from *Captive Kids* (Yonkers, NY: Consumers Union, 1995 Research Report, copyright 1998). Additional content from J. E. Brand and B. S. Greenberg, "Commercials in the Classroom," *Journal of Advertising Research,* January 1994, pp. 18–27; I. Teinowitz, "Marketer Obesity Efforts Get Low Consumer Marks," *AdAge.com,* June 7, 2005; S. Thompson, "Pepsi Hits High Note with Students,"

Advertising Age, October 9, 2000, p. 30; S. Jarvis, "Lesson Plans," *Marketing News,* June 18, 2001, p. 1; M. M. Cardona, "High School Papers Group to Take Ads," *Advertising Age,* March 29, 2004, p. 13; A. Enright, "Food, Drink Firms Take New Path to Reach Youths in, out of Class," *Marketing News,* August 15, 2006, pp. 8–10; A. Ford, "Captive Audience: Has Advertising in School Gone Too Far?," *Time,* November 17, 2010, http://content.time.com/time/magazine/article/0,9171,2028060,00.html, accessed July 27, 2018.

34. "Protecting Your Child's Privacy Online," *Federal Trade Commission,* July 2013, www.consumer.ftc.gov/articles/0031-protecting-your-childs-privacy-online, accessed July 27, 2018.

35. ASRC, "CARU Reviews 'Pottermore' Site, Works with Operator to Address Certain Privacy Practices," press release, September 15, 2015, www.asrcreviews.org/caru-reviews-pottermore-site-works-with-operator-to-address-certain-privacy-practices/, accessed July 27, 2018.

36. ASRC, "CARU Recommends WS Publishing Group Modify Privacy Practices for 'Friendzy' Apps; Company Agrees to Do So," press release, April 6, 2016, www.asrcreviews.org/caru-recommends-ws-publishing-group-modify-privacy-practices-for-friendzy-apps-company-agrees-to-do-so/, accessed July 27, 2018.

37. See, e.g., C. Tucker, "Social Networks, Personalized Advertising, and Privacy Controls," *Journal of Marketing Research* 51 (October 2014), pp. 546–62; L. Bright, S. Kleiser, and S. Grau, "Too Much Facebook? An Exploratory Examination of Social Media Fatigue," *Computers in Human Behavior* 44 (2015), pp. 148–55; K. D, Martin and P. E. Murphy, "The Role of Data Privacy in Marketing," *Journal of the Academy of Marketing Science* 45 (2017), pp. 135–55.

38. *Preliminary FTC Staff Privacy Report* (Washington, DC: Federal Trade Commission, December 1, 2010).

39. Ibid.

40. See, e.g., M. Gillett, "A Company's Ugly Contradition," *Boston Globe,* November 5, 2007.

41. See B. G. Englis, M. R. Solomon, and R. D. Ashmore, "Beauty *before* the Eyes of Beholders," *Journal of Advertising,* June 1994, pp. 49–64; C. R. Wiles, J. A. Wiles, and A. Tjernlund, "The Ideology of Advertising," *Journal of Advertising Research,* May 1996, pp. 57–66; M. C. Martin and J. W. Gentry, "Stuck in the Model Trap," *Journal of Advertising,* Summer 1997, pp. 19–33; M. K. Hogg, M. Bruce, and K. Hough, "Female Images in Advertising," *International Journal of Advertising* 18, no. 4 (1999), pp. 445–73; T. Reichert, "The Prevalence of Sexual Imagery in Ads Targeted to Young Adults," *Journal of Consumer Affairs,* Winter 2003, pp. 403–12.

42. S. Burton, R. G. Netemeyer, and D. R. Lichtenstein, "Gender Differences for Appearance-Related Attitudes and Behaviors," *Journal of Public Policy & Marketing,* Fall 1994, pp. 60–75.

43. R. Gustafson, M. Popovich, and S. Thompson, "Subtle Ad Images Threaten Girls More," *Marketing News,* June 4, 2001, p. 12.

44. For research in these areas, see R. W. Pollay and S. Lysonski, "In the Eye of the Beholder," *Journal of International Consumer Marketing* 6, no. 2 (1993), pp. 25–43; D. Walsh, "Safe Sex in Advertising," *American Demographics,* April 1994, pp. 24–30; R. H. Kolbe and D. Muehling, "Gender Roles and Children's Television Advertising," *Journal of Current Issues and Research in Advertising,* Spring 1995, pp. 49–64.

45. C. Rubel, "Marketers Giving Better Treatment to Females," *Marketing News,* April 22, 1996, p. 10.

46. See L. Langmeyer, "Advertising Images of Mature Adults," *Journal of Current Issues and Research in Advertising,* Fall 1993, pp. 81–91; C. R. Taylor and J. Y. Lee, "Not in *Vogue,*" *Journal of Public Policy & Marketing,* Fall 1994, pp. 239–45; T. H. Stevenson and P. E. McIntyre, "A Comparison of the Portrayal and Frequency of Hispanics and Whites in English Language Television Advertising," *Journal of Current Issues and Research in Advertising,* Spring 1995, pp. 65–74; M. T. Elliott, "Differences in the Portrayal of Blacks," *Journal of Current Issues and Research in Advertising,* Spring 1995, pp. 75–86; J. M. Bristor, R. G. Lee, and M. R. Hunt, "Race and Ideology," *Journal of Public Policy & Marketing,* Spring 1995, pp. 48–59; E. J. Wilson and A. Biswas, "The Use of Black Models in Specialty Catalogs," *Journal of Direct Marketing,* Autumn 1995, pp. 47–56; K. Karande and A. Grbavac, "Acculturation and the Use of Asian Models in Print Advertisements," in *Enhancing Knowledge Development in Marketing,* ed. C. Droge and R. Calantone (Chicago: American Marketing Association, 1996), pp. 347–52.

47. See L. J. Shrum, "Television and Persuasion," *Psychology & Marketing,* March 1999, pp. 119–40.

48. See, e.g., *Fall Colors* (Oakland, CA: Children Now, 2003–04).

49. See A. Simonson and M. B. Holbrook, "Permissible Puffery versus Actionable Warranty in Advertising and Salestalk," *Journal of Public Policy & Marketing,* Fall 1993, pp. 216–33.

50. Insight based on R. J. Harris, "Comprehension of Pragmatic Implications in Advertising," *Journal of Applied Psychology* 62, no. 5 (1977), pp. 603–608; G. J. Gaeth and T. B. Heath, "The Cognitive Processing of Misleading Advertising in Young and Old Adults," *Journal of Consumer Research,* June 1987, pp. 43–54; I. L. Preston, *The Tangled Web They Weave* (Madison, WI: The University of Wisconsin Press, 1994); *Advertising FAQ's: A Guide for Small Business* (Washington, DC: The Federal Trade Commission, 2001).

51. E. Wyatt, "As Online Ads Look More Like News Articles, F.T.C. Warns Against Deception," *New York Times,* December 5, 2013, p. B2; J. DeMers, "Is Native Advertising Sustainable for the Long Haul?," *Forbes,* March 1, 2018, www.forbes.com/sites/jaysondemers/2018/03/01/is-native-advertising-sustainable-for-the-long-haul/#7835b6963733, accessed July 27, 2018; "What Is Native Advertising," www.outbrain.com/native-advertising/, accessed July 27, 2018.

52. C. A. Cole and G. J. Gaeth, "Cognitive and Age-Related Differences in the Ability to Use Nutritional Information in a Complex Environment," *Journal of Marketing Research,* May 1990, pp. 175–84; W. Mueller, "Who Reads the Label?," *American Demographics,* January 1991, pp. 36–40.

53. B. Reid, "Adequacy of Symbolic Warnings," *Marketing News,* October 25, 1985, p. 3.

54. See G. V. Johar, "Consumer Involvement and Deception from Implied Advertising Campaigns," *Journal of Marketing Research,* August 1995, pp. 267–79.

55. Complaint, *In re* Beck's North America, Docket No. C-3859 (FTC March 5, 1999), www.ftc.gov/sites/default/files/documents/cases/1999/03/beckcomplaint_0.htm, accessed August 1, 2018; P. Spencer, "Advertising Battles," *Consumers' Research Magazine,* April 1998; Balance Bar Company, www.company-histories.com/Balance-Bar-Company-Company-History.html, accessed July 31, 2018.

56. "Package Downsizing Proves That Less Is Not More," *Consumer Reports,* September 24, 2015, www.consumerreports.org/cro/magazine/2015/09/packaging-downsizing-less-is-not-more/index.htm, accessed July 27, 2018.

57. See J.-N. Kapferer, "Brand Confusion," *Psychology & Marketing,* September 1995, pp. 551–68; D. J. Howard, R. A. Kerin, and C. Gengler, "The Effects of Brand Name Similarity on Brand Source Confusion," *Journal of Public Policy & Marketing,* Fall 2000, pp. 250–64; A. Aribarg, N. Arora, T. Henderson, and Y. Kim, "Private Label Imitation of a National Brand: Implications for Consumer Choice and Law," *Journal of Marketing Research* 51 (December 2014), pp. 657–75.

58. S. Ellison and B. Steinberg, "P&G Is Settling Disputes on Ads as Suits Pile Up," *Wall Street Journal,* November 26, 2003, pp. B1, B3.

59. See, e.g., A. Mitra et al., "Can the Educationally Disadvantaged Interpret the FDA-Mandated Nutrition Facts Panel?," *Journal of Public Policy & Marketing,* Spring 1999, pp. 106–17; J. A. Garretson and S. Burton, "Effects of Nutrition Facts Panel Values, Nutrition Claims, and Health Claims," *Journal of Public Policy & Marketing,* Fall 2000, pp. 213–27; G. Baltas, "The Effects of Nutrition Information on Consumer Choice," *Journal of Advertising Research,* March 2001, pp. 57–63; S. K. Balasubramanian and C. Cole, "Consumers' Search and Use of Nutrition Information," *Journal of Marketing,* July 2002, pp. 112–27.

60. E. Schultz, "How the FDA's Label Proposal Might Change Food Marketing," *Advertising Age,* February 27, 2014, http://adage.com/article/cmo-strategy/label-proposal-higher-costs-smaller-packages/291904/; FDA, "Changes to the Nutrition Facts Label," May 20, 2016, www.fda.gov/Food/GuidanceRegulation/GuidanceDocumentsRegulatoryInformation/LabelingNutrition/ucm385663.htm#highlights, accessed July 27, 2018; A. Gasparro and H. Haddon, "Food Fight: Brands Clash over Nutrition Facts Labels," *Wall Street Journal,* August 3, 2017, www.wsj.com/articles/why-the-labels-on-your-food-are-changing-or-not-1501758003, accessed July 27, 2018.

61. Schultz, "How the FDA's Label Proposal Might Change Food Marketing"; FDA, "Changes to the Nutrition Facts Label"; Gasparro and Haddon, "Food Fight: Brands Clash over Nutrition Facts Labels."

62. See M. Wilkie, "Rx Marketers 'Test' FDA Guides on Print DTC Ads," *Advertising Age,* April 6, 1998, p. 18.

63. G. R. Milne, M. J. Culnan, and H. Greene, "A Longitudinal Assessment of Online Privacy Notice Readability," *Journal of Public Policy and Marketing,* Fall 2006, pp. 238–49.

64. L. Handley, "People Are Eating Tide Laundry Pods and This Is What Owner P&G Is Doing About It," *CNBC,* January 22, 2018, www.cnbc.com, accessed July 17, 2018; S. Terlep, "P&G Trying to Stop 'Dangerous' Tide Pods Challenge, CEO Says," *Wall Street Journal,* January 22, 2018, online.wsj.com, accessed July 17, 2018.

65. S. Young, "FDA Reveals Bigger, Graphic Warning Labels for Cigarette Packages," *CNN.com,* June 21, 2011.

66. D. Reynolds, "Big Tobacco Returns to Television Advertising by Court Order," *CBS News,* November 27, 2017, www.cbsnews.com/news/big-tobacco-advertising-television-court-order/, accessed July 27, 2018.

6-1 IS CRUDE PUPPET MOVIE HITTING A DEAD END ON *SESAME STREET?*

Sesame Street is a well-known and beloved television program that has brought lessons of kindness, life skills, and education to generations of children across the globe. Highlighted in the show are human actors along with puppets, or rather "Muppets," such as Kermit the Frog, Miss Piggy, Grover, Gonzo, Fozzie the Bear, and more. The Muppets were designed by Jim Henson and then sold to the nonprofit organization Sesame Workshop, which owns the *Sesame Street* television program. Since 1969, Sesame Workshop has worked to build the *Sesame Street* brand to be known as wholesome and educational for children. Jim Henson passed away in 1990, but his creations continue to delight and educate young children, reaching a global audience of 190 million children.

In comes Brian Henson, the son of Jim Henson, with his alternate world of puppets. Brian Henson's puppets are explicitly not Muppets, but they are reminiscent of them. These puppets live in a movie called *The Happytime Murders,* which is produced by STX Entertainment. This movie shows the dark side of puppet life, supposedly what puppets are doing when they are not entertaining children, and takes it to quite the extreme. It is placed in the seedy underbelly of Los Angeles and features puppets engaging in various illicit activities and crimes, including murder, drug use, and prostitution. Melissa McCarthy is the star human actor in *The Happytime Murders* and, ironically, also previously appeared on *Sesame Street* in 2013, albeit in a completely different and more wholesome manner, dancing with Elmo.

Aside from the puppets being styled in a way that resembles the Muppets of *Sesame Street,* the trailer for the movie also implies a connection and even tacit endorsement by *Sesame Street.* For example, the primary tagline is "No Sesame. All Street." In the first several screens of *The Happytime Murders* trailer, the term *Muppet* is explicitly mentioned, as copy reads, "After 35 years of entertaining children . . . The Director of *The Muppet Christmas Carol* . . . The Director of *Muppet Treasure Island* . . . The Director of *Muppets Tonight* . . . is finally ready to reveal what goes down . . . when kids aren't around." While it is true that Brian Henson was the director of those films and is the chairman of

The Jim Henson Company, there was no endorsement of *The Happytime Murders* movie by the *Sesame Street* program or Sesame Workshop.

In fact, quite the opposite. Executives at Sesame Workshop were very unhappy about the implied association between *Sesame Street* and this movie with very adult content. They requested that STX Entertainment remove references from their advertising, but the request was denied. As a result, Sesame Workshop filed a lawsuit against STX Entertainment. The lawsuit claimed that *The Happytimes Murders* movie damages the *Sesame Street* brand by associating its completely unwholesome content with the popular children's program. In particular, the slogan mentioned above that includes the "Sesame" name is particularly repugnant. The Sesame Workshop lawsuit cites extremely vulgar, disgusting, and inappropriate language and behaviors by the characters in the movie as tarnishing the *Sesame Street* brand by appropriating and capitalizing on the *Sesame Street* name and goodwill. According to Sesame Workshop:

> We were surprised and disappointed that *Sesame Street,* a show dedicated to educating young children, is being exploited to market this R-rated film. . . . We take no issue with the creative freedom of the filmmakers and their right to make and promote this movie, rather this is about how our name is being misused to market a film with which we have no association.

Sesame Workshop demanded that STX Entertainment run corrective advertising to make clear that there is no endorsement or association whatsoever and to prevent potential confusion between them.

STX Entertainment disagreed strongly with the Sesame Workshop stance and dug in. Marketers at STX actually turned the lawsuit into an opportunity to create buzz and publicity to spread awareness for the film. Brian Henson quickly developed a puppet attorney named Fred Esq. to speak on behalf of the movie about the case. Fred Esq. got his own Twitter account, where his photograph and statements were distributed. According to Fred Esq.:

STX loved the idea of working closely with Brian Henson and the Jim Henson Company to tell the untold story of the active lives of Henson puppets when they're not performing in front of children. "Happytime Murders" is the happy result of that collaboration and we're incredibly pleased with the early reaction to the film and how well the trailer has been received by its intended audience. While we're disappointed that *Sesame Street* does not share in the fun, we are confident in our legal position. We look forward to introducing adult moviegoers to our adorably unapologetic characters this summer.

The Happytimes Murders was slated to appear in theaters in August 2018. With STX Entertainment just releasing the offensive trailer in mid-May 2018, Sesame Workshop had to act on a short time frame to stop any damage to the *Sesame Street* brand. They filed an emergency restraining order specifically about the "No Sesame. All Street" tagline as an early step. However, in late May, Manhattan federal Judge Vernon Broderick ruled in favor of STX Entertainment, granting them permission to continue to use the tagline while the case proceeded. The judge stated that Sesame Workshop had failed to demonstrate that consumers were really confused about an association, as only a small proportion of parents and other consumers have written in with complaints out of millions of viewers. Also, the judge noted that the tagline does actually indicate there is not a connection by saying "No Sesame."

The fight does not end there though. This initial ruling was only for the emergency restraining order, not the entire lawsuit. At the time of the writing of this case, the lawsuit between Sesame Workshop and STX Entertainment was ongoing.

Discussion Questions

1. Chapter 20 discusses corrective advertising. Sesame Workshop demanded that STX Entertainment run corrective advertising as part of the lawsuit.
   a. Why would Sesame Workshop want the corrective advertising?
   b. Do you think corrective advertising would be effective? Why or why not?

2. Use YouTube to look up and view the trailer for *The Happytime Murders.* (Note: There is some adult and offensive content, so skip viewing it if you feel uncomfortable to do so. You can still answer this question based on the case content alone.) Pay special attention to the written copy that mentions "Sesame" and "Muppets" on the trailer and the style of the felt puppets. Although the tagline says, "No Sesame," would you as a consumer have the impression that there is actually not an association or endorsement by *Sesame Street?* Why or why not?

3. Chapter 20 discusses the CARU guidelines. Examine the actions of STX Entertainment from the perspective of the CARU guidelines. Which of the guidelines (if any) most relate to the situation presented in this case?

4. Chapter 3 discusses several key values in American society. Which of these values is most relevant to the situation described in this case?

5. Chapter 7 describes word-of-mouth (WOM) and buzz marketing. How did STX Entertainment use this type of marketing to capitalize on this legal dispute with Sesame Workshop?

6. At the time of the writing of this case, Sesame Workshop had lost the first round of the lawsuit to STX Entertainment with the denied request for a temporary restraining order from using the tagline "No Sesame. Just Street." However, the lawsuit was set to continue. Perform an Internet search to research the final outcome of this case. What was it? How do you feel about it? Was the final outcome the best decision? Why or why not?

Source: J. Berr, "'The Happytime Murders' May Be Dividing Sesame Street," *CBS News,* May 31, 2018, www.cbsnews.com, accessed July 27, 2018; L. Benson, K. Croffie, and P. Murphy, "'Sesame Street' Loses Lawsuit Against Makers of Raunchy Puppet Comedy 'The Happytime Murders,'" *CNN,* May 31, 2018, www.cnn.com, accessed July 27, 2018; N. Chokshi, "Melissa McCarthy Movie Wins a Round in Sesame Street Lawsuit," *New York Times,* June 1, 2018, www.nytimes.com, accessed July 27, 2018; R. Espinoza, "'Sesame Street' Creators Sue the Henson-Helmed 'Happytime Murders' Puppet Comedy," *Forbes,* May 26, 2018, www.forbes.com, accessed July 27, 2018; A. James, "Happytime Murders Film Successfully Trolls Sesame Street into Marketing the Film," *Boing Boing,* May 31, 2018, https://boingboing.net, accessed July 27, 2018; J. C. Mays, "Makers of 'Sesame Street' Sue to Get Raunchy Puppet Movie to Change Its Advertising," *New York Times,* May 26, 2018, www.nytimes.com, accessed July 27, 2018; M. McCluskey, "Sesame Street Lost a Legal Battle against Melissa McCarthy's R-Rated Puppet Movie Happytime Murders," *Time,* June 1, 2018, http://time.com, accessed July 27, 2018; A. McDonald, "'Happytime Murders' Creators Respond to 'Sesame Street' Lawsuit with Actual Puppet Lawyer," *Huffington Post,* May 28, 2018, www.huffingtonpost.com, accessed July 27, 2018; D. Morris, "'Sesame Street' Producers Sue R-Rated Puppet Comedy for Confusing Audiences," *Forbes,* May 27, 2018, www.forbes.com, accessed July 27, 2018; A. Park, "Judge Sides with Melissa McCarthy's 'The Happytime Murders' after 'Sesame Street' Complaints," *CBS News,* May 31, 2018, www.cbsnews.com, accessed July 27, 2018; B. Pearson, "'The Happytime Murders' Responds to 'Sesame Street' Lawsuit through a Puppet Lawyer," *Film: Blogging the Reel World,* May 29, 2018, www.slashfilm.com, accessed July 27, 2018.

6-2 COPPA EVOLVES, BUT TECHNOLOGY INDUSTRIES EVOLVE FASTER

The Children's Online Privacy Protection Act has evolved and gone through a series of revisions since its inception in 1998 and the Federal Trade Commission's development of the Children's Online Privacy Protection Rule, also known as The Rule, in 1999. There were originally five primary provisions, but with the latest revision, there are now seven provisions of The Rule to adapt to the changing online environment (for more detail on each provision, see Table 20–3).

This evolution of The Rule has become especially relevant as technology progresses and there are many new alternatives for marketers to reach and collect information from children online than simply websites alone. The largest new development is the proliferation of apps. Apps are most commonly found on smart devices such as phones and tablets, but they are even integrated into smart toys that can go so far as to record voices and collect geo-tracking data of children's locations.

There have been several cases where the Federal Trade Commission has found apps to be in violation of COPPA's provisions in The Rule. Stiff consequences are imposed on offending companies, such as lawsuits, shut down of apps, loss of reputation, and fines. For example, in 2015, two app development companies, LAI Systems, LLC, and Retro Dreamer, were found to have allowed advertisers to use persistent identifiers, which are data that are tied to particular devices, to serve advertising to children. This violation was present within a variety of apps from these developers that were targeted to children under the age of 13, such as My Cake Shop, My Pizza Shop, Hair Salon Makeover, Ice Cream Jump, and Happy Pudding Jump, to name a few. LAI Systems, LLC, and Retro Dreamer were forced to pay a combined $360,000 in civil penalties over these violations of The Rule. According to a statement from Jessica Rich, director of the FTC's Bureau of Consumer Protection:

> It's vital that companies understand the rules of the road when it comes to handling children's personal information online. These cases make it clear that we're closely watching this space to ensure children's privacy online is being protected.

However, with the rapid proliferation of apps and the limited regulatory resources of the FTC, much of the compliance with The Rule is falling to self-regulation.

Unfortunately, not all companies are following the letter of The Rule. In fact, a 2018 analysis of 5,885 child-directed Android apps available in the Google Play Store was performed by researchers at the International Computer Science Institute at the University of California, Berkeley. This study revealed shocking results.

- 57 percent are potentially violating COPPA provisions on some level.
- 40 percent shared personal information without reasonable security measures.
- 39 percent displayed ignorance or disregard for contractual obligations aimed at protecting privacy of children.
- 18 percent shared persistent identifiers for prohibited purposes such as targeting advertisements.
- 4.8 percent had clear violations of sharing location or contact information without parental consent.

The researchers of this study, Irwin Reyes, Primal Wijesekera, Joel Reardon, Amit Elazari Bar On, Abbas Razaghpanah, Narseo Vallina-Rodriguez, and Serge Egelman, write:

> Based on our data, it is not clear that industry self-regulation has resulted in higher privacy standards; some of our data suggest the opposite. Thus, industry self-regulation appears to be ineffective.

In response to these findings, a Google spokesperson stated:

> We're taking the researchers' report very seriously and looking into their findings. Protecting kids and families is a top priority, and our Designed for Families programme requires developers to abide by specific requirements above and beyond our standard Google Play policies. If we determine that an app violates our policies, we will take action. We always appreciate the research community's work to help make the Android ecosystem safer.

Table A provides a COPPA Evaluation Grid that can be used to evaluate how well various websites and apps that target children under 13 years of age adhere to The Rule under COPPA (each row represents one of the key provisions). Each website or app can be rated in terms of its adherence to each COPPA provision on the

COPPA Provision	Company A	Company B	Company C
Privacy Policy			
Parental Notice			
Parental Consent			
Parental Access			
Parental Prevention			
Confidentiality			
Data Retention and Deletion			

TABLE A COPPA Evaluation Grid

*Note: The core provisions presented here and in Chapter 20 appear to hold true. However, "The Rule under COPPA" continues to evolve. It is important for every responsible organization to stay current on how those changes affect their efforts to stay complaint with COPPA and to protect the online privacy of children.

following scale: 1 = very poor; 2 = poor; 3 = adequate; 4 = good; 5 = very good. Alternatively, a check-box procedure might be used in which a checkmark is placed in each cell where the provision is met.

Discussion Questions

1. Do you feel that the COPPA provisions found in The Rule are sufficient to safeguard children's privacy online? Why or why not?

2. Do you feel that the Federal Trade Commission's enforcement of COPPA is sufficient? Why or why not? What policy recommendations would you make that could improve industry compliance and government enforcement?

3. What advice would you have for parents of young children in regard to using websites and apps?

4. Visit at least three websites that are designed to appeal to children under 13 and complete the COPPA Evaluation Grid.

5. Download and use three apps that are designed to appeal to children under 13 and complete the COPPA Evaluation Grid.

6. Prepare a report using the COPPA Evaluation Grid results from the previous two questions and discuss the following:
   a. How well did the websites you researched in question 4 appear to be adhering to The Rule under COPPA?
   b. How well did the apps you researched in question 5 appear to be adhering to The Rule under COPPA?
   c. Draw comparisons and contrasts among the websites versus the apps.
   d. Are there areas in which you see room for improvement? Explain.

Source: S. Gibbs, "Thousands of Android Apps Potentially Violate Child Protection Law," *Guardian,* April 16, 2018, www.theguardian.com, accessed July 27, 2018; "Guide to COPPA in Websites and Mobile Apps," *Website Policies: Attorney-Drafted Legal Agreements,* August 7, 2017, www.websitepolicies .com, accessed July 27, 2018; L. Magid, "FTC Clarifies Children's Online Privacy Law (COPPA)," *Forbes,* April 25, 2013, www.forbes.com; I. Reyes et al., "'Won't Somebody Think of the Children?' Examining COPPA Compliance at Scale," *Proceedings on Privacy Enhancing Technologies* 2018, no. 3, pp. 63–83; Federal Trade Commission, "Two App Developers Settle FTC Charges They Violated Children's Online Privacy Protection Act," press release, December 17, 2015, www.ftc.gov, accessed July 27, 2018; Federal Trade Commission, "Complying with COPPA: Frequently Asked Questions," July 2013, www.ftc .gov/tips-advice/business-center/guidance/complying-coppa-frequently-asked-questions, accessed July 27, 2018.

Consumer Research Methods

In this appendix, we want to provide you with some general guidelines for conducting research on consumer behavior. While these guidelines will help you get started, a good marketing research text is indispensable if you need to conduct a consumer research project or evaluate a consumer research proposal.

SECONDARY DATA

Secondary data are basically existing information or data. Any research project should begin with a thorough search for existing information relevant to the project at hand. Internal data, such as past studies, sales reports, and accounting records, should be consulted. External data, including reports, magazines, government organizations, trade associations, marketing research firms, advertising agencies, academic journals, trade journals, and books, should be thoroughly researched.

Computer searches are a fast, economical means of conducting such searches. University and large public libraries, as well as companies, often subscribe to various databases that can be invaluable sources of information, reports, and data. These include, but are not limited to, (a) ABI Inform—electronic access to trade and academic publications, (b) MarketResearch.com—an online source of detailed industry reports, (c) Simmons Research, (d) Gfk Global, (e) Kantar's Standard Rate and Data Service (SRDS), and (f) Mintel global market research and market insight. Publicly available demographic information can be found at the U.S. Census (www.census.gov). And a great source for global information is *The World Factbook* (www.cia.gov/cia/publications/factbook/) or The World Bank.

PRIMARY DATA COLLECTION: ISSUES AND METHODS

If the specific information required is not available from secondary sources, we must gather primary data. Primary data are information or data that we collect for the first time in order to answer a specific research question. Thus, we might use the U.S. Census data to better understand the demographics driving gardening (secondary data) but conduct a survey to collect information (primary data) regarding the specific brand name we will use for our new garden tool.

Sampling

Collecting primary data generally involves talking to or observing consumers. However, it could involve asking knowledgeable others, such as sales personnel, about the consumers. In either case, time and cost constraints generally preclude us from contacting every single potential consumer. Therefore, most consumer research projects require a sample—a deliberately selected portion of the larger group. This requires a number of critical decisions, as described below. Mistakes made at this point are difficult to correct later in the study. The key decisions are briefly described below.

Define the Population   The first step is to define the consumers in which we are interested. Do we want to talk to current brand users, current product-category users, or potential product-category users? Do we want to talk with the purchasers, the users, or everyone involved in the purchase process? The population as we define it must reflect the behavior on which our marketing decision will be based.

Specify the Sampling Frame   A sampling frame is a list or grouping of individuals or households that reflects the population of interest. A phone book and shoppers at a given shopping mall can each serve as a sampling frame. Perfect sampling frames contain every member of the population one time. Phone books do not have households with unlisted numbers or those with no landline; many people do not visit shopping malls, while others visit them frequently. This is an area in which we generally must do the best we can without expecting a perfect frame. However, we must be very alert for biases that may be introduced by imperfections in our sampling frame.

Select a Sampling Method   The major decision at this point is between a random (probability) sample and a nonrandom sample. Nonrandom samples, particularly judgment samples, can provide good results. A judgment sample involves the deliberate selection of knowledgeable consumers or individuals. For example, a firm might decide to interview the social activity officers of fraternities and sororities to estimate campus attitudes toward a carbonated wine drink aimed at the campus market. Such a sample might provide useful insights. However, it also might be biased because such individuals are likely to have a higher level of income and be more socially active than the average student.

The most common nonrandom sample, the convenience sample, involves selecting sample members in the manner most convenient for the researcher. It is subject to many types of bias and generally should be avoided.

Random or probability samples allow some form of a random process to select members from a sample frame. It may be every third person who passes a point-of-purchase display, house addresses selected by using a table of random numbers, or telephone numbers generated randomly by a computer. If random procedures are used, we can calculate the likelihood that our sample is not representative within specified limits.

Determine Sample Size   Finally, we must determine how large a sample to talk to. If we are using random sampling, there are formulas that can help us make this decision. In general, the more diverse our population is and the more certain we want to be that we have the correct answer, the more people we will need to interview.

DATA COLLECTION METHODS

Depth Interviews

Depth interviews can involve one respondent and one interviewer, or they may involve a small group (8 to 15 respondents) and an interviewer. The latter are called **focus group interviews,** and the former are termed **individual depth interviews** or one-on-ones. Groups of four or five often are referred to as minigroup interviews. Depth interviews in general are commonly referred to as qualitative research. Individual depth interviews involve a one-to-one relationship between the interviewer and the respondent. The interviewer does not have a specific set of prespecified questions that must be asked according to the order imposed by a questionnaire. Instead, there is freedom to create questions, to probe those responses that appear relevant, and generally to try to develop the best set of data in any way practical. However, the interviewer must follow one rule: He or she must not consciously try to affect the content of the answers given by the respondent. The respondent must feel free to reply to the various questions, probes, and other, more subtle ways of encouraging responses in the manner deemed most appropriate.

Individual depth interviews are appropriate in six situations:

1. Detailed probing of an individual's behavior, attitudes, or needs is required.
2. The subject matter under discussion is likely to be of a highly confidential nature (e.g., personal investments).
3. The subject matter is of an emotionally charged or embarrassing nature.
4. Certain strong, socially acceptable norms exist (e.g., child care) and the need to conform in a group discussion may influence responses.
5. A highly detailed (step-by-step) understanding of complicated behavior or decision-making patterns (e.g., planning the family holiday) is required.
6. The interviews are with professional people or with people on the subject of their jobs (e.g., finance directors).

Focus group interviews can be applied to (1) basic need studies for product ideas creation, (2) new-product ideas or concept exploration, (3) product-positioning studies, (4) advertising and communications research, (5) background studies on consumers' frames of reference, (6) establishment of consumer vocabulary as a preliminary step in questionnaire development, and (7) determination of attitudes and behaviors.

The standard focus group interview involves 8 to 12 individuals. Normally, the group is designed to reflect the characteristics of a particular market segment. The respondents are selected according to the relevant sampling plan and meet at a central location that generally has facilities for recording the interviews. The discussion itself is led by a moderator. The competent moderator attempts to develop three clear stages in the one- to three-hour interview: (1) establish rapport with the group, structure the rules of group interaction, and set objectives; (2) attempt to provoke intense discussion in the relevant areas; and (3) attempt to summarize the group's responses to determine the extent of agreement. In general, either the moderator or a second person prepares a summary of each session after analyzing the session's transcript.

Observation

Observation can be used when (1) the behaviors of interest are public (or in some way traceable as in behavioral tracking of online patterns via cookies); (2) they are repetitive, frequent, or predictable; and (3) they cover a relatively brief time span. An observational study requires five decisions:

1. *Natural versus contrived situation.* Do we wait for a behavior to occur in its natural environment, or do we create an artificial situation in which it will occur?
2. *Open versus disguised observation.* To what extent are the consumers aware that we are observing their behavior?
3. *Structured versus unstructured observation.* Will we limit our observations to predetermined behaviors, or will we note whatever occurs?
4. *Direct or indirect observations.* Will we observe the behaviors themselves or merely the outcomes of the behaviors?
5. *Human or mechanical observations.* Will the observations be made mechanically or by people?

Physiological Measures

Physiological measures are direct observations of physical responses to a stimulus such as an advertisement. These responses may be controllable, such as eye movements, or uncontrollable, such as the galvanic skin response. Eye-tracking cameras allow researchers to determine how long a consumer looks at each element in a stimulus, such as a point-of-purchase display, ad, or package, and the sequence in which the elements are examined. Galvanic skin response can be measured (via a lie detector) to detect the intensity of emotional responses to ads or packages. Newer measures include brainwave research, conducted using equipment such as electroencephalograms (EEGs), to ascertain what parts of an advertisement connect with a consumer.

Projective Techniques

Projective techniques are designed to measure feelings, attitudes, and motivations that consumers are unable or unwilling to reveal otherwise. They are based on the theory that the description of vague objects requires interpretation, and this interpretation can be based only on the individual's own attitudes, values, and motives.

Table A-1 provides descriptions and examples of the more common projective techniques.

TABLE A-1   Motivation Research Techniques

I. Association Techniques	
Word association	Consumers respond to a list of words with the first word that comes to mind.
Successive word association	Consumers give the series of words that come to mind after hearing each word on the list.
Analysis and use	Responses are analyzed to see if negative associations exist. When the time to respond (response latency) also is measured, the emotionality of the word can be estimated. These techniques tap semantic memory more than motives and are used for brand name and advertising copy tests.
II. Completion Techniques	
Sentence completion	Consumers complete a sentence such as "People who buy a Cadillac _____ _____ _____."
Story completion	Consumers complete a partial story.
Analysis and use	Responses are analyzed to determine what themes are expressed. Content analysis—examining responses for themes and key concepts—is used.
III. Construction Techniques	
Cartoon techniques	Consumers fill in the words or thoughts of one of the characters in a cartoon drawing.
Third-person techniques	Consumers tell why "an average woman," "most doctors," or "people in general" purchase or use a certain product. Shopping lists (describe a person who would go shopping with this list) and lost wallets (describe a person with these items in his wallet) are also third-person techniques.
Picture response	Consumers tell a story about a person shown buying or using a product in a picture or line drawing.
Analysis and use	Same as for completion techniques.

Surveys

Surveys are systematic ways of gathering information from a large number of people. They generally involve the use of a structured or semi-structured questionnaire. Surveys can be administered by mail, by telephone, in person, or online. Personal interviews generally take place in shopping malls and are referred to as mall-intercept interviews. Each approach has advantages and disadvantages.

- **Personal interviews** allow the use of complex questionnaires, product demonstrations, and the collection of large amounts of data. They can be completed in a relatively short period of time. However, they are very expensive and are subject to interviewer bias.
- **Telephone surveys** can be completed rapidly, provide good sample control (who answers the questions), and are relatively inexpensive. Substantial amounts of data can be collected, but it must be relatively simple. Interviewer bias is possible.
- **Mail surveys** take the longest to complete and must generally be rather short. They can be used to collect modestly complex data, and they are very economical. Interviewer bias is not a problem.
- **Online surveys** are increasingly popular because they are highly cost-effective (respondents enter the data), fast, and easy to conduct. A major concern with online survey research historically has been the demographic skew or bias due to income, education, ethnic, and gender gaps. As the online population has become more representative of the general population, such concerns have reduced.

A major concern in survey research is nonresponse bias. In most surveys, fewer than 50 percent of those selected to participate in the study actually do participate. In telephone and personal interviews, many people are not at home or refuse to cooperate. In mail surveys, many people refuse or forget to respond.

We can increase the response rate by callbacks in telephone and home personal surveys. The callbacks should be made at different times and on different days. Monetary inducements (enclosing $1) increase the response rate to mail surveys, as do prenotification (a card saying that a questionnaire is coming) and reminder postcards.

If less than a 100 percent response rate is obtained, we must be concerned that those who did not respond differ from those who did. A variety of techniques are available to help us estimate the likelihood and nature of nonresponse error.

Experimentation

Experimentation involves changing one or more variables (product features, package color, advertising theme) and observing the effect the change has on another variable (consumer attitude, repeat purchase behavior, learning). The variable(s) that is changed is called an *independent variable.* The "change" is called a "manipulation," which simply means that we are systematically varying a factor at different levels. For example, if we presented different groups of consumers with a product priced at $1.00, $1.50, and $2.00, then we would have manipulated price at three levels.

The variable(s) that may be affected by the manipulation(s) is called a *dependent variable.* The objective in experimental design is to structure the situation so that any change in the dependent variable is very likely to have been caused by a change in the independent variable. The way this is done is through high levels of "control," which generally means that we manipulate variables of interest and hold all other factors constant. Thus, we could present three different product concepts that differed only in terms of price. Everything else, including design, package color, and so on, would be held constant (or remain the same) across the different price levels. The logic is that because only the manipulated variable changed, we have high confidence that it was the reason (cause) for any observed changes in the dependent variable.

There are numerous experimental designs depending on the number and level of independent variables the researcher wishes to investigate. There are different kinds of experiments that reflect the level of control that we can achieve. In a laboratory experiment, we carefully control for all outside influences and can conclude with confidence that our independent variables *caused* the changes in our dependent variable(s). Lab experiments thus yield high levels of *internal validity.*

In a field experiment, we conduct our study in the most relevant environment possible. This generally means giving up the pristine control of a lab setting. However, the reason for doing so is to see how consumers actually react in "real-world" settings. Field experiments are important because they help establish *external validity*—which is the extent to which our results are likely to hold true in real-world settings. This can mean that unusual outside influences may distort our results (that is, reduce internal validity). However, careful planning often can avoid these unusual influences.

Conjoint Analysis: Examining Attribute Importance Using Experimentation

Conjoint analysis is an application of experimentation. In conjoint analysis, the consumer is presented with a set of products or product descriptions in which the potential evaluative criteria vary (are manipulated). For example, consider a laptop manufacturer who is interested in the importance of four different attributes: Processor (2 levels: Intel Core i7 processor versus Intel Core i5 processor), Energy Star certified (2 levels: yes versus no), weight (2 levels: 4.2 lbs versus 5.7 lbs), and price (3 levels: $825, $1,200, and $2,000). This would result in 24 different notebook computer configurations ($2 \times 2 \times 2 \times 3 = 24$) that vary on four criteria. Two might be

Intel Core i7 processor	Intel Core i5 processor
Energy Star certified (yes)	Energy Star certified (no)
5.7 lbs	4.2 lbs
$1,200	$825

The consumer ranks all 24 such descriptions in terms of his or her preference for those combinations of features. Based on these preference ranks, sophisticated computer programs derive the relative importance consumers assign to each level of each attribute tested.

For example, in Figure A–1, imagine a consumer was asked to rank in terms of overall preference 24 different computer designs featuring different levels of four key evaluative criteria. The preferences were then analyzed in light of the variations in the attributes. The result is a preference curve for each evaluative criterion that reflects the importance of that attribute. On the basis of the data in Figure A–1, processor is a particularly important evaluative criterion for this consumer while weight (at least in the range examined) is of almost no importance.

Conjoint analysis is limited to the attributes listed by the researcher. Thus, a conjoint analysis of soft-drink attributes would not indicate anything about calorie content unless the researcher listed it as a feature. If an important attribute is omitted, incorrect market share predictions are likely to result. In addition, conjoint analysis is not well suited for measuring the importance of emotional or feeling-based product choices. For example, what types of attributes would you use to perform a conjoint analysis of perfumes?

FIGURE A-1

Using Conjoint Analysis to Determine the Importance of Evaluative Criteria for a Laptop Computer

Design features

Processor
- Intel Core i5 processor
- Intel Core i7 processor

Energy Star certified
- Yes
- No

Weight
- 4.2 lbs
- 5.7 lbs

Price
- $825
- $1,200
- $2,000

Design options

These design attributes produce 24 alternative computer design configurations

One design possibility

Processor: Intel Core i7 processor
Energy Star certified: Yes
Weight: 5.7 lbs
Price: $1,200

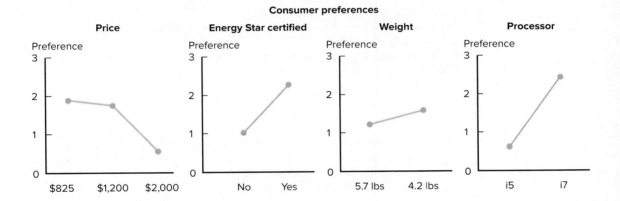

Consumer preferences

Price — Preference: $825, $1,200, $2,000

Energy Star certified — Preference: No, Yes

Weight — Preference: 5.7 lbs, 4.2 lbs

Processor — Preference: i5, i7

Relative importance

Evaluative criteria	Importance
Processor	45%
Weight	5
Energy Star compliant	25
Price	25

■ Processor is the most important feature in this example, and Intel Core i7 processor is the preferred option.

■ While price and Energy Star certified are also important, price becomes important only between $1,200 and $2,000.

Questionnaire Design

All surveys and many experiments use questionnaires as data collection devices. A questionnaire is simply a formalized set of questions for eliciting information. It can measure (1) behavior—past, present, or intended; (2) demographic characteristics—age, gender, income, education, occupation; (3) level of knowledge; and (4) attitudes and opinions. The process of questionnaire design is outlined in Table A-2.

TABLE (A-2)   Questionnaire Design Process

1. *Preliminary decisions*
   Exactly what information is required?
   Exactly who are the target respondents?
   What method of communication will be used to reach these respondents?

2. *Decisions about question content*
   Is this question really needed?
   Is this question sufficient to generate the needed information?
   Can the respondent answer the question correctly?
   Will the respondent answer the question correctly?
   Are there any external events that might bias the response to the question?

3. *Decisions about the response format*
   Can this question best be asked as an open-ended, multiple-choice, or dichotomous question?

4. *Decisions concerning question phrasing*
   Do the words used have but one meaning to all the respondents?
   Are any of the words or phrases loaded or leading in any way?
   Are there any implied alternatives in the question?
   Are there any unstated assumptions related to the question?
   Will the respondents approach the question from the frame of reference desired by the researcher?

5. *Decisions concerning the question sequence*
   Are the questions organized in a logical manner that avoids introducing errors?

6. *Decisions on the layout of the questionnaire*
   Is the questionnaire designed in a manner to avoid confusion and minimize recording errors?

7. *Pretest and revise*
   Has the final questionnaire been subjected to a thorough pretest, using respondents similar to those who will be included in the final survey?

Attitude Scales

Attitudes are frequently measured on specialized scales, as detailed below. The instructions indicate that the consumer is to mark the blank that best indicates how accurately one or the other term describes or fits the attitude object.

Various types of attitude scales exist, including the following:

Noncomparative Rating Scale   Noncomparative rating scales require the consumer to evaluate an object or an attribute of the object without directly comparing it to another object. An example would be
"How do you like the taste of Diet Pepsi?"

Like it very much	Like it	Dislike it	Strongly dislike it
_____	_____	_____	_____

Comparative Rating Scale   Comparative rating scales provide a direct comparison point (a named competitor, "your favorite brand," "the ideal brand"). An example would be
"How do you like the taste of Tom's of Maine compared with Ultrabrite?"

Like it much more	Like it more	Like it about the same	Like it less	Like it much less
_____	_____	_____	_____	_____

Semantic Differential Scale   The semantic differential scale requires the consumer to rate an item on a number of scales bounded at each end by one of two bipolar adjectives. For example:
"Rate the Honda Accord on the following attributes."

Fast _____ _____ _____ _____ _____ _____ _____ Slow
Fancy _____ _____ _____ _____ _____ _____ _____ Plain

The end positions indicate "extremely," the next pair in from the ends indicate "very," the middlemost pair indicate "somewhat," and the middle position indicates "neither/nor."

Likert Scale   Likert scales ask consumers to indicate a degree of agreement or disagreement with each of a series of statements related to the attitude object, such as the following:

1. *Macy's is one of the most attractive stores in town.*

Strongly agree	Agree	Neither agree nor disagree	Disagree	Strongly disagree
_____	_____	_____	_____	_____

2. *The service at Macy's is not satisfactory.*

Strongly agree	Agree	Neither agree nor disagree	Disagree	Strongly disagree
_____	_____	_____	_____	_____

To analyze responses, each response category is assigned a numerical value. For example, in the Likert scales above, we could assign values such as 1 (Strongly agree) through 5 (Strongly disagree). Or a +2 through −2 system could be used with 0 representing the neutral point (Neither agree nor disagree).

Measuring the Three Attitude Components

As we discussed in Chapter 11, attitude can be broken into its cognitive, affective, and behavioral components. Table A–3 provides a detailed set of items for each attitude component.

EVALUATING ADVERTISING EFFECTS

A successful advertisement, or any other marketing message, must accomplish four tasks:

1. *Exposure.* It must physically reach the consumer.
2. *Attention.* The consumer must attend to it.
3. *Interpretation.* It must be properly interpreted.
4. *Memory.* It must be stored in memory in a manner that will allow retrieval under the proper circumstances.

Advertising evaluation covers all these tasks. However, most of the effort is focused on attention and, to a lesser extent, memory.

Measures of Exposure

Exposure to print media is most frequently measured in terms of circulation. Data on circulation are provided by a variety of commercial firms. Frequently, however, these data are not broken down in a manner consistent with the firm's target market. Thus, a firm may be targeting the lower-middle social class, but circulation data may be broken down by income rather than social class.

Diary reports, in which respondents record their daily listening patterns, and telephone interviews are the two methods used to measure radio listening. Television viewing is measured primarily by **people meters** (mechanical observation), which are electronic devices

TABLE A-3   Measuring Attitude Components

Cognitive Component (Measuring Beliefs about Specific Attributes Using the Semantic Differential Scale)

Diet Coke

Strong taste	___	___	___	___	___	___	Mild taste
Low priced	___	___	___	___	___	___	High priced
Caffeine free	___	___	___	___	___	___	High in caffeine
Distinctive in taste	___	___	___	___	___	___	Similar in taste to most

Affective Component (Measuring Feelings about Specific Attributes or the Overall Brand Using Likert Scales)

	Strongly Agree	Agree	Neither Agree nor Disagree	Disagree	Strongly Disagree
I like the taste of Diet Coke.	___	___	___	___	___
Diet Coke is overpriced.	___	___	___	___	___
Caffeine is bad for your health.	___	___	___	___	___
I like Diet Coke.	___	___	___	___	___

Behavioral Component (Measuring Actions or Intended Actions)

The last soft drink I consumed was a _____.

I usually drink _____ soft drinks.

What is the likelihood you will buy Diet Coke the next time you purchase a soft drink?

_____ Definitely will buy

_____ Probably will buy

_____ Might buy

_____ Probably will not buy

_____ Definitely will not buy

that automatically determine if a television is turned on and, if so, to which channel. They allow each household member to log on when viewing by punching an identifying button. The demographics of each potential viewer are stored in the central computer so viewer profiles can be developed.

Websites can automatically record (mechanical observation) the number of total and unique (from distinct computers) visits per time period. Banner ads and the sites on which they appear are often evaluated on the *clickthrough rate*—the percentage of site visitors or total number of people who click on the banner ad.

Measures of Attention

The attention-attracting powers of commercials, packages, and websites can be partially measured in a direct manner using **eye tracking** (mechanical observation) or eye fixations. While a consumer looks at images of print ads, billboards, store shelves, packages, or websites, a camera underneath the screen sends an invisible beam of light off the consumer's pupil. The camera indicates exactly what the consumer is attending to. This technology allows marketers to determine (1) what parts of the message were attended to, (2) what sequence was used in viewing the message, and (3) how much time was spent on each part.

Indirect measures of attention, which also tap at least some aspects of memory, include theater tests, day-after recall, recognition tests, and Starch scores. *Theater tests* involve showing commercials along with television programs in a theater. Viewers complete questionnaires designed to measure which commercials, and what aspects of those commercials, attracted their attention. **Day-after recall (DAR)** is the most popular method of measuring the attention-getting power of television commercials. Individuals are interviewed the day after a commercial is aired on a program they watched. Recall of the commercial and recall of specific aspects of the commercial (assessed through questionnaires) are interpreted as a reflection of the amount of attention.

DAR measures of television commercials have been criticized as favoring rational, factual, hard-sell ads and high-involvement products while discriminating against feeling, emotional, soft-sell ads. However, for many product–target market combinations, the latter approach may be superior. In response, substantial work has been done to develop recognition measures for television commercials. In **recognition tests,** the commercial of interest, or key parts of it, along with other commercials are shown to target market members. Recognition of the commercial, or key parts of it, is the measure.

Starch scores are the most popular technique for evaluating the attention-attracting power of print ads. The respondents are shown advertisements from magazine issues they have recently read. For each advertisement, they indicate which parts (headlines, illustrations, copy blocks) they recall reading. Three main scores are computed:

1. *Noted.* The percentage of people who recall seeing the ad in that issue.
2. *Seen-associated.* The percentage of those who recall reading a part of the ad that clearly identifies the brand or advertiser.
3. *Read most.* The percentage of those who recall reading 50 percent or more of the copy.

Starch scores allow an indirect measure of attention to the overall ad and to key components of the ad.

Measures of Interpretation

Marketers investigating *interpretation* can use any number of the research methods we've discussed, including focus groups, surveys, and projective techniques. A critical task for marketers is to move beyond cognitive interpretation and tap emotions and feelings as well. Techniques such as the AdSAM® discussed in Chapter 11 can be quite useful in this regard.

Appendix B

Consumer Behavior Audit*

In this appendix, we provide a list of key questions to guide you in developing marketing strategy from a consumer behavior perspective. This audit is no more than a checklist to minimize the chance of overlooking a critical behavioral dimension. It does not guarantee a successful strategy. However, thorough and insightful answers to these questions should greatly enhance the likelihood of a successful marketing program.

Our audit is organized around the key decisions that marketing managers must make. The first key decision is the selection of the target market(s) to be served. This is followed by the determination of a viable product position for each target market. Finally, the marketing mix elements—product, place, price, and promotion—must be structured in a manner consistent with the desired product position. This process is illustrated in Figure B-1.

FIGURE B-1 Consumer Influences Drive Marketing Decisions

Consumer influences

External influences
Culture, subcultures, values
Demographics, income, and social class
Reference groups and households
Marketing activities

Internal influences
Needs, motives, and emotions
Perceptions and memory
Personality and lifestyle
Attitudes

Situational influences
Physical, time, social, task, and antecedent

Decision process influences
Problem recognition
Information search
Alternative evaluation
Outlet selection
Purchase
Postpurchase processes

Marketing decisions

Marketing segmentation
Target segment(s)
Single or multiple target segments

Product positioning
Key product differentiation variables
Position relative to competition

Market mix
Product features
Price level
Promotional appeal
Place (distribution)
Services

*Revised by Richard Pomazal of Wheeling College.

MARKET SEGMENTATION

Market segmentation is the process of dividing all possible users of a product into groups that have similar needs the products might satisfy. Market segmentation should be done prior to the final development of a new product. In addition, a complete market segmentation analysis should be performed periodically for existing products. The reason for continuing segmentation analyses is the dynamic nature of consumer needs.

A. External influences
   1. Are there cultures or subcultures whose value system is particularly consistent (or inconsistent) with the consumption of our product?
   2. Is our product appropriate for male or female consumption? Will ongoing gender-role changes affect who consumes our product or how it is consumed?
   3. Do ethnic, social, regional, or religious subcultures have different consumption patterns relevant to our product?
   4. Do various demographic or social-strata groups (age, gender, urban/suburban/rural, occupation, income, education) differ in their consumption of our product?
   5. Is our product particularly appropriate for consumers with relatively high (or low) incomes compared with others in their occupational group?
   6. Can our product be particularly appropriate for specific roles, such as students or professional women?
   7. Would it be useful to focus on specific adopter categories?
   8. Do groups in different stages of the household life cycle have different consumption patterns for our product? Who in the household is involved in the purchase process?
B. Internal influences
   1. Can our product satisfy different needs or motives in different people? What needs are involved? What characterizes individuals with differing motives?
   2. Is our product uniquely suited for particular personality types? Self-concepts?
   3. What emotions, if any, are affected by the purchase and/or consumption of this product?
   4. Is our product appropriate for one or more distinct lifestyles?
   5. Do different groups have different attitudes about an ideal version of our product?
C. Situational influences
   1. Can our product be appropriate for specific types of situations instead of (or in addition to) specific types of people?
D. Decision process influences
   1. Do different individuals use different evaluative criteria in selecting the product?
   2. Do potential customers differ in their loyalty to existing products or brands?

PRODUCT POSITION

A product position is the way the consumer thinks of a given product or brand relative to competing products or brands. A manager must determine what a desirable product position would be for each market segment of interest. This determination is generally based on the answers to the same questions used to segment a market, with the addition of the consumer's perceptions of competing products or brands. Of course, the capabilities and motivations of existing and potential competitors also must be considered.

A. Internal influences
   1. What is the general semantic memory structure for this product category in each market segment?
   2. What is the ideal version of this product in each market segment for the situations the firm wants to serve?
B. Decision process influences
   1. Which evaluative criteria are used in the purchase decision? Which decision rules and importance weights are used?

PRICING

The manager must set a pricing policy that is consistent with the desired product position. Price must be broadly conceived as everything a consumer must surrender to obtain a product. This includes time and psychological costs as well as monetary costs.

A. External influences
   1. Does the segment hold any values relating to any aspect of pricing, such as the use of credit or conspicuous consumption?
   2. Does the segment have sufficient income, after covering living expenses, to afford the product?
   3. Is it necessary to lower price to obtain a sufficient relative advantage to ensure diffusion? Will temporary price reductions induce product trial?
   4. Who in the household evaluates the price of the product?
B. Internal influences
   1. Will price be perceived as an indicator of status?
   2. Is economy in purchasing this type of product relevant to the lifestyle(s) of the segment?
   3. Is price an important aspect of the segment's attitude toward the brands in the product category?
   4. What is the segment's perception of a fair or reasonable price for this product?
C. Situational influences
   1. Does the role of price vary with the type of situation?
D. Decision process factors
   1. Can a low price be used to trigger problem recognition?
   2. Is price an important evaluative criterion? What decision rule is applied to the evaluative criteria used? Is price likely to serve as a surrogate indicator of quality?
   3. Are consumers likely to respond to in-store price reductions?

DISTRIBUTION STRATEGY

The manager must develop a place, or distribution, strategy that is consistent with the selected product position. This involves the selection of outlets (e.g., store-based, online, mobile) if the item is a physical product, or the location of the outlets if the product is a service.

A. External influences
   1. What values do the segments have that relate to distribution?
   2. Do the male and female members of the segments have differing requirements of the distribution system? Do working couples, single individuals, or single parents within the segment have unique needs relating to product distribution?

3. Can the distribution system capitalize on reference groups by serving as a means for individuals with common interests to get together?

4. Is the product complex such that a high-service channel is required to ensure its diffusion?

B. Internal influences

1. Will the selected outlets be perceived in a manner that enhances the desired product position?

2. What type of distribution system is consistent with the lifestyle(s) of each segment?

3. What attitudes does each segment hold with respect to the various distribution alternatives?

C. Situational influences

1. Do the desired features of the distribution system vary with the situation?

D. Decision process factors

1. What outlets are in the segment's evoked set? Will consumers in this segment seek information in this type of outlet?

2. Which evaluative criteria does this segment use to evaluate outlets? Which decision rule?

3. To what extent are product decisions made in the retail outlet?

PROMOTION STRATEGY

The manager must develop a promotion strategy, including advertising, nonfunctional package design features, publicity, promotions, and sales force activities that are consistent with the product position.

A. External factors

1. What values does the segment hold that can be used in our communications? Which should be avoided?

2. How can we communicate to our chosen segments in a manner consistent with the emerging gender-role perceptions of each segment?

3. What is the nonverbal communication system of each segment?

4. How, if at all, can we use reference groups in our advertisements?

5. Can our advertisements help make the product part of one or more role-related product clusters?

6. Can we reach and influence opinion leaders?

7. If our product is an innovation, are there diffusion inhibitors that can be overcome by promotion?

8. Who in the household should receive what types of information concerning our product?

B. Internal factors

1. Have we structured our promotional campaign such that each segment will be exposed to it, attend to it, and interpret it in the manner we desire?

2. Have we made use of the appropriate learning principles so that our meaning will be remembered?

3. Do our messages relate to the purchase motives held by the segment? Do they help reduce motivational conflict if necessary?

4. Are we considering the emotional implications of the ad and/or the use of our product?

5. Is the lifestyle portrayed in our advertisements consistent with the desired lifestyle of the selected segments?

6. If we need to change attitudes via our promotion mix, have we selected and properly used the most appropriate attitude-change techniques?

C. Situational influences

1. Does our campaign illustrate the full range of appropriate usage situations for the product?

D. Decision process influences

1. Will problem recognition occur naturally, or must it be activated by advertising? Should generic or selective problem recognition be generated?

2. Will the segment seek out or attend to information on the product prior to problem recognition, or must we reach them when they are not seeking our information? Can we use low-involvement learning processes effectively? What information sources are used?

3. After problem recognition, will the segment seek out information on the product or brand, or will we need to intervene in the purchase decision process? If they do seek information, what sources do they use?

4. What types of information are used to make a decision?

5. How much and what types of information are acquired at the point of purchase?

6. Is postpurchase dissonance likely? Can we reduce it through our promotional campaign?

7. Have we given sufficient information to ensure proper product use?

8. Are the expectations generated by our promotional campaign consistent with the product's performance?

9. Are our messages designed to encourage repeat purchases, brand-loyal purchases, or neither?

PRODUCT

The marketing manager must be certain that the physical product, service, or idea has the characteristics required to achieve the desired product position in each market segment.

A. External influences

1. Is the product designed appropriately for all members of the segment under consideration, including males, females, and various age groups?

2. If the product is an innovation, does it have the required relative advantage and lack of complexity to diffuse rapidly?

3. Is the product designed to meet the varying needs of different household members?

B. Internal influences

1. Will the product be perceived in a manner consistent with the desired image?

2. Will the product satisfy the key purchase motives of the segment?

3. Is the product consistent with the segment's attitude toward an ideal product?

C. Situational influences

1. Is the product appropriate for the various potential usage situations?

D. Decision process influences

1. Does the product or brand perform better than the alternatives on the key set of evaluative criteria used by this segment?

2. Will the product perform effectively in the foreseeable uses to which this segment may subject it?

3. Will the product perform as well as or better than expected by this segment?

CUSTOMER SATISFACTION
AND COMMITMENT

Marketers must produce satisfied customers to be successful in the long run. It is often to a firm's advantage to go beyond satisfaction and create committed or loyal customers.

1. What factors lead to satisfaction with our product?
2. What factors could cause customer commitment to our brand or firm?

Name Index

Page numbers followed by n refer to notes.

a

Aaker, D. A., 361n, 393n
Aaker, J., 427n
Aaker, J. L., 72n, 109n, 378, 392n, 393n
Abdul-Muhmin, A. G., 75n, 565n
Abinanti, L., 479
Abrams, B., 595n
Abratt, R., 699, 720n
Achrol, R., 638n
Ackerman, D., 256n
Adamowicz, W., 594n
Adams, A. J., 431n
Adams, E., 391n
Adaval, R., 394n, 427n, 511n
Adler, J., 183n
Agnihotri, R., 720n
Agrawal, N., 455n
Ahlusalia, R., 428n
Ahluwalia, R., 318n, 428n
Ahmad, R., 431n
Ahn, H., 358n
Ahuvia, A. C., 72n, 455n
Aikman-Eckenrode, S. N., 316n
Ailawadi, K. L., 635n
Ainscough, T. L., 183n
Alba, J. W., 216n, 256n, 257n, 320n, 361n, 362n, 431n, 456n, 565n
Alden, D. L., 430n, 595n
Aleccia, J., 753
Alexander, D., 317n
Allen, C. T., 146n, 358n, 361n, 427n, 455n, 509n, 511n, 594n
Allen, M., 679
Allenby, G. M., 358n
Allison, S. T., 456n
Allwitt, L. F., 317n
Al-Makaty, S. S., 74n
Almasy, S., 430n
Almquist, E., 721n
Al-Olayan, F. S., 73n
Alreck, P. L., 146n, 636n
Alsop, R., 318n
Alston, D., 533n
Altsech, M. B., 430n
Alwitt, L. F., 394n
Amaldoss, W., 256n
Ambler, T., 360n
Ambruster, A., 315n
Amir, O., 594n
Ampuero, O., 320n
An, J. A., 362n
Anand, A., 689
Anckaert, P., 509n
Anders, K., 754
Andersen, B., 633n
Andersen, P. H., 721n
Anderson, B. B., 75n

Anderson, C. J., 564n
Anderson, E. T., 637n
Anderson, E. W., 671n, 672n
Anderson, J. W., 430n
Anderson, M., 101, 256n, 268
Anderson, P., 148n
Anderson, R., 673n
Anderson, R. E., 673n
Anderson, S., 669n
Andrade, E. B., 638n
Andreasen, A. R., 33n
Andreassen, T. W., 670n
Andruss, P. L., 73n, 76n
Ang, S. H., 360n, 595n
Ang, S. W., 73n
Angelihard, R., 709
Angur, M. G., 109n
Anitha, N., 509n
Ansari, A., 635n
Anstead, M., 672n
Antonetti, P., 107n
Anwyl, J., 684
Apatow, J., 480
Appiah, O., 183n, 429n
Appleton-Knapp, S. L., 360n
Araujo, L., 720n
Arbesman, D. M., 563n
Archacki, R., 719n
Areily, D., 563n
Areni, C. S., 109n, 257n, 392n, 427n, 428n, 456n, 510n, 511n, 637n
Argo, J., 318n
Argo, J. J., 320n, 510n, 637n
Aribarg, A., 216n, 756
Ariely, D., 148n, 564n, 589, 594n, 668n, 753
Armstrong, G. M., 719n
Arnold, S. J., 109n
Arnould, E. J., 225, 256n, 456n, 638n
Aronauer, R., 564n
Arora, A., 428n
Arora, N., 216n, 756
Arora, R., 428n
Arreola, C., 469
Arthur, R., 76n
Artz, N., 429n
Ascarza, E., 672n
Ashley, C., 257n, 673n
Ashmall, K., 76n
Ashmore, R. D., 755
Ashworth, L., 394n, 594n
Au, K., 75n
Auken, S. V., 431n
Aurier, P., 562n
Austin, L., 481
Auty, S., 428n
Aviance, J., 141
Avnet, T., 392n
Axelrod, J., 753
Ayala, G. S., 257n, 672n
Aylesworth, A. B., 317n, 318n

Ayres, C., 268, 670n
Azar, P., 359n

b

Babin, B., 637n
Babin, B. J., 393n
Babin, L. A., 359n, 360n
Baek, T., 393n
Bagozzi, R. P., 146n, 256n, 393n, 511n, 562n
Bagus, B. L., 595n
Bahadur, N., 456n
Bailey, A., 393n
Bailey, A. A., 257n
Bailey, M., 256n
Baiorunos, R., 721n
Baker, J., 317n, 509n, 636n, 637n
Baker, M. J., 429n
Baker, R., 76n
Baker, S. M., 673n
Baker, T. L., 183n
Baker, W. E., 107n, 359n, 360n, 427n, 594n
Bakker, A. B., 318n, 394n
Balabanis, G., 392n
Balachander, S., 362n
Balasubramanian, S. K., 32n, 316n, 756
Baldsare, P. M., 670n
Balfour, F., 75n, 720n
Ballantyne, D., 720n
Ballinger, T. P., 359n
Ballve, M., 562n
Baltas, G., 756
Baluja, S., 564n
Bandyopadhyay, S., 753
Bang, H., 360n
Banister, E. N., 456n
Bansal, H. S., 672n
Barak, B., 73n
Barbopoulos, I., 392n
Barksdale, J. C., Jr., 719n
Barletta, M., 268
Barnes, B. R., 73n, 715, 721n
Baron, S., 637n
Barone, M. J., 108n, 319n, 430n, 431n, 456n, 635n
Barrick, J. A., 565n
Barrios, G., 719n
Barron, C., 316n
Barros, D., 76n
Barry, T. E., 146n
Bart, Y., 563n
Bartlett, B., 33n
Bartlett, J., 478
Barton, C., 147n
Bartos, R., 109n
Bary, E., 255n
Bass, F. M., 258n, 533n
Basuroy, S., 318n
Bathija, A., 482
Batra, R., 384, 393n, 429n, 510n, 636n
Battacharya, C. B., 672n
Bauer, H. H., 720n

Baugh, R., 182n
Baumeister, R. F., 636n
Baumgartner, H., 72n, 392n, 393n, 533n
Baumgartner, J., 595n
Baxter, J., 98
Baxter, S., 429n
Beard, R., 479
Bearden, W. O., 392n, 428n, 637n
Beatty, R. C., 74n
Beatty, S., 428n
Beatty, S. E., 215n, 216n, 635n, 637n, 670n, 671n
Beau, C. L., 256n
Bebko, C. P., 669n
Bechwati, N. N., 670n
Beckham, D., 39, 464
Beckmann, S. C., 392n
Beggan, J. K., 456n
Beggs, R., 671n
Begley, S., 319n
Bejou, D., 672n
Belch, M. A., 215n, 216n
Belk, R. W., 435, 455n, 509n, 511n
Bell, D. R., 636n, 637n
Bell, S. J., 721n
Bellenger, D. N., 669n
Bellizzi, J. A., 509n
Bellman, S., 635n
Beltramini, R. F., 670n
Bendapudi, N., 360n, 673n
Bendixen, M., 720n
Benjamin, B., 634n
Benson, L., 758
Benton, C., 270
Berg, N., 462
Bergen, M. N., 564n
Bergendahl, J., 431n
Berger, J., 256n
Bergiel, B. J., 359n
Bergler, R., 754
Berman, G., 183n
Bernazzani, S., 256n
Bernstein, E., 427n
Bernstein, R., 147n
Bernsten, D., 358n
Berr, J., 316n, 758
Berry, H., 412
Berry, J., 234, 257n, 686
Berry, L. L., 673n
Bertagnoli, L., 75n
Berthon, P., 720n
Best, R., 709
Bettman, J. R., 456n, 533n, 562n, 594n
Bever, L., 391n
Beverland, M., 257n
Bevins, V., 73n
Beward, L., 256n
Beyoncé, 463
Bezos, J., 676–677
Bhagwat, Y., 672n
Bhargava, M., 359n
Bhargave, R., 563n
Bhattacharya, C. B., 108n
Bickart, B., 563n, 669n
Bijmolt, T. H. A., 317n
Biocca, F., 562n
Bioy, A., 427n

Bishop, K., 509n
Bissonnette, Z., 476
Biswas, A., 360n, 428n, 429n, 635n, 636n, 669n, 755
Biswas, D., 428n, 636n
Biswas, S., 73n
Bitner, M. J., 509n, 626
Bitsoie, F., 171
Bittman, M., 465
Biyalogorsky, E., 257n
Bjerke, R., 75n
Bjork, R. A., 360n
Black, J., 635n
Blair, D., 76n
Blair, E., 184n
Blair, M. H., 360n
Blanchard, A. L., 256n
Blankson, C., 362n
Blatt, S. J., 146n
Bleier, A., 317n
Bliss, S. J., 430n
Bloch, P. H., 594n
Block, L., 509n
Block, L. G., 430n, 636n
Blodgett, J. G., 637n, 671n
Bloem, S. G., 258n
Bloom, H. E., 431n
Blumler, J. G., 391n
Boatwright, P., 319n, 594n
Bobinski, G. S., Jr., 636n
Bockenholt, U., 392n
Bodapati, A. V., 257n
Bodey, K., 671n
Bodur, H. O., 216n
Bohn, A., 358n
Bohner, G., 427n, 431n
Boles, J. S., 393n, 669n
Bolton, D., 430n
Bolton, D. L., 670n
Bolton, R. N., 670n, 671n, 673n
Bomkamp, S., 462
Bond, V., 469
Bone, P. F., 428n, 510n, 638n
Boninger, D. S., 428n, 429n
Bonoma, T. V., 719n
Borchard, T., 476
Borin, N., 317n, 637n
Borison, R., 683
Bosanac, A., 687
Boschma, J., 182n, 183n
Bosmans, A., 392n
Bott, L., 359n
Bottomley, P. A., 319n
Bouffard, K., 316n
Bougie, R., 670n
Boush, D. M., 216n
Bower, A. B., 320n, 429n, 669n
Bowman, D., 565n, 637n, 669n
Bowman, J., 72n
Boyd, D. M., 256n
Bozer, A. C., 68
Bradford, K., 675
Bradford, T. W., 215n
Bradley, G. L., 671n
Bradlow, E. T., 319n
Brady, E., 427n

Brady, M., 257n, 671n
Brady, M. K., 671n
Brady, T., 372
Brakus, J. J., 258n
Bramlett, M. D., 673n
Brand, J. E., 754
Brand, R. R., 562n
Brandt, A. M., 430n
Brandt, D., 359n
Brannon, L. A., 428n, 510n
Brasel, S. A., 315n, 316n, 319n, 393n
Braun, K. A., 358n
Braun-LaTour, K. A., 361n
Bray, H., 683
Bremner, B., 476
Brenan, M., 107n
Brenoff, A., 270
Bressler, P., 661–662
Brewer, G., 75n, 673n, 721n
Brewster, S., 465
Bridges, E., 215n
Bridges, S., 362n
Briesch, R., 318n
Briesch, R. A., 215n, 635n
Briggs, J., 359n
Bright, L., 755
Bright, M., 483
Briley, D. A., 72n, 73n
Bristol, T., 216n, 256n, 428n
Bristor, J. M., 565n, 636n, 755
Britton, J. A. E., 431n
Britton, J. E., 318n
Brocato, E. D., 637n
Brock, T. C., 428n, 510n
Broderick, A. J., 109n
Broderick, V., 758
Brodie, R., 511n
Brodowsky, G. H., 74n, 75n
Brody, N., 392n
Broniarczyk, S. M., 361n, 362n, 595n, 638n
Bronn, P. S., 108n
Brooke, Z., 75n, 76n
Brookes, R., 562n
Brooks, A. C., 107n
Brotherton, T. P., 393n
Brough, A., 107n
Brough, C., 272
Brown, A., 183n, 184n
Brown, C. L., 594n
Brown, G., 673n
Brown, S., 361n
Brown, S. P., 670n
Broyles, S. J., 317n
Bruce, M., 755
Bruck, M., 216n, 258n, 318n, 595n
Brucks, M., 74n
Bruemmer, P., 720n
Brumbaugh, A. M., 107n, 109n
Brunel, F., 391n
Brunel, F. F., 109n, 359n, 393n, 510n, 511n
Bruner, G. C., II, 427n, 428n
Bruner, R. E., 563n
Bruno, K., 106n, 360n
Brunsman, B., 394n
Bryan, W., 72n
Bryant, R., 318n

Bryce, W. J., 360n
Buchan, N. R., 74n
Buchanan, B., 431n
Buchanan, G., 32n
Buchanan-Oliver, M., 318n
Bucklin, R. E., 257n
Bues, M., 637n
Bukasa, K. A., 720n
Bukszpan, D., 109n
Bulik, B. S., 145n, 564n
Bulmer, S., 318n
Burgess, T. F., 721n
Burke, E., 675
Burlingham, B., 33n
Burne, T., 360n
Burnett, J. J., 109n
Burnett, S., 687
Burnham, T. A., 671n
Burnkrant, R. E., 318n, 360n, 394n, 428n, 509n
Burns, A. C., 359n, 360n
Burns, E., 183n
Burns, U., 477, 478
Burroughs, J. E., 106n, 147n
Burton, G., 72n
Burton, S., 358n, 429n, 594n, 595n, 635n, 721n, 755, 756
Bush, A. J., 429n
Bush, M., 265
Bush, V. D., 183n, 429n
Busler, M., 429n
Bustos, L., 634n
Butcher, D., 683
Butler, J., 216n
Byron, E., 273, 509n, 634n

C

Cacioppo, J. T., 33n, 428n
Cahill, T., 107n
Caillat, Z., 74n
Cakim, I., 257n
Calantone, R., 563n, 755
Calder, B. J., 593n
Caldwell, C., 510n, 638n
Callan, V. J., 671n
Callow, M., 319n
Cambra-Fierro, J., 671n
Campbell, A. F., 185n
Campbell, M. C., 318n, 360n, 391n, 428n
Campbell-Dollaghan, K., 633n
Campo, K., 638n
Candel, J. J. M., 427n
Capella, L. M., 565n, 638n
Caplan, J., 676
Capo, K. P., 215n
Cardona, M. M., 185n, 754, 755
Carey, R. M., 148n
Carlson, J. P., 428n
Carlson, L., 216n, 429n, 754
Carmona, M., 461
Carone, C., 478, 479
Carpenter, G. S., 594n, 595n
Carroll, D., 265–266, 268, 655
Cartagena, C., 184n
Carter, C., 724

Carter, C. M., 146n, 148n, 215n
Carter, J., 719n
Caruana, A., 75n, 720n
Casey, S., 460
Castiglia, B., 681
Cathy, T., 174
Catterall, M., 256n
Cespedes, F. V., 719n, 721n
Chaey, C., 634n
Chahal, M., 146n, 315n
Chakraborty, G., 316n, 720n
Chakravarti, D., 430n
Chan, K., 72n, 73n, 74n, 456n
Chan, R. Y. K., 74n
Chan, T. S., 74n
Chandon, P., 318n, 361n, 635n
Chandrashekaran, M., 671n
Chandrashekaran, R., 430n
Chandy, R. K., 431n
Chaney, I. M., 257n, 258n
Chang, C., 394n
Chang, J., 508n
Chang, K., 637n
Chang, L., 73n, 74n, 76n
Chang, W. L., 74n
Chao, P., 319n
Chaplin, L. N., 456n
Chapman, M., 75n, 185n
Chartrand, T. L., 317n
Chatterjee, P., 563n
Chatterjee, S., 318n, 635n
Chattopadhyay, A., 316n, 317n, 318n, 358n, 394n, 430n, 431n, 509n, 594n
Chaudhuri, A., 361n, 565n, 636n, 671n
Chebat, J. C., 391n, 510n, 638n, 671n
Chen, B., 455n
Chen, C.-N., 216n
Chen, J., 391n
Chen, K., 74n, 76n
Chen, Q., 318n, 428n, 562n
Chen, S., 147n
Chen, S.-F. S., 635n
Cheney, M. M., 427n
Cheng, M. M.-S., 258n
Cheon, H. J., 316n
Chernev, A., 319n, 392n, 594n
Cheston, V., 721n
Cheyne, A., 464
Childers, T. L., 73n, 216n, 317n, 319n, 393n
Childs, N. M., 32n
Chiou, J.-S., 431n
Chitturi, R., 427n
Cho, C., 72n
Cho, C. H., 316n
Cho, C.-H., 316n, 317n
Cho, H., 148n
Cho, J., 564n
Choi, S. C., 635n
Choi, S. M., 72n
Choi, Y., 455n
Chokski, N., 758
Choong, P., 256n
Chouinard, Y., 458
Chozick, A., 511n
Christakis, N., 255n
Christenson, G. A., 511n

Chu, J., 108n
Chu, S., 106n, 456n
Chun, H., 362n
Chung, B. C., 509n
Chung, H., 430n
Chura, H., 319n
Cialdini, R. B., 358n
Ciarrochi, J., 511n
Cimino, R., 185n
Clancy, H., 683
Clark, J. M., 430n
Clark, L., 564n
Clark, P., 76n
Clark, T., 360n
Claudy, M., 258n
Claxton, J., 564n
Clemons, D. S., 360n
Cleveland, M., 361n
Clifford, S., 255n, 509n, 634n
Cline, T. W., 430n
Clinton, H., 754
Cloud, P., 72n
Clow, K. E., 669n
Clurman, A., 146n
Cockroft, S., 72n
Codjovi, I., 671n
Coe, B. J., 720n
Coggins, E., 74n
Cohn, B., 145n
Cohn, D., 145n
Cole, C., 33n, 146n, 756
Cole, C. A., 755
Cole, N., 455n
Cole, S., 683
Coleman, R., 131, 148n
Colford, S. W., 754
Collen, C., 724
Collins, J. M., 73n
Combs, L. J., 670n
Comm, J., 256n
Compeau, L. D., 318n, 430n, 635n
Conlon, G., 721n
Connelly, S., 468
Conner, C., 258n
Conrad, G. A., 673n
Consoli, J., 107n
Cook, T., 264
Coolbear, N., 318n
Coon, G. S., 511n
Cooper, M. B., 696
Corbett, P., 263
Corfman, K. P., 257n, 358n, 360n, 391n, 455n
Cornwell, T. B., 316n, 430n
Corsten, D., 636n
Corstjens, M., 635n
Cote, J. A., 319n, 320n
Cotte, J., 215n
Coughlan, A. T., 635n
Coulter, K. S., 427n, 511n
Coupey, E., 595n
Cowley, E., 316n, 358n, 361n
Cowley, E. J., 358n, 361n
Cox, A., 636n
Cox, A. D., 360n
Cox, A. J., 456n
Cox, D., 360n, 636n

Cox, J. L., 318n
Coyle, J. R., 428n, 564n, 635n
Craig, C. S., 636n
Craig, V., 391n
Craig-Lees, M., 106n
Craik, F. I. M., 146n
Crawford, E., 724
Crawford, S., 72n
Creamer, M., 672n
Crites, S. L., Jr., 316n
Croffie, K., 758
Cronin, J. J., 562n
Cronley, M. L., 428n
Croson, R. T. A., 74n
Cross, J., 359n
Crowley, A. E., 431n, 509n, 638n
Cui, G., 76n
Culnan, M. J., 638n, 756
Cuneo, A., 672n
Cuneo, A. C., 107n
Cuneo, A. Z., 257n, 316n, 511n, 634n
Curasi, C. F., 456n, 671n
Currie, J., 686
Currie, N., 474
Curry, D. J., 148n
Curry, S., 381
Cushion, D., 15, 33n
Cyrus, M., 281
Czellar, S., 427n, 456n

d

Dabholkar, P. A., 427n
Dabholkar, P. L. A., 595n
D'Agostino, H., 456n
Dahl, D. W., 106n, 255n, 316n, 317n, 359n,
    509n, 510n, 637n
Dahlen, M., 317n, 361n, 431n
Dailey, L., 428n, 637n
Daimler, M., 721n
Dalakas, V., 73n, 215n
D'Amico, M., 75n
Dana, D., 476
Dana, R., 315n
Danaher, P. J., 316n, 320n
Dando, P., 216n
Dandridge, M., 721n
Danguillecourt, L., 564n
Danielova, A., 316n
Danko, W. D., 109n, 215n
Dann, S., 256n
Danova, T., 683
Dant, R., 721n
Danziger, S., 509n
Darbyshire, P., 75n, 636n
D'Arcy, P., 685
Darden, W. R., 393n, 565n, 637n
Darke, P. R., 394n, 594n
Darmon, N., 148n
Das, N., 428n
d'Astous, A., 509n
Daugherty, T., 562n
Daughtery, P. J., 696
Daus, C. S., 109n
Davidow, M., 671n
Davies, G., 315n

Davis, L. M., 637n
Davis, M. A., 670n
Davis, T., 216n
Dawar, N., 362n, 686
Dawes, J., 317n
Dawes, P. L., 719n
Dawidowska, K., 145n
Dawley, H., 315n
Day, E., 719n
Day, G. S., 672n
de Angelis, M., 671n
de Armas, S., 162
De Bellefonds, N., 719n
De Bock, T., 430n
De Hauw, S., 147n
de Juan, M. D., 184n
de Matos, C., 669n
de Mello, G. E., 431n
de Mooij, M., 73n, 74n, 75n, 76n
De Pelsmacker, P., 394n, 509n
de Quinto, M., 67
De Vos, A., 147n
De Wulf, K., 510n
Deal, L., 532n
Dean, D. H., 429n
DeBerry-Spence, B., 183n
DeCarlo, T. E., 257n, 391n
Deighton, J., 317n, 672n
Delevingne, C., 372
Dellaert, B. G. C., 564n, 636n
DelVecchio, D., 362n
Demby, E. H., 456n
DeMers, J., 361n, 755
Demery, P., 720n
Deming, S., 726
Denton, F., 147n
Deponte, A., 392n
Deppa, B., 562n
DeQuine, J., 256n
Deruy, E., 185n
Desai, K. K., 319n, 358n, 361n, 562n
Deshpande, A. D., 317n
Deshpande, R., 182n, 427n, 669n, 721n
Devorak, N., 263
deWolf, M., 106n
Dhar, R., 510n, 594n, 595n
Dholakia, U., 634n
Dholakia, U. M., 257n, 258n, 392n, 565n, 636n
Di Mascio, R., 638n
Diallo, A., 265
Diamantopoulos, A., 392n
Dick, A., 635n
Dickson, J. P., 148n
Dickson, P., 505
Dickson, P. R., 257n, 564n, 637n
Dijksterhuis, A., 317n
Dikshit, S., 483
Dillard, J. P., 430n
Dillon, R., 148n
Dillon, W. R., 361n
Dillow, C., 678
Dingus, R., 720n
D'Innocenzio, A., 509n
Dixon, A., 462
Dobele, A., 257n
Dodd, T. H., 565n

Dodson, K. J., 456n
Dolinsky, A. L., 670n
Doney, P. M., 256n, 719n
Dong, L., 76n
Donthu, N., 72n, 73n, 215n
Dooley, R., 481
Dorris, J., 265
Dotson, M. J., 216n
Dou, W., 317n, 563n
Dougherty, C., 147n
Douglas, R., 154
Douglas, S. P., 109n, 564n
Dowling, G. R., 565n, 636n
Doyle, J. R., 319n
Doyle, P., 721n
Dr. Dre, 263–264
Drewnowski, A., 148n
Drèze, X., 316n, 317n, 358n
Droge, C., 696, 755
Drolet, A., 427n
D'Rozario, D., 564n
Drumwright, M. E., 720n
Dua, T., 462
Dube, L., 393n, 431n, 510n, 638n, 670n
Dublino, J., 674
Duhachek, A., 393n, 637n
Duhan, D. F., 257n, 637n
Dundes, L., 318n
Dunlap, R. E., 107n
Durando, J., 481
Durgee, J. F., 510n, 594n
Dutra, A., 33n
Dutta, S., 564n
Dutta-Bergman, M. J., 107n, 456n
Dutton, S., 461
Dye, R., 257n
Dyer, C. L., 669n

Eagle, L., 145n
Earnhardt, D., Jr., 414
Easterbrook, S., 461
Eastlack, J. O., Jr., 360n
Eastlick, M. A., 636n
Easton, G., 720n
Eaton, J., 359n
Ebenkamp, B., 185n
Echeverria, R., 67
Eckstein, W., 633n
Edmundson, B., 184n
Edvardsson, B., 670n
Edwards, S. M., 147n, 315n, 316n
Edy, C., 75n
Eels, K., 148n
Effron, L., 508n
Egan, C., 147n
Egan, S., 430n
Egelman, S., 759
Ehrenberg, A. S. C., 637n
Ehrlichman, H., 392n
Eikenberry, A., 108n
Eisenbeiss, M., 317n
Eisend, M., 109n, 430n, 431n
Eisingerich, A., 362n
Eismann, O., 358n

Elazari Bar On, A., 759
El-Badry, S., 185n
Elberse, A., 465
Elftman, J., 727
Elkin, T., 317n
Ellen, P., 675
Ellen, P. S., 428n, 510n, 638n
Elliott, K. M., 595n
Elliott, M. T., 316n, 755
Elliott, S., 457n
Ellison, N. B., 256n
Ellison, S., 756
Elpers, J., 430n
Elpers, J. W., 317n
Elrod, T., 595n
Empson, R., 634n
Emrich, O., 256n
Engchanil, N., 564n
Englis, B. G., 755
Enright, A., 755
Ephron, E., 360n
Epp, A. M., 215n
Erb, H.-P., 427n
Erdem, T., 72n, 74n, 362n, 562n, 565n
Erdogan, B. Z., 74n
Erenchun-Podlech, I., 393n
Ergodan, B. Z., 429n
Eriksen, M., 72n
Eroglu, S. A., 510n, 637n
Escalas, J. E., 318n, 456n
Esfahani, E., 33n
Espinoza, R., 758
Essegaier, S., 316n
Esser, A., 76n
Estebaranz, H., 317n
Estelami, H., 671n
Esterl, M., 263, 483
Etcoff, N., 456n
Etkin, J., 392n
Etzioni, A., 106n
Evangelidis, I., 392n
Evans, H., 721n
Evans, K. R., 318n
Evanschitzky, H., 670n
Ewing, M., 75n, 720n
Ewing, M. T., 457n, 720n

f

Faber, R. J., 511n
Fabriger, L. R., 427n
Fajardo, T., 429n
Fam, K. S., 74n
Fan, P., 75n
Farley, J. U., 721n
Farnell, C., 564n
Farrell, M., 725, 726
Farrell, M. A., 719n
Farrell, S., 725, 726
Fattah, H., 73n, 76n, 147n, 148n
Faulds, D. J., 595n
Faulkner, T., 360n
Faw, L., 393n
Fay, B., 257n
Fedorikhin, A., 594n

Feick, L., 257n, 670n
Feick, L. F., 257n
Feiereisen, S., 109n
Feifer, J., 106n
Feinberg, R. A., 636n
Felcher, E. M., 562n
Fellman, M. W., 33n
Fenn, D., 469
Fennis, B. M., 394n
Fenwick, A. E., 261
Ferdman, R., 426n
Fern, E. F., 216n, 720n
Fernandes, D., 361n
Fernandez, A., 638n
Fernandez, C., 255n
Ferree, A., 724
Ferrell, M. E., 257n, 392n
Fetter, R. E., Jr., 565n
Fetto, J., 215n, 358n
Feynman, R., 299
Fielding, M., 72n
File, K. M., 720n
Finn, A., 635n, 636n, 672n
Fiore, A. M., 638n
Fiorletta, A., 683
Fischer, E., 109n
Fishburne, T., 265
Fisher, C., 182n
Fisher, C. M., 564n
Fisher, J. E., 148n
Fisher, M., 669n
Fisher, R. J., 256n, 636n
Fisk, G. M., 109n
Fisk, R. P., 638n
Fitzgerald, B., 563n
Fitzgerald, K., 258n
Fitzpatrick, M., 476
Fitzsimons, G. J., 638n
Flaherty, A., 633n
Flaherty, K., 430n
Fleck, N. D., 430n
Fleming, M., 462
Flint, J., 106n
Folkes, V., 320n, 393n
Folse, J., 670n
Fonda, J., 268
Fong, C. P. S., 594n
Fong, G. T., 430n
Fong, M., 75n
Foote, A., 255n
Ford, A., 755
Ford, G. T., 562n
Ford, J. B., 216n, 533n
Forehand, M. R., 182n, 427n
Forgas, J. P., 511n
Fornell, C., 672n
Forte, D., 391n
Foster, T., 460
Fournier, S., 393n, 671n
Fowler, G., 73n
Fowler, G. A., 76n
Fowler, J., 255n
Fox, R. J., 362n
Fram, E., 564n
France, K. R., 635n
Francese, P., 146n, 147n, 215n

Francis, E., 685, 686
Francis, J. N. P., 72n, 73n, 429n
Frank, B., 320n
Franke, G. R., 289, 318n
Franses, P. H., 638n, 672n
Frary, J., 33n
Freed, J., 678
Freeman, L., 672n
Freeman, S., 319n
Freiden, J. B., 564n
Frels, J. K., 671n
Frey, W. H., 182n
Fridman, A., 721n
Friedman, W., 317n
Friestad, M., 216n, 391n
Fromm, J., 147n, 255n, 469
Fromowitz, M., 72n
Fry, J., 564n
Fugate, D. L., 430n
Fulkerson, J., 673n
Fuller, P., 32n
Fulwood, S., III, 146n
Funk, C., 107n
Furrer, O., 107n
Furst, A., 671n

g

Gaeth, G. J., 428n, 431n, 670n, 755
Gagliordi, N., 683
Gaidis, W., 359n
Gainer, B., 256n, 511n
Gains, R., 678
Gal, D., 456n
Galante, M., 214n
Gallarello, C., 687
Galle, W. P., 720n
Ganesan, S., 672n
Gao, G., 184n
Gao, H., 720n
Gapper, J., 469
Garbarino, E., 669n, 671n
Garber, L. L., 565n
Garber, M., 361n
Garcia, C., 317n
Garcia, J., 184n
Garcia, R., 258n
Garcia, S., 594n
Gardner, M. N., 430n
Gardner, M. P., 511n, 595n
Gardyn, R., 106n, 109n, 146n, 147n, 184n, 215n
Garfield, B., 456n
Garg, N., 511n
Garling, T., 511n
Garretson, J. A., 429n, 635n, 756
Gartner, J., 107n
Garvin, D. A., 721n
Gasparro, A., 689, 756
Gates, B., 132, 599
Gates, G., 108n
Gatti, M., 676
Gegdenk, K., 635n
Gehrt, K. C., 511n, 634n
Geirger-Oneto, S., 183n
Gelb, B. D., 109n, 183n, 431n
Gendelman, V., 319n

Gendron, G., 33n
Gengler, C., 756
Gengler, G. E., 672n
Genson, R., 719n
Gentry, J. W., 755
Gentry, L., 73n, 563n
Gerdes, R., 184n
Gershoff, A. D., 361n, 595n
Gerson, V., 361n
Gerstner, E., 257n
Gesenhues, A., 33n
Geuens, M., 393n, 509n
Ghani, W. I., 32n
Ghosal, T., 594n
Ghose, S., 362n
Ghosh, A., 636n
Gibb, F., 721n
Gibbs, S., 760
Gibson, J., 137
Giebelhausen, M., 257n, 671n
Giering, A., 671n
Giese, J. L., 318n, 319n, 392n
Gigerenzer, G., 593n
Gigliotto, A., 672n
Gijsbrechts, E., 638n
Gil, M., 182n
Gilbert, F. W., 456n
Gilbert, J., 721n
Gilbride, T. J., 216n
Gilgoff, D., 255n
Gill, M., 274
Gill, R., 670n
Gill, T., 510n
Gillett, M., 755
Gilliland, D. I., 215n, 721n
Gilliland, N., 633n
Gillison, S., 216n
Gilly, M., 109n
Gilly, M. C., 75n, 147n, 256n, 257n, 456n, 510n, 563n
Gilmore, J. H., 32n
Gino, F., 753
Ginter, R., 564n
Gips, J., 315n
Gitosudarmo, I., 257n
Glazer, R., 595n
Glover, M., 108n
Gluck, M., 563n
Glum, J., 509n
Godes, D., 257n
Godfrey, A. L., 672n
Godin, S., 32n
Goff, B. G., 669n
Goizueta, R., 68
Goldberg, M. E., 72n, 595n
Golden, L. L., 635n
Goldman, D., 391n
Goldsmith, R. E., 427n, 429n, 564n
Goldsworth, N., 475
Golikeri, P., 362n
Gomez, S., 413
Goode, M. M. H., 673n
Goode, M. R., 359n
Goodhardt, G. J., 637n
Goodman, J., 670n
Goodsmit, J. J., 358n

Goodstein, R. C., 317n, 318n, 428n, 429n
Goodwin, C., 671n
Gopinath, M., 393n, 511n
Gorn, G., 595n
Gorn, G. J., 316n, 318n, 509n, 595n
Gotlieb, J. B., 430n
Gould, S. J., 456n, 511n, 669n
Govind, R., 145n
Grace, D., 510n, 669n, 671n
Grady, E., 460
Graeff, T. R., 456n
Graeth, T. R., 510n
Graham, J. L., 257n
Grandey, A. A., 109n
Grant, K., 687
Grau, S., 755
Grayson, K., 428n
Grbavac, A., 755
Greco, A. J., 637n
Green, C. L., 183n
Greenberg, B. S., 754
Greenberg, K., 393n
Greene, H., 756
Greenleaf, E. A., 637n
Greenlee, T. B., 109n
Greenspan, R., 108n, 109n, 315n
Gregan-Paxton, J., 216n, 317n, 359n
Gremler, D. D., 672n
Grether, M., 720n
Grewal, D., 317n, 318n, 430n, 564n, 635n, 637n, 669n, 672n
Grier, S. A., 107n, 109n
Griffith, D. A., 428n, 562n
Griffith, E., 683
Griffith, R. L., 721n
Grigoriadis, S., 394n
Grigsby, J. S., 109n
Grimm, P. E., 427n
Grisaffe, D. B., 720n
Grisham, L., 508n
Grohmann, B., 427n
Gronhaug, K., 392n, 393n, 670n
Grose, J., 456n
Gross, D., 146n, 678
Grossbart, S., 256n
Grossman, R. P., 359n
Groth, A., 72n
Grove, S. J., 638n
Grunewald, O., 595n
Gu, F. F., 75n
Guesenhues, A., 683
Gulas, C. S., 430n, 456n, 638n
Gullov-Singh, A., 682
Gummerus, J., 673n
Gunelius, S., 362n
Gunther, M., 107n, 108n
Guo, C., 564n
Gupta, A., 261
Gupta, S., 562n
Gurel-Atay, E., 106n, 107n
Gurhan-Canli, Z., 72n, 319n, 362n, 429n, 456n
Gustafson, A. W., 565n
Gustafson, R., 755
Gustafsson, A., 670n
Gustke, C., 270

Guterman, J., 320n
Gwinner, K. P., 146n, 257n, 359n, 670n, 672n

h

Haddon, H., 756
Hadjicharalambous, C., 73n
Hagtvedt, H., 319n, 427n
Hague, M., 676
Hahn, M., 360n
Halfill, M., 238
Hall, E., 73n, 76n, 316n, 594n
Hall, K., 669n
Hallal, P., 74n
Halliday, J., 107n, 147n, 318n, 359n, 361n, 509n, 563n
Hallock, S., 108n
Hamer, L. O., 456n
Hamilton, A., 256n
Hamilton, R., 594n
Hamm, S., 75n
Hammond, D., 430n
Hammond, K., 637n
Hand, C., 316n
Handley, L., 483, 756
Hank, A., 28, 33n, 137
Hansen, D. E., 595n
Hansen, H., 720n
Hansen, S. W., 720n
Hardesty, D., 431n
Hardesty, D. M., 393n, 428n, 637n
Hardy, K., 473
Hargreaves, S., 753
Harmon, H. A., 673n
Harrell, G. D., 257n, 670n
Harrington, K., 465
Harris, E. G., 392n, 670n
Harris, J., 391n
Harris, K., 637n
Harris, L. C., 673n
Harris, R., 358n
Harris, R. J., 755
Hartog, M., 360n
Harwin, S., 476
Hasford, J., 431n
Hass, R., 397
Haubl, G., 595n
Haugen, L., 316n
Hauser, J. R., 562n
Hausknecht, D., 668n
Hawes, J. M., 565n
Hawkins, P., 147n
Hawkins, S. A., 146n, 359n, 360n, 427n
Hayes, G., 562n
Haynes, G. A., 594n
Hays, C., 108n
Hays, S., 563n
Heath, R. P., 148n
Heath, T. B., 318n, 428n, 635n, 755
Heckler, S. E., 317n, 361n
Heide, J. B., 719n
Heilman, C. M., 565n, 637n, 669n
Hein, K., 32n, 319n
Heit, E., 359n
Heitmann, M., 594n, 669n

Helgeson, J. G., 456n, 595n
Helm, B., 265
Hem, L. E., 358n
Hemmes, M., 427n
Henard, D. H., 669n
Henderson, C. M., 672n
Henderson, K. V., 360n, 394n
Henderson, P. W., 319n, 320n, 509n, 638n
Henderson, T., 756
Hendricks, K., 595n
Henley, W. H., 106n
Hennig-Thurau, T., 672n
Henrique, J., 669n
Henry, P., 146n, 148n
Henson, B., 757–758
Henson, J., 757
Henthorne, T. L., 109n, 533n
Heo, K., 108n
Herbig, P. A., 75n
Hernandez, M., 184n
Herper, M., 263
Herr, P. M., 427n
Herrington, J. D., 638n
Herrmann, A., 392n, 594n, 669n
Herzenstein, M., 258n
Hess, R. L., Jr., 672n
Hewett, K., 75n
Hibbard, J. D., 359n
Hibbert, S. A., 510n, 638n
Higgins, E. T., 392n
Higgins, K., 33n
Higgins, M., 680
Higie, R. A., 257n
Hilal, P., 719n, 720n
Hill, C., 106n
Hill, C. J., 533n, 565n
Hill, D., 479
Hill, D. J., 671n
Hill, M. E., 358n, 361n, 393n, 430n, 431n
Hill, R. H., 148n
Hill, R. P., 33n
Hiller, A., 675
Hilton, D. J., 427n
Hilton, P., 413
Hirsch, A. R., 509n, 638n
Hirschhorn, D., 272
Hirschman, E. C., 455n
Hirst, A., 261
Hitchman, S. C., 430n
Hite, R. E., 509n
Ho, B., 562n
Ho, E. A., 562n
Ho, T.-H., 636n
Hobbs, T., 76n, 315n
Hoch, S. J., 216n, 319n, 359n, 360n, 427n, 562n
Hochwald, L., 721n
Hoeffler, S., 317n, 594n
Hoegg, J., 320n
Hoekstra, J. C., 672n
Hoffman, D. L., 428n, 564n, 637n
Hoffman, K. D., 509n
Hofstede, G., 72n, 74n, 76n
Hogan, P., 54
Hogg, M. K., 456n, 755
Holbrook, M. B., 384, 511n, 671n, 755
Holland, J., 673n

Hollingshead, A. B., 139, 148n
Holloway, B. B., 635n, 670n
Holstein, H., 76n
Holt, D., 72n
Holt, D. B., 457n
Holzwarth, M., 638n
Homburg, C., 427n, 671n, 672n
Homer, P. M., 316n, 393n, 427n, 429n, 510n
Homewood, S., 107n
Honea, H., 360n
Honeycutt, S., 429n
Hong, J. W., 392n, 456n
Hope, C., 33n
Hope, K., 75n
Horn, M., 72n, 73n, 455n
Horne, D., 455n
Horovitz, B., 481
Horowitz, D. M., 671n
Horsky, D., 594n
Horton, V., 75n
Hotchkiss, G., 720n
Hough, K., 755
Houston, M. J., 361n
Howard, D. J., 756
Howard, J., 754
Howard, T., 318n
Howe, A. C., 183n
Howe, J., 32n
Howell, D., 183n
Howenstine, J., 476
Hoyer, W., 358n
Hoyer, W. D., 318n, 319n, 427n, 430n, 431n, 533n, 562n, 595n, 672n
Hsee, C., 391n
Hsu, C.-K., 429n
Hu, E., 670n
Hu, M., 427n, 720n
Huang, M.-H., 428n, 431n
Huang, Y., 429n
Huber, F., 392n
Huber, J., 532n, 594n, 595n
Huh, Y., 510n
Huhmann, B. A., 289, 318n, 393n
Hui, M. K., 75n, 670n
Hult, G. T. M., 637n, 721n
Humphreys, J. M., 182n, 184n
Hung, K., 75n, 456n
Hunnicutt, G. G., 754
Hunt, M. R., 755
Hunter, G. L., 392n
Hunter, L. M., 720n
Hurley, D., 215n
Hurley, R. F., 721n
Hurst, B., 636n
Hussain, M., 73n
Hussherr, F. X., 316n, 317n
Husson, T., 682
Hussung, T., 215n
Hutchinson, J. W., 216n, 256n, 257n, 456n, 565n
Hwang, I., 360n
Hyatt, E. M., 216n
Hyde, J., 753
Hyken, S., 669n, 670n
Hyman, M. R., 509n

i

Ifill, G., 214n
Ilfeld, J. S., 563n
Ilicic, J., 429n
Iliff, L., 315n
Inman, J. J., 318n, 391n, 428n, 511n, 533n, 669n
Innis, D. E., 428n
Iovine, J., 263–264
Ippolito, P. M., 754
Irvine, M., 754
Irving, P. G., 672n
Irwin, N., 146n
Isaac, M., 428n
Isen, A. M., 394n
Isidore, C., 106n
Iyengar, R., 672n
Iyengar, S. S., 593n
Iyer, R., 147n

j

Jacob, R., 672n
Jacobson, M., 463, 464, 465
Jacobson, R., 361n, 429n
Jacoby, J., 671n
Jacoby, S., 354
Jagtvedt, H., 316n
Jain, A. K., 635n
Jain, S., 256n
Jain, S. P., 359n, 429n, 431n
Jaju, A., 392n
Jamal, A., 75n, 185n
James, A., 758
James, D., 361n
James, G., 74n
James, L., 222, 243, 264, 412
James, S., 476
Janda, S., 721n
Janiszewski, C., 319n, 359n, 360n, 362n, 595n, 635n, 638n
Janssens, W., 394n
Jarvis, S., 755
Jasper, C. R., 636n
Jass, J., 319n
Javalgi, R. G., 146n
Javalgi, R. R. G., 671n
Jayawardhena, C., 720n
Jean, S., 562n
Jedidi, K., 637n
Jennings, K., 480
Jensen, T., 358n
Jensen, T. D., 429n
Jepsen, A. L., 564n
Jevons, C., 75n, 636n
Jewell, R. D., 361n, 431n
Ji, M. F., 73n, 216n
Jiang, D., 148n
Jin, B., 636n
Jobs, S., 29
Johansson, L.-O., 392n
Johar, G. V., 755
Johar, J. S., 431n
John, D. R., 146n, 216n, 358n, 362n, 456n, 509n, 511n, 594n, 753

John, L. K., 256n
Johns, B., 633n
Johnson, B., 427n
Johnson, D., 595n
Johnson, E. J., 74n, 456n, 635n, 637n
Johnson, J. D., 183n
Johnson, K., 563n
Johnson, L. W., 636n
Johnson, M., 257n, 672n
Johnson, M. S., 669n, 671n
Johnson, R. D., 595n
Johnson, S. D., 257n
Johnson, W. J., 719n
Johnston, L., 265
Johnston, W. J., 721n
Johri, L. M., 72n
Joiner, C., 362n
Joines, J. L., 563n, 636n
Jones, C., 673n
Jones, E., 721n
Jones, J. M., 107n
Jones, J. P., 360n
Jones, M. A., 670n, 671n
Jones, M. Y., 109n
Jones, Q., 256n
Jones, R., 470
Jones, T. O., 671n
Jordan, M., 724
Joy, A., 75n, 511n
Judkis, M., 185n
Jun, S., 509n
Jung, H.-S., 669n
Jung, J. M., 74n
Jurkowitsch, A., 427n

k

Kacapyr, E., 146n
Kadet, A., 676
Kahle, L. R., 257n, 429n
Kahn, B., 316n, 637n
Kahn, B. E., 319n, 320n, 391n, 509n, 510n,
    533n, 594n, 638n
Kahneman, D., 391n, 533n, 668n
Kaiman, J., 72n
Kalafatis, S. P., 362n, 721n
Kalapurakal, R., 257n
Kalliny, M., 73n
Kalra, A., 317n
Kaltcheva, V., 638n
Kalyanaram, G., 594n
Kalyanaraman, S., 316n
Kamakura, W., 671n
Kamakura, W. A., 145n
Kamal, S., 106n, 456n
Kamvar, M., 564n
Kandemir, D., 637n
Kane, L., 147n, 148n
Kang, J., 182n, 184n
Kang, S., 185n, 315n, 393n, 456n
Kanicki, D., 727
Kannan, P. K., 673n
Kanso, A., 76n
Kapferer, J.-N., 756
Kapner, S., 634n

Karande, K., 73n, 635n, 755
Kardashian, K., 243
Kardes, F. R., 146n, 215n, 257n, 359n, 361n,
    428n, 565n, 594n, 669n
Karjaluoto, H., 32n, 145n
Karlsson, N., 511n
Karp, H., 265
Karst, T., 724
Kasper, H., 703
Kass, S., 463
Katerattanakul, P., 635n
Katona, G., 564n
Katrichis, J. M., 669n
Katz, C., 391n
Kauffman, M., 268
Kaufman-Scarborough, C. F., 74n
Kaur, P., 465
Kavovit, B., 100
Keane, M., 476
Keaveney, S. M., 669n
Keefe, L. M., 182n, 183n
Keeling, K., 456n
Keillor, B. D., 75n, 637n
Keiningham, T. L., 672n, 721n
Keith, A., 273
Keith, J. E., 216n
Kell, J., 681
Kellaris, J., 360n
Kellaris, J. J., 74n, 360n, 430n
Keller, E., 234, 257n
Keller, K. I., 319n
Keller, K. L., 360n, 361n, 362n
Keller, P. A., 392n, 430n, 431n, 563n
Kelley, F., 182n
Kelley, S. W., 509n, 670n
Kelso, A., 681
Kemp, M. B., 669n
Kempf, D. S., 318n, 428n
Kennedy, B., 107n
Kennedy, K. N., 671n
Kennedy, P., 272
Kent, R. J., 76n, 361n, 637n
Keown-McMullan, C., 671n
Kerin, R. A., 756
Kern, C., 683
Kerwin, A. M., 148n
Kessler, S., 633n
Keup, L., 184n
Key, W. B., 317n
Khairullah, D. H. Z., 73n, 74n
Khairullah, Z. Y., 73n, 74n
Khan, A., 455n
Khan, H., 634n
Khare, A., 431n
Kharif, O., 633n
Khuraibet, M., 724
Kickul, J., 109n
Kidwell, B., 393n, 431n
Kiecker, P., 109n, 456n, 510n, 511n
Kiekeer, P., 637n
Kiel, G. C., 564n
Kilcourse, B., 634n
Kiley, D., 107n, 315n, 479
Kim, C., 216n, 671n
Kim, D., 74n
Kim, H., 72n, 362n, 563n

Kim, J., 359n, 394n
Kim, J.-O., 636n
Kim, S., 456n
Kim, W. G., 362n
Kim, Y., 360n, 756
Kim, Y. K., 182n, 184n
Kim, Y.-J., 392n
Kindfuller, A., 674
Kindra, G., 753
King, J., 720n
King, M., 358n, 361n, 430n
King, R. L., 184n
King, S. F., 721n
Kirkpatrick, D., 256n
Kirmani, A., 319n, 362n, 391n, 428n, 595n
Kirsch, I., 359n
Kissell, R., 107n
Kitchell, S., 720n
Kivetz, R., 319n, 669n
Klara, R., 634n, 676
Klein, C., 720n
Klein, D., 462
Klein, L. R., 562n
Klein, N. M., 672n
Kleine, R. E., III, 455n
Kleine, S. S., 455n
Kleinman, A., 678
Kleiser, S., 755
Klinenberg, E., 214n
Klink, R., 362n
Klink, R. R., 319n
Knasko, S. C., 509n, 594n, 638n
Knetsch, J. L., 668n
Knight, G. A., 721n
Knight, J. G., 720n
Knorr, C., 754
Knox, G., 636n, 671n
Ko, H., 72n
Koenig, H. F., 255n, 256n
Koetsier, J., 564n
Kohli, A. K., 719n
Kolbe, R. H., 754, 755
Kolko, J., 457n
Konus, U., 359n, 634n
Kopalle, P. K., 635n, 669n
Kornowski, L., 465
Korzenny, F., 184n
Koschate, N., 427n, 672n
Kosmin, B. A., 185n
Koss-Feder, L., 108n
Kotler, P., 33n, 73n
Kovalchik, K., 72n
Kozinets, R. V., 361n, 634n
Krafft, M., 637n, 672n
Kramer, H. E., 75n
Kraus, S. J., 427n
Krauss, C., 109n
Kravets, D., 678
Kreider, R., 214n
Krentler, K. A., 216n
Kripalani, M., 73n
Krishman, H. S., 430n
Krishna, A., 318n, 359n
Krishnamurthi, L., 633n, 635n, 637n
Krishnamurthy, P., 360n, 594n
Krishnamurthy, S., 638n

Krishnan, H. S., 361n
Krishnan, R., 317n, 637n
Krishnan, S., 361n
Krogstad, J., 182n
Krosnick, J. A., 427n, 428n
Krugman, H. E., 296, 317n
Krulwich, R., 358n
Krush, M., 720n
Kuczynski, K., 215n
Kulczynski, A., 429n
Kulik, R. L., 429n
Kulviwat, S., 564n
Kumar, A., 361n, 427n, 720n
Kumar, K., 427n
Kumar, P., 669n
Kumar, R., 721n
Kumar, V., 635n, 672n
Kumard, A., 427n, 428n
Kunis, M., 97
Kurian, V., 73n
Kurtz, D. L., 669n
Kvitastein, O., 670n
Kwak, H., 392n
Kwan, M., 463
Kwon, W., 634n
Kyner, D. B., 671n
Kyung, E., 359n

L

La Ferle, C., 147n
Laaksonen, M., 511n
Labich, K., 148n
Lacey, R., 638n
Lacher, K. T., 393n
Lachman, P., 185n
Lackman, C., 215n
Laczniak, R. N., 216n, 257n, 318n, 391n, 754
Lady Gaga, 222
Lafferty, B. A., 427n, 429n
Lageat, T., 427n
Lages, C., 721n
Lages, L. F., 721n
Lai, C., 721n
Lai, M., 216n
Lal, R., 635n, 637n
Lala, V., 720n
Lam, S. Y., 720n
Lamb, R., 476
Lamberston, D., 464
Lambert, F., 256n
Lambert, J., 595n
Lambert, M., 97
Lanasa, J. M., 215n
Lancaster, C., 183n
Lancastre, A., 721n
Landaum, E., 263
Landers, L., 270
Landers, V., 428n
Landreth, S., 429n
Landry, J. T., 320n
Langdon, J., 562n
Langmeyer, L., 755
Lapierre, J., 721n
LaPorte, N., 594n

Lappe, M., 473
LaReau, J., 315n
Larkin, K. Y., 669n
Laroche, M., 73n, 256n, 361n, 392n, 430n, 510n
Larsen, D., 510n
Larsen, T., 392n
Lassar, W. M., 671n
LaTour, M. S., 109n, 361n, 430n, 533n
Lattin, D., 185n
Lattin, J. M., 637n
Lau-Gesk, L., 455n
Laurent, G., 358n, 361n, 427n, 635n
LaVito, A., 315n
Law, S., 146n, 361n
Lawlor, B., 634n
Lawlor, U., 634n
Lawrence, B., 634n
Lawson, R., 392n, 533n
Layton, R. A., 564n
Leach, M., 720n
LeBlanc, R. P., 636n
Lecleric, F., 595n, 636n
Lee, A. Y., 359n, 392n, 394n, 635n
Lee, B., 317n
Lee, B.-K., 595n
Lee, C. K. C., 216n
Lee, D. H., 215n
Lee, D. Y., 719n
Lee, E.-J., 258n
Lee, H., 216n
Lee, J., 75n, 258n, 358n, 564n, 670n
Lee, J. K. H., 595n
Lee, J. L., 75n
Lee, J. Y., 755
Lee, J.-G., 316n
Lee, J.-H., 315n, 316n
Lee, K., 74n, 594n, 720n
Lee, L., 594n
Lee, M., 75n, 563n
Lee, M. P., 146n, 509n
Lee, M.-S., 256n, 562n, 563n, 564n
Lee, N., 33n
Lee, R. G., 755
Lee, R. P. W., 316n
Lee, S. H., 74n
Lee, T., 72n, 637n
Lee, W., 72n, 147n, 317n
Lee, W.-N., 595n
Lee, Y. H., 317n, 361n, 594n
Leedy, M., 270
Lehann, P., 316n, 320n
Lehmann, D. R., 258n, 318n, 562n, 594n, 669n
Lehrer, J., 257n
Lei, J., 431n
Leigh, J. H., 455n
Leigh, T. W., 256n
Lemmink, J., 703
Lenhart, A., 256n
Lennon, S. J., 634n
Leonard, H. A., 257n
Leone, R. P., 146n
Leong, S. M., 360n
Leonhardt, D., 148n
Leonhardt, M., 473
Leonidou, L. C., 719n
Lepkowska-White, E., 320n, 635n

Lepper, M. R., 593n
Lesly, E., 533n
Leszczyc, P. P., 672n
Leszczyc, P. T. L. P., 671n
Letarte, A., 431n
Leung, W., 318n
Levey, R. H., 109n
Levin, A. M., 319n
Levin, G., 673n
Levin, I. P., 319n, 431n
Lewin, J. E., 719n
Lewis, C., 428n, 676
Lewis, J., 214n
Lewis, J. R., 720n
Li, H., 315n, 316n, 562n
Li, L., 74n
Li, S., 391n, 672n
Li, T., 509n
Libai, B., 257n
Lichtenstein, D. R., 564n, 594n, 595n, 635n, 755
Lieber, C., 391n
Liebowitz, R., 671n
Lii, P., 74n
Lil Wayne, 222
Liljander, V., 671n
Liljenwall, R., 315n, 316n, 636n
Lim, A. L., 392n
Lim, J.-S., 359n
Lim, K. S., 509n
Limbardi, C., 315n
Lin, C. A., 73n, 74n, 107n
Lin, X., 74n
Lindeman, T. F., 257n
Lindquist, J. D., 74n, 612, 635n
Lindsey-Mullikin, J., 318n, 635n
Lingle, S., 672n
Link, A. N., 721n
Linn, R., 317n, 563n
Lino, M., 215n
Linou, N., 362n
Linstrom, M., 675
Linville, D., 360n
Lipka, M., 185n
Lipkus, I. M., 431n
Little, J. D. C., 594n
Little, M., 593n
Liu, B. S. C., 107n
Liu, J., 318n
Liu, M., 73n, 720n
Liu, M. T., 429n
Liu, M. W., 358n
Livingston, A., 106n
Livingston, D., 688
Livingston, G., 106n, 145n
Llopis, G., 276
Loeb, S., 754
Loechner, J., 107n, 563n
Loewenstein, G., 456n
Lohse, G. L., 319n, 635n
Loken, B., 362n
London, B., 476
Long, D., 429n
Long, N., 146n
Lopez, G., 184n
Lord, K. R., 256n, 358n, 360n, 394n, 428n, 509n
Lorenzo-Aiss, J. D., 319n

Lorrenzetti, L., 678
Lotz, S. L., 511n
Lou, Y.-C., 635n
Louie, T. A., 429n
Louviere, J. J., 635n, 636n
Love, L. L., 456n
Lowe, L., 272
Lowrey, P., 315n
Lowrey, T. M., 510n
Luce, M. F., 393n, 533n, 562n, 594n, 668n
Luger, C., 185n
Luhby, T., 106n
Lukas, B. A., 721n
Lukosius, V., 509n
Lumpkin, J. R., 216n, 565n
Luna, D., 184n, 216n, 317n, 359n, 360n
Luna, N., 634n
Luna, T., 32n, 532n
Luo, J., 720n
Luo, X., 510n
Luomala, H. T., 511n
Lurie, N., 564n, 636n
Lutz, A., 255n, 393n
Lutz, K., 362n
Lutz, R. J., 216n, 360n
Lwin, M. O., 76n
Lynch, D. F., 721n
Lynch, J., 315n
Lynch, J. G., 257n, 358n, 360n, 391n, 455n
Lynch, J. G., Jr., 562n, 564n
Lynch, P. D., 76n, 637n
Lynch, R., 465
Lynn, G. S., 720n
Lynn, M., 391n, 594n
Lysonski, S., 755
Lyytinen, K., 669n

m

Ma, J., 60
Maarleveld, M., 565n
Macarthur, K., 361n, 429n, 430n, 635n
MacDonald, E., 359n
MacDonald, J. B., 720n
Machleit, K. A., 456n, 510n, 637n
Maciag, M., 182n
MacInnis, D., 362n, 393n
MacInnis, D. J., 74n, 216n, 258n, 317n, 318n, 431n, 509n, 595n
Mack, E., 678
Mackay, J., 72n
Mackay, M. M., 361n, 671n
MacKenzie, S. B., 318n, 595n
Macklin, M. C., 361n
Mackoy, R. D., 670n
MacLachlan, D. L., 148n
Maclaran, P., 256n
MacMillan, A., 426n
Madden, N., 72n, 73n, 75n, 76n, 563n
Madden, T. J., 75n
Madov, N., 108n
Madran, C., 315n
Madrigal, R., 427n, 429n
Madzharov, A., 509n
Maggiore, D., 479

Magi, A. W., 673n
Magid, L., 760
Mahajan, V., 258n, 427n, 671n
Maher, A., 76n
Maher, A. A., 76n
Maher, J. K., 427n
Maheshwari, S., 272
Maheswaran, D., 72n, 319n, 359n, 362n, 431n, 455n
Main, K. J., 320n
Maklan, S., 107n
Malaviya, P., 360n, 428n, 562n
Malcom, H., 255n
Malhotra, N., 637n
Malhotra, N. K., 437
Malter, A. J., 358n
Malthouse, E., 633n
Manchanda, R. V., 510n, 637n
Mandel, N., 456n, 670n
Mandese, J., 315n
Mandhachitara, R., 73n, 428n
Maney, K., 107n
Manganari, E. E., 509n
Mangleburg, T. F., 216n, 256n, 428n
Mann, R., 465
Manning, E., 464
Manning, K. C., 319n, 430n, 564n, 635n
Manning, P., 39
Mano, H., 394n, 511n, 670n
Manrai, A. K., 74n
Manrai, L. A., 74n
Mantel, S. P., 428n, 510n, 594n, 637n
Mantonakis, A., 563n
Mao, H., 361n
Maoz, E., 361n, 362n
Maravelakis, I., 361n
Marchi, D., 474
Maremont, M., 359n
Marentic, A., 468
Markman, A. B., 258n, 318n
Markus, H. R., 148n
Markus, M. L., 256n
Marmorstein, H., 564n, 635n
Marsden, P., 635n
Marshall, R., 257n, 392n
Martin, B. A. S., 315n
Martin, C. A., 429n
Martin, D., 393n
Martin, K. D., 755
Martin, M. C., 754, 755
Martin, T., 263
Martin, T. W., 753
Martinez, T., 107n
Maslow, A. H., 366–367, 391n
Mason, K., 358n
Mathew, G., 148n
Mathisen, R. E., 319n
Mathur, A., 146n, 509n, 637n
Mathwick, C., 637n
Matisoo-Smith, E., 318n
Matsuo, H., 563n
Matta, S., 320n
Mattila, A., 669n
Mattila, A. S., 109n, 638n, 669n, 671n
Maute, M. F., 670n
Maxham, G., II, 670n

Maxham, J. G., III, 671n
May, C., 466
Mayer, J., 299
Mays, J. C., 758
Mayzlin, D., 257n
Mazumdar, T., 318n, 635n
Mazursky, D., 565n
McAdams, D. D., 317n
McAfee, M., 508n
McAlexander, J. H., 255n, 256n
McAlister, L., 318n, 509n
McArdle, M., 430n
McCabe, D. B., 670n
McCarthy, H., 474
McCarthy, J., 316n
McCarthy, M., 685, 757
McCarthy, M. S., 109n, 428n
McCluskey, M., 758
McColl-Kennedy, J. R., 109n, 394n, 565n
McCorkle, D. E., 636n
McCraken, G., 753
McCrindle, M., 130
McDaniel, S. R., 430n
McDermott, J., 683
McDonald, A., 758
McDonald, B., 273
McDonald, H., 75n, 636n
McDonald, S., 106n
McDonald, W. J., 595n
McGarvey, M., 272
McGill, A. L., 510n, 562n
McGill, B., 185n
McGinty, J., 508n
McGrath, M. A., 510n
McGregor, J., 672n
McGuire, W. J., 366, 367–372, 391n
McIntyre, P. E., 755
McKaig, A., 271
McKeage, K., 456n
McKechnie, S. A., 316n
McKenzie, K., 392n
McLafferty, S., 636n
McLaughlin, E. W., 635n
McLennan, S., 679
McMahon, T. F., 33n
McMurrian, R. C., 719n
McNamara, S., 532n
McNeal, G., 678
McNeal, J. U., 73n, 210, 216n
McNeil, M. M., 564n
McQuade, K., 466
McQuarrie, E. F., 318n, 319n
McQuilken, T., 483
McQuiston, D. H., 701, 721n
McSpadden, K., 75n
Mecia, T., 215n
Meeker, M., 148n
Meenaghan, T., 318n, 429n
Mehta, A., 456n
Mekoth, N., 638n
Mela, C. F., 562n, 635n, 637n
Melero, I., 671n
Meloy, M. G., 318n, 511n
Menon, A. M., 317n
Menon, G., 319n, 428n
Menon, S., 533n, 637n

Mercado, M., 563n
Mergenhagen, P., 33n, 148n
Merlo, L., 262
Merrick, A., 147n
Merrill, C., 564n
Merritt, D., 72n, 73n, 455n
Messinger, P. R., 636n
Meyer, R. J., 216n, 562n
Meyer, T., 183n
Meyer, Z., 473
Meyers, J. G., 393n
Meyers-Levy, J., 75n, 109n, 256n, 319n, 359n,
    360n, 427n, 428n, 431n, 456n, 510n, 563n
Meyvis, T., 319n, 362n
Michell, P., 720n
Mick, D. G., 318n, 319n
Mickelson, P., 239
Midgley, D., 719n
Mike, M., 107n
Miller, A., 107n
Miller, C., 33n, 75n, 148n, 481, 673n
Miller, E. G., 319n
Miller, K. L., 73n
Miller, N., 473
Miller, P., 158, 183n
Milliman, R. E., 495, 509n
Milne, G. R., 638n, 756
Milner, L. M., 73n
Mims, C., 33n
Min, H., 720n
Minaj, N., 281
Minghua, J., 429n
Miniard, P. J., 319n
Miniard, P. W., 319n, 428n, 430n, 431n, 635n
Mirren, H., 118
Mishra, A., 393n
Mishra, S., 360n
Mitchell, A., 638n
Mitchell, A. A., 358n
Mitchell, D. J., 509n, 594n, 638n
Mitchell, E., 270, 673n
Mitchell, P., 715, 721n
Mitra, A., 756
Mitra, K., 257n, 565n
Mittal, B., 594n, 671n
Mittal, V., 145n, 669n, 670n, 671n
Mittelstaedt, J. D., 636n
Mittelstaedt, R. A., 636n
Mittila, M., 145n
Miyazaki, A. D., 108n, 564n, 638n
Mizerski, R., 393n
Moberg, C. R., 671n
Mochon, D., 256n, 563n
Mochon, D. M., 668n
Moe, W. W., 316n, 565n
Mogelonsky, M., 185n
Mogg, T., 678
Mogilner, C., 392n, 393n
Mohammed, F., 270
Mohr, L. A., 108n
Molina, M., 107n
Monga, A. B., 455n
Monllos, K., 109n
Monllos, L., 391n
Monroe, K. B., 317n, 318n, 359n, 510n, 635n
Montague, T., 108n

Montaldo, D., 676
Moody, B., 678
Moon, B.-J., 392n
Mooradian, T. A., 257n
Moore, D. J., 393n, 429n
Moore, D. W., 107n
Moore, E. S., 73n, 216n
Moore, M. C., 318n
Moorman, C., 564n
Moorman, M., 428n
Moran, C., 689
Morash, E. A., 669n
Moreau, C. P., 258n, 359n, 393n
Moreau, E., 258n
Moreau, G. P., 318n
Moreau, P., 359n
Morewedge, C., 510n
Morey, J., 680
Morgan, M. S., 391n, 393n
Morgan, N. A., 671n
Morgan, R. M., 638n
Morin, S., 510n, 638n
Moring, M., 146n
Morrin, M., 358n, 360n, 509n, 510n, 670n
Morris, D., 758
Morris, E., 182n
Morris, H. J., 268
Morris, J. D., 394n, 427n, 431n
Morris, M. W., 72n, 73n
Morrison, K., 256n
Morrison, M., 510n
Morrissey, J., 147n
Morrow, J., 215n
Mort, G. S., 392n
Morton, L. P., 185n
Morwitz, V. G., 636n, 637n
Moschis, G. P., 146n
Moses, E., 457n
Moses, L., 754
Motes, W. H., 359n
Mothersbaugh, D. L., 289, 318n, 428n, 637n,
    670n, 671n
Motley, C. M., 183n
Mourali, M., 256n, 392n, 510n
Mowen, J. C., 74n, 392n, 429n, 455n, 670n
Moye, J., 76n
Mudambi, S. M., 721n
Muehling, D., 755
Muehling, D. D., 754
Mueller, B., 73n, 74n
Mueller, E., 564n
Mueller, W., 755
Mukherjee, A., 430n
Mulhern, F. J., 146n, 635n
Mullarkey, G. W., 316n
Mullen, R., 681–682
Muller, E., 258n
Muller, L. F., 184n
Mulley, S., 72n
Muniz, A., Jr., 225
Muniz, A. M., 456n
Muniz, A. M., Jr., 256n
Murphy, M., 273
Murphy, P., 758
Murphy, P. E., 755
Murray, J. B., 721n

Murray, P., 481
Musk, E., 683, 684
Muthukrishnan, A. V., 358n, 431n, 594n, 595n
Muzellec, L., 315n

n

Na, W., 392n
Nabith, M. I., 258n
Nager, H., 722, 723
Nagpal, A., 431n
Nakamoto, K., 595n, 637n, 638n
Nakamura, Y., 474
Nakata, C., 721n
Nan, X., 108n
Narasimhan, C., 636n
Narayandas, D., 719n, 721n
Narver, J. C., 721n
Nataraajan, R., 109n
Naude, P., 715, 721n
Naughton, K., 185n
Naussaur, S., 676
Naylor, R. W., 319n
Nededog, J., 147n
Nedungadi, P., 358n
Neff, J., 32n, 76n, 107n, 108n, 109n, 273, 393n,
    394n, 456n
Neijens, P. C., 359n, 428n
Nelson, B., 725
Nelson, M. C., 109n
Nelson, M. R., 109n
Nelson, P., 594n
Nelson, R. A., 76n
Neslin, S. A., 634n, 635n, 672n
Nesselroade, K. P., Jr., 456n
Netemeyer, R. G., 359n, 564n, 594n, 635n,
    670n, 671n, 755
Neufeld, J., 721n
Neumann, M. M., 638n
Newell, G., 480
Newell, S. J., 360n, 394n, 427n, 429n, 720n
Newlands, M., 255n
Newman, A. A., 562n
Newman, J., 564n
Newman, K., 359n
Newman, S., 670n
Newport, F., 107n
Ngai, E., 720n
Nguyen, V. T. L., 315n
Nicholls, J. A. F., 509n, 636n
Nichols, E. L., Jr., 721n
Nicholson, J., 429n, 633n
Nicks, D., 678
Niedrich, R. W., 429n, 635n
Nield, D., 669n
Niquette, M., 685
Nisol, P., 638n
Noble, C. H., 456n
Noel, H., 360n
Noguchi, Y., 754
Nordfalt, J., 361n, 509n
Noriega, J., 184n
Norris, V. P., 595n
Norton, M. I., 668n, 753
Novak, T. P., 428n, 564n, 637n

Novellino, T., 687
Nowlis, S. M., 510n, 594n, 637n, 670n
Nudd, T., 106n, 182n, 316n, 669n
Nunes, J., 594n
Nunes, J. C., 319n, 594n
Nyaga, G. N., 721n
Nyer, P. U., 393n, 511n

O

Oakenfull, G. K., 109n
Oakes, S., 510n, 638n
Obama, M., 462–463
Obermiller, C., 428n
O'Brien, K., 724
O'Brien, L., 673n
O'Cass, A., 669n
O'Connor, G. C., 594n
O'Dell, J., 318n
O'Donnel, K., 73n
O'Driscoll, A., 258n
O'Guinn, T. C., 146n, 256n, 318n
Ogunnaike, N., 272
Ohlsson, M., 259
Ohno, A., 412
Okada, E. M., 669n
Okazaki, S., 73n
Okleshen, C., 256n
O'Leary, N., 361n
Oliver, R. L., 670n, 672n
Olsen, G. D., 108n, 317n, 318n, 595n
Olsen, S. O., 427n
Olson, C. A., 510n
Olson, E. L., 428n
Olson, J. C., 392n
Olsson, U., 427n
O'Neal, S., 463–464
Ong, B. S., 669n
Ongley, H., 687
Orbach, S., 456n
O'Reilly, L., 562n
Orendorff, A., 720n
Orsingher, C., 671n
Oser, K., 317n, 565n
Osterheldt, J., 476
Otnes, C. C., 393n, 510n, 511n
Ottman, J., 107n
Ouellette, S. J., 636n
Owyang, J., 685
Ozment, J., 669n

P

Packard, G., 256n
Padgett, D. T., 635n
Paek, H.-J., 106n
Page, C., 360n, 427n, 635n
Page, K. L., 456n
Pak, S., 215n
Palan, K. M., 109n, 216n, 319n, 431n, 456n, 510n, 511n
Paliwoda, S., 391n
Palmatier, R., 721n
Palmatier, R. W., 393n
Palmer, A., 671n, 672n

Palmer, A. T., 33n
Palumbo, M. G., 359n
Pan, Y., 74n
Papatla, P., 637n
Parasuraman, A., 669n
Pardy, S. M., 634n
Parish, W., 107n
Park, A., 758
Park, C. W., 318n, 362n, 392n, 456n, 509n
Park, H. S., 74n
Park, J., 215n, 392n
Park, J. W., 361n
Park, K., 669n
Park, S. Y., 75n, 511n
Parker, G., 74n
Parker, P. M., 595n
Parker-Pope, T., 72n
Parmar, A., 563n
Parsons, A. L., 320n
Parsons, S., 476
Pasquale, C., 672n
Pasquarelli, A., 147n, 391n
Passell, J., 145n
Passingham, J., 673n
Passyn, K., 430n
Patel, D., 148n
Patel, K., 671n
Patel, N., 595n
Patel, S., 258n, 721n
Patrick, V. M., 427n
Patten, E., 147n, 184n
Patterson, P. G., 671n
Patton, T., 256n
Patton, W. E., III, 719n
Paul, I., 72n
Paul, J., 638n
Paul, P., 74n, 107n, 109n, 147n, 215n, 316n
Paulssen, M., 562n
Pauwels, K., 635n
Pawlak, L., 754
Payne, J., 595n
Payne, J. W., 431n, 533n, 562n, 594n
Pearo, L. K., 669n
Pearson, B., 255n, 634n, 758
Pearson, J., 460
Peart, N., 413
Peattie, K., 720n
Pechmann, C., 430n
Pederson, J. P., 273
Pedram, M., 106n
Peerbhoy, A., 354
Peers, M., 320n
Pelley, S., 685
Pelsmacker, P. D., 393n
Peltier, J. W., 431n
Pelton, L. E., 216n
Pennings, J. M. E., 427n
Pennington, G. L., 392n
Penteado, C., 76n
Pento, T., 145n
Pepe, T., 675
Peracchio, L. A., 184n, 216n, 317n, 319n, 359n, 360n, 456n
Perelman, J., 467
Perez, J., 469, 679
Perez, S., 634n

Perkins, L. A., 183n
Perkins-Munn, T., 721n
Perlberg, S., 683
Perri, M., III, 317n
Peters, C., 146n, 256n
Petersen, J., 727
Peterson, A. M., 185n
Peterson, R. A., 183n
Peterson, T., 315n
Petrak, L., 319n
Petrecca, L., 106n, 633n
Petrova, P. K., 358n
Petty, R. D., 318n
Petty, R. E., 33n, 360n, 427n, 428n, 429n
Pham, M. T., 359n, 392n, 428n, 532n, 594n
Phelps, M., 412
Phillips, B. J., 319n
Phillips, C., 633n
Phillips, D. M., 146n, 393n
Phillips-Donaldson, D., 679
Pick, D., 672n
Pierson, D., 671n
Pieters, R., 316n, 317n, 319n, 360n, 510n, 594n, 670n
Pieters, R. G. M., 317n, 360n
Pigato, J., 671n
Pike, J., 475
Pike, N., 429n
Pile, H., 118
Pillutla, M. M., 362n
Pilotta, J. J., 315n
Pine, J. B., 32n
Pinkleton, B. E., 565n
Piron, F., 75n
Pitt, B., 458
Pitt, L. F., 720n
Plank, R. E., 720n
Plato, R., 315n
Podoshen, J. S., 74n
Pogue, D., 258n
Poiesz, T. B. C., 258n
Pol, L. G., 215n, 721n
Polegato, R., 75n
Pollay, R. W., 595n, 755
Pomazal, R., 772
Pomranz, M., 681
Ponnavolu, K., 673n
Pons, F., 256n, 510n
Ponsoda, V., 317n
Popa, M., 318n
Popovich, M., 755
Porac, J. F., 391n
Pornpitakpan, C., 72n, 73n, 74n, 257n, 429n
Portis, B., 564n
Posavac, S., 360n
Posavac, S. S., 258n, 428n, 429n, 431n, 562n, 594n
Posig, M., 109n
Powers, T. L., 720n
Pracejus, J. W., 108n, 318n, 359n
Prasad, V., 636n
Prelec, D., 638n
Prendergast, G. P., 74n
Prensky, M., 75n
Preston, C., 754
Preston, I. L., 319n, 755

Price, L. L., 215n, 257n, 456n, 669n
Price, P. L., 256n
Priester, J. R., 427n, 429n, 430n
Priluck, R., 362n
Priluck, R. L., 359n, 427n
Prince, M., 638n
Prince, R. A., 720n
Pritchard, J., 318n
Protextor, K., 719n
Pruitt, S. W., 430n
Puccinelli, N. M., 393n
Pujari, D., 720n
Pullig, C., 359n
Punji, G., 562n
Puntoni, S., 361n
Puri, R., 636n
Puri, S. J., 719n
Puto, C., 595n
Putrevu, S., 109n, 358n, 360n, 428n, 431n

q

Qu, L., 595n
Quelch, J. A., 72n
Quester, P., 392n, 430n
Qui, C., 594n

r

Rabuck, M. J., 360n
Radtke, R., 358n
Raffel, C. B., 533n
Raggio, R. D., 670n
Raghubir, P., 318n, 320n, 428n
Raghunathan, R., 319n, 427n
Raj, S. P., 318n, 637n
Raj Bhasin, T., 482
Rajagopal, P., 216n
Rajendran, K. N., 635n
Raju, S., 216n
Ram, S., 669n
Ramachandran, S., 315n
Ramanathan, S., 510n
Ramaswami, S. N., 257n, 391n
Ramaswamy, V., 594n
Ramp, D. L., 148n
Ramsey, D., 182n
Rand, E., 753
Rao, A. G., 637n
Rao, A. R., 319n, 595n
Rao, R., 637n
Rao, R. C., 533n
Rao, S. R., 146n
Ratchford, B. T., 562n, 563n, 564n
Ratner, R. K., 391n, 510n, 533n
Ratneshwar, S., 318n, 360n, 361n, 510n, 595n
Raven, P., 74n
Ray, P. H., 457n
Raymond, J., 147n, 215n, 673n
Razaghpanah, A., 759
Razzaque, M. A., 509n
Razzouk, N., 215n
Reardon, J., 76n, 759
Reardon, R., 429n
Reast, J., 720n

Reddy, S. K., 362n
Redlich, F. C., 139
Reed, A., II, 455n
Reichert, T., 755
Reichheld, F. F., 660, 671n, 672n
Reid, B., 755
Reinartz, R. D., 429n
Reinartz, W. J., 635n
Reingold, J., 633n
Reinhardt, A., 33n
Reisenwitz, T., 147n
Reiss, M. C., 216n, 565n
Ren, Y., 33n
Reyes, I., 759, 760
Reynolds, D., 756
Reynolds, S., 685
Reynolds, T. J., 392n
Reynolds-McIlnay, R., 509n
Rhodes, M., 32n
Rice, F., 673n
Rich, J., 759
Rich, S., 724
Richards, K., 636n
Richards, K. A., 721n
Richardson, P. S., 635n
Richins, M. L., 33n, 427n, 455n
Richwine, L., 33n
Ridgway, N. M., 564n, 669n
Riebe, E., 317n
Riegner, C., 74n
Rifon, N. J., 108n, 430n
Rigdon, E., 637n
Rihanna, 413
Rimer, B. K., 431n
Rindfleisch, A., 106n, 146n, 147n, 428n
Ringstrom, A., 261
Ritchi, K., 315n
Ritchie, R. J. B., 317n
Rivlin, G., 316n
Roach, D., 358n
Roach, D. W., 595n
Roberto, N., 33n
Roberts, E., 482
Roberts, M. S., 72n
Robinson, C., 72n
Robinson, H., 316n
Robinson, J. P., 107n
Robinson, M., 360n
Robinson, S., 671n
Robles, P., 634n
Rock, A., 109n
Rodgers, W. C., 257n
Rodriguez, A., 184n, 481
Rodriguez, L., 688
Rodriguez, N., 215n
Rodway, P., 595n
Roehm, H. A., Jr., 358n
Roehm, M. L., 358n, 359n, 360n, 428n
Roethlisberger, B., 414
Rogers, E. M., 258n
Rogers, J., 565n
Rogers, M., 317n
Rohrlich, J., 318n
Rojas-Mendez, J., 315n
Rojas-Mendez, J. I., 393n
Rook, D. W., 511n, 563n, 636n

Roos, I., 670n, 671n
Rosa, J. A., 391n
Rosa-Diaz, M. I. M., 145n
Rosbergen, E., 316n, 360n
Rose, C., 678
Rose, G. M., 216n, 257n
Rose, T., 392n
Rosen, D. L., 319n
Rosen, E., 255n, 257n
Rosenberg, S., 182n
Roslow, S., 509n
Ross, F., 107n
Ross, I., 671n
Ross, W. T., Jr., 670n
Rossi, C., 669n
Rossiter, J. R., 146n, 316n
Roster, C. A., 427n
Rostoks, L., 316n
Rotfeld, H. J., 430n
Roth, M. S., 75n
Roumelis, J., 317n
Rovell, D., 258n
Rowley, I., 72n
Roy, S., 393n
Royo-Vela, M., 394n
Rozensher, S., 108n
Ruan, B., 391n
Rubel, C., 76n, 392n, 755
Rucinski, T., 634n
Rucker, D., 481
Rucker, D. D., 428n
Rude, E., 426n
Rudolph, T., 672n
Ruekert, R. W., 595n
Ruggless, R., 359n
Ruiz, N., 184n
Rundle-Thiel, S., 671n
Rushe, D., 634n
Russak, B., 393n
Russell, C. A., 316n, 360n
Russo, J. E., 595n, 636n
Rust, R. T., 146n, 672n
Ruth, J. A., 318n, 393n, 427n, 428n, 510n, 511n, 594n
Ryu, G., 257n

s

Saad, G., 510n
Saad, L., 106n, 108n, 263
Sabol, B., 672n
Saez, E., 146n
Salpini, C., 33n
Salup, M., 466
Samuelsen, B. M., 720n
Samuelson, R. J., 147n, 148n
Sanbonmatsu, D. M., 562n
Sanburn, J., 255n, 265, 634n
Sanders, L., 183n, 509n
Sands, D., 185n
Sangkhawasi, T., 72n
Sankaranarayanan, K., 638n
Saranow, J., 146n
Sarvary, M., 563n
Sashi, C. M., 719n

Sasser, W. E., Jr., 660, 671n, 672n
Satariano, A., 562n
Sattler, H., 361n, 362n
Sautter, P., 509n
Savage, M., 316n
Sawhney, R., 268, 670n
Sawyer, A. G., 360n, 637n
Sayre, S., 455n
Schaninger, C. M., 109n, 215n
Schap, T., 215n
Schatz, R., 508n
Schau, H., 147n
Schau, H. J., 225, 256n
Schawbel, D., 75n, 147n
Schepman, A., 595n
Scherer, C. W., 563n, 636n
Scheufele, D. A., 563n, 636n
Schewe, D. C., 638n
Schifferstein, H. N. J., 595n
Schiffman, L., 319n
Schindler, R. M., 563n
Schleicher, M., 672n
Schleimer, J., 146n
Schlossberg, H., 362n
Schlossberg, M., 255n
Schlosser, A. E., 562n
Schmidt, L., 147n
Schmitt, B. H., 74n, 319n, 391n, 510n
Schneider, K. C., 257n
Schneider, L., 316n
Schneider, M., 483
Schneider, S. L., 431n
Schneider-Levy, B., 393n
Schneier, M., 429n
Schoefer, K., 72n
Schor, J. B., 216n
Schouten, J. W., 255n, 256n
Schribrowsky, J. A., 431n
Schroder, B., 719n
Schulte, B., 215n
Schultz, D., 315n
Schultz, E., 483, 756
Schultz, E. J., 76n
Schultz, R., 727
Schumann, D., 360n, 428n
Schumann, D. W., 258n
Schwartz, E., 479
Schwartz, J., 256n, 563n
Schwartz, N., 669n
Schwarz, N., 669n
Scommegna, P., 215n
Scott, A., 360n
Scott, J., 148n, 456n
Scott, L., 74n
Scott, L. M., 511n
Scott, M., 754
Scott, R., 147n
Seacrest, R., 480
Seetharaman, P. B., 669n
Sego, T., 510n
Segran, E., 473
Seiders, K., 635n, 672n
Seiler, C. A., 317n
Seitz, V., 215n
Selart, M., 511n
Sellers, P., 73n, 671n, 673n

Selvaraj, C., 509n
Semoff, S., 675
Semons, A., 108n
Sen, S., 108n, 456n, 672n
Sengupta, J., 72n, 106n, 318n, 319n, 428n,
    429n, 509n
Seppela, T., 315n
Sese, F., 671n
Settle, R. B., 636n
Severin, V., 635n, 636n
Sevilla, J., 637n
Shah, R. H., 721n
Shahin, K. N., 317n
Shamdasani, P. N., 320n
Shannahan, L., 73n
Shannon, J. R., 360n
Shannon, R. M., 73n
Shapiro, J., 269, 270
Shapiro, S., 317n, 318n, 509n, 595n
Sharma, A., 509n, 635n
Sharma, S., 392n, 635n
Sharp, L., 753
Shavitt, S., 72n, 73n, 74n, 148n, 315n, 431n
Sheehan, A., 634n
Sheldon, P. S., 456n
Shelton, J., 256n
Shepherdson, N., 148n
Sherman, E., 509n, 637n
Sherman, L., 317n
Sherman, S., 171, 633n
Sherman, S. J., 594n
Sherry, J. F., Jr., 361n
Sheth, J. N., 721n
Shih, C.-F., 258n
Shim, S., 511n
Shimp, T. A., 392n, 394n, 429n, 456n
Shin, J., 392n, 672n
Shiv, B., 431n, 532n, 594n
Shoham, A., 73n, 215n, 257n
Sholl, J., 476
Shrum, L. J., 106n, 755
Shugan, S. M., 564n
Shultz, C. J., II, 510n
Siau, K., 635n
Sidin, S. M., 73n
Sifferlin, A., 466
Silberstein, R. B., 316n
Silseth, P. R., 720n
Silva-Olave, E., 393n
Silver, L., 148n
Simcock, P., 107n
Simester, D., 636n, 638n
Simester, D. I., 637n
Simmons, C. J., 359n
Simon, J. L., 343
Simonson, A., 755
Simonson, I., 72n, 73n, 319n, 595n, 636n,
    637n, 669n
Simpson, E. M., 183n
Sims, T., 315n
Simula, H., 32n
Sin, L. Y., 73n
Sin, L. Y. M., 73n
Singh, J., 670n, 671n, 672n
Singh, M., 316n
Singh, N., 563n

Singh, S. N., 316n, 360n
Singleton, M., 562n
Singley, R. B., 431n
Sinha, I., 318n, 509n, 636n
Sinkula, J. M., 107n, 721n
Siomkos, G. J., 509n
Sirdeshmukh, D., 361n, 428n, 672n
Sirgy, M. J., 431n, 562n
Sirianni, N., 671n
Sirohi, N., 635n
Siu, E., 256n
Siu, N. Y.-M., 258n
Sivadas, E., 148n, 456n
Sivakumar, K., 637n, 721n
Skorinko, J. L., 319n
Slama, M., 565n
Slama, M. E., 431n
Slatalla, M., 107n
Slater, J., 75n
Slater, S. F., 721n
Slattery, G., 216n
Sloan, P., 510n, 638n
Sloot, L. M., 638n
Slote-Graff, R. J., 669n
Slutsky, I., 469
Smeesters, D., 318n, 456n
Smialek, J., 676
Smit, E. G., 359n, 428n
Smith, A., 183n, 256n, 268
Smith, A. K., 670n, 671n
Smith, C. W., 633n
Smith, D., 685, 721n
Smith, D. C., 362n, 456n
Smith, J., 563n
Smith, J. B., 565n, 636n
Smith, J. W., 146n
Smith, K., 720n
Smith, L., 675
Smith, M. C., 318n
Smith, M. F., 636n
Smith, P. K., 317n
Smith, R., 562n
Smith, R. B., 509n, 637n
Smith, T., 32n, 671n
Snelling, S., 145n
Snider, M., 678
Snipes, R. L., 430n
Snyder, K., 719n, 720n
So, S. L. M., 74n
Soberman, D., 319n
Sojka, J. Z., 318n, 319n, 392n
Solomon, M. R., 755
Solsman, J., 265
Soman, D., 358n, 533n, 638n
Sonderup, L., 184n
Song, J. H., 637n
Sood, S., 362n
Sopadjieva, E., 634n
Sorescu, A. B., 431n
Soscia, I., 393n
Sousa, R., 670n
Soutar, G. N., 594n, 636n, 668n, 669n
Souter, G. N., 564n
Spaeth, J., 317n
Spake, D. F., 672n
Spangenberg, E., 456n, 674

Spangenberg, E. R., 215n, 427n, 428n, 509n, 638n
Spangler, T., 562n
Sparks, B. A., 109n, 671n
Sparks, J. V., 106n
Spears, N., 74n, 392n
Spears, N. E., 429n
Speck, P. S., 316n
Spence, M. T., 595n
Spencer, P., 755
Spero, J., 719n
Spiggle, S., 511n
Spilker, B. C., 565n
Spinney, L., 318n
Spira, J. S., 183n
Spitznagel, E., 456n
Spreng, R. A., 670n
Sprott, D., 456n
Sprott, D. E., 456n, 564n, 669n
Srinivasan, S. S., 76n, 594n, 637n, 673n
Srivastava, J., 564n, 636n
Srivastava, P., 720n
Srull, T. K., 670n
St. John, O., 634n
St. Michel, P., 476
Staelin, R., 564n, 565n, 636n
Stafflage, M., 637n
Stafford, M. R., 429n, 635n
Stafford, T. F., 317n, 509n, 635n
Stanaland, A., 76n
Stanaland, A. J. S., 109n, 320n
Stanley, S. M., 359n
Stanley, T. L., 106n, 316n
Stanton, J., 214n
Stanton, J. L., 146n
Stassen, R. E., 636n
Stayman, D. M., 595n
Steckel, J. H., 595n
Steel, E., 563n
Steenkamp, J. E. M., 72n, 74n, 75n, 635n
Steimer, S., 270
Steinberg, B., 107n, 315n, 756
Steiner, M., 637n
Steinman, C., 721n
Stephen, A., 563n
Stephens, N., 146n, 670n
Sterbenz, C., 148n
Stern, B. B., 638n
Stern, J., 509n
Sternthal, B., 360n, 392n, 394n, 428n
Stevenson, J. S., 427n
Stevenson, T. H., 755
Stewart, D. W., 360n
Stinson, L., 634n
Stipp, H., 563n
Stoddard, J. E., 720n
Stojack, C., 669n
Stoner, C., 428n
Strahilevitz, M. A., 456n
Strauss, J., 671n
Streitfeld, D., 258n
Strom, S., 263
Strombeck, S. D., 510n
Strother, S., 74n
Stuart, E. W., 394n
Stutts, M. A., 754

Stutz, C., 360n
Su, C., 216n
Suarez, R., 214n
Sudbury, L., 107n
Sudharshan, D., 107n
Sudhir, K., 672n
Suh, J., 638n, 670n
Sujan, M., 146n, 215n, 257n, 359n, 360n, 361n, 430n, 565n, 594n, 669n
Sullivan, D., 564n
Sun, B., 362n
Sun, T., 72n, 73n, 76n, 455n
Sundaram, D. S., 257n
Sunder, S., 362n
Sunder, S. S., 316n
Sung, Y., 393n
Supphellen, M., 358n, 361n, 392n, 393n, 456n
Suri, R., 510n
Suro, R., 107n
Sustein, C. R., 593n
Suter, T. A., 635n
Sutton, J., 676
Swait, J., 72n, 74n, 258n, 562n, 565n, 594n
Swaminathan, V., 362n, 456n
Swan, I. E., 670n
Swan, J. E., 670n, 720n
Swanson, S. R., 257n
Swayne, L. E., 637n
Sweeney, J. C., 510n, 594n, 636n, 638n, 668n, 669n
Sweet, K., 215n
Swinyard, W. R., 511n
Szymanski, D. M., 669n

 t

Tagg, S., 429n
Talpade, S., 215n
Talukdar, D., 562n, 563n, 564n
Tan, C. T., 73n
Tan, J., 320n, 358n, 428n
Tang, C. S., 636n
Tangari, A. H., 427n
Tanier, M., 481
Tanner, J. F., Jr., 430n
Tansuhaj, P., 215n
Tantillo, J., 319n
Taranto, N., 470
Tarn, D. D. C., 216n
Tarver, E., 483
Tavassoli, N. T., 361n
Tax, S. S., 671n
Taylor, A., 109n, 685
Taylor, A., III, 392n, 457n
Taylor, C. R., 755
Taylor, E. L., 72n
Taylor, G. A., 183n, 637n
Taylor, K., 681
Taylor, K. A., 108n
Taylor, S., 670n
Taylor, S. F., 672n
Taylor, V. A., 320n, 669n
Teinowitz, I., 754
Tellis, G.-J., 635n
Tennis, B. M., 318n

Ter Hofstede, F., 72n, 74n, 75n
Terlep, S., 756
Tewari, S., 483
Thakar, P., 482
Thakor, M. V., 670n
Thaler, R. H., 593n, 668n
Tham, L. L., 360n
Tharp, M., 316n
Tharp, M. C., 184n
Thau, R., 185n
Theil, S., 106n
Thjomoe, H. M., 428n
Thomas, E. G., 146n
Thomas, H., 682
Thomas, J., 466
Thomas, J. B., 146n
Thomas, J. S., 672n
Thomas, K. M., 183n
Thomas, L., 633n
Thomas, M., 359n
Thomaselli, R., 429n
Thompson, B., 256n
Thompson, C., 562n
Thompson, C. J., 595n
Thompson, G. J., 638n, 668n, 670n
Thompson, K., 466
Thompson, K. N., 720n
Thompson, S., 106n, 272, 316n, 319n, 320n, 361n, 362n, 595n, 754, 755
Thornton, C. G., 107n
Thorson, E., 428n, 564n, 635n
Tian, K., 76n
Tian, K. T., 392n
Tibken, S., 72n
Till, B. D., 359n, 362n, 427n, 429n
Tillmanns, S., 672n
Timmerman, L., 257n
Timmermans, H. J. P., 671n
Tinkham, S. F., 393n
Tjernlund, A., 107n, 755
Todd, P. M., 593n
Tohmatsu, K., 474
Toleman, D., 257n
Tollinen, A., 32n
Tom, G., 318n
Tomiuk, M. A., 216n
Tomlin, L., 268
Toncar, M. F., 74n, 430n
Tong, L., 75n
Tootelian, H., 147n
Torelli, C. J., 455n
Townsend, C., 429n, 637n
Tran, L., 72n
Trappey, C., 317n
Travell, C., 468
Trifts, V., 595n
Tripathi, S., 318n, 509n
Triplett, T., 393n
Tripp, C., 429n
Trivedi, M., 391n, 533n
Trosclair, C., 359n
Trump, R., 359n
Trusov, M., 257n
Tsai, C., 720n
Tsao, A., 109n
Tse, A. C. B., 316n

Tse, D. K., 75n
Tsiros, M., 669n
Tucker, C., 755
Tucker, T., 392n
Turano, A., 689
Turley, L. W., 360n, 509n, 636n, 670n
Turnbull, B., 318n
Turner, T., 132
Tuttle, B., 469, 673n
Twain, M., 509n
Tybout, A. M., 359n, 361n, 362n, 429n, 593n
Tyre, P., 107n

U

Ulgado, F. M., 75n
Unnava, H. R., 318n, 360n, 361n, 394n, 431n, 509n
Urbany, J. E., 257n, 564n, 637n
Ursic, M. L., 595n

V

Valentini, S., 671n
Valenzuala, A., 72n, 74n
Vallina-Rodriguez, N., 759
Van Auken, S., 146n
van der Heijden, H., 612, 635n
Van Grove, J., 258n, 563n
van Herpen, E., 319n
Van Ittersum, K., 320n
Van Kenhove, P., 430n, 510n
van Oest, R., 671n
Van Osselaer, S., 361n
Van Osselaer, S. M. J., 361n, 595n
van Putten, M., 637n
van Reijmersdal, E. A., 359n
Van Trijp, H. C. M., 533n
Van Waterschoot, W., 510n
VanBoskirk, S., 563n
Vanhuele, M., 358n
Vanorman, A., 215n
Vargas, P., 315n
Varki, S., 672n
Varshney, S. B., 147n
Vedantam, S., 392n
Vence, D. L., 74n, 108n, 184n
Venkataramani, G., 359n
Venkatesh, A., 258n
Ventakesh, R., 719n
Vergara, S., 412
Verhage, T., 612
Verhagen, T., 635n
Verhoef, P. C., 634n, 638n, 672n
Verlegh, P. W. J., 595n
Verluen, J., 465
Vermeir, I., 430n
Vernellia, R. R., 430n
Vespa, J., 214n
Vetere, B., 271
Vick, M., 413
Vida, I., 76n
Vigar-Ellis, D., 74n
Vila, N., 320n
Villanti, A. C., 430n

Villarreal, R., 183n
Virgillito, D., 634n, 635n
Viswanathan, M., 73n, 216n, 317n
Vlachos, P. A., 108n
Vlahos, J., 676
Vohs, K. D., 393n
Völckner, F., 361n, 362n
Voorhees, C., 637n
Voorhees, C. M., 671n
Vosgerau, J., 510n
Voss, C. A., 75n, 670n
Voss, G. B., 669n, 672n
Voss, K. E., 427n
Voss, Z. G., 672n
Vranica, S., 315n, 469
Vrechopoulos, A. P., 509n, 637n
Vrioni, A. B., 108n

W

Wachtel, P. L., 146n
Wagner, J., 671n
Wagner, T., 672n
Wakefield, K. L. 510n, 636n, 637n
Walford, L. 679
Walker, B. A., 456n
Walker, C., 75n, 457n
Walker, E., 476
Walker, R., 257n, 509n
Wall, K., 261
Wallace, K., 754
Wallendorf, M., 148n
Waller, D. S., 74n
Walliker, A., 147n
Wallis, D., 270
Walliser, B., 429n
Walsh, D., 755
Walsh, G., 257n
Walsh, P. A., 511n
Walsh, T., 685
Walter, A., 721n
Walters, R. G., 701
Walther, E., 394n
Wang, A., 428n, 429n
Wang, C. L., 455n
Wang, H., 72n
Wang, J., 75n, 633n
Wang, L. C., 393n
Wang, R., 633n
Wang, S., 428n
Wang, X., 72n
Wanke, M., 427n
Wansink, B., 318n, 319n, 320n, 358n, 361n, 427n, 509n, 511n, 635n, 668n, 669n
Ward, J., 318n
Ward, S., 147n
Warlop, L., 317n, 359n, 431n, 510n, 594n
Warner, J., 109n
Warner, W. L., 148n
Warren, D., 720n
Warren, D. L., 720n
Warren, M., 393n
Warren, R., 222
Warren, W. E., 456n

Washburn, J. H., 362n
Wasserman, T., 256n
Waters, L. K., 392n
Watson, D., 148n
Watson, G., IV, 721n
Watson, J. J., 510n
Watson, J. L., 73n
Watson, S., 360n
Weaver, K., 594n
Webb, D. J., 108n
Weber, J., 33n
Webley, K., 476
Webster, C., 74n, 183n, 216n, 257n
Wedel, M., 72n, 74n, 75n, 316n, 317n, 360n
Wedell, D. H., 635n
Wee, T. T. T., 393n
Weeks, M., 183n
Weems, C., 316n
Weenig, M. W. H., 565n
Wegener, D. T., 427n
Weinberg, C. B., 595n
Weinberg, T., 257n
Weinberger, M. G., 430n
Weiss, A. E., 593n
Weiss, A. M., 719n
Weiss, M. J., 146n
Weiss, W. M., 719n
Weitz, B., 638n
Wellner, A. S., 33n, 146n, 184n, 185n
Wells, W. D., 107n, 146n, 318n, 456n
Welsh, D. H. B., 74n
Wentz, L., 73n, 184n
Werani, T., 319n
Wergan, R., 477
Wertenbroch, K., 594n
Wertz, J., 258n
West, K., 299
Westbrook, R. A., 564n
Westerman, M., 184n
Wetzer, I. M., 670n
Weun, S., 670n
Wheaton, K., 185n
Whipple, J. M., 721n
White, J., 595n
White, K., 255n, 563n
White, M. D., 72n, 75n
White, N. J., 75n
White, R., 633n
White, T. B., 638n
Whittler, T. E., 183n
Whitwell, G. J., 721n
Wi, J.-Y., 315n
Wickens, T. D., 360n
Widener, S. K., 669n
Widgery, R., 109n
Widrick, S., 564n
Wieseman, E., 679
Wiggins, J. S., 392n
Wijesekera, P., 759
Wilcox, J., 427n
Wilcox, J. B., 257n, 392n
Wilcox, N. T., 359n
Wiles, C. R., 107n, 755
Wiles, J. A., 107n, 755
Wiles, M., 316n

Wilkes, R. E., 215n, 216n
Wilkie, M., 638n, 756
Wilkie, W. L., 216n, 564n
Williams, A., 147n
Williams, A. J., 109n
Williams, E., 633n
Williams, J. D., 76n, 146n
Williams, L., 669n
Williams, P., 393n
Williams, S., 381, 437
Williams, T., 565n
Williams, T. G., 148n
Willis, L. A., 215n
Willis, M., 75n
Willis-Flurry, L. A., 216n
Wilson, A., 257n
Wilson, E. J., 719n, 755
Wilson, H., 359n
Wilson, M., 634n
Wilson, P. H., 184n
Wimalasiri, J. S., 73n
Windels, K., 456n
Windle, K., 483
Winer, R. S., 563n
Winfrey, O., 352–353
Wingert, P., 33n
Winter, C., 318n, 676
Wirtz, J., 638n, 669n, 671n
Wirtz, J. G., 106n
Wise, R., 33n
Wittink, D. R., 595n, 635n
Wolfinbarger, M., 147n
Wolfinbarger, M. F., 257n
Wolin, L. D., 109n
Wolters, G., 358n
Wong, H., 75n, 720n
Wong, N. Y., 72n, 455n
Wong, V., 462, 721n
Wood, S. L., 215n, 258n, 393n, 669n
Woods, T., 413
Woodside, A. G., 359n, 391n, 719n
Wooten, D. B., 510n
Workman, J. E., 74n
Wright, A. A., 562n
Wright, G., 720n
Wright, G. P., 565n
Wright, M., 358n
Wright, P., 216n, 391n, 595n

Wu, B. T., 360n, 394n
Wu, G., 76n
Wuhrer, G., 319n
Wyatt, E., 755
Wyatt, R. J., 183n
Wyber, F., 510n, 638n
Wyer, R., 319n
Wyer, R. S., Jr., 359n, 428n, 594n
Wysocka, A., 316n

X

Xia, L., 318n
Xu, J., 669n
Xu, Y., 563n
Xuan, M. V., 75n

Y

Yadav, M. S., 595n, 635n
Yah, X., 638n
Yalch, R., 391n
Yalch, R. F., 360n
Yale, L. J., 257n
Yan, D., 319n
Yan, R.-N., 634n
Yang, K. C. C., 73n
Yang, S., 317n, 320n, 563n, 594n
Yang, Y., 391n
Yardley, M., 184n
Yarrow, R., 679
Yau, O. H., 73n
Yau, O. H. M., 73n
Yaveroglu, I. S., 72n
Ye, K., 216n
Yeh, C., 216n
Yeo, J., 392n
Yeung, C. W. M., 428n, 594n
Yeung, K. W. Y., 146n
Yi, S., 393n, 533n
Yi, T., 316n, 509n
Yim, C., 456n
Yin, S., 147n
Yoh, E., 638n
Yoo, B., 428n
Yoo, C., 360n
Yoon, C., 146n, 509n

Yoon, S., 393n
York, E., 429n
York, E. B., 430n
Yorkston, E., 319n, 594n
Youn, S., 360n
Young, C., 361n
Young, C. E., 360n
Young, S., 756
Yovovich, B. G., 672n
Yu, D., 263
Yu, J., 719n
Yuan, H., 318n
Yung, Y.-F., 564n

Z

Zaichkowsky, J. L., 392n, 562n
Zakrajsek, T. D., 392n
Zaltman, G., 533n, 719n
Zantal-Wiener, A., 257n
Zavestoski, S., 106n
Zeelenberg, M., 637n, 670n
Zegler, J., 148n
Zeithaml, V. A., 672n
Zhang, J., 72n, 74n, 721n
Zhang, K., 637n
Zhang, M., 455n
Zhang, S., 74n, 319n, 391n
Zhang, X., 672n
Zhang, Y., 430n
Zhao, M., 318n
Zhao, X., 430n
Zhao, Y., 672n
Zhou, J., 316n
Zickhuhr, K., 563n
Zielski, H. J., 343
Zigang, Z., 75n
Zigmond, D., 563n
Zimbres, T. M., 106n
Zimmer, M. R., 635n
Zimmers, B., 510n
Zinkhan, G. M., 257n, 317n, 392n, 430n, 456n, 637n, 672n
Zipkin, N., 361n, 481
Zmuda, N., 146n, 256n, 429n, 564n
Zukin, S., 148n
Zulueta, A., 753

Case Index

a

Albertson's Ditches Self-Checkout in Favor of Human Contact, 687-689
Amazon Prime Air Prepares for Takeoff, 676-678
American Beagle Outfitters: April Fool's Joke Turned Reality, 270-272
Attention, Millennials! Automobile Manufacturers Adapt for You, 466-469

b

Beats by Dre's Rise to the Top, 263-265

c

COPPA Evolves, But Technology Industries Evolve Faster, 759-760
Cuties: How Commodity Fruits Became a Branded Sensation, 722-724
CVS Caremark Discontinues the Sale of Tobacco Products, 261-263

f

Farmers' Brand Loyalty for Heavy Farm Machinery, 724-727

g

Gilt Groupe's Innovative Approach to Loyalty Programs, 685-687
Grace and Frankie: The Invisibility of Baby Boomer Women, 268-270

h

Hello Kitty Mania, 473-476
Hispanic Marketing in Online and Mobile Formats, 274-276
How Social Media Nearly Brought Down United Airlines, 265-268

i

IKEA Uses Market Research to Adapt for Global Markets, 259-261
Is Crude Puppet Movie Hitting a Dead End on Sesame Street?, 757-758

l

Let's Move! Campaign Celebrities Endorsing Soda?!, 462-465

m

Macy's Embraces Beacon Technology, 681-683
Meal Kits Are Shifting How Consumers Shop for Food, 469-473

n

Nissan Goes After the Dog Lover Niche, 678-679

p

Patagonia's Eco-Fashion Push, 458-460

r

Repositioning McDonald's, 461-462

s

Scent Marketing Reaches Consumers' Emotions, 674-676

t

The Tale of Two Emotional Ads, 479-481
Tesla's Novel and Environmental Approach Drives Amazing Brand Loyalty, 683-685
Tide Goes After Green with New Pods, 272-273

w

Wawa Dominates with Its Mobile App, 680-681
The World Shares a Coke, 481-482

x

Xerox's Ongoing Battle to Reposition, 476-479

Subject Index

a

Aad. *see* Attitude toward the ad
AARP, 268
Abercrombie & Fitch, 415, 535
Ability
    in attention, 294–295
    definition of, 294
    lack of, in attitudes, 404
Abr. *see* Attitude toward the brand
Absolut, 302
Abstinence, 51–52, 81–82
Acceptance strategy, 558
Accessibility
    chronic, 376
    of long-term memory, 329
Acculturation, 161–163
Accuracy
    of consumer information, 743–747
    of judgments of price, 577
Ace Metrix, 464
Achievement motivation, 445
Achievement roles, 98
Achievers, in VALS program, 446–447
ACR. *see* Automatic content recognition
ACS. *see* Affiliated Computer Services
Action-oriented approach, 51, 84, 85
Activation, of problem recognition, 526–529
Active coping, 385–386
Active problems, 520–521
Activities, organizational, 705–706
Activity analysis, 523–524
Actual self-concept, 434, 437, 440
Actual state, 518–519
Acura, 353
ADA. *see* American Dental Association
Adaptation level theory, 292–293
Adequacy, of consumer information, 747–749
Adidas, 223, 238, 551
Admire/overcome nature, 86–87
ADM Logistics, 702
Adobe, 711
Adolescents. *see also* Children
    global youth culture of, 60–62
Adopter categories, 248–249
Adoption process, 245–246
AdSAM, 402, 403
Adver-games, 737
Advertisements. *see also specific media and
    types of ads*
    avoidance of, 284–286, 466
    to children (*see* Children, marketing to)
    in importance of evaluative criteria, 579
    measuring effects of, 769–771
    music in, 341
    and opinion leaders, 239
    perception in, 310
    quality of, 295
    reference group influence in, 232–233

    as source of information, 535, 541
    voluntary exposure to, 287
    and word-of-mouth communications, 239
Advertising intensity, 304
Advertising wearout, 344
AEI, 495
Aerie, 234
Aesthetic appeal, 401
Affect, vs. emotion, use of terms, 383
Affect intensity, 298, 383
Affective choice, 569–572
Affective component of attitudes, 398–408
    change strategies for, 406–408
    consistency with other components,
        403–405
    definition of, 401
    measurement of, 401–402, 403, 769, 770
    and smoking, 416
Affective interpretation, 298
Affective motives, 368, 370–372
Affective performance, 652–653
Affective reactions, in schematic memory, 327
Affiliated Computer Services (ACS), 477
Affiliation, need for, 371
African Americans, 154–160
    vs. black Americans, use of terms, 155
    demographic profile of, 155
    marketing to, 158–160
    market segments for, 156, 157
    as percentage of population, 154, 155
    product placement and, 281
    in single-parent households, 190
    subculture of, 151, 154–160
AGCO, 725
Age
    and ability to learn, 207–208
    cognitive, 119
    consumption influenced by, 117–119
    in cultural values, 45–46, 89–90
    and external information search, 554
    of first-time mothers, 191
Age cohorts, 119. *see also* Generation(s)
Age distributions, 64, 85, 117–118
Age-gating, 739
Ageism, and baby boomer women, 268–270
Agreeableness, in Five-Factor Model of
    personality, 379
Agreements, cultural differences in, 58
AI. *see* Artificial intelligence
Ailing outgoers, 120
Air France, 7
Aladdin (movie), 173
Albertson's, 160, 687–689
Alcohol, 23
Alikay Naturals, 99
Allergan, 543
Alternative(s)
    appropriate, 537–540
    evoked set of, 329, 537–540
    in external information search, 552

Alternative evaluation and selection, 566–593
    choice overload in, 567–568
    definition of, 568
    rational choice theory on, 568–569
    types of choice processes in, 569–572
Amazon, 8–9, 242, 243, 411, 600, 604, 612, 627
Amazon Prime, 627
Amazon Prime Air, 676–678
Ambient marketing, 674–676
Ambient scents, 307, 494, 674–676
Ambivalent attitudes, 404
Ambush marketing, 302
American Airlines, 95
American Beverage Association, 463
American Dental Association (ADA), 411
American Eagle, 129, 270–272
American Express, 95
American Girl, 605
American Pistachio Growers, 368, 369, 410
American values, 78–106
    in cause-related marketing, 91–93
    environment-oriented, 81, 84–88
    evolution of, 80–90
    in gender-based marketing, 96–102
    gender roles in, 79–80, 96–98
    in green marketing, 90–91
    in LGBTQ market, 93–96
    other-oriented, 81, 88–90
    Protestant, 175
    self-oriented, 80–84
Ameriprise, 95, 96
Amica, 659
Analogical reasoning, 336
Analytical reasoning, 336, 337
Anheuser-Busch InBev, 281
Ann Taylor, 227
Antecedent states, 499–501
Anthropologie, 605
Antiglobals, 40
Anti-Millennials, 126
Anxiety, in postpurchase dissonance, 643
App(s). *see* Mobile apps
Appeals
    aesthetic, 401
    in attitude formation and change, 415–420
    direct vs. indirect, 374
Apple, Inc., 28–29, 38, 156, 264, 647, 682, 709
Apple Corporation, 38
Approach–approach motivational conflict, 375
Approach–avoidance motivational
        conflict, 375
Appropriate alternatives, 537–540
AR. *see* Augmented reality
Arab American Institute, 172
Arab Americans, 172–173, 176
Arabic language, 173
AriZona Beverages, 464
Arm & Hammer, 513, 644–645
Aromas. *see* Scents
Arousal, emotion, 383–387

Artificial intelligence (AI), 605
Artificial scents, 674
Asch phenomenon, 232
Ascribed roles, 98
Ascribed status, 131
As I Am, 159, 160
Asian Americans, 166–170
  demographic profile of, 155
  languages of, 167–170
  marketing to, 169–170
  market segments for, 168–169
  national background of, 167–168
  origins and use of term, 168
  as percentage of population, 154
  subcultures of, 154, 166–170
Asian Indian Americans, 172
Asics, 386
Aspirational aspects, of celebrities, 413
Aspiration reference groups, 221
Assertion, need for, 371
Association techniques, 764
Associative links, 327–328
Assumptions, in rational choice theory, 568–569
Astroturfing, 243
AT&T, 56, 551, 655–656
ATG, 627
Athleta, 364, 365
AtlasRFID, 692, 693
Atmosphere, store
  in brand choice, 624–626
  definition of, 493
Atmospherics, 493, 625
Attention, 287–297
  celebrity sources and, 412
  definition of, 282, 287
  individual factors in, 294–295
  measurement of, 770–771
  nonfocused, 295–297
  situational factors in, 295
  stimulus factors in, 288–294
Attention reallocation, 290
Attitude(s), 396–426
  affective component of, 398–408
  behavioral component of, 398–408
  changes to (see Attitude change)
  cognitive component of, 398–408
  communication factors in formation
    of, 411–415
  component consistency in, 403–405
  definition of, 26, 398
  globalization of, 39
  as internal influence, 26
  learning of, 208
  in lifestyle, 442
  in market segmentation, 421
  in product development, 421–423
  research on, 768–770
  strength of, 405, 410–411
Attitude-based choice, 569–572
Attitude change, 405–421
  communication factors in, 411–421
  elaboration likelihood model of, 409–410
  individual factors in, 409–411
  situational factors in, 409–411
  strategies for, 397, 405–408

Attitude scales, 768–769
Attitude toward the ad (Aad), 407–408, 412
Attitude toward the brand (Abr), 407–408
Attitudinal loyalty, 660–661
Attraction, in groups, 221
Attractive visuals, 290
Attribute-based choice, 569–589
  decision rules for, 580–589
  definition of, 571
  evaluative criteria in, 572–580
  example of, 569
  vs. other choice processes, 569–572
  stages of, 573
Attribute framing, 421
Attribution, need for, 368
Attribution-oriented consumers, 93
Attribution theory, 368
Audi, 91
Audits, consumer behavior, 772–777
Augmented reality (AR), 605, 610
Authority, in family decision making, 205
Automatic content recognition (ACR), 285
Automobiles. see Car(s)
Autonomy, need for, 369–370
Avatars, 629
Avocados, 396, 397
Avoidance
  ad, 284–286, 466
  as coping mechanism, 385–386
Avoidance–avoidance motivational conflict,
    375–376
Awareness, top-of-mind, 329
Awareness set of alternatives, 537–540
Axe, 742

b

Baby boomers, 122–123
  retirement by, 119, 122
  women, 268–270
Balance Bar, 746
Balancers, 93
Banana Republic, 365, 379
Banner ads
  attention to, 289–292, 294, 296
  involuntary vs. voluntary exposure to, 287
  smart, 294
  as source of information, 546–547
  value-expressive vs. utilitarian appeals in, 420
Bargaining, in family decision making,
    205–206
Barilla, 100, 101, 417
Barkley USA, 126
Bass Pro Shops, 605
Bayer, 336, 351
BCLP Law, 711, 712
Beacons, in-store, 604, 681–683
Beats by Dre, 222, 263–265, 281
Beauty standards, 439–440, 742
Beck's, 746
Behavior. see Consumer behavior
Behavioral component of attitudes, 398–408
  change strategies for, 408
  consistency with other components,
    403–405

  definition of, 402
  measurement of, 403, 769, 770
  and smoking, 416
Behavioral targeting, 13, 294, 547
Beliefs
  adding new, 406
  in attitudes (see Cognitive component of
    attitudes)
  changing, 405–406
  claim-belief discrepancies, 306
Believers, in VALS program, 446–447
Belongingness, 367
Benefit beliefs, 399
Benefit chain, 374
Benefit segmentation, 421
Bermuda, 570
Best Buy, 166
BET. see Black Entertainment Television
Biases
  expectation, 300, 307
  in interpretation, 297, 300
  negativity, 652
  nonresponse, 765
  in postpurchase processes, 641
Big Green Egg, 570, 571
Bilingual consumers, 339, 345
Biyani, 47
Black Americans. see African Americans
Blackberry devices, 307
Black Entertainment Television (BET), 158
Black Friday shoppers, 15
Black-ish (TV show), 281
Black Panther (movie), 281
Blended families, 189–191
Blind tests, 579
Blogging, transparency of advertising in, 227
Blue Bell Creameries, 303, 731
Blue-collar workers, 134
Blue Pet Products, 418, 573–574
Bluesign, 458
BMW, 447
Bonobos, 611
Borden, 526
Born-again Christians, 176
Bosch, 134, 135
Boston Consulting Group, 126
Bots, 545
Bounded rationality, 568
Bounty, 241
Bourjois, 381
Boxfresh, 223, 224
Brain. see also Cognitive development
  hemispheric lateralization in, 295–296
Brand(s)
  importance of retail outlets to, 598
  in-store and online influences on
    choice of, 620–629
  store, 613–614, 746
Brand alliances, 307, 580
Brand ambassadors, 220
Brand awareness, 342
Brand comfort, 658
Brand communities, 219–220, 224–225
Brand delight, 658
Brand effects, 304

Brand engagement, 436-437
Brand equity, 347, 351-354
Brand extension, 307, 351-354
Brand familiarity, 294-295
Brand fests, 225
Brand identification, 658
Brand image, 347-348
    brand personality in, 365-366, 380
    definition of, 327, 347
    vs. product positioning, 348
    usage situations in, 348
Brand leverage, 351-354
Brand loyalty
    of committed customers, 658-659
    definition of, 658
    of farmers, 724-727
    nominal decision making in, 516
    processes for developing, 658
    to Tesla, 683-684
Brand names
    perception of, 307
    as retrieval cues, 346
    as surrogate indicators, 580
Brand performance
    consumer judgments of, 576
    in cultural values, 49-50, 87-88
Brand personality, 380-382
    in brand image, 365-366, 380
    definition of, 365, 380
    dimensions of, 380-381
    strategies for communicating, 381-382
Brand repositioning, 346, 348, 354, 476-478
Brand scandals, 336
Braun, 748, 749
Bribery, 708
Brick-and-mortar stores, 603-606
    beacons in, 604, 681-683
    brand choices in, 620-629
    mobile retailing in, 602-603
    in omni-channel shopping, 606-611
    physical surroundings in, 491-496
    reasons for avoiding, 603
    showrooming in, 607-609, 682
    technology used by, 597-598
    volume of sales in, 603
Buddhist subculture, 177
Budweiser, 235, 236, 480, 535
Buick, 280, 281, 350-351
Burberry, 597-598
Bureau of Labor Statistics, 98
Burger King, 413
Business-to-business (B2B) marketing, 27.
    see also Organizational buying
Buying centers, 694
Buzz
    creating, 241-243, 287
    definition of, 241
Buzzfeed, 467
BzzAgent, 240

C

Café Press, 191
Caffeine, 23
Calgonite, 736

California Walnuts, 526, 527
Calvin Klein, 82
Campbell's, 121, 352, 748
Canada Dry, 301, 329
Capital One, 209, 664
Capture strategy, 556-557
Car(s)
    dog-friendly, 678-679
    electric, 683-685
    hybrid, 323
    luxury sports, 443
    for Millennials, 466-468
    safety regulations for, 731
Cardlytics, 15
Career working women, 100
Care2, 226
CARU. see Children's Advertising Review Unit
Case IH, 725
Casinos, 450
Catalogs, retail, 601
Categorize, need to, 368-369
Caterpillar Tractor Company, 701
Catholicism, 162, 174-175
Cause-related marketing (CRM), 91-93, 94
CBS, 91
CEI. see Corporate equality index
Celebrity endorsements, 412-414
    in attitude formation and change, 412-414
    for Beats by Dre, 264
    in brand personality, 381
    effectiveness of, 412-413, 464
    in Let's Move Campaign, 463-465
    risks with, 413-414, 464
Cellphones. see Smartphones
Census Bureau, U.S., 160, 170-171, 189, 191
Center for Science in the Public Interest
    (CSPI), 463-464
Center-stage effect, 588
Centrality dimension of materialism, 52
Central route to attitude change, 409-410
Centrum, 102
CGC. see Consumer-generated content
Change
    in attitudes (see Attitude change)
    in beliefs, 405-406
    in cultural values, 50, 85-86
    of stimuli, in interpretation, 302-304
ChapStick, 374
Chatbots, 605
Chevron, 710-711
Chick-fil-A, 174
Child care, in household life cycle, 196-197
Child-dominant family decisions, 203
Children
    consumer socialization of, 188-189, 207-210
    cultural values related to, 45-46
    eating disorders in, 736-737
    in family decision making, 203-206
    in household life cycle, 192-200
    in household structure, 189-192
    Let's Move Campaign for, 462-465
    obesity in, 462-463
    online privacy for, 739-740, 759-760
    in PRIZM system, 448-450
    safety regulations for, 732, 750

Children, marketing to, 732-740
    avenues for, 211
    cognitive development and, 210-211,
        733-735
    controversial practices in, 737-739
    effects of content of ads on, 735-737
    regulations on, 208, 732-740
Children's Advertising Review Unit
    (CARU), 733-739
Children's Online Privacy Protection Act
    (COPPA) of 1998, 739-740, 759-760
Children's Online Privacy Protection Rule,
    739-740, 759-760
Chinese Americans, 167-169
Chocolate milk, 228, 229
Choice Market, 612-613
Choice overload, 567-568
Choice paralysis, 567
Choice processes. see also Attribute-based
        choice; Decision process
    types of, 569-572
Choice theory, rational, 568-569, 588
Cholula, 646
Chores, by gender, 98-99
Christian Right, 176
Christians, subcultures of, 174-176
Chronic accessibility, 376
Chrysler, 337
Chunking, 325
Churn, 659-662
Ciba Vision, 334, 335
Cigarettes, 261-263
    antismoking ads and, 416
    e-cigarettes, 738
    end of CVS sales of, 261-263
    marketing outside U.S., 40
    suppression of problem recognition
        with, 529
    warning labels for, 750
Cinnabon, 674
Circulation data, 769
Claim-belief discrepancies, 306
Clairol, 241-242
Clarisonic, 237-238, 241
Claritas, 448-449
Classical conditioning, 331-333
    changing affective component of attitudes
        through, 406-407
    marketing applications of, 331-333
    summary of, 337
Classrooms, ads in, 739
Class to mass strategy, 116, 134
Clean and green Millennials, 127
Cleanliness, as cultural value, 49, 84-85, 86
"Clear and conspicuous" requirements, 734, 749
Clementines, 722
Click-through, 287, 294-295, 546, 770
Clinique, 304-305
Clorox, 79, 85, 86, 344
Closure, 302
Clothing, environmentally friendly, 458-460
Clustering, 15
Clutter, and attention, 295
Coach, 413, 490
Co-branding, 307

Coca-Cola, 67–68, 90, 153, 156, 301, 310–311, 329, 414, 422–423, 463, 481–482
Cocktail party effect, 295
Coding, dual, 344–346
CoffeeMate, 340
Cognition, need for, 379–380
Cognitive age, 119
Cognitive component of attitudes, 398–408
    change strategies for, 405–406
    consistency with other components, 403–405
    definition of, 398
    measurement of, 399–401, 769, 770
    and smoking, 416
Cognitive development
    and marketing to children, 210–211, 733–735
    Piaget's stages of, 207–208, 733
Cognitive dissonance, 368
Cognitive interpretation, 297
Cognitive learning, 335–336
Cognitive motives, 368–370
Cognitive thought, 383
Cohabitation, 190
Cohort analysis, 119
Coleman, 352
Coleman–Rainwater social class system, 131, 132
Colgate-Palmolive, 166, 169, 420
Collection obsession, 475
Collectivist cultures, 44–45, 48–49
Colors
    and attention, 290, 291
    as contextual cues, 301
    cultural differences in meaning of, 57, 494
    interpretation of, 300, 301
    as situational influence, 494
Comcast, 655, 660, 712, 713
Comfort, brand, 658
Commercials. see Advertisements; specific media and types of ads
Committed customers, 657–665
    brand loyalty of, 658–659
    definition of, 658
    marketing strategies for, 662–665
    profitability of, 659–662
Commodity buyers, 716
Common Threads Recycling Initiative, 458
Communications
    with African Americans, 159
    in attitude formation and change, 411–421
    brand personality in, 381–382
    in gender-based marketing, 101–102
    in global marketing, 66
    within groups, 233–242
    with Hispanic Americans, 164–166
    in LGBTQ market, 95–96
    in marketing mix, 18–19
    nonverbal, 53–60, 421
Communications situations, 488–489
Communities
    brand, 219–220, 224–225
    definition of, 224
    online, 221, 226–228
Company image, 347

Comparative ads, 418–419
Comparative rating scales, 768
Comparison shopping, online, 545
Compensatory decision rule, 581, 585–587
Competence, in brand personality, 380–381
Competition
    and attitude change, 409–410
    in cultural values, 48–49, 90
    in importance of evaluative criteria, 579
    market analysis of, 12–13
Competitive advertising, in memory interference, 345–346
Completion techniques, 764
Computers, recycling of, 647
ConAgra, 93
Concepts, in elaborative activities, 326
Conceptual models
    of consumer behavior, 2–3, 24–27
    definition of, 24
Conditioned response, 331–333
Conditioned stimulus, 331–333
Conditioning, 330–334
    classical, 331–333, 337, 406–407
    definition of, 330
    operant, 331, 333–334, 337
Conditions
    market analysis of, 13
    in organizational buying, 702
Conflict, motivational, 375–376
Conflict resolution, in family decision making, 205–206
Confucianism, 168
Congruity, self-image, 438–439
Conjoint analysis, 576–577, 766–767
Conjunctive decision rule, 581–582
Conscientiousness, in Five-Factor Model of personality, 379
Conservative Christians, 176
Conservatives, religious, 175, 176
Consideration set. see Evoked set
Consistency, need for, 368
Conspicuous consumption, 44, 133
Constant-sum scale, 400, 576
Construction techniques, 764
Consumer behavior
    applications of, 8–9
    audits of, 772–777
    definition of, 6, 28
    key aspects of, 6–7
    as learned behavior, 324
    in market analysis, 12
    in marketing strategies, 8–11
    model of, 2–3, 24–27
    nature of, 24–27
Consumer characteristics
    in external information search, 553–554
    in outlet selection, 617–620
Consumer choice, 568. see also Alternative evaluation and selection
Consumer comfort, 658
Consumer cost, 19–20
Consumer decisions. see Decision process
Consumer ethnocentrism, 379
Consumer experience. see Experience
Consumer-generated content (CGC), 234–235

Consumer Price Index (CPI), 487
Consumer Product Safety Commission, 750
Consumer research. see Research
Consumer reviews, 243, 411, 545
Consumer skills
    definition of, 208
    learning of, 208
Consumer socialization, 207–210
    content of, 207, 208
    definition of, 207
    families' role in, 188–189, 207–210
    process of, 207, 208–210
Consumer-to-consumer sales, 648
Consummatory motives, 570
Consumption
    age influences on, 117–119
    education level influences on, 115–116
    meaning of, 27–29
    occupational influences on, 114
Consumption guilt, 643
Consumption-related attitudes, learning of, 208
Consumption-related preferences, learning of, 208
Consumption societies, 9
Consumption subcultures, 221–224
Contact, in groups, 220–221
Contagion, in seeding, 222
Content
    of ads, effects on children, 735–737
    consumer-generated, 234–235
Context effects, on consumer choice, 588–589
Contextual cues, 301
Continuous innovation, 243–244
Contrast of stimuli, in attention, 292–293
Convenience samples, 762
COO. see Country of origin
Cooking lifestyle, 433, 441
Cool colors, 290, 494
Cooperation, as cultural value, 48–49, 90
Coors, 165
Coping, consumer, 385–386
COPPA. see Children's Online Privacy Protection Act
Cord cutters, 284–285
Corporate culture, 705. see also Organizational culture
Corporate equality index (CEI), 95
Corporate-sponsored educational materials and programs, 739
Corrective advertising, 338–339, 746–747, 750
Cost. see also Price
    consumer, 19–20
    opportunity, 627
    vs. price, 19–20
    substitution, 626
    switching, 658
    transaction, 627
Costco, 567
Cotton Incorporated, 458–459
Couch commerce, 535
Counterfeit products, 731–732
Country of origin (COO), 304
Covergirl, 117, 118
Covert marketing, 241
CPI. see Consumer Price Index

Crate & Barrel, 610, 647
Crayola, 203
Creative class, 62, 85–86, 88
Credibility, of sources, 411–412
Credit cards, 629
Crest, 29, 244, 411
CRM. *see* Cause-related marketing
Cross-cultural comparisons. *see* Cultural differences
Cross-cultural marketing strategies, 64–68
Cross-promotions, 306
Crowding
    as situational influence, 495–496
    in store atmosphere, 625
Crowdsourcing
    examples of, 6
    and problem solving, 513
    in relationship marketing, 663–664
CSPI. *see* Center for Science in the Public Interest
Cuban Americans, 161
Cues
    in attitude change, 409–410
    contextual, 301
    decision-relevant, 409
    in interpretation, 298, 299, 301
    retrieval, 346
    sensory, 299
Cultural creatives, 88
Cultural differences, 36–71
    and demographics, 62–64
    vs. emergence of global culture, 60–62
    in gift giving, 59, 499
    globalization and, 38–40
    importance of understanding, 42
    in interpretation, 305
    major categories of, 38
    in marketing strategies, 64–68
    market research on, 259–261
    in meaning of colors, 57, 494
    in nonverbal communications, 53–60
    in organizational culture, 707, 708
    in perception of crowding, 496
    in self-concept, 434–435
    in shopping style, 260
    in source credibility, 412
    in values, 43–53
Cultural values, 39–53. *see also* American values
    definition of, 41, 43, 80
    and demographics, 63
    differences in, 43–53
    environment-oriented, 43, 49–51
    evolution of, 42, 45, 80
    globalization of, 39–40
    in organizational culture, 708
    other-oriented, 43, 44–49
    self-oriented, 43, 51–53
Culture. *see also* Subcultures
    definition of, 40
    as external influence, 24–25
    in family purchase roles, 204
    global, emergence of, 60–62
    globalization of, 38–40
    nature of, 40–42
    organizational, 704–713

Customer commitment. *see* Committed customers
Customer loyalty programs, 664, 685–687
Customer reviews, 243, 411, 545
Customer satisfaction/dissatisfaction, 650–665
    in consumer behavior audits, 777
    definition of, 22
    determinants of, 651–653
    expectations for performance in, 650–653
    and marketing strategies, 22, 654–656
    purchase evaluation in, 650–653
    of repeat purchasers and committed customers, 657–665
    responses to dissatisfaction, 653–656
Customer value, 10
Cuties, 722–724
CVS, 6, 261–263

d

Daisy, 490, 491
Dansko, 381
DAR. *see* Day-after recall
DarkTrace, 694
Data collection, 761–769
    issues with, 761–762
    methods of, 761–769
    privacy issues with, 741
Data mining, privacy issues with, 741
Dave & Buster's, 735
David's Bridal, 492
Day-after recall (DAR), 771
DBS. *see* Direct broadcast satellite
DC Cool, 232, 233
Deception in advertising, 744–745
    inferences in, 306
    through packaging, 746
    regulation of, 744–745
Decision(s), types of, 514–517
Decision makers, family, 202–203
Decision-making units (DMUs), 694–696
Decision process, 512–532. *see also* specific stages
    in development of marketing strategies, 10
    of families, 202–207
    goals of, 567
    for innovations, 245–246
    involvement level in, 27, 485, 514–516, 536
    in model of consumer behavior, 24, 25, 27, 484–485
    of organizational buyers, 694–704
    in outcomes, 20–21
    stages of, 27, 245–246, 485
    types of decisions in, 514–517
Decision-relevant cues, 409
Decision rules, for attribute-based choices, 580–589
Decoy effect, 588–589
Delayed gratification, 53, 82–83
Delight, brand, 658
Dell, 700
Delta, 286
Demand, 372
Demographics, 110–130

characteristics of populations in, 112–119
    definition of, 63, 112
    of ethnic groups, 155
    generations in, 119–130
    global, 62–64
    of green consumers, 460
    in lifestyle, 442
    of mothers, 191
    organizational, 705–708
    in social status, 112
Depend, 123
Dependent variables, 765–766
Depression generation, 119, 120–122
Depth interviews, 762–763
Desire, to resolve recognized problems, 520
Desired lifestyles, 441
Desired state, 518–519
Diageo, 354
Diary reports, 769
Dick's Sporting Goods, 643
Diderot effect, 194
Diet. *see* Food
Differentiation, 336–337, 553
Diffusion, process of, 246–251
Diffusion enhancement, 250
Diffusion inhibitors, 250
Digital natives, 55, 128
Digital video recorders (DVRs), 281, 284–285
Dillard's, 612, 613
Direct appeals, 374
Direct broadcast satellite (DBS), 169–170
Direct claims, 744
Direct contact, in groups, 221
Direct measurement
    of attention, 771
    of evaluative criteria, 575–576
Direct questions, 403
DirecTV, 170, 284–285
Disclosure, in online advertising, 749
Discontinuous innovation, 245–246
DISH Network, 172, 173
Disjunctive decision rule, 582–583
Disney, 20, 111, 736, 738
Disposition, product, 647–650
Disposition situations, 490–491
Disrupt strategy, 555–556
Dissatisfaction. *see* Customer satisfaction
Dissociative reference groups, 221
Dissonance
    cognitive, 368
    postpurchase, 642–644
Distribution
    definition of, 20
    in marketing mix, 20
Distribution strategies, in consumer behavior audits, 774–775
Diversity, as cultural value, 49, 88–89
Divorce
    in household life cycle, 197–198
    step families after, 189–191
DIYVA by Barbara K, 100
DJI Spark, 250–251
DMUs. *see* Decision-making units
Doctors of Osteopathic Medicine, 643, 644
Dodge, 307

Dogpile, 53
Dogs, 678–679
Dolby, 547
Dollar General, 138
Dollar Shave Club, 128, 656, 658
Domenica Fiore, 584, 585
Dominance, as dimension of emotions, 383–384
Domino's Pizza, 661–662
Domino sugar, 746
Dove, 92, 101, 197, 239, 440, 645, 742
Dow Chemical, 53
Drones, delivery via, 676–678
Drugs, advertising for, 748–749
Dual coding, 344–346
Dunkin' Donuts, 490
Duracell, 37
DVRs. *see* Digital video recorders
Dynamic ad placement, 284–285
Dynamically continuous innovation, 244
Dyson, 513

e

Early adopters, 248–249
Early bird shoppers, 15
Early majority consumers, 248–249
Earworms, 341
Eating, mindless, 323
Eating disorders, 736–737
eBay, 121–122, 611
Echo boom, 125
Echoic memory, 345
E-cigarettes, 416, 738
Eco-fashion, 458–460
E-commerce. *see* Internet shopping; Mobile retailing
Economic expansions, 116
Economic outcomes, 23
Economic risk, 617–618
Edge, 387
Educational materials, corporate-sponsored, 739
Education levels, consumption influenced by, 114–116
E-fluentials, 238–239
Ego defense, need for, 370
Elaborate logos, 308
Elaboration, extent of, 326–327
Elaboration likelihood model (ELM), 409–410
Elaborative activities, 325–327
Electric cars, 683–685
Electronic waste, 647–648
Elimination-by-aspects decision rule, 583–584
ELM. *see* Elaboration likelihood model
E-loyalty, 664–665
E-mail, as source of information, 546
Embarrassment, 496–497
Emergen-C, 570
Emotion(s), 382–387
    in attitudes (*see* Affective component)
    coping with, 385–386
    definition of, 366, 382
    in family decision making, 202, 205
    intensity of, 298, 383

in interpretation, 297–298
in marketing strategies, 384–387
vs. mood, 499
nature of, 383
in organizational culture, 713
in problem recognition, 525
in scent marketing, 674–676
types of, 383–384
Emotional ads, 386–387
    characteristics of, 419
    definition of, 419
    effectiveness of, 386–387, 479–480
    popularity of, 387
Emotional appeals, 419
Emotional benefits, 401
Emotional intelligence, 386
Empty-nest households, 198, 200
Endorsements, third-party, 411–412. *see also* Celebrity endorsements
Endowment effect, 436, 641
Enduring involvement, 238
Energizer, 37
Engagement, brand, 436–437
Environmental fragrancing, 494
Environmentalism, as cultural value, 86–87
Environmentally sound products, regulation of, 749–750
Environmental responsibility
    in cultural values, 86–87
    in enviropreneurial marketing, 87
    in fashion, 458–460
    in product disposition, 648, 650
Environment-oriented values
    cultural differences in, 43, 49–51
    definition of, 43
    in U.S., 81, 84–88
Enviropreneurial marketing, 87
Episodic memory, 327
Equity, brand, 347, 351–354
Escort Radar, 583, 584
Essence (magazine), 151
Essence Music Festival, 150, 151
Established Asian Americans, 169
Esteem, in Maslow's hierarchy of needs, 367
Ethical issues, 7
    with activating problem recognition, 529
    with covert marketing, 241
    with fear appeals, 415
    in global marketing, 40, 67, 708
    with group influences, 232, 233
    with inferences, 306
    with marketing to children, 210–211
    with packaging and labels, 311
    with product placement, 286
    with self-concept, 439
Ethnic diversity
    in American values, 88
    of Generation X, 124–125
    and multigenerational households, 111
Ethnic groups. *see also specific groups*
    demographic profiles of, 155
    household structure among, 190
Ethnic subcultures, 154–173
    African American, 151, 154–160
    Arab American, 172–173

Asian American, 154, 166–170
Asian Indian American, 172
    definition of, 154
    Hispanic American, 154, 160–166
    Native American, 170–171
    nature of, 152–153
    size of, 154
Ethnocentrism, consumer, 379
Etiquette, cultural differences in, 59–60
Etsy, 88, 611
Evaluation, purchase. *see* Purchase evaluation
Evaluative criteria, 572–580
    definition of, 537, 572
    and individual judgment, 577–580
    in information search, 537, 540
    measurement of, 575–577
    nature of, 573–575
    in organizational buying, 700–701
    research on, 766–767
Evangelical Christians, 176
Event marketing, 159
Evian, 352
Evoked set of alternatives, 329, 537–540
E-waste, 647–648
Excitement, in brand personality, 380–381
Executional factors, in brand personality, 381–382
Expanded usage situations, 490
Expectation bias, 300, 307
Expectations
    in attention, 292–293
    in customer satisfaction, 650–651
    in interpretation, 300, 301–302
Experian Information Systems, 443–444, 450–451, 548
Experian Marketing Services, 464
Experience, consumer
    evolution of, 5
    in organizational buying, 693
    peak, 436
    as source of information, 540–541
    in total product, 11
    virtual direct, 408
Experience, openness to, 379
Experiencers, in VALS program, 446–448
Experimentation, 765–767
Expertise, of sources, 411–412, 413
Explicit memories, 329
Exposure, 282–287
    definition of, 282
    measurement of, 769–770
    in media strategy, 308–309
    mere, 407–408
    in retail strategy, 306
    selective, 284–287, 309
    voluntary, 287
Expression, need for, 370
Expressive support seeking, 385–386
Extended decision making, 517
    definition of, 517
    with innovations, 245–246
    steps in, 245, 485, 515
Extended families, 46–47, 89
Extended self, 435–437

External influences. *see also specific types*
     in model of consumer behavior,
          24–25, 34–35
     on organizational culture, 705–709
     types of, 24–25
External information search
     amount of, 550–551
     costs vs. benefits of, 552–554
     definition of, 536
     sources used in, 540–541
External motivation, 294
External reference price, 615, 750
External validity, 766
Extinction, 338
Extreme sports lifestyle, 441
Extroversion, in Five-Factor Model of
          personality, 379
Eye movements, research on, 764
EyeSee Mannequins, 492

f

FAA. *see* Federal Aviation Administration
FAA Modernization and Reform Act
          of 2012, 677
Facebook, 226–228, 242, 522, 546, 547
Fair Minimum Wage Act of 2007, 137
Fake reviews, 243
Familiarity, 407–408
Families, 186–214
     in American values, 89
     in consumer socialization, 188–189, 207–210
     decision making by, 202–207
     evolution of, 190–191
     extended vs. limited, in cultural values, 46–47, 89
     gender roles in, 79
     life cycle of, 192
     size of, 191
     step (blended), 189–191
     traditional, 189
     types of, 189–192
Family branding. *see* Brand leverage
Family decision making, 202–207
Family households, 189–192
Farmers, brand loyalty of, 724–727
Fashion, eco-, 458–460
Fatalism, 50, 86
Fathers
     in family decision making, 203–205
     stay-at-home, 79, 98–99
FCC. *see* Federal Communications
          Commission
FDA. *see* Food and Drug Administration
Fear appeals, 415–417
Features beliefs, 399
Febreze, 521
Federal Aviation Administration (FAA), 677
Federal Communications Commission (FCC), 675
Federal Emergency Management Agency
          (FEMA), 419
Federal Trade Commission (FTC)
     on claim-belief discrepancies, 306
     "clear and conspicuous" requirements
          of, 734, 749

on corrective advertising, 747
on covert marketing, 241
on deceptive advertising, 744–745
Green Guides of, 91
on online privacy for adults, 741–742, 749
on online privacy for children, 739–740,
          759–760
on pricing, 750
on transparency in advertising, 227
website of, 730, 731, 739, 740
FedEx, 17
FEMA. *see* Federal Emergency
          Management Agency
Feminine orientation
     cultural differences in, 47–48
     in U.S., 90
Fiat, 86, 468
Field experiments, 766
Figure-ground, 302
Filipino Americans, 167–168
Films. *see* Movies
Firing customers, 662
Firmographics, 705–708
Firm outcomes, 21–22
First-generation Hispanic Americans, 161
First Tee, 367, 368
Fisher-Price, 526
Five-Factor Model of personality, 378–379
Flashbulb memories, 327
Flash sales, 685
Flexjet, 7
Flixable, 542
Focus, of attention, 289–290
Focus group interviews, 762–763
Fonts, 308
Food. *see also* Grocery shopping; Restaurants
     in meal kits, 199, 433, 469–472
     mindless eating of, 323
     mobile ordering of, 680–681
     Native American, 171
     nutrition labels on, 8, 747–748
     safety regulations for, 731
     and social class, 141
Food and Drug Administration (FDA)
     on nutrition labels, 8, 747–748
     on product safety, 23, 749–750
Football, 39
Ford Motor Company, 90–91, 129,
          159, 160, 299, 468
Forgetting, 337–346
     memory interference in, 345–346
     response environment in, 346
     strength of learning in, 339–345
Format of stimuli, in attention, 292
Forrester Research, 443, 524
4imprint, 693
Frail recluses, 120
Frames, sampling, 762
Framing, message, 421
Free samples, 333–334
French's, 746, 747
Frey, 578
Friendships, cultural differences in, 57–58
Frito-Lay, 664
Frugality, in Great Recession, 82, 83

FTC. *see* Federal Trade Commission
Fuel, 371, 372
Fuga Energy, 99
Functional benefits, 401
Fundamentalist Christians, 176
Furman University, 545

g

Gadget gurus, 126–127
Galvanic skin response, 764
Games
     adver-, 737
     video, 286–287, 309
Gap Inc., 365
Garmin, 347
Gatorade, 129
Gay consumers. *see* LGBTQ market
Gay marriage, 94, 95
Geico, 418
Gender
     definition of, 97
     household duties by, 98–99
Gender-based marketing, 96–102
     communications in, 101–102
     gender roles in, 96–102
     market segmentation in, 99–100
     retail strategy in, 102
Gender differences
     in self-concept, 435
     in social media use, 101
Gender identity, 97
Gender orientations, traditional vs.
          modern, 98
Gender roles, 96–99
     definition of, 97
     evolution of, 79, 96–99
     in family decision making, 203–205
     in gender-based marketing, 96–102
     in parenting, 79–80, 98
General Foods, 301
Generalization, 336–337
General Mills, 162–163, 490
General Motors (GM),
          350–351, 406, 731
Generation(s), 119–130
     cohort analysis of, 119
     definition of, 119
     descriptions of, 119–130
     of Hispanic Americans, 161
Generation Alpha, 119, 130
Generation @, 128
Generation X, 119, 123–125
Generation Y. *see* Millennials
Generation Z, 119, 128–129
Generic problem recognition, 526–527
Geo-demographic analysis, 448
Geographic boundaries, 65–66
Gerber, 53
Gerontographics, 120
Gift giving
     cultural differences in, 59, 499
     in extended self, 436
     external information search in, 554
     as situational influence, 498–499

Gillette, 241, 337
Gilt Groupe, 685–687
Global agnostics, 40
Global citizens, 40
Global culture, emergence of, 60–62
Global dreamers, 40
Globalization, of culture, 38–40
Global localization, 64–65, 67–68
Global marketing, 64–68
    considerations in, 65–67
    ethical issues in, 40, 67, 708
    lifestyles in, 450–452
    localization in, 64–65, 67–68
    research in, 259–261
    translation problems in, 53–54
Global youth culture, 60–62
Glocalization, 64–65
GM. see General Motors
Goal framing, 421
Google, 547–549, 677, 711, 759
Go RVing, 298
"Got Milk?" campaign, 346
Government. see also Regulation
    and organizational culture, 708
Grace and Frankie (TV show), 268–270
Gratification
    immediate vs. delayed, 53, 82–83
    sensual, 51–52, 81–82
Gratitude, 384–385
Great Recession of 2007–2009
    frugality in, 82, 83
    gender roles in, 79
    income in, 116
    problem solving in, 86
Green consumers, 90–91
    demographics of, 460
    fashion for, 458–460
    organizations as, 700–701
    segmentation of, 87, 458–459
    stereotypes of, 91
Green Guides, 91
Green household products,
    272–273, 458
Green marketing, 90–91
Green segmentation, 87, 458–459
Greenwashing, 91
Grocery shopping
    meal kits and, 469–472
    self-checkout in, 687–689
    unplanned purchases in, 621
Groups, 218–255. see also Reference groups
    communications within, 233–242
    definition of, 220
    and innovations, 242–251
    membership in, 220
    opinion leaders in, 236–242
    seeding in, 222, 239–240
    types of, 220–228
Growth-related motives, 368–372
Guanxi, 58, 707
Guerrilla marketing, 241
Guess, 492
Guideshops, 611
Guilt, consumption, 643
Guinness, 284

h

Habitual decision making. see Nominal
    decision making
H&M, 605
Hanes Corporation, 575
The Happytime Murders (movie), 757
Harajuku, 39
Hardee, 351
Harley-Davidson, 97, 171, 224, 299, 307, 352
Harm, in injurious consumption, 22–24
Harris Interactive, 464
Hayneedle, 200
Healthy hermits, 120
Healthy indulgers, 120, 121
Hedge words, 745
Hedonic benefits, 401
Hedonic consumption, 493–494
Hello Kitty, 473–476
Hemispheric lateralization, 295–296
Heuristics, 567
Hewlett-Packard (HP), 648, 695, 708, 709
High-awareness brands, 342
High-context cultures, 305
High-impact zones, 292
High involvement. see Involvement
High self-monitors, 439
Hip-ennials, 126
Hip Hop, 158
Hispanic Americans, 160–166
    acculturation among, 161–163
    Catholicism among, 162, 175
    in cohabiting households, 190
    definition of, 160
    demographic profile of, 155
    family purchase roles of, 204
    language of, 161, 163–166
    marketing to, 164–166, 274–276
    media portrayal of, 743
    as percentage of population,
        154, 161, 162, 274
    social media use by, 163, 165, 274
    subcultures of, 154, 160–166
    women, influence of, 162–163
HLC. see Household life cycle
HLC/occupational category matrix, 201
Hoarding, 475
Holidays, as ritual situations, 501–502
Holiday shoppers, 15
Holland America, 198
Hollingshead Index of Social Position (ISP),
    138–139
Home Depot, 135, 136, 547, 605
Home renovations, in household life cycle, 194
Honda, 14, 91, 169, 353, 468, 546, 558
Hormel, 206, 504
Household(s), 186–214
    in consumer socialization, 188–189,
        207–210
    decision making in, 202–206
    definition of, 189
    ethnic differences in, 190
    evolution of, 190–191
    influence of, 188–189
    life cycle of, 192–200

lifestyles of, 441
    multigenerational, 111
    single-parent, 189, 190, 197, 199
    single-person, 187, 198
    types of, 189–192
    unmarried-partner, 191, 193
Household duties, by gender, 98–99
Household life cycle (HLC), 192–202
    definition of, 192
    and external information search, 554
    marketing strategy based on, 200–202
    stages of, 192–200
House of Cards (TV show), 281
Housewives
    traditional, 99–100
    trapped, 100
Housing
    in household life cycle, 194
    micro-apartments, 187
HP. see Hewlett-Packard
HPV, 522, 523
HSN, 534, 535
Human factors research, 525
Human Rights Campaign Foundation, 95
Humor
    in attitude formation and change, 415–418
    cultural differences in, 54
    need for, 415
Humorous appeals, 415–418
Husband-dominant family decisions,
    203–205
Hybrid ads, 284
Hybrid cars, 323
Hygiene, as cultural value, 49, 85
Hyper local approach, 5
Hyundai, 305, 351, 579

i

IBM, 12, 95, 707
Iconic rote learning, 335, 337
Ideal point, in multiattribute attitude models,
    399–400, 422–423
Ideal products, changes to perceptions of, 406
Ideal self-concept, 434, 437, 440
Ideals motivation, in VALS program, 445
Identification
    brand, 658
    need for, 371
Identification influence, of reference groups,
    229, 230, 233
Identity. see also Self-concept
    gender, 97
Identity defense, need for, 370
IKEA, 259–261, 610, 640, 641
IKEA effect, 641
Image
    brand (see Brand image)
    company, 347
    store (see Store image)
Imagery. see also Visuals
    emotional responses to, 383
    in memory, 326, 344–345
    user, and brand personality, 381
Iman, 159

Immediate gratification, in cultural
    values, 53, 82–83
Immigrants, population of, 154–155
Imperatives, juxtaposed, 745
Implications
    logical, 744
    pragmatic, 744–745
Implicit memories, 329
Importance
    of evaluative criteria, 574–575, 576–577, 579
    relative, of problems, 520
    shifting, 406
    in strength of learning, 339
Impression management
    in brand communities, 225
    in family decision making, 205
Impulse purchases, 620–621
Inactive problems, 520–521
Income
    consumption influenced by, 116
    distribution of, 63, 116
    education level and, 115
Income divide, 116
Incongruity, 301
Independent self-concept, 434–435, 441
Independent sources of information, 540–541
Independent variables, 765–766
Index of Social Position (ISP), 138–139
Indian (Asian) Americans, 172
Indirect appeals, 374
Indirect contact, in groups, 221
Indirect measurement
    of attention, 771
    of evaluative criteria, 575–577
Indirect questions, 403
Individual depth interviews, 762–763
Individual development, in problem
    recognition, 521–522
Individual factors
    in attention, 294–295
    in attitude change, 409–411
    in interpretation, 298–300
Individualistic cultures, 44–45, 48–49, 88
Individualized family decisions, 203
Individual judgments, and evaluative
    criteria, 577–580
Individual outcomes, 22–23
Industry categories, and organizational
    buying, 707
Industry structure, and organizational
    buying, 714
Inept set of alternatives, 537–540
Inert set of alternatives, 537–540
Inferences
    and deception in advertising, 744–745
    definition of, 304
    in interpretation, 304–306
Infiniti, 381
Inflated reference prices, 615
Influencers
    in attitude change, 414
    in family decision making, 202–203
    mass, 266
    potential, 266
    social media, 414

Influentials, 238–239, 414
Infomercials, 287
Information
    accuracy of, 743–747
    adequacy of, 747–749
    inferences about missing, 305–306
Informational influence, of reference groups,
    228, 230, 232–233
Information availability, in external
    information search, 552
Information gatherers, in family decision
    making, 202–203
Information overload, 294, 544, 748–749
Information processing. see also Perception
    definition of, 282, 324
    in learning, 324
    steps in, 282, 283
Information quantity, in attention, 293–294
Information search, 534–562. see also External
    information search
    marketing strategies based on patterns of,
        555–558
    nature of, 536
    in organizational buying, 699–700
    sources used in, 540–550
    types of information sought, 536–540
Infrastructure, reference group, 708–709
ING Direct, 17
In-home shopping, 600. see also Internet
    shopping
Initiators, in family decision making, 202–203
Injurious consumption, 22–24
Inner-scope Research, 284
Innovations, 242–251
    adopter categories for, 248–249
    adoption process for, 245–246
    definition of, 242
    diffusion of, 246–251
    marketing strategies for, 249–251
    types of, 243–246
Innovativeness, use, 644–645
Innovators
    characteristics of, 248–249
    in VALS program, 446–447
Instability, in Five-Factor Model of
    personality, 379
Instacart, 498
Instrumental learning. see Operant
    conditioning
Instrumental materialism, 52
Instrumental motives, 570
Instrumental performance, 652
Instrumental training, 208–209
Intel, 299, 307
Intelligence, emotional, 386
Intensity of stimuli, in attention, 289–290
Intercept strategy, 557
Interdependent self-concept, 434–435, 441
Interestingness of stimuli, in attention, 293
Interests, in motivation, 294
Internal influences. see also specific types
    in model of consumer behavior, 24, 25–26,
        278–279
    in organizational culture, 709–713
    types of, 25–26

Internal information search
    definition of, 536
    sources used in, 540–541
Internal motivation, 294
Internal reference price, 304, 615
Internal validity, 766
International lifestyles, 450–452
International marketing. see Global marketing
Internet
    communities on, 221, 226–228
    in global marketing, 66
    identifying consumer problems using, 524
    information searches on, 541–548
    in organizational decision process, 703–704
    social network sites on, 226–228
    surveys on, 765
Internet advertising
    to children, 737
    disclosure in, 749
    growth of, 546
    intrusiveness of, 289
    native, 744–745
    as source of information, 546–547
    voluntary exposure to, 287
Internet privacy. see Privacy, online
Internet (online) shopping, 600–602
    atmosphere in, 625
    barriers to, 601–602
    brand choices in, 620–629
    choice overload with, 567
    dimensions of performance in, 653
    loyalty in, 664–665
    in omni-channel shopping, 606–611
    by organizational buyers, 703–704
    product nonuse with, 646–647
    purchase process in, 629
    reasons for, 600–601
    return policies in, 647
    sales personnel in, 629
    shipping costs in, 676
    store image in, 612
    time pressures and, 498
    top categories of, 600
    volume of, 600
    website functioning and requirements in, 627
Internet use
    by African Americans, 158
    by Asian Americans, 170
    by Asian Indian Americans, 172
    by children, 211
    by Hispanic Americans, 165
    international rates of, 541–542
    reasons for lack of, 543
Interpretation, 297–306
    biases in, 297
    cognitive vs. affective, 297–298
    definition of, 282, 297
    individual factors in, 298–300
    inferences in, 304–306
    measurement of, 771
    situational factors in, 301
    stimulus factors in, 301–304
Interviews
    depth, 762–763
    personal, 765

Intrusiveness, 289
Intuition, in problem recognition, 523
Inventory, brick-and-mortar vs. online, 598
Involuntary exposure, 287
Involvement. *see also* Product involvement
　and attention, 295, 296
　and attitude change, 409–410
　in decision process, 27, 485, 514–516, 536
　definition of, 375
　and discontinuous innovations, 246
　enduring, 238
　in learning, 330–337
　and motivation, 375
　and opinion leadership, 237
　and postpurchase dissonance, 643
　in strength of learning, 339–340
iPad, 401
iPhone, 28–29, 401
IRI/TNS, 87
iRobot, 85, 336
Isolation of stimuli, in attention, 292
ISP. *see* Index of Social Position
iTunes, 38, 96

j

Jaguar, 159, 380
James Trussart, 573
Japanese Americans, 167–168
J. Crew, 374
Jeep, 225
Jewish subculture, 176
Jif peanut butter, 102, 746
Jim Beam, 97
Jingles, 341
j.n.d. *see* Just noticeable difference
Jockey, 571, 572
Joe's Crab Shack, 337
John Deere, 724–727
Johnnie Walker, 354
Johnson's, 124
Johnston & Murphy, 643
Joint family decisions, 203–206
Joule, 444
Judgments, and evaluative criteria, 577–580
Judgment samples, 762
Jump Associates, 12
Just Buy This One, 568–569
Just noticeable difference (j.n.d.), 303, 578
JUUL, 738
Juxtaposed imperatives, 745

k

Kate Spade, 382
Kawaii (cuteness), 474
Keds, 382
Keebler, 330, 331
Keepsake Diamonds, 370
Kellogg's, 56, 57, 67, 79, 412, 522
KFC, 486, 487
Kiehl's, 648
Kimberly-Clark, 199
Kind, 748
Kiton, 369, 370

Knowledge, in interpretation, 298–300
Knowledge structure, 327
Konica, 290, 291
Korean Americans, 167–168
Kraft, 192, 203, 306, 735
Krispy Kreme, 176
Kroger, 604

l

Labeling
　perception of, 310–311
　regulation of, 8, 747–749
　warning, 311, 416, 522, 523, 529, 750
Laboratory experiments, 766
Laddering, 374
Laggards, 248–249
LAI Systems, 759
L&M, 337
Lands' End, 618–619, 627
Languages
　of Arab Americans, 173
　of Asian Americans, 167–170
　challenges of translating, 53–54, 165
　of Hispanic Americans, 161, 163–166
Laser eye surgery, 247
Last-minute shoppers, 15, 378
Late majority consumers, 248–249
Latent motives, 373–374
Latinos. *see* Hispanic Americans
Laundry, green, 272–273
Leaders, opinion. *see* Opinion leaders
Lead users, 708–709
Learn & Master Guitar, 125
Learning, 322–358
　in brand image, 347–348
　in brand leverage, 351–354
　cognitive, 335–336
　of consumption-related skills, 207–208
　definition of, 324
　difficulty of unlearning, 323
　under high vs. low involvement, 330–337
　information processing in, 324
　as internal influence, 24, 25, 35
　and interpretation, 298–300
　memory in, 324–329
　nature of, 324–325
　organizational, 713
　in product positioning, 348–351
　reasons for forgetting, 337–346
　strength of, 339–346
　theories of, 330–337
Legal issues
　with covert marketing, 241
　with packaging and labels, 311
　with product placement, 286
LEGO, 734–735
Leisure, in cultural values, 52, 84, 85
Lennar Homes, 110, 111
Lesbian consumers. *see* LGBTQ market
Let's Move Campaign, 462–465
Levi Strauss, 49, 61, 140, 195, 240, 307, 547
Lexicographic decision rule, 584–585, 700
Lexicon, 307
Lexus, 281, 353

LGBTQ market, 93–96
Life hacks, 513
Lifestyles, 441–452
　definition of, 24, 26, 279, 434, 441
　globalization of, 39
　international, 450–452
　measuring and categorizing,
　　433, 442–450
　in model of consumer behavior, 24, 25,
　　26–27, 278–279
　nature of, 441–444
　organizational, 704–705
　relationship between self-concept
　　and, 441
Lifestyle studies, 442–445
Liggett & Myers, 555
Likert scales, 436, 576, 769
Lilly Pulitzer, 347–348, 604
Limited decision making,
　515, 516–517
Linguistics, in perception, 307
Lipton, 42
Listerine, 382
Living for the Moment Asian
　Americans, 169
Localization, global, 64–65, 67–68
Local mobile search, 548–550
Local relevancy, 5
Location
　of organizations, 707
　of retail outlets, 616–617
Logical implications, 744
Logo(s)
　in brand personality, 381–382
　changes to, 307–308
　perception of, 307–308
Logo network, 95
Long-term memory (LTM)
　definition of, 325, 327
　in learning, 324, 327–329
　retrieval failure in, 338
　retrieval from, 329
　schemas in, 327–329
　scripts in, 329
　types of, 327
L'Oréal, 88, 89, 118, 159, 288, 412
Lotame, 222
Louis Vuitton, 134, 208
Low-context cultures, 305
Lower class, 131, 132, 137–138
Lower-lower class, 137–138
Lower-upper class, 132–133
Low involvement. *see* Involvement
Low self-monitors, 439
Loyalty. *see also* Brand loyalty
　attitudinal, 660–661
　online, 664–665
　service, 658
　store, 658
Loyalty programs, customer,
　664, 685–687
LTM. *see* Long-term memory
Lululemon, 218, 219–220, 224
Lunchables, 21
Luxury sports cars, 443

m

Macrosegmentation, 707–708
Macy's, 166, 604, 608, 681–683
Mail surveys, 765
Maintenance rehearsal, 325
Maintenance strategy, 555
Makers, in VALS program, 446–447
Mall of America, 605–606
Mandarin oranges, 722–724
M&Ms, 292, 310, 414
Manifest motives, 373
Mannequins, 492
Manufacturer's suggested retail price (MSRP), 304
Mapping. *see* Perceptual mapping
Mardel, 174
Market analysis, 11–13
    components of, 11–13
    in development of market strategies, 9–10
Market characteristics
    in external information search, 552–553
    types of, 552
Marketing. *see also specific media and types of ads*
    to consumers vs. for consumers, 5
    evolution of, 5–6
Marketing mix, 10, 17–20
Marketing regulation. *see* Regulation
Marketing research. *see* Research
Marketing sources of information, 540–541
Marketing strategies, 17–20
    consumer behavior in, 8–11
    cross-cultural, 64–68
    customer dissatisfaction in, 654–656
    definition of, 17
    development of, 9–11
    emotions in, 384–387
    evaluative criteria in, 579–580
    family decision making in, 206–207
    household life cycle in, 200–202
    information search patterns in, 555–558
    for innovations, 249–251
    marketing mix in, 10, 17–20
    motivation in, 372–377
    opinion leaders in, 239–242
    organizational buyers in, 714–716
    outcomes of, 10, 11, 20–24
    perception in, 306–311
    problem recognition in, 522–529
    product disposition in, 648–650
    reference groups in, 231–233
    repeat purchasers and committed
        customers in, 662–665
    situational influences in, 502–505
    social class in, 139–142
    word-of-mouth communications in, 239–242
Market mavens, 238–239
Market segmentation, 13–17
    of African Americans, 156, 157
    of Asian Americans, 168–169
    attitudes in, 421
    in consumer behavior audits, 773
    definition of, 13, 773
    in development of market strategies, 10
    of food shoppers, 471, 472

by gender, 99–100
    of green consumers, 87, 458–459
    with innovations, 249–250
    of organizational buyers, 707–708, 714–716
    steps in, 13–17
Market Segment Research, 168
Marriage
    household duties by gender in, 98–99
    in household life cycle, 192–200
    same-sex, 94, 95
    in step families, 189–191
    in traditional families, 189
    traditional vs. modern gender
        orientations in, 98
Marriott, 656
Mars, 53
Marvin Windows, 401
Masculine orientation
    cultural differences in, 47–48
    in U.S., 90, 204
Maslow's hierarchy of needs, 366–367
Mass influencers, 266
MasterCard, 18
Materialism, in cultural values, 52, 83
Mattel, 42, 79
Mature market, 120, 121
Maui Jim, 527–528
Mavens, market, 238–239
Maybelline, 64
McDonald's, 49, 64, 65, 93, 159, 169, 235, 307,
        352–353, 461–462, 723, 737
M-commerce. *see* Mobile retailing
Meal kits, 199, 433, 469–472
Meaning transfer, 413
Means–end chain, 374
Media piracy, 732
Media strategy, perception in, 308–310
Mediation, in consumer socialization, 209
Media usage
    by African Americans, 156–158
    by Asian Americans, 169–170
    by Asian Indian Americans, 172
    by Hispanic Americans, 163–165
    in lifestyle, 442
    by Native Americans, 171
Meishi, 60
Melting pot, 152
Membership, group, 220
Memory, 322–358. *see also* Long-term
        memory; Short-term memory
    in brand image, 347–348
    in brand leverage, 351–354
    definition of, 282, 325
    in learning, 324–329
    of music, 341
    nature of, 324–325
    in product positioning, 348–351
    reasons for forgetting, 337–346
    as source of information, 540–541
    strength of learning in, 339–345
Memory interference, 345–346
Men. *see also* Fathers; Gender roles
    in family decision making, 203–205
Mentos, 645
Mere exposure, 407–408

Mere ownership effect, 436–437, 641
Merrill Lynch, 706
Message framing, 421
Message involvement, in strength of
        learning, 339–340
Message structure, in attitude formation
        and change, 420–421
Metagoals, 568
Metastories, 94
Metropolitan Life, 172
Mexican Americans, 161
MGs, 224
Michael Kors, 382, 439
Micro-apartments, 187
Micron Technology, 706
Microsoft, 299
Micro-targeting, 285
Middle age, in household life cycle, 197–198
Middle class, 131, 132, 134–136
Milk Bone, 573–574
Millennials (Generation Y), 125–128
    car manufacturers targeting, 466–468
    characteristics of, 125–128, 466
    definition of, 119
    gender roles among, 79–80
    as mothers, 126
    organizational buying by, 693, 710
    in organizational culture, 710
    segments of, 126–127
Miller Brewing Company, 64–65, 136
Mindless eating, 323
Mini Cooper, 225, 547
Minigroup interviews, 762
Minimum wage, 139
Mintel, 79, 433, 600
Missing information, inferences about,
        305–306
Mobile apps, 602–605
    in brand choice, 627–628
    children's privacy in, 759–760
    food ordering with, 680–681
    reasons for using, 602–603
    as source of information, 535, 549–550
    technological advances in, 604–605, 759
Mobile marketing
    to children, 738
    growth of, 548
    to Hispanic Americans, 274–276
    information searches and, 548–551
    to Millennials, 466–467
    outdoor, 309–310
    permission-based, 287
    push and pull strategies in, 551, 604
Mobile payments, one-click, 604–605
Mobile retailing, 602–603
    brand choice in, 627–628
    evolution of, 600, 602
    in omni-channel shopping, 606–611
    in organizational buying, 693,
        703–704
    purchase process in, 629
    technological advances in, 603,
        604–605
    volume of, 602
Mobile search, 548–551

Model(s)
    of consumer behavior, 2–3, 24–27
    definition of, 24
    elaboration likelihood, 409–410
    Five-Factor, of personality, 378–379
    multiattribute attitude, 399–401, 422–423
    of organizational buying, 690–691, 695
Modeling
    in consumer socialization, 209
    need for, 372
    vicarious, 335, 337
Modern gender orientations, 98
Modified rebuy, 697
Molson, 382
Momentary conditions, 500–501
Monochronic time perspective, 55
Monster Energy, 414
Montague Bookmill, 625
Mont Blanc, 56
Moods
    definition of, 499
    as situational influence, 499–500
    in strength of learning, 340
Morning Star, 405, 406
Morphemes, 307
Most valuable customers, 716
Mothers
    demographics of, 191
    in family decision making, 203–206
    single, 199
    stay-at-home, 99–100
    working, 84, 98–100, 191
Motivation, 366–377
    in attention, 294
    in choice processes, 570, 571
    definition of, 294, 366
    and emotions, 382
    in learning, 330
    in marketing strategies, 372–377
    in Maslow's needs hierarchy, 366–367
    McGuire's theory of, 367–372
    needs in, 294, 366
    in organizational culture, 713
    regulatory focus theory on, 376–377
    research on, 374, 764
    in VALS program, 445
Motivational conflict, 375–376
Motives
    definition of, 366
    McGuire's categories of, 367–372
Mountain Dew, 307, 327–328, 381
Movado, 447
Movement, and attention, 290
Movies
    ads shown before, 286
    product placement in, 281
Moving target market approach, 249–250
MSRP. see Manufacturer's suggested retail price
Multiattribute attitude models, 399–401,
    422–423, 587
Multigenerational households, 111
Multi-item indexes, 138
Multisensory marketing, 299
Multistep flow of communication, 236
Multitrait personality theory, 378–379

Mumsnet, 47
Muscletech, 571, 572
Music
    in advertisements, 341
    as situational influence, 495, 496
    in store atmosphere, 625
Music streaming services, 264
Music videos, product placement in, 281
Muslims, subculture of, 176–177
Muting, 284–285
Myntra, 604

n

NAD. see National Advertising Division
Names. see Brand names
NASCAR, 414
National Advertising Division (NAD), 733, 746
Nationwide, 480
Native advertising, 744–745
Native Americans, 170–171
Natrol, 525
Natural environment. see also Environment-
    oriented values
    in cultural values, 51, 86–87
    in green marketing, 90–91
    in outcomes of marketing strategies, 23
Natural logos, 308
Necessity consumption, reference groups in,
    229–231, 232
Need(s). see also specific types
    creation of, 372
    and emotions, 382
    lack of, in attitudes, 404
    Maslow's hierarchy of, 366–367
    McGuire's categories of, 367–372
    in motivation, 294, 366
Need for cognition (NFC), 379–380
Need satisfaction, 22
Need sets, 14–16
Negative framing, 421
Negative products, 553
Negative reinforcement, 340
Negative word-of-mouth (WOM), 235–236,
    265–266, 654–655
Negativity bias, 652
Nestlé, 623, 624, 731
Netflix, 281, 542
Net Generation, 128
Net Promoter Score (NPS), 660–661
Neutrogena, 556
New brand strategy, 348
New England Compounding Center, 731
New Holland, 725
New task, 697
New York–Presbyterian Hospital (NYP), 657, 658
NFC. see Need for cognition
Nielsen, 274, 282, 354, 449, 464, 470, 471
Nike, 28, 97, 171, 353, 381, 413, 437, 492, 596,
    597, 742–743
Nintendo, 111
Nissan, 292, 323, 678–679
NLEA. see Nutrition Labeling and
    Education Act
Nodes, memory, 327

Nominal decision making, 515, 516
Noncomparative rating scales, 768
Noncompensatory decision rules, 581–585
Nonfamily households, 189
Nonfocused attention, 295–297
Nonmaterialism, 52, 83
Nonnecessity consumption, reference groups
    in, 229–231, 232
Nonprofits, brand personality of, 380
Nonrandom samples, 762
Nonresponse bias, 765
Nonsatisfaction, 651
Nonuse, product, 645–647
Nonverbal communications
    in attitude formation and change, 421
    cultural differences in, 53–60
    definition of, 54
Nordstrom, 604, 609
Normative influence, of reference groups,
    228–229, 230, 233
Norms, 41, 43
"Notice and choice" approach to online
    privacy, 741
Not of This World, 174
Nouveaux riches, 133
NPS. see Net Promoter Score
Numbers, cultural differences in meaning
    of, 57
NutraSweet, 307
Nutrition labeling, 8, 747–748
Nutrition Labeling and Education Act
    (NLEA), 8, 747
NYDJ, 382
NYP. see New York–Presbyterian Hospital

o

Obesity, child, 462–463
Objectification, need for, 369
Objectives, organizational, 705–706, 710
Observation
    in diffusion of innovations, 247, 250
    in group influences, 237–238
    in research, 763
Occupation
    consumption influenced by, 114
    and household life cycle, 201
Ocean Spray, 746–747
Odors. see Scents
Office Depot, 648
OgilvyAction, 621
Olay, 420
Old Navy, 365
Old-school Millennials, 127
Old Spice, 351
Olympus, 238
Omni-channel shoppers, 606–611
    behaviors of, 607–608
    definition of, 606
    retail strategy for, 608–611
ON Cakebites, 293
One-click mobile payments, 604–605
1-800-PetMeds, 411
One-sided messages, 420

Ongoing information search, 536
Online communities, 221, 226–228
Online shopping. *see* Internet shopping
OnStar, 326, 406
Openness to experience, 379
Operant conditioning, 331, 333–334, 337
Opinion leaders, 236–242
 characteristics of, 238–239
 consumer-generated content by, 235
 definition of, 236
 in marketing strategies, 239–242
Opportunity costs, 627
Optimism, as cultural value, 50
Oranges, 722–724
Orbit, 164
Orbitz, 96
Oreo, 228, 374
Organization, of stimuli, 302
Organizational buying, 27, 690–719
 decision process in, 694–704
 examples of, 27
 marketing strategies for, 714–716
 model of, 690–691, 695
 organizational culture in, 704–713
 stereotype vs. reality of, 691
 trends in, 693–694
Organizational culture, 704–713
 definition of, 704–705
 external factors influencing, 705–709
 internal factors influencing, 709–713
 tips for building positive, 710–711
Organizational values, 708, 709–711
Organization composition, 707
Orthodox Judaism, 176
O That's Good, 352–353
Other-oriented values
 cultural differences in, 43, 44–49
 definition of, 43
 in U.S., 81, 88–90
Otis Elevator, 703
Outcomes, of marketing strategies,
  10, 11, 20–24
Outdoor advertising, 286, 309–310
Outlet selection and purchase, 596–633
 consumer characteristics in, 617–620
 in-store and online influences on, 620–629
 in organizational buying, 700–701
 outlet attributes affecting, 611–617
Overload
 choice, 567–568
 information, 294, 544, 748–749
Ownership, in product value, 641
Ownership effect, mere, 436–437, 641

p

Pabst Blue Ribbon, 351
Pace, 352
Packaging. *see also* Labeling
 cigarette, 750
 deception in, 746
 disposition of, 647
 perception of design of, 310–311
 size effects of, 304
PAD. *see* Pleasure-arousal-dominance

P&G. *see* Procter & Gamble
Panera Bread, 674
Pantene, 52
Paramount Citrus, 722
Parents. *see also* Fathers; Mothers
 cohabiting, 190
 in consumer socialization, 207–210
 in family decision making, 203–206
 gender roles in, 79–80, 98
 in multigenerational households, 111
 single, 189, 190
Partitioned prices, 624
Partner buyers, 716
Partnership for a Healthier America, 462–463
Pass-it-on tools, 239, 242
Passive-oriented approach, 51, 84
Patagonia, 458–460
PBE. *see* Permission-based e-mail
Peak experiences, 436
People meters, 769–770
Pepperidge Farm, 82
Pepsi, 48–49, 171, 463, 547
Per capita income, 63
Perceived fit, 307
Perceived risk. *see* Risk, perceived
Perception, 280–315
 of actual vs. desired state, 519
 attention in, 282, 287–297
 definition of, 279, 282
 exposure in, 282–287
 interpretation in, 282, 297–306
 in marketing strategies, 306–311
 nature of, 282
 in organizational culture, 711–713
Perceptual defenses, 282
Perceptual mapping
 definition of, 349, 575
 in measurement of evaluative criteria,
  575–576
 in product positioning, 349–350
Perceptual relativity, 297
Performance. *see also* Brand performance
 in customer satisfaction, 650–653
 dimensions of, 651–653
Peripheral route to attitude change, 409–410
Permission-based e-mail (PBE), 546
Permission-based marketing, 287
Permission-based text messaging, 551
Personal interviews, 765
Personality, 377–382. *see also* Brand
  personality
 definition of, 366, 377
 and emotions, 382–383
 in family purchase roles, 204–205
 trait theories of, 377–380
Personal sales, 231–232, 240–241
Personal sources of information, 540–541
Personal space, cultural differences in, 56
Persuasion. *see also* Attitude change
 consumer resistance to, 410–411
Pet ownership, 270–272, 678–679
Pew Hispanic Center, 161
Pew Research Center, 87, 111, 549
Pharmaceutical drugs, advertising for, 748–749
Phased decision making, 572

Phonemes, 307
Phone numbers, 325
Physical environment outcomes, 23
Physical exercise, in cultural values, 51
Physical surroundings, as situational
  influence, 491–496
Physiological changes, with emotions, 383
Physiological measures, in research, 764
Physiological traits, in interpretation, 298
Piaget's stages of cognitive development,
  207–208, 733
Picture superiority, 290
Piracy, 732
Pistachios, 368, 369, 410
Pizza Hut, 664
Plated, 199, 470
Pleasure-arousal-dominance (PAD),
  383–384, 402
Point-of-Purchase Advertising International
  (POPAI), 620–623
Point-of-purchase (P-O-P) materials, 622–623
Polaroid, 51
Polychronic time perspective, 55
Pomegranates, 406
P-O-P. *see* Point-of-purchase
POPAI. *see* Point-of-Purchase Advertising
  International
Population, research, 762
Population, U.S. *see also* Demographics
 characteristics of, 112
 immigrants in, 154–155
Population distribution, 63, 112
Population growth, U.S.
 immigrants in, 154–155
 patterns of, 112
Population size, 63, 112
Population structure, 63
Pop-up ads
 attention to, 289
 avoidance of, 285–286
 involuntary vs. voluntary exposure to, 287
Porsche, 372, 443
Position of stimuli, in attention, 290–292
Positive framing, 421
Positive products, 553
Positive reinforcement, 340
Possessions, in extended self, 435–437
Postponed gratification, 53, 82–83
Postpurchase dissonance, 642–644
Postpurchase processes, 641–668. *see also*
  Customer satisfaction
 biases in, 641
 dissonance as, 642–644
 of organizational buyers, 702–703
 product disposition as, 647–650
 product use and nonuse as, 644–647
 purchase evaluation as, 650–653
 types of, 641, 642
Potential influencers, 266
Pottery Barn, 95
Power distance, 49–50
PPP. *see* Purchasing power parity
Pragmatic implications, 744–745
Pre-Depression generation, 119, 120
Preferences, learning of, 208

Preference strategy, 557–558
Preservation-related motives, 368–370
Prevention-focused motives, 376–377, 378
Price
    accuracy of judgments of, 577
    in consumer behavior audits, 774
    vs. cost, 19–20
    definition of, 19
    in global markets, 260
    in marketing mix, 19–20
    partitioned, 624
    perceived range of, in external information
        search, 552
    reference, 304, 615, 750
    regulation of, 750
    retail advertising of, 614–616
    as surrogate indicator, 578–580
Price-perceived quality, 304
Price premium, 659–660
Price reductions, in brand choice, 623–624
Primary data collection, 761–769
Primary groups, 221
Primary motivation, in VALS program, 445
Print ads
    attention to, 289–294
    interpretation of visuals in, 304–305
Printer cartridges, 648
Print media, LGBTQ, 95–96
Privacy, consumer, 741–742
Privacy, online, 739–742
    for adults, 741–742
    for children, 739–740, 759–760
    definition of, 739
    website policies on, 749
Private consumption, reference groups in,
        229–231, 232
Private firms, organizational culture of, 706
Private self-concept, 434
PRIZM, 443, 448–450, 451
Proactiv Solution, 735–736
Probability samples, 762
Problem(s)
    relative importance of, 520
    types of, 520–521
    use of term, 27
    work-around, 513
Problem analysis, 524–525
Problem recognition, 512–532
    activation of, 526–529
    definition of, 518
    marketing factors in, 522–529
    nature of, 518–520
    nonmarketing factors in, 521–522
    in organizational buying, 698–699
    process of, 517–521
    suppression of, 529
Problem solving
    in cultural values, 50, 86
    social media in, 513
Procter & Gamble (P&G), 66, 94, 158, 272–273,
        387, 512, 513, 747, 750
Product(s)
    adaptations for cultural differences,
        259–260
    for African Americans, 158–159

in consumer behavior audits, 776
    definition of, 17–18
    emotion arousal as, 384–385
    in extended self, 435–437
    for Hispanic Americans, 166
    inferences about quality of, 304
    in marketing mix, 17–18
    primary or core services as, 17, 20
    total, 11
Product analysis, 523–524
Product assortment optimization, 568
Product characteristics
    in external information search, 553
    in schematic memory, 327
Product development, attitudes in, 421–423
Product disposition, 647–650
    in marketing strategies, 648–650
    through recycling, 647–648
Product involvement
    and motivation, 294
    vs. purchase involvement, 515–516
Product nonuse, 645–647
Product placement
    definition of, 281, 286
    rise of, 281–282, 286
Product positioning, 348–351
    vs. brand image, 348
    in consumer behavior audits, 773–774
    definition of, 21, 348, 773
    as outcome of marketing strategies, 21
    perceptual mapping in, 349–350
    repositioning, 350–351
    self-concept in, 438–439
    usage situations in, 503–505
Product-related need sets, 14–15
Product repositioning, 350–351
Product safety. see Safety regulations
Product sampling, 239–240
Product use, 644–645
    biases in, 641
    innovativeness in, 644–645
    lack of (nonuse), 645–647
    by organizational buyers, 702–703
Product value, 641
Profits
    as outcome of marketing strategies, 22
    from repeat purchasers and committed
        customers, 659–662
Program context effects, 500
Program involvement, and attention, 295, 296
Projective techniques, 374, 575, 764
Promotional deals, in brand choice, 623–624
Promotion-focused motives, 376–377, 378
Promotions, cross-, 306
Promotion strategies, in consumer behavior
        audits, 775–776
Prom ritual, 487
Protestant subcultures, 175
Proximity, 302
Psychographics, 442–445
Psychological meanings, 297
Psychological needs, 367
Psychological traits, in interpretation, 298
Public firms, organizational culture of, 706
Public Health Service, U.S., 24

Public self-concept, 434
Puerto Ricans, 161
Pull strategies, 546, 551, 604, 722, 723
Pulsing, 343
Puma, 302
Punishment, in strength of learning, 341
Purchase(s). see also Outlet selection and
        purchase
    definition of, 629
    repeat (see Repeat purchases)
    unplanned, 620–622
Purchase evaluation, 650–653
    in organizational buying, 700–701
    process of, 650–653
Purchase implementation, in organizational
        buying, 701–702
Purchase involvement, 514–516
    definition of, 514–515
    and discontinuous innovations, 246
    and opinion leadership, 237
    vs. product involvement, 515–516
Purchasers
    in family decision making, 202–203
    repeat, 657–665
Purchase situations
    for consumers, 489–490, 588
    for organizational buyers, 696–697
Purchasing power parity (PPP), 63, 64
Purina, 330, 331, 518, 555, 556
Push-based apps, 604
Push strategies, 546, 551, 604, 722, 723

q

Quaker Oats, 399
Qualitative research, 762
Quality
    of ads, 295
    of products, signals of, 304
Questionnaires, 767–768
Quinceañera, 502
Quiznos, 235

r

Racial diversity, in American values, 88
Racial subcultures. see Ethnic subcultures
Radian6, 524
Rage episodes, 386
Rakuten, 612
Ram Trucks, 14, 97, 166, 447, 449
Random samples, 762
Rank ordering scales, 576
Rating scales, attitude, 768–769
Rational choice theory, 568–569, 588
Rationality, bounded, 568
Rational thought, 295–296
Rawlings, 413
Ready.gov, 521
Reasoning
    analogical, 336
    analytical, 336, 337
    in family decision making, 205
Recall, in long-term memory, 329

Recession of 2007-2009. *see* Great Recession
Recognition tests, 771
Recycling, 647-648
    of clothing, 458
    rates of, 647
Red Baron, 197
Reebok, 380, 441, 442
Reference groups
    aspiration, 221
    changes to situation and, 220-221
    definition of, 220
    degree of influence of, 229-231
    dissociative, 221
    infrastructure of, 708-709
    marketing strategies based on, 231-233
    nature of influence of, 228-229, 230
    in organizational culture, 708-709
Reference price, 304, 615, 750
Referent state, 304
Referral reward programs, 240-241
Referrals, in profitability, 659-660
Regency planning, 345
Regional subcultures, 177-179
    consumption differences among, 178
    definition of, 177
    examples of, 112-113, 177-178
    in organizational culture, 707
Regulation(s), 728-760
    on drone traffic, 677
    examples of, 8, 731-732
    in global marketing, 66
    on marketing to adults, 741-750
    on marketing to children, 208, 732-740
    and model of consumer behavior, 27
    and organizational culture, 708
Regulatory focus theory, 376-377
Reinforcement
    definition of, 340
    need for, 370
    in operant conditioning, 333-334
    in strength of learning, 340-341
Relational exchanges, 714
Relationship marketing, 663-665
    definition of, 663
    elements of, 663
    and loyalty, 664-665
    with organizational buyers, 714-716
Relationships, cultural differences in, 57-58
Relative attitudes, 404
Relative importance of problems, 520
Relativity, perceptual, 297
Relevance, of cues, in attitude change, 409
Religion
    in American values, 80-81, 173
    in cultural values, 53
    subcultures based on, 173-177
Religious Right, 176
Reminder purchases, 620-621
Remodeling, 194
Renovations, 194
Repeat purchases, 657-665
    definition of, 657
    marketing strategies for, 662-665
    nominal decision making in, 516
    profits from, 659-662

Repetition
    in attention, 289
    in maintenance rehearsal, 325
    in strength of learning, 341-344
Repositioning
    brand, 346, 348, 354, 476-478
    product, 350-351
Research, 761-771
    in global marketing, 259-261
    in market analysis, 12
    methods of, 761-771
    on Millennials, 466-467
    on motivation, 374, 764
    need for, 7
    on problem recognition, 525
Research in Motion, 307
Resources, in VALS program, 445
Response environment, 346
Restaurants
    mobile ordering at, 680-681
    music in, 494
Retail advertising, 614-616
Retail attraction model, 617
Retail gravitation model, 617
Retail outlets
    attributes of, 611-617
    brick-and-mortar (*see* Brick-and-mortar
        stores)
    definition of, 599
    importance of brands to, 598
    loyalty to, 658
    mobile, 602-603
    online (*see* Internet shopping)
    perceived risk of, 618-619
    selection of (*see* Outlet selection)
    types of, 599
Retail shopping
    evolution of, 599-611
    in-home, 600
    omni-channel, 606-611
    socialization of, 210
    U.S. volume of, 600
Retail strategy
    for African Americans, 160
    in gender-based marketing, 102
    for Hispanic Americans, 166
    omni-channel, 608-611
    opinion leaders in, 240-241
    perceived risk in, 618-619
    perception in, 306-307
Retirement, by baby boomers, 119, 122
Retrieval, 337-346
    from long-term memory, 329
    memory interference in, 345-346
    response environment in, 346
    strength of learning in, 339-345
Retrieval cues, 346
Retrieval failure, 338
Retro Dreamer, 759
Return policies, online, 647
Reviews
    customer, 243, 411, 545
    fake, 243
Revlon, 17, 352
Reward programs, customer, 664

Rhetorical figures, 302
Riders by Lee, 742, 743
Risk, perceived
    in diffusion of innovations, 247, 250
    in external information search, 554
    in outlet selection, 617-619
    social vs. economic, 617-618
Risk taking, in cultural values, 50, 86
Risk tolerance, of organizational buyers, 714
Ritual situations, 487, 501-502
R. J. Reynolds, 138
Robitussin, 501
Rogaine, 246
Roku, 285
Role specialization, in family decision
        making, 204
Roman Catholicism, 162, 174-175
Rote learning, iconic, 335, 337
Royal Caribbean, 85
Rub-off effect, 337
Ruggedness, in brand personality, 381
Rules, decision, 580-589

S

Sabian, 413
Safety
    in Maslow's hierarchy of needs, 367
    in organizational culture, 710-711
Safety regulations, 749-750
    and children, 732, 750
    examples of, 23, 731
Saks Fifth Avenue, 604
Sales, as outcome of marketing strategies, 22
Sales personnel, in brand choice, 628-629
SAM, 402, 576
Same-sex marriage, 94, 95
Samples, product, 239-240, 333-334
Sample size, 762
Sampling, in research, 761-762
Sampling frames, 762
Samsung, 243
Sanctions, 41
Sandals Resort, 195-196
Sanrio, 473-474
SAP, 700, 702
Satisfaction. *see* Customer satisfaction
Saturn, 337, 348
SBI. *see* Strategic Business Insights
Scandals, brand, 336
Scent marketing, 674-676
Scents, 674-676
    ambient, 307, 494, 674-676
    artificial vs. natural, 674
    emotions and, 674-676
    in memory, 339-340
    as situational influence, 494-495
    in store atmosphere, 625
Schemas, 327-329
Schematic memory, 327-329, 347-348
Schools, commercialization of, 738-739
S.C. Johnson, 8
Scripted fonts, 308
Scripts, memory, 329
Scrubbing Bubbles, 557

SDI. *see* Subjective discretionary income
Search, information. *see* Information search
Search engine optimization (SEO), 547–548
Search engines, 543–550
Sears, 170
Seating technology, virtual, 542
Secondary data, 761
Secondary groups, 221
Second-generation Asian Americans, 169
Second-generation Hispanic Americans, 161
Second screen, 535, 546
Secret, 370, 371, 522
Secular societies
    cultural values of, 53
    U.S. as, 80–81, 173
Security, in cultural values, 50, 86
Seeding, 222, 239–240
Segmentation. *see* Market segmentation
Selective exposure, 284–287, 309
Selective problem recognition, 526–527
Self-actualization, 367
Self-checkout, 687–689
Self-concept, 434–440
    cultural differences in, 434–435
    definition of, 24, 26, 279, 434
    dimensions of, 434–435
    ethical issues with, 439
    measurement of, 437
    in model of consumer behavior, 24, 25,
        26–27, 278–279
    organizational, 704–705
    and possessions, in extended self, 435–437
    in product positioning, 438–439
    relationship between lifestyle and, 441
Self-expression motivation, in
        VALS program, 445
Self-image congruity, 438–439
Self-monitors, high vs. low, 439
Self-oriented values
    cultural differences in, 43, 51–53
    definition of, 43
    in U.S., 80–84
Self-referencing, 340
Self-selection, in consumption
        subcultures, 222–223
Self-service
    in organizational buying, 693
    in self-checkout, 687–689
Semantic differential scales, 437, 576, 768–769
Semantic meanings, 297, 307
Semantic memory, 327
SEMs. *see* Sponsored educational materials
SeniorNet, 122
Sensory cues, 299
Sensory discrimination, 303, 577–578
Sensual gratification, in cultural values,
        51–52, 81–82
SEO. *see* Search engine optimization
Service failures, 652
Services
    definition of, 20
    in marketing mix, 20
    primary or core, as products, 17, 20
Servicescape, 493, 625
Sesame Street (TV show), 757–758

7-Eleven, 498, 612
7-Up, 45, 46
Sex, definition of, 97
Sexual orientation. *see* LGBTQ market
Shaping, 334
Sharps, 451, 452
Shazam, 535
Sherwin Williams, 407
Shipping costs, 676
Shiseido Co., 45
Shopkick, 682
Shoppertainment, 597–598
Shopping bots, 545
Shopping orientations, 554, 619–620
Shopping style, cultural differences in, 260
Shopzilla, 545
Short-term memory (STM)
    capacity of, 325
    definition of, 325
    duration of, 325
    elaborative activities in, 325–327
    in learning, 324, 325–327
Shout, 244
Showrooming, 607–609, 682
Simplicity, voluntary, 83
Simulation, of opinion leaders, 239
Sincerity, in brand personality, 380–381
Single individuals, in household life cycle,
        193–200
Single-item indexes, 138
Single Mothers by Choice, 199
Single-parent households, 189, 190, 197, 199
Single-person households, 187, 198
Single-trait personality theories, 379–380
"Sin" products, 138
Situational factors
    in attention, 295
    in attitude change, 409–411
    in attitude inconsistency, 405
    in external information search, 554
    in interpretation, 301
    in motivation, 377
    in organizational buying, 696–697
    in reference group influence, 220–221
    in schemas, 327, 328–329
Situational influences on behavior, 486–508
    antecedent states as, 499–501
    definition of, 488
    in external information search, 554
    in marketing strategies, 502–505
    nature of, 488–491
    physical, 491–496
    ritualistic, 501–502
    social, 496–499
    task definition as, 498–499
    temporal, 498
Size
    of families, 191
    of organizations, in organizational
        culture, 705
    of populations, 63
    of retail outlets, in outlet selection, 616–617
    of stimuli, in attention, 288–289
Skeptical consumers, 93
Skittles, 299

Skyline Chili, 177–178
Skyscanner, 550
Slang, 53
Sleep Number, 526, 527
Slotting allowances, 288–289
Smart banner ads, 294
Smartphones. *see also* Mobile apps; Mobile
        marketing; Mobile retailing
    children's use of, 738
    Hispanic American use of, 274–276
    mobile search on, 548–551
    recycling of, 647–648
    types of users, 548
    U.S. rates of ownership, 548, 602
Smashburger, 177
Smell. *see* Scents
Smith & Wesson, 100
Smithfield, 502
Smoking. *see* Cigarettes
Snapchat, 129, 242
Snapple, 557
Sneakerheads, 223–224, 644
Soccer, 39, 47–48
Social broadcasters, 266
Social class, 130–142. *see also specific classes*
    Coleman–Rainwater system of, 131, 132
    as continuum, 131
    definition of, 130
    demographics in, 112
    and diet, 141
    in marketing strategy, 139–142
    measurement of, 138–139
    U.S., descriptions of, 131–138
Social class system, 130
Socialization. *see* Consumer socialization
Socially concerned consumers, 93
Social marketing
    vs. cause marketing, 91, 92
    definition of, 8, 91
Social media
    ads on, 546, 547
    African American use of, 158
    and children, 738
    consumer power on, 6
    gender differences in use of, 101
    Hispanic American use of,
        163, 165, 274
    identifying consumer problems using, 524
    marketing via, 226–228
    Millennial use of, 466–467
    negative word-of-mouth on, 265–266
    number of active users of, 265, 267
    in problem solving, 513
    as source of information, 546
    viral marketing on, 242
Social media influencers, 414
Social networks
    in brand communities, 225
    in seeding, 222
Social network sites, online, 226–228
Social risk, 617–618
Social standing, 130. *see also* Social class
Social status
    demographics in, 112
    and external information search, 554

Social surroundings, as situational influence, 496–498
Social ties, strength of, 220–221
Social welfare, 23–24
Societal rank, 130
Societies
    consumption, 9
    secular, 53, 80–81, 173
Society outcomes, 23–24
Socioeconomic status. see Social class
Sonic Drive-in, 738–739
Sony, 227, 648
Sony Ericsson, 241
Sophistication, in brand personality, 381
Sounds
    in interpretation, 299
    memory of, 345
Sources
    in attitude formation and change, 411–415
    credibility of, 411–412
Sour Patch Kids, 242
Southwest Airlines, 710
Souvenirs, in extended self, 436
Space, cultural differences in views of, 56
Spam, 546
Spanish language, 161, 163–166
Spillover, from scandals, 336
Spillover sales, 614
Spokescharacters, 414
Sponsored educational materials (SEMs), 739
Sponsorship, 414–415
Sports. see also specific types
    globalization of, 39
    masculine vs. feminine orientation in, 47–48
Sprint, 662, 738
Sprite, 380
Starbucks, 4, 5, 18, 19, 42, 235, 664
Starch scores, 771
Status, in cultural values, 49–50, 87–88
Status continua, 131
Status crystallization, 131
Stay-at-home parents, 79, 98–100
Steady shoppers, 15
Step families, 189–191
Stereotypes
    of Arab Americans, 172, 173
    of green consumers, 91
    of organizational buying, 691
Steroids, 731
Stimulation
    need for, 370
    of opinion leaders, 239
Stimulus discrimination, 336–337
Stimulus factors
    in attention, 288–294
    definition of, 288, 301
    in interpretation, 301–304
Stimulus generalization, 337
Stitch Fix, 566, 567–568
STM. see Short-term memory
Stockouts, 626–627
Store(s). see Retail outlets
Store atmosphere
    in brand choice, 624–626
    definition of, 493

Store-based retailing. see Brick-and-mortar stores
Store brands, 613–614, 746
Store distribution, in external information search, 552
Store image
    definition of, 347, 611
    dimensions of, 611–612
    in outlet selection, 611–613
Stouffer's, 585, 586
Straight rebuy, 697
Strategic Business Insights (SBI), 45
Streaming services
    music, 264
    product placement in, 281
    rise in use of, 284
    techniques for advertising on, 281, 284–285
Strength
    of attitudes, 405, 410–411
    of learning, 339–346
Strivers, in VALS program, 446–447
STX Entertainment, 757–758
Subcultures, 150–182
    African American, 151, 154–160
    Arab American, 172–173
    Asian American, 154, 166–170
    Asian Indian American, 172
    consumption, 221–224
    definition of, 152
    in family purchase roles, 204
    Hispanic American, 154, 160–166
    Native American, 170–171
    nature of, 152–153
    regional, 112–113, 177–179, 707
    religious, 173–177
Subjective discretionary income (SDI), 116
Subjective feelings, 383
Subjectivity, of interpretation, 297
Subliminal advertising, 296–297
Subscription video-on-demand (SVOD) services, 281. see also Streaming services
Substitution costs, 626
Subway, 235, 463
Success dimension of materialism, 52
Sugar, 746–747
Suggested list prices, 615
Sunbeam, 577
Sunkist Growers, 348–349
Sun Pacific, 722–724
Super Bowl, 287, 535
Superconnectors, 61
Supergirl (TV show), 40
Suppression, of problem recognition, 529
Surrogate indicators, 578–580
Surveys, 765, 767–768
Survivors, in VALS program, 446, 448
Suspense, 340
SVOD. see Subscription video-on-demand
Swanson, 401, 402
Sweet 'N Low, 298
Switching costs, 658
Symbolic performance, 652
Symbols, cultural differences in, 56–57

Symmetrical logos, 308
Synesthesia, 299
Synners, 298, 299

t

TAG Heuer, 133, 372
Tang, 165
Target, 12, 36, 37, 94, 116, 166, 344, 347–348, 405, 604, 616, 746, 747
Target Australia, 37
Targeting, behavioral, 13, 294, 547
Target market, 16–17, 309
Task definition, 498–499
Technology use, in lifestyle, 443–444
Telemundo, 164, 165
Teleological need, 370
Telephone surveys, 765
Television
    interactive, 599–600
    measures of viewership, 769–771
    multitasking with, 467
    product placement inside shows, 281
    second screen use with, 535, 546
Television commercials
    effects on children, 735–737
    interactive, 599–600
    and Millennials, 466–467
    skipping, 284–286
    as source of information, 535
Temporal perspectives, 498, 554
Tension reduction, need for, 370
Terminal materialism, 52
Terms and conditions, in organizational buying, 702
Tesco, 42
Tesla, 224, 245, 683–685
Testimonial ads, 411
Text messaging, permission-based, 551
TFI. see Total family income
TGI Fridays, 604–605
Theater tests, 771
TheraBreath, 598, 599
Things, cultural differences in meaning of, 59
Thinkers, in VALS program, 446–447
Thinking
    cognitive, 383
    with emotions, 383
    rational, 295–296
    short-term memory as, 325
Third-generation Hispanic Americans, 161
Third-party endorsements, 411–412
Third screen, 738
Ticketmaster, 542
Tide, 272–273, 352, 750
Tie-ins, 293
Tiffany and Co., 95
Timberland, 610
Time
    cultural differences in views of, 54–56
    as situational influence, 498
Time perspective, 54–55
Tinder, 286
Tobacco. see Cigarettes
Tommy Hilfiger, 25, 26

Toms Shoes, 93, 94
Tone, in brand personality, 381–382
Top-of-mind awareness, 329
Toro, 349
Total family income (TFI), 116
Total product, 11
Toyota, 353, 731
Tracking consumers, in brick-and-mortar stores, 598
Trademark law, 37–38
Tradition, in cultural values, 50–51, 85–86
Traditional families, 189
Traditional gender orientations, 98
Traditional housewives, 99–100
Traditionalist Asian Americans, 168–169
Training, instrumental, 208–209
Traits, in interpretation, 298, 301–302
Trait theories of personality, 377–380
Transactional exchanges, 714
Transaction costs, 627
Translations, challenges of, 53–54, 165
Transparency in advertising
    and covert marketing, 241
    on social media, 227
Transportation, U.S. Department of, 417
Trapped housewives, 100
Trapped working women, 100
Trialability, in diffusion of innovations, 247, 250
Tricycles, 750
Trust, in organizational culture, 711
Trustworthiness, of sources, 411–412
Truth in Lending Act, 577
Tumblr, 129
Twitter, 226–228, 242–243, 546
Two-sided messages, 420
Two-stage decision process, 700
Two-step flow of communication, 236
Tylenol, 96, 97, 528
Tyler's, 606, 607
Typographics, perception of, 307–308
Tyson, 347

U

UberEATS, 462
Umbrella branding. see Brand leverage
Unconditioned response, 331–333
Unconditioned stimulus, 331–333
Underperforming buyers, 716
Uniformity, as cultural value, 49, 88–89
Unilever, 440, 742
UniMás, 164
Uniqueness, need for, 380
United Airlines, 265–268, 655
Unit pricing, 577
Univision, 164
Unlearning, difficulty of, 323
Unmarried-partner households, 191, 193
Unplanned purchases, 620–622
Upper class, 131–134
Upper-lower class, 137
Upper-middle class, 133–134
Upper-upper class, 131–132

Upward-pull strategy, 134
Urban blight, 142
Urbanization, in PRIZM system, 448–450
Usage situations, 490
    in brand image, 348
    definition of, 490
    in evoked set of alternatives, 538
    expanded, 490
    in importance of evaluative criteria, 579
    in product positioning, 503–505
    in schematic memory, 327, 328–329
Use, product. see Product use
Used-product market, 648
Use innovativeness, 644–645
User-generated content. see Consumer-generated content
User imagery, and brand personality, 381
Users
    in family decision making, 202–203
    lead, 708–709
Use situations. see Usage situations
Utilitarian appeals, 419–420
Utilitarian benefits, 401
Utilitarian consumption, 493–494
Utilitarian influence, of reference groups, 228–229
Utilitarian need, 370

V

Validity
    external, 766
    internal, 766
VALS program, 443, 445–448, 450
Value-expressive appeals, 419–420
Value-expressive influence, of reference groups, 229
Values. see also American values; Cultural values
    globalization of, 39
    impact of advertising on, 736–737, 742–743
    in lifestyle, 442
    in marketing to children, 736–737
    in organizational culture, 708, 709–711
Vanity numbers, 325
Variables, 765–766
Verbal communications, cultural differences in, 53–54
VeriSign, 627
Verizon, 351
Via Spiga, 300
Vicarious learning, 335, 337
Video games, advertising in, 286–287, 309
Vietnamese Americans, 167–168
View-throughs, 546–547
Vionic, 537, 538
Viral marketing, 242, 287
Viral videos, 265–266
Virgin Mobile, 96
Virtual direct experiences, 408
Virtual seating technology, 542
Visa, 487
Visible consumption, reference groups in, 229–231, 232

Visuals
    in antismoking ads, 416
    attractive, 290
    interpretation of, 304–305
    in memory, 326, 344–345
    regulation of, 746
    words combined with, 326, 345
Vodafone, 50
Voluntary exposure, 287
Voluntary simplicity, 83
Volvo, 125

W

Walmart, 166, 170, 173, 550, 604, 627–628
Walnuts, 526, 527
Warby Parker, 610
Warm colors, 290, 494
Warning labels, 311, 416, 522, 523, 529, 750
Warranties, 304
Waste, electronic, 647–648
WD-40, 645
Wearout, advertising, 344
Weber, 18, 19
Webrooming, 607–608
Websites. see Internet
Weedex, 745
Weighting out, 303
Well-being, in organizational culture, 710–711
Wells Fargo, 95
Western Union, 170, 172
Whirlpool, 94
White Americans, demographic profile of, 155
White-collar workers, 134
WHO. see World Health Organization
Wife-dominant family decisions, 203–205
Windex Effect, 268
Window displays, 597
WOM. see Word-of-mouth
Women. see also Gender roles; Mothers
    baby boomer, 268–270
    beauty standards for, 439–440, 742
    in family decision making, 203–206
    Generation X, 124
    Hispanic American, 162–163
    market segments for, 99–100
    portrayal in ads, 742–743
    self-concept of, 435, 439–440
    working, 84, 98–100
Word-of-mouth (WOM) communications, 233–243
    from committed customers, 659
    consumer-generated content and, 234–235
    definition of, 233
    from dissatisfied customers, 654–655
    in marketing strategies, 239–242
    negative, 235–236, 265–266, 654–655
    in Net Promoter Score, 660–661
    situations for, 237–238
Work, in cultural values, 52, 84
Work-around problems, 513
Working class, 131, 132, 136

Working-class aristocrats, 136
Working memory. *see* Short-term
    memory
World Bank, 64
World Health Organization (WHO), 40
Worldwide Breast Cancer, 242
Wrangler, 496, 497
Wyndham Hotels, 95

X

Xerox, 476–479

Y

Yelp, 243
Yeti, 435
Yoplait, 79, 500
Young adults
    in household life cycle, 193–197
    in multigenerational
        households, 111
Youth, in cultural values, 45–46, 89–90
Youth culture, global, 60–62
Youth trend, 45–46

    among Asian Americans, 169
    among Hispanic Americans, 164–165
YouTube, 228
YouTube TV, 285

Z

Zaoboa.sg, 167
Zapping, 284–285
Zappos, 299, 647
Zero Vitamin Water, 582
Zipping, 284–285